HISTORIC
CITIES
OF THE
AMERICAS

HISTORIC CITIES OF THE AMERICAS

An Illustrated Encyclopedia

Volume 2: North America and South America

David F. Marley

A B C · C L I O

Santa Barbara, California · Denver, Colorado · Oxford, England

Library of Congress Cataloging-in-Publication Data

Marley, David.
    Historic cities of the Americas : an illustrated encyclopedia / David F. Marley
        p. cm.
    Includes bibliographical references and index.
    ISBN 1-57607-027-1 (hardback : alk. paper)   ISBN 1-57607-574-5 (e-book)
1. Cities and towns—America—History—Encyclopedias. 2. City and town life—America—
History—Encyclopedias. 3. Urbanization—America—History—Encyclopedias. I. Title.
    HT121.M37 2005
    307.76'097—dc22

                                                                2005019012

07 06 05   10 9 8 7 6 5 4 3 2 1

This book is also available on the World Wide Web as an e-book. Visit http://
www.abc-clio.com for details.
ABC-CLIO, Inc.
130 Cremona Drive, P.O. Box 1911
Santa Barbara, California 93116–1911

This book is printed on acid-free paper.
Manufactured in the United States of America

To my mother, Lilly May Marley (née Rolston),
who created loving homes in:

Angola, Indiana
Sudbury, Ontario
Rosario, Honduras
El Dorado, Salvador
Camborne, England
Caquipec, Guatemala
Stamford, Connecticut
Mexico City, Mexico
and Windsor, Ontario

Contents

Volume 2: North America and South America

NORTH AMERICA

Oh, what a thing had be, then
if they that be Englishmen
might have been the first of all
that there should have taken possession
and made first building and habitation.

—John Rastell, *Interlude of the*
***Four Elements* (ca. 1519)**

Canada

HALIFAX
Originally an advance naval base, which evolved into the principal seaport for Atlantic Canada.

Foundation and Early Development (1749–1755)
The strategic importance of this vast, ice-free anchorage was first recognized after an army of New England militiamen under Lt.-Gen. William Pepperrell captured the great French Canadian frontier fortress of Louisbourg at the tip of Cape Breton Island during King George's War in the spring of 1745, only to be outflanked by a counterexpedition of sixty vessels and 11,000 men under Adm. Jean-Baptiste Louis de la Rochefoucauld de Roye, Duc d'Anville, which in September 1746 put into an uninhabited bay 200 miles to its southwest, known as Chibouctou, or Chebucto (from the local Mi'kmaq word *chebookt,* meaning "chief harbor"). All communication with Massachusetts through the forward British outpost of Annapolis Royal—Nova Scotia's capital, situated 100 miles due west inside the Bay of Fundy—was consequently disrupted, and Louisbourg's isolated New Englander garrison was to be spared only by the ravages suffered by D'Anville's

force after its stormy, two-and-a-half-month transatlantic passage.

In the first two weeks after dropping anchor in Chebucto Bay, 2,300 of his soldiers and sailors succumbed to scurvy or smallpox, including the admiral himself, on 27 September 1746. His successor, Commo. Constantin Louis d'Estourmel, knight of the Orders of Malta and Saint Louis, also fell ill and attempted suicide, while Commo. Pierre Jacques Taffanel de la Jonquière was able only to detach four warships from the sickly formation to threaten Annapolis Royal—and they had to turn back after encountering turbulent weather. Disheartened, De la Jonquière disembarked his survivors, then steered back toward Brest by early November 1746.

Yet notwithstanding this expedition's failure, the thrust had revealed the strategic value of Chebucto Bay. When Anglo-French hostilities ceased in 1748 and Louisbourg was restored to France, the colonial governor in Boston, William Shirley, and the British secretary of state in London—John Russell, 4th Duke of Bedford—pressed Parliament to have this crucial halfway point occupied and secured for Britain, even designating it as the new capital for a revitalized Nova Scotia. Some

Panoramic view northwestward across the city in 1887, with old Fort George perched atop Citadel Hill at left, and the Narrows—leading into Bedford Basin—hazily visible in the distance at right. (National Archives of Canada)

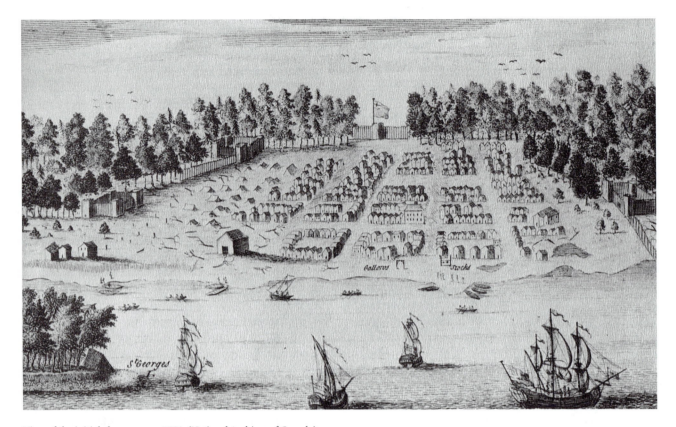

View of the initial clearance, ca. 1750. (National Archives of Canada)

2,500 settlers were rapidly recruited in England, and by 21 June 1749 ("Old Style," or "O.S."; 2 July according to our "New Style," or modern Gregorian calendar) the sloop of war *Sphinx* was entering Chebucto Bay, followed over the next couple of weeks by thirteen more transports bearing the colonists and their thirty-seven-year-old private governor, Edward Cornwallis.

An initial settlement was chosen near the open sea (modern Point Pleasant), but this site was soon discarded in favor of the eastern slopes of a 225-foot-high drumlin—today's Citadel Hill—which sat astride a small peninsula jutting into the bay, being deemed more defensible. By midsummer enough trees had been felled to clear a grid of five-by-seven town blocks around a central Grand Parade, the resultant logs being used to erect five primitive stockades around its perimeter, as well as the first few homes and blockhouses. Cornwallis opted to christen the new settlement "Halifax" in honor of George Dunk, Lord Halifax and president of London's influential Board of Trade, the Crown agency responsible for maintaining his fledgling colony. Chebucto Bay's sheltered inner harbor—known briefly as "Torrington Bay"—was renamed "Bedford Basin" in honor of the secretary of state.

Migratory bands of Mi'kmaq tribesmen viewed these developments with foreboding, being aware of earlier displacements of indigenous peoples in New England, as well as being incited by French missionaries living among them. In September 1749, local hostilities erupted when a warrior band killed several English log-cutters clearing a mill site on the harbor's eastern side (soon to become known as Dartmouth), which in turn caused Cornwallis to offer bounties for Indian scalps; he also imported a contingent of veteran Massachusetts "Indian fighters" under Capt. John Gorham.

A protracted guerrilla struggle smoldered, bottling the English settlers—as well as successive immigrant groups such as the "Foreign Protestants," several hundred German migrants brought from the Upper Rhine Valley in 1750–1752—along the rocky shores of Chebucto Bay, unable to establish homesteads amid the more fertile terrain of the Nova Scotian hinterland. Further discouraged by the long, damp winters, many farmers soon began quitting Halifax for other North American colonies; Cornwallis himself resigned as governor and returned home disillusioned and ill in 1752.

However, a few Anglo-Americans reversed this population decline. Men such as Bostonian John Bushell, who launched the *Halifax Gazette* as Canada's first newspaper in 1752, or Jonathan Belcher, who became Nova Scotia's chief justice two years later, were enticed into Halifax by financial inducements offered by the Crown. There were also other, more disreputable figures, simply fleeing their creditors. Still, the greatest impetus to the fledgling town was to be provided by a renewed round of Anglo-French warfare.

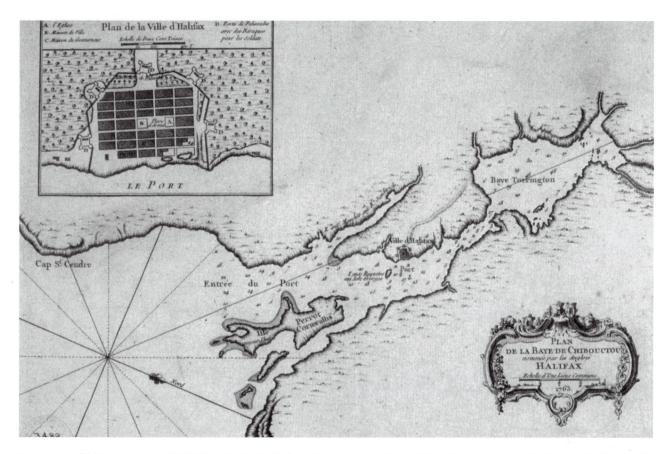

French map of "Chibouctou Bay, called 'Halifax' by the English"—with north toward lower right—plus an insert showing the town itself; originally published in Paris as Plate 28 in the first volume of Jacques Nicolas Bellin's *Petit atlas maritime,* 1764. (Metropolitan Toronto Reference Library)

Emergence as a Naval Base (1756–1840)

Friction flared again in western Pennsylvania as of 1754, and although no official declaration of war emanated from Europe, colonial armies marched into disputed wilderness areas the next spring. One such column consisted of 2,000 Anglo-American militiamen under Brig. Robert Monckton, who disembarked at the head of the Bay of Fundy on 3 June 1755 and ten days later invested the principal French stronghold in the region, Fort Beauséjour (near modern Sackville, New Brunswick). Its defenders quickly capitulated, after which Halifax's governor, Charles Lawrence, and his council—grimly determined to eradicate all enemy influence from their territory—ordered every French subject forcibly removed from their homes and expelled down the Atlantic seaboard as far as Louisiana over the next few weeks. This heartless measure effectively depopulated the interior, and formal hostilities soon erupted between London and Paris.

As the forwardmost base for conducting large-scale operations deeper into French Canada, Halifax benefited from the resultant upsurge in military construction and expenditures. Shore batteries were installed, and a sprawling complex of wharves and buildings began taking shape about a mile north of town, evolving rapidly into "His Majesty's Naval Yard." The original, insubstantial defenses atop Citadel Hill were replaced by an impressive array of trenches and wooden walls, while two massive barracks were added below. By 1758, Halifax boasted 6,000 residents—most crowded into extemporized wooden housing, dotting the steep slopes of Citadel Hill "like seats in a theater," according to one visitor. The majority of civilians catered to the needs of the 22,000 military personnel massed in encampments for another assault against Louisbourg; liquor was so prevalent that one councilor noted ironically: "The business of one half the town is to sell rum, and the other half to drink it."

The great French fortress fell again that same year, followed by Quebec City in 1759 and Montreal the year afterward—a string of victories that secured Canada for Britain. Yet it also abruptly curtailed the presence of large expeditions at Halifax, so that the town's population plummeted back under 3,000 people. Before peace could be consummated in Europe in the spring of 1763, Haligonians were already casting about for alternative means of livelihood to compensate for their lost military revenues. A treaty having been signed with the Mi'kmaq two years previously, properties wrested from the expelled

View northwestward from George's Island in 1759, showing Citadel Hill and the town of Halifax at left, Bedford Basin in the center distance, plus Dartmouth at far right; etching by James Mason, based upon a drawing copied by Richard Short from an original oil painting by Dominic Serres "the Elder." (Metropolitan Toronto Reference Library)

The town of Halifax as seen from Dartmouth opposite in 1759; etching by James Mason, based upon a drawing copied by Richard Short from an original oil painting by Dominic Serres "the Elder." (Metropolitan Toronto Reference Library)

The Governor's House and Saint Matthew's Church—better known as "St. Mather's Meeting House"—on Holles Street in 1759, with Citadel Hill visible farther up George Street; etching by François-Antoine Aveline, based upon a drawing copied by Richard Short from an original oil painting by Dominic Serres "the Elder." (Metropolitan Toronto Reference Library)

View northwestward from Barrington Street in 1759, looking at Saint Paul's Church—built nine years previously—as well as at troops drilling before the Old Artillery Barracks in the right background; etching by John Fougeron, based upon a drawing copied by Richard Short from an original oil painting by Dominic Serres "the Elder." (Metropolitan Toronto Reference Library)

French Acadians could now be safely taken over by settlers migrating up out of New England, who became known as the Planters. Yet they were few in number: the 1767 census revealed only 8,104 inhabitants in all of Nova Scotia, of whom 3,685 resided at Halifax. Moreover, most provincial inhabitants were clustered around the Bay of Fundy, so distant from Halifax that they preferred trading by sea with Boston.

Nova Scotia's isolated capital therefore remained mired in poverty and neglect, until the Thirteen American Colonies rebelled against Crown rule in the spring of 1775. Although sympathetic to patriot grievances—many of which they shared—Haligonians nonetheless became immersed in the resurgence of their naval traffic as British squadrons resumed use of local facilities for sorties against Boston, a mere two days' sail away. Merchants profited enormously as subcontractors throughout the ensuing eight years of this conflict, along with most other citizens in more menial capacities, while losses to American privateers gradually eroded sympathy for the insurgent cause. Halifax had received its first wave of Loyalist refugees when the Massachusetts capital fell to rebel besiegers in March 1776; an even greater exodus arrived after America's full independence was achieved early in 1783, a total of 100,000 people quitting the United States over the next few years rather than remain under republican rule.

Many of these émigrés passed through Halifax, yet only a fraction resettled in town; Gov. John Parr estimated some 1,200 had done so by 1784. Although the capital's economy had once more been plunged into a postwar depression, these new arrivals encouraged a few urban improvements, such as construction of the New Grand Theater, which opened near the central waterfront in February 1789, as well as the establishment of a university (King's College) in the nearby community of Windsor. But under such straitened financial circumstances and with a tight housing market, tensions inevitably rose, culminating with violent riots between the two groups that were supporting rival candidates during a provincial assembly by-election in 1788. Another noteworthy group of Loyalist refugees were American blacks, many of whom had gained their freedom through fighting for the Royalist cause during the Revolutionary War. Several hundred chose to stay in Halifax before trickling away to take up small landholdings in the outlying rural districts of Preston and Hammonds Plains; another 1,200 black Nova Scotians also departed in 1792 to attempt to forge new lives in Sierra Leone (West Africa).

The town's population had stabilized at 3,932 people by 1791, and two years later their fortunes were revived for a third time by an outbreak of hostilities, this time against Revolutionary France. On 7 May 1793 a small convoy cleared port, escorted by the 28-gun frigate HMS *Alligator* of Capt. William Affleck and the armed schooner *Diligente,* capturing the nearby French islands of Saint Pierre and Miquelon without resistance a week later. However, Halifax's true role during the ensuing two decades of warfare was to serve as the Royal Navy's main North American station, its vastly expanded yards refitting and resupplying a steady stream of visiting warships.

These efforts were furthermore bolstered by the arrival in 1794 of Prince Edward Augustus, fourth in line to the British throne and later created Duke of Kent, who, having served in the conquests of the West Indian islands of Martinique and Saint Lucia, spent the next six years in Nova Scotia's capital. Energetic, well connected, and determined to regain the favor of his father, George III, through public service, Edward threw himself into a bold program of harbor refortification that saw Citadel Hill retrenched, five stone "Martello" towers erected at strategic points around the harbor, and a string of semaphore stations built along the coast. He furthermore encouraged numerous other architectural innovations, such as the magnificent St. George's Anglican Church—built in the round Mason's Hall on the waterfront—and a huge ornate clock atop the city garrison, whose four faces were visible from every point in town, so as to satisfy the prince's mania for punctuality.

Haligonians profited noticeably, their number more than doubling to 8,532 residents by 1802, while simultaneously achieving greater social stability, refinement, and confidence. When the French emperor Napoleon I instituted his Continental System in Europe and interdicted timber supplies reaching Britain's shipyards from the Baltic, Nova Scotia and other Canadian Maritime Provinces stepped in to satisfy the demand, adding to their economic boom. Wealthy local merchants now began actively seeking business opportunities in the hinterland, so that by the time that the War of 1812 erupted against the United States, Halifax had become Eastern Canada's leading commercial port.

Despite some initial fears about a possible U.S. invasion, plus regrets over their lost New England trade, Haligonians soon benefited from this new conflict as well: numerous prizes were brought in over the next three years for adjudication and disposal by the local vice admiralty court. One of the most celebrated captures was the 38-gun frigate USS *Chesapeake* of Capt. James Lawrence, beaten 20 miles outside of Boston in June 1813 and towed into Halifax by Capt. Philip Bowes Vere Broke's victorious 38-gun frigate HMS *Shannon.* Several hundred black slaves were also brought back from the unsuccessful British campaign into Chesapeake Bay and Washington, D.C., being granted their freedom and forming the core for a permanent new Afro-Canadian community called Africville, just northwest of Halifax.

The cessation of global hostilities in 1815 resulted in another slump, Haligonians—who now numbered 11,156, according to a census taken two years later—being left with a shrunken garrison and a mothballed navy yard; even their new university, founded in 1818 by Gov. George Ramsay, 9th Earl of Dalhousie, proved to be stillborn. Some revitalization occurred when the British government unexpectedly financed a massive refortification program starting in the mid-1820s, replacing the old wooden defenses atop Citadel Hill with a huge new stone stronghold called Fort George, leading the town to be temporarily referred to as the "Gibraltar of British America."

Yet more significantly, Halifax now possessed enough entrepreneurs to diversify its own business, starting with the establishment of its first commercial bank in 1825; the digging of Shubenacadie Canal to link up with the Bay of Fundy; and the erection of a growing cluster of water-powered mills, foundries, factories, tanneries, and shipyards at Dartmouth. The *Sir Charles Ogle,* Halifax's first steam-powered ferry, was launched in 1830 to provide better access to the eastern shore, followed the next year by the oceangoing *Royal William,* furnishing regular steam service deep into the Saint Lawrence River. (Nine years afterward, Halifax-born Samuel Cunard made Nova Scotia's capital a stopover for his newly inaugurated coal-powered, transatlantic traffic when his paddle-wheeler *Unicorn* glided into harbor from Liverpool on 1 June 1840, bound toward Boston on its maiden voyage.)

The town's population had reached 14,439 people by 1827, and despite a devastating cholera epidemic and economic depression seven years later, its emergent middle class soon began demanding a greater say in civic affairs. Eventually, their plurality in the Nova Scotia House of Assembly allowed them to pass an act of incorporation in 1841, elevating Halifax to the status of a city with its own elected mayor and council.

Growth (1841–1914)

A few municipal reforms were rapidly instituted, such as the naming and numbering of all streets in 1843, construction of a privately owned waterworks the following year, the laying of gas lines and the installation of eighty gas lamps to replace the old oil ones by 1849, assignation of new public cemeteries, and the enactment of a primitive building code. Yet the cost of renovating and maintaining an entire urban infrastructure soon proved too much, retarding progress on other worthy projects such as a general hospital, schools, paved streets, sewers, and markets. Halifax moreover remained a relatively small coastal community of limited resources and no great agricultural potential, so that it could not keep pace with cities such as Montreal, Toronto, Boston, or New York in attracting large numbers of migrants.

Despite its lack of spectacular growth, however, overseas traffic still persisted, so that the city's warehouses and transport remained in steady demand, while insurance and banking concerns also flourished. Britain's shift to free trade in the 1840s and 1850s meant an end to protective tariffs and most-favored shipping status, yet such changes did not drastically curtail Halifax's port movements, and its military presence remained a reliable source of income. Telegraphic service was inaugurated in 1849, and two years later the combined population of Halifax and Dartmouth was measured at 19,165 residents; that number grew to 25,026 by 1861, thanks to an improved birthrate and increased rural-urban migration. A commercial treaty signed with the United States seven years

George Street on Bedford Row, ca. 1870; note its muddy, unpaved condition. (National Archives of Canada)

previously had also improved trade, as did enormous demand engendered by the U.S. Civil War, during which neutral British vessels serviced both Union and Confederate clients.

During the mid-1850s, the city's first railway station had also been established on the shoreline of the harbor narrows at Richmond, with lines radiating as far as Windsor, Truro, and Pictou over the next dozen years. Thanks to this slow but consistent growth, a public hospital was finally erected in 1859 (although it remained vacant for another eight years because of funding disputes). The city council furthermore purchased some steam-powered fire engines in 1861—as well as expropriating the private Halifax Water Company to ensure reliable hose pressures and passing regulations designed to create a brick-and-stone downtown core—so as to combat the frightening outbreaks of conflagrations amid the city's old wooden structures. Dalhousie College reopened on a permanent basis as of 1863, patrols by constables and night watchmen were supplanted by a professional police force the next year, free public education was introduced in 1865, and the first horse-drawn streetcars appeared the year after.

On 1 July 1867, Nova Scotia somewhat grudgingly became a province in the newly independent Confederation of Canada, yet Halifax was to retain much of its British flavor because certain treaty provisions meant that it was to continue to serve as home port for several thousand English sailors and soldiers, thereby maintaining its long-standing imperial connections. (One of the most famous people to resettle in the city as a result of this global embrace was Anna Leonowens, whose service as a teacher to the king of Siam's children was later immortalized

Anna Leonowens—nicknamed "Anna of Siam"—as she appeared while residing in Halifax, 1903. (McCord Museum, McGill University)

in Rodgers and Hammerstein's musical play *The King and I*, as well as other works.)

The first Canadian federal census in 1871 recorded 31,773 Haligonians, two-thirds of whom had been born within the province; their ethnic origins broke down as 38.9 percent Irish; 32.4 percent English; 16 percent Scottish; 4.9 percent German; 3.2 percent African; and 1.6 percent French. Light industry continued to expand with the erection of the city's first cotton mills, and a new railway depot was opened at the foot of North Street in 1877 to service the new Deep Water Terminus being built on Upper Water Street to receive ever larger ocean steamers.

However, despite adding a grain elevator in 1882, Halifax was increasingly hard pressed to compete with Portland, Maine, and suffered through some harsh economic times during the 1880s. Eventually a measure of prosperity was fomented by the completion of the biggest dry-dock on the Atlantic Seaboard at the foot of Young Street in 1889. Two years later the city's population was measured at 44,688, its physical boundaries having also been pushed outward. Electric streetlights had been introduced as of 1886, and a decade later electric trams—nicknamed "Birneys"—made their appearance, servicing the new suburbs.

The British military presence finally drew to a close in 1905–1906, leading to the temporary closure of Halifax's Naval Yard. When the port was made Canada's principal naval base four years later, its new military establishment proved to be very small, only a single warship being on station—an elderly former cruiser renamed HMCS *Niobe*. Still, Halifax benefited when the federal government financed the blasting of a major new railway route westward and southward across its rocky peninsula. Municipal services for its 51,677 residents (according to the 1911 census) had also been significantly enhanced, even movies making an appearance; the premiere of the Amer-

Two views southeastward across Halifax's anchorage, showing the devastation left by the cataclysmic munitions-ship explosion of 6 December 1917. See following page for another view. (National Archives of Canada)

ican film *Birth of a Nation* was delayed for a year by protests from black Haligonian church leaders.

World War I Calamity (1914–1918)

When Canada was drawn into European hostilities as a member of the British Commonwealth in August 1914, Halifax responded eagerly to this mobilization, local patriotism being underscored by hopes of achieving full employment. In addition to its traditional role as a naval base, the city also served as the sole embarkation point for Canadian troops bound overseas, its resources being strained to the very limit during the ensuing four years of struggle as almost 285,000 personnel transited through the port, in addition to many visits made by thousands of Allied sailors and soldiers.

Harbor defenses remained unthreatened by German U-boats until September 1917, when the United States entered the conflict, so that merchant convoys began gathering in the safety of the inner bay of Bedford Basin before striking out across the Atlantic. Ironically, this decision was to result in the worst disaster in the city's history, for at 8:50 A.M. on 6 December 1917, an outward-bound Norwegian freighter (chartered for Belgian relief) collided in the Narrows with the inward-bound French munitions ship *Mont-Blanc* because of heavy traffic, misunderstood whistle blasts, and possibly some sun glare off the water. More than 240 tons of highly flammable benzyl stowed on *Mont-Blanc*'s deck consequently ignited; with another 2,750 tons of picric acid, guncotton, and TNT from New York aboard, its panic-stricken crew abandoned their burning vessel and rowed toward Dartmouth, while unwary onlookers watched from ashore.

Seven courageous volunteers from HMCS *Niobe* attempted to board and scuttle the stricken ship, only to be vaporized when it suddenly detonated with a tremendous roar at 9:15 A.M. The resultant fireball—described as "the greatest man-made explosion in history to that point"—leveled a square mile of Halifax, its working-class neighborhood of North End bearing the brunt of the blast. Dartmouth, directly opposite, was also hard hit, while anchored vessels sank and smaller boats were tossed ashore by the resultant tidal wave. Telephone poles as far as a mile inland were snapped off, windows shattered in Truro (60 miles distant), and the noise was even heard on Prince Edward Island. Fires from ruptured ovens and furnaces embraced the ruins, after which a blizzard set in the following day, complicating efforts by rescuers who rushed in from throughout Eastern Canada and Massachusetts. The official casualty toll came to 1,963 Haligonians dead, 9,000 injured, and 6,000 left homeless at the onset of winter; more than 13,500 structures had been leveled or damaged. Even the city's massive sugar refinery, a foundry, and a cotton mill were entirely lost. The dry-dock was severely damaged, and the roof of the Intercolonial Railway Station collapsed onto its tracks.

Modern Era (1918–Present)

The city's recuperation proved to be quite painstaking, for within a year of this dreadful devastation, global hostilities ceased, bringing an abrupt halt to the city's boom. The peacetime Canadian Navy was to be so minute as to be unable to significantly buoy the local economy, while shipyards laid off 95 percent of their 2,000 workers within the next several months; many civilian factories had also been lost to the great explosion and were never rebuilt. Large corporations preferred investing directly in central Canada, where Halifax could not compete because of increased freight rates and new tariffs. Lumber from British Columbia and European fish also

Two views southeastward across Halifax's anchorage, showing the devastation left by the cataclysmic munitions-ship explosion of 6 December 1917. See previous page for another view. (National Archives of Canada)

flooded North American markets, adding to the city's woes by undercutting demand for much of its traditional produce.

During such bleak times, when half its manufacturing jobs were lost, the population of metropolitan Halifax nonetheless swelled from 67,726 people in 1921 to 79,352 a decade later, as desperate people arrived from the countryside seeking work. Racial tensions escalated, the situation worsening further after the New York stock market crash of October 1929. One of the few bright spots during the 1930s was provided by the modernization of harbor facilities to better receive passenger liners, as well as the erection of tourist hotels. Harbor races by the famed fishing schooner *Bluenose* proved particularly popular.

Two decades of economic malaise were dramatically reversed by the outbreak of World War II in September 1939, as Halifax was once more thrust into its traditional role as a major naval base. But the intervening Depression had left it ill prepared to cope with a massive influx of conscripts; the region's already limited resources would become further curtailed by wartime rationing. In short order the city's peacetime complement of 1,800 servicemen mushroomed to 75,000, the federal government commandeering numerous hotels and even the King's College campus to accommodate officers, while huts and tents were erected on fairgrounds and other open spaces to supplement its elderly, Victorian-era barracks. These throngs of incoming personnel, plus transient merchant seamen and laborers, naturally competed with Halifax's 96,636 civilians (according to the 1941 census) for housing and other services. Municipal authorities pleaded with Ottawa for assistance, pointing out that their public water system was scarcely adequate to cope with such heightened demand, while only 51 of their 114 miles of streets had been paved and no traffic lights were installed; yet no relief was forthcoming.

Although individual Haligonians profited from this resurgence, it proved impossible to invest any such gains into permanent civic improvements because of the chronic wartime shortages. Meanwhile, tens of thousands of soldiers and sailors passed through the city—150 troop convoys setting sail during the course of the conflict, plus a huge merchant convoy every eight days—so that resentment gradually escalated against its overpriced, overcrowded conditions.

On the eve of Tuesday, 8 May 1945 ("Victory-in-Europe," or V-E Day), when Nazi Germany's defeat was to be officially announced, a destructive outburst exploded at 10:30 P.M. Sailors on a streetcar bound toward downtown Halifax threw out its driver, then set it ablaze with the help of hundreds of comrades walking along Barrington Street. Liquor stores were ransacked, and 10,000 angry seamen—plus large numbers of thrill-seeking civilians—rampaged all the next day on Tuesday, before the sailors were recalled into barracks by the port's senior naval officer, Rear Adm. Leonard W. Murray, who drove through the streets that evening of 8 May with nine truckloads

Merchant convoy assembled within Bedford Basin, prior to venturing out through the Narrows and past the city of Halifax into the perilous North Atlantic beyond; 1 April 1942. (National Archives of Canada)

of naval policemen and a loudspeaker. A heavy overnight rain furthermore dampened ardors, and 1,000 soldiers arrived the next day from Debert, Nova Scotia; however, an estimated $5 million in damages had already been inflicted.

With the restoration of peace, Halifax once again endured a slump, until federal funding for military and social programs revived its economy during the 1950s—especially through funding the construction of two cross-harbor suspension bridges and a modern international airport 30 miles away, at Kelly Lake. The population of what had now become Canada's thirteenth largest city blossomed from 138,427 residents in 1951 to 193,353 a decade later and 222,627 by 1971—two years after the western suburbs of Jollimore, Purcell's Cove, Spryfield, Armdale, Kline Heights, Fairview, Rockingham, and Kearney Lake had all been annexed. Port traffic rebounded modestly after Halifax's terminals adapted to the use of standardized containers, yet manufacturing continued its slow decline; the employment market instead became dominated by wholesale-distribution jobs and government payrolls. Federal cutbacks during the mid-1970s created a minor downturn, but Halifax nevertheless revived once more into an even more modern, diversified city with a population of 338,971 people by 1994.

For additional sources on the history of Halifax, as well as sources on North American and Canadian urban history, please consult the Select Bibliography at the end of this volume.

MONTREAL
Strategically placed crossroads that has evolved into a major world metropolis.

Early Contacts (1535–1641)
On his second reconnaissance into the North American interior in quest of a "northwest passage" to Asia, the French explorer Jacques Cartier ventured up the Prairies River—a subsidiary of the Saint Lawrence River—and on 2 October 1535 was greeted at some rapids (later known as Gros-Saut, or Sault-au-Récollet) by Iroquois tribesmen, who the next day conducted him and his twenty men overland into their principal settlement of Hochelaga. This proved to be a large, circular town, whose three tiers of wooden palisades—accessible only through fortified ramps—encircled about fifty huge longhouses covered in bark, accommodating a total of some 3,500 residents. The surrounding fields were also extensively cultivated.

Hochelaga stood approximately on the site now occupied by McGill University; it dominated canoe traffic ascending the Saint Lawrence River or descending from what would later become known as the Ottawa and Richelieu rivers, because all craft had to portage round the turbulent rapids at this confluence. Cartier climbed the 700-foot heights of an adjacent promontory and decided to call this vantage point Mont-Réal

(Mount Royal). The exact reasoning behind this choice of name remains a subject of scholarly debate, popular legend attributing it to its panoramic view, although it has been suggested that King François I of France had expressed a desire for the first settlement founded in Canada to be named in honor of Cardinal Ippolito de Medici, archbishop of the old Norman town of Monreale in Sicily, as he had been instrumental in persuading his uncle, Pope Clement VII, to modify the original Hispano-Portuguese monopoly over the New World.

Cartier and his party remained in Hochelaga overnight, then departed on 4 October 1535 to retrace their route downriver, spending the winter with their companions near present-day Quebec City. No more French contingents penetrated inland for several decades, until Samuel de Champlain appeared on another reconnaissance late in June 1603, discovering that the Iroquois town of Hochelaga had since disappeared—whether because of an attack by rivals or in favor of a better site remains unknown.

Recognizing that the river bend constituted an ideal spot for a trading outpost, Champlain returned eight years later to barter with local bands, as well as to clear a flat space that he dubbed Place-Royale on the north bank of the Saint Lawrence; there he planted experimental gardens to determine the fertility of the soil. The explorer also felt that the large island in midriver represented the safest point on which "a good and strong town could be built," so he named it Île Sainte-Hélène (Saint Helen's Island), presumably in honor of his youthful bride, Marie-Hélène Boullé, who had not yet joined him from France. Lastly, he drew upon a deposit of "earth thick with clay, very good for making bricks," from which to construct a 60-foot-long wall that he left standing upon his departure, so as to determine later what damage it sustained from winter ice or spring floods.

But although Champlain revisited the Place-Royale site in the summers of 1613 and 1615, and continued to use it as a staging base from which to develop fur-trading contacts deeper in the wilderness, no permanent settlement was attempted. His main stronghold at Quebec was then captured in the summer of 1629 by an English expedition out of Boston under the Kirke brothers, who held that place for three years. Champlain could not return to Canada until May 1633, and he died two years afterward.

France set about resurrecting its North American colony in the wake of this British occupation, and a group of high-minded promoters formed an association in Paris called the Société de Notre-Dame de Montréal (Society of Our Lady of Montreal), forming a private company with the aim of dispatching volunteers to this remote inland site to reclaim it for France and convert its inhabitants to Christianity. Inspired by a visit to the shrine of the Virgin in Notre-Dame Cathedral, the pious members decided to name their new outpost Ville-Marie (Town of Mary). Money was raised from among wealthy subscribers, and equipment was shipped ahead for storage at

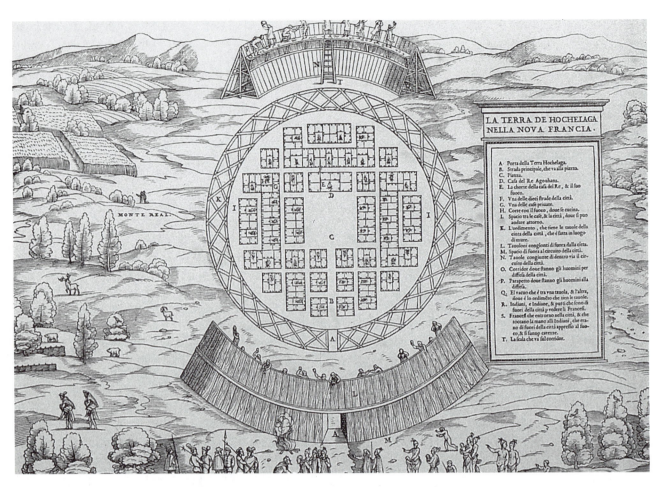

Woodcut supposedly depicting Hochelaga, based upon Jacques Cartier's written description and published more than twenty years later in Venice in the third volume of Giovanni Battista Ramusio's *Delle Navigationi et Viaggi*. (Metropolitan Toronto Reference Library)

Panoramic view southward across the city from atop Mont-Royal, ca. 1900–1910. St. Helen's Island appears at left, the Victoria Bridge at center, and Nun's Island to the right. (*Montreal in Halftone*)

Quebec, followed in the summer of 1641 by the first fifty to sixty colonists under their designated leader, Paul de Chomedey, Sieur de Maisonneuve.

These newcomers realized that the season was too far advanced to commence house building, so they visited their future site briefly in October 1641 before wintering at Quebec. They also learned that the Iroquois were now so unremittingly hostile against the French and their Huron and Algonquin allies that the notion of erecting a tiny and exposed settlement deep within the wilderness—at a time when there were not 200 Frenchmen in all of Canada—was deemed a *folle enterprise* (foolish venture) by the private colony's governor, Charles Huault, Sieur de Montmagny. Yet despite being offered comparable properties around Quebec, Maisonneuve and his followers constructed a pinnace and barge over the winter of 1641–1642; an advance group then used them to strike up the Saint Lawrence on 8 May 1642.

Foundation and Early Struggles (1642–1662)

Nine days later, the first forty settlers under Maisonneuve and Montmagny reached Champlain's old Place-Royale clearance, laying claim to a vast municipal tract extending between the Prairies and Saint Lawrence rivers with the name of Ville-Marie de l'Île-de-Montréal (Town of Mary on the Island of Montreal). After a brief Mass celebrated that same 17 May 1642 by the Jesuit priest Barthélemy Vimont, the colonists erected tents above the high-water mark, then began constructing "a small fortress of large stakes to keep themselves protected against their enemies" beside a small natural harbor enclosed by a projecting point of land—later called Pointe-à-Callière—and a small island that was to become known as Ilot-Normandin, or Market Gate Island.

This stockade and the rudimentary homes within its compound were improved after a dozen more settlers arrived from France and Quebec that same summer, including a skilled carpenter named Gilbert "le Minime" Barbier. Governor de Montmagny further helped the fledgling town by ordering a border fort constructed at the mouth of the nearby Richelieu River—then still known as the Iroquois River—to keep enemy war bands in check. The only setback occurred late in December 1642, when ice damming caused the Saint Lawrence to overflow and flood Ville-Marie's moat, threatening to bring down its gate before finally receding on Christmas morn.

Early in June 1643, forty Iroquois warriors materialized nine miles west of Ville-Marie at La Chine Rapids (so called because waters on the far side flowed west, supposedly toward Asia), slaying five woodcutters. These losses were offset by the arrival from France that same September of another forty settlers, including an engineer named Louis d'Ailleboust, who replaced the original stockade with more solid wooden walls, flanked by four bastions crowned with artillery pieces. D'Ailleboust also recommended that the inhabitants supplement their plantings of peas and corn with wheat, so as to provide more substantial harvests.

These innovations paid dividends when 200 Iroquois warriors beset the town on 30 March 1644, defeating a sally led across its snowy fields by Maisonneuve; for despite being pent inside their stronghold over the next several weeks, the French were able to survive by sending out armed parties to gather wheat. A few more settlers and soldiers arrived, and a truce was concluded with the Iroquois by September 1645, allowing sufficient respite for a Jesuit hospice and a *hôtel-dieu* (charity hospital) to be completed (at the intersection of

A continuation of the panoramic view from the previous page.

modern Saint-Sulpice and Saint-Paul streets), plus a few other urban amenities.

The first town plots outside Ville-Marie's walls were granted in January 1648, and two years later its population was measured at 196 inhabitants. But hostilities with the Iroquois soon resumed, allied Huron villages and Jesuit missions being gradually exterminated throughout the region until Ville-Marie was once more attacked on 6 May 1651. Its outlying farms were torched and the population declined to slightly more than 50 individuals, yet the garrison's stubborn resistance under Sergeant-Major (military commander) Raphaël Lambert Closse allowed the outpost to survive until another uneasy truce could be concluded in the autumn of 1653. Shortly thereafter more than 100 new settlers reached Ville-Marie from France, providing enough strength and stability to resist future Iroquois threats.

Four priests of the Order of Saint-Sulpice also arrived in the summer of 1657 under a newly appointed *grand vicaire* (grand vicar) for New France, Gabriel de Thubières de Queylus, assuming the duties of Ville-Marie's parish clergy while its Jesuits concentrated upon missionary work. Two years later, warnings were received of another planned Iroquois offensive, being confirmed when Adam Dollard des Ormeaux and sixteen companions, plus forty Huron allies and four Algonquins, were surprised at nearby Long-Sault by a vanguard of 300 hostile warriors on 2 May 1660. The outnumbered contingent resisted desperately inside their extemporized redoubt for the next several days, until Iroquois numbers swelled to 800 warriors and the French were overwhelmed. But the raiders suffered so heavily that they decided not to attempt Ville-Marie, which now had a population of 470 inhabitants.

Crown Rule (1663–1759)

Disappointed by the meager benefits obtained from France's privately owned colonies, the new king, Louis XIV, and his chief minister, Jean-Baptiste Colbert, moved to unite all overseas possessions under a single royal administration in the spring of 1663. Alexandre de Prouville, Marquis de Tracy, set sail the next year with the titles of civilian "governor-general" and military "lieutenant-general"; after imposing Crown authority over the scattered dominions of the Caribbean, he reached Quebec on 30 June 1665 with 650 settlers and four companies of French troops. Eleven days previously, the first of 1,000 more soldiers of the Carnigan-Salières Regiment had also begun disembarking from France, providing the Canadian colony with its first significant military force.

The security of Montreal—as Ville-Marie was to henceforth be known—improved greatly as the new governor-general detached contingents early in July 1665 to construct a chain of forts along the Richelieu and other rivers, deterring Iroquois incursions. A treaty was concluded with three of their nations (Onondaga, Cayuga, and Seneca) by December of that same year, while a sweep through Mohawk and Oneida territory in

the autumn of 1666 subdued the latter. By the time De Tracy visited Montreal in May 1667, the frontier settlement's population had blossomed to 766 residents, with many new properties being apportioned. Over the next five years, Montreal's population doubled to 1,500 inhabitants, and the notary Bénigne Basset surveyed and registered residences along its first thirteen streets. Work also started on a new stone church to replace its original wooden structure at the urging of New France's bishop, François de Montmorency Laval.

Although Quebec remained the colonial capital and principal seaport, Montreal grew into its most significant inland trading post, prospering from a rich flow of pelts, as well as its own agricultural and forestry products. When hostilities with the Iroquois—now allied to the English—resumed during the late 1680s, Montreal proved too formidable for a direct assault, although its neighboring village of Lachine was surprised and burned by 1,500 warriors on 5 August 1689. Even when a large body of Anglo-American militiamen and Indians advanced up the Hudson River in 1690, they were unable to press any closer than Lake George before having to turn back.

For the remaining eight years of that conflict—known as the War of the League of Augsburg, or King William's War—Montreal was spared any threats, instead serving as a springboard for counteroffensives into English territory. The town grew as a result, its first Récollect missionaries arriving in 1692 to found a monastery, while the Charron brothers (members of a religious fraternity created by the merchant François Charron de La Barre) appeared two years later to erect Montreal's second hospital, at Pointe-à-Callière. As the seventeenth century drew to a close, French influence spread ever more deeply into the continent, a string of outposts being erected from Detroit as far south as Louisiana.

Events during the next round of European hostilities—the War of the Spanish Succession, or Queen Anne's War, which commenced in May 1702—were duplicated for Montreal in that its population size of 3,500 inhabitants precluded any Iroquois attacks; nor could its remote site be reached by Anglo-American offensives. Indeed, its worst losses occurred when a viral epidemic claimed about 250 lives the next year. Col. Francis Nicholson led an army up the Hudson River to the foot of Lake Champlain in the summer of 1709, hoping to invest Montreal while his colleague Samuel Vetch descended upon Quebec with a seaborne expedition out of Boston. But the French governor-general, Philippe de Rigaud de Vaudreuil, dispatched Montreal's governor, Claude de Ramezay, southward with 1,500 men to check Nicholson's incursion, after which Vetch's campaign was canceled; the demoralized and ill Anglo-American militiamen once more trudged home. A similar effort two summers later also ended badly, when the fleet of Rear Adm. Sir Hovenden Walker wrecked in the Gulf of Saint Lawrence, obliging Nicholson's 2,300 new volunteers—mostly Palatine Germans and Indian warriors—to retire yet again.

But ironically, the Treaty of Utrecht that concluded this war

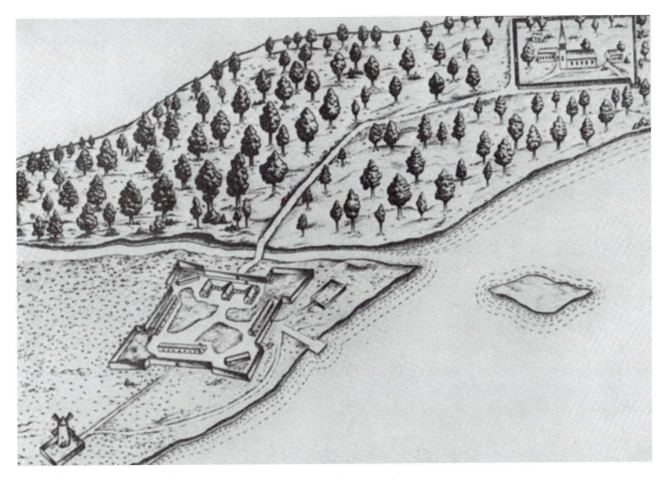

The early seventeenth-century compounds at Montreal. (*Jesuit Relations of New France*)

in 1713 proved more detrimental to Montreal, as Hudson's Bay was ceded to Britain and trading posts there soon began siphoning off many beaver pelts. Eight years afterward, the Jesuit priest Pierre François-Xavier de Charlevoix noted: "There are still now and then companies, or rather flotillas, of Indians arriving at Montréal, but nothing in comparison to what used to resort hither." A calamitous fire sparked by an accidental musket discharge during the religious procession of Pentecost gutted the town on 19 June 1721, the flames racing through its wooden structures and reducing 138 of them to ashes. The royal military engineer Gaspard Joseph Chaussegros de Léry was sent from Quebec to supervise Montreal's reconstruction, realigning and widening numerous streets. An ordinance promulgated on 8 July furthermore altered the town's appearance by directing that all future homes be constructed of stone, without mansard roofs or large roof frames; that attic floors be thickly covered with tiles or bricks; and that tiles or slates be used instead of wooden shingles on rooftops.

The authorities also took advantage of the spaces cleared by this conflagration to have Chaussegros de Léry design a stone fortification to replace Montreal's decrepit old wooden

stockade, resulting in a rectangular compound roughly equivalent to modern Berri, Commune, McGill, and Saint-Antoine streets. Its stone ramparts—although almost 20 feet high—were only 3 feet thick and intended to repel lightly armed Indian attacks, not heavy siege artillery. The engineer added a small battery and powder magazine on a rise east of town (later becoming known as Citadel Hill), as well as devising a beautiful façade of cut stone for Notre-Dame Church in 1723.

Eight years later, an enumeration revealed that there were 1,211 houses scattered around the Île-de-Montréal, 266 being made of stone. A smallpox epidemic struck in January 1733, Gov. Jean-Baptiste Bouillet de La Chassaigne falling among its first 900 victims. A second dreadful conflagration then swept through the reconstructed town on 10 April 1734, when the black slave Marie-Josèphe Angélique set fire to her mistress's house—the widow Thérèse de Couagne—in the hope of escaping with her lover during the resultant confusion. Instead, the blaze spiraled out of control, burning down the Hôtel-Dieu and forty-six other houses, so that the intendant, Gilles Hocquart—in charge of New France's civilian administration—issued another ordinance on 12 July that created Montreal's

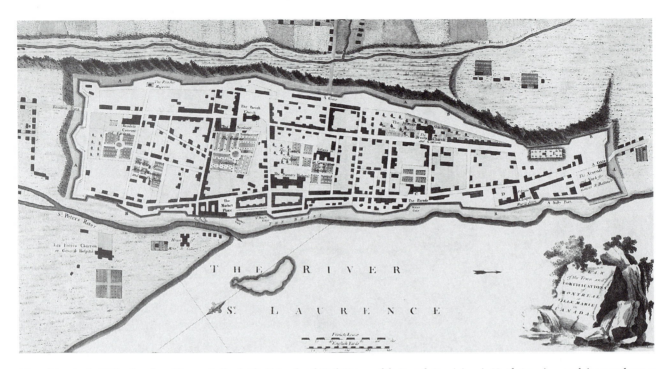

Map of the city in 1758, taken from Thomas Jeffery's *The Natural and Civil History of the French Dominions in North America;* north is toward upper right. (Metropolitan Toronto Reference Library)

first volunteer firefighting brigade. Two squads of carpenters, masons, and roofers were to assemble upon the sounding of an alarm, using four strategically placed depots of buckets, axes, shovels, hooks, and ladders (all marked with the royal fleur-de-lis) to put out the flames.

Later that same August 1734, the "chief road-master of New France"—Jean-Eustache Lanouiller de Boisclerc—departed Quebec in a sedan chair, inaugurating the *Chemin du Roy* (King's Highway) by traveling to Montreal without once setting foot in a canoe, as the intervening 180 miles had now been linked by a series of bridges and ferries. Trips between the two towns grew in frequency, governors-general and intendants routinely wintering in milder Montreal before returning to the capital to resume their official posts once the spring thaw came; also, royal warships and dispatches began arriving from overseas. Both communities were spared any direct threat during King George's War of 1744–1748, as the main Anglo-American military thrust was directed against Louisbourg on the Atlantic coast; only a few Mohawk raids along the Saint Lawrence created some minor concern at Montreal. The Swedish naturalist Peter Kalm described the town and its 8,200 inhabitants in glowing terms during his 1749 visit.

Yet commercial friction in the wilderness borderlands escalated throughout the early 1750s, prompting London and Paris to dispatch troops to reinforce their respective North American garrisons. Maj.-Gen. Louis Joseph, Marquis de Montcalm, reached Montreal in late May 1756, pushing inland to capture Fort Oswego once hostilities erupted, then taking Fort George

the next summer. But the outnumbered French gradually became hard pressed because of the Royal Navy's Atlantic blockade, as well as the severing of all supply lines when Louisbourg fell in 1758. A huge British seaborne expedition then advanced up the Saint Lawrence in the summer of 1759 under Maj.-Gen. Sir James Wolfe, defeating Montcalm's army at Quebec by mid-September.

Surviving French units regrouped at Montreal under his second-in-command, Brig. François Gaston, Chevalier de Lévis, who led almost 7,000 troops out of winter quarters in April 1760 to attempt in vain to dislodge the British garrison holding the capital under Wolfe's successor, Brig. James Murray. Pushed back, Lévis retired into Montreal a few weeks later and braced to repel the three British armies now closing in: 2,500 redcoats from Quebec under Murray, 3,400 troops pressing up Lake Champlain from Crown Point (New York) under Lt.-Col. William Haviland, and 10,000 men approaching from Oswego under Maj.-Gen. Jeffery Amherst.

Murray's small army materialized at Varennes near the east end of Île-de-Montréal on 27 August 1760, digging in to await the other two British contingents. Many disheartened French-Canadian militiamen had already begun surrendering or deserting, reducing Lévis's effective strength to only 2,100 regulars within Montreal. Haviland's army took Chambly and reached the south shore of the Saint Lawrence by 5 September, while Amherst's 6,500-man main army materialized at Lachine the following day. Surrounded, Gov.-Gen. de Vaudreuil requested terms from Amherst and two days later agreed to surrender Montreal and all remaining portions of New France. The actual capitulation was consummated when English troops marched into the town on 9 September, as Lévis's soldiers laid down their weapons in its Place d'Armes.

British Occupation (1760–1774)

Over the next two weeks, all French officials and troops were deported to New York as prisoners of war, while Amherst announced to Montreal's civilian population on 22 September 1760 that a provisional military government would be established. For administrative purposes, the newly conquered Canadian territories were subdivided into three military districts—Quebec, Montreal, and Trois-Rivières—each with an English governor. Amherst's subordinate Thomas Gage was duly installed at Montreal, and despite a mediocre reputation as a soldier, he proved to be an able and just administrator who left French civil, social, and ecclesiastical arrangements virtually intact, a benign policy that reassured both the *seigneureal,* or aristocratic, class as well as *habitants,* or ordinary residents. A census taken in 1761 revealed 24,957 people scattered throughout the town and its islandwide jurisdiction.

According to the Treaty of Paris, which ended hostilities two years afterward, the British retained possession over their North American conquests. Civilian rule was re-established by proclamation that same autumn of 1763, at which time the three former military subdistricts were reunited into a single province called Quebec. Because of its strategic position in the interior, Montreal was furthermore designated as the British Army headquarters for the Northern Department, with the task of supplying outposts throughout the Great Lakes region.

The town's prosperity quickly revived under British rule, despite accidental blazes on 18 May 1765 and 11 April 1768 that each claimed more than 100 houses—roughly a quarter of Montreal's total. The so-called Quebec Act was passed by the English Parliament in June 1774, recognizing the legitimacy of French civil law throughout the province while at the same time maintaining English criminal law and freedom of religion. By that time, Montreal's population had stabilized at approximately 8,000 residents.

American Occupation (1775–1776)

The loyalty of the recently conquered French constituency was to be tested when the Thirteen American Colonies revolted against London the next summer and a rebel army mustered at Crown Point (New York) to invade Canada in the hope of supplanting its British rulers. Brig. Richard Montgomery disembarked at Île aux Noix on the Richelieu River with 1,500 American troops on 30 August 1775; Maj.-Gen. Philip John Schuyler then assumed command of that invasion force on 4 September and pushed forward the next day to assail the advance British outpost at Saint-Jean—20 miles south of Montreal—which was stoutly defended by 200 English

Panoramic view, looking westward toward Montreal from its Saint Lawrence River approaches, ca. 1762; etching by Pierre-Charles Canot, based upon an original drawing by Thomas Patten. (Metropolitan Toronto Reference Library)

regulars and several cannon under Maj. Charles Preston and an Indian contingent.

Deeming the stronghold too difficult to carry, Schuyler's force retired to Île aux Noix, then made a second unsuccessful assault on 10 September 1775. But as the rebel army was continually reinforced, Montgomery reassumed command on 16 September and attempted to circumvent the deadlock by sending 110 men under Col. Ethan Allen to surprise Montreal, landing directly below the town at Longue-Pointe on 24 September while Col. John Brown was to lead another 200 rebels ashore above Montreal. The latter failed to appear, however, so that Allen's contingent found itself alone the following dawn, surrendering to 35 British regulars and 200 Canadian volunteers rushed into position by British Maj.-Gen. Sir Guy Carleton.

Yet the American siege of the 500 men now holding Saint-Jean and another 90 at nearby Chambly nonetheless persisted, until the latter capitulated on 18 October 1775, allowing Montgomery to tighten his investment around Saint-Jean. Carleton tried in vain to relieve this pressure by a diversionary attack on 30 October, but the half-starved garrison finally gave up three days later. The rebels advanced, and a strong force landed above Montreal on 11 November, compelling Carleton's 150 British regulars and a few local militiamen to evacuate down the Saint Lawrence aboard eleven ships the next day. Intercepted off Sorel, most surrendered except for Carleton and a few officers, who escaped ashore in a small boat and eventually reached Quebec.

Montgomery meanwhile landed troops on Île des Soeurs just below Montreal and received a citizens' delegation on 12 November 1775—including such local luminaries as James McGill and Pierre-Méru Panet—before peaceably entering the town the next day, not wishing to alienate either republican sympathizers or conservative Loyalists. The rebel general soon proceeded downriver with several hundred men to besiege Quebec, while Benjamin Franklin and Samuel Chase visited Montreal as part of a Continental Congress commission intended to win French-Canadian support. But despite being accompanied by the Catholic Charles Carroll of Maryland and his Jesuit cousin John Carroll (future archbishop of Baltimore), this delegation met with a cool reception.

Montgomery was killed attempting to storm Quebec at dawn of 31 December 1775, and his disheartened subordinate Benedict Arnold retired into Montreal, leaving David Wooster in command of siege operations. The next spring, heavy Anglo-Hessian reinforcements arrived from overseas under Gens. "Gentleman Johnny" Burgoyne and Friedrich, Baron von Riedesel, allowing the British to mount a counteroffensive out of Quebec. Wooster retreated and succeeded Arnold in command at Montreal, his rigid and sometimes arbitrary rule further dampening republican sentiments, so that after British Lt.-Col. Simon Fraser won a resounding victory at Trois-Rivières on 8 June 1776 and Carleton massed 8,000 troops, he was able to reoccupy Montreal without opposition on 17 June.

American survivors reeled back into Fort Ticonderoga (New York) by late July and did not threaten Montreal again for the remainder of the conflict.

British Administration (1777–1836)

Some normalcy returned to Montreal, despite the battles that would rage south of the border for another seven years. New firefighting and police ordinances were issued in 1777, and its first newspaper—the *Gazette du Commerce et Littéraire Pour la Ville et District de Montréal (Commercial and Literary Gazette for the Town and District of Montreal)*—was issued on 3 June 1778 by Fleury Mesplet, a French-born printer who had arrived with Franklin, then been briefly detained upon the departure of the Americans. (Mesplet was rearrested and his *Gazette* closed down on orders from Gov. Frederick Haldimand in early June 1779, during a renewed invasion scare.)

Montreal prospered by serving as a military depot until the conclusion of the American War of Independence in 1783, then received numerous displaced Loyalists; its fur trade also resurged once peace returned, although exports were now controlled by Scottish immigrant merchants. Every spring flotillas of large canoes—some capable of carrying up to 5 tons of merchandise—would sail west from Lachine, powered by eight to ten *coureurs de bois* (backwoodsmen), who bartered and returned in late summer or early autumn with tens of thousands of pelts. (The average annual haul for the North West Company, for example, was 100,000 beaver skins, 50,000 martens, 12,000 buffalo hides, and nearly 20,000 of other species.) The town mushroomed thanks to such booming trade volumes, dealing directly with such prominent international clients as John Jacob Astor of New York. By the early 1790s, the population of Montreal and its district had risen to 18,000 inhabitants, two and a half times that of the capital, Quebec.

So many transplanted Anglo-American Loyalists and British immigrants had begun settling in the country that Britain's prime minister, William Pitt, announced in late February 1791 that the colony was to be divided into two provinces, called "Lower Canada" and "Upper Canada" (modern Ontario), according to their respective positions along the Saint Lawrence waterway. A governor-general was to rule over both, with a lieutenant-governor appointed for each province, plus separate legislative assemblies. Montreal's first election was held in June 1792, six representatives being chosen from among its six wards to sit in the legislature of Lower Canada at Quebec. One of that assembly's earliest acts, passed in July 1793, restricted the importation of slaves in anticipation of a complete abolition of slavery; at the time, there were perhaps 200 individuals being held in bondage at Montreal.

Montreal had emerged as Canada's largest town and commercial hub by the close of the eighteenth century, thanks to busy waterborne traffic between New York, Quebec, and the

Farmers holding market on a wintry Saturday in Jacques Cartier Square, ca. 1900; city hall looms in the background. (William Notman Collection, McCord Museum, McGill University)

Great Lakes. Almost 9,000 people now lived within its original core, and the town had sprawled well beyond its ancient fortifications (which would gradually be torn down). Its two main arteries were paved over in 1800—Notre-Dame Street, where most public buildings stood, and Saint-Paul Street, with its concentration of private warehouses—while construction of a new courthouse was also commenced. Joseph Frobisher, one of the retired founders of the North West Company, created the Montreal Water Works Company in April 1801 to divert spring water down from Mount Royal through bored tree trunks.

Two years later an accidental fire consumed the stately Collège Saint-Raphaël (the former Château de Vaudreuil, once the residence of France's governors), as well as the Jesuit residence, part of the jail, and a score of houses. Municipal authorities decided not to allow the sector to be rebuilt, instead converting its cleared space into a much-needed public market named Place Jacques-Cartier. More significantly, the local brewer John Molson—who had emigrated from Lincolnshire in England a quarter century earlier and prospered handsomely—financed the construction of a steamboat, only two years after Robert Fulton's *Clermont* had sailed up the Hudson River from New York to Albany. The 75-foot paddle-boat *Accomodation* was launched just below Montreal in August 1809, steaming down to Quebec three months later to inaugurate a service that would dramatically improve the speed and volume of traffic.

Such progress was interrupted, though, in late June 1812,

when it was learned that Britain and the United States were once again at war, so that Montreal was likely to be invaded. Notwithstanding being heavily outnumbered, British and Canadian forces were able to fend off such a penetration until October 1813, when Maj.-Gen. James Wilkinson departed Sackets Harbor in New York State with 8,000 U.S. troops aboard 300 craft, pushing east along the Saint Lawrence to join Maj.-Gen. Wade Hampton, who crossed the border from Four Corners, New York, and pressed up the Châteauguay River with another 4,000 infantrymen, 200 dragoons, and ten field-pieces. On 26 October, however, Hampton was checked 14 miles short of Montreal by 1,650 well-entrenched Franco-Canadian troops under Swiss-born Maj.-Gen. Louis de Watteville and Lt.-Col. Charles Michel d'Irumberry de Salaberry. Despite suffering only fifty casualties, the U.S. commander retreated without informing his colleague Wilkinson, whose army was then overtaken near Cornwall, Ontario, by pursuing Anglo-Canadian columns and so badly mauled in the Battle of Crysler's Farm on 11 November that it too veered south into winter quarters two days later.

Montreal had been saved, and when hostilities ceased in 1815, its core population exceeded 15,000 residents, who soon resumed their former rapid growth and modernization. Water service was improved by drawing directly from the Saint Lawrence with steam pumps and distributing the flow through cast-iron pipes; private citizens also paid to hang twenty-two whale oil lamps along Saint-Paul Street, which service was extended into Notre-Dame Street by 1816. Municipal authorities assumed responsibility over lighting two years later, and the thirty lamplighters became night watchmen as well. Canada's first chartered banking institution—the Bank of Montreal—opened its doors on Saint-Paul Street in November 1817, almost half its capital having been raised from U.S. investors, while the British government furthermore purchased Île Sainte-Hélène next year and transformed it into a midriver stronghold by constructing barracks, arsenals, powder magazines, and so forth. Charitable donations funded the establishment of a general hospital on Craig Street (modern Sainte-Antoine Street) in 1819, while another such institution opened its doors three years later on Dorchester Street.

By 1820 the number of inhabitants had increased to 25,000, and outlying satellite communities were becoming increasingly populated—many members of high society preferring to live in the eastern and less crowded Faubourg Québec (Quebec Suburb), so called because it lay on the road leading toward the capital). In March 1821 an endowment left by McGill bequeathed

St. James' Club on Dorchester Street—modern René-Lévesque Boulevard—showing a horse-drawn sleigh on winter runners in the foreground, ca. 1875–1880. Many of the Victorian-era houses along this street were torn down during the city's urban expansion of the 1950s. (National Archives of Canada)

his Burnside estate on the lower slopes of Mount Royal, plus £10,000, for the creation of a college to bear his name. In July, work started on the 7-mile-long Lachine Canal to aid navigation; Citadel Hill was leveled that same year on orders from Gov.-Gen. George Ramsay, Earl of Dalhousie, to fill in a swamp at the end of Notre-Dame Street and extend the urban boundaries (in the process creating Dalhousie Square). The first cathedral—Saint-Jacques-le-Majeur—was commenced in May 1823 and completed twenty-eight months later at the corner of Saint-Denis and Sainte-Catherine streets, a magnificent episcopal palace being added later, designed by the architect John Ostell. Molson also financed construction of the Théâtre Royale, which opened shortly before Christmas 1825.

Montreal's population stood at 30,000 inhabitants by June 1832, when it was granted a royal charter of incorporation so that it could legally be recognized as a city and replace its old system of management by magistrates, with elected municipal councilors from eight wards. Unfortunately, the passenger vessel *Voyageur* arrived from Quebec that same month with Irish immigrants sick with cholera, unleashing a deadly epidemic that claimed an estimated 4,500 lives in the city before abating that autumn.

The next year, Jacques Viger was selected from among Montreal's councilors as its first mayor, but there remained much discontent against other outdated aspects of British imperial rule. The desire for more democratic representation was widely held, but with special acuteness among the half million French-Canadians scattered throughout the province, who resented their under-representation in Anglo-dominated institutions and felt increasingly marginalized by the recent waves of immigrants. Leaders such as Louis-Joseph Papineau therefore began identifying themselves as *patriotes* and appealed to their countrymen's pride, forming an association called the Société Saint-Jean-Baptiste in Montreal on 24 June 1834 to press for political and social reform. (Irish immigrants had already formed their own group on 17 March, the Saint Patrick's Society.)

The first Canadian railway—and fourth in all of North America—was inaugurated when a tiny locomotive chugged 14 miles south from Laprairie to Saint-Jean on 21 July 1836, initiating a notable improvement in commercial haulage with New York by bypassing the Chambly Rapids. That same year the city's first gas company was formed, its old kerosene street lamps being replaced by 1837; however, such gains were overshadowed by escalating political agitation and repression, climaxing in armed revolt.

Lower Canada Rebellion and Aftermath (1837–1866)

The growing number and size of political protests finally goaded Gov.-Gen. Archibald Acheson, Lord Gosford, into issuing a proclamation in mid-June 1837 that exhorted the public not to entertain any "seditious" notions. Antigovernment rhetoric nonetheless deepened, while some Anglo Tories

formed Loyalist countergroups. On 6 November a meeting of 5,000 *patriotes* on Saint-Jacques Street ended in clashes between ardent young French-Canadians called *Fils de la Liberté* (Sons of Liberty) and an Anglo countergroup called the Doric Club. Gosford responded by issuing arrest warrants for Papineau and *patriote* leaders only, a one-sided reaction that galvanized opposition throughout the surrounding countryside.

When twenty Anglo Tory militia troopers seized two wanted *patriotes* in Saint-Jean on the night of 16 November 1837, they were intercepted the next morning at Longueuil while riding back into Montreal by 150 rebels under Bonaventure Viger (a close relative of the city's first mayor), who freed the prisoners amid a hail of shots. Gen. Sir John Colborne, British commander-in-chief for Lower Canada, sent two columns to crush this apparent insurgency, the first—300 soldiers and a 12-pound howitzer under the elderly Col. Sir Charles Gore—reaching Saint-Denis early on 23 November after marching overnight from Sorel through a heavy snowstorm. They were obliged to withdraw by 800 poorly armed *patriotes* under Dr. Wolfred Nelson, who suffered twelve killed and seven injured, compared with six dead and ten wounded among the redcoats. Two days later a second British column of 425 men and two cannon from Chambly under Lt.-Col. George Augustus Wetherall reached the main rebel stronghold of Saint-Charles, overrunning its 200 to 250 *patriote* defenders under Thomas Storrow Brown while killing forty, wounding thirty, and capturing twenty-eight.

The waterfront, 1875; the opening of the Saint Lawrence River to oceangoing ships twenty years previously had greatly enhanced Montreal's development. (National Archives of Canada)

Gosford proclaimed martial law in Montreal on 5 December 1837, detaining so many *patriote* sympathizers that the newly completed Pied-du-Courant Prison and old jail on Notre-Dame Street were soon overflowing; an old building at Pointe-à-Callière therefore had to be pressed into service as well. Learning of another concentration of 800 to 900 rural dissenters north of the city at Saint-Eustache, Colborne led 1,280 British regulars, 220 Anglo Tory volunteers, and five field-pieces against them. When the British vanguard appeared on 14 December, the overconfident *patriote* defenders sallied across Saint-Eustache's frozen river, only to flee when Colborne's main force suddenly materialized behind them. Approximately 70 *patriotes* died and 100 were captured, after which Colborne destroyed neighboring Saint-Benoit the following day, effectively bringing an end to all armed resistance as *patriote* leaders fled into the United States.

During that ensuing winter, 112 insurgents were tried before a military tribunal, 12 being condemned to death, 58 sentenced to exile in Bermuda or Australia, 30 released on bail, and a dozen acquitted; another 500 detainees were eventually amnestied in April 1838. A second *patriote* uprising south of Montreal in early November of that same year failed because of a lack of weaponry, as well as internal dissension and effective Loyalist opposition. Yet the dissatisfaction underlying such outbursts prompted London to send a royal representative to Montreal to investigate local grievances and propose a constitutional solution. The result was Westminster's passage of the Act of Union in February 1841, which brought Lower and Upper Canada together into a single and more equitable government.

Gov.-Gen. Charles Poulett Thomson had in the meantime handpicked Montreal's councilors from among the city's Anglo elite, who in turn selected the wealthy Peter McGill as mayor. He overhauled the municipal taxation system and ushered in a vigorous program of public works intended to improve roads, markets, and the water supply. Yet when open elections were once again held in 1842, the 40,000 residents—more than 50 percent now being English speakers—nonetheless elected a majority of French-Canadian councilors, and Joseph Bourret as mayor. Sufficient stability was restored to commence dredging a ship channel in May 1844, as well as construction of a lavish new municipal building and market (Bonsecours Market) that same September; in addition, the new Canadian legislature was transferred from Kingston into Montreal by November. The city was struck by a calamitous typhus epidemic in the spring and summer of 1847 that claimed 6,000 lives, yet its first telegraph line also went into operation by August of that same year and a new railway line was inaugurated around the Lachine Rapids by November.

Unfortunately, legislative sessions were disrupted on 18 January 1849 when reformist Gov.-Gen. James Bruce, Lord Elgin, announced that French would once again be employed in Lower Canada's official texts; that exiled *patriote* leaders would

be amnestied; and that all citizens would be compensated for their losses during the recent rebellion, regardless of their faction. Some Anglos angrily complained that such a measure treated Loyalists and rebels alike, rewarding even those guilty of attempting to overthrow the government; a riot consequently ensued, and arsonists torched the legislative building that night. The assembly consequently met behind a screen of soldiers the next day and voted to forsake Montreal in favor of Toronto.

Despite losing its status as British Canada's capital, the city continued to flourish, especially after the vigorous Scottish-born John Young was nominated to Montreal's Harbour Commission in 1850 and improved dredging operations so dramatically—principally by directing that the natural channel of the Saint Lawrence River's clay bed be followed—that oceangoing ships would soon be berthing directly at city wharves. That same year of 1850, Montreal's two railway companies also merged and initiated construction of a new line running from Kahnawake to the U.S. border, greatly augmenting traffic volumes. The city's charter was amended the following year so that mayors could be directly elected by voters, rather than from among its councilors, and a hardware store owner from Coteau-du-Lac named Charles Wilson was duly voted into office. A new reservoir was furthermore opened in June 1851 at the top of Côte à Baron (the section of Saint-Denis between Sherbrooke and Ontario) to better meet the needs of what were now 60,000 urban residents.

Tragically, the reservoir had been temporarily drained so that water mains might be installed when a fire broke out on 8 July 1852 on Sainte-Catherine Street, between Saint-Laurent and Saint-Dominique. Gusting westerly winds quickly propelled the blaze through the city, utterly destroying the neighborhoods of Saint-Jacques, Saint-Louis, Sainte-Marie, and part of Montreal East, before burning out the next day at Pied-du-Courant (De Lorimier Street). Some 1,100 homes—roughly a quarter of the city's total—had been reduced to smoldering ruins, including Notre-Dame Basilica, the bishop's palace, and Molson's brewery; 10,000 people were left homeless, so that tents were erected for those unable to find shelter among family or friends. In response to this catastrophe, Wilson and his council decided to finance a new aqueduct, which began pumping water from the Lachine Rapids into a reservoir at McTavish Street four years later. (Although a distinct improvement over previous efforts, it was found that this new aqueduct became blocked by ice during winter.)

Montreal was able to recuperate thanks to its ever-growing commerce, the first transatlantic steamship arriving in the spring of 1853, inaugurating regular oceanic service. Rail links also expanded, a new line to ice-free Portland, Maine, going into service by June of that same year, while the following month construction of the Victoria Bridge commenced under the supervision of the famous engineer James Hodges, seeking to span the milewide Saint Lawrence. Not even a

Panoramic view across the city, ca. 1851, with Craig—modern Saint-Antoine—Street in the foreground. The distant spires marked the Congregationalist and Saint Andrew's churches, as well as the Catholic cathedral at the corner of Saint-Denis and Sainte-Catherine streets. (National Archives of Canada)

cholera epidemic, which struck in 1854 and claimed more than 1,000 lives within two months, could deflect the city's revival. A new courthouse was opened by May 1855, while Molson's Bank was founded that same October, and rail service with Toronto began with a torch-lit parade and banquet for 4,000 people at Point Saint-Charles in October 1856.

By the time Victoria Bridge opened to rail traffic in 1860, Montreal's population had swollen to 90,000 residents, making it the tenth-largest city in North America. This expansion entailed some problems, however, as spring ice thaws now threatened its built-up areas. When the Saint Lawrence rose more than 20 feet in 1861, a quarter of the urban area was flooded, many streets being inundated so swiftly that people abandoned their possessions, while worshippers stranded in Saint Stephen's Church on Dalhousie Square and the Wesleyan Chapel on Ottawa Street had to be rescued by boats. Still, the hardy residents shrugged off such setbacks, and that same summer the first horse-drawn streetcars were introduced by a private company, whose shareholders included William Molson and John Ostell. (During snowy winter months, this service required the use of sleighs.) A professional fire department was moreover established in 1862, with thirty-five hydrants and an alarm system distributed throughout the city.

Confederation and Modernization (1867–1966)

The legislatures of Nova Scotia, New Brunswick, and Prince Edward Island hosted a conference at Charlottetown in the summer of 1864 that forged a union from their individual Maritime Provinces, then they in turn were joined by a delegation from Upper and Lower Canada to suggest a national confederation. After lengthy debate, this measure was approved by all five bodies at a second conference held in Quebec City that same October, subsequently winning a favorable vote from Parliament in London.

Canada peaceably became an independent nation as of 1 July 1867, and Montreal continued to prosper as its leading city. The first streets were paved with tarmac in 1870, while other urban amenities for its 115,000 citizens also appeared: its first golf club, for instance, was founded three years later, while a team from McGill University played one of the first intercollegiate football games against Harvard in 1874. (Seven years later, McGill students and members of the Victoria Club also codified rules for the game of ice hockey.)

Of more practical benefit, the first catchment sewers were dug under Craig Street in 1875, improving health standards; a grand new *Palais Municipal* (city hall) was completed three years later; the first telephones were installed by 1879; rail lines continued to multiply; and so many new industries sprang up that Mayor Jean-Louis Beaudry even annexed the neighboring municipality of Hochelaga in 1883, so as to allow Montreal to expand beyond its ancient boundaries. This appropriation started a trend, and the metropolis absorbed an average of one town a year as it sprawled outward over the next four decades, altering the city's linguistic composition as these outlying rural communities were almost invariably French speaking; thus Montreal's Anglophone percentage dwindled from almost 50 percent in the early 1880s to 25 percent by 1920.

A smallpox epidemic claimed 3,164 lives in 1885, then heavy flooding occurred the next April. Still, progress could not be stemmed. The first Pacific-bound train departed on 28 June 1886 toward the distant Rockies, so that Montreal became the headquarters and railhead for the powerful Canadian Pacific Railway Company, whose Angus Shops—an industrial complex in the city's east end named after the financier Richard Bladworth Angus—eventually employed 5,000 workers. Montreal's first electric streetlights were illuminated on 17 July 1886 (despite the rival gas lamp company's assertion that such lighting would be detrimental to women's complexions), and the population stood at a robust 216,650 people by 1891. The city was now receiving a daily average of 130 trains, plus 6,000 annual ships, 725 from overseas; its first electric streetcar ran in September 1892, while the single-track Victoria Bridge across the Saint Lawrence was doubled in width seven years later.

Urban boundaries continued to expand as municipal authorities purchased Saint Helen's Island from the federal government in 1907, converting the small park that had been leased there ever since the nineteenth century into a much larger sanctuary, accessible by ferry. Digging also commenced in July and August 1912 at opposite ends of a railway tunnel through Mount Royal for a northward-running line envisaged by the private entrepreneurs William Mackenzie and Donald Mann; this passage—considered a remarkable engineering feat by the technological standards of that era—was com-

McGill Street, looking southward from Notre-Dame Street, during the spring flood of April 1886. (National Archives of Canada)

pleted when a train chugged into the terminal on Dorchester Street (modern René-Lévesque Boulevard) on 10 December 1913, inaugurating regular service out of the model town of Mount Royal. The Sulpician Order the next May finished a grand new library—the Bibliothèque Saint-Sulpice, which would later evolve into the Bibliothèque Nationale du Québec—and encouraged the city fathers to found a municipal library as well.

When World War I broke out in Europe in August 1914, Canada immediately joined the Allied cause as a member of the British Empire, although French-Canadian sentiments were more lukewarm; notwithstanding the invasion of France, their long insularity had made them detached from such distant conflicts. Individual Montrealers nonetheless volunteered and fought bravely in such famous units as the 22nd Regiment, but casualty figures eventually rose so high that the Conservative government of Prime Minister Robert Borden in Ottawa had to reverse its campaign pledge and introduce national conscription in July 1917. That act provoked violent protests in the city (including an attempt on the night of 8 August to blow up Elmwood, the sumptuous Cartierville estate of Hugh Graham, Lord Atholstand, owner of the Montreal *Star* and a vocal British imperialist).

The city nevertheless prospered as a manufacturing and transportation hub throughout the war, airmail service being inaugurated when Brian A. Peck took off in a JN-4 Curtiss on 24 June 1918 from a polo field used by amateur flying clubs at Bois-Francs to deliver 120 letters to Toronto—pausing twice en route to refuel, then landing at Leaside to drive the mailbag into the main post office. More grievously, an epidemic called the "Spanish influenza"—because it was first detected in Spain—reached Montreal that same year when the Indian vessel *Somali* arrived with two sick crew members on 19 July; despite being quarantined off distant Grosse-Île, it infected the general population by late September and caused more than 3,000 deaths.

The first city buses appeared in 1919, proving more economical and flexible than streetcars in servicing the many disperse neighborhoods. The next year, the wooden carriageway of the old Victoria Bridge was badly damaged by fire, so that thousands of commuters had to be shuttled back and forth across the Saint Lawrence by the steamer *Longueuil,* an inconvenience that roused demands for a better span. The result was to be Harbour Bridge—now known as the Jacques-Cartier Bridge—whose construction commenced in May 1925. Occasional fires, and a flood in the Village Turcot area on 17

Aerial photograph of the inauguration of Harbour Bridge on Île Sainte-Hélène in the Saint Lawrence River, 24 May 1930, looking northward across the east end of Montreal; this span was renamed the Jacques-Cartier Bridge during Canada's 400th anniversary celebrations four years later. (National Archives of Canada)

November 1927, also galvanized efforts at further urban improvements. The decades-old bylaw forbidding structures taller than 130 feet was rescinded that same year, allowing for the first skyscrapers to appear and encouraging the drive toward modernization.

Progress was abruptly curtailed by the Great Depression of October 1929, which closed scores of plants throughout Montreal and left thousands unemployed. The government attempted to ease the crisis by massive public works projects, including the completion in June 1934 of a third span across the Saint Lawrence—the Honoré-Mercier Bridge—to service the city's west end from Ville LaSalle across to Kahnawake. Slowly, the global economy revived, although the greatest impetus to Montreal's recovery was to be provided by the outbreak of World War II in early September 1939.

Again, French Canadian volunteers flocked to join the two local regiments (the Fusiliers Mont-Royal and Régiment de Maisonneuve), although the region as a whole showed itself less committed to the struggle than their Anglo compatriots—especially after the fall of France in June 1940 and the emergence of the collaborationist Vichy regime. Montreal's rightist mayor, Camillien Houde, even expressed such vocal opposition to Ottawa's national registration drive—seen as a prelude to conscription—that he was arrested at City Hall on the morning of 5 August and shipped to an internment camp. Montreal nonetheless remained calm and served as a manufacturing center and transportation crossroads for the duration of these hostilities, profiting accordingly.

When World War II ended in 1945, Montreal gradually began a concerted drive toward its modern configuration. Six years later the population within its urban boundaries was measured at 1,021,520 residents (64 percent identifying themselves as being of French origin, 22 percent British, 5 percent Jewish, and 9 percent from other nationalities); outlying suburbs and enclosed municipalities such as Verdun, Outremonte, Westmount, and Mount Royal contained an additional 374,000 people. Anglos tended to be clustered in the best residential area below the mountain, especially in Westmount and Notre-Dame-de-Grace, while several eastern wards near the river were almost entirely Francophone. The Montreal Transportation Commission was formed in June of that same year to overhaul public transit, and urban redevelopment gathered headway after lands were expropriated in 1958 for the construction of Place Ville-Marie, a beautiful complex of downtown offices and shops that were to form the new city core.

A construction boom followed during the early 1960s under the vigorous leadership of Mayor Jean Drapeau, a fourth span—the Champlain Bridge—linking Montreal to the south shore of the Saint Lawrence by June 1962, while the city was furthermore selected to host the World's Fair the following March, launching a massive four-year effort to prepare for that event. Île Sainte-Hélène was artificially united with Moffat's Island, Île Verte, Île Ronde, plus the wholly new Île Notre-

Dame, to produce a single connected parkland on which pavilions might be erected; landfill was provided by the already ongoing Metro subway project, completed in October 1966. The World's Fair opened the next April, proving to be a great success, the only discordant note occurring when President Charles de Gaulle of France visited in May 1967 and—carried away by effusive greetings from an ecstatic Francophone crowd—shouted in reply from Montreal's city hall balcony: *Vive le Québec libre!* (Long Live Free Quebec!).

Current Events (1967–Present)

French-Canadian nationalism had revived strongly since World War II, many Quebecers now wishing to emerge from their previous insularity. Resentful of Anglo domination, some even sought secession from Canada, while a few extremists detonated letter bombs in the English enclave of Westmount. De Gaulle's outburst was therefore regarded as an unwelcome inducement to such secessionists by the federal authorities in Ottawa, who abruptly curtailed the president's visit. Yet violent acts by fringe groups within the separatist movement escalated over the next few years, until a senior British trade commissioner named James Richard Cross was kidnapped in Montreal on 5 October 1970 by armed members of a group calling itself the Front de Libération du Québec (Front for the Liberation of Quebec, better known by its acronym FLQ).

Their demands included a ransom of $500,000 in gold, freedom for twenty-six "political prisoners," safe passage out of the country, and publication of a quasi-Marxist mishmash of grievances. Five days later, Quebec's provincial labor and immigration minister, Pierre Laporte, was also snatched from in front of his home, deepening the sense of shock. Although there was virtually no public support for the kidnappers' methods, opinion makers among the new French-speaking news media, the trade unions, and the political elite were divided as to how to resolve the crisis. Prominent figures such as René Lévesque, leader of the mainstream separatist Parti Québécois, and *Le Devoir* newspaper publisher Claude Ryan, issued a statement on 14 October 1970 calling for an "exchange of the two hostages for the political prisoners"; at the same time, radical students called for a strike in support of the FLQ.

Fearing that the situation was spiraling out of control, the provincial premier, Robert Bourassa, the next day asked the federal prime minister, Pierre-Elliot Trudeau, to send troops into Montreal and Quebec City. The War Measures Act—a 1914 statute giving the authorities extraordinary powers to arrest anyone deemed a threat to public order—was proclaimed on 16 October 1970, and more than 250 individuals were detained that first day. Polls in Quebec and Canada showed enormous support for Trudeau, but the FLQ responded by murdering their captive Laporte on 17 October, his body being found in the trunk of a car in the Montreal suburb of Saint-Hubert. Troops remained in the city until a negotiated deal finally freed

Panoramic view of the city as seen from atop Mont-Royal in 1865, with the Saint Lawrence River and Victoria Bridge visible in the far distance. (National Archives of Canada)

Cross on 3 December, allowing his kidnappers to go into exile in Communist Cuba; Laporte's murderers were caught by the police on 28 December.

This incident besmirched the reputation of the separatist movement, at a time when Montreal's status as the largest and most influential city in Canada was being challenged by Toronto. Commercial shipping patterns had begun to shift as far back as 26 June 1959, when Queen Elizabeth II and President Dwight D. Eisenhower of the United States had jointly inaugurated the Saint Lawrence Seaway, a series of deep-water locks and canals extending hundreds of miles inland, that allowed oceangoing ships to sail directly into the Great Lakes to unload or receive cargoes. Although Montreal's highly developed infrastructure prevented any immediate decline in its fortunes, and the city successfully hosted such events as the summer Olympic Games in 1976, its preeminent trading position was nonetheless being bypassed.

That trend accelerated after Lévesque's Parti Québécois was elected into office in the 1980s, so worrying financial institutions and international corporations—notwithstanding the premier's more restrained calls for a quasi-separatist "sovereignty-association" with the rest of Canada—that they began transferring their business operations elsewhere. Montreal nonetheless remained a rich and diverse metropolis, its population within the old city limits being virtually unchanged at 1,017,666 inhabitants by 1991, although the greater metropolitan area now encompassed a total of 3,127,424 people. As of 1 January 2002, the twenty-eight diverse municipalities still existing on the island of Montreal were reorganized into a single administrative entity.

For additional sources on Montreal urban history, please consult the Select Bibliography at the end of this volume.

QUEBEC CITY

Seaport set upon a major inland waterway, which for centuries linked Atlantic traffic with the interior of North America.

Initial Contacts (1535–1543)

During his second exploration of the continental coastline in search of a "northwest passage" leading toward Asia, the Frenchman Jacques Cartier entered a broad gulf on 10 August 1535 that he christened "Saint-Lawrence Bay"—being that particular feast day on the Church calendar—then was piloted deeper upstream by two young Hurons, who assured him that it was "the great river of *Hochelaga* [modern Montreal] and road to *Canada* [actually an indigenous term denoting any sizable community]." After probing for 300 miles, Cartier and a boat party reconnoitered past a large island on 8 September that he dubbed Île d'Orléans in honor of King François I's son Charles, Duc d'Orléans; 4 miles beyond, he sighted "a forking of the waters, fair and pleasant" that was dominated by a 333-foot-high promontory towering above a village named Stadaconé. Its populace greeted him with songs and speeches.

Crude wooden engraving of l'Habitation at Quebec, based upon an original drawing by Champlain. (*Les Voyages du Sieur de Champlain,* 1613)

Realizing that penetrating beyond this milewide strait could not be accomplished by ship, Cartier decided to return to his anchored trio of vessels and secure them in the small and shallow harbor beside Stadaconé, fed by a Saint Lawrence tributary that he dubbed the Sainte-Croix River (modern Saint-Charles). Therefore, his 120-ton flagship *Grande Hermine* and 60-ton *Petite Hermine* were weighed on 14 September 1535, to be gingerly warped past Île d'Orléans and into this "port of Sainte-Croix" two days later, after which the 40-ton *Émerillon* towed Cartier's boat parties farther up the Saint Lawrence on 19 September. The crews of both anchored ships meanwhile erected a log fort ashore and installed artillery, where Cartier's group rejoined them on 11 October, having visited Hochelaga.

The 110 Frenchmen spent that ensuing winter ensconced near Stadaconé, their vessels becoming immobilized by thick ice as of mid-November 1535, after which twenty-five members succumbed to scurvy and the harsh living conditions before spring finally brought a thaw in mid-April 1536. While preparing to depart on his homeward passage toward France, Cartier lured Stadaconé's friendly chieftain Donnaconna into his stockade on 3 May—the feast day of the Holy Cross—on the pretext of attending a ceremonial erection of a wooden cross bearing a Latin inscription and the arms of France, then kidnapped the chief, his two sons, and a few other Indians to be conveyed as curiosities before François I. *Grande Hermine* and *Émerillon* set sail for Saint-Malo three days later, *Petite Hermine* having been abandoned.

Delays occasioned by an outburst of Franco-Spanish hostilities in Europe did not permit Cartier to regain Stadaconé until 23 August 1541, accompanied by an advance contingent of settlers aboard five ships who were to establish a toehold in anticipation of a larger colonizing expedition under the Huguenot (French Protestant) nobleman Jean-François de La Rocque, Seigneur de Roberval—newly appointed lieutenant-general of Canada. Although not ill received by Stadaconé's inhabitants, Cartier's party nonetheless pressed 9 miles farther up the Saint Lawrence to Cap-Rouge, where mineral samples were gathered to be sped back toward France aboard two ships; the few score settlers meanwhile disembarked their livestock, planted seeds, and cleared a palisaded compound called Charlesbourg-Royal. Cartier ventured farther upriver on 7 September but returned a few weeks later to find that the Hurons were no longer as friendly. Over that ensuing winter, thirty-five Frenchmen died in ambushes outside the stockade, so that when Roberval's reinforcements failed to materialize the next spring, Cartier razed his camp and sailed away in early June 1542.

Despite chancing upon Roberval's belated trio of ships and several hundred more colonists in Saint John's harbor (Newfoundland), Cartier and his disheartened survivors refused to reverse course. Undismayed, Roberval's contingent reached the ruined Charlesbourg-Royal site by the end of July 1542—without having paused at Stadaconé—and reestablished that outpost under the name of France-Roy. After suffering through yet another bitter winter, though, during which about fifty of his party died, Roberval made a half-hearted probe inland the following spring, then withdrew altogether with his survivors. France was not to regain a presence in these northern climes until the very end of that century, when a fur-trading base was licensed farther down the Saint Lawrence River at Tadoussac.

Tentative Foothold (1608–1631)

Samuel de Champlain visited Tadoussac and explored up the Saint Lawrence again in the summer of 1603, noting that the indigenous communities at Stadaconé and Hochelaga had in the interim disappeared. After an abortive attempt to create a coastal settlement at modern Annapolis Royal (Nova Scotia), Champlain persuaded his superior, Pierre du Guast, Sieur de Monts, to finance a new trading outpost up the Saint Lawrence. Given command over a ship and some artisans, Champlain reached Tadoussac by 3 June 1608, then exactly one month later arrived off Cartier's old Stadaconé anchorage and:

> searched for a suitable place for our residence [*habitation*], and I did not find any more convenient, nor better sited than *Quebecq* Point—so called by the savages—which was covered with walnut trees. I immediately employed a party of our workers in felling them, so as to make our dwelling.

The resultant strong-house (located not far from what would later become the Church of Notre-Dame-des-Victoires) took the remainder of that year to complete, becoming known simply as l'Habitation. Sixteen of Champlain's twenty-five companions died during that ensuing winter, yet he refused to be deterred, setting out the next spring to reconnoiter a vast expanse of territory, and even winning a battle near present-day Ticonderoga (New York) against the Iroquois, traditional foes of his Huron and Algonquin allies.

Leaving Pierre Chauvin, Sieur de la Pierre, in command at Quebec, Champlain returned to France in the autumn of 1609 to seek reinforcements, reappearing the following spring for further barter and campaigns. He repeated this procedure over the next several years, making annual transatlantic peregrinations to shore up his wilderness base, which remained dependent upon Tadoussac for most of its supplies. On 8 October 1612 the boy-king Louis XIII enhanced the private colony's status by appointing the nobleman Charles de Courbon, Comte de Soissons, as titular viceroy of New France, with Champlain becoming its subordinate lieutenant-general shortly thereafter. The tireless pioneer also helped create com-

mercial companies at Rouen and Saint-Malo two years later to market the furs that were being exported out of Canada.

Quebec began to evolve into something beyond a lone trading outpost when Champlain returned in the spring of 1615 with four Récollet missionaries from Rouen—Denis Jamet, Joseph Le Caron, Jean Dolbeau, and Pacifique Duplessis—who celebrated its first Mass on 25 June, then started their own separate chapel and residence in the Saint-Charles Valley. Champlain also reappeared on 11 July 1616 after wintering among the Hurons and ordered l'Habitation expanded before sailing on his annual trip to France nine days later. Louis Hébert reached the Quebec compound in 1617 and planted the first crops on the 8-mile expanse of flatlands above l'Habitation, as well as serving as apothecary to its tiny community; his wife, Marie Rollet, taught school.

Champlain and the Récollets attempted to recruit farmers from France for a new settlement farther up the Saint-Charles Valley to be called Ludovica, but its town plots went unclaimed.

Modern panorama northeastward across the core of Quebec City's upper town, demonstrating its dominant position overlooking the Saint Lawrence River. (Tourism Department, Ville de Québec)

Consequently, when Champlain returned with his young bride, Marie-Hélène Boullé, in the spring of 1620, he initiated construction of a small log redoubt on the escarpment above L'Habitation, despite complaints from company directors on the far side of the Atlantic as to this unwarranted expense. A few municipal ordinances and a simple judicial system were also enacted for the community at Quebec, although it consisted of only fifty residents by 1622.

Next year, Hébert—now promoted to *procureur du Roi* or king's attorney—received extensive grants of flatlands above the settlement (around the future basilica and seminary in the Upper Town, plus Hébert and Couillard streets, the latter named for his son-in-law Guillaume Couillard, Sieur de Lespinay). A steeply winding road up to the redoubt was completed by 23 November 1623 that—along with the Habitation—was torn down and replaced by larger structures as of

1624. The first Jesuit missionaries—Jean de Brébeuf, Enemond Massé, and Charles Lalemant, plus the lay brothers François Charton and Gilbert Burel—arrived in June 1625, being assigned the already existing seigncy of Notre-Dame-des-Anges the next year.

Louis XIII's chief minister, Cardinal Armand-Jean du Plessis de Richelieu, reorganized the colony's private ownership in Paris into a Compagnie des Cent-Associés (Company of the Hundred Associates) in 1627 but was unable to dispatch timely assistance to Quebec's seventy isolated *hivernants*— that is, "winter residents" or year-round inhabitants—before hostilities with England erupted the next year. As a result, a three-ship privateering expedition materialized from Boston under the brothers David and Lewis Kirke, ravaging hapless Tadoussac and Cap-Tourment before appearing off Quebec in the spring of 1628 to demand Champlain's surrender. He

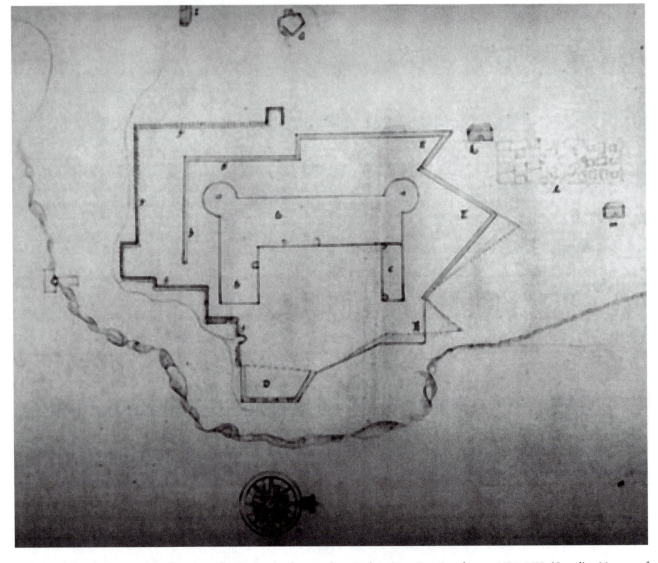

Diagram of the rebuilt *Magasin* or "Storehouse" at Quebec, by the recently arrived engineer Jean Bourdon, ca. 1634–1635. (Canadian Museum of Civilization)

refused, so the Kirkes withdrew but captured the annual relief convoy from France on 18 July.

The Kirkes were therefore easily able to subdue Tadoussac upon resuming their offensive the next spring, then intercepted a lone French relief ship under Émery de Caën, before dispatching three vessels under Lewis and Thomas Kirke to compel Champlain finally to capitulate his starving Quebec garrison on 19 July 1629. Next day, Thomas Kirke came ashore with 150 men to oversee the outpost's evacuation, officially installing an English administration under his brother Lewis by 22 July. All French company officials and Catholic missionaries were to be repatriated via London; Champlain and the first batch of deportees reached Tadoussac by 1 August, followed by a second group that departed Quebec on 9 September. A few dozen French inhabitants remained behind as English subjects, suffering through a lonely winter, while Kirke's garrison lost fourteen men as a result of disease and want.

Resurrection (1632–1662)

Less than three years later, Quebec was restored to French control by the terms of the treaty signed at Saint-Germain-en-Laye on 29 March 1632, so that a forty-man contingent reached the outpost and supplanted its English occupiers. De Caën temporarily assumed office as acting lieutenant-general until Champlain could return with more colonists on 22 May 1633. In gratitude for their colony's recuperation, the French initiated construction of Notre-Dame-de-la-Recouvrance (Our Lady of the Recovery) Chapel atop the Cap-Diamant promontory, then channeled the bulk of renewed company support into the redevelopment of Quebec rather than Tadoussac, which had proven to be more vulnerable to enemy attacks.

L'Habitation, now referred to as the Vieux Magasin (Old Storehouse), was consequently rebuilt, yet most of the community's expansion occurred beyond its immediate vicinity. The doctor Robert Giffard, Sieur de Moncel, for example, was granted extensive holdings at Beauport on the far banks of the Saint-Charles River in 1634, while the fifteen-year veteran resident Abraham Martin—nicknamed L'Ecossais, or "The Scotsman"—received more of the flatlands around Cap-Diamant the next year, which thus became known as the Plains of Abraham.

When Champlain died on Christmas Day 1635, he was succeeded as private governor and lieutenant-general by Charles Huault, Sieur de Montmagny, who arrived from France on 11 June 1636 with instructions from the company to transform Quebec from a cluster of disperse dwellings into a community capable of evolving into a future city. Although Montmagny was able to assert the company monopoly over the riverfront area around L'Habitation, his task proved somewhat more difficult atop the heights. Painstakingly, he had to exchange outlying properties with the Hébert-Couillard families, as well as various religious orders, in order to clear a central core to lay out a street plan radiating from the old log redoubt, which he began to rebuild in masonry as Fort Saint-Louis.

Three Urseline nuns arrived from Tours under Marie-Madeleine de Chauvigny de La Peltrie on 1 August 1639 to found a vast convent compound on the promontory, completed two years later (between modern Saint-Louis, des Jardins, Sainte-Anne, and Sainte-Ursule streets), as well as a small contingent of Augustinian Hospitalers under Marie Guenet, Mère de Saint-Ignace, who established a *hôtel-dieu* (or charity hospital) 2 miles upriver at the new satellite community called Sillery. Quebec itself, however, proved slow to coalesce, most *engagés* (or indentured) workers sent out by the company preferring to migrate elsewhere once their contracts expired. Two years afterward, Montmagny even tried to persuade the colonizing expedition of Paul de Chomedey, Sieur de Maisonneuve—destined to found Montreal, 180 miles farther inland—to instead accept properties around Quebec. Hostilities with the Iroquois erupted shortly thereafter, adding to the sense of unease throughout New France as numerous Huron villages and Jesuit missions were exterminated.

Quebec's status improved after the company allowed a colonial council to be created in 1647, whose sessions attracted business and visitors into town and justified the foundation of its wooden Notre-Dame Cathedral, as well as the expansion of Fort Saint-Louis into a much larger stone castle and governor's residence called Château Saint-Louis, as well as the erection of a vast new trade storehouse in 1648. Still, the Jesuit priest Raguenau wrote derisively two years later

Modern rendering of the map of the spreading city in 1660, by Bourdon; north is toward upper right. The Urseline convent to its west-southwest had been rebuilt following an accidental fire on 30 December 1650, while the low wooden hospital to its northwest had been completed in 1654. (National Archives of Canada)

about this rough-hewn, backwater community's pretensions as a capital, dismissing Quebec as "a miserable burgh of some thirty scattered houses"; Marguerite Bourgeoys reported shortly after her own disembarkation in September 1651: "Everything is so poor as to cause pity."

Renewed Iroquois offensives added to the residents' fears within their unfortified settlement, while economic misery deepened as fur trading became paralyzed. When François de Montmorency Laval landed as New France's "apostolic vicar" on 16 June 1659, he counted scarcely 1,200 people in the entire colony, of whom approximately 550 lived around Quebec, mostly crowded into seventy dwellings in its Basse Ville (Lower Town) and a few more scattered upon its heights. Many structures suffered considerable damage from an earthquake that struck on 5 February 1663.

Entrenchment (1663–1689)

That same spring, the new monarch, Louis XIV, and his chief minister Jean-Baptiste Colbert—disappointed by the meager benefits derived from France's privately owned overseas colonies—decided to impose direct Crown rule over all such possessions in the New World; thus Augustin de Saffray, Sieur de Mézy, disembarked at Quebec on 15 September 1663 as its first royal governor. Joyous citizens attempted to elevate their community to the status of a town by electing a mayor and two aldermen, but that act was voided a month later because of their meager numbers.

All French colonies were united under a single administrative rule the next year when Alexandre de Prouville, Marquis de Tracy—bearing the titles of civilian governor-general and military lieutenant-general—toured the island outposts of the Antilles, then reached Quebec on 30 June 1665 with 650 new settlers and four companies of troops. Eleven days previously, more of what would prove to be a total of 1,000 soldiers of the Carnigan-Salières Regiment had also begun disembarking from France, providing the Canadian colony with its first significant military force. An intendant (civilian administrator) named Jean Talon moreover arrived on 12 September.

Thanks to those reinforcements, the town population jumped to 747 inhabitants by 1666 (91 being clerics), and the energetic Talon invigorated and diversified its economy through the importation of looms to produce thread and cloth, as well as by encouraging the manufacture of boats, ropes, cordage, shoes, hats, tar, potash, and soap, plus the cultivation of hemp, flax, hops—for a brewery he established—and many other edibles. A limited form of parish government called *syndicat municipal* was also introduced for the town in 1667, while the next year the intendant furthermore persuaded the Crown to disband the Carnigan-Salières Regiment in New France rather than upon its return to Europe, so as to augment the colony's sparse population base, as well as to transport out 1,000 *filles du Roi* (king's wards—that is, orphan girls) to marry among the largely male society. Talon proved

so excellent an administrator that he was reappointed for a second term from August 1670 to November 1672, during which time he developed a significant shipbuilding facility at Quebec, plus a sawmill and two brickyards.

By now, a seasonal routine had evolved whereby once the spring floods of melting snow and ice receded, fur traders and Indians congregated in the town to participate in the commercial fair, which was celebrated when the annual supply convoy arrived from France at the end of July. Royal officials and the garrison received their payrolls and provisions on that occasion, as well as stipends for the religious orders, while lesser residents profited by serving as boatmen, stevedores, teamsters, innkeepers, warehousemen, retailers, shipwrights, tanners, smiths, and the like. Outlying farmers and ranchers also sold their produce to this concurrence in an assigned marketplace every Tuesday and Friday—according to the municipal reorganization of 1676—rather than roaming unsupervised through the streets. Activities tapered off with the departure of the last transatlantic merchantman at the end of October or early November, prior to the onset of winter. For year-round residents, the ensuing months of cold would be brightened every February by a carnival (a tradition maintained after an exceptionally felicitous ball hosted in 1667 by Louis-Théandre Chartier de Lotbinière).

Economic troubles gripped the town when overseas traffic from La Rochelle and Bordeaux was disrupted during the Franco-Dutch hostilities of 1672–1678; then a devastating fire swept through the tightly packed lower town on 4 August 1682, reducing fifty-five edifices to ashes. Henceforth, the *colombage* (half-timbered) architectural style was to give way gradually to more fire-resistant stone structures, and although Montreal surpassed Quebec in size around that same time, the capital of New France nonetheless regained sufficient commercial vigor that its population could grow from 1,354 inhabitants in 1683 to 1,611 only two years later.

In order to free up lots in the core of the burgeoning Haute Ville (Upper Town)—increasingly attractive because it was less prone to springtime floods—the old cliff-top battery above L'Habitation was shifted down to Pointe-aux-Roches, directly beside the Cul-de-Sac anchorage at the base of the escarpment, eventually becoming known as the Batterie Royale. Construction of a grand new *Intendance* (intendant's palace) was also undertaken on the northwestern side of the Upper Town, overlooking the Saint-Charles River.

Fortification (1690–1711)

Frictions with rival traders pushing into North America's hinterland out of New England contributed to the outbreak of the War of the League of Augsburg in the summer of 1689, remembered among Anglo-Americans as King William's War. After vainly awaiting arms and ammunition from London, Gov. Sir William Phips set sail from Massachusetts on 19 August 1690 with 2,000 volunteers aboard thirty-two vessels,

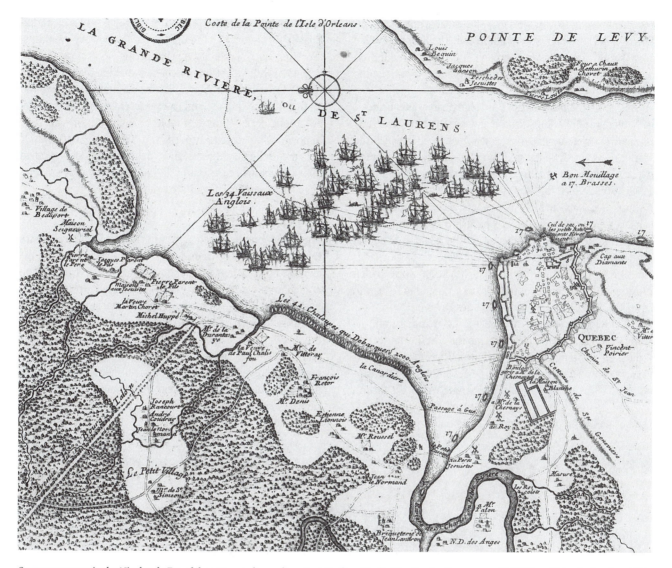

Contemporary print by Nicolas de Fer of the attempted assault against Quebec City by New England's governor, Sir William Phips, in October 1690; north is toward the left. (Bibliothèque Nationale de Québec)

determined to assault New France's capital in concert with another large force of militia and Indians advancing up the Hudson River against Montreal. Hampered by a lack of knowledgeable pilots, however, Phips's expedition did not grope within sight of Quebec until 15 October.

Its garrison of fewer than 200 troops and twelve guns under the seventy-year-old Gov. Louis de Buade, Comte de Frontenac et Palluau, had recently been reinforced from Montreal, as the Americans' Hudson River thrust had turned back. Phips, his men now racked by smallpox, anchored 3 miles below Quebec and sent an officer to demand its surrender on 16 October 1690, which Frontenac refused. Next morning, Phips forged upriver with four ships to create a diversion by bombarding the battlements, while 1,300 New Englanders were disembarked at Beauport under Maj. John Walley. But Phips's wooden ships were promptly obliged to retreat, while

Walley's poorly accoutered troops suffered intensely from the cold and re-embarked by 22 October. The entire expedition withdrew when heavy gales blew up a few days later, being swept back out to sea by blinding snowstorms.

The exultant defenders renamed their incomplete Church of Saint-Enfant-Jésus—whose cornerstone had been laid only on 1 May 1688—as Notre-Dame-de-la-Victoire (Our Lady of the Victory) to commemorate this providential deliverance, then turned to strengthening their capital's defenses through such measures as erecting an additional battery in 1692–1693, completing a circuit of wooden palisades connected by eleven bastions across the promontory (nicknamed l'Enceinte de Beaucours or "Beacours's Enclosure" because it had been designed by the royal military engineer Boisberthelot de Beaucours), as well as demolishing and rebuilding Château Saint-Louis with stouter stone walls and a new two-story wing in

1693–1695, so as to provide a more formidable gun platform. Even sanitary problems were addressed, a *tombereau* (waste cart) being hired to wend through the couple of hundred dwellings in the Lower Town every week, gathering and tipping refuse into the river.

Peace briefly ensued once a European treaty was concluded in September 1697, but disease and famine hampered any immediate economic resurgence for Quebec, after which the War of the Spanish Succession, or Queen Anne's War, erupted five years later. A smallpox epidemic that same winter of 1702–1703 claimed the lives of 260 townspeople, and the survivors—measured at 1,939 inhabitants, according to the 1707 census—endured considerable hardship because of more implacable Royal Navy actions out in the Atlantic. The local population compensated through privateering, blockade-running, and another round of fortification work, which included the installation of the northern Dauphine Battery to cover the dockyard on the Saint-Charles River.

The town was spared any direct military threat until the summer of 1709, when a New England militia army under Col. Francis Nicholson pushed up the Hudson River to attack Montreal, in conjunction with a seaborne descent against the capital of New France by his colleague Samuel Vetch. Yet Nicholson's incursion was checked, and Vetch's campaign against Quebec was subsequently canceled. A more serious offensive was launched when Rear Adm. Sir Hovenden Walker departed Boston in August 1711 with eleven Royal Navy warships, escorting sixty-seven transports bearing 7,500 troops under Brig. John Hill. Nicholson marched up the Hudson River again with 2,300 volunteers, but Walker's expedition blundered too far north in the Gulf of Saint Lawrence, crashing on the breakers around Île aux Œufs near modern Baie Trinité in early September, losing eight transports and 885 men. That disaster halted both English thrusts, and Quebec's defenders renamed their Church of Notre-Dame-de-la-Victoire as Notre-Dame-des-Victoires (Our Lady of Victories).

Revival (1712–1759)

The town nonetheless struggled to revive economically once this conflict ceased, trade losses being exacerbated by the expense of replacing the Intendant's Palace—destroyed by an accidental fire on 5 January 1713—and a widespread monetary devaluation. A yearlong outbreak of measles also claimed 302 lives starting in July 1714. Crown subsidies for enlarging the Upper Town's defensive perimeter in accordance with plans drawn up by the royal military engineer Gaspard-Joseph Chaussegros de Léry were also halted in 1720, then diverted altogether the next year into Montreal's reconstruction, following a major conflagration. Quebec's population consequently remained virtually stagnant throughout this

The Intendant's Palace in Quebec City, showing how it had been "reconstructed after the fire of 5th January 1713"; drawn in 1759 by Richard Short, then engraved by William Elliot and published in September 1761 in London. (Metropolitan Toronto Reference Library)

interlude, census numbers rising from only 2,408 inhabitants and 165 clerics in 1716—two-thirds of whom were still crammed into the Lower Town—to 2,704 people a decade later.

Trade resurged during the latter half of the 1720s, however, as agricultural produce came into great demand for the huge new French stronghold at Louisbourg on Cape Breton Island. Quebec's Haute Ville began to expand as a result, clusters of new houses appearing around its seminary and other major compounds. Overseas traffic was also reanimated by bountiful exports of fur pelts to France, as well as lumber and wheat to the Antilles, while a half dozen small ships (averaging 100 tons in displacement) were launched every year from Quebec's slipways during the 1730s. This combined commercial boom came to be reflected by a population spurt, the number of inhabitants rising to 4,721 people by 1737, despite a smallpox outbreak that had claimed almost 300 lives four years previously. By 1739, Intendant Gilles Hocquart could count more than 100 small stores, 22 flour mills, 11 sawmills, 6 tanneries, and 2 brickyards around the bustling town, while 5,010 residents and 197 clerics were recorded by 1744—a majority now residing in the Upper Town.

Unfortunately, the wheat harvests of 1742 and 1743 had proven so disappointing as to require the imposition of rationing, after which war with Britain erupted again in March 1744, interrupting oceanic trade—especially after Louisbourg fell to an expedition out of New England in June 1745. Nevertheless, Quebec diverted much energy into a new naval dockyard called the Quai du Roi (King's Wharf), established the next year amid expropriated properties below the Intendant's Palace on the Saint-Charles. It turned out ships as of 1747 and attracted so many impoverished rural migrants into town that a new suburb had to be created on the low marshy terrain of Saint-Roch. All these labors, plus extensive fortification works subsidized by the Crown, provided the bulk of urban employment for the remainder of the conflict. Anglo-French disputes for control over the North American wilderness resumed so swiftly that Quebec's 169-man garrison was augmented to 650 soldiers the next year, while large-scale naval construction and fortification projects were furthermore revived by the Crown in 1751.

When the Swedish naturalist Pehr (Peter) Kalm visited Quebec on 5 August 1749, a year after peace had been restored, he described it in these words:

> The mountain on which the upper town is situated reaches above the houses of the lower town—notwithstanding the latter are three or four stories high—and the view from the Palace is enough to cause a swimming head. Most of the merchants live in the lower town, where the houses are built very close together. The streets in it are narrow, very rugged, and almost always wet (because of water runoff from the rocky escarpment above). The upper town is inhabited by people

of quality, by several people belonging to the different offices, tradesmen, and others. The Palace is the lodging of the Governor-General of Canada, and a number of soldiers mount guard before it, both at the gate and in the courtyard; and when the Governor or the Bishop comes in or goes out, they must all appear in arms and beat the drum.

Four years later, the urban population having swollen to 7,215 residents, an ominous escalation in international tensions occurred when a British fleet under Vice Adm. Edward Boscawen off Newfoundland intercepted a French formation that was bringing an additional 3,000 troops into Canada. Two transports were taken, but Rear Adm. Emmanuel Auguste de Cahideuc, Comte Dubois de la Motte, reached Quebec safely with fifteen other vessels and deposited several battalions of regulars. Maj.-Gen. Louis Joseph, Marquis de Montcalm, followed with two more battalions—1,200 men—of La Sarre and Royal Roussillon regiments on 8 May 1756; ten days afterward, Britain declared war against France.

Conditions for Quebec's civilians quickly deteriorated as the Royal Navy imposed an Atlantic blockade, restricting trade and supplies at a time when 1,300 Acadian refugees began fleeing into the capital to escape offensives emanating out of Nova Scotia and New England. Another 1,500 to 1,600 dispossessed people straggled in the next year, as well as a couple of thousand English captives, straining the town's limited resources and contributing to an outbreak of disease; the outbreak was exacerbated by the fact that the Charity Hospital had been destroyed by an accidental fire in 1755, so that only the General Hospital remained operational, treating 3,500 patients over the next four years. Louisbourg fell in the summer of 1758, and although a convoy of twenty French supply ships won through to Quebec early in May 1759, the British were now massing for a major offensive against the forlorn capital of New France.

Devastation (1759–1784)

Maj.-Gen. Sir James Wolfe and Vice Adm. Sir Charles Saunders set sail from Louisbourg on 6 June 1759, forging up the Saint Lawrence with 8,500 soldiers crammed aboard 119 transports. Advance elements of this invasion fleet reached Île d'Orléans twenty days later, from where Wolfe sent Brig. Robert Monckton on ahead to occupy strategic Pointe-Lévis—variously spelled as Pointe-Lévy, Pointe-de-Lévis, Pointe-des-Lévis—on the eastern headland opposite Quebec. Montcalm loosed fire-ships downstream on 28 June to scatter the British formation, but they proved ineffectual, the enemy host anchoring within sight of the capital. A few days later, they pushed 2 miles west of Pointe-Lévis to install siege artillery and initiate a cross-river bombardment. Wolfe meanwhile probed for a disembarkation point on the western shoreline, but his initial efforts were repelled east of Montmorency Falls on 9 July, as well as at Beauport on 31 July.

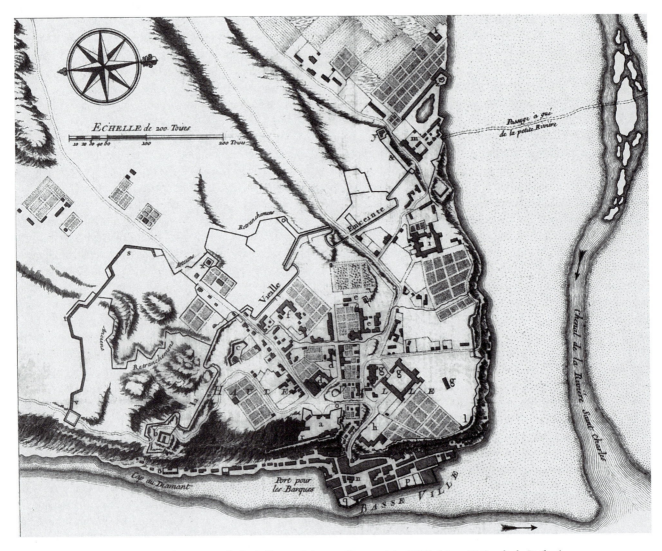

Map of the flourishing city in 1744, by Jacques Nicolas Bellin; north is toward upper right. (Bibliothèque Nationale de Québec)

Hoping to sap the garrison's morale, the English torched all nearby villages, then sent columns upstream to sever communications with Montreal. A lengthy stalemate ensued, punctuated by sporadic artillery exchanges or sallies. Wolfe fell ill in late August 1759, and by early September he had decided on the gamble of landing troops at a tiny cove called Anse-au-Foulon southwest of Quebec, emerging onto its heights so as to surprise Montcalm from the rear. News that relief ships would soon attempt to reprovision Quebec goaded Wolfe into action, setting across the darkened river with 1,700 troops aboard thirty boats at 1:00 A.M. on 13 September, followed by a second wave of another 1,900 men. Three hours later, under cover of a diversionary attack launched by Royal Navy warships in the direction of Beauport, the British vanguard under Capt. William Howe slipped ashore at Anse-au-Foulon, picked its way up a footpath to the 175-foot summit, overwhelmed a sentry post, then fanned out onto the Plains of Abraham. More

soldiers were hastily ferried across to consolidate this breakthrough, until Wolfe had 4,500 redcoats arrayed for battle.

Montcalm assumed that only a small contingent had come ashore, until he galloped across to view the enemy lines at 6:30 A.M. on 13 September 1759; he thereupon summoned out 4,250 of his own troops from behind Quebec's ramparts within the next three hours. Believing he could still dislodge the British flanking force, the French general attacked at 10 A.M., but his charge was checked by long lines of redcoats unexpectedly rising from the grass (where they had been lying prone to avoid galling fire from Indian and Franco-Canadian snipers), plus volleys of grape fired from British guns manhandled to the cliff tops by hardworking Royal Navy parties. Montcalm's army was shattered, suffering 500 killed and 350 captured before melting back into the town and surrounding countryside, compared with only 58 British dead—including the mortally wounded Wolfe—and 600 injured.

Quebec City as it had been seen in 1759 from the British encampments on Pointe-Lévis on the eastern bank of the Saint Lawrence River; from an original eyewitness drawing by Richard Short, engraved by Pierre Charlos Canot and published in London two years later. (Metropolitan Toronto Reference Library)

Carried back inside Quebec, Montcalm expired the next day from a wound, and Lt.-Gov. Nicolas Roch de Ramezay agreed to surrender the devastated town on 17 September 1759 to Wolfe's successor, Brig. George Townshend, who entered the following day to find only 1,300 surviving defenders, 1,200 hospitalized invalids, and 2,600 civilians, mostly women and children. At least 180 buildings had burned during the protracted siege, while many others were damaged; only two days' rations remained for the starving inhabitants. Brig. James Murray was appointed military governor and addressed the widespread distress by discharging all Franco-Canadian militiamen into the countryside and recommending that civilian refugees remain at their rural sanctuaries. British troops were then billeted in Quebec's least damaged structures, settling in amid its depleted civilian populace for a miserable winter—interrupted when a small French force attempted to recapture Pointe-Lévis in February 1760, only to be chased away by troops that Murray dispatched across the frozen Saint Lawrence.

The remaining French armies had meanwhile reconcentrated around Montreal, from where Brig. François Gaston, Chevalier de Lévis, advanced down the Saint Lawrence in late April 1760 to amass 7,000 troops at Saint-Augustin (15 miles from Quebec), in hopes of dislodging the capital's weakened British occupiers. Murray emerged with his healthiest 2,500 redcoats to erect defensive works along the Plains of Abraham, but he was interrupted when the French vanguard suddenly materialized along the road from Sainte-Foy, pressing the outnumbered British back inside Quebec for a second siege. Both sides maintained close watch toward the ocean to see whose springtime relief ships arrived first, the frigate HMS *Lowestoft* appearing by 9 May, cheering Murray's garrison. The French redoubled their bombardment, pouring so many shells into the town's relatively undamaged northwestern sector that a blaze consumed most of its quartier du Palais around the Intendant's Palace, yet they could not prevent more British ships from arriving with two fresh regiments a week later. Lévis was obliged to retreat, and Murray in turn counterattacked inland by 14 July, eventually overrunning Montreal in conjunction with two other British offensives out of New York, subduing all French resistance in Canada.

Civilian refugees were permitted back into Quebec that same autumn of 1760, but only a few hundred chose to resume permanent residence because of its ruinous condition and the

The Bishop's House and other damaged buildings in the occupied city; drawn in 1759 by Short, then engraved by John Fougeron and published in London two years later. (Metropolitan Toronto Reference Library)

presence of large numbers of redcoats. Two years afterward the urban population was still measured at only 3,497 inhabitants. But when Canada was formally annexed into the British Empire by the peace treaty signed at Paris in the spring of 1763, citizens grudgingly returned to initiate the painstaking task of reconstructing their town. A couple of hundred masons were kept gainfully employed over the next dozen years replacing many stone edifices, while poorer homes were rebuilt in wood—especially in Saint-Roch and the new western suburb of Saint-Jean (formerly a military preserve, but now partitioned by the British for private usage). Signs of progress appeared, such as the courier mail service to Montreal and New York implemented by Postmaster-General Benjamin Franklin.

Quebec's garrison was reduced to a peacetime establishment of only 900 redcoats, but the English nonetheless maintained a high profile—especially in the Upper Town—by conducting a great deal of fortification work, as well as refurbishing such older structures as the Château Saint-Louis. Several score English and Scottish merchants also arrived to supplant Quebec's merchant class, who had been bankrupted by wartime losses and severed overseas contacts. The Scotsmen William Brown and Thomas Gilmore, for example, imported the town's first printing press and issued the *Quebec Gazette*

as of 21 June 1764. Centuries-old British practice prohibited office to Catholics, so that these newcomers furthermore secured all appointed posts when Quebec's civil administration was reconstituted that same autumn, performing a few days' unpaid service every month as "justices of the peace." They moreover erected fine homes around the Upper Town's main square, as well as along Notre-Dame and Saint-Pierre streets in the Lower Town, plus country villas at Sillery and other choice inland estates while Anglican services were held in the damaged Récollet convent.

Because the cathedral and Notre-Dame-des-Victoires Church had been gutted during the siege, Catholic Masses were temporarily celebrated in the Urseline chapel and later at the seminary, until Jean-Olivier Briand could return as bishop in June 1766 and initiate the cathedral's resurrection two years later. (He also rented the devastated episcopal palace out to the Crown.) But thanks to continuous reconstruction efforts, the urban populace at least rebounded to roughly 6,000 people among 1,200 households by 1770. Sports such as cricket and regattas even appeared, as well as horse races on the Plains of Abraham, plus skating, tobogganing, and curling in winter. Sea traffic resurged once London eased trade restrictions three years later, so that more than a hundred vessels were soon anchoring off Quebec every year to load lumber and other agricultural exports (although furs were now monopolized by Montreal). The Quebec Act passed by Britain's Parliament in 1774 furthermore recognized the Franco-Canadian legal system, language, and mores; however, before any significant number of Quebeckers could be appointed to offices, the town underwent yet another ordeal.

A few months after the Thirteen American Colonies had revolted against Crown rule in the spring of 1775, rebel armies mustered in upstate New York and at Cambridge (Massachusetts) to invade Canada, hoping to dislodge its British administration. The first American army under Brig. Richard Montgomery occupied Montreal by 12 November, its garrison commander—British Maj.-Gen. Sir Guy Carleton—escaping down the Saint Lawrence into Quebec with a few subordinates.

Three days previously, 600 to 650 half-starved rebel troops under Col. Benedict Arnold had also arrived opposite, after a difficult 230-mile trek through the wilderness from Massachusetts. Traversing the Saint Lawrence from Pointe-Lévis, Arnold attempted to invest the capital's British garrison under Lt.-Col. Allan Maclean out of the west but proved unable to breach its ramparts without a siege train; he therefore retired on 19 November 1775, to be reinforced by Montgomery. But even with an additional 600 troops and some artillery, the Americans could still not encircle Quebec, whose garrison had since risen to 1,700 men under Carleton. The invaders consequently decided to surprise the defenders by approaching from two directions in the early hours of 31 December, under cover of a blizzard. Montgomery led 500 men out of the southwest and reached Près-de-Ville by 4:00 A.M., only to be suddenly killed along with two dozen of his soldiers by a pair of British 3-pounders, at which his second-in-command, Col. Donald Campbell, ordered a retreat. Arnold meanwhile advanced out of the northwest through Saint-Roch with another 700 rebels, drawing fire and being wounded in a knee; his second-in-command, Kentucky Col. Daniel Morgan, nonetheless pressed forward, only to become trapped at Sault-au-Matelot and captured along with 425 survivors at 9:00 A.M.

The Americans had suffered a total of thirty killed and forty-two wounded during these repulses, compared with only five dead and thirteen injured among the defenders, so that a halfhearted investment was continued until 6 May 1776, when the British ship *Surprise* entered Quebec with supplies, effectively putting an end to the besiegers' hopes. Soon afterward a sally chased away the demoralized rebels, after which a large Anglo-Hessian expedition disembarked on 1 June under Maj.-Gen. "Gentleman Johnny" Burgoyne and Friedrich, Baron von Riedesel, advancing under Carleton's command to reclaim Montreal and eventually counterattack into the American Colonies.

Residents of Quebec were meanwhile left to begin the task of replacing another couple of hundred destroyed homes, at least fifty being in the Saint-Roch suburb—including the ancient Intendant's Palace, although its charred ruins would never be rebuilt—plus another three dozen dwellings at Saint-Jean. The town even prospered over the remaining six and a half years of this conflict by serving as a major British base, receiving and provisioning thousands of troops (one famous visitor in 1782 being a youthful Horatio Nelson, commander of HMS *Albemarle*). The Lower Town's dockyard facilities were enhanced as a result, yet depression set in once peace was restored in the spring of 1783, as Quebec's sea traffic collapsed by at least half. The population was also decimated by a scarlet fever epidemic that same winter, suffering 1,100 deaths and the flight of many residents into safer rural areas, so that only 6,491 inhabitants remained to be enumerated the following year.

Resurgence (1785–1855)

This depletion of residents was countered by the arrival of dispossessed American Loyalists and other British immigrants, while the town's faltering economy was alleviated by such public projects as expansion of its Château Saint-Louis and erection of a grand new reception hall in 1786; there was also extensive decorative work done on the Catholic cathedral's interior, while limited commerce with the newly independent United States was furthermore restored the next year. A pedestrian bridge across the Saint-Charles River—dubbed Pont Dorchester in honor of Carleton, now ennobled as Lord Dorchester and reappointed as Canada's governor-general—was inaugurated as of September 1789, improving access to the northern satellite towns of Charlesbourg and Beauport, while military defenses continued to be strengthened throughout the Upper Town.

So many settlers were now arriving that Britain's prime minister, William Pitt, announced in late February 1791 that the entire colony was to become divided into two provinces, called Lower Canada and Upper Canada (modern Ontario), according to their respective geographic positions along the Saint Lawrence waterways. The governor-general was to rule over both on behalf of the Crown, with a lieutenant-governor appointed to each province, plus their own separate legislative bodies. The town of Quebec was consequently divided into two electoral districts in May 1792, each voting a pair of delegates to the fifty-member assembly of Lower Canada, which convened in its former Bishop's Palace by mid-December.

A mere five weeks later, however, hostilities erupted in Europe between the British Empire and Revolutionary France, so that Quebec's port traffic and ship construction grew accordingly. Its population had stabilized at 7,162 inhabitants by 1795 (of whom 1,267 were now British-born, not including 1,000 garrison troops), who furthermore benefited economically when the Jay Treaty was signed the next year, permitting increased trade with the United States. The town prospered steadily throughout these decades of distant warfare, exemplified by such improvements as professionalization of piloting and charting services, lengthening of piers, construction of more wharfs, and addition of floors to existing edifices in its Lower Town. The Upper Town became more completely enclosed by stone ramparts and gatehouses designed by the military engineer Capt. Gother Mann, while a new Hall of Justice was designed by the architect François Baillairgé. A police force was created, and the magnificent Anglican Cathedral of the Holy Trinity was consecrated by 1804 (atop the remains of the old Récollet convent, consumed by an accidental fire on 6 September 1796). The suburbs of Saint-Jean and Saint-Roch also experienced considerable growth.

But the greatest commercial upsurge occurred after the French emperor Napoleon I imposed the so-called Continental System in Europe two years later, denying Baltic wood products to British yards, so that vast quantities of Canadian lumber had to be substituted. Quebec's exports mushroomed in consequence, 340 huge rafts of logs being floated into its harbor for sale by 1807, while 500 of 661 departing ships three years later were all conveying white pine. The Lower Town's waterfront doubled in size to accommodate this expanded traffic, with edifices becoming tightly packed from Anse-au-Foulon as far as the mouth of the Saint-Charles. Ship construction boomed as well, seventeen vessels being launched along the banks of the Saint-Charles during the spring of 1811 alone. That same summer, a visitor noted that there were about 200 sailing ships anchored off Quebec, whose forest of masts was "three or four rows deep for a distance of six miles."

The War of 1812 against the United States briefly interrupted this seagoing traffic, but export losses were offset by increased demand for provisioning British expeditions, as well as the erection of round, stone "Martello" defensive towers. All these endeavors were so labor intensive that the permanent population almost doubled, from 8,968 residents in 1805 to 15,839 by 1818—of whom 3,340 were British-born, and not counting 1,250 garrison troops or 3,450 transient sailors. The first paddle steamers coming down the Saint Lawrence from Montreal further augmented the flow of goods. Despite a brief postwar recession, a new Catholic cathedral, as well as a Presbyterian and a Methodist church, plus a new jail on Saint-Stanislas Street, had all been erected within the town, while the Bank of Quebec and a fire insurance company were moreover created by 1818. That same May, the 310-ton *Lauzon* began regular ferry service across to Pointe-Lévis. The first public lamps were suspended shortly thereafter from corner posts throughout the capital, and a new bridge across the Saint-Charles was inaugurated by 1820.

Ship traffic revived in intensity over the next couple of decades, hundreds of vessels arriving annually during the ice-free season to deposit thousands of immigrants and receive cargoes, so that Quebec came to rank behind only New York City and New Orleans in volume of trade. A major refortification effort was also undertaken by the Crown in May 1820. Work commenced on a massive *Citadelle* atop Cap-Diamant,

followed by a system of heavy ramparts and gatehouses throughout the Upper Town, as well as launchings of ever larger vessels from the yards. Lumber exports expanded thanks to the introduction of steam tugs capable of hauling in enormous log rafts, and tanneries multiplied along Saint-Vallier Street on Saint-Geneviève Hill. The urban population, bolstered by numerous Irish Catholic arrivals, grew from 22,101 inhabitants in 1825 to 27,141 by 1831, making Quebec the sixth most populous community on the North American continent.

The next year, Lower Canada's assembly officially granted the capital its charter of incorporation as a city on 5 June, so that its first councilors could be elected on 25 April 1833; they in turn chose the lawyer Elzéar Bédard from among their number as the first mayor. Unfortunately, though, a cholera outbreak had also struck that same year of 1832 and claimed the lives of 2,200 residents and 800 transients within a month, despite the quarantine anchorage created for arriving vessels at Grosse-Île, 25 miles east-northeast of Quebec. The Château Saint-Louis was moreover consumed by an accidental fire on 23 January 1834. Some 2,000 more citizens succumbed to a second cholera epidemic that same year; British military headquarters were transferred to Montreal as of 1836; forty structures around Sous-le-Fort and Saint-Pierre streets in the Lower Town burned on 10 September; and martial law was imposed when a Franco-Canadian revolt occurred outside Montreal in November 1837.

Quebec nonetheless recovered from these vicissitudes thanks to a boom in ship production, launchings multiplying from sixteen vessels in 1838 to forty-five a couple of years later, providing employment for 2,800 urban workers (although at such low wages and long hours that a shipwrights' union was formed by December 1840). Four years later the population was measured at 32,876 people, and some steps had been taken to improve urban amenities through upgrading the police force and street paving. But a catastrophic fire erupted on the hot and windy morning of 28 May 1845 in the Osborne & Richardson tannery on Arago Street, destroying 1,650 dwellings in the Saint-Roch suburb by evening and leaving 12,000 people homeless. A second conflagration burst from a shed beside Saint-Jean Gate at 11:00 P.M. that same 28 June, consuming another 1,300 abodes and rendering another 8,000 people homeless in the Saint-Jean suburb. Hundreds of these unfortunates chose to resettle west of the General Hospital or north of the Saint-Charles River, unwittingly expanding the urban boundaries.

These devastating material losses were exacerbated by the deaths of seventy people in the Saint-Louis Theatre fire of 12 June 1846, plus a typhus and cholera epidemic the next year that killed several thousand more (not including 5,000 Irish immigrants at the distant Grosse-Île quarantine station). Ship traffic nevertheless remained so vigorous that Quebec quickly recuperated, its first telegraph line being completed to Montreal by August 1847 and its first public gaslights being installed by November 1849. Despite another epidemic that claimed 1,200 more citizens that same year, the census of 1851 enumerated 45,940 inhabitants spread among 4,549 dwellings, serviced by 810 stores and 66 inns, plus the new Finlay public market in the Lower Town. The city's old seminary was also elevated to the rank of Laval University in December 1852 by royal charter.

Quebec was to enjoy one last great economic boom during 1852–1854, thanks to heightened demand for its summertime lumber exports and wintertime ship construction, the latter soon employing more than 5,000 laborers. An aqueduct providing citywide water distribution was completed and the Saint-Paul market wharf was replaced, both by 1854, while streets were paved and plank sidewalks laid the next year. A new Champlain market was started in the Lower Town, but the city's harbor was now so cluttered as to scarcely be able to contain the enormous log rafts and ever larger vessels that were arriving.

Diminished Circumstances (1856–Present)

More ominously still, oceangoing steamers were now able to proceed directly past Quebec City to Montreal, as the Saint Lawrence had been successfully dredged during the early 1850s. That larger rival metropolis had also concentrated upon laying multiple rail links—including a line to Portland, Maine, a seaport that remained ice-free year-round—while Quebec counted upon only a single spur of the Grand Trunk, laid in 1852 through Lévis and serviced by four small cross-river steamboats. As a result, Montreal's commerce would quickly begin to far outstrip that of Quebec, whose more seasonal economy experienced a noticeable downturn by 1857. Even though it was to be temporarily designated as capital of Canada once again on 24 September 1859, and construction even started on a new Parliament building designed by F. P. Rubidge, more centrally located Ottawa had already been chosen to succeed Quebec.

A census taken two years later indicated that its population had risen to 57,375 residents spread among 8,200 dwellings. Yet Quebec now ranked as only the sixteenth-largest city in North America, and it was so palpably slipping in influence that local authorities moved to reverse the decline by completing a new customshouse and financing an 875-foot breakwater at Pointe-à-Carcy in 1860–1861. They also hired a steam dredger to deepen the waters off the Saint-Charles shipyards the next year and imported a grain silo from Montreal in May 1863. The U.S. Civil War renewed demand for lumber and other exports, so that Quebec enjoyed another brief burst of prosperity. Its first horse-drawn streetcars appeared in the Lower Town by 1863; the Porte Saint-Jean (St. John's Gate)—a 7-foot-wide

Review of militia volunteers on the Champ de Mars or "Parade Ground," ca. 1866; Canada's forthcoming independence from Great Britain the next year required the substitution of local forces to replace the departing British garrisons. (National Archives of Canada)

A tugboat hauling a raft of logs past Quebec City's north shore to the nearby lumber mills, ca. 1890. (Bibliothèque Nationale de Québec)

bottleneck to traffic in the Upper Town—was redesigned to permit easier access as of October 1864; and five 140-foot motorized ferries provided regular service to Lévis. The entire city now encompassed 3 square miles.

This bubble of resurgence burst with the Union victory in the spring of 1865, and the resultant depression was deepened by the transfer of the capital to Ottawa in anticipation of Canada's forthcoming independence from Great Britain, 1,000 functionaries and their dependents being withdrawn from Quebec. Another calamitous fire then erupted in a grocery store on Saint-Joseph Street and swept through the Saint-Roch suburb and village of Saint-Sauveur on 14 October 1866, consuming 1,800 dwellings and seventeen churches, while leaving 20,000 people homeless.

While fire stations and a citywide electric fire-alarm system were being installed, Quebec's citizenry struggled to recuperate. Yet the volume of ship tonnage proceeding directly to Montreal doubled, local lumber exports fell by half, most arriving passengers disembarked at Lévis to board trains, and the launchings of wooden vessels at the Saint-Charles yards diminished because of a new preference for iron hulls. (Scarcely 800 shipwrights remained employed by 1873.) Then the Saint-Roch suburb was swept yet again by another large conflagration on 24 May 1870, 422 homes and part of the shipyards being destroyed, after which the 60th Royal Rifles Regiment of the Duke of Connaught, plus the Royal Artillery and

Royal Engineer battalions garrisoning Quebec's Citadel, departed on 11 November 1871 to the tune of "Goodbye, Sweetheart, Goodbye." The withdrawal of those 1,000 soldiers and their families represented the loss of an additional 3,000 urban residents.

That same year, a census revealed that the city population had virtually stagnated at 59,699 people, Quebec having now lost out as Canada's principal seaport, main military stronghold, and national capital. Only 9 percent of its residents were now British-born, wealthy entrepreneurs and lesser English-speaking tradesmen having migrated to Montreal or other inland cities in quest of better prospects. That left French-Canadian manufacturers to keep Quebec's economy alive through increased output of less profitable items such as shoes and leather goods—seven large factories employing 2,200 workers in this business that same year of 1871—as well as furniture and other light industrial production. The Parliament building had been converted into the provincial legislature four years previously, and a new post office was erected at the intersection of Buade and Du Fort streets by 1873. Still, the city remained sidelined because of its lack of a large-scale access system: the Quebec North Shore Railway did not even go into operation until 1878, and it did not link up with other lines until the next year. By 1880 Quebec had slipped to Canada's third-largest city and was surpassed by Toronto.

Quebeckers have centuries-old traditions of enjoying winter; an outdoor ice hockey rink, illuminated with electric lights for nighttime play during the 1890s. (National Archives of Canada)

The provincial government's Hôtel du Parlement (Parliament Building) was nevertheless constructed on the old Cricket Field grounds near the Saint-Louis Gate in the Saint-Jean suburb during 1882–1884, followed by a new Palais de Justice (Hall of Justice) in 1887. The Saint-Sauveur suburb—also known as Boisseauville or Bijouville—was absorbed into Quebec's municipality two years afterward; yet the city's total population still only stood at 63,090 people by 1891. Three years afterward, the enormous Château Frontenac Hotel was erected, and a grandiose Hôtel de Ville (City Hall) in 1895. The suburb known as Saint-Roch Nord, located on the far bank of the Saint-Charles River, was absorbed into Quebec's jurisdiction as well, in 1909, followed by the town of Montcalm the following year.

However, the greatest boon to the modern city's economy was to be the Quebec Bridge across the Saint Lawrence, which was commenced nine miles away at Cap Rouge in 1907 and completed a decade later despite two serious accidents during its construction. This new span would allow a half dozen railways ready access from the southern shore, greatly augmenting traffic volumes and shortening travel distances. Quebec prospered as a result and soon exported vast amounts of

paper products garnered from throughout its forested district, processing and handling being facilitated by plentiful amounts of hydraulic power generated at the nearby Montmorency and Shawinigan Falls. Quebec experienced a particular boom by serving as a major transportation hub and naval construction center after Canada entered World War II in September 1939, and even hosted a pair of famous Allied conferences between the British prime minister Winston S. Churchill and the U.S. president Franklin D. Roosevelt: the first—code-named "Quadrant"—in August 1943, discussed the fate of Italy after Benito Mussolini's overthrow and numerous other strategic matters; the second was held in September 1944 and concerned itself with the imminent fall of Nazi Germany.

Another economic downturn inevitably ensued once this conflict ceased in 1945, to which Quebec adjusted by concentrating upon its regional pulp and paper output as well as light industrial manufactures. By 1951 the population within its old city limits was measured at 161,439 residents, but a total of 271,236 were now recorded throughout its burgeoning metropolitan area. This sprawl would continue to develop over the next several decades as rural-to-urban migration trends and the growth of automotive transportation caused new suburbs

View of the Chateau Frontenac Hotel looming above Quebec's Lower Town on a snowy day in 1922. (National Archives of Canada)

Aerial view looking westward across the historic Upper Town and Lower Town of Quebec City, 1937. (National Archives of Canada)

to expand well beyond the narrow, 8-mile-long tableland upon which the original city core had been created. By 1991 Quebec's population figure remained virtually unchanged at 167,517 inhabitants—while the total for its metropolitan area had mushroomed to 645,550. As the great majority were Francophone descendants of past generations of *habitants,* their consciousness and pride in the city's unique heritage eventually helped to make Quebec the heartland of the province's sovereignty movement.

For additional sources on Quebec's urban history, please consult the Select Bibliography at the end of this volume.

TORONTO
Despite its modest origins, the largest and wealthiest city in modern Canada.

Antecedents (900–1719)
Primitive hunters began forsaking their nomadic way of life to settle along Lake Ontario's shoreline as early as 900 C.E., their villages gradually evolving into circular, palisaded strongholds on defensible, well-drained pieces of ground. Preferably, a site with a spring nearby that would flow year-round was chosen, as well as trees to supply saplings and other construction materials for their elongated "longhouses." Some of these structures attained 150 to 175 feet in length and were frequently aligned so as to present the smallest possible surface area to the prevailing winds. Typically, such settlements had to be shifted 3–6 miles every eight to twelve years because of the depletion of local soils and firewood, yet inhabitants remained in the general vicinity because of its fertile, well-irrigated, and forested landscape, as well as its strategic value as a portage point.

During the early seventeenth century the local Seneca tribe (a branch of the larger Iroquois nation) learned of the arrival of French settlers farther to their east, and Étienne Brûlé—a subordinate of Samuel de Champlain—passed through this spot in September 1615 with a dozen Huron allies on his explorations. Yet Iroquois hostility prevented these foreign interlopers from gaining a foothold in Lake Ontario until 1673, when the French finally established Fort Frontenac (modern Kingston), followed by Fort Niagara to its southwest five years later; it was during this period that the name *Toronto,* or Meeting Place, first appeared on French maps. Although the possibility of installing a trade outpost at its often visited river mouth was suggested as early as 1686, such a project could not be put into practice until after the Iroquois had finally been defeated in 1701 and had retreated into what is today upstate New York.

French Outposts (1720–1759)
With a fresh influx of traders and settlers moving across Lake Ontario during the early decades of the eighteenth century,

the Crown authorities decided to establish a few more outposts in 1720, including a new *magasin royal* (royal storehouse) at Toronto. However, this particular stronghold was intended to conduct commercial activities with Native American travelers rather than serve as a settlement center, and it was furthermore intended to remain subordinate to Fort Niagara. The officer assigned to this duty was Alexandre Dagneau Douville, who built a small storehouse, probably on the east bank of the Humber River mouth. But because of more competitive prices being offered by English traders at Albany, this *magasin* had to be abandoned as unprofitable within the next decade, although French voyageurs continued using the Toronto portage for their transits.

In 1744 the chief engineer in French Canada, Gaspard Chaussegros de Lézy, conducted a survey of the north shore of Lake Ontario, and a few years later the notion of re-establishing an outpost at Toronto was revived to counteract the appeal of a new English trading house installed at Oswego. France's minister of marine, Antoine Louis Rouillé, who was also in charge of overseas colonies, approved this recommendation in April 1750, so that a detachment consisting of a sergeant and four soldiers was duly sent out from Fort Frontenac under Ens. Pierre Robineau, Chevalier de Portneuf. They arrived on 20 May 1750 and within two months had constructed a "small stockaded fort and a small house for safekeeping of His Majesty's effects" near Baby Point, on the east side of the Humber.

This structure, commonly called Fort Toronto, quickly developed a brisk trade, so much so that the erection of a larger structure was approved that same summer, to be installed farther east and nearer the harbor (on what are today the grounds of the Canadian National Exhibition). This latest stronghold—officially named Fort Rouillé upon its completion in 1751, but that soon inherited the title of Fort Toronto—was a sturdy compound constructed of squared logs and with 80-foot-long walls, enclosing several official dwellings. Its tiny garrison toiled to clear away another 300 acres of brush just beyond the palisades, so as to prevent any surprise attacks and provide a good field of fire, as well as for planting gardens.

When the French and Indian War erupted against the British four years later, garrison commander Charles Joseph de Noyelles was initially able to discourage an attack by local Mississauga tribesmen in 1757, thanks to the timely arrival of 60 reinforcements from Fort Niagara. The next summer, though, communications with Montreal and Quebec City were effectively severed when Lt.-Col. John Bradstreet pushed north from Fort Stanwix (modern Rome, New York) and Oswego with almost 3,000 British troops and colonials, besieging and destroying Fort Frontenac by the end of August 1758. Then, on 6 June 1759, another British expedition under Sir William Johnson laid siege to Fort Niagara, while a still larger host under Maj.-Gen. James Wolfe invested Quebec City shortly thereafter. Fort Niagara fell by 25 June, and when the victorious English sent a detachment to attack Fort Toronto, they found this subsidiary stronghold already reduced to smoldering embers; its vastly outnumbered fifteen-man garrison having torched their outpost and retired toward Montreal. Johnson interviewed the Mississauga chieftain Tequakareigh on 2 August to receive his submission, then all of French Canada was finally conquered by September 1760. The outpost at Toronto, however, remained virtually deserted for the next three decades.

Refoundation as "York" (1793–1811)

Following the American War of Independence and the subsequent partition of the Great Lakes system between the new nations called the United States and British Canada, considerable numbers of Loyalists chose to emigrate rather than remain under republican rule. Many of those displaced individuals began resettling in the eastern counties of what would later become the Province of Ontario, Fort Frontenac being re-established as Kingston in 1783, from whence British colonization expanded westward along the north shore of Lake Ontario.

By 1786, Canada's governor-general, Guy Carleton, Baron Dorchester, was actively considering the acquisition of the old French portage at Toronto, because its nearly circular bay—3 square miles of water protected by a long, low, narrow spit of land jutting out from the east—was regarded as the best natural harbor on the lake. The next year, the purchase of its surrounding terrain was arranged between Deputy Surveyor-Gen. John Collins and three Mississauga chiefs in exchange for an estimated £1,700 in goods and cash (although a second purchase was made in 1805, because of uncertainties regarding the original boundaries). Collins thereupon conducted a survey in 1788, even outlining a proposed grid for a future town, while Dorchester promised large land grants to several prominent French-Canadian figures.

But by 1791 the number of English pioneers settled along Lake Ontario had grown sufficiently for Parliament in London to create a separate legal entity, so that the entire colony was split into Upper Canada and Lower Canada (modern Ontario and Quebec). The able veteran New World campaigner Lt.-Col. John Graves Simcoe, educated at Eton and Oxford, came out from England with his wife, Elizabeth, the next year to assume office as lieutenant-governor of the Upper Canada territory. Pausing at Kingston to consult with regional officials, Simcoe decided to install a temporary administration at Niagara-on-the-Lake while Toronto was being converted into a viable naval base, after which he could transfer to oversee the creation of a permanent provincial capital farther inland at London (Ontario).

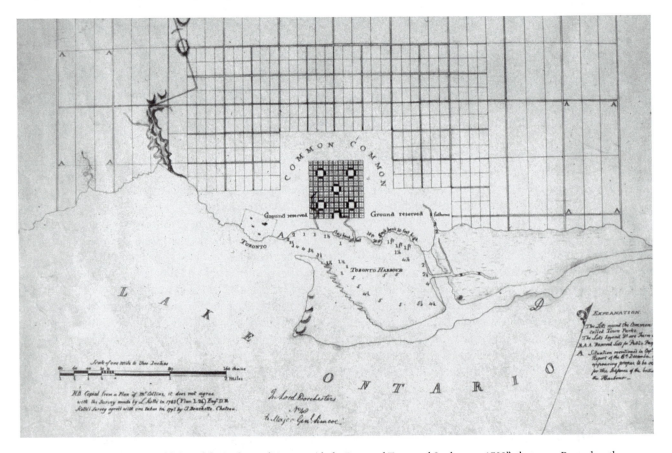

Detail from John Collins's original "Plan of the Harbour of Toronto with the Proposed Town and Settlement, 1788"; that same December, the survey was copied and further refined by Capt. Gother Mann of the British Royal Engineers at Quebec City. (Metropolitan Toronto Reference Library)

A unit from his Queen's Rangers Regiment therefore quit Niagara-on-the-Lake in late July 1793, traveling across Lake Ontario in flat-bottomed bateaux to begin cutting down trees and throwing up crude huts for the forthcoming winter. Simcoe followed a month later with his family and entourage aboard the 6-gun, fourteen-man, 120-ton schooner *Mississauga*, piloted by Capt. Jean-Baptiste Bouchette. Upon disembarking the new governor had a special canvas tent unfurled, complete with wooden floors, doors, and windows. It had originally been designed for Capt. James Cook's Pacific voyages and now would serve as the new settlement's interim Government House. By the end of that same August, a formal ceremony could be held with the assistance of Chief Justice William Osgoode, at which the future town was christened York in honor of Frederick, Duke of York—the second son of King George III, who had just won a victory over French Revolutionary forces in The Netherlands (and is still derisively remembered today as the "Grand Old Duke of York" of a children's rhyme). The surveyor Alexander Aitken then laid out a ten-block grid of private lots bounded by George, Berkeley, Palace (modern Front), and Duke (now part of Adelaide) streets, as well as additional plots farther north for cultivation; the harbor front remained reserved for the Crown.

Col. John Graves Simcoe, founder of "York" or Toronto; disappointed when its lakeshore site was chosen as Upper Canada's new capital rather than London, farther inland in Ontario, he consoled himself by observing that at least York's salmon fishing was good. (Metropolitan Toronto Reference Library)

Over the next few years, more settlers arrived—mostly "late Loyalists," Americans with a greater interest in free land than monarchical principles—who joined the struggle to clear properties and erect better dwellings and soon formed a majority of the civilian population. By 1797 there were 241 permanent residents, with another 196 scattered throughout the surrounding rural townships of York, Scarborough, and Etobicoke. More importantly, enough of a town had been carved out for Upper Canada's government to be transferred across from Niagara-on-the-Lake that same year, and "Little York" (as it had become known, to distinguish it from the more famous cathedral city in England) even expanded westward to Peter Street and the Military Reserve—an area dubbed New Town, although it was to remain sparsely populated for some time thereafter. A simple two-wing legislature was also constructed on Parliament Street, land was set aside for St. James Cathedral, while a jail was completed by 1798, consisting of a tiny log structure with accommodations for only a keeper and three prisoners.

Gradually, this wilderness garrison town began taking on more permanent trappings as its stability and prosperity grew, 5.5 acres of land being set aside for a public market in 1803 (today's Saint Lawrence Market at King and Jarvis streets). The earliest Georgian-style, brick mansion was built at the corner of King and Frederick streets four years later by the French royalist refugee Laurent Quetton de St. George, while the first high school was established and Saint James Cathedral was consecrated that same year of 1807. A limestone lighthouse was raised at Gibraltar Point two years afterward, while water-powered saw- and gristmills had been installed along the banks of the nearby Don River, and breweries and tanneries had also materialized. A troupe of traveling New York actors even performed Richard B. Sheridan's play *School for Scandal* in February 1809, to the delight of the town's nearly 600 inhabitants.

U.S. Invasions (1812–1815)

However, the fledgling community was shocked on 27 June 1812 by news that the United States had declared war against Great Britain nine days previously. Heavily outnumbered in their isolated corner of North America, and with the Crown engrossed in a protracted struggle against Napoleon in Europe, tiny Canadian outposts such as York felt considerable trepidation about the forthcoming hostilities. Remarkably, though, the war began well, as the gifted regional commander Maj.-Gen. Isaac Brock was able to counter an invasion of southwestern Ontario and capture Detroit that same summer, then successfully repel another incursion into the Niagara peninsula that autumn, although at the cost of his own life. Reassured by such victories, York prospered from greatly increased demand for war supplies, as well as the construction of vessels at its new Provincial Marine dockyard (where modern Union Station stands).

Georgian mansion on the corner of King Street East and Frederick Street, originally owned by Laurent Quetton de St. George, as it appeared after being purchased as a regional office for the British "Canada Company" during the latter half of the nineteenth century. (Metropolitan Toronto Reference Library)

U.S. forces regrouped, however, and the next spring, after the ice had broken on Lake Ontario, launched a more effective offensive when Commo. Isaac Chauncey exited Sackets Harbor, New York, on 25 April 1813 with his 24-gun flagship *President Madison* and thirteen lesser consorts, conveying Maj.-Gen. Henry Dearborn's army on a sweep of the Canadian shoreline—starting with a surprise attack against York. The landing force consisted of 1,700 troops, mostly regulars from the 6th, 15th, and 16th U.S. Infantry regiments. The next afternoon, their approaching convoy was sighted from Scarborough Bluffs, and Maj.-Gen. Sir Roger Hale Sheaffe hastily rallied York's 750 defenders: two companies of the 8th, or King's, Infantry Regiment; two companies from the Royal Newfoundland Regiment; a company of Glengarry Light Infantry Fencibles; perhaps 300 volunteers of the 3rd York Militia; 50 to 100 Mississauga, Chippewa, and Ojibway warriors; plus assorted dockyard workers. The town itself lay exposed and indefensible, its unfinished "Fort York"—sprawled along both banks of the Garrison Creek mouth—consisting of little more than some wooden barracks, a powder magazine, and the Governor's House, behind a partial screen of palisades and earthworks.

Yet the invaders steered west of the harbor entrance on the

morning of 27 April 1813, intending to disembark a mile away, near the old Fort Rouillé ruins. Such a decision meant that they would have to fight their way back past the twin-gun Western Battery (near Princes' Gate on the modern Canadian National Exhibition grounds), as well as Half-Moon Battery. The wind in fact carried the invaders so far west that they forged ashore around 8:00 A.M. at Sunnyside (near the present western junction of King and Queen streets), brushing aside some Indian snipers before scattering Capt. Neale McNeale's 8th Grenadier Company with a bayonet charge. Brig. Zebulon Montgomery Pike—the famed prewar explorer—came ashore and marched 1,000 soldiers eastward to engage the Western Battery by 10:00 A.M., supported by fire from Chauncey's armed schooners offshore. After an hour's exchange, one of the battery's portable magazines exploded accidentally, killing twenty defenders and wounding fifteen others, so that the redoubt was evacuated.

Pike's contingent resumed its advance, being briefly checked at 12:30 P.M. by the two 12-pounders of Half-Moon Battery, while Chauncey sailed into the bay and began bombarding Fort York. Having suffered 62 dead and 94 wounded, Sheaffe instructed his surviving regulars to begin retiring east toward Kingston, while simultaneously ordering Fort York's magazine blown and the 30-gun frigate *Sir Isaac Brock* and marine stores in the dockyard torched, so as to prevent their falling into U.S. hands. In the chaos, Pike halted his victorious column a few hundred feet short of Fort York, only to be mortally wounded—along with 37 of his men, plus another 222 injured—when its magazine suddenly detonated and pelted them with falling debris. (Casualties were also inflicted among equally startled British units.) With the withdrawal of Sheaffe and his regulars, the town's actual surrender had to be negotiated by local militia Lt.-Col. William Chewett and Maj. William George Allan, as well as the Reverend John Strachan and acting Attorney-Gen. John Beverley Robinson. Their task was complicated by Pike's unexpected death and the destruction of the *Brock* and dockyard as talks were proceeding, thus depriving the U.S. side of valuable spoils of war.

Yet despite their annoyance, Chauncey and Dearborn offered generous terms, agreeing to respect private property when their troops marched into York at 4:00 P.M. on 27 April 1813. Good discipline was generally maintained, seven eminent citizens later writing: "We must acknowledge that they behaved much better than expected." Government properties, however—including the public library—were thoroughly ransacked over the next few days, while the Fort York compound and house of assembly, or legislature, were burned to the ground on 30 April–1 May, as the disappointed U.S. forces began re-embarking to sail for Niagara a week later.

Chauncey's squadron returned two and a half months later, sailing into the harbor on 31 July 1813 after apparently being informed of some valuable British stores recently deposited at York. Powerless to resist, citizens fled into the interior, while the Reverend Strachan confronted the U.S. commodore amid Fort York's burned remains that same afternoon and was assured that pillage was not the Americans' objective. Finding no military materiel, they sailed away that same night, although some schooners reappeared the next morning, having learned that two British ammunition scows were anchored up the Don River. Attorney-Gen. Robinson and some British dragoons managed to hide them, so that the frustrated raiders then looted and burned some storehouses at Gibraltar Point, before sailing away at daylight on 2 August. The British authorities suspected U.S.-born subjects of having provided intelligence to the enemy during both invasions, yet they were never able to prove such allegations.

For the remainder of the War of 1812, York was to serve as a hospital for convalescent British troops, an average of 400 recuperating from their wounds at any given time. On 15 February 1815, news was received that peace had been restored as of that previous Christmas, so that the town could begin laboriously returning to its previous existence.

Incorporation as "Toronto" (1816–1834)

One of the town's earliest postwar stimulants was the reconstruction of Fort York, whose seven buildings were rebuilt and enclosed by a triangular stockade, plus three protective strong-houses; a military road called Yonge Street was also extended 90 miles due north to the strategically important base at Penetanguishene on Georgian Bay, opening up the

Bird's-eye view northeastward from the approximate foot of modern Parkside Drive, depicting the American fleet bearing down upon York, 27 April 1813; painted a century later by Owen Staples. (Metropolitan Toronto Reference Library)

hinterland for development. And despite their recent difficulties, Yorkers retained sufficient influence to successfully challenge a Crown decision to transfer Upper Canada's capital into larger Kingston: Gov. Francis Gore was persuaded that such upheaval would be needlessly wasteful, so that York's claim as seat of the provincial government was reconfirmed by the official *Gazette* of 12 June 1816.

Trade slowly struggled back to life, aided by the appearance the following year of the first Canadian steamer on Lake Ontario: the *Frontenac*. Nevertheless, York's population rose only from 720 people in 1816 to 1,240 five years later; growth might have been greater, except that the authorities now restricted the influx of U.S. migrants, because of lingering doubts regarding their loyalty. Symptomatic of the town's stagnation was the erection of its brick General Hospital in 1820, which—through lack of funds to furnish and operate it—remained vacant for a number of years, being temporarily taken over by the legislature in 1824 after their own assembly house accidentally burned down.

It was to be the completion of the Erie Canal in 1826 that truly galvanized York, like all other Great Lakes communities, by facilitating mass exports of regional produce to the Atlantic Seaboard, as well as the cheaper importation of manufactured goods from as far away as Europe. Attracted by the district's rising economic prospects, British immigrants began reaching York in growing numbers, its population increasing from 1,719 people in 1826 to 2,235 two years afterward, to 2,860 by 1830, to 5,505 two years later, then 9,252 by 1834. The town blossomed accordingly, a new three-building legislature having been inaugurated in 1829, freeing the General Hospital to become properly activated. A new two-story market made of bricks was completed two years afterward, and fine mansions and churches began to multiply, along with tenements and factories.

In order to regulate such rapid growth, an act of incorporation was passed by the legislature on 4 March 1834 and received royal assent from Lt.-Gov. John Colborne two days later. Curiously, when the bill to incorporate the town of York was sent by the house of assembly for ratification in the upper house—the legislative council—it was returned as a bill to incorporate the "City of Toronto." A debate thereupon ensued among puzzled house members about this name change, ending with a vote in favor of accepting the city's original Indian name, because it was unique and "more musical" than York.

The city's central nucleus was to be delimited on the west by Crookshank's Lane (modern Bathurst Street), by Parliament Street on its east, and to its north by a line drawn 400 yards above Lot (today's Queen) Street. However, there were also sparsely populated city territories called "liberties" beyond these lines, the outer boundaries having actually been fixed at the Don River to the east, Second Concession Road (modern Bloor Street) to the north, and what is today Dufferin Street to the west.

Rebellion and Victorian Evolution (1834–1903)
The recent influx of immigrants had also generated an undercurrent of political unrest, as the city's original English property owners—a close-knit oligarchy derisively dubbed the "Family Compact," because of their frequent intermarriages—sought to monopolize power and impose a conser-

Litho-tint of a rooftop view by John Gilespie, looking westward up King Street East from Victoria Street, toward Yonge and Church streets, 1841. (Metropolitan Toronto Reference Library)

vative, British-style model upon society. Their efforts were resented by leaders among the immigrant communities, who desired a more open approach based upon the U.S. experience. Two rancorous factions soon emerged, known as the Tories and Reformers. The new city was subdivided into five wards, named for the patron saints of the British Isles—Saint Andrew of Scotland, Saint David of Wales, Saint George of England, and Saint Patrick of Ireland—as well as Saint Lawrence, to add a Canadian flavor. Each ward was to elect a pair of aldermen and two common councilmen annually, who would select a mayor from among the aldermen.

Both factions viewed the first municipal election of 27 March 1834 as a test of political wills and so rushed forth candidates, the Reformers defeating the Tories 12–8; the victors thereupon bypassed the moderate Reformer Dr. John Rolph as mayor and instead selected the radical William Lyon Mackenzie—a contentious son of Scottish immigrants who edited the Tory-baiting newspaper *Colonial Advocate*. A political tug-of-war ensued over the next three years, the Tories winning a majority in 1835. The Reformers returned to power in 1836, and then the Tories formed a new government in 1837. In such an unstable atmosphere, organizing better municipal services for the city's 10,871 people proved difficult, furthermore hampered by inadequate financing. The first large, brick sewer had nonetheless been laid from King Street as early as 1835 (greatly stimulated by fears resulting from the cholera epidemic that had ravaged the city in June 1832), while plank sidewalks also began to be installed, and the unpaved streets were "macadamized" or resurfaced with pounded gravel.

Political wrangling finally climaxed when an economic depression gripped the province in 1837, and the supposedly neutral governor, Sir Francis Bond Head—nicknamed "Bonehead" by his many detractors—campaigned to defeat the Reform government at the polls. Incensed by his loss, Mackenzie called for an insurrection at the end of that same year, which was enthusiastically yet ineptly organized. Some 150 rebels mustered prematurely on the evening of 4 December at John Montgomery's tavern, 4 miles north of Toronto on Yonge Street (near the modern intersection with Eglington Avenue). Alerted as to this mutinous assemblage, militia Lt.-Col. James FitzGibbon called out Loyalist volunteers that same night in the city and sent scouts to reconnoiter.

The next day, the high-strung Mackenzie advanced down Yonge Street, his ill-disciplined followers swelling to 1,000 men, most wearing white armbands for identification. After burning the country homes of several prominent Tories, the rebel vanguard was scattered around 4:30 P.M. by a volley from twenty-seven Loyalist pickets under Sheriff William Botsford Jarvis, concealed near the present McGill Street (on the edge of today's Ryerson Polytechnic campus). Both groups fled into the night, after which FitzGibbon was reinforced in Toronto by Loyalist units arriving by steamer. They marched up Yonge Street on 7 December 1837 at the head of 1,000 men in three

columns, supported by two 6-pounders. Brushing aside 200 insurgent pickets at Paul Pry Inn (between Mount Pleasant Cemetery and modern Davisville Avenue), the Loyalists routed the few hundred disheartened insurgents still at Montgomery's tavern, killing two before torching the building and bringing the "Upper Canada Rebellion" to an end. Mackenzie escaped to Buffalo, New York, leaving behind all his papers, so that his comic-opera revolt resulted in scores of subsequent arrests and the execution of two of his lieutenants.

Public disapproval over this ill-judged grab for power doomed the Radical Reform movement to political exile, so that Tories monopolized city government for more than a decade, providing stability during a period of considerable transition. In order to improve Canada's administration, the British government decided to unite both Upper and Lower Canada into a single province in February 1841, choosing Kingston as a new capital. Many Torontonians were dismayed, fearing that such a transfer—with its resultant loss of prestige for their city—would precipitate a business flight, depreciation of property values, and depression. However, their city's importance as a commercial hub for an increasingly prosperous hinterland (being rapidly developed thanks to generous grants directed toward rural public works) assured a steady flow of traffic, so that its economic prospects did not diminish. The English novelist Charles Dickens even commented upon his visit to Toronto in 1842: "The town itself is full of life and motion, bustle, business, and improvement. The streets are well paved and lighted with gas (an innovation introduced only late that previous year); the houses are large and good; the shops excellent."

Civic confidence was moreover encouraged by the inauguration of the University of Toronto and reorganization of the public school system in 1843, as well as by the opening of a grand, multistory city hall the next year; a moderate Reform newspaper called the *Globe* also appeared in 1844 (eventually evolving into today's *Globe and Mail*), while the city's first telegraph went into service by December 1846. Toronto's population increased appreciably as well, growing from 14,249 people in 1849 to 19,706 only four years later, then being further augmented by a great wave of Irish emigration following the Potato Famine, which caused 40,000 refugees to stream through Toronto during 1847 alone.

With the completion of a Canadian canal system in 1848, Toronto's rise was assured, as vessels could thereafter sail as far as the Atlantic and return unimpeded. The city's vitality was now such that it could shrug off a devastating predawn fire on 17 April 1849 that ignited just northeast of the modern intersection of King Street East and Jarvis, consuming six entire blocks of the congested downtown area—including Saint James Cathedral—before finally being extinguished by volunteer firefighters and a fortuitous rain shower. Losses were promptly replaced by stout brick buildings, and this dislocation did not prevent Toronto from serving as national capital

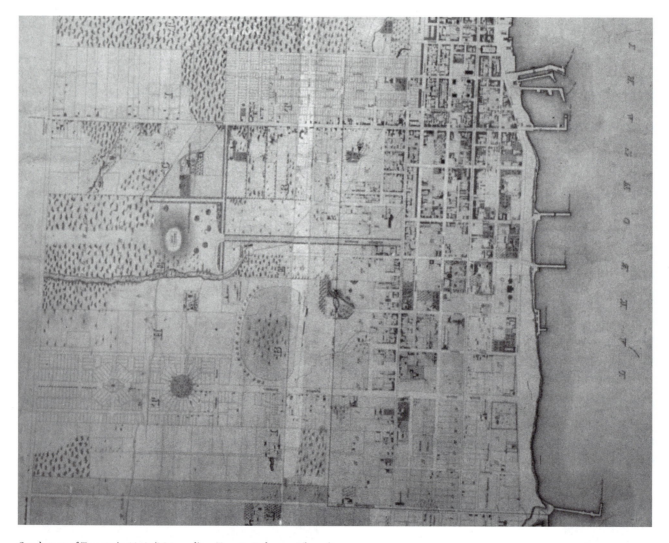

Cane's map of Toronto in 1842. (Metropolitan Toronto Reference Library)

again as of 1849 until 1851, then again from 1855 to 1859, in alternation with Quebec City. Toronto's population had surged to 25,166 residents by 1850 and 30,775 a year afterward.

An even more welcome boost to local prosperity was provided by the laying of Toronto's first railroads: the Northern Railway, which extended as far as Aurora by May 1853, Barrie by October, and Collingwood on Georgian Bay by January 1855; a link with the Great Western Railway at nearby Hamilton, which was connected the latter year; plus Montreal's Grand Trunk Railway, which reached Toronto by 1856. Such a network allowed the city to receive and distribute goods more effectively than before, without becoming overly dependent upon any single source, as tracks radiated out in all directions. Rail lines moreover penetrated into rural areas previously inaccessible to ship traffic, and they operated year-round, regardless of winter ice, thereby enhancing overall economic performance. Toronto's harbor nevertheless remained highly useful for cheap shipments of bulk items, and a new channel

called the Eastern Gap was rather fortunately cut through its narrow peninsula by a spring storm in April 1858.

Canadian produce experienced a slump when global demands eased with the conclusion of the Crimean War in 1856, a downturn felt most acutely in Toronto because local capital was overextended because of the recent flush of investments. The ensuing depression lasted only until 1861, however, after which the economy temporarily revived with the outbreak of the U.S. Civil War. The city's first horse-drawn streetcar service was inaugurated along Yonge, King, and Queen streets that same year, and modern conveniences such as piped water through indoor plumbing, central heating with more efficient stoves, and indoor gas lighting began appearing in many homes.

By the time Canada achieved its independence from Britain via the Act of Confederation of 1 July 1867, Toronto's population stood at 49,016 residents, and it was declared the capital of the newly created Province of Ontario. Despite another depression, which struck in 1873, the city emerged as a banking and insurance leader, gradually expanding beyond its physical boundaries—past Ossington Avenue in the west, the Don River to its east, and engulfing Yorkville to its north. At the same time, it exhibited all the strengths and weaknesses of a conservative, Puritanical society of the high Victorian era: for although now sufficiently stable and secure to survive business slowdowns, Toronto was also palpably divided into upper and lower classes, its increasingly flamboyant mansions, corporate headquarters, and churches standing in stark contrast to lowly tenements. Wages were meager and labor conditions in many factories were primitive, so that well-intentioned reformers struggled to alleviate living conditions for the poor through such efforts as the foundation of the Home for Incurables (modern Queen Elizabeth Hospital) in 1874 and Sick Children's Hospital the next year, as well as setting aside public recreational areas such as 335-acre High Park, opened in 1873–1877.

Progress continued apace, the city's first telephone exchange being introduced in 1879, while a permanent Industrial Exhibition was established in September of that same year (reconstituted as the Canadian National Exhibition, or CNE, as of 1904). Torontonians also took great pride in the rowing exploits of their world champion sculler Ned Hanlan, as well as the more intellectual accomplishment of Sir Sandford Fleming, who invented standard global time. (When it was adopted by the Washington Conference, Toronto had to advance its own clocks by seventeen minutes on 18 November 1883.) Starting that same year, a series of annexations absorbed several outlying suburbs, so that Toronto increased in physical size by about 50 percent, and its population jumped from 81,372 inhabitants in 1882 to 181,215 by 1891. The University of Toronto also grew significantly, with the incorporation of several smaller theological colleges in 1884, and electric power became widely available throughout the city for the first time. Horse-drawn streetcars began to be supplanted by electrified ones as of 1892; a grand new provincial legislature building and city hall were also unveiled in 1892 and 1899, respectively.

View of the devastation left by Toronto's great fire of 19 April 1904; photograph taken eight days later from atop the customshouse at the corner of Yonge Street, looking west along Front Street. (Metropolitan Toronto Reference Library)

Panoramic view of Toronto's harbor in 1856 by the civil engineer William Armstrong, looking north from Hanlan's Point on the peninsula opposite; the long, low building at center was the Provincial Parliament. (Metropolitan Toronto Reference Library)

The first locomotive manufactured in Ontario, completed at James Good's factory in May 1853 and named the Toronto, as photographed ca. 18: (Metropolitan Toronto Reference Library)

Second Great Fire and Modern Era (1904–Present)

Another economic boom as of 1896 propelled the city into the twentieth century, its population climbing to 208,040 people by 1901. Then, on 19 April 1904, a fire broke out in a neckwear manufactory in the Currie Building on the north side of Wellington Street West, in the heart of Toronto's warehouse district, rapidly spreading to other structures as firefighters found water pressure too low and not enough hydrants available. As the flames spiraled out of control, Mayor Thomas Urquhart telegraphed neighboring cities for help, and rail lines were cleared for special trains to rush in additional firefighters and equipment from Hamilton, Niagara Falls, Buffalo, London, and Peterborough.

Eventually the blaze was brought under control through their combined efforts, aided by a few buildings that contained privately installed sprinkler systems and the fact that the wind was blowing out toward the lake. Almost 20 acres and 100 structures were nonetheless consumed, representing more than $10 million in damages and 5,000 to 6,000 temporarily idled workers. Still, no lives had been lost, and reconstruction was initiated forthwith. Adoption of more up-to-date techniques, such as the use of structural steel frames and high-speed elevators in buildings, meant that taller structures could be erected to replace the old, resulting in the emergence of grand edifices such as Union Station and a new customshouse, while a high-pressure water system went into operation by 1909.

Other civic improvements followed in rapid succession, the Royal Alexandra Theater having opened its doors in 1907, the same year in which a 15,000-seat sports stadium was built on the Canadian National Exhibition grounds. A symphony orchestra was founded the next year; a magnificent new public library was inaugurated in 1909 (thanks to generous financial assistance from the American philanthropist Andrew Carnegie); a Board of Harbor Commissioners was appointed two years later to improve channels and wharves, so as to receive ever larger shipping; 900 acres were set aside on the peninsula opposite for recreational parks (today's Toronto Islands, still accessible via ferry); and a new general hospital was unveiled in 1913, as was the magnificent Royal Ontario Museum two years later.

The city successfully weathered dislocations occasioned by the outbreak of World War I in 1914—prospering from increased industrial demands, yet sacrificing some 10,000 young men to that European conflict—as well as the transition

University College at the University of Toronto on a snowy Friday, 24 January 1896. (Metropolitan Toronto Reference Library)

to a peacetime economy four years later. Urban transport was significantly enhanced by the establishment of the Toronto Transit Commission, or TTC, in 1921, which so standardized and modernized the many competing services that it was possible to travel throughout the entire city system on a single ticket as of two years later. Another major scientific accomplishment was the discovery of insulin at the University of Toronto that same year of 1921 by a four-man team led by Dr. Frederick Banting (who was knighted and received the 1923 Nobel Prize). Harbor facilities and highways continued to be improved, but prosperity was abruptly curtailed by the stock market crash of October 1929, which ushered in the Great Depression. A most difficult decade ensued, which, however, culminated with a few noteworthy innovations, such as the creation in 1937 of Trans-Canada Airlines (today's Air Canada), fomenting the construction of Malton International and Toronto Island airports over the next couple of years. The nation's first superhighway was created, complete with night lighting, and it was named the "Queen Elizabeth Way" when officially inaugurated in May 1939 by the visiting monarch, George VI, and his consort.

The eruption of World War II in September of that same year proved another mixed blessing for Toronto, restoring prosperity because of heightened demand—by 1943, more than two-thirds of the city's laborers were engaged in war-related work—while simultaneously straining municipal services and housing. After peace was restored in 1945, authorities began addressing such problems by initiating work on a subway system four years later, then hammering out an agreement that annexed outlying townships and created "Metropolitan Toronto" in 1953, a single square-mile entity embracing 1.25 million residents (of whom less than 680,000 lived within the old city boundaries).

Such amalgamation permitted a more efficient use of funds and more rational planning, so that large-scale projects could now be undertaken, such as expanding the old harbor facilities to receive the larger oceangoing ships that had begun entering the Great Lakes through the new Saint Lawrence Seaway as of June 1960. Toronto also became increasingly cosmopolitan, a post–World War II immigration wave transforming it from a city with 59 percent residents of British descent in 1941 to a multiethnic metropolis a generation later. Such change was even exemplified by its new city hall, designed by Viljo Rewell of Helsinki and opened in 1965 to look down upon Nathan Phillips Square, named for Toronto's first Jewish mayor.

By 1967, Toronto's population had reached 1,887,798 people, and nine years later it surpassed Montreal as Canada's most populous city. The Francophone nationalism and socialist policies accompanying the election of the first separatist government in the Province of Quebec in 1976 further accelerated this trend, as large multinational firms transferred their operations into more stable Ontario, with a resultant boom in Toronto's economy and job market. By 1991 its residents numbered 3,893,046—almost 775,000 more than in Montreal—while it had furthermore become the undisputed financial and commercial leader for Canada, as well as a prominent international city.

For additional sources on the history of Toronto, please consult the Select Bibliography at the end of this volume.

United States

*[H]alfway up the hill, I see the Past
lying beneath me with its sounds and sights,
a city in the twilight dim and vast,
with smoking roofs, soft bells, and gleaming lights.*

—Henry Wadsworth Longfellow (1807–1882)

BOSTON
Seaport that evolved into early America's leading city and still today retains a significant cultural and political influence.

Exploration (1614–1629)
Although the rugged shoreline of Massachusetts had been known to transatlantic fishermen and seamen since the six-teenth century, no permanent European settlement was attempted because of its inhospitable winters, stubborn soils, and lack of readily exploitable resources. Bartholomew Gosnold visited Massachusetts Bay and named Cape Cod in 1602, while Samuel de Champlain also reconnoitered the area for France two years afterward. John Smith conducted an even more detailed survey from Penobscot to Cape Cod during

Aerial view looking west-southwestward across modern Boston. Note the skyscrapers clustered atop its original Shawmut Peninsula, as well as the extensive commercial development of its Back Bay area. (City of Boston)

521

July–August 1614 with two ships financed by the Virginia Company of English merchants, assigning various place-names and dubbing the entire stretch of coastline "New England."

Yet no actual colonization effort was made until 1620, and then merely by chance, when a band of religious idealists bound for Virginia aboard the *Mayflower* were driven off course and disembarked at Plymouth. About half their number perished over that ensuing winter, yet the survivors remained and were joined by others, who carved out small settlements along the coastline. One individual, named Robert Gorges, founded a tiny community at Wessagusset (modern Weymouth) in the summer of 1623, and when that toehold failed two years later, one of its members—an eccentric and unmarried Anglican clergyman and master of arts from Cambridge University named the Rev. William Blaxton, or Blackstone—ventured north into the rock-lined bay known among local Indians as Shawmut. There he erected a house and planted an orchard near an excellent spring on the western slope of a hilly peninsula jutting across the inner recesses of its bay (near modern Beacon and Spruce streets). Over the next several years, a handful of neighbors appeared nearby, such as Thomas Walford on the mainland opposite and Samuel Maverick on Noddle's Island.

Meanwhile, adherents of a religious fundamentalist sect back in England called Puritans became interested in immigrating to the West Indies or North America, so as to pursue their beliefs without official constraint. A commercial patent was obtained by one such group in 1628 to revive a defunct fishing outpost at Cape Ann, so that a 180-person advance party set sail under John Endicott to secure a foothold. Another royal patent was then procured from King Charles I on 4 March 1629 (according to the "Old Style" [O.S.] Julian calendar then in use; 14 March according to our "New Style," or modern Gregorian calendar), authorizing the establishment of a distinct Massachusetts Bay commercial colony that would extend from 3 miles south of the Charles River to 3 miles north of the Merrimack River. John Winthrop was elected "governor" that same October over this second Puritan band, who furthermore agreed to shift their entire "commercial" enterprise—directors, managers, stockholders, and so forth—across the Atlantic, so that 700 settlers struck out aboard eleven ships in April–May 1630.

Upon arriving in Massachusetts, Winthrop and his Puritan latecomers judged Endicott's sickly advance base camp at Salem to be unsatisfactory, so he proceeded to the north shore of the Charles River mouth in July 1630, to a site christened "Charlestown." Yet owing to a lack of freshwater and defensive vulnerabilities at this second locale as well, plus the need to husband their scant resources against the forthcoming winter, they opted to disperse into smaller groupings—the largest single band accepting an invitation from Blaxton to shift over to his lonely Shawmut outpost, also known as "Trimount" or "Trimountain" Peninsula because of its distinctive triple peak.

(This eminence was later to become dubbed "Beacon Hill," as a bonfire was kept in constant readiness to alert the district of any approaching dangers; the term "Trimount" became garbled into "Tremont" or "Tramount.") During one final meeting celebrated at Charlestown on 17 September, this group of colonists furthermore agreed to call their new community Boston, in honor of the Lincolnshire town from which so many of them had come.

Foundation as Puritan Capital (1630–1684)

The first official settler meeting—known as a "General Court"—was held at Boston on 19 October 1630 (O.S.), during which 108 male members applied to become "freemen," or enfranchised citizens, while toiling to complete their rudimentary homes against the onset of winter. Of the 1,000 Puritans now dispersed around Massachusetts Bay, some 100 deserted when their ships weighed for the return passage to England; malnourishment and disease claimed another 200 over that ensuing winter. Fears of a possible French raid—England having only recently concluded peace with that nation—prompted a resolution for the erection of a single fortified Puritan stronghold a mile east of Watertown the next spring, yet no such effort was ever seriously undertaken.

Instead, the central cluster of Boston, Charlestown, and "New Towne" (modern Cambridge) flourished in about equal measure over the next couple of years, before the former was finally recognized as de facto capital in 1632. Two years later, it was agreed that a pair of representatives would be elected every year from all other Puritan townships to attend quarterly sessions at Boston's "Great and General Court." That town's predominance owed much to its wide and deep anchorage—ensconced at the "bottom" of Massachusetts Bay, 6.5 miles distant from the ocean—which allowed seagoing ships to anchor close enough inshore to offload their cargoes easily; redistribution inland was then by riverboat. Boston's defensive capabilities also played a significant role in its select status, as its narrow approach channel was lined with menacing rocks, and its peninsula was accessible from the mainland only via a narrow neck of land that could be easily fortified. Batteries enclosed by log ramparts filled with earth were also erected atop Copp's and Fort hills to cover the anchorage.

Because of a growing rift between the king and Parliament back in England, the Massachusetts Bay colony was to exist as an almost semiautonomous private commonwealth over the next few decades, developing its own laws, tax system, and judiciary, all strongly shaped by Puritan zealotry. Its settlers also began to spread inland, virtually eradicating the Pequot Indians during a war in 1637, while a strong earthquake rattled the area the next year. Nevertheless, another 14,000 mostly Puritan immigrants streamed into the colony via Boston before the English Civil War finally erupted in 1642. The next year, a loose confederation called the "United Colonies of New England" was formed by Massachusetts, Connecticut, Plymouth, and New

Haven, in which Boston was to exert considerable influence before that association gradually faded.

Ironically, the triumph of Oliver Cromwell's Puritan forces in the English Civil War slowed the pace of immigration to North America, although Massachusetts was by now quite self-sufficient, its strategic position at the northeastern tip of the continent allowing it to dominate most seaborne contacts with New England, the Grand Banks, and Europe. (Early in 1650, Bostonian sympathizers were even able to send a shipload of provisions to a struggling group of coreligionists in the Bahamas, who reciprocated with a gift of 10 tons of braziletto wood—which, upon being sold at auction, provided a substantial portion of Harvard College's endowment.) In July 1654, Massachusetts also raised a substantial military expedition under Maj. Robert Sedgewick to assault French "Acadia" (modern Nova Scotia) in reprisal for attacks against British shipping.

But the Puritan colony's chosen isolation began to be breached after Cromwell died and his successor state collapsed in England, paving the way for the exiled Charles II to be peacefully installed on the throne in London as of spring 1660. This restoration of the Stuart monarchy was unenthusiastically acknowledged at Boston as of 7 August 1661 (O.S.), after which the king's privy council—seeking to impose stricter royal control over all overseas dominions—created a committee in London to look into New England's peculiar self-governing status. A Crown commission made an inspection tour in 1665; the next year Charles addressed a circular to all inhabitants of New England, expressing particular dissatisfaction with affairs in Massachusetts. That feeling was echoed by many of its own Puritan citizenry, known as "Moderates" for deploring the extreme pretentiousness of their theocratic leaders, as well as the intolerance directed against non-Puritan traders settling in Boston, who were denied the right to become enfranchised or establish churches in their own faith.

New England was moreover shaken when the Algonquian tribes rose in revolt in June 1675 against the unremitting expansion inland by settlers, igniting a conflict known as "King Philip's War" because of the Christian name applied to the sachem (chieftain) Metacomet. Hundreds of militiamen, aided by loyal Mohican allies, had to be rushed into the interior of Massachusetts, Connecticut, and Rhode Island as remote communities went up in flames, and an Indian counteroffensive during that unusually mild winter even razed Weymouth, Groton, parts of Plymouth, and finally Sudbury—just 15 miles outside Boston. The colonists' fortunes did not revive until the spring and summer of 1676, when the hostiles were decimated by famine and disease, so that Capt. Benjamin Church was at last able to surprise Metacomet's camp near Mount Hope that same August and slay him, carrying his head into Plymouth upon a pole.

Some 600 New Englanders had nonetheless succumbed during these hostilities, representing one out of every sixteen men of military age in Massachusetts and Connecticut; overseas reinforcement was needed, and Puritan intransigence became weakened. The exasperated royal commissioner, Edward Randolph, had on 10 March 1676 (O.S.) informed the most hard-line theocratic leaders at Boston that they were acting in contempt of Crown authority; he sailed for England on 30 July to so advise the privy council. Transatlantic litigation ensued, the Puritan leaders ignoring or delaying compliance with many royal orders in hopes of retaining as much of their "old charter" intact, until quo warranto proceedings were finally instituted in London's Chancery Court as of 1683. Massachusetts reverted to a royal colony—temporarily bereft of any charter at all—as of 16 June 1684 (O.S.).

Royal Capital of New England (1685–1763)

When Charles II died early the next year and was succeeded on the throne by his brother James II, London redoubled its efforts to assert Crown authority over all of New England by melding its diverse private colonies into a single "Dominion of New England," to be administered from Boston by a new royal governor. Sir Edmund Andros arrived in 1685 with 100 soldiers aboard the frigate HMS *Rose* of Capt. John George, supplanting Joseph Dudley—son of one of the original settlers. Next year, the visiting bookseller John Dunton described the capital of Boston as a "rich and very populous" town, "much frequented by strangers," and whose edifices mostly faced onto its bay and were crowded close together on streets that were:

> many and large, paved with pebbles; the materials of the houses are brick, stone, lime, handsomely contrived (especially along the High Street towards the Common), and when any new houses are built, they are made conformable to our new buildings in London (whose construction regulations had been revised and more strictly enforced as a result of the Great Fire of 1666).

Dunton also noted Boston's two bustling markets; its "three fair and large meeting-houses or churches"; its Town Hall "built upon pillars in the middle of the town, where their merchants meet and confer every day"; its fine gardens and orchards in the southern sector, especially around the "small but pleasant Common, where the gallants a little before sunset walk with their Marmalet Madams . . . till the nine o'clock bell rings them home; after which the constables walk their rounds to see good order is kept, and to take up loose people."

The Puritan seaport's commercial life depended upon shipbuilding, Grand Banks fishing, and trade as far abroad as the West Indies, Europe, and even Africa. Politically, its moderate and theocratic factions had been reunified by the imposition of the unpopular "tyrant" Andros, so that when the Protestant prince William of Orange and his consort Mary Stuart landed in England in November 1688 to unseat the pro-Catholic James in a bloodless coup known as the "Glorious Revolution," disgruntled Bostonians availed themselves of the opportunity to depose their own royal governor. On the morning of 18 April 1689 (O.S.), a mob seized Captain George and numerous other dignitaries, before sending a surrender demand to Andros within the fort, which he grudgingly accepted that same afternoon and became confined. A wave of anxiety ensued when reports arrived that August from England that the former king, James, had landed in Ireland with a French army to attempt to regain his throne; the news prompted a few counterrevolts around Boston, which were promptly squelched.

Conflict with France erupted as well, known as King William's War, so that Andros was deported to London the following spring and New England's native-born "provost-marshal," Sir William Phips—once a rough-hewn Boston carpenter, who had struck it rich by salvaging a Spanish wreck in the Caribbean—organized a 700-man seaborne expedition to raid French Acadia in May 1690, returning triumphantly one month later. Inspired by this easy success, he led a second offensive of 2,000 men and thirty-two vessels against Quebec City that August, which limped back into Boston by the end of November missing six ships, which led to many bankruptcies.

The town also suffered a destructive conflagration that same year, yet these setbacks began to be reversed once King William granted Massachusetts its long-delayed charter in 1691, expanding its territory to incorporate the disputed province of Maine and Plymouth. More important, while Puritans retained their original liberties and freedom of worship, equal rights and enfranchisement were extended to other faiths, leading to a more open and vigorous civic life. Still, when Rear Adm. Sir Francis Wheler arrived at Boston from the West Indies in June 1693 with a Royal Navy fleet to participate in another venture against the French at Quebec, he found no New England contingent assembled; his own crews quickly became so diseased that after a series of consultations with Phips and members of the council, it was decided to forgo any invasion attempt.

Peace with France was restored by 1697, and Boston entered a period of considerable growth as overseas commerce boomed, despite a smallpox epidemic that struck the town five years later. By the early 1700s, its waterfront and Charlestown opposite boasted fourteen shipyards and more than seventy-five wharves. The outbreak of the next European conflict—Queen Anne's War—began with border skirmishes against the French in Acadia in the summer of 1704. It grew three years later into a major offensive when a Bostonian expedition sailed against Port Royal (modern Annapolis Royal, Nova Scotia), only to return in disgrace. That failure, coupled with Adjutant-Gen. Samuel Vetch's inability to support a land invasion of French Canada by Col. Francis Nicholson's militia army advancing up the Hudson River in the summer of 1709, convinced the New England authorities to request royal troops and warships from London.

Nicholson himself visited the English capital, returning to Boston in July 1710 with a small Royal Navy squadron under Commo. George Martin. A local militia contingent was then raised to mount a second attempt against Port Royal in conjunction with the anticipated arrival of an army of British regulars under Maj.-Gen. Viscount Shannon. Although that force failed to materialize, Nicholson, Vetch, and Martin nonetheless sailed from Nantasket by September with thirty-one transports bearing 3,500 troops in five regiments (two from Massachusetts, plus one each from Connecticut, New Hampshire, and Rhode Island). Port Royal's French garrison was surprised and overwhelmed a month later, Nicholson renaming it "Annapolis Royal" in honor of Queen Anne, before installing Vetch with 500 men as a garrison and returning to Boston one week later.

Elated by his success, Nicholson visited London again to persuade the Crown to engage in a much larger military effort deep into French Canada; he reappeared by June 1711 with eleven Royal Navy warships under Rear Adm. Sir Hovenden Walker, plus fifty-one transports bearing 5,300 redcoats under Brig. John Hill. An additional 1,300 New England militiamen were raised, and the expedition set sail in early August to invest Quebec City; Nicholson would push northward from Albany a month later with another 2,300 volunteers to threaten Montreal. However, Walker's fleet lost eight ships and 900 men in a calamitous shipwreck, so that both operations were canceled; hostilities ceased a couple of years later.

Boston emerged from this war commercially invigorated, especially by the completion of its privately financed Long Wharf in 1710—so named because it thrust for an impressive 800 feet out into the anchorage from the warehouse district at the foot of King's Street (modern State Street), thereby allowing multiple ships to be received and processed "without the assistance of boats." Another significant improvement, emblematic of the port's rise to regional prominence, was the inauguration in September 1716 of the first lighthouse in Colonial America: the so-called Boston Light, a stone tower with large whale oil lamps erected on Great Brewster Island and maintained by fees garnered from ship traffic. (Great Brewster Island subsequently became known as "Beacon Island," because its light tower would signal the approach of any large number of vessels to the harbor fort, called Castle William, which in turn would advise the warning fire above Boston to be lit.)

The town continued to prosper despite setbacks such as the arrival of a vessel from the Caribbean in late April 1721 bearing a slave infected with smallpox, which spread among Boston's 10,000 inhabitants until perhaps half became diseased; 800 had died by the end of that year. The town was also rattled by another earthquake in 1727, yet members of its increasingly affluent shipowners' elite, such as Peter Faneuil, Charles Apthorp, Thomas Boylston, and Thomas Amory, were able to indulge in the construction of fine mansions filled with imported luxuries, as well as country estates at such outlying retreats as Milton or Cambridge. Yet despite Boston's growing

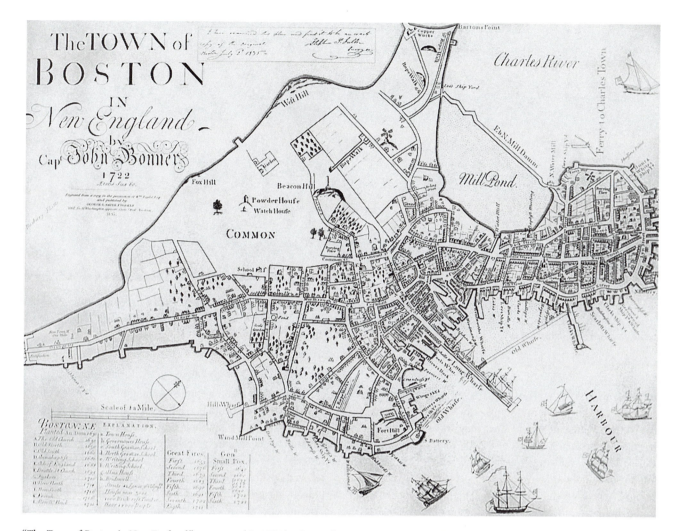

"The Town of Boston in New England," as surveyed in 1722 by Capt. John Bonner; reprinted in 1867. North is toward upper right. (Massachusetts Historical Society)

sophistication, its Puritan "Congregational" churches still received regular grants from the municipal government, and a strong Puritan ethic governed social conduct. The 1740 visitor John Bennet, for example, noted how Boston's observance of the Sabbath was "the strictest kept that ever I yet saw anywhere."

Bennet found much to admire in "the capital of New England," describing it as being "as dry and clean" as any town he could remember, with enhanced harbor facilities at that time handling 300 to 400 vessels annually; Long Wharf had by then almost doubled to 1,600 feet in length. He especially admired the way in which buildings rose "with an easy ascent westward about a mile," adding that there were "a great many good houses and several fine streets." He estimated the total number of edifices at 3,000, of which fifteen were churches; there were "several booksellers' shops, and there are four or five printing-houses which have full employment in printing and reprinting books . . . brought from England or other parts of Europe." Bulk exports of lumber and provisions to the Carolinas and West Indies were reciprocated with rum, sugar, spices, and logwood for re-export to England, further supplemented by the local whale and cod fisheries, plus a great deal of shipbuilding. Citizens recreated on "[w]hat they call the Mall . . . a walk on a fine green Common adjoining to the southwest side of the town. It is near half a mile over, with two rows of young trees planted opposite to each other."

Ferry service from the North End communicated with Charlestown, and mainland roads were "exceeding good in summer, and it is safe traveling night or day, for they have no highway robbers to interrupt them." About 6 miles distant, the cluster of Harvard College, Stoughton Hall, and Massachusetts Hall composed "a University called Cambridge."

Boston's commerce was to be bolstered when tensions with France erupted into King George's War in May 1744, many of its merchants, shipwrights, chandlers, and sailors profiting when the port became a major marshaling point for a renewed

Panoramic view of Boston in 1743 by William Price, based upon a view executed eighteen years previously by William Burgis. Roxbury and Fort Hill appear at the left, Charlestown at the far right, while beyond the mouth of the Charles River can be faintly discerned Harvard College. Note the prominence accorded Long Wharf at center, which jutted almost 1,600 feet out into the busy anchorage. (American Antiquarian Society)

offensive against Canada. Gov. William Shirley spent that ensuing winter raising funds and supplies for a large New England expedition against the main French bulwark of Louisbourg at the tip of Cape Breton Island, until 2,800 volunteers under the militia Lt.-Gen. William Pepperrell and militia Brig. Samuel Waldo set sail aboard fifty-one transports on Sunday afternoon, 4 April 1745; they subdued that French citadel a month and a half later. A huge counterexpedition of sixty ships and 11,000 men out of France under Adm. Jean-Baptiste-Louis de la Rochefoucauld de Roye, Duc d'Anville, briefly severed contact with those New England occupiers by putting into uninhabited Chebucto Bay (modern Halifax) in September 1746; yet there was too much illness in the French fleet after its stormy transatlantic passage to seriously discomfit either Louisbourg or Boston.

However, the New England capital—whose structures were made mostly of wood—suffered an accidental fire in 1747. The following year Louisbourg was restored to French control with the signing of the peace treaty, so that Shirley persuaded the British Crown to settle Halifax quickly as an advance naval base in case of future conflict. When the French and Indian War erupted in 1756, Boston was no longer to serve as the principal marshaling area for expeditions bound against Canada; James Campbell, Earl of Loudoun, reached Massachusetts with two British infantry regiments that same July and succeeded Shirley as New England's governor, only to use New York City as his rallying point for convoys bound toward the new advance base of Halifax. Boston nonetheless profited from the ensuing round of warfare until Quebec City was conquered in 1759, ending Britain's major military efforts in North America.

Another devastating conflagration gutted a portion of the town in 1760, and Boston's economy sputtered for the final two years of the war against France. When the Treaty of Fontainebleu's signing revealed that Canada was not to be restored to French control, the removal of this perennial threat relieved Boston of the need for constant military preparedness, unleashing long-simmering political, economic, and social grievances.

Patriot Tinderbox (1764–1776)

Although the city was no longer the largest metropolis in British North America, Boston's tradition of independent thinking was to spearhead an emergent national movement that would culminate with the rupture between London and the Thirteen Colonies. When Parliament passed the Sugar Act in 1764 and the Stamp Act the next year, New Englanders reacted angrily against both unilateral impositions. In Boston a riotous mob even destroyed the home of Lt.-Gov. Thomas Hutchinson on 26 August 1765, and the refusal by local merchants to affix the requisite stamps to their transactions brought trade and the courts to a virtual standstill. Parliament consequently repealed the Stamp Act the following year, yet it sought to reaffirm its right to tax the colonies by passing the Declaratory Act, under which policy the Townshend Acts placed new duties upon lead, glass, papers, paint, and tea.

Bostonians were once again galvanized into opposition, well-to-do merchants making common cause with such proletarian leaders as Samuel Adams, whose "Liberty Party" clashed openly with revenue collectors and Loyalist subjects. With civic defiance threatening to become more than local magistrates and watchmen could contain, the Crown dispatched two infantry regiments to garrison the town; they landed on 1 October 1768. Denied the usual accommodations among citizens' homes, the redcoats encamped upon the Common, and frictions escalated until an angry throng of agitators confronted a heavy-handed British sentinel guarding the customshouse on King Street at 8:00 P.M. on 5 March 1770. The squad sent to his support opened fire, killing five people and wounding six, and only prompt intervention by Hutchinson in promising to try the offending troops prevented the so-called Boston Massacre from igniting a bloody insurrection. Nonetheless, at a town meeting convened by Adams, 3,000 of his Sons of Liberty roared for the immediate expulsion of both regiments to Castle William, far out in the harbor, to which Hutchinson reluctantly assented.

Tensions moderated somewhat once a trial exonerated most of the soldiers and Parliament repealed all duties—except for the tax on tea, retained to reassert that body's sovereignty. Consequently, resistance revived anew until Samuel Adams and some of his radical adherents decided to act against three ships that had arrived late in 1773 with cargoes of East India Company tea, moored at Griffin's Wharf. At the conclusion of a town meeting on 16 December, they donned disguises as Indians, boarded the vessels, opened the chests of tea, and threw the contents into the harbor. In retaliation for

this so-called Tea Party, Parliament passed the Boston Port Bill the next year, ordering that the harbor be closed to all trade until the East India Company had been compensated for its losses and "reasonable satisfaction" had been extended to the revenue officers and others injured during the outburst.

Upon being promulgated on 1 June 1774, this punitive bill fanned even greater resentment—not only among Bostonians but also among all the other colonies as well, contributing to the calling of the first Continental Congress in protest at Philadelphia that same September. As antiroyalist sentiment escalated, more redcoats were sent to garrison Boston under Maj.-Gen. Sir Thomas Gage, while colonists in outlying communities countered by forming a skeleton militia organization dubbed the Minutemen, which began gathering ammunition and supplies.

Finally, Gage—under mounting pressure from London to take more direct action against this spreading sedition—decided on 14 April 1775 to stealthily detach a column to destroy the supplies stockpiled at nearby Concord and arrest delegates bound for the Second Continental Congress. Paul Revere and William Dawes carried forewarnings of this intended sally, so that when Lt.-Col. Francis Smith emerged from Boston with 800 men on the night of 18–19 April, his vanguard—six companies of light infantry under Maj. John

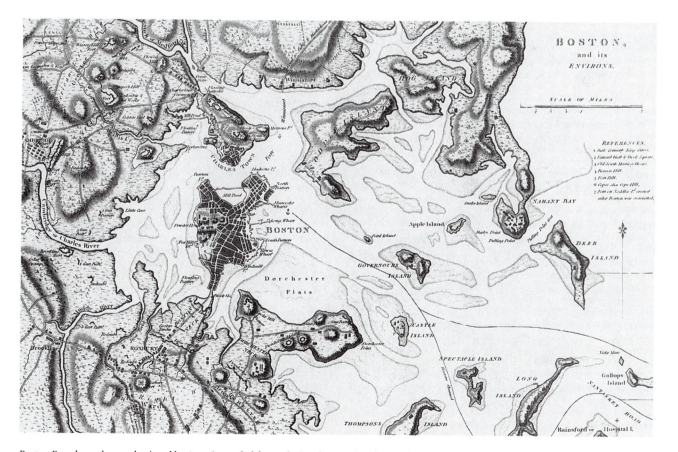

Boston Bay, shown here as besieged by American rebel forces during the opening phases of the Revolutionary War in 1775–1776. Note how the original city occupied only a peninsula within the bay, joined to the mainland by a narrow "neck" of land. (William Faden, *North American Atlas*)

Pitcairn, some 200 redcoats in all—were met at dawn by a hastily assembled company of Minutemen at Lexington, 6 miles short of Concord, and armed resistance exploded. Despite fighting their way through to Concord and reversing their march by noon, the British were harassed by constant sniper fire, suffering some 250 casualties before Brig. Lord Hugh Percy could push out of Boston with 1,400 men and two 6-pounders to reinforce Smith's bloodied column at Lexington, helping it regain the safety of the naval guns at Charlestown Neck.

Widespread American outrage over this bloody sortie led Boston to become besieged within a week, while Gage's garrison was reinforced from sea on 25 May 1775 by other British contingents under Maj.-Gens. "Gentleman Johnny" Burgoyne, William Howe, and Henry Clinton, bringing their total strength to 6,500 troops—soon opposed by some 15,000 militiamen from throughout Massachusetts and other colonies, who, although short of ammunition and heavy equipment, installed their headquarters at Cambridge and began erecting a half ring of redoubts in the encircling countryside. On 12 June, Gage offered a royal pardon to all insurgents except Adams and John Hancock, an offer ignored by the besiegers. Then, the Americans learned the next day that the British intended to seize the Charlestown Peninsula on 18 June, so that Gen. Artemas Ward countered by sending Col. William Prescott with 1,600 men on the evening of 16 June to dispute that design by digging in atop Breed's Hill.

At dawn of 17 June 1775, HMSS *Glasgow, Lively, Somerset,* and *Falcon* opened fire against Prescott's trenches in anticipation of the sally, Howe disembarking by noon with 2,400 heavily burdened redcoats, who were twice repulsed as they advanced upon the American lines. Bolstered by an additional 400 troops under Clinton, and with the patriots running low on ammunition, Howe's third attack finally succeeded in driving the provincials off Breed's Hill, and the even higher Bunker Hill. The Americans retreated toward Cambridge, and Howe halted his pursuit at the neck of the Charlestown Peninsula, British casualties totaling 1,050 men, as opposed to only 100 colonials killed and 270 wounded. More important, the indiscriminate Royal Navy bombardment of Charlestown had further deepened animosity against the Loyalist cause, so that Gage was obliged to abandon his plan of marching upon Cambridge by way of Dorchester.

George Washington was appointed commander-in-chief of all colonial forces by the Continental Congress, and on 2 July 1775 he assumed command over the besieging forces—whose numbers now had risen to 17,000 men. However, with the investiture of Boston stalled because of its natural impregnability and ease of resupply thanks to the Royal Navy's supremacy at sea, he used the ensuing stalemate to begin recruiting and training a more professional Continental Army for a protracted struggle: many of his volunteer militiamen's terms of enlistment were due to expire with the new year. On

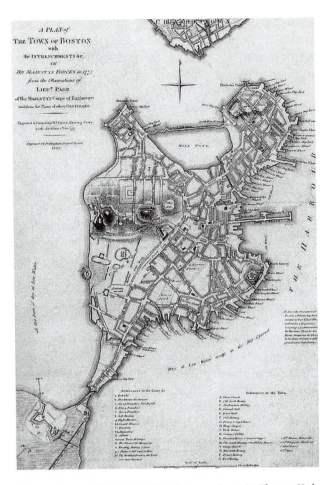

Boston as surveyed by the British military engineer, Lt. Thomas Hyde Page, during the patriot siege of 1775–1776, and published the next year by William Faden. (Library of Congress)

12 September, Col. Benedict Arnold was also detached from Cambridge with 1,100–1,200 American volunteers to advance up the Kennebec River and help invest the British stronghold at Quebec City. Less than a month afterward, on 10 October, Gage was replaced by Howe as commander-in-chief of all British forces in North America; although his garrison— whose numbers had also swollen to 12,000 men—could not be dislodged from Boston, they were powerless to penetrate inland and reimpose Crown control.

Federalist Era (1776–1821)

Eventually, this eleven-month siege culminated when American forces gained Dorchester Heights overlooking Boston, at which point Howe decided to evacuate his army for New York, ordering Castle William blown as the last of his redcoats sailed out of the harbor on 17 March 1776. Many Loyalist citizens also fled the half-deserted town, while others endured reprisals as jubilant patriots swarmed back in, securing valuable cannons and military stores for their cause. The successful conclusion of the siege moreover inspired the Continental

Congress to declare outright independence from Britain that same 4 July.

Yet despite its having been reclaimed, the town's revival initially proved slow, as port traffic was reduced to blockade-runners or raiders dodging Royal Navy patrols. On 26 September 1778, for example, the 32-gun frigate *Raleigh* of Capt. John Barry was intercepted by the 50-gun HMS *Experiment* of Capt. Sir James Wallace and 28-gun *Unicorn* of Cmdr. Matthew Squire, being crippled, beached, and captured the next morning. However, as most other major ports along the Atlantic Seaboard were either in British hands or likewise blockaded, Boston profited disproportionately from what it was able to import as the principal patriot sea outlet, its prospects brightening still further with France's entry into the war as an ally that same year, diverting Royal Navy activities into more far-flung theaters.

Boston's commerce, population, and infrastructure rebounded quickly as a result, so that it was even capable by the summer of 1781 of welcoming allied vessels such as Jean-François de Galaup, Comte de Lapérouse's, 32-gun frigates *Astrée* and *Hermione,* which put in with some prizes to refit. Little more than a year later, a full battle fleet of thirteen ships-of-the-line materialized from the West Indies on 10 August 1782 under Commo. Louis-Philippe Rigaud, Marquis de Vaudreuil, being all received except *Magnifique,* which was wrecked while being piloted into Nantasket Bay. (A grateful Congress would offer to replace this loss with the brand-new, 74-gun USS *America.*)

Brahmin Era (1822–1884)

By 1820, the population of Boston stood at 43,298, yet fewer than 8,000 enjoyed the right to vote. All previous efforts to upgrade Boston's legal status from that of a town governed by a board of selectmen elected every year—into a full-fledged city with a mayor, board of aldermen, and common council—had been rejected, largely based upon the premise that "the pure democracy of a town-meeting" better suited New England's traditions. Nevertheless, the state legislature finally approved an act in February 1822 that established "the city of

Map of the burgeoning city in 1838; note how the once-narrow neck of the peninsula was gradually being widened, as land was filled and reclaimed in the adjacent Back Bay. (Harvard University)

Boston," granting the first municipal charter in Massachusetts history (largely the work of Lemuel Shaw). It was accepted by an election in which 4,678 Bostonians voted on 2 March, so that the new administration was inaugurated on 1 May, John Phillips becoming the first mayor. Effective implementation and modernization of municipal services did not really occur during the 1823–1827 tenure of Josiah Quincy.

In 1860, Boston gave Abraham Lincoln only 9,723 votes in the presidential election, almost 1,000 fewer than his opponents, yet sentiment swung firmly behind the Union cause once Fort Sumter was fired upon by Confederate batteries in April 1861 and Massachusetts regiments began suffering their first heavy casualties of the Civil War. City businesses boomed thanks to increased wartime demand, although textile mills experienced shortages of cotton and military riots erupted in 1863 and 1864. In that latter year its urban population was measured at 164,788 inhabitants (not including men absent on military service), and Boston gave Lincoln a 5,000-vote plurality during his reelection bid. The final Union victory in the spring of 1865 confirmed Massachusetts abolitionists in their belief as to the righteousness of their cause, and wealthy businessmen as to the superiority of their capitalist system of "free labor" over the inequities of the South's slave-driven economy.

Although now outstripped in size and strength by New York, Boston nonetheless experienced a golden age during the immediate postbellum era, exerting considerable political, financial, and cultural influence upon the nation. Substantial estates were erected by rich Brahmins in the Back Bay area, as well as summer homes along the North Shore and South Shore, while the city enjoyed the benefits of a great symphony orchestra and many musical entertainments, wonderful parks, and the first subway in the United States. Its wholesale district was gutted by a blaze that erupted at 83–85 Summer Street on the Saturday night of 9–10 November 1872, spreading rapidly until it engulfed 767 buildings, encompassing some 67 acres and claiming fourteen lives; material losses were estimated at $75 million, yet a quick recovery ensued, with a new, better-built district of wider and straighter streets soon re-emerging. (The old Protestant Trinity Church, for example, that had been consumed in the conflagration, was replaced four years and three months later by a magnificent edifice in Copley Square, designed by the talented architect Henry H. Richardson and set upon reclaimed land of the filled-in Back Bay area.)

Divided Rule (1885–1945)

The swelling numbers of Irish Catholic voters in the teeming city eventually resulted in Hugh O'Brien being elected as city mayor in 1885, despite opposition from the entrenched Protestant Brahmins, who viewed him as an upstart and suspected the slick backroom deals and cronyism that had propelled his rise to power. Unable to prevent O'Brien from actually assuming office, the Commonwealth nonetheless made swift changes to Boston's regulations so as to sheer the mayor's office of much

of its patronage power by passing laws to regulate the hiring and promotion of employees, as well as by placing the police department and liquor licensing board under the jurisdiction of a special commission appointed by the state governor. Boston was to become politically and socially paralyzed by this divide over the next several decades, the antagonism between frustrated working-class voters and the fading Brahmin power brokers hampering much municipal business, while preventing state and city officials from acting in concert against a rising tide of corruption and graft that tainted city politics.

O'Brien was succeeded in office in 1905 by John "Honey Fitz" Fitzgerald, but the most spectacular antagonist of the elite stranglehold on power was to be Mayor James Michael Curley, who led the city's Irish political machine throughout much of the 1920s, 1930s, and 1940s. He was to introduce numerous progressive social measures that endeared him among the electorate, as well as improving living conditions and beautifying the city; yet he was brazenly corrupt, receiving kickbacks from municipal contracts that allowed him to build a grand private mansion overlooking Jamaica Pond, while taxes quintupled during his tenure. The city was hard hit by the Great Depression ,which started in October 1929, and any hopes of recovery were hampered by its declining infrastructure, departing businesses, reduced port traffic, and crime. It nonetheless remained a crowded but impoverished city, with a population measured at 770,816 residents in 1940.

Modern Revival (1946–Present)

Boston emerged from World War II to 1950 with a population of 801,444 or 2,369,986 if its entire metropolitan district was considered, encompassing an area roughly within 24 miles of the State House.

Conditions in Boston began to improve with the election of unassuming John Hynes as mayor in 1967, who brought an end to machine politics and was to be aided by an infusion of billions of federal dollars, which funded a series of massive municipal projects under the aegis of the Boston Redevelopment Authority or BRA, as well as a gradual economic revival. A group of several prominent civic leaders greatly helped in this development, being nicknamed "The Vault" as they held their regular meetings in the basement of the Boston Safe Deposit and Trust Company.

An early attempt to replace the tenements of the West End with the Charles River Park apartments had ended badly in 1958, as entire neighborhoods had been demolished, amid bitter antagonism. The efforts a decade later to restore Faneuil Hall and Quincy Market as part of a larger program of preserving the city's historic past fared much better, clearing the squalid old red-light district of Scollay Square so as to make way for an expanded and redesigned Government Square.

As in other urban centers drained by "white flight" to a new ring of suburbs, the ethnic neighborhoods remaining in Boston's core were to be the scene of explosive racial tensions

Bird's-eye view across Boston, ca. 1870, looking eastward toward the bay entrance; lithograph by F. Fuchs. (Library of Congress)

in 1974, when the School Committee was directed by court order to end de facto segregationist policies by busing 15,000 African American students every day out of Roxbury and Dorchester into predominantly white schools in Charlestown and South Boston. Animosity was so severe as to require constant police protection to avert major outbreaks of violence, and throughout the 1970s Boston—once one of the most tolerant towns in the country and birthplace of abolitionism—was to be derided as "the most racist city in America."

With time, however, Boston overcame these and many other problems, not the least being its need to adapt its severely limited geographical constraints to the advent of modern automotive volumes and patterns. The city nonetheless enjoyed a remarkable recovery, blending modern innovations with a proud historical past. The population within its old limits contracted to an estimated 547,725 residents by 1994, yet the entire metropolitan area was now home to 5.5 million.

For additional sources on the history of Boston, as well as sources on North American and U.S. urban history, please consult the Select Bibliography at the end of this volume.

CHARLESTON

Outlet for a fertile agricultural hinterland that has endured numerous natural and man-made catastrophes, most notoriously during the U.S. Civil War.

Initial Settlement (1670–1671)

Despite halfhearted attempts by the Spaniards and French to colonize the low marshy coastline north of Florida during the sixteenth century, only Virginia had actually become populated by English settlers by the time that Charles II ascended the throne in London in 1660. Three years later, eight of his most influential supporters persuaded the king to name them "lords proprietors" over a vast expanse in this uncharted wilderness area that was to be privately settled and operated under the name of Carolina in their monarch's honor.

A couple of hundred disgruntled Barbadians were the first to be attracted by the prospect of immigrating into this virgin preserve, believing that their experience in West Indian cultivation would prove useful in such an environment; they therefore sent Capt. William Hilton to explore northeastward from Portus Regalis (Port Royal)—a natural harbor so named by

Bird's-eye view looking southwestward across the city of Charleston, 1872. (Library of Congress)

the sixteenth-century French explorer Jean Ribault—up Carolina's coast as far as Cape Fear. Hilton's favorable report encouraged a short-lived Barbadian settlement at the latter point, as well as a visit to Port Royal by Capt. Robert Sandford in 1666.

Returning to England, Sandford recruited his own band of colonists, then set sail in August 1669 aboard three ships. Only his flagship, *Carolina,* survived the traverse through the Caribbean, the other two being replaced by *Three Brothers* and an unnamed sloop. Reaching Port Royal early the following year with his flagship and sloop—*Three Brothers* having become separated by a storm—Sandford and his followers were greeted with news of recent attacks by a rival tribe called the Westoes. They consequently allowed themselves to be persuaded by the chief of Kiawah (another natural harbor, 60 miles farther up the coast) to settle among his tribe for mutual protection.

Carolina and the sloop duly arrived off this harbor in April 1670, steering gingerly inland until they had moved beyond sight of the sea. Following a curved river channel, they dropped anchor before the Kiawah village at the mouth of a creek on the western bank of what Sandford would soon christen the Ashley River. (This waterway, along with its twin—the Cooper

River—were named in honor of the most influential lord proprietor back in London, Anthony Ashley-Cooper, later the 1st Earl of Shaftesbury. The disembarkation spot also became known as Albemarle Point, in honor of the eldest lord proprietor, George Monck, Duke of Albemarle.)

About 150 British colonists came ashore and with aid from the Kiawahs enclosed a 10-acre compound with palisades and moats on a low bluff near the village as a defensive precaution. The measure proved justified when three Spanish ships and fourteen piraguas (dugouts) suddenly materialized in mid-August 1670 under Juan Menéndez Marques, having coasted northeastward from St. Augustine to expel the intrusive settlement. Forewarned by their Indian allies, the English repaired inside their stronghold and waited until Menéndez withdrew after a storm dragged his ships' anchors.

With the danger having receded, the colonists turned to planting crops to relieve the hunger that threatened their fledgling community. Plots were assigned under the direction of the surveyor Florence O'Sullivan, a surly former Irish soldier who performed his task so erratically, and proved so personally disagreeable—being described as an "ill-natured buggerer of children"—that he was banished to man the lookout station and signal gun at the distant harbor entrance, a lonely outpost known ever afterward as Sullivan's Island. Besides food crops, the settlers furthermore planted cotton, indigo, and tobacco to determine their commercial viability, while cattle were bred and furs obtained through barter with the local tribes of the coastal Cusabo Confederation.

More than 100 Barbadian émigrés reached the outpost in mid-February 1671, claiming to be "weary of the (West Indian) hurricanes," along with some rich New Yorkers who had come south to escape their "taxes and hard winters." Lord Ashley-Cooper wrote to express his satisfaction with the establishment of this tentative foothold, although he requested that a permanent site be selected on high ground and named "Charles Towne" in honor of the king. He even enclosed a plan—known as the Grand Model—that indicated the generous lot sizes and street widths he envisioned, so as to "avoid the undecent and incommodious irregularities which other English colonies are fallen into for want of an early care in laying out the Townes."

Foundation (1672–1682)

Having familiarized themselves with their surroundings, the settlers attempted to comply with the lord proprietor's wishes by laying out a street plan and surveying town lots in 1672 on the southeastern side of the flat, narrow peninsula known as Oyster or White Point, which enjoyed a commanding view over the Cooper River mouth and distant harbor entrance. Although the peninsula stood only 16 feet above water level at its highest point, the new site was nonetheless deemed more accessible for oceangoing sailing ships than having to navigate the curving Ashley River channel, while its more exposed position facing the bay meant that dwellings would be "refreshed with

"A particular draught" for navigating the harbor approaches, drawn ca. 1685 by the Charlestonian Maurice Mathews; north is to the right. (Library of Congress)

a continued cool breathing from the sea" during the hot and humid Carolina summers.

Most colonists transferred their households across only slowly, concentrating instead on developing their inland clearances. Charles-Town, as it was then spelled, nevertheless evolved thanks to its strategic locale, boats being used to off-load cargoes from arriving vessels and ferry them up the various river branches, while seasonal harvests were gathered and warehoused there for easy export. By 1680 the seat of the private colony's government (consisting of a London-appointed governor and grand council, plus elected deputies from among local property owners) had been installed at the new site, although no church, town hall, or wharves had as yet been completed.

Immigrants continued to arrive from Barbados, as well as hundreds of English Dissenters and French Huguenots attracted by Carolina's freedom of religion, so that the colony grew and became subdivided into three counties two years later. Charles-Town, with numerous brick houses now under construction—including Saint Philip's Anglican Church, a large black cypress structure on a solid foundation—became the capital for Berkeley County, in addition to serving as Carolina's capital.

Survival (1683–1720)

The bustling little community and its outposts scattered among the surrounding coastal plain—known as the Low Country—were startled in August 1686 to learn that a Spanish expedition out of St. Augustine had annihilated a new Scottish establishment at Port Royal, then had pushed northeast as far as the Edisto River to plunder plantations, before being struck by a hurricane that compelled it to turn back. Although uneasy in their frontline existence, residents were nonetheless heartened by the introduction shortly thereafter of rice to Carolina as a cash crop, proving so amenable to its watery terrain that planters were having difficulty finding ships at Charles-Town on which to export their bumper crops by the 1690s; in fact, rice become so plentiful that it was commonly used to pay quitrents.

The town suffered a smallpox outbreak in 1697; then a fire consumed most of its dwellings, disease broke out among its cattle, and an earthquake rattled through the next year. Before Charles-Town had fully recuperated, a yellow-fever epidemic struck in 1699, claiming the lives of 160 citizens (including half the Carolina assemblymen); a few months later a tidal wave also swept into its harbor and flooded the low-lying streets, compelling "inhabitants to fly for shelter to the second stories of their houses." Still, exports exceeded imports for the first time that same year, a favorable balance of trade that would continue over the next several years and greatly facilitate the town's reconstruction.

By 1703, Gov. Nathaniel Johnson could report to the lords proprietors that Carolina had a total population of 3,800 white residents, 3,000 black slaves, and 350 Indian slaves. Charles-Town had been spared any direct foreign threat for a generation, but England became embroiled in Queen Anne's War, or the War of the Spanish Succession, so that Johnson ordered his militia subordinate Col. William Rhett to reinforce the defenses against any possible Spanish or French descent. Ramparts were strengthened and armaments augmented to 83 guns; a triangular, 22-gun fort was also erected on the harbor's southern shoreline to cover the anchorage from Windmill Point on James' Island.

These preparations proved timely, as five French privateer vessels under Capt. Jacques Lefebvre and a few hundred Cuban troops under Esteban de Berroa were sighted by lookouts from Sullivan's Island on 7 September 1706 (the date is "New Style," or modern Gregorian calendar, not the "Old Style" [O.S.], Julian calendar then in use among the English). Despite a yellow-fever epidemic gripping Charles-Town, militiamen rallied to its defense from throughout the district. The raiders anchored off Sullivan's Island by nightfall, then sent a surrender demand inshore the next morning, which Johnson rejected.

An enemy landing party disembarked on James' Island by the morning of 9 September 1706 and set fire to a house, before being driven back to their demigalley by Carolina militiamen and Indian allies. Another 160 Spanish soldiers meanwhile disgorged onto a narrow stretch of land between the Wando River and the ocean, burning two small launches and a storehouse before encamping for the night. They were surprised, while eating dinner, by 100 defenders, who killed a dozen Spaniards, captured 60, and drove the rest back out to their craft. Then, on 11 September, Johnson ordered Rhett to take six small launches and a fireship and bear down upon the anchored enemy vessels off Sullivan's Island; when they scattered out to sea, Lefebvre and Berroa decided to retire altogether for St. Augustine.

No sooner had this enemy formation disappeared over the horizon than the laggard French ship *Brillante* appeared, having become separated during the initial approach. Unaware that the defense was now fully aroused, it landed another 200 soldiers farther east, who were rapidly defeated near Holybush Plantation by militiamen. Another group of Carolinians meanwhile rowed out to the *Brillante* and secured it. Charles-Town's garrison had won a resounding victory, killing 30 invaders and capturing 320, which would discourage future raids from St. Augustine.

By 1708, Johnson could report that Carolina's population had reached 4,080 whites, 4,100 black slaves, and 1,400 Indian slaves, trade resuming once peace was restored five years later. But the colony's expansion unwittingly worsened relations with local tribes, which complained of ever deeper penetrations into their territory, and most especially of the ruthless practices of certain unscrupulous English traders who sold rum and other goods to the local population against promised payments of skins, then seized their families and sold them into bondage when debts fell forfeit.

Edward Crisp's survey of "Charles-Town" and its rivers, ca. 1704; north is toward right. Note how Fort Johnson and other defenses had recently been completed, plus the relatively few civilian dwellings outside the city walls. (David Ramsay, *History of South Carolina*)

On 12 April 1715 (O.S.), two traders hastened into Charles-Town to warn Gov. Charles Craven that a Yamasee uprising was imminent; it exploded three days later—at daybreak on Good Friday—when warriors surprised various plantations between the Combahee and Edisto rivers, slaughtering more than 100 people. Fires could be plainly discerned from Charles-Town's walls, and a stream of frightened refugees began arriving. Craven ordered out his militia, advancing into rebel territory the following week with 250 volunteers and settlement Indians to disperse a Yamasee concentration; he then established a defensive perimeter some 30 miles around Charles-Town. Raid and counter-raid ensued until late July 1715, when Craven marched north with 100 militiamen and 100 black fighters and Indians to join North Carolinian forces in a sweep. But no sooner had the governor crossed the Santee than he was advised that 500 to 700 Apalaches had slipped through the Edisto perimeter, obliging him to hasten back to defend his capital.

Fortunately, those raiders stopped short of Stono Island, after which the Virginia guard ship *Valour* entered Charles-Town harbor with 160 muskets and other military supplies, greatly easing local fears. Guerrilla warfare persisted in the interior until that autumn, when the Cherokee finally joined the English, helping to expel the rebel Yamasee and Creeks southwestward by late January 1716. After a few minor skirmishes, a treaty was concluded in 1717, and Charles-Town felt sufficiently reassured to expand by creating several new streets and a civic square west of its walls.

The next spring, its port was unexpectedly blockaded by the renegade Edward Teach (Blackbeard), the most notorious of a band of lawless privateers driven from the Bahamas by its conversion to Crown rule. In previous wars, Carolinians had often purchased booty from such rovers, yet Blackbeard—bereft of legitimate prizes and outlawed in the West Indies—brazenly took up station outside the port, intercepting eight or nine English merchantmen during a week in May 1718. A member of Carolina's council, Samuel Wragg, and his four-year-old son William, were among the hostages whom the pirates threatened to behead—and furthermore to "burn the ships that lay before the town and beat it about our ears," according to Gov. Robert Johnson—if a ransom of medicines and other sundries were not forthcoming. These items were surrendered and the captives released, although Blackbeard continued to prowl the North Carolina coast.

When word reached Charles-Town that same autumn of another pirate ship off Cape Fear, Johnson commissioned Colonel Rhett to sail in pursuit with two sloops. After a five-hour gun battle he returned with thirty rogue privateers, whose commander—Maj. Stede Bonnet of Barbados—was hanged at White Point in November 1718, then buried in disgrace in the marsh below the low-water mark (near modern Meeting and Water streets). Shortly thereafter, Johnson himself sortied to battle yet another pirate off the coast, returning with the captive Richard Worley.

The Commons House of Assembly—an expanded, bicameral South Carolina legislature—had requested assistance amid these difficulties from the lords proprietors in London, to no avail; local leaders had also grown increasingly exasperated at having their decrees vetoed by the distant owners. Consequently, the frustrated assembly declared itself in 1719 to be "a convention, delegated by the people to prevent the utter ruin of this government, if not the loss of the province," and so petitioned King George I to assume direct Crown control over Carolina.

Crown Rule (1721–1774)

Sir Francis Nicholson, the province's first royal governor, received a tumultuous welcome when he arrived aboard HMS *Enterprise* on 22 May 1721 (O.S.), being greeted by fired salutes and a petition signed by more than 500 delighted citizens. The lords proprietors contested this change of government, but after eight years of litigation, they agreed to be bought out. Carolina was henceforth to be a Crown colony, and the name of its capital became more commonly rendered as "Charlestown." Trade, cultivation, immigration, and slavery all expanded exponentially after the changeover, and the town benefited accordingly—despite setbacks such as the hurricane that struck in August 1728, driving twenty-three ships ashore and damaging fortifications, wharves, and houses.

As inland plantations grew into vast commercial operations, wealthy owners began building fine mansions in Charlestown, while city merchants also grew rich off the increased maritime traffic. Long, narrow homes—only a single room in width, thus known as "single houses"—began to appear, laid out facing south or west so that cool breezes might blow through their entire length, easing the heat and humidity of summer. (Later, open galleries called piazzas were added along the exteriors, for that same reason.) Creeks and marshes west of Charlestown began to be filled in, while Church, Meeting, and King streets were extended beyond the old urban perimeter. North of the neighborhood known as Rhettsbury, a new suburb called Ansonborough appeared (on land that naval Capt. George Anson had allegedly won from Thomas Gadsden in a card game). Scottish, Irish, German, and French immigrants continued to arrive, pushing inland to establish homesteads, while thousands of African slaves were also brought in to be sold.

Urban amenities multiplied, the town's first newspaper—the *South Carolina Gazette*—being issued after Benjamin Franklin sent Thomas Whitmarsh to Charlestown for that purpose in 1732. Three years later the York Course for horse races was opened, and the first theatrical play (Thomas Otway's *The Orphan or the Unhappy Marriage*) was performed in the long-room of a tavern at the corner of Broad and Church streets. The performance was so well received that the New Theater was built on Dock Street by 1736, opening with Farquhar's bawdy favorite *The Recruiting Officer.*

Yet as plantation society grew more genteel, racial policies became harsher, with large-scale commercial operations dehumanizing the treatment of slaves. Now heavily outnumbered by its retainers, Charlestown responded fearfully when a rebellion erupted at Stono Bridge in September 1739, prompting a restrictive new slave law to be promulgated the following year. The War of Jenkins's Ear, or King George's War, had also begun in October 1739, but Charlestown was not threatened; its worse suffering came from a fire that started in a saddler's house on Broad Street on 18 November 1740 (O.S.), consuming 300 houses between Church and East Bay streets, as far as Granville Bastion. Losses were so extensive that the British Parliament allocated £20,000 to help with reconstruction.

Charlestown recuperated sufficiently to help muster a relief force of almost 1,100 men, who sailed in August 1742 aboard four Royal Navy warships and eight armed South Carolinian vessels to aid the new frontline province of Georgia against a Spanish invasion. Arriving to find the enemy gone, Capt. Charles Hardy reversed course four days later with the bulk of the expedition, on the unfounded belief of a Spanish assault against Charlestown during their absence. But the town was not to be menaced throughout this conflict, and when hostilities ceased six years later, the Charlestown Library was founded—to prevent residents from sinking into "the gross ignorance of the naked Indian," according to its seventeen charter members.

By 1750 indigo had been added to the list of lucrative

Map of Charleston as surveyed by Bishop Roberts in 1737, then engraved in London two years later by W. H. Toms; north is toward right. Note how the city had expanded westward, beyond its original enclosure of ramparts. (Library of Congress)

exports, and Charlestown's citizens now enjoyed the highest per capita income in the Thirteen Colonies. Their port was also the fourth busiest, bringing in many luxury items in addition to its regular commercial traffic; wagon movements inland had also increased, and exotic produce such as limes and oranges were plentiful. Plantation owners such as Henry Middleton and John Drayton were among the wealthiest men in North America, constructing palatial town houses and country estates. Not even the hurricane and tidal wave that struck Charlestown on the morning of 15 September 1752, running 10 feet higher than the previous high-water mark and driving ships right into the streets while terrified residents fled into their upper stories, could stall the town's rise to prosperity.

Repairs were swiftly made, and William Gerard de Brahm was hired to raise a new seawall—standing 4 feet above the new high-water mark to run from Granville's to Broughton's Bastions (modern corner of South Battery and Church Street), then westward to the vicinity of Gibbes Street (named for the Goose Creek merchant William Gibbes, who owned a wharf and house at that shoreline juncture). The New Market Course was

opened just a mile beyond the town limits in 1754, its weekly horse races becoming an elegant highlight of the social season. The Anglican community was also divided because of overcrowding at Saint Philip's, which prompted the construction of a new parish called Saint Michael's south of Broad Street.

Charlestown was unaffected by the French and Indian War of 1754–1763, known locally as the Cherokee War, and its trade grew even stronger at the conclusion of those hostilities when an English bounty was offered on indigo exports while the town was furthermore authorized to ship rice directly to Spain, Portugal, and the Mediterranean. The resultant boom financed still deeper inroads into South Carolina's backcountry, bringing yet more land under cultivation, so that slave imports and crop exports swelled. Merchants scarcely noticed the restrictions imposed by Parliament's Navigation Acts that so enraged New England, and Charlestown expanded yet again; once desolate White Point became "almost covered with houses, many of them very elegant," while its suburb of Harleston Village was surveyed and numerous streets extended or newly created.

Charleston as seen from its sea approaches, as painted in 1774 by Thomas Leitch. (Library of Congress)

Reaction against the 1765 Stamp Act, which Parliament passed in order to have colonies contribute more toward imperial defense, proved much more adverse. South Carolina's Commons House adopted resolutions against such "taxation without representation," and despite the act's repeal the following year, political dissatisfaction had taken deep root at Charlestown, and the will for independence gained momentum.

Revolutionary War (1775–1782)
Lord William Campbell reached Charlestown aboard HMS *Scorpion* to assume office as its new royal governor in late April 1775, one week after fighting had erupted between Massachusetts "Minutemen" and British regulars outside Boston. His local reception was subdued, being viewed with suspicion. Less than three months later, Campbell was charged with attempting to arouse the inland settlements against the coastal colonists; he subsequently fled aboard the British sloop *Tamar*, taking the province's great seal with him.

Although bereft of a Crown representative, South Carolina did not immediately secede from Britain, despite considerable debate toward that end. Fighting meanwhile spread out of New England into Virginia and North Carolina, and nine days after Boston fell to Gen. George Washington's patriot besiegers, an independent government was promulgated at Charlestown on 26 March 1776, with John Rutledge serving as provincial "president." South Carolina even unveiled a flag bearing a silver crescent upon a blue field, derived from the uniforms of Col. William Moultrie's Second Regiment.

Scarcely two months later, Commo. Peter Parker's fifty-five Royal Navy vessels appeared off Sullivan's Island, intent on recouping Charlestown by depositing Gen. Henry Clinton's army and former governor Campbell on Long Island (today known as the Isle of Palms); the reoccupied port would then be used as a springboard from which to subdue Carolina's coastline and interior. Maj.-Gen. Charles Lee, commanding Charlestown's defenses, began feverish fortification works, while doubting whether Moultrie could hold the harbor entrance with his 1,200-man garrison on Sullivan's Island. Only the front and one side of the small, square, open fort had been completed, and it was now being hastily finished by using palmetto logs and sand, which Lee was convinced could not resist a British bombardment.

He therefore withdrew half of Moultrie's powder and men. But as the British delayed their assault for almost three more weeks, the colonel had time to increase his fort's ordinance to 31 guns and brace for action. Parker's warships finally bore down upon the morning of 28 June 1776, while Clinton attempted to cross Breach Inlet from Long Island with a couple of thousand redcoats in support, only to be checked in the shallows by 780 well-placed defenders under Lt.-Col. William Thomson. The British bomb vessel *Thunder* opened fire against Moultrie's low stronghold from a mile and a half distance, while the 50-gun HMSS *Bristol* and *Experiment,* frigates *Active* and *Solebay,* plus the smaller consorts *Syren, Actaeon,* and *Sphinx* closed to within 400 yards. Surprisingly, the fort's porous palmetto logs absorbed rounds remarkably well, so that

A contemporary British engraving of the British naval bombardment of Charleston's harbor defenses, 1776. (Library of Congress)

the Carolinian defenders could inflict heavy punishment without themselves being discomfited. *Actaeon* and *Sphinx* collided during the afternoon, then ran aground along with *Syren* on the Middle Ground shoal (where Fort Sumter would later be built), *Actaeon* sticking fast. Parker eventually drew off at 9:30 P.M., his vessels having suffered 420 total casualties as opposed to negligible losses among Moultrie's triumphant garrison.

To the delight of anxiously watching Charlestonians, the British expedition steered northward for New York by 2 August 1776, leaving them to celebrate by adding a palmetto symbol to their state flag and naming Moultrie's fort after him. Their port's trade nevertheless languished, even though major campaigning shifted elsewhere over the next few years. Charlestown experienced another accidental fire in 1778 that consumed more than 250 houses in the Church Street area, from Queen Street to Stoll's Alley. Then the next summer a British army under Gen. Augustine Prevost pushed northeastward from recently reconquered Georgia to threaten the South Carolinian capital again, being turned back in mid-June 1779 when a Continental relief column drew near under Maj.-Gen. Benjamin Lincoln. To cover his retreat, Prevost left a 900-man rear guard under Col. John Maitland entrenched at Stono Ferry, 8 miles from the Ashley River, which Moultrie—now promoted to brigadier—surprised with 1,200 troops from Charlestown on 20 June 1779. But despite being caught off guard and suffering 130 killed or wounded, Maitland drove Moultrie off with 150 casualties, plus another 150 men missing, so that the British rear guard could be safely evacuated three days later.

At the end of August 1779, a huge French fleet anchored offshore under Vice Adm. Charles-Henri, Comte d'Estaing, who proposed a joint offensive against Georgia. Charlestown's authorities accepted, the thirty-nine allied warships creating a sensation when they appeared off the town on 3 September

to escort Moultrie, Lt.-Col. Francis Marion, and a host of South Carolinians against Savannah. A protracted siege failed to reduce that British garrison, so that it was lifted by 18 October 1779 and the provincial soldiers returned.

On the day after Christmas 1779, a British fleet under Vice Adm. Marriot Arbuthnot quit New York with a 7,500-man army under Clinton to campaign in warmer climes while the north was gripped by winter. Less than two weeks after being reinforced at Savannah by another 3,700 men, this British expedition made for the Edisto River, intending to invest Charlestown while Arbuthnot menaced it from the sea. Clinton's army disembarked and on 29 March 1780 slipped across the Ashley River, 4 miles farther north than its patriot defenders had anticipated, then pressed within a few hundred yards of Charlestown's outer defenses by the next day, trapping 5,600 troops inside under Maj.-Gen. Lincoln.

Siege batteries were installed over the ensuing fortnight, and they opened fire by 13 April 1780. Tory Lt.-Col. Banastre Tarleton was detached with irregulars of his so-called British Legion to seize Biggins' Bridge from an American unit the following day, thereby cutting off the beleaguered capital's last important supply route. Maj. James Moncrieff accelerated the British siege operations by using prefabricated mantelets, so that his lines advanced to within 250 yards of the American ramparts by 19 April, prompting Lincoln to offer to surrender two days later—although his insistence on full honors of war was rejected by Clinton. At dawn on 24 April, the British right overran Charlestown's outer lines, and after increased bombardments from both land and the river, its garrison finally gave up. On 12 May, 5,500 Americans—including seven generals—marched out to lay down their arms, having suffered 230 casualties during the course of the siege, compared with 270 among the British ranks.

Some 200 prominent citizens greeted the victors as they entered; another 163 later swore allegiance to the Crown, while several score rebel sympathizers were deported. Clinton installed Lt.-Gen. Charles, Marquis Cornwallis, as military governor before returning to New York with a third of his army for a spring campaign. Cornwallis then proceeded inland with 2,500 British troops on 18 May 1780 to stamp out the last vestiges of Revolutionary resistance in South Carolina, but he soon found that his cumbersome army could not overtake their more nimble foes, and a protracted guerrilla struggle ensued. Charlestown, despite the lifting of the Royal Navy blockade, remained commercially hamstrung because of the turmoil gripping its hinterland.

An army of 4,000 patriots under Maj.-Gen. Horatio Gates was defeated by Cornwallis at Camden on 16 August 1780, so that Maj.-Gen. Nathanael Greene succeeded to command of all local Continental forces, gradually eroding British strength before Cornwallis marched north into Virginia, becoming trapped at Yorktown. Greene's 2,200 soldiers defeated the last major British concentration in rural South Carolina—1,800 men at Eutaw Springs—on 8 September 1781, but they did not possess sufficient strength to reclaim the capital. It was not until British forces had been beaten elsewhere that Charlestown's occupiers at last marched out of the town gates to the wharf at the foot of Boundary (modern Calhoun) Street on 14 December 1782, allowing Greene and his Continentals to lead Gov. John Mathews and his council back through a cheering throng to their old chambers on Broad Street.

Antebellum Era (1783–1860)

The town had emerged battered and diminished, so that some years of depression ensued as patriot exiles slowly returned, Loyalists were banished, and reconstruction commenced. Charlestown was incorporated as a city on 13 August 1783, Richard Hutson being elected its first intendant, or mayor, and its name was officially changed to Charleston. Three years later, the legislature—wishing to create a safer and more centrally located state capital—chose an inland site, laying out a street plan in a forested area that by 1790 had become Columbia.

Life gradually returned to normal in the coastal port-city of Charleston, although merchants worried about their vanished English commerce; most especially, they mourned the lost bounty on indigo. There were nonetheless signs of progress: the College of Charleston was chartered (fifteen years after its actual foundation, in 1770), while Scottish residents even organized the South Carolina Golf Club to play on Harleston's Green; thoroughbred horse racing also revived. President Washington lifted spirits by paying a visit in 1791, being greeted by some 16,000 people, half of who were black. He noted in his journal the city's "unpaved streets of sand," as well as the "number of very good houses of brick and wood, but most of the latter." That same year refugees began reaching Charleston from the French sugar colony of Saint-Domingue (Haiti), having been driven out by a massive slave revolt that heightened fears of a similar insurrection in South Carolina.

The local politician Charles Cotesworth Pinckney was one of three U.S. delegates sent to Paris by Pres. John Adams in 1797 to complain about captures made by French Revolutionary privateers, and who angrily rebuked a requested bribe of $250,000 for three unnamed French ministers with the words: "No, not a sixpence!" (more elegantly rendered by Congressman Robert Goodloe Harper as: "Millions for defense, not a cent for tribute!"). Because of his defiant stand in this so-called XYZ Affair, Pinckney returned to a hero's welcome at Charleston, and a new harbor fort—erected to resist French raiders during the ensuing Quasi-War—was named Castle Pinckney in his honor. The city's "mechanics" (a term then applied to blue-collar construction workers and tradesmen) also donated their labors toward building Fort Mechanic on East Battery, while a patriotic subscription helped finance the launching of the frigate *John Adams*.

Once peace with France was restored, Charleston's commerce surged during the early nineteenth century; it was discovered that cotton made a lucrative substitute for indigo exports, while rice planters furthermore increased their productivity by adapting the "tidal method" of cultivation—whereby tides were used to push freshwater into irrigation canals and to power mills. Retail stores in the city multiplied as a result, along with new wharves and warehouses, these improved urban amenities encouraging rich planter families to reside in Charleston for more extended periods (usually from May to November). The boom was curtailed by the War of 1812, during which the port was sporadically blockaded by Royal Navy warships, although no direct assault occurred.

When hostilities ceased three years later, Charleston's drive toward prosperity quickly resumed. Its first few principal avenues were paved over with stone ballast, while sidewalks were covered in brick and shade was provided by planting "Pride of India" trees (known locally as "Chinaberry"). The population of the city and its suburbs—which now included Sullivan's Island, accessible by steam ferry—was estimated at 17,000 whites, 3,000 free "colored," and 20,000 slaves by 1826; more than half its houses were made of brick, with tile or slate roofs, and Charleston exuded a refined and fashionable air. Local celebrities included the well-traveled Joel R. Poinsett, a former cabinet member who had served as U.S. ambassador to Mexico and had brought the first "fire-plants," or poinsettias, back from that country as a Christmas tradition.

On 25 December 1830 the city's first steam locomotive went into service, whose line would extend 136 miles to Hamburg by October 1833 and divert so much farm produce from the Upper Savannah River that it was jocularly nicknamed the "Best Friend of Charleston." A grand new theater opened in 1837 on the west side of Meeting Street, just south of Market, followed four years later by a Roman-style public market

The city of Charlestown. ca. 1850. (Corbis)

designed by the local architect Edward Brickell White. Exotic structures in Greek Revival style became popular as well, especially during the building boom that followed another destructive conflagration in 1838.

Yet despite its genteel society and bountiful traffic, the city was becoming too dependent upon cotton exports; suggestions for agricultural diversification and industrial development fell upon deaf ears, manufacturing being particularly resisted by planters for fear that it would undermine slavery in a state that now consisted of more than 50 percent black laborers. Such panic gripped the city when a purported rebellion was discovered in 1842 that 131 black "conspirators" were arrested, 35 hanged, and the rest deported. A state arsenal was installed on Boundary Street as a precaution (evolving into the Military College of the South, better known today as the Citadel), while guard units patrolled Charleston's streets at night and free blacks were banned from re-entering the state if they departed. Even free blacks on arriving vessels were jailed until their ships weighed in the harbor.

But abolitionism and modernization were gaining hold elsewhere in the nation, while South Carolina clung stubbornly to its old ways. Sen. Robert Y. Hayne of Charleston had already engaged in heated debates with Sen. Daniel Webster of Massachusetts in the national Senate, arguing that states that had signed the Constitution had acted as sovereign entities and so could secede if they wanted. Charleston had also been the scene of angry confrontations between local "Unionists" and "Nullifiers," and when the General Assembly passed the Ordinance of Nullification by a narrow margin in 1832—declaring certain federal tariffs void within the state—Pres. Andrew Jackson threatened an invasion and blockade, until Sen. Henry Clay of Kentucky forged a compromise and South Carolina repealed its ordinance.

Passions became inflamed again after the western territories annexed during the war against Mexico of 1846–1848 were declared "free" states by a majority vote in Washington; many Carolinians felt that their Palmetto Regiment's participation in that campaign had been insultingly negated. Similar indignation festered in Alabama, Florida, Georgia, Louisiana, Mississippi, and Texas, coalescing into a movement to withdraw altogether from the federal government.

Annihilation (1861–1865)

Because of a smallpox epidemic in the state capital of Columbia, Charleston hosted the "Nullification Convention," which passed the Secession Act on 20 December 1860, initiating the

Union's dissolution in favor of a breakaway "Confederate States of America." The federal commander at Fort Moultrie, Maj. Robert Anderson, moved his slender force under cover of darkness out to the still incomplete Fort Sumter in the bay on 26 December, prompting South Carolina's governor, Francis W. Pickens, to authorize state units to occupy the U.S. arsenal in the city, as well as Fort Moultrie and Castle Pinckney. Work also commenced on installing a battery called Fort Morris at the harbor entrance, which fired upon the federal supply ship *Star of the West* when it tried to reinforce Anderson's garrison on 9 January 1861.

A tense standoff ensued, with Confederate president Jefferson Davis appointing the Louisiana military engineer Brig. Pierre G. T. Beauregard to strengthen the encircling batteries. Matters finally came to a head when Abraham Lincoln was inaugurated as president and informed local authorities on 8 April 1861 that the isolated federal outpost would be resupplied, by force if necessary. Beauregard consequently demanded Fort Sumter's outright surrender on the evening of 11 April, and when rebuffed opened fire at 4:00 A.M. on 12 April. After thirty hours of artillery exchanges, Anderson's 111-man garrison gave up, being allowed to evacuate for New York aboard a federal warship by 14 April.

Charleston's euphoria at initiating Civil War hostilities soon changed to concern, however, as the U.S. steam warship *Niagara* arrived outside on 11 May 1861 to impose a blockade. That stranglehold tightened considerably after Commo. Samuel F. Du Pont and Gen. Thomas W. Sherman captured

Charleston's ruins, April 1865: at left, scaffolding has been erected around the Circular Church's damaged steeple. (Miller and Lanier, *Photographic History of the Civil War*)

nearby Port Royal Sound with a large expedition that same November, transforming it into an advance Union naval base. Charleston moreover suffered its worst conflagration when a fire flared out of control at 8:30 P.M. on 11 December in William P. Russell's sash-blind factory at the foot of Hasell Street on the Cooper River waterfront. Propelled by gale-force winds, the flames roared westward through town, consuming five major churches and more than 500 residences across 540 acres, before finally sputtering out in the Ashley River marshes. Northerners viewed this wholesale destruction—and in particular of the South Carolina Institute Hall, where the Secession Act had been signed—as a sign of divine judgment.

With their overseas commerce at a standstill, Charlestonians could not begin righting such widespread devastation. Scarcely a week later Union blockaders added to their woes by deploying the so-called Stone Fleet: sixteen old whaling ships sailed down from New England, ladened with granite, and were towed into position and scuttled so as to block the main channel off Morris Island. A second flotilla was then used to bottle up Maffitt's Channel in January 1862, leaving only two small entrances for blockade-runners, which were constantly patrolled by federal warships. Charleston's sea communications were virtually severed, and hopes of regaining any significant traffic faded.

On 7 April 1863, Union ironclads penetrated the bay and dueled for two and a half hours against Forts Moultrie and Sumter, as well as Batteries Bee and Beauregard. The damaged twin-turreted *Keokuk* sank the next morning in about 18 feet

Remnants of the Circular Congregational Church on Meeting Street at left, with Secession Hall at right, after reconstruction had begun in April 1865. (Miller and Lanier, *Photographic History of the Civil War*)

The Circular Church's steeple enclosed with scaffolding, while across the street stand the gutted remains of the once-famous Mills House—the first building in the city to boast running water and steam heat when opened a dozen years earlier—plus rubble-strewn foundations from former mansions. (Miller and Lanier, *Photographic History of the Civil War*)

of water while limping back around Morris Island, allowing Confederate salvors to retrieve its pair of 11-inch Dahlgren guns and install them in the defenses. But undeterred, a federal army under Gen. Quincy A. Gillmore disembarked at the lower end of Morris Island on 10 July, intending to outflank the Confederate batteries from the landward side. The first major assault by 6,000 Union troops—including Col. Robert Gould Shaw's black regiment, the 54th Massachusetts Infantry—failed to carry Fort Wagner and resulted in 1,500 fatalities, compared with only 174 Confederate dead; Gillmore's army thereupon settled down for a protracted bombardment. Blockading warships added their salvos as of 17 August, battering Fort Sumter into silence four days later, so that Gillmore called upon Beauregard to evacuate this mid-island stronghold and Morris Island—threatening to shell the city if his demand was not accepted.

The Confederate general refused, so that an 8-inch Parrott gun that the besiegers had skidded across the marshes into a new emplacement opened fire by 1:30 A.M. on 22 August 1863, lobbing incendiary rounds 4 miles across the bay into Charleston's lower reaches, precipitating a civilian flight. Other batteries were added as the Union army spread out over Morris Island and dug in, supported by their fleet. Desperation drove the Confederate engineer David Ebaugh to design a

semisubmersible wooden boat at Stony Landing on the Cooper River near Moncks Corner that could steal upon enemy warships anchored offshore, then use the tip of a spar to imbed an explosive charge called a "torpedo" into their hulls. Four volunteers under Lt. William T. Glassell slipped out of Charleston after nightfall on 5 October aboard that tiny craft and badly damaged the Union ironclad *New Ironsides*—although the resultant blast also swamped and almost sank their own boat.

Inspired by this success, the defenders experimented with a complete submersible, made from a 25-foot iron boiler that had been brought in by rail from Mobile; it was called the *Hunley* in honor of its principal financial backer, Horace L. Hunley. The first trials in Charleston Bay failed, claiming the lives of Hunley and three crewmen, but the privately owned submarine was eventually prepared to sortie—although Union ironclads now routinely anchored with chain fenders and weighted nettings, guarded by watchful picket boats, so that the *Hunley* was instead directed against a less valuable wooden warship. Stealing out of Battery Marshall on Sullivan's Island on the evening of 17 February 1864 under the command of Lt. George E. Dixon of the 21st Alabama Infantry, it rammed a torpedo into the 13-gun, 1,240-ton sloop-of-war USS *Housatonic* of Capt. Charles W. Pickering outside the bar and sank it, although the submarine never resurfaced.

The Federals refused to be deterred by such attacks, grimly maintaining their investiture of the city for more than a year because Charleston was widely hated throughout the North as the "cradle of secession" and thus seen as the source of so much suffering. Gen. William T. Sherman finally began to march out of Georgia through the interior of South Carolina in February 1865 with 60,000 Union troops, cruelly ravaging the hapless countryside. Some measure of the venom felt was expressed in a letter to Sherman from Gen. Henry W. Halleck: "Should you capture Charleston, I hope that by some accident the place may be destroyed; and if a little salt should be sown upon the site, it may prevent the growth of future crops of nullification and secession."

Ironically, Sherman had to hasten past the city to disperse a last-gasp Confederate concentration under Gen. Joseph E. Johnston at Durham, North Carolina, so that it was Charleston's own garrison that set fire to thousands of unexported cotton bales throughout the city on the evening of 17 February 1865, determined to leave nothing behind for their foes before retreating northwestward. The magazine at the Northwestern Railroad Depot also exploded, killing 150 people, and flames soon engulfed the riverfront, anchored vessels, and the Ashley River bridge. Union troops disembarked shortly thereafter, black troops of the 55th Massachusetts Infantry leading a triumphal march up Meeting Street to the strains of "John Brown's Body."

Reconstruction (1865–1894)

Once-proud Charleston had been left a gutted shell, described by one visitor as "a place of widowed women and rotting wharves, of buzzards perched in melancholy rows upon the roofs of deserted warehouses, of weed-grown gardens and miles of grass-grown streets." South Carolina's interior lay equally devastated, thousands of inhabitants being either dead, displaced, or bankrupt. The old plantation-based economy had been eradicated, and although tens of thousands of field hands were emancipated, they had no means of support and so thronged toward the federal garrison towns.

Charleston was occupied by the 21st U.S. Colored Troops and 127th New York Volunteers, who clamped an iron discipline upon the ruined city, rationing food supplies so as to avert any famine as inhabitants slowly trickled back, some facing arrest as former secessionists. White citizens were traumatized by their straitened circumstances and irrationally hostile to even the most mundane liberties accorded blacks— such as access to Battery Promenade, which had formerly been segregated. Racist attitudes hardened and intermingled with the shame of defeat, so that when a constitutional convention dominated by prewar white leaders assembled in Columbia to request South Carolina's readmission to the Union, it refused to consider a petition by 103 black Charlestonians that no color bar be placed upon their rights or privileges. The white legislators instead inserted a vindictive Black Code into their new constitution, so that a Colored People's Convention met in Zion

Ruined mansions along Battery Promenade, April 1865. (Miller and Lanier, *Photographic History of the Civil War*)

Church in Charleston and appealed directly to the U.S. Congress to be granted equal suffrage.

The latter responded by refusing to seat the white delegates, and furthermore overturned their authority by enacting the First Reconstruction Act. South Carolina's Black Code was voided as of 1 January 1866 by Gen. Daniel E. Sickles, military commander for the district, after which federal authorities assumed control over all state affairs. Although intended to rectify past wrongs, such heavy-handed intervention exacerbated the whites' sense of grievance, especially through such punitive riders as denying office to former Confederate officials unless they had obtained a congressional pardon or requiring voters to swear an oath of allegiance to the Union. Northern reformers also offended local sensibilities by attempting to dictate social change, while greedy speculators—nicknamed "carpetbaggers" because they arrived carrying carpetbags, forerunners of modern suitcases—sought to exploit Charleston's prostrate economy; inexperienced and illiterate black voters were easily swayed into supporting such opportunists.

With two-thirds of the state electorate now black and former Confederates restricted, more than half of the delegates who assembled in the city for a new constitutional convention on 14 January 1868 were black, and all but four were Republicans. The resultant legislation contained numerous positive elements, such as provisions for a public school system, with nonsegregated and free elementary schools. Yet, unfortunately, South Carolina's economy had not recuperated sufficiently to finance such innovations, while whites remained bitterly aloof from the new administration, obstructing its plans, deriding Southern-born white members as "scalawags" or traitors, and idealizing their lost antebellum existence.

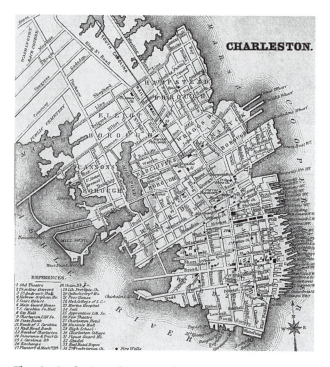

The city in the immediate postbellum era, 1869. (Univ. of Texas Archives)

Charleston's struggle to revive commercially was aided by the fortuitous discovery of rich phosphate-rock beds along the Ashley River banks, supplementing cotton or rice exports, which now faced stiffer competition on international markets. An undercurrent of racial animus became entrenched as the Ku Klux Klan appeared among whites, while a serious split developed between radical Republican blacks and more moderate elements, who—disappointed by their continuing poverty and apparent lack of advancement—were willing to consider an alternative. When the popular former Confederate general Wade Hampton ran for governor on the Democratic ticket in 1876, his broad appeal provoked an attack by black agitators against the Colored Democratic Club in Charleston's Fourth Ward on 6 September, inflicting many injuries and damages around Citadel Green and requiring the imposition of martial law.

Hampton subsequently won the election by garnering virtually every white vote, as well as those of 15,000 black South Carolinians; yet the sitting governor, Daniel Chamberlain, refused to vacate office in December 1876, provoking a four-month constitutional impasse. (Born in Massachusetts, Chamberlain had come to South Carolina after the Civil War to settle a friend's estate, then had parlayed his service as a lieutenant in the Negro Union cavalry into a political career.) President Rutherford B. Hayes finally mediated a settlement that saw federal troops withdrawn from the state by 11 April 1877, so that Chamberlain grudgingly made way for Hampton. His personal integrity and wartime prestige seemed to augur

well, but Hampton lost a leg during a hunting accident immediately after his 1878 re-election, requiring a lengthy convalescence. When he was later elected to the U.S. Senate, state Democratic polls—bereft of a suitably esteemed champion—betrayed their black supporters by enacting discriminatory legislation in 1881 that imposed certain conditions for registration, effectively disenfranchised illiterate voters, and restored a white plurality.

Charleston had still not recuperated when a massive hurricane struck on the evening of 25 August 1885, crashing through its seawall to flood the city. A heavy earthquake followed at 9:51 P.M. on 30 August 1886, felling or damaging 90 percent of its remaining edifices and sparking a score of fires; twenty-seven people lost their lives outright plus another eighty-three who died later from injuries, shock, or exposure. Gas lines were ruptured and telegraph lines came down, so that there was no communication with the outside world until the next day, and rumors circulated that the city had been swallowed by a tidal wave; aftershocks also prompted many fearful residents to sleep outside in tents for several more weeks. Finally, an even more deadly hurricane occurred on 25 August 1893, leaving the entire western section of Charleston under 10 feet of water by the time it blew itself out five days later; everything south of Tradd Street was inundated, and thousands lost their lives on South Carolina's offshore sea islands. Clara Barton and Red Cross volunteers subsequently established their headquarters in Charleston the next June.

Modern Era (1895–Present)

Despite its suffering and poverty, the city nonetheless began to show some modest signs of progress, such as replacement of its old wooden boardwalks with concrete sidewalks and the laying of a "modern" cinder roadway along Saint Philip Street. Charleston's economy was given an unexpected boost when 7,000 soldiers arrived by rail in July 1898 to transfer aboard transports and sail for Cuba during the Spanish-American War. More important, the U.S. Naval Station was transferred from its Civil War–era base at Port Royal Sound into Charleston three years later, as its more spacious harbor could better accommodate the huge battleships then being launched. When Adm. F. W. Dickens arrived aboard the U.S. Coast Squadron's flagship *Texas,* he noted that sixty-five warships could easily anchor 1,000 feet apart in its 30-foot-deep waters while the naval base was taking shape on the west bank of the Cooper River north of Charleston.

A higher city seawall was completed by 1910, running from King Street to Chisholm's Mill at the west end of Tradd Street; 47 acres of mudflats were also filled in west of Charleston, being subdivided into residential lots. A long-deferred plan of constructing a pair of lengthy stone jetties to facilitate loading and off-loading was undertaken, the city approaches having been nearly sealed off by a crescent-shaped bar 10 miles long that extended from Sullivan's Island to Mor-

Windswept curiosity seekers viewing hurricane debris along Battery Promenade, late August 1911. (South Carolina Historical Society)

ris Island. A new convention center and police headquarters were inaugurated as well, and the city developed a considerable reputation as a year-round resort.

Another hurricane struck Charleston on 27–28 August 1911, causing seven fatalities and much damage within the city, along with delivering a mortal blow to South Carolina's rice industry: so many inland dikes burst that it was not economically feasible to replace them all, given that commodity's low price on international markets. The state's cotton industry was wiped out at almost that same time by boll weevils, which ruined its most lucrative strain, the "long-staple" cotton grown in the Sea Islands region. Phosphate fertilizers, lumber, and fishing remained Charleston's principal industries.

Fortunately, World War I saved its economy, its port serving as a major transshipment point for outward-bound materiel and soldiers. Additional private wharves were constructed to handle the excess, and many rural people moved into the city to obtain new jobs. The first suburbs appeared in North Charleston, while Reynolds Avenue—running from Meeting Street Road to the main gate of the U.S. Naval Station on the Cooper River—became the first stretch of paved concrete highway in the state. After the war concluded in November 1918, municipal authorities took over these new docks and railway spurs, agglomerating them into a Port Utilities Com-

mission so as to compete for more commercial harbor traffic; a huge tipple was also erected on the Cooper River that could lift an entire railway coal car and dump its contents into a ship's bunkers, so that Charleston became a port of call for ocean-going steamers.

City finances were reformed after the 1923 election of Mayor Thomas Porcher Stoney, permitting a few urban improvements such as replacing gas lamps with electricity; opening Union Pier at the foot of Market Street; and completing a bridge westward across the Ashley River by 1926, so that new subdivisions might spring up on its far banks. Three years later a new municipal airport was also opened, and the John P. Grace Memorial Bridge spanned the Cooper River (named in honor of Charleston's previous mayor, who held office from 1911 to 1915 and 1919 to 1923).

Unfortunately, the Great Depression, starting in October 1929, plunged Charleston into poverty once more, so that slums multiplied and owners of stately old mansions complained that they were "too poor to paint, and too proud to whitewash." Consciousness of the city's past at least led to a 1931 zoning ordinance to preserve many of its historic landmarks and feature them as tourist attractions. The city was battered by a series of tornadoes on the morning of 29 September 1938, inflicting hundreds of casualties and widespread damage. Charleston's population was measured at 71,275 residents by 1940, but since it now sprawled well beyond its original boundaries—which had not been officially extended to match beyond the old 5-square-mile area in almost a century—the true total for its metropolitan area exceeded 100,000.

The military buildup prior to the entry of the United States into World War II was reflected by increased construction at the city's naval station, shipyard, dry dock, and airport facilities; some slum clearance was also undertaken, making way for low-cost housing projects. After the Japanese attack on Pearl Harbor on 7 December 1941, Charleston once again served as a major departure point for outgoing troops and supplies, a training base for Army Air Transport personnel, and an attractive convalescent area for servicemen wounded overseas.

The brief economic downturn after peace returned in August 1945 was compensated for by numerous urban projects, such as street paving, drainage and sewage projects, as well as more slum clearance; industrial growth by the private sector at the northern end of the peninsula beyond the city boundaries also grew substantially. By 1950 the population for the entire metropolitan area stood at 159,838 residents—of whom only 68,243 now lived within the old city core—and raw material imports increased through its modern port terminals (installed

10 miles north of the customshouse), especially as containerization became more prevalent. Hurricane Able howled ashore just south of Charleston on Labor Day weekend 1952; Hurricane Hazel almost eradicated the nearby Myrtle Beach resort area when it crashed by, two years later; Hurricane Gracie struck land on 19 September 1959; and Hurricane Donna struck the following year—yet none could stem the city's commercial growth. Thanks to its wartime road and rail systems, Charleston had become a regional distribution hub, particularly for the new textile factories in the state's Piedmont area.

Urban industrialization was also encouraged by the clearing of several thousand acres on the Cooper River banks, which became the Bushy Park development. City boundaries were also expanded by the annexation of part of Saint Andrew's Parish in 1960 and the completion of the Silas Pearlman Bridge six years later, which facilitated the development of the East Cooper area. Grain elevators had moreover been erected in North Charleston to speed the state's agricultural exports (now principally soybeans), and Charleston became a major military contractor as well, constructing Polaris missiles and berthing nuclear submarines.

Yet, regrettably, Charleston remained so steeped in its historical past that racial segregation had also become deeply entrenched, sullying the city's reputation by its resistance to the

Panoramic view across the modern Navy Yard, ca. 1993. (U.S. Naval Historical Center, Washington, D.C.)

national drive toward greater social justice and equality during the 1960s. On a more positive note, nostalgic pride in their heritage led the city council to declare the entire urban core as far north as Calhoun Street a historic preserve in 1966, thereby tripling the size of its thirty-five-year-old Old and Historic Area, which today remains a popular architectural and tourist destination.

For further reading materials on the history of Charleston, as well as sources on North American and U.S. urban history, please consult the Select Bibliography at the end of this volume.

CHICAGO

Great midwestern metropolis that experienced a meteoric rise from a minor crossroads into the "Second City" of the United States during the course of the nineteenth century.

Frontier Outpost (1673–1802)

At its inception, this marshy and inhospitable stretch of terrain with its hot, humid summers and bitterly cold winters seemed to offer scant promise. Few if any Native Americans chose to settle in the spot they dubbed Chicagou (The Wild-Garlic Place). About 4 miles inland from its lakefront, the mud and bogs gave way to a 12-mile-wide prairie swamp whose soil was not especially fertile and whose lack of hills or trees offered scant shelter against the harsh winter winds. Moreover, the surrounding flatlands routinely flooded during spring thaws. Local Illiniwek, or Illinois, tribesmen therefore traversed this area only during summertime, preferring to reside on drier land, amid stands of trees that could be felled to fashion log cabins and be heated.

Around 1650 the Illiniwek were defeated by Iroquois war bands pushing out of the east and so became displaced around Chicagou by Miami tribes. Some years afterward the first French fur traders began paddling down Lake Michigan out of Canada, and they noted how waters to one side of its river mouth (near modern Midway Airport) flowed eastward, while the Des Plaines River ran westward. Because waterborne transport was so crucial during this era before any roads could be driven overland, Chicagou's intersecting river systems promised a vital connection between the Great Lakes and the midwestern prairies that lay beyond. French voyageurs soon learned that they could span the Continental Divide by paddling through Chicagou's flooded delta during the wet season or by the portage (carrying) of canoes and goods across short stretches of ground during the dry season.

Aerial view looking southward down the Lake Michigan shoreline of the modern city of Chicago. (Urban Studies, University of Toronto)

The importance of this new link was confirmed when the Jesuit missionary Jacques Marquette and the explorer Louis Joliet made an extended reconnaissance from Lake Superior through Wisconsin and down the Mississippi as far as the Arkansas River in the summer of 1673, before reversing course. Rather than forge several hundred more miles upstream against the powerful Mississippi flow, a Native American boy among their party suggested that they follow the Illinois and Des Plaines rivers in a shorter, easterly detour toward Lake Michigan. Emerging at Chicagou, both explorers recognized the strategic value of the shorter route, so that Marquette returned the next autumn to begin indoctrinating its friendly Miami residents. Becoming snowbound, he spent the winter of 1674–1675 in a cabin built on a riverbank by two French traders (near where the Damen Avenue Bridge stands today) and died there the following year.

Meanwhile, news of this discovery prompted the Crown authorities to send two officers—Robert Cavelier, Sieur de La Salle, and Henri de Tonty—to establish a chain of forts from the Chicagou portage all the way down the Mississippi Basin, so that France might lay claim to the middle portion of North America and prevent their British rivals from expanding inland from the Atlantic Seaboard. Both men passed through Chicagou in 1681–1682, erecting a stockade and cabin, as well as several other strong-houses nearby, before proceeding down the Mississippi as far as the Gulf of Mexico. They named that distant territory "Louisiana," in honor of King Louis XIV.

The French settlement at Chicagou flourished over the next decade and a half, comprising at its peak perhaps 300 tiny, crude cabins inhabited by a few royal officials and fur trappers, plus several hundred Christianized Indians. Nevertheless, the number of Frenchmen willing to reside permanently that deep in the wilderness never amounted to more than a handful, so that the Crown eventually regarded such advance bases as too costly to staff and maintain, and Gov.-Gen. Louis Frontenac curtailed government support by the close of the seventeenth century.

Consequently, Chicagou remained a private trading outpost, yet so debilitated that hostile Fox Indians were able to cut off all access to the southern end of its portage by 1720. Only a few French frontiersmen and Native Americans were still residing in this imperial backwater when Canada was conquered by Maj.-Gen. James Wolfe's expeditionary force in 1759, meaning that Chicagou legally passed under British control once a treaty was signed in Europe four years later. Much the same occurred during the American War of Independence, when twenty-six-year-old George Rogers Clark—with a commission from the Virginia House of Burgesses—led 175 Kentucky militiamen in a sweep that bypassed Chicagou yet nonetheless resulted in the entire "Northwest Territory" being claimed by Virginia in 1778.

Six years later, after the Thirteen Colonies had gained their freedom from Britain, Virginia ceded this claim to the new U.S. government; protracted negotiations ensued with London over where the new international boundary with Loyalist Canada was to run, while serious opposition also fermented among the Great Lakes tribes, which banded together to contest this transfer of their ancestral homelands to U.S. control. Indigenous resistance suffered a serious setback with their defeat at the hands of Maj.-Gen. "Mad Anthony" Wayne's army on 20 August 1794, in the so-called Battle of Fallen Timbers on the banks of the Maumee River (near modern Toledo, Ohio). Hostilities were officially concluded by the signing of the Treaty of Greenville a year later, so that American occupiers moved into the Northwest Territory during the summer of 1796; however, seven more years were to elapse before Chicagou received a U.S. Army garrison.

Fort Dearborn (1803–1812)

Irish-born Capt. John Whistler reached the 6-mile-square tract of land—thereafter spelled "Chicago"—with sixty-eight soldiers in 1803, finding its dwellings reduced to a mere four "dilapidated log huts, covered with bark." Over the next year he and his men erected a stockade with 12-foot-high palisades on the southern bank of the Chicago River mouth (near the modern intersection of Michigan Avenue and Wacker Drive), naming the structure Fort Dearborn in honor of Secretary of War Henry Dearborn. The troops resigned themselves to bored isolation on the farthest fringe of the American frontier, Fort Wayne (Indiana) being a week's travel away, Fort Detroit (Michigan) two weeks distant, while St. Louis (Missouri) was almost three. Fur trading with the local Miami and Pottawatomie tribes nonetheless revived, as did some small-scale farming, but frictions with outlying tribes such as the Winnebago gradually grew—especially after Indian resentment against further American encroachments began to coalesce under the leadership of the Shawnee chieftain Tecumseh, with covert support from the British in Canada.

Regional tensions finally exploded in late autumn of 1811, when Gov. William Henry Harrison of the "Indiana Territory" advanced with a mixed force of 900 regulars and militiamen against Tecumseh's home village of Tippecanoe (near modern Lafayette, 100 miles southeast of Chicago), destroying it on 7 November. War preparations accelerated throughout that winter, and hostilities touched Fort Dearborn the following spring, when a Winnebago party raided Charles Lee's farm—4 miles south of Chicago—killing and scalping two workers and sending the entire community of fewer than 100 white settlers fleeing within the shelter of its stockade. They huddled inside over the next few months while war bands prowled the countryside, plundering and torching farms; Washington moreover declared war against Great Britain as well on 19 June 1812 because of a host of other international grievances.

Hundreds of Native Americans marshaled around Chicago that same summer, until its defenders realized that it would be impossible to resist in the event of an assault or siege. The new garrison commander, Capt. Nathan Heald, was therefore authorized to evacuate Fort Dearborn. After destroying its munitions and liquor supplies, as well as hiring a small escort of loyal Miami warriors, his fifty-four U.S. regulars, twelve militiamen, and twenty-seven noncombatants emerged from the stockade on the morning of 15 August 1812, hoping to slip past and reach Fort Wayne. Tribesmen thronged into the fort to plunder it, while others menaced the refugees. Several hundred warriors under Chief Blackbird then sprang an ambush about a mile and a half farther south, massacring twenty-six soldiers, all the militiamen, two women, and a dozen children, while capturing the rest; a few whites were rescued from this killing frenzy by friendly Pottawatomie. The gutted stockade was subsequently torched, marking an end to the first U.S. presence at Chicago.

Revival and First Shipping Boom (1816–1870)

Four years later, victorious U.S. authorities were able to dictate terms to the defeated tribes and reoccupy the entire Northwest Territory. Fort Dearborn was re-erected during 1816–1817, while Chicago's fur trade rebounded quickly thanks to renewed demand back east, fed by such monopolies as John Jacob Astor's American Fur Company. Although enough settlers arrived so that Illinois could boast 40,000 inhabitants and achieve statehood by 1818, virtually none of those migrants chose to take up residence at Chicago. Three years later a visitor reported that its settlement still consisted of only the military stockade and "about nine or ten houses and families, mostly French traders."

That same year of 1821, the energetic Gov. Lewis Cass of neighboring Michigan held a conference with approximately 3,500 natives at Chicago, purchasing 5 million acres in the southwestern corner of his territory from them for $100,000, spread out over twenty annual payments, plus other nonmonetary aid, all to be disbursed at Chicago. Thousands of Indians therefore converged upon the tiny settlement every autumn to collect these annuities over the next few years, being greeted by a crowd of itinerant salesmen peddling liquor and other goods. Yet the village itself benefited little from such transitory commerce, a report in 1825 recording a mere fourteen permanent taxpayers and thirty-five eligible voters. The following year, another visitor noted that Chicago "contained about fourteen houses, and not more than 75 to 100 inhabitants at the most."

Yet since more migrants continued pouring into the state (the population of Illinois rising from 55,000 people in 1820 to 157,000 by 1830), the hamlet became transformed. Chicago's first formal land survey was conducted in 1830; streets were named and a few lots sold by auction. A year later it became the seat of justice for the newly created Cook County, and its first river bridges and a jail were erected by 1832. By the next year, its population had doubled to roughly 350 people; it

Joshua Hathaway's 1834 plat map of Chicago's original land plots, most of which were still unoccupied; note the two branches of the Chicago River, plus the sandbar obstructing access to Lake Michigan. (Chicago Historical Society)

became incorporated as a town, and its first newspaper appeared: the *Chicago Democrat*.

The short-lived Black Hawk War against a small tribe in the northwestern corner of the state unwittingly stimulated further growth, as ships bearing federal reinforcements had been unable to enter the harbor and off-load because of Chicago's silty, shallow shoreline. Government engineers consequently cut a channel directly through the sandbar obstructing the Chicago River mouth and dredged a passage up to a 1,260-foot pier, which they completed by July 1834. Such improvements not only eased ship movements—255 major vessels entering harbor that very next year—but they furthermore provided so many new jobs that the town's population leapfrogged from 1,800 residents in 1834 to more than 3,200 a year later.

Construction began in 1836 on a portage canal just south of Chicago at Canalport (modern Bridgeport) to link with another stretch joining the South Branch of the Chicago River to the Illinois River, so that steamships might transport goods as far as the Mississippi. Despite sporadic economic downturns throughout this boom period, the town became a city in 1837 and continued to develop and attract a steady stream of migrants; its population increased to 6,200 inhabitants by 1842, 8,000 two years later, and 20,000 by 1848, the year in which the canal project was finalized. Business increased dramatically the very first year it went into operation, with corn shipments, for example, multiplying eightfold and lumber volumes doubling; farmers could now market their produce in Chicago by simply conveying it to the nearest riverbank. Steamship service as far as New York had already become regularized, travel times being reduced to a mere six days, and East Coast manufactures could also be imported inexpensively into Chicago, then delivered to rural customers.

The city's population therefore leaped to 30,000 people by 1850, a spectacular gain accompanied by the introduction of Chicago's first streetlights and the founding of Northwestern University the next year. Unfortunately, overcrowding contributed to a cholera epidemic that killed 6 percent of Chicagoans in 1854, but that tragedy at least served to encourage the digging of its first sewer system two years later. Economic progress was further boosted by the laying of its first railway lines, which initially supplemented—and eventually replaced—canal traffic. Ten miles of track laid in 1848 blossomed into 3,000 within the next nine years, nearly 100 trains using the city's central rail hub daily by 1857. Three years later, Chicago was the ninth-largest metropolis in the United States, and its population had skyrocketed to 109,260 people, fully

Street scene near the Chicago River mouth, encapsulating its nineteenth-century economic life: a grain elevator in the background towers above steamers, sailing schooners, railway cars, and oxcarts; note that the two men at center are also sitting upon a lumber shipment. (Chicago Historical Society)

half of whom were foreign-born (including 21,000 Germans, 20,000 Irish, and 2,200 Scandinavians).

Rail transport, unaffected by winter freezes that paralyzed waterborne traffic, also allowed early industrialists such as Cyrus McCormick to ship the first mechanical wheat reapers directly to his farm clients, while furthermore accelerating the handling of wheat harvests—a lucrative commodity that would spoil if stored for too long. Steam-powered grain elevators installed as of the 1850s began removing wheat from railcars, depositing it in huge warehouses, then transferring it onto outward-bound ships or trains more efficiently than ever before. Where a crew of stevedores might have previously toiled all day to load a ship with 7,000 bushels, a single man could now do the same in an hour by operating a mechanized grain elevator; volumes therefore increased from 2 million bushels a year in 1856 to 50 million five years later. Railways moreover facilitated the extraction of vast quantities of lumber from forests in Wisconsin, Michigan, and Minnesota, where lumberjacks preferred working during the winter months so as to move heavy logs more easily across the frozen ground.

The huge demands engendered by the Civil War years of 1861–1865 spurred all of Chicago's industries, especially clothing and boot manufactures, yet perhaps none profited more spectacularly than meatpacking. During the initial phases of the conflict, the number of pigs imported by rail increased sixfold, being slaughtered and cured in a myriad of private stockyards scattered throughout the city before being shipped out to feed Union forces. However, the Chicago Pork Packers' Association held a conference with the city's nine principal railroad companies in 1864 and agreed to jointly purchase a half-mile-square tract 4 miles south of downtown (west of Halsted Street, between 39th and 47th streets) to be developed into a purpose-built complex.

When completed late the next year, this vast new spread—patriotically named the "Union Stock Yards"—contained 3 miles of water troughs, 10 miles of feed troughs, and nearly 30 miles of drainage pipes. Trains had easy access, and every necessity was present on-site, including a posh 260-room hotel for buyers and sellers. Thanks to such large-scale investments, Chicago's economy continued to expand even after hostilities ceased, so that the city's population grew from 190,000 people in 1865 to more than 306,000 five years later.

The Great Fire (1871)

Much of this rapidly erected urban infrastructure consisted of wooden buildings, while planks had also been used to line its sidewalks and even pave over 55 of its 530 miles of muddy streets; fire therefore posed a continuous hazard, serious outbreaks having occurred in 1857 and 1868. On the night of Saturday, 7 October 1871, half of Chicago's 185 firefighters spent fifteen hours extinguishing a 20-acre blaze just west of the city, at the end of an unusually dry summer. The next evening, at 9:00 P.M., another conflagration began less than a mile southwest of downtown, in the O'Leary's barn near the intersection of Jefferson and Taylor streets—although whether started, as legend has it, by Mrs. O'Leary's cow kicking over a lantern cannot today be verified. Lamentably, the exhausted firemen responded slowly, then were diverted to the wrong address, so that by the time seven companies finally mustered forty-five minutes later, a huge blaze had been whipped up by 20-mile-per-hour winds.

Throughout that night of 8–9 October 1871, flames raced from block to block and across wooden bridges, precipitating a citywide panic. The inferno's glow could be seen as far away as Indiana, and hydrants ran dry the following dawn when the city waterworks burned to the ground. A cold rain eventually quenched the flames at 3:00 A.M. on Tuesday morning, but not before a swath of destruction a mile wide and 4 miles long had been carved. Almost every structure between Harrison Street to the south and Chicago Avenue on the north, and between the two branches of the Chicago River to the west and Lake Michigan on the east, had been consumed—a total of some 17,000 buildings, representing a material loss of $250 million, which would bankrupt several local insurance companies. Some 300 people had also perished, and another 90,000 to 100,000 of the city's 335,000 residents had been left homeless, with winter about to set in.

Resurgence (1872–1892)

Incredibly, Chicago would be rebuilt within two years, good fortune having spared its most valuable components—the Union Stock Yards, railways, lumberyards, and most grain elevators—so that its business remained unaffected, helping speed this remarkable recovery. In the year immediately following the Great Fire, 13,000 ships put into Chicago harbor—more than all the arrivals at New York, Philadelphia, Baltimore, Charleston, San Francisco, and Mobile combined. So much

Some of the devastation left by the Great Fire: panoramic view eastward up Randolph Street in late October 1871, after the rubble had been cleared away. Note the temporary wooden shacks and stacks of bricks at curbside for the colossal reconstruction effort that was about to commence. (Chicago Historical Society)

Ruined southern façade of the Great Central Union Passenger Depot at the foot of Lake Street; note the railcars and Grain Elevator "B" in background, miraculously spared by the flames. (Chicago Historical Society)

money was raised by charitable donations from sister cities— $600,000 in New York; $400,000 in Boston; $160,000 in Cincinnati; $100,000 in Buffalo; $500,000 in England; and so forth— that within a fortnight, civic authorities "had to telegraph them to stop."

The eradication of the old downtown core even allowed for a more rational upgrading, its previous jumble of offices, dwellings, warehouses, factories, and barns being replaced by mostly commercial buildings, while residences were relocated to more outlying areas. Downtown property values soared as modern new structures began to emerge, many rising into skyscrapers so as to maximize the return upon now expensive lots; terra-cotta was also applied to many metal-frame exteriors, so as to render the structures more heat resistant, although the city nonetheless endured another frightening fire in 1874.

Chicago's economy was also bolstered by a young entrepreneur named Aaron Montgomery Ward, who had learned

that many Midwestern farmers felt exploited by traveling salesmen who bought their produce cheap and then sold it at a markup in Chicago—only then to purchase consumer goods and sell them back to the farmers at inflated prices. Ward contacted this disgruntled clientele in 1872 by mailing lists of items that he had bought in mass quantities, offering to cut out the middlemen by shipping directly to the countryside at wholesale prices, with an unconditional money-back guarantee: any client unsatisfied upon examining a purchase at the post office could simply return it for a full refund. Montgomery Ward and Company proved to be an overnight success, and it spawned numerous Chicago imitators in the lucrative "mail-order" business (the most famous being Richard Sears and Alvah Roebuck, who founded their own rival company in 1893).

Another significant boost to the city's economy occurred later during the same decade of the 1870s, when Gustavus F.

An example of the citywide reconstruction effort, here at the corner of Lake and La Salle streets, ca. 1872; the Marine Bank Building is going up at left. (Chicago Historical Society)

Swift perfected the refrigerated railway car. Previously, live prairie cattle had to be shipped on the hoof from Chicago to be butchered in eastern markets. By cleverly packing ice and brine into the rooftops of specially designed cars—with vents that allowed incoming air to become chilled and drop through the lighter, warm air on to the vehicles' floor—Swift was able to ship processed beef as far as the Atlantic coast without spoilage.

The rebuilt downtown core by 1878, looking westward from Dearborn Street up the north side of Lake Street. (Chicago Historical Society)

Such consignments were not only more remunerative, but—when embraced by his chief competitor, Philip Armour, in 1880—created a huge new butchering and processing industry in Chicago, as well as many ancillary businesses derived from by-products, such as the manufacture of brushes and combs, fertilizers, glue, and margarine. By the early 1880s, the volume of eastbound beef had exceeded that of live cattle.

The metropolis now began to swell to enormous proportions, becoming the third largest in the United States, its population being measured at 503,185 inhabitants in 1880. The city's first 4-mile electric streetcar track appeared two years afterward, expanding into an 86-mile system within the next decade. Frictions also developed between the rich capitalists who dominated civic life and the ever more numerous urban masses. A nationwide work stoppage known as the Great Railroad Strike of 1877 sparked three days of running street battles in Chicago between gangs of workers and police, resulting in 30 dead and 200 wounded, as well as prompting George Pullman—inventor of the luxurious railway sleeping car—to transfer his entire corporation to a custom-built "company town" 15 miles south of the city.

Leading industrialists' suspicions of leftist activities worsened during the 1880s, especially when the first unionization efforts began among the throngs of new laborers reaching the United States—most of whom were non-English speakers and were falsely believed to harbor violent anarchistic tendencies. With the job market tight because of this sudden influx of cheap labor, workers felt that they had no other recourse than to organize in order to obtain better wages, safer working conditions, compensation for injuries or death, and better living conditions.

On 1 May 1886, workers struck Cyrus McCormick's International Harvester factory, demanding an eight-hour workday. Having already experienced considerable labor strife, McCormick hired a host of replacement workers, who were set upon two days later by 6,000 strikers just outside the factory gates. Policemen and company guards intervened, and two people were killed and several injured during the resultant melee. Labor thereupon held a protest rally in Haymarket Square on the evening of 4 May, but at its conclusion 150 police arrived to disperse the 300 remaining participants; a bomb was tossed out of the crowd, killing 7 officers and wounding 60. The surviving officers opened fire and later arrested 8 known German-born anarchists on charges of having incited the attack. Despite lack of evidence, seven were condemned to death and four executed, a fifth committing suicide in prison. The funeral cortege for these so-called Haymarket Martyrs was followed by 20,000 mourners, while another 200,000 onlookers lined Chicago's streets; yet the bombing nonetheless gravely tarnished the young labor movement in the United States, so that the union striking McCormick's plant—the Knights of Labor—saw its national membership plunge from 730,000 members in 1886 to only 260,000 two years later.

The Great Fair (1893)

Notwithstanding these difficulties, the brash young city successfully bid in 1890 to host the World's Columbine Exposition two years later, a fair intended to commemorate the 400th anniversary of Christopher Columbus's discovery of the New World. Such grand international exhibits had originated with London's Crystal Palace Exposition of 1851, the most recent having been celebrated in Paris in 1889 (at which the Eiffel Tower had been unveiled). Despite widespread skepticism, Chicago had secured this prestigious prize by raising $10 million in financing and by hiring the renowned architects Frederick Law Olmstead and Daniel H. Burnham to design the most impressive venue possible. A marshy, undeveloped scrubland of sand dunes called Jackson Park, located 7 miles south of the city center, was chosen as the exposition site; a three-year construction project transformed it into a splendid convention center. The number of laborers engaged soon rose to 12,000—including Elias Disney, father of Walt Disney—and they often worked round the clock, thanks to newly installed electric lights.

Chicagoans and visitors alike were dazzled by the size and beauty of this World Fair when it opened on 1 May 1893. The steel-frame exhibition halls, their exteriors covered in gleaming plaster that shone like marble, led to the grounds being nicknamed the "White City," while its 600 acres—three times bigger than any previous exhibit—welcomed a total of 27 million people before closing on 30 October. Among its most memorable displays was a huge, rotating metal wheel designed by bridge builder George Washington Ferris for lifting sightseers aloft—remembered today as a "Ferris wheel"—and the Electricity Building, dazzlingly illuminated by nearly 130,000 bulbs. Having hosted one of the most successful and memorable of World Fairs, Chicago's reputation as a great international metropolis was solidly entrenched.

Ironically, though, the White City did not survive long. A period of acute national depression followed, and many of Chicago's poor and unemployed moved into the now-vacant buildings as squatters. In July 1894 soldiers and striking rail workers clashed on its grounds, sparking a huge fire that engulfed almost the entire complex. Only two structures remain today: the former Fine Arts Palace—now converted into the Museum of Science and Industry—and the Art Institute.

Progressive Era (1894–1930)

By the end of the nineteenth century, Chicago had exploded into a bustling metropolis of 1,698,575 people, the second largest in the United States, and with its commercial predominance ensured. Yet such spectacular and unbridled growth had also produced a congested agglomeration of streets, factories, and slum housing that would become ever more crowded as millions of Eastern European immigrants continued to press into the United States. Well-intentioned reformers—middle-class citizens, women, journalists such as Upton Sinclair, small businessmen, and college professors—condemned the social ills and injustices that had been engendered through relentless industrialization and urbanization, believing that some of the city's enormous wealth could be diverted into the amelioration of living conditions, so as to make Chicago better for all.

Regrettably, these noble designs often ran counter to the interests of petty officeholders, who represented the many ethnic enclaves of which the city was now composed. New migrants customarily settled amid tightly knit groups of their own nationality or religion, compliantly electing neighborhood leaders as aldermen to the powerful Chicago city council. Corrupt figures such as Joseph "Bathhouse" Coughlin and Michael "Hinky Dink" Kenna from the Irish South Side—who derived much of their income and patronage power from the "boodle," or graft, paid by brothels and other illegal establishments in the First Ward—could therefore not be turned out of office, nor did they have any incentive to embrace social engineering.

Carter Harrison II achieved some modest civic improvements during his two terms as mayor by rescinding several crooked utility company contracts; significantly bettering the safety record of railways running through city streets; denying a monopoly over streetcar service to the disreputable Charles Tyson Yerkes; and encouraging Burnham's 1909 plan for rationalizing and beautifying Chicago through the construction of landscaped parks, boulevarded roads, and the like. The urban population also grew impressively during his tenure, reaching 2.7 million by 1920, with another 693,000 living just outside the city limits. But more substantive reforms made scant headway, especially after the highly unpopular prohibition on liquor was passed by Washington in January 1920. Criminal gangs expanded from their traditional prostitution and gambling rackets into bootlegging as well, spearheaded by Johnny Torrio and a young hired thug from New York City named Alphonse Caponi—better known as Al "Scarface" Capone.

After a series of gangland killings derisively dubbed the "Beer War" in local newspapers, Capone emerged as overlord of a citywide syndicate that controlled all illegal liquor sales, allegedly grossing $70 million a year by 1930. The populist mayor William "Big Bill" Thompson turned a blind eye to such activities, ignoring the criticisms from Chicago's wealthy and middle-class reformers and instead wooing blue-collar voters through a series of public works projects and jobs. During his first administration, for example, 441 miles of streets and 230 miles of sidewalks were paved; 221 miles of sewers were laid; and the city's teeming population climbed to 3,376,000 inhabitants by 1930, with more than a million others residing in outlying communities.

"Machine" Politics (1931–1975)

Dependence on patronage jobs became ever more acute during the Great Depression following the stock market crash of

October 1929, and inadvertently helped solidify the Cook County Democratic Party's stranglehold over power. Ward bosses traditionally brokered the outcome of any municipal election by channeling block votes from their ethnic followers; given the harsh economic climate, this decisive influence meant that private businessmen had to contribute to party coffers in hopes of gaining or retaining city contracts. Such extracurricular funding in turn meant that the party did not have to draw upon the depleted municipal treasury for its own needs and could hand out construction projects and civic services as a reward for precinct loyalists.

Because of the infallibility with which this system churned out the necessary votes in any given election, it became known as the "Machine," and its adherents came to rely heavily upon the resultant largesse. The first Machine boss—Czech-born Mayor Anton J. Cermak—accompanied Franklin D. Roosevelt on a visit to Miami in March 1933 and was accidentally killed when an assassin missed the president-elect. Edward J. Kelly (who had amassed a tidy fortune in kickbacks as president of the South Park Board and chief engineer of the Sanitary District) replaced Cermak and led Chicago out of the difficult Depression years, aided by generous financial assistance from the Democratic administration in Washington. World War II poured $9.2 billion into the city, reviving its overall prosperity thanks to a massive infusion of industrial, manufacturing, construction, and high-tech jobs. (One example is provided by the local Douglas Aircraft Corporation, which built test runways at Orchard Park—2 miles beyond Chicago's northwestern border—that were eventually purchased by the city and transformed into O'Hare Airport.)

Yet societal expectations also changed in the immediate postwar era, as the electorate was no longer as tolerant of the Machine's blatant cronyism and organized crime connections; as a result, the Cook County Democratic Party fielded the incorruptible Martin H. Kennelly as its candidate to deflect such criticisms and burnish its image. Soon afterward, though, a noticeable migration also began toward the ring of brand-new suburban developments, Chicago's population declining for the first time from 3,621,000 inhabitants in 1950 to 3,550,000 a decade later, while its suburbs almost doubled from 1,557,000 people to 2,671,000 during that same span, and many of those new suburbanites represented the city's younger, more upwardly mobile, professional families.

Like other older U.S. metropolises, Chicago now faced the specter of inner-city stagnation, a trend strongly contested by the Machine's next leader: Richard J. Daley. Born to working-class parents in the tough Irish neighborhood of Bridgeport, the diligent yet uncharismatic Daley was elected mayor in 1955 and immediately launched a massive construction program of new highways, public housing projects, dock facilities, convention centers, and an airport, as well as public parking garages to entice suburban commuters back into the downtown core. He simultaneously overhauled the city's medical,

police, fire, lighting, and sewage services. Such large-scale municipal spending not only revitalized the local economy, but also persuaded corporations to invest in downtown showpieces such as the John Hancock Building, Sears Tower, and Water Tower Place. As a result of such widely trumpeted civic improvements, Chicago even became dubbed "the city that works" by the national press.

Yet although Daley's application of a traditional public works solution had successfully reversed Chicago's economic downturn, it failed to rectify more deep-seated social ills. African Americans in particular had long been marginalized, their original "Black Belt" neighborhood along State Street on the South Side and near West Side having been kept confined and underserviced, despite its growth from 30,000 black residents in 1910 to 813,000 by 1960. Territorial clannishness and bigotry by other ethnic groups denied African Americans access to a broader housing market, resulting in de facto segregation—so much so that the civil rights activist, the Rev. Dr. Martin Luther King, Jr., traveled from the Deep South to campaign against discrimination and overcrowded conditions in Chicago ghettos during 1965–1966.

In August 1968 the national Democratic Party celebrated its presidential convention in the city, attracting thousands of delegates, news media representatives, and activists from across the country. Given the heightened state of sociopolitical tensions that summer—Dr. King and Sen. Robert F. Kennedy having both been assassinated just a few months previously, while resistance to the unpopular Vietnam War was peaking—Daley geared his 12,000-man police force for trouble, backed by 6,000 Illinois National Guardsmen. On the last night of the convention, several thousand protestors marched from Grant Park toward the old Chicago Amphitheater, where delegates were preparing to nominate Vice Pres. Hubert H. Humphrey to the party ticket. The marchers were halted at the intersection of Michigan Avenue and Balbo Street by a phalanx of helmeted policemen, who after several minutes of tense confrontation waded into the crowd and began clubbing participants. Television networks cut away from their live coverage inside the hall to show 90 million viewers the scenes of brutality outside, which were subsequently labeled a "police riot."

Both Chicago and Daley became deeply tainted by this event, the Machine's stranglehold over power being advanced as proof of the innate corruption and injustice prevailing within its city government. White flight to the suburbs increased, so that population figures were reversed by 1970: there were now 3,612,000 suburbanites as opposed to 3,369,000 urban Chicagoans. Simultaneously, African American support for the Cook County Democratic Party fell away, but Daley nonetheless won re-election in 1971 and 1975, thanks to his ethnic white base and his undoubted skills at providing good public services. At a time when other major U.S. cities such as New York, Philadelphia, Detroit, Cleveland,

A block of burnt-out buildings standing in the wake of the riots following the assassination of Martin Luther King, Jr. (Bettmann/Corbis)

and Cincinnati were undergoing financial crises, Chicago remained efficient, well managed, and fiscally sound.

Modern Era (1976–Present)

A more noticeable transformation began after Daley died of a heart attack in 1976, being succeeded by the shy and unremarkable Michael Bilandic. In January 1979 the city was hit by a series of record-breaking blizzards, and snow removal efforts proved slow and ineffectual. Chicagoans crawled through a difficult winter over roads made impassable by frozen mounds of ice, while businesses suffered and garbage piled up. Unused to such a breakdown in municipal services, voters turned against Bilandic and the Cook County Democratic Party when he stood for election later that same year, so that he was upset by Jane Byrne, a charismatic Irish American Chicagoan who attracted significant numbers of disaffected black and white liberal voters because of her anti-Machine platform.

Yet despite being a talented campaigner, Byrne proved a disappointing city manager, her administration furthermore being hobbled by a downturn in the national economy. Transit workers, teachers, and firefighters all went on strike during her term, while the business community fretted over her inability to provide stable leadership. In order to pass bills through the powerful city council, she eventually abandoned her reformist stand and forged an alliance with Alderman Edward Vrdolyak, new head of the Cook County Democratic Party, and she subsequently alienated many black supporters by courting the white ethnic vote when her 1983 re-election bid was challenged by Daley's son, Richard M. Daley.

Frustrated, the historically fragmented black electorate rallied behind their own candidate—Harold Washington—who won the Democratic primary by 425,000 votes to Byrne's 388,000 and Daley's 345,000. Normally such a victory meant an automatic win during the ensuing mayoral election, yet racial animosity ran so deep that many white Chicagoans threw their support behind the Republican candidate, Bernard Epton, a wealthy Jewish lawyer from the liberal Lakefront area—who often found such unsolicited backing uncomfortable. Washington eventually won the 1983 election by a slim majority of 46,000 votes out of 1.3 million cast, the city's growing Hispanic population—measured three years previously at 422,000 people—apparently providing the margin of victory. But bitter white resistance continued in city council chambers, where Washington's proposals were routinely voted down by a majority of twenty-nine aldermen led by Vrdolyak; a counterproposal would then be passed, 29–21, by that same group, only to be vetoed by Washington. Four years of acrimonious deadlock ensued, until Washington at last routed Vrdolyak in the Democratic primary of 1987 and was returned as mayor with an effective majority in the city council. He died unexpectedly in office that same November, at the age of sixty-five.

An early mayoral election was called for 1989, during which Richard M. Daley defeated Washington's unpopular interim successor, Eugene Sawyer, then installed a moderate administration that set about addressing the city's most pressing problems—crime, poor schools, substandard public housing, segregation, and an aging industrial infrastructure. The younger Daley succeeded by applying his father's old hallmarks of efficiency and fiscal responsibility, tempered with much greater sensitivity toward Chicago's social needs and racial harmony. By 1994 the dwindling urban population had stabilized at 2,731,743 residents, with 5.8 million people now living amid its encircling sprawl of suburbs. Six years later the population of Chicago had rebounded slightly, to 2,896,016.

For further reading materials on the history of Chicago, as well as sources on North American and U.S. urban history, please consult the "Select Bibliography" at the end of this volume.

DETROIT
Major industrial center, so famous for its automotive output as to have earned the sobriquet of "Motor City."

Foundation (1701–1760)
As early as the 1630s, French fur traders from Quebec had pushed deep into the Upper Great Lakes wilderness to barter for pelts from regional tribesmen, eventually establishing an outpost at Sault Ste. Marie. Crown officials came to regard such inland bases as too costly to staff and maintain, so that Gov.-Gen. Louis Frontenac decided to curtail the fur trade in 1696. One disappointed trader named Antoine de la Mothe Cadillac sailed to France three years later to petition King Louis XIV for permission to found a new fur-trading outpost in the territory, his authorized project prospering even further upon his

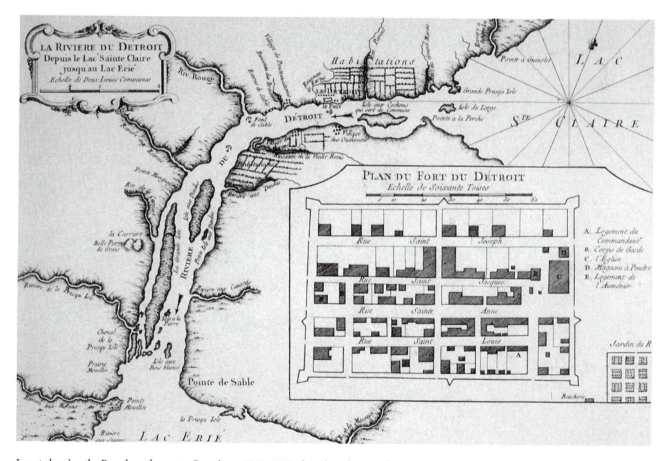

Insert showing the French settlement at Detroit, ca. 1749–1755, plus a broader map depicting its position on the curving river narrows; published in 1764 as part of the naval engineer and cartographer Jacques Nicolas Bellin's *Petit atlas maritime*. (Metropolitan Toronto Reference Library)

return, when a peace treaty was also signed with the previously hostile Iroquois in 1701.

Armed with his royal license, Cadillac and a small band of followers departed up the Ottawa River from Montreal in June of that same year, across Georgian Bay, down Lake Huron, then through Lake Saint Clair until they at last espied an ideal location for their new trading post and on 24 July 1701 established a tiny settlement on the northwestern shore of a narrow river curve that was to become dubbed Détroit, or the "Strait." Subsequent attempts to lure more French migrants to the remote locale from eastern Canada proved largely unsuccessful, but Huron, Ottawa, Miami, and Chippewa did congregate around its rustic stockade called Fort Pontchartrain.

Disheartened by his lack of support and profits, Cadillac quit a decade later, and by the middle of the eighteenth century, Detroit's territory was being encroached upon by English traders pushing inland from the Atlantic Seaboard. The major French-Canadian strongholds of Quebec City and Montreal then fell to British invaders in 1759–1760, during the French and Indian War, so that the commandant of isolated Detroit was compelled to capitulate in November 1760 to a British detachment led by Maj. Robert Rogers of Rogers's Rangers fame (the inspiration for Kenneth Roberts's novel *Northwest Passage*).

British Occupation (1761–1796)

The next year, regulars of the 60th, or Royal American, Regiment arrived to take up residence, but local Indian allies of the French were reluctant to forsake their ancient loyalties; thus the Ottawa chieftain Pontiac spent the winter of 1762–1763 secretly forging a confederacy to drive the British back out of the Great Lakes region and Ohio Valley. Their campaign was to be launched by a surprise springtime attack against the Detroit garrison, yet its commanding officer, Maj. Henry Gladwin, forewarned by a Native American woman, received Pontiac and 300 braves when they appeared for a conference and ritual dance on 7 May 1763 with fully armed troops, so that Pontiac had to withdraw and initiate a siege two days later.

Despite failing to surprise Gladwin, the Indians did annihilate almost every other British outpost within little more than a month, only Detroit and Fort Pitt holding out, until indigenous hopes gradually faded that France might resume its former role in North America. A number of tribes thereupon withdrew from the confederacy, causing dissension among the rest. As the rebellion lost momentum, Pontiac lifted his siege of Detroit, and in the spring of 1765 he accepted British rule.

When the Thirteen Colonies subsequently revolted against London in 1775, Detroit remained loyal to the Crown, its garrison commander Henry Hamilton even encouraging nearby Native American war bands to raid patriot territories (thereby earning the nickname "Hair Buyer Harry Hamilton" among resentful Americans, who falsely believed he offered bounties

for scalps). More practically, a new stronghold called Fort Lernoult was also erected north of the small town in 1778–1779 to better resist any potential patriot counterattack.

No assault ever occurred, though, and even after the United States won its freedom from Britain in 1783, Detroit remained in British hands: there remained considerable confusion as to how deep into the wilderness the new international boundary with Loyalist Canada was to run, or even whether Detroit was to pass under U.S. control at all. The question was apparently resolved after four years' protracted negotiations, when it was agreed that 250,000 square miles west of the Alleghenies and north of the Ohio River—the so-called Northwest Territory, including modern Ohio, Michigan, Indiana, Illinois, Wisconsin, and part of Minnesota—was to be opened up for American settlement. But the Miami, Shawnee, Pottawatomie, and Chippewa residents banded together to contest such a transfer, with covert support from the British.

Seven years of intransigence by the indigenous population finally culminated with their defeat at the hands of Maj.-Gen. "Mad Anthony" Wayne's army on 20 August 1794, in the so-called Battle of Fallen Timbers on the Maumee River (near modern Toledo, Ohio). Hostilities were officially concluded by the signing of the Treaty of Greenville on 3 August 1795, after which the British garrison withdrew from Detroit when a U.S. regiment under Col. John Hamtramck marched into its village

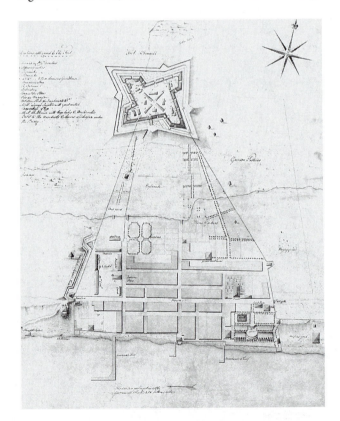

A 1799 survey by John J. Rivardi of the riverside town of Detroit and its Fort Lernoult stronghold, erected in 1778–1779. (William L. Clemens Library, University of Michigan, Ann Arbor)

on 11 July 1796 and occupied the citadel, renaming it Fort Wayne. When the major-general himself paid a visit a few weeks later to help set up a U.S. civil authority, the newly created county was furthermore named in his honor as well.

Early American Development (1796–1859)

Yet despite the installation of a U.S. garrison, Detroit remained a tiny French-speaking community, separated from all other major population centers by several weeks' travel through often hostile Indian territory. Its evolution into a city was fomented by two key figures: Father Gabriel Richard, a priest who had escaped from revolutionary France in 1798 and established Detroit's first school and printing press, among many other innovations, and Judge Augustus B. Woodward of Virginia, one of five men appointed in 1805 by President Thomas Jefferson to help organize the newly named "Michigan" into a U.S. territory and who was the only one of the five to participate actively in the task.

On 11 June 1805, a baker named John Harvey accidentally set a hay pile on fire, and within minutes, strong winds fanned a conflagration that consumed almost all of Detroit. This calamity allowed Woodward two years later to lay out a unique new street plan of broad boulevards, interlocking hexagons, and spacious plazas—a radial, "wheel-spoke" pattern inspired by Maj. Pierre L'Enfant's recent designs for Washington, D.C.— that were to define the city's future form, although never adopted in their entirety. Despite the best efforts of Woodward and Richard, the 1810 census revealed only 1,650 people liv-

ing in the reconstructed town, plus another 3,112 settlers scattered throughout Michigan.

These pioneers were to endure yet another ordeal when the War of 1812 broke out against the British and their Indian allies, although local campaigning started promisingly enough when sixty-one-year-old Gov. and U.S. Brig. William Hull— uncle to the USS *Ironsides*'s captain, Isaac Hull—crossed the Detroit River into Ontario with 1,200 troops and 1,000 auxiliaries on 12 July, occupying the tiny Canadian hamlet of Sandwich (modern Windsor). However, Hull did not then press southward against the main British stronghold of Fort Malden in Amherstburg, so that his volunteer army soon began to dissipate.

On 2 August 1812, Fort Michilimackinac's defeated U.S. garrison retreated into Detroit, and that same day local Wyandotte Indians crossed over into Amherstburg to join the British. Three days later, the Native American leader Tecumseh threatened a U.S. supply train approaching Detroit from Ohio, prompting Hull to contemplate a strike against Fort Malden. But he reversed his decision when informed on 8 August of an approaching British relief column under Maj.-Gen. Isaac Brock, instead recrossing the Detroit River with the bulk of his army. The next afternoon, the 600-man escort that Hull had delegated to meet the supply train was ambushed near the village of Maguaga, suffering eighteen killed and sixty-four wounded; then, while retiring into Detroit the following day, that same mauled detachment was shelled by the brig *Queen Charlotte* and schooner *General Hunter,* prompting Hull to order the last

Anonymous wash drawing looking east-northeastward along Detroit's riverfront in 1794 when the town was still in British hands. (Burton Historical Collection, Detroit Public Library)

of his troops to evacuate Sandwich on 11 August—a retirement that so exasperated some subordinates that they openly circulated petitions demanding his recall.

With his army's morale broken and Michigan militiamen deserting back into their homes, the U.S. brigadier decided that he could not resist when Brock's smaller force disembarked nearby on 16 August 1812, surrendering his citadel and being marched off into captivity along with his 582 U.S. regulars, while 1,600 Ohio volunteers were paroled. The British major-general—created a knight of the Order of the Bath for this unexpectedly easy success—gained Detroit's fort along with its thirty-three cannon, 2,500 muskets, and the 14-gun brig *Adams,* holding on to the prize for slightly more than thirteen months against repeated U.S. counterthrusts out of Ohio.

Commo. Oliver Hazard Perry at last defeated Amherstburg's squadron in the Battle of Lake Erie on 10 September 1813, paving the way for William Henry Harrison—governor of the Indiana Territory and a major-general in the Kentucky state militia—to advance against occupied Detroit with his 4,500 troops. Vastly outnumbered, the British garrison commander Brig. Henry A. Procter torched his supply dump and many of Detroit's buildings two weeks later, before retreating cross-river to destroy Fort Malden as well. He then slowly retired eastward through Ontario as Perry's victorious warships entered the Detroit River from the south on 26 September, covering Harrison's occupation of Amherstburg the next day and the smoldering remnants of Detroit by 29 September.

The U.S. major-general quickly installed a garrison under Gen. Duncan McArthur to begin rebuilding its burned defenses, while pursuing the retreating British column with 3,000 troops. Reinforced by 500 mounted Kentucky riflemen under Lt.-Col. and U.S. congressman Richard Mentor Johnson, Harrison overtook and crushed Procter's weary redcoats and Tecumseh's warriors on the north bank of the Thames River, 5 miles southwest of Moraviantown (modern New Fairfield, Ontario) on 5 October 1813, his cavalry returning triumphantly into Detroit four days later, followed by his infantry on 10 October.

Harrison concluded regional operations by dictating terms to the Pottawatomie, Wyandotte, Miami, and Chippewa tribes, which had fought as British allies on 14 October 1813, receiving numerous hostages against their future good behavior. He then appointed Brig. Lewis Cass as Michigan's new governor and departed on a victorious progression toward Washington. (With his military reputation thus enhanced, Harrison was eventually elected ninth president of the United States, serving only a single month, while his subordinate Johnson— wounded five times at the Battle of the Thames—became ninth vice president under Van Buren, having run under the slogan "Rumpsey, dumpsey, Johnson killed Tecumseh.")

Detroit was never again to be threatened by an invasion, yet its remoteness continued to stunt development once peace with Britain was restored early in 1815. According to a census conducted five years later, its population had shrunk to 1,422 residents, with only another 7,474 spread throughout the entire Michigan Territory—compared with almost 600,000 thriving settlers in neighboring Ohio. This predicament was altered dramatically by Robert Fulton's application of steam power to boats—the first Great Lakes paddle steamer, *Walks-Upon-Water,* having reached Detroit on 27 August 1818—and most especially by the completion of the Erie Canal in 1826. That waterway permitted agricultural produce to be shipped directly from Detroit across Lake Erie as far as New York City, while goods and migrants could also travel out along that same route.

Territorial officials soon began pressuring Michigan's Indians, still regarded with much lingering hostility and suspicion on account of the recent wars, to make way for a new wave of homesteaders. Typically, tribes were offered an annual payment to restrict themselves to a single area, thereby allowing whites to take over virtually all other lands within the next decade. (Surviving tribesmen either moved westward or resettled on reservations, of which seven still exist in Michigan today.) Enough migrants displaced the indigenous inhabitants that Michigan was able to achieve Washington's minimum population requirement for statehood—30,000 residents—by January 1837. Detroit also blossomed, expanding from 2,222 inhabitants in 1830 to 9,102 a decade later, as well as serving as temporary state capital until a wilderness site could be chosen in central Michigan in 1848 (the modern city of Lansing).

State and federal funds soon began underwriting significant development projects as well, such as drainage of swamps, clearance of farmlands, building of canals and railroads, and so forth. By 1848 a railway line ran 175 miles westward from Detroit as far as the shores of Lake Michigan, while a Chicago–New York link was completed seven years later, including a ferry service across the Detroit River into Ontario to link up with an existing Canadian track as far as Buffalo. Detroit's population had multiplied to 21,019 inhabitants by 1850, with another 376,635 spread throughout the state, figures that were to soar more impressively still—to 45,619 and 702,494, respectively—within the next ten years.

Industrialization (1860–1899)

Detroit transformed into a major manufacturing hub thanks to the enormous demands generated during the U.S. Civil War, its riverside setting allowing it to receive weighty cargoes— such as iron and copper ores from Michigan's Upper Peninsula or timbers and other heavy bulk items—directly from lake steamers; this feature meant it could handle much larger tonnages than could be conveyed into less favored centers by horse-drawn wagons traversing the region's primitive, unpaved roads. Factories and workshops consequently mushroomed all along the city's waterfront during the early 1860s, turning out a vast assortment of wood and metal products, railroad equipment, paints and varnishes, plus hundreds of industrial and pharmaceutical chemicals, all of which could then be shipped out via the same steady stream of paddle vessels or the increasingly sophisticated rail system.

This upsurge in productivity also caused Detroit's population to swell as laborers were attracted from rural areas, Canada, or even as far away as Europe. In this era before any effective public transit, many settled into densely packed ethnic enclaves within easy walking distance of their workplaces. Frictions increased, and the city experienced its first major race riot. Although blacks represented only 3 percent of Detroit's inhabitants, they nonetheless bore the brunt of public opprobrium when President Abraham Lincoln—his Union armies faring badly against the Confederacy—called for an additional 300,000 conscripts in late 1862. Draftees might buy an exemption for $600, but no migrant could afford such a sum, and many resented serving a cause that they assumed was being fought exclusively on behalf of African American slaves.

As a result, anger flared when a black restaurant owner named William Faulkner was arrested early the next year, accused of molesting two young girls. On 6 March 1863 a mob of dock workers—primarily recent Irish, Dutch, or German immigrants—surrounded the jail to lynch the prisoner, but they were foiled when the Wayne County sheriff was reinforced by troops hastily summoned from Fort Wayne. The crowd nonetheless pelted the soldiers with stones, provoking them into opening fire and killing a rioter. The outraged mob thereupon torched numerous black-owned businesses and homes,

causing two more deaths before order could finally be restored. Troops remained in Detroit's streets for several more weeks, while Mr. Faulkner was released after seven years, receiving restitution from the state legislature for wrongful incarceration, as one of his accusers had recanted.

The city's industrial base continued to expand even after the Civil War concluded in 1865, its population soaring commensurably from 79,577 inhabitants five years later to 116,340 by 1880 and 205,876 a decade afterward. Detroit had now become such a prosperous and well-established midwestern metropolis that it could even afford the luxury of hiring the nation's premier landscape architect—Frederick Law Olmsted—to design Belle Isle Park opposite its riverfront; its leading industrialists had furthermore become so technically adept and confident as to be ideally positioned to take advantage of the next great technological opportunity in the United States.

Automotive Capital (1900–1966)

At the dawn of the twentieth century, Detroit had a population of 285,704 residents, ranking it fifteenth among the nation's cities. Within the next two decades it would leapfrog to fourth—behind only New York, Chicago, and Philadelphia—thanks to its successful adaptation to the demanding automobile industry. Although many other urban centers had their own infant car companies—as well as the same combination of industrial elements, such as access to large quantities of

Packard S-24 Victoria, 1906; priced at over $5,000, this model was typical of the custom-built, luxury automobiles produced before the advent of the more efficient assembly line. (Detroit Public Library)

wood, steel, and coal, experienced engineers and machinists, and capital investors—Detroit nonetheless came to excel because its manufacturers proved to be more determined and resourceful. Henry Ford's innovative use of the assembly line, which introduced standardized parts and an integrated production system to build his Model T, is today remembered as an outstanding example of such creativity. Yet many other local entrepreneurs made significant contributions, such as Ransom E. Olds, William C. Durant, Walter P. Chrysler, the Dodge brothers, and Alfred P. Sloan.

Although early vehicles were unreliable and expensive, U.S. production figures nonetheless rose from 6,400 cars in 1908 to 78,000 four years later, because such purchases represented status symbols among the urban upper class. However, the greatest impetus to Detroit's automotive industry came as a result of the outbreak of World War I in Europe in 1914, which—besides increasing export demands for traditional manufactures such as chemicals and steel—furthermore required an expansion of the U.S. highway system as railroad companies could not keep up with the excessive freight loads bound toward the East Coast. Trucks therefore provided an alternative solution, Detroit's annual production of such vehicles multiplying from 25,000 at the beginning of the conflict to 227,000 by its conclusion in 1918. And once world peace was restored, many states still continued paving thousands of miles of new highways, so that trucks eventually came to dominate the short-haul freight business, ensuring an apparently inexhaustible market for Detroit's output.

The city's population had doubled again between 1910 and 1920, while urban boundaries expanded from encompassing 28.35 square miles to 142.1 square miles by 1926. Four years later the number of residents was measured at 1.6 million people, making it the fastest-growing metropolitan area in the country. This upsurge naturally entailed a building boom as well, with monumental new structures such as the Detroit Public Library being completed by 1921; the 1,200-room Book-Cadillac Hotel the next year; a magnificent Institute of Art by 1927; and the forty-seven-story Penobscot Building, twenty-eight-story Fisher Tower, Fox Theater, and Music Hall the following year.

Demand for vehicles collapsed with the Wall Street stock market crash of October 1929, then revived spectacularly in the mid-1930s, after which production of cars was suspended altogether by Washington in favor of weapons manufacture when the United States was drawn into World War II in December 1941. Such sharp drops and resurgences were to prove an ominous harbinger of future development, for although Detroit would continue to prosper, it always remained vulnerable—unlike most other major U.S. cities—to "boom-and-bust" cycles brought on by fluctuations in the national economy, alterations that were quickly reflected in abrupt sales declines for its high-ticket products.

Detroit's City Hall Square, 10 June 1925. (National Archives of Canada)

Aerial view northwestward across Detroit in 1920; note the pollution caused by numerous small factories, still clustered around its waterfront and rail yards. (National Archives of Canada)

Resentment against working conditions in its ever larger and more depersonalized factories also led to the formation of strong unions, while residential shortages created further frictions—especially among the black minority, which now constituted roughly 9 percent of the total population yet faced a host of discriminatory "Jim Crow" practices in both labor and housing markets. Racial animus finally exploded on a hot Sunday afternoon, 20 June 1943, when crowds of white and black youths began fighting on the bridge leading out to Belle Isle Park. State militia and U.S. Army units had to be deployed the next day to quell the spiraling violence, which ended on Monday night with a death toll of thirty-four people. An inquiry impaneled by Michigan's governor blamed the outburst on the African American community, although a National Association for the Advancement of Colored People, or NAACP, counter-report prepared by Walter White and future Supreme Court justice Thurgood Marshall laid bare many underlying grievances—including such details as how seventeen of the twenty-five dead blacks had been shot by city police, at a time when all but 43 of Detroit's 3,400 officers were white.

Tensions eased somewhat after World War II ended in 1945 and millions of U.S. servicemen returned home from abroad, creating a national consumer boom. Detroit's factories suffered little from peacetime transition, because once the wartime ban on car production was lifted, they could cater to a tremendous pent-up demand. The National Defense Highway Act of the 1950s furthermore financed the largest con-

struction project ever undertaken in the United States, resulting in thousands of miles of new concrete expressways. Vehicular production surged to record highs, and Detroit experienced its last great influx of job seekers, including many impoverished blacks from the South.

The 1950 census recorded nearly 1.5 million whites and 351,000 blacks living within the city limits; many of the former now began moving to new suburban tracts, while the latter remained confined into old, segregated neighborhoods, despite their steadily increasing numbers and an overall decline in the urban population to 1,670,144 people by 1960. Less affluent ethnic whites and recent arrivals from Appalachia or other southern states refused all inducements to share their Detroit enclaves, while discriminatory practices also permeated the educational system and daily commerce, to say nothing of the police department. At a time of rising social expectations for African Americans throughout the country, municipal politicians unwittingly added to black Detroiters' resentment because—with the white electorate usually split between two competing white candidates—they espoused liberal civil rights platforms to attract crucial black voters, yet failed to implement any such policies once in office.

The mayoral election of 1961 saw black voters join with a white minority to elect a distinguished yet inexperienced liberal politician, Jerome Cavanagh. Backed by generous federal grants from Washington, he sought to revitalize what was now becoming an aging inner city. He furthermore appointed

Michigan Supreme Court Justice George Edwards—a former union organizer and prominent liberal activist—as police chief, in the hope of diffusing the escalating tension between frustrated blacks and an increasingly authoritarian force. Tragically, little could be effected against such entrenched attitudes, and Cavanagh's unsuccessful effort to pass an "equal housing opportunity ordinance" two years later galvanized a backlash among white homeowners, so that—despite healthy automotive sales—the stage was set for a devastating upheaval.

Race Riot and Divide (1967–Present)

At 4:00 A.M. on a Sunday morning, 23 July 1967, two undercover vice squad officers gained access to a "blind pig" at 9125 Twelfth Street, being an establishment illegally offering entertainment and liquor after hours. Expecting to arrest perhaps a dozen patrons, they instead detained a crowd of eighty-two people who were celebrating the safe return of two black servicemen from the Vietnam War. As there were not sufficient police vans available to shuttle so many prisoners quickly in for booking, the throng was held on the street for more than an hour, while an angry crowd gathered. By the time the last detainees were removed, bottles were being hurled at the police and windows broken.

Rather than subsiding at dawn on Sunday, the rioting instead escalated, with such vehemence that Cavanagh mobilized the city police, as well as alerting the Michigan State Police and National Guard, but even their combined strength could not contain such a massive disturbance. Matters worsened after nightfall, stores being looted and fires started, while unruly mobs prevented firefighters from combating the flames. The city remained paralyzed throughout Monday as well, and despite sweeps by heavily armed patrols with tanks, looting and sniper fire persisted after dark, convincing President Lyndon B. Johnson to order in an integrated contingent of 2,700 U.S. Army paratroopers. Yet these veteran soldiers were deployed into relatively calm areas east of Woodward Avenue, while National Guardsmen—mostly untested white Michigan militiamen, untrained in riot duty—were sent into the much more troubled areas to its west.

Consequently, although this overwhelming show of force in black neighborhoods eventually brought an end to the worst excesses by Wednesday, 26 July 1967, the toll had been heavy:

The gutted remains of buildings (left) attest to the destruction caused by two days of rioting in Detroit's west side. A service station continues to burn (right), pouring smoke and flames onto other structures. At least twenty-three persons were killed and more than a thousand injured in the two days of violence, July 25, 1967. (Bettmann/Corbis)

forty-three people dead, thirty-three blacks and ten whites—of whom twenty-one had been slain by city police, nine by National Guardsmen, and one by a paratrooper. Millions of dollars in damages had also been inflicted and more than 7,200 arrests made, primarily for property offenses (although most detainees were released shortly thereafter because the judicial system simply could not process so many charges).

Detroit was polarized by this dramatic confrontation, a majority of whites departing to resettle in the suburbs beyond Eight Mile Road over the next few years, while the city's crime rate simultaneously skyrocketed. The population of its urban core plunged to 1,514,063 residents by 1970, and blacks achieved a plurality, electing the city's first African American mayor—Coleman A. Young—three years later. However, Detroit's economic infrastructure and best technical jobs had also shifted out to the suburbs, so that Young's two decades in office would be hampered by economic depression and deep-seated urban blight as the city's central core stagnated and its urban population contracted to 1,203,368 people by 1980.

Despite mutual involvement in the auto industry and occasional expressions of goodwill, the two constituencies viewed each other with suspicion, white suburbanites convinced that they would be selectively preyed upon in Detroit—even after its crime wave had abated—while blacks often encountered instances of overt racism during their visits to the suburbs. By 1990 more than 925,000 of Detroit's 1,027,946 inhabitants were black, while most of the 3.3 million suburbanites in its outer rings were uniformly white. The city was now reduced to the tenth-largest metropolis in the United States, and the most segregated. The census of 2000 revealed that its population had contracted to 951,270 inhabitants.

For further reading materials on the history of Detroit, as well as sources on North American and U.S. urban history, please consult the Select Bibliography at the end of this volume.

NEW ORLEANS
Seaport ensconced deep amid swampy savannas that lend it to dominate the Mississippi River and Delta.

Antecedents (1682–1717)
This region's low, bleak stretch of Gulf coastline was roamed for centuries by seminomadic tribesmen who resided seasonally in one spot before moving on to another. The Spaniards, despite regular galleon traffic sailing between Veracruz and Havana ever since the mid-sixteenth century, did not mount any sustained colonization efforts along this bordering fringe of steamy shoreline. Rather, it was the French explorer Robert Cavelier, Sieur de La Salle, who descended from Canada with a small expedition in 1682, hoping to lay claim to the entire 2,500-mile length of the Mississippi River valley so as to deny it to rival British traders pushing inland out of the Atlantic Seaboard, by establishing a colony astride its strategic drainage basin.

La Salle consequently dubbed the featureless landscape near the delta outlets as Louisiana, in honor of King Louis XIV, before visiting the royal court in France and returning into the Gulf with four ships bearing settlers in 1685—only to miss all three of the main river apertures (which were often shrouded with fog as their cold, muddy discharges met the warmer Gulf Stream). The first French colonists were therefore doomed to establish an ill-fated toehold in the vicinity of Matagorda Bay in Texas that succumbed to disease, want, hostility by local tribes, and mutiny.

It was not until February 1699 that a second expedition arrived, four ships from Brest under the veteran French-Canadian fur trader Pierre Le Moyne, Sieur d'Iberville, whose 200 would-be colonists were accompanied by cattle, horses, and supplies. Tiny communities were duly carved out of the wilderness at Biloxi, Natchez, and Mobile, yet they remained such remote and unappealing outposts—especially after Queen Anne's War erupted against Britain in May 1702, hampering transatlantic and West Indian traffic—that the Louisiana colony struggled to survive. D'Iberville died four years later in Havana and was succeeded as governor by his younger brother Jean-Baptiste Le Moyne, Sieur de Bienville, who granted land titles in 1708 to a band of residents that wished to relocate more than 100 miles inland from the Gulf. Their aim was to

De la Tour's original 1720 layout for New Orleans, as copied by the British army captain Pittman for publication in London by Thomas Jefferys in November 1759; the road at top leads toward Bayou Saint John and Lake Pontchartrain. (New York Public Library)

settle among the docile Houma Indians along a 4-mile-long bayou renamed in honor of Saint John, and near a large lake that D'Iberville had earlier christened Pontchartrain in honor of his French sponsor, Louis de Phélypeaux, Comte de Pontchartrain.

D'Iberville had considered the area to be a promising site for a new establishment, as it lay only 2 miles from a half-mile-wide bend on the east bank of the Mississippi; yet he had lacked resources for such an undertaking. His brother had also remained equally handicapped until the astute Scottish-born financier John Law persuaded the regent of France—Philippe, Duc d'Orléans, reigning on behalf of the sickly seven-year-old Louis XV—that the most effective means for the bankrupt Crown to develop Louisiana's untapped economic potential was by creating a corporation in August 1717 called the "Company of the West" or "Mississippi Company," which would raise capital by selling shares to private investors.

Initial response proved so bountiful that Bienville was confirmed as the company's colonial governor and authorized to attempt his brother's proposed relocation inland. As a result, Bienville reached the site in February 1718 with an advance party of eighty convict salt smugglers to begin clearing the thick, mosquito-infested cane breaks and cypresses atop a slightly elevated, narrow riverside ridge beside an Indian village called Tchoutchouma—near modern Esplanade Avenue—in anticipation of several hundred more settlers who would follow to found a new city.

French Colonial Era (1718–1765)

Bienville employed a half dozen carpenters in extemporizing crude barracks and single-room huts from the felled trees to shelter these first migrants, some 800 disembarking from three ships that same June 1718. Urban plots and outlying farmlands were duly assigned, while the western shoreline opposite was reserved for company use. Although the fledgling community was flattened by a hurricane and inundated by a flood the next year, the directors in France nonetheless continued to dispatch slaves and people to Louisiana, including a small band of architects, engineers, and craftsmen who reached Biloxi in 1720 under Pierre Le Blond, Sieur de la Tour.

Despite misgivings about Bienville's low-lying clearance beside the Mississippi, de la Tour drafted a simple grid pattern for the city's orderly development, which John Law had furthermore decreed was to be christened Nouvelle Orléans (New Orleans) in honor of the French regent. (Its streets were to be given similarly fawning names: Bourbon, Royal, St. Louis, Burgundy—for the young king's father, the Duke of Burgundy—Du Maine and Toulouse for two of that previous monarch's illegitimate sons, and so forth.)

De la Tour's assistant engineer, Adrien de Pauger, was delegated to lay out the city in 1721, although Law's speculative schemes had led to a crash in France that previous October, compromising the company's finances. Nevertheless, 1,265 res-

idents were already installed at the pioneer outpost, categorized as 290 free white men, 140 women, and 96 children; 156 indentured white servants; plus 533 black and 50 Indian slaves. The provincial administration, known as the Superior Council, was moreover to be transferred out of Biloxi after that Gulf Coast town burned down in 1722, despite another hurricane that had also swept through New Orleans. When the itinerant Jesuit priest Pierre François-Xavier de Charlevoix visited the new riverside community, he found only thirty rebuilt log cabins, a warehouse, and a shed temporarily serving as a church, although he rather charitably noted that "this wild and deserted place shall one day become the capital of a large and rich colony."

De Pauger was able to use the dislocations occasioned by this latest disaster to realign all urban plots into a more uniform grid pattern, nine blocks wide by six blocks deep, with 38-foot-wide streets radiating inland from a single riverfront plaza dubbed the Place d'Armes (modern Jackson Square). Each 60-foot-wide individual plot was to be marked off by a low circuit of stakes, unwittingly initiating the practice of surrounding homes with decorative hedges, while each city block was to have a trench dug around it to divert the free-flowing waters. Although some fortifications were planned, none were raised, as relations with the district's tribes were at first quite harmonious. By 1723, De Pauger was writing with satisfaction that New Orleans was "growing before [his] eyes."

Inasmuch as wooden edifices quickly rotted in such humid environs, a brickyard was created on the city outskirts two years afterward, yet even single-story structures in that heavier material soon cracked, tilted, or collapsed because of the spongy terrain; thus a style evolved combining the old Norman "split-timber" fashion of exposed diagonal and horizontal beams set atop firm footings of brick pilings. When the young Ursuline sister Marie-Madeleine Hachard reached the emergent community in 1727, she noted many such *colombage et mortier* (split-timber and mortar) dwellings—although with soft local bricks substituted for the traditional European stones, and clay mixed with Spanish moss as insulation. She added that many houses were furthermore whitewashed with lime, "paneled and very sunny," as well as boasting wooden-shingle roofs in a low, sloping pitch and curved at the eaves.

In order to protect the city against floods, the natural levee along its waterfront—formed by centuries of alluvial deposits—was raised to a height of 15 feet and strengthened along its entire half-mile length by 1727, although breaches would persist. Every springtime the Mississippi would rise as melting snow and ice surged downstream, while hurricanes occasionally roared inland from the Gulf, both phenomena resulting in frequent inundations. The subsoil remained so saturated year-round that wells became tainted, and tombs had to be erected aboveground.

Bienville was recalled to France, and Étienne de Périer

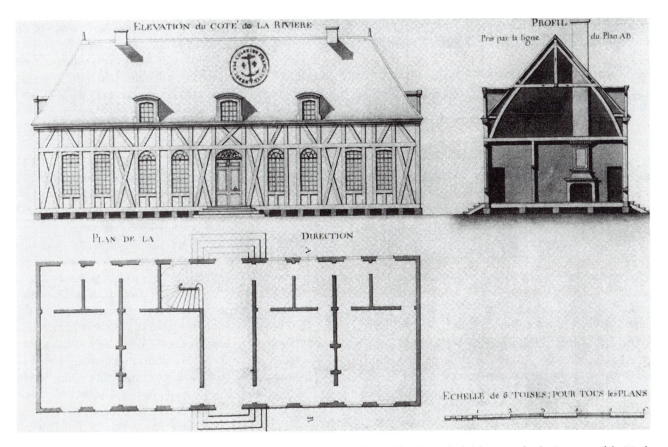

De la Tour's and De Pauger's diagrams, prepared early in January 1723 for erecting La Direction—the headquarters for the Company of the West's personnel in New Orleans, which would face the waterfront near the intersection of Toulouse and Decatur streets. (Archives Nationales, France)

became governor, weathering a major crisis when the Indians around Natchez assaulted Fort Rosalie in 1729, massacring 235 men, women, and children. Although shaken, New Orleans was able to endure the resultant hostilities, thanks in part to the reinstatement of Bienville and the reversion of Louisiana to royal control after the crippled company surrendered its grant in 1731. Life in the isolated colony improved significantly after Bienville was supplanted for a second time in 1742, his successor as governor—the aristocratic Pierre de Rigaud, Marquis de Vaudreuil—invigorating local trade in indigo, tobacco, unrefined sugar, and even a little cotton, which in turn allowed for a few gracious refinements to be introduced at the frontier outpost.

The Grand Marquis, as he was to be remembered, popularized lavish entertainments such as balls and banquets, and he even staged the first theatrical production in New Orleans: the play *The Indian Father,* performed at his own mansion. A new slate-roofed Ursuline convent was commenced as of 1745, and when Jean-Bernard Bossu visited Louisiana a few years afterward, he noted that plantation owners and skilled artisans now enjoyed many imported luxuries. Upon being promoted to the governorship of Canada, Vaudreuil received his successor—the former naval captain Louis Billouart,

Chevalier de Kerlerec—in high-flown style in February 1753; New Orleans's two public water fountains in the Place d'Armes gushed red wine throughout a spectacular dinner and fireworks display.

Unfortunately, the French and Indian War erupted the next year deep within the North American wilderness, and although Louisiana was to be spared any direct British assaults, its tenuous overseas links were almost completely disrupted. The population of the city and its 200-square-mile parish was estimated at 5,200 residents by 1760, of whom 3,200 were classified as whites. Their numbers rose slightly after all the other French colonies in North America fell to British arms and Paris surrendered all its continental aspirations upon signing the peace treaty in February 1763. The first few Acadian refugees reached New Orleans from Nova Scotia in April 1764, followed by 230 more in late February of the next year, with hundreds more still to come. Local officials provided them with some material assistance before resettling most along different inland river properties in Attakapas country.

But it was then learned, in October 1764, that the French Crown had secretly ceded the entire province of Louisiana to Madrid almost two years before to compensate its Spanish allies for the loss of Florida to the British during the conflict.

A delegation traveled to Paris to petition King Louis XV's chief minister, Étienne François, Duc de Choiseul, to no avail.

Spanish Era (1766–1803)

Louisiana's 5,552 residents greeted the naval captain Antonio de Ulloa y de la Torre Guiral so coolly when he arrived at New Orleans with ninety troops to assume office as their first Spanish governor on 5 March 1766 that he initially ruled through the French proxy Philippe Aubry. Although a distinguished scholar, the fifty-year-old de Ulloa was ill equipped to win over the resentful residents, and after two and a half years of frustration, a mob rose and spiked the city guns on 27 October 1768, before swarming through the streets again the next afternoon and driving the governor aboard the Spanish frigate *Volante*, which set sail for Havana on 1 November.

The rebellious Creole leaders thereupon offered their allegiance to the English colony at Pensacola, and even briefly contemplated outright independence, before two dozen Spanish vessels arrived below New Orleans from Havana on the afternoon of 17 August 1769, disembarking 2,000 troops who marched into its main square with music and salvos to officially reimpose Spanish rule two days later under the Irish-born inspector-general and knight of the Order of Alcántara, Alejandro O'Reilly y McDowell.

Thanks to this overwhelming show of force, O'Reilly was able to arrest the twelve Creole ringleaders at a breakfast on 21 August 1769, half being publicly executed and the remainder transported to Cuba. The first Spanish-style *cabildo* (city hall) meeting was duly celebrated on 1 December, O'Reilly and his troops ensuring full acceptance of the new administration, while digging a moat and erecting four guardhouses around the urban perimeter to discourage any future uprisings. He also ordered a census taken, which revealed a total of 3,190 people residing within New Orleans proper, of whom 1,225 were slaves. Finally, as no further hints of resistance had appeared, the general departed early in March 1770, leaving Luis de Unzaga y Amézaga behind as interim governor with a 400-man garrison.

Louisiana's small capital once more slipped back into its former state of benign neglect, the British Army captain Philip Pittman noting during his visit in the mid-1770s that it still had no official residence for the provincial governors, who had to rent a house from a former agent of the Company of the Indies, while its cathedral was so dilapidated that services were being celebrated in a storehouse. Conditions improved modestly after the vigorous, youthful, and politically well-connected Bernardo de Gálvez arrived as governor in 1777, encouraging a few municipal improvements—such as the city council's approval of erecting a wooden market shed in 1779 to prevent food spoilage in the sun.

The pace of progress quickened after Spain aligned itself with the Thirteen American Colonies in their rebellion against Britain that same year, de Gálvez raising a mixed force of 667 men and departing northwestward from New Orleans on 28 August 1779 to overwhelm an intrusive British outpost at Fort Manchac. De Gálvez followed up that success with two more years of Gulf Coast campaigns that climaxed with his capture of Pensacola. The triumphant governor was eventually promoted to viceroy of Mexico, while Louisiana benefited from enhanced trade contacts with Spanish, American, and other foreign vessels, which continued even after peace was restored. The English visitor John Smyth described New Orleans in 1784 as "rather a disagreeable place," although he admitted that it now boasted some 300 to 400 "pretty good" houses, not including lesser dwellings, while a census the following year indicated that its population had grown to 4,980 residents.

Unfortunately, New Orleans was to be leveled by a terrible conflagration that burst from the Chartres Street home of military treasurer Vicente José Núñez on Good Friday, 21 March 1788, after a taper had fallen against lace drapes in his household altar. Although no fatalities were reported among the inhabitants—now numbering 5,338—the blaze nonetheless raced so swiftly through the crowded wooden core that within five hours, 816 of the 1,100 edifices were consumed. Andrés Almonaster y Roxas, the wealthiest man in the colony, was to distinguish himself by personally financing much of the reconstruction of the gutted urban core, including its *cabildo* at the north end of the Place d'Armes; the parish church, redesigned by Gilberto Guillemard and reconsecrated as of 24 December 1794; an improved hospital; a Capuchin rectory; a chapel for the ancient Ursuline Convent (miraculously spared by its surrounding wall and lush gardens); and an elementary school, although the latter would be attended only by some thirty Spanish-speaking pupils, as well-to-do French parents still preferred hiring tutors fluent in their own language.

This wholesale reconstruction effort also altered the city's appearance, its traditional French structures being supplanted by many more Spanish-style, fire-resistant, tile-roofed brick edifices with enclosed courtyards, iron-wrought adornments, and plastered walls in pastel hues, thus giving a distinctly Hispanic architectural flavor. As work proceeded, New Orleans furthermore began receiving the first waves of French refugees escaping from the slave revolts exploding on Saint-Domingue (Haiti), who brought their West Indian skills and even some artistic innovations, such as the public theater, which they established at 732 Peter Street in 1791. At the end of that same December, the French-born Francisco Luis Héctor, Barón de Carondelet, also arrived from San Salvador as Louisiana's new Spanish governor and intendant, initiating a series of municipal reforms with his very first *bando de buen gobierno* (good government decree) issued on 22 January 1792.

In it, Carondelet directed that the city's two barrios, or wards, were to be increased to four, each administered by a pair of alcaldes, or commissioners, while streets were to be illuminated with eighty oil lamps imported from Philadelphia; the indigenous population and slaves were to be well treated; and

Historical landmark known as "Madame John's Legacy," a private dwelling originally erected by the Provençal sea captain Jean Pascal in 1726 at the corner of Bourbon and Dumaine streets, then rebuilt after the citywide conflagration of March 1788. Note its broad gallery under shady eaves, intended to provide respite against the oppressive heat, as well as its louvered shutters or jalousies. (Curt Bruce)

the levee was to be better maintained, trees being planted along its length as reinforcement (although frequently uprooted when boats tied up to them). When the Revolutionary Republic of France declared war against Spain early in 1793, the governor furthermore bolstered military defenses, while striving to stifle any pro-Jacobin sentiments among the Francophone populace. A new slaughterhouse was erected that same year on the road leading toward Bayou Saint John, as well as a drawbridge in 1794, followed by the initiation of labor upon a 1.5-mile canal with towpaths for boats to be hauled through the marshes right up to the northern edge of New Orleans.

Unfortunately, another fire swept through the city on 8 December 1794, destroying 212 buildings—mostly warehouses, barracks, and stores. As residents once more bent their attentions on recuperation, events overseas further complicated their fate when French armies invaded Spain and forced it to capitulate by July 1795, after which Madrid realigned itself with Paris, so that Britain's powerful Royal Navy imposed a constrictive naval blockade one year afterward. A yellow fever outbreak also claimed 638 of New Orleans's 8,756 residents in the summer of 1796—including Carondelet's own brother, a cleric.

However, the application of West Indian agricultural techniques now permitted Louisiana's plantations to produce small

yet lucrative amounts of refined sugar, while the distant Crown ministers had furthermore agreed to grant trade privileges to neutral Americans with the signing of the Treaty of Madrid in October 1795. Soon, swelling numbers of rough-hewn frontier boatmen would begin drifting downstream from as far away as Pittsburgh and Cincinnati with cargoes of furs, grains, pickled pork, cornmeal, and whiskey aboard large log rafts called "flatboats." The latter were broken up and sold as lumber upon reaching New Orleans, after which the boatmen returned north with their profits via overland trails known as the Natchez Trace.

Although this arrangement augmented Louisiana's trade, the hard-pressed Spanish Crown eventually grew so reluctant to sustain the backwater province that it was returned to its French allies in October 1800. As Paris proved equally ill prepared to resume control over its former colony, First Consul Napoleon Bonaparte entertained offers from an expansionistic U.S. government toward outright purchase. A temporary truce in the struggle against Great Britain allowed Pierre-Clement de Laussat to reach New Orleans in March 1803 as its new commissioner, officially accepting the colony's retrocession from Spain.

Yet the joy of the city's 8,056 inhabitants at being reclaimed by France proved short-lived, as hostilities against Britain resumed that same May 1803, after which news furthermore arrived that the so-called Louisiana Purchase had been struck with Washington and would be consummated by year's end, leaving New Orleans's French residents—"that is to say, nine-tenths of the population," according to Laussat—"stupefied and disconsolate; they speak only of selling out and fleeing far from this country."

U.S. Annexation, British Assault (1804–1815)

Yet despite their disappointment, most New Orleanians spent the next three months being wooed by a series of festivities, until finally the newly named "Mississippi Territory" passed on 20 December 1803 under the control of Washington's appointed commissioners, William C. C. Claiborne and Gen. James Wilkinson. Notwithstanding an imposition of rather unsettling administrative changes—such as the city's incorporation and elections of aldermen in 1805, a prohibition against slave imports, and the separation of Orleans and Jefferson parishes two years afterward—Claiborne went out of his way to accommodate local French leadership within the new municipal government. Trade also revived as the Royal Navy blockade was lifted, so that the city expanded beyond its original boundaries for the first time when the planter Bernard de Marigny hired the engineers Nicolas de Finiels and Bartholemy Lafon to subdivide his downriver plantation so as to create the eastern Faubourg Marigny (Marigny suburb), inhabited mostly by Creole artisans or workers, many of them "free persons of color."

By 1806 the population of the city and its parish stood at a robust 17,001 inhabitants—6,311 being classified as whites, 2,312 as free mulattoes or blacks, plus 8,378 slaves—so that Lafon began devising a more elegant residential subdivision with ample lots that would eventually become the Lower Garden District. The 700-seat Saint Philip Theater opened its doors between Royal and Bourbon streets by 1808, followed by the even more opulent Orleans Theater the following year. The city's Gallic character was further reinforced when another wave of 10,000 refugees—having earlier been resettled around Santiago de Cuba, after being chased from Saint-Domingue by the Haitian Revolution—were compelled to relocate as of

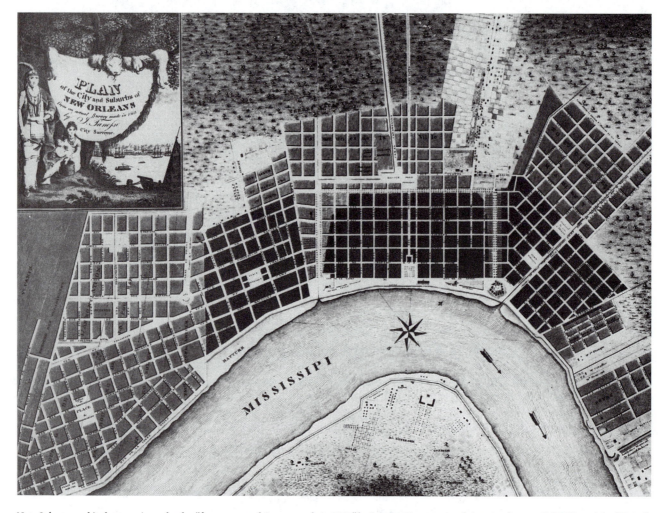

New Orleans and its burgeoning suburbs, "from an actual Survey made in 1815" by Jacques Tanesse; north is toward upper right. The original French Quarter lies at center, with Faubourg Marigny at right and Faubourg Ste. Marie at left. (Library of Congress)

May 1809 because that Spanish island no longer welcomed them after Napoleon invaded Spain.

The U.S.-appointed mayor of New Orleans, James Mather, called upon its council to adopt emergency measures to receive these latest refugees, such as removing the city fish market to a vacant lot so that its five storerooms might be used as temporary shelters and encouraging the formation of welfare committees. Most of the newcomers, divided numerically almost equally between whites, free mulattoes, and slaves, adapted well to New Orleans, a majority settling in its environs; the census of 1810 recorded a palpable population boost to 24,552 inhabitants, of whom 8,001 were categorized as whites, 5,727 as free persons of color, and 10,824 as slaves.

Their skills soon began contributing significantly to commercial life, as well as to the plantation economy and artistic endeavors. The next year the state legislature appropriated $20,000 to establish the Collège d'Orléans (College of Orleans), although its five faculty members—three being former refugees—would struggle to attract students; most well-to-do parents still preferred sending their children to private tutors or abroad for higher education. Other, less reputable ventures also arrived with the refugees, such as the smugglers' nest created at Grande Terre (Barataria Bay) south of the capital by the veteran rover Jean Lafitte, which became connected to the hamlet of Algiers opposite New Orleans by its own canal as of 1814.

The minority of American residents was displeased by this latest influx, sensing an entrenchment of French predominance. Properties in the crowded urban core had already proven difficult to obtain, while municipal leaders showed themselves unresponsive to many proposed innovations. A few cultured American individuals such as the youthful, French-speaking architect Henry Latrobe profited by designing private homes and public buildings, yet more rough-hewn frontiersmen and traders plying down the Mississippi in ever larger pine flatboats—some now measuring more than an acre across—or the narrower keelboats that could be poled back upstream found the old Vieux Carré especially unwelcoming and "foreign" to their tastes. They preferred tying up to the west of the city, along the shallow landings of the natural Batture (Bank) beyond its old moated fortifications, amid the more sparsely populated Faubourg Ste. Marie (St. Mary Suburb). One particular American vessel, of course, received a much more distinguished reception: Robert Fulton's steamboat *New Orleans,* which arrived from Pittsburgh on Christmas Eve 1811.

Therefore, notwithstanding its nominal U.S. administration, its small coterie of permanent American residents, and the elevation of the state of Louisiana in the Union as of 30 April 1812, New Orleans remained a predominantly French and black city when the War of 1812 erupted that same spring, bringing a halt to most overseas commerce because of renewed Royal Navy blockades. Worse still, once Britain bested Napoleon two years afterward, it was able to redeploy its con-

siderable military resources for a summer offensive along the Atlantic seaboard, followed by a winter strike against Louisiana.

As early as 3 September 1814, Capt. Nicholas Lockyer of the sloop HMS *Sophia* contacted Lafitte at Barataria Bay, offering inducements for his freebooters' aid in the forthcoming campaign. Despite his brother Pierre's incarceration in New Orleans by U.S. authorities, which were furthermore about to extirpate Barataria itself, Lafitte revealed this design to the Americans. The regional commander-in-chief—brevet Maj.-Gen. and former senator Andrew Jackson—reached New Orleans on 1 December 1814 to begin strengthening Louisiana's coastal defenses against an anticipated British invasion. One week later, a fifty-ship expedition bearing 8,000 redcoats under Maj.-Gen. John Keane weighed from Pensacola and anchored north of the Chandeleur Islands by 12 December, brushing aside five U.S. gunboats before ferrying Keane's army across shallow Lake Borgne to circumvent the U.S. strongholds and advance directly overland against the unfortified capital.

Although surprised by this unexpected thrust, Jackson reacted vigorously by proclaiming martial law—much to the dismay of New Orleans's French legislators—and summoned all possible units to converge upon the city. The 1,800-man British vanguard disembarked 9 miles away at the mouth of Bayou Bienvenu by the evening of 22 December 1814, being checked when Jackson counterattacked the next night at the Mississippi's Villeré Canal, supported by fire from the schooner *Carolina* of Capt. John Henley. This respite allowed the defenders time to extemporize a line of earthen ramparts behind Chalmette Plantation, 5 miles short of New Orleans proper.

Gen. Sir Edward Michael Pakenham—brother-in-law to the famed Arthur, Duke of Wellington—reached the advance British encampment and assumed command from Keane on Christmas Day 1814, after which both armies built up their strength for a major confrontation. Pakenham probed the U.S. line on 28 December, then pounded it again with long-range artillery fire on New Year's Day, failing to find any exploitable weakness. Brig. John Adair entered New Orleans with 2,300 Kentucky militia reinforcements on 4 January 1815, while 1,700 more redcoats joined Pakenham two days later, bringing the invaders' frontline strength to almost 8,000 soldiers. However, unable to conceive of a maneuver around Jackson's line—which now extended for a mile from the Mississippi directly into dense cypress swamps—the British general opted to storm straight at it.

Despite failing to shift 1,400 redcoats across to the western shore of the river in time to distract the main U.S. Army with a flanking attack, Pakenham ordered his redcoats at dawn of 8 January 1815 to march in twin columns across open country against Jackson's waiting 4,000 men, safely ensconced behind 10-foot earthen ramparts bristling with eight artillery emplacements. The mixed agglomeration of defenders included the 7th and 44th U.S. Infantry regiments, Thomas Beale's Orleans Riflemen, Maj. Jean-Baptiste Plauché's Louisiana *Carabinière* Militia, two battalions of free black troops under Maj. Pierre-Robin Lacoste, Lafitte's Baratarians, Maj.-Gen. William Carroll's Tennessee Rifles and Adair's Kentuckians, plus a screen of sixty Choctaw warriors in the swamps. Together they mowed down the advancing British, and when the first wave faltered, Pakenham was mortally wounded trying to rally his men. Of the 6,500 assault troops, 858 were killed, 2,468 injured, and 500 captured—compared with only 13 dead and 39 wounded among Jackson's ranks.

Although the British flanking attack against the west bank belatedly succeeded in scattering Brig. David B. Morgan's 1,200 U.S. defenders, and a British naval squadron moved in from the Gulf on 9 January 1815 to bombard the 366-man garrison holding Fort Saint Philip, 45 miles southeast of New Orleans, nothing could offset the devastating losses sustained by the main British army. After a fortnight of paralyzed inactivity, the survivors withdrew on the evening of 18 January, re-embarking and sailing away. Jackson was paraded through a triumphal arch in New Orleans's Place d'Armes and repeatedly feted at banquets, despite some lingering resentment among French legislators against his high-handed actions during the mobilization. It was subsequently learned that the war had actually concluded before the battle was fought, yet the resounding nature of this victory was nevertheless long commemorated.

Cotton Boom (1816–1860)

With the resumption of peace and trade, Louisiana entered into a period of almost unbridled agricultural development, its plantations multiplying in number, size, and wealth, while a great westward migration by U.S. settlers swept ever more deeply into the Mississippi Valley. A half dozen steamboats visited New Orleans in 1816—of a superior design created by Henry Shreve, with reversible side paddles so as to make them more maneuverable. Despite the disastrous flood caused by the Macarty *Crevasse* (crack) in the levee just above the city that year, opposite the Macarty sugar plantation (modern Audubon Park, named in honor of the naturalist John James Audubon, who lived in a wooden cottage on Dauphine Street from 1821 to 1822), an urban boom had undeniably commenced. In 1817 some 1,500 flatboats and 500 barges visited the so-called Crescent City, while the famous architect Benjamin H. Latrobe arrived in January 1819 to complete his deceased son Henry's waterworks project. Latrobe also found so many potential commissions, such as the design of the Louisiana State Bank building, which was to be raised on the northeast corner of Royal and Conti streets, that he moved his entire household to the bustling riverside community before dying of yellow fever in September 1820.

New Orleans's population was measured that same year at 27,176 inhabitants, of whom 13,584 were classified as whites, 6,237 as free persons of color, and the remainder as slaves. (The

One of the early American commercial houses—the ship chandlers Hoover & Pearce—which occupied a narrow lot on Levee Street, along the crowded city riverfront. (Notarial Archives, New Orleans Public Library)

total parish figure was 41,000.) An export bonanza surged through its waterfront, most especially lucrative shipments of cotton and sugar, which were transported in bulk down various Mississippi waterways aboard improved steamboats. In 1821, 287 such vessels were received at the docks, along with 441 flatboats and 174 barges, plus a commensurate number of oceangoing ships bearing imported goods and manufactures for sale; even ballast stones were purchased from arriving ships to pave some of the muddiest waterfront streets.

The state capital was nominally transferred to Donaldsonville for six years as of 1825, while New Orleans's traditional French leaders struggled to contend with so much vigorous growth. Recently arrived entrepreneurs such as the English-born James Caldwell and the New Englander Samuel Peters were frustrated by the authorities' refusal of practical improvements, such as extending the crowded wharf district beyond the Vieux Carré. These newcomers therefore bought up large tracts of Faubourg Ste. Marie, beyond the newly created Canal Street, to develop that district privately. Despite the cholera and yellow-fever epidemics that struck in 1832, a New Basin Canal was commenced to run the 6.5 miles from Rampart Street along Poydras Street to Bayou Saint John and Lake Pontchartrain, bypassing the clogged old Carondelet Canal. As commercial activity accelerated, flatboats were obliged to land ever farther upstream, around the three plantation villages that had coalesced into the "city" of Lafayette by 1833. A new three-story, 500-bed Charity Hospital was erected the following year on Common Street (modern Tulane Avenue).

By the time New Basin Canal was inaugurated in 1835, Faubourg Ste. Marie had come to exceed the original city in wealth and rival it in population, and Caldwell that same November superseded his twelve-year-old, 1,100-seat American Theater on Camp Street with the spectacular new Saint Charles Theater on Saint Charles Street. Located between Natchez and Poydras streets, it was designed by the Italian set designer Antonio Mondelli with a capacity for 4,100 spectators, illuminated by gas, and thrown together since the preceding May, despite ninety days of rain. The equally magnificent, white-domed, six-story Saint Charles Hotel—its bar capable of serving 1,000 patrons at a time—was completed the next year near Saint Charles and Canal streets by the renowned architect James Gallier, who with his colleague Charles Dakin also created the elaborate Merchants' Exchange on Royal Street in the French Quarter. Some 1,600 to 1,700 riverboats and 2,000 ships now called every year at the levee between Julia and St. Louis streets with prodigious harvests of cotton, sugar, molasses, coffee, rice, and so forth. And despite the U.S. government's prohibition against the importation of African slaves, New Orleans had become the largest slave mart in the South, with numerous holding yards along Camp Street.

At Peters's suggestion, the city administration was subdivided in 1836 into three separate municipalities, so as to minimize frictions among factions: the First was to be composed of the old French Quarter, the Second of Faubourg Ste. Marie, and the Third of Faubourg Marigny below Esplanade Avenue. Each municipality would expend funds at its discretion, although a single mayor and council would continue to be elected for the whole city. A financial crash the next year temporarily halted development, fourteen of New Orleans's sixteen banks being forced to close their doors; yet the American-dominated Faubourg Ste. Marie soon made a full recovery. Canal Street became the prime commercial thoroughfare, instead of Royal and Chartres streets, while innovations such as gas lights replaced the old oil lamps, and waterworks were upgraded by a private firm that pumped water from the Mississippi through iron pipes into a reservoir to settle out sediments before being redistributed to wealthy subscribers' homes. Feeder railways also began radiating out—5 miles to Lake Pontchartrain, as well as the length of Saint Charles

Avenue to the new resort town of Carrollton—while a rudimentary sewer system was introduced, as well as mule-drawn omnibus service.

Thousands of immigrants continued to be attracted into the vibrant river city, so many Irish laborers settling in the vicinity of lower Tchoupitoulas Street that it became known as the Irish Channel, while so many German artisans escaped their politically troubled homeland a decade later for Faubourg Marigny that it was nicknamed Little Saxony. Slums also sprang up along the "back of the town," its swampy northern fringes. By the early 1840s, New Orleans had become the country's third-largest city and a popular winter resort because of its warm climate and genteel cosmopolitanism. The wealthy lavished money upon mansions and churches, especially in the Garden District on the river side of Saint Charles Avenue, while Creole high society hosted the visiting Henry Clay at a magnificent ball in the recently reconstructed St. Louis Hotel, complete with music provided by the French Opera Company's orchestra. Ornamental ironwork became a popular decorative feature, as it did not decay, like wood.

Seven local doctors combined in 1843 to create a medical school in a splendid Greek Revival–style edifice designed by James Dakin at Common Street and University Place, to which was added a law school two years afterward, constituting the nucleus for the University of Louisiana's creation in 1847. Tragically, medical science was unable to stem a dreadful cholera outbreak two years later, which claimed one-seventh of the urban population after another major upriver flood submerged 2,000 tenements for almost three weeks, leaving 12,000 people homeless. More space being required for internments, the Metairie Ridge Cemetery came into being, while the state government was transferred out to Baton Rouge.

In 1846, New Orleans furnished men and supplies for the war against Mexico, while its commercial traffic simultaneously received 2,763 steamboats and 2,670 riverboats, plus 1,342 oceangoing ships; the former often tied up four deep opposite the city center, while the less maneuverable sailing ships anchored downstream. The influx of so many new ethnic groups had transformed New Orleans well beyond its French origins, although the insatiable labor demands of Louisiana's agricultural and shipping industries required a constant turnover of slaves; thus its black identity was retained—albeit severely restricted, as fears of a potential uprising produced ever stricter racial dictates. Great wealth permitted the old Spanish-era cathedral to be torn down and replaced by the Basilica of St. Louis as of 1849, yet the city's municipal infrastructure in other regards remained quite primitive—a public school system not even being initiated until the reclusive plantation owner John McDonogh died the following year, bequeathing his $2 million fortune toward education in both New Orleans and his native Baltimore; with these funds, forty-five schools were created throughout the Crescent City.

Canal Street as photographed in 1842 by Jules Lion, a "free man of color" and early daguerreotypist. The building at right was the Bank of Orleans; note the wooden cones in the foreground, protecting freshly planted saplings along its "neutral ground" or boulevard. (Louisiana State Museum)

In 1852, New Orleans's three municipalities were reunited and its administration occupied a new city hall designed by Gallier (modern Gallier Hall, facing Lafayette Square), while the metropolis expanded upriver by absorbing Lafayette with its 15,000 inhabitants the next year. Another terrible yellow-fever epidemic that same summer of 1853 claimed 12,000 lives, almost exclusively among recently arrived migrants. Steamboats and ships nonetheless continued to line the city waterfront, the former bringing in cotton harvests every March–April to be compressed by steam presses for accommodation and export before the heat, humidity, and torrential downpours of summer caused New Orleans to empty again for the season. Many wealthy businessmen went north at that time with their families to White Sulphur Springs or other spas, or even as far as Newport, while the middle class went to the Gulf Coast or the far shores of Lake Pontchartrain to escape the unpleasant and unhealthy summer climate.

Volunteer fire companies were supplanted by salaried employees, and New Orleans's first steam fire engine was purchased in 1855; and despite its plunging through a bridge while being hauled to a conflagration, another half dozen were soon added. Two years later, the escapist Mardi Gras (Shrove Tuesday) festivities—practiced ever since the earliest French

days preceding the denials of Lent—were organized for the first time into a formal "Comus" parade based upon the "Demon Actors from John Milton's *Paradise Lost*," initiating the colorful pageantry and tableaux that would eventually evolve into the spirited celebrations of modern times, complete with costly costumes and socially prestigious "krewes," riders atop floats tossing baubles into the crowd.

By 1860, New Orleans's population stood at 168,675 residents—of whom only 11,133 were now categorized as "free persons of color" and 15,204 as slaves—yet its ranking had slipped to sixth-largest city in the United States, as midwestern produce was being increasingly diverted by canals such as the Erie and Ohio, as well as railways, both networks connecting more directly and securely to the great seaports of the Atlantic Seaboard. The Crescent City was not as well favored for receiving the ever larger ships now traversing the Atlantic, which would otherwise have to be towed across the shifting Belize sandbars at the Mississippi River mouth and up the twisting, 100-mile river ascent, only to find cotton bales and merchandise lying exposed to the elements and thievery upon New Orleans's levee because of a lack of warehouses. Northern banking institutions had furthermore come to dominate the nation's financial markets, as would their emerging industrial complexes.

New Orleans, by way of contrast, had grown overdependent upon agricultural exports—especially cotton, which constituted 60 percent of its total traffic—and otherwise enjoyed little diversification in its trade or industry, as well as the handicaps of a slave-based economy. Resentment was furthermore coalescing in rural Louisiana and other Southern states against the abolitionist strictures being enacted by the North's predominance in the federal legislature, until a secessionist movement finally emerged in December 1860, favoring separation from the Union to create a breakaway "Confederate States of America."

Although secessionist sentiment was not as pronounced in the more cosmopolitan port city of New Orleans, tensions between the rival national groups escalated over the next several weeks, until Louisiana state militiamen occupied the U.S. Marine Hospital at McDonoghville across the river from the city on 10 January 1861, in addition to the federal installations at Forts Saint Philip and Jackson farther down the Mississippi. Hostilities exploded openly with the shelling of Fort Sumter outside Charleston, South Carolina, by rebel batteries on the evening of 12 April, and the conflict became fully joined.

Civil War and Reconstruction (1861–1878)

As the South's largest metropolis and the nation's second-busiest seaport, New Orleans was blockaded when the Union sloop *Brooklyn* took up station in the Gulf off its Mississippi outlets on 26 May 1861, abruptly curtailing all economic activity. Businesses closed, banks collapsed, and unemployment soared, while in another ominous portent, the Marine Hospital at McDonoghville—having been converted into a powder magazine—detonated with a colossal blast on 28 December, further shaking the worried city populace.

New Orleans's symbolic importance to the Confederacy also made it a prime strategic objective, when Commo. David Glasgow Farragut penetrated the Mississippi less than a year later with his West Gulf Squadron, spearheading an invasion force of 13,000 soldiers under Gen. Benjamin F. Butler. On 18 April 1862, Farragut's mortar boats opened fire against Forts Saint Philip and Jackson; then his warships dashed through a gap in the Confederate boom six days later, defeating the ram *Manassas* and some armed steamers, before proceeding upstream to hove within sight of New Orleans by the morning of 25 April. Bereft of defenses or troops—5,000 having been raised to serve in other frontline theaters—the city fell prey to panic, its outnumbered Confederate garrison and private citizenry resorting to the "scorched-earth" tactic of torching everything of value before decamping. Steamboats were ignited and released downstream as fireboats, while 15,000 bales of cotton were set ablaze on the levee, along with many hogsheads of sugar and molasses, and the customshouse contents were thrown on to a massive bonfire at the end of Canal Street.

After forging past some cable booms stretched below the city, Farragut viewed the waterfront and described it as a "scene of desolation; ships, steamers, cotton, coal, etc., were all one common blaze." Union forces took three days to bring the conflagration under control, before disembarking in strength to occupy the entire city. Butler commandeered the Saint Charles Hotel as his headquarters, deposed the mayor and city council on 1 May, then imposed a rigid military administration aimed at preventing any outbreaks of disease. He put many of the unemployed to work removing garbage, scouring the French Market in Jackson Square, clearing open drains (there being virtually no sewers in the city), and many other sanitary measures. Starvation was averted by rationing the flow of Union supplies, so that New Orleans not only survived but even attracted a steady flow of runaway black slaves from throughout Confederate-held territories.

Yet Butler also issued many harsh dictates against Confederate sympathizers, such as closing schools that refused to use Union textbooks or closing churches for refusing to pray for President Abraham Lincoln; arresting people for not saluting the Stars and Stripes; inscribing a pro-Union slogan upon Andrew Jackson's statue in Jackson Square; and most notoriously, threatening to flog women who spat at federal troops, earning him the sobriquet of "the Beast." He also ordered rail lines laid along Saint Joseph Street through Faubourg St. Mary, ruining that once fine neighborhood, and detained foreign nationals on suspicion of abetting the enemy—which precipitated his recall by Washington in December 1862.

His successor, Maj.-Gen. Nathaniel P. Banks, adopted a more conciliatory attitude toward the white civilian population, before pushing up the Mississippi and—in conjunction

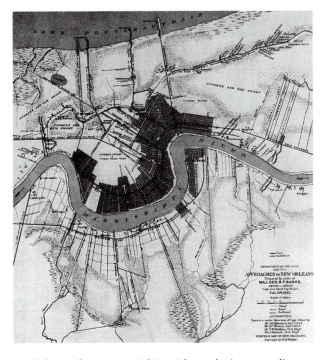

Detailed map of Union-occupied New Orleans, plus its surrounding waterways and rail-links, as surveyed in February 1863 by Capt. Henry L. Abbot of the "Topographical Engineers." Note the subsidiary communities of Algiers, McDonoghville, and Gretna on the opposite shoreline. (U.S. Army Corps of Engineers)

with Gen. Ulysses S. Grant pressing down out of Illinois—besting the last Confederate river strongholds at Vicksburg and Port Hudson by July 1863, so that the Mississippi's trade links were restored. Banks was moreover directed by Washington to convene a Louisiana state convention in April 1864 to draw up a new constitution; among other matters, it abolished slavery, yet did not enfranchise black voters before adjourning. On 11 June of that same year, a great celebration was staged in New Orleans's black-patronized Congo Square (modern Beauregard Square), attended by the highest-ranking Union officers, at which Lincoln's "Emancipation Proclamation" was read to an ecstatic throng of 20,000 listeners, then followed by a parade of black regiments.

However, once the Civil War campaigns concluded the next spring, Pres. Andrew Johnson issued a blanket amnesty for most former rebels as of May 1865; they were then voted back into office in New Orleans, as Louisiana's electoral rolls remained exclusively white. Looking to overturn this ballot-box defeat by disenfranchising former Confederates and empowering black voters in turn, delegates from the adjourned constitutional convention sought to reconvene and rewrite the state laws. Yet when they assembled in the Mechanics' Institute on Monday, 30 July 1866, and a procession of black supporters attempted to push through an angry white crowd gathered outside on University Place, a bloodbath ensued that left 48 dead and more than 200 injured before federal troops were able to restore order.

Washington responded to such reactionary sentiments by passing the Reconstruction Act of 1867, and New Orleans was moreover struck by a serious yellow-fever epidemic that same summer, adding to the crippled city's woes. A Republican-controlled constitutional convention then disenfranchised many former Confederates and empowered blacks as of 1868, although any hopes of true social progress were squandered when the Crescent City plunged into a period of corruption and violence as avaricious Northern speculators—nicknamed "carpetbaggers" because they commonly arrived with carpet-bags, forerunners of modern suitcases—sought to garner economic advantages by manipulating the inexperienced and often illiterate black electorate. Prime municipal properties along Decatur Street and the levee were consequently sold to unscrupulous developers, who erected unsightly warehouses and factories, as well as laying rail lines through the French Quarter—now so dilapidated as to attract only penniless Italian migrants, the latest wave of refugees arriving from Europe. Algiers on the opposite bank of the river and Jefferson City (formerly Lafayette) were formally annexed in 1870, becoming New Orleans's Fifth and Sixth municipal districts—raising the total metropolitan population to 191,418—and followed by Carrollton as the Seventh District in 1874.

Graft became so blatant that a splinter group separated against Gov. Henry Warmoth during the state Republican convention of 1871, some 4,000 armed men gathering on Canal and Rampart streets the next January to chant "Down with Warmoth and his thieving crew!" Gangs and vigilantes ruled many neighborhoods, while unempowered Democrats formed supremacist associations such as the White Leagues, more than 14,000 such individuals being enrolled just prior to the March 1873 elections. And when the unhappy city's Republican administration believed that a ship was arriving bearing weapons, many Democrats barricaded themselves at the river end of Canal Street and resisted fiercely against policemen sent against them on 14 September 1874, suffering twenty-one deaths in an inglorious clash remembered as the "Battle of Liberty Place."

It was not until the tightly contested presidential election of 1876 that Rutherford B. Hayes finally agreed to withdraw federal troops from Louisiana by 20 April 1877, restoring some semblance of local government. Debilitated New Orleans was struck shortly thereafter by yet another yellow-fever outbreak, when a ship's purser from Brazil died in his boarding-house on 29 May 1878, starting an epidemic that claimed 4,046 lives and left another 27,000 ill before abating at the end of summer. Hopes of commercial resurgence were so blighted by this calamity that a group of private businessmen, frustrated by the city council's impotence under its staggering municipal debt (inherited from its carpetbag regimes), organized an

Auxiliary Sanitary Association during the winter of 1878–1879 to help the Board of Health combat disease. The Saint Charles Hotel privately installed the city's first underground sewer in 1880, discharging directly into the Mississippi, while a shadowy "Committee of Public Safety" was also formed two years afterward, sending shotgun-toting patrols into the most lawless areas.

Recuperation (1879–1894)

The census of 1880 revealed that although New Orleans's population had increased to 216,090, its ranking had nonetheless declined to ninth-largest city in the United States. It was also not as well positioned as metropolises along the Atlantic Seaboard to receive the mass exodus of migrants streaming out of Europe— it possessed too little industry and too few financial resources—and its administration was too debt ridden to undertake even the most basic enhancements to its infrastructure. For example, 90 percent of streets still remained unpaved. As late as 1949 that figure still stood at 50 percent, a serious problem in such a humid environment.

Nevertheless, the engineer Capt. James B. Eads had succeeded in 1879 in clearing a channel at the muddy Mississippi River mouth sufficiently for larger oceangoing ships to enter and exit fully laden, thanks to his newly designed jetties, so that trade volumes would gradually resurge. Telephone service was introduced into New Orleans that same year, while electric streetlights were fully functional by 1882. Freight rail traffic was extended as far as California when the Southern Pacific Railroad completed a fifth link out of the city the next year; cotton exports rebounded to antebellum figures by 1883; and the real estate magnate Paul Tulane bequeathed his fortune to the struggling University of Louisiana in 1884, prompting the institution to change its name to Tulane University and move into much larger quarters on Saint Charles Avenue as of 1895.

Therefore, despite having lost the title of Louisiana's state capital to Baton Rouge as of 1882, New Orleans was reviving economically—a resurrection seemingly confirmed when the vast Cotton Centennial Exposition was hosted in December 1884, attracting thousands of visitors to a 234-acre site that would later become Audubon Park.

Negatively, however, this economic rebirth was accompanied by a hardening of segregationist legislation; the Louisiana state government enacted increasingly harsh Jim Crow laws after 1890, which reduced the number of enfranchised black voters from more than 125,000 to 5,000 within a decade and entrenched segregationist attitudes. About half of the shabby dwellings at Algiers Point opposite New Orleans were furthermore consumed by a fire in 1895, a tragedy compounded by the collapse of a pier near the ferry house under the weight of excited onlookers. The Southern Pacific Railroad, the community's single-largest employer and property owner, soon started reconstruction efforts.

The third version of the famous Saint Charles Hotel, erected in 1896 after the second had burned down two years previously; note the prominent fire-escape ladders, plus streetcar tracks running up Canal Street in the right foreground. (Historic New Orleans Collection)

Modern Era (1895–Present)

More significantly, municipal authorities in New Orleans—in order to relieve the city of its perennial problems of flooding and soft subsoil—established a commission in 1895 to address such matters through a comprehensive, technological approach. As a result, dozens of pumping stations were installed throughout its district over the next two decades to extract waters from the trough of encircling swamps and divert them into Lakes Pontchartrain or Borgne; at the same time, old canals were cleared, and 95 miles of new ones were dug. Thousands of miles of pipes and drains were also laid, and a gigantic electric plant was erected to provide the requisite power. Clamshell dredged from Lake Pontchartrain was used to provide firmer foundations for bigger and more modern structures.

By 1900 the city's population stood at 287,104 inhabitants, and despite now being ranked as only the twelfth-largest city in the United States, New Orleans had at least regained its sta-

tus as the second-busiest seaport after New York—thanks in part to the effective work of the state-created Dock Board, which had assumed responsibility over wharf operations from a variety of private agencies. Disease had moreover become less of a threat—once a definitive link had been proven between mosquitoes and the spread of yellow fever—so that officials were able to curtail an outbreak for the first time, in the summer of 1905, by eradicating all depositories of stagnant water. As swamplands north of the city around Bayou Saint John were drained and rendered habitable, urban expansion moved beyond Marais Street as well, while a grand new railway terminal was inaugurated at Canal and Basin streets in 1908, designed by the nationally renowned architect Daniel Burnham. A purification plant was installed the next year to provide the city with safe drinking water.

The clearance and development of a vast Industrial and Inner Harbor Navigation Canal commenced as of 1912, linking up the Mississippi with Lake Pontchartrain from a point

5 miles below the city; it eventually added 11 miles of frontage to New Orleans's docklands. That same year, the city administration was overhauled by an act of the state legislature, so that its mayors were thenceforth to become "commissioners of public affairs," directing the activities of four other similarly titled colleagues. A distinct new musical style, dubbed "jazz"— allegedly derived from the Mandingo term *jasi,* meaning "to act out of the ordinary"—emerged from the black nightclubs of the city's Storyville red-light district on Basin Street (so named in 1897 in mock honor of its representative before the city council, alderman Sidney Story). Thanks to the transit of thousands of troops through New Orleans during World War I, jazz would sweep the nation and world, finding its greatest exponents in such gifted local practitioners as Louis Armstrong and Ferdinand "Jelly Roll" Morton.

The yearlong participation of the United States in World War I in 1917–1918 proved a further economic boon, as the U.S. Corps of Engineers not only constructed a huge dock unit below Faubourg Marigny but also poured resources into maintaining the 70- to 100-foot depths out in New Orleans's river, as well as a navigable passage all up and down the Mississippi. Once peace returned, such improvements continued to facilitate barge traffic bearing increasingly large bulk shipments of grain that could be housed in the concrete grain elevators that now lined the waterfront immediately above and below the city core.

The population had surged to 387,219 inhabitants by 1920, while the discovery of oil along Louisiana's Gulf Coast fueled an additional boom over the ensuing decade, during which New Orleans's first skyscrapers appeared in its old "American Quarter"; fine mansions once again began to sprout to designs by such talented architects as Thomas Sully. Record rainfalls during the winter of 1926–1927 produced massive spring flooding all down the Mississippi Valley, the Crescent City being spared by the desperate expedient of blasting the levee 15 miles below it at Caernarvon near Poydras on 29 April— although unfortunately at the cost of inundating large portions of Saint Bernard and Plaquemines parishes.

To avert such calamities in the future, the U.S. Congress voted an act that financed an intricately planned maze of cutoffs, spillways, and dams to bring the river gradually under control—the Bonnet Carré Spillway 30 miles above New Orleans being used on several occasions to release rising waters into Lake Pontchartrain. The 4.5-mile, concrete New Orleans–Pontchartrain Bridge was also opened to traffic as of 1928 (to be followed by the Chef Menteur and Rigolets bridges), while the Harvey Canal and its lock upriver from Algiers were also added to connect Mississippi barge traffic with the Intracoastal Waterway, so that vessels might travel along sheltered inland waterways as far as Brownsville, Texas, further augmenting trade volumes flowing through New Orleans.

City politicians had a contentious relationship as of 1928 with the populist, erratic, backcountry lawyer Gov. Huey P. "the Kingfish" Long, who invigorated and expanded state powers, while New Orleans and the nation reeled from the effects of the Great Depression, which started the following October. After Long's assassination, his chosen successor, O. K. Allen, even invoked martial law against the opposition concentrated in New Orleans.

By 1940 the urban population numbered 494,537 inhabitants, who enjoyed another economic upsurge when the United States was drawn into World War II as of December 1941, increasing the transit of troops and materiel. Because of its secure position deep inland, New Orleans was untroubled by the few German U-boats that attempted to interdict oil tanker traffic out in the Gulf, only a single submarine succeeding in laying a dozen mines off the Mississippi River mouth in August 1942, before being sunk by planes of U.S. Coast Guard Squadron 212.

Once that conflict had ended, the Crescent City evolved much as did other modern North American metropolises, regional rural-to-urban migration patterns to take advantage of new industrial-based jobs and an enhanced quality of life accelerating its demographic explosion. Already crowded with 567,257 inhabitants by 1950, and with shipping facilities monopolizing 41 miles of frontage along both sides of the Mississippi, residential development shifted to the West Bank after the Greater Mississippi Bridge was inaugurated in 1958, providing better access for the increasingly prevalent automotive traffic. A large new ship channel called the "Gulf Outlet" was opened two years afterward, reducing the distance to the sea by 40 miles; it soon became lined with gigantic industrial installations, such as the Michoud complex, where even Saturn moon rockets would be manufactured for shipment to Cape Canaveral in Florida.

New Orleans embraced select facets of its heritage during this period, justly proud of its French character, unique architecture, and joyous celebrations of life in its music, cuisine, and Mardi Gras festivals—which as tourism grew into a nationwide industry, attracted millions of revelers from chillier northern climes. The tiny old airport had been replaced by Moisant International, 10 miles west of the city, as early as 1946, while new national highway links further facilitated visits by voluminous numbers of travelers. Yet the city and state also struggled with continued poverty, neglect, and corruption, plus a painful transition from its segregationist past, while new suburbs mushroomed around the original urban core. By 1994 the population within the old city limits was reduced to an estimated 484,000 residents, while the entire metropolitan area consisted of 1.3 million.

For further reading materials on the history of New Orleans, as well as sources on North American and U.S. urban history, please consult the Select Bibliography at the end of this volume.

NEW YORK CITY

Sheltered seaport, which thanks to its river-borne access deep into the continental interior, has grown into one of the great metropolises of the world.

Initial Probes (1524–1623)

The first European to sight this magnificent natural harbor was Giovanni da Verrazano or Verrazzano, a Florentine-born navigator in the service of France. His capture of a pair of Spanish ships in 1522, while they were bound from recently conquered Mexico bearing exotic Aztec spoils, had helped to persuade King François I to sponsor his own independent exploration of North America.

Consequently, Verrazano had made his landfall around what would later become known as the Carolinas in late February or early March 1524, coasting northward and eventually peering into what is today called the Upper Bay, because he had noted that from inside there "flowed to the sea a very great river." Hoping that this waterway might lead to the ephemeral Northwest Passage and the riches of distant Asia, he passed through the Narrows (spanned since 1964 by the Verrazano Bridge) and conducted a brief survey of the Upper Bay, being greeted by feather-clad Lenape tribesmen before exiting and continuing his continental exploration as far northeastward as Newfoundland. Regaining Dieppe in France by 8 July, Verrazano submitted a favorable report to the king, although subsequent French colonization efforts were to be directed elsewhere.

It was not until early in the seventeenth century that European interest in this stretch of coastline revived, after Henry Hudson—an English sailor commissioned by the Dutch East India Company of Amsterdam—arrived offshore to reconnoiter, entering the bay with his ship *Half Moon* on 3 September 1609 and pushing 150 miles upriver to near present-day Albany, before finally acknowledging that it could not possibly reach the Pacific, so that he reversed course and re-emerged out into the Atlantic by 4 October.

Panoramic view looking northward up New York City, ca. 2000. At left are the New Jersey shoreline and the Hudson River; at center, Manhattan Island, with Central Park prominently featured in the distance; while the East River and Brooklyn appear at right. (City of New York)

Nevertheless, Hudson's belief that a lucrative trade in furs might be struck with the local Iroquois inspired the Dutch master Adriaen Block to make a trading visit two years afterward, during which he bartered with the indigenous inhabitants of Manhattan Island for beaver pelts, then sold them at such a high profit in Europe that more contacts ensued. In the spring of 1614, Block's ship *Tijger* burned at anchor within the harbor, so that he and his crew came ashore near modern Wall Street to spend the next couple of months extemporizing a 44-foot "yacht," with which they ventured along Long Island Sound that same summer to rejoin another Dutch vessel, which conveyed them home to Holland. (In remembrance, an island between the tip of Long Island and Narragansett Bay bears Block's name to this day.)

Encouraged by the commercial promise of this vast hinterland, a consortium of Amsterdam and Hoorn merchants formed the New Netherland Company, and on 10 October 1614 obtained an exclusive charter from the States-General to dispatch four trading voyages over the next three years to tap this North American wilderness in an unclaimed area between the French colony of New France in Canada and the English colony of Virginia to the south.

Dutch traders therefore erected a storehouse at the southern tip of Manhattan Island and a tiny outpost called Fort Nassau farther inland near Albany by 1615, from which footholds they conducted a more regularized traffic with regional tribes. However, no all-out colonization effort was made until the United Provinces resumed their global struggle against the Spanish empire as of spring 1621, simultaneously creating a unified *Westindische Compagnie* or West Indian Company that same May to coordinate all their American commercial ventures over the next two dozen years.

New Netherland officially became designated as an overseas province to be administered by the Amsterdam chamber of the WIC in June 1623, so that early next May the ship *Nieuw Nederland* arrived at Manhattan with 30 Protestant Walloon families to lay the foundation for a permanent settlement under the "director" or governor, Cornelis Jacobszoon Mey. Only eight of these first migrants chose to reside on Nut Island (modern Governor's Island), most families instead opting to proceed up what was then called the *Noort* or North River (today's Hudson) to create Fort Orange at Albany. More settlers arrived in 1625 aboard another three vessels under a new director, Willem Verhulst, bringing the colony's total Dutch population to some 200 residents, many of whom were now congregated upon Manhattan proper.

New Amsterdam (1626–1663)

Yet it was not until the director-general Pieter Minuit arrived with yet more settlers on 4 May 1626 that a regulated form of

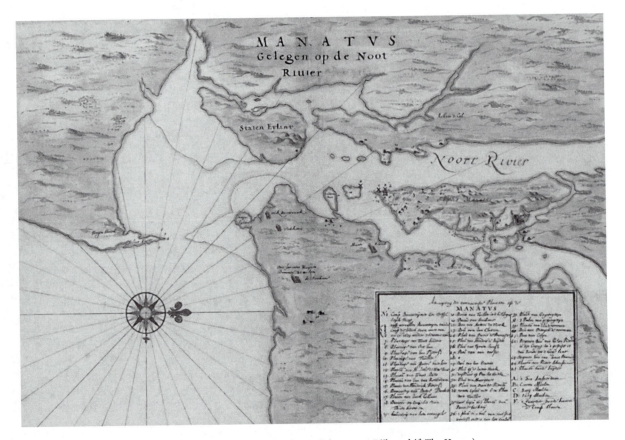

"Manatus" situated on the North River, 1639, by Johannes Vingboon. (Algemeene Rijksarchif, The Hague)

municipal governance was imposed upon this strategic island community, and the decision was taken to designate it as the capital for the entire Dutch colony of New Netherland. Urban lots were duly allocated at Manhattan's southernmost tip for a blockhouse, warehouse, and mill, a cluster destined to constitute the core of the future town of New Amsterdam. Minuit also summoned local tribal chieftains to a meeting six months afterward, at which he arranged to "purchase" all of the island in exchange for cloth, beads, and other trinkets valued at roughly 60 guilders or $24.

This fledgling outpost failed to flourish, though, despite the WIC's granting of a "charter of privileges and exemptions" to all its members in 1629, so as to encourage the clearance and operation of more lucrative estates inland. Resentment against Minuit's efforts in favor of the landholder elite—known as patroons—led to his recall three years afterward, while his successor Wouter van Twiller adhered so narrowly to the commercial interests of the company that his 1633–1637 administration also ended ruinously. The disillusioned WIC even relinquished its trade monopoly over New Netherland as of the next year and instructed its new director-general, Willem Kieft, to relax many immigration and manufacturing restrictions so that a few more settlers—some of them foreign-born—began to trickle into New Amsterdam. However, Kieft's attempts to collect tributes from the Algonquians in the vicinity of Manhattan and other indiscretions provoked an Indian uprising by 1641, which laid waste to most outlying settlements. A board of eight disgruntled residents therefore petitioned the States General for his recall in 1644, and he was succeeded by the peg-legged, veteran West Indian administrator Pieter Stuyvesant.

This latest director-general was joyously received at New Amsterdam on 11 May 1647, and he and the local council even agreed to appoint a consultative board of nine burghers that same September. Prosperity resurged, and the town stabilized into a tightly packed community of roughly 100 sturdy houses, most of a typical Dutch design: two and a half stories tall and with their façades of stepped gables squeezed into the few blocks lying between the sheltered Upper Bay anchorage and the WIC fort, which itself contained the governor's residence, offices, barracks, and a church. However, the Board of Nine soon became alienated by some of Stuyvesant's more arbitrary decisions, as well as by company opposition to even the most limited form of self-government, as had been suggested by the States General in 1650.

That same year, Stuyvesant was furthermore compelled to contract New Netherland's boundaries into Oyster Bay on Long Island when he signed the Treaty of Hartford with John Winthrop and other neighboring commissioners from the expansionistic United Colonies of New England, and in 1651 Stuyvesant built Fort Casimir at what is today Newcastle (Delaware) to contain a rival Swedish colony. When the First Anglo-Dutch War erupted in Europe as of May 1652, the physical appearance of New Amsterdam became transformed as its residents—now numbering close to 1,000—felt the need the next year to complete a palisade of sharpened tree trunks facing northward and bristling with seven bastions, so as to impede any sudden enemy descent (a defensive line that would later give rise to the name of "Wall Street"). The first legally constituted municipal government was also established for the community in 1653, modeled upon similar city charters in Holland.

Upon the cessation of hostilities against England, Stuyvesant visited Amsterdam and returned in July 1655 to

A Dutch view of New Amsterdam, ca. 1643. (Stokes, *Ichnography*)

lead seven Dutch vessels and several hundred men in a military sweep that recaptured Fort Casimir, then occupied Fort Christina (modern Wilmington, Delaware), thereby attaching the entire colony of "New Sweden" to Dutch rule. However, the much more populous and vigorous English colonies along the Atlantic seaboard could not be so easily subdued, and their conflicting claims to North American primacy gradually closed in upon New Amsterdam.

Seizure and Reoccupation (1664–1674)

The English finally moved to impose their authority over the small Dutch outpost when King Charles II commissioned Col. Richard Nicolls on 2 April 1664 (O.S.) to sail to the New World with a small peacetime expedition to unify the disparate New England colonies and "reduce" New Netherland—whose coastal jurisdiction extended from the west side of the Connecticut River to the east side of Delaware Bay, plus all of Long Island—into a new English province that was to be granted to his royal brother James, Duke of York and Albany. Nicolls, backed by the battle squadron of Commo. Robert Holmes, paused at Boston long enough during his outward passage to order an additional force of New England militiamen to assemble at the west end of Long Island, before reaching Gravesend Bay himself on 25 August.

Unable to defend sparsely fortified New Amsterdam against such overwhelming odds, Stuyvesant grudgingly entered into negotiations with Nicolls, who spoke fluent Dutch and soon won over the *burgomaster* and several other prominent citizens with promises of fair treatment under English rule. Stuyvesant was obliged to concede when, as Drisius reported, "the frigates came up under full sail on the 4th of September, with guns trained to one side." Under the direct menace of Holmes's warships, the Dutch governor agreed to the articles of surrender at his Bowery home two days after-

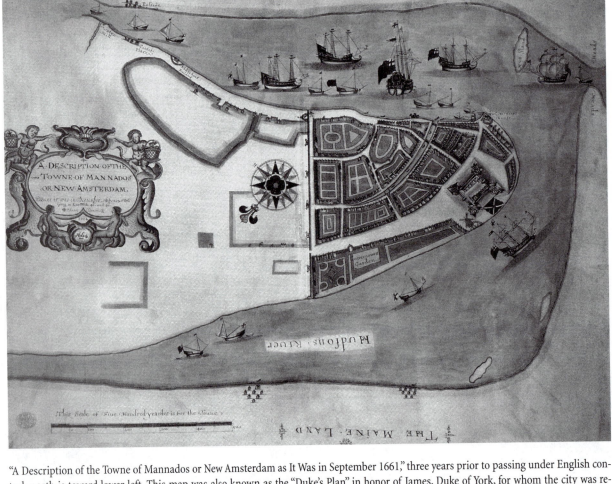

"A Description of the Towne of Mannados or New Amsterdam as It Was in September 1661," three years prior to passing under English control; north is toward lower left. This map was also known as the "Duke's Plan" in honor of James, Duke of York, for whom the city was renamed. Several modern landmarks can be clearly discerned, such as the fort that gave its name to Battery Park, plus the palisaded ditch along which Wall Street runs today. (British Library)

ward, which were then ratified by the council the following Monday morning, 8 September.

Nicolls took possession of New Amsterdam that same day, the Dutch garrison marching out of its fort without incident. An English flag was substituted, and Nicolls promptly renamed the territories in honor of his royal patron James: the city and southern portion of the province being renamed New York, Fort Orange and the northern portion changing into Albany, and so on. The charismatic English governor even got Stuyvesant and the city's other civic leaders to swear fealty to Charles II on 25 or 26 October 1664, before winter set in.

Next spring, Nicolls promulgated the so-called "Duke's laws" to a convention of provincial delegates assembled at Hempstead on 8 March 1665 (O.S.), which reassuringly retained many of the traditional rights and mores of the Dutch inhabitants. On 12 June, he furthermore reorganized the municipal government of New York along English lines by replacing its offices of *burgomaster* and *schepens* with one-year appointments for a mayor, aldermen, and a sheriff, while its urban boundaries were expanded so as to encompass all of Manhattan Island. Liberal trade policies were implemented as well, helping the city merchants to quickly gain a vigorous new trade with other ports in New England, the West Indies, and throughout the English maritime empire, so that traffic and prosperity returned to the seaport.

Nicolls's familiarity with Dutch customs helped ensure a smooth transition until his departure in August 1668, while the role played by many leading Dutch citizens and clergymen in the city's capitulation had undermined any will to resist among the general population. Consequently, New York was to remain peaceably under English rule until the Third Anglo-Dutch War erupted overseas in March 1672, during which the city was unexpectedly reoccupied by a twelve-ship expedition under Commos. Jacob Binckes of Amsterdam and Cornelis Evertsen de Jongste of Zeeland. After sweeping through the West Indies and along the Virginia coast, this fleet suddenly materialized outside New York's harbor on 28 July 1673. Faced with such superior numbers, it was now the turn of the English governor to be intimidated into surrendering without a shot being fired on 9 August, so that Dutch rule was temporarily reinstated under Acting Governor Anthony Colve.

However, when both commodores sailed home, they found that their unauthorized reoccupation of New Amsterdam met with disapproval at The Hague, which was already deep into negotiations to conclude a peace with England. New York was therefore ordered to be restored to English domination, an act that was consummated as of 9 November 1674, when Colve submitted to the newly arrived governor, Sir Edmund Andros.

British Restoration (1675–1688)

English municipal practices were once again imposed, and the city resumed its peaceful existence as a commercial entrepot for its inland territories. As commerce revived, merchants came to resent certain duties being exacted under the "Duke's laws," so that Governor Thomas Dongan called for an election among freemen to the first New York assembly on 17 October 1683 (O.S.). He also granted the city "Dongan's charter" as of April 1686, which placed its future evolution on a firmer footing by confirming all previous rights and privileges; by vesting sources of income in the city corporation; and by conveying proprietorship of the city hall, marketplaces, bridges, wharves, docks, cemeteries, ferries, unoccupied lands, and all waterways to the municipal authorities. Even a city seal was created.

However, after the pro-Catholic Duke of York succeeded his brother onto the English throne as King James II in February 1685, the Protestant burghers of New York—like most other subjects throughout the empire—lived rather uneasily with this tilt in policy, until thrown into outright ferment by their province's annexation into the dominion of New England. Then came news during the winter of 1688–1689 of the deposal overseas of James in favor of the Protestant usurpers William and Mary.

Leisler's Revolt (1689–1691)

Availing themselves of this change in royal government, the citizens of Boston unilaterally imprisoned Andros, who had since been elevated to the post of governor-general for all of New England. When he in turn attempted to send a message to his lieutenant-governor at New York, Francis Nicholson, local resentments began to coalesce into a rebellious stance on 22 May 1689 under the reluctant leadership of the wealthy, German-born merchant Jacob Leisler. After eight days of uncertainty, matters came to a head when Nicholson threatened to "fire the town," so that Leisler's militia company angrily retaliated by seizing Fort James on 31 May. Leisler joined them two days later, vowing to hold it until a new royal governor arrived, appointed by the new monarchs William and Mary.

His intervention was seemingly justified when word arrived on 3 June 1689 that they had indeed been crowned in England, after which Nicholson fled, and Leisler assumed his office upon seizure of letters from William that he interpreted as authorization. For the next several months, he acted as governor, being acclaimed as commander-in-chief on 16 August by his followers at the council of Albany, although bitterly opposed by the province's aristocratic faction. Leisler nonetheless maintained power through military force, and even convened an intercolonial congress in May 1690 to plan concerted action against the French and Indians.

New York's experiment with self-rule ended when William finally commissioned Col. Henry Sloughter as the new royal governor, and an advance contingent of troops were dispatched from England under Maj. Richard Ingoldesby. This force arrived in January 1691 and Ingoldesby sided with the local faction opposing Leisler, eventually demanding the surrender of the strategic fort guarding Manhattan's vital anchorage and waterfront. Leisler refused, and fighting broke out on

17 March, during which two soldiers were killed and several others wounded. Two days afterward, Sloughter himself appeared and Leisler surrendered the fort to him, being tried as a traitor and hanged by 16 May, amid public lamentations.

Late Colonial Evolution (1692–1775)

New York resumed its former peaceful existence under English rule, and its original Dutch character gradually faded under the influx of migrants from other colonies and Europe. Only its initial layout and unique names were to remain, such as the Bowery, Staten Island, the Bronx—named for its earliest Dutch landowner, Jonas Bronck, who had cleared a farm upon this land claim as long ago as 1636—and even *Conyne Eylandt* or "Rabbit Island," which would devolve into Coney Island.

As the disparate colonies along the Atlantic seaboard slowly expanded and coalesced during the first decades of the eighteenth century, New York grew and prospered as well, its first newspaper, the *Gazette*, being issued in 1725, and refinements such as its first fire company being formed a dozen years afterward to battle the constant threat of blazes amid its many wooden structures. King's College (now Columbia University) was founded by 1754, and six years later the population was measured at a robust 14,000 residents, easily spread among the urban concentration at the southernmost tip and ample surrounding farmlands of Manhattan Island.

The colonial city was to undergo a cruel ordeal after the patriot insurrection erupted around Boston, and an eleven-month siege finally ended in mid-March 1776 when Gen. William Howe evacuated the last of his redcoat occupiers from that port to inaugurate a new offensive against New York. Martial law was consequently declared as of 4 April, with Maj.-Gen. Israel Putnam designated as its military governor, batteries installed along the East River and other strategic points, while George Washington—commander-in-chief of the Continental army—relocated his headquarters for the forthcoming encounter. News of the passage of the Declaration of Independence by the Continental Congress in Philadelphia reached New York City on 9 July, its announcement—under the strained circumstances of an impending siege—leading some soldiers to tear down the equestrian statue of George III in Bowling Green and other excesses.

Capture and Occupation (1776–1783)

Three days later, advance elements of Adm. Richard Howe's Royal Navy fleet began pushing into the bay, gradually disgorging his brother's army onto Staten Island. Unable to impede this massive British buildup, the city's defenders braced to repel an assault. On 22 August 1776, an outpost on Long Island reported movement toward Gravesend Bay, from where Howe's 20,000 redcoats and Hessians marched north-

View of Fort George and New York in 1739, by John Carwitham. (U.S. Naval Historical Center, Washington, D.C.)

ward against the 10,000 Americans holding Brooklyn Heights under Putnam. The intervening ridge of Guian Heights was stoutly defended by a 3,500-patriot vanguard under Major-General John Sullivan, until the American reserves were consumed and Howe swung behind their line with his main body, collapsing the defense. Patriot losses totaled more than 1,400 dead, wounded, or captured, compared to 380 Anglo-Hessian casualties; and when Howe pressed on against Brooklyn Heights on 27 August, Washington ordered Putnam to abandon that position on the night of 29 August, so as to regroup within New York City.

(During the ensuing two-week lull after this Battle of Long Island was fought, a one-man American submersible called the *Turtle*—designed by David Bushnell of Westbrook, Connecticut—was released into New York harbor by two whaleboats on the night of 6 September 1776, in a bid to blow up Admiral Howe's anchored flagship, the 64-gun HMS *Eagle.* The lone submariner, Sgt. Ezra Lee, reached his target by patiently turning hand cranks, yet could not attach his "torpedo"—a cask filled with 150 pounds of powder, plus a timer—against the warship's barnacle-encrusted hull, so that he retired behind Governor's Island. Lee narrowly avoided capture at daybreak, his mine exploding harmlessly in the water.)

General Howe resumed his offensive on the morning of 15 September 1776, when five Royal Navy warships took up station in Kip's Bay and covered the disembarkation onto Manhattan of 4,000 redcoats ferried out of Newton Creek on Long Island. Realizing that the British could not be contained within this new bridgehead, Putnam galloped southward to start bringing as many American troops and artillery out of doomed New York, while Washington extemporized a three-line defense around Harlem Heights. Howe had the bulk of his invasion force across by evening, pressing three-quarters of a mile inland to establish a front line from Horn's Hook to Bloomingdale (modern East 90th Street). Next morning, a 150-man American reconnaissance company under Lt.-Col. Archibald Crary clashed against the advance British elements—two infantry battalions and some men of the Black Watch under Brig. Alexander Leslie—near present-day East 105th Street, briefly driving them back, until the redcoats returned in overwhelming strength that same afternoon to effectively bring an end to all organized resistance within New York.

Yet although the city fell, Howe had failed to destroy Washington's army, which still held numerous strongpoints along Harlem Heights and both riverbanks, while Continental forces were being reconstituted on the mainland. The British therefore fortified New York so as to create a secure base of operations, being hampered when a fire broke out at Whitehall Slip about a week later, almost completely destroying the lower part of the hapless city. Trinity Church burned during this conflagration, although Saint Paul's and King's College were saved by a miraculous shift in the wind. (That same evening, Nathan Hale was captured on Long Island, facing a summary trial in

New York City and its environs as surveyed in 1767 by John Montresor and engraved by Peter Andrews. (Stokes, *Ichnography*)

New York for espionage and being hanged shortly thereafter near modern 45th Street and First Avenue.)

Howe did not push across the Hudson to Pell's Point until 13 October 1776, cornering and bloodying Washington's outnumbered American army at White Plains two weeks later, although without being able to crush the main rebel force before it retreated. A month afterward, the British again sallied from New York to eliminate a rebel stronghold called "Fort Washington"—a crude pentagonal earthwork atop 200-foot Mount Washington, at the northern tip of Manhattan Island. Major-Generals Putnam and Nathanael Greene reassured its 2,900 defenders under Col. Robert Magaw, unaware that the spy William Demont had already revealed its weaknesses. Before dawn of 16 November, 3,000 Hessians under Maj.-Gen. Wilhelm, Baron von Knyphausen, glided from King's Bridge aboard 30 flatboats to circle up the Hudson and attack upon the position's weak northern side; Brig. Lord Hugh Percy led another 2,000 redcoats up from the south to dislodge the 800 Americans under Lt.-Col. John Cadwallader who were holding a rise a mile and a half below Fort Washington. Brig. Edward Mathew's 2,000 men and Cornwallis's reserves were to then cross the Harlem River out of the east at midday to complete the Americans' rout.

Von Knyphausen's troops, supported by heavy artillery fire from British batteries and the frigate *Pearl,* pushed Fort

Washington's outlying defenders back amid hand-to-hand combat; Percy—subsequently supported by Mathew, Cornwallis, and two more battalions under Colonel Sterling—drove the Americans up Harlem Heights, securing 170 prisoners. Magaw was called upon to surrender his overcrowded redoubt, and agreed at 3:00 P.M. American losses totaled 59 killed, 96 wounded, 2,837 prisoners, plus nearly 150 cannon and 2,800 muskets taken, compared to 136 dead and 646 injured among the Anglo-Hessians. The fall of Fort Washington also meant that the 2,000-man American garrison holding Fort Lee on the opposite bank of the Hudson evacuated on 18 November 1776, so that when Cornwallis crossed the river two days afterward with 4,500 redcoats, he found that Washington's entire army had escaped into New Jersey.

Most American patriots nonetheless endured a difficult winter, conditions being especially bleak in occupied New York. Its shrunken population endured military occupation and the loss of their regular inland commerce, while most surviving edifices had been commandeered as barracks, storehouses, or hospitals for thousands of British officers and troops, as well as jails for thousands more American prisoners. Hunger and illness were so rife that more than 11,000 captives would die over the next few years aboard the prison hulk *Jersey*, anchored in Wallabout Bay in the East River. Shacks and tents also mushroomed throughout the burnt lower sector, which became derisively nicknamed "Canvas Town," and lawlessness abounded.

In the spring of 1777, British forces sailed up the Hudson to destroy American depots at Peekskill and Danbury (Connecticut). They enjoyed less success, however, after Howe shipped out with his main army to attack Philadelphia, and his subordinate left behind in New York City, Lieutenant-General Sir Henry Clinton, attempted to lead a belated relief column of more than 3,000 troops upriver that same October to rescue an expedition descending out of Canada under General John Burgoyne, who was obliged to capitulate at Saratoga. When Howe was recalled from Philadelphia to England in May 1778 and Clinton succeeded him as theater commander-in-chief, he ordered that New York become the main headquarters for British efforts.

The unhappy city consequently endured five and a half more years of military occupation and economic depression, the suffering of most inhabitants not being alleviated until Clinton was also recalled in May 1782 and was succeeded as military governor by the more humane Sir Guy Carleton, who restored good municipal government. America's independence was finally won by the combined efforts of Continental and French forces elsewhere, culminating with the implementation of the Treaty of Versailles in March 1783. As de facto Loyalist capital, New York City was not ceded until thousands had been allowed to emigrate by 25 November of that same year, in an act later commemorated as Evacuation Day. The victorious Washington witnessed this event and then bid farewell to his officers at Fraunces Tavern on Pearl Street on 4 December, before departing Whitehall wharf aboard a barge for Paulus Hook, traveling on to Annapolis to resign his commission before the Continental Congress.

Recuperation (1784–1824)

James Duane was appointed mayor of the depleted city by Gov. George Clinton, and business gradually revived, abetted by the implementation of some modest municipal enhancements. By an act of the legislature passed on 1 May 1784, King's College became transformed into the state university under the name of Columbia College, while Alexander Hamilton founded the Bank of New York. The city's urban populace had rebounded to roughly 24,000 inhabitants by the time the seatless U.S. Congress voted to take up residence in its dilapidated city hall as of 11 January 1785, the national Constitution being crafted and passed here a couple of years later. When George Washington was elected first president and traveled to New York for his inaugural in late April 1789, the old city hall was hastily torn down and replaced at the corner of Broad and Wall streets by a grand new "Federal Hall," designed by the engineer and architect Pierre-Charles L'Enfant (a French volunteer who had risen to the rank of major in the Continental Army). Nevertheless, a political compromise with southern delegates the next year saw Philadelphia temporarily designated as the seat of government while a new capital was being created beside Georgetown, so that the president and national legislators departed by August 1790.

New York nonetheless had blossomed into the largest city in the United States, with a population measured that same year at approximately 33,000 residents, which rose to 60,515 by 1800. A most significant economic advancement began when the young inventor Robert Fulton installed a steam engine imported from England into a boat launched at the Charles Brownne shipyards at Paulus Hook, then plowed up the Hudson on 17 August 1807 toward Albany, unimpeded by contrary winds or currents. Although not the first vessel to boast such a means of propulsion, this particular steamboat—popularly called the *Clermont*—was not only better designed than most others, but financially backed by the wealthy chancellor of New York State, Robert R. Livingston, a scientific enthusiast who held the exclusive privilege of operating all such craft within the state.

The immense potential of this new means of locomotion was nonetheless initially restricted to relatively small volumes, as the pair sought to stifle all imitators, as well as to extend their monopoly to include the Mississippi River in the Territory of Orleans as of April 1811. That same year, plans were adopted for regularizing most streets on Manhattan Island into a rational grid pattern, but when war with Great Britain erupted the next summer, a crippling overseas blockade was imposed. The economy was slowed until peace returned three years later, yet New York quickly recuperated—its population having

Anchored ships at left greet the flotilla arriving down the Hudson River from Albany in November 1825, the steamer *Chancellor Livingston* with Gov. DeWitt Clinton aboard having towed the first boat to pass through the Erie Canal. (Museum of the City of New York)

nearly quadrupled between 1790 and 1820—and it was now ideally poised to enter into its greatest era.

Boom (1825–1897)

The opening of the Erie Canal late in 1825 marked a significant watershed in New York City's history, as this lengthy waterway into the Great Lakes system permitted its steamboats to carry produce and passengers deep into North America's vast heartland, an advantage that rival Atlantic ports did not enjoy. New York's burgeoning array of financial institutions, industrial plants, and overseas contacts were furthermore ideally positioned to service this ever-expanding flow, which was to be further supplemented by other technological innovations such as the laying of the New York and Harlem Railroad in 1832.

The city consequently entered into a period of almost unbridled commercial and demographic growth, largely shaping the modern metropolis. Two years afterward, its mayoralty became an elective office, while not even a massive fire that destroyed much of Lower Manhattan in 1835 could curtail the upsurge. Instead, its losses were quickly replaced, and the calamity even inspired passage of new building laws, as well as the construction of the vast Croton water system.

Having clearly emerged as the busiest and wealthiest seaport in the nation, New York received a massive influx of refugees from Europe during the 1840s, so that large numbers of Irish and German immigrants began settling everywhere in its vicinity and increasingly affected the character of urban life and politics. Many of these newcomers were welcomed into the Tammany Society, an eighteenth-century organization originally founded to promote patriotism and democratic suffrage, yet which would soon turn to apply its influence in dominating electoral outcomes.

As New York blossomed, a large tract of land bordered by 59th Street on the south, Fifth Avenue on the east, and 110th Street on the north was acquired in 1856 by the city government and cleared of its few small hamlets, so as to create a broad communal space known as Central Park. Over the next twenty years, it was to become developed according to plans designed by the landscape architects Frederick L. Olmsted and Calvert Vaux to incorporate lakes, ponds, bridle paths, and walkways for the recreational needs of the general public. Points of interest would eventually come to include a formal garden, a zoo, an Egyptian obelisk popularly dubbed "Cleopatra's Needle," a reservoir, the Metropolitan Museum of Art, and the Mall. Such outlets for outdoor activities were becoming increasingly necessary on the fast-filling island, whose population stood at 808,651 people by 1860.

Prior to the eruption of the Civil War, many of these citizens shared Mayor Fernando Wood's pro-Southern proclivities, yet once hostilities erupted, most strongly backed the Union under the leadership of Gov. Horatio Seymour and voted Wood out of office in 1861. However, violent antidraft riots nonetheless broke out in New York on 13 July 1863 to protest against the highly unpopular federal Conscription Act. A tremendous mob, many being disgruntled Irish American laborers unable to purchase exemption from military service, overpowered the city police and militia, then seized the Second Avenue armory containing rifles and guns. Blazes multiplied and people were randomly attacked, blacks and abolitionists being especially singled out. Many were beaten to death, and even a black orphanage was burned. Civic life was completely paralyzed, while robbery and looting flourished. The Tammany-controlled city government tried to contain the outburst by voting to pay the necessary $300 for anyone who might be drafted, but order was not restored until New York

View of Wall Street, ca. 1850. (New York Historical Society)

troops (including the famous 7th Regiment, which had been sent to the front for the Gettysburg campaign) were rushed back and aided other forces in restoring order by 16 July. Casualty figures for these riots were estimated as high as 1,000 people, with property damage ranging between $1.5 million to $2 million.

Following the Union victory, the pace of industrial and commercial development accelerated in New York—exemplified by such vast undertakings as construction of the Brooklyn Bridge as of 1869—although its city government was in the clutches of the corrupt Tammany Hall leader, William M. "Boss" Tweed, who defrauded it of millions before being turned out of office and convicted of felony during the early 1870s. New York nonetheless continued to attract so many more migrants that the Tammany organization promptly regained its influence, while the first expansion of urban boundaries beyond Manhattan Island proper was necessitated in 1874, when portions of Westchester were annexed. By 1880, the population had reached 1,206,299 inhabitants, and it would continue to experience an exponential growth as the waves of emigration out of Eastern and southern Europe peaked over the next few decades. Hundreds of thousands were

to be processed as of 1892 at the government installations on Ellis Island, southwest of Manhattan.

Modern Era (1898–Present)

Because of such continuous and unbridled growth, New York became a city of five boroughs with the adoption of its new charter in 1898: the original island administration being split into the Manhattan and Bronx boroughs, while the independent city of Brooklyn was annexed, as were the western portions of Queens County and Staten Island. As a result of this expansion, the total population for the city was recorded two years afterward at 3,437,202 residents. Improved engineering techniques also allowed the first subway line to open in 1903 and for taller buildings to appear, so as to take better advantage of land values in the increasingly crowded and expensive city.

As New York's influence now extended well beyond its boundaries, the need for rational regional planning resulted in the nation's first zoning legislation in 1916, as well as the formation of such bodies as the Port of New York Authority five years afterward to administer the more than 900 miles of meandering shorelines with a myriad array of bridges and

Maze of suspension cables being installed on the Brooklyn Bridge, ca. 1878. (Bettmann/Corbis)

tunnels. The Regional Plan Association was also created in 1929, the Municipal Housing Authority a half decade later, and the City Planning Commission in 1938. Such broader scope furthermore weakened the influence of the Tammany Hall political machine within the city, especially during the administration of the popular reformist Mayor Fiorello H. LaGuardia, who won three consecutive terms that saw great improvements in urban conditions and the adoption of a new city charter.

Although immigration from overseas had become curtailed, labor shortages occasioned by the universal mobilization during World War II attracted another wave of migrants from rural areas of the United States, many being poor southern blacks seeking employment, so that the traditional Harlem enclave expanded from its old core between 110th and 150th streets and between Fifth Avenue on the east and Saint Nicholas Avenue on the west. New arrivals were soon followed into the east Harlem and Bronx slums by some 300,000 Puerto Ricans, displacing their original black residents into other areas of Brooklyn, the Bronx, and Queens.

City politics underwent a change when the war concluded in 1945 and LaGuardia did not run for reelection, a Democrat named William V. O'Dwyer—a former patrolman and district attorney who had risen to the rank of brigadier general—being elected mayor and who inaugurated a vigorous building program with great emphasis upon schools, hospitals, freeways, and public housing. O'Dwyer also overhauled the administration by creating professionally advised committees to oversee the billion-dollar annual budget and twenty-four major municipal departments. New York experienced its first serious water shortage during the winter of 1949 through the summer of 1950, stimulating projects to draw upon a more reliable supply from upland sources.

That same year of 1950, the urban population was measured at 7,891,957 inhabitants, of whom 1,960,101 lived on Manhattan; 1,451,277 in the Bronx; 2,738,175 in Brooklyn; 1,550,849 in Queens; and 191,555 in Richmond. However, the city was in effect already sprawling into adjacent counties, as well as into parts of Connecticut and New Jersey, so that the

New York in the immediate post–World War II era. (City of New York)

total metropolitan population was estimated at more than 12.9 million people. As highway and mass transit systems continued to be enhanced, increasing numbers of residents and companies began forsaking the urban core for a new fringe of suburbs, their departure gradually contracting the city's tax base, infrastructure, and services until New York nearly went bankrupt in 1975.

A brief but spectacular boom in the stock and real estate markets during the 1980s brought some limited relief, although the national recession of the early 1990s caused considerable hardship. In 1994, the population within the old city limits had diminished to an estimated 7.33 million, although the entire metropolitan area now held 19.8 million. New York was no longer the industrial and corporate leader of previous decades, yet specialized manufactures and high-tech products helped supplement its traditionally strong financial, legal, and communication services, which helped inject a considerable

measure of vigor and prosperity into the economy, so that the census of 2000 even registered a resurgence of its population to 8,008,278 inhabitants.

The city's worldwide fame made it the target of a terrorist attack on 11 September 2001, during which its tallest buildings—the twin towers of the World Trade Center—were destroyed and 2,700 people were killed. This loss represented 10 percent of all available commercial office space, saddling the city with months of expensive cleanup, plus years of reconstruction.

For further reading materials on the history of New York City, please consult the Select Bibliography at the end of this volume.

PENSACOLA
Centuries-old naval base, strategically located inside one of the Gulf of Mexico's most sheltered bays.

First Colonization Attempts (1519–1560)
While Hernán Cortés was initiating his conquest of the Aztec empire in central Mexico in the summer of 1519, four other Spanish vessels under Alonso Alvarez de Pineda simultaneously coasted along the Florida shoreline and noted a vast harbor with a narrow entrance that they dubbed Bahía del Espíritu Santo (Holy Ghost Bay)—possibly because it had been sighted on 25 May, that particular feast day of the Church calendar. A more detailed exploration of the Gulf was ordered by Cortés once Mexico City fell two years later, which confirmed the presence of a fine anchorage somewhere along that body of water's desolate north shore, protected from storms and currents by a low, sandy, offshore island. However, as the few thousand conquistadors were to remain engrossed in despoiling the central Aztec empire, no immediate effort was made to occupy this remote and vaguely charted port.

It was not until late February 1528 that the veteran Pánfilo de Narváez set sail northward from Jagua, Cuba, with five vessels, intent on subduing the seminomadic tribes of the Florida peninsula. But his squadron was driven deep into the Gulf by bad weather and an inexperienced pilot, so that his 240 sol-

Panoramic view northwestward across Pensacola, ca. 1909; note the flat coastal terrain. (Library of Congress)

diers came ashore and struck blindly inland. Only Alvar Núñez Cabeza de Vaca and three others staggered back out of the desert into northern New Spain nine years later.

Another expedition was not attempted until early in 1540, when the Cuban governor, Hernando de Soto, wintered near modern Tallahassee with more than 500 men. One of his detached brigantines explored westward and rejoined him in February with news of an excellent anchorage, apparently called Ochuse by its indigenous residents: modern Pensacola Bay. Hoping to use it as his base of operations, de Soto sent his ships back to Cuba with instructions to resupply and rendezvous with his main body at Ochuse that same autumn. Although they did so, de Soto did not appear, a mere 311 of his emaciated survivors emerging at the Pánuco River in northern Mexico by 10 September 1543.

Despite the failure of these first two privately mounted ventures, the voluminous growth of cross-Gulf traffic between Veracruz and Havana convinced the Crown to finance a larger-scale enterprise, with the aim of creating a permanent presence upon this vital lee shore. Tristán de Luna y Arellano, a forty-nine-year-old survivor of Coronado's expedition, was therefore delegated to found the new colony, and after a preliminary reconnaissance in September 1558 by Guido de Bezares, Luna recruited 500 soldiers, 240 horses, and 1,000 settlers and departed Veracruz on 11 June 1559. His thirteen vessels reached Bezares's suggested landfall of Bahía Filipina (modern Mobile Bay) that same July, but Luna rejected it as a potential settlement spot and instead disembarked his cavalry near present-day Bon Secour to proceed overland toward Ochuse while his ships circled round by sea.

Luna arrived and laid claim to Pensacola Bay on 14 August 1559, detaching two ships to convey news of this event to Spain, while a camp was initiated inside its harbor and contingents probed the hot and humid hinterland. Unfortunately, a hurricane destroyed this fledgling settlement shortly thereafter, along with most of the Spaniards' provisions and ships (modern archaeologists have uncovered one such wreck off Emanuel Point). This disaster obliged Luna to transfer his half-starved followers to the banks of the Alabama River, into an indigenous village that they rechristened Santa Cruz de Nanipicana.

Word of the colonists' plight reached Mexico City by 27 September 1559, yet although a relief squadron was quickly sent out, Luna's enterprise was essentially doomed. After enduring a sickly winter at Nanipicana, the Spaniards migrated down the Alabama River to set up another temporary encampment on the lower eastern shores of Mobile Bay, surviving off fish and clams until disease and want drove the unhappy settlers back into Pensacola Bay a few months later. Disillusioned and ill, Luna departed for Mexico that same summer of 1560, being succeeded as governor by Jorge Cerón. Angel Villafañe later assumed the mantle of leadership and oversaw the actual disbandment of Pensacola's first Spanish settlement.

Renewed Interest (1685–1697)

The bay reverted to its natural state for more than a century, being visited only occasionally by seasonal bands of indigenous hunters, gatherers, and fishermen until Spain's concerns over this vulnerable coastline adjacent to their main plate-fleet route was revived in 1685, when authorities in Mexico learned that the French explorer Robert Cavelier, Sieur de La Salle, had penetrated the Gulf with a small seaborne expedition. Worried about this potential threat, the pilots Juan Enrique Barroto and Antonio Romero were dispatched from Havana on 3 January 1686 aboard Capt. Juan Rodríguez Manzano's forty-two-man frigate *Nuestra Señora de la Concepción y San José* to reconnoiter the Gulf Coast and locate the intruders.

Concepción stood into "the bay the Indians call Panzacola" on 6 February 1686, peacefully parleying with the fishermen in its shoreside village, before continuing westward two days later. The Spaniards were unable to find any French settlement, so additional reconnaissance missions were sent out—including one under Capts. Francisco Gamarra and Andrés de Pez y Malzarraga, which probed the mile-and-a-half-wide entrance to Pensacola Bay again on 16 August 1687 but espied only empty huts and untended fields inside.

Eventually, it was learned that most of La Salle's followers had succumbed in the vicinity of Matagorda Bay (Texas), but de Pez nonetheless traveled to Madrid early in 1690 to propose that Pensacola Bay—with its easily defensible entrance, broad anchorage, abundant timber, freshwater, fertile soil, and large game animals such as buffalo—be settled as a preventive measure against future French encroachments. War having meanwhile erupted against that nation, the Crown assented by the summer of 1692, instructing de Pez to return to Veracruz and organize a probe to identify suitable sites for a stronghold and town. The Mexican viceroy, Gaspar de la Cerda, Conde de Galve, further added the services of the cleric and cosmographer Dr. Carlos de Sigüenza y Góngora, a philosophy and mathematics professor at the Royal University of Mexico, to compile the actual survey and written report.

The reconnaissance force set sail from Veracruz on 25 March 1693, reaching their objective a few days later. De Sigüenza, recalling how Luna y Arellano had originally claimed the harbor on 14 August—Saint Mary's day of the Church calendar—renamed it Bahía de Santa María de Galve (Bay of Saint Mary of Galve), thereby linking the name of the Virgin with that of the viceroy. The low headland opposite its harbor entrance was christened San Carlos in honor of Spain's reigning monarch, Charles II, while the western tip of its offshore island became Sigüenza Point (near where Fort Pickens would later stand). Other geographical names were assigned as the inner harbor and waterways were explored; distant bands of Indians were sighted twice, although they fled before they could be contacted.

De Pez's and Sigüenza's scouting party erected a large wooden cross on the offshore island and departed a few days

The bespectacled Mexican scholar Dr. Carlos de Sigüenza y Góngora, who surveyed Pensacola Bay in the spring of 1693. (Museum of History, Chapultepec Castle, Mexico City)

later to coast westward, before returning into Veracruz to report by 13 May 1693. Two days afterward, a second twenty-five-man reconnaissance unit under Laureano de Torres y Ayala and Fr. Rodrigo de la Barreda disembarked at Apalache from Havana, traveling overland into Pensacola Bay by 2 July. Their guides informed them that its local tribesmen had been exterminated by repeated clashes with warriors from Mobile Bay, so that Pensacola's shoreline lay uninhabited. This second Spanish probe also did not remain, but de Pez traveled to Madrid and secured royal permission in June 1694 to colonize the harbor. However, men, ships, and resources proved scarce because of the ongoing war with France, after which de Pez was accused of cowardice and dereliction of duty for an unsuccessful clash against buccaneers off the Cuban coast; he subsequently became engrossed in litigation to clear his name.

Foundation as "Santa María de Galve" (1698–1719)

Once peace with France was restored in September 1697, the Crown issued a new directive the next April, urging that Pensacola Bay be claimed. Capt. Juan Jordán de Reina—an experienced pilot who had visited the harbor with Barroto and Romero—consequently departed Havana with fifty soldiers in late summer 1698 to hold the site, until a larger colonizing expedition from Veracruz could join on 21 November under the veteran naval officer Andrés de Arriola. The latter was accompanied by the Belgian-born military engineer Jaime

Franck, who installed a 16-gun pine-log stronghold dubbed Carlos de Austria in honor of the Archduke Karl of Austria among the *barrancas* or ravines overlooking the entrance channel (several hundred yards east of where Fort Barrancas would later stand among the Red Hills); he then laid out a town outside its ramparts. A second fort planned for Sigüenza Point opposite was deemed impractical because of that island's low and swampy terrain.

However, both Arriola and Franck deemed the Santa María de Galve venture to be placed too far eastward to effectively counteract French efforts near the Mississippi River. Living conditions at Pensacola moreover proved to be very harsh, especially for the Mexican *forzados* (transportees)—convicts who made up many of the initial settlers—of whom some forty deserted en masse, necessitating recapture. Quarrels erupted frequently, and the fledgling community's misery deepened when a fire on 3 January 1699 leveled eight crude buildings—including the main storehouse, chapel, and Jordán's quarters.

A vessel was dispatched to Veracruz to plead for aid, but before that same month was out, five French ships under Pierre Le Moyne D'Iberville materialized outside the bar. Startled, the Spaniards manned their damaged log stronghold and two anchored vessels, but these visitors proved to be peaceful, alleging that they were merely searching for French renegades and requesting permission to recuperate within Pensacola Bay. Arriola refused, correctly surmising that D'Iberville's 1,000-man expedition—encumbered with cattle, horses, and supplies—was actually planning to found a permanent new settlement along the Gulf Coast. The French steered westward on 30 January 1699, eventually coming ashore at Biloxi (Mississippi).

Leaving Francisco Córcoles y Martínez as Santa María de Galve's *sargento mayor* (garrison commander), Arriola hastened for Veracruz three days later to report on the intruders' arrival. During his absence, starvation so afflicted the unhappy outpost that Jordán's Cuban contingent mutinied and separated from Córcoles's command, before Arriola at last returned in December 1699 with a 26-gun frigate and 100 more Mexican *forzados*. He thereupon probed westward the following March with four vessels, discovering D'Iberville ensconced at Biloxi. But after he lodged a protest, three of the Spanish vessels were wrecked in a storm on their homeward passage to Santa María de Galve; the survivors were rescued by the French.

At the end of November 1700, Spain's Hapsburg king Charles II died without issue, leaving his empire to the young French Bourbon princeling Philip of Anjou, grandson to Louis XIV. This unexpected Franco-Spanish union precluded any attack against D'Iberville's toehold; instead, the French commander was welcomed upon visiting Pensacola Bay again with four vessels in late December 1701 to advise his new-found allies that he had been instructed to occupy Mobile Bay

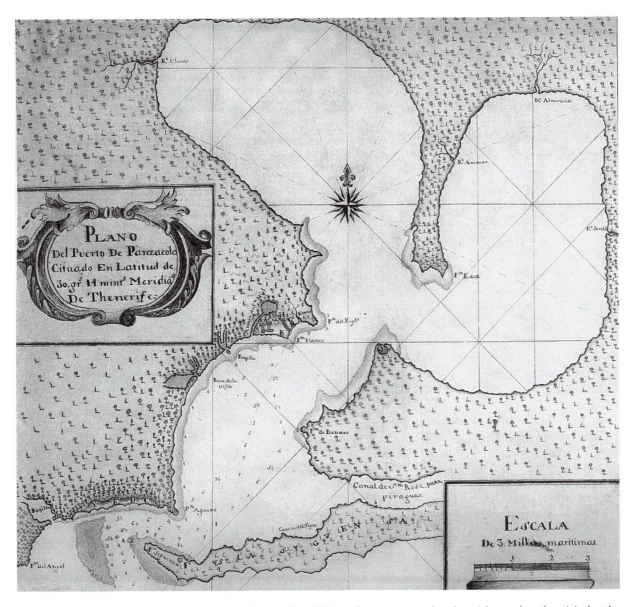

Santa María de Galve Bay as "inspected, surveyed and fortified" in 1698 by its first governor, Andrés de Arriola; note how the original settlement was sited directly opposite its entrance channel. (Archive of Indies, Seville)

so as to deny it to their mutual rivals, the English. Santa María de Galve's 180 destitute inhabitants, of whom 60 were convicts, even borrowed one of D'Iberville's craft to sail to Veracruz for supplies; yet although France and Spain were further bonded the next year by war against England, Holland, and other European powers, Madrid rebuffed all diplomatic overtures from Paris to incorporate Santa María de Galve into Louisiana.

In November 1703, the viceroy of New Spain was directed to offer tax exemptions and other inducements to Mexican families who might wish to immigrate to this isolated frontier outpost, as the tapping of Santa María de Galve's cypress and pine forests to supply the shipyards in Cuba and Mexico had been frustrated by a lack of skilled labor, uncertain sea communications, and simmering hostility from the indigenous

inhabitants. The few score colonists eked out a miserable subsistence, exacerbated when another fire swept through their rudimentary settlement in February 1705. Their plight was not alleviated until Vice Adm. Antonio Landeche arrived late that same August with munitions, provisions, and 200 more convicts aboard his *Nuestra Señora del Rosario* (which sank the following month during a hurricane).

Santa María de Galve's lack of appeal worsened when several hundred Talapoosa Indians—incited by English traders pressing out of Carolina—surprised the town in the summer of 1707, almost carrying Fort Carlos before its garrison could expel them. Eleven Spaniards were nonetheless killed, fifteen captured, a dozen slaves carried off, and the houses outside its stockade went up in flames. A second assault by 1,500 Indians and Carolina frontiersmen was averted when Louisiana's new French governor, Jean-Baptiste Le Moyne, Sieur de Bienville, arrived from Mobile with a relief column on 8 December. José de Guzman, the Spanish garrison commander, subsequently traveled to Mexico to complain about his inadequate defenses, so that some reinforcements arrived on 29 January 1708 and helped strengthen Fort Carlos. Outlying dwellings were henceforth prohibited, but the residents crowded inside the garrison compound developed yellow fever, which claimed fifty-five lives by early October.

Peace was eventually restored, but when hostilities against other European powers threatened early in 1719, the Crown directed Mexico's viceroy to dispatch an engineer to construct an additional fortress at Sigüenza Point, the westernmost tip of Santa Rosa Island. Before those instructions could be received, however, France joined the War of the Quadruple Alliance against Spain, and Louisiana—learning of this realignment before their Spanish neighbors—launched a devastating surprise attack against Santa María de Galve. Joseph Le Moyne de Sérigny et de Loire materialized offshore on 14 May with four warships and 600 men, calling upon Gov. Juan Pedro Matamoros to surrender. He refused, but after a token three-day resistance from behind the town's partially com-

pleted fortifications, his 200-man garrison and 800 noncombatants sued for terms. French citizenship was extended to all who chose to remain, while de Sérigny assigned the 22-gun frigate *Comte de Toulouse* and 20-gun *Maréchal de Villars* to transport the defeated governor and Spanish troops to Havana.

As those vessels approached Cuba on 4 July 1719, they were captured—notwithstanding their flags of truce—by fourteen Spanish privateer vessels exiting under Lt.-Col. Alfonso Carrascosa de la Torre to raid Louisiana. Apprised of Santa María de Galve's fall, this expedition instead steered on 29 July to reconquer the West Florida outpost, two companies of regulars and 900 volunteers disembarking by 24 August outside its bay under *sargento mayor* Estéban de Berroa to subdue the 400 French occupiers under Capt. Antoine Le Moyne de Châteauguay, appropriating two vessels and 160 black slaves as booty. De Berroa subsequently attempted to raid Louisiana but was dissuaded by the high state of alert maintained by Governor de Bienville.

Strongly reinforced when Commo. Marquis Desnots de Champmeslin reached Louisiana on 2 September 1719 with five warships and almost 2,000 men from Saint-Domingue (Haiti), local French militia also struck out overland with indigenous auxiliaries, jointly investing the 800-man Spanish

New harbor castle at the western tip of Santa Rosa Island, as proposed by the Havana-based military engineer Bruno Cavallero, after Pensacola's original mainland fort had been destroyed by a French force advancing out of Louisiana in 1720. (Archivo General de la Nación, Mexico)

garrison within reconquered Santa María de Galve shortly thereafter. A two-hour assault against a couple of the stockade's weakest points persuaded the defenders to capitulate by 17 September, 600 Cuban volunteers being repatriated to Havana while the Spanish officers and two companies of regulars were carried off as prisoners of war. Not wishing to reinstall a French garrison, Champmeslin razed Santa María de Galve's stockade before sailing away for France.

Relocations (1721–1762)

By the terms of the subsequent peace treaty, the town was restored to Spanish control, so that expeditions were ordered across from Veracruz and Havana to reoccupy Pensacola Bay in 1721. Given the ease of Santa María de Galve's fall, the authorities moreover decided to revive their earlier plan of erecting a stronghold at the western tip of its offshore island and transfer the entire mainland settlement over to this more defensible site.

Work on a redoubt to cover the entrance channel commenced in 1723 and was completed three years later, the town that sprang up just east of it becoming known as Santa Rosa Punta de Sigüenza. (Florida State University archaeologists excavated this site in 1964, estimating its total number of buildings to be thirty-five.) The tiny military garrison and civilian populace were sustained by semiannual dispatches of arms, provisions, medicines, and payrolls from Mexico—although deliveries were often delayed by Gulf storms or enemy threats. *Presidiarios* (convicts) were also transported out to provide a labor force, as well as to permanently bolster the community once their sentences were served.

Most of the few hundred residents operated farms on the mainland and in addition started felling large numbers of tall, straight, limber pines during the 1730s to export to Havana's shipyard. Because of their isolation, inhabitants furthermore indulged in clandestine trade with Louisiana. The War of Jenkins's Ear against Great Britain complicated sea movements for a decade as of 1739, after which low-lying Santa Rosa Punta de Sigüenza was leveled by a prolonged hurricane on 3–5 November 1752 that drove the survivors to seek refuge on the mainland.

Relief soon arrived from Havana and Veracruz, but it was agreed to transfer the entire town and its defenses back off the exposed offshore island to the mainland; the military engineer Felipe Feringán Cortés consequently drew up plans for a new quadrilateral stockade with twin towers and four gates, enclosing a new civilian community. This proposal was approved by the Crown and implemented in 1756 by the military engineer Agustín López de la Cámara Alta, supported by funds and 200 additional convict laborers from Mexico, as well as 50 cavalrymen and 100 women to help reinvigorate the population base. The new mainland town was dubbed San Miguel de Panzacola, and its new citadel became known as Fort San Carlos.

The community had scarcely settled into its new surroundings when Gov. Miguel Román de Castilla was succeeded by Diego Ortíz Parrilla in October 1761, bearing news of heightened tensions back in Europe. Madrid, after maintaining neutrality during the past five years of the French and Indian War, now secretly promised to join Paris against Britain the next spring. But London learned of this covert Bourbon alliance and preemptively declared war against Spain, unleashing a huge expedition against Havana in June 1762. Pensacola was cut off from both Cuban and Mexican support, then early the following year learned that according to the terms of the peace treaty that had been signed at Paris, the conquered Cuban capital was to be restored to Spain in exchange for Florida, so that Pensacola would be surrendered to the English.

Ambrosio Funes de Villalpando, Conde de Ricla, reached Havana on 6 July 1763 to reassume Spanish rule over Cuba from its British occupiers. He then dispatched the royal officials José Bernet and Lázaro Alberja across to West Florida to expedite Pensacola's evacuation, assuring residents that the expenses of their passage to Veracruz would be defrayed by the Crown. Gen. William Keppel, commander of the British force departing Havana, in turn directed Lt.-Col. Augustine Prevost to take possession of Pensacola with his Third Battalion of the 60th "Royal American" Infantry Regiment, the flotilla materializing off the harbor mouth by 5 August.

Prevost landed the next day to inform Ortíz Parrilla that all Spanish citizens who did not wish to remain under British rule must depart for Mexico within a month; as no transports had yet arrived, his 350 British troops—many weakened by disease—encamped outside Pensacola's stockade. Prevost presumed that all buildings inside would devolve to the British Crown and so permitted sales of homes and lots outside the wooden palisades to English officers, soldiers, or speculators. Eight transport ships soon appeared, the town being formally ceded to the colonel's control on 2 September 1763, after which 622 Spanish subjects—including 160 soldiers, 108 Christianized Yamasee Indians, and 105 convicts—sailed out of the bay the following day. Only a single Spaniard remained behind, guarding the cargo of a wrecked vessel until it could be salvaged.

British Occupation (1763–1781)

Prevost ruled as military governor for more than a year, his exhausted redcoats—joined by Maj. William Forbes's 35th Foot Regiment as of 30 November 1763—finding few attractions within Pensacola's "rotten stockade" or the humid, pestilential landscape. The town languished until the Scottish-born naval officer George Johnstone arrived from London and Jamaica aboard the frigate HMS *Nautilus* on 24 October 1764 to assume office as the first civilian governor of West Florida. He described his capital of Pensacola as:

> An assembly of poor despicable huts, to the number of one hundred and twelve; but it has all the advantages which a

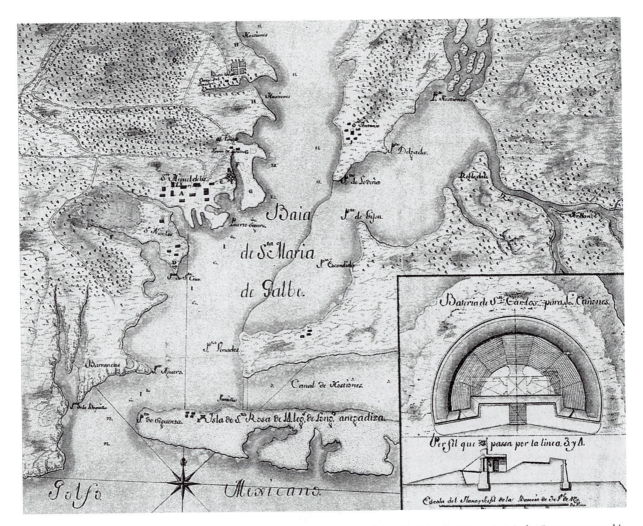

Map pinpointing the third and final Spanish establishment at Pensacola, plus an insert depicting its 10-gun San Carlos Battery, surveyed in March 1756 by the military engineer Agustín López de la Cámara Alta. (Servicio Geográfico del Ejército, Madrid)

sandy soil can afford, namely health, good water, a noble port, beautiful situations surrounding it, infinite communications by water, capable of easy communications by land, great plenty of fish, and excellent vegetables.

After appointing a council—including the surveyor-general, Elias Durnford, plus Pensacola's customs collector and postmaster—the governor reconnoitered its bay, then decided to lay out a new town grid upon the old Spanish site. Confusion regarding land titles complicated this procedure, and a few months later Johnstone reported that there were only 1,473 white residents and 842 blacks in all of West Florida. Over the ensuing decade, those numbers slowly trebled as trappers, traders, settlers, and speculators flowed through the province, although Pensacola did not expand commensurately because of its poor agricultural terrain and its lack of a navigable river into its hinterland. Disease claimed 119 lives between August and November 1765, so that even the Anglican minister

William Dawson fled to South Carolina early the next year. Johnstone compared his capital's development unfavorably with that of Spanish New Orleans in a complaint to the London Board of Trade in November 1766:

To see the fortifications, churches, hospitals, and public buildings which are everywhere erecting in the Spanish dominions since the arrival of Don Antonio de Ulloa [as governor of Louisiana], whilst nothing is undertaken on our part, is extremely mortifying.

Some local improvement began after the Swiss-born Brig. Frederick Haldimand arrived as Pensacola's garrison commander on 24 March 1767. He extended Fort George and widened its streets to improve air circulation, as well as draining nearby swamps and tapping a freshwater supply. He also initiated construction of a hospital, storehouses, magazines, gardens, a signal house at the tip of Santa Rosa Island, and a road leading toward Mobile. Having been recalled early in 1767, Johnstone was succeeded the next year as governor by John Eliot, who hanged himself in his study, so that Lt.-Gov. Montford Browne headed up an interim administration as of May 1768. Haldimand and the bulk of West Florida's 3,500 redcoats were withdrawn that same September–November, yet he returned early in 1770, after the Spaniards had heavily reinforced New Orleans.

Peter Chester arrived at Pensacola as governor of West Florida that same 10 April 1770, erecting a new Government House, while Haldimand concentrated upon completing a new barracks, brick batteries, and blockhouses around the harbor with the assistance of military engineer Thomas Hutchins. Haldimand was eventually promoted to major-general and departed Pensacola in April 1773 to become acting commander-in-chief at New York two years before the American War of Independence erupted in New England.

West Florida remained loyal to the Crown throughout this struggle, welcoming numerous monarchist refugees. Commerce sagged, and Pensacola was briefly perturbed when a rebel army under James Willing descended the Mississippi to despoil Natchez early in 1778, but a few hundred redcoats were sent across from Jamaica that same autumn to bolster its garrison. The "severest hurricane ever known or felt in this part of the world" then roared through Pensacola on the night of 9–10 October 1778, killing seven people and leveling most buildings and defenses; tidal surges even carried anchored vessels a mile into the woods. Maj.-Gen. John Campbell therefore hastened from New York to the flattened town's relief with 1,200 troops—a detachment of Hessian mercenaries of the 3rd Waldeck Regiment, plus Pennsylvania and Maryland Loyalists—arriving on 18 January 1779 to commence rebuilding its fortifications.

Spanish Reoccupation (1781–1813)

That same autumn, word arrived that Spain had joined the American rebels in their war against Britain, so that Gov. Bernardo de Gálvez advanced out of his headquarters at New Orleans to overrun West Florida's advance outpost of Baton Rouge in September 1779, followed by Mobile in February 1780. Campbell vainly attempted to relieve this latter garrison by a cross-country march with 500 troops and 600 Indian allies, but he returned into Pensacola unsuccessfully on 18 March. Nine days later, ten Spanish warships and twenty-six transports under Commo. Joaquín de Cañaveral hove into view, creating alarm before they steered westward to unite with de Gálvez. But having lost the element of surprise, the Spanish governor decided not to invest Pensacola immediately.

Instead, he traveled to Havana, departing on 28 February 1781 with five warships and twenty-seven transports bearing 1,500 soldiers. Dispatch vessels were sent ahead to arrange a rendezvous with units from New Orleans and Mobile; de Gálvez's fleet then appeared off the eastern end of Santa Rosa Island by dawn of 9 March, slipping grenadier and light infantry companies ashore that same night. When Col. Francisco Longoria's column approached the signal house at its western extremity the next morning, they found that redoubt abandoned—although the anchored frigates HMSS *Mentor* of Capt. Robert Deans and *Port Royal*, along with the battery atop Red Cliffs, opened fire from inside the bay and peppered the Spaniards. De Gálvez landed two 24-pounders to respond, driving the English frigates deeper into the bay by the afternoon of 11 March. But the Spanish governor could not persuade Commo. José Calvo de Irrazábal to lead his fleet across the shallow entrance bar because the 74-gun flagship *San Ramón* drew too much water.

After a week spent disgorging equipment and importuning the commodore, de Gálvez finally boarded his private brig, *Gálveztown,* and dashed past the Red Cliffs battery on 18 March 1781, followed the next afternoon by the entire fleet (except for *San Ramón,* which stood away toward Havana). An additional 905 Spanish troops arrived overland from Mobile on 22 March, followed the next afternoon by 1,348 more aboard fourteen vessels from New Orleans, raising de Gálvez's total strength to 3,553 soldiers. He began ferrying his army across from Santa Rosa Island two days later, disembarking on the mainland to swing around the Red Hills and Moore's Lagoon and encamp southwest of Sutton's Lagoon. Chester and Campbell concentrated their defenders outside indefensible Pensacola, around their Fort George strongpoint.

On 30 March 1781, another Spanish advance edged their base closer to that British citadel. Yet de Gálvez did not institute a close siege until Adm. José Solano y Bote and the French commodore François Aymar, Baron de Monteil, arrived from Havana on 19 April with two dozen more warships, adding 1,600 Spanish and 725 French soldiers as well as 1,350 sailors, swelling the invading host to 7,400 men. Nine days later Spanish sappers commenced digging a covered trench or tunnel toward a small hill that commanded the Queen's Redoubt, Fort George's advance outpost. Despite English countersallies, siege batteries were installed over the ensuing fortnight; a chance Spanish round detonated the magazine within the Queen's Redoubt by 8 May, leveling it with a blast that claimed seventy-six lives and wounded two dozen. Spanish light troops immediately occupied the smoldering ruins, moving their artillery within point-blank range of Fort George, so that Chester and Campbell requested terms that same afternoon.

Pensacola's actual capitulation took place on the afternoon of 10 May 1781, when 1,113 Englishmen surrendered, giving up 193 artillery pieces and 2,100 muskets. De Gálvez appointed Lt.-Col. Arturo O'Neill as military governor, initiating the evacuation of all prisoners to Havana for eventual repatriation to St. Augustine, Charleston (South Carolina), or New York. All royal properties within Pensacola were to devolve to the Spanish Crown, while English civilians had eighteen months' grace to sell their holdings to Spanish purchasers. Yet there were to

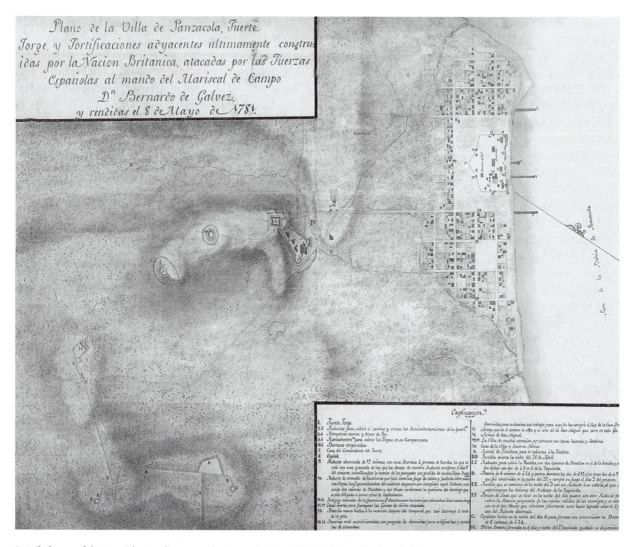

Detailed map of the Spanish siege lines outside Pensacola, May 1781. (Archive of Indies, Seville)

be no buyers among the invading army, so that most residents simply abandoned their town houses. (Lt.-Gov. Durnford further lamented the loss of his own Belle Fountain Plantation, with its 1,400 cattle and horses.) Inland plantations were also destroyed by a wave of local uprisings, after the British capitulation became widely known.

Madrid, elated by the victory, instructed O'Neill a few weeks later to rename the harbor Bahía de Santa María de Gálvez, "to the honor and glory of the Holy Virgin, and in memory also of the conqueror who has recovered it"; the fort atop Red Hills was to become San Carlos de Barrancas, and Fort George was to be dubbed San Miguel, "since it surrendered on the day of the appearance of the Holy Archangel (Michael), General of the God of armies." According to the general peace treaty concluded at Versailles early in 1783, Spain retained possession over West Florida and therefore reactivated its old colonial administration for Pensacola, sustaining its tiny garrison and population with annual ship-

ments of money, provisions, and troops from Veracruz or Havana. Heavily outnumbered by the indigenous population, the Spaniards moreover concluded defensive alliances with Sewanee, Talapuche, Alibamon, Chickasaw, and Choctaw chieftains as early as 1784, agreeing to recognize Creek sovereignty over all tribal lands south of 32 degrees, 28 minutes north latitude, in exchange for their help in fending off territorial encroachments by American frontiersmen.

The military engineer Joaquín de Peramas reached Pensacola in 1784 to study the refurbishment of its defenses, noting fewer than 300 townspeople spread among its eighty-four households—most being either French-speaking Creoles who had migrated out of Louisiana or recently arrived Canary Islanders. Given their feeble numbers, de Peramas suggested strengthening Fort San Carlos de Barrancas and shifting the town 6 miles west into its shadow for greater protection. His colleague Gilbert Guillemard arrived from New Orleans three years later to draw up the actual plans for the fort's transformation; yet although that project was initiated shortly thereafter, the town of Pensacola was never relocated below its walls.

When the Englishman John Pope visited in 1790, he noted that there were still "elegant buildings in this place, particularly the palace, barracks, and chapel," although the town itself was "in a ruinous state." Life became even more difficult for the isolated outpost once Spain allied itself with Revolutionary France and declared war against England on 6 October 1796: Pensacola suffered a surprise descent by Indians allied to the British early the next year. A shaken Gov. Vicente Folch instructed the military engineer Francisco de Paula Gelabert early in February 1797 to draw up new plans for strengthening the town's defenses, and construction of an outer palisade with seven bastions was initiated; work was ordered to cease a few months later, though, by the penniless government in Madrid. However, as Indian dangers persisted, a more modest proposal was drafted in August 1799 and approved by the Crown the next January.

The frontier outpost's status became enhanced after overseas hostilities were briefly interrupted by a European truce, and neighboring Louisiana was purchased by the United States in 1803—a sale that meant that all regional Spanish administrations, formerly headquartered at New Orleans, were shifted across into Pensacola. Subsidies and sea traffic grew proportionately to the town's new role, while the number of its residents trebled to 3,063 by June 1813—although a majority remained French-speaking Creoles, plus some Scottish and Irish immigrants, ruled over by a few hundred Spanish officials and troops.

The latter's authority had been shaken by the overthrow five years previously of King Ferdinand VII by the French emperor Napoleon I. Then, American resentment against the sanctuaries afforded fugitive slaves and Creek raiders out of Florida sharpened once the War of 1812 erupted, as the nominally neutral Spaniards—allies of the British in Europe—welcomed Royal Navy vessels into their Gulf ports. U.S. columns pushed out of Georgia and Tennessee into northern Florida in late September 1812 and early February 1813 to punish Seminole and black border raiders, while Maj.-Gen. James Wilkinson advanced from New Orleans to displace the tiny Spanish garrison holding Mobile Bay (which Washington claimed as part of its earlier Louisiana Purchase).

After a year of clashes between U.S. regiments and Creek warriors throughout the Alabama wilderness, Pensacola became directly embroiled when Royal Navy Capt. William Henry Percy and Royal Marine Lt.-Col. Edward Nicolls recruited 600 Creek and Choctaw warriors at the Apalachicola River mouth in the summer of 1814, marshaling them in the Spanish capital of West Florida for an assault against the U.S. occupiers of Mobile. This attack was repelled in mid-September by the 130-man garrison of U.S. regulars holding Fort Bowyer under Maj. William Lawrence, who killed 162 and wounded 72

of the 730 attackers, as well as destroying Percy's 28-gun flagship *Hermes*. But more significantly, this aggression so incensed the U.S. theater commander—Maj.-Gen. and former senator Andrew Jackson—that he marched against Pensacola, notwithstanding the supposedly peaceful relations existing between the United States and Spain.

Uncertainty (1814–1820)

Jackson appeared outside the small city on 6 November 1814 with 700 U.S. regulars, 2,000 mounted Tennessee militiamen under Maj.-Gen. John Coffee, a detachment of Mississippi dragoons under Maj. Thomas Hind, plus other auxiliaries. Maj. Henry D. Peire of the 44th U.S. Regiment was sent forward under flag of truce to demand that Pensacola's San Miguel citadel and more distant Fort Barrancas—both now manned by British garrisons—be surrendered by Spanish governor Mateo González Manrique. But Peire's party was fired upon by redcoats, so that Jackson carried the city at bayonet point, encountering scant resistance. Percy's small warships briefly opened fire from out in the bay, while British sappers demolished Fort Barrancas before the occupiers withdrew eastward to Apalachicola.

Jackson installed a U.S. garrison and returned into New Orleans by 21 November 1814, yet his unsanctioned seizure of Pensacola proved short-lived, as the city was soon relinquished to the Spaniards; British forces again used it as a staging area that same December for their ill-fated assault against Louisiana's capital. The cessation of Anglo-American hostilities by early 1815 resulted in the Royal Navy's entire withdrawal from Gulf waters, after which American migrants started to infiltrate the northern fringes of Spanish West Florida with greater impunity. As Madrid was distracted by the independence movements raging throughout its Latin American empire, Pensacola remained an unimportant and neglected outpost. Lacking troops or resources, Gov. José de Callava tolerated the American settlers who began establishing homesteads—some complete with water-powered mills and slave laborers—along the Escambia River north of Pensacola, because their production at least enhanced local food supplies and trade.

The city again passed under direct U.S. control when the First Seminole War erupted in November 1817. The next spring, Jackson launched a major offensive into Florida with 500 U.S. regulars, 1,000 Tennessee militiamen, and 2,000 Creek allies, easily driving through enemy territory and—determined to eradicate Seminole resistance once and for all—pressing on to seize San Marcos de Apalache by early April; Pensacola and St. Augustine followed one month later. Upon regaining Tennessee on 30 May 1818, Jackson found that his high-handed actions were cheered by the general public, yet they had met with disapproval in official circles. That same August, President James Monroe offered to restore Florida to Spain, but Spain instead chose to sell its increasingly untenable province to the United States the next year for several million dollars.

U.S. Annexation (1821–1860)

Once the treaty of cession was ratified, Jackson returned to Pensacola as Florida's newly appointed governor in June 1821, formally taking possession of the provincial capital from Governor de Callava during a ceremonial exchange held on 17 July. American settlers began arriving in large numbers to join the few hundred Spanish inhabitants who had remained behind, while Jackson created an interim administration before departing for Tennessee that same October, leaving George Walton as acting governor. The U.S. Congress recognized Pensacola as capital of the newly consecrated Territory of Florida on 30 March 1822.

Although the city's population quickly resurged to almost 2,000 residents, their numbers were thinned to 1,200 to 1,400 by a yellow-fever epidemic that struck in mid-August 1822, claiming 237 lives and causing many others to flee. Many recent American arrivals had moreover been discouraged by the district's sparse agricultural potential, while urban problems were compounded because the departed Spanish officials had taken all the existing land titles among their records, causing considerable difficulty for the Board of Land Commissioners in disentangling and authenticating claims. Neverthe-

less, undeterred residents petitioned Congress to be granted a tract containing the worn remnants of old English "Fort George" in which to construct a school and other public buildings, while a road leading overland to Blakely, Alabama, was also recommended by the assistant quartermaster-general of the U.S. Army in October 1823; a contract to commence a second road eastward to St. Augustine was let by December 1824.

More important, the Florida Legislative Council petitioned President James Monroe to establish a major U.S. naval station within Pensacola's vast anchorage and to replace its badly decayed Spanish harbor forts with new defenses. The bill was duly passed by Congress early in March 1825, so that three months later Commo. Lewis Warrington of the U.S. West India Squadron was ordered to begin transferring all stores and personnel from the base on Thompson's Island (Key West) into temporary housing within Fort Barrancas. Naval captains William Bainbridge and James Biddle arrived from Norfolk, Virginia, aboard the sloop-of-war USS *Hornet* on 25 October to select the actual site for a permanent naval yard and depot; the citizenry hosted them at a banquet one week later, presided over by Judge Henry M. Brackenridge of the Superior Court of West Florida and the city's mayor, John Jerrison.

Despite its broad expanse, much of Pensacola Bay proved to be quite shallow, so that a deep-water anchorage was selected off Tartar Point—a mile and a half east of Fort Bar-

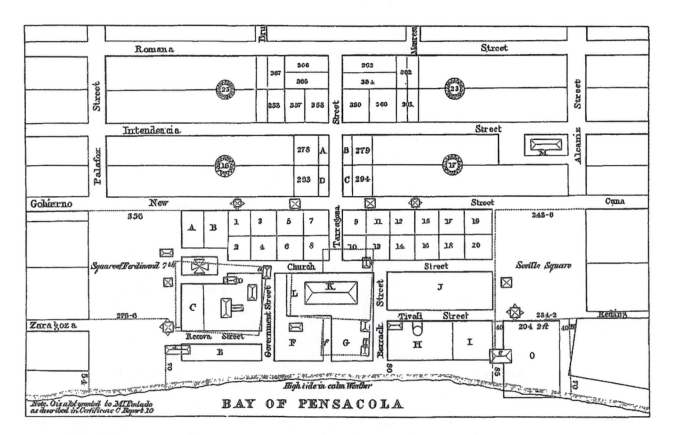

Map attempting to clarify conflicting property claims around Pensacola's main square, January 1825. (American State Papers, Class 8: "Public Lands," Volume 4)

rancas on the western shoreline; construction of brick houses and a stone wharf commenced by March 1826. Local resources proved so limited, however, that materials and craftsmen had to be imported from New York and Boston, while slaves supplemented the local labor pool. Another outbreak of yellow fever in the summer of 1827 retarded progress, but a few buildings nonetheless emerged, lots and streets being laid out beside the navy yard for workers' quarters, later evolving into the villages of Warrington and Woolsey. (The latter was named for the depot's first commandant, Capt. Melancthon T. Woolsey, who was obliged to serve without salary because of financial irregularities at his previous station on Lake Ontario.)

An arsenal and hospital were added over the next few years, while work also commenced in 1829 on a major fortification project to replace Fort Santa Rosa at the mouth of the bay, being completed five years later and named Fort Pickens in honor of the Revolutionary War general Andrew H. Pickens. Fort McRee was begun opposite, named "in compliment to the late Colonel William McRee of the Engineers." Thanks to this construction boom, as well as the regular provisioning and repair of warships and a steady influx of immigrants, Pensacola's population more than doubled to 3,000 residents by 1831; one observer, however, noted that its "public and private buildings' [were still] in a very dilapidated state," its streets remaining quite sandy and with few sidewalks.

A newspaper—the *Pensacola Gazette*—and a college had nonetheless appeared, while the Bank of Pensacola was founded by December 1833. Another yellow-fever epidemic then struck the following summer, and the Second Seminole War erupted by the end of 1835, creating such uncertainties that the city's development lagged behind that of Mobile and New Orleans. The growth of lumberyards at Black Water at the northeastern end of Pensacola Bay (modern Milton on the Blackwater River) helped the city survive economically, while local magistrates even tolerated the excesses committed when hundreds of sailors were given liberty during the West India Squadron's summertime layovers. (On a more positive note, a detachment from the frigate USS *Macedonia* helped bring a devastating city fire under control in February 1841; it nevertheless consumed all structures along both sides of Intendencia Street, from the Old Coffee House to Baylen Street.)

Florida became a state of the Union in 1845, and the desultory pace of naval construction accelerated when the Mexican-American War erupted in May of the next year. Because of its strategic position on the Gulf, Pensacola was expected to serve as the main supply base for U.S. naval operations in Mexican waters, yet it proved ill prepared for the ensuing two years of conflict. Officers complained that its repair facilities were inadequate, coal stocks meager, while "thirty days were required to bake enough bread to last the flagship [the 480-man frigate *Potomac*] three months, and even fresh water was difficult to obtain in sufficient quantities." As a result, major expenditures were authorized once hostilities ceased in 1848,

leading to the installation of a floating dry dock, a properly seated wharf, a machine shop, and other improvements.

The city itself furthermore benefited from the resurrection of a failed proposal to lay a railway track from Pensacola to Montgomery, Alabama, while a plank road was also added in 1850. Local materials were used to strengthen harbor defenses, as well as to build and launch the naval sloops *Pensacola* and *Seminole* nine years afterward—although they had to be sailed to Norfolk to receive their engines and armament. A new lighthouse with a revolving beacon was inaugurated at Pensacola's harbor entrance on 1 January 1859.

Civil War Abandonment (1861–1865)
Passions regarding states' rights and slavery rose so sharply that when the USS *Supply* entered Pensacola Bay on 7 December 1860 to refurbish its navy yard, one officer found meetings being openly held calling for secession and the seizure of all federal installations. "Men, women, and children seemed to have gone mad," he added, and large numbers of volunteers were drilling in the streets. When news arrived in early January 1861 that prosecessionists had taken the U.S. arsenals at Chattahoochee, Florida, and Fort Morgan on Mobile Bay, Lt. Adam J. Slemmer received permission from Washington to withdraw his forty-six gunners of G Company, 1st U.S. Artillery Regiment, into empty Fort Pickens at Pensacola's harbor mouth. The artillery in Fort McRee opposite was spiked by 10 January when Florida passed its own secession act.

Two days later, Confederate governor Madison Starke Perry directed 550 troops under retired colonel William H. Chase to occupy the federal navy yard and mainland fortifications, encountering no opposition from the elderly base commandant, Commo. James Armstrong. An uneasy standoff ensued, with Fort Pickens's federal garrison—now totaling 82 men—observing 1,500 Confederates on the mainland; merchantmen all the while continued to enter harbor, unchallenged by the federal men-of-war anchored outside in support of Slemmer. Confederate brigadier Braxton Bragg eventually relieved Chase and tightened the island's isolation as tensions escalated throughout the nation that spring. Newly inaugurated President Abraham Lincoln ordered Fort Pickens reinforced, so that federal troops disembarked from the frigates *Brooklyn* and *Sabine* of Capt. H. A. Adams at dawn on 12 April 1861.

Rebel batteries opened fire against Fort Sumter (outside Charleston, South Carolina) that same evening, and the Civil War became fully joined. More federal troops and artillery under Col. Harvey Brown landed at Fort Pickens over the next few days, but Adams delayed imposing a naval blockade until 13 May 1861. Bragg responded by attempting to scuttle the floating dry dock in the entrance channel, but that ungainly structure grounded on a shoal and was eventually burned during a nocturnal foray by Brown's garrison on 2 September.

Pensacola, having been placed under martial law, experienced great hardship as a result of its interrupted trade.

Fort Barrancas amid the Red Hills after its occupation by Confederate troops in late January 1861; note the rebel "Stars and Bars" flag above its ramparts, plus the fully installed heavy artillery. (Miller and Lanier, *Photographic History of the Civil War*)

Famine even appeared as overland food shipments failed to meet its requirements, in addition to those of thousands of Confederate soldiers. On the moonless night of 14 September 1861, a 100-man boat party from the Union warship *Colorado* rowed stealthily into its bay and burned the 250-ton blockade-runner *Judah*, which was being armed at the naval dockyard. Bragg replied by allowing Brig. Richard H. Anderson to land 1,000 Confederates 4 miles east of Fort Pickens before dawn of 9 October and attempt to surprise the federal garrison from its rear; this attack was foiled, however, when they blundered into the encampment of Col. William Wilson's "Bloody 6th" Regiment of New York Zouave Volunteers.

Union artillerists sustained a protracted exchange with the Confederate shore batteries on 22–23 November 1861, causing part of the village of Warrington and the navy yard to go up in flames; more damage was inflicted during another such duel on 2–3 January 1862. Realizing that the stalemate was a waste of the Confederacy's meager resources, Bragg transferred to Mobile and on 27 February ordered his subordinate, Brig. Samuel Jones, to prepare to abandon Pensacola. Over the next couple of months, everything of value was surreptitiously removed inland from Pensacola, and two nearly completed gunboats on the Milton stocks were torched. A majority of the citizenry also joined the exodus, municipal authorities reconvening their "government-in-exile" at Greenville, Alabama.

The Confederate colonel Thomas M. Jones's rear guard set fire to all fortifications and the remnants of the navy yard shortly before midnight on 9–10 May 1862, which the Federals across the bay recognized as a signal of the city's abandonment. Union lieutenant Richard Jackson came ashore at the deserted Pensacola waterfront the next dawn from the schooner *Maria A. Wood*, arranging surrender terms with its few remaining residents. Brig. L. G. Arnold meanwhile occupied Forts Barrancas, McRee, and the navy yard, before his 1,000 troops marched triumphantly into the city on the evening of 12 May, hoisting the Stars and Stripes in its main plaza (Ferdinand Square).

Federal commanders refurbished the gutted yard so as to receive the Western Gulf Blockading Squadron of Rear Adm. David G. Farragut, which had been using extemporized facilities at Ship Island, Mississippi; however, Union strategists were not interested in pressing into Pensacola's interior to secure the hinterland, so that the city did not revive. Instead, its roughly 1,000 remaining residents—mostly impoverished blacks or Spanish descendants—were encouraged to resettle around the yard, where their labor was urgently needed, espe-

View south-southeastward from Pensacola's lighthouse, taken early in 1861 by the Confederate photographer J. D. Edwards of New Orleans. Two miles across the water lies Fort Pickens, on the western tip of Santa Rosa Island, with federal warships anchored in support out in the Gulf. (Miller and Lanier, *Photographic History of the Civil War*)

cially after the 1,300 federal troops garrisoning Pensacola were redistributed around the harbor defenses in March 1863. As most inhabitants did not wish to be left behind at the mercy of Confederate raiders, Pensacola was reduced to desolation. A Union soldier who visited a couple of months afterward found grass growing in its empty streets, while the Spanish vice consul, Francisco Moreno, informed him that "the whole population of Pensacola, white and black, is less than forty."

Yellow fever struck the crowded navy yard in August–September 1863, claiming three score victims; then, on 8 October, a couple of hundred Confederate raiders under Brig. James Holt Clanton appeared from Pollard, Alabama, skirmishing near Big Bayou or Bayou Grande with pickets of the 82nd U.S. Colored Infantry Regiment. Clanton's column, though, was too weak to pose any real threat to the fortifications.

Afterward, a few citizens even drifted back into Pensacola, living uneasily between the distant Union garrisons and occasional Confederate cavalry forays. Southern fortunes eventually faded so badly that Washington declared Pensacola's port reopened to commercial traffic as of 1 December 1864, although local federal officers only implemented this policy at Woolsey and Warrington, without allowing vessels to venture "above the Navy Yard limits until such time as Pensacola itself is garrisoned by our troops." When Gen. Robert E. Lee finally surrendered the main Confederate army at Appomattox, Virginia, on 9 April 1865, Union brigadier Alexander Asboth traveled up Pensacola Bay fifteen days later from his headquarters in Fort Barrancas aboard two armed Navy launches to receive Clanton's surrender at Milton.

Resurrection (1865–1905)

Pensacola remained the principal U.S.N. base on the Gulf, although federal authorities ordered an immediate curtailment of work at its yard as part of the general demobilization, paying off its employees and closing many workshops. This economic dislocation complicated the revival of the decayed city, whose municipal authorities had by now returned from exile. Yellow-fever epidemics in the summer and fall of 1867, and in 1873, further retarded development, and when that disease reoccurred in 1874, it was reported that 354 of Pensacola's

3,347 citizens died and 1,947 fled. Another outbreak occurred in August–September 1882, and the village of Warrington suffered a devastating fire on 6 October that consumed its Catholic church and forty other structures.

Pensacola nonetheless survived and even managed to prosper modestly thanks to a late nineteenth-century national boom that increased demand for such local produce as seafood—especially red snapper—and lumber. The separate Saint Joseph's Parish for African American Catholics was established by 1890, while the outbreak of the Spanish-American War in April 1898 created further work at the navy yard, although the bulk of the U.S. expeditionary force sent against Cuba actually embarked from Tampa because of its superior rail connections. Guantánamo was subsequently acquired by the U.S. Navy and became its new Caribbean base.

Still, Pensacola's population had grown to 17,747 residents by 1900, whose civic leaders encouraged annual peacetime visits by battleship squadrons over the next few years. Even another yellow-fever epidemic in late August 1905 was overcome, as mosquitoes had now been identified as carriers of the disease; thus effective fumigation countermeasures could be deployed.

Cataclysm and Modern Evolution (1906–Present)

The small, somnolent city was struck by a devastating hurricane and tidal wave on 26 September 1906 that inundated waterfront properties and washed away many homes. Survivors later averred that had it not been for the protective bulwark of Santa Rosa Island, Pensacola would have been utterly destroyed. The navy yard also suffered serious damage, most anchored vessels being either sunk or driven aground, while Fort McRee at the harbor mouth was leveled; Forts Pickens and Barrancas also sustained injury. Major repairs could not commence until the Hurricane Damage Act was passed on 2 March 1907, appropriating the requisite funds for reconstruction, as well as modernization of sewers, drains, pavements, and sidewalks.

Despite this natural catastrophe, the city nonetheless managed to export more than half a million tons of commodities that same year—mostly cotton, naval stores, tobacco, and

Wide-angle photograph of Pensacola's main plaza and park, with city hall visible at right, ca. 1909. (Library of Congress)

lumber—and its population rebounded to 22,982 people by 1910 as neighborhoods began expanding into the surrounding hills. Still, residents were shocked when the navy yard was closed by Washington on 20 October 1911, although Asst. Sec. of the Navy Franklin D. Roosevelt announced during a visit on 17 November 1913 that the site was to be converted into a Marine base; the transport *Prairie* arrived fifteen days later to disgorge 800 Marines under Col. John Archer Lejeune. A small "Aeronautic Center" to train young officers in the new science of naval aviation had also been authorized, inaugurating operations with a flight across Pensacola Bay on 2 February 1914—and suffering its first fatality when Lt. (jg) J. M. Murray's Burgess D-1 flying boat plunged into the water thirteen days later during an exercise. Five submarines arrived with their tender *Tonapah* on 25 February; then more warships followed in April, when the United States intervened in Mexico by seizing Veracruz, using Pensacola for logistical support until that occupation ended the same year.

Although not as beneficial to the local economy as a major naval yard, the city nonetheless profited from catering to this reduced Navy presence. Pensacolians also witnessed the first catapult launch of an airplane from a warship—an AB-2 flying boat off the stern of the armored cruiser USS *North Carolina* in November 1915—as well as several altitude records. The city was battered by another heavy hurricane and tidal surge on 5 July 1916; this time its recuperation was accelerated by a huge demand for labor, supplies, and accommodations once the United States was drawn into World War I in April 1917. Naval installations mushroomed outside their compound to engulf the villages of Warrington and Woolsey, so as to accommodate a massive influx of thousands of servicemen. (The complement of the Naval Air Station, for example, swelled from 500 peacetime officers and men to 6,000 by the conclusion of the conflict, a year and a half later.)

Once again, an abrupt postwar demobilization caused considerable local dislocation. Among the few construction projects undertaken by the government was the razing of the town of Woolsey to clear an airstrip in 1922; the Pensacolian authorities furthermore donated another "outlying landing field about 5 miles north of the city, near the fertilizer plant," which was to be named Corry Field in honor of the first Floridian trained as a naval aviator: Lt. W. M. Corry, Jr. (This second airstrip was located near the present Booker T. Washington High School. In order to retain Washington's patronage, city and county commissioners also purchased a 500-acre tract west of Pensacola and turned it over to the Navy Department, so that Corry Field might be expanded.)

The U.S. Navy's commitment to the port was confirmed when the first American aircraft carrier, USS *Langley*—converted from the collier *Jupiter*—was deployed at Pensacola to perfect takeoff and landing procedures within the sheltered waters of its bay during 1923–1924. The city also enjoyed a minor tourist boom after the completion of the Gulf Beach Highway, drawing tourists with such major new attractions as the 500-room Hotel San Carlos. Bootlegging and movies added to Pensacola's allure, but another hurricane and tidal wave wreaked considerable havoc on 20 September 1926. The Great Depression, initiated by the stock market crash of October 1929, retarded the city's recovery, as government expenditures were restricted.

The collapse of Pensacola's land boom, and failure to replace its outdated timber companies with modern industries, meant that about one-fourth of all urban salaries were derived from the Naval Air Station by 1930, when the population stood at 31,579 inhabitants. Budgetary cutbacks began to ease once the national economy recuperated during the late 1930s, so that Washington could concentrate emergency-relief construction programs—such as the Works Project Administration (WPA) and Public Works Administration (PWA)—into upgrading the station's military preparedness because of deteriorating relations overseas. Pensacolian contractors and laborers profited during this military buildup from improving or erecting vast new hangars, airstrips, barracks, hospitals, and other training facilities, as millions of dollars were expended.

Pensacola served as a major marshaling and recuperation area throughout World War II, and the emergence of naval airpower as a dominant strategic weapon during that conflict ensured a continuation of operations for its Naval Air Station once hostilities ceased. The city economy blossomed and diversified thanks to such demands, as well as from a regional tourism and retirement boom; thus Pensacola's population exploded from 43,479 inhabitants in 1950 to more than 250,000 by the late 1960s (although only 60,000 actually lived within the old city limits, the remainder being scattered about its now sprawling metropolitan area). The University of West Florida and Pensacola Junior College had furthermore been established, while in order to preserve an illustrious heritage, a thirty-six-block downtown area—stretching from Plaza Ferdinand past Seville Square to North Avenue on the east and from the waterfront to Saint Michael's Cemetery on the north—was declared the Pensacola Historical District.

For further reading materials on the history of Pensacola, as well as additional sources on U.S. urban history, please consult the Select Bibliography at the end of this volume.

PHILADELPHIA

Seaport established deep amid the fertile valleys of the Delaware watershed, which would evolve into Colonial America's largest city and the first national capital.

Antecedents (1609–1680)

Seminomadic Lenni-Lenape tribesmen had hunted for generations throughout the forested, well-irrigated wilderness area where this city would eventually rise, dubbing it Coaquannock (Grove of Tall Pines). However, no permanent presence was created, and no European explorers penetrated this far inland. Eventually, the Englishman Henry Hudson—sailing under Dutch colors in 1609—probed its sea outlet 88 miles away on the Atlantic coast. It was christened Delaware Bay the next year when the Englishman Samuel Argall called, while sailing toward Virginia; he named it in honor of his own provincial governor, Lord de la Warr.

It was not until 1616 that the Dutch sea captain Cornelis Hendricksen actually ventured up the Delaware River from that bay, establishing friendly contacts with some local inhabitants near the mouth of a tributary called Manayunk, which was to become better known among the newcomers as the Schuylkill (Hidden River). The first European settlement in the region was a tiny Dutch enclave installed on Burlington Island in the Delaware River by 1624, which served as a springboard for further expansion inland—including the creation of an outpost on the east bank of the Schuylkill by 1633. Some fifty Swedish émigrés arrived five years afterward and were the first to begin settling what is today Delaware County, establishing an outpost at Tacony on the Tinicum lowland, 5 miles south of Philadelphia's future core. (This suburb would eventually become dubbed "Southwark," in honor of a similar shipbuilding sector of London.) Handfuls of Finnish and English migrants continued to trickle into the district, all eking out an agricultural-based subsistence along diverse riverbanks, while trading and intermingling with the dwindling numbers of Lenape.

After England had displaced The Netherlands from North America, this thinly populated territory was solicited from the Crown in June 1680 by the wealthy English patrician William Penn, a leading member of a dissenting pacifist, Protestant movement known as Quakerism; Penn sought it in repayment for a loan of £16,000 that his father—the famous Adm. William Penn—had extended to King Charles II. Imbued with religious idealism, the younger Penn hoped to convert this almost virginal North American territory into an earthly utopia, where people of diverse persuasions might live in harmony as "an example to all nations." He furthermore envisioned its future capital as an unfortified "green country town," carefully laid out in a grid pattern beside a beautiful river, welcoming vessels from all around the world and becoming known as the city of Philadelphia (the Greek term for "brotherly love," as well as the name of one of the seven earliest church sees founded at Lydia in Asia Minor).

Conflicting boundary claims with adjacent North American properties already held by James, Duke of York, and Lord Baltimore delayed the consummation of Penn's proposal until 14 March 1681 (O.S., or "Old Style"; nine days afterward, according to our "New Style," or modern Gregorian, calendar). On that date he received a royal grant to a new private colony that was to measure roughly 300 by 160 miles and be christened Sylvania (Woodlands)—but Charles amended the name to Pennsylvania in honor of Penn's seafaring father. That same September, William Markham was appointed deputy governor, and he departed aboard the ship *Bristol Factor* with an advance party to begin laying the groundwork for the imminent Quaker transfer.

Foundation and Early Evolution (1681–1713)

After landing at Chester in October 1681, Markham selected a site at the narrowest point of the peninsula, between the Schuylkill and Delaware rivers, where Philadelphia could be installed. He directed the efforts of work parties felling trees throughout the winter of 1681–1682, as well as negotiating the purchase of some 100 square miles of present-day Bucks County from the Lenape later that same summer. As Penn had specified that a symmetrical gridiron pattern of blocks was to be created, with streets spaced far enough apart for substantial individual plots, his friend and "surveyor-general," Thomas Holme, crafted just such a layout. The urban area measured 1 mile high by 2 miles wide, with generous commons or "Liberty lands" attached.

The future capital's waterfront was to overlook the Delaware River and be concentrated around an inlet dubbed "Dock Creek," whose tiny anchorage would contain a public wharf (this inlet later became Dock Street, after its waterline receded and it was filled in, running northward from near modern Spruce Street as far as Market Street at Fifth). The city boundaries were envisioned as eventually reaching as far as the Schuylkill River to its west, to Vine Street on its north, and to South Street on its south. Space for five public squares was allotted: one central one, plus one each in its northeastern, southeastern, southwestern, and northwestern quadrants (which in turn would evolve into Franklin, Washington, Rittenhouse, and Logan squares, while the central one—originally intended to serve as Philadelphia's civic core—was not actually fully occupied until the early nineteenth century, becoming Penn Square and occupied by a massive new city hall and other public edifices as of 1871). One main thoroughfare called High Street was to bisect the urban grid from east to west, traversed at Centre Square by another north-south thoroughfare called Broad Street, although Penn decreed that all other east-west streets were to be named after indigenous trees, while north-south streets were to be numbered.

Penn himself disembarked at New Castle on the Delaware from the ship *Welcome* on 27 October 1682 (O.S.), one-third of his 100 travel companions having succumbed from smallpox during their transatlantic crossing. Upon reaching Markham's clearance sometime thereafter, he was received at the Dock Creek shoreline's first tavern—the Blue Anchor, located on the west side of Front Street—before making a regional inspection tour, establishing peaceful relations with local tribesmen (allegedly sealed with a wampum belt) and convening a general assembly at Chester. That body partially diluted his powers, before officially constituting Pennsylvania into a province on 7 December, with Philadelphia as its designated capital.

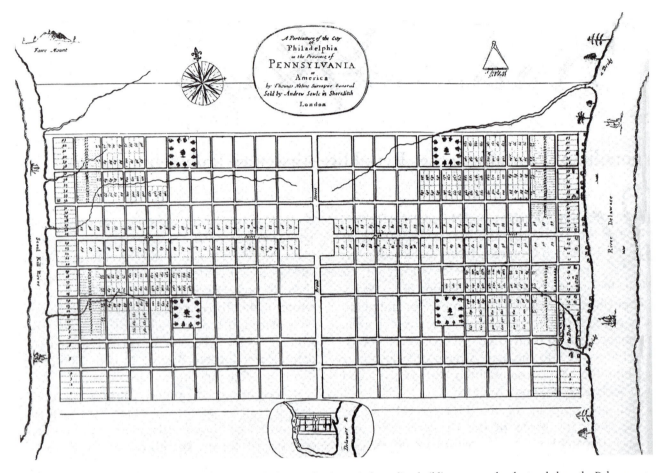

Thomas Holme's original grid plan for the city, as published in London in 1683; the earliest buildings were to be clustered along the Delaware waterfront at right. (Library Company of Philadelphia)

Many of the city's earliest citizens sheltered temporarily inside its shoreline caves, until spring could permit the erection of more fitting abodes. Penn nonetheless was able to chair a meeting of the Provincial Assembly in his pioneer community as early as 10 March 1683 (O.S.). Philadelphia quickly began taking shape, impelled by a steady stream of migrant ships arriving with more European coreligionists—often from Holland or Germany, because of Penn's lifelong contact with those countries, his mother having been Dutch-born. Skilled tradesmen such as carpenters, bricklayers, tanners, coopers, weavers, cobblers, tailors, wheelwrights, and brewers helped accelerate the settlement's evolution, one of its first public edifices being a market shed erected near the waterfront on High Street (hence later renamed Market Street) to receive farm produce brought in by riverboat.

One group of settlers from Crefeld in Germany, headed by Francis Daniel Pastorius, founded a separate municipality 5 miles away dubbed Germantown that same year of 1683. Philadelphia's first private school was also opened, the Provincial Assembly having enacted a compulsory education law that required all children to be taught to read and write by the age of twelve. (Six years afterward, George Keith of the Quaker Society of Friends opened a free Public Grammar School beside their Meeting House on the east side of Fourth Street south of Chestnut; it would become chartered as of 1701 and eventually evolve into the William Penn Charter School, being relocated into the East Falls section.)

As early as 1684, Philadelphia—although still hemmed in by dense forest—boasted 2,500 residents spread among 300 wooden houses and a few hundred nearby farms, serviced by a variety of shops and stores selling imported goods. The printer William Bradford established its first press the next year, and sturdy brick edifices began to appear for wealthier inhabitants. The city's first fire-resistant slate roof was commenced as of 1687 on Penn's mansion at the corner of Norris Alley, on the east side of Second Street north of Walnut. (He was also to build a magnificent estate at Pennsbury on the upper Delaware River, complete with fine furnishings, servants, and slaves, from whence he could be rowed into his capital to attend to political or business affairs.)

However, his dream of having Philadelphia evolve into an open community of broad streets with individual dwellings

Penn's once grand slate-roof home as it appeared, ca. 1864, after having been reduced to commercial usage; it was abandoned shortly thereafter and demolished by 1867. (Free Library of Philadelphia)

centered amid ample plots was soon compromised by the influx of many less affluent migrants, whose modest resources required that some blocks be subdivided by alleys so as to accommodate smaller landholdings. (One surviving example would be Elfreth's Alley, located just north of Arch Street, running a block westward from Front Street to Second Street and named after the blacksmith Jeremiah Elfreth—one of about 120 craftsmen toiling in the settlement by 1690.) Many people disembarked from ships penniless, having been given free passage by sea captains in exchange for performing several years' manual labor, as indentured servants for any citizen willing to discharge their fares. Slaves had also been imported as early as November 1684, when the Bristol ship *Isabella* appeared with 150 African captives—although a few local purists decried such trade in a community supposedly dedicated to human freedoms; the first abolition petition was circulated four years afterward by a quartet of recently arrived German immigrants.

Regular ferry service was inaugurated from the waterfront to the New Jersey shoreline opposite in 1688, greatly facilitating the traffic in goods and people, for in an era when roads were unpaved tracks, ill suited for hauling heavy loads, the ability to receive both small riverboats and oceangoing ships proved to be a distinct commercial advantage. And unlike other, more exposed coastal cities or frontier outposts in northern New England or the Carolinas, often threatened by French or Spanish raiders during times of war, pacifist Philadelphia lay at a relatively safe remove and so did not have to shoulder the additional expense of major fortification projects. Its gravest dangers were posed by disease and fire, which Penn's vibrant young community were able to withstand, so that some 2,200 residents were clustered in Philadelphia by the close of the seventeenth century, servicing another 15,800 settlers scattered throughout Pennsylvania.

The small Quaker capital continued to flourish, although without expanding westward from the Delaware shoreline up into its vacant upper reaches, above the slopes known as the Fall Line. In 1701 it became a chartered city, packet boat service being inaugurated five years afterward as far upriver as Burlington. From there, passengers could take a stagecoach on to Perth Amboy (New Jersey), then another ferry on to New York City. In 1707 a new courthouse was erected on Philadelphia's High Street for the Provincial Assembly to meet in, and private merchants also gathered there to conduct business. As forestry products were so abundantly available, the capital's shipbuilding and carpentry trades were expanding, while salt could furthermore be obtained for curing fish, pewter and clay for making pottery, furs for export, and so forth. Skilled artisans such as silversmiths, furniture-makers, glaziers, and clock makers began to acquire a reputation for excellent craftsmanship, along with bakers, distillers, and other more humble trades.

Colonial Expansion (1714–1775)

Transatlantic traffic had been disrupted by England's participation in King William's War from 1688 to 1697 and Queen Anne's War from 1702 to 1713; yet once peace was restored, the volume of migration into North America accelerated noticeably. Although a majority of the people disembarking at Philadelphia were destined to settle into rural counties on the Piedmont Plateau west of the city, the provincial capital nonetheless absorbed such a significant percentage that its population swelled to roughly 10,000 inhabitants by the mid-1720s, including so many more Germans that bilingual newspapers and broadsheets were published routinely. The first iron ores from hinterland mines were also smelted in Germantown smithies as of 1717, while a seventeen-year-old journeyman printer named Benjamin Franklin immigrated to Philadelphia from Boston in 1723, launching the *Pennsylvania Gazette* six years later as a vehicle for civic improvement. In its pages, he espoused such useful measures as creation of a proper fire company, better paved and illuminated streets, as well as a public hospital. (Franklin's genius would eventually add such innovations as America's first fire insurance company and even lightning rods to reduce accidental blazes.)

Most British colonies along the Atlantic seaboard blossomed during the mid-eighteenth century, and Philadelphia, which lay conveniently between the primary concentrations of New England and Chesapeake Bay, found itself well situated to satisfy the swelling demand for goods and manufactures. Port traffic grew as a result, 140 ships calling at Philadelphia in 1725, in turn helping to fuel a significant period of refinement and sophistication—symbolized by such endeavors as the commencement of Christ Church by the amateur architect John Kearsley in 1727, the founding of Philadelphia's Library

Company four years afterward, and initiation of a splendid new legislative hall in 1732 on Chestnut at Sixth streets to a design by the local builder Edmund Woolley. (Although not completed until two dozen years later, that imposing structure—whose brick tower would enclose a bell cast in England in 1753, later dubbed the Liberty Bell—eventually anchored a clump of public edifices that together would become known as the State House Group, today a National Historic Site overlooking Independence Square.)

Some 427 ships called at Philadelphia in 1735, and its soaring exports of lumber, grain, meat, horses, and furs—often as far as London or the West Indies—meant that the few original city wharves multiplied into more than three score sturdy jetties plus a dozen busy shipyards; the old ramshackle collection of public market stalls were also replaced as of 1745 by fine purpose-built sheds, which extended in a line for two blocks southward on Second Street as far as South Street. That same year, James Logan began collecting materials for what a decade and a half later would become a free public library.

The bustling port's vigor and prosperity continued to attract ever more diverse ethnic migrants, so that the city lost much of its original Quaker austerity and began to address the needs of a broadening population base. In response to three dreadful yellow-fever outbreaks in the 1740s, the Pennsylvania Hospital for the Sick Poor was completed on the capital's outskirts in 1756, while a public water system was also created to more efficiently draw that resource from the Schuylkill River. By 1753 the total number of inhabitants for the city and its adjoining county stood at 14,563, and the following year non-Quaker settlers pushed Pennsylvania's boundaries so far inland as to exacerbate frictions with indigenous tribes and French traders, so that open conflict erupted.

Philadelphia largely benefited from the nine ensuing years of the French and Indian War, especially during that struggle's earliest phases, as local merchants and artisans reaped windfall profits as Crown contractors; labor demands also escalated so rapidly as to provide higher wages and more employment for working-class tradesmen. Some Philadelphian seafarers even achieved notable successes as privateers, the Scottish-born John Macpherson amassing such a bonanza in prize money as to lavish £14,000 upon the construction of Mount Pleasant, his magnificent, 160-acre riverfront estate just above the city (today part of Fairmount Park).

The urban population soared to almost 19,000 inhabitants by 1760—including roughly 1,500 slaves—while its built-up area had also expanded for the first time with the absorption of an adjacent hilled property, once deeded by Penn to the Free Society of Traders, that ran eastward from Front Street and westward from Seventh Street and between Walnut and South streets. This eminence was graded and transformed into a new, prestigious, residential area dubbed Society Hill, dotted with the town houses of such prominent citizens as Mayor John Stamper. One of its most beautiful structures was to be Saint

Peter's Anglican Church, erected at the intersection of Pine and Third streets during 1758–1761, where such future luminaries as the naval hero Stephen Decatur and the painter Charles Wilson Peale would be interred.

An economic downturn occurred after French Canada was conquered by British arms in 1759, and military efforts were shifted into more distant theaters, further embittered for Philadelphians by the particularly harsh winter endured in 1761–1762. And when hostilities ceased altogether the next spring, the city suffered an additional scare when a rowdy mob of Scotch-Irish farmers from Paxton Creek massacred a hapless band of Conestoga Indians at Lancaster, then marched upon Philadelphia late in 1763 to demand that the assembly bolster the security of frontier outposts. City militia companies were mustered to confront these so-called Paxton Boys, and although no great violence thereupon ensued, the election of 1764 proved to be so hotly contested as even to cost Franklin his seat. The unpopular Stamp Act passed by Britain's Parliament further inflamed political passions, leading to violent boycotts by working-class residents against all English goods.

Yet despite such outbursts, Philadelphia's sea trade and urban development resumed and proceeded unabated throughout much of the period, the number of its edifices almost doubling from 2,969 to 5,470 between 1760 and 1777, while its total population surged to 28,043 inhabitants by 1769, making it the largest city in the Thirteen Colonies and second only to London in the entire British Empire. By now Philadelphia was exuding a cosmopolitan and affluent air, with many handsome homes and straight, tree-lined streets with even-numbered addresses on one side and odd-numbered on the other (then considered an exceptional refinement). Wealthy citizens were erecting sumptuous country estates along nearby banks of the Schuylkill and Delaware rivers, far removed from the increasingly crowded confines of the urban core.

Traditional exports of bulk produce were regularly supplemented by skilled manufactures, such as furniture of cherry, oak, walnut, and even mahogany (imported from Central America), as well as countless lesser commodities and printed works. Philadelphia had furthermore become North America's premier publishing, scientific, and artistic center. The elegant

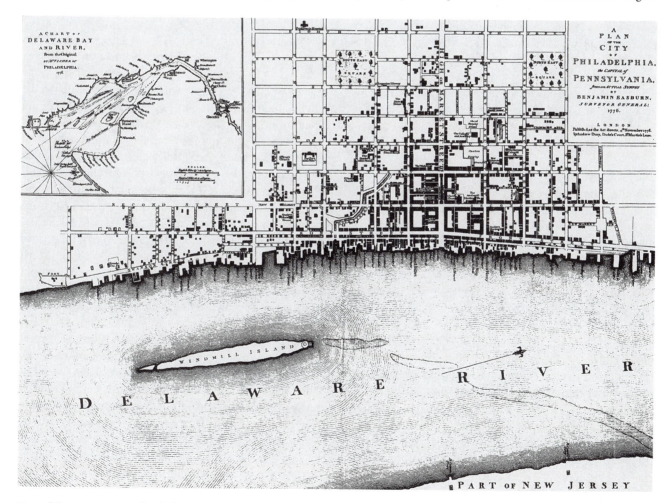

Copy of the surveyor-general Nicholas Scull's 1762 plan of Philadelphia, re-issued in London by Andrew Dury in November 1776, as the American Revolutionary War was raging; north is toward upper right. Note how the eighteenth-century city still remained clustered along its waterfront. (Metropolitan Toronto Reference Library)

Southwark Theater was opened in 1766 on the south side of South Street west of Fourth—situated, for moralistic reasons, just outside the city limits—and a vast new "Bettering House," or almshouse, was also raised by private subscription and completed the next October on Spruce Street, acknowledged as the largest single edifice in the Thirteen Colonies. Sixteen creeks had been dammed around the city environs to provide an abundance of hydraulic power, the Wissahickon alone sustaining eleven mills.

And because of the city's undisputed commercial prominence, wide-ranging seaborne contacts, polyglot ethnic mix, and vigorous press, it came to serve as the cradle for a nascent national consciousness, initially coalescing around demands for a stronger North American voice in Britain's policy making. Most Philadelphians yearned for varying degrees of political reform, yet working-class members proved to be especially motivated, organizing such radical bands as the Committee for Tarring and Feathering in October 1773 to protest against the Tea Act by reimposing a citywide boycott against that commodity, as well as threatening Delaware pilots who brought British ships upriver to off-load tea. Less than a year later, delegates from throughout the Thirteen Colonies assembled for the first so-called Continental Congress in Carpenters' Hall on Chestnut Street at Fourth to begin debating Americans' role in their own governance. When Crown officials in Massachusetts attempted to detain delegates bound toward the second Congress in the spring of 1775 on charges of sedition, the Revolution flared openly with the first exchanges of gunfire at Lexington and Concord.

Patriot Capital (1776–1800)

At a safe remove from these opening hostilities, Philadelphia hosted the second Continental Congress, which—swayed by impassioned local opinion makers such as the immigrant stay maker and author of *Common Sense,* Thomas Paine—adopted a series of resolutions leading toward greater autonomy. However, it was not until the British garrison was expelled from Boston in March 1776 that delegates were faced with the prospect of actually declaring outright separation from Britain, which many feared would lead to social disintegration and anarchy. At this crucial juncture, Philadelphian commoners moved that June to dismiss Pennsylvania's hesitant government leaders, then instructed the state's delegates in Congress to vote in favor of a Declaration of Independence on 4 July.

When the so-called Liberty Bell was pealed four days later for this historic document to be read to a jubilant throng assembled on the state house steps, the royal crest was torn from above its door and thrown into a celebratory bonfire. Yet considerable segments of Philadelphian society recoiled at such a wholesale transition, including many members of its upper classes, as well as the pacifist Quakers (whose refusal to take up arms would make them suspect in patriot eyes). Slaves were also tempted by British promises of individual

freedom, while Pennsylvania's inland tribes supported the Royalist cause as a counterweight against American expansionism. Ship traffic had already become slowed by Royal Navy blockades, so that the city economy had worsened, after which Philadelphia became the object of a major British land offensive when Gen. Sir William Howe disembarked in Delaware Bay the next summer with 15,000 troops from New York, intent upon pressing inland in twin columns to overrun the patriot capital, then pushing detachments farther north to link up with Maj.-Gen. John Burgoyne's smaller army descending out of Canada.

The vanguard of Howe's invasion force clashed with an American unit guarding Cooch's Bridge at the Christiana River crossing on the morning of 3 September 1777, scattering it back toward Washington's main encampment at White Clay Creek. The American commander-in-chief opted to make a stand at Brandywine with his 10,500 troops, yet was outflanked on 11 September, and so retreated toward Chester. Even Brig. "Mad Anthony" Wayne's attempt to cover this retirement by springing an ambush ten days later, 2 miles southwest of Paoli Tavern on the west bank of the Schuylkill River, was detected and dispersed by the advancing British columns.

Philadelphia consequently fell without resistance on 26 September 1777, Maj.-Gen. Charles, Lord Cornwallis, being installed as its garrison commander; Howe's main army encamped around Germantown, being headquartered in the Cliveden mansion of wealthy Loyalist landowner Benjamin Chew. Realizing that the invaders were now dispersed—3,000 redcoats still guarding the overland supply routes from Delaware Bay, plus another 2,000 holding Philadelphia, so that only 9,000 remained with Howe—Washington reversed his retreat and massed 11,000 men to assault the British cantonments at Germantown out of the southwest. His vanguard crested Chestnut Hill at dawn of 4 October, Maj.-Gen. John Sullivan and Brig. William Alexander's columns being assigned to sweep along Shippack Road, while Maj.-Gen. Nathanael Greene was to lead an encircling movement. Instead, the first patriot units were repelled from Airy Hill by Capt. Allen McLane's Light Horse, while Sullivan was checked at Chad House by Lt.-Col. Thomas Musgrave's heavily outnumbered 40th Regiment. Then, just as Washington was about to commit to a general attack, two American regiments mistakenly fired upon each other in the fog, so that a withdrawal instead commenced—without any vigorous pursuit by the British. Only Cornwallis emerged from Philadelphia with three battalions to hound Washington for 5 miles before giving up the chase.

Yet despite its being repulsed, Washington's surprise counterattack had proven that patriot resistance was still dangerous, so that Howe subsequently remained ensconced at Philadelphia, dooming Burgoyne's unsupported army to encirclement and defeat at Saratoga by mid-October 1777. And when the capital's British occupiers detached Col. Carl von Donop downstream to Haddonfield with 2,000 Hessians and

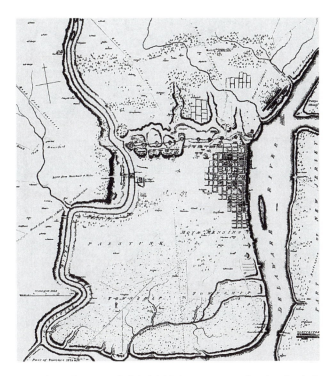

Map of British-occupied Philadelphia in 1777–1778, showing the city's strategic placement on the peninsula between the Schuylkill and Delaware rivers. (William Faden, *North American Atlas*)

two fieldpieces on 21 October to clear the last American troops from Forts Mercer and Mifflin near Mud Island on the Delaware River, so as to free up the flow of waterborne supplies from their fleet anchored in Delaware Bay, they too encountered stiff opposition the following noon.

Von Donop vainly called for the surrender of Fort Mercer's 400-man American garrison under Lt.-Col. Christopher Greene, before launching two of his Hessian grenadier battalions and the Von Mirbach Regiment out of the north at 4:30 P.M. against this crude earthwork at Red Bank on the New Jersey shoreline; simultaneously, more Hessian units closed in out of the west. Yet although the fort's northern defense seemed to be only a weak brush abatis, quickly abandoned by its defenders, the French military engineer Du Plessis had reinforced its interior with a stone wall lined with some American guns, so that when the Hessians attempted to cut their way through the branches, they were dispersed by a withering counterfire. A second assault led by Von Donop in person also failed, at the cost of his life. Hessian casualties totaled 400 killed, wounded, or captured, plus the loss of the British support ships *Augusta* and *Merlin* out in the Delaware, compared with only 40 dead or injured Americans.

The surviving Hessians therefore settled down to a loose siege, being reinforced a fortnight later by a British contingent that opted to redirect all efforts against Fort Mifflin on the opposite, or Pennsylvania, side of the river (in what is today

southwest Philadelphia). However, as that island stronghold boasted eighteen 10-pounders and four blockhouses bristling with four guns apiece, manned by 450 equally determined patriots under Col. Samuel Smith, the British had to install five Royal Navy batteries on Province Island, as well as a floating battery of almost two dozen 24-pounders upstream, before initiating a long-range bombardment on 10 November 1777. Four days later they were joined by ten warships from Adm. Richard Howe's battle fleet, together raining so many shells into Fort Mifflin's interior that its huddled defenders sustained 250 casualties—compared with only 7 British dead and 5 wounded—before retreating across the Delaware into Fort Mercer on the night of 15–16 November.

The patriots abandoned that latter stronghold as well, on 20 November 1777, thus opening up the Delaware for supplies to flow into occupied Philadelphia; thus while Washington's army endured a bitter winter 20 miles northwest in grim quarters at Valley Forge, Howe lived luxuriously in a four-story red-brick mansion at Germantown (now vanished from the southeast corner of Sixth and Market streets), his officers being well entertained by Loyalist adherents and his troops comfortably housed. Their conditions even allowed his staff and members of Philadelphia's high society to stage an elaborate medieval ball, when Howe was ordered back to England in May 1778, called the *Mischianza* or *Meschianza* and celebrated—complete with jousting and fireworks—at the Walnut Grove estate of Joseph Wharton on the city's southern fringe.

Yet news then arrived that same spring that France had allied itself with the patriot cause and was dispatching a battle fleet across the Atlantic under Vice Adm. Charles-Henri, Comte d'Estaing. This deployment caused the Royal Navy supply vessels to forsake their vulnerable anchorage in Delaware Bay and in turn led Philadelphia's British occupiers to march out by 18 June 1778; they were subsequently chased back toward New York by an American column. The patriot capital was therefore recuperated four days later, Maj.-Gen. Benedict Arnold being appointed as its garrison commander and the Continental Congress reinstated into Independence Hall, although economic woes persisted once the British blockade was reimposed. State authorities had to enact various price controls and other unpopular measures in an attempt to stem the rampant inflation of 1779, widespread disaffection leading its citizenry to vote many radical members out of office the next year. Philadelphians were cheered only when Washington arrived to winter in their city after his Yorktown victory of late October 1781.

Upon finally securing independence from Great Britain in the spring of 1783, problems continued to plague Philadelphia and the fledgling nation. Some 300 soldiers, angered at being furloughed from the disbanding Continental Army—rather than being discharged with back pay, as no funds were available—marched from Lancaster on 17 June to demand their arrears from Congress. Despite appealing for protection from the Executive Council of the state of Pennsylvania, which was in session in the same building, the federal legislators were left to endure a day of menaces from the mutinous soldiery outside before voting to adjourn and reconvene eight days later in Princeton (New Jersey)—thus shifting the national capital out of Philadelphia. Although invited to return shortly thereafter, they instead appointed a committee under James Madison to consider the creation of a permanent government seat elsewhere.

Philadelphia nevertheless managed to host the Constitutional Convention, which assembled in its state house in the summer of 1787 to better organize the federal government and whose deliberations in turn inspired Pennsylvanians to do much the same with their own state administration three years later. In the process, they restored many of Philadelphia's municipal powers, so that the city at last began to revive from its recent dislocations. And as its commerce resurged, Congress also voted in July 1790 to restore temporarily the federal seat of government to Philadelphia until "the first Monday in December 1800," while a new national capital was being completed in the District of Columbia.

National legislators therefore returned in December 1790 to find a city that now boasted 28,522 inhabitants, plus another 26,000 scattered throughout its adjoining county and that would continue to blossom throughout this Federalist interlude. President Washington rented the Germantown mansion of the influential Robert Morris as his private residence, while the first bank of the United States was charted the following year and opened its doors in a magnificent neoclassical building at the corner of Third and Dock streets. The first U.S. Mint was erected at 37–39 North Seventh Street in 1792, with the famous Philadelphian scientist and inventor David Rittenhouse—a personal friend of both Washington and Franklin—being appointed as its director.

A dreadful yellow-fever epidemic the next August paralyzed many activities as thousands of Philadelphians fled, while 4,000 to 5,000 of those who remained behind died, including many grave diggers infected while burying cadavers. The capital nonetheless rebounded quickly, its elegant Chestnut Street Theater—inspired by a playhouse in Bath, England—being inaugurated near the intersection of Chestnut and Sixth streets in 1794. And when the Zion Lutheran Church on Fourth Street at Cherry burned down that same year, it was replaced within a couple of years by a fine brick edifice, deemed the largest church in the United States. The publisher Thomas Dobson also issued the first American edition of the *Encyclopaedia Britannica*, in twenty-two volumes, while French Royalist refugees added to the sophistication of Philadelphian social life. Seaborne trade boomed thanks to the neutrality of the United States during the global conflict between Britain and Revolutionary France; more than 1,400 vessels berthed at the bustling Philadelphia waterfront in 1797 alone, helping finance another noteworthy construction surge as well as the digging of canals and clearing of roads into the hinterland.

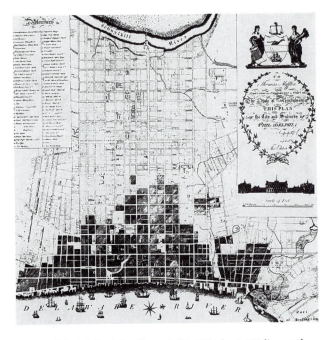

Engraved plan of the Federalist capital in 1794, by A. P. Folie; note how its built-up area was now expanding inland through Penn's original grid pattern of orchards and empty lots, toward the distant Schuylkill. (Historical Society of Pennsylvania)

Early Republican Heyday (1800–1853)

The city suffered a loss of its political status when the Commonwealth of Pennsylvania legislature was shifted to Lancaster in 1799 and the federal administration departed for the District of Columbia in mid-November 1800. In addition, New York City was emerging as a formidable financial rival, and Baltimore was rising as a challenger in flour exporting. Nevertheless, Philadelphia's 41,220 citizens would retain considerable commercial and cultural impetus even after 1800, reflected in improved urban amenities.

Benjamin H. Latrobe created the city's first steam-powered water system in 1801, using an engine to pump river water from the Schuylkill through an underground culvert to Centre Square, where a second engine elevated it into a tank to drain through wooden pipes into subscribers' homes. Within a decade the service would be furnishing more than 7 million gallons daily, through 35 miles of mains. Latrobe also helped to initiate a nationwide "Greek revival" style in architecture with his magnificent Bank of Pennsylvania building, completed that same year. The University of Pennsylvania—originally founded with Franklin's assistance as the nonsectarian College of Philadelphia—was relocated in 1802 into College Hall at the corner of Ninth and Chestnut streets; the old floating bridges across the Schuylkill were supplanted by the permanent Market Street Bridge as of 1804, permitting year-round access; and a beautiful Academy of Fine Arts was inaugurated by 1805–1806. The wealthy merchant Paul Beck even built a shot tower at distant Cherry and 21st streets in 1808, visible for several miles around and becoming a notable landmark. The 1,500-seat New Circus Theater moreover opened the following year at the corner of Walnut and Ninth.

When Congress refused to renew the charter of the First Bank of the United States in 1811, the wealthy Philadelphia businessman Stephen Girard was able to take it over as Girard's Bank. The largest single-span bridge in the world was completed in 1812 about a mile west of the city center, across the Schuylkill, and financed by Jacob Ridgway and designed by the German-born engineer Lewis Wernwag. War against Britain erupted that same spring, causing an economic downturn as a Royal Navy blockade was once again imposed. Yet Philadelphians could take pride in the victories won by the frigate USS *Constitution*, or "Old Ironsides," launched from a city yard. The cessation of hostilities in 1815 was followed by another half dozen years of national depression, severely hampering recuperation.

Still, the old Board of Control gave way to a new Board of Education in 1818, so that the first tax-supported public schools could be opened. And as the overall trade of the United States gradually revived, the nation entered into a period of remarkable economic and demographic growth—greatly spurred, in Philadelphia's case, by the full embrace of industrial methods. Its old agglomeration of water-powered craft workshops would soon give way to larger, steam-driven, multistoried factories whose mass production would greatly increase export volumes. The first 300 tons of anthracite coal had been received out of Piedmont mines as early as 1820, encouraging the conversion of many industries over to mechanization and helping to power the increased numbers of steamships and riverboats. Iron and steel foundries also multiplied in number and capacity.

This upsurge in productivity came to be reflected in municipal enhancements, such as the new market terminus—complete with a clock and bell—erected in 1822 at the intersection of Market and Front streets to better regulate operations of the public produce sheds (that now stretched far westward into the city, eventually reaching 18th Street). Work also commenced the next year on the massive State Penitentiary for the Eastern District of Pennsylvania, atop Cherry Hill in the northern district, resulting in a forbidding fortress intended as a more enlightened place of confinement. The architect William Strickland unveiled his neoclassical Second Bank of the United States on Chestnut Street as of 1824, while the Schuylkill Canal was completed the next year, freeing riverboats to bring in ever heavier cargoes of lumber, wheat, farm produce, and coal. The annual tonnages of the latter commodity skyrocketed from 6,500 that same year to 227,000 only nine years afterward.

The Arch Street Theater opened in 1828 just off Sixth Street, later to be managed by the famed Irish comedian John Drew, precursor of the Barrymore acting family, and Flat Rock Dam was completed the following year on the Schuylkill, providing power for a new generation of large mills that would

spring up in the Manayunk district. The beautiful First Independent Presbyterian Church was completed at Broad and Sansom streets by 1830, and the first railway to Germantown and Norristown opened for service two years later. An imposing new U.S. Mint was installed overlooking Centre Square as of 1833, and Strickland completed his magnificent Merchants' Exchange Building at the intersection of Third and Walnut streets the next year, while his Philadelphia Bank building at Chestnut and Fourth was finished by 1836. The first city gasworks appeared that same February, and in a historical footnote, the Liberty Bell cracked on 8 July 1835, while tolling a knell for the deceased chief justice of the U.S. Supreme Court, John Marshall.

Despite the fact that the city had now been eclipsed by New York as the premier metropolis of the United States—thanks to the direct access to the heartland afforded to that rival seaport by the Erie Canal—Philadelphia had nonetheless emerged as the nation's most highly industrialized city. It stood first in metal output because of huge plants such as the Alfred Jenks factory in Bridesburg, the Samuel V. Merrick facility in Southwark, and the Morris Iron Works, which together produced not only bulk items but also a sophisticated array of steam engines, pumps, lathes, precision tools, presses, and other equipment. Locomotive manufacture was to become a particular Philadelphian specialty, engines from the plants of Richard Norris, the Baldwin Locomotive Works at Broad Street and Spring Garden, the American Steam Carriage Company,

The Merchants' Exchange Building at 3rd Street and Walnut, ca. 1859, with the offices of the *Saturday Evening Post* and the First Bank of the United States visible in the right background. Note the streetcar tracks laid atop the older cobblestone streets. (Library Company of Philadelphia)

as well as Garrett and Eastwick being exported nationally and internationally. Busy shipyards also extended from Kensington as far as League Island, while hundreds of textile manufacturers were dotted throughout the urban area, providing an abundance of low-paying employment in the poorer Kensington, Germantown, and Manayunk neighborhoods.

Yet although industry was thriving, and mansions and expensive shops were multiplying in well-to-do areas, factories and shanty-filled slums blighted working-class districts as the population grew from 63,802 inhabitants in 1820 to 93,665 two decades later. Impoverished Irish laborers tended to cluster around their Schuylkill workplaces, while free blacks and escaped slaves from the South gathered in Moyamensing. (As the southernmost "free" city of the North, with considerable abolitionist sentiment among its Quaker minority, Philadelphia had become a busy terminus for the Underground Railway.) Yet as migrants continued to crowd into the city, living conditions deteriorated even further, provoking strident strikes and intolerance, exacerbated by job competition when another nationwide depression occurred in 1837.

On the night of 17 May 1838, a white mob burned the abolitionists' hall on Sixth Street near Franklin Square, as well as a Quaker-run black orphanage and church in the city's northeastern sector the next night; the state constitution was even amended to disfranchise free black voters. A massive influx of more Irish Catholic immigrants fleeing the Great Potato Famine of the early 1840s generated still more friction, especially after some complained about the reading of the Protestant King James version of the Bible in public schools. The reactionary Native American Party emerged on a platform of denying citizenship to anyone not born in the United States, leading to ugly street brawls, such as the Battle of Nanny Goat Market in 1842. Fights also spilled out of Kensington during the spring and summer of 1844, leaving twenty people dead, hundreds wounded, and two Catholic churches torched before 5,000 militiamen under Gens. George Cadwalader and Robert Patterson restored some semblance of order and passions cooled.

Philadelphia's title as the City of Brotherly Love was now openly derided abroad, so that municipal leaders responded to the recent collapse of public order by obtaining legislative approval in April 1845 to organize a 1,000-man professional police force, as well as to initiate the lengthier task of consolidating the city and its twenty-eight adjacent communities into a single metropolis. Urban tensions eased somewhat once national prosperity returned and the country became unified by the Mexican-American War of 1846–1848, a conflict for which thirty companies of young Philadelphians volunteered. Direct police authority was extended in 1850 over Northern Liberties, Spring Garden, Kensington, Moyamensing, Southwark, and other troublesome working-class suburbs. A census taken that same year revealed a population of 121,000 inhabitants within the 2 square miles of Penn's original city, plus more than 287,000 others in its adjoining communities, soon to be annexed.

Industrial Boom (1854–1945)

Philadelphia's boundaries were enlarged to engulf the entire 129.7 square miles of its county according to the Consolidation Act of 1854, twenty-eight municipalities being absorbed to create a single metropolis extending from Poquessing Creek in the northeast to Darby and Bow creeks in the southwest, with a waterfront now running for almost 24 miles. Numerous municipal reforms and enhancements followed, including the installation of a second water pumping station to draw from the Delaware, plus replacement of many rowdy volunteer fire companies with better-disciplined professionals. Despite another nationwide depression, which began in 1857, the city's 2,700-seat Academy of Music was nonetheless opened that same year, while business and residential development continued to radiate west toward the Schuylkill, as well as northward and southward. In 1859 the sheds were removed from the center of Market Street by city ordinance, so as to improve traffic flows along that principal thoroughfare, while the census of the next year recorded a population of 565,529 residents, ranking Philadelphia as the second-largest city in the United States.

Despite pockets of considerable pro-Southern sentiment, most Philadelphians rallied to the Union cause after Fort Sumter was bombarded by Confederate batteries in April 1861, the Walnut Street mansions of the rich militia generals Patterson and Cadwalader—both owners of large plantations in the South—being stoned by mobs before police could restore order. During the ensuing four years of the Civil War, some 90,000 to 100,000 Philadelphians served in the federal forces, and there were no riots when conscription was imposed in the summer of 1863, although largely because the city had only recently been relieved by the repulse in central Pennsylvania of Gen. Robert E. Lee's invading Army of Northern Virginia by Union defenders commanded by Bucks County's own Gen. George G. Meade. (Black Philadelphians, whose offer to serve in Pennsylvanian regiments had initially been rejected by the state governor, were grudgingly welcomed into the ranks after this rebel incursion of June 1863.)

More significantly, the city—as a major seaport and railroad hub, strategically located just north of the Mason-Dixon Line—had been transformed into a vital staging area for most Northern armies bound toward the front, as well as a readily accessible convalescent center for the returning wounded. Some 150,000 such injured soldiers were to be treated during the course of this conflict at its twenty-four military hospitals, the largest being the 4,000-bed Mower Hospital erected at Chestnut Hill. Huge contracts were also awarded by the federal government for war production, creating an economic bonanza for Philadelphia's factories, shipyards, and a host of lesser suppliers. The Civil War even shook the moneyed elite's traditional stranglehold over city politics: its Democratic Party officeholders—many obliquely sympathetic to Southern attitudes regarding race and slavery—were defeated in the midwar elections of 1864, the populist Union League leader Morton McMichael becoming the city's first Republican mayor the next year.

Philadelphia emerged from this conflict as an industrial and commercial powerhouse, its rail connections and port facilities, having been augmented for strategic reasons, providing enhanced distribution outlets for its enlarged factories, foundries, and first major department stores, such as John Wanamaker's, opened in 1861. Seven years later, the equally famous Strawbridge and Clothier opened its doors, followed eventually, Gimbel Brothers. The return to a peacetime economy moreover spawned numerous municipal projects, work commencing in 1868 on clearing Centre Square to make way for a massive new city hall. The University of Pennsylvania's College Hall was relocated from Ninth and Chestnut streets to a more ample campus in West Philadelphia in 1872, so that

construction might begin the next year on a huge new U.S. Post Office and federal building stretching as far as Market Street. Despite another economic downturn in 1873, and large pockets of slums and fractious ethnic neighborhoods blighting many parts of the city, Philadelphia was able to open the first zoo in the United States by 1874, and it successfully bid to host the World Exposition from 10 May to 10 November 1876. This grand international fair to mark the centenary of the nation's independence was held on a 450-acre riverside site above the city, and the next year a fine museum was also created.

By 1880, Philadelphia's population stood at 847,170 inhabitants, still ranking it second in size in the United States, and its growth would continue apace. Electric lighting was introduced the following year, and passenger service inaugurated from the Pennsylvania Railroad Company's ornate new Broad Street Station—deemed an engineering marvel because of its huge, arching, wrought-iron roof and elevated track beds, which permitted traffic to flow underneath. (When finally completed more than a decade later, Broad Street Station was

View looking east toward the Delaware River from atop George's Hill, over the 1876 World Exposition grounds in Fairmount Park. (Free Library of Philadelphia)

also considered the largest railroad terminal in the world.) Baronial estates and exclusive country clubs multiplied west and northwest of the city, telephone services appeared, and the horse-drawn trolley cars along Market Street from the ferry terminal at Delaware Avenue became fully electrified as of 1892. Heavy industry impelled the local economy, foundries and factories producing scores of vessels, such as the battleship USS *Maine,* plus thousands of locomotives, as well as staggering amounts of textiles and other goods.

Because of its vibrant economy, Philadelphia attracted a tremendous influx of European and rural U.S. immigrants during the 1880s and 1890s, so that Italian, Greek, Pole, Hungarian, Ukrainian, Lithuanian, Latvian, and Russian enclaves were added to its already diverse ethnic mix. The residential construction boom to accommodate this wave produced thousands of low-cost row houses, while public transit became even more effective as the former butcher boy Peter A. B. Widener and former grocery clerk William L. Elkins bought up dozens of small traction companies, consolidating them into the Philadelphia Rapid Transit Company. Their company developed an interconnected network of more than 264 miles of urban streetcar lines, providing swift access throughout the city. White Protestant families consequently felt freed to move out to the suburbs and commute back into work, leaving their old neighborhoods to migrant communities. For example, forty-five synagogues had sprung up south of Spruce Street by 1895, as the city's tiny original Jewish population was swollen by the arrival of 100,000 coreligionists, two-thirds of them from Russia.

Widener and William Pepper, one of the city's wealthiest lawyers and benefactors, jointly furnished funds to create the Free Library in 1891, which stocked reading materials in scores of different languages. Pepper also financed the expansion of the University of Pennsylvania's law and medical schools, while the Baptist evangelist Russell H. Conwell used proceeds from his famous Acres of Diamonds speech to charter Temple University in 1888, intended to educate students from less privileged backgrounds at its campus at Broad and Montgomery. Four years afterward, the financier Anthony J. Drexel furthermore founded the Drexel Institute for technical training, while the Quaker institutions of Bryn Mawr, Haverford, and Swarthmore all flourished in the wealthy western and southwestern suburbs.

By 1900 the population had mushroomed to 1,203,697, and although now ranked third behind New York and Chicago, Philadelphia nevertheless retained its primacy in industrial output. Volumes had risen so appreciably that river pollution required the introduction of sand-filtration plants at its municipal waterworks in 1901, while harsh labor conditions sparked a huge textile strike two years afterward in which more than 100,000 Philadelphian workers—some 10,000 being children as young as ten years old—shut down that industry to demand a fifty-five-hour workweek. The seventy-eight-year-old Mary

Harris Jones ("Mother Jones") even led a band of impoverished youngsters on a 125-mile trudge from the Kensington mills to President Theodore Roosevelt's mansion in Oyster Bay, Long Island, to highlight the need for reform of the child labor laws.

The ordinary citizen's quality of life was nonetheless slowly improving. Movement throughout the metropolitan area became easier after all its intraurban roads and services were contracted by the city in July 1907 to the Philadelphia Transportation Company, or PTC. The Frankford "L" and Bustleton surface line, along with the Broad Street subway, were built and equipped by the city, then leased by that firm, while the transportation company independently dug the Market Street subway. Residents therefore had more options for finding work, as well as shopping at fine consumer emporiums in the urban core such as Wanamaker's or traveling out to the new amusement and sports parks that were multiplying around the periphery.

The population rose to 1,549,008 inhabitants by 1910, and chlorination treatment was added at all municipal waterworks three years afterward. Increased demands in Europe for manufactured goods after the eruption of World War I in 1914 indirectly benefited the city's economy, being further spurred by the entry of the United States into that conflict in 1917. The tradition of celebrating an annual Army-Navy football game in Philadelphia even dates from that era, the metropolis being regarded as a "neutral" site, roughly equidistant between the academies of West Point (New York) and Annapolis (Maryland), as well as being able to handle the mass transit of thousands of cadets, midshipmen, and their supporters.

In the postwar era, municipal government was overhauled by the Charter Act, passed by the Pennsylvania State Assembly in 1919, and Philadelphia's population was found the next year to have swelled to 1,823,779 people. And as the global economy changed with the advent of more modern technologies, the city adapted, oil refineries sprouting to its southwest, as well as chemical plants along its riverfront—although its textile industry continued to dominate its poorer Kensington and Germantown areas. More sophisticated construction methods allowed for the erection of ever larger and taller buildings, better paved roads, and colossal spans such as the 1.8-mile Delaware River suspension bridge (later renamed the Benjamin Franklin Bridge). Upon its inauguration on 1 July 1926, it offered easier access for the 100,000 passengers traversing that river every day from the New Jersey shoreline aboard the centuries-old ferry service.

Yet because of its reliance upon heavy industry, Philadelphia suffered cruelly from the Great Depression, which was precipitated by the stock market crash of October 1929. The ensuing decade proved difficult for many citizens, and the city's economy did not rebound fully until the entry of the United States into World War II after the Japanese attack against Pearl Harbor on 7 December 1941. The vast Cramp Shipyard in Kensington, for example, was brought back up to

Pennsylvania Railroad Station, overlooking Penn Square at the intersection of Filbert Street, in 1889. This imposing structure was demolished in 1952 as part of an urban renewal project, train travel having become superseded by the automobile and aircraft. (Free Library of Philadelphia)

full capacity after having lain idle for years, while the ship channel leading out to the open sea was deepened to 40 feet along its entire length in 1942. Because of its huge navy yard and industrial plants, the city toiled around the clock for the next three years producing war materiel, its shortage of laborers a result of the nationwide mobilization being filled by a resurgence of job seekers from small towns and rural areas, often in the South.

Modern Era (1946–Present)

Not even the restrictions imposed by wartime rationing and lack of consumer goods, nor the temporary slowdown after victory was achieved in August 1945 and manufacturers readjusted to meet peacetime demands, could halt Philadelphia's demographic growth. The city successfully hosted the Republican Party nomination of Thomas Dewey and the Democratic Party nomination of Harry S. Truman as presidential candidates in 1948, and its municipal administration became

more fully empowered after a reformist Democrat movement got the state assembly to grant Philadelphia the right to draft its own charter the next year. That initiative climaxed with the approval by a majority of electors in 1951, the seventy-year Republican stranglehold on office being broken when Joseph S. Clark, Jr., was elected mayor of a twenty-two-member council. (A leading member of the Democratic reformers was the former bricklayer, Olympic rowing champion, and millionaire businessman John B. Kelly—father of the actress Grace Kelly, later Princess Grace of Monaco.)

An ambitious program of urban renewal was promptly implemented, such as removing the unsightly cluster of dilapidated buildings that had sprung up before Independence Hall, making way for an attractive mall to showcase these historic treasures. However, the urban core was also to become increasingly forsaken as part of a national trend in favor of modern suburban development, many of Philadelphia's industrial concerns opting to relocate their operations into

Boats dot the modern Schuylkill River, while the Philadelphia Museum of Art and city skyscrapers rise in the distance, 1982. (Ted Spiegel, Corbis)

more ample grounds in its virgin northeastern reaches, thus initiating a migration of the most upwardly mobile segments of its society. Although the city's population had peaked at 2,071,605 inhabitants in 1950, another 1.6 million already resided outside its boundaries and would continue to use their newfound automotive access to spread into the five contiguous Pennsylvania and three New Jersey counties, which together contained more than 3,400 square miles of new metropolitan expanse.

The city consequently became polarized as white residents decamped into these burgeoning suburbs, while poor rural blacks flocked into the urban core. Philadelphia's population base shrank to 1,949,996 residents by 1970, of whom 34 percent described themselves as black, compared with 2,874,000 mostly whites now living in outlying areas. Like other older northeastern metropolises, the City of Brotherly Love had also entered into a difficult interlude during which its industrial base was regarded as outdated and uncompetitive. Philadelphia declined from the third- to the fifth-largest city in the United States, while its social frictions worsened. White flight accelerated, dramatically reflected in census figures that recorded a further contraction in Philadelphia's population from 1,688,210 inhabitants in 1980 to 1,585,577 a decade later

and 1,517,550 by 2000. By then, there were almost 4.5 million living within the 150 newly incorporated cities, towns, or boroughs that composed the rest of its metropolitan area.

For further reading materials on the history of Philadelphia, as well as additional sources on North American and U.S. urban history, please consult the Select Bibliography at the end of this volume.

SAN FRANCISCO
Late-blossoming city that sprang up around one of the world's greatest natural harbors along the Pacific coast.

Antecedents (1542–1774)
After the Spaniards conquered the Aztec capital of Tenochtitlán in 1521 and fanned out to subdue its vassal kingdoms in central Mexico, they soon encountered more primitive and seminomadic tribes in the arid territories to its north, so they did not seek to penetrate and colonize much beyond the original core states. As a result, California remained unvisited by Europeans until a seaborne exploration by Juan Rodríguez Cabrillo mapped its coastline in the winter of 1542–1543, although without entering what would later become known as San Francisco Bay, nor attempting any nearby disembarkations.

Panoramic view across modern San Francisco. (Author's Collection)

Once the Spaniards' transpacific galleons began circulating between Acapulco and Manila in the late 1560s, a few passing vessels sighted the California shoreline during their return legs toward Mexico, although without actually approaching its unfamiliar shoal waters. The first descent occurred in June–July 1579, after the English privateer Francis Drake had pushed up the coast from Cape Horn and then careened his ship *Golden Hind* in a desolate cove a few miles north of the bay entrance. He ventured a short distance inland among the Miwok-speaking Penutian Indians and dubbed the region "Nova Albion" before departing across the Pacific for Mindanao. (Drake also left behind a commemorative plaque, which has never been found.)

The Manila galleon of Capt. Sebastián Rodríguez Cermeño was wrecked in "Drake's Bay" in 1595, its seventy survivors proceeding southeastward past the main harbor entrance in their launch. Yet despite another extended reconnaissance made by three Spanish ships and almost 200 men under Capt. Sebastián Vizcaíno in the winter of 1602–1603—who named Monterey Bay in honor of the reigning Mexican viceroy, Gas-par de Zúñiga y Acevedo, Conde de Monterrey, and proposed occupying it as a refuge for crippled galleons—the Crown did not endorse any colonizing effort until concern grew in Madrid about a Russian fur-trading outpost ensconced in Alaska during the mid-eighteenth century.

Fearful that such a toehold might be expanded so as to challenge Spain's unexercised claim over the Pacific Northwest, a counterexpedition was dispatched northward from Baja California early in 1769 by the energetic Crown *visitador* (inspector) José de Gálvez to rendezvous at San Diego that same July and found a military *presidio* (garrison), as well as a religious mission to begin indoctrinating the region's seminomadic fishermen, hunters, and gatherers. The next year a similar Spanish base was created farther north at Monterey, and both would be used to sustain the subsequent development of a chain of missions throughout the intervening territory, which was dubbed Nueva or Alta California—"New" or "Upper California," to distinguish it from the older communities at the tip of Baja California.

The coastal stretches visible from out at sea above Monterey offered an attractive contrast to the more arid shorelines of California's southern reaches, consisting of well-irrigated forests and pasturelands with abundant wildlife. Consequently, after the veteran Mexican frontier officer Juan Bautista de Anza reached Monterey in April 1774 with a group of colonists that he had led overland from the province of Sonora, preparations began to create yet another outpost inside the huge bay still farther to the north.

Stillborn Foundation (1775–1810)

The royal packet *San Carlos* of Lt. Juan Manuel de Ayala became the first Spanish vessel to enter through the milewide harbor entrance on 24 July 1775, spending the next two months making a detailed survey of its extensive shorelines and waterways before departing to report favorably to the Crown about its potential use as a future port. De Anza also arrived overland with some troops and a second group of Mexican settlers that same year, so that the San Francisco mission was founded by 1776.

For tactical considerations, a presidio was to be erected behind the red-rock hills and sand dunes at the northeastern tip of the bay's southern headland so as to overlook its entry and guard its anchorage, while a community called Yerba Buena was intended to evolve beneath its adobe walls. However, foreign enemies were nonexistent, and despite being heavily outnumbered by the seminomadic tribesmen who roamed the bayside, the most immediate concern for the few score Spanish settlers proved to be subsistence. Although some crops were planted and cattle would soon be imported from northern Mexico, the remote community had to rely upon packets sailing out of San Blas for their provisions throughout much of the first decade of Spanish rule.

Fortunately, the pastures round Yerba Buena proved to be ideally suited for grazing cattle, while many of the narrow coastal strips at the base of the Coast Range opposite were ripe for cultivation. Some colonists even explored as far inland as the San Joaquín and Sacramento valleys shortly after their arrival, yet did not relocate from the bayside, because much of that region was covered by a shallow lake dubbed Los Tulares. The Spaniards instead preferred clearing ranches around San Francisco Bay proper, retaining easy access to Yerba Buena's presidio, mission, and beaches without clustering into its town. The climate proved to be benign, albeit often producing nocturnal fogs, as well as considerable precipitation during the rainy seasons every November to March.

Yerba Buena was to remain Spain's northernmost base over the next few decades, with the exception of a short-lived occupation of Nootka (Vancouver Island). The title of capital for both Californias was conferred upon Monterey as early as 1777, while the entire territory became subordinated two years afterward to the *Comandancia de Provincias Internas* (Interior Provinces' Command), headquartered at Chihuahua in northern Mexico; judicial matters were referred to the even

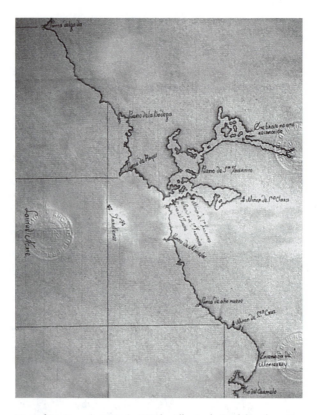

Map of San Francisco Bay in 1796 by Alberto de Córdoba, plus some of its adjacent coastline. (Archivo General de la Nación, Mexico)

more distant *Audiencia* of Guadalajara. Overland travel was severed because of the revolt of the Yuma Indians in 1781, so that the San Blas packets became California's sole means of communication. Isolated at the empire's most extreme fringe, San Francisco's garrison commanders often served as deputy governors for local affairs.

By 1790 there were still only approximately 220 Spaniards scattered from Yerba Buena as far southeast as Santa Clara, such a tiny population base as to preclude the emergence of any significant town. Their numbers more than doubled over the next decade, and, more important, they became largely self-sufficient thanks to increased yields from their cattle herds and wheat harvests—mostly belonging to the missions—so that a few sturdier edifices came to be erected at lonely Yerba Buena. A measles epidemic decimated the natives in 1806, and four years afterward communication with San Blas was halted by the eruption of Mexico's War of Independence from Spain.

Foreign Interest and Conquest (1811–1847)

Cut off from their previous suppliers in Mexico, the few thousand *Californio* residents turned to clandestine contraband trade with the foreign vessels that had begun flocking to the Pacific Northwest ever since Capt. James Cook had bartered for some sea otter pelts in 1778, then sold them at a huge profit in

China. San Francisco's authorities simultaneously upheld a wary adherence to Spain, especially where it coincided with their own local self-interest, such as resisting any direct territorial encroachments: when Russian traders built a permanent new base at Rossiya (Fort Ross) in the Coast Miwok area in 1812, for example, the Spaniards mustered enough strength to install their own counteroutpost at San Rafael five years afterward. A similar policy was maintained even after Mexico and California achieved their independence from the Crown in 1821; the San Francisco Solano Mission was created at Sonoma two years later, although plans for other inland centers at Tulares and elsewhere could not be realized.

President Andrew Jackson consequently made an offer in 1835 to purchase Upper California, including San Francisco Bay, which was refused by the Mexican government. Foreign interest in acquiring the vast, underdeveloped territory nonetheless intensified over the next few years, Great Britain and France manifesting designs of supporting their nationals dotted throughout California, although the greater percentage of American settlers seemed to ensure that the United States would eventually win out. When a Texas border war was rumored to have erupted between Washington and Mexico City in September 1842, Commo. Thomas ap Catesby "Tac" Jones rushed up the Pacific coast from Callao with the frigate *United States* and sloop *Cyane* to preemptively seize the main Mexican stronghold at Monterey on 19 October—only to discover the next day that no state of belligerency as yet existed.

Still, the U.S. consul at Monterey, Thomas O. Larkin, was instructed three years later to discreetly begin encouraging the 700 American residents in California to begin working toward their province's eventual secession from Mexico, so that when the explorer John C. Frémont—already famous as "the Pathfinder," and son-in-law to the influential Missouri senator Thomas Hart Benton, a close adviser to newly inaugurated President James K. Polk—approached Monterey with a sixty-man survey party in March 1846, he was ordered to leave California by its suspicious Mexican authorities and hastened on his way by a 350-man force under Gen. José María Castro.

However, because of Brig. Zachary Taylor's advance to the Texas border that same month, the government in Mexico City

Depiction of the handful of edifices that constituted newly named San Francisco, formerly Yerba Buena, March 1847. (California Historical Society)

declared war, to which Washington corresponded by 13 May 1846. When news of this long-anticipated outbreak reached Upper California, a half dozen American settlers seized 150 horses on 10 June destined for Castro's camp at Santa Clara; four days later, two score Americans arrested the province's titular Mexican commander, Gen. Mariano Guadalupe Vallejo, at his Sonoma home. Castro moved to crush this insurrection by dispatching 160 men northward across San Francisco Bay on 24 June; they were easily repulsed. Frémont, having returned into California, countered by leading some men across the bay on 1 July to spike the ten guns of the deserted San Joaquín Battery on its southern shore.

The rebellious American settlers at Sonoma under former Vermonter William B. Ide thereupon proclaimed independence from Mexico on 4 July 1846, devising a new country dubbed the "Bear Flag Republic"; three days afterward, U.S. commodore John D. Sloat set 85 Marines and more than 140 sailors ashore at Monterey to claim California. When the 22-gun, 210-man, 1,020-ton sloop USS *Portsmouth* of Cmdr. John B. Montgomery subsequently entered San Francisco Bay on the morning of 9 July and set 70 men ashore at Clark's Point to march into Yerba Buena, planting the Stars and Stripes before "the whole of the male population"—some 25 or 30 souls—in its windswept main square (modern Portsmouth Plaza), this event caused the newfangled republic to become dissolved that same afternoon, allegiance being formally sworn to the United States.

Some unease occurred two days later, when the British sloop *Juno* of Capt. F. J. Blake entered harbor, galvanizing Montgomery into manning its defenses for fear that Rear Adm. Sir George F. Seymour's Pacific squadron—spearheaded by the powerful 80-gun, 2,600-ton flagship HMS *Collingwood*—might attempt to appropriate some portions of California during this volatile transition from Mexican rule. *Juno*, however, merely observed the Americans' proceedings before exiting on 17 July 1846: Washington had already struck a diplomatic compromise with London by agreeing to recognize the 49th parallel as the future boundary with British Canada.

U.S. forces used Monterey as their base to subdue flickering Mexican opposition throughout the rest of the province, while Yerba Buena was officially renamed "San Francisco" as of 1847. Santa Anna's defeat resulted in the cession of California and all other northern Mexican territories to the United States the next spring, the last U.S. occupiers departing Mexico by the end of July 1848.

"Gold Rush" and Railhead Boom (1848–1905)

San Francisco's evolution, as well as that of all of California and the western United States, was to be dramatically spurred by the discovery of gold and the subsequent onrush of immigrants. In the nearby Sacramento Valley, a Swiss immigrant named John Sutter had earlier received a largely empty, 49,000-acre estate from the Mexican government that he continued to

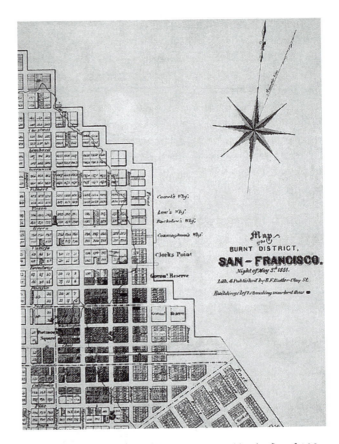

Map showing the portions of the city consumed by the fire of 4 May 1851. (California Historical Society)

administer under U.S. rule from his main settlement of Sutter's Fort (modern Sacramento). In the summer of 1847, he sent a carpenter named James Marshall with a crew of workmen up the South Branch of the American River as far as Coloma to build a sawmill, and when they loosed water into its race mill for the first time on 23 January 1848 to wash clear the debris, they noticed gold nuggets glinting in its bed next morning.

Worried about potential work disruptions and an influx of lawless prospectors, Sutter asked the construction crew at the mill to keep their discovery secret for another six weeks, so that his other laborers might at least not desert before the spring planting was done. Marshall's crew agreed, continuing their regular employment at the site while panning for gold on Sundays, until the sawmill was completed in March 1848. News of this strike had nonetheless trickled into San Francisco and been reported in both its newspapers, yet the 850 to 900 residents had not succumbed to any undue excitement. Yet when reports and samples began arriving from a second, richer lode being worked by several Mormons about 25 miles from Sutter's Mill—soon dubbed Mormon Diggings—it began to be realized that gold might be more plentiful and widespread than previously believed. By the end of April, men were slipping into

San Francisco from up the American River with caches of gold nuggets to replenish supplies and hasten back.

But the so-called California gold rush truly began when the Mormon businessman Sam Brannan visited San Francisco on 12 May 1848, brandishing a quinine bottle full of gold dust that he showed to as many people as possible, so as to excite interest and then sell supplies and mining equipment to prospectors disembarking at his strategically placed store on the landing below Sutter's Fort. Within two days fleets of boats were headed up the American River, and by the end of June it was estimated that fewer than 100 inhabitants remained in San Francisco. Even its municipal alcaldes (magistrates) had departed, along with its sheriff, while other California communities soon began to empty as well. Word spread rapidly as far as Hawaii, Oregon, Utah, and the Mexican state of Sonora, before finally reaching the eastern United States. President James K. Polk corroborated the wealth of this discovery in his annual address of 5 December, so that thousands of easterners also took ship for the 17,000-mile, six- to eight-month voyage round Cape Horn—or the riskier six-week traverse across the Isthmus of Panama.

Most vessels crowded with these so-called Argonauts converged upon San Francisco Bay, disgorging so many transients as of 1849 that the town quickly replenished the population it had lost to the mines, plus gaining many thousands more. Crude wooden-frame shanties and canvas tents sprawled along muddy thoroughfares in every direction, oftentimes supplemented by the beached ships themselves, whose crews had deserted upon gaining port. Severe fires raced through the ramshackle city on 4 May 1850, 14 June 1850, 17 September 1850, 4 May 1851, and 22 June 1851.

Throngs continued to disembark over the next three years, yet the vast majority of these amateurs who pressed up into the goldfields along the banks of the Sacramento and San Joaquin tributaries failed to find their fortunes, as only those operators who combined together to process many tons of ore a day through mechanical means succeeded in amassing significant amounts.

Thousands of individuals nevertheless settled and prospered in San Francisco itself, whose population was calculated to have swollen to 25,000 people by 1851, the city serving as the main depot for the masses of seaborne goods and equipment required inland. Miners would also return into the bustling bayside community to replenish their supplies and

View looking northwestward across the city's crowded waterfront and anchorage, 1855. (California Historical Society)

enjoy their profits, most often in its colorful array of taverns, gambling halls, or bordellos. One such visitor remembered San Francisco in his journal with these words: "Of all the cities in the world, this is the greatest one, composed of all nations and colors, and the hairiest set of fellows that ever existed." Lawlessness flourished in such a wide-open environment, to the extent that honest citizens banded together to form a Vigilance Committee and mete out rough justice to the gangs of toughs who dominated many neighborhoods. In 1859, the Comstock Lode was furthermore discovered in what is today Nevada, so that another onrush of prospectors headed up into the Sierra Nevada passes.

A major earthquake struck San Francisco on 21 October 1868, wreaking havoc among its structures—especially those built of unreinforced masonry or atop unstable landfills. Still, the huge volumes of wheat being harvested inland from the fertile Central Valley held the promise of immense future profits, coupled with the completion the next year of the transcontinental railroad emanating from Sacramento, whose operation was to be monopolized by four rich San Franciscan owners. Expectations for a new upsurge in prosperity were not to be immediately realized, though, as the sudden influx of cheaper eastern manufactures glutted local markets and collapsed wholesale prices, while the completion of the railroad itself had released thousands of workers into a saturated labor market. By 1875, San Francisco's building boom was winding down, although the city entered into a period of relative stability. As the waterfront area south of Market Street became increasingly commercialized with growing clusters of small factories, warehouses, and workshops, crowded residents began migrating into more attractive neighborhoods.

The quartet of wealthy railway barons—Leland Stanford, Mark Hopkins, Charles Crocker, and Collis Huntington—erected sprawling mansions atop the crest of the hill originally known as the California Street Hill, overlooking San Francisco. Being commonly referred to because of their huge fortunes as "nabobs," the title of ostentatiously extravagant governors of the Mogul empire in India, this term soon became shortened into "nobs," so that their elite enclave was dubbed Nob Hill. The railway owners' enormous resources not only allowed them to dominate far-flung economic interests through their monopoly of the Southern Pacific Railroad but also municipal and state politics. Their corrupt stranglehold over local offices came to be contested by such individuals as Adolph Sutro, who ran on an antimonopoly platform and was elected mayor of San Francisco in 1894. When Huntington tried three years later to defer repaying the millions in federal loans for the building of the transcontinental railroad, the U.S. Congress's refusal led the governor of California to proclaim a public holiday in celebration. In 1901, the novelist Frank Norris furthermore published his best-selling book *The Octopus* as a denunciation of the exploitation of California wheat farmers by Southern Pacific.

Yet by the early twentieth century, San Francisco had undoubtedly benefited by serving as the main sea outlet for this transportation network and emerged as a regional financial center and manufacturing hub.

Earthquake and Resurrection (1906–1929)

At 5:12 A.M. on Wednesday 18 April 1906 the city was rocked by a violent earthquake emanating from the Pacific and North American tectonic plates along the San Andreas Fault. Buildings throughout the city collapsed, gaping fissures opened in its streets, sidewalks buckled, and water and gas mains snapped. Within an hour, over fifty fires quickly began spreading among the thousands of damaged wooden structures, creating a firestorm that could not be combated because of the lost water pressure. Despite resorting to the desperate expedient of dynamiting some large buildings in order to check the advance of the flames, almost 4 square miles of San Francisco's central business and residential districts—encompassing 28,188 edifices spread among 497 blocks—were entirely lost, along with as many as 3,000 lives. The conflagration could not be entirely stemmed until a spring shower doused the smoldering embers on Saturday, 21 April.

Rescue crews dug through the rubble and eventually put up 200,000 tents at the Presidio and in Golden Gate Park to act as temporary shelters for the many thousands left homeless.

Bustling intersection below San Francisco's Call Building, ca. 1905. (Joseph Collier)

Smoldering ruins left by the devastating earthquake and fire of 18 April 1906. The gutted frame of the Call Building rears at left center, while the distant city hall dome can be faintly discerned at far right. (William Graham)

Municipal resources and private insurance companies could seemingly not cope with such cataclysmic devastation, despite the vast amounts of aid being rushed to the stricken city from throughout the nation and abroad. However, in an astonishing display of resilience, San Francisco was to be very swiftly rebuilt, a fact that prideful citizens commemorated by adopting a new city emblem, depicting a phoenix rising from the ashes. The old corrupt practices at city hall were also exposed and reformed by public-spirited San Franciscans, leading to the removal from office of officials who had previously profited from dishonest dealings with gas, electric, telephone, and water companies.

Hiram Johnson, a special assistant in the district attorney's office, as a result won the Republican nomination for governor in 1910 on the Progressive ticket, the hope being that he would clean up corruption in the state just as he had helped to do in San Francisco. That same year, the population for the port city was measured at 416,912 inhabitants, and five years later it was able to showcase its miraculous recovery by hosting the Panama Pacific International Exposition. The PPIE, as it was affectionately known, opened its gates on the morning of 20 February 1915, Mayor James "Sunny Jimmy" Rolph leading a procession of 150,000 eager patrons onto the grounds amid

the shrieks of factory whistles, clanging cable-car bells, and cannons booming from the Presidio. Over the next nine months, the exposition would attract 18 million visitors. When the United States entered World War I in 1917, U.S. Navy "boot camps" and installations around San Francisco Bay were vastly expanded to receive an influx of conscripts, and the city's influence expanded.

Depression (1930–1941)

Unfortunately, San Francisco's remarkable revival from its cataclysmic earthquake losses was to be abruptly curtailed by the worldwide effects initiated by the stock market crash of October 1929, which brought on the worst depression in the history of California or the nation. Businesses and banks closed their doors, while thousands of investors and depositors lost everything, even their homes. Thousands of unemployed workers and their families were reduced to living in makeshift encampments, one such village near downtown Oakland sheltering a couple of hundred squatters inside 6-foot sections of concrete sewer pipes stored aboveground. Desperate out-of-work laborers turned upon foreign workers, Filipinos and Asians being among the first in San Francisco to bear the brunt of such xenophobic riots.

Panoramic photograph of San Francisco's city square, reconstructed with remarkable speed by 1910. (Author's Collection)

Unemployment in the Golden State reached a staggering 28 percent by 1932, and the federal administration of newly elected Pres. Franklin D. Roosevelt tried to help by underwriting such massive public works projects as the constructions of both the San Francisco–Oakland Bay Bridge and Golden Gate Bridge next year. The former, an 8-mile structure recognized as the world's longest steel span upon its completion in November 1936, was hailed as an engineering marvel, although the particular challenges posed by extending the Golden Gate Bridge across the entrance of the bay proved even more formidable. One of its twin 746-foot towers had to be seated 65 feet below the ocean surface upon an offshore ledge before it was successfully inaugurated on 27 May 1937.

The state economy nevertheless remained so crippled that many Californians were still dependent upon public relief, and San Francisco had been the scene of a long and bitter strike starting in early May 1934, when the militant labor leader Harry R. Bridges of the International Longshoremen's Association demanded improved wages and working conditions, coastwide bargaining rights, and the establishment of union-controlled hiring halls. Employers and local officials denounced him as a dangerous radical, and on the morning of 5 July—remembered as "bloody Thursday"—a thousand police officers attempted to clear pickets from the waterfront so that strikebreakers might go to work at the docks. Sixty-four people were injured and two strikers were killed during the resultant melee, and the state governor sent in national guardsmen to prevent further violence. The ILA responded by calling for other unions to go on a general strike in support of the dockworkers, so that virtually all work in San Francisco and Alameda counties ceased for four days as of 16 July. Public opinion was alienated, yet the original waterfront strike was eventually resolved when federal arbitrators granted the ILA most of its demands. The city also witnessed an unusual calamity when the U.S. Navy's two-year-old, helium dirigible USS *Macon* was returning to its home-base of Moffett Field on the San Francisco peninsula on the evening of 12 February 1935, when it was caught in a rain squall off Point Sur. A freakish gust of wind collapsed its upper tail fin, ripping holes in three of its helium cells, so that the huge airship quickly lost altitude and hit the water. The mist-shrouded wreckage floated just long enough for all but two of its eighty-three crew members to escape before slipping beneath the waves.

The Depression gradually lost its economic grip as the decade progressed and the global economy revived, so that San

Shadow cast over the city by a passing dirigible, 1935. (Author's Collection)

Francisco was able to expend vast amounts a few years later in preparing for the Golden Gate International Exhibition, pumping millions of cubic yards of mud up from the bottom of the bay to form a special venue called Treasure Island, in honor of when Robert Louis Stevenson lived on Bush Street in the city. Over 10 million visitors streamed through its grounds between the exhibition's opening on 18 February 1939 and its closure that same October.

Modern Era (1942–Present)

The Japanese bombing of Pearl Harbor on 7 December 1941 not only drew the United States into World War II, it was to also feature San Francisco prominently during the forthcoming Pacific campaigns, as well as the economic expansion toward Asia in its aftermath. Another period of intense urban building characterized this phase in the city's history, beginning around 1960 and lasting for a quarter century, with the emergence of many taller skyscrapers. Notwithstanding the heavy earthquake that rattled through on 17 October 1989, spectacular growth continued all around the bay—for although the population within the old city confines remained static at an estimated 735,000 by 1994, the entire metropolitan area had swollen to 6.5 million.

For further reading materials on the history of San Francisco, please consult the Select Bibliography at the end of this volume; additional sources can be found in the reference section on North American and U.S. urban history.

ST. AUGUSTINE

Lonely coastal stronghold, which has the distinction of being the oldest European settlement within the modern boundaries of the United States.

Initial Probe (1513)

After being displaced as governor of Puerto Rico by a rival, the Spanish adventurer Juan Ponce de León organized a three-vessel expedition that materialized off this low stretch of shoreline on 27 March 1513, having traversed the Caicos and Bahamas archipelagos in quest of a mythical land called *Bimini*, which according to Indian legend had waters of marvelous curative powers: the so-called "Fountain of Youth." Because that particular date coincided with Easter Sunday—in Spanish, *Pascua Florida*—Ponce de León disembarked on 2 April and formally laid claim to this new territory as "Florida" six days later.

No colonization was immediately attempted, though, the explorer continuing south to round the peninsula and reconnoiter its western or Gulf side as well, before regaining Puerto Rico by 15 October 1513. Next year, Ponce de León traveled to Spain to receive a knighthood and appointment as governor of this newly discovered "island of Florida," but did not actually try to secure a foothold until spring of 1521—and then

only upon its Gulf side. Repulsed by Calo tribesmen, the badly wounded Ponce de León was conveyed into Havana to die that same June, after which his followers joined Hernán Cortés's more alluring campaign against the Aztecs of Mexico.

Foundation and Early Vicissitudes (1565–1594)

Sporadic efforts were made over the ensuing four decades to colonize Florida's peninsula, yet all concentrated upon its Gulf coast and ended in failure. No European tried to settle its Atlantic side until a trio of vessels under the *Huguenot* or "French Protestant" Jean Ribault of Dieppe installed a rival base camp at what is today Parris Island (South Carolina) in the summer of 1562. This toehold was soon deserted, but a follow-up expedition materialized on 22 June 1564 at the Saint John's River mouth (near modern Jacksonville) under his subordinate René Goulaine de Laudonnière, who disgorged 300 settlers and erected a triangular compound called "Fort Caroline" before enduring a year of disease, mutinies, starvation, and native hostility.

On 28 August 1565, Ribault arrived at Fort Caroline with an additional 600 Huguenot settlers aboard a half-dozen vessels, accompanied by a privateer ship from La Rochelle, plus two small Spanish prizes seized off Santo Domingo; but the implicit threat posed by this French presence beside the Bahama Channel—exit route for richly ladened, homeward-bound Spanish galleons emerging out of Havana—had also galvanized Madrid, so that a counterexpedition of 2,600 men and thirty vessels had been sent out under Adm. Pedro Menéndez de Avilés, Knight of the Order of Santiago.

Depleted by desertions and a storm, Menéndez's remaining ships appeared at dusk of 4 September 1565 to chase the anchored French vessels out to sea, then reversed course to another narrow entrance that he had spotted 35 miles farther south. A reconnaissance party was set ashore two days later, being well received by the local Timucuan chieftain Seloy, who gave the Spaniards his large, palm-thatched communal lodge (at the north end of what would soon become known as Santa Anastasia Island), which Capts. Andrés López Patiño and Juan de San Vicente fortified by digging a ditch "with a strong breastwork of earth and faggots." Realizing that this harbor constituted one of the few sheltered anchorages along the otherwise exposed coastline, Menéndez began ferrying troops, colonists, and equipment across its shallow sandbar from his heavy galleons, then came ashore himself amid salvos and musical fanfare on Saturday, 8 September, to found a municipality called *San Augustín de la Florida*—St. Augustine being the patron saint of his birthplace of Avilés in Spain.

Ribault had meanwhile taken the desperate gamble of hastening almost all his soldiers aboard his four largest ships—which had rejoined after their nocturnal escapade—to attempt a seaborne descent against Menéndez's position before it became too strong, but when the Huguenots came within sight of St. Augustine's entrance on 10 September 1565, they

Aerial photograph over modern St. Augustine. (Charles Rotkin/Corbis)

were driven southward by a storm. Six days later, the Spanish admiral advanced overland against Fort Caroline with 400 troops, overrunning it on the rainy morning of 20 September, butchering 112 hapless settlers and capturing 70 women and children, without suffering a single casualty. Only 27 survivors managed to flee through the marshes and swim out to join the 40 seamen aboard a pair of anchored vessels, getting under way for France by 25 September. Menéndez renamed Fort Caroline as Fort *San Mateo* or "Saint Matthew" in honor of the particular feast day on which this brutal assault had taken place, then installed Capt. Gonzalo de Villarroel as garrison commander with 300 troops.

Returning to St. Augustine, the admiral then learned that Ribault had been shipwrecked south of this stronghold, so that over the next several days, 600 survivors were pitilessly hunted down and exterminated by the Spaniards. Ribault's own party of 200 exhausted men eventually surrendered on 10 October, only to have their throats slit at a place 13.5 miles south of the Spanish base, forever remembered as *Matanzas* or "Slaughter."

As the sandy marshlands around St. Augustine and San Mateo seemed incapable of sustaining all 1,500 Spanish colonists, Menéndez allowed many to disperse to other tiny oases, before departing himself with three ships on 30 October 1565 to patrol the region for further enemies. The Ticumuans turned hostile during his absence and burned St. Augustine's log fort with flaming arrows early the next year, so that when the admiral returned, he and its *cabildo* or "town council" decided to erect a new fort at the very harbor entrance, 170 colonists toiling to complete this structure and install its artillery within ten days. However, as the sea quickly began "eating away" its foundations, Menéndez selected a more inland site on Santa Anastasia Island for a third fort in July 1566, after more reinforcements had arrived from Spain under Adm. Sancho de Arciénega (alternatively spellings: "Arciniega" or "Archiniega").

Menéndez sortied once again with his fleet that same October 1566, while St. Augustine's townspeople struggled to plant crops and breed livestock along the banks of its inner harbor. Disease also began taking a toll, and Jesuit missionaries had little success in converting Florida's fierce and seminomadic tribesmen, so that mutinies erupted and a supply ship was stolen, after which the fledgling colony was further shocked when the Gascon rover Dominique de Gourges's trio of vessels and 180 Huguenot rovers surprised the depleted garrison at San Mateo on 24 April 1568, killing 30 and capturing 38 of Villarroel's men when they attempted to flee under cover of darkness toward St. Augustine. To avenge Ribault's massacre, Gourges put all his prisoners to death before sailing away on 3 May.

Settlers soon began quitting Florida in disillusionment, less than 300 Spanish residents remaining by 1570 and reduced to such extreme want that the garrison at Santa Lucía (halfway between modern Fort Pierce and West Palm Beach) even ate their own belts and shoes, while the disgruntled soldiery at St. Augustine torched their fort. Because of the shrunken number of townspeople now left, it took garrison commander Diego Maldonado eight months to erect a new log-fort on the mainland opposite Santa Anastasia Island (modern North Beach), while St. Augustine's town council was furthermore suspended as of 1571 because of a lack of members.

Menéndez's sons-in-law Hernando de Miranda and Diego de Velasco tried to reanimate the moribund private colony by bringing their families and a few more settlers to Florida in 1573, while the Spanish Crown instructed Mexico's viceroys to bolster its populace by deporting undesirables, and the Franciscan Order supplanted the Jesuits as missionaries; yet the settlement's decline was not to be checked until the old admiral died at Santander (Spain) in September 1574, and his ownership rights reverted to the Crown.

Wishing to maintain this outpost for their own strategic reasons, imperial administrators at Madrid sent the royal *visitador* or "inspector" Baltasar del Castillo y Ahedo to tour St. Augustine in November–December 1576, followed by a second inspector in September–November 1578, who suggested that Florida's 150 troops be doubled in number and succored by regular shipments of *situados* or "subsidies" from the Mexican Exchequer via Havana, plus provisions, armaments, and clothing. Such assistance at least helped stabilize St. Augustine's economy, although the town did not recuperate its civilian standing, being instead declared a *real presidio* or "royal garrison." Prospects nonetheless brightened sufficiently for the remaining residents to plant maize fields and orchards around their community inside the bay, as well as to come to terms with the local natives.

But in the spring of 1585, Spain's relations with Elizabethan England deteriorated so badly that warnings were received that Sir Francis Drake intended to lead a large priva-teering sweep through the Antilles. His fleet burst upon Santo Domingo next January, spurring St. Augustine's Gov. Pedro Menéndez Márquez (nephew of its founder) to commence a 14-gun redoubt of cedar logs dubbed Fort San Juan del Pinillo, directly opposite the harbor entrance. Drake meanwhile devastated Cartagena (Colombia) and steered around Cuba on his homeward passage, wishing to assist Sir Walter Raleigh's recently established colony at Roanoke by attacking the Spanish outpost at Santa Elena (South Carolina). Unfamiliar with the Atlantic Seaboard, Drake's twenty-three large ships and nineteen lesser consorts chanced upon St. Augustine first, anchoring off its entry by evening of 6 June 1586.

Apprised from the beacon station at the harbor mouth, Menéndez Márquez mustered 80 troops inside Fort San Juan, while sending St. Augustine's 200 to 250 noncombatants inland by boat. More than a thousand British rovers forged ashore the next day under Drake and his land commander, Lt.-Gen. Christopher Carleill, advancing across the half-mile breadth of Santa Anastasia Island to install a battery in the dunes opposite Fort San Juan by nightfall. Outnumbered and distrustful of their native vassals, who had begun pillaging empty Spanish homes, the defenders abandoned their stronghold as British boat-parties stole across the harbor under cover of darkness, so that both the empty fort and town were taken without opposition on 8 June.

The invaders described St. Augustine as "a little town or village without walls, built of wooden houses." Local Indians were well treated, but bitter memories of Ribault's fate led the English Protestants to punish Menéndez's descendants: St. Augustine was sacked and torched when the occupiers withdrew four days later, even its fruit trees—"which were numerous and good"—being chopped down. Fort San Juan was also stripped of its artillery and everything of value before being set ablaze as well, so that Menéndez Márquez and his Spanish colonists returned to smoldering ruins, being left with nothing more than six hogsheads of flour, a little powder, plus "the clothes we stood in." A boat was sent to Havana to beg for "help in food, supplies and equipment, nails, iron, augers, axes, saws, smithy, in order to reestablish the settlement and fortify it." Such assistance was soon provided, the Cuban Gov. Gabriel de Luján even suggesting that St. Augustine's women and children might be temporarily evacuated to Havana.

The survivors meanwhile extemporized wooden shelters, while San Juan de Pinillos was hastily replaced by a new log-stronghold called Fort San Marcos, although it was hoped that the Crown would provide masons to tap the *coquina* quarries recently discovered on Santa Anastasia Island to create a stouter citadel. (This material consisted of sandstone impregnated with shells, malleable enough to be cut and shaped upon its removal from lagoons, yet that hardened dramatically after protracted exposure to the sun and air.) A town gradually re-emerged, its new Franciscan convent being completed by 1588.

Permanent Configuration (1595–1701)

Enough confidence and prosperity were regained that Gov. Domingo Martínez de Avendaño sent Hernando de Mestas as an emissary to Spain five years later to suggest moving the fort "140 paces nearer the town" and constructing it entirely of stone, so as to provide the unwalled community with a reassuring stronghold. This proposal was approved by 1595, so that two stonecutters and a mason were hired from Havana, and a permanent new grid pattern was laid out so as to cluster St. Augustine's church, six-bed hospital, fish market, public well, and approximately 120 shops and dwellings under the protective bulk of a triangular, moated castle at the northern tip of its mainland peninsula.

Unfortunately, this fortification project was suspended when a hurricane and tidal surge occurred on 22 September 1599, the town being "entirely flooded and many houses knocked down." Disheartened by this latest calamity, residents talked of relocating to a new site, although after an evaluation by yet another royal inspector, they chose to remain. The Crown's resolve to sustain St. Augustine was also reinvigorated after a rival English colony was founded at Virginia in 1607, so that payrolls and supplies for its military and Church personnel were maintained—albeit erratically.

The tiny and remote frontline outpost enjoyed several decades of relative peace, during which its community took permanent root as long-serving Spanish soldiers began intermarrying among native women, so that the immediate environs became pacified and modest farming, fishing, and barter could develop. Franciscan missionary work into the interior furthermore became increasingly effective, making such

Crude map of the reconstituted town and its proposed new stone castle, February 1595; north is toward right. Because of a major flood four and a half years later, this fortification project was deferred until 1672. (Archive of Indies, Seville)

inroads among once-hostile tribesmen that by 1655, fifty friars presided over a string of two score friendly villages radiating north as far as St. Catherine's Island (Georgia) and across the peninsula to the Apachicola River, encompassing 26,000 native vassals. Outbursts occasionally occurred, such as the Timucuan reaction in May 1656 against Gov. Diego de Rebolledo's orders concerning food deliveries into St. Augustine, but were swiftly put down.

More worrisome was to be the onset of Caribbean buccaneering during the latter decades of the seventeenth century, as these roving mercenaries—unconstrained by European conventions—sought out "soft" targets such as St. Augustine. The Jamaican rover John Davis struck in 1668, prompting Madrid to augment the garrison from 300 to 350 soldiers and authorize the replacement of Fort San Marcos's old wooden ramparts with stone walls. This project took on greater urgency after the English colony of Carolina was furthermore established in April 1670, posing such a potential challenge to Spanish sovereignty along the eastern seaboard that Gov. Juan Menéndez Márques ventured northeast from St. Augustine that same August with three ships and fourteen piraguas or "dugouts" in a vain attempt to mount an attack.

Maj. Manuel de Cendoya succeeded as governor next year and initiated construction of St. Augustine's stone Castillo or "Castle" of San Marcos by October 1672, ferrying *coquina* blocks across from Santa Anastasia Island to complete two seaward bastions to a height of 11 feet by the time he died the next March. Work was reanimated after the French *flibustier* Capt. Abraham Bréhal—seconded by the New York freebooters John Markham and Jan Corneliszoon, plus Thomas Paine and Conway Wooley—stole across from the Bahamas into Matanzas Inlet with their five ships and 300 men in March 1683, seizing one of three watchtowers and looting the countryside before withdrawing. (This descent provoked a Cuban counter-raid against the Bahamas that same May.) Another buccaneer attack portended when a captured Spanish galliot under Nicolas Brigaut approached Matanzas under false colors on 30 April 1686, hoping to gather intelligence for the pirate chieftain Grammont, lurking farther south with his 180-man flagship *Hardi* and a sloop, but Brigaut was wrecked in heavy weather and Grammont driven north three days later to be lost with all hands.

St. Augustine's defenders mounted their own counterstrike by dispatching a galley and two piraguas that same August 1686 with 100 troops, plus native and mulatto auxiliaries, to raze Anglo-Scottish establishments in South Carolina, threatening Charleston itself before two of their vessels were lost in a hurricane and Capt. Tomás de León was drowned. (The Carolinians wished to retaliate by issuing commissions to two French privateers, but were forbidden by their newly arrived Gov. James Colleton.) The veteran Spanish soldier Juan de Ayala Escobar was furthermore dispatched from St. Augustine to Madrid early in 1687 to request additional aid from the Crown, as well as an overhaul of the unreliable support provided from Mexico.

Spain and England were allied during the War of the League of Augsburg or King William's War, which erupted in Europe in the spring of 1689, so that St. Augustine was not invested by Carolina forces. The total population for its garrison and town was measured at 1,444 people that same year, while its Castillo de San Marcos was considerably strengthened over the ensuing seven years. Yet when Anglo-Spanish relations deteriorated early the next century, fears of a potential British colonial offensive prompted Gov. José de Zúñiga y la Cerda to again send Ayala Escobar in March 1702 to Madrid to request help.

Regional hostilities commenced when a Creek war party, abetted by English traders, exterminated the North Florida mission of Santa Fe de Toloco in May 1702; Governor de Zúñiga retaliated by dispatching 800 Apalache allies into Creek territory under Capt. Francisco Romo de Uriza, who met defeat at the Flint River. Carolina's Gov. James Moore thereupon disembarked at the Saint John's River mouth with 580 militiamen under Col. Robert Daniel and 370 Yamasee allies by the end of October, laying waste to everything as they advanced against St. Augustine by both sea and land.

Frontline Stronghold (1702–1762)

Lookouts sighted Moore's approaching thirteen vessels on the morning of 7 November 1702, so that the town and its 400 defenders under elderly *sargento mayor* or "garrison commander" Enrique Primo de Rivera braced for an assault. Next day, the small frigate *Gloria* was able to slip down toward the Matanzas exit to carry word of this impending assault to Havana. On 9 November, De Zúñiga learned from two Apalache scouts that Daniel's land column was also nearing, so that more than 1,400 people and several hundred livestock crowded into the Castillo de San Marcos, while adjacent buildings were razed to clear a field of fire. Daniel's army entered the deserted town on 10 November, establishing their headquarters in its Franciscan convent; yet they lacked heavy artillery to batter a breach in the stone castle, so instituted a loose investment while Moore detached Daniel to procure a siege train from Jamaica.

A lengthy stalemate ensued, the Carolinians digging trenches and exchanging shots with the fort until they were resupplied by a British brigantine and sloop on Christmas Day 1702, causing morale within San Marcos to sag, but the defenders' spirits revived when four Spanish relief ships were sighted offshore two days later, having been dispatched from Havana with 212 troops under Capt. Lope de Solloso. Moore thereupon torched St. Augustine's buildings and abandoned four vessels in the harbor before retreating overland from Vilano Beach by dawn of 30 December.

Casualties had been light on both sides, yet material losses were considerable, more than forty of St. Augustine's buildings having been destroyed, including its main church and convent.

Residents were reduced to living in tents and shacks, as well as being afflicted by a smallpox outbreak, so that the community struggled to survive. Even special funds provided from ecclesiastical sources in Mexico and Guatemala would be inadequate to replace its church, which was not rebuilt for another three decades, so that Masses had to be celebrated in the crowded confines of Nuestra Señora de la Leche Hermitage.

Worse still, the town's defensive string of northern missions vanished when Moore and 1,500 Creek allies ruthlessly exterminated the Ayubale outpost in January 1704, carrying 325 surviving families off as slaves. Another 1,300 tribesmen meekly migrated into British-controlled Savannah (Georgia), while thousands more simply melted into the wilderness, so that the Spanish garrisons at Fort San Luis and San Marcos de Apalache had to be withdrawn as well by mid-July, so that the borderlands passed under the control of English traders. The Franciscans' patiently crafted network had dissolved and would never recuperate as the order became riven by dissent between Spanish-born and Creole clergymen, never again exerting the same influence in the colony. Starvation spread as well, Florida's best agricultural pockets having been lost with this native dislocation, while St. Augustine's few tilled plots were insufficient to sustain its populace, and lone hunters or fishermen fell prey to roving war bands.

Defensively, new bulwarks were raised at the northern and southern entrances of St. Augustine's harbor, while a new cavalry company and naval patrols were also created, and the Crown dispatched a little ordinance and equipment, while trying to ensure that payrolls and provisions arrived more promptly from Mexico. When six allied French privateer vessels appeared from Havana under Capt. Jacques Lefebvre in late August 1706, bearing 200 Cuban troops and two fieldpieces under Estéban de Berroa for an attack against Charleston, St. Augustine's new Gov. Francisco de Córcoles y Martínez, could only furnish a few score additional men, and this expedition ended in failure.

Even after peace with England was restored in 1713, the town still struggled to recuperate, royal building funds being diverted into the purchase of such essentials as food. Circumstances were further complicated when the Yamasee—angry at being victimized by dishonest Carolina traders and encroachments upon their lands—revolted against their former British allies in April 1715 and met defeat, so that bands of Yamasee, Creek, Choctaw, and Cherokee refugees furthermore began moving into St. Augustine's already overcrowded jurisdiction by next January, straining resources and spreading disease. It was even proposed that Florida's gutted capital be transferred to Apalache, although this project ended in disappointment, while the English meanwhile encroached ever nearer by creating Georgia.

A smallpox epidemic claimed 300 lives in unhappy St. Augustine in late 1727, after which a punitive expedition of 100 English militiamen and 200 native allies disembarked under Col. John Palmer at the mouth of the Saint John's River in March 1728, destroying the fortified Yamasee village of Nombre de Dios and chasing its survivors into the Castillo de San Marcos. Desperate because of their unremitting neglect, the forlorn garrison sought to ease their poverty by making a few discretionary purchases from such English merchants as New York's William Walton in 1731, but this tactic—technically illegal in the eyes of the Crown—was expanded so blatantly under Gov. Francisco del Moral Sánchez that spiteful residents wrote to Madrid to complain in the autumn of 1736, declaring that a half dozen English vessels could be found moored in the harbor at any time, while "English merchants walked the streets of the Florida capital as if they were in London." (Their cheap goods had also driven several Spanish shopkeepers out of business.)

Consequently, Manuel José de Justís suddenly materialized from Cuba on 11 March 1737, bearing a royal order to supplant Moral, who resisted for two days—even seeking sanctuary in the Franciscan convent—before being deported to stand trial. Madrid attempted to improve economic conditions by authorizing a fur-trading station at Apalache, as well as by encouraging the sale of local produce such as tar, pitch, and masts into Havana. The garrison was also reinforced by 400 Cuban troops and more than 90 skilled laborers, while the auxiliary bishop, Francisco de San Buenaventura Tejada (better known as the "Bishop of Trical," presumably being his nominative see from ancient times), visited St. Augustine and succeeded in having its church roof and belfry completed.

However, progress was halted by the outbreak of the War of Jenkins's Ear in late 1739, so that a British expedition once again invested the town the next summer. Initially, 300 regulars under Gov. James Edward Oglethorpe of Georgia and 400 South Carolina provincials under Dutch-born Col. Alexander van der Dussen seized Fort Mosa (an earthen redoubt encircling a deserted black village a mile north of St. Augustine) on 13 June 1740, hoping to lure Gov. Manuel de Montiano y Luyando out from behind San Marcos's stone ramparts; his 366-man garrison and more than 1,000 noncombatants refused to sally, though, so Oglethorpe temporarily retired.

The British resumed their offensive when Van der Dussen landed at Point Quartell or Point San Mateo at St. Augustine's harbor mouth with 500 South Carolinians on 17 June 1740, after which 137 rangers, highlanders, and Indians under Col. John Palmer reoccupied Fort Mosa five days later, while Oglethorpe disembarked on Santa Anastasia Island with 200 more men of his own 42nd Regt. of Foot, plus 200 seamen and a like number of Indians, on 23 June. Their intent was to weaken the defenders by cutting off all supplies, but at dawn of Sunday, 26 June, 300 Spaniards under Capt. Antonio Salgado surprised the English occupiers of Fort Mosa, slaughtering 63 men—including Palmer—before marching two score prisoners back into their citadel.

Spanish morale soared, so that when Oglethorpe called upon De Montiano to surrender four days later, he was rebuffed. The British rearranged their siege lines, but a storm on 7 July 1740 drove the blockading warships of Commo. Vincent Pearse out to sea, so that seven Cuban relief boats could slip into the Matanzas River to deliver 300 men and much-needed succor into Castillo de San Marcos one week later. Discouraged, the besiegers started melting away as of 15 July, after which the triumphant Spaniards spent that next year erecting a small stone blockhouse just inside Matanzas Inlet, while privateers brought numerous English prizes into St. Augustine's harbor.

Early in June 1742, a storm-tossed Spanish fleet arrived from Havana for a major counteroffensive against the British outpost of Saint Simon's Island (Georgia); De Montiano quickly marshaled more than 50 craft bearing 1,950 men, setting sail on 1 July to ravage this enemy shoreline. His expedition returned in August, closely pursued by Oglethorpe with a dozen warships, who attempted to force St. Augustine's entrance on 9 September, then the Matanzas River the next day, only to be repelled.

Oglethorpe returned stealthily on 17 March 1743 to establish a base on the southern banks of the Saint John's River (near modern Mayport), from which a Creek war party stole upon St. Augustine and ambushed a Spanish boat bearing 40 laborers, scalping 5 before being driven off by San Marcos's guns. Oglethorpe then tried to surprise its garrison by concealing his 200–300 regulars and provincials 3 miles north on the evening of 27 March, only to be betrayed by a deserter. Finally, two bands of Indian allies probed the town's outskirts without result, after which the British governor materialized off Santa Anastasia Island with 80 troops aboard four vessels on the afternoon of 8 April, sailing away for Georgia a few days later because of the high seas.

Although not directly threatened again for the remaining five and a half years of this conflict, St. Augustine—whose peacetime allotment of 350 soldiers was strained by an extra 700 troops and laborers—suffered from a lack of supplies, only Spanish privateers providing some solace by bringing in prizes. Once peace was restored, manpower was reduced, and the needs of St. Augustine's 2,446 permanent troops and inhabitants could once again be supplemented by English traders. The Crown also tried to improve living conditions by enhancing subsidies, as well as by paying for the reedification of Castillo de San Marcos by 1756. The first barrels of pitch and tar were also exported to Havana that same spring, while Florida's population was modestly reinvigorated when Madrid facilitated the immigration of over 700 Canary Islanders into the colony by 1761, in hopes of redeveloping farms as far inland as Apalache.

Madrid even agreed to approve creation of a *cabildo* or "town council" for St. Augustine, although its elderly Acting-Governor Alonso de Cárdenas, demurred at doing so immediately because there were not enough "distinguished men with a long record of community service" available—as required by law—

to be appointed to fill its nine positions: two alcaldes or "magistrates," six *regidores* or "councilors," plus a single clergyman. He was then superseded as of 4 March 1762 by Col. Melchor Feliú, while war had erupted back in Europe, with the British unleashing a huge expedition against Havana three months later. St. Augustine was cut off by Royal Navy operations, then learned in mid-March of the next year that according to the terms of the peace treaty signed at Paris, the Cuban capital was to be restored to Spain in exchange for Florida, so that St. Augustine would be surrendered to the English.

British Interlude (1763–1783)

Ambrosio Funes de Villalpando, Conde de Ricla, reached Havana on 6 July 1763 to reassume Spanish rule from its British captors, while the departing Gen. William Keppel directed Capt. John Hodges to take possession of St. Augustine with his 1st Regt. of Foot. They arrived on 21 July and received the garrison from Acting-Governor Feliú, Hodges being superseded nine days later by Maj. Francis Ogilvie of the 9th "Norfolk" Regt. of Foot. All Spanish citizens who did not wish to remain under British rule were to have the expenses of their passage to Havana defrayed by the Crown and were granted eighteen months' grace to sell their properties to British buyers.

The first of 3,100 Spanish subjects departed St. Augustine for Havana aboard three schooners on 12 April 1763, while the laborious task of ferrying cannons and other heavy equipment to vessels anchored outside its shallow bar slowly proceeded. (After two centuries of Spanish occupation, the latter still continued to pose such an obstacle to navigation that Ogilvie wrote his superior, Gen. Thomas Gage, that same December, stating that if a pilot, large boat, and schooner were not procured to aid ships' entry, St. Augustine would "have no trade.") Acting-Governor Feliú and the parish priest Juan José Solana were among the last 350 evacuees to sail away aboard the seven vessels that departed on 21 January 1764; less than twenty Spanish subjects remained behind to corral the king's scattered horse herds from the nearby woodlands. The ex-comptroller Juan José Elixio de la Puente also returned on 7 May to attempt to sell almost three-quarters of the 400 Crown, Church, and private properties within the town, eventually turning the bulk over to Jesse Fish, resident agent of the William Walton Exporting Company of New York.

Consequently, when the Scottish-born Col. James Grant arrived as East Florida's first civilian governor in February 1764, he was irked to find that everything within his capital "was claimed as private property except the Governor's house and the hospital; I have (therefore) declared the Bishop's palace, the convent of Franciscans, and all the churches to be the King's, and also some other houses about which I picked up information from the officers who came to take possession of the town."

As a result, the bishopric became transformed into the

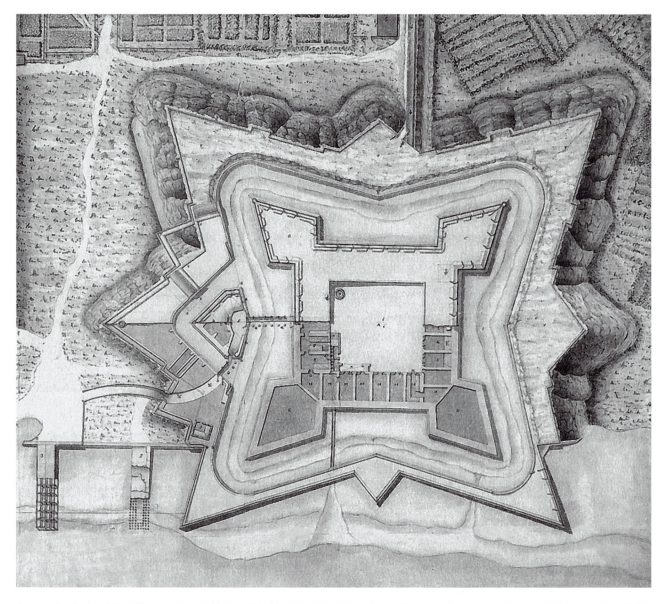

Diagram by the Spanish military engineer Pablo Castelló of Castillo de San Marcos's condition upon being surrendered to British control on 21 July 1763; north is toward right. (Servicio Geográfico del Ejército, Madrid)

Anglican Church, while Nuestra Señora de la Leche Hermitage was converted into a hospital, and the Franciscan convent became the "St. Francis" army barracks. Rev. John Forbes was also appointed Anglican minister in May 1764, while Enoch Hawksworth became St. Augustine's first English schoolmaster.

Development of East Florida proved to be slow, though, trade through its capital being hampered by the shallow sea entrance: only 35 tiny vessels visited St. Augustine in 1764, augmenting modestly to 52 three years later and 56 by 1768. To compensate, the London-based Board for Trade and Plantations auspiced construction of the King's Road into Georgia, and by February 1768 Johnstone was able to write to his

friend, Brig. Frederick Haldimand, "Our plantations here go fast, numbers of people have of late crowded into the province, and I can count from 600 to 800 working slaves in the country, which is a tolerable beginning—and I am looking out for Dr. (Andrew) Turnbull with 500 Greeks every day."

This latter comment referred to a Scottish medical doctor who had served as British consul in Greece, married a local merchant's daughter, and was now bringing 1,400 Greek and Minorcan refugees to found a community dedicated to indigo cultivation 70–75 miles south of St. Augustine, to be named "New Smyrna" in honor of his Greek wife's birthplace. St. Augustine also welcomed the transfer of more than 3,000 redcoats from West Florida that same October–December, being quartered in shacks outside the town until ordered back to Pensacola, Mobile, and Natchez early in 1770.

When the American Revolutionary War erupted in the spring of 1775, St. Augustine remained a staunchly Loyalist outpost, harried by rebel privateers out of South Carolina until the Royal Navy schooner *St. Lawrence* was assigned to its station that same October. Invasion scares gripped the small town almost every summer, although exports of lumber, hides, tar, pitch, indigo, coffee, rice, and salt continued—mostly to British-held Charleston. East Florida's capital even experienced a modest population boom after the New Smyrna agricultural colony collapsed when 450 indentured Minorcan workers rose against their intolerable conditions and fled with their families into St. Augustine to be granted asylum by Gov. Patrick Tonyn in the summer of 1777. Waves of Loyalist refugees also began arriving as monarchist fortunes faltered throughout the South, most especially after West Florida's conquest by the Spaniards in 1781, plus Georgia's and South Carolina's fall to rebel forces the next year.

The latter colonies contributed 2,925 displaced whites and 4,448 blacks to East Florida's populace, swelling the total to more than 17,000 residents. A contemporary observer estimated the number of resettled monarchists and their dependents at "upwards of 10,000," most of whom initially congregated either in St. Augustine or near the mouth of the Saint John's River, which they developed into a new community called "Saint John's Bluff." The capital also expanded as wood cabins with palmetto roofs were extemporized around its periphery to accommodate this sizable influx of people, until it became known late in May 1782 that East Florida was to be evacuated to make way for Spanish reoccupation.

Lack of shipping temporarily postponed this withdrawal, and St. Augustine even acquired a few urban niceties, such as a few fine neoclassical edifices and its first newspaper: the *East-Florida Gazette,* which was issued in February 1783 by the Charleston refugee Dr. William Charles Wells. But the necessity of abandoning the colony in compliance with the European peace treaty became inevitable, so that disappointed residents began looking elsewhere: on 30 March 1783, a 24-year-old militia colonel exiled from Beaufort (South Carolina) and named Andrew Deveaux sortied with 70 followers, being joined at sea two days later by a pair of well-armed privateer brigantines to reconquer the Bahamas.

Spanish Reoccupation (1784–1821)

Peace was declared and St. Augustine's evacuation order was repeated in earnest by April 1783, after which a Spanish delegation arrived to initiate the handover. Although departing British residents had the right to sell their properties to Spaniards, there were no buyers, and because of the shallow bar, many emigrants preferred going north to Amelia Harbor near the Saint Mary's River mouth to load their goods, so that the town began to empty.

A Spanish expedition finally quit Havana on 11 June 1784 under Brig. Vicente Manuel de Zéspedes y Velasco, bringing a few thousand settlers and the Irish Catholic "Hibernia" Regt. of Capt. Carlos Howard to reoccupy East Florida. Zéspedes arrived outside St. Augustine's bar aboard the brig *San Matías* by 26 June, coming ashore the next day to officially assume office as Governor on 12 July. Two days later, he advised the few thousand remaining Britons that they might remain as Spanish subjects if they converted to Catholicism, and three months afterward reported to Madrid that 1,992 foreigners were still left in and around town—of whom 656 intended to stay permanently, 155 were undecided, and the rest determined to emigrate.

Troops had meanwhile garrisoned Castillo de San Marcos north of town and the barracks and hospital to its south, while Crown functionaries and well-to-do citizens occupied the plaza and San Carlos Street. Merchants—the most prominent being ex-British Loyalists—lived along the waterfront, while the slaughterhouse and public market were at the main square's east end. Some new construction was undertaken by the Spaniards, a five-year basilica-cathedral project being commenced as of 1786, while the old wooden lookout tower at the harbor entrance was replaced by a twelve-sided beacon. That same year, a census found that St. Augustine's civilian population now consisted of only 772 people: 216 Spaniards, Cubans, or returned Floridians; 87 white foreigners, mostly ex-British Loyalists; and 469 Minorcans who, having previously been Spanish subjects, adapted quite well to the new regime and lived as fishermen or tradesmen in the northwestern sector (modern Cuna Street).

St. Augustine's last Spanish-era church, erected in 1791, as it appeared, ca. 1864. (Miller and Lanier, *Photographic History of the Civil War*)

The community once again depended upon subsidies from distant Mexico, but also maintained commercial contact with neighboring provinces, especially through St. Augustine's Anglo firm of Panton, Leslie and Company, which was permitted to send a pair of ships annually to trade in British ports. Complaints against this monopoly caused the privilege to be broadened in 1793 so as to include all St. Augustinian merchants, trading solely with nations allied or friendly to Spain. English trade diminished after Madrid realigned itself with Revolutionary France in August 1796 and declared war against London on 6 October, so that American traffic came to predominate—especially with Charleston, which soon surpassed Havana as St. Augustine's largest trading partner, plus Savannah, Philadelphia, and New York. East Florida became economically dependent upon the United States as a result, exporting produce such as oranges, lumber, and cotton while importing fish, grains, and foodstuffs.

St. Augustine's populace moreover began to diversify because of a steady stream of French, Irish, British, American, and black migrants—including the rebel Haitian chieftain Georges Biassou and his followers—who arrived as of 1796–1797. The total population of St. Augustine and its outlying villages rose to 1,592 people by 1792, the town itself embracing 851 whites, 85 free mulattoes and blacks, plus 312 slaves.

When war erupted between the United States and Great Britain in the spring of 1812, Washington asked the Spanish authorities to permit an American occupation of East Florida, so as to deny its neutral anchorages to Royal Navy warships. Although refused, U.S. forces nonetheless broke the northern border and seized Fernandina, and sympathizers organized a breakaway "government" at Saint Mary's. When U.S. Marine Capt. John Williams advanced upon St. Augustine that same September with a company of marines and militiamen, he was defeated by black and Indian ambushers at Twelve Mile Swamp, after which Washington repudiated its occupation strategy and in February 1813 canceled a planned invasion by militia Maj.-Gen. and ex-Sen. Andrew Jackson.

Almost unnoticed in this tense atmosphere, the promulgation of Spain's first constitution in 1812—a liberal document that promised restive Spanish American colonies limited self-rule, plus other reforms—had allowed for the creation of St. Augustine's first town council in 240 years, although practical constraints restricted its effectiveness. Friction with the United States resurged once peace with Britain was restored in 1815, until Pres. James Monroe authorized American forces from Fort Scott (southwestern Georgia) on 16 December 1817 to pursue hostile Seminoles back deep into Spanish territory. The aggressive Jackson assumed overall command early the next March, striking south with a 3,500-man army that drove through the tribe lands and seized the Spanish outpost of San Marcos de Apalache by early April 1818, followed by Pensacola, while directing his subordinate Brig. Edmund P. Gaines to capture St. Augustine as well.

Map of St. Augustine and its coastline in August 1817, by the Spanish military engineer Capt. Francisco Cortazar; north is toward left. (Servicio Histórico Militar, Madrid)

Such high-handed action met with disapproval in Washington, so that Monroe offered to restore Florida to Spain in August 1818. However, that country's royal ministers—distracted by their losing efforts to resist the rising tide of rebellions in other, much more valuable New World viceroyalties—agreed the next year to sell the peripheral, unprofitable, and increasingly untenable Florida peninsula back to the United States for several million dollars.

Antebellum and Civil War Eras (1821–1865)

Jackson assumed office as interim governor at Pensacola as of June 1821, while the 4th U.S. Artillery Regt. arrived to occupy St. Augustine's Castillo de San Marcos, which was renamed "Fort Marion" in honor of South Carolina's Revolutionary War hero, Lt.-Col. Francis Marion—the fabled "Swamp Fox." That same autumn, a yellow-fever epidemic swept through the town, so many lives being lost that a new public burial ground had to be created just north of its city gate (later becoming known as the "Huguenot" Cemetery).

Congress formally recognized the newly constituted "Territory of Florida" as of 30 March 1822, after which Col. José Coppinger y Gámarra—the last Spanish governor—withdrew with his men to Havana. St. Augustine failed to flourish under its new U.S. administration, though, as its narrow harbor and sparse hinterland offered relatively poor prospects for homesteaders entering the region. The census of 1830 recorded an urban populace of only 2,544 residents, subcategorized as 1,335 whites, 172 free "colored," plus 1,037 slaves. Uncertainties unleashed with the eruption of the Second Seminole War late in 1835 compounded the city's lack of allure, although the U.S. government's efforts to sustain Fort Marion's garrison and military forays into the peninsula did indirectly benefit the city—most especially through improvements and extensions of steamboat service across its bar and into adjacent waterways.

St. Augustine's population nonetheless declined to 2,352 people by 1840 and a mere 1,938 ten years later, as other areas of Florida continued to prove more amenable. The forlorn city was therefore scarce contested when Florida became one of the first Southern states to secede from the Union in January 1861, Fort Marion being peacefully occupied by rebel militia. After hostilities erupted in earnest that same spring, Commo. Samuel F. Du Pont seized Hilton Head (South Carolina) in October with his federal fleet, then detached Cmdr. C. R. P. Rodgers early in 1862 to do the same at St. Augustine.

Already weakened by the extensive Union blockades and without any hope of Confederate reinforcement, its few defenders withdrew upon Rodgers's approach, taking Fort Marion's light artillery with them, as well as more than 400 civilian sympathizers—approximately one-sixth of the city's total population. Those who stayed behind hoisted a white flag over one of the fort's bastions as the federal squadron sailed into their harbor on the evening of 8 March 1862, and the mayor met Rodgers upon his disembarkation, conducting him to city hall to meet with the assembled municipal officials. The commander assured them that their local authority would be respected, and the Stars and Stripes were duly raised over Fort Marion; the mayor even temporarily assigned guards to hold the stronghold until federal troops could arrive and properly secure it.

Rodgers reported to his superiors that there remained in town "many citizens who are earnestly attached to the Union, a large number who are silently opposed to it, and a still larger number who care very little about the matter." The Union garrison held Fort Marion for the duration of this struggle, as well as patrolling the nearby Saint John's River. A feeble Confederate advance against the city was easily repulsed on 30 December 1863, but a federal counter-offensive into the interior of the state early the next year also failed when the small Union army disembarked at Jacksonville met defeat at Clustee on 20 February 1864. Federal warships moreover proved powerless to prevent small Confederate blockade-runners nicknamed "wildcatters" from making runs to and from the neutral Bahamas, so that St. Augustine stagnated as an isolated federal foothold until the Civil War concluded a year later.

Reconstruction and Tourism Evolution (1866–Present)

The city emerged from this prolonged occupation yet more diminished, its civilian population being measured at only

Fort Marion's inner courtyard under Union occupation, ca. 1864; note the stacked artillery rounds and tents pitched atop the encircling ramparts. (Miller and Lanier, *Photographic History of the Civil War*)

1,700 inhabitants as late as 1870. A few innovations were attempted, such as the inauguration of a new lighthouse at its harbor mouth four years later, but St. Augustine remained such an isolated coastal garrison town that hostile western Indians were even brought to Fort Marion to serve out their imprisonments as of 1875.

Five years afterward, the city's population had painstakingly rebounded to 2,295 residents, whose fortunes would begin to improve thanks to the regional development of the Florida East Coast Railway Company, as well as an upsurge in tourism all along the Atlantic Seaboard. For decades, winter-weary northern tourists had ventured south to enjoy vacations in the sun, and St. Augustine's pristine beaches, warm breezes, and exotic tropical vegetation would prove especially appealing as the volume swelled. (One very early visitor had been the 23-year-old Ralph Waldo Emerson, who wintered in Florida as long ago as 1827, in an attempt to ease his tuberculosis.) The tourist trade would give St. Augustine new life, even bolstering the development of its library association.

The tourist boom accelerated most notably once the wealthy oil magnate Henry Morrison Flagler—enamored of the notion of transforming the sleepy Florida port into another fashionable Newport—built the huge Spanish Renaissance-style "Grand Hotel Alcazar" in 1885, thus elevating St. Augustine into a major destination for wealthy travelers. That same year, he furthermore founded the Model Land Company—a residential project that would shape the future growth of the city—then had the renowned architect Bernard Maybeck design the even grander "Hotel Ponce de Leon" by 1887, whose interior was decorated by Louis C. Tiffany (a magnificent edifice that eventually formed the core of Flagler College). Privately, the millionaire also funded a beautiful Presbyterian church as a personal memorial to his daughter, while train traffic was simultaneously enhanced throughout the entire South by the adaptation of a standard railway gauge.

For a time, St. Augustine became the country's foremost luxury resort, but its tourist business went into decline because of a nationwide depression during the early 1890s, plus unusual cold snaps, so that many seasonal visitors instead sought out southern Florida. The city's populace consequently receded to 4,100 permanent residents by 1895. It remained mired in that somnolescent existence, catering to occasional tourist upsurges, one of the few municipal innovations being the introduction of its first electric trolleys in 1907. Still, the permanent populace struggled back to 6,200 people by 1920, and four years later Fort Marion was declared a national monument, after which tourism made such a dramatic resurgence all along the Atlantic Seaboard that the number of residents had almost doubled again by 1930.

The onset of the Great Depression as of October 1929 reversed all these gains, though, but local officials remained committed to their city's historic allure.

In order to provide work and revive the desolate economy,

Fort Marion was transferred to the National Parks Service in 1933, opening to the public as a tourist attraction two years later. (It was also officially renamed "Castillo de San Marcos" by an Act of Congress, passed on 5 June 1942.) Attractions include the "Colonial Spanish Quarter" Museum, which re-creates life in the city during 1740, while Castillo de San Marcos receives some 600,000–700,000 annual visitors.

For reading materials on American urban history, please consult the Select Bibliography at the end of this volume, including "General Works on Latin America," as well as "General Works" on North American urban history.

WASHINGTON
City specifically created as the national capital and whose evolution has mirrored the growth of the United States into a global superpower.

Antecedents (1783–1790)
Upon securing their independence from Great Britain in the spring of 1783, the fledgling government of the thirteen former colonies did not possess an acknowledged capital. Rather, its Continental Congress had been obliged to shift between various locales during the Revolutionary War, and although Independence Hall in Philadelphia had served as its seat for the past five years, it was forsaken when some 300 soldiers—disgruntled at being furloughed from the disbanding army, rather than discharged with their back pay, as no funds were available—marched upon Congress from nearby Lancaster on 17 June 1783 to demand their arrears. Despite appealing for protection from the executive council of the state of Pennsylvania, which was in session in the same building, the federal legislators were left unsupported, enduring a day of menaces and offensive language from the mutinous soldiery outside. Finally, they voted to adjourn and reconvene in Princeton, New Jersey, eight days later.

Although subsequently invited to return to Philadelphia, the congressional legislators demurred and instead appointed a committee chaired by James Madison to consider the question of a permanent and autonomous seat of government. Many municipalities expressed a willingness to shoulder the responsibility of becoming the national capital—Boston, New York, Yorktown, Kingston, Newport, Wilmington, Trenton, Reading, Lancaster, Annapolis, and Williamsburg—yet in order that no city might be favored over others, it was decided on 7 October 1783 to build an entirely new capital on a site along the Delaware River, near the falls above Trenton, New Jersey. However, delegates from southern states complained about the great distances that they would have to travel into these northerly climes to attend sessions, so that an alternative site was also approved ten days later, near Georgetown on the lower falls of the Potomac River. The latter was regarded by some as the geographical center of the nation, as the thirteen original

Aerial view looking southwestward across Washington, ca. 1938, with Union Station in the right foreground, plus the Capitol at left; the Washington Monument and Potomac River also figure in the distance. (Fairchild Aerial Surveys, Inc.)

states all faced out onto the Atlantic and were interconnected by ship traffic.

Neither project prospered, however, as the legislature remained engrossed in its many other nation-building problems over the ensuing years. After sitting at Annapolis, Maryland, from 26 November 1783 to 3 June 1784, then at Trenton in November–December 1784, Congress finally took up residence in New York's dilapidated old city hall as of 11 January 1785. The Constitution was crafted and passed here on 17 September 1787, including—among its many other articles—a section that once again called for the creation of a permanent capital, situated within its own autonomous district.

When George Washington was elected the nation's first president and traveled to New York for his inaugural in late April 1789, the old city hall was torn down and hastily replaced by a grand new Federal Hall, designed by the engineer and architect Pierre-Charles L'Enfant (a French volunteer who had risen to the rank of major in the Continental Army). With the federal government now properly constituted and public funds at last beginning to be raised, the question of a permanent capital could be addressed. This time, southern members were able to hammer out a compromise whereby Philadelphia would serve temporarily as seat of government until "the first Monday in December 1800," while a new capital was being built beside Georgetown. Apparently this deal was clinched when Thomas Jefferson agreed to back Alexander Hamilton's proposal for an assumption of state war debts, in exchange for Hamilton's support of the southern site.

Creation and Early Growth (1790–1814)

The legislature voted 14–12 on 1 July 1790 in favor of a bill to set aside a 100-square-mile federal district somewhere between the eastern branch of the Potomac and one of its smaller tributaries, the Connogochegue. The president was moreover authorized to appoint three commissioners to survey and define this area, as well as to purchase the necessary lands and erect "suitable buildings for the public offices of the United States." The chief executive thereupon named Daniel Carroll of Frederick, Maryland, and Thomas Johnson of Rock Creek, Maryland, as well as David Stuart of Hope Park near Fairfax Court House, Virginia, as his commissioners on 24 January 1791. He furthermore asked Congress whether the future federal district should extend far enough south to include Alexandria; this latter proposal was approved, the southernmost point being defined as Jones Point on Hunting Creek.

A preliminary survey was conducted by Andrew Ellicott, resulting in a diamond-shaped pattern straddling both states so as to encompass the prescribed geographical features—Alexandria, plus both branches of the Potomac—as well as running as far north into Maryland as the modern Sixteenth Street Heights. Washington arrived at Suter's Tavern in Georgetown on 29 March 1791; the next day, he personally inspected the designated terrain, accompanied by Ellicott and L'Enfant. Given that the U.S. Treasury was empty, the president also drew up an agreement that persuaded nineteen reluctant local property owners to convey their land to the federal government in trust, in return for compensation once the capital began to take shape. Specifically, stretches destined for future avenues and streets were to be ceded outright by fee simple title. Spaces to be used for public buildings and parks were to be remunerated at a price of $25 per acre; the remaining plots were to be divided equally between the government and original landowners, for resale as individual homesites.

L'Enfant was put in charge of the new city's actual design and spent the next few months drawing up plans before submitting a sketch to the president on 7 August 1791; it was approved with minor alterations. The capital was to be erected on the Maryland side of the Potomac, with a congressional building at its center, atop an 88-foot eminence formerly

Andrew Ellicott's map of the 100-square-mile, diamond-shaped District of Columbia, ca. 1800; north is toward upper left. At lower right appears the survey's starting point below Alexandria, which meant that some 32 square miles of Virginia were originally included within the District's jurisdiction. (Caemmerer, *A Manual on the Origin and Development of Washington*)

known as Jenkin's Hill (which the French architect described as "a pedestal waiting for a monument"). The President's House was to be set atop another low ridge about a mile farther west and connected to the legislature by a 160-foot-wide avenue, one of many that were to radiate out from the Capitol in ingenious "wheel-spoke" patterns, crisscrossing so as to form squares, circles, and triangles at various intersections. Thanks to this unusual layout, the new capital was subdivided into four sectors: Northeast, Northwest, Southeast, and Southwest. Even a small local stream called Tiber Creek was to cascade into a reservoir, then pass through a mile-long esplanade of decorative gardens before discharging into the Potomac.

A month later, Secretary of State Thomas Jefferson and James Madison furthermore announced that the new capital was to be named the "City of Washington," and its surrounding district the "Territory of Columbia." Future streets were to be named "alphabetically one way and numerically the other," so as to facilitate visitor orientation. L'Enfant meanwhile continued drawing up a more comprehensive plan, which was officially submitted to Congress by the president on 13 December 1791. There were now to be two great focal points—the President's House and Capitol—while broad, straight avenues radiating out from each were to provide easy access to even the capital's most distant points. (There was also to have been a third focal point for the judiciary branch, thus complementing the executive and legislative centers.) L'Enfant envisioned a city eventually expanding as far as modern Florida Avenue NW and accommodating some 800,000 residents, the size of late eighteenth-century Paris. The president was more modest in his assessment, believing that a capital "not as large as London" would emerge, while Jefferson thought that it might attain a population of 100,000 within a century, and possibly 200,000 ultimately.

Construction soon commenced, but the temperamental L'Enfant withdrew from the project in March 1792, vexed by the many commentaries and criticisms about his design. The practical details for its implementation therefore fell to Ellicott, who set aside 3,606 acres for avenues and streets, plus another 540 for public buildings and grounds, before splitting the 20,000-plus remaining plots with the former property owners. Speculators such as Robert Morris, James Greenleaf, Thomas Law, John Nicholson, and Samuel Blodgett invested heavily in the new city's development, yet the task of creating an entirely new urban area progressed only slowly.

By the time the federal government moved from Philadelphia in mid-November 1800, the city of Washington contained only 109 brick and 263 frame houses, holding perhaps 3,000 inhabitants. Delegates who arrived by sailboat were disappointed to see only two painted sandstone structures rearing above the Potomac tree line: the partially completed President's House amid its 20-acre park and the incomplete Capitol about a mile away. (The former had been designed by the Irish-born James Hoban, modeled after the Duke of Leinter's palace near Dublin—Hoban being rewarded with a prize of $500 and a plot of land—while the latter building was designed by the more celebrated architect Dr. William Thornton; at this early date it still comprised only a small rectangular edifice, which became the north wing, or "Supreme Court section," of what is today a vast and modern complex.)

Pennsylvania Avenue—named by Congress as a compliment to the Keystone State—was but a dusty road, running through a swampy landscape so low lying that it often flooded. Other major arteries were merely primitive cuts, although bearing the names of states toward which they generally pointed, such as Massachusetts Avenue, New York Avenue, and so forth. The only government departments in existence were State, Treasury, War, Navy, Attorney-General, and the Postal Service, employing a total of 137 clerks; private structures were restricted to a height of no more than 40 feet. Newspaper correspondents and foreign diplomats, accustomed to the sophisticated refinements of much larger Philadelphia, derided the sleepy town with its unpaved streets and widely spaced clumps of low buildings, seemingly lost among the lush foliage. Its climate furthermore proved dank and dreary during the winter and debilitatingly warm and humid during the summer.

Still, the arrival of the federal administration spurred greater development, as well as the personal attentions of the multitalented President Thomas Jefferson, who served from March 1801 to March 1809 and procured funds from Congress for numerous beneficial projects, including the planting of fast-growing poplar shade trees along the length of Pennsylvania Avenue. Another of his projects was the expansion of the legislative building, which was further accelerated by Jefferson's appointment of the energetic Benjamin H. Latrobe as "Architect of the Capitol" in March 1803, resulting in a second southern wing joined to its original northern wing by a wooden passageway four years later.

By 1810, the city of Washington could boast a neat collection of two-story public offices and a considerable navy yard, while its population had grown to 8,028 residents; another 5,000 lived in adjacent Georgetown and 7,250 more a little farther down the Potomac at Alexandria. Demand for office space was becoming such that the government even purchased a three-story hotel from Blodget to convert it into the first U.S. Patent Office. However, increased friction with Great Britain led to a declaration of war in June 1812, and two years later a British expedition swept through the Virginia Capes and up Chesapeake Bay to mount a devastating strike against the young republic's capital.

Conflagration and Resurrection (1814–1860)

The fleet of Vice Adm. Sir Alexander Cochrane disgorged 4,000 redcoats under Maj.-Gen. Robert Ross at Benedict, Maryland, on 19 August 1814, which army pushed north up the Patuxent River the next day, with support from a light naval division under Rear Adm. George Cockburn. The invaders veered west toward Washington on 23 August, while President Madison concentrated several militia regiments at Bladensburg, hoping to make a stand. Yet despite outnumbering their approaching foe, the 7,000 citizen-soldiers proved no match for the seasoned British regulars. Shortly after midday on 24 August, a British column easily drove the defenders from the lone bridge across the eastern branch of the Potomac, then panicked the entire U.S. Army by their inexorable advance. So many American volunteers ran that the redcoats later remembered this battle as the "Bladensburg Races."

With the road into Washington now lying open, 1,500 British troops entered unopposed around 6:00 P.M., finding President and Mrs. Dolly Madison already fled westward, along with most of the capital's inhabitants. A few snipers fired upon Ross's party out of the gloom, provoking sporadic exchanges throughout the night, while U.S. naval Capt. Thomas Tingey had furthermore set the navy yard ablaze—along with the new 44-gun frigate *Columbia* and sloop *Argus*—so as to prevent their falling into enemy hands; the mile-long pile bridge across the Potomac had been torched as well. The next day, 25 August 1814, British parties added to this devastation by burning the President's House, Capitol, Treasury, State, and Navy Department buildings, allegedly in revenge for similar torchings of Canadian towns by U.S. forces. The occupiers thereupon exited that same night, retracing their steps and re-embarking by 30 August.

When Madison returned to the smoldering capital, he took up temporary residence two blocks west of his gutted executive mansion in the Octagon House at Eighteenth Street and New York Avenue. Congress held sessions in the U.S. Patent Building, while other departments sought whatever accommodations they could find. Peace with Great Britain was concluded by the signing of the Treaty of Ghent on 24 December 1814, being officially received by Madison on 14 February 1815, then ratified by Congress three days later. Both the nation and its capital could now begin to recuperate from the ravages of war, Madison moving into a complex known as the Seven Buildings at the northwest corner of Pennsylvania Avenue and Nineteenth Street, while Congress occupied a building at First and A streets NE (later remembered as the Old Capitol Building). Hoban meanwhile supervised repairs to the President's House, while Congress—in order to begin replacing their lost library—purchased 6,760 volumes from Thomas Jefferson's library at Monticello the next year.

The presidential residence was sufficiently restored for partial rehabitation by the time James Monroe was inaugurated in March 1817, and as the scorch marks on its sandstone exterior had been whitewashed, it became known as the White House. Three years later, Washington's population had rebounded to 13,247 people, and the city was entering a period of modest yet steady growth, Monroe's administration being remembered as the Era of Good Feeling. The cornerstone for a new city hall was laid (later becoming the District of Columbia Supreme Court Building), George Washington University was founded in 1821, the first few miles of streets began to be paved over with brick, height restrictions on private structures were eased, and Congress reconvened in its reconstructed Capitol by 1827.

More importantly, President John Quincy Adams turned the first spadeful of earth at Georgetown on 4 July 1828 for the new mile-long Chesapeake and Ohio Canal, which would allow access into the continental interior—a long-held dream of President Washington—and greatly benefit local commerce. The city's progress was further spurred by the completion of its first railway line in July 1835, with a depot located at the northwest corner of Pennsylvania Avenue and Second Street. As pioneers pushed inland to develop the vast virgin territories of the Midwest, the early nineteenth-century economic boom in the United States came to be reflected in Washington, where a huge, neoclassical post office was commenced by 1830, occupying an entire block between Seventh and Eighth streets and E and F streets NW. (Fourteen years afterward, Samuel F. B. Morse opened the world's first telegraphic office on the premises, later converted into the "Old Land Office Building.") A fine new patent office was started in 1837 on two whole blocks

between Seventh and Ninth and F and G streets NW, later to become converted into the Civil Service Commission Building; the old Treasury Building just east of the White House had burned down four years previously, and so it was therefore replaced as of 1839 by an even more magnificent four-story, granite edifice. Thanks to the impatience of President Andrew Jackson, some of its employees were installed into this building well before it was actually completed in 1842.

By 1840, Washington's population had swelled to 23,364, and the nation continued to expand so vigorously across the continent that Congress voted on 1 March 1845 to accede to American settlers' wishes and annex the Republic of Texas, although that decision led to a diplomatic rupture with Mexico. Hostilities broke out the following spring, and Washington prospered by serving as the national headquarters for this war effort. The Mexicans were soon defeated, and by the Treaty of Guadalupe Hidalgo of February 1848, the United States acquired the territories of New Mexico, Arizona, Colorado, Utah, Nevada, and California.

Ironically, the District of Columbia had contracted in size during this same interval, when its Virginian citizenry at Alexandria and other villages along the western banks of the

Granite blocks and columns for the new U.S. Treasury Building, having been off-loaded from sailing ships from Maine, are delivered by mule and oxen teams just east of the White House, 1839. Note the "Billiard Room & Coffee House" in right background, as well as the sparse clumps of dwellings in the early national capital. (National Photo Company)

Potomac—disgruntled because the capital and all public buildings were, by law, to be erected only upon the Maryland side of the river—held a congressionally approved plebiscite on 1–2 September 1846, in which they had voted 763–222 in favor of reincorporation into their original state. President James K. Polk concurred with this retrocession by issuing a proclamation on 7 September, which declared that the 36-square-mile portion of the District was to be officially re-ceded to Virginia.

In January 1848, Congress at last authorized the long-delayed project of erecting a memorial to President Washington, and work commenced that same 4 July—on a slight rise near the Potomac, south of the White House and west of the Capitol—on a 550-foot obelisk that would become the Washington Monument (although not actually completed until almost forty years later). That same year of 1848, the White House was illuminated by gas for the first time, and the census of 1850 revealed that the urban population had increased to a total of 51,687 inhabitants.

As the number of states comprising the nation had increased, work commenced on 4 July 1851 to expand Congress by building a large Senate chamber at its north end and a House of Representatives chamber at its southern end, a vast undertaking that was not completed for some years: the House extension was not occupied until December 1857 and the Senate extension fourteen months later, while the cast-iron dome that replaced the older wooden, copper-sheathed one was not finished until the very last year of the Civil War.

Union Capital (1861–1899)

Washington's population had been counted at 61,122 residents in 1860, but that number quickly mushroomed with the eruption of the Civil War the next spring, as the city was to become the focus of great wartime concentrations. Given its symbolic importance to the federal cause, as well as its exposed position on the very front line—scarcely 100 miles from the Confederate capital of Richmond in Virginia—it was felt imperative that large Union armies be maintained in and around Washington to ensure its survival. One of the earliest regiments to appear—the 6th Massachusetts Volunteers—had even been attacked by a mob while passing through Baltimore on 19 April 1861, and secessionist sympathizers in Maryland had also destroyed several bridges along the Northern Pennsylvania Railroad the next day, in the vain hope of stemming the passage of more troops.

Union regiments nonetheless continued to pour into the capital, and they succeeded in reoccupying Baltimore on 13 May 1861, after which a 13,000-man army pushed across the Potomac eleven days later to seize Alexandria and Arlington Heights. An incursion deeper into rebel territory ended badly when the federal army was defeated on 21 July at the First Battle of Bull Run, Gen. George B. McClellan assuming command over the beaten force one month later and beginning to mold

it into the Army of the Potomac. By 20 November he could parade 70,000 Union troops near Washington, who spent that ensuing winter digging well-planned defenses. The next spring, though, his halfhearted bid to invest Richmond by sea—the so-called Peninsula Campaign—ended in failure, allowing Confederate Gen. Robert E. Lee to counterattack against another smaller federal army in northwestern Virginia, sending it reeling back into the fortifications around Washington by early September 1862, after the Second Battle of Bull Run.

On 7 September 1862, Lee crossed the Potomac at Leesburg with 40,000 men, overrunning Harper's Ferry and sowing panic in the Union capital before being checked at Antietam Creek near Sharpsburg, Pennsylvania, on 16 September by McClellan's slower-moving 70,000 Federals. A ferocious exchange resulted in 12,000 Union casualties, as opposed to 9,000 Confederates. Lee might well have been crushed if McClellan had renewed action the following day, but the Union commander instead allowed the rebels to retire westward uncontested and recross the Potomac on the night of 18 September. Despite the 252,000 federal soldiers now massed in and around Washington, and the capital's enormous ring of fortifications, President Abraham Lincoln could not persuade McClellan to commit the Army of the Potomac to a renewed offensive, and so relieved him of command on 7 November.

McClellan's successor, Gen. Ambrose E. Burnside, advanced into Virginia only to be mauled by Lee at the Battle of Fredericksburg in December 1862. Then Gen. Joseph Hooker led the Union army to another defeat at Chancellorsville in late April–early May 1863, which freed Lee to counterinvade the

The U.S. Capitol during wartime, ca. 1863. (Miller and Lanier, *Photographic History of the Civil War*)

Locomotives marshaled in Washington yards for protection during the approach of Gen. Jubal Early's small Confederate army, July 1864; note the recently completed U.S. Capitol dome in the background. (Miller and Lanier, *Photographic History of the Civil War*)

next month by circling through Maryland and Pennsylvania in the hope of threatening Washington again. Hooker was supplanted by Gen. George Gordon Meade, whose forces at last found the main Confederate body near the small Pennsylvania town of Gettysburg on 30 June 1863, fighting a great battle over the next four days in which the 82,000 federal troops suffered 23,000 killed, wounded, or missing, while inflicting 30,000 casualties among their 75,000 foes. Defeated, Lee retired into Virginia, trailed by Meade's battered army.

It was not until Ulysses S. Grant—the most successful Union commander in the West—was finally brought east by Lincoln in March 1864 and promoted to commander-in-chief of all federal forces that a concerted offensive could be launched into the rebel heartland. After reorganizing the Army of the Potomac, Grant pushed south into Virginia in early May with 120,000 men, encountering Lee's 70,000 in a large forest dubbed the Wilderness in Spotsylvania County, then doggedly pressing him back into Petersburg. In hopes of easing Grant's iron grip upon the main Confederate army, which was being bled white, a small rebel detachment in the Shenandoah Valley under Gen. Jubal A. Early was ordered to divert attention by launching a thrust toward the Union capital. Early therefore bested his local Union opponents and moved into Maryland, his 3,000-man vanguard under Gen. Bradley T. Johnson crossing the Potomac on 5 July, followed shortly thereafter by his own 10,000-man main force.

View northeastward across the Potomac River in 1864, with the Long Bridge visible at left and the Capitol faintly in the distance at right. (Miller and Lanier, *Photographic History of the Civil War*)

Union regiment assembled on F Street, just prior to marching in the second day of the Grand Army's victory parade through the national capital, 24 May 1865. (Miller and Lanier, *Photographic History of the Civil War*)

Consternation once more gripped Washington, so that Grant was obliged to detach the Sixth and part of his Nineteenth Corps to bolster the city's defenses, all the while maintaining his pressure upon Petersburg. As suspected, Early's small army proved to be no real menace, passing through Rockville on 10 July 1864 to probe the massive network of Union defenses the next morning, 6 miles north of Washington at Fort Stevens (Brightwood, D.C.; the approximate site of modern Walter Reed General Hospital). That same afternoon, the scratch force of rear-echelon troops and convalescents holding these positions were reinforced by the veteran 1st and 2nd divisions of Sixth Corps under Gen. Horatio G. Wright, who easily repulsed a more determined Confederate assault the following day—under the gaze of Lincoln himself, who had come from the White House to witness Fort Stevens's defense. Having suffered 500 casualties and lacking heavy siege artillery, Early could not penetrate farther, so he withdrew on 13 July to recross the Potomac and return into the Shenandoah Valley.

This was to be the last offensive directed against the Union capital during the conflict. The next spring, Lee's shrunken army at last surrendered, and the War of Secession was over. Washington had been transformed by its leading role during these hostilities, both materially and symbolically. Because of the war, little public work had been undertaken, with the exception of the Capitol expansion and completion of its dome—at Lincoln's insistence. However, the massive influx of troops had led to the erection of hundreds of temporary structures, at least seventy of which had served as hospitals, tending to as many as 30,000 sick or wounded men at a time. In order to regularize its water supply, the Washington Aqueduct had also been developed to bring in a steady stream from Great Falls on the Potomac, while the Long Bridge had been more sturdily rebuilt as well, so as to ensure easy passage for Union columns. Naval construction had increased, and even public transit had been upgraded, the first horse-drawn streetcars having been inaugurated on 2 October 1862, running from the navy yard all the way across the city into Georgetown. Population figures had multiplied, as munitions and other supplies had to be manufactured and stockpiled in record amounts, requiring thousands of laborers, while the number of permanent government employees had more than doubled from 3,466 in 1861 to 7,184 by 1865.

Still more significantly, however, Washington had emerged as the widely recognized core of the Union, tens of thousands of troops returning to their homes with cherished memories of having defended the national capital. Such sentiments were made even stronger by the shocking assassination of Lincoln while attending a play during the closing stages of the war on 14 April 1865. (Ford's Theater, where the murder occurred, was located on the east side of Tenth Street, between E and F streets NW; immediately after the assassination, the building was taken over by Secretary of War Edwin M. Stanton and never again used to stage theatrical productions. Its ill fame was further perpetuated when its three floors collapsed while undergoing repairs on 9 April 1893, killing twenty-two clerks and injuring sixty-eight.)

As armies dispersed and Washington's defenses were dismantled, its buildings were restored to civilian use; the lumber from temporary structures was used to begin constructing new houses in a subdivision called Mount Pleasant. Nonetheless, it was not until Grant was inaugurated as president in March 1869 that a concerted effort was made to improve the capital (whose population had stabilized at 109,199 people by the next year). Some individuals had suggested that the capital be relocated farther west—such as at St. Louis—but Grant instead persuaded Congress to pass an act on 21 February 1871 that did away with the old, ineffectual government of the District of Columbia by three commissioners, replacing it with a governor and board of public works appointed by the president, plus an elected legislative assembly consisting of an eleven-member council and a twenty-two-member house of delegates. These officials in turn issued bonds to finance a host of civic improvements, some 180 of 300 miles of city streets being paved, 128 miles of sidewalk laid, a system of sewers commenced, 3,000 gas lamps installed, the waterway known as Tiber Creek filled in, scores of parks created or beautified, 60,000 trees planted, and so forth. Even Georgetown was incorporated into the District, its charter having been revoked, although its name would continue to be featured as a topographical designation.

Unfortunately, these improvements were accompanied by a great deal of graft and corruption, centered around Grant's choice for governor—Alexander R. "Boss" Shepherd—who was eventually banished from the city, while the District's new governmental arrangement was also temporarily rescinded on 20 June 1874. A new municipal corporation was created by 1 July 1878, to be governed once again by three commissioners appointed by the president, with half of its budget borne by the federal government, and half by local taxes. (These percentages have since varied.

A separate Library of Congress building was initiated on two city blocks east of the Capitol in 1886, and L'Enfant's old city plan was rediscovered the next year in the offices of the Geodetic Survey, revealing that developers and property owners had routinely ignored or violated his design over the past century, especially with regard to roads—which many subdividers had simply laid out according to whim, perpetuating such changes by recording a plat. As many original avenues had consequently become blocked off, reduced in size, or even ignored, a new highway plan was approved in 1893 in the hope of better regulating development.

Modern Evolution (1900–Present)

It was not, however, to be until the city's centennial was observed in 1900 that a second great reconstruction effort was actually undertaken. Flush with euphoria from the recent

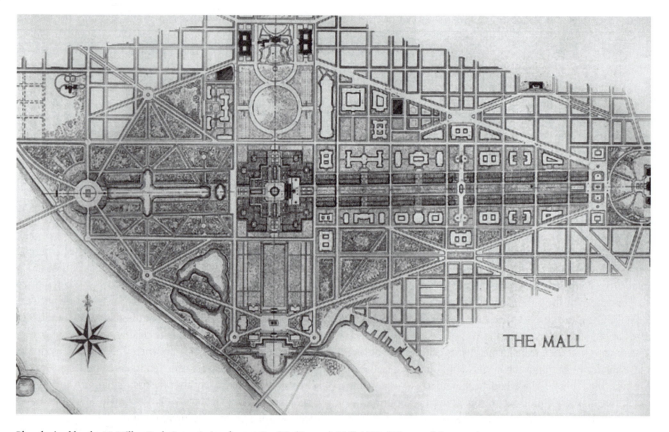

Plan devised by the McMillan Park Commission for creating Washington's Mall, 1902. (Library of Congress)

Chicago World's Fair and the victory in the Spanish-American War, many people felt that it was appropriate to elevate the grandeur of the capital—whose population had grown to 218,196 inhabitants, with another 60,500 living just outside its boundaries—so as to better reflect the nation's newfound global prestige. Accordingly, the wealthy James McMillan of Michigan—Republican chairman of the Senate Committee for the District of Columbia—enlisted the services of the eminent architects Daniel H. Burnham and Charles Follen McKim, the landscape architect Frederick Law Olmstead, Jr., and the sculptor Augustus Saint-Gaudens to jointly devise a sweeping plan for modernizing and beautifying the capital in keeping with L'Enfant's original vision.

This so-called McMillan Park Commission report was submitted to Congress by 15 January 1902, outlining an ambitious program of clearances, creation of green areas, and street realignments. Its first success was to persuade the Pennsylvania Railroad Company to remove its tracks from the Mall—originally intended as a common pastureland—and combine them with those of the Baltimore and Ohio Railroad Company into a magnificent new Union Station, designed by Burnham. Work on this relocated terminal commenced in August 1902, along with other projects such as remodeling of the White

House, addition of legislative office space beside the Capitol, and the planting of elms along part of the proposed new 2-mile-long National Mall. The cornerstone for a Gothic-style, limestone Episcopal cathedral—originally dubbed Saint Peter and Saint Paul, but that would later become better known as the National Cathedral—was furthermore laid in 1907 atop 400-foot Mount Saint Alban, with a superb view across the capital. (Several decades would elapse before this huge edifice could be entirely completed, having been designed for a seating capacity of 7,500 congregants or a standing crowd of 27,000.) In 1909, L'Enfant's body was reverentially removed from its pauper's grave in Maryland to be reinterred in the most prominent spot of the 612-acre Arlington Cemetery.

Yet the scope of these proposed improvements entailed so much expense and reclamation of property—particularly to extend the Mall and its reflecting pools as far as the Potomac, where a new Lincoln Memorial was to be erected—that the overall pace slowed. President William Howard Taft appointed a Commission of Fine Arts in 1910 to guide future development, yet significant progress was frequently interrupted by changes of administration and other transcendent events, such as when the United States was unexpectedly drawn into World War I late in 1917. Public works were consequently suspended,

Aerial view over the White House, ca. 1938. (Fairchild Aerial Surveys, Inc.)

and the capital furthermore suffered from a sudden influx of government workers, some departments becoming so overcrowded that 30,000 to 40,000 employees had to be housed in temporary accommodations.

Once hostilities ceased a year later, Congress—after prolonged study and debate—finally passed the Public Buildings Act of 25 May 1926, which authorized large-scale erection of numerous agencies throughout the city, so as to avert such complications during future crises. In addition to the widespread new construction that resulted, older edifices were also upgraded and modernized under this program—such as the Library of Congress, Supreme Court, Government Printing Office, Social Security Building, War Department, Navy Department, Walter Reed Hospital, and so forth—while the grounds of the Capitol, Union Station, and the Mall were expanded and beautified as well, and access roads were improved by the completion of the Arlington Memorial Bridge, Mount Vernon Highway, and the George Washington Memorial Parkway. By 1930, the city boasted a population of 486,869.

As the national capital, Washington has been the scene of numerous petitions and protests, one of its first mass demonstrations occurring in early June 1932, when widespread unemployment throughout the country caused 20,000 to 30,000 former servicemen to descend upon the city from all states to urge Congress to pass adjusted compensation certificates or "soldiers' bonuses" (a name that resulted in this group becoming derisively known as the "Bonus Expedi-tionary Force," or BEF). The indigent petitioners were greeted by the sympathetic police chief, Pelham D. Glassford, a retired brigadier, who provided temporary housing and food. But the desired bill was voted down by the Senate on 17 June, after which Congress recessed for the summer. Weary of the BEF petitioners who remained in shanties, the District of Columbia's commissioners requested that President Herbert Hoover send in federal troops to disperse the throng. A cavalry squadron, infantry battalion, and tank platoon appeared on the afternoon of 28 July under Gen. Douglas A. MacArthur, Maj.-Gen. George Van Horn Moseley, and Brig. Perry Miles (with Maj. Dwight David Eisenhower serving as a liaison to the police), driving the BEF out of Washington in short order, inflicting a pair of fatalities and numerous injuries.

In September 1941, a long-proposed plan for consolidating the many scattered offices of the War Department into a single building was commenced by U.S. Army engineers on an oddly shaped site in Arlington. The resultant five-sided structure was completed by 15 January 1943, at a cost of $83 million—resulting in a 29-acre "Pentagon," which accommodated about 3.7 million square feet of office space for 23,000 employees, making it the largest building in the world at that time.

For further reading materials on the history of Washington, please consult the Select Bibliography at the end of this volume; additional sources can be found in the reference sections on North American and U.S. urban history.

SOUTH AMERICA

In this hidden empire bathed by the sun,
more of pious Bacchus than of Alcydes,
between a frozen tropic, and another which burns . . .

—the anonymous seventeenth-century
Peruvian poetess "Amarilis"

Argentina

BUENOS AIRES

Capital at the confluence of several important waterways dominating a rich agricultural hinterland, which has emerged as one of the most cosmopolitan cities in the world.

Failed Settlement (1536–1541)

Buenos Aires's origins were quite inauspicious, for after the nearby shorelines were probed by competing Spanish and Portuguese explorers during the 1520s—most notably by Sebastian Cabot—Spain's emperor Charles V granted his wealthy courtier Pedro de Mendoza, knight of the Order of Santiago, license to found a colony. Traversing the Atlantic ahead of a rival expedition believed to be preparing in Portugal, de Mendoza's eleven vessels and 1,300 colonists rendezvoused in early January 1536 off San Gabriel Island (modern Colonia del Sacramento, Uruguay), before pressing deeper into the estuary to come ashore south of the Riachuelo River on 2 February. They named their new establishment Nuestra Señora Santa María del Buen Aire (Our Lady Holy Mary of the Fair Breeze)—a popular patron saint among sixteenth-century Spanish sailors, soon contracted into Buenos Aires.

The settlers quickly threw up earthen ramparts to enclose their extemporized shacks, and within the next couple of weeks they skirmished against local Querandí, Guaraní, and Pampa nomads. Yet hunger proved to be a much greater threat, so that de Mendoza detached 300 men in late May 1536 to venture up the Carcarañá River under his subordinate Juan de Ayolas in quest of a source of provisions. The remaining Spaniards meanwhile built an advance outpost on the banks of Conchas Creek near the Luján River, then weathered a

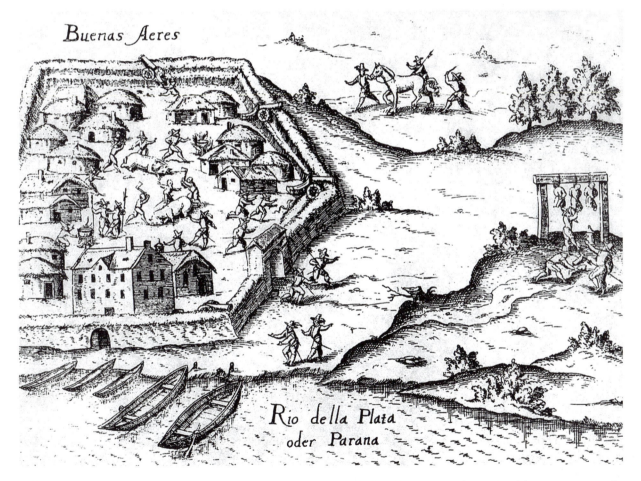

Pedro de Mendoza's first settlement on the River Plate, ca. 1536; engraving published thirty-one years later in Frankfurt, accompanying the memoirs of Ulrich Schmidel, a Bavarian soldier who had participated in this enterprise and returned to Europe in 1554. (Schmidel, *Derrotero y viaje a España y las Indias*)

major confrontation against its local population on 15 June, during which their 40 cavalrymen and 300 infantrymen suffered numerous casualties.

An Indian army several thousand strong thereupon gathered over the next few days to besiege Buenos Aires proper, pelting the thatched roofs inside its earthworks with flaming arrows and exhausting its weakened defenders, before finally lifting their siege by mid-July 1536. As a result of these repeated vicissitudes, de Mendoza—apprised by a returning vessel at the end of that same month of more bountiful lands farther inland—led 400 men up the Paraná River in late August to secure a new foothold within that more promising territory, while leaving only 100 men behind to hold Buenos Aires. Most settlers would eventually be lured still farther north by reports of legendary Incan mines high up in the distant Andes, nicknamed the Sierra de la Plata (Silver Range) by local Spaniards so that Buenos Aires's estuary also became known as the Río de la Plata (River of Silver), later rendered as the "River Plate" by the English.

Sick and disheartened, de Mendoza staggered back into his Buenos Aires base camp in November 1536, sailing for Spain on 22 April 1537 and dying at sea. By now, scarcely seventy Spaniards remained in the original settlement under Capt. Francisco Ruiz Galán, who—beset by unremitting want, discord, and indigenous hostility—decided to abandon this site in 1541 and relocate all surviving inhabitants upriver.

Refoundation (1580–1617)

It was not until the veteran conquistador Juan de Garay pushed 1,000 miles back down the Paraguay River from Asunción and Santa Fe early in 1580, with sixty-four mostly mestizo (mixed-heritage) families aboard his caravel *San Cristóbal de Buena Ventura*, plus two brigantines and a flotilla of canoes, that Buenos Aires was reclaimed as a Spanish settlement. On Sunday, 29 May—feast day of the Most Holy Trinity on the Church calendar—de Garay anchored in the muddy, shallow waters at the Riachuelo River mouth, reconnoitering the landscape over the next few days before selecting a new site, three-quarters of a mile northwest of de Mendoza's old ruins.

The locale was chosen as it sat atop one of the few pieces of high ground on an otherwise flat alluvial plain, offering some protection against floods or attacks; it also lay adjacent to a *pozo* (deep-water anchorage), suitable for receiving small oceangoing vessels. By 11 June 1580, de Garay's followers had cleared sufficient space to assign lots and to formally constitute a new community, which was dubbed the Ciudad de la Santísima Trinidad y Puerto de Santa María de Buenos Aires (City of the Most Holy Trinity and Port of Saint Mary of the Fair Breezes). A grid of fifteen-by-nine blocks was to radiate out from a central square (modern Plaza de Mayo), which was to be lined with a fort, church, jail, and a *cabildo* or "municipal hall." Multiple plots were assigned to each of the sixty-four founding families, plus ample outlying pasturelands for *quintas* (farms) for the planting of corn, beans, squash, and wheat, as well as for grazing livestock.

Initially, the number of inhabitants totaled perhaps 300 people, although households dwindled over the next five years to roughly fifty, as some families quit the primitive outpost in discouragement. One unwilling visitor to the struggling settlement was to be John Drake—nephew of the famed English circumnavigator Sir Francis—who after his 40-ton bark *Francis* had been wrecked on the Uruguayan coast early in 1583 escaped captivity among its Charrúa Indians with some surviving crewmen aboard a boat. Despite its lonely isolation, a small Franciscan monastery came to be erected in Buenos Aires by 1589, and a square, riverside citadel made of adobe bricks and christened Fort San Juan Baltasar de Austria was completed six years later. Its foundations are still visible today on the south side of the basement of the Casa Rosada Presidential Palace.

Buenos Aires's population had rebounded to roughly 500 persons by 1600, yet because they lived at such an immense remove from the main imperial mainstream, development remained lethargic: for despite the bountiful landscape abundantly irrigated by seasonal rainfalls, most Spanish maritime traffic still sailed through the Caribbean to service the wealthier viceroyalties of Mexico, Peru, or Colombia, while Buenos Aires lay at the farthest extreme of that traffic flow, separated

Buenos Aires as seen from its sea approaches in 1817, by the visiting British naval officer Emeric Essex Vidal; note the extremely flat terrain and low silhouette of the city. (Metropolitan Toronto Reference Library)

from Peru by the Andean barrier. Its inaccessibility meant that what little European merchandise such as clothes, wine, oil, or weaponry chanced to arrive were usually only poor-quality leftovers offered at exorbitant prices.

Porteños (port residents), as they were coming to be known, had consequently initiated their own backdoor trade with the Portuguese in neighboring Brazil as of the early 1580s after both monarchies had become unified in Europe. Sun-dried hides, beef jerky, tallow, cotton, wheat, and flour would be brought into Buenos Aires by cart from as far away as Córdoba or Tucumán, plus a little silver from Potosí, to be shipped out aboard coastal craft for barter in Brazilian ports in exchange for African slaves or European goods. Despite the illegality of such proceedings, the Crown authorities in Madrid turned a blind eye to these minor transgressions, realizing that they represented insignificant losses to the Exchequer, while ensuring the remote outpost's survival.

Slowly, Buenos Aires began taking on a more permanent feel, its crude church being demolished in 1603 to make way for a sturdier edifice of adobe bricks. Its fort was expanded the next year, and a combined *cabildo* and jail was created in 1607. That next year, the Jesuit Order arrived in the city, joining the Franciscans and Dominicans—who began work on a new Santo Domingo Church in 1610—while the city's first hospital, a military establishment dedicated to the patron saint San Martín, was inaugurated in 1611.

Regional Capital (1618–1775)

Buenos Aires's population may have reached 1,000 people by 1618. There were perhaps a total of 1,800 Spaniards scattered throughout the entire River Plate estuary by that time, most living in simple, low housing built of stone and mud with thatched roofs, although a few boasted tiled roofs. The city was furthermore designated as the region's capital, with governors to be appointed directly from Madrid, rather than to continue being administered from Asunción. Two years afterward, Buenos Aires was also elevated into the see for a bishopric, and its brand-new church thus became a cathedral.

Thanks to this enhanced status, a few more "permission" ships, or slavers, were authorized to visit Buenos Aires's anchorage, as well as distressed foreign ships seeking repairs, which helped supplement the existing clandestine trade. Indeed, some leading citizens had proven adept intermediaries for inland ranchers, while the *porteños* themselves had become so comfortable with foreign visitors that a few Portuguese traders even settled and intermarried among them. The population was further augmented when 200 Spanish soldiers arrived in 1631 to bolster the garrison.

When Portugal rebelled and threw off the Spanish yoke in Europe in 1640, Dutch merchants quickly supplanted Brazilian traders in Buenos Aires, so that the city's prosperity continued its slow but steady ascendancy. Business grew so notably that the French warships *Gaspard* of Capt. Timoléon

Hotman, Chevalier de Fontenay—former governor of the notorious buccaneer stronghold of Tortuga Island, Haiti—and his consort *Renommée* under Dutch-born Capt. Job Forant blockaded Buenos Aires's anchorage in April 1658, engaging three anchored Dutch vessels that were loading cargo. After a lengthy exchange during which de Fontenay was killed and *Gaspard* captured, *Renommée* emerged with a single prize.

The first official census, undertaken in 1664, revealed that the capital's population had not increased appreciably, recording slightly more than 1,000 inhabitants distributed among 211 households. But its fertile hinterland—ideally suited for breeding cattle, horses, and sheep—soon began attracting so many more migrants that the total figure exploded to 4,600 people within the next ten years, 300 of whom were garrison soldiers. A fine new cathedral with twin spires was inaugurated in 1671, plus a new Jesuit church four years afterward.

The Portuguese also noticed the territory's growth and so attempted to lay claim to half of the River Plate estuary by sending an expedition from Rio de Janeiro in January 1680 to establish a rival foothold called Colônia do Sacramento opposite Buenos Aires. The city's Spanish authorities and residents naturally regarded such an incursion as an encroachment upon their dominions, so they massed 480 troops and 3,000 indigenous auxiliaries under *maestre de campo* Antonio de Vera Múxica, who made a bloody dawn assault on 7 August that razed the stockaded Colônia outpost. But the Portuguese persisted, so that Gov. Alonso Juan de Valdés Inclán had to dispatch a second counterexpedition from Buenos Aires on 2 October 1704 of more than 800 Spanish regulars, 600 militiamen, and 4,300 indigenous auxiliaries under Gen. Baltasar García Ros to beset that resurrected outpost. Colônia do Sacramento's exhausted defenders finally withdrew on the night of 14–15 March 1705, after which the Spaniards once more leveled the intrusive settlement.

Buenos Aires meanwhile continued to thrive, being designated as one of the few Spanish-American ports authorized to receive French slavers under the terms of Madrid's newly reorganized *real asiento* (royal monopoly). After 1715, the *asiento* was assumed by England's South Sea Company, which would eventually establish large barracoons at Barracas. The city population had furthermore grown impressively to 8,900 residents by 1720, while exports of cattle hides from its surrounding district had also multiplied from 45,000 in 1716 to 60,000 by 1724; also, many major buildings were now being routinely erected in a sturdy bricks-and-mortar design.

The Portuguese again reoccupied Colônia do Sacramento and established a secondary base at Montevideo in November 1723, to which Buenos Aires's new governor, Bruno Mauricio de Zabala, knight of the Order of Calatrava, responded by sending 250 soldiers aboard two warships under Commo. Salvador García Pose, who compelled the trespassers to evacuate by 19 January 1724. Less success was enjoyed eleven years later, when Gov. Miguel Salcedo, knight of the Order of Santiago,

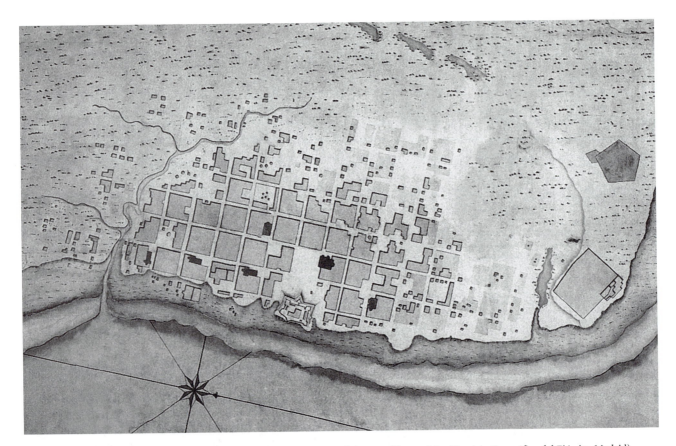

Anonymous, watercolor map of the burgeoning city during the 1720s; north is toward lower right. (Servicio Geográfico del Ejército, Madrid)

mounted yet another protracted siege of Colónia do Sacramento in October 1735—for despite massing 500 soldiers, 4,500 indigenous auxiliaries, and 36 siege pieces, he was unable to dislodge its 935 defenders and 80 guns. Salcedo therefore withdrew the bulk of his forces into Buenos Aires by mid-February 1736, leaving behind only a token unit to harry the interloper garrison. But the Portuguese made several successful sallies, and even installed yet another new outpost at Maldonado, before diplomats finally signed a truce in Paris in October 1737.

Notwithstanding such distractions, Buenos Aires's population easily surpassed 10,000 people by 1744 (being estimated by modern scholars at 11,600), then continued to rise in numbers, so that the city had clearly emerged as the most significant Spanish administrative and commercial center along the South Atlantic coast by the mid-eighteenth century—despite its rather poor port facilities, which required larger oceangoing vessels to anchor in the outer roads and ferry cargoes and passengers across its muddy shallows, depositing them onto oxcarts waiting amid the surf. By now, the city's 14,000 inhabitants included prominent regional bureaucrats and merchants, the latter dominating all trade passing in and out of the interior. When Buenos Aires's old cathedral suddenly collapsed on the night of 23 May 1752, leaving only its twin spires

still standing, construction was promptly commenced on a magnificent new structure.

Ten years later, when Spain declared war against Portugal during the closing phases of the French and Indian War, or Seven Years' War, the city furthermore mounted a much more creditable offensive against Colónia do Sacramento. Gov. Pedro de Cevallos Cortés y Calderón—forewarned of the impending outbreak—marshaled 700 Spanish regulars, 200 dragoons, 1,800 militiamen, plus thousands of indigenous laborers at an advance staging area in Uruguay, then marched swiftly against Colónia upon receiving final confirmation from Madrid on 1 October 1762. The ramparts were encircled and a breach battered, compelling the 2,355 Portuguese defenders and 1,600 civilians to capitulate by 2 November. Then, de Cevallos and his army drove still farther east and eliminated other frontier outposts as far as Rio Grande, before finally being advised on 8 April 1763 that hostilities had ceased in Europe.

Buenos Aires's newfound power—its population now standing at more than 20,000 people, having become the fastest-growing city in Spanish America—manifested itself even more ambitiously when naval Capt. Felipe Ruiz Puente set sail early in 1767 with the French adventurer Louis Antoine de Bougainville to consummate a prearranged exchange whereby Spain was to assume ownership over his fledgling French

Typical *bonarense* oxcart, here depicted by Vidal while hauling watercasks in 1817; note the oversized wheels, designed to roll into shallow waters. (Metropolitan Toronto Reference Library)

colony, located 1,100 miles farther south on the Falkland Islands. This settlement, called Port Louis, was handed over to the Spanish on 1 April, but its new proprietors then over-reached by attacking the English settlers at nearby Port Egmont as well, when four frigates and a xebec sent from Buenos Aires by Gov. Francisco Bucareli surprised its few score British residents by disgorging 1,400 soldiers and a siege train under Col. Antonio Gutiérrez on 10 June 1770. This force overwhelmed the inhabitants after a token exchange of shot. However, news of this seizure created such a diplomatic furor back in Europe that Madrid had to back down by January 1771, alleging that the assault had been conducted without King Charles III's consent and so would be rescinded.

Viceregal Capital (1776–1805)
Notwithstanding this lone reverse, the swelling volume of goods and people now flowing through Buenos Aires to service its rich hinterland led to the city's elevation in 1776 into a viceregal capital—the fourth in Spanish America, joining Mexico City in the viceroyalty of New Spain, Bogotá in the viceroyalty of New Granada, and Lima in the viceroyalty of Peru.

The arrival from Spain of the River Plate's first viceroy also proved highly dramatic. This official—Pedro de Cevallos, now promoted to lieutenant-general and knight in the orders of Santiago and San Genaro—materialized off Brazil in February 1777 with a 116-ship, 19,000-man expedition to overrun Santa Catarina Island. He then disembarked 4,500 troops outside Colônia do Sacramento and compelled its 1,000 Portuguese defenders to surrender by 4 June. De Cevallos permanently eradicated that intrusive outpost by scuttling block ships to close up its entrance, before finally learning on 27 August that peace had been restored back in Europe. According to the subsequent Treaty of San Ildefonso, Portugal renounced all future claims over the estuary, and one month after ratification on 24 March 1778, the huge Spanish expedition quit the River Plate.

More important for the new viceregal capital, however, were the Bourbon economic reforms implemented around that same time, which so liberalized imperial trade over the ensuing decade that Spain became Buenos Aires's chief trading partner for the first time in the city's history. About sixty transatlantic merchantmen called every year with manufactured goods,

Anonymous, watercolor map of the city, ca. 1800; north is toward right. (Servicio Histórico Militar, Madrid)

cloths, ironwork, slaves, mercury for the Bolivian mines, and the like. Millions of pesos in silver bullion were also extracted from Potosí, while exports of local produce surged as well, cattle ranching in particular expanding so rapidly that the volume of outgoing hides multiplied from 150,000 in 1778 to almost 875,000 by 1796; dried or salted beef also rose from 158 metric tons in 1787 to 1,785 tons a decade later.

Buenos Aires boomed as a result of this upsurge and its enhanced administrative standing. The result was a commensurate rise in municipal standards—starting with the capital's first sanitation and building ordinances; the establishment of a *protomedicato* (medical board) in February 1779; the importation of a government printing press one year later; the erection of a brick bullring with a capacity for 8,000 spectators in the Recio suburb by 1781; and the inauguration of a fine new theater called the Ranchería as well as the Colegio San Carlos (Colegio Carolino), both in November 1783. Oxcart traffic was restricted in January 1784 to only Monserrat Plaza in the city's west end or Plaza Nueva (Amarita) to its north, as their heavy burdens left deep ruts through the unpaved streets, especially

during the rainy season. Some main thoroughfares around Buenos Aires's central plaza were moreover leveled and paved shortly thereafter, while a tree-lined alameda promenade was cleared north of the main citadel for recreation. A *real audiencia* (royal tribunal) was established by 1785, a wooden city bridge was erected in 1791, and public lighting was switched over from 100 *velas de cebo* (animal-fat candles) to more efficient *grasa de potro* (horse grease) lamps the next year.

Despite the handicap of an inadequate water supply—a commodity routinely hawked through the streets by *aguateros* (water sellers), as few houses boasted cisterns—as well as chronic shortages of wood, so many Spanish immigrants and African slaves arrived that the population grew from at least 24,000 inhabitants in 1778 to 42,500 by 1810, although even those official census figures appear to be low, the actual totals probably measuring closer to 29,900 and 61,100, respectively. *Bonarense* merchants were additionally granted the privilege of forming their own *consulado* or guild by the Crown in 1794, augmenting their ability to conduct trade.

But the twenty-year bonanza came to an abrupt halt when

Spain, hard pressed in a European conflict against Republican France, was compelled to realign itself with the radical French Directorate in August 1796—which in turn prompted Britain to impose an embargo against Spanish shipping the next month, then declare war by 6 October. Its all-powerful Royal Navy promptly paralyzed overseas traffic with Cadiz, so that Buenos Aires's annual exports plummeted from 5 million pesos to a mere 500,000 by 1797. Neutral carriers such as Portuguese, German, Scandinavian, and Turkish vessels attempted to fill this void, as well as American vessels: forty-three ships from Boston, New York, or Philadelphia called at Buenos Aires in 1800 alone, bearing slaves from Mozambique and other goods. Argentine yards also launched at least ten ships between 1796 and 1800 in an attempt to make up for this overseas downturn, while Buenos Aires's first newspaper—*El Telégrafo Mercantil* (*The Mercantile Telegraph*)—appeared in May 1801; construction of its *recova* public market also commenced the following year.

British Invasions (1806–1807)

On the evening of 24 June 1806, the Viceroy Rafael, Marqués de Sobremonte, was summoned from a theatrical production to receive the shocking news that an English expedition had arrived in the River Plate estuary from Africa's Cape of Good Hope. Next morning, eight vessels were sighted at anchor off distant Quilmes, disgorging 1,200 redcoats, sixteen horses, and eight field-pieces under Brig. William Carr Beresford, supplemented by 340 marines and 100 sailors from Commo. Sir Home Riggs Popham's Royal Navy squadron. These invaders quickly advanced to invest the panic-stricken capital, brushing aside hastily assembled militia units sent to bar their path, as well as the 400 Spaniards manning the Riachuelo River's 6-gun battery on Sunday morning, 27 June.

Sobremonte exited Buenos Aires with 600 troops, allegedly to take the English from the rear, but actually fleeing inland toward Córdoba; thus the British encountered no resistance as they dashed through a rainstorm that same afternoon to seize several strongpoints within the hapless city. Its official capitulation was signed on 2 July 1806 and dispatched to London two weeks afterward, along with a request for British reinforcements. This unexpected seizure had been the brainchild of English Commo. Riggs Popham, who believed reports that Platine residents were so disenchanted with Madrid's misrule and their lost trade that they would acquiesce to such foreign intervention.

View through the archway of Buenos Aires's *recova* or "public market"—completed in 1803—into the muddy main square beyond, with its *cabildo* or "city hall" at the far end, reconstructed in 1791. Sketched by Vidal in October 1817. (Metropolitan Toronto Reference Library)

Yet *bonarense* pride would hardly abide occupation, so that upon perceiving the invaders' numerical weakness, rural units began mustering secretly with the aim of expelling them. At 1:30 A.M. on 1 August 1806, Beresford sallied from Buenos Aires with 550 redcoats and six field-pieces, defeating one such concentration at Perdriel Manor outside the city. But a relief force from Montevideo disembarked 20 miles away at Las Conchas three days afterward under the French-born commander of the Ensenada de Barragán garrison, naval Capt. Santiago de Liniers y Bremond, knight of the Order of Malta, who incorporated local contingents into his own force to produce a combined total of 2,500 troops.

De Liniers marched upon Buenos Aires through a cold rain and on 11 August 1806 encountered Beresford's defenders drawn up in an open space north of the capital called the Retiro; the attackers therefore deployed their artillery and threw a cavalry screen around the city. The next day, in a sharp two-hour fight during which the Spaniards suffered 205 casualties as compared with 157 British, the attackers pressed the outnumbered English back inside Buenos Aires. Beresford and his 1,300 men surrendered at 3:00 P.M. on 12 August, eventually being interned at Luján, while the victorious de Liniers was acclaimed acting viceroy in place of the disgraced Sobremonte.

However, Popham's warships still controlled the River Plate estuary, and two months later they were joined by 2,200 additional redcoats from the Cape of Good Hope. After an abortive thrust against Montevideo, they seized Maldonado on 29 October 1806, then were further reinforced when 3,600 more troops appeared on 5 January 1807 under the American-born Loyalist Brig. Sir Samuel Auchmuty, who carried Montevideo by storm on 3 February. The British built up their strength, Lt.-Gen. John Whitelocke arriving as new commander-in-chief, before finally launching a second attempt against the viceregal capital.

On the rainy Sunday morning of 28 June 1807, 9,000 redcoats, 350 horses, and 16 field-pieces were disembarked 30 miles southeast of Buenos Aires at Ensenada de Barragán. Leaving behind 5 field-pieces and many horses mired in the mud, the invaders' vanguard overran the abandoned Spanish battery at Reducción de Quilmes by 1 July. They then forded the Riachuelo the next morning and outflanked the 6,900 men and 53 field-pieces that de Liniers had entrenched south of this river at Barracas, precipitating a hasty redeployment toward Misere Ranch to prevent an immediate assault against the capital. The British vanguard nonetheless broke through, although—unaware that Buenos Aires lay helpless before them—they then encamped to await the arrival of the main British body, thereby allowing de Liniers time to organize resistance within the capital's barricaded streets.

By 3 July 1807, the English had massed 6,900 men in the city's western suburbs and the next day called upon its 7,000 defenders to surrender. Rebuffed, Whitelocke sent 8 battalions—5,800 men in 13 columns—into Buenos Aires's

streets at 6:30 A.M. on 5 July, his right wing wresting possession of the Hospicio de la Residencia, while his left took the bullring. Yet the 88th Regiment and Light Brigade met stout resistance in the city center from Spanish regulars and militiamen firing from rooftops, gradually becoming enveloped and forced to surrender. English losses totaled 311 killed, 679 wounded, 208 missing, and 1,600 prisoners, compared with the defenders' 600 casualties and 700 captives. That same evening, de Liniers proposed a cessation of hostilities and mutual restoration of prisoners if the British agreed to evacuate the entire River Plate region within the next 2 months—including their 1,500-man garrison at Montevideo—to which Whitelocke acceded, convinced that his remaining strength was insufficient to subdue both Buenos Aires and its district. His troops therefore bivouacked at Retiro and began re-embarking by 9 July, sailing away 3 days later, while Montevideo was relinquished in September 1807.

Independence and Early Republican Strife (1808–1852)

Ironically, these allegiances were to be reversed less than a year later, when the new French emperor, Napoleon I, sent an army into Spain to depose King Ferdinand VII in favor of his brother Joseph Bonaparte on 7 June 1808, so that the Spaniards and British became allies. With the consequent lifting of the Royal Navy's blockade, hundreds of British merchantmen descended upon the River Plate, offering such an array of goods that its market quickly became saturated and consumer prices collapsed, resulting in heavy losses for traders of both nationalities. One of the few bright spots remained overseas demand for beef, leather, and tallow, so that bulk exports remained persistently strong—although large-scale ranchers out of the interior now began gaining an ascendancy over the *porteño* commercial elite. By the end of the decade, Buenos Aires boasted a secondary school—the Colegio de San Carlos—and ten primary schools, in addition to two hospitals, an orphanage, and a home for "wayward" women.

More important, though, the climate of economic and political self-interest unleashed throughout the Spanish empire by Ferdinand's deposal fed a growing sentiment within the port city in favor of outright independence. A coup attempt against Viceroy de Liniers on 1 January 1809 had been easily put down, yet unsubstantiated doubts as to his loyalty to the captive Bourbon monarch—simply on account of his French birth—led to his replacement by Adm. Baltasar Hidalgo de Cisneros, a veteran of the Battle of Trafalgar. Popular opinion also coalesced behind the notion of creating a semiautonomous Creole junta (council) at Buenos Aires, similar to the body spearheading resistance against Napoleon in occupied Spain.

Hidalgo de Cisneros finally bowed to the pressure of a great public assembly in Buenos Aires's main square on 20 May 1810 that called for his resignation and the convocation of a *cabildo abierto* (open town meeting). Two days later he authorized the convening of such a body, expecting to serve as its president. Yet after becoming constituted, the royal official found himself deposed on 25 May by militia Col. Cornelio Saavedra and the radical politician Mariano Moreno in the so-called May Revolution, which, although still professing a token loyalty to the captive king, marked the beginning of Argentine independence. Some 1,500 volunteers marched out of Buenos Aires a month and a half later under Col. Francisco Ortiz de Ocampo and Lt.-Col. Antonio González Balcarce to spread their revolutionary philosophy into the viceroyalty's interior, and when a Loyalist countercoup was uncovered that same August, the radical junta ordered its ringleaders shot—including the former viceroy de Liniers.

Buenos Aires consequently served as a regional patriot springboard, its so-called Army of the Andes pressing up into upper Peru (modern Bolivia) under González Balcarce before finally being repelled at the Battle of Huaqui the following year. The same fate befell the revolutionary force sent into Paraguay under Gen. Manuel Belgrano. Still, the port city's adherence to the insurgent cause kept the struggle for independence alive throughout the region, while also denying the strategic advantage of the capital's position to the viceregal successors designated by Madrid, so that Francisco Javier de Elio and Gaspar Vigodet were constrained to attempt to govern while besieged inside Montevideo.

Buenos Aires suffered economically throughout this protracted conflict, as well as from an absence of proper municipal development. The chaotic revolutionary administration known as the First Triumvirate, for example, was overthrown on 8 October 1812 in favor of a so-called Second Triumvirate. Two and a half years later, the same occurred to the "supreme director," Gen. Carlos María de Alvear, at the hands of his rival, Gen. José Manuel Rondeau. Still, the city and its inland provinces proved sufficiently self-reliant to weather all royalist attempts at reconquest; thus by 9 July 1816, despite other unconcluded insurgencies raging in South America, a republic called the United Provinces of the River Plate could be officially proclaimed.

Unfortunately, the emergent nation was to be riven over the next several decades by bitter factional fighting between Buenos Aires's leadership, who strove to impose a "Unitarian," or centrist, vision of republicanism upon the country, and Argentina's inland provinces. The divergent economic interests, more conservative sociopolitical outlook, and long-simmering resentment held by the latter against the *porteño* stranglehold over trade would lead them to contest the capital's unilateral assumption of primacy a mere three days later, when they formed a rival "Federalist," or anticentralist, government at the city of Santa Fe. Rondeau retaliated by dispatching 1,500 troops from Buenos Aires up the Paraná River under Gen. José Miguel Díaz Vélez; despite gaining that largely deserted city by 4 August, they could not bring Federalist resistance to heel and retreated at month's end.

Santo Domingo Church in 1817, with typical congregants, as seen by Vidal. (Metropolitan Toronto Reference Library)

Defeats inland at the hands of Federalist forces in 1817–1818 threatened Buenos Aires itself, when Estanislao López's counterattack against the capital was checked in February 1819 by 2,400 *bonarense* soldiers marching north to San Nicolás de los Arroyos under Gen. Viamonte. Yet despite being deflected and contained, López recouped by annihilating Viamonte's vanguard on 10 March and driving his survivors back into Rosario, from where Viamonte agreed to a truce by 12 April. When Buenos Aires's "Supreme Director" Rondeau subsequently attempted to resume the civil war that same November, several of his units mutinied or defected, dooming his demoralized 2,000 followers to be dispersed from the banks of Cepeda Creek southwest of San Nicolás by 1,600 Federalists under López on 1 February 1820, so that Rondeau resigned a fortnight later.

Two weeks afterward, the Treaty of Pilar was signed, seemingly bringing an end to Argentina's strife with a Federalist triumph. Yet as early as 6 March 1820, disgruntled elements within the capital deposed the interim governor, Manuel de Sarratea, in favor of their former Unitarian champion, Gen. Juan Ramón Balcarce, obliging López's Federalist army to intervene six days later. Fighting spread anew, so that López and the Chilean-born Federalist Brig. José Miguel Carrera marched upon Buenos Aires in late June with slightly more than 1,500 troops to restore their ally Alvear as its governor. The 1,750 *bonarense* soldiers that the rival Gov. Miguel Estanislao Soler brought out to offer battle were defeated at Cañada de la Cruz, 12 miles southwest of Campana, so that he resigned a few days later.

The Federalists were unable to gain the capital, however, so that Manuel Dorrego was instead named as his successor; he sallied from Buenos Aires with a small army on 18 July 1820 to drive away López. Two weeks later, Dorrego made a rapid nocturnal march to fall upon 700 unsuspecting Federalists under Col. José M. Benavente at San Nicolás on 2 August. At a cost of 7 dead and 42 wounded, Dorrego destroyed this unit, killing 60 and capturing 450. The governor then achieved a second victory ten days later, when he crossed Pavón Creek with 1,500 riders and dispersed 500 troopers encamped on its north bank under López himself. At Gamonal, however, Dorrego's luck ran out when he overtook the fleeing López with 600 riders and a field-piece on 2 September. Not realizing that his opponent had been reinforced and now commanded 1,000 cavalrymen, both armies collided in a frontal charge that saw Dorrego enveloped and compelled to surrender after suffering 320 killed and 100 captured.

Because of Dorrego's capture, Gen. Martín Rodríguez proclaimed himself governor of Buenos Aires on 26 September 1820. Five days later, Brigadier Pagola rose against him, his faction being put down after two days of heavy fighting in the city streets. The 5th Colorados del Monte Militia Cavalry Regiment proved crucial in its support of Rodríguez, winning its twenty-seven-year-old commander, Juan Manuel de Rosas, promotion to colonel.

The Treaty of Benegas was signed on 24 November 1820, bringing a halt to the fratricidal struggle between Buenos Aires, Santa Fe, and Córdoba. On 2 December, General Carrera, dissatisfied with its terms, sacked and burned Buenos Aires's suburb of Salto in conjunction with Indian warriors, then retired southward. He was pursued two weeks later by General Ramírez in the so-called *expedición al desierto* (expedition into the desert), which failed to catch this renegade. But after capturing San Luis and laying siege to Córdoba in March 1821, Carrera was defeated.

Yet notwithstanding such political flare-ups, Buenos Aires remained the troubled young republic's sole outlet to the world. By 1822, its population was officially tallied at 56,416 inhabitants, although the true figure was estimated as high as 68,900. With old mercantilist restraints removed, the city inevitably prospered as the sole importer of cheap European goods, as well as being the traditional exporter of hides and other cattle by-products. In fact, the latter trade escalated noticeably in both volume and value, thanks to improved methods of animal husbandry introduced on outlying ranches, as well as better preservation techniques practiced at the *saladeros* (meat-salting plants) that sprang up around the capital's periphery, especially along both banks of the Riachuelo and in the neighborhood of Barracas. *Estancieros* (ranchers) grew increasingly wealthy as a result, expanding their operations by claiming vast new stretches of the Pampas to graze their ever larger herds; sheep were introduced into Argentina around that same time, eventually resulting in a significant wool industry.

Sea traffic became compromised after the government of President Bernardino Rivadavia supported the expedition led in the spring of 1825 by Uruguayan patriot Juan Antonio Lavalleja to free his homeland from Brazilian occupation and who—despite failing immediately to wrest Montevideo or other major cities from enemy control—nonetheless agreed to incorporate his unreclaimed country into Rivadavia's Argentine union as of 24 October. Rio de Janeiro retaliated by declaring the so-called Cisplatine War on 10 December, so that a Brazilian squadron moved into the River Plate estuary eleven days later to impose a blockade against Buenos Aires. Argentine Adm. Guillermo Brown sortied from Los Pozos naval base in February 1826 to launch a yearlong series of attempts to drive the enemy out of the waterway, and a Brazilian squadron under Adm. James Norton counterattacked Los Pozos itself on 11 June 1826.

Unprepared for prolonged hostilities, the Argentine government virtually collapsed within a year, further sapped by simmering resentment expressed by many interior provinces against the traditional primacy still being exerted by the capital. The disgraced government finally sought terms from Brazil in the summer of 1828, and five days after the first embittered Argentine contingents had returned into Buenos Aires on 26 November, Gen. Juan Galo Lavalle led a revolt that deposed President Dorrego. The latter united with the influential rural landowner Juan Manuel de Rosas while marching with 2,000 ill-armed volunteers toward Santa Fe for more help, prompting Lavalle to appoint Admiral Brown as interim governor of Buenos Aires on 6 December, then sally in his opponent's pursuit.

The capture and summary execution of Dorrego a few days later exacerbated resistance, so that Lavalle was obliged to defend Buenos Aires by again emerging with 1,900 troops and four guns to confront more than 2,000 approaching foes under Rosas and Estanislao López. They fought an indecisive action on 26 April 1829 at Márquez Bridge over the Reconquista River, before Lavalle retreated to Altolaguirre—a mere dozen miles outside the capital—to conduct protracted negotiations with Rosas. The latter was to emerge as the national strongman and dominate politics for the next 23 years, routinely placing the interests of Buenos Aires above those of the interior, so that tensions continued. The inland provinces of La Rioja, San Juan, Mendoza, San Luis, Santiago del Estero, Tucumán, Catamarca, Salta, Jujuy, and Córdoba consequently formed the Liga Unitaria or Unitarian League, also known as the Liga del Interior or Interior League, in July 1830, to which Buenos Aires, Corrientes, Santa Fe, and Entre Ríos responded by signing the Pacto Federal in January 1831. They thereby created the so-called Liga del Litoral or Coastal League, which subdued its opponents by the end of that same year.

Buenos Aires was to be once more threatened militarily in August 1840, after Lavalle's 2,700 rebel troopers, 300 infantrymen, and four field-pieces had pushed down the Paraná River. But when this army began its final offensive against the capital on 29 August, Lavalle hesitated because of his lack of local support and the apparent strength of Rosas's defenses (greatly exaggerated through false intelligence reports). Five days later at Cañada de la Paja, near the headwaters of Morales Creek, only 3 miles southwest of the capital, the invaders' 400-man cavalry vanguard scattered 200 Rosist troopers and took Merlo by 5 September. Yet Lavalle again halted his advance, convinced that he was too weak to storm Buenos Aires, and so reversed course upriver the next day to attack Santa Fe instead.

Eventually, though, the iron-fisted rule of the conservative Rosas was to be overwhelmed by widespread opposition. On 3 February 1852, he made his last stand, with 12,000 cavalry troopers, 10,000 infantrymen, and 1,000 gunners manning 56 artillery pieces at Caseros Estate on the banks of Morón Creek, southwest of Buenos Aires. His opponent, the rebel general Justo José Urquiza, crossed over that same morning with his own slightly larger army, launching a devastating charge with 10,000 riders on his right wing that destroyed Rosas's left and consumed the Rosist reserves in a vain attempt to stem the onslaught. Individual units resisted tenaciously, but the bulk of Rosas's army disintegrated after suffering 1,500 casualties and 7,000 men captured, as well as the loss of all its artillery, provisions, and equipment, compared with 600 dead and wounded among Urquiza's ranks. Rosas fled to the British embassy in the capital with his daughter, departing to live out the remaining twenty-five years of his life as an exile in Southampton. Meanwhile, the victorious Urquiza designated Vicente López y Planes the next day as the new governor of Buenos Aires, and a new era in its urban evolution was about to commence.

Transition (1853–1879)

Buenos Aires initially fared badly under this new regime, as Urquiza and delegates from the interior moved to reorganize the national government along confederate lines in the hope of diminishing the capital's influence. Governor López and other ministers subsequently resigned in protest on 23 June 1852, clearing the way for Gen. Manuel Guillermo Pinto to assume office. Urquiza voided this gesture, then dissolved the legislature and compelled his most vocal critics to leave. A second insurrection occurred on 11 September, three days after Urquiza had quit Buenos Aires to attend the national congress at Santa Fe, compelling his outnumbered garrison under the military governor, Gen. José Miguel Galán, to retreat toward

San Nicolás, thereby allowing Pinto to be proclaimed president and Buenos Aires's rebellion to take full hold. Yet rather than plunge the country back into civil war, Urquiza instead sent emissaries into the city on 18 September, offering to recognize its separation from the other provinces.

Unable to hammer out a compromise, a rival confederate capital was thereupon created at Paraná early in the spring of 1853, after which Urquiza as confederate president returned and besieged Buenos Aires with 12,000 troops. This encirclement grew tighter on 17 April, when a squadron under American-born Commo. John H. Coe destroyed its Buenos Aires counterpart, then imposed a close blockade. But Coe was bought off on 20 June, bringing his warships into Buenos Aires in exchange for 26,000 ounces of gold. The confederate congress then passed a resolution federalizing Buenos Aires as part of its constitutional overhaul, which prompted numerous besieging units to switch loyalties, so that Urquiza was obliged to lift his siege by 13 July and retreat into Entre Ríos Province, temporarily retiring from public life.

Street carnival in Buenos Aires, 1837; engraving by the visiting French artist Auguste Borget. Note the architecture, little changed from Spanish colonial times. (*Fragments d'un voyage autour du monde*)

Despite being left as a separate capital, considerable resentment lingered among the 90,000 inhabitants of Buenos Aires because three days before withdrawing, Urquiza had signed a treaty with France, England, and the United States promising free navigation up the Paraná and Uruguay rivers, thus bypassing the city's monopoly over inland traffic. Yet this confederate agreement nonetheless opened the doors to a broad influx of foreign capital and technologies into both the strife-torn republic and its seaport capital, especially helping to benefit and modernize the latter. Buenos Aires enjoyed an economic resurgence and its first few modern enhancements, such as its first railway—the Ferrocarril del Oeste, which was laid down westward toward Flores and Merlo as of 1854—as well as gas lighting, which was introduced the next year. However, frictions persisted with the interior confederation over such contentious issues as customs duties and free passage, until Urquiza was finally authorized by the confederate congress on 29 May 1859 to use any means necessary to bring Buenos Aires back into the national fold. The city countered by dispatching the steamers *General Pinto* and *Buenos Aires* up the Paraná River on 7 July to contest any immediate confederate descent, yet marines aboard the former vessel mutinied against their commander, Col. José Muratore, and switched loyalties.

Urquiza mustered a large army and arrived north of Pavón Creek by 22 October 1859 with 10,000 confederate troopers, 3,000 infantrymen, and 1,000 gunners manning thirty-two field-pieces. To his south awaited Gen. Bartolomé Mitre with 4,700 Buenos Aires infantrymen, 4,000 cavalrymen, and 300 artillerymen with twenty-four guns. A *bonarense* cavalry detachment crossed Medio Creek and clashed near Rica Canyon with the advance confederate elements, only to retire once reinforcements were rushed to the scene. The next day, confederate Gen. Benjamín Virasoro drove in Mitre's skirmishers from the east bank of Medio Creek, clearing the way for Urquiza's main army to cross and take up position. Their final attack did not start until 6:00 P.M., the confederate cavalry on both flanks soon defeating their outnumbered opponents, after which Mitre's infantry on the left was annihilated. By 11:00 P.M., *bonarense* survivors were streaming off in defeat, Mitre reeling back into San Nicolás with only 2,000 men and six cannon after a thirty-six-hour, 50-mile forced march.

Urquiza retained 2,000 prisoners, twenty field-pieces, and all the baggage trains, so that when his confederate army—now swollen to an intimidating 20,000 men—halted at San José de Flores on 7 November 1859, hapless Buenos Aires had no choice but to agree to become reincorporated into the Argentine Union four days later. Yet despite its capitulation, the city continued to prosper from a rising tide of trade and manufacture, so that by 1862 it was functioning as de facto capital for both its provincial and the national governments. Its rail lines and industrial plants multiplied, while a swelling wave of European immigrants virtually doubled its population to 177,787 by 1869. The first tramways appeared in the urban core that same year, so improving public transportation that poorer residents began to congregate in the city's southern working-class neighborhoods, while the elite came to prefer the northern barrios of Palermo, Belgrano, and Barrio Norte—particularly after a yellow-fever epidemic gripped the southern neighborhoods of Constitución, San Telmo, and La Boca in 1871.

The burgeoning city was to undergo another ordeal in April 1880, after War Minister Gen. Julio A. Roca won the presidential elections, although his opponent, Dr. Carlos Tejedor—the governor of Buenos Aires—refused to concede, thereby threatening a renewal of Argentina's civil wars. The two men met aboard the gunboat *Pilcomayo* on 10 May to attempt to resolve this impasse, yet failed. On 2 June a shipment of 3,500 Mauser rifles was brought ashore and distributed among Tejedor's followers, so that two days later Roca declared Belgrano to be his new capital, and Tejedor was in a state of rebellion. After a few minor skirmishes, Roca's forces closed in upon Buenos Aires on 20 June, an 800-man cavalry column under Col. Nicolás Levalle probing Barracas Bridge. The next day, Col. Eduardo Racedo's troops stormed Alsina Bridge from the south, compelling Col. José Inocencio Arias's 7,000 defenders to redeploy at Los Corrales (modern Patricios Park) after a bloody engagement costing 1,200 casualties on both sides. The defenders then retreated into Buenos Aires proper that same afternoon, which was also blockaded on its seaward side by warships. Tejedor requested terms two days later; after a week's negotiations he resigned as governor, Roca being officially inaugurated as president on 12 October.

Demographic Boom and Physical Expansion (1880–1946)

That same year of 1880, Buenos Aires was reorganized as a federal district with the incorporation of the adjoining *partidos* or counties of Belgrano and Flores, as well as part of San Martín, and officially became designated as the capital of the republic. After lengthy debate, its harbor facilities were upgraded with the dredging and construction of modern dockyards in 1887 at Puerto Madero, on former mudflats east of the center. Increasingly wealthy civic leaders also poured their money and efforts into renovating Buenos Aires along European lines, most often drawing upon the designs of such contemporary French architects as Baron Georges Haussmann for inspiration. Thanks to the profits being generated by the myriad railway companies, factories, banks, shipping firms, and cultural institutions such as publishers, Buenos Aires underwent a dramatic transformation. The two plazas adjacent to its cathedral were reunited to create the Plaza de Mayo, while many older streets were widened and its urban core was cleared to make way for four parallel avenues: Santa Fe, Córdoba, Corrientes, and Avenida 25 de Mayo. The latter, upon its inauguration in 1894, became the major dividing line between the city's northern and southern sectors and sym-

Modern docks installed at Buenos Aires, as they appeared, ca. 1900. Such enhanced facilities had greatly increased the city's volume of sea traffic. (Dawson, *The South American Republics*)

bolically linked the presidential palace or *Casa Rosada* with a new congressional complex a mile to its west.

Another political flare-up had occurred on 26 July 1890, while the feverish Argentine economy had been in the grip of one of its periodic downturns. Gen. Manuel J. Campos gathered 1,300 troops—three infantry battalions, the 1st Artillery Regiment, an engineering battalion, plus senior cadets from the military academies—in Artillería Park (site of the modern Tribunales Palace) to proclaim a revolt against President Dr. Miguel Juárez Celman. The naval squadron offshore also joined in, prompting Juárez Celman to leave the capital by train for Rosario, while delegating his vice president—Dr. Carlos Pellegrini—to deal with the crisis. Loyal troops quickly attacked the rebels, trapping them and setting off a night of bloody exchanges, during which more than 1,000 people were killed. At dawn of 27 July, Campos requested a truce to tend to his wounded, then surrendered two days later; Juárez Celman nevertheless resigned on 6 August, being succeeded by Pellegrini.

The pace of commercial and demographic advances continued unabated despite this incident, and the census of 1895 revealed that Buenos Aires's population had mushroomed into 663,854 inhabitants. Impressive public and private build-

ings were now being erected throughout its downtown core, as well as scenic parks and promenades, while the British-owned railway companies created English-style stations named Constitución and Retiro to service the city's southern and northern sectors, respectively. The first automobiles were already circulating, the first elevator was installed by 1898, and the first bus appeared in 1904. Some avenues became lined with beautiful jacaranda trees, some sidewalks were laid in Swedish marble, while Parisian-style cafés, hotels, theaters, and bookshops multiplied. The first subway was dug in 1913, and new port facilities called Puerto Nuevo were added north of Madero near Retiro the next year. Commercial activity remained concentrated west and north of Plaza de Mayo, while recent European arrivals—precluded from buying even small farms on the surrounding pampas because of the monopoly enjoyed by an oligarchy of large landowners—toiled instead in the meatpacking plants, factories, and service industries that ringed the city, especially along its southern periphery.

By 1914, the population of Buenos Aires stood at 1,575,814 inhabitants, with another 458,217 scattered among its nineteen adjoining counties, which together now comprised the

Buenos Aires's splendid 25 de Mayo Avenue, ca. 1905, boasting some of its new Parisian-style edifices. (Keane, *Central and South America*)

Federal District's greater metropolitan area. Of this mass of people, almost half were foreign-born, and 80 percent lived in cramped, single-room dwellings because the housing industry could not hope to keep pace with such a relentless influx. Sanitation, lighting, water supplies, and paving were equally laggard. Well-to-do *bonarenses* of the northern sector sought to escape this increasing congestion by creating additional suburban *quintas* (estates) along the River Plate shoreline at San Isidro, Vicente López, and Olivos, effectively expanding the urban boundaries toward Tigre. Middle-class neighborhoods clustered around the city center and westward beyond Flores, while to the south lay the industrial, manufacturing, and working-class areas of Nueva Pompeya, Barracas, Avellaneda, and La Boca.

Buenos Aires continued its dynamic growth throughout the 1920s, its financial, cultural, and industrial infrastructures attracting visitors from throughout South America. Displays of great opulence nonetheless coexisted around the sprawling slum tenements known as *conventillos,* until the volatile fluctuations of Argentina's economy were dealt a crippling blow by the stock market crash of October 1929, which plunged the entire world into the Great Depression. Less than a year later, the effects of this calamity embroiled the capital once more in political conflict.

On the Saturday morning of 6 September 1930, after several weeks of civil unrest, Lt.-Gen. José Félix Uriburu launched a carefully planned military uprising against the second term of seventy-eight-year-old President Hipólito Yrigoyen, receiving support from the Campo de Mayo Army Base, Palomar Air Base, and the senior military college outside Buenos Aires. At noon the mutinous general marched into the capital, and he had occupied all government buildings by 5:30 P.M., encountering only sporadic opposition around the congress. A burst of fighting erupted during the night of 8 September, when nervous sentries at the Casa Rosada mistakenly fired upon another rebel contingent in the gloom, killing one soldier and seven civilians, as well as wounding twelve soldiers and thirty-six civilians. Yrigoyen meanwhile went into exile from La Plata, after which Uriburu imposed martial law and purged the government. But upon the holding of new provincial elections on 5 April 1931, Yrigoyen's Radical Union Party still emerged victorious, much to the general's dismay—prompting him to annul its results. When presidential elections were held on 8 November 1931, the Radical Unionists boycotted, and Uriburu engineered the victory of his fellow conspirator, Gen. Agustín P. Justo.

Economic recovery was nonetheless slow to follow for Argentina, and poverty became so acute throughout its countryside that many rural dwellers also began migrating into the capital in search of jobs, so that Buenos Aires's population continued to swell beyond the 2,413,829 residents recorded in

1936. The numbers of these newest arrivals proved so weighty as to eventually influence political developments. On 3–4 June 1943, a military coup spearheaded by Gens. Arturo Rawson and Pedro Pablo Ramírez deposed President Ramón S. Castillo, and by 18 June they had installed a new pro-Fascist administration under Ramírez. It soon became apparent, though, that the real driving force behind this regime was a clique of nationalistic army colonels with totalitarian leanings known as the Grupo de Oficiales Unidos (Group of United Officers, or GOU), dominated by the forty-seven-year-old Col. Juan Domingo Perón, who was furthermore very aware of the need for mass appeal and control. In September, more than seventy newspapers were forced to suspend publication for criticizing this military dictatorship.

However, Washington pressured Ramírez into severing diplomatic relations with Nazi Germany and Japan on 26 January 1944, leading to his ouster by a clique of GOU officers, who were concerned that he was about to declare war against the Axis powers. Although replaced by his vice president, Gen. Edelmiro J. Farrell, Perón now emerged as the government's true power broker, being appointed war minister by 4 May and vice president on 8 July. When hostilities were finally declared against the Axis on 27 March 1945, in a belated attempt to placate the United States, a faction led by Gen. Eduardo J. Avalos and Adm. Héctor Vernengo Lima arrested Perón on 9 October,

stripping him of his titles. Eight days later, though, he engineered a countercoup with support from organized labor, then married his staunchest backer—the charismatic and politically astute actress María Eva, or "Evita," Duarte—and was subsequently elected president on 24 February 1946, launching an ultranationalistic program of reforms backed by both the army and the newly powerful unions.

Modern Sprawl (1947–Present)

Buenos Aires was to be the centerpiece of Perón's domestic policies, which were tailored to cater to the urban masses by improving social benefits, housing, and public sector jobs. Transit, utilities, and many other major industries were all nationalized, while imports became restricted, measures designed to benefit a population, which by 1947 had grown to 2,982,580 city dwellers—although the actual total was 4,798,670 when the entire metropolitan area was taken into account. Two years afterward, Argentina's constitution was even amended so that the president was granted complete power over the Federal District, appointing its *intendente* or mayor without any input from the electorate.

In September 1951, Perón stifled a military coup just two months prior to another presidential election, in which he was easily reelected—although because of army disapproval, his wife Evita's name had been removed from the vice presidential

The city of Buenos Aires, Argentina. (Yann Arthus-Bertrand/Corbis)

slate; she died of cancer that following year. The president's unrealistic policies then began to experience difficulties, as the lavishing of so many public jobs eroded the value of currency, so that the buying power and standards of living declined sharply among the middle and working classes. Fraud, featherbedding, inefficiency, reduced foreign commerce, and a relentless rural-to-urban migration pattern further aggravated the city's woes, and unrest grew.

Relations between Perón's faltering government and the Catholic Church reached such a low ebb that he was excommunicated, prompting an abortive coup on 16 June 1955 by the navy and part of the air force, but which was suppressed by the army. However, with the Argentine economy in ruins, Perón was compelled to declare martial law by 1 September, although another military revolt nonetheless erupted in the interior two weeks later, causing him to resign by 19 September and go into exile aboard a Paraguayan gunboat anchored off Buenos Aires. Four days later, Maj.-Gen. Eduardo Lonardi was provisionally installed into office as president, yet he too was deposed, on 13 November, by Gen. Pedro E. Aramburu, because of his tolerant attitude toward former Peronistas and appointment of ultranationalistic Catholic ministers to the cabinet.

Both the city and nation fell into a cycle of recurrent economic and political crises, set against a backdrop of continued metropolitan sprawl and demographic growth. Foreign invest-ment resurged, especially by U.S. multinational firms in the local petrochemical, metallurgical, mechanical, pharmaceutical, and electronics industries. Soon, a second industrial belt began to encircle Buenos Aires, especially along the principal axes of communications. By 1970, its population stood at 5,380,447—or 8,352,900 if the greater metropolitan area was included. To accommodate the expanding business demands, the municipal government developed the Catalinas Norte office complex opposite the old Retiro railway station, deactivated the decades-old docks of Puerto Madero, and pushed back the River Plate shoreline with landfill and reclamation projects. Construction of major freeways also commenced during the 1970s to try to ease the frequent traffic jams caused by many more circulating automobiles and trucks.

Despite such efforts, the fragile national economy lurched through boom-to-bust cycles, resulting in heavy foreign debts, currency devaluations, collapses, and uncertain standards of living. Political repression became particularly acute after the so-called Dirty War against leftist urban guerrillas erupted in 1976, and Buenos Aires was to remain the scene of outbursts into present times. By 1991, the population for the entire metropolitan area had stabilized at 10,686,163 inhabitants.

For further reading materials on the history of Buenos Aires, please consult the Select Bibliography at the end of this volume.

Bolivia

LA PAZ

Ancient mining center that evolved into an Andean crossroads and the highest metropolis in the Americas.

Origins (1185–1547)

Nestled at 12,000 feet above sea level, La Paz lies sheltered on the floor of a deeply eroded valley that spans some 10 miles long by 3 miles wide and whose flanks rise 1,500 feet on three sides to the edge of another vast plateau. Farther east loom still higher snowcapped peaks crowned by the 21,000-foot dormant volcano Illimani. It is believed that the valley has been populated since at least 1185 by inhabitants who eked out an existence by panning for gold washed down from the multicolored valley faces into streams below.

La Paz's early inhabitants passed under the domination of the Collas or Cullawas, a branch of the Aymara tribe of the larger Tiahuanaco or Tiwanacu nation. They named this particular valley Chuquiapu Marka (Place of the Goldfields). About 1511, the Aymaras were in turn subjugated by the Incas after a series of military campaigns. Little more than two decades later, the Incan capital of Cuzco was conquered by a Spanish army under Francisco Pizarro, whose subordinate Diego de Almagro was then detached to subdue all southern vassal states.

During his southward progression toward Chile, Almagro sent a company of conquistadores under Capt. Juan de Saavedra to reconnoiter the densely populated Chuquiapu or Chuquiabo Valley in 1535, yet they did not establish any formal Spanish settlement. A few individual prospectors arrived three years later and began exploiting its native gold miners

An Aymara Indian, ca. 1900–1923. (Library of Congress)

A "Chola" or Colla woman, ca. 1900–1923. (Library of Congress)

667

until most of these early colonizers were slain during an uprising. Pizarro reimposed Spanish rule in 1540, drafting Indian conscripts, dubbed *yanaconas,* from other regions to begin reworking the valley's gold deposits. However, Pizarro was assassinated shortly thereafter in his palace at Lima, and the Spaniards splintered into bickering factions, thus ignoring the valley as civil war gripped Peru.

Eventually, an army rallied around the royal emissary Lic. Pedro de la Gasca and defeated Gonzalo Pizarro's adherents near Cuzco on 9 April 1548, thereby restoring Crown rule. In honor of this triumph, De la Gasca authorized his loyal backer Capt. Alonso de Mendoza to found a new town halfway along the wending mountain trails between Cuzco and the recently discovered silver mines at Potosí, on condition that this community be named after Nuestra Señora de la Paz (Our Lady of the Peace) to commemorate the restoration of harmony among the Spaniards.

Foundation and Early Vicissitudes (1548–1568)

De Mendoza duly reached the town of Laja and drew up a charter for his new settlement by 20 October 1548. He then pushed 25 miles south with nine Spanish settlers and penetrated the Chuquiabo Valley as far as *hoya del Choqueyapu* (Choqueyapu Dell), where on 23 October he selected a site near the existing Aymara hamlet of Churubamba—on an *isla* (island) between the confluence of the Choqueyapu and Mejavira rivers—to establish his Pueblo Nuevo de Nuestra Señora de la Paz (New Town of Our Lady of the Peace). Individual plots were assigned around a central square (modern Murillo Plaza), each property being marked off with crude fences and within which compounds adobe huts were to be erected.

The displaced Aymaras were recongregated into a new community named San Sebastián, while Yanacona conscripts were gathered the following year around a new Franciscan mission created by Fr. Francisco de los Angeles on the southern bank of the Choqueyapu River in an area that became known as the San Pedro y Santiago suburb. The former Ayllu Inca overseers were resettled east of the Mejavira River into yet another new community called Santa Bárbara de los Alcañices. All these Indian satellites consisted of circular dwellings laid out in a haphazard pattern and were much more densely populated than the Spanish core.

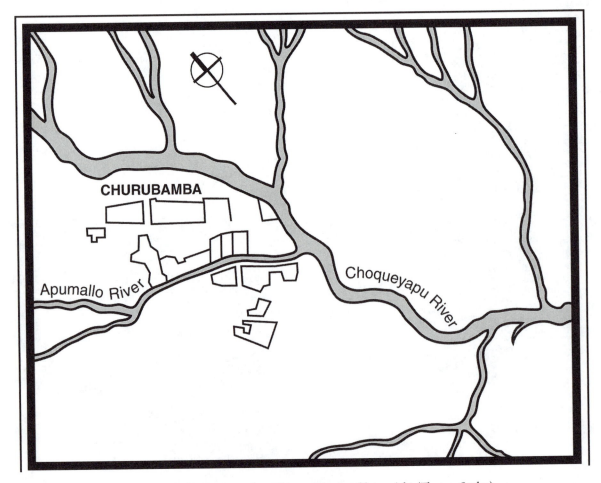

Modern sketch map of La Paz's original layout, November 1548; north is toward lower right. (Thomas Conley)

Within a very few years, construction began on a main church, hospital, and *tambo*, the Incan word for travelers' inn. La Paz's *calle real* (royal street) was paved over with cobblestones, others streets were leveled, and a public fountain was installed. Unfortunately, though, the fledgling town was still subject to raids out of the north by unsubjugated war parties of Yungas (Chunchos). The town was also sacked early in 1554 when the disgruntled Cuzcan landowner Francisco Hernández Girón led a revolt against the Crown's pro-Indian legislation, delegating the hardened adventurer Antonio Carrillo to occupy La Paz. He mistreated the inhabitants and even dug up hidden treasures from the grounds of the Franciscan convent, before being murdered by four *Paceños* inside the town's best two-story house—which Carrillo had commandeered as his residence—on 11 June 1554. A few months later, his chief Hernández Girón was also defeated and beheaded, thus bringing the insurrection to an end.

Work resumed on La Paz's town hall, treasury, and jail in 1556, yet due to the more compelling allure of Potosí's rich silver bonanza—as well as the rather bleak nature of La Paz's own landscape—the town did not thrive. With only forty-two Spanish householders and a like number of other inhabitants recorded in a census five years later, the Crown stripped La Paz of its salaried office of municipal *corregidor* by a royal decree issued on 18 October 1561, instead leaving regional administration to a few locally elected and unpaid *alcaldes ordinarios* (magistrates). Four years later, the president of the viceregal *Audiencia* (tribunal) at Lima attempted to reinstate La Paz's title of *corregidor* so as to reduce jurisdictional disputes that had already resulted in some disturbances and deaths, yet this request was refused by Madrid.

Emergence (1569–1660)

The Peruvian viceroy Francisco de Toledo was at last able to restore La Paz's status in 1569, as a reward for the 130 of 200 municipality residents who had volunteered to confront a rogue band of Spanish soldiers that roamed through the Camata Valley the previous summer under the renegade Capt. Gómez de Tordoya. Moreover, an economic purpose had also been found for La Paz—to cater to the stream of travelers bound to and from the sprawling mining camps at Potosí. Over the next century, the city would evolve into a crucial way station for such traffic, providing lodging and sustenance for Crown and Church officials, merchants and traders, soldiers

Street scene in La Paz, ca. 1905, with stagecoaches gathered before one of its famous *tambos* or "inns." (Keane, *Central and South America*)

and teamsters, as well as thousands of *mitayos* or conscripted Indian laborers being marched for a year's work in the mines and smelters.

Despite the chilly highland climate, arid terrain, and meager rainfall, *Paceños* were able to develop some farming to supplement the meager food supplies that otherwise had to be imported from Cuzco or other more distant districts. A few Castilians in particular found conditions upon this gray and windswept *meseta* (plateau) similar to central Spain, and they gradually began harvesting coca, potatoes, *quinuas,* and *cañahuas* as well as raising sheep and goats. In addition, some mining activity commenced at the nearby silver deposits of Sicasica and Berenguela, while gold placer mining was conducted at Tipuani. Both helped to spur the small city's growth.

When market-bound produce was diverted into other competing jurisdictions during a food shortage fifteen years later, Vasco de Contreras, one of La Paz's eldest residents, was able to use the city's enhanced importance as a strategic way station to petition the Peruvian viceroy Fernando de Torres y Portugal, Conde de Villar, to extend its municipal boundaries so as to encompass up to 30 miles in every direction on 25 September 1586. Two years later, La Paz's urban population was estimated at 260 Spanish residents and 5,820 Indians. *Paceños,* moreover, sought financial relief from King Philip II in 1590 by claiming that, because of the cost of conveying goods into the Andes, work on their church had been suspended for more than twenty years and their hospital remained without medicines.

(In a minor historical sidelight, the crippled Spanish veteran and struggling playwright Miguel de Cervantes Saavedra—hopeful of securing a livelihood through a Crown posting in the Americas—had solicited appointment as La Paz's *corregidor* from Seville on 21 May 1590; had this petition been granted, the immortal *Don Quixote* might never have been published fifteen years later.)

La Paz's allotment of Indian tributaries, who were obliged to perform services for its Spanish residents, was reduced from 1,500 to 700 in 1593 after all Andean tribes had been decimated by an epidemic. The city nonetheless continued its modest growth, spreading southeast into several new blocks between the Mejavira and Choqueyapu rivers by 1603 and boasting five small convents tended by perhaps thirty monks. In October of that same year, the Crown even decided to elevate La Paz into its own separate episcopal see, as the regional bishop was unable to visit all his parishes from his headquarters at La Plata (formerly Chuquisaca; modern Sucre). Rome approved this measure via the Papal bull *Super specula militantis ecclesiae,* issued on 4 July 1605, and La Paz's first bishop, the Dominican Domingo de Valderrama Centeno, arrived from the island of Santo Domingo five years later. He promptly spurred work on the city's partially completed cathedral, whose interior lay exposed to the elements.

Some flannel- and wool-making operations had also developed privately throughout the municipality. In addition, some

The city crest, as depicted in a report submitted by Bishop Antonio del Castro y Castillo in May 1651. Around the edge appears the original sixteenth-century motto *Los discordes en concordia, en paz y amor se juntaron, y Pueblo de Paz fundaron para perpétua memoria* or "The discordant gathered in concord, in peace and love, and Town of Peace founded in perpetual memory." (Archive of Indies, Seville)

silversmithies were created, so that most Spanish *Paceños* ate off silverware that was exempt from royal taxes and cheaper than imported European tableware. Despite its unprepossessing appearance, the city had become a well-established community and center of its own distinct administrative region, as well as the main stopover for travelers traversing the Andes.

Stagnation (1661–1780)

A commercial slowdown and economic depression set in as Potosí's silver production gradually tapered off during the seventeenth century, fueling the simmering resentment felt by locally born mestizos (offspring of whites and natives, a derivation of the Latin term *mixticius* or mixed) against the powers monopolized by Iberian-born Spaniards. A revolt therefore exploded on 10 December 1661 with the arrest of Antonio Gallardo, a popular mestizo mine owner from Puno. That same night, a dozen armed men forced their way into the residence of La Paz's *corregidor,* Gen. Cristóbal de Cañedo, slaying him along with another peninsular companion and wounding three more.

The next morning, to cries of *¡Viva el Rey!* and *¡Muera mal* *gobierno!* ("Long live the King!" and "Death to bad government!"), several hundred mestizos gathered in the city streets, while the outnumbered Spaniards fled or sought sanctuary within its churches. On 20 December 1661, a small army of 300 mestizos and 150 Indians set off with 800 mules up the winding trail toward Lake Titicaca, 42 miles away, hoping to recruit further adherents and depose the hated *corregidor* of Paucarcolla, Pedro de Herquinijo Velarrinaga. The rebels, however, were defeated eight days later outside Puno and their ringleaders were slain, after which more than sixty fugitives who slipped back into La Paz were arrested and tortured, six eventually being executed.

With peace reimposed, the city's new San Juan de Dios Hospital opened three years later, and by 1675 La Paz's population was measured at 12,600 residents of whom the vast majority were Indians. Eight years later, the cathedral was finally completed, and an organ was installed thanks to the wealthy new bishop, Juan Queipo del Llano y Valdés. Shortly thereafter, small gold deposits were discovered in the foothills below Illimani, sparking a brief onrush of prospectors. Yet, as profits soon petered out, the city remained a rustic and impoverished Andean outpost well into the eighteenth century.

Siege and Reform (1781–1808)

Another rebellion gripped northern Peru after José Gabriel de Condorcanqui, Marqués de Oropesa—an Incan descendant better known as *Tupác Amaru,* chief of Tungasuca—executed a cruel Spanish *corregidor* in November 1780, sparking another widespread outburst. The distant viceroy Agustín de Jáuregui y Aldecoa attempted to placate popular discontent from Lima by banning all forced native labor, as well as dispatching 200 regular troops into the Andes. Tupác Amaru was defeated the next spring outside Cuzco and put to death on 18 May 1781. However, his brother Diego Cristóbal or *Tupác Katari* continued the struggle, overrunning Chucuito and threatening Puno and La Paz later that same summer.

As a result of such unrest, the city was strengthened by a defensive perimeter of adobe walls, while La Paz's five gates and ten bridge crossings were converted into military strongpoints. Diego Cristóbal arrived outside with perhaps 40,000 Indians to besiege the terrified Spanish inhabitants, but after 109 days—during which the natives even attempted to subdue its garrison through unleashing floodwaters—La Paz was rescued by a Spanish relief column in June 1781. When the rebels later attempted a second encirclement, they were scattered by 7,000 reinforcements from Oruro under Lt.-Col. José Reseguín. Diego Cristóbal eventually surrendered on 10 September 1781 to meet his fate.

In this rebellion's aftermath, as the extemporized city defenses began to come down, La Paz's forty-eight blocks and streets were realigned, the latter becoming paved to the very edge of urban boundaries. Other aspects of living conditions were upgraded in accordance with the reformist Bourbon spirit then sweeping the empire. Numerous new, two-story, private mansions in the Baroque style subsequently appeared, while Acting Intendant Fernando de la Sota inaugurated La Paz's first public lighting system in 1796. Iron-encased glass lamps were installed throughout the city, and their candles were tended after dark by hired watchmen. De la Sota also authorized the construction of the Coliseo Theater and a new bridge and had a census taken that revealed that La Paz's population had restabilized at 21,120 residents, comprised mostly of Indians, segregated into suburbs around a core of roughly 500 Spanish households.

De la Sota's successor, Antonio Burgunyó y Juan, furthermore rebuilt the San Juan de Dios Hospital, then directed that the principal city fountain—fed, like all lesser ones, from a covered *caja de agua* (cistern) in Riosinho Plaza—be replaced by a beautiful, white alabaster design created by the architect José Núñez del Prado. Commercial activity still centered around the eight city *tambos*—respectively named Quirquincho, Tejada, San José, San Miguel, San Antonio, Santiago, Carmen, and Cochabambinos or Remedios—where all imported merchandise was received and resold from stores, and through which all regional exports were shipped. Public entertainment consisted of bullfights in the main square, cockfights, and theater plays, while some private establishments also offered gambling and billiards.

Independence Struggle (1809–1825)

Like all other Spanish-American communities, the remote Andean city was astonished by news that the French emperor Napoleon I had sent an army into Spain early in 1808, deposing King Ferdinand VII in favor of his brother Joseph Bonaparte. Although such a crude usurpation of power was rejected, resistance quickly coalescing around an interim junta (council) established at Aranjuez in September 1808 to uphold their captive monarch's cause, the resultant climate of political uncertainty and loosened imperial ties did allow La Paz to experience its first taste of liberty.

On the morning of 16 July 1809, several hundred men under the republican mestizo agitator Pedro Domingo Murillo seized the city barracks in an almost bloodless coup and arrested both Intendant Tadeo Dávila and Bishop Remigio de la Santa y Ortega. An autonomous local junta was thereupon constituted, whose members—while still professing fealty to the imprisoned Ferdinand VII—rescinded numerous unpopular Crown decrees and raised 3,000 militiamen as a "national army." Such measures went well beyond the more conservative inclinations of their Andean neighbors, so that Murillo's faction soon found itself isolated. A counterexpedition of 3,200 troops advanced upon the city under Brig. José Manuel de Goyeneche, president of the Cuzcan *Audiencia,* so that La Paz's junta dissolved amid rancorous debate, and Murillo was detained by a rival on 11 October. Drunken and unpaid Creole militiamen looted La Paz's stores and homes before fleeing,

Map of the realigned and reconstructed city, as surveyed in 1796 on orders from Acting Intendant Fernando de la Sota, so as to plan for its first regulated public lighting system. (Archive of Indies, Seville)

Goyeneche entering on the morning of 25 October to restore order. Nine ringleaders were subsequently tracked down and executed, eighty-five received lesser punishments, and more than 500 *Paceños* remained under surveillance as suspected radicals.

The uneasy city endured a second occupation when a revolutionary Argentine army pushed up into the highlands under Col. Antonio González Balcarce, defeating a monarchist concentration at Suipacha on 7 November 1810. Nine days later, as Spanish royalists fled La Paz, Gov. Domingo Tristán Moscoso gathered sixty-five Creole citizens into a body and agreed to submit to the authority of the Buenos Aires junta. However, when their political deputy Juan José Castelli finally arrived on 10 April 1811, he immediately offended local sensibilities by interrupting La Paz's Ash Wednesday festivities, then alienated most inhabitants through his haughty demeanor, severity toward monarchists, and extremist ideology. When González Balcarce's army was subsequently defeated at the Battle of Huaqui or Guaqui on 20 June, the junta dissolved a fortnight later, and La Paz was looted again before returning to royalist rule.

The unhappy city was threatened by roving insurgent guer-rillas under Juan Manuel de Cáceres, then suffered a direct assault when an insurrection dubbed the "Pumacahua Rebellion" erupted at Cuzco in August 1814, its adherents calling for the reimplementation of Spain's liberal constitution of March 1812. A *cuzqueño* throng pushed southeast under Juan Manuel Pinelo and the priest Ildefonso de las Muñecas, overrunning Desaguadero by 13 September, before materializing outside La Paz with eight captured artillery pieces nine days afterward. Its defenses were stormed on 24 September and the heavily outnumbered Spanish garrison surrendered after a token resistance, many buildings once again being pillaged. Then on 28 September, while untrained insurgent troops were man-handling some powder barrels, an accidental detonation leveled the city barracks, and a hysterical mob murdered seventy-two monarchist captives—including Intendant Gregorio de Hoyos Fernández de Miranda, Marqués de Valde Hoyos, whose nude body was left dangling from a balcony opposite the main plaza.

Less than two weeks later, when a small royalist army approached from Oruro under Brig. Juan Ramírez, the main rebel force sortied to make a stand at Desaguadero, but were scattered on 2 November 1814. The next day, a vengeful

Ramírez allowed his victorious soldiers to sack La Paz as a reward, then summarily executed 108 patriot captives. A garrison of 350 royalist troops and twenty-five gunners was subsequently installed to hold the gutted city for the Crown, retaining it uncontested over the next nine years. However, trade remained moribund as virtually all overseas trade was paralyzed by warfare and the monarchist cause eventually faltered elsewhere in South America, the Peruvian viceroy José de la Serna e Hinojosa eventually being driven from Lima in the summer of 1821, retreating up into the Andes to reinstall his government at Cuzco.

A two-pronged insurgent pursuit penetrated the highlands two years later, patriot Gen. Andrés de Santa Cruz entering deserted La Paz without resistance by 8 August 1823, after Gen. Pedro Antonio de Olañeta's 2,500-man royalist army had retired toward Oruro. This liberation proved short-lived, though, for Viceroy de la Serna's 4,000 royalists soon united with Olañeta's contingent, driving Santa Cruz's and Agustín Gamarra's 4,500-man army hastily back toward Lake Titicaca. Overtaken near Ayo Ayo on 17 September, the insurgent retirement degenerated into a wholesale rout with some 2,000 being taken prisoner and with all their artillery and supplies being seized at Desaguadero Ford on 20 September. La Paz was then restored to monarchist rule for a fourth time.

The end of colonial rule came little more than a year later, when insurgent Gen. Antonio José de Sucre Alcalá, a subordinate of the Venezuelan-born "Liberator" Simón Bolívar, smashed the last royalist army and captured Viceroy de la Serna at the Battle of Ayacucho on 9 December 1824, after which monarchist resolve evaporated as Sucre marched higher into the Andes to receive the surrenders of Cuzco, Arequipa, and Puno. Olañeta reconcentrated 5,900 Loyalist troops around La Paz in a desperate bid to continue resisting, but his detached commanders began switching allegiances, so that the republican guerrilla chief José Miguel Lanza was able to occupy La Paz unopposed on 29 January 1825, while Olañeta was retreating toward Potosí.

Republican Strife (1825–1898)

Nine days later, Sucre's triumphant army entered half-deserted La Paz, and a decree was issued on 9 February 1825 calling for a representational assembly to decide the nation's future course. Olañeta was mortally wounded while attempting to put down a mutinous contingent and died on 2 April, bringing the struggle for independence to a close. At a congress celebrated at the former *Audiencia* capital of La Plata from July to August of the same year, it was decided to proclaim a new sovereign nation called the *República Boliviana* in honor of its liberator, who along with Sucre were offered its two top elected posts. Bolívar refused and instead drafted a national constitution before leaving on a triumphal departure tour, but his youthful subordinate was acclaimed Bolivia's first president on 25 May 1826.

According to its new constitution, four cities—La Plata,

Oruro, Cochabamba, and La Paz—would share the title of national capital in rotation, so as to avoid discord. La Paz also changed its official name to *La Paz de Ayacucho* in 1826 to pay additional homage to Sucre's great victory, yet its impoverished inhabitants soon tired of the Venezuelan born leader and his 2,000 Colombian troops. Viewed as foreign occupiers, they were driven from La Paz by the end of 1827, and a second mutiny the following spring by La Plata's garrison finally convinced Sucre to resign. He was succeeded in office by Marshal Santa Cruz, who was in turn challenged by Gen. Pedro Blanco in 1829, touching off a civil war. Santa Cruz emerged victorious two years later, promulgating a national code of laws that solidified his grip upon power.

A census taken in 1831 revealed that La Paz's population stood at 30,463 people, packed among 2,343 dwellings—an average of 13 residents per edifice, some of which were even spreading up the perilous valley inclines. Still, the city was fortunate to be somewhat self-sufficient agriculturally, given the unstable political and commercial climate elsewhere throughout Bolivia that hampered commercial traffic. A border conflict with Peru ten years later brought an invading army under President Gamarra into the Department of La Paz that attempted to besiege its capital in August 1841 in hopes of annexing the territory. The new Bolivian strongman, Gen. José Ballivián, succeeded in routing these invaders and slaying Gamarra, thereby retaining La Paz for Bolivia.

Despite its suffering, the city had nonetheless continued to grow. The architect Núñez del Prado completed a new *Palacio de Gobierno* (Government Palace) by 1841, as well as a new *Teatro Municipal* (Municipal Theater). A vast new cathedral was also commenced two years later, intended to become the largest in South America. The census of 1845 revealed that La Paz's population had rebounded to 42,842 inhabitants, its former Indian satellite communities now having become engulfed into the city. Throughout the remainder of the nineteenth century, Bolivia was wracked by a succession of military coups and countercoups that greatly hampered urban development.

In 1879, Bolivia's bankrupt national government launched a disastrous conflict against Chile—a four-year struggle dubbed the War of the Pacific that ended in defeat and cost the mountainous republic its last outlet to oceanic commerce at Arica. This setback was further exacerbated by a series of droughts, famines, and epidemics throughout the Andes that decimated the residents of La Paz's department. The city population had climbed to only 56,849 people by 1886—a modest 32 percent increase over 40 years—yet La Paz was still better off than its three rival capitals, as it lay closest to secondary export markets in Peru.

Modern Era (1899–Present)

Jealous of La Paz's influence and relative prosperity, frictions escalated into an attempt by Pres. Severo Alonso to rescind the

View of Santo Domingo Church on La Paz's public square, ca. 1868; note the stark and arid landscape. (Library of Congress)

old system of shared leadership among Bolivia's four major cities by elevating Sucre to the sole status of national capital. A *Paceño* army under Col. José Manuel Pando defeated a rival force some 40 miles away on 17 January 1899, then seized Oruro by 11 April. Alonso fled into exile and a new provisional government was formed that decreed three days later that Bolivia's federal government would henceforth reside at La Paz—although in a conciliatory gesture, Sucre would retain the nominal title of "national capital" and remain home to the supreme court. Pando was elected president without opposition and assumed office on 26 October, inaugurating a vigorous new Liberal regime that began transforming La Paz into a more modern metropolis.

Such efforts were greatly abetted by the belated peace treaty concluded with Chile in 1904, whereby the latter agreed in exchange for retaining their wartime conquests to pay a cash indemnity and construct a 273-mile railway up into the Andes from their captured port of Arica, thus linking La Paz via a 20-mile spur so that the Pacific once again became accessible to city merchants. The Bolivian capital blossomed as government agencies expanded and light textile industries were established over the ensuing twenty-five years, then experienced a further boom as demand for metal exports soared during World War I. La Paz's population mushroomed from 60,331 inhabitants in 1902 to 78,856 by 1909 and 135,768 by 1928. This growth was largely attributed to the influx of migrants from the impoverished countryside. Foreign expertise was also sought, such as that of the German military officer Hans Kundt who was hired along with two dozen colleagues in 1910 to establish Bolivia's first military academy.

The old city was almost entirely rebuilt during this period of growth, and many new French-style structures were introduced by Emilio Villanueva and other European-trained architects. No sixteenth- or seventeenth-century buildings remained, and only a dozen or so from the eighteenth century, such as a few churches and the National Art Museum. Even the shape of La Paz's streets was altered, as modern paving and sewer systems were installed. Previously, no sidewalks had existed, and streets tilted in toward a central trough called an *arroyo* or *albañal,* which carried raw sewage and rainwater toward the Choqueyapu River. Because of this malodorous flow, the northern end of the city, at a slightly higher elevation, had always been the preferred residential area. La Paz was also beautified by public works such as the Prado, a handsome promenade lined with rows of exotic trees, shrubs, and flowers—plantings not easily maintained in such an inhospitable climate.

Yet despite such gains, development was still handicapped by a lack of readily available fuel and power and the grinding poverty of a majority of residents—most still being illiterate Indians, many not even fluent in Spanish. The worldwide effects of the Great Depression precipitated by the New York stock market crash of October 1929 also injured Bolivia's economy. The calamitous war against Paraguay in 1932–1935, during which Bolivia's government unsuccessfully disputed ownership over a wedge of territory east of the Andes known as the *Chaco,* further hurt the national economy.

Yet, this unsuccessful conflict nonetheless encouraged considerable small-scale industrialization around La Paz, so that the city began expanding beyond its original boundaries. The wealthy Miraflores and Obrajes suburbs were officially incorporated as of 1938; Calacoto, Irpavi, Següencoma, and Villa Hugo Zalles (modern La Florida) were added in October 1942; while Villa Dolores was annexed five years later, and the windy heights of El Alto above the valley's *Ceja* (Brow)—where the city airport had been installed, being inhabited by as many as 48,000 people—were taken over by 1950. The Bolivian economy had furthermore received a major impetus when it became the Allies' principal source for tin throughout World War II, after mines in Malaya and Indonesia had fallen into Japanese hands as of December 1941.

La Paz's metropolitan population was measured at 301,450

Panorama across the modern city nestled within its valley, looking east toward the towering Illimani Volcano. (Turismo Bolivia)

residents by 1942 and 321,073 in 1950. Violent outbursts of political instability nevertheless continued to slow progress, as the white elite's military domination was increasingly challenged by populist groups sprung from its impoverished slums—such as the Fascistic *Movimiento Nacional Revolucionario* (National Revolutionary Movement), which overthrew the dictator Gen. Enrique Peñaranda in December 1943. Maj. Gualberto Villarroel became president, although real power rested with the MNR leader Victor Paz Estenssoro, who acted as finance minister. However, the party was in turn swept from office by a countercoup on 21 July 1946. Villarroel was hanged from a lamppost, and Paz Estenssoro, having escaped into Argentina, was eventually elected president from exile in 1951.

As rural-to-urban migration patterns gathered speed throughout Bolivia and Latin America during the latter half of the twentieth century, La Paz's population skyrocketed from 410,116 people in 1967 to 562,682 only three years later (of whom 50–60 percent remained illiterate). The metropolitan area now occupied the entire valley floor, except for a small, central hill. Industries and poorer neighborhoods, such as Pura-Pura, tended to cluster in La Paz's northeastern sector, while well-to-do residential areas moved south and southwest,

away from the malodorous factories and frequent mud slides plaguing the steeply inclined valley periphery. Numerous high-rise edifices were also privately erected during the 1970s. They were nicknamed "cocaine buildings," as they were allegedly financed from the proceeds of illegal drug exports.

Direct vehicular access to Bolivia's main *altiplano* highway system out of the low-lying city basin was at last perfected when a modern, 7-mile route up to the heights was inaugurated in 1978. Under mounting pressure because of its unbridled growth, lower-income housing radiated out so dramatically from the upper town of El Alto that it was declared a separate city as of 1988, absorbing most of the continuing influx of rural migrants—euphemistically referred to as *relocalizados* (relocatees). Ten years later, there were an estimated 713,000 residents crowded into the rich lower city, in addition to another 406,000 living above.

Modern La Paz consequently contains considerable differences in elevation, its airport at El Alto lying at 13,380 feet above sea level, while the Calacoto suburb to the southeast lies at only 10,500 feet. Such contours provide many spectacular urban vistas, yet also trap a great deal of pollution within the valley, which now contains roughly two-thirds of Bolivia's entire industrial output and 75 percent of all its commercial

Team of llama pack-animals in the streets of La Paz, ca. 1917. (Franck, *Vagabonding Down the Andes*)

activity, resulting in a maze of traffic congestion, smog, and blight among its narrow cobblestoned streets. And despite considerable modernization, La Paz still retains a strong native influence, some residents dressing to this day in traditional garb and speaking their ancient dialects.

For further reading materials on the history of La Paz or Bolivia, please consult the Select Bibliography at the end of this volume; additional sources on South American urban history can also be found under "Regional Studies," as well as under "General Works on Latin America."

POTOSÍ

The world's most populous mining center during the sixteenth century and nicknamed "the jewel in the crown of the Spanish kings."

Discovery and Early Boom (1544–1571)

Lying on a windswept, inhospitable terrace called *Potoc Umu* in the local Quechua dialect, Potosí is perched at 13,189 feet above sea level in the eastern Andes, inland from the Bolivian *altiplano* (plateau) and surrounded by still higher 20,000-foot peaks. Although mineral strikes had been made much earlier at Porco and other nearby Incan sites, Potosí's history dates from 1544, when a Chumbivilca native named Diego Huallpa

discovered an almost pure silver-ore outcrop atop the upper reaches of the 15,380-foot, reddish-colored *Sumaj Orko* (Beautiful Hill).

Huallpa informed Diego de Villarroel, a Spanish soldier, and he in turn registered the first official property claim on behalf of his superior, Capt. Diego Centeno, at Porco on 21 April 1545, precipitating an onrush of prospectors to what quickly became known as *Cerro Rico* (Rich Hill). Within a year, there were at least 170 Spaniards and 3,000 Indians toiling upon its heights, and by 1547 a sprawling mining encampment of 14,000 people called *Villa Imperial* (Imperial Town) had coalesced nearby on a sloping site some 2 miles north of this barren dome. Although some initial attempts had been made to administer this ramshackle boomtown from nearby La Plata (formerly Chuquisaca; modern Sucre), Potosí expanded so swiftly as to gain a measure of autonomy as early as 1546.

Potosí's deposits proved to be among the richest in world history. *Tacana* ores from Cerro Rico's uppermost tip required nothing more than simple selection and crushing before being smelted in small, clay wind ovens called *guayras*. Yet this unusually rich outcrop of surface ore was almost entirely depleted by 1561, so that many of the camp's initial prospectors and 20,000 Indian laborers began abandoning the site in discouragement. It was not until a more effective method of

View southward across Potosí's ancient Calvimonte *ingenio* or "mill" in the foreground, with Cerro Rico looming in the distance, ca. 1940. (Academia Nacional de Bellas Artes, Buenos Aires)

treating lower-grade ores—the *patio* or amalgamation process—was developed in Mexico and introduced to Potosí ten years later that the camp's fortunes revived and a more substantive city took shape.

Emergence (1572–1625)

The Peruvian viceroy Francisco de Toledo conducted a detailed inspection of this district during the winter of 1572–1573, enacting numerous measures that were to transform Potosí from an undisciplined boomtown into a viable community with well-regulated industrial practices. First, he arranged for the vital *azogue* (quicksilver) fluxing-agent—essential to the amalgamation process—to be extracted from the Santa Bárbara mercury mine at Huancavelica in central Peru, then conveyed from Chincha to Arica by sea and into the Andes by relays of teamsters.

De Toledo also codified the *mit'a* system—a Quechua word signifying "turn" or "period of service"—whereby one-seventh of the 90,000 adult Indian males between the ages of 18 and 50 found in sixteen *altiplano* provinces extending almost as far north as Cuzco were to be drafted on a rotating annual basis

and marched under the supervision of a *kuraka* (nobleman) to Potosí to provide its mine and mill operators with a reliable labor pool. Indians on frontiers bordering the hostile Chiriguano territories or in cities that required their services for other purposes were exempt from this service. The first distribution of 3,200 *mitayos* (conscript laborers) was made at Potosí on 1 April 1573. Each worker toiled in the mines for a week, then rested for two, during which time many chose to earn additional *kapcha* (profit), trebling their weekly stipend of two and a half *pesos* by working as *mingas* (voluntary laborers) in the city mills.

During a subsequent inspection tour of Potosí in the winter of 1574–1575, the viceroy moreover suggested that city water allocations—a requisite commodity for treating ores, yet scarce in a region notorious for nine-month droughts, followed by three months of torrential downpours—be properly harnessed through the construction of reservoirs called *lagunas*, caulked with lime. From these reservoirs, water could be more equitably distributed among all operators via paved flumes or aqueducts controlled by sluice gates. And last, De Toledo commanded that the unplanned community be reorganized by

Woodcut published in Antwerp in 1554, depicting Potosí only a decade after its discovery; despite the simplicity of this rendering, the early city's appearance is accurately represented. (Pedro de Cieza de León, *Chronica*)

replacing its original winding and narrow lanes with streets laid out in a proper grid pattern. De Toledo also called for the erection of a cathedral, *Casa Real de la Moneda* (Royal Mint), government offices, and other public buildings.

By early 1577, 6,000 native laborers had completed the vast reservoir network, which was to make the city's riverbank—the so-called *Ribera de la Vera Cruz* (Shoreline of the True Cross)—universally famous. Some eighty water-powered *ingenios* (mills) were eventually installed along the length of this shore to grind Cerro Rico's ores, before passing them on to amalgamation *patios* and placer-style basins to separate out their precious metals, which were then smelted into crude bars in adobe retort-kilns or *desazogadoras*. The decade between 1575 and 1585 was to prove the most lucrative in Potosí's history, witnessing a fivefold increase in production, as its old *remontes* (slag heaps) were profitably reexploited and new ore bodies were tapped. A few years later, the Jesuit author José de Acosta noted in his *Historia natural y moral de las Indias:*

This site is arid, cold, very unpleasant, and quite sterile. It yields no fruit or grain or grass, and is naturally uninhabit-

able . . . But the power of the silver, which calls forth other things than greed, has peopled that hill with the largest population of all those kingdoms and has produced such quantities of foods and supplies that everything one wants can be found there in abundance.

A true city had evolved once the rudimentary practices of individualistic prospectors had given way to large-scale investment in permanent structures and equipment by a few hundred wealthy owners, supplemented by enhanced municipal services. The Spanish population had not only rebounded tenfold by 1577 from the 200 impoverished residents of a decade earlier, but they now directed the economic fortunes of 20,000 permanent Indian dwellers in addition to more than 14,000 seasonal conscripts. The highest-yielding year was to be 1592, when 7.1 million ounces of silver were declared at Potosí's treasury.

In the century between its discovery and 1650, the city and its district produced roughly half the entire silver output for the Americas—an amount calculated at more than 450 million ounces. As the Crown received 20 percent in a special tax called the *quinto real* (royal fifth), Potosí contributed significantly to Spain's rise as a global power. The catchphrase *Vale un Potosí* or "He's worth a Potosí," to denote anyone of great wealth, even figured in the works of Miguel de Cervantes Saavedra, author of *Don Quixote.*

Potosí's populaton—while fluid because of the constant ebb and flow of traders, adventurers, teamsters, and other transients—may well have exceeded 100,000 by the end of the sixteenth century, making it one of the most populated cities in the world. By 1611, the number of residents was calculated at 160,000. Of this number, 3,000 were actual property owners, while the rest consisted of 40,000 Spanish and 35,000 Spanish-American hopefuls, 76,000 permanent or seasonal Indian laborers, and 6,000 black slaves.

Mine and refinery owners, merchants, Crown officials, and priests lived in the city core, a rectangular area of streets running north to south and east to west, radiating out for three or four blocks in every direction from a main plaza. The cathedral, *cabildo* (town hall), mint, treasury, and other official edifices faced on to this square, yet most remained unprepossessing in appearance—despite the community's immense wealth—because all interest was fixated upon mineral extraction rather than urban amenities. A *Coliseo de Comedias* (public theater) did appear by 1616, while extravagantly expensive celebrations were also held on festival days, such as the popular bullfights of Carnival Week, during which the rich attempted to outdo each other in ostentation.

Most inhabitants huddled in miserable *rancherías* around the periphery, the densest concentrations being on the city's south side, directly beneath Cerro Rico. In spite of noxious and often dangerous working conditions, many *mitayo* conscripts—who frequently arrived accompanied by their wives and children for their yearlong stay—preferred to remain in Potosí as permanent wage earners once their service was complete, rather than make the long trek home to even more meager prospects. Otherwise, the stark and remote landscape—constantly chilled by the Tomahavi wind and without any agricultural or ranching potential—attracted few

migrants, most foodstuffs still having to be imported up the 100 miles of winding road from La Plata.

Property owners (particularly the Basque refinery operators, despised by most other residents) furthermore guarded their monopoly jealously, greeting new arrivals with suspicion and disdain. The total number of rights holders was estimated at only 2,750 by 1614, some early entrepreneurs having departed once they amassed a fortune, while others leased or delegated their day-to-day operations to local managers. As dust expelled by the mills covered everything in grit, while sanitation and other civic services were nonexistent, family life was unpalatable for rich Spaniards and their dependents, who preferred leaving to enjoy their profits at such agreeable spots as Chuquisaca. Poorer residents resorted to gambling, drink, or prostitution, the wide-open atmosphere of the remote mining city attracting numerous runaways and delinquents from throughout the region, vainly hoping to strike it rich.

Downturn (1626–1749)

Potosí was swept by a major flood when its huge Cari Cari *laguna* burst on 15 March 1626, resulting in the death of roughly 4,000 people, plus the eradication of 110 city blocks and 120 mills. Although the latter were quickly rebuilt, production nonetheless tapered off gradually during the remainder of the seventeenth century due to lower-quality ores, problematical quicksilver deliveries, deepening labor shortages, plus continual water crises. Discoveries in the highland district of the *Audiencia* of Charcas helped to offset these losses for the Crown, the most important occurring 170 miles south-southwest of Potosí at San Antonio del Nuevo Mundo—which was exploited as of 1647 by the dynamic Galician émigré Antonio López de Quiroga—as well as 100 miles northwest at Oruro.

Yet such rival bonanzas helped accelerate Potosí's decline and depopulation, especially the strike at Oruro, which drained the shrinking number of *mitayo* laborers away from Potosí. The city's surviving mine owners grew so desperate that they even murdered the viceregal emissary Fr. Francisco de la Cruz (bishop-elect for Santa Marta, Colombia) and La

Drawing depicting the improvements made to Potosí's *Casa Real de la Moneda* or "Royal Mint" in 1770–1772, by Acting Superintendent Pedro de Tagle. The original edifice had been commenced in 1759, to a design by the Aragonese architect Salvador Villa, and remains in use today. (Casa Pardo)

Plata's Audiencia Pres. Francisco Nestares Marín with cups of poisoned hot chocolate on the evening of 23 April 1660, because they were threatening to drastically curtail the allotments of conscript laborers. A decade later, the Peruvian viceroy Pedro Fernández de Castro y Andrade, Conde de Lemos, recommended to the Crown that the *mit'a* system be abolished altogether, but this suggestion was rejected; his successors Melchor de Navarra y Rocafull, Duque de la Palata, and Melchor Portocarrero Laso de la Vega, Conde de la Monclova, consequently attempted to overhaul the increasingly untenable system during the 1680s and in 1692, respectively, without great success.

The number of annual laborers dwindled and Potosí's lowest output was registered in 1712, when only 915,000 ounces of silver were extracted throughout its entire province—an economic depression exacerbated by the typhus epidemic that decimated its indigenous population during 1719–1720 and claimed 22,000 lives. The once-preeminent city had been eclipsed by Oruro, a well as by enormous silver strikes at Guanajuato and Zacatecas in Mexico, which would come to dominate Spain's imperial mining industry for the remainder of the eighteenth century.

Resurgence (1750–1809)

Despite three decades of flat output, worsened by a prolonged drought, the Potosí district managed to stage a modest recovery during the late 1740s, its silver exports slowly doubling in volume, although still barely half the totals of two centuries previously. This revival was aided by a renewed demand for precious metals abroad, by a halving of the royal tax from a fifth to a *diezmo* or tenth in July 1736, as well as by increased pressure upon the less than 3,000 annual *mitayos* to increase their productivity.

Potosí's access to quicksilver and other essential shipments from Spain improved once the new Viceroyalty of the River Plate was created in 1776, coalescing what are today Bolivia, Paraguay, Argentina, and Uruguay into a single administrative entity, serviced by the seaport at Buenos Aires. Three years later, a census revealed that Potosí's population stood at 22,622, subdivided into 350 clerics; 3,502 Spanish-born residents; 4,902 Spanish-American Creoles; 560 mulattoes; 422 blacks; 7,170 permanent Indian dwellers; plus 5,716 seasonal *mitayo* laborers and their dependents. A large new *socavón real* or drainage adit was started that same year of 1779 to lower underground water levels within Cerro Rico; a mining acad-

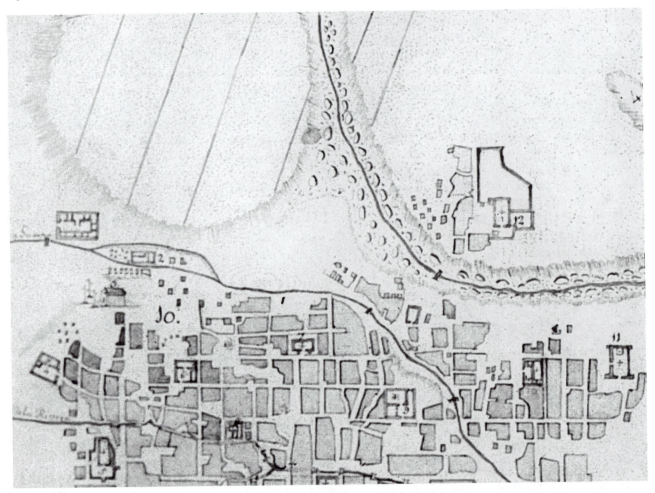

Map of the city and its environs, as surveyed in April 1779 by Hilario Malaver. (Archive of Indies, Seville)

emy was created by Gov. Jorge Escobedo y Alarcón; and blasting-powder began to be used to reach ever-deeper bodies of ore.

A delegation of German miners also reached the city in January 1789 under Thaddeus, Baron von Nordenflicht, having been hired by Madrid to disseminate European mining and metallurgical techniques throughout South America; yet despite making various suggestions, they were unable to contribute much to local technology before continuing their trip toward Lima in September 1790. The *Real Banco de San Carlos* or Royal San Carlos Bank enhanced lending practices by extending free credit to operators at Potosí; yet as a Crown institution monopolizing the purchase of all silver production, its presence was quite often resented.

Devastation (1800–1825)

The population had resurged to almost 40,000 by the closing decade of the eighteenth century, and the city's output represented a significant percentage of the viceroyalty's wealth and commercial traffic. Suddenly, Madrid realigned itself with the Revolutionary French government in August 1796, joining the ongoing hostilities against England that same October. The tight Atlantic blockade imposed by Royal Navy squadrons plunged Potosí back into another economic slump, especially as its crucial mercury imports became severed. Because of its former glory, the city was also to be repeatedly contested once King Charles IV was deposed by a French invasion of Spain in the spring of 1808, unleashing the first stirrings toward outright independence in South America.

During the early stages of this insurrection, 1,500 Argentine revolutionaries under Col. Antonio González Balcarce marched north from Jujuy in the autumn of 1810, being checked at Cotagaita on 29 October by 2,000 Loyalists under Gen. José de Córdoba; but when the latter pursued the retreating rebels, he was defeated by a sudden Argentine stand at Suipacha on 7 November, resulting in de Córdoba's execution along with that of Potosí's royal intendant, Francisco de Paula Sanz. The revolutionaries therefore entered Potosí uncontested on 25 November, being initially greeted as liberators; yet once González Balcarce continued his invasion of upper Peru, the political commissar Juan José Castelli and other radical colleagues offended local sensibilities through their arrogance, severity toward defeated monarchists, and extremist ideology. González Balcarce's army was eventually smashed on the shores of Lake Titicaca in June 1811, precipitating a wholesale insurgent retreat into northern Argentina, so that Potosí was reclaimed for the Crown by Pres. José Manuel de Goyeneche of the *Audiencia* of Cuzco that same 20 September. Commerce, though, remained in a state of utter collapse.

Two years later, the revolutionaries marched north again from Salta under Gen. Manuel Belgrano, reoccupying Potosí by 21 June 1813, before being obliged to relinquish their prize for a second time after meeting defeat at Vilcapugio on 1 October,

as well as at Ayohuma a month and a half later. To add to Potosí's woes, Belgrano attempted to blow up its mint as his beaten forces streamed southward, and the royalists reentered a devastated city. They in turn were distracted by the outbreak of the so-called Pumacahua rebellion at Cuzco and other problems in their rear the next summer, so that Argentine forces were able to regain Potosí for a third time on 1 May 1815, retaining it until the Peruvian viceroy Joaquín de la Pezuela y Sánchez beat the main insurgent army at the Battle of Sipesipe or Viluma Heights on 27 November, driving Potosí's occupiers into yet another retreat toward northern Argentina by January 1816.

Over the next nine years, the battered city was retained by Loyalist forces, its economy prostrate because the independence movement gradually spread across the entire continent and thus restricted its access to both the Atlantic and Pacific coasts. Finally, the last viceroy, José de la Serna, was driven out of Lima and the Peruvian lowlands, leading his remaining forces high up into the Andes during the summer of 1821 to make a last stand by reinstalling his government at Cuzco in late December. The end came three years later, when patriot Gen. Antonio José de Sucre Alcalá defeated the viceroy's army

Ornate Baroque portico leading into the *Casa de Moneda,* as it appeared, ca. 1940. This beautiful structure—today declared a World Heritage site—has been fortuitously spared from destruction during Potosí's long history. (Academia Nacional de Bellas Artes, Buenos Aires)

at Ayacucho on 6 December 1824, wounding and capturing de la Serna, so that monarchist resistance collapsed and Sucre advanced uncontested into upper Peru to accept the surrender of most garrisons.

The last royalist holdout, Gen. Pedro Antonio de Olañeta, fell back upon Potosí from La Paz in early February 1825, only to be mortally wounded while attempting to quell a mutinous subordinate at Tumusla a month later. The patriot army of Irish-born Gen. Francisco Burdett O'Connor consequently marched into the silent, gutted shell of the once-wealthy city of Potosí on 29 March, followed by the English-born Gen. William Miller on 25 April, bearing orders from Simón Bolívar to head up its new municipal administration.

At an assembly celebrated in the former *Audiencia* capital of La Plata in July and August of that same year of 1825, it was decided to proclaim a new sovereign nation called the *República Boliviana* or Bolivian Republic in honor of its liberator, who refused the top elected post, although he did draft a national constitution before departing on an inspection tour that brought him to Potosí that same autumn.

Republican Era (1826–Present)

Despite an influx of English speculators eager to participate in the revival of the mining city's collapsed fortunes, Potosí remained too diminished by its protracted wartime ordeal. Longtime owners and its most skilled operators had vanished, overseas suppliers and markets had been lost, mines and refining plants lay neglected or were being disputed by greedy claimants, and the mint and *lagunas* were unattended. Bolívar attempted to rectify matters at a single stroke by offering monopoly rights over the district to the highest-bidding consortium from the London market, then departed the Andes in early January 1826, leaving his youthful Venezuelan-born subordinate Sucre to be acclaimed as Bolivia's first president on 25 May.

Unfortunately, the investment fever had already broken across the Atlantic, so that no significant funds could be subscribed to reanimate and modernize Potosí's businesses. According to a census taken in 1827, its population stood at a mere 9,000 inhabitants, while the abolition of the *mit'a* system had ended the annual peregrinations of conscripts. Sucre and his 2,000 Colombian troops were then driven from La Paz at the end of that same year, and his successor, Marshal Santa Cruz, was challenged by Gen. Pedro Blanco in 1829, inaugurating a prolonged period of internal and external strife for the fledgling republic.

Potosí and the Bolivian mining industry did not truly begin their slow resurgence until cheap mercury began to be made available in large quantities from California after 1850; nevertheless, the nation as a whole continued to be wracked by a succession of military coups and countercoups, which greatly hampered development. In February 1865, a rebel army under José Mariano Melgarejo defeated and deposed Pres. José M. de Achá in a confrontation near the city, yet despite such upheavals, foreign engineers were eventually brought in to improve treatment methods and introduce new technical innovations—such as the steam-driven mills installed in 1878 at Huanchaca, 75 miles southwest of Potosí, which augmented ore-crushing capacity so dramatically that this single camp was yielding over 1 million ounces of silver by 1895.

Shortly thereafter came an abrupt drop in the world price for this precious metal, yet demand for tin rose sharply, which Potosí and its department proved well suited to meet—having large deposits, among the most famous being those located 100 miles northwest at Uncía that were developed from 1897 onward by Simón I. Patiño, the first of Bolivia's so-called "tin barons." Potosí also shared in this boom, partly through tapping the tin veins of Cerro Rico, partly through reprocessing older waste-dumps left from centuries of silver extractions. By 1906, its population had rebounded to approximately 23,000 inhabitants, doubling to 45,758 by 1950, 77,000 by 1976, and slightly more than 123,000 by 1993.

For further reading materials on Potosí or Bolivia, please consult the Select Bibliography at the end of this volume; additional sources on South American urban history can also be found under "Regional Studies," as well as under "General Works on Latin America."

Brazil

RECIFE

Uniquely shaped natural harbor dominating a rich agricultural delta, which blossomed as the capital of seventeenth-century Dutch Brazil.

Discovery and Settlement (1535–1629)

European explorers charted this lush stretch of tropical coastline during the early 1500s, yet the Portuguese did not actually establish a tiny trading outpost called Conceição on Itamaracá Island—20 miles farther to the north—until 1515. Its colonists eked out an existence by bartering with the local inhabitants for dyewoods, amber, cotton, and exotic wildlife, and in a venture southward reconnoitered a distinctive estuary formed by a long and tapering peninsula that they nicknamed the Lingueta (Tongue) and a prominent offshore reef. A channel between these two barriers led into a narrow anchorage, 1,600 feet wide by 2 miles long, that in turn was fed by a pair of rivers called the Capibaribe and Beberibe, providing access to a broad expanse of fertile tablelands radiating out in every direction and known as Pernambuco.

When the Portuguese Crown finally began dispensing hereditary *capitanias* (captaincies) to secure Brazil two decades later, one of the first such titles was issued to Duarte Coelho Pereira, who—as *donatário* (grantee)—was to populate and administer Pernambuco's vast territory at his own expense from a coastal capital whose municipality would extend as far inland as the Spanish-American border. He and his band of settlers arrived at the reef-lined harbor in 1535, examining its inner shoreline before deciding to establish their community atop a hill at the north end of the estuary. This site was chosen because it afforded a good vantage point and protection against attacks by the primitive and hostile local tribesmen; it also lay amid rich farmland, offered some respite against the oppressive heat and humidity with its cooling southeast ocean breezes, and was at a safe remove from the insalubrious marshes farther to its southwest. Pleased with their choice, the colonists named their new city Olinda (The Fair One), establishing its first *casa de misericordia* or charity hospital by January 1540, thanks to a legacy from Pedro Fernandes Vogado.

The jungly expanse below contained few mineral resources, yet the settlers soon discovered that the alluvial soils along the *várzea* (riverside plain) beside the Capibaribe were ideal for cultivating sugarcane, a highly prized commodity in Europe. The indigenous residents were pushed back and decimated by diseases, such as the 1563 smallpox epidemic, so that ten water-powered *engenhos* (mills) were soon operating along the riverbanks, refining harvests from plantations tended by several thousand African slaves. Visits by oceango-

ing merchantmen increased accordingly in number, although the channel running 3 miles north up the Beberibe to Olinda's *varadouro* (landing beach) had proven so shallow as to be navigable only by small boats—and then only at high tide. Most bulk cargoes were consequently lightered down to the *poço* (deep-water anchorage) called Corpo Santo at the southwestern tip of the Lingueta Peninsula to be hoisted directly into ships' holds.

Another tiny community therefore sprang up on that spit of land, consisting of a crude cluster of warehouses and inns plus a few fishermen's shacks; it was referred to simply as Recife, a contraction of the term *arrecife,* or reef. Despite its unprepossessing size and appearance, the Lingueta's seaside hamlet bustled with the arrival and departure of each seasonal convoy; the patron saint of its diminutive chapel soon came to be São Frei Pedro Gonsalves, venerated by Portuguese sailors, and as the easternmost stopover for all transatlantic traffic between Portugal, Africa, and other Brazilian settlements, it also received many transient vessels.

The city of Olinda nonetheless remained Pernambuco's capital, as well as the preferred residence for its landowning elite, who continued to expand their operations by clearing new sugar plantations along waterways as far south as the São Francisco River. Cattle ranches also appeared between the headwaters, as well as among the less fecund *tabuleiros* (tablelands) north of Olinda, while dyewood loggers felled trees throughout the jungles. As no roads existed beyond a few rustic tracks, virtually all of these enterprises depended upon waterborne communication with Recife, thereby keeping its few score stevedores, warehousemen, and boatmen gainfully employed.

In 1580, Portugal and its overseas empire became absorbed by Spain after the epileptic cardinal-king Henrique died, leaving Philip II as nearest claimant to his throne. Olinda—although technically subordinate since 1549 to Brazil's colonial capital of São Salvador at Bahia—remained sufficiently influential and autonomous, even under the new Hispanic regime, to organize its own huge expedition four years later under Adm. Diego Flores de Valdés and expel a group of French interlopers from Paraíba Bay (modern João Pessoa). And notwithstanding the commercial dislocation caused by the union with Spain and subsequent outbreak of hostilities against Elizabethan England, Olinda's growth continued; its urban area sprawled down from the original promontory into a maze of steeply winding lower streets. A magnificent new Carmelite convent was also commenced in 1588, followed by the São Pedro Mártir Church two years later and the Benedictines' São Bento monastery in 1599.

Yet in contrast to the burgeoning Pernambucan capital atop

Panorama taken in 1855 by the visiting German photographer Augustus C. Stahl, looking southwestward across Olinda, down the Lingueta Peninsula toward distant Recife; the *varadouro* appears at right. (Ferrez, *Velhas fotografias pernambucanas*)

its scenic hill, low-lying Recife remained a functional ancillary, so insignificant a sea outlet that a lone English privateering ship under John Lancaster was able to seize the hamlet briefly in 1595, ransacking its warehouses before escaping. To prevent such future penetrations, a pair of fortresses were painstakingly erected to guard the harbor entrance in 1614: Fort São Francisco da Barra at the northern tip of the offshore reef, which became known as the Castelo do Mar (Sea Castle), and Fort São Jorge on the Lingueta Peninsula opposite, which became the Castelo do Terra (Land Castle). By the close of the sixteenth century, Olinda's population stood at a robust 4,800 residents, while Recife had scarcely 200 permanent inhabitants as late as 1627—a circumstance that would be dramatically reversed by a foreign invasion.

Dutch Conquest and Transference (1630–1636)

Dutch merchants had discreetly controlled Pernambuco's sugar industry for many years, furnishing covert investments and equipment, as well as monopolizing export sales through-

out Europe. Despite repeated injunctions from Madrid, vessels from The Netherlands had routinely visited Brazil to conduct clandestine trade. Such a long-standing relationship persuaded the Westindische Compagnie (West Indian Company, or WIC)—constituted at Amsterdam when war was declared against Spain in April 1621—to consider conquering their own commercial colony in Brazil, furthermore believing that such intervention would be welcomed by Portuguese residents weary of Spanish misrule.

After an abortive occupation of the Bahian capital of São Salvador in 1624–1625, a second Dutch colonizing expedition of fifty-two ships and fifteen sloops bearing 3,780 sailors under Adm. Hendrick Loncq and 3,500 soldiers under Col. Diederik van Waerdenburch materialized northeast of Olinda on 14 February 1630. Landing parties were quickly disgorged at Pau Amarelo, pushing southward the next day across the Doce and Tapado rivers, while Pernambuco's Spanish governor, Matías de Alburquerque, Conde de Alegrete, ordered all noncombatants to torch their properties and flee inland, then

View southwestward down the length of Recife's mudstone reef, as photographed from Fort Picão by Marc Ferrez in 1875. The open Atlantic lies at left, with the city in the distance at far right. (Ferrez, *Velhas fotografias pernambucanas*)

braced to meet an assault with his small garrison. The invaders easily overran the city's Casa de Misericordia hospital—converted into a strongpoint because its new Forte Real citadel had not yet been completed—then swept down the Lingueta Peninsula to seize Forts São Jorge and São Francisco da Barra, as well as the empty Recife on 16 February, at a total cost of only sixty casualties.

Bent upon permanent annexation, the Dutch formally laid claim to the entire captaincy of Pernambuco on 2 March 1630, renaming it Nieuw Holland (New Holland), while Waerdenburch was installed as governor. Yet Hispano-Portuguese resistance coalesced 3 miles beyond Recife at Fort Arraial do Bom Jesus, repulsing an inland incursion by 2,000 Dutch troops two weeks later. A counterthrust by Alburquerque against the Dutch enclave at Recife also failed, though, after which its occupiers—now becoming ill and worried about a possible Hispano-Portuguese counterexpedition out of Europe—decided on 19 March to concentrate all their strength around Recife's crucial anchorage: Waerdenburch opined that

the larger hilltop city of Olinda could "only be defended through great expense and a very considerable military force."

The Dutch therefore dug in at the port, adding a new redoubt called Fort Bruijn, or Brum, on Lingueta Peninsula to help defend Recife. The twenty-year-old Franciscan convent of Santo Antônio—lying across the anchorage on Antônio Váz Island—was also enclosed by a stockade to become Fort Ernestus, while a new pentagonal fort was started farther south on the island that same autumn to guarantee access to the mainland's *cacimbas* (water wells) and prevent shallow-draft vessels from sneaking across Afogados Bar. When finished, its moat being flooded with seawater in December 1630, this stronghold was christened Fort Frederik Hendrik in honor of the Prince of Orange, although nicknamed Vijfhoek or Five-Point by its Dutch garrison and Cinco Pontas by the Portuguese. To resist riverborne descents out of the interior, a small water fort dubbed Fort Waerdenburch, or Waardenburg, was initiated at the confluence of the Capibaribe and Beberibe, while lesser defenses were scattered along both banks.

A relief convoy arrived from Holland in the spring of 1631 under Adm. Adriaen Janszoon Pater and Vice Adm. Maarten Thijssen, so bolstering Recife's occupiers that they sailed a detachment north to seize the southern tip of Itamaracá Island as well. Pater furthermore sortied with eighteen ships on 31 August to battle a Hispano-Portuguese fleet under Adm. Antonio de Oquendo that had reinforced São Salvador, mauling this formation so severely that de Oquendo merely deposited 700 troops at distant Barra Grande of Porto Calvo before proceeding toward Europe.

Having weathered that danger, the Dutch turned to erecting a few permanent dwellings at Recife, in the process stripping deserted Olinda of construction materials, before torching the former capital's ruins in late November 1631. Over the next several years, vessels from The Netherlands would deposit an additional supply of bricks and tiles, which they carried as ballast, so as to supplement the local woods, stone, and adobe. All municipal activities had been effectively shifted down from Olinda's heights by the occupiers' decision to center their circuit of defenses around Recife's anchorage, where a WIC warehouse was soon installed. Being accustomed to river life in the Low Countries, the new occupants remained undaunted even when the Capibaribe overflowed its banks in July 1633.

Over the next couple of years, Hispano-Portuguese forces were ejected from Fort Arraial do Bom Jesus, so that the Dutch could begin venturing deeper inland. Some Pernambucan estate owners torched their plantations and retreated into the neighboring captaincy of Bahia rather than submit to foreign rule, yet most of Pernambuco's sugar-growing territory passed under the invaders' control, while the number of defiant Portuguese *moradores* (residents) dwindled to scarcely 7,000. Concerned about their loosening grip on the occupied captaincy, Madrid dispatched another fleet of thirty warships under Spanish Adm. Lope de Hoces and Portuguese Adm. Rodrigo Lobo, who sighted Jaraguay Point on 26 November 1635 and examined Recife's defenses from a distance before steering southward to deposit 2,500 sickly troops at the Lagunas under veteran Gen. Luis de Rojas y Borja. Assuming military command from Alburquerque, de Rojas was defeated and killed by a Dutch army under Col. Christovam Artichoksky, or Arciszewsky, at the Battle of Mata Redonda on 18 January 1636. His 500 surviving troops retreated into a hilltop fortress at Porto Calvo, while 8,000 noncombatants retreated 80 miles from Recife into Alagoas.

Emergence of "Mauritsstad" (1637–1653)

The energetic Johan Maurits, Graaf or Count van Nassau-Siegen, reached Recife as the new governor-general for New Holland on 23 January 1637, promptly spearheading an offensive that captured Porto Calvo in early March. He then laid waste Alagoas and drove all guerrilla bands as far back as Sergipe del Rey. The next spring, Maurits launched an even more ambitious strike by setting sail with 3,600 Dutch troops and 1,000 indigenous allies aboard forty-five vessels to besiege São Salvador, withdrawing on 25 May 1638 after a forty-day siege that had cost him 500 dead and 1,500 ill.

Portion of a map drafted by the cartographer Cornelis Sebastiaanszoon Golijath, ca. 1640, and engraved eight years later by Claes Janszoon Visscher alias Nicolaus Ioannis Piscator. The old Portuguese capital of Olinda appears to the north at right, while the new Dutch capital of "Mauritsstad" is taking shape within the distinctive, reef-lined harbor at left. (Algemeen Rijksarchief, The Hague)

Yet despite that setback, the count's vigorous campaigns had pacified the Pernambucan interior, so that the Dutch could now start converting their coastal foothold into a viable colony. Former estate owners were enticed into returning and resurrecting their mills and plantations (few Dutchmen initially participating in sugar cultivation; they concentrated instead upon trade and administration). Taxes were abated to boost economic revival, and the West India Company initiated large-scale importations of African slaves and European goods.

Maurits also deemed Recife's untidy agglomeration of narrow houses—many three stories tall, because land was at such a premium upon the spit—to be unsuitable as a future capital. After discarding suggestions from Pernambucan residents to rebuild Olinda, as well as Dutch proposals for a new town on Itamaracá Island, he decided to create a wholly new city on low-lying Antônio Váz Island, on the western side of the anchorage. Specifically, a strip of marshland was to be cleared between the triangular Dutch military enclosure attached to Fort Ernestus—known as the Groot Kwartier (Great Quarter)—and five-point Fort Frederik Hendrik farther to its southwest, an area corresponding to the modern metropolis's São José district as far as the Taborda enclosure.

The terrain was reputedly surveyed in 1638 by Maurits's personal architect, Pieter Post, resulting in an oblong grid of streets enclosed by their own set of ramparts, bisected by a canal and a triangular inner basin to permit boat access. Locks were included to control tides rising out of the Capibaribe, as the ground stood only 7 feet above water level and was so spongy that heavy oxcarts were forbidden. A Walloon-Reformed Church was to be erected at its core, shade trees were to be planted against the sun's oppressive heat, and a private

Cruz Street in old Recife, ca. 1855, as photographed by Stahl. Fifteen years later, it would be renamed Bom Jesus Street; note the Dutch-inspired layout and architectural style, plus the unpaved streets, recently installed gas lamps, and horses gathered around its nine-year-old public fountain. (Ferrez, *Velhas fotografias pernambucanas*)

cross-harbor ferry service was inaugurated with Recife. As an inducement for citizens to move over into his new capital, the governor-general even commandeered a former Portuguese estate near Santo Antônio Church to serve as his official residence. In honor of its founder, the city was named Mauritsstad (Maurits City), sometimes Latinized as Mauritia.

The count moreover initiated construction in 1639 of a splendid private villa just outside Fort Ernestus's moated ramparts, amid a garden spot on the island's northeastern side, that was to become the Palladian-style, U-shaped Vrijburg Palace. One of its twin towers would serve as the harbor lighthouse, the other as an observatory for the scientist Georg Markgraf, a favorite among Maurits's retinue (although it was not completed in time for him to study the partial solar eclipse of 13 November 1640). When they learned of such grandiose schemes, the West India Company directors—known as the Heren XIX—reprimanded Maurits for his extravagance yet took no further action, as Vrijburg had been paid for out of his own funds.

A Hispano-Portuguese convoy attempted to disembark 1,200 more troops under Luis Barbalho Bezerra to revive Pernambucan resistance in January 1640, but it was driven so far north by twenty warships exiting Recife under Adm. Willem Corneliszoon Loos and Vice Adm. Jacob Huygens as to pose no danger. Yet when Portugal revolted against Spain that same December—acclaiming the seventh Duke of Bragança as their King João IV in place of Philip IV—the tenure of Brazil's Dutch occupiers became more complicated; for although this schism was welcome and the Spaniards soon withdrew, The Netherlands refused to restore any territories conquered during the war. A ten-year truce was arranged in Europe in June 1641, whereby Lisbon grudgingly acknowledged Dutch sovereignty over Pernambuco in exchange for The Hague's assistance against Spain.

Mauritsstad and Recife therefore enjoyed a brief spurt of peaceful growth, and in a goodwill gesture intended to assuage latent Pernambucan resentment, the count even allowed some citizens to resettle at Olinda in 1640, resurrecting its Casa de Misericordia hospital and church. The next year, the Capibaribe again overflowed its banks, causing considerable damage to the new capital. Yet the Dutch remained ensconced on Antônio Váz Island, most especially once Maurits's magnificent Vrijburg Palace became habitable the following year and he ceded his older residence to Dirck Codde van der Burch, high councilor of the chamber of North Holland. The gardens of the governor-general's new villa would eventually boast 2,000 transplanted coconut trees in seventy different strains, 252 orange trees, numerous botanical specimens, ponds for raising fish and shellfish, and a small zoo.

Mauritsstad and Recife also had a combined population of almost 6,000 inhabitants, plus a new municipal hall and other official edifices and low-cost housing for recent immigrants in a suburb dubbed Nova Mauritia. A wooden trestle bridge was completed to connect Antônio Váz Island northwestward across the Capibaribe with the mainland as of 1643, which Maurits strengthened by commissioning yet another Italianate-style villa at one end, called Boa Vista (Fair View). The stone span linking Mauritsstad eastward with Recife was inaugurated on 28 February 1644, although its central portion could be made only of suspended wood, as the midchannel waters had proven too deep to seat stone columns. Pedestrians alighted beside the governor-general's old residence, able to proceed as far on Brugstraat as the rectangular Cocosplein clearance in the city's northern quarter.

Yet the popular count was abruptly recalled by the WIC board because of his willfulness and profligacy, after which Pernambucan discontent—against their subordinate status, as well as Dutch monopolies and liberal social practices—flared into open rebellion when the planter João Fernandes Vieira ignited a rural uprising at Ipojuca in mid-June 1645. The council in Mauritsstad responded by dispatching 400 to 500 troops and 300 to 500 Tapuia, or Tarairiu, Indian allies under Lt. Col. Hendrik van Haus, who confronted these rebels 30 miles outside the Dutch capital on 3 August. But although scantily armed, the 1,000–1,200 insurgents were well entrenched atop Tabocas Hill—highest point in the Comocim Range—and repelled every assault, inflicting more than 200 casualties.

Van Haus's subsequent retreat imparted even greater impetus to the so-called War of Divine Liberty, as Fernandes Vieira united with the black guerrilla leader Henrique Dias of Rio Grande do Norte and the Petiguar Indian chieftain Antônio Filipe Camarão of Paraíba. Two regiments sent by the Portuguese governor of Bahia—supposedly to help contain this outburst—instead reoccupied the Serinhaém district and Fort Nazaré, further fanning the revolt. The Dutch retaliated by sending a squadron from Recife under Adm. Jan Corneliszoon Lichthardt, who annihilated the sixteen Bahian transports still anchored off Tamandaré under Vice Adm. Jerônimo Serrão de Paiva on 9 September 1645. But the rebellion continued to make gains inland, the provinces of Paraíba and Sergipe del Rey soon falling, along with Porto Calvo and Fort Maurits on the São Francisco River.

By the end of that same year, the Dutch had lost control over most of the sugar-producing territory, while their seaside capital became crowded with refugees and closely invested by enemies. Civilians were reduced to a starvation ration of a pound of bread per week by June 1646, until the supply vessels *Valk* and *Elizabeth* made a providential entry. Adm. Joost "Banckert" van Trappen tried to ease the pressure by sortieing from Recife in February 1647 with twenty-six ships bearing 2,400 troops under Von Schoppe to occupy Itaparica Island and counterthreaten São Salvador. Yet this escalation of hostilities galvanized Lisbon into sending out another large fleet, while Von Schoppe's army took ill and forsook Itaparica by mid-December.

The next March 1648, Adm. Witte Corneliszoon de With

Photo southeastward from Santo Antônio's waterfront across the Beberibe River toward Recife by Stahl, ca. 1855. The bridge appears little changed from the seventeenth-century span and would be replaced ten years later by the iron *Sete de Setembro* or "Seventh of September" Bridge and by the Maurício de Nassau Bridge in 1917. (Ferrez, *Velhas fotografias pernambucanas*)

straggled into Recife with 6,000 sickly sailors and soldiers aboard two score vessels, prompting Pernambuco's governor, Francisco Barreto de Meneses—recently escaped from Dutch captivity—to attempt to subdue the hard-pressed garrison before this reinforcement could recover. Detachments were therefore left to hold the encircling siege camps at Olinda, Arraial, and Bateria, while 2,200 picked troops closed in upon Mauritsstad out of the south in four columns. Von Schoppe countersallied on 16 April with 5,500 infantrymen, 500 sailors, 300 Indian allies, and five field-pieces, hoping to break the Portuguese encirclement altogether by overrunning Fort Barreta in their rear, while Colonel van Haus's regiment was delegated to destroy encampments in the Várzea.

Barreto de Meneses entrenched his troops in narrow Guararapes Plain, 9 miles south of the Dutch capital, against which Von Schoppe launched a diversionary assault on 19 April 1648 while circling a flanking column through the hills on the Portuguese right. Barreto sent the guerrilla chieftains Fer-

nandes Vieira and Dias to ambush this stealthy approach, the Dutch being defeated in the jungle. Von Schoppe's bloodied army was meanwhile reinforced by Van Haus, after which a second Dutch flanking maneuver also ended in failure, so that 1,500 dead, injured, or missing were left behind when they retreated, compared with only 80 killed and 400 wounded among Barreto's ranks.

Still, the Pernambucans were incapable of storming the Dutch capital's defenses, despite being reinforced in August 1648 by another infantry regiment from Madeira and the Azores under Francisco de Figueiroa. The Dutch also retained sufficient naval superiority to send a fleet from Recife to raid Bahia that same December. Yet when 3,500 troops again marched out of Mauritsstad in mid-February 1649 to confront Barreto's 2,600 men—now even more strongly entrenched on Guararapes Plain—they were beaten once more, with the loss of another 1,045 dead, wounded, or captured. Despite compensating by recapturing Ceará in April 1649, Mauritsstad's resolve was further tested when the Capibaribe overflowed its banks the next year.

It would not be until after The Netherlands became distracted by the First Anglo-Dutch War in May 1652 that the besiegers could finally overcome the last vestiges of resistance. A fleet of seventy-seven ships under Pedro Jacques de Magalhães and Francisco de Brito Freire appeared outside Recife on 20 December 1653, severing its sea links, while depositing thousands more troops to combine with Pernambucan forces and together press home a close siege. Desperate, the defenders razed many buildings—Nova Mauritia being almost utterly consumed—while countless rare tropical specimens were also felled to bolster their ramparts. Yet hunger and thirst sapped Dutch will until they agreed to capitulate on 27 January 1654, their 1,500 surviving troops and residents being granted three months' grace to depart Brazil.

Reversion (1654–1709)

The Portuguese promptly restored Olinda to its former status as Pernambuco's capital, while the enemy-created city of Mauritsstad along the harbor front was shorn of all recognition. Yet a survey conducted by the victors counted 290 edifices still standing in both the gutted former Dutch capital and the less damaged Recife—200 being two stories high, 50 of three stories. The presence of such a permanent infrastructure at least ensured that both seaside towns would continue to function and even to thrive modestly once the captaincy's sugar exports and commercial traffic resumed.

And although local estate owners had resurrected their traditional urban mansions at Olinda, the emergent merchant class would find advantages in maintaining residences at Santo Antônio—as Mauritsstad became known—so as to better attend to seasonal business at their warehouses and shops in Recife. The survival of both seaside communities seemed confirmed when the Carmelite Order initiated construction in 1685 of a magnificent new baroque church dedicated to their patron saint Nossa Senhora do Carmo, on the grounds of Maurits's former villa of Boa Vista—notwithstanding the yellow-fever epidemic that swept through the port that same year.

Resurgence (1710–1822)

The Crown finally acknowledged the significant commercial role being played by Recife upon its spit of land, as well as Santo Antônio opposite on Antônio Váz Island, so that both communities were combined and reconstituted into a single town in 1710 with the joint name of Santo Antônio do Recife de Pernambuco. Its administration nonetheless remained subordinate to Olinda, while the captaincy's overall prosperity furthermore sagged after its sugar monoculture was undercut during the late 1730s by an export boom out of Saint-Domingue (Haiti) and other French Caribbean islands. That boom so saturated European markets that prices and profit margins contracted dramatically.

A quarter century of depression ensued for Brazil, and when Portugal's chief minister, Sebastião José de Carvalho e Mello, Marques de Bompal, overhauled its colonial government in 1763, the shift southwestward of wealth and influence was fully recognized when Rio de Janeiro was granted the title of viceregal capital. Yet estate owners in the northeastern captaincy of Pernambuco nevertheless recuperated from their financial reverses by developing alternative export crops, such as tobacco and coffee to supplement sugar, while Santo Antônio do Recife enjoyed a commensurate rise in prosperity. Its first theater—the Santa Isabel (Saint Elizabeth)—was built on Cadeia Nova Street by 1772, while an additional church was commenced at Boa Vista twelve years later.

Yet the most significant efforts to improve Santo Antônio do Recife's urban infrastructure occurred during the 1786–1798 tenure of Gov. Tomás José de Melo, who started paving its main streets, established the São José public market, and had rows of shade trees replanted. The city's resurgence was even more strongly abetted by the collapse of sugar production in the French Caribbean because of the emergence of a radical new revolutionary government in Paris, which dislocated transatlantic movements as of 1791. Prices therefore skyrocketed, so that Pernambuco and its seaport reaped a considerable bounty. The population of Santo Antônio do Recife had blossomed by the conclusion of de Melo's term to roughly 15,000 inhabitants, spread among more than 1,100 stone buildings, many two stories high.

Despite sporadic setbacks, trade was to flow relatively unimpeded for the next several years, as Portugal and its overseas colonies were allies of Great Britain and thus spared any blockades by the Royal Navy. Municipal circumstances improved still further after a truce was arranged in Europe in October 1801, as Lisbon remained neutral once fighting resumed a year and a half later. Such close commercial contacts with England eventually goaded the French emperor Napoleon I into sending an invasion army to depose Portugal's royal family early in 1808, who fled to re-establish a government in exile at Rio de Janeiro.

Rather than return after Napoleon's defeat seven years later, Prince Regent João chose to remain in Brazil, proclaiming it a kingdom in December 1815; upon the death of his deranged mother, Maria, three months afterward, he became ruler of Portugal's vast empire. Because of the popular young monarch's presence, many Brazilians chose not to join their Spanish-American neighbors in seeking independence from European rule, although a secessionist outburst did occur at Pernambuco when Gov. Caetano Pinto de Miranda Montenegro ordered the arrest of several conspirators at Olinda early on 6 March 1817.

One, a sexagenarian militia veteran named José de Barros Lima, killed the officer sent to detain him, and then sparked an immediate uprising that drove Governor Pinto into hiding inside Brum harbor-castle on the Lingueta Peninsula. Some

Count Mauritz's Gate and Recife's slave mart; engraving attributed to Edward Finden, from an original 1821 drawing by the English traveler Maria Dundas Graham. (*Journal of a Voyage to Brazil*, 1824)

800 rebels—a mixed brigade of local white and mulatto militiamen, plus half an artillery regiment—then released other captive leaders, descended to cut off all access to Antônio Váz Island by seizing its bridges, and occupied both Santo Antônio and Recife by sunrise of 7 March 1817. Outflanked and isolated, Pinto arranged a safe conduct to Rio de Janeiro five days later, from where King João VI ordered forth an expedition to reconquer the rebellious province.

Loyal warships arrived off Recife to initiate a blockade by early April 1817, followed two weeks afterward by a full battle squadron under Adm. Rodrigo Lobo, who vainly called upon the insurgents to surrender. Four Portuguese regiments meanwhile approached overland under Luiz do Rêgo—Pernambuco's new governor-designate, recently arrived from Lisbon—and when the rebel leader Domingos José Martins marched south from Santo Antônio do Recife to confront them, he was defeated and captured at Serinhão on 17 May. His colleague Domingos Teotônio Jorge fled inland with the city garrison two days later, so that Lobo entered Recife's anchorage uncontested to restore monarchist rule. The rebels eventually disbanded at Engenho Paulista in the interior, many being hunted down and executed over the next few months, while royalist rule was reimposed and a few improvements

were made at the seaport—such as the inauguration of a lighthouse on Recife's mudstone reef by 1 February 1822.

Short-Lived Independence (1823–1824)

Republican sentiment nonetheless remained strong, and after Brazil seceded from Portugal and installed young Prince Pedro as its emperor in 1823, Santo Antônio do Recife assumed the full status of a city and once again displayed autonomous tendencies. English mercenary Capt. John Taylor was consequently dispatched from Rio de Janeiro with the imperial frigates *Niterói* and *Piranha* to attempt to persuade Gov. Manoel de Carvalho País de Andrade to install a royalist candidate into office. Taylor appeared outside Recife on 8 April 1824, but his proposal was rebuffed. He therefore instituted a blockade until ordered to withdraw on 28 June by his superior Adm. Thomas, Lord Cochrane, so as to reconcentrate all Brazilian imperial forces against an anticipated Portuguese invasion.

Four days later, de Carvalho proclaimed Pernambuco to be an independent republic and sent two vessels under John Mitrovich (a Maltese deserter from Britain's Royal Navy) to invest neighboring Barra Grande as well. However, the pair were soon captured by an imperial Brazilian schooner, after which Cochrane's entire squadron set sail from Rio de Janeiro on 2 August 1824, transporting 1,200 troops to put down Pernambuco's separatist regime. After depositing the soldiers eight days later at Alagoas, 80 miles short of Recife, his squadron arrived offshore on 18 August to impose a blockade. Having failed to come to terms with de Carvalho, the admiral shelled the city with his schooner *Leopoldina* until the 1,200 troops arrived overland, effectively bringing an end to the short-lived republic by mid-September. De Carvalho fled into exile aboard HMS *Tweed*, while a few executions ensued. The emperor—as punishment for Pernambuco's rebelliousness—stripped it of the southern Comarca de São Francisco district.

Provincial Capital (1825–1888)

The city of Santo Antônio do Recife officially supplanted Olinda by becoming elevated to the status of Pernambucan capital in 1827, its commercial growth having now far outstripped the last vestiges of power and influence exercised by the rural-based plantation aristocracy. As a result, a few modest urban improvements began to be made, in keeping with the city's newfound prominence: its bridges were repaired and streets upgraded in 1837, for example, while a magnificent new

Photo by Stahl, ca. 1857, looking southwestward across the Capibaribe River toward Boa Vista. The white domed building at left center was the new *Casa de Detenção* or "Penitentiary," inaugurated on 25 April 1855, while the Dom Pedro II Hospital appears on the opposite bank. (Ferrez, *Velhas fotografias pernambucanas*)

Palácio da Presidência da Província (Provincial Presidential Palace) was commenced four years later near the site of Maurits's former Vrijburg Palace. Widespread backwardness and poverty, though, as well as Brazil's political uncertainty and natural calamities, retarded progress until foreign firms were encouraged to invest more than a decade later.

The city's Santo Antônio and Boa Vista sectors were heavily flooded by rising river waters on 22 July 1854, after almost two weeks of torrential rain. Yet steamship service was inaugurated up the Capibaribe that same year with the purchase of the English-built, 967-ton *Marquez de Olinda,* while the English-backed Recife & San Francisco Railway Company also commenced operations in 1855. Both innovations would greatly augment the flow of regional produce through the seaport and indirectly help finance the completion of another new span—the Santa Isabel Bridge—across the Beberibe by December 1863, as well as the replacement two years later of the wooden cross-channel span linking Recife to Santo Antônio with the much sturdier iron Sete de Setembro (Seventh of September) Bridge. Mule-drawn streetcar tracks were moreover laid to the outlying suburbs of Apipucos and Caxangá by 1866, extending as far as Olinda shortly thereafter.

The burgeoning capital suffered an even worse flood in early February 1869, yet when Brazil's first national census was taken three years later, a robust figure of 117,000 urban residents was recorded. Santo Antônio do Recife's first sewerage system was installed in 1873; its old colonial-era São José Market was replaced by a more modern enclosure in September 1875; and its new Assembléia Provincial (Provincial Legislature) was completed that following year. Despite more than 2,500 deaths during the great epidemic of 1878–1879, another new stretch of railroad track was completed as far as Paudalho. And when slavery was officially abolished throughout Brazil in 1888, there were only 41,000 such rural vassals remaining to be set free.

Modern Era (1889–Present)

Marshal Manuel Deodoro da Fonseca overthrew Emperor Pedro II in a bloodless coup at Rio de Janeiro in mid-November 1889, installing a shaky republican regime. The ensuing political and economic turmoil were worsened at Recife—as its entire metropolitan area was now commonly known—by another epidemic that claimed 2,200 lives in 1890, after which the Capibaribe again overflowed its banks in May 1894. Disease claimed a further 2,500 victims in 1895–1896; almost 5,000 more people in 1904–1905; 2,575 in 1907–1908; and 3,872 in 1910–1911.

The city finally began to emerge from its doldrums when the government hired a French company in 1908 to overhaul and modernize its port facilities. This vast project commenced two years later with the demolition of Fort Picão and the Laje Lighthouse at the tip of the reef, so as to extend that natural barrier with the addition of a 3,600-foot breakwater. Despite

Panoramic view northeastward up the anchorage, ca. 1913. To the left lies Antônio Váz Island, connected to Recife—at center—by a bridge, while to the right lies the open Atlantic. (*Lloyd's Twentieth Century Impressions of Brazil*)

interruptions caused by the eruption of World War I in 1914, plus a few local difficulties, a second 2,500-foot breakwater, dubbed the Olinda Mole, was also driven out from the low Lingueta Peninsula in a southeasterly direction, creating a 900-foot protected entry channel. The anchorage was meanwhile dredged to a low-water depth of 32 feet, while city dockyards were enhanced by the installation of modern cranes, conveyor belts, rail spurs, and a coaling plant. Even the old iron Sete de Setembro Bridge across to Santo Antônio was replaced by the more modern Maurício de Nassau Bridge in 1917, the entire harbor complex being inaugurated when a 15,000-ton Dutch merchantman entered to berth directly at Recife's quayside in October 1924.

Unfortunately, heavy rainfall had raised river levels that same spring, obliging 5,000 people to abandon their homes in the city's most low-lying areas before the waters receded on 26 April 1924. Tens of thousands of migrants had also begun forsaking the Pernambucan countryside in favor of the capital, attracted by its better job prospects and impelled by the utter collapse of their traditional rural livelihoods, mechanization having driven farmland prices up and seasonal wages down. Recife's population consequently mushroomed from 239,000 inhabitants in 1920 to 313,150 only three years afterward (although that latter figure included 52,200 people from the recently incorporated Olinda), and it would continue with exponential growth.

A majority of these impoverished new arrivals were crowded into slums of miserable huts known as *mocambos*—originally an African word denoting "caves"—scattered among the insalubrious mangroves and floodplains around the city periphery, where public services were virtually nonexistent. Epidemics occurred frequently and infant mortality remained cruelly high, helping fuel a Comintern-inspired revolt in November 1935 in which soldiers rose at Recife and throughout northeastern Brazil. Forces loyal to President Getúlio Dor-

nelles Vargas rushed in from neighboring states to crush these mutineers, Recife's own three-day ordeal ending when its rebels were expelled from the city center, then finished off in the hinterland.

Recife was rated the nation's third-largest and most densely populated city by 1940, with 384,000 inhabitants. Its economy was briefly stimulated by Brazil's participation in World War II, during which port, rail, and highway networks were all upgraded, along with a few other ancillary municipal services. Its population reached 512,370 by 1950, the same year in which rising river waters again compelled 4,000 residents to temporarily abandon their homes (400 of which were destroyed by the floods). The city recuperated and resumed its traditional, low-yield exports of sugar, cotton, and agricultural produce, while importing coal, petroleum, and wheat. Some large-scale public work projects were undertaken by the federal government during the 1950s, the ancient Buraco Fortress being torn down, while Beberibe was transformed into a huge Brazilian naval base. Yet the metropolis declined until it became only the country's seventh-largest city, with a population of 1,296,995 in 1990.

For further reading materials on Recife or Brazil, please consult the Select Bibliography at the end of this volume; additional sources on South American urban history can be found under "Regional Studies," as well as under "General Works on Latin America."

RIO DE JANEIRO

Vast natural harbor dominating a rich agricultural hinterland that has spawned a sprawling metropolis characterized by extremes of wealth and poverty.

Initial Contacts (1502–1554)

Despite Christopher Columbus's inauguration of a new westerly route across the Atlantic in 1492–1493, and the subsequent

Sweeping panorama southeastward across the sprawling modern metropolis toward its harbor entrance and the open Atlantic beyond. (City of Rio de Janeiro)

papal mediation of conflicting claims between Spain and Portugal to any discoveries, the Portuguese did not exhibit any interest in examining their allotted New World sphere until almost a decade later. On 10 August 1501, an expedition commanded by André Gonçalves and piloted by the veteran Florentine navigator Amerigo Vespucci finally appeared off Brazil, slowly reconnoitering down its coast until they sighted the milewide mouth of an enormous bay called Guanabara by its Tamoio and Tupinambá inhabitants—but which the explorers christened as *Rio de Janeiro* or January River, because its entrance had been espied on 1 January 1502.

They did not disembark, but a second Portuguese expedition under Gonçalves Coelho landed in 1503, examining the vast inner harbor that measured 15 miles wide by 16 miles long, and they even erected a whitewashed stone building that the Tamoios dubbed as the *carioca* or white house. Yet Portugal's interest remained engrossed in their existing trade around the Cape of Good Hope to Asia, so that no permanent settlement was contemplated in Brazil. It is believed that the Spanish explorer Ferdinand Magellan may have entered Rio de Janeiro's bay on 13 December 1519 and temporarily renamed it Santa Lucía, while refreshing his five ships' crews before departing two weeks later around the tip of South America on his circumnavigation.

However, it was not until rival French explorers began exhibiting interest in Brazil's southern portion that the Portuguese Crown moved to act upon their own unexercised claim. A small colonizing expedition under Martim Afonso de Sousa consequently entered Rio de Janeiro Bay on 30 April 1531 to erect a tiny fortification and try to establish peaceful relations with the Tamoios. He remained for only three months, before charting the coast as far as the River Plate and returning to take up residence instead at São Vicente (Santos).

King João III decreed on 28 September 1532 that Brazil was to be administratively subdivided into *capitanias hereditárias* or hereditary captaincies extending inland from different stretches of coastline, and the province of Rio de Janeiro was allocated to Sousa. Yet he returned to Lisbon shortly thereafter and was promoted to a better position in India, so that Rio de Janeiro Bay was once again forsaken by the Portuguese. Other outposts farther to its northeast were colonized instead, such as Salvador or Olinda, as they lay closer to Europe and the routes of homeward-bound East Indiamen, so were the preferred choices for settlement. Rio's Guanabara Bay was consequently to be visited only sporadically by a few Breton or Norman vessels, who dubbed it Iteronne or Genève and eventually sought to essay a permanent foothold.

French Settlement (1555–1564)

Two well-armed vessels entered on 10 November 1555 with a few hundred Calvinist colonists under the seasoned Nicolas Durand, Chevalier de Villegagnon and Vice-Admiral of Brittany, bearing orders from Admiral Gaspar, Comte de Coligny, to found a new settlement to be called *France Australe* or Southern France—or *France Antarctique,* Antarctic France. They disembarked on rocky Laje Island in the middle of the channel, then transferred to nearby Sergipe Island (modern Villegaignon Island), erecting a redoubt named Fort de Coligny, as well as a smaller two-gun battery to command the entrance channel. A town christened Henryville was duly founded, and a couple of relatively prosperous years ensued for the community, some crops being planted and goods peaceably bartered with the seminomadic Tamoio and Tupinambá tribesmen.

In March 1557, a second expedition of three French ships arrived, bringing an additional eighteen cannon and 300 people under Villegagnon's nephew Paris Legendre, Sieur de Bois le Compte le Meaux. Yet religious dissension erupted shortly thereafter, fracturing the remote outpost's harmony, prompting Villegagnon to revert to Catholicism, appoint his nephew as his successor, and return homeward by late 1559.

Around that same date, ten Portuguese warships under Adm. Bartolomeu de Vasconcellos da Cunha reached Salvador to provide the energetic new Brazilian governor-general, Mem de Sá, the nucleus for an expedition to dislodge the French. They set sail in early February 1560, arriving outside the bay and advancing upon the interlopers' trenches so swiftly that the defenders were easily overrun, aided by the fact that Governor Bois le Compte was exploring inland with his best troops, a company of Scottish Calvinists. Only the 74-man garrison at Fort de Coligny managed to resist for two days, before being outflanked on the night of 15 March by de Sá with 120 Portuguese soldiers and 140 Indian auxiliaries under their chieftain Martim Affonso.

However, the victors only blew the fortifications and sailed back to Salvador by mid-June 1560 with a hundred captives, leaving the French survivors to reemerge from the jungle and build new defenses at Uruçumirim outside Glória Bay (modern Flamengo Beach) and on Paranapuan (modern Governador) Island with the aid of their indigenous allies. A few minor counterstrikes were also launched against São Paulo and other frontline Portuguese outposts, while Villegagnon vainly attempted to organize a relief force back in France that following year, handicapped by the growing religious dissension

View westward across the entrance into Rio's bay, ca. 1890; in the right foreground can be seen a portion of Fort Santa Cruz, while on the opposite shore can be faintly discerned Fort São João, completed only ten years previously. (Marc Ferrez)

within the home country. The survivors remained unchallenged until two Portuguese galleons bearing 300 soldiers and a host of Brazilian auxiliaries under the governor-general's nephew, Estácio de Sá, arrived outside on 6 February 1564 to make another sweep. On that occasion, though, they were repelled by Tamoio resistance.

Portuguese Foundation (1565–1579)

After gathering greater strength, Estácio de Sá set sail again on 27 January 1565 to mount yet another attack, disembarking on 1 March and quickly establishing a fortified camp below the 1,200-foot-high *Pão de Açúcar* or Sugarloaf Hill, where he optimistically proclaimed the creation of the new city of São Sebastião do Rio de Janeiro, named in honor of the Portuguese monarch Dom Sebastião. However, this position was invested five days later by Tamoio Indians loyal to the French, after which three ships arrived from France with reinforcements, so that a stalemate ensued: the Portuguese controlling the harbor entrance, while the French remained unchallenged inside the bay.

Estácio de Sá even allotted the first few *sesmarias* or land grants in an official ceremony held on 24 July 1565, and the Portuguese grip gradually spread inside the bay. A municipal government was constituted that same September, with Francisco Dias Pinto appointed by Governor-General Mem de Sá as first *alcaide-mor* or senior magistrate, but it was not until the governor-general led the three recently arrived galleons of Cristóvão de Barros from Salvador in January 1567 that the French presence could at last be totally eradicated. Arriving by 18 January, the governor-general and his nephew's forces jointly fell upon the heavily outnumbered French two days later, easily overrunning their defensive positions at Uruçumirim—held by only eleven Frenchmen and a handful of Tamoio warriors—plus nearby Paranapuan.

De Sá consummated his victory by better fortifying the harbor entrance and officially confirming his nephew—badly wounded by an arrow in the face during the Uruçumirim assault—as the new city governor. Estácio de Sá died of his injury on 20 February, being succeeded by another of the governor-general's nephews, Salvador Correira de Sá e Benevides. The original, extemporized city was transferred that same August to a permanent site at the point of Glória Bay, where the governor-general recognized his nephew's earlier land grants and construction began on a fort, churches, and other edifices. A street grid was laid out, and commons for planting and grazing allocated. When four French ships belatedly materialized offshore in late June 1568, they found the Huguenot colony completely extirpated and Rio firmly in Portuguese hands. Their attempt to disembark was repelled, and the four interlopers were chased as far west as Cabo Frio, where one was overwhelmed.

When some French trespassers subsequently established contacts ashore with the natives at Cabo Frio, Admiral de Barros was able to sortie from Rio de Janeiro on 27 August 1575 with a small expedition and destroy their base. The fledgling city enjoyed an interlude of peace and even developed a modest trade in sugar from its bayside plantations, although its physical remove from the main Brazilian sea-traffic lanes farther to its northeast hampered any significant growth in its commerce.

Spanish Neglect (1580–1620)

The small city's standing was also affected by the death of the epileptic Portuguese king Henrique on 31 January 1580, which left Philip II of Spain as nearest claimant to the throne. Although his succession was disputed by force of arms, a Spanish victory at Alcántara compelled Lisbon to surrender by 25 August, so that Philip was proclaimed king by the Cortes or Portuguese parliament on 15 April 1581, and Brazil became incorporated into Spain's empire. The remote port city of Rio de Janeiro was consequently drawn into Madrid's strategic policies.

As early as 25 March 1582, a storm-tossed and sickly Spanish fleet under Pedro Sarmiento de Gamboa and the veteran Admiral Diego Flores de Valdés entered the bay, landing more than 200 convalescents and slowly setting about repairs, before eventually exiting seven months later in a doomed attempt to colonize the Strait of Magellan. The survivors staggered back into Rio on 9 May 1583, to be met by Admiral Diego de Alcega with another four galleons bearing supplies and reinforcements to mount a second unsuccessful try that same December.

Spain's wars against The Netherlands during the late sixteenth and early seventeenth centuries furthermore came to embroil Rio de Janeiro. When four Dutch ships under Olivier van Noort arrived offshore on 9 February 1599, hoping to buy provisions before attempting to round the Strait of Magellan, they were discreetly greeted before being reluctantly driven off by Brazilian residents. A similar reception befell the half dozen vessels of Joris van Spilbergen in December 1614, who were allowed to spend almost a month covertly refreshing their provisions and tending to their sick before setting sail for the Strait.

Emergence (1621–1709)

A much more serious threat arose after the United Provinces renewed their hostilities against Spain in April 1621. Dutch merchants of the Westindische Compagnie (West Indian Company) were persuaded that their long-standing covert contacts with Brazilian sugar traders meant that a seaborne expedition to secure a permanent commercial enclave would be welcomed by the Portuguese inhabitants, who had grown resentful of indifferent Spanish rule. A Dutch fleet consequently seized São Salvador in May 1624, and although expelled the next year, another invasion force occupied Recife as of February 1630. The Dutch then expanded out of that foothold and over the ensuing two dozen years came to control as much as 1,000 miles of northeastern Brazil's coastline.

Rio de Janeiro, being 850 miles safely removed from the destructive cycle of raids and counterraids being conducted by local and Hispano-Portuguese forces against the Dutch interlopers, benefited as a haven for displaced refugees and overseas traders. The war became even more complicated after Portugal revolted against Spain in December 1640, acclaiming the seventh duke of Bragança as King João IV. The Luso-Brazilians expelled their former Spanish allies shortly thereafter, yet were disappointed when the Dutch refused to restore any of the territories that they had won. A truce was arranged in Europe whereby Lisbon grudgingly recognized Dutch sovereignty over Pernambuco in exchange for The Hague's continued assistance against Spain. Yet dissatisfied Portuguese residents in northeastern Brazil rose against the Dutch presence in June 1645, so that more fighting ensued. Even Rio de Janeiro was ineffectually blockaded four years later by Admiral Witte Corneliszoon de With before the Dutch finally acknowledged defeat and evacuated Brazil in the spring of 1654.

Rio de Janeiro emerged undamaged from this protracted struggle, and more prosperous and vigorous than before it had erupted. Although the Portuguese authorities sought to reimpose the same administrative practices that had existed prior to the Dutch intervention, restoring São Salvador to its status as overall Brazilian capital, that devastated city was to be clearly superseded in growth, size, and wealth as the seventeenth century progressed. Although the Crown steadfastly clung to its traditional arrangements, Rio de Janeiro was recognized as the capital of the southern captaincies in 1680, and the subsequent discovery of gold in neighboring Minas Gerais ensured its prominence. In fact, the southwestern seaport's ascendancy was to be most unmistakably confirmed when Portugal was drawn into Europe's War of the Spanish Succession in April 1704, Rio being assaulted twice while Bahia was ignored.

French Attacks (1710–1712)

During the closing phases of that conflict, eight ships bearing 1,500 men suddenly appeared outside Rio de Janeiro's bay on 16 August 1710 under Jean-François du Clerc, recently promoted to captain in France's royal navy. Although falsely flying the colors of Portugal's ally, England, his vessels were nonetheless fired upon by 44-gun Fort Santa Cruz as they attempted to stand into Rio's harbor, so that they veered westward and anchored in Ilha Grande Bay. After a few desultory disembarkations around Guaratinguetá and Sepetiba Bay on 27 August, du Clerc returned eastward and four days later landed 1,200 men 6 miles southwest of the city at Barra da Tijuca, hoping to circle round Orgãos Range.

Fighting their way up the Desterro road past Praya Vermelha, the invaders' small army stormed the capital on 18 September 1710, only to be thrown back from Carmo Square by Gov. Fran-

cisco de Castro Morais's militiamen—spearheaded by Bento do Amaral's student company—plus artillery fire from Fort São Sebastião on nearby Cobras Island. Having lost 380 men, the French tried to occupy São Bento Hill, only to again be repulsed and obliged to seek shelter in a sugar plantation. Cornered, outnumbered, and threatened with being burnt alive, du Clerc surrendered his army's remnants and became imprisoned in the city's Jesuit college. Three of his warships materialized outside Rio's entrance on 21 September and opened fire, desisting when the captive French commander sent out a message advising of his fate. The French vessels then sailed away, yet du Clerc was murdered on 11 March 1711 by a frenzied mob outburst, while his senior commanders were manhandled.

To avenge this loss and mistreatment, the famed Saint Malo privateer René Trouin, Sieur Duguay, appeared offshore on 12 September 1711 with fifteen ships and 6,000 men. His approach masked by mists, he decided to burst directly into Rio's harbor, braving Fort Santa Cruz on the eastern side of its entrance and the 48 guns of Fort São João and Praya Vermelha on the western side. Shooting their way in behind Captain Chevalier de Courserac's 74-gun *Magnanime*, who was familiar with the roadstead, the French immediately attacked six recently arrived Portuguese warships inside under Commodore Gaspar da Costa, who cut his cables and grounded his ships beneath the protection of Rio's ramparts. At a cost of 300 total casualties, Duguay has penetrated the harbor.

The next dawn, these invaders seized Cobras Island, installing a battery of almost two dozen guns and mortars. Duguay meanwhile circled the city on 14 September 1711 and deposited 2,800 soldiers within a half mile of its walls, who repelled a counterattack by 1,500 militia defenders the next sunrise. On 19 September, Duguay called upon Governor de Castro to capitulate and commenced a bombardment when it was rejected. The demoralized garrison withdrew and at 1:00 A.M. of 21 September, a French prisoner slipped out of Rio de Janeiro to advise the besiegers that the Portuguese had abandoned their city. Duguay consequently entered and freed 360 survivors from du Clerc's failed expedition, while his second in command accepted the capitulation of the harbor batteries.

Governor de Castro attempted to regroup 5 miles inland in the vain hope of being reinforced from other Brazilian provinces. However, the French were firmly ensconced and demanded a ransom to spare Rio's buildings upon their departure, which the Portuguese reluctantly paid on 10 October 1711—although only 610,000 cruzados, far less than Duguay expected. The French therefore stripped many buildings setting sail on 13 November, having incorporated the 56-gun *Nossa Senhora da Encarnacão* and 44-gun *Reinha dos Anjos* into their fleet, and torched more than 60 Portuguese vessels.

Recuperation (1713–1762)

In the aftermath to this devastating assault, the first major calamity endured by Rio de Janeiro, Governor de Castro was tried and condemned to life imprisonment in India for his undistinguished role in the defense, while other senior officers received similar sentences. Antônio Albuquerque Coelho de Carvalho, the governor of Minas Gerais, was temporarily installed into office and initiated the city's slow and painful recovery from its sack.

The fertility of the inland plantations helped ensure a revival within the next decade and a half, so successfully that Rio de Janeiro even spilled beyond the confines of its original perimeter of walls, and the century-old proposal for constructing the Santa Tereza aqueduct to bring it water from the Carioca River was accelerated and began discharging through sixteen bronze faucets into the new marble Fonte da Carioca by 1723. (Twenty-one years later, Gov. Gomes Freire de Andrade, Conde de Bobadela, ordered the aqueduct reconstructed of more sturdy materials and covered over with tiles four years afterward.)

Brazil's prosperity sagged after its sugar monoculture was undercut during the late 1730s by an export boom out of Saint-Domingue (Haiti) and other French Caribbean islands, an upsurge that so saturated European markets that prices and profit margins fell dramatically. A quarter century of depression ensued, yet Rio de Janeiro rebounded better than most other Brazilian cities. A new cathedral was built in 1761, and

Rio served as the springboard for Portuguese expeditions pushing the boundaries southwestward into the River Plate estuary, furnishing provisions and logistical support to such frontline garrisons as Colônia do Sacramento in Uruguay. A joint Anglo-Portuguese expedition entered Rio's harbor on 2 November 1762, for example, led by the 50-gun English vessel *Lord Clive* and 28-frigate *Ambuscade* under a former East India Company captain named John Macnamara, escorting seven Portuguese transports bearing 500 troops under Lt.-Col. Vasco Fernandes Pinto Alpoim, who continued less than three weeks later for the River Plate in the company of the 38-gun Portuguese frigate *Glória*.

Viceregal Capital (1763–1807)

When these hostilities ceased the next year and Portugal's chief minister, Sebastião José de Carvalho e Mello, Marques de Bompal, set about overhauling Brazil's outdated colonial administration, the shift of wealth and influence southwestward was so palpable that Rio de Janeiro was declared the new viceregal capital. Antonio Álvares, Conde da Cunha, arrived in October 1763 to assume office as its first viceroy, immediately setting about to improve the capital city's hygienic standards, and he furthermore transformed the former Jesuit monastery at São Christóvão into a hospital for lepers. The next year, the

Onlookers gazing southeastward from São Bento heights across Rio toward the harbor entrance, ca. 1821–1825; lithograph by Godefroy Engelmann published in Paris in 1835, from an original drawing by the young German artist, Johann Moritz Rugendas. (*Malerische Reisen in Brasilien*)

arsenal at the Casa do Trem beside Forte de Santiago was expanded, and three royal regiments arrived from Portugal in 1767 to be quartered within the city: the Bragança, Estremoz, and Elvas or Mora regiments. A navy yard was moreover properly constituted at the base of São Bento Heights.

When Luiz de Almeida Portugal Soares Mascarenhas, Marquês do Lavradio, assumed office as the third viceroy in 1769, he initiated a further round of military construction that produced the São Clemente redoubt and Picos fortress, as friction with Spain for control over the River Plate continued to escalate until a border was finally fixed with the signing of the Treaty of San Ildefonso in October 1777. The Marquês also initiated the reclamation of marshlands on the alluvial plain beside Rio de Janeiro (where Lavradio Street runs today), as well as creating the slave mart at Valongo and a public slaughterhouse at Santa Luzia Beach.

The viceroy José Luiz de Castro, Conde de Resende, was able to reclaim more swamps around the city and prolong streets such as Largo do Paço, as well as to transform the Campo de Santana into a *passeio público* or public promenade in 1783, where an exuberant religious festival dubbed the Folias do Divino would become the precursor of the city's modern carnivals. The collapse of sugar production in the French Caribbean because of the rise of a radical new government in Paris in 1791 greatly benefited Brazil, as prices skyrocketed and its trade was to flow relatively unimpeded over the next several years, as Portugal was allied to Great Britain and thus spared any blockade by the Royal Navy. Lisbon even remained neutral as of 1803, until its close commercial contacts with England goaded the French emperor Napoleon I into sending an army to depose the royal family early in 1808, who fled to reestablish their government in exile at Rio de Janeiro.

Imperial Capital (1808–1888)

Prince Regent João arrived at his Brazilian capital on 7 March 1808, accompanied by a large fleet bearing virtually the entire Portuguese government and treasury, as well as several thousand refugees. This wholesale reinstallation of the imperial apparatus was to have a profound effect not only upon Rio de Janeiro, but the future course of Brazil. The city had to expand and upgrade so as to absorb this influx of Crown agencies, while its commerce was simultaneously enhanced by closer

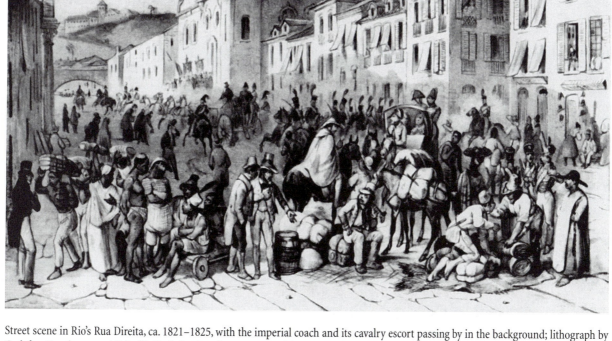

Street scene in Rio's Rua Direita, ca. 1821–1825, with the imperial coach and its cavalry escort passing by in the background; lithograph by Godefroy Engelmann published in Paris in 1835, from an original drawing by the young German artist, Johann Moritz Rugendas. (*Malerische Reisen in Brasilien*)

contacts with the British allies of the throne, who introduced new products and technologies. A permanent naval base was even offered to the Royal Navy, complete with storehouses and support facilities. When Napoleon was defeated seven years later, the prince regent chose to remain in Brazil and proclaimed it a kingdom as of December 1815; and upon the death of his deranged mother, Maria, three months afterward, he became King João VI and ruler of Portugal's global holdings. His presence persuaded many Brazilians not to join their Spanish-American neighbors in seeking independence from European rule.

Rio de Janeiro's position as capital of the Portuguese overseas empire concluded when the twenty-three-year-old successor prince, Pedro, refused to acknowledge his recall to Lisbon in January 1822 by the Cortes, as well as their peremptory relegation of Brazil to secondary status within the empire. Citizens rallied when the Voluntarios d'El Rei Regiment of Lt.-Gen. Jorge Avilez—2,000 Portuguese regulars homeward-bound from recent garrison duty at Montevideo—proclaimed their intention of embarking for Europe with the prince. Thousands of Brazilian militiamen, black Henriques guerrillas, and Indian contingents consequently massed along Rio's waterfront to contest this threat, prompting Avilez to call for their disbandment. Pedro refused, attempted to replace the general, then ordered the regiment to withdraw to Praia Grande on the opposite side of the bay on 14 January. After a monthlong standoff, the Portuguese general grudgingly sailed away, leaving Brazil to assume independence with Pedro as its emperor.

The city nonetheless remained blighted by poverty throughout most of its neighborhoods, with an economy overly dependent upon the fluctuating fortunes of agricultural exports. A 451-square-mile federal district was created around the city in 1834, authority being invested in an appointed prefect and a municipal council. Despite a yellow-fever outbreak in December 1849, Rio entered into a half century of considerable foreign investment and modernization. In May 1852, its first experimental telegraph line was strung, and a single line was operating to the imperial suburb of Petropolis by July 1858. The first railway had also been inaugurated as of 1854, initially running between Mauá and Petropolis, although it was soon more practically extended into rural areas. The urban population climbed spectacularly from 154,764 residents in 1860 to 191,000 a decade later, to 297,983 by 1880, and to 429,848 by 1890.

Turmoil (1889–1924)

However, the backwardness perpetuated by the imperial government's traditionalist policies finally culminated in a series of revolts, during which Rio de Janeiro was to be prominently featured. First, some 2,500 troopers of the 1st and 9th Cavalry regiments, as well as the 2nd Artillery Battalion, rebelled at dawn of 15 November 1889 at São Cristóvão, marching into the

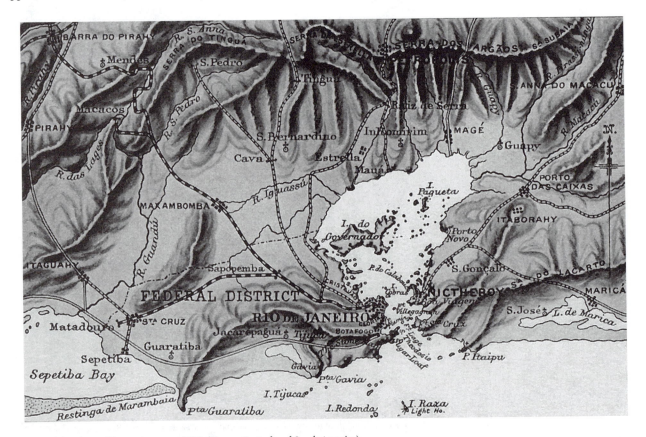

Map of the city and its environs, ca. 1905. (Keane, *Central and South America*)

View of Rio, ca. 1905. (Keane, *Central and South America*)

The heavy cruiser *Aquidabã,* flagship of the 1893–1894 naval rebellion, as it appeared while lying at anchor in Rio's harbor during peacetime. (Marc Ferrez)

capital. Liberal Prime Minister Affonso Celso, Visconde de Ouro Prêto, dispatched units to check these rebels, yet they instead joined the mutineer ranks. Even the arrival of Pedro II from his palace at Petrópolis that same afternoon failed to quell the insurrection, the emperor being informed the next day that he was to be banished into exile aboard a Brazilian warship by 17 November.

This toppling of the decayed imperial apparatus had been engineered by Marshal Manuel Deodoro da Fonseca, who temporarily replaced it with a provisional government, aiming to constitute a republic. Yet the transition was to be plagued by Brazil's continuing economic deficiencies and political bickering, until Fonseca sent troops to dissolve the congress on 3 November 1891. Rear Adm. Custódio José de Melo reacted to this intervention twenty days later, when his anchored 5,700-ton battleship *Riachuelo* fired a single shell into Rio de Janeiro, signaling the outbreak of another revolt. Surrounded by enemies, the dictator resigned rather than mount a futile resistance, being succeeded in office by his vice president, Adjutant-Gen. Floriano Peixoto.

The troops at Fort Santa Cruz then mutinied on 19 January 1892, being joined shortly thereafter by Fort Laje's garrison, before both groups were crushed by forces loyal to Peixoto. A group of thirteen high-ranking officers sent Peixoto a threatening manifesto on 31 March, urging quick presidential elections, which resulted in their dismissal from the service. When they organized a riot in Rio de Janeiro ten days afterward, most of the ringleaders were arrested and deported. Centralist and anticentralist insurrections continued to erupt throughout the country; Adm. Eduardo Wandenkolk, one of the thirteen dismissed officers, even commandeered the ammunition ship *Jupiter* outside Rio on 6 July 1893, diverting it to the port of Rio Grande in hopes of fomenting a more widespread anti-Peixoto revolt.

Finally, Admiral de Melo went aboard the English-built, 4,950-ton cruiser *Aquidabā* on the evening of 5 September 1893 with his staff and some disaffected federal deputies, raising the white flag of revolt. The 1,400 officers and men aboard the other 15 warships and 18 auxiliaries anchored before the city, as well as the naval base of Niterói opposite, supported this initiative; yet instead of an easy capitulation, the mutineers were disappointed when the harbor castles remained loyal to Peixoto, and no widespread insurrection ensued. Moreover, their squadron was in such poor condition that only five vessels could actually maneuver under their own power, while foreign warships banded together to protect their nationals' interests, restricting de Melo's actions (although not before he managed to commandeer about 30 merchantmen as supply ships).

Fighting flared between rebel and federal forces on 10 September 1893, then again on 13 September. Four days afterward, the mutinous admiral detached his cruiser *República* and torpedo boat *Primeiro de Março*, covering their escape past the batteries with a bombardment by *Aquidabā* so that they might proceed south to Destêrro (modern Florianópolis) to foment more rebellions. Meanwhile, Peixoto patiently mustered 5,000 troops at Santana and reinforced Rio's defenses, so that a lengthy stalemate ensued, punctuated by occasional exchanges with de Melo's anchored squadron. Foreign powers rushed warships to Rio, most notably the United States, Pres. Grover Cleveland being determined to uphold American influence against European interference.

Hoping to revive his flagging fortunes by personally heading southwestward for more help, de Melo broke out of Rio de Janeiro's harbor on 1 December 1893 with his flagship *Aquidabā*, leaving his fellow conspirator Adm. Luís Filipe de Saldanha da Gama to maintain pressure upon the capital. The latter grew increasingly frustrated at his idled squadron's impotence against Loyalist encroachments around Rio, so led 500 men ashore on 9 February 1894 under covering fire from his ships to attempt to capture the eastern town of Niterói. Although initially successful, Saldanha was soon thrown back by loyal troops, then driven back aboard ship from Armação Point. This action marked a virtual end to resistance within the harbor, the remaining mutineers learning on 11 March that a small loyal squadron—many of its vessels recently purchased,

Jornal do Commercio newspaper offices on Rio's magnificent new Avenida Rio Branco, ca. 1913. (*Lloyd's Twentieth Century Impressions of Brazil*)

Roundhouse at Rio's central railyard, ca. 1913. (*Lloyd's Twentienth Century Impressions of Brazil*)

armed, and manned in the United States—was approaching from Pernambuco under retired Adm. Jerônimo Gonçalves.

Their morale shattered, Saldanha and almost 500 of his men sought asylum aboard the tiny Portuguese corvettes *Mindelo* and *Afonso Albuquerque,* so that when Gonçalves entered Rio de Janeiro's harbor two days later, he thought its lengthy naval rebellion was already ended. Peixoto demanded the return of the mutineers, but the Portuguese commander refused, instead exiting the harbor and setting sail for the neutral River Plate. As a result, Peixoto severed diplomatic relations with Portugal.

Rio de Janeiro was to be shelled once more in the spring of 1910, when crew members of the 19,250-ton Brazilian battleships *Minas Gerais* and *São Paulo* overwhelmed their officers, mutinied against the newly installed government of Marshal Hermes da Fonseca, then opened fire. These rebels were eventually granted amnesty, but when a second rebellion erupted a few days later aboard another warship and at the Cobras Island barracks, it was more severely repressed. Fort Igrejinha's garrison at Copacabana revolted against President Epitácio Pessoa on 5 July 1922, being joined by cadets from the military academy. A few rounds were lobbed against strategic targets within Rio, before being put down by loyal troops and warships. And lastly, the warship *São Paulo* mutinied at its anchorage in Guanabara Bay on 6 November 1924, threatening to shell the presidential palace, before these mutineers changed their minds and sailed out of port under fire from the batteries to surrender to the Uruguayan authorities at Montevideo.

Modern Era (1925–Present)
Despite the volatility of its political life and unremitting pockets of poverty, Rio de Janeiro continued to attract a steady influx of migrants from its surrounding districts and slowly sprawled around its extensive bay shore into a massive modern metropolis. Its population mushroomed from 544,917 inhabitants in 1900 to 708,669 eleven years later and to 1.1 million by 1920, finding work hard to find in a city with such limited industrialization or manufacturing infrastructure. The first unserviced and unregulated squatter slums known as *favelas* began to appear, and the pattern of growth for the modern metropolis became established, a city of contrasts between great wealth and dire poverty, between beautiful panoramas and squalid tenements.

SALVADOR
Sea outlet for a rich agricultural delta, which became the earliest Portuguese capital in the Americas and the modern heartland of Afro-Brazilian culture.

Discovery and Settlement (1501–1545)
This beautiful and commodious natural harbor was sighted by the Florentine-born explorer Américo Vespucci on 1

Panoramic view looking northwestward across Salvador's lower city and anchorage, as photographed in 1860 by the English visitor Benjamin R. Mulock. (Ferrez, *Bahia: velhas fotografias*)

November 1501, who named it Baia de Todos os Santos (All Saints' Bay), because that particular date coincided with All Saints' Day on the Church calendar. After proceeding southwestward with his initial reconnaissance, Vespucci is believed to have returned two summers later, sheltering inside Bahia's deep and ample anchorage—25 miles in length by 20 in breadth—for more than two months while charting its islands and inland waterways, as well as recording the name of the temporary camp established ashore as São Salvador (Holy Savior).

Yet Portugal's interest remained fixated upon trade around the Cape of Good Hope with distant India, so that only a few passing ships touched at this harbor over the next quarter century. It was not until all Portuguese hopes of Far Eastern commerce were extinguished that the Crown turned to securing and exploiting its New World claim by issuing hereditary *capitanias* (captaincies)—long, narrow strips of territory extending inland from a coastal capital, as far as the Spanish-American border. Each was assigned to a specific *donatário* (grantee), usually an aristocrat or distinguished soldier or navigator, who would populate and administer this vast wilderness property at his own expense.

Consequently, the first permanent foothold was not founded atop the 250-foot-high bluff peninsula enclosing Baia de Todos os Santos from the Atlantic Ocean until 1530; its few score colonists could eke out a meager subsistence only by bartering with regional tribesmen and harvesting a few crops, before their tiny outpost was destroyed by a Tupinambá civil war fifteen years later.

Relocation and Flourishment(1549–1623)

Bahia's private title was rescinded and Tomé de Sousa arrived as Brazil's first Crown-appointed governor-general on 29 March 1549, accompanied by three large ships, two caravels, and a brigantine bearing 500 new Portuguese colonists—including a Jesuit mission under Fr. Manuel Nobrega and the Jewish physician Jorge Valadares. They found fifty survivors ensconced near the burned remnants of their original outpost (henceforth known as Vila Velha or Old Town); a more defensible site was therefore chosen on a promontory facing west-

Panoramic view looking northwestward across Salvador's lower city and anchorage, as photographed in 1860 by the English visitor Benjamin R. Mulock. (Ferrez, *Bahia: velhas fotografias*)

ward across the interior of the bay, which the military engineer Luis Dias fortified by erecting a stockade to enclose what was destined to become the new *cidade do São Salvador* (city of the Holy Savior)—capital for both the captaincy of Bahia and all other Portuguese settlements in Brazil. Its Casa de Misericordia do São Cristóvão (St. Christopher Charitable Hospital) was founded that same year with donations from Gama de Andrade, plus support from the first city mayor, Diogo Munis Barreto. Three years afterward, São Salvador also became the captaincy's ecclesiastical center, when Sé parish was founded.

Citizens meanwhile conducted a series of forays inland, gradually wresting control over the fertile and flat wetlands opposite—known as the Recôncavo (Back Bay)—from their Tupí, Je, and Cariri inhabitants, who were furthermore depleted by an influenza epidemic in 1551 and by smallpox introduced aboard a slave ship a decade afterward. The settlers' expansion culminated with the establishment of Sergipe do Conde deeper in the interior in 1559, so that the next year the energetic new governor-general, Mem de Sá, could even use Bahia as a springboard from which to assault the French Huguenot set-

tlement at Rio de Janeiro, setting sail on 21 February 1560 with ten galleons under Adm. Bartolomeu de Vasconcellos da Cunha. A follow-up expedition of two galleons departed four years later with 300 soldiers under the governor-general's nephew, Estácio de Sá, but the French interlopers were not entirely eradicated until Mem de Sá himself led one final effort against Rio in January 1567, with the recently arrived squadron of Cristóvão de Barros.

The citizens of São Salvador—also commonly referred to as Salvador, or Baía—had meanwhile cleared more farm tracts and discovered that sugarcane was especially well suited to this sun-baked tropical setting; thus large-scale importation of Angolan slaves commenced as of the 1570s. The city proved to be a strategically placed clearinghouse for this valuable cash crop, as well as cotton and tobacco, harvests being lightered from the Recôncavo's *engenhos* (mills) by *alvarengas* (boats), then stored in city warehouses to await the ships that anchored in its sheltered roadstead. Upon their arrival, they also ferried slaves and European goods ashore for sale, while crews and passengers recuperated in hostels and vessels underwent repairs at the shipyard. Imported goods would be distributed back into the Recôncavo, until eventually the ships were ladened and supplied for departure, and the annual cycle began anew.

The population of the city and its extensive municipality (ruled through a *Câmara* or council) more than doubled to 1,100 Portuguese residents by 1576, plus several thousand indigenous inhabitants and black laborers toiling around the bay shore and the interior. Four years later, after the death of the epileptic cardinal-king Henrique, Portugal and its overseas empire became absorbed by Spain. Frictions with Elizabethan England then precipitated São Salvador's first seaborne raid, when the privateers Robert Withrington and Christopher Lister led a small squadron past its batteries on 21 April 1587, ransacking four of nine anchored merchantmen in the bay on the moonlit night of 23–24 April, before the English finally tired of their blockade and vanished on 1 June.

Full-scale Anglo-Spanish hostilities erupted in Europe the following year, so that the city's role as a commercial entrepot became further upgraded, Atlantic depredations requiring the assembly of annual convoys in its bay to protect outward-bound merchantmen. Its defenses and shipyard facilities expanded as a result, and food supplies were regularized. São Salvador itself, though, was not directly threatened until after a smallpox epidemic had been unwittingly introduced by two neutral French ships in 1597. A squadron of Dutch interlopers under Hartman and Broer hovered around its bay for twenty-five days in 1599, and four Dutch ships under van Caarden mounted another forty-day blockade five years later, immediately after the cessation of the English conflict. São Salvador had emerged from this ordeal rather well, its jurisdiction containing perhaps 8,000 Portuguese and black inhabitants, several hundred of whom would succumb to a measles epidemic in 1616–1617.

Bahia's captive 48-year-old Gov. Diego de Mendoza Hurtado and 61-year-old Jesuit provincial Domingo Coinia, as they arrived at Amsterdam in October 1624; engraving by Claes Janszoon Visscher, alias Piscator, who witnessed their disembarkation. The conquered city is featured as a backdrop. (Algemeen Rijksarchief, The Hague)

Invasion and Reclamation (1624–1625)

A more serious threat arose after the United Provinces of The Netherlands declared war against Spain in April 1621. For decades, Amsterdam merchants had discreetly financed Brazil's sugar industry and sold its exports throughout Europe, while vessels from The Netherlands made regular clandestine visits. Their friendly reception persuaded the Westindische Compagnie (West Indian Company) to raise an expedition to secure a permanent commercial colony, São Salvador being targeted because its Portuguese inhabitants were believed to be especially resentful of Spanish rule.

Twenty ships and five yachts consequently materialized outside its bay on 8 May 1624 under Adm. Jacob Willekens of Amsterdam and Vice Adm. Pieter Pieterszoon Heyn of Rotterdam, bearing an invasion army of several thousand troops under Col. Johan van Dorth, Lord of der Horst and Pesch. Bahia's Spanish governor, Diego de Mendoza Hurtado, was taken by surprise, the landward approaches to his capital being protected only by Fort Santo Antônio to its north and a few lesser defenses, while a 6-gun battery lay incomplete along its waterfront. The Dutch fleet swept into the bay and split into two squadrons, one under Heyn pausing opposite São Salvador to open fire, while the second disembarked van Dorth's troops at Santo Antônio Beach, 3 miles farther north. Next morning, the 3,000 city defenders—mostly reluctant peasant levees and black slaves—beheld more than 1,000 well-armed Dutch soldiers with two field-pieces circling into the hills above their barricades. Fearful of being cut off, the defenders deserted in droves, leaving de Mendoza with only sixty troops inside his main citadel, so that São Salvador was overrun at a cost of only fifty Dutch casualties.

Van Dorth was installed as governor and began strengthening the defenses through deepening the moat and erecting additional bulwarks, while Willekens and Heyn landed equipment and provisions for a long-term occupation in anticipation of departing with their squadrons on further commissions. Four ships carried prisoners and booty away toward The Netherlands, while Brazilian slaves were tempted to switch allegiance through promises of freedom and land. By the time Willekens and Heyn set sail in early August 1624, São Salvador's new Dutch garrison had three to four months' provisions, plus the promise of timely relief from Holland.

Yet the Recôncavo shoreline opposite remained hostile, guerrilla resistance having sprung up at the behest of Bahia's bishop, Marcos Texeira, who had fled inland before the capital fell. Van Dorth was killed shortly thereafter while leading a probe inland, and disease appeared as well, sapping Dutch morale. A Hispano-Portuguese counterexpedition had also been swiftly raised in Europe—news of São Salvador's fall having reached Madrid before The Hague—and appeared outside Bahia on 29 March 1625 (Easter Saturday), composed of twenty-two galleons and forty consorts with 2,700 sailors under Spanish Adm. Fadrique de Toledo y Osorio, Marqués de Villanueva de Valdueza, and Portuguese Adm. Manuel de Meneses, knight of the Order of Cristo, as well as bearing 4,000 soldiers under Pedro Rodríguez de Santiestéban, Marqués de Cropani and knight of the Order of Calatrava.

Forming a wide crescent to impede escape, the fleet disgorged its troops at Santo Antônio Beach by the next afternoon, linking up with guerrilla bands to occupy the São Pedro high ground. The outnumbered Dutch meanwhile warped their eighteen remaining ships beneath São Salvador's batteries, then launched sporadic sallies over the next few weeks as siege lines were driven toward their ramparts. The defenders loosed two fireships against the anchored Spanish fleet one night, without success, and Heyn's depleted squadron reappeared from West Africa but was powerless to assist. When the siege lines finally reached São Salvador's moat, the Dutch commander Willem Schouten requested terms, a capitulation being signed on 30 April 1625 whereby 1,912 Dutch, English, German, and French occupiers surrendered, being allowed to exit with their baggage and travel back to Holland; the victors—who had suffered 120 dead and 144 wounded—retained 260 cannon, 500 quintales (hundredweight) of gunpowder, 600 black slaves, and much other booty.

A belated Dutch relief convoy of thirty-three ships under Adm. Boudewijn Hendricksz and Vice Adm. Andries Veron approached the harbor mouth on 22 May 1625, galvanizing the Spaniards and Portuguese into herding the surrendered garrison aboard five anchored German storeships, then sortieing with only a half dozen men-of-war—in hopes of luring the Dutch into a murderous cross fire within the bay. But Hendricksz spotted de Toledo's waiting fleet and refused to be drawn, instead steering northeastward to ravage Pernambuco. The Hispano-Portuguese fleet essayed a halfhearted pursuit, ending abruptly when the galleon *Santa Teresa* ran aground, so that both commanders were later reprimanded—Hendricksz for forsaking São Salvador without a fight, de Toledo for suffering an enemy fleet to roam unchallenged along Brazil's coast.

Disputed Stronghold (1626–1648)

Despite its timely rescue, the gutted and half-empty city of São Salvador—so thoroughly pillaged by the 1,000 Spanish troops left on garrison duty as to discourage Portuguese civilian refugees from even returning—was to endure another quarter century of misfortune, bearing the brunt of future Dutch offensives. Heyn stormed its Forte do Mar or Sea Castle (today's island fortress of São Marcelo) in March 1627, penetrating into the bay to sink or capture twenty-six merchantmen, then returned to inflict yet more damage later that same summer. A second huge Dutch colonizing expedition also seized the Pernambucan cities of Olinda and Recife early in 1630, which—being only 450 miles from São Salvador—perpetuated its predicament, as Madrid designated the battered Bahian capital as a military base to expunge this enemy enclave.

The first counterexpedition of twenty-seven Hispano-Portuguese warships under Adm. Antonio de Oquendo entered Bahia's anchorage from Lisbon on 11 July 1631, depositing troops under a Neapolitan-born commander named Giovanni Vincenzo de San Felice, Conde de Bagnuoli, to reinforce its garrison and assail the distant Dutch intruders. De Oquendo's fleet stood back out on 3 September to escort a twenty-ship sugar convoy across to Europe, successfully defending this charge—nine days later and 200 miles out at sea off the Abrolhos—against eighteen Dutch warships out of Recife under Adm. Adriaen Janszoon Pater. It proved impossible to prevent the enemy from expanding their beachhead deeper into Pernambuco, however, so that many residents were obliged to resettle in Bahia. Adm. Lope de Hoces deposited more reinforcements at São Salvador in December 1635, before having his fleet mauled in February 1636, and then exiting again on 26 March to safely escort yet another sugar convoy.

Recife's able new Dutch governor-general, Johan Maurits, Graaf van Nassau-Siegen, drove Bagnuoli's forces back upon Sergipe del Rey in March 1637; then a second offensive by Col. Sigismund von Schoppe pressed them to within 40 miles of São Salvador itself that same November. Convinced that Hispano-Portuguese resistance was on the verge of collapse, Maurits set sail on 8 April 1638 with 3,600 Dutch troops and 1,000 Brazilian auxiliaries aboard forty-five vessels, hoping to overrun the capital. Yet despite disembarking 6 miles to its north at Ponta de São Braz on 16 April, then carrying its small outlying Forts of São Bartholomeus and Monserrate, Maurits was finally checked by São Salvador's 1,200-man garrison under Gov. Pedro da Silva and Bagnuoli. Timely infusions of manioc flour and cattle allowed the defenders to manage a monthlong resistance, climaxed with a Dutch assault against the Santo Antônio citadel on the moonlit night of 18–19 May, which was repelled with 237 deaths. Maurits sailed away in defeat six nights later, São Salvador having been spared at a cost of 60 defenders slain and 90 wounded, compared with a total of 500 dead and 1,500 ill among the invaders' ranks.

However, hopes of turning this victory into a successful counterattack against Recife evaporated when forty-six Hispano-Portuguese ships staggered into Bahia early in 1639 under the Portuguese Adm. Fernão de Mascarenhas, Conde la Torre, having lost 3,000 of 8,000 troops to yellow fever during a terrible transatlantic crossing. The survivors could do nothing more than recuperate within depleted São Salvador, de la

Drawing of São Salvador as seen from its inner harbor, ca. 1629, attributed to the Portuguese military architect, Christovão Alvares. (Algemeen Rijksarchief, The Hague)

Torre's fleet not sortieing again until a year later and depositing 1,200 soldiers under Luis Barbalho Bezerra too far beyond Pernambuco, before continuing toward Europe with the annual sugar convoy. That same April 1640, a Dutch squadron under Adm. Jan Corneliszoon Lichthardt burst into São Salvador's bay and destroyed twenty-seven valuable mills throughout the Recôncavo.

Hostilities became more complicated after Portugal revolted against Spain in December 1640, acclaiming the seventh Duke of Bragança as their King João IV. The Dutch welcomed this schism, expecting the Brazilians to turn against their Spanish allies. Yet although the latter were soon expelled from the Portuguese realm, regional differences did not abate, as the Dutch refused to restore any territories won during the war. A ten-year truce was arranged in Europe on 12 June 1641, whereby Lisbon grudgingly recognized Dutch sovereignty over Pernambuco in exchange for The Hague's assistance against Spain.

This uneasy accommodation was ruptured when disgruntled Portuguese residents rose against Dutch rule in northeastern Brazil in June 1645. The governor of Bahia pretended to help contain this outburst by ordering Adm. Salvador Correia de Sá e Benevides, commander of that year's sugar convoy, to disembark 800 soldiers in passing by Tamandaré. But their regimental field commanders, Martim Soares Moreno and André Vidal de Negreiros, then fanned the unrest by reoccupying the Serinhaém district and Fort Nazaré, so that a Dutch squadron under Lichthardt retaliated by annihilating the sixteen Bahian transports still anchored off Tamandaré under Vice Adm. Jerônimo Serrão de Paiva.

Nonetheless, the Dutch were driven back inside Recife by the end of that same year, and in desperation they launched their third great invasion of Bahia in February 1647, when Adm. Joost "Banckert" van Trappen set sail with twenty-six ships and 2,400 troops under von Schoppe to occupy Itaparica Island. From a foothold won at Ponta das Baleias, they hoped to subdue São Salvador and its district, but their aggression had galvanized the Portuguese government into authorizing a counterexpedition, fifteen ships and almost 4,000 men departing Lisbon on 18 October under Gov.-Gen. Antônio Teles de Meneses, Conde de Vila Pouca de Aguiar; the next month they were followed by seven more ships under Salvador de Sá. Von Schoppe's army grew ill and was obliged to forsake Itaparica Island by mid-December. Hoping to divert pressure from closely invested Recife, a Dutch fleet then penetrated São Salvador's bay again in December 1648, destroying another twenty-three mills in the Recôncavo.

Mid-Colonial Era (1649–1762)

A stalemate ensued over the next five years, with no more major operations being conducted around São Salvador, so that it enjoyed a modest recuperation—further spurred when The Netherlands shifted their global strategy away from maintaining large overseas colonies to instead retaining small out-posts for their merchant marine, by now the world's largest and most lucrative. When the First Anglo-Dutch War erupted in May 1652, the Portuguese availed themselves of this distraction to send seventy-seven ships from São Salvador in December 1653 under Pedro Jacques de Magalhães and Francisco de Brito Freire, compelling Recife's last holdouts to capitulate by 27 January 1654. The Hague and Lisbon settled all outstanding differences through a treaty signed on 6 August 1661, whereby the latter agreed to pay 4 million cruzados as indemnity for the reconquest of Netherlandic Brazil.

At last free from invasion fears, São Salvador henceforth began its revival in earnest, the volume of its trade increasing so notably as even to finance certain urban improvements. Civilian edifices, for example—traditionally made of crude adobe brick covered in painted plaster and with red-tile roofs—improved in sturdiness and appearance, some two-story warehouses and homes acquiring imported wrought-iron window latticework, tile decorations, and plaster ornamentation in classical motifs. Brazil's first nunnery, the Convent of Santa Clara do Destêrro, was founded by 1677, while São Salvador's urban population rebounded to approximately 20,000 residents spread among 2,000 dwellings by the end of the seventeenth century—notwithstanding losses caused by sporadic epidemics and other calamities. Its mili-tary garrison, now that foreign dangers had receded, dwindled to scarcely 400 troops.

Much of this demographic upsurge was attributable to increased importation of slaves for Recôncavo *fazendas* (estates), plus the more distant Minas Gerais goldfields, so that blacks and mulattoes soon came to outnumber the tiny Portuguese elite, especially in rural areas. An ecclesiastical survey conducted throughout the captaincy of Bahia in 1709 listed a total of 21,601 white *almas de confissão* (confessional souls)—that is, communicants—compared with about 100,000 slaves. Most of the latter were employed as plantation field hands, although when the French traveler Amédée-François Frézier visited São Salvador five years later aboard the frigate *Saint Joseph,* he was so struck by its African omnipresence that he labeled the city a "New Guinea."

Rio de Janeiro, having been 850 miles farther removed from the destructive cycle of raid and counterraid against the Dutch, now emerged to rival the nominal Brazilian capital in both size and wealth. That ascendancy was underscored when Portugal became drawn into Europe's War of the Spanish Succession in April 1704, Rio being assaulted twice during the ensuing hostilities by French expeditions, while Bahia was ignored. (After that struggle ceased, however, São Salvador's anchorage was penetrated in September 1719 by the pirate Bartholomew Roberts with his 32-gun *Royal Rover,* who

Paço Municipal or "Municipal Palace," as photographed by Mulock, ca. 1860. This edifice had been rebuilt two centuries previously from the original building's ruins, burnt in 1625 during the struggle against the Dutch. (Ferrez, *Bahia: velhas fotografias*)

plundered the forty-two assembled sugar merchantmen preparing to clear for Lisbon.)

Its prosperity linked to the sugar monoculture, Bahia suffered another quarter century of economic depression starting as of the late 1730s, once French exports from Saint-Domingue (Haiti) and other Caribbean islands began flooding European markets, lowering prices and profit margins. When Portugal's chief minister, Sebastião José de Carvalho e Mello, Marques de Bompal, subsequently overhauled the imperial administration, he acknowledged Rio de Janeiro's undisputed primacy by granting it the title of viceregal capital in 1763.

Late Colonial Resurgence (1763–1807)

Yet despite its economic downturn and diminished political status, São Salvador's prospects nevertheless recovered once more. Its captaincy general of Bahia—which already encompassed the modern state of Sergipe—had expanded in 1759 to include the adjoining captaincy of Ilhéus to its north, plus Pôrto Seguro to its south two years later; both eventually contributed significant rice and coffee harvests to its overall exports, as well as their traditional production of manioc, the staple food for plantation slaves. Forestry products from these two districts moreover supplemented the hard *vinhatico* and *potomujú* planks brought across São Salvador's bay from the town of Jaguaripe on its southwestern shore, both for export and use in its Royal Arsenal and Dockyard, as well as several private yards and carpentry shops. Within the next three decades, most of Portugal's largest warships and merchantmen were launched from Bahian yards. The influential Recôncavo *senhores de engenho* (mill owners) had also diversified their crops to include more lucrative tobacco and coffee.

According to a census taken in 1775, São Salvador's population stood at 35,253 inhabitants, of whom 12,720 were classified as whites, 7,837 as free mulattoes or blacks, and 14,696 as slaves. This total rose to 39,209 people only five years later, for whom urban conditions and services continued to improve through such measures as the inauguration of a *cepeiro público* (public granary) in 1785. Rich inhabitants now increasingly resided in beautiful, pastel-hued mansions atop the bluff, cooled by sea breezes and well above the narrow and fetid streets of the lower city, which were often inundated with muddy effluence during heavy rainfalls. Visitors to the port commented upon its high incidence of crime, poverty, and public sexuality—typified by mulatta prostitutes plying their trade from curtained *cadeiras* (sedan chairs)—in contrast to the great number and variety of churches, allegedly numbering 365, one for every day of the year.

But the greatest stimulus to São Salvador's development proved to be the collapse of French sugar production in the Caribbean as of 1791 because of the emergence of a radical new revolutionary government in Paris that dislocated all transatlantic sales. Prices skyrocketed so dramatically upon European exchanges that Bahia's plantation owners profited enormously, and their sea outlet and financial capital shared in this bounty. Ship launchings at São Salvador also increased once Lisbon joined in the general wars against the new Republic of France, creating such an unforeseen boom that local food prices spiked, creating considerable hardship and unrest.

As allies of Great Britain, Portugal's colonies were spared any blockade by the Royal Navy, so that Bahian trade flowed relatively unabated over the next few years. Circumstances improved even further after a truce was arranged in Europe in October 1801: Portugal was to remain neutral when fighting resumed a year and a half later. Thanks to this second interlude of almost completely unimpeded trade, much of it aboard friendly English vessels, the city's population surged from 40,992 residents in 1801 to 51,112 a mere six years later, most of the increment occurring among its black and mulatto labor pool. And finally, because of Portugal's continued close commercial ties with Britain, the French emperor Napoleon I sent an invasion army into that country late in 1807, chasing its royal family across the Atlantic.

Independence Struggle (1808–1823)

Prince Regent João arrived at São Salvador to a warm reception from his colonial vassals on 22 January 1808. Virtually the entire Portuguese court, government, and treasury—10,000 to 15,000 people in total—had been crammed aboard the flagship *Principe Real,* sixteen lesser men-of-war, thirty merchantmen, and four English warships delegated as escorts by Rear Adm. Sir Sidney Smith. After a few weeks' respite, João proceeded to the viceregal capital of Rio de Janeiro to reinaugurate his administration in the New World.

Rather than return to Portugal after Napoleon's defeat and abdication seven years later, the prince regent chose to remain in Brazil and proclaimed it a kingdom as of December 1815. Upon the death of his deranged mother, Maria, three months afterward, he became King João VI and ruler of Portugal's global holdings. His decision to remain in turn persuaded many Brazilians not to join their Spanish-American neighbors in seeking independence from European rule, although a minor antimonarchist revolt did erupt at Recife in March 1817. The Conde dos Arcos, Bahia's governor, promptly sent two corvettes and a schooner to blockade that rebel port, then helped raise and direct regiments to subdue the mutinous province. When its insurgent leader Domingos José Martins marched south from Recife, he was defeated and captured on 17 May at Serinhão by 800 loyal Bahian militiamen (nicknamed Scipios in honor of the famous Roman general).

São Salvador endured a *bicha* (yellow-fever) epidemic in 1819, then three years later the widening schism between Brazil and Portugal finally ruptured when João's successor—the twenty-three-year-old Prince Pedro—refused to acknowledge a recall by the Cortes (parliament) at Lisbon, nor their legislative relegation of Brazil to subservient status. When a homeward-bound Portuguese regiment threatened to take

A thirty-oared royal galliot, constructed at São Salvador in 1808 for use by the prince regent, then transferred to Rio ten years afterward; note its dragon-shaped bowsprit, emblematic of the Bragança dynasty. Here, the boat was still being employed to greet Argentina's president Julio Roca during a state visit in 1899. (Marc Ferrez)

the prince with them, thousands of Brazilian volunteers defied and isolated the contingent within Rio de Janeiro Bay, until they departed empty-handed on 15 February 1822.

Four days afterward, Portuguese Gen. Inacio Luiz Madeira de Melo—alarmed by the rising tide of Brazilian nationalism—seized control of Salvador at a cost of 100 lives, intending to at least retain it in Lisbon's name. An ineffectual blockade was instituted by Brazilian Commo. Rodrigo Lamare, failing to prevent a trio of Portuguese warships from disembarking 600 more troops on 27 August 1822. Upon learning of this provocative escalation eleven days later, Pedro proclaimed Brazil's outright independence from Portugal. Then another 1,200 Portuguese reinforcements reached Salvador on 6 November, escorted by Commo. Félix de Campos's 74-gun flagship *Dom João VI* and the frigate *Perola.*

Pedro was officially crowned emperor of Brazil less than one month afterward, and the land siege of Salvador tightened. Yet no complementary sea blockade could be imposed until the former Royal Navy officer Thomas Alexander, Lord Cochrane (later tenth Earl of Dundonald), assumed command over Brazil's ramshackle navy in mid-March 1823. Setting sail from Rio with a quartet of vessels on 1 April, Cochrane skirmished inconclusively against de Campos's Portuguese warships outside Bahia on 4 May, neither side gaining any advantage because of their green and disaffected crews. The Portuguese commodore retired inside the harbor, while Cochrane withdrew 30 miles southward to São Paulo Fortress to reconcentrate his veteran British and American sailors

aboard his 74-gun flagship *Pedro Primeiro* and 26-gun corvette *Maria da Gloria,* so as to have two reliable vessels.

Resuming his watch outside Bahia, Cochrane was joined at the end of May 1823 by Capt. James Thompson's 44-gun frigate *Real Carolina,* then toward the end of June by Capt. John Taylor's 38-gun frigate *Niterói* and the brig *Bahia.* Gen. Madeira and Commo. de Campos eventually decided to evacuate their starving and half-empty city, especially once Cochrane threatened a fireship attack against their anchored vessels—their only means of escape. A flotilla of 75 to 85 sailors therefore exited Bahia on 2 July 1823, bearing away with 2,000 soldiers and thousands of noncombatants, while jubilant Brazilian irregulars surged into Salvador's deserted streets. Cochrane's five warships pursued this fleeing convoy northward, crippling many craft by boarding and cutting down their masts or staving in water casks, so as to compel them to return into Bahia, where sixteen ships and 1,000 troops were obliged to surrender.

Imperial Era (1824–1888)

Salvador struggled to revive from this debilitating ordeal and the loss of all its Portuguese contacts, which plight was exacerbated over the next decade and a half by a seething discontent: on 31 March 1824, for example, a group of military officers browbeat its city council into ordering all Portuguese citizens expelled. The mostly black 3rd Battalion rose on 25 October against a rumored disbandment of their unit, storming the regional headquarters to slay their commander in chief,

Gen. Felisberto Gomes Caldeira. Although the city's two other battalions and artillery company joined in a monthlong spree of looting and murder, they eventually surrendered to loyal troops without resistance—an uprising remembered as the *Periquitos* (Parakeets) Rebellion, because of the 3rd Battalion's distinctive bright green uniforms. Another outburst occurred on the morning of 10 April 1830 in the city slave mart, being swiftly repressed; sailors aboard the anchored warship *Carioca* also mutinied against their officers out in the harbor on 31 January 1831.

A much more serious revolt began when hundreds of soldiers and armed civilians occupied Fort Barbalho on 4 April 1831, calling for the ouster of the provincial commander in chief, Portuguese-born João Crisóstomo Callado. As their numbers swelled to 8,000 within the next three days, the authorities gave in—only to have more bloody riots ensue on 13 April, spreading across the bay into the Recôncavo before dissipating. The Piauí Battalion occupied Fort São Pedro on 12 May to demand freedom for political detainees, the ouster of the provincial president and interim commander, as well as the expulsion of all Portuguese-born citizens. The artillery company seized that same citadel on the night of 31 August to protest against their abysmal service conditions; then two months later, a group of officers seized Fort São Pedro yet again, as part of a growing nationwide movement against the centralizing tendencies of the imperial regime, these rebels being dispersed shortly thereafter into the wilds of the Recôncavo. A band of prisoners also rose and took the Forte do Mar sea castle on 26 April 1832 before being pounded into submission three days later.

Although the institution of Brazilian slavery remained legal, the importation of further transatlantic captives had been banned by an imperial decree issued on 7 November 1831, so that the number of African arrivals at Salvador declined. Smugglers nonetheless flouted this law by clandestinely discharging thousands of slaves amid its many harbor islands or at the mouth of the Una River to supply the Bahian plantations from a major new illegal depot on the west side of Itaparica Island. Hundreds of African-born Muslim slaves—known locally as *Malês*—took to the streets of Salvador on the night of 24–25 January 1835, holding off counterattacks by imperial soldiers and local militiamen for more than three hours before finally being crushed with the deaths of nearly 70 rebels, more than 500 prisoners being subsequently executed, imprisoned, flogged, or deported. That same year of 1835, the urban population was measured at 65,500 inhabitants—of whom 18,500 were classified as whites, 19,470 as free mulattoes or blacks, and 27,500 slaves.

Another anticentralist coup erupted when the 3rd Artillery Battalion mutinied at Fort São Pedro on 17 November 1837, taking on added gravity when they then threw their support behind the separatist preachings of the radical newspaper editor and medical doctor Francisco Sabino Álvares da Rocha Vieira—more commonly called "Sabino," this revolt becoming known as the *Sabinada*. Within hours the 3rd Infantry Battalion also joined, while Brazilian marines and part of the city militia remained loyal to the imperial government. The province of Bahia was acclaimed an independent republic, while many pro-centralists fled out into the Recôncavo to begin organizing a counterrevolutionary force called the Restorationist Army.

By the end of November 1837, 1,900 Restorationists—mostly national guardsmen—returned to lay siege to Salvador, soon being reinforced by blockading imperial warships. Starvation gripped the rebel garrison by December, while their besiegers swelled to 5,000 men. An all-out assault was mounted by the Restorationists against the debilitated city defenses on 12 March 1838, hundreds of casualties being inflicted during two days of close-quarter combat. Capitulation finally came on 16 March, Sabino being captured a week later and exiled to remote Goiás, while thousands of mulatto and black rebels were condemned to hard labor on Fernando de Noronha Island.

Despite this defeat, the rate of private manumissions rose in the city within the next couple of years, especially among female house servants; some 5 to 6 percent of Salvador's urban slaves were freed by their owners over the ensuing decade, although many faced no better prospects than living in a thatched-roofed, clay hut in the slums. A yellow-fever epidemic swept through the unhappy port during the 1840s, overwhelming such charitable institutions as the Monte Serrat Infirmary, which often lacked running water. Sanitary conditions were further hampered by the still unpaved streets, seasonal floods of muddy effluence cascading down from the promontory. Carrion buzzards called *urubus* were ubiquitous, while whale-oil lamps provided only dim illumination. The lower city remained largely commercial, crowded with quays, warehouses, and small factories; its craftsmen and other skilled laborers resided around its periphery in mud-brick edifices called *separadas* or *retiradas*. Most public buildings and the mansions of the elite were in the more prestigious upper city, painstakingly reached up a few sharply inclined access streets by sedan chairs carried by porters or by burro carts.

Some progress began after the cholera outbreak of the late 1850s abated, foreign firms being encouraged to invest in such modernization projects as paving over a few streets and inserting steel tracks to operate animal-drawn trolleys (nicknamed *Bonds,* after the method by which they were financed). An English concern also laid a railway line inland, so as to better tap the agricultural hinterland. According to the first national census, taken in 1872, the population of Salvador had grown to 108,138 residents, with another 21,000 people scattered among such satellite communities as Bomfin and Ribeira. The census also revealed that only forty-nine male and fifteen female slaves were literate out of a total of 167,760 living throughout the province; slavery was not abolished in Brazil

The São João Municipal Theater in the upper city, as photographed by Camillo Vedani in 1865, showing its spectacular view across the lower city and anchorage. Italian opera companies performed annually in Bahia during their off-seasons. (Ferrez, *Bahia: velhas fotografias*)

until 1888. Urban improvements continued when the upper and lower halves of the city were connected in 1873 by a huge, hydraulic-powered pedestrian lift—officially named the *Elevador Lacerda,* although nicknamed the Parafuso (Screwdriver) because of its unique traction method—while telegraph service appeared shortly thereafter, as well as a few telephones by the 1880s.

During the last two decades of the nineteenth century, wealthy families began forsaking their traditional rural existence, leaving estates or mills under the supervision of managers so as to take up year-round residence in their upper-city mansions and send their sons to Salvador's medical or law schools. A new elite soon began to emerge featuring bankers, commodity brokers, merchants, and newspaper editors (although circulation within the city totaled only about 22,000) and who would prove to be quite active in Brazilian politics—despite Bahia's declining influence in comparison with the booming southern provinces.

Republican Era (1889–Present)

The backwardness and isolation of imperial Brazil finally began to be lifted after Marshal Manuel Deodoro da Fonseca overthrew Pedro II in a bloodless coup at Rio in mid-November 1889, installing a republican regime. However, his administrative reorganization failed to significantly improve conditions for Salvador da Bahia's inhabitants—enumerated at 173,879 people by the census of 1890, most being poor and illiterate—while the city's modest light-industrial output of food products, matches, soap, and candles came to a virtual halt as the nation descended into economic and political turmoil. Municipal authorities furthermore tried to contain an onslaught of rural refugees fleeing from Bahia's drought-stricken interior, while a major epidemic also gripped the seaport from 1891 to 1893.

Efforts by the federal government three years later to eradicate a conservative religious sect led by the firebrand Antônio Conselheiro and ensconced in the remote rural hamlet of Canudos, 200 miles north of Salvador, created a brief outburst of prosperity, the port serving as transportation hub and supply base for the several thousand troops who were transported upriver as of June 1897. Ambushes by their fanatical Guarda Católica (Catholic Guard) opponents inflicted so many casualties that hundreds of extra beds had to be crammed into Salvador's Medical School that same September to handle the

São Bento Church as photographed by Marc Ferrez in 1884; note the steeply inclined street leading down toward the lower city. (Ferrez, *Bahia: velhas fotografias*)

exports of cacao, hides, tobacco, coffee, sugar, rubber, and hardwoods. The upper city, though, boasted more modern boulevards, parks, mansions, shops, hotels, theaters, and schools, as well as electric car lines radiating out to ever more distant suburbs.

Many colonial structures had unfortunately been lost to decay, as well as swarms of indigenous termites that consumed their wooden ceiling beams, collapsing the roofs. On the other hand, a majority of streets were now paved, and electric service for domestic purposes had been extended throughout most of the city by the national Companhia Brasileira de Energia (Brazilian Energy Company). Urban development also stretched well beyond the ancient municipal boundaries to include light manufacturing plants, a pair of large shipyards, a coaling station, and a petroleum refinery around the bay's periphery.

The core population rose to 393,207 residents by 1960, then—thanks to the effects of accelerating industrialization and rural-to-urban migration patterns—exploded to 1.5 million inhabitants by the mid-1980s and an estimated 2.1 mil-

flood of wounded. An estimated 5,000 Brazilian soldiers, including one-third of Bahia's state militia, perished before the campaign finally concluded with Canudos being overrun and burned on 5 October.

Another epidemic gripped Salvador at the conclusion of those hostilities, after which it slipped back into its antebellum lethargy. Agriculture continued to decline in value, industry stagnated, and few foreign investors could be attracted. The electrification of the city's streetcar system was one of the few urban improvements instituted until 1909, when efforts also commenced to upgrade its harbor facilities, channels being dredged and a concrete waterfront poured so that ships might dock and transfer their cargoes directly at Salvador's wharves, rather than continue the outdated and tedious practice of lightering goods to and from the anchorage. The population experienced a modest upsurge by 1920, although neither the city nor state was any longer a major player in national politics.

Another population increase began in the early 1940s, the stimulus of Brazil's participation on the Allied side during World War II pushing the number of Salvadorian residents to 274,910 by 1950 (or 389,422 if its entire metropolitan area was included), while a 350-mile railway would soon be completed as far as Joazeiro on the São Francisco River. The lower city's dockyard area was still to be characterized by narrow colonial-era streets and crowded with warehouses handling bulk

"A Liberian Plutocrat of Bahia," covered in ornaments of pure gold, ca. 1900. (Wright, *The New Brazil*)

lion by 1993. Despite such notable modernization and expansion, the city's Afro-Brazilian character nonetheless adapted and thrived to these changes, mostly in the form of spiritist cults that were opposed to orthodox Catholicism, as well as such cultural outlets as popular music and fashion.

For further reading materials on the history of Salvador or Brazil, please consult the Select Bibliography at the end of this volume; additional sources can be found in the reference section on South American urban history under "Regional Studies," as well as under "General Works on Latin America."

Chile

CONCEPCIÓN

Centuries-old military base that has withstood attacks, earthquakes, and tidal waves during its colorful history.

Initial Settlement (1550–1554)

The first Spanish explorer to sight the mouth of the Bío-Bío River and neighboring Talcahuano Bay was the Italian-born Capt. Juan Bautista de Pastene aboard the passing galleon *San Pedro,* while returning northward in late September 1544 from reconnoitering the Chilean coast. However, when his superior, Pedro de Valdivia, subsequently led a small army overland from Santiago to attempt to subjugate the territory two years later, his expedition encountered such stiff resistance from the fierce Araucanian Indians that the conquistadors soon become beleaguered inside an extemporized base camp at a seaside valley called Penco (or, alternatively, Pemuco or Peguco) in the southeastern corner of the broad bay, from whence they eventually managed to escape at night.

It was not to be until January 1550 that Valdivia could re-enter this district with a stronger contingent of 200 Spaniards and 2,000 indigenous auxiliaries, smashing several Araucanian concentrations while driving toward the coast and re-emerging at Penco by 24 February. His men then felled trees from its dense stands to erect a large, moated stockade within the next eight days atop a prominence called Alto de Pinto (Pinto Height), before settling down to await the arrival of seaborne reinforcements being brought by Capt. de Pastene. Four columns of Araucanians swarmed out of the hills under Chief Ainavillo on 12 March to challenge this establishment, but they were decimated by Spanish cavalry sallies and artillery salvos; the galleon and its consorts then arrived eight days later. Thus strengthened, Valdivia began a series of punitive sweeps inland from his coastal foothold, gradually eroding Araucanian resistance by carrying off or destroying their food crops.

When the first regional chieftains began coming into Penco to submit to these invaders, Valdivia—aware of Talcahuano Bay's strategic importance as a sea link, as well as its rich fishing banks, abundant trees for shipbuilding or repairs, and the district's great agricultural potential—decided to transform his initial base camp into a permanent settlement by distributing land plots and indigenous vassals among his followers. He reconstituted it into a formal city under the name of La Concepción de María Purísima del Nuevo Extremo (The Conception of the Most Pure Mary in New Extremadura). A Mass was duly celebrated in a crude church by 11 May 1550, and its first mayor and municipal councilors were officially installed into office by 5 October. Valdivia thereupon spent the next four months ensuring the residents' security by replacing its original log stockade with a small adobe fort, before finally leaving

Panoramic view across Concepción, ca. 1950, with the Bío-Bío River visible at far left and Talcahuano Bay lying just out of sight at right. (Author's Collection)

behind fifty-two soldiers with twenty horses to act as both garrison and the new city's titled property owners, while pressing southward with the remainder of his army.

These first inhabitants erected private dwellings on the flat terrain below its hilltop citadel, their efforts becoming better regularized once Valdivia returned later that same spring of 1551 and issued a set of ordinances on 30 September to ensure the expanding city's *buen gobierno* (proper administration); he even financed the erection of its hospital the following year. Although still only a tiny and remote enclave on the extreme southern fringes of the Spanish empire, Concepción's title was nonetheless confirmed by the Crown and a coat-of-arms was granted via a *real cédula* (royal patent) issued at Madrid on 5 April 1552.

More ambitious construction projects were undertaken at Concepción as of 1553, such as the San Francisco convent, although all work was interrupted that same December by reports of a huge Araucanian insurrection inland. Valdivia quickly gathered fifty Spanish riders and more than 1,000 indigenous auxiliaries to put down this rebellion; however, his force was overwhelmed and massacred at Tucapel on 1 January 1554 by a 6,000-man Araucanian army under the brilliant *toqui* (war chief) Lautaro. A second army of 180 Spaniards and six artillery pieces that ventured inland under Valdivia's successor, Francisco de Villagrán, also suffered more than two-thirds killed when they too were surprised and scattered on 24 February along the Marihueñu Heights.

Terrified by these twin disasters, the city's remaining inhabitants abandoned their establishments that same day, joining the flood of refugees already streaming northward into Santiago, while behind them the triumphant Araucanians slaughtered stragglers and put every Spanish property to the torch. It was not until twenty-one months later—24 November 1555—that a Peruvian naval squadron under Capt. Juan de Alvarado sailed back into Talcahuano Bay and erected a new stockade near Concepción's burned remnants. Yet that contingent too was engulfed on 12 December by an Indian onslaught spearheaded by Lautaro, the few survivors either fleeing overland or seeking refuge aboard the tiny vessel *San Cristóbal* anchored in its harbor.

Refoundation (1558–1575)

Lautaro was eventually slain in April 1557 while defending Mataquito against a Spanish counteroffensive out of Santiago, and that same summer García Hurtado de Mendoza—the twenty-two-year-old son of Peru's viceroy, Andrés Hurtado de Mendoza, Marqués de Cañete—reached Talcahuano Bay with 600 troops aboard a small flotilla, throwing up a new hilltop stockade between the old Penco site and Playa Negra (Black Beach) by late August. Again, this stronghold was beset by an Araucanian army on 7 September, led by Lautaro's successor, Caupolicán, but this time the garrison repulsed the warriors with ease, inflicting heavy casualties. When Hurtado de Mendoza was reinforced eight days later by another 300 Spanish horsemen who had been advancing overland, he completed his coastal defenses, then crossed the Bío-Bío River into Araucanian territory on 18 November with 600 troops, 4,000 auxiliaries, and a herd of 1,000 horses and cattle.

His ensuing sweep through the Araucanian heartland proved so devastating that the youthful governor was able to send word back into Concepción early the next year, authorizing its formal reconstitution as a city. This ceremony was duly performed on 6 January 1558, the new "citizens" consisting mostly of officers and soldiers from its garrison (including Antonio Vargas, a Portuguese soldier dismissed from the front lines for cowardice, who apparently planted the first grapevines at the foot of Cayumangue Hill, inaugurating Concepción's lucrative wine industry). Previous residents later complained that their original land titles had been ignored, Hurtado de Mendoza dismissing all former deeds as voided because of the citizenry's precipitate flight four years earlier.

Few civilians chose to seek out this tiny resurrected city, as South America now offered more comfortable prospects elsewhere, while Araucanian raiding parties continued to pose a threat around Concepción. Early in February 1564, one such band materialized in the nearby hills under the leaders Loble and Millalemo, prompting Gov. Pedro de Villagrán—Francisco's nephew and heir—to hasten every resident inside his

The city crest—a black Hapsburg eagle upon a goldfield, with a golden sun above and a silver moon below, etc.—as issued by the Spanish Crown in April 1552. (Author's Collection)

6-gun stockade (emplaced where La Planchada Fort would later rise). Unable to breach its ramparts, the warriors satisfied themselves with pillaging and burning all outlying buildings, then settled down to a protracted siege. Two months later, the half-starved garrison was heartened by the arrival of a pair of supply vessels from Valdivia and Valparaíso, while the Araucanians withdrew in frustration. A few private dwellings were soon rebuilt by the Spaniards, yet Concepción was not truly safe until Governor de Villagrán traveled to Santiago for reinforcements and fought his way back into his coastal city by 15 April 1565—Palm Sunday—at the head of 150 fresh troops and 800 indigenous porters.

In order to bolster the beleaguered frontier outpost, King Philip II decreed on 27 August 1565 that it was also to become the seat for Chile's first *real audiencia* (royal tribunal). A pair of *oidores* (justices) arrived from Spain two years later, followed on 4 November 1568 by the chief magistrate *(presidente)* Melchor Bravo de Saravia, who immediately launched forays against the Araucanians, with mixed success.

The small city was then flattened by an earthquake at 9:00 A.M. on Ash Wednesday, 8 February 1570, a calamity made much worse by the funneling of the subsequent tidal wave that rushed across the shallow waters of semicircular Talcahuano Bay directly into the ruined city itself. The painstaking reconstruction process was additionally complicated when Gov. Pedro de Pantoja was lured away from Concepción in March

1572 by rumors of an Araucanian concentration near Talcahuano, only to have a surprise attack descend upon the hapless city during his absence; this assault was repelled with considerable difficulty. And finally, disappointed by its meager achievements, the king suppressed Concepción's *Audiencia* in March 1575, thereby diminishing the city's status.

Stagnation (1576–1598)

Yet despite this string of setbacks, Concepción's tenacious populace had at least gained some respite from Araucanian attacks by repeated Spanish thrusts ever deeper into their territory, as well as outbreaks of contagious disease. Because of its lack of sea traffic, the port was also spared any raids by the English rovers who penetrated the Strait of Magellan into the Pacific Ocean during this period: Francis Drake in 1578, Thomas Cavendish in 1587, and Richard Hawkins in 1594. (Only the detached Dutch vessel *Hendrik Frederick* of Olivier van Noort's expedition would eventually intercept a single vessel off Talcahuano Bay on 2 May 1600.) More promising still, a truce had been arranged with the nearest Araucanian tribes as of 1592, permitting a few of Concepción's residents to begin cultivating inland properties.

Stronghold (1599–1750)

This arrangement collapsed six years later amid a renewed outburst of regional hostilities known as the Great Araucanian War. The city was relieved once again on 28 May 1599 by yet another Peruvian expedition under Gov. Francisco de Quiñónez, who augmented its meager population by resettling all people driven out of La Imperial and Arauco. With the destruction of the much larger southern city of Valdivia later that same year, Concepción became the main frontline outpost for all future campaigns against the tribesmen, hundreds of troops being dispatched under an able new governor—Alonso de Ribera—in 1601 to bolster its garrison. A regular system of *situados* (subsidies) was also instituted as of the next year to provide a small but steady stream of income from the royal Exchequer at Lima.

Concepción's evolution into a viable city truly dates from this era, Governor de Ribera installing its first mill for use by both his troops and civilians. Skilled tradesmen were soon released from his ranks to become the community's first shoemakers, haberdashers, and saddlers. On 31 December 1602, the city was even temporarily elevated into an ecclesiastical see when its main San Pedro Church was reconsecrated as a cathedral for the recently arrived Bishop Reginaldo de Lizárraga, whose predecessor had died after fleeing from his see at La Imperial. Despite its enlarged garrison, though, civilians were still relatively few in number, a report in 1610 by the *oidor* Gabriel de Celada indicating that there were only seventy-six dwellings at Concepción, a mere forty being permanent adobe structures with tiled roofs, the rest being extemporized wooden shacks with thatched coverings. Although some small

Araucanian woman, ca. 1920. (Franck, *Working North from Patagonia*)

farms or ranches dotted the surrounding landscape, most citizens still lived very modestly, depending upon their herds for almost all of their needs.

But as the city remained safe from Araucanian raiders, its citizenry gradually began gaining a few urban improvements. A Jesuit school was commenced in 1612 and their monastery was completed next year, followed in 1616 by the Real Hospital de Nuestra Señora de la Misericordia (Royal Hospital of Our Lady of Mercy), which soon became more popularly known as the San Juan de Dios Hospital after a group of brothers from that charitable order under Father Gabriel de Molina took over its administration in 1617. Concepción's first streets were paved four years later, during the administration of Gov. Cristóbal de la Cerda, while a new Governors' Palace was commenced by 1633 under his successor, Francisco Lasso (or Lazo) de la Vega. Seaborne exports of wheat, wine, and leather increased throughout this period, so that by the mid-seventeenth century the city's buildings totaled approximately ninety.

Such moderate progress came to an abrupt halt when laborers on inland estates rose in rebellion on 14 February 1654, driving 3,000 frightened refugees into Concepción. Anger against the ineffectual leadership of Gov. Antonio de Acuña y Cabrera led to his deposal six days later, although he was eventually restored into office by the Crown; fortunately,

the crisis passed without any direct assault against the overcrowded city. But the residents' morale received a further shock when a second heavy earthquake struck at 5:30 P.M. on 15 March 1657, followed by a tidal wave roaring across Talcahuano Bay that killed forty persons. Material damage proved so extensive that it was suggested rebuilding Concepción at a safer remove from the sea, although that notion was soon forgotten as residents began reconstituting their homes so as to remain near its protective garrison, which had been resurrected and reinforced within a month of the disaster. Fears eventually eased somewhat after the rebel chief Alejo perished in September 1660, so that some limited agricultural activity could resume.

Full-blown prosperity did not return, however, until Chile's great wheat export boom at the end of the seventeenth century, although even then the city still remained so poor when compared with other South American ports that it did not experience a single enemy descent during the buccaneer incursions into the Pacific of the 1680s. Nonetheless, disembarkations elsewhere encouraged Gov. José de Garro to erect a low, U-shaped, moated battery with twin hexagonal bastions to cover the city's anchorage in 1687. (Because it was not topped by crenellated embrasures, but rather had its ancient artillery pieces exposed upon the roof—to be protected in battle by

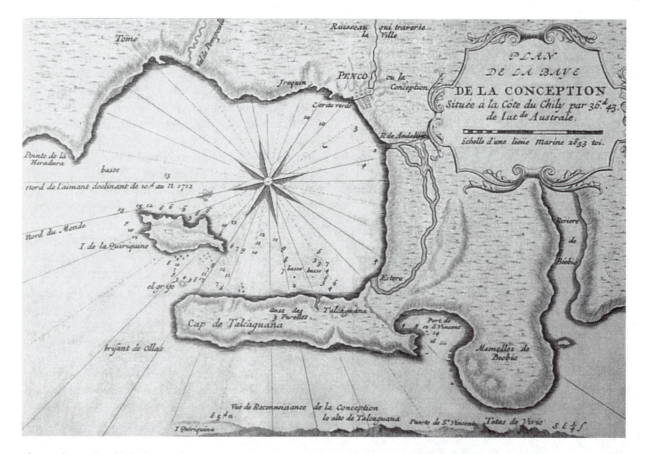

Chart and coastal profile by the French visitor Amédée-François Frézier, showing the city of Concepción at its original Penco site in the southeastern corner of Talcahuano Bay, ca. 1712; north is toward left. (Metropolitan Toronto Reference Library)

movable stone blocks, called *bonetes*—this structure was nicknamed La batería planchada or The Flattened Battery, also being referred to as the Fuerte de Penco, Fuerte de Castillo, and Batería de Bóvedas de Penco.) Its presence failed to deter a lone pirate craft from cutting out the anchored vessel *Santo Cristo* at dawn on 29 January 1694.

Regional wheat harvests nevertheless continued to multiply so satisfactorily that by 1700 they were being routinely stockpiled in low adobe warehouses at Cantarranas to be shipped aboard vessels calling at Concepción. Coupled with its traditional wine and cattle products, plus Crown subsidies to its garrison, the burgeoning local economy attracted a few more migrants, as well as the first French visitors entering the Pacific. They were made welcome because the Bourbon princeling Phillip of Anjou, sixteen-year-old grandson to Louis XIV, had allied both Crowns by ascending the vacant throne at Madrid. The priest Louis Feuillée, for example, spent more than a month at Concepción in early 1709, describing his impressions in a *Journal des observations physiques et mathematiques de les cotes Orientals de l'Amerique Meridional;* Amédée-François Frézier appeared three years later and did much the same in his *Relation du voyage de la mer du Sud aux cotes du Chily et du Perou.* French merchants also began entering the port, quickly establishing a brisk trade in contraband luxuries. The city's first brick buildings appeared around that same time, brick now replacing adobe as the preferred construction material.

Concepción's newfound tranquillity was scarcely ruffled when former Royal Navy Lt. George Shelvocke slipped into Talcahuano Bay on 16 January 1720 with his 24-gun English privateer *Speedwell,* taking the supply ship *San Fermín* as part of a renewed round of European hostilities known as the War of the Quadruple Alliance. A decade later, however, the city's 200 buildings swayed gently when a mild tremor ran through at 4:00 P.M. on 8 July 1730, apparently posing little danger. Yet that proved to be merely an aftershock from a much more powerful quake farther up the coast that soon caused the water to drain ominously out of Talcahuano Bay, then rush back in and destroy the city in three massive tidal waves. Citizens and soldiers alike were reduced to replacing their lost dwellings, the Governors' Palace being extensively expanded during the subsequent reconstruction. A large new brick-and-mortar cathedral with a cypress-wood roof was commenced under the direction of Lugardo Bravo in 1743, being completed shortly thereafter.

Relocation (1751–1807)

However, the city's 5,500 inhabitants were alarmed by a series of light tremors on the night of 23–24 May 1751. Then a much heavier jolt struck at dawn of 25 May, followed ten minutes later by a massive tidal wave rushing across the darkened bay. Disheartened by their repeated sufferings at the original Penco site, survivors now began seriously entertaining the notion of shifting to a safer locale. On 1 September, Chile's *Audiencia*

president, Domingo Ortiz de Rozas, wrote to advise its leading 131 citizens to meet in a *cabildo abierto* (open council meeting) to consider some alternatives, so that by the time he reached the ruined city on 18 December, four new inland sites were being contemplated: Dichato, Rinconada, the Landa Hills, and Mocha or Mendoza's Valley.

The next day, the president and a large body of advisers rode 10 miles south to the banks of the Bío-Bío River and, after reconnaissances and deliberations, finally announced on Christmas Day 1751 that a new city was to be erected 7 miles from the river mouth, sheltered on the level plain of the Mocha Valley (temporarily renamed "Rozas Valley" in the president's honor). The French-born surveyor Diego de Villeau-Brun drew up a grid pattern of nine-by-eleven blocks, subdivided into individual plots, some of which were preassigned to institutions or eminent individuals on 5 January 1752, after which the remainder were distributed among ordinary citizens by a lottery held over the next three days.

However, opposition to this allocation arose one month later, spearheaded by the redoubtable Bishop José de Toro y Zambrano, who had apparently been miffed at receiving only a single block for his ecclesiastical purposes, while the Jesuit Order had been assigned two. Poorer citizens, dismayed at the expense entailed in any move, rallied behind their prelate and delayed the transfer. A report in March 1753 indicated that while numerous official structures had already been erected at Nueva Concepción (New Concepción)—such as Crown offices, the Jesuit convent and college, the San Francisco convent, the San Juan de Dios convent and hospital, the Trinitarian nunnery, as well as numerous well-to-do homes—a large percentage of plebeians were still "offering great resistance against abandoning the hovels" that they had reerected at Penco. And when the authorities sought to pressure those laggards, the bishop retaliated by excommunicating the bailiffs on 23 September 1754, then stubbornly rebuffed all attempted suasion until his death in May 1760.

The impasse was finally resolved when Chile's new *Audiencia* president, Antonio de Guill y Gonzaga, arrived in September 1764 on an inspection tour, summoning the Irish-born military engineers Juan Garland y White and Ambrosio O'Higgins from Valdivia to advise upon defensive matters. As a result of their combined assessments, the president issued a series of decrees on 3–13 November, directing that Penco be abandoned within the next three months and all inhabitants recongregated into thirty-one additional blocks at Nueva Concepción. The new area was furthermore to be rechristened Concepción de la Madre Santísima de la Luz (Conception of the Most Holy Mother of the Light). Citizens, however, up to the present day have continued to refer to themselves as *penquistas* or people of Penco. Only a token garrison was to remain behind in La Planchada Fort, while the seaside hamlet of Talcahuano on the bay's southwestern shore was to become the city's new anchorage and be ringed with batteries.

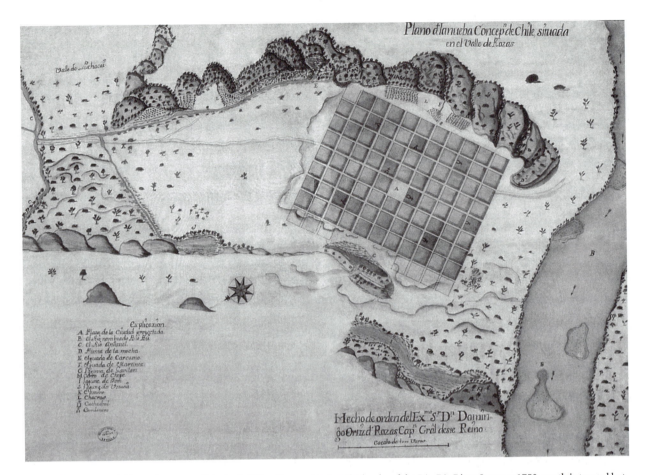

Villeau-Brun's map of the newly surveyed blocks for "New Concepción," on the banks of the Bío-Bío River, January 1752; north is toward bottom left. (Archive of Indies, Seville)

The civilian transfer out of Penco was at long last complete by early March 1765, and Concepción's citizens were still adjusting to living together once again when a major Araucanian uprising erupted in December 1766 and plunged the interior into renewed strife. Another sensation occurred at dawn on 26 August 1767, when troops surrounded the Jesuit buildings and arrested every member of that order on secret instructions from Charles III, deporting them one month later as part of the king's sweeping eradication of their influence. Their vacated premises at New Concepción were subsequently taken over by the Franciscan Order. Yet despite these incidents, the number of residents had grown to 6,078 people by 1778, whose prosperity truly began to flourish once peace with the Araucanians was restored by the 1784 Treaty of Santiago de Tapihuc, and the able O'Higgins assumed office as regional intendant that following year. Soon, the city would be considered the virtual capital of southern Chile.

On 23 February 1786, French Rear Adm. Jean-François de Galaup, Comte de La Pérouse and knight of the Order of Saint-Louis, entered Talcahuano Bay with his frigates *Astrolabe* and *Boussole,* having rounded Cape Horn to explore the Pacific in a peacetime expedition funded by Paris's Académie des Sciences. Spanish naval Capt. Alejandro Malaspina brought in his corvettes *Descubierta* and *Atrevida* four years later, on a similar commission from Madrid. Both groups noted that Concepción—located 8 miles from the port—was now bustling with activity, its exports of agricultural produce having been increased by the liberalization of Spain's imperial trade policies under the Bourbon regime, while major new buildings and defenses were also being installed. Such material improvements—including the city's beautiful new San Agustín convent, commenced in 1804—were to continue until the very end of the colonial era, by which time the total population of the city and its municipal district had swollen to perhaps 25,000 people.

Independence Struggle (1808–1819)

Like all other South American vassals, Concepción's 10,000 urban residents were astonished to learn that the French emperor Napoleon I had sent an army into Spain in the summer of 1808, deposing Ferdinand VII in favor of his brother Joseph Bonaparte. Most subjects rejected this crude usurpa-

Concepción as seen from its *almacén de pólvora* or "powder magazine" on the city outskirts, 1790; sketch by José del Pozo, an artist who joined Capt. Alejandro Malaspina's scientific expedition in the Pacific. (Braun Menéndez Collection, "Andrés Bello" Central Archive, University of Chile at Santiago)

tion of power, yet the ensuing period of political uncertainty and loosened imperial ties also allowed for stirrings toward outright independence. Thus when news was received on 12 October 1810 that an autonomous Chilean junta (council) had been acclaimed at Santiago, Concepción's inhabitants exploded into spontaneous celebration, driving out their elderly monarchist intendant—Col. Luis de Alava—and dispatching delegates to attend the first national congress.

Soon, Concepción adopted an even more radical policy than Santiago, 180 of its most prominent democrats meeting on 5 September 1811 to create their own local junta, which in turn enacted laws that went well beyond the more conservative line being pursued at the Chilean capital. (Concepción's assembly, for example, promulgated the total abolition of slavery on 15 October and entered into their own separate negotiations with the Araucanians.) This republican experiment ended on the night of 8–9 July 1812, when Col. Pedro José Benavente arrested its leaders and proclaimed martial law, acknowledging Santiago's authority. An ecclesiastical census that same year revealed 10,512 people living within the city and its immediate environs.

On the night of 26–27 March 1813, a small royalist counterexpedition disembarked from Peru under naval Brigadier (Rear Admiral) Antonio Pareja, capturing the 150-man garrison holding Talcahuano from the rear next afternoon, then calling upon Concepción to capitulate. Most troops having

become so disillusioned with republican rule as to be willing to switch sides, Benavente and his adherents fled inland, allowing Pareja to enter the city uncontested on 29 March. A ceremony was held in its main square on 4 April to swear fealty to the Crown once more, after which Pareja marched north with his main army four days later to invest the Chilean capital. However, he was defeated by the chief of Santiago's junta, Gen. José Miguel Carrera, so that the royalist garrison of 60 regulars and 300 militiamen left behind to hold Concepción under Andrés de Alcázar, Conde de la Marquina, decided to retire into Talcahuano by mid-May to brace for the inevitable patriot counterattack. Their vanguard appeared by 23 May, followed two days later by Carrera's main body, which chased the royalists out to sea by launching a dawn attack against Talcahuano on 29 May.

Concepción had been considerably battered by these operations, as well as suffering from its interrupted trade, which was further exacerbated when Carrera failed to stamp out all royalist resistance in the interior. Patriot resolve was gradually sapped by infighting, inept administration, and piecemeal defeats. Eventually, royalist guerrillas under Matías de la Fuente advanced upon Concepción in several columns from their inland stronghold of Chillán, subduing its debilitated defenders by 12–13 April 1814, after which Crown rule was reimposed and a couple of hundred republican sympathizers were exiled to Quiriquina Island in Talcahuano Bay. Santiago

Watercolor by Fernando Brambila of Talcahuano's anchorage, as it appeared in 1793. (Braun Menéndez Collection, "Andrés Bello" Central Archive, University of Chile at Santiago)

also fell that same October, and it was not until two years later that insurgent hopes revived when youthful Argentine Gen. José Francisco de San Martín crossed the Andes with an army and reconquered the capital by February 1817. (A year earlier, Concepción had also been visited by the neutral Russian warship *Rurick* of Lt. Otto von Kotzebue on a scientific exploration of the Pacific.)

San Martín's subordinate Col. Juan Gregorio de Las Heras led the 1,300-man División del Sur (Southern Division) down from Santiago to drive out the 1,000 royalists holding Concepción under Col. José de Ordóñez, who gathered his main force behind the entrenchments at Talcahuano rather than attempt to defend the unfortified city. On 3 April 1817, the approaching patriot army reached Curapaligüe or Curapalihue Hacienda, 10 miles east of Concepción, repelling a surprise attack by the monarchists at 1:30 A.M. on 5 April. Las Heras followed up this success by entering the deserted city that same afternoon, then awaited an additional 800 patriot troops and two field-pieces under the new Chilean "supreme director," Bernardo O'Higgins (son of Concepción's former Irish-born colonial intendant, Ambrosio O'Higgins). Before this contingent could appear, however, Ordóñez was reinforced on 1 May by four ships bearing 1,600 royalist troops from Peru, sortieing from Talcahuano four days later to assault the advance patriot redoubt northwest of Concepción, atop Gavilán (modern Amarillo) Hill.

The royalists intended to attack in twin columns, one thrust of 800 men and three field-pieces advancing directly from Chepe, plus another 600 men and two guns coming down the old Penco road in a flanking maneuver. Action commenced at 6:45 A.M. on 5 May 1817, when nine royalist gunboats opened fire upon the insurgents within Concepción. Ordóñez then launched his main assault, but it was decimated before his second column could intervene an hour and a half later. Broken by the loss of 118 dead, plus 80 men and four field-pieces captured, the monarchists reeled back inside their trenches, while O'Higgins arrived that same night to assume overall command of the patriot forces. Because of the onset of heavy winter rains, nothing more could be done beyond detaching Chilean Lt.-Col. Ramón Freire Serrano with 300 men to destroy the royalist keeps south of the Bío-Bío River, which were resupplying the beleaguered Talcahuano garrison. This sweep nonetheless proved insufficient to starve out the defenders, whose sea communications remained open.

After seven months' siege, O'Higgins finally deployed his 3,700 Chileo-Argentine troops for an all-out assault, although Ordóñez's 1,700 defenders had seventy cannon and several warships concentrated to protect the swampy, half-mile-wide isthmus leading out onto the Tumbes Peninsula, where Talcahuano lay. In an assault commencing at 2:45 A.M. on 6 December 1817, Las Heras carried the royalists' easternmost bastion of El Morro with four battalions, despite heavy losses. His subsequent attempt to drive northwest and overrun Cura Hill failed, though, obliging a retirement by dawn on 8 December. Another diversionary attack against San Vicente Castle at the opposite end of the royalist line had also been repulsed, the patriots suffering a total of 156 killed and 280 wounded, compared with 100 royalist casualties. When word arrived shortly thereafter that Spanish Brig. Mariano Osorio had sailed from Callao to relieve Talcahuano with 3,276 troops and ten field-pieces aboard ten vessels, O'Higgins lifted his siege and abandoned Concepción on 1 January 1818, retreating toward Santiago with thousands of civilian evacuees and harassed by royalist guerrillas.

Ordóñez reoccupied Concepción two days afterward and on 10 January 1818 was joined by Osorio's expedition. The Spanish general promptly detached his naval squadron to blockade Santiago's seaport of Valparaíso, while gathering mounts and supplies for his own army to march overland against the patriot capital. His offensive, however, was smashed by San Martín at the Battle of Maipó on 5 April, so that Osorio hastened back through Concepción eight days later with a few dozen survivors, intending to quit Talcahuano. But the exhausted patriot forces had not pursued, so that the Spanish commander remained uneasily in possession of Concepción and its harbor. At last he received a recall order from the viceroy of Peru, and on 25 August he instructed his subordinates to throw down all fortifications, fill in trenches, and spike all artillery pieces that could not be embarked, before sailing away on 8 September. As no patriot occupiers appeared, Col. Juan Francisco Sánchez's royalist guerrillas held the district.

Belated reinforcements arrived from Spain when the 50-gun frigate *Reina María Isabel* and three transports dropped anchor in Talcahuano Bay on 24 October 1818, part of a larger troop convoy that had made a lengthy passage across the Atlantic and through the Strait of Magellan. They disgorged 600 convalescents and were disappointed to find Concepción's royalist garrison already withdrawn; four days later, they were surprised by a pair of large vessels standing into the bay under English colors. Suspicious, the Spanish Commo. Dionisio Capaz opened fire, and the intruders revealed themselves as two patriot warships from Valparaíso under twenty-eight-year-old Commo. Manuel Blanco Encalada: the 56-gun former Indiamen *San Martín* under the English mercenary Capt. William Wilkinson and the 44-gun *Lautaro* under Capt. Charles Wooster. Without shore batteries, the monarchists were powerless to prevent these raiders from making off with *Reina María Isabel* the next day (soon recommissioned as the insurgent *O'Higgins*); they also watched impotently as most of their convoy stragglers were intercepted over the next few weeks.

Colonel Sánchez was furthermore disheartened to learn on 17 November 1818 that a 3,400-man patriot army had advanced into Chillán under Argentine Brig. Antonio González Balcarce, so that his monarchist guerrillas would have to forsake both Talcahuano and Concepción. González Balcarce pushed these fleeing units still deeper south, before finally declaring an amnesty for all former monarchists in the region and installing Freire as Concepción's new republican intendant with a garrison of 600 men in mid-February 1819. Royalist

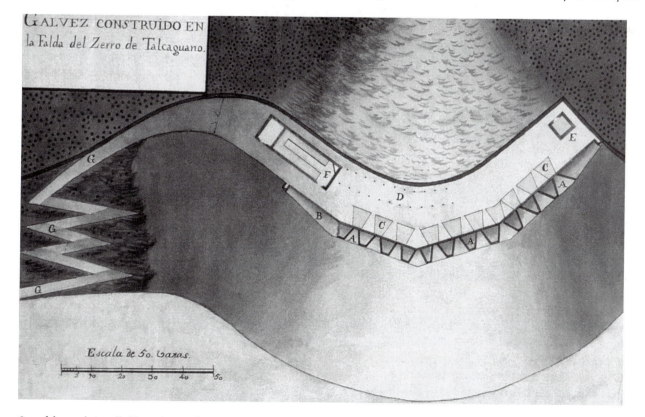

One of the newly installed batteries at Talcahuano Bay, 1785. (Archive of Indies, Seville)

renegades under a pardoned leader called Vicente Benavides soon resumed depredations in the interior, though, eventually becoming so emboldened as to steal an anchored frigate out of Talcahuano Bay in late August 1819 and menacing Concepción itself one month later.

Freire retired with his patriot troops behind Talcahuano's defenses on 30 September 1819, allowing Benavides to seize the city two days later—the eighth time it had changed hands during that turbulent decade. Although close pressed, the republicans sallied on 25 November and surprised a guerrilla contingent near San Vicente, killing 150 and capturing 30. Freire then followed up this success by marching upon Concepción two days later, defeating its monarchist occupiers and expelling Benavides, who was run to earth less than two years later and hanged.

Vicissitudes (1820–1860)

The city had been so ravaged by invasions and counterinvasions that it was now largely deserted, most of its churches and major edifices having been reduced to gutted shells. When Capt. Basil Hall of HMS *Conway* visited late in 1821—hoping to rescue some British and American seamen held hostage by monarchist guerrillas—he found entire blocks of Concepción burned and reduced to rubble, while its outlying suburbs had disappeared back under vegetation. Living conditions were so primitive that the years 1821–1823 were later remembered as El Hambre (The Famine); yet despite such desperation and the civil wars that were to ensue between Chile's Liberal and Conservative factions—nicknamed *pipiolos* (greenhorns) and *pelucones* (bigwigs)—the city nonetheless survived.

Concepción's resurrection was initially aided by English merchants, who revived its flour milling and industrial capacity by importing modern equipment and specialists, restoring some semblance of food production and an export trade. The city struggled back to life, neighborhoods and buildings gradually reemerging, while even its first newspaper was published by October 1833: *El Faro del Bío-Bío (The Bío-Bío Beacon)*. However, many reconstructed dwellings suffered damage from an earthquake that struck at 6:00 P.M. on 24 December 1832; then ominous tremors were felt at 11:30 A.M. on 20 February 1835, quickly escalating into a major seismic event that brought down numerous edifices and claimed eighty-one lives. Much of the city was leveled, the cathedral's spires plunging into the main square, rock slides cascading down Caracol Hill, and a 35-foot tidal wave rumbling through Talcahuano Bay a half hour later. (Less than two weeks afterward, HMS *Beagle* entered its desolate harbor with the naturalist Charles Darwin on board, who penned numerous observations in his journal.) Concepción once again began a painfully slow recovery, debris still littering its streets more than a dozen years later.

Yet Chile's overall situation nonetheless improved during the early 1840s under the Conservative presidency of Gen. Manuel Bulnes, the national debt being liquidated and cus-

toms collection better regulated. These improvements in turn attracted more foreign investors and settlers—Britons, Americans, and Germans—who developed profitable coal-mining operations at Lota, 25 miles farther to the south of Concepción, as well as other deposits throughout its province. That exploitation spurred national output of copper and silver, as well as providing fuel for factories, oceangoing steamships, and riverboats.

An unsuccessful Liberal revolt against Bulnes's Conservative successor, Manuel Montt, was hatched at Concepción on the night of 13–14 September 1851, but the 3,400 poorly equipped rebel troops of Gen. José María de la Cruz met defeat at the Battle of Loncomilla on 8 December; thus the city was peacefully reoccupied eleven days later. When a second revolt against Montt erupted in the rural hinterlands early in 1859, Concepción was briefly imperiled when 700 to 800 rebels under Juan Alemparte surprised Talcahuano on the evening of 7 February 1859. But Concepción's hastily reinforced government garrison under *Intendente* (Provincial Governor) Rafael Sotomayor was able to repulse a rebel assault the next day, some 50 people being killed and 300 wounded in house-to-house fighting on the city outskirts.

Modernization (1861–1938)

The election of compromise candidate Joaquín Pérez as president in 1861 inaugurated a period of unprecedented national growth and prosperity. Concepción endured a brief interruption in its trade when a Spanish battle squadron penetrated the Pacific a few years later and imposed a blockade in the summer of 1865. Tensions escalated further when the 20-gun Chilean corvette *Esmeralda* of Capt. Juan Williams Rebolledo sortied from Papudo near Valparaíso on 26 November and captured the Spanish auxiliary *Covadonga*, sparking an outright declaration of war. Warships prowled offshore for the next several months, and Adm. Casto Méndez Núñez's flagship *Numancia* and consort *Blanca* even made some captures at Arauco and Coronel—southwest of Concepción—in March 1866. Soon afterward, though, his entire fleet bombarded Valparaíso and steamed north in frustration, marking an end to the blockade. Talcahuano also suffered considerable damage when its water level suddenly rose at 8:15 P.M. on 13 August 1868, only to drain out frighteningly over the next hour as the result of an unfelt earthquake farther up the coast. The water rushed back in at 9:15 P.M., and a 10-foot wave engulfed the town and its adjacent shoreline.

Concepción nevertheless began to enjoy the fruits of the nation's newfound political stability and economic prosperity, boasting 2,800 dwellings—mostly single-story structures with large patios and gardens—radiating out from its main square among 146 blocks by 1872. They were serviced by three banks, a like number of newspapers, and two public markets; gas lighting had replaced kerosene that previous year, while the inaugural run of the first railway to Chillán occurred on 18

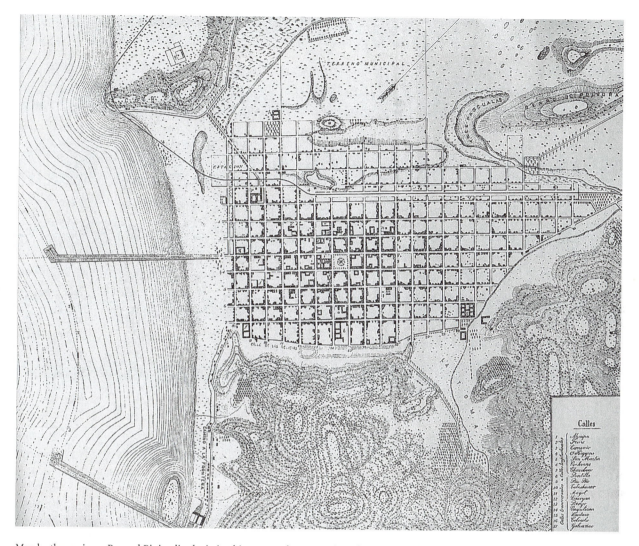

Map by the engineer Pascual Binimelis, depicting his proposed construction of twin jetties along Concepción's riverfront, 1856; north is toward upper right. (Author's Collection)

September 1874 (although it ended tragically when the train derailed into a ravine, with hundreds of casualties). Ironically, it was to be a similar disaster—a conflagration that consumed the state railway's *maestranza* workshops in March 1883—that led to the creation of Concepción's first volunteer fire brigade on 13 April, George Blackburn being selected as first captain. Mule-drawn streetcars were also introduced by 1885.

The city was again rattled by a strong tremor at 10:17 P.M. on 22 July 1898, some fifty buildings suffering damage. Still it continued to grow, the population increasing from 55,330 residents in 1900 to 60,676 five years later. Another quake struck at 4:00 A.M. on 13 June 1907, and electric streetcars were introduced a year later. The worldwide effects of the Great Depression after the New York stock market crash of October 1929 incited a mutiny by the Chilean fleet during its winter exercises while lying at anchor in Tongoy Bay near Puerto Aldea, 15 miles south of Coquimbo, on 1 September 1931. Outraged by

the pay reductions enacted by the bankrupt government at Santiago that would hurt family members living in home ports, the junior officers and seamen detained the fleet's senior commanders, then radioed an ultimatum to naval headquarters in the capital.

In order to underscore their demands, the rebel warships *Riveros* and *Capitán Arturo Prat* materialized off Talcahuano—which now sprawled for almost 5 miles along the inner beaches of the Tumbes Peninsula, northwest of the original town—and persuaded more than 3,000 naval and civilian personnel to join their insurrection. At dawn on 5 September 1931, however, two infantry and one cavalry regiments under Gen. Guillermo Novoa, plus a company of loyal naval officers, advanced upon this base's Los Leones Gate, eventually using artillery to overwhelm the complex by afternoon, securing more than 2,000 prisoners while crippling both rebel warships offshore and driving *Riveros*'s crew into Fort Rondizzoni on

Talcahuano naval base, ca. 1950; Concepción lies several miles farther southeast, just out of sight beyond the hills. (Author's Collection)

Quiriquina Island. Threatened the next day with aerial bombardment by float planes, these last holdouts surrendered, the confrontation having cost the lives of nine mutineers and a dozen Loyalists.

Concepción's tranquillity was also broken by freakish weather at 4:30 A.M. on Sunday, 27 May 1934, when a tornado suddenly blew out of the Bío-Bío River mouth and cut a swath of destruction through the sleeping city, before disappearing toward Caracol Hill and Las Cruces—leaving behind two dead, thirty injured, hundreds homeless, and darkness because of downed power lines. Still worse was to ensue at 11:24 P.M. on 24 January 1939, when the city suffered the most dreadful earthquake in its history. It was later estimated that 80 percent of its 15,000 structures either collapsed or were so badly damaged by this catastrophe as to be rendered uninhabitable. Casualties ran well into the thousands, exact numbers proving impossible to tally.

Overcoming this calamity, the city recuperated and its population grew from 85,813 inhabitants in 1940 to 119,887 a dozen years later. In addition to its traditional role as Chile's main naval base, urban industrial and manufacturing output supplemented the produce from its agricultural hinterland to ensure commercial activity well into the twenty-first century.

For further reading materials on Concepción or Chile, please consult the Select Bibliography at the end of this volume; additional sources on South American urban history can be found under "Regional Studies," as well as under "General Works on Latin America."

Military rescue party picking through the debris on Colo-Colo Street after the city's destruction by an earthquake on 24 January 1939. (Author's Collection)

SANTIAGO

Village set on a beautiful and fertile plain that evolved into an austere Spanish American capital.

Foundation and Colonial Evolution (1541–1809)

An army of 150 Spanish conquistadors and 1,000 indigenous auxiliaries penetrated the Mapocho River valley under Pedro de Valdivia late in 1540, having been detached eleven months previously by Peru's conqueror, Francisco Pizarro, to push down the Pacific shoreline and occupy vassal Incan states. Pleased by the bountiful terrain and mild climate he encountered within this enclosed basin at 1,860 feet above sea level, framed by snowy Andean peaks to its north and the lesser heights of Cuesta del Prado to its south, Valdivia received the submission of local tribal chieftains and rested his weary column. A camp was duly established amid a small Indian farming community between the foot of rocky Huelén (modern Santa Lucía) Hill and the southern bank of the Mapocho River, itself a tributary of the larger Maipó, or Maipú, River.

Realizing the spot's strategic value—as its easiest approaches were through the Maipó River valley and a narrow passage called the Angostura de Paine leading into the central Valle de Chile—Valdivia opted to transform his temporary base camp into a permanent capital. He therefore renamed it on 12 February 1541 as Santiago del Nuevo Extremo (Saint James of the New Extremadura), in honor of his and Pizarro's natal province in Spain. Valdivia then formally distributed 126 land plots among his followers over the next twelve days. The first dwellings were the soldiers' straw or daub-and-wattle shacks, yet this legal fiction of creating a "town" was maintained with the appointment of a municipal "council" on 7 March and Valdivia's own installation as governor by 10 August.

He thereupon struck southward with 60 riders, leaving behind 32 horsemen, 18 harquebusiers, and 350 Peruvians to hold his base camp. This garrison was surprised at 3:00 A.M. on 11 September 1541 by an Indian army under Chief Michimalonco, who burned down the huts and killed four Spaniards and fifteen mounts before finally being repelled after nine hours' desperate fighting. The surviving Spanish residents spent the next couple of years eking out a miserable existence under constant threat from roving war bands, yet tenaciously defended their adobe strong-house because of the region's undoubted agricultural potential. Indigenous attacks eventually dwindled as disease and enslavement took their toll, while the Spanish garrison was reinforced by the arrival of Lucas Martínez Vegaso's ship at Valparaíso in September 1543, who sent a column inland under Capt. Alonso de Monroy that reached Santiago by that same December.

The settlers' wheat harvests soon became so plentiful that the town had two mills in operation by 1545, one owned by the German immigrant Bartholomeus Blumenthal (better known by his Hispanicized name of Bartolomé Flores). Santiago was tentatively recognized as Chile's capital four years afterward, its first few two-story, brick-and-mortar structures appearing around a rectangular plaza by 1550. Governor Valdivia erected the Hospital de Nuestra Señora del Socorro on La Cañada's riverbank two years later. Emperor Charles V elevated the settlement to the full status of a city via a *real cédula* dated at

Panoramic view of Santiago as seen from atop Blanco Hill, 1793; lithograph based upon an original watercolor by Fernando Brambila, one of the artists who served as a member of Capt. Alejandro Malaspina's scientific expedition in the Pacific. (Braun Menéndez Collection, "Andrés Bello" Central Archive, University of Chile at Santiago)

Madrid on 4 March 1552; livestock multiplied so quickly throughout the surrounding pasturelands that residents celebrated their first bullfight as early as 1554 (although fresh meat would not be made directly available from a city slaughterhouse for thirteen more years). By 1558, there were forty households within the small city, a new cathedral was under construction, its first few vineyards had taken root, and the discovery of a nearby gold deposit three years later ensured Santiago's livelihood. The population swelled to 350 to 400 householders by 1571.

The inhabitants' resolve to maintain their remote highland capital was tested when the Mapocho overflowed its banks in July 1574, after which most buildings were further leveled by a major earthquake that struck on the morning of 17 March 1575—Easter Thursday—so that the total population was reduced to a mere 1,100 Spaniards eight years later. Santiago remained unappealing to most immigrants when compared with the more accessible and splendid viceroyalties of Peru or Mexico, there even existing a catchphrase among other sixteenth-century Spanish-Americans: *Guardáos, que os enviarán a Chile* (Beware, lest you be sent to Chile). This inland community moreover had to compete with rival coastal centers within its own jurisdiction, Concepción farther to the south being where the *real audiencia* (royal tribunal) had been established in 1565, while the bulk of Spanish troops were concentrated at Valdivia to contend with Araucanian uprisings, as well as intrusions by foreign ships rounding the Strait of Magellan. To the north, La Serena was the commercial and communications hub for seaborne traffic out of Peru.

Santiago's closest outlet to the Pacific lay 85 miles westnorthwest at Valparaíso, and the Andean city quickly developed a reputation as a peaceful yet uninfluential breadbasket, safely isolated behind the barrier of its mountains. Its chill and rainy summers, plus warm and mild winters, nonetheless provided such an abundance of harvests and livestock that when a great Araucanian revolt erupted in southern Chile late in December 1598 and destroyed Valdivia and its district over the next few years, Santiago benefited by receiving a stream of Spanish refugees fleeing northward. Initially it proved difficult to absorb so many people, Santiago's edifices multiplying in number from 160 in 1601 to 285 only thirteen years later. Yet this transition was eased by financial support from the viceregal Exchequer in Peru, and soon the city began to manifest renewed signs of prosperity: on 8 September 1609, for example, the *Audiencia* was reinaugurated in the capital, although Chilean governors would still continue to spend much of their terms on the coast.

That same autumn of 1609, the city suffered a major flood, reputedly claiming 200,000 head of livestock throughout its ranch lands and prompting the authorities to undertake construction of a series of *tajamares* (dykes) to regulate water flow. The city quickly resurged, having 1,700 Spanish residents

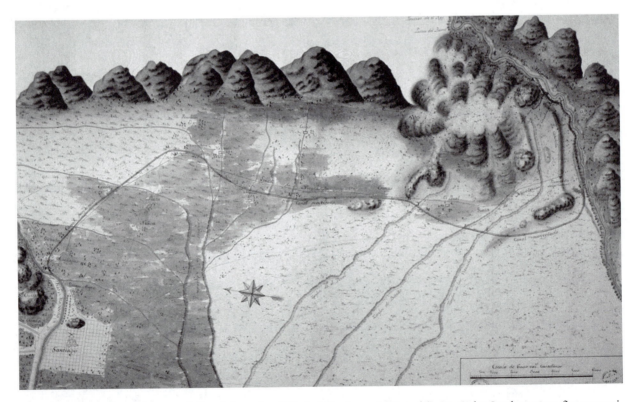

Map signed by the engineer Agustín Caballero in December 1800, depicting the completion of the San Carlos Canal, a seventy-five-year project intended to divert water from the Maipó River into the Mapocho River so as to better irrigate the vast tracts of farmland eastward and southeastward of Santiago; north is toward left. (Archive of Indies, Seville)

by 1613, as well as 8,600 Indians and 300 blacks. The number of Spaniards multiplied to 3,500 by 1630, although its indigenous population dwindled as a result of epidemics. Schools were now well established, the Jesuits having 400 pupils enrolled, their original Colegio Máximo de San Miguel, founded in 1593, having been granted the title of Pontifical University by 1625. In addition, the *cabildo*'s (city council's) public school beside the plaza (run since 1580 by the Dominicans) taught another 100, and the Franciscan and Mercedarian orders maintained their own private institutions.

Santiago boasted a dozen fine churches and 300 stone buildings when another massive earthquake struck at 10:30 P.M. on Monday, 13 May 1647, killing more than 600 people and destroying virtually every major structure, while claiming several hundred more lives throughout its district. This time, the city recuperated much more slowly, its material damages being exacerbated by an outbreak of *chavalongo* (typhus). Ten years later, the total population stood at a mere 4,896 people, when it was again shaken by a lesser quake and had but eighty dwellings left standing by 1662. The number of Spanish householders was still only 700 by 1671, although a boom in wheat exports to Peru gradually helped Santiago to revive, especially during the tenure of Gov. Juan Henríquez, from 1670 to 1682.

The Dominicans' Colegio de Santo Tomás de Aquino (Saint Thomas of Aquinas College) was elevated into the city's second ecclesiastical university by 1685, while the reconstructed cathedral was reconsecrated two years later, a magnificent bronze water fountain was installed in its main square, and many more streets became paved. Not even a minor earthquake at 1:00 P.M. on 9 July 1690, nor further outbreaks of disease, could stem Santiago's resurgence. Its first theater—the Salón de Comedias—was opened in the Governors' Palace by 1709. When the French military engineer Amédée-François Frézier visited three years later, he found a provincial capital of roughly 3,000 Spanish and 7,000 other residents living in low adobe houses encircled by fences, most with attached orchards or gardens, all well irrigated by water.

Santiago's inhabitants withstood a huge flood in 1723, a minor earthquake the following year, a drought in 1725, and then another massive earthquake at 4:45 A.M. on 18 July 1730 that brought down almost half their buildings; there were only four or five deaths, however, because of the light construction materials employed. The laborious process of rebuilding began once more, a new stone cathedral being commenced by July 1747, as well as a stone bridge across the Mapocho the next year. These efforts were complemented by the beautification

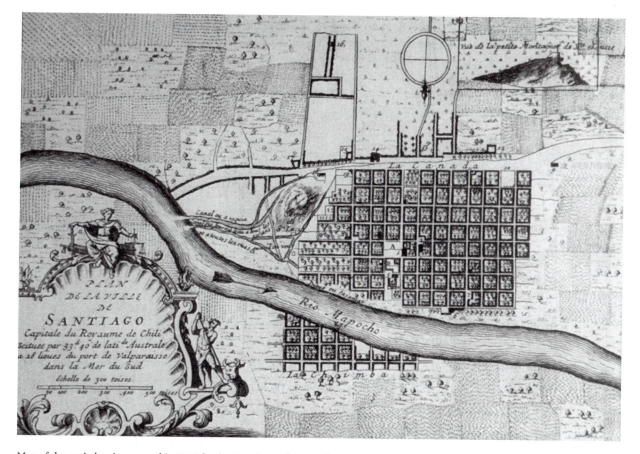

Map of the capital as it appeared in 1712, by the French traveler Amédée-François Frézier; north is toward bottom. (Metropolitan Toronto Reference Library)

projects of interim President Félix de Berroeta—who erected a circular wooden bullring in the city's wooded *tajamar* area in 1760 and a 400-seat cockpit nearby two years later—as well as the more professional structural designs introduced by the Roman-born architect Joaquín Toesca. Still, Santiago suffered another setback when its new cathedral burned down on 22 December 1769.

The census of 1778 revealed 24,318 inhabitants in the capital, who were rattled by another quake on 13 April 1783, then endured a major flood on 16 July of that same year—after nine days of continuous rainfall that had swept away its bullring, among many other structures. Yet Santiago nevertheless continued to expand, thanks to a general economic upturn engendered throughout Spanish America by the Bourbon economic reforms. By 1802, there were approximately 30,000 inhabitants distributed among the city's 2,900 dwellings, covering 179 blocks.

Independence Struggle (1810–1818)

When Spain's King Charles IV abdicated under pressure from the French emperor Napoleon I in March 1808, Chile was among the first South American nations to begin loosing its ties to distant Madrid. An independent Creole junta (congress) was acclaimed at Santiago on 18 September 1810 that remained largely unchallenged by Loyalist authorities for the next three and a half years, until a counterexpedition was launched out of Peru. Weakened by factional infighting among their leaders, Bernardo O'Higgins and José Miguel Carrera, Chile's patriots suffered a crushing defeat on 1 October 1814 at the Battle of Rancagua, 50 miles south of Santiago. Since their unwalled capital could not withstand an assault, many insurgents fled into Argentina, while those who remained behind suffered harsh repression at the hands of the triumphant monarchists.

A little more than two years later, youthful Argentine Gen. José Francisco de San Martín crossed the Andes with an army, accompanied by O'Higgins. Having swiftly traversed its mountain passes, these 3,600 insurgents surprised Brig. Rafael Maroto's 2,500 royalists on 11 February 1817 as they were digging in around Chacabuco Hill to block the road into Santiago. At 2:00 A.M. the next morning, the revolutionaries advanced from Manantiales in two divisions, O'Higgins being on the left to distract the defenders with two infantry battalions, three squadrons of cavalry, and two cannons, while Brig. Miguel Estanislao Soler was to circle behind with a larger contingent on the right and attack the Spaniards from the rear. Instead, O'Higgins rashly charged without awaiting his colleague, destroying the royalist squadrons. When Soler advanced upon the flank, Maroto's army was routed, suffering 600 fatalities and 550 captives. Patriot casualties were 11 killed and 110 wounded, allowing San Martín to enter Santiago unopposed two days later and restore O'Higgins as Chile's ruler.

Statue dedicated to Bernardo O'Higgins, ca. 1888. (Curtis, The Capitals of Spanish America)

The insurgents had to fight to retain the capital in 1818, O'Higgins and San Martín formally proclaiming Chile's independence on 12 February, before sallying to engage a royalist counterexpedition approaching out of the south under Gen. Mariano Osorio. Learning that this army of 4,600 troops and fourteen cannons was nearing Talca on 19 March, the 8,000 Argentino-Chilean defenders made a forced march down Tres Montes Road with thirty-three guns to intercept. They began to deploy a mile and a half northeast of Talca at Cancha Rayada, but Osorio shrewdly launched an immediate nocturnal thrust, sowing panic among the revolutionary ranks. The 3rd Chilean Battalion disintegrated, O'Higgins was wounded in an elbow, and other insurgent units fired wildly upon each other in the darkness. By midnight they were streaming north in confusion, having lost 120 killed, plus hundreds of deserters or prisoners, and twenty-six artillery pieces. Royalist casualties were only 300, so that five days later Osorio resumed his drive against Santiago.

San Martín quickly regrouped and emerged from the capital once more on 1 April 1818 with 5,300 troops, taking up position 6 miles to its south atop Blanca Hill. Osorio had hoped to capture Valparaíso first so as to resupply his army by sea, but he discovered the patriots to be so close upon reaching Lo Espejo Hacienda three days later that he prepared his 4,900 royalists and twelve cannons for battle the next day. After both armies moved into position near Maipó, San Martín ordered a general advance by his entire line at noon on 5 April, his cavalry emerging victorious on the flanks and the royalists being annihilated after a six-hour, seesaw clash in which they suffered almost 2,000 dead and 2,400 prisoners, along with the loss of their artillery. Osorio escaped with fewer than 600 men, fleeing south toward Talcahuano, never to return.

Republican Era (1819–1891)

The last Spanish viceroy was not defeated high up in the Andes until six and a half years later, but Santiago remained unthreatened by monarchist counteroffensives for the remainder of the conflict, and so began to blossom into its role as capital of an independent nation. Its primacy was initially challenged by La Serena and Concepción, although it quickly outstripped both in size and wealth, a growth in power that was reflected by a rapid expansion in Santiago's population from approximately 46,000 residents in 1820 to 65,665 ten years later, 67,777 by 1835, and 95,795 by 1844.

Many foreigners also took up residence or visited the capital during these early republican decades, and Chile's overseas commerce multiplied exponentially with the elimination of the old Spanish trade barriers. English influence proved especially strong, thanks to the leading role played by Adm. Thomas, Lord Cochrane, and other British mercenaries in helping to secure Chilean independence. American contacts were also fostered by the presence of an astronomical observatory atop Santa Lucía Hill from 1849 to 1852 under U.S. naval Lt. James M. Gillis. (The Jesuits had also studied the heavens from the city since the early eighteenth century, using an 8-foot telescope.)

Because of such external influences, as well as Santiago's growing importance as the national capital, it soon began to adopt a few modern improvements and amenities: embankments were raised to better contain the Mapocho, more bridges were built, a police force of vigilantes (watchmen) was created in June 1830, the Universidad de San Felipe was reopened in 1842 as the Universidad de Chile, gas lighting was introduced by August 1856, and horse-drawn streetcars that following year. Still the city remained vulnerable to disaster, the entire nation being horrified when its splendid old Jesuit church was consumed by fire during a well-attended evening service on 8 December 1863, claiming more than 2,000 lives, mostly women.

The urban population was measured at 115,377 people by 1865, when a 5-mile-long aqueduct was inaugurated. That population figure swelled to approximately 140,000 residents by March 1872, when the former political refugee Benjamín Vicuña Mackenna was appointed Santiago's *intendente* (mayor). Having resided in Paris while in exile, Vicuña Mackenna returned with exalted notions as to what constituted a great capital, and he immediately implemented a series of welcome improvements: the digging of deeper channels and

The *Gran Hotel Inglés* or "Grand English Hotel," ca. 1883, looking out over Santiago's *Plaza de Armas* or "Main Square." (Dawson, *The South American Republics*)

raising of levees along the Mapocho River to prevent flooding in the lower sections of the city; demolition of Santiago's worst slums, replacing them with low-income housing based upon U.S. designs; a broader-based distribution of potable water; construction of a central market—whose iron framework was imported from Europe—as well as other new plazas and streets; beautification of Santa Lucía Hill; and the planting of tens of thousands of trees. By the time Vicuña Mackenna left office only three years later, Santiago was well on its way to becoming a more modern metropolis.

Such progress was briefly interrupted when—after months of bitter diplomatic wrangling—Chile's president, Aníbal Pinto Garmendia, led the nation into hostilities against Bolivia and Peru in April 1879 to settle disputed ownership over the Atacama Desert in the north. Despite the great strain placed upon its limited resources, Chile emerged victorious from this War of the Pacific five years later, vastly expanding its territory by annexing the provinces of Atacama and Tarapacá, thereby gaining a monopoly over the world's largest nitrate deposits. Santiago, as the capital of a now strongly centralized government, benefited from the resultant upsurge in national pride, international prestige, and war profits. Electric lighting had been introduced late in 1882, while the census three years later revealed a population of 177,271 inhabitants.

As the undisputed political, cultural, and societal leader for Chile, Santiago was also transformed into the main stage for its internal politics. On 1 January 1891, the flamboyant, Liberal president, Dr. José Manuel Balmaceda—nearing the end of his five-year term in office—announced that he would rule without congress, which had refused to approve his budget. The latter body replied by attempting to depose Balmaceda that very same day, then on 6 January it placed the navy under the command of Commo. Jorge Montt, who was loyal to their interests. Balmaceda responded by declaring martial law the next day, and civil war erupted on 8 January. The congressionalist faction, controlling most of the fleet, retreated into the northern part of the country and set up its headquarters at Iquique, while Balmaceda retained the support of the army in the south and held Santiago. This impasse was not resolved until August 1891, when a congressionalist army disembarked at Quintero Bay north of Valparaíso, driving Balmaceda from power by the end of that same month and prompting him to commit suicide on 18 September.

Modern Boom (1892–Present)

Such turmoil remained relatively rare, however, and Santiago was able to resume its development in peace, sprawling ever farther as its population reached 252,629 by 1895, approximately 378,000 by 1905, and 460,603 by 1920. The following year a Chilean enterprise, having expropriated the German

Streetcar in Santiago, ca. 1920; note the woman conductor at right. (Franck, *Working North from Patagonia*)

streetcar and lighting company during World War I, began a hydroelectric project to supply the entire city with power, as well as the railway running down to Valparaíso. In 1924 the government furthermore granted a concession to a local firm to drive an underpass, 5.5 miles long and 33 feet below the congested city center.

On 5 September 1924, after a prolonged period of economic decline, Gen. Luis Altamirano was appointed interior minister. He in turn named Col. Juan P. Bennett and Adm. Francisco Neff to the cabinet along with three civilians. The beleaguered president, Arturo Alessandri, at that point proffered his resignation, but the Congress refused to accept it, instead granting him a six-month leave of absence. The military ministers thereupon passed a popular labor legislation bill and in the resultant euphoria compelled their civilian colleagues to resign on 10 September. Altamirano, Bennett, and Neff subsequently annulled Alessandri's leave of absence, accepted his original resignation, and dissolved the congress in a bloodless coup. (A group of young Chilean army officers mounted a liberal countercoup against this conservative military junta on 23 January 1925, almost plunging the nation into a renewed civil war. However, cooler heads prevailed and President Alessandri was restored to office by 20 March.)

Despite severe economic dislocation caused by the stock market crash and Great Depression of October 1929, Santiago's population continued to soar from 725,306 residents the next year to 943,689 in 1940 and 1,348,283 a dozen years afterward. By that time, more than 50 percent of the country's manufacturing industries were located in the capital, including breweries, flour mills, foundries, machine shops, woodworking plants, tanneries, knitting mills, soap factories, and so forth.

On 11 September 1973, shortly before noon, a military coup erupted in the very heart of Santiago, following three years of ruinous leftist rule by Marxist Pres. Dr. Salvador Allende Gossens. At 11:52 A.M., two Hawker Hunter fighter jets fired salvos of rockets into La Moneda Palace, setting parts of it ablaze. From his command post in Peñalolen (a suburb in the Andean foothills), the recently promoted Gen. Augusto Pinochet Ugarte thereupon ordered tank and infantry columns under Gen. Javier Palacios to descend upon Allende's presidential residence, fighting their way inside after an hour and a half, in spite of resistance from civilian bodyguards and nearby snipers. Allende was found dead, after which other units fanned out throughout the country and arrested thousands of activists. Pinochet meanwhile established a junta with Air Force Gen. Gustavo Leigh, Adm. José Toribio Merino, and Gen. César Mendoza of the *carabinero* paramilitary police, ushering in a prolonged period of repression.

Modern Santiago's basin stretches out at the foot of the

"A Chilean belle dressed for morning mass," ca. 1888. (Curtis, *The Capitals of Spanish America*)

Andes, serving as a majestic backdrop to the eastern segments of the city. Well ventilated by mountain winds, this area—called Barrio Alto—is the preferred place of the wealthy class. Among numerous parks and wide avenues are located the boroughs of Providencia, Vitacura, Valdivia, Los Leones, Los Condes, and La Reina, as well as the largest malls, diplomatic residences, the military academy, and the medical school.

For further reading materials on Santiago or Chile, please consult the Select Bibliography at the end of this volume; additional sources on South American urban history can be found under "Regional Studies," as well as under "General Works on Latin America."

Colombia

BOGOTÁ

Indigenous stronghold that became transformed into the viceregal capital of New Granada and has since evolved into one of the great metropolises of South America.

Conquest (1536–1538)

A detached company of conquistadors probed up the Opón River in October 1536, emerging onto an elevated and lush plateau that was home to a highly developed Indian civilization. This patrol retraced its steps to report to their commander, the *licenciado* (licentiate) Gonzalo Jiménez de Quesada, who over the previous seven months had been attempting to lead an expedition up the Magdalena River into its Andean headwaters, so as to link up with the newly subjugated Incan empire of Peru. With only 220 exhausted survivors left from the 600 men who had set out with him from Santa Marta, Jiménez de Quesada opted to digress eastward from his jungle base camp at La Tora, pushing up the Opón on 28 December 1536 with his healthiest 60 cavalrymen and 110 foot soldiers. Eventually, they gained the fertile highlands after passing through a mountain valley early the next March, south of Chipatá, which was renamed San Martín.

After the disappointingly primitive and poor river tribesmen encountered along the Magdalena, the Spaniards were delighted by the wealth and sophistication of these mountain peoples, whom they erroneously dubbed Muiscas or Moxcas (actually a word in the local dialect that signified "persons," rather than their correct tribal name, Chibchas). There were five tribal groupings—Panche, Yarigui, Agate, Muzo, and Colima—spread throughout an interconnected series of high valleys, living off their bountiful harvests as well as a brisk barter in gold, salt, coca, pottery, fine cotton weaves, emeralds, and the like. The invaders pressed forward in easy stages against sporadic opposition, for although the 1 million Chibchas maintained a professional warrior caste and large conscript armies, they were overawed by the strangers' horses and weaponry. Tribal leadership was also riven, Tunja's *zaque* (chieftain), Quemuenchatocha, being then at war with the dominant *zipa* (overlord), Tisquesusa of Bacatá, or Bogotá.

Consequently, Jiménez de Quesada was able to forge into the latter's territory by 22 March 1537, christening it the Valle de los Alcázares (Valley of the Forts) before overrunning its stockaded, yet largely vacant capital of Bogotá one month later. Having suffered few injuries, the conquistador army split off

View across the rooftops of Bogotá, ca. 1905. (Keane, *Central and South America*)

737

secondary units to raid lesser Chibcha communities, while the main force stormed Tunja on 20 August and the religious center of Sogamoso by 4 September.

Jiménez de Quesada returned into the burned remnants of Bogotá on 16 February 1538, being rejoined on 12 May by the contingent of his brother Hernán Pérez de Quesada, to make a joint division of spoils. Legend has it that a new Spanish capital was created on 6 August, when some conquistadors began erecting a dozen shacks at a spot called Teusa, or Teusaquillo, on the western riverbank, opposite the devastated former indigenous capital. Yet Jiménez de Quesada had most probably not taken any formal steps toward legally constituting a city, when he was surprised to learn early in 1539 of the approach of two rival expeditions: 90 horsemen and 140 soldiers advancing out of the southeast from Venezuela under the German-born Nicolaus Federmann, plus 150 men under Sebastián de Belalcázar (alternate spellings: Benalcázar, Velalcázar) descending from Popayán in the Andes in quest of the reputed indigenous kingdom of Cundirumarca (Land of the Condors).

Early Colonial Evolution (1539–1739)

Spurred by the necessity of staking a recognizable claim over his conquered territory, Jiménez de Quesada declared it to be the Nuevo Reino de Granada (New Kingdom of Granada), while simultaneously distributing town plots among his 164 soldiers and creating a proper capital that was to bear the name Santa Fé de Bogotá (Holy Faith of Bogotá); both provincial and city names were chosen in honor of his birthplace of Santa Fé de Granada in Spain. Federmann arrived by March 1539, after which Santa Fé's municipal council celebrated their first official session on 27 April, and Indian vassals were brought in from Guatavita shortly thereafter to provide the necessary labor force to create a permanent Spanish settlement.

Once Belalcázar joined, Jiménez de Quesada departed down the Magdalena River early in June 1539 with his two rival leaders to make the lengthy peregrination across the Atlantic and have the Crown arbitrate their jurisdictional differences. During this absence, Santa Fé commenced to take shape, the urban grid pattern usually required in Spanish-American foundations having to conform to its sloping terrain and bisecting streams. Individual lots were nonetheless assigned around a central plaza for a future cathedral, *cabildo* (municipal hall), and so forth, while a suburb for the local population also sprang up opposite, on the original Chibcha site—although nowhere near as large nor as populous as the ancient Indian capital had been. In 1540, Charles V decreed that the new Spanish community should be recognized as a "most noble and most loyal city," to be commonly referred to as Santa Fé throughout its colonial reign.

Most of the region's rural inhabitants had been spared and became docile tributaries to their new Spanish masters, although they remained prey to occasional outbreaks of measles or smallpox. Despite being devoid of mineral wealth, the fertility of Santa Fé's adjacent plateau—well irrigated by cool streams of freshwater descending out of the mountains—held great agricultural potential, so that livestock and cereal crops, vegetables, and fruits soon came to flourish under the supervision of a few dozen major landholders. Standing at 8,563 feet above sea level and sheltered by the enclosing mountain ranges, the new city furthermore enjoyed a mild and bracing climate that proved more amenable to Castilian immigrants than had New Granada's torrid equatorial coastline or the low-lying, swampy, and pestilential Magdalena Valley.

Yet notwithstanding such attractive geographical features, the wealthier viceroyalties of Mexico and Peru continued to lure the bulk of transatlantic travelers and traders, while New Granada's capital lay so deep amid its upland setting that only a trickle of Spaniards proved hardy enough to endure the weeks-long river ascents from the Caribbean or Pacific coasts, a trip that meant traversing at least 750 miles over formidable terrain and past other equally tempting agricultural or mining pockets. Santa Fé's administrative status, agricultural self-sufficiency, and peaceful surroundings nevertheless ensured the city's survival, furthermore becoming elevated to an archiepiscopal see by 1561, after which its religious institutions

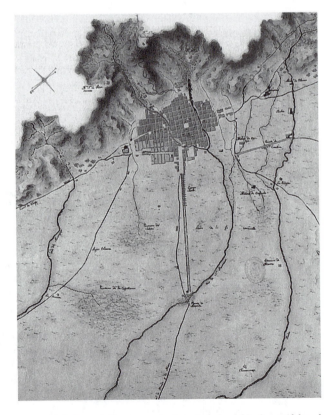

Santa Fé de Bogotá, shown perched on the edge of its bountiful and well-irrigated plateau in a survey conducted by Carlos Francisco Cabrer, April 1797; north is toward lower left. (Servicio Histórico Militar, Madrid)

multiplied and a college was founded eleven years later. Gifted individuals such as the Spanish music master Gutierre Fernández Hidalgo also visited as early as 1584, briefly serving as cathedral choirmaster. And in contrast to other communities nearer the coasts, Santa Fé was also spared any danger from foreign sea raiders, so that its physical evolution was to be unconstrained by the expense of erecting a military enclosure. Disease and earthquake posed the greatest threats to its residents, so that most dwellings were single-story structures made of whitewashed adobe bricks, with thatched or red-tile roofs.

An observer in 1616 calculated that New Granada's capital contained 3,000 inhabitants, as well as boasting wide streets and three urban parishes. A few score rural aristocratic families maintained larger mansions, which they visited seasonally from their haciendas (estates). Safely ensconced within its mountain retreat, the city by 1670 consisted of some sixty-eight blocks radiating out from its Plaza Mayor (Main Square), encompassing from present-day Calle 4 North to Calle 23 South and from Carrera 2 East to Carrera 12 West. A few large, two-story edifices were clustered around its core, although the majority of residences still remained only single-story adobe huts with thatched roofs. A half dozen gristmills lined the San Francisco River banks, while the tiny capital's peaceful and bucolic remove allowed it to enjoy a modest reputation as a center of learning; its artistic pursuits were exemplified by such outstanding locally born composers as José Cascante (1630–1702) and Juan de Herrera (1670–1738), both of whom produced many fine musical works. Architectural innovations included the imposing Guadalupe and Monserrate churches, which were set atop a pair of mountains towering above the city.

Spain's imperial decay during the latter half of the seventeenth century nevertheless added to Santa Fé's sense of isolation and neglect, until the enfeebled Hapsburg dynasty at last died out and was replaced overseas by a more vigorous French Bourbon offshoot. An administrative overhaul initiated by these reform-minded new rulers recognized that the provinces, which today comprise Colombia, Panama, Ecuador, and Venezuela, had by then become so productive and populous that it was decided in 1717 that they no longer warranted subordination to Lima (Peru). Rather, they were to become merged into a newly constituted "Viceroyalty of New Granada." This entity was temporarily suppressed six years later, by which time the city had blossomed to roughly 22,000 inhabitants; yet regional growth continued so impressively that the office was resurrected in July 1740.

Viceregal Capital (1740–1819)

Once the British naval blockade from the War of Jenkins's Ear was lifted late in 1748, a resumption of peacetime trade from across the Atlantic and Caribbean to the Spanish Main helped finance Santa Fé's rise into its new jurisdictional status,

although not without certain setbacks as the eighteenth century progressed. Local discontent grew especially acute in mid-March 1781 against new royal taxes imposed by Insp.-Gen. Juan Francisco Gutiérrez de Piñeres, until a mob finally ran riot in Socorro and other rural towns. When 6,000 *comuneros* (commoners) gathered the next month and selected Juan Francisco Berbeo as their leader, Gutiérrez responded by sending a company of troops from Santa Fé to scatter them. Yet the soldiers were defeated at Puente Real outside Vélez, and their sortie so inflamed the uprising that Berbeo countermarched upon the capital. Gutiérrez was compelled to flee for Honda by 13 May, after which the *comuneros* were joined at the end of that same month by the Indian chieftain Ambrosio Pisco, who assumed the ancient Chibcha title of Lord of Chía and Prince of Bogotá. The rebels presented their demands to the remaining Crown authorities on 4 June, who acceded to Gutiérrez's dismissal, repeal of all taxes, and a greater Creole participation in government by signing the so-called Zipaquirá Pact three days later.

Berbeo's tens of thousands of adherents thereupon dispersed, yet another leader called José Antonio Galán persisted with a revolt north of Santa Fé, even slaying the governor of rural Neiva. The capital was finally reinforced by 500 Spanish troops on 15 August 1781, after which Viceroy Manuel Antonio Flores declared the Zipaquirá Pact null and void, and a series of military sweeps brought an end to regional unrest as Galán and many others were arrested, executed, or incarcerated.

Santa Fé enjoyed the apex of its colonial splendor during the last two decades of the eighteenth century, with numerous fine Baroque *Neogradino* (New Granadian) buildings and churches being erected within the city, as well as a flourishing of its arts and learning. A new highway was even added, running northward from its San Diego parish toward the Torquita Hills and distant Chía (modern Carrera 7 to Usaquen), plus a second extending from the communal bridge and running parallel to the old Camino Real or "Royal Highway" as far as Zipaquirá (modern Carrera 13). The capital's population was measured at 21,394 according to the census of 1801, now occupying approximately 150 blocks. Yet conflict unleashed overseas by the French Revolution had already led to the imposition of a debilitating British naval blockade upon the viceroyalty's coastline, after which the Emperor Napoleon I sent a French army into Spain in the spring of 1808 to depose Ferdinand VII in favor of his own brother Joseph Bonaparte.

Such a crude usurpation of power was repudiated by most Spanish-American vassals, who instead rallied behind an interim junta (council) established at Aranjuez to uphold their captive monarch's cause. Nevertheless, the loosening of imperial ties also fired aspirations of independence among the viceroyalty's many mixed-heritage Creoles, who had long grown resentful of the preferments accorded peninsular-born Spaniards by Crown or Church officials in distant Madrid.

As subordinate juntas multiplied throughout the Americas,

Exterior view of the viceregal palace at Santa Fé de Bogotá as drafted by Juan Ximénez Donoso, ca.1775–1781. (Servicio Histórico Militar, Madrid)

advocating various degrees of autonomy, one such body came to be created at Santa Fé on 20 July 1810. Initially, it included the participation of Viceroy Antonio Amar y Borbón, although dispensing with his services five days later. Broad-based sentiment in favor of outright independence led to the creation of a new national union called the United Provinces of New Granada by November 1811, although Santa Fé refused to join that breakaway confederation and was instead ruled by its own local strongman, Antonio Nariño.

Border disputes soon erupted between the factions, after which a Loyalist counteroffensive reconquered Popayán for the Crown in September 1813. In order to dispute that reversal, Nariño forged a temporary alliance with his insurgent rivals elsewhere in New Granada and marched out of Santa Fé at the head of a small army, winning a few minor victories over the royalists before being defeated and captured. Shorn of its leader and best troops, the city of Santa Fé waited uneasily under Nariño's elderly successor, Manuel Bernardo Alvarez, until a rival insurgent column moved to intervene.

The Venezuelan-born Gen. Simón Bolívar, having been given command of Col. Rafael Urdaneta's division, arrived outside Santa Fé on 8 December 1814 to subdue its government

for the republican cause. After calling for its surrender and being refused, he attacked two days later, pushing the city defenders back into its main square by 11 December before accepting the final capitulation the next day. However, despite having secured New Granada's capital, Bolívar was obliged to depart a month and a half later to attempt to control the bitter factional wrangling that had gripped republican forces elsewhere.

Battered Santa Fé remained only briefly under republican control, as the fall of Napoleon in Europe and restoration of a Bourbon monarch to the Spanish throne had freed the Crown to address the rebellion in its American colonies more effectively. An expedition of 10,500 soldiers duly disembarked in eastern Venezuela by early April 1815 under Gen. Pablo Morillo y Morillo, who bore instructions to pacify the entire Spanish Main and assume office as its military governor, before striking even more deeply into other insurgent theaters. Republican jealousies drove Bolívar into exile shortly thereafter, after which Morillo's army gradually pushed westward to secure the vital seaport of Cartagena, then proceeded up the Magdalena River.

This royalist thrust disgorged into New Granada's central

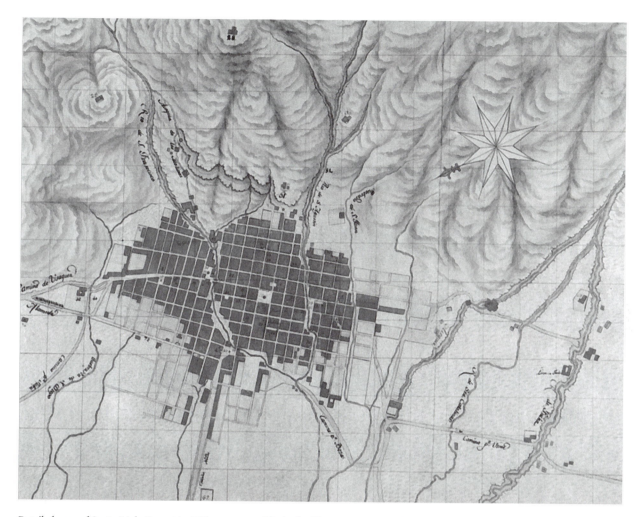

Detailed map of Santa Fé de Bogotá in 1791, as surveyed by its "artillery commander," Lt.-Col. Domingo Esquiaqui, on orders from Viceroy José de Ezpeleta; north is toward lower left. (Servicio Geográfico del Ejército, Madrid)

highlands when Gen. Custodio García Robira's 3,000-man patriot division was pulverized at Cachirí on 22 February 1816, no prisoners being taken. Frightened patriot citizens consequently began fleeing from defenseless Santa Fé toward the viceroyalty's eastern *llanos* (plains), until Col. Miguel de la Torre's Spanish division at last entered the half-deserted capital on 5 May, followed three weeks later by Morillo's main force. Suspect patriot sympathizers were arrested and executed over the next few months, as virtually all of New Granada had passed under Crown control by the end of that same year.

Bolívar nonetheless managed to regain the wilds of eastern Venezuela from exile and so reanimated its rebel guerrillas that Morillo and de la Torre were compelled to march from Santa Fé with the bulk of their troops by December 1816, leaving the city under a military administrator. The viceroyalty struggled to resurrect its shattered economy, until the protracted guerrilla struggle in Venezuela eventually ended with royalist setbacks, so that Bolívar was able to ascend into the Andes and penetrate Pisba Plain by June 1819. On 7 August he achieved

a crushing victory as Col. José María Barreiro's royalist army was recrossing the Boyacá River bridge for Santa Fé, which freed the *Libertador* (Liberator) to hasten toward the capital with his *Llano-arriba* (Lancer) Regiment.

On the morning of 9 August 1819 the last viceroy, Juan Sámano, decided to abandon Santa Fé, so that Bolívar entered triumphantly the next afternoon and spent the following month and a half installing a new republican administration (after which he withdrew to Venezuela, where a coup by Arismendi had challenged his title as president).

Early Republican Era (1820–1921)
The city was officially declared the capital of Bolívar's newfangled "Republic of Gran Colombia" on 17 December 1819, and its name was reduced to its original Chibcha name of Bogotá only, in repudiation of the name Santa Fé employed during the colonial regime. However, little else was to change in the city's fortunes during the chaotic decades immediately following independence, as political and economic instability

gripped the emergent nation, along with the entire South American subcontinent. English seaborne commerce—especially in cloth and garments, exchanged along the coastlines for Neogranadian agricultural produce—supplanted some of the nation's lost Spanish trade, yet Bogotá was too far inland to benefit significantly from such traffic; its status as capital of Bolívar's insolvent and far-flung administration moreover brought no appreciable material gain.

The valley's agricultural self-sufficiency at least allowed the city to survive the ensuing period of internecine struggle between Conservative Party advocates of a strong centralized government and Liberal Party proponents under Santander who favored greater regional autonomy for Gran Colombia. As late as 1848, Bogotá's layout still consisted of a mere 160 blocks—only 8 new ones having been added north of the San Francisco River, plus another 2 south of the San Augustín River, after three decades of republican rule. Pres. Tomás de Mosquera changed the country's name to the United States of Colombia in 1861 and oversaw the expropriation of Church properties, while Bogotá was officially subdivided into four administrative *parochias* (parishes) six years later. Yet it still

contained no more than 2,620 houses, thirty churches, and six public baths for its 40,000 inhabitants.

Those figures would remain virtually static, at 3,000 residences and eight baths, as late as 1881, although thanks to a national upsurge in lucrative coffee exports, they then had to service 94,723 urban residents. A significant increase in bureaucratic jobs and ancillary domestic industries had been derived from the national coffee exports, reflected in such construction innovations as Bogotá's first three- or four-story edifices (supposedly capable of resisting earthquakes), as well as the introduction of its first telephone line northward to the resort town of Chapinero in 1884, followed by animal-drawn streetcars two years later.

The latter service was supplemented by a railway line in 1890, by which time the city encompassed 193 blocks lying between modern Calle 26 Norte and Calle 25 Sur, with Parque del Centenario as its northernmost fringe and "Kopp's Bavaria" brewery and a military academy lying just beyond. Conditions in the crowded and underserviced capital proved so volatile that on 16 January 1893, a mob of artisans and laborers—offended by an author who had complained about their alleged

View along Calle Real, ca. 1880; note the suspended street lamp, which could be lowered to be ignited at nightfall. (*América pintoresca*, 1884)

gambling and alcoholic excesses—ran riot and destroyed every police station except for one, before being put down at a cost of fifty dead, countless injuries, mass arrests, and considerable property damage.

Rail connections with more distant Facatativa, Zipaquirá, and Sibate were inaugurated in 1894, while the capital's population was measured the next year at 95,813 inhabitants. But progress was interrupted when Gen. Jorge Moya Vásquez, the garrison commander at Soacha west-southwest of Bogotá, marched upon the capital and toppled the national Conservative government on 31 July 1900 in favor of another faction, called the Historical Conservatives, of Vice Pres. José Manuel Marroquín. The main Liberal army was subsequently defeated at the Battle of Palonegro; they therefore resorted to rural guerrilla warfare, especially in the departments of Cundinamarca and Tolima. A vicious irregular campaign known as the Thousand Days War cost the lives of some 100,000 of Colombia's 4 million people, before the rebels finally capitulated in exchange for amnesties and limited political reforms late in 1902.

The first automobile was imported into Bogotá that same year, and modernization efforts resumed when the streetcar line toward Chapinero along Carrera Santander (formerly Calle Real, modern Carrera 7) was electrified in 1909, and the capital's main roads were paved in macadam the following year. The urban population was measured at 121,257 inhabitants by 1912, who were to receive a noteworthy impetus from Colombia's economic upsurge at the end of World War I.

First Urban Boom (1922–1947)

After an especially violent electoral campaign, Gen. Pedro Nel Ospina assumed office as president in August 1922 and initiated an ambitious program of public works that would begin to end Bogotá's traditional geographic isolation deep within its mountain vastness, as well as upgrade its antiquated infrastructure. A concession had already been granted two years previously to a German-Colombian consortium called Sociedad Colombiana Alemana de Transportes Aéreos, or SCADTA, to initiate air service on a commercial scale, yet the most significant innovations under Nel Ospina and his successor Miguel Abadia Méndez from 1926 to 1930 were to be a series of new railways and roads connecting the capital to other regions, as far down as the coasts.

Urban water service was also expanded, but as this commodity was drawn from wells or mountain streams around Chapinero, Bogotá's northern sectors benefited first. Commerce and industry increased, a modern sewage system was laid down, and the city endured an intense interlude of construction. The effects of the worldwide Depression precipitated by the New York stock market crash of October 1929 led to a significant downturn for Colombia's capital by 1931–1932, although the government of the aristocratic Liberal Pres. Enrique Olaya continued to invest scant resources in urban

projects, so as to contain proletarian discontent and the rise of militant unionism. Despite such difficulties, the population nonetheless multiplied from 235,421 inhabitants in 1928 to 272,714 a half decade later and 336,996 by 1938.

The latter census furthermore recorded the existence of 144 factories in Bogotá, plus 503 workshops and 106 warehouses or garages. Under the guidance of Mayor Germán Zea and the Austrian-born urban engineer Karl H. Bonner, residential areas continued to spread northward along the main transportation arteries, almost as far along Calle 81 as the wealthy neighborhood of El Chico, while industrial plants were concentrated to the west around the transportation hub of Sabana Railway Station. Raw materials for brick or cement making were extracted from the loamy and sandy soils around the southern suburbs of Las Cruces, San Cristóbal, and "20 de Julio." (No expansion could occur northwestward because of the presence of Bogotá's public cemetery and Techo Airfield, plus several large private landholdings.)

Social distinctions became entrenched as more and more well-to-do citizens began forsaking the narrow confines of the old colonial core for attractive new developments north of the capital, although banks and luxury stores were to remain

Blazing streetcar in the Plaza de Bolívar on the evening after Gaitán's assassination, 9 April 1948. (Foto Tito)

clustered for some time along Calle Real or Avenida de la República in the city center, with jewelers and silversmiths along Calle 12 and Carrerra 6. In contrast, laborers and poorer families congregated in swelling numbers around their industrial workplaces in the lower-lying southern or western sectors, despite their being underserviced and prone to floods during the rainy seasons.

"Bogotazo" and Municipal Expansion (1948–1954)

Once World War II concluded, repressed political aspirations resurged, resulting in more bitter animosity between the Liberal and Conservative parties. On 9 April 1948 the populist Liberal leader and chosen presidential candidate, Jorge Eliécer Gaitán, was shot by a lone assassin upon leaving his office for lunch. Although Bogotá's 513,681 residents had by then become inured by the decades of rural strife known as *La Violencia*—which had claimed almost 14,000 lives that previous year alone—the brazen murder of such a beloved figure in the capital's streets unleashed a torrent of wrath against the administration of Conservative president Mariano Ospina Pérez, at a time when the Ninth Pan-American Conference was being celebrated and the capital was hosting such prominent international visitors as the U.S. secretary of state, George Marshall, and the secretary of commerce, Averell Harriman; the Venezuelan president, Rómulo Betancourt; and even the young Fidel Castro.

The assassin was beaten to death by a mob and his body dragged into Calle Real, being hurled against the doors of the Presidential Palace in reproach. Shots rang out, and eighty presidential guardsmen managed to clear the street, before eventually opening fire into the increasingly frenzied crowds in Plaza de Bolívar. An orgy of vandalism thereupon erupted, government ministries and churches being gutted and burned throughout the city core, while many stores were looted in the downtown commercial sector before calm could be restored the next day. The total number of dead was calculated at 1,000, with another 2,500 injured and more than 100 buildings destroyed between Calle 21 Norte and Calle 10 Sur and Carrera 3 to the east and Carrera 10 to the west.

As the capital turned to recuperating from this devastation

Some of the widespread destruction left amid Bogotá's downtown core, late April 1948. (Foto Lunga)

(as well as undertaking a great deal of new private or public construction with the assistance of the famed French architect Charles-Edouard Jeanneret "Le Corbusier," many old colonial streets being widened), *la violencia* flared ever more dramatically in the countryside. Another 43,000 lives were claimed that same year, plus 19,000 in 1949, and 50,000 after the Liberals abstained from the 1950 elections and Ospina Pérez installed the Conservative Laureano Gómez as president. An uneasy state of siege was maintained over the 648,000 inhabitants of the capital even after Gómez resigned for health reasons in November 1951; Acting Pres. Roberto Urdaneta Arbeláez was deposed on 13 June 1953 by the dissident Conservative general Gustavo Rojas Pinilla, chief of the armed services.

The latter imposed numerous changes by convening a national constituent assembly a year later, which among many other reforms expanded Bogotá's jurisdiction by annexing the neighboring townships of Bosa, Engativa, Fontibon, Suba, Usme, and Usaquen from the *departamento* (state) of Cundinamarca to create a 1,000-square-mile *distrito especial* (special district), bringing poor and fractious rural suburbs under more direct control of a chief executive appointed by the president, with an elected council. Railway gauges had been stan-

dardized as of 1952, improving traffic into the capital by eliminating the necessity of transferring cargoes en route, while an oil pipeline was completed into Bogotá three years afterward from Puerto Salgar, providing direct access to petroleum products and derivatives.

Modern Sprawl (1955–Present)

As in many sister Latin American nations, emigration from impoverished rural areas into the major cities accelerated exponentially during the latter half of the twentieth century, especially given the persistently high level of violence throughout Colombia (although numerous other cities grew commensurately as well, without the capital becoming a dominant national megalopolis, as was to occur in other South American republics). Bogotá's population consequently soared to 1,271,700 residents by 1960, 1,697,311 only four years afterward, 2,526,000 by 1970, and 2,862,000 three years after that.

The capital's ancient residential patterns also changed, its colonial-era core no longer serving as a focal point; modern development projects instead attracted wealthier residents northward, while lower-income slums multiplied to its south. The demand for property became so intense that evictions and

Young woman in the streets of Bogotá, ca. 1880. (*América pintoresca,* 1884)

land disputes in the eastern foothills even led to armed clashes. During this transformation Bogotá became dramatically polarized between the fine upper-income neighborhoods to its north and ever more slums around its southern fringes. Pollution and crime increased as a result, the population reaching 3,983,000 inhabitants by 1985—or 4,207,657 if all suburbs were included—which compounded the already existing array of socioeconomic and environmental problems.

For further reading materials on the history of Bogotá or Colombia, please consult the Select Bibliography at the end of this volume; additional sources on South American urban history can be found under "Regional Studies," as well as under "General Works on Latin America."

CARTAGENA

Seaport nicknamed Reina de las Indias or "Queen of the Indies" during its great colonial heyday and that was repeatedly invested by enemies before almost fading into oblivion.

Antecedents (1501–1532)

The explorer Rodrigo de Bastidas, commanding two ships piloted by Juan de la Cosa, reconnoitered the South American shoreline from Cape de la Vela as far southwest as the Gulf of Darien early in 1501, in the process sighting a broad natural harbor formed by two long, low-lying islands parallel to the coast, called Calamar or Calamari by its indigenous residents (not to be confused with the modern city of the same name, located almost 50 miles due east on the Magdalena River). Because of its approaches' similarity to the ancient Mediter-

ranean port of Cartagena in Spain, de la Cosa gave this harbor that same name on his charts before proceeding with his reconnaissance.

Three summers later, a small colonizing expedition appeared offshore under Cristóbal Guerra, hoping to found a settlement inside the vast and sheltered anchorage. But Guerra was soon slain and his survivors ejected by Indian counterattacks. In mid-November 1509, Alonso de Ojeda—also seconded by de la Cosa—chanced to arrive offshore with 225 men aboard two ships and a pair of brigantines, intending to establish another new outpost at San Sebastián de Urabá (near the modern border between Colombia and Panama). Wishing to kidnap local inhabitants to serve as slave laborers, de Ojeda slipped ashore with 100 soldiers, surprising the village of Calamar and securing some sixty captives amid terrible slaughter. Yet when his men pressed toward the larger inland town of Turbaco, 12 miles farther southeast, they became separated in the jungly, hilly terrain and were destroyed piecemeal—suffering seventy deaths, including that of de la Cosa, who was captured and tortured before succumbing. De Ojeda was extricated only with difficulty, and after being joined a few days later by the five-ship, 700-man expedition of Diego de Nicuesa, he threw 400 men ashore to vindictively raze Turbaco before departing.

Such ferocity nonetheless gave Calamar a reputation for bloody resistance, so that its harbor was spared any further invasions over the next couple of decades; the Spaniards concentrated instead upon claiming easier footholds elsewhere along that coast, now commonly referred to as Tierra Firme

Cartagena's vast harbor, as surveyed in 1735 by the military engineer Carlos Desnaux; the city lies at its northern extreme, at left. (Servicio Geográfico del Ejército, Madrid)

(the "Mainland," later becoming translated into the "Spanish Main" in English). Finally, Lt.-Gov. Pedro de Heredia of nearby Santa Marta—a hard-bitten adventurer whose nose was missing as a result of a Madrid street brawl—traveled to Spain in 1530 to obtain permission from the Crown to subjugate the recalcitrant port, setting sail from Seville two years later with a small flotilla.

Foundation and Early Vicissitudes (1533–1560)

De Heredia appeared outside Calamar's bay with a ship, two caravels, and a lesser consort bearing a total of 150 soldiers and twenty-two horses on 13 January 1533. The next day he came ashore and rested his cavalry until 17 January, before pushing along its low and sandy peninsula. He found that the main village—protected by a thick stockade of spiny *guamacho* tree trunks—had been abandoned by its frightened inhabitants. To proclaim his title as new territorial governor, de Heredia went through the legal fiction of constituting a "city" amid Calamar's empty huts on 20 January, although no actual residence was established; rather, his caravels were detached to explore the nearby port of Zamba and coastline around Cenú or Sinú, while he and his troops clashed with the inhabitants of Canapote and Turbaco before rejoining their flotilla at Zamba.

After a harrowing twenty-two-day ascension upstream as far as the Magdalena River, the Spaniards returned into their original seaside conquest. On 1 June 1533, de Heredia formally "named the first *alcaldes* [magistrates] and *regidores* [aldermen] for the town of Calamar, in which he had his seat, and ordered that the city be called *Cartagena*"—soon changed to Cartagena de Indias or "Cartagena of the Indies," so as to distinguish it from its namesake in Spain. Town lots were distributed among its first citizen-soldiers, their initial dwellings consisting of simple straw huts or wooden shacks clustered inside a stockade, with farmlands also assigned around the encircling bay.

Despite its torrid and unhealthful climate, the community evolved rapidly, migrants being attracted by news of gold strikes in its hinterland, as well as reports of Francisco Pizarro's conquest of the rich Incan empire of Peru. So many people arrived to begin clearing and cultivating estates and ranches amid Cartagena's fertile lowland delta that a religious see was created by 1534, with Fr. Tomás de Toro appointed as first bishop. (Another notable early resident was the canon Juan Pérez Materano, a gifted musician and composer who arrived two years later and who wrote a treatise entitled *Canto de órgano y canto llano*.) The island named Getsemaní beside the burgeoning city had been ceded to de Heredia's accountant, Rodrigo de Durán, and a slaughterhouse was installed on it once animal husbandry multiplied. Some years afterward, Durán's widow, Beatriz de Cogollos, also granted a portion of the island to the Franciscan Order to erect a monastery ministering to the indigenous population.

The fledgling city's first foreign enemy also materialized, as Spain was embroiled throughout the first half of the sixteenth century in a dynastic struggle against France known as the Hapsburg-Valois Wars. A lone French corsair vessel therefore prowled past Cartagena toward the Panamanian port of Nombre de Dios early in 1537, prompting the Crown to order harbor defenses augmented throughout the Antilles. Yet Cartagena's modest increment of three artillery pieces proved woefully inadequate, as four large French corsair vessels and a smaller consort—piloted into the bay on the night of 24–25 July 1543 by a Spanish turncoat embittered at a punishment received from Lt.-Gov. Alonso Vejines—deposited 450 raiders, who overran the city with ease in a three-pronged surprise attack. According to Spanish sources, these rovers bore commissions from Jean-François de La Rocque, Seigneur de Roberval and Lieutenant-General of Canada, and extorted a ransom of 35,000 pesos from Bishop Benavides and the overawed populace, as well as commandeering another 2,500 from the royal coffers and a mass of goods before withdrawing.

The next year, the Crown decreed that all transatlantic departures from Seville must be coalesced into two annual convoys with naval escorts, a temporary wartime expedient that would eventually evolve into the plate-fleet system. In 1550, Spain's "Captain-General of the Ocean Sea," Adm. Alvaro de Bazán, furthermore began increasing the size of shipping from 150- to 200-ton vessels into 500- to 600-ton galleons that would prove much better suited to resisting storms and enemy privateers—yet would also require wider and deeper anchorages in the Americas, such as at Cartagena.

The city had recuperated and received its first transatlantic convoy in December 1550, which paused for a few days to refresh provisions before proceeding across to the more exposed and reef-lined roadstead at Nombre de Dios to celebrate the annual commercial fair with Peru's merchants. Hostilities with France resumed in 1552, the same year in which Cartagena was swept by an accidental fire, so that no more convoys visited until 17 January 1556, again remaining only six days and taking on 60,000 pesos in local taxes before proceeding to Nombre de Dios. Such sporadic stopovers meant that Cartagena still remained so insignificant a community that when five French privateer ships under Jean-Martin Cotes and Jean Bontemps set 300 harquebusiers ashore on 11 April 1559, they easily brushed aside its three dozen Spanish defenders and pillaged its dwellings; Bishop Juan de Simancas paid to have them spared for a meager ransom of 4,000 pesos.

Emergence as Plate-Fleet Terminal (1561–1585)

The city's resurrection was greatly spurred when the Crown codified all transatlantic sailing patterns in 1561, designating Cartagena's anchorage as a major port of call, so that it was thereafter to be visited regularly. Such enhancement in its strategic role also provided royal funds for construction of defenses, while Adm. Bartolomé Menéndez—brother of the

Crude pen-and-ink sketch of the unfortified city, with vessels sheltering inside its harbor, ca. 1570–1573; north is toward left. (Real Academia de la Historia, Madrid)

founder of St. Augustine, Florida—added a further refinement by touching at the harbor in late July 1562 on his outward passage toward Nombre de Dios, then making a second call on his homeward leg toward Havana and Spain. Finally, Adm. Diego Flores de Valdés not only returned into Cartagena from Nombre de Dios in late September 1567, but also wintered over the next four months with his fifteen galleons and crews.

The city was so bolstered by such increased traffic that when the English slaver John Hawkins arrived outside with ten ships on 16 July 1568, having already overawed the Spanish defenders at Ríohacha and Santa Marta, his request for trade was rebuffed by Gov. Martín de Salas. Although these interlopers subsequently bombarded Cartagena's new defenses from long range and penetrated into its bay in boats to scrounge for provisions—scrupulously paying for everything with goods, in hopes of encouraging further barter—Hawkins was nevertheless obliged to quit the coast empty-handed by 24 July.

The port had now become a major lynchpin in Spain's convoy system, with a repair yard called La Machina opposite the tiny Pastelillo (Little Cake) fortress at El Boquerón and a swelling number of Neogranadian officials, traders, boatmen, and teamsters crowding in every year to receive the *galeones.* (In order to distinguish between the two *flotas de galeones* or "fleets of galleons" that annually plied from Seville toward Mexico or Tierra Firme, it became customary to call Mexican convoys *flotas,* while referring to those bound for Cartagena as *galeones.*) Ever larger amounts of European imports and African slaves began to be off-loaded at the city wharf for distribution or resale into the interior, while exports of regional produce also grew, supplementing the allure of Peruvian specie flowing out of the Pacific.

As a haven and crossroads for this rich commercial traffic, Cartagena became elevated to a "very noble and very loyal" city by a royal decree issued on 12 December 1574, complete with its own coat-of-arms. Its strategic role was further confirmed when a small naval squadron was assigned to it two years later, emerging from its harbor to patrol Caribbean waters and using captives as oarsmen in its *galeras* (galleys). The inadequacy of Nombre de Dios's anchorage as a commercial entre-

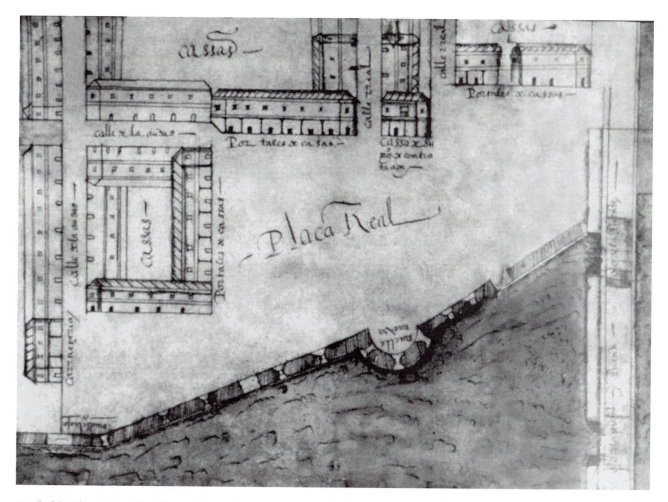

Detail of the *Plaza Real* or "Royal Square" facing the city's waterfront in 1571, depicting some of the stout, two-story edifices erected to handle its blossoming traffic in goods. (Archive of Indies, Seville)

pot was underscored when transatlantic galleons eventually grew so heavy that they had to be lightened merely to cross its reef-lined bar, so that more goods instead came to be off-loaded at Cartagena. Despite chronic shortages of food and water, plus inflated prices whenever a plate-fleet entered, the city's overall prosperity nonetheless allowed for a grand new cathedral to be commenced, along with fine new Dominican and Franciscan convents in its Getsemaní suburb.

Drake's Descent (1586)

Yet the city's newfound prominence also drew unwelcome attention from abroad, as Spain's relations with Elizabethan England deteriorated. Warnings were received in 1585 that Sir Francis Drake intended to lead a large privateering sweep through the Antilles. This enemy force burst upon Santo Domingo the following January, then steered directly toward Cartagena. Drake's approaching twenty-three ships were sighted from Santo Domingo Beach (also known as Playa Grande or "Big Beach") on 19 February 1586, prompting Gov.

Pedro Fernández de Bustos to order all civilians evacuated inland. Only 54 riders, 450 harquebusiers, 100 spearmen, 20 armed black slaves, and 400 Indian archers remained to defend the city, along with two anchored galleys under the veteran commander Pedro Vique Manrique.

Drake led his fleet straight into the inner harbor, disgorging 600 troops that same evening to advance overland under Christopher Carleill, while Martin Frobisher's pinnaces probed the tiny Boquerón fortress held by Pedro Mexía de Mirabal after nightfall. The next morning, Carleill's column pushed past a line of trenches and broke the morale of Cartagena's garrison, which fled; Vique's galleys also were run aground, and their crews abandoned ship as the slave oarsmen revolted. All resistance had ceased by 21 February 1586, only seven or eight Spaniards having died, as opposed to thirty Englishmen. The vacant city was thereupon ransacked, its buildings eventually being ransomed by Bishop Juan de Montalvo and other leading citizens for 107,000 ducats—against which Drake extended a receipt before departing early in May.

Recuperation (1587–1633)

A battle fleet of twenty ships and 4,500 men hastened out from Spain that same year under Adm. Alvaro Flores de Quiñones to rescue the battered city, followed by the annual plate-fleet, which arrived in December 1586 accompanied by two new coast guard galleys with a combined complement of 233 troops and 384 slaves. City defenses were strengthened and Cartagena resumed its traditional role, receiving plate-fleets roughly every other year throughout the ensuing decade and a half of the Elizabethan War. However, regular business did not truly revive until peace was confirmed in August 1604, after which the port's economy thrived.

A splendid tribunal for the Holy Office of the Inquisition was created in 1610, while work on Cartagena's cathedral was completed two years later. The Dominican, Franciscan, and Augustinian monasteries were also expanded or beautified during these prosperous first decades of the seventeenth century, while many new churches furthermore emerged: La Trinidad, San Roque, Santo Toribio, Santa Teresa, La Merced, Santa Clara, San Diego, and a Jesuit monastery. The most famous was to be Santa Cruz Church, erected east of the city

so that its statue of the Virgin of the Candelaria—venerated by sailors—might be visible from out at sea atop La Popa Hill (a derivation of that eminence's earlier nickname of Popa de la Galera or "Galley's Poop" because of its resemblance to a vessel's stern).

Military construction also kept pace, the Italian-born royal engineer Cristóbal de Roda laying the foundation for a new star-shaped bastion on Carex Island by 8 September 1614 that was to be called San Felipe in honor of the reigning Spanish monarch, Philip III. It was built to supplant the elderly Santangel redoubt and overlap its new field of fire with Fort San Matías at Hicacos Point opposite, so as to better protect the sea entrance into the inner bay as well as the city's Santo Domingo land gate. However, its design was deemed inadequate, and a royal order dated 19 April 1626 called for the demolition of both, their materials being combined to construct Fort Santa Cruz. The name of the city land gate was subsequently changed to Santa María, then eventually into Santo Domingo during the mid-eighteenth century.

Much of Cartagena was leveled by a hurricane in 1618, but the city quickly rebuilt thanks to its healthy commerce, plate-

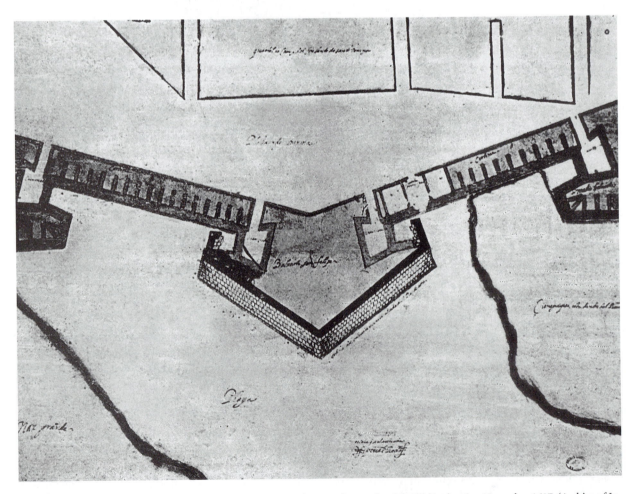

Diagram by the military engineer Cristóbal de Roda of a portion the recently completed San Felipe bastion, November 1617. (Archive of Indies, Seville)

fleets being received every single year between 1616 and 1640. Its eastern bulwarks were strengthened during the governorships of García Girón de Loayza from 1618 to 1626 and Francisco de Murga from 1629 to 1636, while some clusters of dwellings were also rebuilt farther from the sea, beyond the original perimeter on other adjoining islands, some even as far inland as San Lázaro Hill. Fears of a potential Dutch raid—Madrid having been at war against The Netherlands since 1621—prompted the fortification of the city bridge connecting to its Getsemaní suburb with a Media Luna (Half Moon) gatehouse in 1631, erected with the labor of 800 prisoners brought in two years previously by Adm. Fadrique de Toledo after having eradicated the Anglo-French colonies on the Antillean islands of Nevis and St. Kitts.

Beleaguered Stronghold (1634–1696)

As Spain's power was fading and becoming increasingly challenged by rival West European settlements in South America and the Caribbean, Cartagena's role changed from a plate-fleet terminal into a base for regional defense—especially after the Dutch seized the strategically placed island of Curaçao in 1634. That very next summer, the one-legged privateer, Capt. Cornelis Corneliszoon Jol—famous among the Dutch as Houtebeen (Peg Leg) and among Spaniards as Pie de Palo—materialized outside Cartagena with two vessels, defeating four coast guard frigates sent to chase him away. Jol returned in August 1637 and trailed the battle fleet of Adm. Carlos de Ibarra as it escorted twenty-six merchantmen across to Havana; because of such growing perils, the city's Santa Catalina and San Lucas bastions (facing north toward La Boquilla) were completed by de Roda in 1638 to designs created by his colleague Juan Bautista Antonelli "the Younger."

Another major change occurred when the flagship and two large galleons of Portuguese Adm. Rodrigo de Lobo y da Silva—vassals of the Spanish king—were wrecked in Bocagrande Channel on 17 March 1640, blocking that shallow passageway once their remnants began accumulating silt. After lengthy deliberation, Cartagena's authorities decided to close the channel off altogether rather than underwrite costly dredging operations, so that this original entrance into the bay was filled in with stone and debris; smaller Bocachica Channel, 7 miles farther south, was instead activated as the only access point.

That same spring of 1640, two Spanish galleons and six frigates had sortied from Cartagena under Antonio Maldonado in a vain attempt to expel an English settlement from Santa Catalina, or "Providence" Island (150 miles east of Nicaragua's Mosquito coast). Determined to fulfill that operation, the Spanish Crown ordered Adm. Francisco Díaz Pimienta to take his anchored battle fleet from Cartagena Bay the next spring—where it was awaiting the Portobelo treasure convoy—and expunge the intruders. Upon returning triumphantly into port with 770 English prisoners, news of Por-

tugal's overthrow of sixty years of Spanish rule was received, so that the commander of Díaz Pimienta's Portuguese contingent—Juan Rodríguez de Vasconcellos Sousa, Conde de Castel Melhor—was arrested on 29 August 1641, charged with plotting to seize Cartagena for his new monarch, João IV. Eventually he escaped, but the captain-general of New Granada refused to honor the repatriation promise extended to the English captives from Santa Catalina, instead putting more than 500 to work clearing El Dique Channel, which led inland to the Magdalena River.

Spain's decay had by now become so palpable that Cartagena experienced a significant economic downturn: plate-fleets arrived only every other year until 1654, after which problems deepened. A heavy storm destroyed much of the city seawall and Santa Clara convent that same year, while the following spring a huge English expedition conquered Jamaica, from where Vice Adm. William Goodson ventured across to sack Santa Marta and threaten Cartagena by the autumn of 1655. He devastated Ríohacha and blockaded Cartagena again in May 1656, prompting city officials to have Irish-born Richard Carr design and Pedro Zapata de Mendoza erect a small castle called San Felipe de Barajas atop a 100-foot eminence east of Cartagena, as well as Fort San Luis and a gun platform to protect the Bocachica entrance.

Jamaica's station commander, Commo. Christopher Myngs, hovered outside the bay in the summer of 1658, while plate-fleet traffic became ever more erratic. Spain's naval weakness even tempted the rover Henry Morgan to pulverize Portobelo with a few hundred buccaneers in July 1668, in anticipation of a surprise descent against Cartagena itself with 900 to 1,000 freebooters the next January—prevented only by the accidental explosion of his flagship, *Oxford*, off the Haitian coast. Gov. Pedro de Ulloa of Cartagena countered by issuing a privateering commission in January 1670 to the corsair Manuel Rivero Pardal to attack English interests throughout the West Indies, which goaded Morgan into sacking Panama City a year later.

Transatlantic movements were furthermore hampered by France's declaration of war against Spain in October 1673, while Cartagena was unable to reconstitute its old Armada de Barlovento (Windward Fleet) under the veteran commander Antonio de Quintana until the 200-ton warships *San Juan, Nuestra Señora del Camino,* and *Santo Cristo del Buen Viaje,* or *Mogoleño,* arrived in July 1677. They were immediately dispatched—along with two hired merchantmen and 500 troops—to rescue Santa Marta from an occupying force of French *boucaniers.* Even after peace was restored the next year, the city was alarmed by a visit from a powerful French squadron under Adm. Jean, Comte d'Estrées, in the spring of 1679.

The port's debility was such that when the pirate chieftain Laurens de Graaf and his minions Michiel Andrieszoon, Jan Willems, and François Le Sage began snapping up prizes outside Cartagena in late November 1683, Gov. Juan de Pando Estrada was obliged to commandeer the private slavers *San*

Francisco of 40 guns, *Paz* of 34, and a 28-gun galliot to chase the rovers away. However, when the Spanish vessels exited on 23 December—manned by 800 soldiers and sailors under naval Capt. Andrés de Pez y Malzarraga—the seven smaller pirate craft captured them, with 90 Spaniards and 20 freebooters being slain. De Graaf deposited his prisoners ashore with an insolent note on 25 December, thanking Governor de Pando for his Christmas presents before blockading the entrance for another three weeks.

French Siege and English Blockade (1697–1713)
When the War of the League of Augsburg, or King William's War, erupted in April 1689, Cartagena was initially not imperiled. Spain was arrayed with Britain and other powerful European allies against France, so that no buccaneer descents occurred, and a commercial fair was even held in 1691. However, during that conflict's closing phases a half dozen years later, fourteen French warships and 4,000 men stole across the Atlantic under Adm. Bernard Jean-Louis de Saint-Jean, Baron de Pointis, to mount one last surprise attack against Spanish interests—by securing Cartagena as a prize before any peace treaty could be concluded.

Bolstered by a dozen French West Indian *boucanier* vessels under Gov. Jean-Baptiste Ducasse of Saint-Domingue (Haiti), Pointis arrived off Cartagena on 13 April 1697, probing its reef-lined shoreline near Hicacos Point for a possible disembarkation point, before steering south to force the Bocachica entrance. On the afternoon of 15 April, 1,700 French troops and 1,100 *boucaniers* came ashore at Los Hornos to besiege the 150 Spaniards holding 33-gun Fort San Luis (of whom only 15 were regular troops, under Capt. Sancho Jimeno de Orozco). That stronghold surrendered upon being stormed the next day, Pointis installing a 170-man garrison before working his fleet inside the lower bay, then pressing north toward the city.

Gov. Diego de los Rios y Quesada ordered Fort Santa Cruz—also called Castillo Grande—vacated, so as to concentrate his 750 regulars around Cartagena proper. French buccaneers meanwhile moved across the bay to seize La Popa high ground, while the main French army pressed overland to outflank Fort San Lázaro. The two columns reunited on 20 April 1697 to commence siege works against the city's Getsemaní suburb, which was defended by 700 men under aged, gout-ridden Capt. Francisco Santarén. The invaders dug trenches and ferried artillery ashore, Pointis—wounded in a leg by a sharpshooter's round—supervising work from a litter until a bombardment could be initiated on 28 April. During a lull two days later, Ducasse visited a Spanish officer at the Media Luna Gate and noticed that a breach had been battered; he therefore urged Pointis to order a general assault for 4:00 P.M. French grenadiers and buccaneers fought their way into Getsemaní and reached the very edge of Cartagena itself in bloody fighting, at which point the defenders' morale collapsed; white flags were displayed upon the ramparts by the evening of 2 May.

While negotiating the final capitulation terms, Pointis sent Ducasse's buccaneers with several hundred soldiers, supposedly to oppose a 1,000-man relief column approaching out of New Granada's interior; actually, it was to prevent the unruly irregulars from spoiling his peaceful occupation of the city on 4 May 1697. Ducasse and his men returned to find Cartagena's gates closed to them, being billeted instead in its devastated Getsemaní suburb, while Pointis tallied booty inside; it eventually totaled 8 million crowns, which were transferred aboard his men-of-war. The freebooters expected to receive a quarter as their share, and so were outraged to learn on 25 May that they had been allotted only 40,000. They swarmed into the hapless city on 30 May to inflict tortures upon its few surviving inhabitants, thereby extorting an additional 1,000 crowns per buccaneer.

The French admiral meanwhile quit the bay on 1 June 1697 with his heavily ladened fleet, the rovers not reboarding their own vessels until 3 June, then weighing four days later. At sundown on 6 June, Pointis's ten warships and two auxiliaries had been sighted by an Anglo-Dutch battle fleet under Vice Adm. John Neville, sent to counter this French venture. Outnumbered, overburdened, and with most of his crews sick, Pointis nevertheless outran his pursuers by dawn on 10 June, after which Neville visited Cartagena before resuming his chase and overtaking Ducasse's eight buccaneer vessels on 25 June. He captured three, the prisoners being brought back and put to work rebuilding shattered Cartagena.

The city struggled to recuperate from this destructive ordeal, despite a plate-fleet visit in 1698, once peace had been restored. When an expedition of Scottish colonists sailed past the harbor later that same year, bound to establish a settlement at Darien on the Isthmus of Panama, it took Gov. Juan Díaz Pimienta y Zaldívar sixteen months to scrape together sufficient men and ships to counter the incursion. King Charles II then died in November 1700 and left the French princeling Philip of Anjou as his heir, so that the War of the Spanish Succession, or Queen Anne's War, erupted across the Atlantic, disrupting Cartagena's traffic once more.

Ironically, Ducasse—now promoted to commodore and bearing a Spanish commission as an ally—fought his way past the blockading Royal Navy squadron of Vice Adm. John Benbow to enter Cartagena with a small relief convoy on 5 September 1702. However, no plate-fleet could traverse the Atlantic until the winter of 1707–1708; the Jamaican station commander Commo. Charles Wager maintained stealthy watch off Baru Island for several months, in the hope of intercepting this rich formation upon its return leg into Cartagena from Portobelo.

Two vessels were finally sighted standing into Cartagena's bay at daybreak on 8 June 1708, the seventeen-ship convoy of Adm. José Fernández de Santillán, Conde de Casa Alegre, coming within view by noon. Only his 64-gun, 600-man flagship *San José* and the 64-gun, 500-man vice flagship *San*

Joaquín were men-of-war; the remaining Spanish vessels consisted of a 44-gun hired merchantman bearing 400 men under naval Capt. Nicolás de la Rosa, Conde de Vega Florida, a 40-gun merchantman, and eight lesser craft accompanied by five French privateers. Awaiting them were Wager's 70-gun flagship *Expedition,* Capt. Timothy Bridges's 60-gun *Kingston,* Capt. Edward Windsor's 50-gun *Portland,* and the fireship *Vulture.*

The English concentrated against the three Spanish capital ships, while the convoy scattered northward round Baru Island to escape into Cartagena. *Expedition* gained upon *San José* by sunset, the Spanish flagship exploding and going down with almost all hands an hour and a half later. Wager then overhauled de la Rosa and obliged him to strike by 2:00 A.M. on 9 June 1708, before sending *Kingston* and *Portland* in pursuit of the Spanish vice flag *San Joaquín* the next dawn. *San Joaquín* won free by running through the dangerous Salmedina Channel, where the English dared not follow. When Bridges and Windsor rejoined on 10 June, the commodore detached them again along with *Vulture* to probe for the 40-gun Spanish merchantman behind Baru Island. But upon seeing them approach, the Spaniards beached their ship, set it ablaze, and escaped ashore. Wager therefore sailed for Port Royal with but a single prize, court-martialing and cashiering Bridges and Windsor for their lackluster performance.

The British nonetheless maintained such close watch upon Cartagena that when local traffic with Portobelo was cautiously resumed three years later, Commo. James Littleton arrived outside with five two-deckers and a sloop on 6 August 1711, chasing five large vessels up to its Bocachica entrance, as well as another four the next morning—during which pursuits the 50-gun HMS *Salisbury* of Capt. Francis Hosier and 50-gun *Salisbury Prize* overtook the 60-gun Spanish vice flagship, while a second vessel was captured by Edward Vernon's 60-gun *Jersey.* Littleton maintained his close blockade of Cartagena for another few weeks, after which the unhappy city was devastated by hurricanes in 1713 and 1714.

Recovery (1714–1740)

Once hostilities ceased, Cartagena could begin both private and public reconstruction, abetted by a partial resumption in its trade and some Crown funding. That same year of 1714, work started on a new San José Battery at the northern tip of Baru Island to cover the southern side of Bocachica entrance, while the city's damaged northern bastions also began to undergo extensive repairs two years later under the direction of the military engineer Brig. Juan Herrera y Sotomayor. The empire's new reform-minded Bourbon rulers also recognized that the provinces that today comprise Colombia, Panama, Ecuador, and Venezuela had by then become so much more productive and populous that they no longer warranted subordination to Lima (Peru); thus they were merged in 1717 to become the "Viceroyalty of New Granada." Cartagena's status as the regional naval base and principal seaport was conse-

quently enhanced, a plate-fleet moreover visiting in 1721, the same year in which segments of its city seawall underwent expensive reconstruction.

However, the viceroyalty decision was reversed in 1723, and another plate-fleet did not call until three years afterward, being further obstructed from making its return leg from Portobelo when London—once more angry at Madrid—dispatched an English fleet under Vice Adm. Francis Hosier to

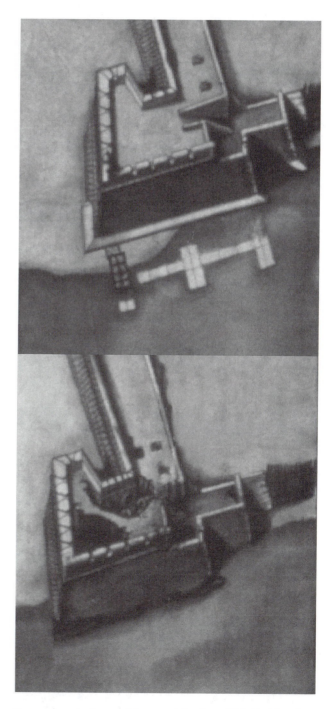

Proposed repairs to one of Cartagena's bastions, 1725. (Archive of Indies, Seville)

hover menacingly offshore in late June 1726, postponing the convoy's reappearance at Cartagena until early 1727. War was narrowly averted, but once peaceful relations were restored, another more successful plate-fleet visit was made in 1730, while Herrera y Sotomayor set about reinforcing the city's century-old Media Luna gatehouse by erecting the new Santa Teresa and Santa Bárbara bastions.

The plate-fleet visit scheduled for 1737 was canceled when a huge fire destroyed two-thirds of Panama City. Two years later the War of Jenkins's Ear erupted against England, and a British naval expedition under Vice Adm. Edward Vernon pulverized the defenses at both Portobelo and Chagres during the initial operations in 1739–1740, rendering them useless as havens for anchored merchantmen. That operation effectively diverted the flow of South American commercial traffic away from Panama altogether, toward the safer venues of Cartagena and other ports.

English Siege (1741)

As Spain's principal naval base for South America, Cartagena was to be prominently featured during the War of Jenkins's Ear. A Royal Navy squadron under Vice Admiral Vernon materialized on 13 March 1740, taking soundings for four days before the bomb vessels *Alderney* and *Terrible* began shelling the city in an attempt to lure out the anchored Spanish squadron of Vice Adm. Blas de Lezo. When that gambit failed, Vernon delegated HMSs *Windsor* and *Greenwich* on 20 March to maintain watch, while steering the remainder of his squadron away the next day to attack the secondary Panamanian port of Chagres.

One year later, a French sloop ran into Cartagena Bay on 14 March 1741, bringing word from the governor of Saint-Domingue (Haiti) of an approaching British invasion fleet under Vernon, whose 176 warships and troop transports appeared the next afternoon, anchoring between Hicacos Point and Playa Grande by 16 March. Smaller English vessels feinted a disembarkation north of Cartagena, while the main fleet reconnoitered the shoreline around Bocagrande before shifting 7 miles south toward Bocachica. The twenty-seven-year-old viceroy, Sebastián de Eslava, meanwhile rallied the city garrison of 1,100 regulars, 300 militiamen, 200 free blacks, and 600 indigenous archers raised by Col. Melchor de Navarrete. Admiral de Lezo also transferred four of his six warships—the 70-gun *Galicia* and *San Felipe*, 66-gun *San Carlos*, and 64-gun *San José* or *Africa*—to bolster Bocachica's defenses, sending many of his 600 sailors and 400 marines ashore to help man guns and stretch its log boom. The Spaniards mustered perhaps 4,000 men in total.

On the morning of 20 March 1741, the 80-gun HMSs *Norfolk*, *Shrewsbury*, and *Russell* opened fire against the Santiago and San Felipe batteries; the 80-gun *Princess Amelia* and smaller *Litchfield* engaged the Chamba battery, bomb vessels rained shells upon Fort San Luis, and Commo. Richard Lestock's squadron feinted against Cartagena. *Shrewsbury* suf-

fered sixty casualties before limping out of range, yet the British otherwise silenced the Spanish defenses by noon, allowing Brig. Thomas Wentworth's 8,000 soldiers to land north of Fort San Luis and slowly begin installing siege artillery. At dawn on 1 April, 300 British sailors and 200 soldiers (including Virginia militia Capt. Lawrence Washington) temporarily overran and spiked the 15-gun Abanicos battery, although its commander—naval Lt. José Campuzano—cleared several and resumed fire.

At first light on 3 April 1741, Lestock ventured inshore with a half dozen warships to commence a two-day exchange with Fort San Luis and the nearby San José Battery, eventually retiring with numerous casualties. Eslava and de Lezo were wounded by shell fragments from a round that struck *Galicia* on 4 April, although neither was seriously incapacitated. The Spaniards had already resolved to abandon Fort San Luis, so that when Wentworth ordered an assault at 5:30 P.M. on 5 April, its 500 exhausted defenders beat for a parley, then fled out the far side in confusion as *San Carlos*, *San Felipe*, and *Africa* were scuttled to block the channel. A party of Royal Navy seamen secured the San José Battery on the southern bank by 10:00 P.M., rowing out to capture the Spanish flagship *Galicia* intact. More importantly, they cut the log boom so that Vernon's fleet could begin working past the scuttled Spanish warships the next morning, gaining the safety of the lower harbor by evening on 7 April.

The British admiral then pressed north against the inner Spanish defenses, so confident of victory that he dispatched a sloop toward England to announce Cartagena's imminent fall. But its defenders scuttled their last two warships—the 64-gun *Santa Rosa de Lima* or *Dragón* and 62-gun *Conquistador*—along with all merchant shipping on 10 April 1741 to block the Manzanillo Channel into the upper harbor, while evacuating Fort Santa Cruz after nightfall. Its seizure allowed the English to clear the block ships and commence shelling the city proper with bomb vessels by 12 April. Four nights later, a large-scale disembarkation was effected 3 miles south of La Popa at Tejar de Gracias, from where Anglo-American colonial militiamen gained the heights unopposed by next noon, cutting Cartagena off from its hinterland.

Wentworth nevertheless closed in upon the city ramparts very sluggishly, as illness was now sapping his main army. The 24-gun San Felipe de Barajas fortress, manned by 250 Spanish marines and soldiers under military engineer Carlos Desnaux, bloodily repulsed an assault by 1,500 English troops under Brig. John Guise at 3:00 A.M. on 20 April 1741, killing, wounding, or capturing 645 of the invaders. Disheartened, Wentworth announced a few days later that Cartagena could not be carried with his remaining strength of 3,569 soldiers, so that notwithstanding the bitter recriminations of his naval counterpart, the English expedition prepared to withdraw.

At dawn on 27 April 1741, the captive *Galicia*—transformed into a floating battery—approached Cartagena's walls, exchanging broadsides with its garrison for seven hours before sinking. This action allowed the debilitated English army to decamp so as to reembark, their transports setting sail for Jamaica that same day; Vernon and his men-of-war remained behind until 17 May to raze the harbor fortifications and load booty. Cartagena's defenders had endured some 600 deaths, plus many others wounded or lost, yet they exulted at their success in defeating the invasion. De Lezo unfortunately succumbed to his wounds on 7 September, being posthumously ennobled as Marqués de Ovieco, while Eslava was created Marqués de la Real Defensa.

Late Colonial Era (1742–1807)

Although plate-fleet traffic was discontinued, once peace was restored late in 1748 Cartagena was nonetheless able to revive thanks to an invigorated overall trade, as well as continued Crown subsidies for its naval installations and shipyard. In November 1761 another hurricane breached its northwestern ramparts, allowing the sea to flood into the city streets as far as the Santo Domingo Plaza before receding. News arrived shortly thereafter of renewed hostilities against England, prompting the erection of extemporized fortifications such as Angel Battery, thrown up atop a hill north of Fort San Fernando. Once peace returned in the spring of 1763, the Crown authorized a major reconstruction of all defenses via a royal order issued on 7 June 1764 that resulted in the enlargement of San Felipe de Barajas Castle by the addition of several collateral batteries and other works. A huge new *escollera* (breakwater) was also constructed north-northwest of Cartagena's

Map of the city in August 1744, by Juan Bautista MacEwan; copy made in December 1769 by Antonio de Arévalo. (Servicio Histórico Militar, Madrid)

waterfront between 1765 and 1771 by the military engineer Antonio de Arévalo, successfully deflecting many storms.

Fearing renewed hostilities against Britain, Fort San Fernando and the earthen Angel Battery just to the north of it, as well as the San José Battery covering the Bocachica entrance, were transformed into complete stone strongholds by November–December 1778. A complex of twenty-three large storerooms, 40 feet high by 50 to 60 feet wide, were also built into a section of the city ramparts in 1789 to store ammunition and supplies against any potential siege. Cartagena had consequently fared rather well during the closing phases of its colonial era, enjoying one final flush of prosperity before Spain was unwillingly driven into an alliance with revolutionary France in October 1796, so that a dozen years of intermittent blockades ensued by the Royal Navy.

Independence Struggle (1808–1821)

The beleaguered port was furthermore surprised by news early in 1808 that the French emperor, Napoleon I, had sent an army into Spain, deposing King Ferdinand VII in favor of his own brother Joseph Bonaparte. Such a crude usurpation of power was widely rejected, resistance coalescing around an interim junta (council) established at Aranjuez that same September to uphold the captive monarch's cause. Cartagena additionally benefited from a resurgence in its own local traffic, as the British blockade was lifted when both nations became allied in Europe. Yet despite its brief economic revival, the city would soon enter another difficult interlude, for the loosening of New Granada's imperial ties also gave rise to the first stirrings toward outright independence.

Subordinate, but semiautonomous juntas had multiplied throughout the Americas, one such triumvirate forming at Cartagena on 22 May 1810, seconded by another such body at the highland capital of Santa Fé de Bogotá on 20 July; the latter initially included even Viceroy Antonio Amar y Borbón, although his services were dispensed with five days later. Sentiment among the port city's Spanish-American Creoles soon escalated into demands for their own complete autonomy, leading to the creation of a new national union called the United Provinces of New Granada by 11 November 1811; Bogotá refused to join Cartagena's breakaway confederation, however, being instead ruled by its own strongman.

The port's influence over the interior was therefore limited by this split, and border disputes erupted until the Venezuelan-born Gen. Simón Bolívar finally subdued the highland regime with a republican army in mid-December 1814; he then marched down to the coast to subjugate Cartagena and its local chieftain, Brig. Manuel del Castillo. Such infighting among independence-minded Creoles proved ill timed, as Napoleon's fall and the restoration of Ferdinand VII back in Europe had at last enabled Spain to dispatch significant reinforcements to its American possessions, so that one week after Bolívar's besieging troops had occupied La Popa high ground outside Cartagena on 27 March 1815, a fleet deposited 10,500 Spanish soldiers in eastern Venezuela under the veteran Gen. Pablo Morillo y Morillo to spearhead the restoration of the viceroyalty.

Bolívar's siege was consequently lifted and Venezuelan resistance collapsed, after which Morillo seized Santa Marta in mid-July 1815, detached columns up the Magdalena River, and then sailed against Cartagena while the royalist Col. Francisco Tomás Morales advanced overland. The Spanish commander in chief landed outside the port unopposed on 1 September, joining Morales to invest del Castillo's garrison. Conditions within the city deteriorated so gravely that he was deposed by 17 October in favor of Gen. José Francisco Bermúdez, while many residents starved. The Spaniards finally made a triumphal entry on 6 December, Morales vengefully conducting summary executions at San Fernando de Bocachica Fortress. It was estimated that 3,000 civilians had died of malnutrition, disease, or in reprisals after this 108-day siege.

Having restored Cartagena to its traditional role as a major Spanish naval base, columns penetrated inland and defeated insurgent concentrations until Bogotá was reclaimed on 5 May 1816, so that Morillo was able to reimpose Crown rule over all of New Granada by the end of that same year. Smoldering patriot resistance nonetheless persisted in the wilds of eastern Venezuela, gradually eroding Loyalist gains, until Bolívar could lead a counteroffensive into New Granada's Andes by the summer of 1819. The last viceroy, Juan Sámano, was compelled to abandon Bogotá by 9 August, retreating into Cartagena as the royalist forces were slowly pressed back down upon the coast.

Next spring, the patriot Adm. Felipe Luis Brion (originally born on Dutch Curaçao as Philippus Ludovicus Brion) took nearby Ríohacha with his sixteen vessels and Col. Mariano Montilla's division. Morillo was thereupon ordered by a new Liberal administration in Madrid to repromulgate the constitution of 1812, which he reluctantly did by declaring a forty-day truce as of 6 May 1820; he realized, however, that its articles would only sap demoralized royalist spirits and increase desertions. When the cease-fire lapsed and Montilla advanced with his troops into Turbaco on 1 July, supported by Brion's squadron outside Cartagena's harbor, the city's 1,150-man Spanish garrison was so rent by dissension that it did not react; instead, Viceroy Sámano and other officials were deposed through a coup engineered by disgruntled Brig. Gabriel de Torres.

Still, the insurgents lacked a siege train or sufficient numbers to breach Cartagena's defenses, and so could not mount a direct assault. But the city in turn remained cut off from the interior, its commercial life at a virtual standstill. In an attempt to break the rebel encirclement, de Torres delegated 420 Spanish soldiers of the León Regiment and 60 gunners to set sail at midnight on 1–2 September 1820, disembarking at Cospique and surprising the 1,000 patriots holding Bellavista under Col. Ramón Ayala at dawn. The latter suffered 125 killed

and 50 wounded before fleeing in disarray, after which the Spaniards spiked the guns and retired into Cartagena.

Yet this lone sortie could not cause patriot resolve to slacken, so that when royalist fortunes faded the following year and Bocachica fortress had to be abandoned, an insurgent squadron under Commo. José Padilla gained the inner roads of Cartagena Bay and captured eleven anchored Spanish ships at dawn on 25 June 1821—abetted by a feint against the city's landward defenses by troops under Col. Friedrich de Adlercreutz, a Swedish count serving the republican cause. Now bereft of all hope of relief or reinforcement, de Torres agreed to surrender the empty city to Montilla's 2,500 patriot besiegers on 1 October, being allowed to sail away to Cuba with more than 700 surviving royalist officers and men.

Collapse (1822–1906)
On this occasion, Cartagena would fail to revive from its protracted sufferings, its economy plunging into a free fall as a result of forever losing all its royal subsidies, while its commercial monopoly was breached and local traffic had long since shifted elsewhere. Bolívar's newfangled "Republic of Gran Colombia," headquartered at Bogotá, had neither funds nor interest in compensating for such lost income, while influential regional property owners chose not to rejoin the few thousand survivors still residing within the pestilential port city. Rather, they remained more comfortably on their rural estates amid the cooler Turbaco hills or emigrated abroad. The city's permanent populace was reduced to a few thousand citizens, largely impoverished blacks or mulattoes.

Political unrest continued to hamper Cartagena's fortunes during the postindependence era, such as when the British brig *Jane and Sarah* and the sloop *Little William* were ransacked by five rebel Colombian warships off Zapote on 6 February 1842. The 6-gun Royal Navy brig *Charybdis* of Lt. Michael de Courcy retaliated by defeating those transgressors, then briefly blockaded Cartagena's entry. Farther inland, the ancient Dique Canal providing waterborne access to the Magdalena River at Calamar had been allowed to silt up, and although dredged and reopened by 1846, it soon became obstructed again by floods.

The disgraced Mexican dictator Antonio López de Santa Anna, having fled into exile on Jamaica after his defeat during the U.S. invasion of 1846–1848, retired in 1850 to an estate at Turbaco once owned by Bolívar. Its landscape being reminiscent of his home state of Veracruz, the former Mexican president whiled away his days by cultivating sugar, tobacco, and gamecocks, until recalled to reassume his country's leadership from 1853 to 1855. A further nine years of enforced retirement then ensued for him at Turbaco, before Santa Anna eventually made another failed attempt at reentering Mexican politics early in 1864; he quit his Colombian refuge for the last time two years afterward.

At its nadir Cartagena was reduced to little more than a

ghost town, real estate owners offering properties rent-free to any occupants, merely to keep their buildings inhabited and maintained. A modest regional revival occurred once the *cartagenero* Rafael Núñez was elected Colombia's president in 1880, so that some funds began to become available for public works and industrial subsidies. A 65-mile railway was even laid running inland toward Calamar, so as to once more provide commercial access to the Magdalena River. But although a British company also received a concession in 1906 to supply the city with fresh water from springs among the Turbaco hills, Cartagena's population had been measured that previous year at a paltry 9,681 inhabitants.

Modern Resurgence (1907–Present)

The enormous undertaking of the Panama Canal dig during the first decade of the twentieth century greatly reinvigorated Cartagena's fortunes, as well as the effective countermeasures being discovered and adopted against tropical diseases, so that both factors combined meant that its population almost quadrupled to 36,632 inhabitants by 1912. Commercial traffic out of the Colombian interior—consisting largely of coffee bean exports—continued to increase after the canal was inaugurated two years later; after that, oil was discovered in the middle Magdalena basin and piped directly into Cartagena's

suburb of Mamonal for export aboard tankers, fueling yet another population upsurge from 51,382 people in 1918 to 92,494 a decade later. Wealthy white residents now began forsaking the cramped colonial-era quarters in the city core—with its contiguous dwellings and narrow streets pent behind ancient walls—in favor of the broad new residential suburb of Manga, characterized by ample gardens and more healthful air.

The effects of the stock market crash of October 1929 and subsequent Great Depression throughout the world slowed Cartagena's development and caused its municipal population to contract to 84,937 residents by 1938—72,767 being registered as living within its old core. But prosperity eventually returned, spurred especially by the increased demand for petroleum during World War II. Petrochemical and light manufacturing plants came to be installed around the bay's inner shoreline, the city's population escalating from 97,680 people in 1943 to 128,877 eight years later.

That figure doubled to 242,085 inhabitants by 1964 and to 297,173 five years afterward, as rural-to-urban migration patterns accelerated throughout Colombia and Latin America. Cartagena's tourism industry furthermore boomed as of the early 1970s, Caribbean cruise ships routinely beginning to call and disgorge thousands of passengers to enjoy the city's historical attractions and tropical allure. Many colonial-era

Modern luxury hotels facing the inner harbor all along the Bocagrande Peninsula. (Colombian Department of Tourism)

structures were restored and the metropolitan area expanded as a result of the particular demands of of this traffic, in particular along the Bocagrande Peninsula where luxury hotels, restaurants, mansions, and apartment blocks were added to cater to visitors.

However, access to this wealthy, largely white enclave from the older, mostly Afro-Latino neighborhoods in the city and around the bay was controlled by a strategically placed police station and marine base, the feeling of segregation increasing after the onset of leftist guerrilla activity throughout Colombia. Cartagena's population was officially measured at 513,986 people according to the census of 1985, although that figure soon approached 1 million, especially if the entire shoreline was included. Criminality around the ancient port city deepened when a cocaine exporting syndicate was challenged by Colombian forces as of 1989 at the behest of antidrug agencies in Washington, D.C.

For further reading materials on the history of Cartagena or Colombia, please consult the Select Bibliography at the end of this volume; additional sources on South American urban history can be found under "Regional Studies," as well as under "General Works on Latin America."

Ecuador

GUAYAQUIL

Sheltered seaport that also dominates the fertile Guayas River Basin, making it the largest and busiest city in this republic, although not its national capital.

Foundation and Early Evolution (1537–1623)

The most commonly given date for the establishment of Santiago de Guayaquil—25 July 1535, feast day of Spain's patron saint Santiago (Saint James) on the Church calendar—is now held in considerable doubt by most modern historians. Rather, it is believed that during the mopping-up operations after the Spanish conquest of Quito and the northern Incan empire in 1534, a detachment under Sebastián de Belalcázar, or Benalcázar (also Velalcázar), slew a coastal subchieftain named Guayas, then concluded its campaign by encamping at the mouth of the Babahoyo River.

This initial base was subsequently shifted southwestward to Dima—later known as Estero de la Ataranza (Shipyard Inlet)—before finally being relocated for a third time to its present site, when Francisco de Orellana's expedition arrived from Peru in 1537 and pushed 33 miles upriver from the Gulf to disembark. His troops chose a comparatively level plain on the western bank of the muddy Guayas River on which to lay out their encampment, beneath three hills known collectively as Santa Carmen de la Cruz (although the steep Santa Ana and Carmen hills are its most prominent peaks). This temporary military establishment quickly evolved into a permanent shantytown, despite the fact that its dwellings stood only 30 feet above sea level and so flooded frequently during the rainy seasons of January through May.

The flat and marshy surroundings, as well as the wet and torrid climate, proved an ideal breeding ground for lethal respiratory and digestive afflictions, as well as yellow fever, malaria, bubonic plague, cholera, typhoid, and smallpox, so that this community attracted far fewer Spanish settlers than other, more temperate South American environments. Freshwater also proved to be a problem, ocean tides working their way far upriver, tainting the water tables along both shorelines. (The Guayas River reverses flow twice daily past the city waterfront, currents and countercurrents running at speeds of up to 5 miles per hour.) Yet Guayaquil was too good a seaport not to survive—being generally fog-free and calm year-round, facilitating ocean access—while its 25,000 square miles of wild hinterland was well irrigated by regular rainfalls.

Guayaquil's *Malecón* or "Waterfront," ca. 1909, looking north toward Las Peñas, with Santa Ana Hill looming in the far distance. (*El Ecuador: guía comercial*)

Juan Montalvo Square, ca. 1909, looking north toward the Santa Carmen de la Cruz Hills in the distance. (*El Ecuador: guía comercial*)

During its earliest years, the town served merely as a stopover for vessels circulating between Panama City and Callao, as well as a way station for passengers and cargoes disembarking to ascend into the Andes. However, its ready access to multivaried stands of oak, cedar, laurel, mulberry, ebony, hawthorn, plus many tropical woods—such as the highly durable *guachapeli*—would soon transform Guayaquil into the most important shipyard along the Pacific coast.

A few Spanish carpenters and caulkers arrived, using indigenous and black slaves to fell timbers to build ships for the Peruvian traffic, which burgeoned exponentially as of the mid-sixteenth century because of the discovery of rich silver deposits at Potosí (Bolivia). Everything from tiny coastal traders to large galleons were soon being contracted from the *ataranzas* (shipyards) along Guayaquil's northern fringe, as well as refits and repairs for existing craft, so that the small yet bustling community became elevated to the status of a city by the early 1570s. Most of the thirty-five to forty Spanish vessels plying the Pacific by 1590 had been launched at Guayaquil, and when the Crown subsequently began commissioning pairs of royal galleons for Peru's Armada del Mar del Sur (South Sea Fleet), the entire city population would become engaged in such a project: Indian laborers felled and ferried trees out of the interior to be fashioned into ships by Spanish shipwrights and mulatto craftsmen.

In addition to its shipbuilding industry, the port also began exporting significant amounts of produce from small outlying farms, especially cacao—which was highly coveted as far

north as Mexico, despite Venezuela's supposed monopoly over that commodity. Clandestine traffic was possible because Guayaquil had regular visitors and few permanent Spanish residents, mostly lower-class tradesmen with little interest in upholding viceregal decrees emanating from Lima, 700 miles farther to the southeast. The lengthy shoreline along its shelving Gulf estuary moreover provided numerous quiet inlets for smugglers to handle cargoes, as larger oceangoing ships now routinely anchored 40 miles below Guayaquil in the lee of Puná Island, lightering their legitimate goods to and from its customshouse, rather than risk the shifting sandbanks and currents.

Guayaquil grew modestly and its population multiplied thanks to these combined activities, although most early seventeenth century homes still consisted of simple wooden structures with thatched roofs. A few of the more elaborate had protruding balconies and planted palm trees as a respite against the oppressive heat.

Enemy Raids (1624–1709)

The city had nonetheless gained sufficient prominence to suffer its first attack, when a Dutch squadron under Jacques l'Hermite "the Younger" of Antwerp circled Cape Horn to invest Callao in the spring of 1624. The Peruvians repelled the assault and l'Hermite died of an illness, but his successor, Gheen Huygen Schapenham of Rotterdam, detached his vice adm., Jan Willemszoon, on 6 June to raid Guayaquil with the 32-gun, 560-ton *Mauritius* and the 14-gun, 260-ton *Hoop.* This small

Modern rendering of Guayaquil's coat-of-arms, originally issued during the early 1570s. (Author's Collection)

force arrived offshore undetected, seizing three frigates, two brigantines, and four lesser craft in the Gulf before falling upon the mainland towns of Guarmey, Cherrepe, and Santa Fe. The surprised local *corregidor*, Diego de Portugal, and his 200 ill-prepared militiamen could do little more than cover their civilians' flight. The Dutch then ransacked a few dwellings, although their retirement toward their boats was harried by riders, resulting in some losses. After plundering Puná Island and burning most of his prizes, Willemszoon departed to rejoin the main Dutch squadron.

The defenders acquitted themselves somewhat better when Schapenham subsequently forsook his blockade of Callao and stole upon Guayaquil with his full complement of four ships and 600 men. Having penetrated as far as Ataranza Inlet, the Dutch launched a dawn attack on 5 August 1624 by igniting two brigantines that they found upon its stocks, plus other vessels anchored close inshore. The resultant conflagration helped illuminate their assault (while also consuming the city's Santo Domingo and San Agustín churches, as well as many other wooden structures along its waterfront). But Schapenham was checked in the streets by black and mulatto residents under the municipal *corregidor*, José de Castro y Grijuela. The rovers tried several more landings on 25–28 August, again without success, before finally suffering twenty-eight men taken captive and disappearing northward.

Guayaquileños were to remain largely undisturbed for the next half century, until a group of West Indian buccaneers hacked their way across the Isthmus of Panama and began wreaking havoc in the Pacific. Underestimating the danger, a small vessel put out from Guayaquil in early September 1680 under Capt. Tomás de Argandoña, bearing thirty "merry blades, gentlemen, who drinking in a tavern" had made a vow to confront the freebooter flotilla of Bartholomew Sharpe. Instead, the marauders captured these young Spaniards and summarily shot their chaplain, "casting him overboard before he was dead," thereby inaugurating a blockade of Guayaquil that was to diminish its traffic greatly for the remainder of the decade.

Early in December 1684, four vessels and 200 English rovers under Edward Davis, John Eaton, Peter Harris, and Charles Swan entered the Gulf, seized three Spanish slavers, and then mounted an attempt against the city itself—which was foiled only when a captive Indian guide escaped as they were approaching overland, alerting the lookouts posted downriver at Fort San Carlos on 18 December.

Two and a half years later, a combined force of French *flibustiers* under François Grogniet—alias "Chasse-Marée"—and English buccaneers under George Hout, or Hutt, materialized opposite Puná Island, depositing three columns on 16 April 1687 who also stole inland toward Guayaquil: Grogniet led one company through some marshes called Estero Salado (Salt-Water Inlet), while Hout advanced against a small bastion guarding the city's outskirts; Grogniet's subordinate Pierre le Picard led a third company against another. The *corregidor* Gen. Fernando Ponce de León had been forewarned about strange sails offshore, yet when no attack had immediately ensued, he had assumed it to be a false alarm. Therefore, the buccaneers burst upon an unprepared city early on the rainy Sunday morning of 20 April 1687, overrunning it after an eight-hour, house-to-house melee in which two to three score residents were slain and many others captured, compared with nine pirate dead and a dozen wounded. Plunder totaled "134,000 pesos, much precious jewelry, a large amount of wrought silver, and a great deal of merchandise and goods."

Among the injured attackers was Grogniet, who was carried back aboard his anchored flagship off Puná when the raiders departed four days later, dying of his wounds by 2 May 1687 while still awaiting payment of ransoms for his four principal hostages—including two city aldermen. Picard assumed overall command of the French *flibustiers*, who along with their English allies were joined a few days later by Davis. They then learned that a Peruvian relief squadron was on its way. These rescuers—two 20-gun vessels under the Biscayan privateers Dionisio López de Artunduaga and Nicolás de Igarza, plus a small *patache* (auxiliary)—hove into view on 27 May, engaging the freebooters at long range and scattering them over the next five days.

The buccaneer menace finally abated when the War of the

League of Augsburg, or King William's War, erupted in Europe in 1689, luring most rovers back into their original Caribbean hunting grounds. The only unusual visitor to the Gulf of Guayaquil was to be the private English salvor John Strong, who materialized off Puná on 20 August 1690 after rounding the Strait of Magellan with his 40-gun, 270-ton ship *Welfare*. He had come to work the wreck of the 900-ton Peruvian galleon *Jesús María de la Limpia Concepción,* which had gone down off Chanduy on the night of 26 October 1654 with millions in silver still aboard. Yet despite anchoring over the site by 7 September 1690, Strong could not find any trace of the galleon's remains, so he stood away for the Juan Fernández Islands some weeks later.

An accidental conflagration reduced most of Guayaquil's buildings—bleached dry by the fierce tropical sunlight—to ashes in 1692, then again in 1707. The War of the Spanish Succession, or Queen Anne's War, had also commenced, and several boats were sighted offshore on the night of 1–2 May 1709; daybreak revealed 238 Englishmen who had rowed upriver from Woodes Rogers's anchored 30-gun, 320-ton privateer frigate *Duke* and Stephen Courtney's 26-gun, 260-ton *Duchess.* A surrender demand was presented to the 24-year-old *corregidor,* Jerónimo de Boza Solís y Pacheco, and after two days of tense negotiations during which the English seized two newly launched ships and other lesser prizes in the river, the raiders finally stormed ashore at 4:00 P.M. on 4 May, carrying Guayaquil at a cost of three dead and four wounded.

The Spaniards retreated inland and two days later agreed to pay 30,000 pesos so that the invaders would peaceably retire

to their frigates off Puná Island by the next evening. But when that entire sum could not be raised, the English sailed away on 18 May 1709 without releasing their hostages, Capts. Manuel Jiménez and Manuel de la Puente. A rover later described Guayaquil as consisting of perhaps 500 edifices, a few made of brick but mostly of wood, housing some 2,000 people in "a low boggy ground."

Late Colonial Era (1710–1819)

The city revived slowly after peace was restored, and Madrid furthermore shifted its entire *Audiencia* jurisdiction—headquartered at Quito, 280 miles farther northeast in the remote Andes—from Peruvian control by 1717 to instead merge it along with Panama, Colombia, and Venezuela to create the "Viceroyalty of New Granada." That new administrative entity was temporarily suppressed six years later, so that the *Audiencia* of Quito and its southern Pacific outlet port once more reverted to Peruvian control. But the viceroyalty was then resurrected in July 1740, so that Guayaquil once more passed under its aegis.

Of more practical benefit to the city, its local *corregidor,* Juan Miguel de Vera, had erected two small stockades in 1730 to protect the approaches to its anchorage: a 12-gun redoubt at Punta Gorda, covering the main channel between the Ubilla Islands, plus another 8-gun fortress on Sono Island. Four years later, the total population for Guayaquil's district was measured at 12,000 Spaniards, plus many thousands of mulatto and Indian laborers, as well as black slaves. The city itself remained quite small, however, while its shipbuilding

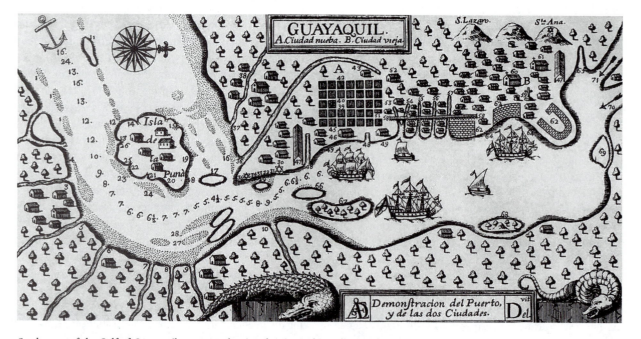

Crude map of the Gulf of Guayaquil, ca. 1730, showing the city and its adjacent shipyard disproportionately large; north is toward right. (Alsedo y Herrera, *Compendio histórico,* 1741)

industry—employing many skilled mulatto craftsmen—went into a steep decline as larger and better-built vessels began reaching the Pacific from France.

The governorship of Guayaquil was separated from that of Quito in 1763, allowing for some small measure of local autonomy, and a census taken the next year enumerated 4,914 inhabitants living within its city limits. Unfortunately, another accidental fire swept through Guayaquil's tight concentration of wooden structures that same year of 1764, requiring extensive reconstruction. The economy nevertheless prospered and the number of its inhabitants steadily increased, thanks to a series of reforms implemented throughout South America by Madrid during the 1770s that eased many trade restrictions, so that the seaport and its district began to enjoy an export boom of cacao. The entire delta's population grew as impoverished Indians were lured down out of the Andes, hoping to win a better life by working as manual laborers or gaining a small *huasipungo* (land plot) to cultivate as indentured farmers. The Crown's liberalization efforts culminated when Guayaquil was declared a limited *puerto de comercio libre* (free port) early in 1800, and the first large-scale cacao haciendas (estates) began appearing throughout its interior.

Partly because of its newfound prosperity and partly because of its backward setting, Guayaquil remained loyal to the Crown when Latin America's struggle for independence erupted in 1808. The city was spared any direct involvement until early February 1816, when three insurgent warships—the 28-gun, 200-man Argentine frigate *Hércules* of Irish-born Capt. William Brown; the brig *Trinidad* under his younger brother, Michael Brown; and the 16-gun, 130-man Chilean corvette *Halcón* under French-born Hipolite Bouchard—entered the Gulf with seven prizes, detaching a contingent upstream that captured the small defenses near the city during a nocturnal assault, before Michael Brown's crew were taken prisoner after the *Trinidad* ran aground. These captives were exchanged on 16 February, when *Hércules* and *Halcón* arrived to directly threaten the city with a bombardment.

Strife (1820–1834)

Eventually, however, resentment against burdensome royalist war taxes and conscription, as well as news of rebel victories elsewhere throughout the Americas, sparked a popular uprising against Spanish rule on 9 October 1820, so that Guayaquil and its outlying district proclaimed themselves an independent state. The city now boasted approximately 13,000 inhabitants spread over eighty urban blocks, and it raised a volunteer militia division to march northeastward under Luis Urdaneta and Febres Cordero to help liberate Quito. But although this force defeated a monarchist contingent under *Audiencia* President and Gen. Melchor Aymerich near Guaranda on 9 November, they were crushed thirteen days later at Huachi near Ambato by a royalist counterexpedition

Map of the city, as surveyed in July 1770 by the military engineer Francisco Requena. (Servicio Histórico Militar, Madrid)

under Col. Francisco González, who compelled the survivors to retreat toward the coast.

Guayaquil was nonetheless retained for the insurgent cause when Simón Bolívar's most trusted and able subordinate—Antonio José de Sucre—arrived in mid-May 1821 with 700 troops, a reinforcement that enabled the city's patriot authorities to weather two mutinies. One, on 17 July, began when a garrison company rebelled and commandeered the anchored corvette *Alejandro*, shelling Guayaquil's wharf before being driven out to sea by its batteries. Nicolás López's infantry battalion then revolted at Babahoyo two days later, marching east up into the Andes in the hope of joining Aymerich at

Guaranda, only to be overtaken and decimated at Palo Largo by several of Sucre's pursuing dragoon squadrons. The year concluded with Sucre signing a temporary armistice on 19 November with Aymerich's representative, Col. Carlos Tolrá, whereby the royalists agreed to retire up into the mountains around Riobamba, while the patriots remained concentrated around their coastal stronghold of Guayaquil.

On 11 January 1822, the Spanish frigates *Venganza* and *Prueba* contacted Sucre, offering to switch allegiance and bring their vessels into Guayaquil in exchange for payments to their disgruntled crews. Four days later they received 80,000 pesos, and the warships became incorporated into the fledgling Peruvian navy. But the most significant event for the city occurred after Bolívar won a smashing victory against the last royalist army outside Quito on 24 May 1822, securing the *Audiencia* capital and then rushing down to the coast with a large contingent of Colombian troops by 11 July to abolish Guayaquil's independent status two days later, his aim being eventually to annex it into his newfangled "Republic of Gran Colombia." The "Liberator" had acted thus swiftly so as to establish full control over the port before receiving rival Argentine Gen. José Francisco de San Martín at Guayaquil on 26 July to discuss the thorny question of South America's future political development.

As a result of his intervention, Guayaquil became incorporated into Bolívar's Gran Colombia, serving as a provincial subcapital within the Department of the South (modern Ecuador) as of 1824. Yet the port economy had been devastated by trade dislocation and population flight during the war of independence, while the new republic proved spectacularly ineffectual; uncertainty and depression gripped the entire postindependence era.

Jurisdictional disputes also arose with Peru, until Lima dispatched the corvette *Libertad* of Capt. Carlos García del Postigo to intercept vessels off the mouth of the Gulf of Guayaquil in the summer of 1828; the Ecuadorian warships *Pichincha* and *Guayaquileña* counterattacked against the intruders off Punta Malpelo on 31 August, full-scale hostilities being inaugurated when a Peruvian squadron under the French-born Vice Adm. Martín-Jorge Guise imposed a tight blockade and bombarded Guayaquil's defenses on 22 November. His flagship, *Presidente,* grounded and was raked, resulting in the commander's death, but Guise was soon succeeded by Hipólito Bouchard, who maintained this stranglehold until the city offered to capitulate at the end of January 1829, being occupied by the Peruvians from 1 February through 21 July.

Widespread national disillusionment against the chaotic maladministration provided by distant Bogotá encouraged

Cacahueros or "cacao handlers" in a commercial house's sorting yard, ca. 1909. (*El Ecuador: guía comercial*)

secession from Gran Colombia in May 1830, a breakaway "Republic of Ecuador" being created by that same September, with the Venezuelan-born Gen. Juan José Flores elected as its first president. But his attempts to concentrate power in the highland capital of Quito were resented at Guayaquil, fueling continuous frictions, until the coastal strongman Gen. Vicente Rocafuerte finally defeated a Quitan army at Miñarica early in 1835 and advanced up into the Andes to seize the presidency for the next four years.

Revival and Reoccupation (1835–1860)

Guayaquil benefited from this ascension of its local champion, as well as from a simultaneous boom in cacao demand overseas that began transforming the port and its district into one of the leading suppliers to the world market. Rocafuerte's regime meanwhile allocated more revenues to the coastland and initiated a few modest reforms in public education and social welfare for the Indians before Flores could regain office in 1839.

Progress nonetheless continued unabated at Guayaquil, whose urban population rose from only 13,093 residents the next year—a figure virtually unchanged from the late-colonial numbers of two decades previously—to 14,740 people by 1843, despite a yellow-fever epidemic that had claimed 4,000 lives and caused almost half the inhabitants to abandon their homes temporarily in 1842. This upsurge was encouraged by the introduction of steam-driven paddle boats (the first having been launched at a Guayaquil shipyard on 7 August 1841), which greatly facilitated river traffic deeper into the delta, opening up its 25,000 square miles of fertile terrain for development.

Flores was driven into exile by a revolution in 1845, and the young republic slid into a period of weakened central rule, with autonomous town governments coming to predominate. Guayaquil's population grew to 23,207 residents by 1857, when the bankrupt national authorities in Quito sought to pay off some British debts by granting Amazonian border areas for exploitation. But as these territories were also claimed by Peru, Lima retaliated by sending a squadron under Rear Adm. Ignacio Mariátegui to blockade the mouth of the Gulf of Guayaquil in early November 1858. A tense standoff ensued until the Peruvian president—Field Marshal Ramón Castilla—concluded an anti-Ecuadorian pact with Colombia that ensuing September, freeing him to disembark with more than 5,000 troops and to capture the seaport and its district by mid-November.

Castilla signed the so-called Treaty of Mapasingue with Guayaquil's local strongman, Gen. Guillermo Franco, on 25 January 1860, seemingly signaling the port district's permanent annexation by Peru. But, galvanized by the threat of possibly losing both Ecuador's wealthiest province and its best outlet to the Pacific, nationalist forces rallied behind Dr. Gabriel García Moreno, who marched down from Quito into the coastal lowlands and reclaimed Guayaquil that same 24 September after a series of military clashes with Franco.

Tentative Modernization (1861–1894)

As a result of his victory, García Moreno became president the next year, then settled down to unify Ecuador through an iron-fisted and austerely religious regime. The Catholic Church received complete charge over national education, while a concordat signed with the Vatican in 1863 ensured a prominent clerical representation in civic affairs. The clergy, army, and prisons were all reformed, while roads were improved and a rail line commenced to supplement the inadequate wagon trail running between the capital and Guayaquil—it was known as Vía Flores and was passable only three to six months each year because of frequent rainfalls.

Despite being relegated to a subordinate political status under this new conservative administration, the seaport nonetheless continued its commercial rise toward prosperity and modernity, especially after its first riverboat company was formed in 1866, ushering in an era in which 100- to 250-ton paddle steamers—many prefabricated in Wilmington, Delaware—began radiating ever more deeply into the delta, opening up vast new tracts for exploitation. Such a swift and inexpensive means of bulk transport allowed cacao production to flourish on to a much larger scale, at a time when international demand was furthermore skyrocketing: milk was being mixed with chocolate for the first time in Switzerland during that same decade to produce an insatiable global appetite.

Guayaquil served as a commercial hub for the haciendas mushrooming all along the silted banks beyond the city, while already-existing small or low-yield operations made way for bigger, more industrialized plantations. River access to Guayaquil became so paramount that if a stream course shifted, as oftentimes occurred, an estate might simply be abandoned by its owner in favor of a better site. The introduction of a heartier Venezuelan strain of cacao plant also helped accelerate this expansion, as operations could now spread into the previously unprofitable hill country. Impoverished migrant workers came down out of the Andes in droves to participate in this boom, swelling the labor base all along the coastline.

Soon, roughly two-thirds of the world's cacao was being shipped out of Guayaquil, and the city continued to expand as a result. Gas streetlights made their appearance by 1870, with slightly brighter electric ones being installed three years later. The first sewers were dug in 1881, the first streetcars circulated the next year, and an aqueduct to bring freshwater was commenced as of 1886—although all of these projects proceeded fitfully and could scarcely keep pace with the population influx, whose numbers escalated from 25,866 residents living among 169 blocks in 1880 to 36,000 crowded into 182 blocks only two years later and 43,460 residents by 1887. The piers receiving oceangoing ships, river steamers, and smaller *balsas*

The steamer *Lautaro* idling off Guayaquil, ca. 1909; such small riverboats opened up Guayaquil's fertile hinterland for large-scale commercial exploitation during the second half of the nineteenth century. (*El Ecuador: guía comercial*)

(boats) also grew from fifteen that same year to thirty-seven by 1896, while businesses became densely packed all along the waterfront. French and German agents controlled most of the exports, while the British monopolized shipping and imports.

Ascendancy (1895–1925)

Guayaquil's newfound wealth and progress even came to resound in national politics, as its Liberal sentiments coalesced behind the *costeño* (coastal) strongman, Gen. Eloy Alfaro—who had previously been engaged in Liberal movements in Central America—and that led to his successful revolt against Ecuador's Conservative *serrano* (highland) rulers in 1894. Alfaro's army captured Quito the next year, and he assumed the presidency in 1897 under a new Liberal constitution that severely curtailed the Conservative policies and influence of the Church, while diverting funds to the seaport for improvements in public health, utilities, and other services.

Guayaquil was in considerable need of such assistance, as a major fire had erupted at 7:45 P.M. on 5 October 1896 in La Joya boutique near its waterfront, gutting 92 blocks by the following evening with a loss of 36 lives, and leaving as many as 18,000 out of some 55,000 residents homeless. Scarcely had the city commenced to recuperate, when a second conflagration started in the San Agustín Church on 16 July 1902, consuming another 26 of the city's 417 blocks. These twin disasters prompted municipal authorities to purchase the most modern firefighting equipment available from the United States and to revise their building codes so as to create wider streets, as well as lower and less flammable structures. This new equipment

went into service on 1 January 1905, water pressure being heightened by three large new holding tanks installed atop Santa Ana Hill, measures that effectively ended the city's centuries-old threat of fire.

That same year of 1905, Guayaquil's urban population was measured at a robust 81,650 people, and the next year Alfaro—who had been succeeded by his rival, Gen. Leónidas Plaza Gutiérrez—seized the presidency again through dint of arms. The seaport benefited materially from his second term, with new public buildings being constructed and the lengthy railway to the capital at last being completed in 1908 (although at such immense expense and burdened with such heavy operating costs as to render it virtually unprofitable). Visits to the austere Andean capital also underscored traditional regional prejudices, many Guayaquileños viewing their Quitan counterparts as cold, sanctimonious snobs whom they derisively dismissed as *longos* (obsequious houseboys), while the Quitans in turn regarded their swarthier and wealthier coastal cousins as immoral, money-grubbing *monos* (monkeys).

Although Alfaro and his top supporters were murdered by an angry mob at Quito in 1912, and Plaza finished a second term amid formidable opposition, Guayaquil nonetheless continued to dominate the nation economically through the strength of its foreign trade, as well as such influential institutions as its Commercial and Agricultural Bank. Sugar cultivation and light manufacturing had also increased, while Ecuador's petroleum industry was born thanks to overseas demand generated by World War I. Guayaquil's first movie theater—The Eden—had opened in 1912, followed four years

Rare photograph of new firefighting equipment being tested in Rocafuerte Plaza on 1 January 1905, with San Francisco Church barely visible at upper right; this innovation ended the recurrent threat of conflagrations racing through the city's mostly wooden structures. (*El Ecuador: guía comercial*)

later by a soccer stadium, while a census taken in 1919 revealed that its population had increased to 91,842.

The post–World War I recession, agricultural blight, and collapse of international prices for cacao created such hardship in the city, however, that Guayaquil's trolley and power company employees—inspired by an earlier and successful railroad strike—walked off their jobs in the autumn of 1922, soon being joined by virtually all other labor associations. This protest was crushed when a massive downtown rally was dispersed on 15 November by indiscriminate gunfire from the police and army, resulting in at least 300 deaths, so that the city economy struggled to rebound. In 1925, the Ecuadorian army—composed chiefly of *serranos*—toppled President Gonzalo Córdova in a coup at Quito, ending the seaport's domination of the nation by substituting rule through military junta.

Modern Evolution (1926–Present)

Although Guayaquil continued to grow, it suffered considerable economic and social problems because of the global effects of the Great Depression which started in October 1929, as well as a lack of assistance from the capital. The Liberal candidate Car-

los Arroyo del Río was elected president in 1940, but he became embroiled in a costly border dispute with Peru in July of the next year, so that a blockade was imposed upon Guayaquil and its trade suffered until that conflict could be concluded through the surrender of a large section of Ecuador's Amazonian claims in January 1942.

Arroyo del Río stifled all internal dissatisfaction against this defeat, but when he attempted to engineer the election of his handpicked successor in 1944, he was overthrown and replaced by the coastal-based Conservative populist and former president, José María Velasco Ibarra. His administration too was hampered by the post–World War II recession and political infighting, resulting in Velasco Ibarra's ouster by the army in August 1947. Guayaquil nevertheless continued to grow exponentially over the ensuing decades, as rural-to-urban migration accelerated throughout Latin America. The city population mushroomed from 315,000 in 1950 (266,000 within the municipal boundaries proper) to slightly more than half a million by 1962 and 861,000 by 1974. Authorities struggled to meet the needs of such unbridled expansion, many residents still living in grinding poverty. The official measure for 1994 estimated a population of 1,500,000,

La Infatigable or "The Indefatigable" steam-driven sawmill at Guayaquil, ca. 1909. (*El Ecuador: guía comercial*)

although it was believed the actual figure stood closer to 2.4 million due to severe undercounting among many unregulated slums.

For further reading materials on Guayaquil or Ecuador, please consult the Select Bibliography at the end of this volume; additional sources on South American urban history can be found under "Regional Studies," as well as under "General Works on Latin America."

QUITO

Ancient Incan capital that, because of its remote highland setting and devout Catholicism during the Spanish era, earned the sobriquet of "cloister of the Andes."

Indigenous Origins (900 B.C.E.–1533 C.E.)

The small Hoya del Guayllabamba (Guayllabamba Dell), a bottleneck lying at 9,350 feet above sea level amid the great central plateau of the inter-Andean basin, has been inhabited since at least 900 B.C.E. because of its stable water supply and fertile surroundings. During the second half of the fifteenth century, the powerful new Incan empire began making inroads into the tribal lands of the first inhabitants, called the Shiri, out

of the south through a series of military campaigns, strategic alliances, and cultural assimilation. Emperor Túpac Yupanqui's reign from 1471 to 1493 saw a renewed offensive establish a string of Inca garrisons at Quinchicaxa, Azuay, Pomallacta, and Tiocajas. Then, during a second major drive, Incan armies finally overran Quito itself, despite desperate resistance from the local *sinche* (chieftain) Pillaguaso and his Tumibamba allies under the rebel Inca leader Pisar Cápac.

Impressed by his newly conquered and densely populated valley, Emperor Túpac Yupanqui decreed that Quito should be transformed into a central stronghold commanding its own circuit of fortresses, and so he installed a sizable garrison and imported numerous *mitimas* (vassal workers) to upgrade its rather primitive urban layout and infrastructure. His son Huayna Cápac then crushed a revolt in the northern territories and expanded Incan influence still further by subjugating the hostile Cayambi and Caranqui nations by 1520–1521, in the process improving and developing Quito.

Huayna Cápac's demise in 1527 resulted in a succession struggle between the elder princeling, Huáscar, headquartered in the old imperial capital of Cuzco far to the south, and Atahualpa, who transformed Quito into a new northern capi-

Panoramic view across Quito, ca. 1920. (*Monografía ilustrada de la provincia de Pichincha,* 1922)

tal by erecting monumental structures to service his own particular administrative and religious elite. Within the next few years, this northern faction defeated its southern opponents, so that Atahualpa's armies occupied Cuzco and took Huáscar captive. Yet before he could fully consummate his hold upon power, Atahualpa learned late in 1532 of the disembarkation of a small yet powerful new force out of the northwest: 60 Spanish riders and 106 foot soldiers from Panama under hard-bitten Francisco Pizarro, who pushed boldly up into the Andes.

The emperor met these strangers at Cajamarca on 15 November 1532, surrounded by one of his vast armies. Yet the following evening, he was seized while visiting Pizarro's lodgments, and his awestruck troops did nothing when several thousand courtiers were massacred, after which the Incan army dispersed. The empire remained supine for the next nine months, although the northern general Rumiñahui seized partial power by marching into Quito with his army and deposing the captive emperor's uncle and regent, Cozopangui, as well as holding the imperial offspring. Finally, Pizarro—well informed about conditions in the empire and reinforced by

more Spanish troops—executed Atahualpa and marched into the southern realm from Cajamarca on 11 August 1533. The conquistadors encountered hostility from its Quitan occupiers, yet they were greeted as liberators by the oppressed Cuzcan inhabitants; they therefore entered the southern capital without resistance on 15 November, while the main Quitan army fled northward under its general Quizquíz or Quisquís.

Quito became the core of Incan resistance until Pedro de Alvarado—famous for his earlier role in defeating the Aztecs of Mexico—landed at Caráquez near Portoviejo (Ecuador) in February 1534 with 500 rival conquistadors and 4,000 auxiliaries from Guatemala, striking inland toward Guayaquil. Concerned that this redoubtable challenger might appropriate the northern portion of the Incan empire, Pizarro's subordinate Sebastián de Belalcázar (alternate spellings: Benalcázar, Velalcázar) set out from San Miguel de Piura early in March with 200 Spanish soldiers and several hundred Cañari allies, hoping to conquer Quito preemptively, in advance of the intruders. His column smashed through several Quitan outposts, then defeated Rumiñahui's main concentration on the plains outside Tiocajas on 3–4 May, before detouring down into the

Young Huasicana native woman, ca. 1876; engraving by E. Ronjat, from an original photograph by Edouard André. (*Le Tour du Monde*)

lowlands and reascending the Andes around Lake Colta and Riobamba.

Spanish Conquest (1534)

Powerless to deflect the superior weaponry and cavalry of Belalcázar's approaching conquistadors, Rumiñahui ordered Quito's main edifices torched and his capital evacuated on 17 June 1534. The Spanish army fought its way in five days later, pressing eastward in pursuit of the fleeing Incas, while vassal tribes began switching allegiance and turning against their former overlords. After a monthlong sweep, Belalcázar returned into Quito, which was devastated once again when Rumiñahui launched a sudden attack out of the mountains: a

stealthy nocturnal descent by 15,000 warriors, who were checked at its ramparts by the defenders, then scattered by a cavalry charge the next dawn as numerous thatched-roof adobe neighborhoods went up in flames.

Belalcázar's superior, Diego de Almagro, then recalled him and his army almost 100 miles south to Sicalpa (near Riobamba) in August 1534 to jointly confront Alvarado, who was expected to emerge near Ambato. In a legal move designed to underscore his exclusive claim over all northern Incan territories, Almagro went through the fiction of founding a new Spanish municipality on 15 August called Santiago de Quito—even to the point of granting land plots to sixty-seven of his soldiers, although noting that these titles were "to be transferred later to a more advantageous spot." By these means, he could appeal any disputed ownership to Madrid. Yet when Alvarado's host finally materialized shortly thereafter, it had been greatly debilitated by its harsh trans-Andean crossing, losing eighty-five men and almost all its horses; a deal was therefore struck on 26 August, whereby Almagro agreed to buy Alvarado's ships and equipment for 100,000 pesos, while the latter returned to Guatemala and left his survivors in Peru under Pizarro's orders.

Almagro decreed two days later that the former north Incan capital should be repopulated as a Spanish town and be renamed San Francisco del Quito; municipal officers were even appointed in anticipation of that event, while Belalcázar was named lieutenant governor for its entire province, with 400 to 500 soldiers under his command. Almagro and Alvarado departed toward Peru, clashing en route with Quizquíz's retreating army, whose morale collapsed upon sighting Quito and finding it destroyed and its remnants occupied. When the Inca general ordered his officers to march on into another remote Andean sector to continue resistance, he was murdered. Belalcázar hunted down or dispersed all remaining native contingents over the next several weeks, marking a virtual end to Incan rule.

Refoundation and Early Colonial Era (1535–1562)

It was not until 6 December 1534 that Belalcázar reached Quito. He began reconstituting it as a Spanish town by chairing the first meeting of its *cabildo* (town council), which represented 204 would-be citizens. Indian vassals were to be resettled into adjoining suburbs, while a diagram of a proposed new central core was drafted a few days later—today, unfortunately, lost. Quito's first alcalde (magistrate), Juan de Ampudia, was assigned more than 10,000 indigenous laborers to begin leveling the remnants of Incan buildings, replacing them with Spanish-style structures made of recycled masonry and wood hewn from nearby copses.

This work effectively erased all vestiges of the old Incan capital, a Spanish gridiron pattern being superimposed upon its ancient street layout. The new Franciscan monastery, for example, was erected atop several former indigenous palaces,

One of the city's characteristic *quebradas* "or ravines," ca. 1917. (Franck, *Vagabonding Down the Andes*)

The brisk mountain climate and verdant, somewhat treeless landscape—reminiscent of Toledo or Valladolid in central Spain—proved attractive to migrants and preferable to the pestilential tropical coasts. Yet Quito's single greatest allure was to be its vast expanse of farmlands and villages, whose residents (variously estimated at 750,000 to a million inhabitants at contact) had previously been serfs of the Incas; they now were reassigned among the victors in land grants known as *encomiendas* (protectorates), an arrangement whereby each Indian community was obliged to pay taxes and perform personal services for a specific Spanish *encomendero* in exchange for protection and rudimentary religious indoctrination. Missionaries quickly set about this evangelization: one such was the Belgian-born Franciscan superior Jodoco Ricke, who furthermore gathered indigenous artisans under the tutelage of Spanish instructors into what became the first art school in the Americas and also introduced wheat cultivation to the district.

The valley's seemingly inexhaustible labor pool and fertile terrain tempted many conquistadors into settling down, using Quito as a central spot to develop outlying haciendas (estates)—although not without difficulties, for Incan raids continued, while the serf population soon began a calamitous decline because of the appearance of epidemic diseases. Government authority also remained chaotic, Belalcázar departing Quito in January 1536 to explore, so that Pizarro replaced him as lieutenant governor on 8 March with Pedro Puelles. But although the latter arrived by 28 May and was ceded all of Belalcázar's properties, this decision was overturned and Belalcázar was reinstated by 7 July 1537. Almagro feuded even more seriously with Pizarro over distribution of spoils, being killed in July 1538; Belalcázar had already departed eastward again that same February with the bulk of his troops and 5,000 auxiliaries to help conquer Colombia. Yet despite this and other misadventures that reduced Quito's Spanish householders to a mere 160, the fledgling town thrived and was elevated to the status of city by a royal decree issued in Spain on 14 March 1541.

Quito even reverted to its former role of northern capital when the first Crown-appointed Peruvian viceroy—Blasco Núñez Vela, in office scarcely four months—was deposed by Lima's *Audiencia* (high tribunal) in September 1544 for his heavy-handed zeal in implementing Spain's new laws to protect the Indians, then was banished the next month by the usurper Gonzalo Pizarro. Freed while being conducted toward Panama, Núñez Vela disembarked at Piura and made his way inland to Quito, vainly attempting to organize a rival administration. He departed Quito on 4 March 1545, but was chased back through the city by Pizarro, who finally defeated and killed the luckless viceroy on 18 January 1546 at the Battle of Añaquito (modern spelling: Iñaquito, a low and marshy plain just north of Quito). The city naturally suffered from these campaigns, but another Crown emissary—Lic. Pedro de la Gasca—arrived from Spain that same autumn and advanced through its district in 1547,

even taking over their aqueduct from the Pichincha Springs. Pizarro confirmed the new town's legal status by a decree issued at "Pachacamac" (modern Lima) on 22 January 1535, so that plots could be duly allocated to citizens in a formal ceremony, celebrated that same 12 July.

These early inhabitants were pleased with their surroundings, although somewhat hampered by two deep *quebradas* (ravines) and a river running through their settlement, as well as numerous lesser gullies and ridges radiating down from the dormant, 15,550-foot Guagüa-Pichincha Volcano to its west. The town also lay at the heart of an already existing network of Incan roads and outposts, while its low position within the Guayllabamba Basin afforded some protection against the chill Andean winds. Municipal boundaries would eventually stretch as far north as Carlosama and as far south as Tixán, while Belalcázar's administrative scope as lieutenant governor proved still broader: south as far as the province of Pomallacta or Alausí, north to the Quillacinga River (near the modern border with Colombia), west to the Pacific plains, and east to Hatun-Quijos Province.

Modern rendering of Quito's coat-of-arms, originally issued in March 1541. (Author's Collection)

winning adherents. He eventually used Quito as a springboard to overwhelm Pizarro near Cuzco in April 1548.

Audiencia Seat (1563–1764)

The city having been ruled since its inception by governors appointed from Lima, Quito's residents petitioned the Crown on 4 July 1560 to have their own separate *Audiencia* created, with a jurisdiction extending from the Pacific port of Buenaventura in the north to Paita in the south. That measure was duly approved at Guadalajara, Spain, on 29 August 1563, the small city gaining greatly in prestige from this new court's activities, which encompassed administrative, political, and military functions, beyond mere civil and criminal cases.

Ten years later, the city had 1,500 inhabitants spread among 300 dwellings in an eight-block circuit around its main square, serviced by fourteen stores. But only its cathedral and Franciscan church had been completed in stone, while the Domini-

can and Mercedarian convents were still modest structures; most other edifices consisted of brick-and-adobe walls topped with thatched roofs. There were only 100 heads of Spanish households, a garrison of 300 soldiers, and eight priests. The indigenous population continued to decline, the overall population of Quito and its district falling from 240,670 people in 1561 to 118,141 by 1586. Its isolation was such that its *Audiencia* was reduced to only three members and no president for a half dozen years before replacements could arrive.

Quito was then struck by a damaging earthquake in August 1587, after which an epidemic swept down from Cartagena (Colombia), claiming thousands of lives within the next couple of months. Quito's district moreover did not possess the great mineral wealth found in southern Peru, nor did it lie on any major trade routes, so that its exports were limited to rough woolen textiles from rural mills that brought little money into the depressed capital. When the Crown informed Quito's *cabildo* at the end of July 1592 that a 2 percent *alcabala* sales tax was to be imposed upon even these few transactions, popular outrage coalesced behind the spokesman Alonso Moreno Bellido.

His incarceration on orders from the unpopular *Audiencia* president, Dr. Manuel Barros de San Millán, was breached by an angry mob of disgruntled citizens and soldiers on the night of 28 September 1592, so that the Peruvian viceroy, García Hurtado de Mendoza, Marqués de Cañete, dispatched sixty troops under Capt. Pedro de Arana to Guayaquil to advance up into the Andes and quell the rebellion. Excitement gripped Quito upon the expedition's approach that same December; the freed Moreno Bellido was murdered, after which a mob hunted down and imprisoned the *Audiencia* president in retaliation. Negotiations through the royal *visitador* (inspector), Esteban Marañón, finally hammered out an agreement by March 1593 whereby the city would accept the new tax and peacefully receive Arana's troops in exchange for a general pardon. But when the force entered on 10 April, they initiated a dozen summary executions the following dawn.

Quito resigned itself to a period of peaceful development, its agricultural self-sufficiency and safe remove from foreign seaborne raiders along the coast precluding any necessity for expensive military defenses. As the the seventeenth century progressed, its educational institutions such as the Real Colegio de San Fernando and the Universidad de Santo Tomás attained considerable prestige as regional centers of learning. Commercially, its district also became a renown textile exporting region, although these were usually rural operations, not necessarily headquartered in Quito.

During the early eighteenth century, the city economy further improved by shifting from overdependence upon exports of rough woolen textiles to more profitable crops such as sugarcane, only to then undergo another marked slump during the 1750s. A heavy earthquake in 1755, plus outbreaks of epidemics in 1759 and 1765, worsened this plight, so that when

Panorama looking westward across the city, drawn by Dionisio Alsedo y Herrera in 1734, with the Pichincha Volcano serving as backdrop; north is toward upper right. (Archive of Indies, Seville)

a Crown official named Juan Díaz de Herrera arrived to implement more changes in the imperial revenue collection system, specifically by transferring the *aguardiente* (cane liquor) monopoly from local licensees back under treasury control, as well as expanding the scope of the *alcabala* sales tax, he was met with worried resentment.

Civic leaders expected a loss of income as a result of this former reform (which furthermore threatened to increase the sales price of *aguardiente*), while the lower classes feared additional burdens during a period of economic depression; many of those who had been left unemployed by the closure of textile mills had found new jobs in the burgeoning "underground" trades, such as small-time grocers, butchers, tanners, barkeeps, and the like, which would now become subject to the new *alcabala*. Outlying haciendas and farms would also see their levies raised.

Revolt and Late Colonial Era (1765–1807)

In spite of such widely expressed objections, the new *alcabala* was instituted on 21 May 1765 and immediately affected many people who had previously been exempt, such as ecclesiastics and the Indians who supplied Quito's marketplace. The

following evening, therefore, a mob several thousand strong—summoned out of the poorer neighborhoods by pealing church bells and fireworks—demolished the royal customshouse and a distillery in Santa Bárbara Square, then plunged the city into several weeks of uncertainty and turmoil. The heavily outnumbered Spanish authorities attempted to restore order a month later by arresting more than two score troublemakers and punishing them with public floggings and duckings in water. Yet that served only to incite a second major outburst on the evening of 24 June that quickly escalated into mob violence when some peninsular Spaniards fired into a group in the San Sebastián suburb, killing two or three people.

The *Audiencia* building and homes of many prominent peninsulars were stormed, the crowd even overrunning the armory and calling for the expulsion of every unmarried Spanish resident from Quito. Effective government rule having collapsed, a broad-based popular coalition of local Creoles appointed "captains" throughout the neighborhoods and surrounding district in early July; they attempted to contain the occasional signs of unrest, although wilder spirits even called for full independence from Spain. However, once passions cooled, political differences began to emerge between each affected class and ethnic group, along with fears regarding the city's vulnerability to an Indian descent out of the hinterland. Over the course of the ensuing year, these latent divisions slowly sapped the coalition's unity and hastened the peaceful return of royal control, so that when a column of viceregal troops finally entered Quito on 1 September 1766 under the conciliatory governor of Guayaquil, Antonio de Zelaya, they were received enthusiastically.

Quito gradually resumed its somnolent existence, although feelings of autonomy were to remain intact in their isolation high up in the Andes and manifest themselves once more a generation later.

Insurgency (1808–1821)

Like every other Spanish-American city, Quito was shaken by news that a French army had entered Madrid in March 1808 and that King Ferdinand VII had been deposed two months later in favor of Joseph Bonaparte. Most Spaniards chose to resist this foreign usurpation of power, their resistance coalescing around an interim junta (council) established at Aran-

juez in September 1808 to uphold their captive monarch's cause. Yet the ensuing interlude of political uncertainty also allowed for the first stirrings toward full independence throughout the empire. Already, many mixed-heritage Creoles had grown weary of the preference routinely afforded peninsular-born Spaniards, as well as trade and taxation measures intended to favor the home country. Now, in this new unfettered climate, they began contemplating nationhood.

As a result, around 10:00 P.M. on the night of 9 August 1809, a group of Liberal conspirators led by Dr. Juan de Dios Morales launched an uprising at Quito by first securing the adherence of its 180-man garrison, then the next dawn detaining the elderly *Audiencia* president, Manuel Urriez, Conde de Ruiz de Castilla, replacing him with their own junta under the titular leadership of the wealthy landowner Juan Pío María de Montúfar y Larrea, Marqués de Selva Negra, and Bishop José Cuero y Caicedo. However, neighboring districts refused to acknowledge this abrupt change of administration, despite the junta's claim to be acting in the name of Ferdinand VII. Moreover, Quito's 30,000 residents soon found themselves cut off, and the

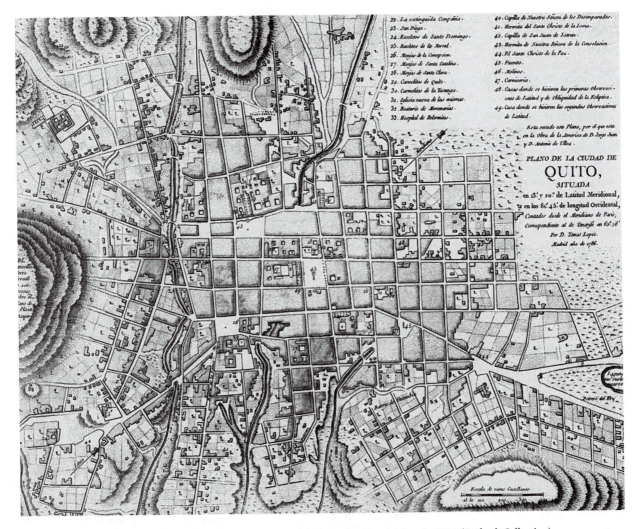

Map of the city, published in Madrid by the royal geographer and cartographer Tomás López in 1786. (Author's Collection)

Peruvian viceroy, José Fernando de Abascal y Sousa, dispatched 500 troops under Lt. Col. Manuel Arredondo toward Babahoyo, who were heavily reinforced by other regional militias as they advanced up into the Andes. Faced with such widespread opposition, the Quito assembly dissolved amid much bickering, Selva Alegre resigning by 13 October, after which Ruiz de Castilla was allowed to reassume office twelve days later. When Arredondo's column finally arrived on 24 November, numerous arrests and trials ensued.

Less than a year later—on the afternoon of 2 August 1810—a desperate attempt was made to free the captives, but it was bloodily put down by the Peruvian garrison at a cost of more than 200 lives (including 70 prisoners). Shortly thereafter, however, the Peruvian contingent was withdrawn and Carlos Montúfar, a Quiteño, arrived from Spain with a mandate to resolve local issues. He sided with those local leaders favoring autonomy, so that a second junta was peacefully convened on 22 September 1810, again containing many Liberal members. Fighting once more erupted with Quito's neighbors, however, and although a new constitution was eventually promulgated in February 1812, a royalist army under Gen. Toribio Montes fought its way past the Quitan strongpoint atop 600-foot Panecillo Hill and into the largely deserted city by 7 November of that same year, ending this brief experiment in self-government.

Despite other insurgent eruptions elsewhere, the capital remained firmly in royalist hands throughout much of South America's ensuing struggle for independence, although somewhat isolated from Spain because Colombia was controlled by rebel factions until the spring of 1816. Then Guayaquil, too, opted for independence as of October 1820, dispatching a volunteer division northeastward under Luis Urdaneta with the intent of assaulting Quito, until they were defeated on 22 November at Huachi near Ambato by a royalist counterexpedition under Col. Francisco González. Nevertheless, the insurgent foothold at Guayaquil was fully secured when Simón Bolívar's most trusted and able subordinate, Antonio José de Sucre Alcalá, arrived there in mid-May 1821 with 700 patriot troops as a seaborne reinforcement. The next year, the two patriot commanders began closing in upon royalist Quito, Bolívar by pushing southwestward out of Popayán (Colombia) with 3,000 troops, while Sucre advanced northeastward up out of Guayaquil, overrunning Riobamba by 21 April 1822.

One month later, Sucre came within sight of Quito, marching along the Machachi road on 23 May 1822 with his 2,160 infantrymen, 400 cavalrymen, plus forty gunners for two artillery pieces. As night fell, he circled westward to avoid its Panecillo defenses, instead taking up position in the Pichincha foothills and thus compelling the outflanked *Audiencia* president, Gen. Melchor Aymerich, to redeploy his own 1,700 royalist troops and brace for an assault. The so-called Battle of Pichincha began at 9:30 the next morning, and by noon the royalists had been defeated, suffering 400 dead and 200

wounded, compared with 200 killed and 140 injured among the patriot ranks. The city having being lost, Aymerich and his surviving soldiers remained ensconced within their Panecillo redoubt until 25 May, at which time they capitulated.

Departmental Capital (1822–1830)

In the popular euphoria following this triumph, it was decided on 29 May 1822 to submit to Bolívar's wishes and incorporate Quito and its entire jurisdiction into the newfangled Republic of Gran Colombia, the former *Audiencia* territory consequently becoming known for a while as the Departamento del Sur (Southern Department). However, within the next few years discontent spread against the chaotic maladministration provided by this inexperienced and self-serving government in distant Bogotá, so that on 13 May 1830 the Quitans separated and formed their own independent Republic of Ecuador, exactly one week after the Venezuelans had also withdrawn from the same untenable union.

The austerely Conservative Dr. Gabriel García Moreno seized control of the national government in 1860, quieting opponents with repressive measures over the next fifteen years

The presidential residence, ca. 1909, with an honor guard wearing Prussian-style helmets stationed outside. (*El Ecuador: guía comercial*)

Quito's *Plaza Independencia* or "Independence Square," ca. 1920. (*Monografía ilustrada de la provincia de Pichincha*, 1922)

Quito's University, ca. 1920. (*Monografía ilustrada de la provincia de Pichincha*, 1922)

Typical street scene in Quito, ca. 1920; note the *Peluquería La Americana* or "The American Barbershop" sign at left. (*Monografía ilustrada de la provincia de Pichincha,* 1922)

and thereby providing some measure of stability to the impoverished nation and its capital. However, he was assassinated on the steps of the capitol in 1875, and Gen. Ignacio Veintemilla emerged as his successor the following year, ruling until he too was driven from office by dint of arms in 1883. Up until that point, Quito—with its population of approximately 40,000 people in 1880—had merely been a political prize to be contested and held by rival national factions. There then ensued an interlude of three presidential terms that were all decided by elections, a so-called Progressive Era during which urban amenities increased and some attempts at modernization were introduced to the city.

But civil war resumed in 1895, the Liberal faction spearheaded by Guayaquil's strongman, Gen. Eloy Alfaro, capturing the capital and holding the presidency for the next six years, only to be succeeded by his rival, Gen. Leonidas Plaza Gutiérrez. When the latter named a successor and left the country in 1906, Alfaro again seized office by force of arms. That same year, Quito's population stood at 51,858 people, yet national unrest resurged when Alfaro attempted to retain the presi-

dency in 1911, igniting an especially bloody round of renewed fighting and anarchy. Events finally concluded when Alfaro and his top supporters were murdered by a mob in a most gruesome and public manner in Quito in 1912.

Modern Capital (1922–Present)

It was not until the advent of the centennial of the Battle of Pichincha on 24 May 1922, which commemorated Ecuador's independence from Spain, that a concerted effort was at last undertaken by municipal authorities to modernize and beautify their capital through new building projects, statues, and parks; by extending its water system to service all neighborhoods; and by paving over most streets. Despite a coup that toppled Pres. Gonzalo Córdova three years later, these peaceful innovations in turn attracted more migrants into the city, so that Quito's population swelled from 80,702 people in 1922 to approximately 123,000 ten years later and 150,000 spread among 6,230 dwellings by 1938. The latter year, a precise count was also taken that revealed that the growing metropolis boasted eight banks, five libraries, eighteen churches and ten convents, four hospitals and five medical clinics, a university plus eighteen colleges and schools, nine theaters, seven hotels, three newspapers, three markets, five barracks, but only three factories.

An urban development plan was drafted by the architect Guillermo Jones Odriozola in 1941 that attempted to channel and control future growth, as the expanding city would henceforth find itself increasingly constricted into a confined area between its mountains. Indeed, over the past few decades these geographic features have caused Quito to evolve into a narrow, tapering city, 9 miles long but less than 2 miles wide, as its population has mushroomed from 212,873 people in 1950 to 355,000 by 1962, 687,304 by 1974, and an estimated 1.2 million by 1989. However, despite such rapid growth, Quito still remains one of the smallest capitals in Latin America, and it is not even the largest city in Ecuador; that honor belongs to Guayaquil. To this day, Quito contains relatively little heavy industry, while many of its beautiful colonial-era buildings have survived intact.

For further reading materials on Quito or Ecuador, please consult the Select Bibliography at the end of this volume; additional sources on South American urban history can be found under "Regional Studies," as well as under "General Works on Latin America."

French Guiana

CAYENNE

Tiny capital—not of an independent South American republic, but of an overseas *département* or county of France.

Tentative European Settlements (1568–1663)

It is believed that Galibi war bands migrated northwestward out of the Amazon River Delta into this area as early as 900 C.E., displacing the Caribbean Arawak tribesmen who had lived there for more than a millennium. A fishing village has probably existed in the lee of what is today Cayenne's peninsula since the very earliest times, being sheltered against the prevailing Atlantic winds and currents by its shallow bar.

Christopher Columbus sighted the Guyanese coastline in 1498, yet the main colonizing efforts of both the Spanish and Portuguese crowns were to be subsequently directed into other regions of the continent. The Spaniard Gaspar de Sotelo apparently established a short-lived settlement of 126 families in this district in 1568, only to be driven out five years later by its Galibi inhabitants. English, Dutch, and French seamen therefore found this particular stretch of low, humid coastline still unclaimed at the beginning of the seventeenth century, when passing captains began bartering with local inhabitants for tobacco and other produce. Soon, reports by these transitory visitors encouraged the arrival of permanent settlers of all three nationalities, who wished to establish footholds ashore in order to begin harvesting their own cash crops, warehousing goods, and receiving ships from their homelands. As a result, minor outposts were to be founded throughout the Guianas over the next several decades by private West European companies, most of which succumbed to disease, neglect, the torrid climate, or Indian hostilities.

French efforts began in April 1604, when the explorer Daniel de la Touche, Sieur de la Ravardière, charted the coastline northwestward from Cap du Nord (North Cape, the name then given to the Araguari headland of the Amazon River mouth) before steering for home by 18 May. That same month, the Englishman Charles Leigh came ashore on the western banks of the Oyapock River, establishing a colony that survived for little more than two years. Robert Harcourt revived this English settlement in May 1609, then in August of that same year dropped anchor off of what was later to become Cayenne, reconnoitering its river ways. In the spring of 1615, a group of

The sleepy tropical port of Cayenne, as seen from its sea approaches, ca. 1920. (Franck, *Working North from Patagonia*)

280 Dutch colonists also disembarked near here under Theodore Claessen of Amsterdam before transferring farther west into Surinam.

Although numerous establishments had now come to dot the entire Guyanese shoreline, the first formal attempt to implant a French outpost did not occur until the arrival from Rouen on 25 November 1643 of Charles Poncet, Seigneur de Brétigny, with 400 Norman colonists raised by his Compagnie du Cap Nord. This expedition initially disembarked in the adjacent estuary called Mahoury, or Mahury, finding five Frenchmen already living in its district, plus a few Dutch settlers occupying the Mont Cépérou height to its northwest, which commanded the best anchorage. Legend has it that Cépérou had been the name of the local Galibi chieftain who had ceded this spot to these settlers; Poncet soon reached a like accommodation with this chieftain's son "Caïenne" or Cayenne and was allowed to install his own colony. Plots were duly distributed, and a temporary Capuchin temple was erected at Montabo (modern Conobé Bay); however, the sweltering heat, epidemics, and starvation led to a revolt against Brétigny's hardfisted rule on 4 March 1644, after which some sixty of his disgruntled followers left to join the more promising Anglo-Dutch settlement at Surinam. Freed from incarceration two and a half months later, Brétigny could no longer stem the deterioration of his reduced colony, and he was killed during an Indian insurrection on 14 June 1645. Some forty survivors eventually fled to the West Indian island of St. Kitts, leaving behind another thirty scattered members.

The next French colonizing effort fared no better, beginning when a party of sixty men returned on 24 March 1652 under Captain de Navarre to rebuild the stockade atop Mont Cépérou and plant new crops. But on 28 September of that same year, the ships *Charité* and *Grand Saint-Pierre* also appeared directly from Havre, bearing 800 fresh colonists raised by the rival Compagnie de la France Equinoxiale (more commonly referred to as the Compagnie des Douze Seigneurs, because its finances had been provided by a dozen noblemen). This expedition's original leader—Etienne Le Roux, Sieur de Roiville—was murdered in his bunk during the voyage by his subordinate Vertaumont; the latter came ashore the next day and assumed office as Mont Cépérou's new governor, renaming its stronghold Fort Saint-Michel in honor of Saint Michael's feast day (which falls on 29 September in the Church calendar). Vertaumont began his rule by having its wooden ramparts replaced by a 10-gun stone structure designed by his military engineer, Captain d'Aigremont; then, after installing a 70-man garrison into this completed structure, Vertaumont proceeded to lay out an entirely new residential area that November at Rémire, on the southeastern side of Cayenne's peninsula (which because it is interspersed by numerous waterways and marshes, seemingly separating it from the mainland, became widely known as the Île de Cayenne or "Island of Cayenne").

Disease and miserable living conditions soon took their toll among these newcomers as well, after which they began squabbling among themselves and so antagonized the Galibis that another major uprising erupted on 8 July 1653. Five months later, 400 discouraged survivors set sail westward to seek shelter amid the new English colony of Surinam. Learning of Cayenne's abandonment, a group of Dutch refugees from Recife (Brazil) arrived early in 1654 under Quirijn Spranger, repairing and reoccupying Fort Saint-Michel, which they renamed "Fort Nassau." They were soon reinforced by other independent groups, including sixty experienced Jewish settlers who arrived with eighty slaves in 1656 and erected the first ox-driven sugar mill at Rémire; their leader, David Nassy, then invited more Jews to migrate into this area in September 1659, being joined the following year by another 152 coreligionists from Livorno (Leghorn, Italy).

French Conquest (1664–1678)

At this point, Louis XIV's ambitious new finance minister, Jean-Baptiste Colbert—displeased with the meager inroads

Depiction of the fledgling community of Cayenne in May 1679 by Jean Barbot, who visited aboard the slaver *Soleil d'Afrique*. (British Library)

being achieved by private enterprise—began throwing the full weight of the Crown behind such colonizing ventures, convinced that his government must compete with Holland and Britain through an active mercantilist policy overseas. Consequently, seven vessels bearing more than 1,000 men appeared off Cayenne from La Rochelle on 11 May 1664 under Alexandre de Prouville, Marquis de Tracy, who had been designated as lieutenant-general for all of France's New World territories, with instructions to impose government rule over its various competing companies. Two days later his subordinate Samuel Le Picard, Sieur de Flavigny, demanded that Spranger restore Cayenne to French control, which the outnumbered Dutch were constrained to do by 15 May, marching out of Fort Nassau twelve days later with all of their belongings to transfer to Surinam. Antoine Lefebvre, Seigneur de la Barre, was temporarily installed as governor, Fort Nassau was renamed Fort Saint-Louis, and by the time Tracy's expedition steered northwestward into the Lesser Antilles to continue his tour, it left behind 350 French settlers and 50 black slaves living in approximately 200 thatched-roofed shacks at Cayenne; 100 settlers and 45 slaves, respectively, at nearby Mahoury; 60 and 25 at Rémire; plus another 60 and 25 scattered inland.

Having returned to France in 1665, de la Barre was then promoted to lieutenant-general and secured the appointment of his brother, Ciprien Lefebvre, Chevalier de Lézy, as Cayenne's governor from the newly created Crown corporation, the Compagnie Royale des Indes Occidentales (Royal West Indies Company). However, his fledgling colony was almost extirpated by a destructive English raid during the closing stages of the Second Anglo-Dutch War, in which France had fought on the side of Holland. On 22 September 1667, vessels were seen approaching Cayenne, which Lefebvre de Lézy assumed to be reinforcements sent from Martinique by his brother. Upon circling round from his residence at Mahoury into Fort Saint-Louis at Cayenne, however, he learned that these were actually English warships out of Barbados under Rear Adm. Sir John Harman pursuing a lone French supply frigate, with the further intention of disembarking 850 troops. Alarmed, the governor led 200 men back to join another 100 hastily marshaled at Rémire, then watched as fourteen boatloads of invaders gathered offshore at Père or Cabrittes Isle in anticipation of a landing. But when Harman's fleet shifted menacingly overnight toward Romana (modern Bourda Beach) nearer Cayenne, Lefebvre de Lézy followed this feint, allowing the boat parties to disgorge unopposed the next day at Rémire.

Panic gripped the defenders, who spiked their guns and fled in every direction. It took the English at Rémire six days to discover that Fort Saint-Louis lay abandoned, after which they circled round and leisurely stripped its citadel and surrounding district of everything of value—as well as seizing numerous captives and 250 slaves—before finally torching the plantations and departing on 9 October to visit a like treatment upon Dutch Surinam. When Harman eventually regained Barbados

that November, he learned that a peace treaty had already been concluded at Breda in Europe as of 31 July 1667, and so released all his prisoners. Lefebvre de Lézy was subsequently resupplied by his brother from Martinique and returned to Cayenne in late May 1668 with 200 followers. They found some forty French survivors who had emerged from hiding places in the jungle, and together began reconstructing Fort Saint-Louis and their devastated properties.

Cayenne had not yet fully recuperated when it was again attacked eight years later, this time by the Dutch. At 2:00 P.M. on Sunday, 3 May 1676, lookouts at Montjoly spotted an approaching fleet—ten warships and sixteen transports under Vice Adm. Jacob Binckes of Amsterdam—who sent in a flag-of-truce boat the next morning, calling on the French to capitulate. When no reply was received, Binckes disembarked 900 troops at Queslin Cove on 5 May who advanced upon Rémire, while his three heaviest warships circled round, traversed Cayenne's 12-foot bar, and anchored opposite Fort Saint-Louis to commence a bombardment by 2:00 P.M. Rémire was quickly overrun, and Lefebvre de Lézy surrendered his battered stronghold (which contained only 180 defenders), being immediately deported to France while his French colonists were carried away aboard Binckes's vessels when they proceeded against their next Antillan target, Marie-Galante. Some 120 Dutch settlers remained in their stead under the reinstalled ex-governor Spranger, with expectations of being strongly reinforced from Holland.

However, the French Crown retaliated most swiftly, a fleet of fifteen sailors under Vice Adm. Jean, Comte d'Estrées, materializing before Rémire by 17 December of that same year,

Map of the fortified headland of Cayenne in May 1679, by the visiting slaver Barbot. (British Library)

guided by Lefebvre de Lézy in person. The next day, 800 troops were disembarked at Conobé Bay and entered the deserted town of Cayenne by 19 December, its outnumbered Dutch residents having retreated inside Fort Saint-Louis without resistance. After vainly calling upon Spranger to surrender, the attackers stormed its ramparts at 9:00 P.M. on 21 December, carrying the citadel a half hour later at a cost of 25 French dead and 92 wounded, compared with 20 killed, 38 injured, and 219 captured among its defenders. D'Estrées quickly restored Lefebvre de Lézy into office as governor, detached 150 soldiers to reconstitute its garrison, and then departed northwestward to continue his New World campaign. Lefebvre de Lézy spent the next several months razing smaller Dutch outposts inland, before general hostilities finally ceased with the signing of the Treaty of Nijmegen in Europe on 10 August 1678, whereby France retained undisputed possession of Cayenne.

Early Difficulties (1679–1713)

With this peace Cayenne and its surrounding district experienced a modest rebirth, some sugar mills and plantations being reestablished, while the burned ruins of its original Saint-Sauveur Church were replaced with the consecration of a magnificent new wooden temple on 6 August 1680. A few skilled craftsmen such as masons and blacksmiths were even sent out from France by the Royal Company, along with some convict laborers, while an ever-increasing number of African slaves also were imported. Fort Saint-Louis was expanded and became the governors' official residence (instead of Rémire) starting in the late 1680s, while West Indian rovers, *flibustiers,* such as Capt. François Le Sage, chose to settle in this out-of-the-way colony as well, so as to discreetly dispose of their ill-gotten booty by purchasing lands.

Yet Guiana never proved as attractive to migrants as larger French colonies such as Martinique, Guadeloupe, or Saint-Domingue (modern Haiti), which were greatly to outstrip it both in population and production; also, Cayenne's development suffered a further setback when French naval Capt. Jean-Baptiste Ducasse arrived in mid-April 1689 with four royal frigates to announce a renewed conflict against the Dutch. Having been directed to assist in a surprise assault against neighboring Surinam, Gov. François de la Barre felt that Ducasse's strength was insufficient for such a task, so he added the commandeered merchantman *Diligence* to this force, along with the 40-gun, 180-man privateer *Dauphin* out of Dunkirk. In his enthusiasm, the governor further committed most of Cayenne's garrison under its commander, Remy Guillouët, Seigneur d'Orvilliers, as well as raising a host of local volunteers; that left French Guiana virtually denuded of men when this squadron set sail by 2 May.

One week later Ducasse approached the Surinamese capital of Paramaribo, only to find its Dutch defenders already alerted; they therefore compelled his attack columns to withdraw, after leaving behind thirty-four prisoners. As his main force was scheduled to continue directly toward Martinique, 200 of Cayenne's volunteer contingent attempted to beat back upwind toward home aboard *Dauphin,* only to become shipwrecked near Berbice and surrender to the Dutch after much suffering. The few survivors were eventually exchanged in November 1689, yet Cayenne had been deprived of many of its best troops and residents through such misadventures. Its economic stagnation deepened further when the military engineer Paquine committed every resource to a reconstruction project of Fort Saint-Louis in 1690, spurred on by fears of a potential counterinvasion; also, ten houses were consumed by an accidental fire on 16 September 1696. (After a similar conflagration in November 1701, palm thatch was banned as a roofing material at Cayenne, being replaced by shingles.)

Some small measure of prosperity was reclaimed once peace returned in September 1697, allowing for the importation of 1,000 slaves the next year—which raised the colony's total population to 352 whites, 13 free mulattoes and blacks, plus 1,399 African and 121 Indian slaves (compared with 319 whites and 4,756 slaves in neighboring Surinam around that same time). But such gains were quickly reversed by a renewed interruption in maritime traffic during 1702–1713, occasioned by the War of the Spanish Succession, or Queen Anne's War; the resultant naval blockade and other complications even meant that the royal patent of 6 June 1701, authorizing Cayenne to establish its own self-governing *conseil supérior* (high tribunal), could not be implemented for more than two years.

Colonial Capital (1714–1788)

When peace at last returned once more, French Guiana's white population had been reduced to a mere 296 individuals, yet shipments of African slaves quickly increased the latter group's numbers to 2,536 by 1716. Over the next two decades, the plantation system became fully implemented throughout the colony, abetted by a commensurate rise in passing maritime traffic bound toward the West Indies. Local planters benefited especially from the development of coffee as a cash crop during the early 1720s, which supplemented their traditional exports of sugar, tobacco, cotton, indigo, and vanilla. (Cocoa was also introduced as of the 1730s, while the colony's most famed agricultural export—albeit never that voluminous—came to be the so-called Cayenne pepper, an extremely spicy condiment produced by repeatedly drying and finely grinding the bright red pods of its *Capsicum frutescens* chili shrub.) Thanks to this increased activity, the total population reached 484 whites by 1735—not including 200 soldiers garrisoning Fort Saint-Louis—plus 13 free mulattoes or blacks and 4,416 slaves; these figures rose to 777 whites and 5,471 slaves by 1749 (again compared with 2,129 whites and 25,135 slaves in neighboring Surinam).

As a result of this modest boom, Cayenne came to be improved by additions to its jetty and fortifications, while

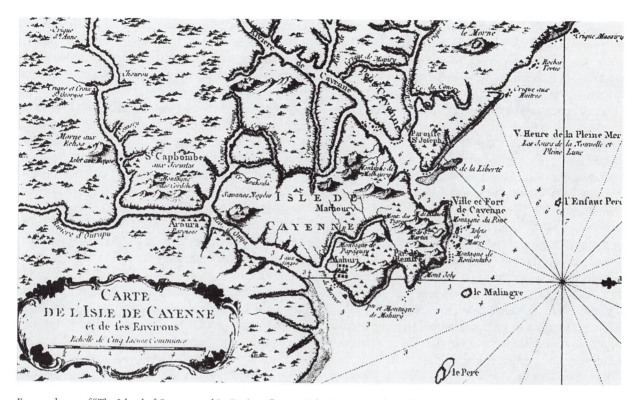

Engraved map of "The Island of Cayenne and Its Environs," ca. 1763, by Jacques Nicolas Bellin. (*Description géographique de la Guyane*)

amenities such as a public market, shops, and even a resident doctor also appeared. Nevertheless, the colony remained such an imperial backwater that its officials did not learn of the outbreak of the War of the Austrian Succession, or King George's War, until November 1744, eight months after the actual commencement of hostilities in Europe—and that merely because the privateer *Prince Charles* of Capt. Simon Potter, commissioned by Gov. William Green of Rhode Island, chanced to make a descent upon Guiana's unguarded coastline. Still, the return to peace four years later saw Cayenne expand even further, as a new cluster of houses dubbed the Nouvelle Ville (New Town) materialized outside its walls by 1753, in what had formerly been known as La Savane (The Swamp). Some dislocation in trade was again experienced during the Seven Years War or French and Indian War from 1756 to 1763, although Cayenne continued to be sporadically serviced by neutral Dutch or Italian vessels, as well as receiving English prizes brought in by French privateers. Three years into this conflict, French Guiana's population still remained virtually unchanged at 456 whites, 21 free mulattoes or blacks, plus 5,571 slaves; with the restoration of peace in 1763, it quickly grew to 575 whites, 64 free mulattoes or blacks, and 6,996 slaves.

Yet France had fared badly elsewhere, forfeiting its North American empire. In an attempt to counterbalance this loss, the king's chief minister, Étienne-François, Duc de Choiseul, began shipping 14,000 European migrants into a large new clearance at Kourou, 20 miles northwest of Cayenne, in hopes of transforming western Guiana into a thriving new commercial enterprise to compensate for the loss of Canada and Louisiana. But that effort ended in calamitous failure, more than 10,000 settlers quickly succumbing to malnourishment, yellow fever, and other diseases, and its survivors mostly either returning to Europe or seeking refuge on the three Îles du Diable (Devil's Islands) offshore—ironically renamed the Îles du Salut (Salvation Islands)—before scattering elsewhere.

One of the few benefits accrued from this massive influx of people through Cayenne was the reorganization of its Nouvelle Ville suburb by Gov. Étienne-François, Chevalier de Turgot, who realigned its streets early in 1765, then ordered its 200 dwellings enclosed within a large new hexagonal perimeter of walls. Wealthy citizens maintained fine wooden homes—some two stories high—nearest the seashore in Rue Royale and Rue de Choiseul (modern Avenue du Générale de Gaulle), although most preferred residing on their estates year-round except for occasional business visits. Poorer residents lived in adobe huts clustered farther away from Cayenne's waterfront. This entire new sector came to be encompassed by ramparts interconnected with five bastions and a moat, further protected on its western flank by the old Saint-Louis citadel.

But despite the recent migration wave, French Guiana's total population had increased only to 977 whites, 200 free mulattoes or blacks, and 8,499 slaves by 1776. The following year its new colonial intendant, Pierre-Victor Malouet, instituted a few urban improvements at Cayenne by importing the Swiss engineer Pierre Guizan (or Guisan) to begin digging the Sartines (modern Laussat) Canal, demolish some older structures, transfer Fort Saint-Louis's magazine beyond its walls, and erect a new prison and some public parks. Still, only one street in the city had been paved by the time those labors concluded.

Revolutionary Upheaval (1789–1808)

Thanks to peace and a steady growth in agricultural production throughout the region, the colony's population had increased to 1,307 whites, 494 free mulattoes or blacks, and 10,748 slaves by 1789. Yet this prosperous interlude was about to be shattered by the radical changes unleashed in distant Paris during the spring of that same year, as well as the three ensuing decades of blockade and occupation. After some initial uncertainty in the aftermath of the storming of the Bastille, anarchy really began taking hold at Cayenne with the arrival of a contingent of 100 soldiers on 14 November 1789, who increased its garrison to 700 men. Imbued with republican ideals, these newcomers led a revolt shortly thereafter that cowed the recently installed governor, Jacques-Martin de Bourgon; then, the following summer, the National Assembly in Paris ordered the election of a separate Guyanese Assemblée Coloniale, whose libertarian deputies quickly clashed with their more conservative predecessors from Cayenne's royal Conseil Supérior, culminating in numerous arrests on 9–10 August 1790.

Contradictory directives continued to arrive from France as contending factions succeeded each other in office, after which a half million slaves on Saint-Domingue (Haiti)—impatient to achieve the Revolution's promised freedoms—revolted during the autumn of 1791, raising the specter of a similar insurrection at Cayenne. Finally, the captive Louis XVI was executed on 21 January 1793 and the republican government declared war against Britain, Spain, and Holland, provoking a precipitous decline in transatlantic ship movements. On 11 April 1793, Nicolas-Georges Jeannet-Oudin—nephew of the formidable head of Paris's Committee for Public Safety, Georges-Jacques Danton—arrived at Cayenne from France as *commissaire* to "republicanize" the colony. Yet he too fled to North America only nineteen months later, after learning that his uncle had been guillotined and that slavery had been abolished by the Directorate; for when that latter decree was promulgated throughout French Guiana three months later, it caused an utter economic and social collapse, most planters fleeing into Cayenne while their slaves devastated the plantations and scattered into the jungle.

Desperation eventually drove the beleaguered French colonists to extreme measures, such as sorties out of Cayenne to capture and execute renegade slaves, as well as the illegal interception and detention of passing neutral vessels (German, Swedish, Danish, American, and so forth) so as to procure supplies. Among the very few vessels that arrived from France were a pair during 1797–1798 bringing out more than 200

Women street sweepers in Cayenne, ca. 1920, wearing wicker hats against the scorching heat of the sun. (Franck, *Working North from Patagonia*)

deportees: political opponents of the Directorate, such as Jean-Marie Collot d'Herbois, Jacques-Nicolas Billaud-Varenne, and Jean-Charles Pichegru, as well as other lesser outcasts condemned to exile. As a further cause for woe, Cayenne's garrison mutinied on 30 August 1798 because of their eight months' arrears in pay, being placated five days later by a forced contribution raised from its unhappy merchants.

Eventually some measure of order was reestablished, and French privateers even began bringing in some prizes. The able Brig. Jean-Baptiste Victor Hugues (familiar with New World conditions because he had been born on Saint-Domingue) assumed office as the new governor on 9 January 1800, and so improved matters that Cayenne's extemporized land defenses could be removed a few months later; only its citadel and seaside batteries remained.

European hostilities ceased shortly thereafter with the signing of the Treaty of Amiens on 27 March 1802, which reinvigorated the colony's trade—as well as the reimposition of slavery in all French territories as of 20 May of that same year, which resurrected its old plantation-based economy. Yet this commercial revival proved to be short-lived, as the newly crowned Emperor Napoleon I resumed hostilities against Britain a mere fourteen months later, and the Atlantic blockade was reimposed. As Saint-Domingue was now lost to black Haitian rebels, some displaced planters from that island resettled in French Guiana, while Cayenne furthermore resumed its former role of privateer base. In the spring of 1806, it was even visited by Commo. La Marre La Meillerie's four large frigates during a dash across the Atlantic.

Portuguese Occupation (1809–1817)
Eventually, the British determined to remove the naval threat posed to their own transatlantic trade routes by Cayenne, and so proposed a joint operation to their Portuguese allies at Belem, who had long wished to eradicate this French presence near their Amazonian frontier. Consequently, the Royal Navy clamped a close blockade against Cayenne starting in November 1808; then a 1,200-man expedition led by Capt. James Lucas Yeo of the 22-gun sloop HMS *Confiance* and the Portuguese artillery Lt. Col. Manoel Marques entered the Oyapock River on 3 December, overrunning its French outpost with little resistance. Twelve days later, the French settlement in the adjacent Approuage River was also taken.

Although Hugues had been apprised of this steady enemy approach, Yeo and Marques nonetheless managed to appear undetected on the evening of 6 January 1809 with a contingent of 550 Portuguese troops and 80 British marines and sailors crammed aboard several vessels. They surprised the French batteries at Grande Cane and Fort Diamant at 3:00 A.M. the next morning, before occupying Père Isle a mile away, and then capturing the Dégrad des Cannes and Trio batteries on the mainland. Hugues sallied from Cayenne and massed several hundred defenders near the windmill at the former Jesuit con-

vent of Loyola on the morning of 8 January, watching impotently as the invaders burned his plantation on Torcy Canal opposite. At 6:00 P.M. that same evening, he launched a 150-man counterattack against the Anglo-Portuguese beachhead at Dégrad des Cannes, only to be repulsed after a three-hour firefight and pressed back inside Cayenne by 10 January. With the invaders now outside his city gates, Hugues requested terms and pointedly capitulated to the Portuguese—not to the British—by 12 January. Yeo and Marques paraded through the muddy streets of Cayenne two days later as 400 French regulars, 600 militiamen, and 200 black auxiliaries laid down their arms. (For this exploit, Yeo was later knighted by the British Crown, while silver medals were issued to all Portuguese officers by their government and bronze ones to their troops.)

Ironically, Cayenne came to thrive once more under this foreign occupation, both because it was no longer subject to the strangling Royal Navy blockade and because its Portuguese administrators—unlike their British allies—allowed local planters to resume importing African slaves to work their estates. Indeed, the Portuguese implemented very few changes during their interregnum, being distracted by larger issues abroad. Some portions of Cayenne's stone ramparts were toppled to fill in defensive ditches, and the Jesuits were allowed to reclaim some of their former properties; otherwise, life went on much as in peacetime. One of the few untoward incidents occurred on the night of 5–6 March 1811, when a Portuguese company mutinied and was driven back inside its Cayenne barracks by grapeshot, after which full discipline was reimposed.

When Napoleon finally fell and went into exile on the Mediterranean island of Elba late in April 1814, having first abdicated in favor of Louis XVIII, Guiana was to be returned to France as part of the European restoration of the Bourbon monarchy. But when the emperor escaped confinement the next spring and plunged the world back into conflict, this restitution was postponed until after his final defeat at Waterloo and deportation in July 1815 to Saint Helena in the South Atlantic. Thus it was not until the following summer that Louis's plenipotentiary could at last travel to Rio de Janeiro and work out the details with the Portuguese; a French expedition under Cayenne's new governor, Jean-François, Comte de Carra Saint-Cyr, did not actually arrive to take formal possession until 8 November 1817.

Reclamation (1818–1851)
The French found their colony relatively prosperous and quite unchanged from nine years previously: according to the census of 1807, French Guiana's total population had been 969 whites, 1,040 free mulattoes or blacks, and 13,474 slaves; upon being restored, the figures stood at 989 whites, 1,698 free mulattoes or blacks, and 13,369 slaves. The next governor, Pierre Clément, Baron de Laussat, instituted numerous civic improvements at Cayenne during his administration from July 1819 to March 1823, such as a new Palais de Justice

(courthouse), a new cathedral, a botanical garden, and its first printing press; he also removed the last ramparts so as to allow for more expansion and had the canal dredged. These efforts increased the city's population from 3,764 residents in 1822 to 5,899 a mere two years later, yet Cayenne still remained rather dilapidated in appearance and blighted by empty, overgrown lots. Moreover, wealthy planters continued to reside in the countryside; as late as 1836, only twenty-eight maintained households in the capital, its inhabitants being mostly impoverished blacks and mulattoes. Low by the sea and hemmed in by steamy mangroves, many of its buildings—mostly built of wood—deteriorated in the unremitting sunlight and humidity.

The total population of French Guiana slowly rose to 20,000 people, then stagnated. In November 1842, the royal government in Paris ordered a new survey and reorganization of Cayenne, which resulted in a somewhat better alignment of its

A former Parisian lawyer digging a street sewer in Cayenne, ca. 1920. (Franck, *Working North from Patagonia*)

streets, as well as the creation of five new ones; public education was also encouraged in anticipation of softening the forthcoming transitional period, as slavery was once again slated to be abolished. Six years later, though, when this measure was rather abruptly enacted throughout all French dependencies in April 1848 after the toppling of the monarchy and restoration of republicanism in Paris—the so-called Second Republic—this precipitate decision caused an economic freefall in Guiana. Trade was crippled by bankrupting most old colonial-era plantations, while at the same time no new form of livelihood was substituted for thousands of suddenly freed slaves, leading to widespread poverty. It was not to be until a few years later, after the conservative coup in Paris of 1–2 December 1851 led by President and Prince Louis Napoleon, which resulted in the establishment of his Second Empire as Emperor Napoleon III, that Guiana was once again provided for—and in a most unexpected fashion.

Penal Colony (1852–1939)

One of the many reactionary measures adopted by this new imperial regime included closing the penitentiaries at the French seaports of Brest, Rochefort, and Toulon in March 1852, as local authorities and citizens alike had grown weary of the continuous threat of escapes or riots—as well as the unseemly sight of convicts, clad in their red-and-yellow-striped jackets and green caps, shuffling through the streets to perform manual labor. Instead, these 2,000 prisoners were to be deported to Guiana. Not only would the danger of violent outbreaks or clandestine contacts be curtailed by this transfer to such a remote locale, serviced only rarely by vessels calling at its lone port of Cayenne, but parolees who completed their sentences could furthermore be compelled to stay on for an additional time period equal to that of their original incarceration. They could even be compelled to remain indefinitely if sentenced to more than eight years, thus precluding the return of undesirables to France, while simultaneously swelling the colony's thin population figures.

Consequently, the first frigate set sail from Brest on 25 April 1852 with 360 convict laborers, 240 parolees who had agreed to be released overseas, plus 30 political prisoners. Deportation soon proved so popular an expedient that the rubber-stamp imperial legislature voted on 30 May 1854 to close virtually every penitentiary in France, ridding the nation of 6,000 inmates at a stroke, while furthermore approving the transportation of all future felons as well. Therefore, Cayenne (along with Saint-Laurent du Maroni, farther to its west) was to become one of the main ports of entry for this considerable influx, holding some *bagnards* (convicts) in its own local compound, while dispersing others up the coast to Kourou to isolated jungle clearances or to the offshore Îles du Salut—the most notorious destination being Devil's Island.

Disease so ravaged the enfeebled deportees thrust into this steamy equatorial climate that yellow fever quickly claimed

1,057 of the first 6,000, while malaria weakened the rest, making their forced labors a cruel ordeal. In short order, Guiana was to acquire a sinister reputation on account of its unhealthful penal depots, further heightened by its exotic landscape and mysterious remove from Europe, which—in the absence of any organized political opposition to the emperor—fired the imagination of a few intellectuals opposed to such a heartless policy. (Jules Verne's fictional Captain Nemo, for example, in the 1869 novel *Twenty Thousand Leagues under the Sea,* was an embittered, half-mad escapee from an unnamed tropical prison modeled after Devil's Island.)

Unfortunately, this prison traffic so benefited Cayenne that its citizens soon grew dependent upon it, the somnolent town of slightly more than 7,000 inhabitants in 1852 coming alive as its wholesalers were called upon to supply the vast new camps, stevedores and boatmen to tend to the ships, landlords to rent homes and offices to transplanted officialdom, storekeepers and tavern owners to cater to the personnel, while many other minor jobs abounded. Cayenne's own depot came to be erected at Buzaré, or Buzaret Point, just northeast of the town, consisting of three huge barracks designated "Europe," "Asie," and "Afrique," so as to subdivide French, Arab, and black inmates into their respective linguistic groupings. No containment wall was erected, only an encircling drainage ditch was dug, as these prisoners—mostly trustees or parolees—performed their daily labors within Cayenne anyway, and so posed little threat. More dangerous or controversial convicts were forwarded to Devil's Island or to some other distant coastal camp.

Thanks to this infusion of fresh activity and people, the city's first public lighting system was inaugurated in 1854 (oil lamps being lit every evening by an artillery company detachment, then extinguished every dawn by a trio of early-rising military defaulters); decorative palm trees were planted three years later around its main square—the Place de l'Esplanade, henceforth known as the Place des Palmistes—while water and drainage systems were commenced as of 1861, along with the paving of a few more streets. Convicts provided a pool of cheap yet skilled labor to install and maintain many such improvements; nevertheless, Cayenne's development continued to be hampered by its shallow, silty harbor, which compelled larger vessels to unload at Larivot, 2 miles away.

The colony's fortunes were also further raised by the discovery of gold in the Upper Approuage River in 1855, sparking an onrush of prospectors and the emergence of Guiana's first millionaires. Attracted by such improved business prospects, large commercial houses began appearing at Cayenne throughout the 1870s, while Guiana's sudden upsurge in wealth also meant that a few thousand Chinese and Far Eastern coolies could be imported during this same decade, reviving some of its former plantations. The colony's newfound prominence during this "golden era" also came to be reflected at Cayenne, where brick housing began to appear; a new bar-

Some of the French officers charged with prisoners at Cayenne, ca. 1920. (Franck, *Working North from Patagonia*)

racks was erected in 1876 between the old fort and its seashore; a Conseil Général (County Council) was approved two years later by the French authorities; and the city's first colonial representative to Parliament in Paris was elected in 1879. By 1903, Cayenne boasted perhaps ten automobiles, and its first electric lights were installed the next year on the Rue du XIV Juillet and Rue Nationale (prior to 1881, Rue Royale; modern Avenue Léopold Heder).

Nevertheless, most wealthy citizens still resided in country villas far removed from the town, so as to avoid its shabby districts and omnipresent convict laborers. Despite its role as business entrepot, Cayenne—like the rest of Guiana—still relied heavily upon the penal traffic, some 52,000 convicts eventually being transported to its shores over a span of eight decades, before deportation was finally stemmed in 1936 and then halted entirely during World War II. Among its most celebrated detainees was to be Capt. Alfred Dreyfus, a Jewish officer wrongly accused of betraying military secrets to Germany in the autumn of 1894, who was to spend five years on Devil's Island before finally being retried and exonerated. His memoirs, published in 1901, were entitled *Cinq années de ma vie— Five Years of My Life.*

World War II (1940–1945)

Because of its physical remove from Europe, Cayenne remained largely unaffected by the World War I campaigns of 1914 to 1918, although some of its citizens fought in defense of France. However, the entire colony was to undergo considerable hardship during World War II and then benefit from its outcome. The conflict began disastrously when France was overrun by a sudden Nazi blitzkrieg, surrendering on 22 June 1940 and being left with only the central portion of its homeland, its

Mediterranean coastline, overseas colonies, and navy. When delegates—driven out of Paris—gathered at the small French city of Vichy on 10 July to ratify this capitulation, Pierre Laval persuaded them to create an entirely new government the next day, with the elderly Marshal Henri Pétain as president.

French Guiana's Gov. Robert Chot and other local officials acquiesced with this decision, although maintaining contact with this new administration in the home country proved somewhat problematical because of the ferocious Anglo-German naval struggle that ensued in the Atlantic. Moreover, both the British and later the U.S. government remained distrustful of this Vichy enclave in South America, suspecting it of harboring pro-German proclivities.

These fears of collaboration with the enemy became fully aroused when German submarines suddenly unleashed a new Caribbean offensive in early March 1942, the *U–129* of Lt. Cmdr. Nicoli Clausen even sinking the American freighter *Steel Age* 60 miles off of French Guiana itself. When U.S. forces landed in Morocco and Algeria on 8 November of that same year, encountering no resistance from its French defenders, many Vichy units began switching loyalties to the Allies, in turn prompting the Germans to overrun the remainder of France and incorporate it into their Reich. Given these changed circumstances—their homeland now completely in German hands, its remaining Vichy figures openly cooperating with the Nazis—Washington grew increasingly frustrated with the continual refusal of French Guiana, Martinique, and Guadeloupe to align themselves with the Free French cause. The U.S. Navy consequently instituted a full-scale blockade of Cayenne by mid-November.

By spring of the next year, French Guiana's economy was so crippled that unrest and starvation began spreading among the populace, until at last Gov. René Verber resigned on the morning of 17 March 1943, allowing a provisional committee to cable Gen. Henri Giraud in North Africa two days later and offer to join the Free French cause. With U.S. assistance a Giraud representative arrived on 22 March, and four days later his superior, Gov. Jean Rapenne, assumed control over the entire colony (despite a conflicting appointment of Maurice Berthaud as governor by the original Free French leader, Gen. Charles de Gaulle). Toward the end of March, U.S. troops also appeared and stationed a few antisubmarine aircraft at the

Aerial view over modern Cayenne. (Cayenne Tourism)

two-year-old Pan American Airways strip at Gallion Field, while simultaneously commencing work on a much larger airfield 10 miles outside Cayenne on the road toward Matoury, which was to become the Aérodrome de Rochambeau. The U.S. Corps of Engineers brought in 1,500 Puerto Rican laborers to toil on this huge project, in addition to hiring thousands of local Guyanese, who were greatly impressed by the scope and wealth of this operation. The United States maintained this vast base until after the end of the war, ceding it to the French authorities on 25 January 1949.

Departmental Capital (1947–Present)

With the conclusion of hostilities, a movement quickly emerged at Cayenne—spearheaded by the former Radical Socialist Party deputy, Gaston Monnerville—to have Guiana elevated from a territorial dependency into a full *département* of France, thus equal with all other regions of the homeland. It was hoped to thereby improve local conditions, as the Guyanese economy lay shattered, with businesses shuttered and misery abounding. On 26 February 1946, even Cayenne's once-loyal 140-man garrison of black Tirailleurs Sénégalais rioted, venting their frustration against the Creole citizens who so openly despised them. Nine people were killed and more than 100 wounded amid widespread destruction, while terrified residents fled for the protection of the U.S. air base. Gov. Jules Surlemont defused this crisis by ordering all the Senegalese troops to board the steamer *Saint-Domingue* and set sail for Dakar that same afternoon.

Very slowly, subsidies from the French government began to raise the overall standard of living, although commercial self-subsistence would prove elusive, beyond the traditional exports of lumber, fish, rum, and so on. Despite continuous difficulties, Cayenne's population more than doubled from 13,362 inhabitants in 1954 to 18,635 seven years afterward to 24,581 by 1967 and 30,461 by 1974. A significant boost for both the city and its district occurred the next year, after various nations had combined to form the European Space Agency so as to launch satellites independent of U.S. restrictions. The French government contributed by creating a company called Arianespace to develop the actual rockets, and the former penal outpost of Kourou had already been selected as the actual launch platform, because it lay close to the equator (thereby adding extra velocity to missiles thanks to the Earth's rotation), because it had open water to its east to receive splashdowns, and because its remote locale enhanced security.

The first Ariane rocket lifted off on Christmas Eve 1979, and ever since the Kourou facility has benefited Cayenne's economy considerably, as well as making French Guiana of strategic importance to France. By 1982, the city had grown to 38,091 inhabitants (or 47,396 if the adjacent towns of Rémire-Montjoly and Mahoury were included), a figure which would continue to swell along with the overall standard of living in French Guiana, in turn attracting thousands of impoverished migrants from neighboring Brazil, Surinam, and even Haiti. Resentment against lingering unemployment problems and a pernicious racial divide provoked some street violence during the 1990s as Cayenne continued to grow.

For further reading materials on the history of Cayenne or French Guiana, please consult the Select Bibliography at the end of this volume.

Peru

CUZCO

Ancient Incan capital that has today been resurrected as a world-famous archaeological center.

Origins (1000–1533)

According to Indian legend, this city was founded ca. 1000 C.E.—during the reign of the first Inca emperor, Manco Cápac—when a band of Quechua-speaking settlers migrated north from Pacaritampu on the shores of Lake Titicaca to displace even more primitive tribesmen living in the enclosed, fertile Huatanay Valley, whose encircling ranges afforded some shelter from the harsh Andean winds. Perched at 11,380 feet in the mountains, this new community's climate proved bracing, with regular rainfalls occurring during the summer months of November through March.

Cuzco (alternate Spanish spelling: Cusco) remained a relatively insignificant agricultural town until the first half of the fifteenth century, when the ninth emperor, Pachacútec Inca Yupanqui, defeated a Chanca invasion army at the nearby Carmenca (modern Santa Ana) heights, then launched a series of expansionistic campaigns that vastly increased Incan territory. During his long reign from 1438 to 1471, as well as that of his son and successor, Túpac Inca Yupanqui from 1471 to 1493, Cuzco became transformed into a grand imperial capital, a project that was carried out in accordance with a clay-and-stone model kept at Pachacútec's court. Imposing new temples to adore the sun were erected around the city center, as well as fine palaces and other lesser homes, while outlying fields were drained and given over to a regular rotation of food crops. Nobles from throughout the empire were expected to maintain residences in Cuzco, living there at least four months every year to attend its most important religious festivals, while their sons remained year-round so as to become fully assimilated and imbued with Incan administrative practices.

Beyond its politico-religious significance, the city's central geographic position also contributed to its importance; it

Cuzco's main square, city hall, and surrounding mountains, ca. 1975. (Organization of American States)

served as a commercial crossroads for tribute and trade arriving from up and down the empire—which by the early sixteenth century extended more than 3,000 miles along the Pacific coast, from what is today Colombia in the north to Chile in the south. Cuzco's strategic position astride one of the lower sections of the Andean range moreover made it a significant military base as well to check incursions by hostile Amazonian tribesmen pushing westward up the Urubamba River. An imposing stone fortress called Sacsayhuaman (also spelled Sacsaihuaman or Sacsahuaman) loomed northwest of imperial Cuzco to maintain permanent guard over this pass.

Yet despite its many strengths, the capital fell to an army of rival Incan warriors out of Quito early in the 1530s, marking an end to a civil war that had erupted between two claimants to the throne: Atahualpa and Huáscar. A brutal occupation was imposed by the Quitans, and still worse followed a few years later, when a Spanish expedition arrived on the northwestern fringes of the empire from Panama under Francisco Pizarro and commenced a remorseless drive inland. Having allied himself with the anti-Quitan Inca faction of the nineteen-year-old fugitive Prince Manco, this foreign conqueror reached Cuzco and was greeted as a liberator on 15 November 1533, while its former Quitan occupiers retired in disarray toward the Condesuyo Mountains. Manco was proclaimed emperor the following day, and some 5,000 Cuzcan auxiliaries were thereupon raised to support the fifty Spaniards who set off in pursuit of the retreating enemy.

Spanish Conquest (1534–1554)

The Cuzcans soon came to resent their new overlords as well: the conquistadors greedily stripped them of their riches and proclaimed Cuzco a Spanish city on 23 March 1534, subdividing its properties among their ninety most senior members. Pizarro furthermore chose to establish a new coastal capital at Lima the next year, thus threatening to diminish Cuzco's prestige. Followers of his disgruntled subordinate, Diego de Almagro, almost staged a revolt in the ancient Incan capital in March 1535, being placated by a visit from Pizarro in late May, who authorized his lieutenant to lead a new expedition farther south to conquer Chile. Almagro consequently quit Cuzco on 3 July at the head of 570 Spanish riders and foot soldiers, 12,000 Incan warriors under Paullu—the puppet emperor's brother—and great trains of porters; Pizarro meanwhile returned to the coast to continue organizing his other vast dominions.

Because of continued Spanish excesses in the hapless city and his own lack of power, Manco slipped away from his handlers early in November 1535 to attempt to raise a revolt in Cuzco's district, only to be ridden down and cruelly imprisoned by Juan and Gonzalo Pizarro. Isolated Spanish land-

Remnants of the ancient Sacsayhuaman fortress northwest of Cuzco, as seen from the so-called *Silla del Inca* or "Inca's Chair" in the foreground; drawn ca. 1864 by the amateur American archaeologist E. George Squier. (*Peru: Incidents of Travel,* 1877)

owners also began to be murdered, prompting the two brothers to lead a punitive expedition against the remote Incan stronghold of Ancocagua. When Hernando Pizarro returned to Cuzco from Spain in January 1536, he had Manco released from bondage because Madrid disapproved of disrespect shown toward any indigenous monarchs; yet the young emperor resumed planning to drive out the occupiers by having weapons secretly stockpiled and troops alerted in the countryside to fall upon Cuzco once the rainy season ended.

On 18 April 1536, Manco left Cuzco with Hernando Pizarro's permission, supposedly to attend some religious ceremonies in the nearby Yucay Valley; actually, he left to mobilize his secret army. News of this plot reached the old capital on 21 April—Easter Saturday—so that Juan Pizarro immediately sallied with seventy riders to disperse the gathering Incan forces, fighting his way into Calca and capturing part of their train. Yet three or four days later, his detachment was abruptly recalled when an immense indigenous army began encircling Cuzco itself under General Inquill. The cavalry fought their way back inside the capital, then watched as perhaps 50,000 warriors slowly deployed outside.

Hernando Pizarro had only 110 Spanish soldiers and 80 riders as his total garrison, dividing the latter into three companies under Gabriel de Rojas, Hernán Ponce de León, and Gonzalo Pizarro. They were too few to scatter such a host, so Inquill was emboldened to institute a close siege and mount a massive dawn assault on Saturday, 6 May 1536, preceded by a hail of heated stones that ignited many of the city's thatched roofs. Through sheer weight of numbers, the Incan army fought its way into the narrow and winding streets, pushing the desperate defenders back into two buildings opposite each other at the eastern end of its main square.

After several days of ferocious thrusts and counterthrusts, Juan Pizarro led fifty riders in a wild dash at sunrise on 16 May 1536 that succeeded in circling out into the countryside; he almost captured Sacsayhuaman citadel from the rear before he died from a head wound. His brothers Hernando and Gonzalo Pizarro nonetheless pressed home infantry assaults over the next few days that eventually carried the fortress, virtually all of its 2,000 Incan defenders being either slain or committing suicide. Indigenous reinforcements appeared and attempted to recapture Sacsayhuaman for three days more before finally giving up at the end of May. Still, the city's siege persisted until late August, when Hernando Pizarro finally fought his way out with 70 horsemen, 30 foot soldiers, and a large contingent of indigenous auxiliaries to attack Manco's headquarters in the formidable fortress of Ollantaytambo (30 miles downstream in the Yucay Valley). It proved impossible to assault, however, so that Pizarro retreated into Cuzco, then scattered a renewed Incan offensive in the open countryside; both sides thereupon retired in exhaustion into their respective bases for the rainy season.

Cuzco remained isolated by other rebellions flaring throughout highland Peru, until Almagro—having failed in his Chilean venture—finally reappeared by early April 1537 and sent a peace embassy to call upon Manco at Ollantaytambo, listening to his grievances against the Pizarro brothers. The emperor seemed inclined to make peace with this rival conquistador, but he changed his mind once Almagro reached Calca with a vanguard of 200 riders, who were attacked by 5,000 to 6,000 warriors under the young Inca commander Paucar. The Spaniards therefore battled their way into beleaguered Cuzco by nightfall on 18 April, where Almagro immediately deposed and imprisoned Hernando and Gonzalo Pizarro along with a handful of their supporters, assuming overall command of the city and its district.

In order to retain control, Almagro even dispatched his subordinate Rodrigo Orgóñez with a strong Spanish contingent and 10,000 indigenous auxiliaries under Paullu on 12 July 1537 to defeat an approaching pro-Pizarro relief force under Alonso de Alvarado the next dawn. Despairing of ever besting the Spaniards upon the battlefield, Manco furthermore abandoned Ollantaytambo shortly thereafter, being pursued into Peru's interior by Orgóñez, who returned into Cuzco by the end of that same month with enormous booty and many thousands of prisoners, while Paullu was crowned new puppet emperor. However, Almagro's self-anointed rule proved to be short-lived, as he opened negotiations with Francisco Pizarro on the coast by mid-September, only to have his position weaken when Gonzalo Pizarro escaped confinement and Hernando was exchanged.

Close-up view of the foundations of Sacsayhuaman's ramparts, ca. 1864, showing the enormity of their construction. (Squier, *Peru: Incidents of Travel,* 1877)

Fighting between the two Spanish factions erupted the following spring, and Hernando Pizarro invaded the central highlands, pressing the infirm and elderly Almagro's followers back into Cuzco before crushing his lieutenant Orgóñez in a bloody clash a few miles south of the city on 26 April 1538. Cuzco was thereupon reoccupied and Almagro tried and garroted by 8 July, after which Hernando Pizarro and Paullu marched to put down an Incan offensive in Collasuyu Province. Manco subsequently menaced Jauja and Ayacucho as well, so that Francisco Pizarro himself entered Cuzco with his main army by November and detached columns to deal with the threat. These columns were unsuccessful until Pizarro finally sortied on 22 December with seventy riders, compelling the fugitive emperor to retire. A year of campaigns against remote Incan holdouts and elusive raiders ensued, so that Cuzco began a modest recuperation from these devastating onslaughts, as well as the dislocation of all its agricultural and commercial activity.

Political anarchy among the Spaniards flared anew when Blasco Núñez Vela, the first Crown-appointed Peruvian viceroy, was deposed in Lima by Gonzalo Pizarro in September 1544 for his heavy-handed attempts to implement Spain's new laws protecting Indian serfs. Another royal emissary, Licentiate Pedro de la Gasca, eventually came out from Spain and pushed into northern Peru by the autumn of 1546, gathering sufficient adherents to pronounce Gonzalo Pizarro guilty of treason that same December. The rebel leader was pressed back into Cuzco, until de la Gasca's royalist army finally fought its way on to Jaquijahuana, or Sacsayhuana, Plain, a few miles west of the city, for a decisive confrontation on 9 April 1548. Some forty-five of Pizarro's closest supporters were killed during that battle, while most others simply ran across the field to join the opposing ranks, permitting de la Gasca to enter Cuzco and have Pizarro executed the following day, thereby restoring Madrid's hold over all of Peru.

But resentment against the Crown's renewed efforts to introduce pro-Indian legislation prompted the *hacendado* (estate owner) Francisco Hernández Girón to lead Cuzco's Spanish citizens into yet another revolt on 13 November 1553, joined shortly thereafter by the citizens of Huamanga and Arequipa. For another year the southern Andes remained in a curious state of rebellion, while simultaneously proclaiming unswerving loyalty to Charles I, until an army raised by the *real audiencia* (royal tribunal) at Lima finally defeated Hernández Girón north of Lake Titicaca on 8 October 1554, capturing and beheading him by that same December. One last plot was to be foiled when some mestizos—offspring of whites and indigenous inhabitants, this word being a garbling of the Latin term *mixticius* (mixed)—who referred to themselves locally as *montañeses* (mountaineers), planned to assassinate peninsular-born Spaniards and seize their lands around Cuzco, only to in turn be discovered and arrested by January 1567.

Transformation and Stagnation (1555–1779)

The ancient Incan capital had been severely maltreated and depleted by these protracted troubles, yet when Spanish residents and migrants began resurrecting the city once peace and prosperity were restored during the 1560s, they uncharacteristically chose to use the original foundations and outlines of its burned structures to erect new edifices, thereby retaining the meandering street layout of Incan times, rather than creating a new grid pattern. (Spanish property owners did, however, move indigenous neighborhoods into outlying ghettos.) New Hispanic-style churches and residences soon began to rise around the former Huacaypata and Cusipata squares, while the Dominican convent, for example, was erected atop the ruins of the old Coricancha (Temple of the Sun).

Repopulation and development were to be encouraged when Viceroy Francisco de Toledo ended the long-standing truce with die-hard Incan refugees still holding out in the Andes by declaring war against their newly crowned emperor Tupác Amaru on 14 April 1572 and dispatching 250 mounted conquistadors under Martín Hurtado de Arbieto, as well as thousands of indigenous warriors and auxiliaries, from Cuzco a few weeks later, to overwhelm those last holdouts at their

A street in Cuzco, ca. 1972; note how the ancient Incan wall at left was used as the foundation for a superimposed Spanish colonial-era edifice. (Organization of American States)

remote stronghold of Vilcabamba. A summerlong campaign concluded when this force returned triumphantly on 21 September and beheaded the captive emperor three days later.

Red tiles came to be substituted for thatched roofs throughout the city, its first public fountain was inaugurated on 1 October 1583, and Cuzco regained enough prestige that when the unpopular royal *alcabala* sales tax was introduced to Peru in April 1592, the viceroy, García Hurtado de Mendoza, Marqués de Cañete, sought the support of its *cabildo,* "being the head of this kingdom and on whom many had their eyes to see what it did."

A local university was created by 1598 and a theater by 1622; the city's population had been estimated to have stabilized at 3,100 inhabitants in 1614. With the passage of time, colonial Cuzco—although now relegated to a mere district capital—came to thrive once more as a manufacturing center for woven cloths and as an exporter of sugar, coca, and corn. However, its prosperity was shattered at approximately 2:00 P.M. on 31 March 1650, when a heavy earthquake killed thirty-six people and left survivors in a state of fear for many months afterward because of hundreds of aftershocks. Most of the city's sixteenth-century structures were leveled at that time, so that many of Cuzco's oldest buildings today date only from the second half of the seventeenth century. According to a report prepared by Bishop Mollinedo in 1689–1690, its population by his time stood at 13,600. Other, lesser earthquakes occurred on 30 December 1702, 23 May 1707, 24 March 1742, and 19 November 1744.

Tupác Amaru Rebellion (1780–1781)

By 1770, Cuzco's population had risen to an estimated 26,000 people, and ten years later it was briefly threatened by the great Indian revolt raised throughout neighboring districts by José Gabriel de Condorcanqui, Marqués de Oropesa—an Incan descendant better known as Tupác Amaru, chief of Tungasuca. Cuzco's Spanish garrison commander, Joaquín Valcarce, although initially able to scrape together barely 3,200 men (few of them trained soldiers), nonetheless sallied with a picked unit and in January 1781 inflicted some 300 casualties upon Tupác Amaru's much larger host while it hesitated 6 miles outside the city. Further reinforcements subsequently arrived from the coastal lowlands on 23 February 1781 under Field Marshal José del Valle y Torres, who set about reorganizing the district militias and soon commanded more than 15,000 defenders. The royal forces defeated the insurgents at Tinta, Tupiza, and La Paz (Bolivia), bringing an end to Tupác Amaru's rebellion by September of that same year.

War of Independence (1814–1824)

Upon the outbreak of South America's much more protracted struggle for independence from Spain in 1808, Cuzco's 35,000 inhabitants initially remained loyal to the Crown. However, on 2 August 1814—after almost a year of political wrangling—

the liberal Creole councilors of its *cabildo* escaped the confinement imposed upon them by its more conservative *oidores* (justices) and in turn arrested many peninsular Spaniards and called for the full implementation of Spain's liberal constitution of March 1812. These rebels were led by the middle-class citizens José and Vicente Angulo, plus Gabriel Béjar, although their insurrection has somewhat erroneously become better known as the Pumacahua Rebellion, after one of its military leaders—the elderly *curaca* (local Indian official) Mateo García Pumacahua. Tens of thousands of poorly armed peasants advanced quickly against Huamanga and Huancavelica in the north, as well as La Paz and Arequipa in the south, and also allied themselves with the revolutionaries who were invading upper Peru from Argentina. But when the latter were defeated toward the end of that same year, Pumacahua's followers were brutally repressed.

Ironically, the final years of Peru's struggle for independence saw Cuzco transformed into its last royalist capital. Having been driven out of Lima and the coastal districts during the summer of 1821, Viceroy José de la Serna led his remaining forces high up into the Andes to make a stand. By late December, Cuzco had been officially designated as his new headquarters, leading to the installation of a mint, armaments factories, and even the city's first printing press. In October 1824 the viceroy marshaled 13,000 troops at nearby Paruro to repel an approaching patriot army under Gen. Antonio José de

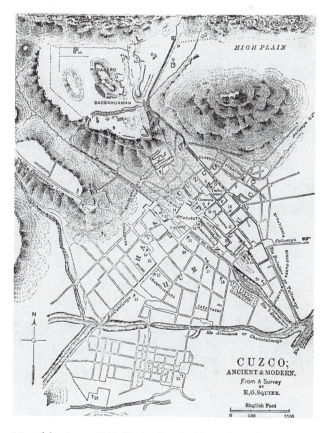

Map of the city, ca. 1864. (Squier, *Peru: Incidents of Travel,* 1877)

Sucre Alcalá, then left behind 1,800 men to garrison Cuzco, while his main body departed to seek battle on 22 October. However, after overtaking Sucre's 5,800 insurgents at Ayacucho on 9 December 1824, la Serna was defeated, wounded, and captured, thus bringing an end to organized royalist resistance in South America. When Sucre resumed his eastward push over the Andes, a patriot detachment under his subordinate Gen. Agustín Gamarra quietly accepted the surrender of Cuzco the day after Christmas.

Republican Era (1825–Present)

The postindependence period proved especially difficult for Cuzco, as its textile products could no longer compete with cheaper, shipborne imports arriving directly at Peru's more populous coastlands from abroad. A brief Cuzcan revival occurred during the period of the confederation between Peru and Bolivia (1836–1839), but when this trans-Andean union was dissolved the city again fell into decline, its population plummeting from 40,000 people in 1840 to a mere 20,000 six years later.

It was not until railway lines extended high into the mountains in 1908, followed within the next couple of decades by paved highways, that Cuzco's remaining 18,600 residents could at last begin shipping out significant amounts of commercial goods, especially wool. Its population consequently grew steadily from 15,000 inhabitants in 1903 to 24,000 in 1927, 30,000 in 1930, and 46,000 by 1940.

An earthquake rumbled through the city on 18 September

View across the city's traditional red-tile rooftops toward the Plaza de Armas and cathedral, whose construction was commenced in 1564. (Organization of American States)

1941. But at 1:39 P.M. on Sunday, 21 May 1950, there occurred the second such great catastrophe in Cuzco's history, when a much heavier quake killed approximately 80 people and injured another 100—remarkably light casualties considering that some 3,000 buildings collapsed. Nonetheless, as many as 30,000 to 40,000 of its 63,000 inhabitants were left temporarily without shelter, and thousands chose to abandon the city altogether. By now, Cuzco's importance as a regional commercial center was so well established, however, that it rebounded from this setback, its population increasing from a low of 59,918 people in 1953 to 82,265 by 1961, 127,057 by 1972, and an estimated 302,700 by 1991.

For further reading materials on Cuzco or Peru, please consult the Select Bibliography at the end of this volume; additional sources on South American urban history can be found under "Regional Studies," as well as under "General Works on Latin America."

LIMA

Incan religious center that became transformed into the Spanish viceregal capital, then mushroomed into a modern metropolis.

Foundation and Early Vicissitudes (1535–1548)

Prior to the arrival of the Spaniards, the narrow valley bordering the Rímac River—one of the few fertile strips set amid a vast, rainless, coastal desert—was dominated by the small temple at Pachacamac, whose god was believed to control earthquakes. Although it is situated in a tropical latitude, its climate is humid and cool from April through November because of continual cloud cover generated by the cold offshore current (later named the Humboldt Current); it remains sunny and hot during the summer months of December to March.

Pachacamac was first visited by twenty mounted Spaniards and some foot soldiers under Hernando Pizarro in late January 1533, who had been detached from Cajamarca by his brother and commander in chief, Francisco Pizarro, to conduct a reconnaissance. Finding most of the temple's gilt decorations already removed, they vainly searched for this treasure until early March before rejoining the main army. Less than two years later, after the Incas had been vanquished and their imperial capital of Cuzco overrun high up in the Andes, Francisco Pizarro decided to create a new capital at Pachacamac. Its seaside setting would allow unimpeded access to Spanish reinforcements and supplies sailing down from Panama, his few thousand troops still being heavily outnumbered by millions of restive new vassals.

Consequently, on 6 January 1535—Epiphany, or the Day of the Three Kings on the Church calendar—the Ciudad de los Reyes (City of the Kings) was founded on the southern banks of the Rímac River, just north of the old Indian town of Pachacamac. Throughout the early colonial era, the capital was to remain known as Ciudad de los Reyes, the name Lima appar-

Pencil sketch looking south past the seventeenth-century Montesclaros Bridge toward the city spires, dated "Dec. 20 de 1842" by the famous visiting German artist, Johann Moritz Rugendas. (National Museum, Lima)

ently being a later corruption of the word *Rímac,* or perhaps derived from the original indigenous town of Limatambo, 3 miles distant. On 18 January a dozen large urban plots were distributed among the first Spanish citizens, and a *cabildo* (city council) was constituted four days afterward. Another fifty-seven families arrived in March 1535 to receive more allotments, while construction was initiated on a simple adobe church, Pizarro's fortified mansion, and numerous private residences—most being stout blockhouses surrounded by vegetable gardens and orchards. Ten miles downstream lay the port of Callao, one of few sheltered anchorages along Peru's otherwise exposed Pacific coastline.

Pizarro's precaution paid dividends when the captive emperor Manco II organized an uprising in the mountains, his victorious general Quizo Yupanqui descending into the coastal plateau with a huge Incan army in August 1536 to invest the fledgling Spanish capital. Capt. Pedro de Lerma sortied with seventy riders to check this approach, fighting a sharp engagement in which one Spaniard was killed and many others wounded, before being pressed back into the city through sheer weight of numbers. Another sally by Pizarro's cavalry compelled Quizo Yupanqui to retreat north of the Rímac River into defensive positions atop 2,789-foot San Cristóbal Hill, from where—after six days of seesaw fighting—the indigenous commander launched a desperate, three-pronged assault against the Spanish defenses. Personally leading the eastern column with his senior staff, Quizo Yupanqui received the brunt of two cavalry squadrons streaming out of the City of the Kings under Pizarro, being slain along with most of his Incan

officers and countless followers, so that his army melted away that same night.

The Spaniards reconquered the Andes shortly thereafter, yet because of lingering fears regarding a possible recurrence of a revolt, the capital's dwellings remained stout adobe blockhouses, clustered around its main square, or Plaza de Armas, for mutual protection. Nor were Indian rebellions the only danger, for on 26 June 1541, twenty embittered supporters of the disenfranchised Spanish leader Diego de Almagro "the Younger" forced their way into Pizarro's palace and hacked the sixty-three-year-old *marqués* to death, sparking a civil war between rival Spanish factions that was not put down until fifteen months later.

Then in September 1544, the first Crown-appointed viceroy for Peru—Blasco Núñez Vela, installed in the City of the Kings scarcely four months previously—was deposed by its *Audiencia* (high tribunal) for his heavy-handed zeal in trying to implement Spain's new laws to protect Indian serfs. Gonzalo Pizarro subsequently entered the capital, having rallied popular support against a purported indigenous uprising, and he compelled the viceroy to flee to Ecuador. Núñez Vela tried to install a counter-administration at the old northern Inca capital of Quito, but Pizarro defeated him again in January 1546, thus becoming undisputed master over all Peru—despite professing unswerving loyalty throughout this episode to the Spanish monarch. That same autumn, another Crown emissary—Licentiate Pedro de la Gasca—arrived in Ecuador from Spain and won over many Peruvian adherents by 1547, so that he was eventually able to defeat Pizarro near Cuzco in April 1548.

View looking northward across the Rímac River toward San Cristóbal Hill, ca. 1900; note the modern lampposts adorning Montesclaros Bridge, plus the railway tracks in the foreground. (Dawson, *The South American Republics*)

Viceregal Capital (1549–1745)

Notwithstanding this political anarchy and the dislocation of all its trade, the farmland around the City of the Kings had ensured its survival, and many more Spanish migrants began disembarking from overseas once Crown rule was peacefully restored. The tiny capital's original urban core expanded as a result, a span of bricks replacing the old rope suspension bridge across the Rímac by 1560, so that such unpalatable municipal institutions as the slaughterhouse and San Lázaro leper colony could be transferred across to its northern bank. A 2-mile-long aqueduct was also initiated by 1562, extending northeastward to bring water from the Incan-era spring of Cacahuasi (soon renamed La Atarjea or "The Conduit" by the Spaniards), while the small city infirmary was supplanted the next year by the Real Hospital de San Andrés (Royal Saint Andrew's Hospital). A royal mint was completed by August 1565, work on a magnificent new cathedral commenced the next year, the first inquisitorial officers arrived from Spain by late November 1569, and street paving was commenced in 1570.

This urban boom had been bolstered by the discovery of rich mines at Potosí (Bolivia), whose silver output increasingly flowed through the viceregal capital. Early every year a pair of galleons would depart southeastward from Callao, pausing at Chincha to take on *azogue* (mercury) from the Huancavelica mines to be delivered at Arica for use in processing Potosí's raw ores. The galleons would be met at the latter port by teamsters bringing down Potosí's annual silver output, which was to be conveyed into the treasury in the City of the Kings for assay and the levying of royal taxes, then subsequently forwarded to Spain aboard another pair of galleons that sailed northward every May or June for Panama to meet the annual plate-fleet traversing the Atlantic.

This second pair of Peruvian galleons would be accompanied from Callao by a convoy of merchantmen, who sold South American produce at Panama's commercial fair, then returned by the end of that same year with their purchased European goods to be resold throughout the viceroyalty. The City of the Kings soon developed a reputation for ostentatious luxury thanks to its monopoly over this rich traffic, many of its flat-roofed, single- or double-story, whitewashed homes becoming embellished with elaborate Moorish balconies and carved stone portals. (Most decorative elements, such as wrought iron, sculptures, colored tiles, even architectural plans, still had to be imported from Spain during the late sixteenth century.) Its churches also became increasingly ornate and eventually glittered with gold and silver adornments, while its Real y Pontif-

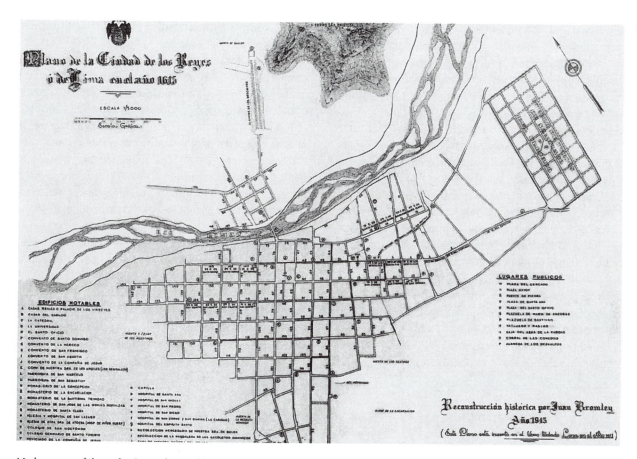

Modern map of the early viceregal capital by Juan Bromley and José Barbagelata B., showing its configuration, ca. 1613. (National Library, Lima)

ica Universidad de San Marcos (Royal and Pontifical University of Saint Mark)—officially accredited as of May 1551, although initially confined to only a few rooms in the Dominican monastery—moved into resplendent new quarters by 1576.

An earthquake brought down several major edifices on 9 July 1586, while numerous other damaged buildings had to be either demolished or repaired, after which an outbreak of measles and smallpox claimed more lives three years later. The capital nonetheless resurged, its commerce continuing to flourish despite the first foreign rovers to round the Strait of Magellan and raid the Pacific coast: Francis Drake in 1579, Thomas Cavendish in 1587, Richard Hawkins in 1594, and the Dutchmen Olivier van Noort and Simon de Cordes in 1599. Such single-ship ventures were little more than a transitory nuisance, so that the urban population had grown to a robust 14,262 inhabitants by 1599. Three of the six arches of its brick bridge across the Rímac were washed away by heavy flooding in 1607, so that the entire span was replaced in stone, under the supervision of the engineer Juan del Corral (resulting in Montesclaros Bridge, named in honor of the reigning viceroy, Juan Manuel de Mendoza y Luna, Marqués de Montesclaros and knight grand cross of the Order of Santiago).

Another quake rattled the City of the Kings in 1610, but the number of residents nevertheless soared to 25,434 people by 1614, categorized as 9,616 Spaniards, 2,518 clerics, 10,386 blacks, 1,978 Indians, 744 mulattoes, and 192 mestizos. The capital now boasted six convents, five monasteries, a half dozen hospitals, five colleges, and a theater, yet its citizens were unexpectedly alarmed by the defeat—virtually within sight of shore—of Callao's battle squadron by five Dutch men-of-war under Commo. Joris van Spilbergen in July 1615. The city's vulnerability to foreign attack was further underscored when the ten-ship expedition of Jacques l'Hermite materialized off Callao in May 1624 and attempted to disembark several hundred heavily armed Dutch soldiers; despite being discouraged by the sight of three hastily assembled infantry companies and two cavalry squadrons under Viceroy Diego Fernández de Córdoba, Marqués de Guadalcázar and Conde de las Posadas, these interlopers nonetheless hovered offshore with impunity for another 100 days, impeding all commerce.

Municipal authorities were therefore galvanized into requesting the erection of a wall around their unfortified capital, yet royal funds were allocated only for a temporary strengthening of Callao's shore batteries, after which Limeños were distracted when another devastating earthquake struck at 11:30 A.M. on 27 November 1630, so that all defensive measures were shelved. The City of the Kings was painstakingly resurrected and enjoyed several decades of relative peace and stability, although overall silver output declined, and Spain's power was eclipsed in Europe.

Another cataclysmic quake occurred on 17 June 1678, after which it was furthermore learned that buccaneer contingents were pushing out of the Caribbean and around the Strait of Magellan to raid Spanish America's vulnerable Pacific coastline, so that demands for Lima's fortification were revived. The first section of a 7-mile circuit connected by thirty-four bastions was consequently started on 30 June 1684, being completed three and a half years later, after considerable deviation from the original plans devised by the Flemish-born Jesuit priest Jean-Raymond Coninck. This project was carried through despite another triple earthquake that struck between dawn and dusk of 20 October 1687, damaging structures such as the viceregal palace so badly that only its ground floor could be restored, while its upper level was eliminated altogether; Archbishop Melchor de Liñán y Cisneros's residence had to be

entirely demolished and rebuilt, while that prelate recuperated from his injuries at Callao.

Although Lima was to remain enclosed by its circuit of ramparts for the next couple of centuries, the city did not entirely occupy this vast enclosure, sufficient space having been left for parks and private orchards. By 1700, the number of residents had risen to 37,234 and—thanks to an overhaul of Spain's decayed administrative apparatus and other modest reforms enacted by the new Bourbon monarch at Madrid—the Peruvian capital was to embark upon another period of prosperity and peaceful development, reflected by the appearance of its first baroque-style buildings.

Devastation and Resurrection (1746–1820)
Most of Lima was leveled by yet another heavy earthquake at 10:30 P.M. on Friday, 28 October 1746, which claimed 2,000 lives—plus 5,000 more at Callao and 3,000 others throughout the district—and was to be remembered as the worst catastrophe in the city's history. Because of such widespread destruction, the capital recuperated more slowly, while many of its most ancient buildings were lost forever when Viceroy

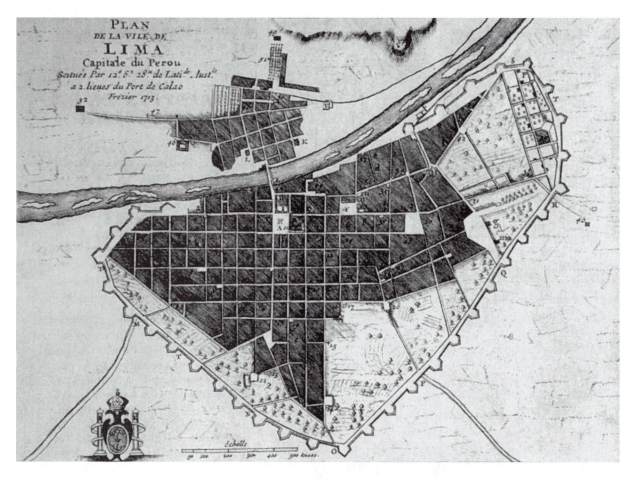

Map of Lima as it appeared in October 1713, by the French traveler Amédée-François Frézier; published in Paris three years later as an insert to his book *Relation du voyage de la mer du Sud aux cotes du Chily et du Perou*. (Metropolitan Toronto Reference Library)

José Antonio Manso de Velasco, Conde de Superunda, ordered all damaged structures torn down and replaced by simpler yet sturdier edifices, rather than risk repairing or reconstructing vulnerable designs.

Confidence gradually revived among the citizenry, while Peru's economy—along with that of the entire Spanish empire—continued to blossom throughout the late eighteenth century. Urban amenities such as a new bullring in the San Lorenzo sector were added by 1766–1768, public oil lamps were introduced as of 1776, streets were named and numbered during the early 1780s, a police force was created by 1787, fine rococo-style mansions multiplied, and so forth. By 1791, Lima's population had rebounded to 52,627 residents (including 17,215 Spaniards and 13,479 slaves), while a grand new highway to its seaport of Callao was also completed by January 1799, and a public cemetery—deliberately sited downwind of the capital—was inaugurated by 1808.

That same summer, Limeños were astonished to learn that the French emperor, Napoleon I, had sent an army into Spain to depose Ferdinand VII in favor of his brother Joseph Bonaparte. This crude usurpation of power was repudiated by Peruvian subjects, yet the subsequent loosening of imperial ties sparked the first aspirations toward independence elsewhere in the Americas, as many mixed-heritage Creoles had grown resentful of the preferments routinely accorded peninsular-born Spaniards by Crown or Church officials in Madrid. Rebellions consequently exploded throughout the continent, but because of its large permanent garrison and conservative inclinations, Lima remained a loyal bastion of the Crown, serving as a springboard for expeditions dispatched to other endangered monarchist outposts.

The capital's population grew to 63,900 people by 1812, and its defenses were bolstered by the completion of Fort Santa Catalina by artillery colonel and future viceroy Joaquín de la Pezuela y Sánchez, as well as by the creation of a new military college, artillery foundry, an improved gunpowder factory, and the San Fernando College of Medicine. Still, Loyalist reverses elsewhere in South America eventually allowed insurgent Gen. José Francisco de San Martín to sail past Callao at the end of October 1820 with a Chileo-Argentine fleet, disembarking his army 30 miles farther northwest at Ancón. Although this force proved insufficient to storm Lima's defenses, San Martín's presence on Peruvian soil nonetheless drained royalist resolve, as outlying detachments began surrendering or switching allegiance and Creole sentiment coalesced around these would-be liberators.

Insurgent Conquest (1821–1825)

Debilitated by its isolation, starvation, and disease, Lima was finally abandoned by Viceroy José de la Serna in favor of more impregnable Callao at dawn on 5 July 1821, leaving behind 1,000 troops who were too ill to march. Monarchist adherents also took flight, and looting gripped the half-deserted city until

an insurgent force entered four days later, proclaiming Peruvian independence by 28 July. The city's commercial traffic nonetheless remained obstructed by the royalists holding Callao, so that great want and unemployment persisted, while the 5,900 insurgent troops assigned to reclaim the seaport soon became infected by diseases emanating out of Lima. On 10 September, 3,200 royalist troops descended out of the Andes under Gen. José de Canterac to relieve Callao of its vital military stores, after which the empty stronghold was surrendered to the patriots.

This capitulation of its sea outlet at least permitted San Martín to receive fifty-three Peruvian delegates at a swearing-in ceremony in Lima's cathedral on 20 September 1822, who then retired into the University of San Marcos chapel to celebrate the nation's first republican congress. Yet the gutted city remained otherwise supine, a mere symbolic prize for the two contending sides. During a temporary absence of the main patriot armies farther southeast in June 1823, Canterac and his subordinate José María Valdéz again descended from Huancayo in the central highlands with 9,000 royalist troops, driving Gen. Antonio José de Sucre Alcalá's surprised 5,000-man insurgent garrison back out of Lima into Callao. But these monarchists could not hold the capital for want of provisions, and so disappeared toward Jauja and Huancavelica on 1 July.

Lima reverted to republican control by default, until Callao's unpaid garrison mutinied on 5 February 1824 and Canterac dispatched yet another column down from Jauja under Brig. Juan Antonio Monet, who closed in upon the unhappy capital by 29 February and compelled Simón Bolívar's weak and divided government to flee. The monarchists chose to retain the city's shell only until 18 March, while ensconcing a strong garrison in Callao; consequently, the unwanted capital remained unclaimed once more, until Gen. Luis Urdaneta's republican army reappeared in late October, followed shortly thereafter by Bolívar himself—fresh from his smashing victory at Junín—who deployed 3,000 troops to besiege the 2,700 monarchists entrenched in Callao. The monarchists finally agreed to capitulate on 23 January 1826, and thus brought an end to Spanish America's eighteen-year struggle for liberty.

Early Republican Era (1826–1880)

Lima's recovery from its five years of evacuations, invasions, and occupations was subsequently further complicated by factional infighting among the victors, whose disputes often entailed military coups and countercoups enacted within the capital. The Bolivian strongman Andrés de Santa Cruz eventually imposed a confederation in 1836 that united both impoverished republics, yet drew them into conflict against Chile and Argentina that same November. This war was concluded when a 6,000-man Chilean expedition and numerous Peruvian dissidents defeated Santa Cruz in the highlands north of Lima in January 1839, some measure of the capital's

Part of Lima's main square, as it appeared during the mid-nineteenth century; note the general air of dilapidation following several decades of difficulties, plus the open sewers in the street. (National Library, Lima)

diminution being gauged by a census taken that same year, which revealed that its population had shrunk to 55,627.

The strongman Marshal Ramón Castilla restored some measure of stability during his reign in the late 1840s, while the city and coastal economies were simultaneously spurred by an export boom of guano (a nitrate fertilizer deposited on offshore islands by seabirds, greatly coveted by international markets). Thanks to this revival of trade and enhanced foreign investments, the capital began to modernize through the introduction of such innovations as its first gas lamps—illuminated in May 1855—as well as by the completion that same month of the Ferrocarril Inglés (English Railway), running from the new urban terminal (formerly the San Juan de Dios Convent) westward to Callao. Iron tubing also replaced the old colonial-era, baked-clay water pipes, while telegraph service appeared by 1857, the same year in which a census indicated that Lima's population had rebounded dramatically to 94,195 people.

An economic blockade was imposed in April 1864 by a Spanish squadron, which persisted until Peru's president Juan Antonio Pezet acceded to their terms early the next year, after which Colonel Mariano Ignacio Prado launched a rebellion that drove the discredited Pezet from Lima in November 1865, and the Spaniards returned to shell Callao the next summer. A yellow fever outbreak also occurred in 1868–1869. Nevertheless, a vast new sewerage system was installed in the city, while Lima's emergent civilian elite furthermore began erecting splendid new urban residences, as well as fine summer homes at the nearby resort towns of Miraflores and Chorillos, effectively expanding the capital's boundaries southward beyond its old ramparts. This growth was greatly facilitated when the American entrepreneur Henry Meiggs was hired to tear down the crumbling old defensive walls during the late 1860s and early 1870s, making way for broad avenues and rail lines radiating up into the Andes.

Chilean Occupation (1881–1884)

Unfortunately, this progress was to become severely curtailed when Peru and Bolivia became jointly embroiled in a conflict against Chile in April 1879, the so-called War of the Pacific. At first, battles were confined far to the south of Lima, but a Chilean naval blockade was eventually imposed, after which the Peruvo-Bolivian armies were defeated; a 24,000-man Chilean expedition under Gen. Manuel Baquedano then disembarked near Pisco in November 1880, driving against the capital.

Its 101,000 residents pinned their hopes upon a hastily constructed line of fortifications north of the Lurín River, extending for 8.5 miles through the San Juan foothills and held by 22,000 Peruvian troops—mostly raw militiamen and civilian recruits under Gen. Miguel Iglesias. The invaders reached the opposite banks by mid-December, forging across into the town of Chorrillos at dawn on 13 January 1881. They killed almost 4,000 defenders and captured 1,500, while sending the survivors reeling back toward Lima in disarray. Only the fact that the Chilean troops paused to loot the wealthy summer homes, then inflicted a like treatment upon Barranco the next day, permitted the Peruvians sufficient time to reassemble 5,000 men in a shaky 4-mile line of defenses along the Surco River, 2.5 miles outside their capital.

A delegation of international diplomats headed by Salvadorian ambassador Jorge Tezanos Pinto arranged a ceasefire and conference at Miraflores in the no-man's-land between both armies for 15 January 1881. But the meeting between Peru's president, Nicolás de Piérola, and the Chilean commander in chief, Baquedano, was interrupted by gunfire shortly after 2:00 P.M., the invaders having continued to deploy their units for a final assault: a jittery Peruvian company had consequently opened fire when a Chilean artillery battery began unlimbering within point-blank range. Spontaneous fire erupted all up and down both battle lines, as well as from the Chilean warships offshore, while the diplomats fled.

The Peruvian army was shattered by nightfall, defeated troops retreating through the capital as rioting and pillage erupted. De Piérola galloped toward Tarma and Jauja to continue resisting from the mountainous interior, leaving Mayor Rufino Torrico to offer to surrender Lima to the victors on the morning of 16 January 1881. A select regiment of 3,000 Chilean troops entered at 2:00 P.M. the next afternoon under Gen. Cornelio Saavedra, restoring order. But the ensuing two and a half years of occupation proved extremely bitter for Limeños, as the Chileans stripped their city of its industrial base and cultural heritage to help defray their war costs. Among much damage, the University of San Marcos was looted and the National Library destroyed.

Eventually, the Peruvian lawyer Dr. Francisco García Calderón—defying the discredited de Piérola—created a provisional government in the La Magdalena suburb of occupied Lima on 12 March 1881, then entered into negotiations with the Chileans. However, it was not until the war hero Iglesias was acclaimed as president at Cajamarca and sat down with Chilean intermediaries at Ancón that a treaty could be hammered out and the damaged capital restored to Peruvian control on 23 October 1883. Even then, other Peruvian factions refused to ratify this agreement until June 1884—Bolivia concurring only after being threatened by a Chilean invasion—

Some of the ruins left by the 1881 Chilean invasion and occupation, as they appeared once the city had started to recuperate a few years later. (Curtis, *The Capitals of Spanish America*)

so that an actual suspension of hostilities was not finally achieved until August 1884. Nor did Lima's sufferings end there, for on 27 August 1884 a guerrilla army under Andrés Avelino Cáceres descended out of the Andes to assault the capital, sparking a year-long struggle to drive the "traitor" Iglesias from office.

Modern Era (1885–Present)

Lima had stagnated because of this protracted ordeal, the number of its inhabitants rebounding to 103,956 only by 1891; it was not to be until de Piérola returned to power four years later and launched an ambitious reconstruction and modernization scheme—financed by the exploitation of heretofore untapped rubber and petroleum resources in Peru's eastern jungles—that the capital at last began its long climb back to prosperity. Electric power became widely available throughout the city as of 1902, in turn allowing for the introduction of a streetcar system for its 139,400 citizens.

Unrest resumed when the radical politician Augusto Durand led an unsuccessful uprising against Pres. José Pardo y Barreda in May 1908, which was suppressed through hundreds of arrests; after that, two dozen of de Piérola's backers stormed the national palace on 29 May 1909 and seized the recently installed president Augusto B. Leguía, parading him through the streets in a vain attempt to foment a popular insurrection. A military coup spearheaded by Col. José Urdanivia Ginés on 4 February 1914 proved more successful, unseating President Guillermo Billinghurst (the grandson of an English naval officer who had served in the war of independence) on its second assault directed against the national palace.

Starting during the 1920s, Lima's economy began to grow exponentially, reflected by a demographic explosion as its urban population rose from 173,007 residents in 1920 to 273,016 by 1931. Such a dramatic increase naturally precipitated a real estate boom, banks and financial institutions funding the construction of an ever-widening ring of suburban neighborhoods that eventually engulfed many outlying communities and farms. The global effects of the Great Depression, which started in October 1929, abruptly curtailed development and precipitated another military uprising, the Arequipa garrison of Lt.-Col. Luis M. Sánchez Cerro revolting against Leguía in August 1930. When this opposition spread into the capital itself, the president fled out to sea aboard the cruiser *Almirante Grau*, leaving Sánchez Cerro to reach Lima by airplane and receive a tumultuous welcome before establishing a junta.

Politics became increasingly volatile in the needy and underserviced metropolis when Victor Raúl Haya de la Torre of the Alianza Popular Revolucionaria Americana (Popular American Revolutionary Alliance)—better known by its acronym of APRA, members being referred to as Apristas—called for a leftist reaction against the colonel's installation as president on 8 December 1931. Violence escalated until Sánchez Cerro was wounded in an assassination attempt on 6 March 1932, after which a major Aprista revolt was crushed that summer at Trujillo. Resistance subsequently moved underground, until the president—after reviewing 25,000 troops at Lima's San Beatriz racetrack on 30 April 1933—was murdered by an Aprista gunman.

The Peruvian military nonetheless retained a grip on power, while urban conditions worsened as the city's population more than doubled from 402,976 people in 1940 to 835,400 a decade later, many new residents being rural migrants attracted by the industrial and trade jobs being generated during World War II. Social discontent and economic difficulties in the aftermath of that global conflict encouraged yet another revolt by the Arequipa garrison, this time led by Brig. Manuel A. Odría against President José Luis Bustamante y Rivero on 27 October 1948. When the commander of Lima's troops refused to obey a presidential order to march against the rebel, Bustamante realized that all was lost, and so withdrew from the national palace two days later. Odría assumed power thanks to this so-called Restorative Revolution, then set about stamping out leftist opposition.

Lima continued its rampant growth as the population skyrocketed to 1,578,298 residents by 1961, the first major slums

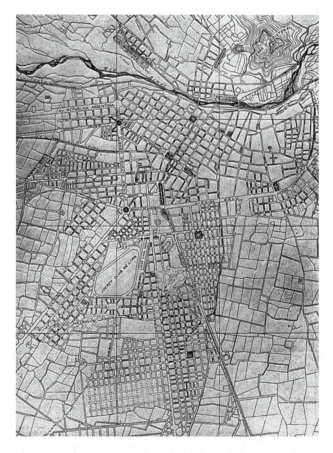

The city as it began to expand, ca. 1935. (National Library, Lima)

appearing around its periphery; the housing market could no longer keep pace with the massive influx from Peru's impoverished rural areas. Like many other Latin American megalopolises, the Peruvian capital would continue to expand, as it was now the undisputed industrial, commercial, and political center for the nation, handling roughly 80 percent of all imports and 50 percent of all exports. No other Peruvian city could take in the streams of people seeking better prospects.

Once again, economic difficulties and festering social unrest encouraged Gen. Ricardo Pérez Godoy to topple President Manuel Prado y Ugarteche in a dawn coup on 18 July 1962, ten days before the latter's term in office was to expire. Pérez Godoy was in turn unseated by Gen. Nicolás Lindley in early March 1963, while the elected president, Fernando Belaúnde Terry—beset by political scandal—was deposed by yet another military coup on 3 October 1968, engineered by the reform-minded Gen. Juan Velasco Alvarado. The coastal capital sprawled ever farther afield and its population doubled yet again to slightly more than 3,317,000 inhabitants by 1972, discontent festering among the poverty and political corruption of its illegal slums, which now held 25 percent of all residents. That figure swelled to almost 33 percent by the 1990s, as the total urban populace mushroomed from 6.98 million by the beginning of that decade to more than 8 million by its conclusion.

Municipal management could no longer cope with such widespread needs, so that these slum enclaves became hotbeds of extremism, whose demands could even affect Peru's domestic and international agenda. Leftist urban movements such as the Sendero Luminoso (Shining Path) guerrillas spread out from universities into the countryside, the most dramatic confrontation in Lima occurring when seventy-two hostages were seized in the Japanese embassy by fourteen gunmen of the Movimiento Revolucionario Tupác Amaru (Tupác Amaru

Milkwoman on horseback, ca. 1900. (Dawson, *The South American Republics*)

Revolutionary Movement, or MRTA). A four-month standoff ended when 140 Peruvian commandos successfully stormed the building on the afternoon of 22 April 1997.

For further reading materials on Lima or Peru, please consult the Select Bibliography at the end of this volume; additional sources on South American urban history can be found under "Regional Studies," as well as under "General Works on Latin America."

Surinam

PARAMARIBO

Capital and only major city in this nation, whose ethnic and racial diversity reflects the multifaceted history of this former Dutch colony.

Initial Settlement (1651–1666)

Although explorers had sighted the coast of the Guianas as early as Christopher Columbus in 1498, subsequent Spanish and Portuguese colonizing efforts were directed into other regions of the continent. Dutch, English, and French masters therefore found this stretch of low, hot coastline still unclaimed at the beginning of the seventeenth century and so began bartering with local tribesmen for tobacco and other produce. Dutch merchants referred to these territories collectively as the Wild Coast, and it is recorded that Dirck Claeszoon van Sanen and Nicolaes Baliestel penetrated the milewide, silty mouth of the Surinam River—often spelled Suriname, apparently being named after a particular flower that proliferates along its banks—to establish a temporary trading post as early as 1613 at an Indian village variously called Purmerbo, Paramaru, or Paramurubo by the Caribs or Simarabo by the Arawaks. This site was located on the northwestern bank of the winding river, 7 miles from the sea.

Soon, these first visitors sought to establish permanent footholds ashore to begin harvesting their own cash crops, warehousing goods, and reprovisioning ships from their homelands; all three nationalities therefore installed numerous tiny bases in the Guianas over the next several decades, most of which succumbed to starvation, disease, abandonment, Indian attacks, or Hispano-Portuguese counterexpeditions. It is believed that a group of sixty English settlers ventured up the Surinam River to begin carving out some small plantations in 1630, being joined two years later by a few Jewish colleagues and more Dutch colonists in 1633.

The inland territory proved to be vast, the Surinam River being navigable up to 100 miles inland by vessels drawing up to 10 feet of water. Most inhabitants lived tolerantly with each other for companionship during these early days, often being spread far apart throughout this coastal alluvial zone, doing their best to support one another amid the difficulties of this tropical isolation. They soon realized that Surinam's shoreline consisted of some 12 to 15 miles of flattish, steamy swamps and mangroves crisscrossed by waterways that gave way to another 20 or so miles of undulating, grassy savannas before finally turning into impenetrable, mountainous jungle farther south in the highlands. Its equatorial climate was uniformly

Paramaribo as it appeared shortly before the devastating fire of 21 January 1821; note the low marshy terrain. (Atlas van Stolk Foundation, Rotterdam)

807

hot and humid, eased only by occasional sea breezes, as well as copious rainfalls from May through August.

In 1643, a certain Captain Marshall arrived from Barbados with a significant new number of English colonists, and in March 1644 a French ship from Cayenne deposited another sixty settlers at Paramaribo. Yet after dispersing to begin their farming activities, most of these newcomers were lost to illness or hostilities among each other or against the local Indians. Consequently, Surinam was not to be fully secured until seven years later, when the energetic Francis, Lord Willoughby of Parham, the governor of Barbados, raised an expedition of 300 men under Anthony Rowse, who disembarked and negotiated a land treaty with the coastal tribes early in 1651. Rowse then set about developing a proper colony, headquartered 20 miles inland at Thorarica yet with its river approaches protected by a wooden stockade enclosing a stone strong-house at Paramaribo, in whose shadow a town soon began to evolve (its nearby land being cleared of trees, whose trunks were subsequently used to erect some fifty crude huts outside that structure). When a ship under Commander Vertammon appeared on 10 April 1653 from Fort Cépérou (later to become Fort Saint Michel at Cayenne) to reclaim the original abandoned French settlement at Paramaribo, he instead found a thriving English community of perhaps 350 people.

Willoughby had also toured this new territory in 1652, bringing more English and Jewish settlers, although Surinam was not to be officially granted to him until a decade later— once Charles II was restored to England's throne—at which time the territory became briefly known as Willoughby-Land. It prospered still more thanks to the arrival from Brazil of yet further Dutch and Jewish refugee planters, whose experience of New World conditions so enhanced sugar production that by 1663 Surinam boasted a population of 1,000 whites, 2,000 African slaves, and 1,000 natives scattered among fifty large and several hundred smaller plantations. When the Second Anglo-Dutch War erupted early in 1665, the English sensibly transferred their administrative center from Thorarica into Paramaribo and were even strong enough to conquer most of the weaker Dutch outposts to the northwest—a campaign that in turn provoked a counterstroke out of Europe.

Dutch Conquest (1667)

Zeeland was the province responsible for Dutch settlements in the Guianas, so in December 1666 it fitted out an expedition "to reconquer, with God's help, the territory the enemy have taken from us." Commo. Abraham Crijnssen—soon to become known among the English as "Captain Crimson"—materialized unexpectedly before Paramaribo on the afternoon of 26 February 1667 with his 34-gun flagship *Zeelandia* and a half dozen other warships, manned by almost 1,000 sailors and soldiers. William Byam, the English governor, rebuffed Crijnssen's initial call for surrender, so the next morning the Dutch squadron bore down and opened fire on 21-gun Fort

View northeastward across Paramaribo, ca. 1946. (Van de Poll, *Suriname: Een fotoreportage,* 1949)

Willoughby (as yet incomplete), then set 700 men ashore who quickly obliged its outnumbered garrison to lay down their arms.

After haggling over terms for five days, Byam agreed to allow Surinam to pass under Dutch rule, its multinational residents either switching fealty to the States General or emigrating to an English colony. These articles were signed aboard *Zeelandia* by 6 March 1667, after which Crijnseen improved Paramaribo's defenses—in the process renaming its citadel Fort Zeelandia and installing a 250-man garrison under Maurits de Rame—before departing toward Berbice (modern New Amsterdam, Guyana) on 17 April to continue his New World campaign.

Meanwhile, English forces in the Leeward Islands under William Willoughby—younger brother of the now-deceased Francis, as well as his successor as governor of Barbados— quickly massed to recoup Surinam, a large fleet reaching Paramaribo by 13 October 1667 under Rear Adm. Sir John Harman and Willoughby's son, Henry. Disembarking a half mile from Fort Zeelandia, the English troops surrounded it, then called for de Rame's capitulation at nightfall. The Dutch commander refused, yet after a four-day lull caused by a lack of wind, Henry Willoughby and Harman launched a combined land-sea assault on 17 October that drove the demoralized Dutch from their guns and obliged de Rame to request terms. Before they could be finalized, some English soldiers swam ashore and occupied

Fort Zeelandia, seemingly consummating the reconquest of Surinam. A new garrison and governor—James Bannister—were installed before this fleet returned toward Barbados.

Two weeks later, however, a trio of vessels arrived at Paramaribo from The Netherlands with news that a general peace had already been concluded by the signing of the Treaty of Breda on 31 July 1667, whereby Surinam was to be retained by the Dutch in exchange for New Netherland (modern New York). A new governor—Willem Hendricksen—had even come out to take possession, yet Bannister refused to comply without confirmation from his superiors. Frustrated at the prospect of losing his prize, Henry Willoughby soon arrived from Barbados and delayed matters further, before finally resorting to the burning of sugar mills, the inducement of settlers to emigrate, and the appropriation of slaves and cattle in order to render the colony useless to the Dutch. Eventually, Commodore Crijnssen reappeared on 25 April 1668 with 270 sailors and 180 soldiers aboard his frigates *Suriname* and *Zeelandia,* plus the flute, or transport, *Land van Beloften* ("Promised Land"), threatening to bombard Fort Zeelandia if its recalcitrant English occupiers did not immediately decamp. At long last, they agreed to submit and Crijnssen temporarily assumed office as Surinam's new governor, Henry Willoughby and his father, William, later being compelled to pay for all their property damages.

Early Sugar Capital (1668–1711)

Nevertheless, some 1,200 residents had forsaken Surinam, and its economy was therefore crippled, a mere 564 slaves being left to work its remaining twenty-three plantations. In order to underscore their exclusive claim over this territory, its new rulers renamed Paramaribo "New Middelburg," after the famous port in Zeeland (although its original Indian name proved impossible to dislodge; a subsequent attempt to rename the capital Surinaamsburgh toward the end of the seventeenth century also failed). In March 1673, when the Third Anglo-Dutch War broke out, Surinam was reinforced by a small squadron out of Zeeland under Commo. Cornelis Evertsen de Jongste—nicknamed "Kees the Devil"—yet it remained such an impoverished, untempting target that it did not even warrant a single enemy attack during the ensuing five years of conflict (which was fortunate, as a letter by Pieter Versterre in 1675 claimed that the colony could count upon only "123 able-bodied men of the Dutch nation and 58 able-bodied men of the Jewish nation"). Reporting from Paramaribo toward the end of December 1678, its new governor, Johannes Heinsius, described the capital as merely "an open borough with some scattered houses."

Because of such poor prospects, Zeeland sold its unprofitable colony to the West Indische Maatschappij (West India Company) for 260,000 florins in June 1682. Then, the next year, the city of Amsterdam and Cornelis van Aerssen, Lord van Sommelsdijck, each acquired a third share as well, combining to create the Geoctroyeerde Societeit van Suriname (Chartered Society of Surinam). That same September of 1683, Sommelsdijck set sail for Paramaribo as Surinam's new governor, determined to revive its fortunes. Upon his arrival, he found pentagonal Fort Zeelandia totally dilapidated and the capital "consisting of only 27 or 28 houses," many of which also served as taverns.

The English had originally established their stronghold atop a low, stony ridge to protect it from incoming tides. Sommelsdijck therefore delegated Fort Zeelandia's soldiers to begin replacing its wooden stockades with ramparts made from local "shell-stone" (whose softness would help absorb cannonballs), while further ordering the construction of a new "Fort Sommelsdijck" at the confluence of the Commewijne and Cottica rivers. He also ordered a fortified outpost on Para Creek to resist the increasingly frequent Indian raids out of the interior. Only fifty to sixty plantations were in operation, but with admirable drive, Sommelsdijck was able to reinvigorate the colonial administration and economy. In 1684 alone, fifty-two new estates were laid out, while the following year the French Crown's revocation of the Edict of Nantes brought a fresh wave of Huguenot refugees into Surinam; in 1686, Sommelsdijck signed a treaty with the inland tribes that restored some measure of peace. Sugar exports quickly rose from 3.5 million pounds to more than 5 million by 1687 and 7 million by 1688.

Unfortunately, Sommelsdijck's heavy-handed reformist zeal had also provoked much local resentment, and on 17 July 1688 he was approached by spokesmen for the 60 soldiers toiling on Fort Zeelandia's defenses, who complained about their meager rations and harsh work conditions. Outraged, the governor drove them from his mansion with a cane, only to be shot two days later by their aggrieved comrades. The mutineers thereupon gathered 140 to 150 disgruntled men, disarmed the local militia, and seized two ships in the roadstead to sail away before their resolve finally collapsed and they were recalled to order by the arrival of a new governor, Johan van Scharphuysen. Notwithstanding this outburst, Paramaribo's garrison responded well when nine French vessels under Capt. Jean-Baptiste Ducasse appeared offshore from Cayenne and threatened a disembarkation on 6 May 1689 during the opening phases of the War of the League of Augsburg, or King William's War. Fort Zeelandia's 69 soldiers were quickly reinforced by 84 Jewish volunteers under their veteran Capt. Samuel Cohen Nassy, as well as another 78 Dutch militiamen, compelling the attackers to withdraw without attempting an assault. A similar incursion seven years later also ended anticlimactically.

Although Surinam's white civilian population stood at only 319 by 1693, its black slaves now numbered 4,756, and the plantation system had become firmly entrenched. In addition to sugar, exports through Paramaribo included tobacco, letter wood, cotton, indigo, various gums and resins, plus indigenous goods such as hammocks and cassava. The city began to reflect this newfound prosperity by expanding westward over

A palm-lined street in Paramaribo. (Van de Poll, *Suriname,* 1959)

the next decade and a half, the sixty or so original homes along its Waterkant (Waterfront) no longer being primitive wooden huts with thatched roofs but two- or three-story dwellings in the Dutch style, spaced well apart on good-size lots. By draining adjacent marshlands with small, brick-lined canals, further terrain was freed up for expansion, and broad new streets could be laid out in a rectilinear pattern, many even lined with orange or tamarind trees against the sun's heat.

By the first decade of the eighteenth century, Paramaribo boasted perhaps 500 houses, from magnificent palaces built of shell-stone with baked-tile roofs and glass windowpanes to more modest thatch-roofed shacks with windows covered in wooden blinds or coarse wire netting. Fort Zeelandia remained isolated by its now half-empty moat, as well as its adjacent Oranjeplein parade ground (the modern Onafhankelijkheidsplein). Paramaribo's greatest drawbacks were its high percentage of wooden structures, which were always threatening to succumb to sudden outbreaks of fire, plus the poor quality

of its drinking water, which was drawn from a few brackish wells. There was also considerable drunkenness and licentiousness among its inhabitants and carousals by visiting sailors.

Cassard's Raid (1712)

Still, Surinam had grown so wealthy that in June 1712—during the closing stages of the War of the Spanish Succession, or Queen Anne's War—Commo. Jacques Cassard appeared off Paramaribo with eight French warships and two auxiliaries lent to him by the Crown, his financing having been raised by private subscribers with the specific intent of securing prize money before the final cessation of hostilities. Daunted by the Dutch batteries guarding the capital's approaches, Cassard reversed course and stood back out into the Atlantic, steering northwest toward Martinique.

But after being reinforced by thirty privateer vessels in the West Indies and ransacking English Montserrat, Cassard returned, disembarking 1,100 men on 10 October 1712 to advance overland against Paramaribo, while he himself led the remaining 1,900 men upriver aboard his squadron. Every able-bodied Dutch militiaman had rallied inside the capital under Gov. Willem de Goyer, and the invaders once again proved reluctant to storm its defenses. However, a French contingent slipped past and threatened to wreak havoc among Surinam's unguarded plantations, so that the beleaguered Dutch requested terms. Although Paramaribo itself was never taken, its defenders gave Cassard 700,000 florins' worth of sugar, 730 slaves, plus some cash in order for their properties to be spared. After visiting a like treatment upon neighboring Berbice, the French departed by December.

Recovery and Decay (1713–1798)

Wealthy planters felt aggrieved by their lack of support from the States General prior to this invasion, while they had also resented its ongoing efforts to block their imports of much-needed goods aboard British North American vessels (mostly sailing out of Boston). As a result, local resentments hardened against governors appointed from The Netherlands. The colony's economy gradually recuperated, as ever more slaves began to be imported, and a new cash crop was introduced: coffee, whose first consignment was sold in Amsterdam in 1724. Twenty years later, Surinam boasted a population of 2,129 whites and 25,135 blacks working among approximately 450 plantations. Yet this rapid growth had also displaced the old paternalistic interaction between gentlemen farmers and their small bands of loyal retainers, replacing it with a much more heartless arrangement whereby managers oversaw vast enterprises for absentee owners; the single-minded drive for profit made the slaves' existence so hellish as to incite frequent rebellions and escapes, which no amount of punishment could stem.

Paramaribo was now dominated by its planter elite, mostly

A Djuka or *bosneger,* ca. 1920, descended from the Maroons or runaway slaves who had long ago sought sanctuary in Surinam's interior. (Franck, *Working North from Patagonia*)

banks, the treatment of their slaves worsening because of ever-spiraling demands for increased production.

During Mauricius's time, the capital had evolved into a city of approximately 750 buildings, despite an outbreak of smallpox in 1743 and a fire that consumed several blocks two years later. Late in December 1772, Holland dispatched 800 soldiers—plus the gunboats *Charon* and *Cerberus*—to Surinam under Swiss-born Col. Louis Henry Fourgeoud to subdue several thousand Maroons settled along its Upper Cottica River. When united with locally raised black militiamen of the *Vrijkorps* (Free Corps, now reorganized as *Jagers,* or Hunters), they gave the colony a total of 2,300 armed men. But despite repeated campaigns over the next several years, the Maroons proved too elusive to be brought to battle.

By 1791, Paramaribo was receiving and dispatching seventy to eighty Dutch merchantmen a year, and its population was estimated at almost 13,000 people living in approximately 1,700 buildings: 950 white Christians, 1,050 Jews (620 "Portuguese" or Sephardic Jews, and 430 "German" or Ashkenazic Jews), 1,760 free mulattoes and blacks, plus approximately 8,000 slaves. Inland were another 1,080 white Christians, 280 Jews, and 45,000 slaves distributed among 600 plantations. The colony's ruling class were now increasingly divided between conservative traditional Orangists and more liberal Patriots,

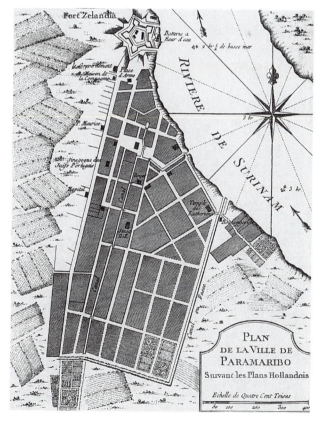

French map of Paramaribo, ca. 1763, drawn from Dutch sources. (Jacques Nicolas Bellin, *Description géographique de la Guiane,* Volume 2, Plate 36)

descended from early settlers, who increasingly lived idle existences amid garish displays of opulence. Their influence proved so great that even such a talented reformist governor as Jan Jacob Mauricius, who arrived late in 1742, was recalled nine years later because of their vociferous complaints. (Among the improvements left by his administration were to be Fort New Amsterdam, constructed between 1743 and 1747 opposite the strategic sea entrance at the confluence of the Surinam and Commewijne rivers, as well as a peace treaty with the thousands of hostile Maroons or black runaways living deep within the interior.) As the century progressed, many planters furthermore became heavily mortgaged to Dutch

the latter having been influenced by the egalitarian ideals of the recent French Revolution. When The Netherlands was overrun during the winter of 1794–1795 by French revolutionary armies, Prince Willem V fled to England and wrote to all Dutch governors overseas, ordering them to allow free entry to their British allies. The French Revolutionary Directorate, in turn, simultaneously reorganized Holland into the puppet "Batavian Republic," dissolved the seventeenth-century Geoctroyeerde Societeit, and instead created the Comité tot de Zaken van de koloniën en bezittingen op de kust van Guinea en in Amerika (Board for the Affairs of the Colonies and Possessions on the Coast of Guinea and in the Americas) to administer these territories. Surinam's governor, Jurriaan François de Friderici—despite being a large plantation owner and considered an Orangist sympathizer—consulted with his own local *raad* (council) before finally recognizing the authority of the Batavian Republic.

British Interregnums (1799–1815)

As a result of this alignment, nine English warships under Vice Adm. Lord Hugh Seymour appeared off Surinam on 11 August 1799, bearing a small invasion army under Lt. Gen. Thomas Trigge. Cut off from support by the Royal Navy's Atlantic blockade and heavily outnumbered, Governor de Friderici agreed to capitulate by 20 August, Fort New Amsterdam's garrison marching out the next day with full honors of war, Paramaribo and all other important points deeper inside Surinam being officially occupied by the British two days later. The colony remained under foreign rule, although with de Friderici

retained in office, until a temporary truce was forged between England and France back in Europe on 27 March 1802, at which time the territory was restored to Batavian control on 23 November, and de Friderici was arrested as a collaborator.

Hostilities nonetheless resumed overseas a scant fifteen months later, though, so that on 25 April 1804, Commo. Hood arrived off Surinam with nine British warships, escorting a convoy bearing 2,000 troops under Maj.-Gen. Sir Charles Green. A division of 700 men was immediately disembarked at Warapa Creek, then three vessels crossed the bar the next evening and bombarded the 7-gun Dutch battery at Braam Point, allowing another division to wade ashore and subdue its forty-three-man garrison. On the morning of 27 April, Hood and Green personally proceeded up the Surinam River to call upon Paramaribo's authorities to surrender, but French-born Commissioner-General Pierre Berranger, Lt.-Col. B. A. Batenburg, and Commo. Willem Otto Bloys van Treslong refused the next day; thus the English squadron slowly pushed upstream while Hughes's division also pressed overland, overrunning Leyden Redoubt on the morning of 30 April, after being disembarked at Resolution Plantation by a Royal Navy boat party. The Dutch garrison fired this magazine and withdrew, inflicting numerous casualties when the British entered unwarily and it detonated. Meanwhile, Maitland closed in from the west, and Hood's shallow-draft warships arrived off Fort New Amsterdam by the evening of 5 May. Batenburg had already requested terms that previous evening, and the Dutch capitulated on 6 May, surrendering their colony along with the 32-gun frigate *Proserpine,* 18-gun corvette *Pylades* (captured

Panoramic view of Paramaribo's waterfront, ca. 1880, from a photograph by the French traveler, Dr. Jules Crevaux. (*América pintoresca,* 1884)

from the English earlier in the war), three merchantmen, the 10-gun sloop *George,* and seven gunboats.

Green was installed as military governor, and Paramaribo and Surinam were to remain under a succession of British rulers for the next dozen years. It was not until Napoleon was at last defeated that London and The Hague resolved their differences, so that Willem Benjamin van Panhuys arrived and reasserted Dutch rule as of 27 February 1816.

Colonial Backwater (1816–1939)

With Holland now reduced to a minor world power and Surinam's sugar trade greatly diminished because of larger international competitors, the early decades of the nineteenth century passed unremarkably for the neglected colony. A ban on the importation of more African slaves after 1818 effectively restricted expansion of the plantation system, while an economizing move by The Hague ten years later directed that Surinam be melded into a single jurisdictional unit with the islands of The Netherlands Antilles (Curaçao, Aruba, Bonaire, Saba, Sint Eustatius, and the southern half of Sint Maarten). They were thus governed jointly by a governor-general resident at Paramaribo until this arrangement was rescinded in 1848, and both groups became separate again. As a result of all these general economic downturns, more than eighty Surinamese plantations closed between 1816 and 1832; even the number of Dutch troops assigned to the forlorn colony declined from 873 in 1825 to 620 by 1833.

Paramaribo naturally stagnated throughout this interlude, its population slowly rising from 15,265 inhabitants in 1830 to 16,336 two decades later and 18,666 distributed among 1,643 permanent dwellings (not including shacks) by 1863. That same year, the institution of slavery was finally abolished throughout all Dutch colonies, obliging Surinam's dwindling number of planters to turn to indentured workers and coolies from the Far East as an alternative pool of cheap labor for their plantations; they even entered into a formal arrangement with British purveyors in 1870 to import workers from India. Soon, so many of these contracted estate laborers arrived from British India and Dutch Indonesia, often remaining after their terms had expired, that they became a significant new presence among Surinamese society.

In addition to the traditional harvesting of sugar and coffee, some gold placer mining also began farther inland in 1876, reaching its peak production by 1912 and then gradually tapering off. It was supplemented shortly thereafter by bauxite mining, which was commercially exploited as of 1916 (spurred by increased international demand engendered by World War I). This ore soon developed into one of the colony's most valuable exports, oceangoing vessels steaming directly up the Cottica River as far as Moengo to take on their cargoes. Nevertheless, Surinam—like most other overseas dependencies—was to suffer drastically as a result of the global effects caused by the Great Depression of October 1929. From 1935

Chinese woman in Paramaribo's marketplace, ca. 1920. (Franck, *Working North from Patagonia*)

to 1939, the colony operated at an average annual deficit of several million florins, requiring heavy subsidization from The Netherlands.

World War II (1940–1945)

The final shipload of Javanese coolies reached Paramaribo in 1939, for like other European colonies in the Americas, Surinam was about to become transformed by the events surrounding World War II. When that conflict first broke out in September, Holland professed its neutrality. Yet the small country was nevertheless overrun by a lightning Nazi offensive on 10–17 May 1940, aimed at outflanking the powerful military defenses in adjacent France. Queen Wilhelmina and the Dutch cabinet fled into exile in London and directed their overseas possessions to support the Allied cause; for Surinam, this meant that 151 local Germans were interned and a detachment of British auxiliaries arrived, although the main European conflict still seemed very remote.

Almost two years later, however, Surinam became fully

embroiled when German submarines inaugurated a surprise transatlantic offensive code-named Operation *Neuland,* which (among other things) was intended to cut off the vital flow of bauxite shipments from the Guianas. On 27 February 1942, *U–129* of Lt. Cmdr. Nicoli Clausen—having earlier attacked Allied shipping off Trinidad—sank the small freighter *Bayou* off the Surinamese coast, thus instituting a blockade. Less than two weeks later, the U.S. Air Corps's 99th Bomber Squadron reached the Pan Am airfield of Zandery and commenced anti-submarine patrols by 12 March.

Through poor intelligence, however, the U.S. forces sent to reinforce Dutch Guiana mistakenly came to believe that its Dutch governor was hostile to Allied interests. They therefore attempted his ouster, leading to soured relations. Bauxite exports nonetheless soared—increasing from 504,062 tons in 1939 to 2.71 million tons by 1952—until they came to represent about 75 percent of Surinam's total export values, dominating its economy.

Modernization (1948–1974)

The extended residence of so many troops from democratic countries had inevitably stirred a desire to overhaul Surinam's outdated colonial administration, so that on 3 September 1948 The Hague officially declared its former colony part of The Netherlands. Nine months later, Surinam held its first general election for a twenty-one-member assembly that was to

Bauxite ship steaming inland. (Van de Poll, *Suriname,* 1959)

be called the States of Surinam. This experiment in limited self-government went into full effect with the first assembly session, on 20 January 1950, although real power continued to be exercised by a governor appointed directly from Holland, plus his eleven-member advisory council.

Although well intentioned, such marginal power sharing could not hope to satisfy the aspirations of so many diverse ethnic groups. In 1953, Surinam's population was estimated at 240,000 people, of whom 86,000 were identified as Creoles (descended from free mulattoes and blacks), 70,000 "Hindustanis" (born either in India or Pakistan, or descended from such migrants), 40,000 Indonesians (mostly of Javanese origin), 22,000 Djukas or *bosnegers* (descended from the runaway Maroons who had long ago sought sanctuary in the interior), 5,390 whites (mainly Dutch), 3,700 aboriginal Amerindians (subdivided into Caribs and Arawaks), and 3,068 Chinese. Of the total, some 90,000 people resided in Paramaribo, while the next-largest town was the western port of Nieuw Nickerie at the mouth of the Corentijn River, with a mere 3,100 inhabitants. Dutch remained the official language, although the Creole dialect known as Sranan Tongo was also widely spoken, and English was beginning to make considerable inroads. Each Asian community furthermore spoke its own indigenous tongue among themselves. Religious affiliations included Protestant, Catholic, Hindu, Muslim, Confucian, and Jewish worshippers. The countryside had few paved roads, and fewer railroads, most transportation still depending upon river traffic—which was uncertain during periods of drought or the floods occasioned by heavy rainfalls.

Independence (1975–Present)

On 25 November 1975, Surinam at last became an independent republic, its severance treaty with The Netherlands being further backed by an economic aid program worth $1.5 billion that was to be distributed over the ensuing decade. However, so many people emigrated to Holland because of uncertainty and unrest in the fledgling nation that the population had declined to 352,041 by 1980, and on 25 February a military coup led by Col. Desi Bouterese overthrew the elected government—despite open disapproval from both The Hague and Washington. When fifteen opposition leaders were subsequently executed on 8 December 1982, The Netherlands broke off relations and suspended its aid program, while even the vital Moengo bauxite mines were closed during the mid-1980s because of continuing civil strife.

Bouterese's ban on political parties was not lifted until 1985, when a new constitution was drafted. A guerrilla movement called the Jungle Commando, led by Ronny Brunswijk—a former bodyguard of Bouterese—then launched a campaign in 1986 to overthrow his rule, further delaying political and economic plans. Elections for the National Assembly were not celebrated until November 1987, but although a three-party coalition called the Front for Democracy and Development won forty of fifty-one seats, differences between Assembly President Ramsewak Shankar and Bouterese led to the bloodless deposition of this government on 24 December 1990 (in the so-called Telephone Coup).

Eventually, a military-backed administration was installed, with Johan Kraag as president, and a New Front of four traditional parties won thirty seats in the elections of 25 May 1991, compared with only twelve for Bouterese's National Democratic Party, or NDP; nine went to the Democratic Alternative (which favored closer links with The Netherlands). Ronald Venetiaan of the New Front was duly installed as president by 6 September, leading to a resumption of Dutch aid in the latter half of 1992 and a peace treaty with the Jungle Commando by August 1992. However, a severe economic slump and corruption charges then dimmed the New Front's popularity, so that a coalition of the NDP and five other parties elected the army-backed Jules Wijdenbosch as president in September 1996; he in turn appointed Bouterese as "Adviser of the State" the following year—despite an arrest warrant issued by Interpol in his name on suspicion of drug trafficking. The ruling coalition was weakened by the departure of the Hindustan Party after its minister of finance, Motilal Mungra, was sacked for refusing to increase government spending; a plot to overthrow the government was also uncovered in October 1997.

Today, Paramaribo holds approximately 257,000 residents, out of a national population of approximately 460,000 (although official statistics listed only 402,000 in the census of 1995 because of spotty undercounting). Overall, 35 percent of this total identify themselves as Creole, 33 percent as Hindustani, 16 percent Javanese, 10 percent *bosnegers,* 3 percent whites and Chinese, plus 3 percent Amerindians. Descendants of Asian immigrants dominate the countryside, but 90 percent of all inhabitants now live either in Paramaribo or the northern coastal towns. Some racial tension persists, although not as severely as in neighboring Guyana. In the capital city, many eighteenth- and nineteenth-century Dutch colonial buildings remain intact, such as the old Governor's Mansion—now the Presidential Palace—although some private dwellings are decaying. A new harbor facility has been constructed about a mile upstream, while Fort Zeelandia has been converted into the Surinam Museum and been largely restored with financial assistance from Holland. Paramaribo's most prominent religious edifices include its Roman Catholic cathedral (built in 1885, and said to be the largest wooden building in the Americas), plus several Hindu temples, mosques, and a pair of synagogues.

For further reading materials on the history of Paramaribo or Surinam, please consult the Select Bibliography at the end of this volume.

Uruguay

MONTEVIDEO

Seaport and national capital and one of the most densely populated cities in all of the Americas.

Early Visits (1514–1520)

The low, rocky headland from which Montevideo radiates was originally sighted in 1514 by the Portuguese explorers Nuño Manuel and Juan de Haro, who named the sheltered, circular harbor that it dominates Monte de Santo Ovidio (Saint Ovid's Mount). The Spaniard Juan Díaz de Solís also visited in 1516, and four years later Ferdinand Magellan did the same, allegedly making the comment *"Monte vide eu"*—"I saw Monte"—which gave the bay its curious name, before proceeding on his famous circumnavigation. (Another legend insists that Magellan's Basque lookout made this cry from the crow's nest, indicating that he had sighted hills rising above the horizon. Whichever version is correct, the city's name would continue to be written as two words, "Monte Video," well into the nineteenth century.)

Despite its protected harbor, moderate climate, and a fertile and rolling landscape, no permanent settlement was to be founded for another two centuries, partly because of the ferocity of the seminomadic Charrúa Indians, but mostly because of a lack of readily available water or firewood at the point. A few vessels paused occasionally inside its bay for provisions, but otherwise, most migrants reaching the River Plate region preferred colonizing the district farther to the west around Buenos Aires.

Portuguese Outpost (1723–1724)

The uninhabited bay finally took on significance when Portugal pushed Brazil's frontier westward during the late seventeenth century, establishing a rival outpost deep within the River Plate estuary at Colonia del Sacramento. In order to support this frontline base against recurrent Spanish counterattacks out of Buenos Aires, Lisbon ordered the creation of subsidiary forts at Montevideo and Maldonado in 1701. However, the theater's Portuguese military commander, Manuel de Freitas da Fonseca, was unable to put this directive into effect until 4 November 1723, when he set sail from Colonia with 150 troops and 100 colonists aboard the 50-gun warship *Nossa Senhora da Oliveira* under Capt. Manuel Henriques de Noronha, transport *Chumbado* under Francisco Dias, and two lesser consorts. They reached Montevideo Bay on 22 November and six days later came ashore to commence erecting a small, square redoubt on its narrow eastern peninsula.

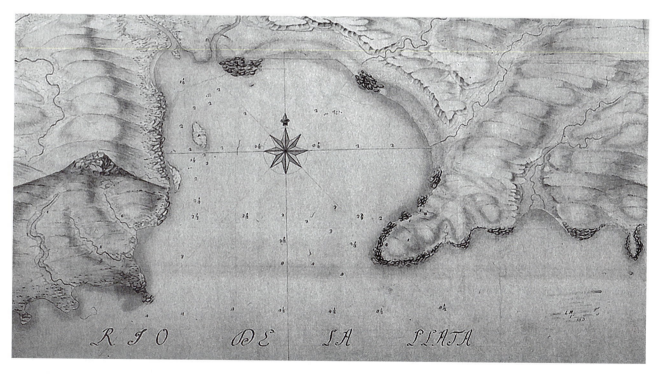

Map with watercolor highlights of Montevideo's uninhabited bay in 1719, by the Spanish military engineer Capt. Domingo Petrarca. (Servicio Geográfico del Ejército, Madrid)

Upon learning of this Portuguese disembarkation on 1 December 1723, Buenos Aires's governor, Bruno Mauricio de Zabala, knight of the Order of Calatrava, responded by dispatching 250 soldiers under Lt. Alonso de la Vega aboard the two warships of Commo. Salvador García Pose to evict the new garrison. A protracted blockade and siege ensued, culminating with a Portuguese agreement on 19 January 1724 to withdraw from Montevideo Bay. Triumphant, the Spaniards then furthermore decided on 9 November of that same year to install their own stronghold, both to preclude any possible Portuguese reoccupation as well as to threaten sea communications with Colonia farther to the west. On 16 April 1725, King Philip V expanded upon Zabala's original directive by also allowing civilians to immigrate into Montevideo, receiving legal land grants so as to transform that military outpost into a permanent community.

Spanish Foundation and Early Struggles (1726–1777)

The first six families, a total of thirty-four people brought from Buenos Aires and Santa Fe, joined the Spanish soldiery by late autumn 1726, soon to be followed by another ninety-six individuals in thirteen families from Tenerife in the Canary Islands. A new town called San Felipe y Santiago de Monte Video was officially constituted by 24 December 1726, with plots facing onto its bay. Yet most construction efforts continued to be focused upon completing the stone San José fortress, initiated by the troops two years previously. Civilian labors lagged in consequence, only two permanent homes being

built within the first year, so that most families still lived inside cowhide tents.

When Zabala inspected the new settlement during the winter of 1729–1730, he felt compelled to decree that "decent houses" be erected within fifteen days, made of mud walls, with cowhide or thatched roofs. A sense of community began to emerge, especially after the first town council meeting was celebrated in Zabala's presence on 1 January 1730; a church was commenced shortly thereafter to replace the original, tiny, interim Jesuit chapel.

Yet notwithstanding such slow progress in civilian matters, Montevideo's 800-man garrison was able to hold its own when Hispano-Portuguese hostilities revived, and Brig. José da Silva Paes materialized offshore from Colonia on 29 December 1736 with 720 Portuguese troops aboard the galleys *Leão Dourado* and *Santana do Pôrto*, brigantine *Piedade*, corvette *São Francisco Xavier*, and royal sloop *Nossa Senhora da Conceição*. Even after being reinforced two days later by the 500-man squadron of Commo. Luiz de Abreu Prego, the attackers still did not feel sufficiently strong to storm Montevideo's defenses, which were supported by a 42-gun Spanish frigate anchored in the roads. Silva Paes therefore withdrew on 13 January 1737, continuing eastward to land at Punta del Este and install a 130-man detachment at Maldonado before retiring toward Brazil with his main body.

Once peace was restored in Europe, Montevideo's garrison completed Fort San José by 1741, then in February of that same year started work under the direction of the military engineer

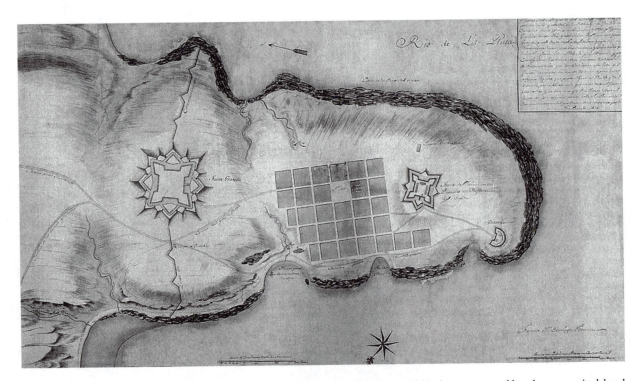

A 1730 map of Montevideo's peninsula by Petrarca, demonstrating how its inhabitants would be better protected by a large new citadel and line of ramparts; north is toward lower left. (Servicio Geográfico del Ejército, Madrid)

Diego Cardoso, or Cardozo, on a much larger Ciudadela (Citadel) that would command the entire peninsula. The next year additional walls were extended from the citadel in both directions to eventually seal off Montevideo's landward approaches. (Today, Fort San José has disappeared from near the modern intersection of Cerrito and Guaraní streets, while the Ciudadela's last vestiges were torn down in 1879, only its main entrance façade having been relocated as a historical monument.) Lesser bastions and batteries were added around the shoreline over the passage of time, as well as atop 400-foot Cerro Hill across the bay.

Although trade continued to be quite limited because of the restrictive monopolist dictates imposed from Madrid, as well as by Buenos Aires's regional dominance, Montevideo's grasslands nonetheless proved so lush that cattle ranching flourished farther inland, creating an export boom for the port in hides, salt meat, tallow, and similar produce. After repeated requests, Montevideans also succeeded in getting their governors appointed directly from Spain in 1749, rather than remaining subordinate to the Buenos Aires authorities. The first such royal appointee arrived two years later, and Montevideo experienced quite rapid growth throughout the remainder of the eighteenth century—most noticeably after the Portuguese relinquished all claims to Colonia in 1777 and Madrid freed up South American commerce by liberalizing its trade policies the following year.

Late Colonial Era (1778–1806)

Such an upsurge meant that Montevideo's dwellings now began to become transformed into solid, single-story structures made of baked brick, with gardens and orchards surrounded by cactus hedges, plus cisterns atop their roofs (although water would still be brought by oxcart from La Aguada and sold through the streets for many decades to come). A visitor in 1783 commented that even residents were "bewildered at the speed at which their city has gone up," while four years later another new arrival counted 1,560 buildings within Montevideo's walls, plus 400 shacks outside. When a portion of its fifty-year-old Iglesia Matriz (Main Church) collapsed in June 1788, a magnificent new temple was promptly commenced; two years later, Fort San José was also replaced by a new Casa del Gobernador (Governor's House), while the city also got its first theater—the Casa de Comedias—by 1791. Three years afterward, labors started on a vast network of reinforced casements called Las Bóvedas to store gunpowder and other provisions, as well as to cover Montevideo's inner harbor.

By 1796 the city's population stood at 15,245 people, roughly a third the number residing at Buenos Aires, and work was initiated in November 1804 on a grand new city hall made of granite. Unfortunately, though, the River Plate's rise to prominence was also to attract unwelcome attention from abroad, a small British expedition under Commo. Sir Home Riggs Popham materializing in mid-June 1806, fresh from hav-

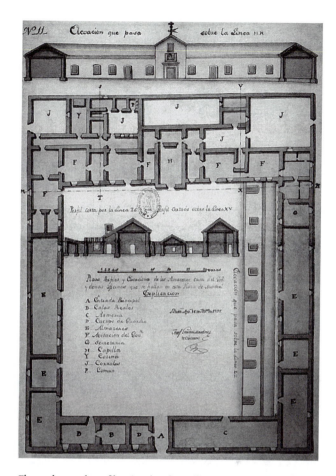

Floor plan and profile view by the military engineer José García Martínez de Cáceres of the recently completed governor's palace at Montevideo, February 1797. (Servicio Histórico Militar, Madrid)

ing conquered Holland's Cape of Good Hope colony in South Africa. Leaving his 64-gun flagship HMS *Diadem* to blockade Montevideo, Popham reached Buenos Aires by 25 June and disembarked 1,200 redcoats under Brig. William Carr Beresford, who overran the unprepared viceregal capital two days later. However, a relief force from Montevideo succeeded in uniting at Las Conchas with surviving Argentine contingents under the leadership of naval Capt. Santiago de Liniers to reconquer Buenos Aires by 12 August.

British Occupation (1807)

Popham's warships nevertheless remained in command of the River Plate estuary, and after being reinforced, bore down upon Montevideo on the morning of 28 October 1806, exchanging fire with its batteries for three hours while probing for a landing spot. Discouraged, the British retired to set up a temporary base camp at Maldonado, where they were joined early the following year by a fresh army under the New York–born American Loyalist, Brig. Sir Samuel Auchmuty.

Around noon of 16 January 1807, operations against Montevideo resumed when Auchmuty landed his troops 6 miles east at Mulata, or Verde Beach, between Manzo and Gorda points; 800 Spanish riders and six field-pieces attempted to bolster the few regulars resisting from atop Carretas Point, but their efforts proved ineffectual. Over the next two days, the British brought their 5,500-man army ashore, plus six guns, as well as 800 marines and sailors. Opposing them were 3,500 mostly untried militiamen inside Montevideo under Gov. Pascual Ruiz Huidobro, plus 2,500 irregulars roaming the countryside under the River Plate's viceroy, Rafael, Marqués de Sobremonte—disgraced after his pusillanimous retreat out of Buenos Aires the previous summer.

Auchmuty initiated his drive against Montevideo in three columns on 19 January 1807, Sobremonte's 1,300 infantrymen and some cavalry being incapable of preventing the invaders from gaining Tres Cruces Heights that same afternoon. Ruiz Huidobro therefore sent out 2,350 men under Brig. Bernardo Lecoq the next dawn to mount a pincer attack against the advancing English in conjunction with Sobremonte's 1,700 riders closing in from behind, but Lecoq's infantry blundered into the British left at Cristo del Cordón and were decimated by cross fire from adjacent cornfields; Sobremonte's demoralized cavalry simply viewed this action from a safe distance before retreating into their Las Piedras cantonment to disband.

That same afternoon of 20 January 1807, a British detachment had seized the vital La Aguada water wells across Montevideo Bay, while their main body arrived directly outside the city's eastern ramparts. With insufficient men to isolate the defenders, nor trenching equipment to dig through the flinty subsoil, Auchmuty opted to install heavy siege batteries and pound a breach, ferrying hundreds of sailors ashore for that purpose. The first guns opened fire by 23 January, and although more than 500 Spanish reinforcements under Brig. Pedro de Arce slipped into Montevideo from Buenos Aires on 2 February, an 11-yard gap had already been battered along the southern walls. Auchmuty therefore launched his final assault the next dawn and assumed control of the city after two hours of hand-to-hand combat in which 800 Spanish troops perished, 500 were wounded, and 2,000 were captured.

The British were to remain in possession over the next seven months, using Montevideo as a staging area for a second major effort against Buenos Aires, which was eventually defeated in the streets of the viceregal capital on 5 July 1807. By the terms of their capitulation, the English agreed to evacuate the entire River Plate, so that the last 6,500 redcoats sailed away from Montevideo on 9 September. While glad to see them depart, Montevideans nevertheless long remembered the stream of inexpensive goods that had entered their port during this brief interregnum.

Beleaguered Stronghold (1808–1814)

Six months later the city was again shaken by news that the French emperor, Napoleon I, had sent a huge army into Spain to depose King Ferdinand VII in favor of his own brother Joseph Bonaparte by early June 1808. Like most other Span-

Auchmuty's British troops successfully storm Montevideo's ramparts before dawn of 3 February 1807; original drawing by George Robinson, engraved by Edward Orme. (National Maritime Museum, Greenwich, London)

ish-American vassals, Montevideans resisted such an unsolicited change of rulers, instead throwing their wholehearted support behind a temporary junta (assembly) formed at Aranjuez to spearhead resistance against the usurpers. A similarly ultra-Loyalist junta was even formed at Montevideo on 21 September to uphold their captive monarch's cause, and most citizens resisted the sentiments that subsequently developed among disgruntled Creoles elsewhere in South America for outright independence.

Still, Viceroy Baltasar Hidalgo de Cisneros was arrested in Buenos Aires on 25 May 1810 by its radical new junta, which thereupon began delegating Argentine armies to foment a full-fledged war of independence throughout the district. In Uruguay the wealthy inland cattle owner José Gervasio Artigas and other rural patriots echoed such feelings by raising their own revolt at Asencio on 28 February 1811, quickly mustering 1,100 men who pulverized a force of 1,200 royalists under José de Posadas at Las Piedras Mill 12 miles north of Montevideo on 18 May, then permitted a small Argentine army under Gen. José Rondeau to arrive on 1 June to loosely besiege the Crown garrison holding the port city—although rather ineffectually, as its seaward approaches remained open.

This investment dragged on for more than a year and a half, and despite the revolutionaries' lack of heavy artillery or blockading ships, Montevideo nonetheless suffered by being cut off from its economic hinterland. The River Plate's new viceroy designate, Gaspar Vigodet, took up residence and led a three-pronged sally of 2,300 men and three field-pieces at dawn of 31 December 1812, which surprised the encircling Argentines. Yet the Loyalists were thrown back after heavy fighting around El Cerrito, 3 miles north of the city. The insurgents subsequently redoubled their pressure, particularly once Artigas patched up his differences with his Argentine allies in February of the next year, and a severe drought set in. Thirst, exacerbated by the tainting of La Aguada and Las Canarias wells by animal carcasses flung in by the besiegers, compelled many civilians to evacuate the forlorn city under flag of truce, while its royal garrison hung on only by bringing in water at night in launches from El Buceo.

The arrival offshore of seven Argentine warships on 20 April 1814 under Commo. Guillermo Brown (born in Ireland and raised in Philadelphia) brought Montevideo's three-year ordeal to a head. When thirteen Loyalist vessels sortied on 14 May under Miguel Sierra to chase them away, Brown defeated his pursuers near El Buceo in a three-day running fight, thus effectively severing Montevideo's sea communications. Shortly thereafter, Rondeau's 4,000 besiegers were furthermore reinforced by 1,500 fresh Argentine troops under Gen. Carlos María de Alvear, prompting Vigodet to request terms by 20 June. Three days later the city surrendered, the Argentines unilaterally seizing it along with 500 artillery pieces, 9,000 muskets, 100 anchored ships, and 7,000 prisoners—most of whom were repatriated to Spain.

However, Montevideo's suffering was not yet at an end, for when a rural Uruguayan militia company reached Las Piedras under Colonel Ortogués on 25 June 1814 to request that Alvear cede control to local authorities, the Argentine general not only refused but also dispatched 800 cavalrymen overnight to disperse the Uruguayan formation, capturing 200 men along with all their artillery and baggage. The gutted city therefore spent the next several months still isolated from its hinterland, being nominally under the rule of the revolutionary junta out of Buenos Aires, while Uruguayan forces marshaled inland to dispute ownership.

On 6 October 1814, Alvear detached Col. Manuel Dorrego with 600 men to disperse another 1,000 Uruguayan militiamen gathered at Marmarajá, 18 miles northeast of Montevideo. But when the Argentines attempted to duplicate this tactic early the next year, Dorrego's column—now augmented to 800 men by the incorporation of 200 former royalists—was defeated at Guayabos on 10 January 1815 and scattered toward Entre Ríos by 1,200 Uruguayan troops under Bernabé Rivera. Realizing that they could no longer sustain Montevideo's garrison, the Buenos Aires leadership agreed on 15 February to cede the battered city to Artigas. Its occupiers withdrew ten days later—although, as Alvear's soldiers were determined to leave behind nothing of military value, they hastily dumped gunpowder into the bay from Las Bóvedas casements on 23 February; as a consequence of their actions, a shovel sparked a sudden blast that claimed 120 lives, injured scores of others, and left widespread destruction throughout the core of the unhappy city.

False Liberty (1815–1816)

Resentful of the inland ranching class represented by Artigas, which had for so long invested Montevideo and now showed scant interest in aiding its recuperation, the few surviving urban residents greeted their new rural occupiers with distrust. Revival was further blighted by the unformed young nation's political anarchy, commercial uncertainty, and lack of government funds or infrastructure, which together would characterize the brief interlude of nominal independence known today as the Patria Vieja.

Montevideo remained so at odds against its new administration, and suffered so acutely while attempting to recover economically, that residents even tacitly welcomed the news that the Portuguese had launched a two-pronged offensive out of Brazil in early August 1816, availing themselves of the collapse of Spanish royalist rule in South America and the fratricidal rifts between republican forces in Uruguay, Argentina, and Paraguay to reestablish their dominion over the eastern half of the River Plate estuary.

Lt.-Gen. Carlos Frederico Lecor, Barão de Laguna and knight grand cross of the Order of Torre e Espada, marched southwestward from Rio Grande do Sul along the coast with his main body, while a second army penetrated westward from Porto

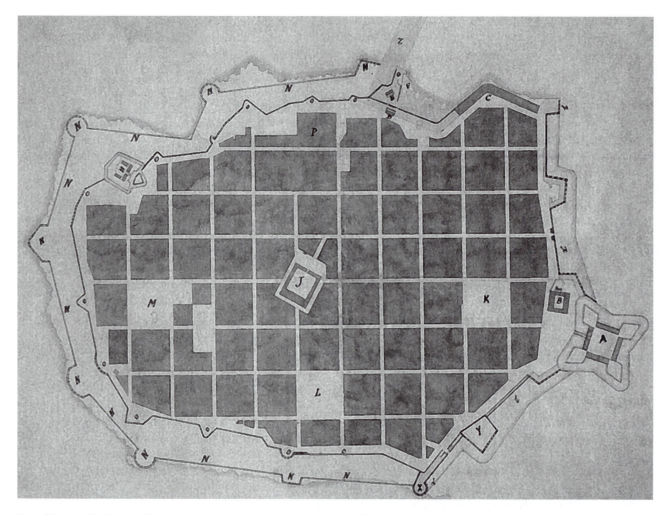

Map of Montevideo by the military engineer, José Antonio del Pozo y Marquy, showing proposed improvements to its seaside defenses, December 1808. (Servicio Geográfico del Ejército, Madrid)

Alegre toward the headwaters of the Uruguay River. The invaders' strength totaled some 10,000 troops, half being Portuguese regulars, against whom the ill-prepared Uruguayan guerrillas could offer scant resistance. Lecor swept into Maldonado with little opposition by 18 September 1816, then his advancing units defeated a succession of Uruguayan concentrations organized by

Artigas in October–November, until the desperate republican leader requested aid from his political foes in Buenos Aires— who were themselves distracted by a Spanish royalist invasion out of the north and other internal uprisings.

Artigas and his 400 most loyal adherents were surprised and scattered by a 600-man Portuguese flying column on 3

Panoramic view of Montevideo as seen from out at sea, by the visiting British naval officer, Emeric Essex Vidal, 1817; note Cerro Hill at far left. (Metropolitan Toronto Reference Library)

January 1817 from a hilltop north of the Arapey River, 60 miles east of Belén, while the main inland Uruguayan army was also soundly beaten the next morning on the western banks of Catalán Creek (headwaters of the Guareim River), so that effective resistance collapsed. Therefore, as their unpopular rural occupiers melted inland, Montevideo prepared to greet the invaders almost as liberators.

Portuguese Occupation (1817–1828)

Lecor entered the city on the morning of 20 January 1817 with his 7,000 to 8,000 troops, installing a garrison before proceeding to pacify the coast and interior. Shortly thereafter, Montevideo was proclaimed the capital of Brazil's newly created "Cisplatine Province," and once all Uruguayan resistance ceased, its port traffic resurged modestly thanks to renewed visits by foreign vessels. However, the citizenry soon wearied of Portuguese misgovernment and indifference, while Brazil itself was to secede from Portugal five years later, so that Montevideo's garrison split into two contending factions: a proseparatist Brazilian group headed by Lecor from inside the Casa del Gobernador (old Fort San José) arrayed against a Loyalist, pro-Portuguese group represented by Gen. Alvaro da Costa's 2,000 troops quartered within the city. The latter finally agreed to cede command to Lecor in February 1824, setting sail for Lisbon with his regiment.

Most of the Uruguayan interior was subsequently gripped by revolt, as the patriot leader Juan Antonio Lavalleja led a thirty-three-man guerrilla band back from Argentine exile, landing at Rincón de la Agraciada on 19 April 1825 to raise an insurrection against the Brazilian occupation. A rival government was extemporized in the interior, which voted on 25 August to join with Argentina to form the so-called United Provinces of the River Plate. Lavalleja's 2,000 troops then crushed a 2,200-man Brazilian army at Sarandí on 12 October of that same year, so that Lecor's garrison found itself isolated within Montevideo. On 24 October, Buenos Aires furthermore recognized Uruguay's request for incorporation and advised Rio de Janeiro of this fact.

Yet despite such dramatic developments, the city itself was to remain under Brazilian control, as Rio de Janeiro countered by officially declaring hostilities against Buenos Aires on 10 December 1825; the Cisplatine War became fully joined when a Brazilian squadron arrived off Montevideo eleven days later to blockade the River Plate. An Argentine squadron responded under Adm. Guillermo Brown, battling on 11 April 1826 a mile off El Cerro against the 42-gun Brazilian frigate *Nichteroy,* then attempting to cut the 52-gun *Imperatriz* out of Montevideo's anchorage on 27 April. The struggle eventually shifted much deeper inland and became quite protracted as the impoverished combatant nations lacked adequate resources to deliver a knockout blow, until finally Buenos Aires and Rio de Janeiro—almost equally exhausted—signed a peace treaty on 27 August 1828.

Brief Boom (1829–1837)

Despite the fact that Uruguayan forces had failed to reconquer Montevideo, Brazilian resistance had nonetheless been bled white by the punishing Cisplatine conflict, so that the city's occupiers were glad to withdraw. The alliance with Argentina was moreover in abeyance, as the government in Buenos Aires had been toppled and the "United Provinces" plunged into civil war. Montevideo therefore passed under full Uruguayan control as of 1 May 1829. Efforts were immediately implemented to assist in its resurrection, the city being sadly deteriorated after twenty years of repeated investments and foreign occupation, with only 9,000 people still residing inside its walls, plus another 5,000 scattered about outlying communities; its port traffic now depended entirely upon British and French commerce.

The new provisional government decreed as early as 25 August 1829 that Montevideo's old ramparts should be torn down, so that the capital might not only rebuild but also expand eastward along its peninsula. (Previously, no edifices had been tolerated within this clearance, so as not to mask the Ciudadela's field of fire.) Uruguayan independence was promulgated on 18 July 1830, the war hero Gen. Fructuoso Rivera being elected as first president, who adopted a policy of benign neglect toward the resurgent city, trusting its municipal authorities to make the necessary changes and improvements. A suburb called Ciudad Nueva (New City) soon appeared beyond the Citadel, which bulky structure was also largely torn down in 1833 to make way for a public market, while Montevideo welcomed a flood of European immigrants—who increased not only its population base but also its cosmopolitanism. By 1836 the 11,400 native-born residents found themselves outnumbered by almost 20,000 foreigners—of whom 8,000 were transient visitors—and the economy was once again booming.

Great Siege (1838–1851)

Unfortunately, Montevideo's revival was cut short when Rivera—irked that his handpicked successor, Gen. Manuel Oribe, had passed a series of laws affecting rural matters—rebelled and defeated him on 15 June 1838 in the Battle of El Palmar, forcing Oribe back inside Montevideo. After a four-month siege, the latter abdicated and on 25 October set sail for exile in Buenos Aires.

Rivera was thereupon reelected president and on 24 February 1839 declared war against the Argentine dictator Juan Manuel de Rosas for having granted Oribe asylum and support. That decision plunged the entire region back into a conflict known among Uruguayans as the Guerra Grande (Big War) and would eventually draw in international powers such as Britain and France. Despite some initial successes, Rivera's army was shattered three and a half years later at the Battle of Arroyo Grande south of Concordia (Argentina), clearing the way for Oribe to counterinvade Uruguay. His victorious army

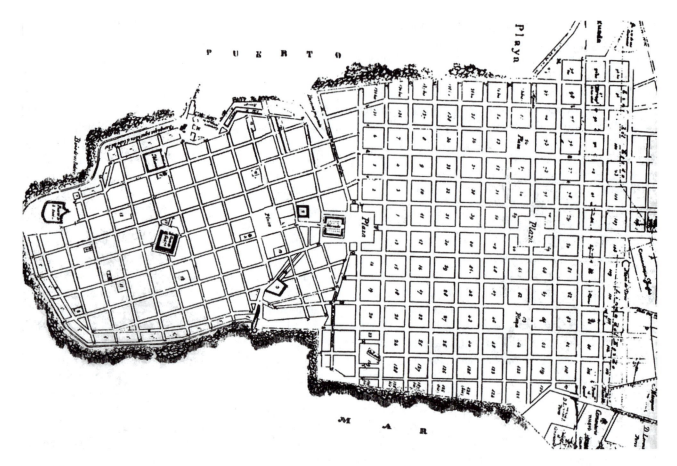

Map of the resurgent city in 1839 by Carlos Zucchi—perhaps based upon an original survey by the military engineer, José María Reyes—showing the city's projected expansion eastward along its peninsula, beyond its old confining ramparts. (Author's Collection)

reached Cerrito by 16 February 1843, while Montevideo braced for yet another siege, most of its foreign colony rallying to its defense: 2,000 Frenchmen under Col. Jean Thiebaut, 600 Italians under Col. Giuseppe Garibaldi (later to become his homeland's unifier), plus 500 Argentine exiles under Eustaquio Díaz Vélez, swelling Gen. Gregorio Paz's total garrison to 7,000 men.

The anchored British squadron of Commo. Brett Purvis furthermore refused to allow Argentina's Adm. Brown to blockade Montevideo, declaring that any British subject found aboard any of his warships—a goodly percentage of Brown's most skilled seamen—would be condemned as traitors if they fired upon the Union Jack. This threat caused Brown to retire, although London soon revoked Purvis's directive, and a half-hearted Argentine blockade ensued. Oribe's troops had meanwhile thrown up breastworks and began pounding the city's landward defenses by 10 March 1843, while Rivera attempted to harry the invaders with guerrilla raids out of the interior by his mounted irregulars—frequently countered by cavalry sweeps from Oribe's main body under Argentine Gen. Justo José de Urquiza.

Life in the Uruguayan capital continued with considerable difficulty, one eyewitness describing how "Italian laborers tilled the soil amid battery-fire outside the walls, in garden patches, criss-crossing all day amid the rounds from both armies." A year later, two battalions sallied on 15 February 1844 to damage Oribe's siege works; then on 28 March, Gen. Venancio Flores reinforced Montevideo's garrison with an additional 2,000 men and four field-pieces, which in turn encouraged Paz to mount a major sortie on 24 April with 7,800 troops in three columns. His plan was to cut off Gen. Angel Pacheco's Argentine contingent holding Cerro Hill across the bay, then annihilate Oribe's reserves near Arroyo Pantanoso as they hastened to the rescue. But the operation broke down, the 2,000 men sent by boat to outflank Pacheco disembarking so noisily as to forewarn their enemy, after which the main infantry thrust out of the city fell back in disarray when threatened by an Argentine cavalry charge. On 4 July, Paz resigned as garrison commander and emigrated from the encircled city to Rio de Janeiro.

A year later, British and French plenipotentiaries protested before Rosas in Buenos Aires about the protracted siege of Montevideo, which affected their citizens' commercial interests. Receiving no satisfaction, an Anglo-French squadron

Panoramic view of the city in 1840 as seen from its *Cemeterio Nuevo* or "New Cemetery," as reproduced in the French naval officer Adolphe d'Hastrel's *Album Río de la Plata;* note Cerro Hill in the far distance at extreme right. (National Historical Museum, Montevideo)

seized Brown's three blockading warships on 22 July 1845, handing the vessels over to the Montevideans. One month later Garibaldi used these prizes to launch a successful counteroffensive up the Uruguay River, while the British and French clamped their own naval blockade upon Argentina. But for the city, the removal of Brown's warships simply meant an easing of living conditions, as Oribe's army still remained ensconced at Cerrito, controlling much of the surrounding countryside with his 14,000 troops.

The stalemate dragged on for another six years, until Urquiza finally switched sides and moved against Oribe with his 9,000 troops in the summer of 1851, backed by a

Montevideo's cathedral, ca. 1900. (Dawson, *The South American Republics*)

The Solis Theater, ca. 1900; note the *Cambio de Monedas* or "Money Exchange" office in left foreground. (Dawson, *The South American Republics*)

16,000-man Brazilian army. Oribe agreed to capitulate by 8 October, bringing the eight-and-a-half-year siege of Montevideo to an end.

Resurgence (1852–1869)

Some measure of its stultifying effects was reflected by the census of 1852, which found a population of 34,000 inhabitants, scarcely more than sixteen years previously. By way of contrast, another 24,000 people would appear on the city rolls over the next eight years of peace. Some outlying towns, long occupied by Oribe's besieging host, had grown appreciably and now became thriving new suburbs, while the capital itself received its first gas lines and a new customshouse by 1853 and a sewer system the next year.

Fortunately, Montevideo was able to weather its next crisis much more easily, after the exiled former president, Venancio Flores, slipped a small rebel force into the country in April 1863 to reinstall his Liberal Colorado (Red) Party, deposed nine years previously by the rival Blancos (Whites). His Brazilian backers massed troops on the border and sent a squadron into the River Plate by autumn of 1864, followed by a full-bore invasion starting on 21 September. The Paraguayan dictator Francisco Solano López declared war against Rio de Janeiro in support of his Uruguayan allies, but to no avail: Flores came into power by 10 February 1865, joining both Brazil and Argentina in the subsequent War of the Triple Alliance, which annihilated the hapless Paraguayans. During the four remaining years of this conflict, Montevideo served as a major supply depot for the Brazilian expeditionary forces fighting far inland, and profited accordingly.

Modern Era (1870–Present)

The city now entered a period of almost unbridled growth, during which most vestiges of its original infrastructure were torn down and replaced with promenades, wide avenues, and some magnificent buildings in southern European styles. Its outer boundaries expanded as well, as modern services multiplied: the first system of horse-drawn streetcars was inaugurated in 1868, piped drinking water three years later, a primitive telephone system by 1878, and electric power in 1887. The population multiplied exponentially from 164,000 residents in 1884, to 215,000 by 1889, 309,231 by 1908, and more than half a million by 1922—the vast majority being immigrants of Italian or Spanish origin. The only serious impediments to Montevideo's urban boom were rampant land speculation along its outer ring, as well as government corruption and mismanagement, which provoked several financial collapses.

Still, Montevideo was able to host the first-ever World Cup

The German pocket battleship *Graf Spee* quitting Montevideo on the evening of 17 December 1939. (National Archives of Canada)

soccer tournament in 1930 (which its national team won in the city's new 80,000-seat stadium). On the evening of 13 December 1939, the capital was also witness to one of the most dramatic incidents early in World War II, when Capt. Hans Langsdorff's 16,200-ton German "pocket battleship" *Admiral Graf Spee* sought sanctuary inside its bay after dueling with British Commo. Henry Harwood's heavy cruiser *Exeter,* plus the light cruisers *Ajax* and *Achilles.* Although legally permitted to remain in a neutral port for only twenty-four hours, Langsdorff received a seventy-two-hour extension to repair his damaged ship and refuel. In the meantime, Harwood maintained a stream of false wireless traffic, suggesting that strong reinforcements—the aircraft carrier *Ark Royal* and 32,000-ton battle cruiser *Renown*—had joined him, rather than being several hundred miles distant. Convinced that he could not break out against such odds, the German captain weighed at 6:15 P.M. on 17 December and stood out past the city's thronged waterfront, trailed by the German merchantman *Tacoma* and two Argentine tugs. A short distance out, he and his crew transferred aboard their consorts, then *Graf Spee* was scuttled at 7:56, exploding shortly thereafter. (Three days later,

amid criticism of his performance, Langsdorff committed suicide in Buenos Aires.)

Today, Greater Montevideo extends all around its bay and encroaches upon the neighboring Department of Canelones, being delimited by the Santa Lucía River to its west, as well as Las Piedras, Toledo, and Carrasco creeks to its north and east. The population of 746,181 inhabitants in 1941 topped 850,000 by 1950, 954,723 by 1956, 1 million inhabitants by 1959, 1,154,500 in 1963, 1.25 million in 1990, and 1,311,976 by 1994. High-income housing tended to follow the River Plate shoreline eastward—the so-called Rambla Costañera—while low-income sectors radiated eastward from the Cerro, north toward Canelones, and west into the industrialized sectors. Communications with Buenos Aires are extremely busy, with hourly services by ferries and hydrofoils, plus numerous commuter flights from the Carrasco Airport, located some 13 miles from downtown.

For additional background information on Uruguayan and Spanish-American urban history in general, please consult the Select Bibliography at the end of this volume.

Venezuela

CARACAS

One of the last South American capitals to become established during the Spanish colonial era, not truly flourishing until two centuries later.

Foundation and Early Evolution (1567–1640)

Central Venezuela—which possessed no highly evolved native civilization such as in Mexico, Peru, or Colombia to attract the sixteenth-century conquistadors pushing out of the Caribbean Basin—was among the last territories to be subdued. After landing and securing a coastal foothold at Coro in western Venezuela in 1529, a majority of its settlers then moved eastward out of this arid coastal strip to establish a new settlement in 1545 in the more fertile El Tocuyo Valley, amid the Segovia highlands. Gradually expanding this foothold by wresting arable lands from hostile tribes so as to create a string of cattle ranches and farms, these pioneers founded Barquisimeto seven years later, and Valencia on the edge of the even richer Aragua Valleys complex by 1556. From the latter town, exploratory columns probed still farther east and eventually pushed up into the rich valleys beyond, despite such stubborn opposition from local warriors under Chief Guaicaipuro that the Aragua Valley became known for a time as the Valle del Miedo (Valley of Fear).

The earliest Spanish encampments in this new, roughly triangular, 580-square-mile series of valleys were thrown up by transient prospectors seeking gold from deposits such as Los Teques, resulting in no permanent presence. In 1560, however, a mestizo (mixed-blood) conquistador named Francisco Fajardo and thirty of his followers cleared a cattle ranch in this frontier district that he dubbed Hato de San Francisco (San Francisco Ranch); it had to be abandoned shortly thereafter but was revived into a short-lived hamlet of that same name under Fajardo's successor, Juan Rodríguez Suárez. San Francisco was soon evacuated for a second time after the latter's death at the hands of a war party under Guaicaipuro; it was not to be resettled until Crown officials in Madrid—desirous of imposing their control over the entire Venezuelan shoreline between Coro and Cumaná, so as to preclude occupation by seaborne foreign interlopers—commanded that an expedition be sent up into this territory to populate it for Spain.

The fifty-four-year-old veteran conquistador Diego de Losada consequently left El Tocuyo early in 1567 with approximately 20 Spanish cavalrymen, 50 harquebusiers, 80 foot soldiers, 800 Indian auxiliaries, and a large herd of livestock. He forged into the narrow, 15-mile-wide valley of the Caracas Indians to found Santiago de León de los Caracas (Saint James of León among the Caracas Indians) by 25 July of that same

Panoramic view across Caracas, ca. 1905. (Keane, *Central and South America*)

829

summer, Santiago de León being the name of a medieval Spanish military order. His chosen site—near the former San Francisco hamlet—was located at the highest point of Chacao Plain, 3,300 feet above sea level on the northern bank of a wide bend in the Guaire River. Its surrounding landscape—renamed San Francisco Valley—was spectacularly beautiful, lush pasturelands being enclosed on three sides by the Central Littoral Mountains, with twin peaks towering to a height of 8,622 feet some 2 miles farther to the northeast (which prominence was nicknamed La Silla or "The Saddle" for its resemblance to a horse's mount). The valley's climate proved to be benignly dry and warm, although interspersed with frequent showers and elevated humidity levels during the summer months of June through September.

The initial town consisted of twenty or so mud-wattle huts with thatched roofs, clustered around four streets cleared and leveled by Losada's subordinate Diego Henares Lezama; the neighboring Indian lands and peoples were distributed as *encomiendas* (vassal estates) among 136 Spanish property owners, a few of whom began planting crops and tending livestock. The next April, this fledgling community held its first *cabildo* (municipal council) meeting and sent a detachment to scale the mountain barrier to its north, so as to gain access to a Caribbean outlet (initially selecting the harbor at Nuestra Señora de los Remedios de Caraballeda, although shifting westward in 1585–1588 to the port of La Guaira, which lay less than 7 miles from Caracas in a direct line—although accessible only via a twisting, 20-mile descent to the coast).

Most of the conquistadors soon proved unwilling to settle down to an agrarian subsistence, preferring to continue campaigning against the confederacy formed against them by outlying tribes, which vainly strove to expel the Spaniards from the Caracas Valley. For the better part of a decade, Losada's dwindling band of followers conducted slave-catching raids against these elusive tribesmen, in the process pushing out the settlement's boundaries.

In May 1576, a new royal governor—Juan Pimentel, knight of the Order of Santiago—reached Caraballeda and ascended the Avila River, opting to install his administration at Santiago de León rather than at either El Tocuyo or Coro, allegedly because the former was better situated to monitor local gold production; it is more likely, however, that he had been favorably impressed by Caracas's superior climate and landscape. During his tenure, the rudimentary rural hamlet grew into Venezuela's true capital, expanding into a dozen blocks laid out in a grid pattern around a central square, while its population rose to roughly 300 Spanish residents spread among sixty households (of which only 14 were original property owners, left over from Losada's contingent), as well as another 4,000 Christianized vassals scattered throughout its neighboring haciendas (estates).

The city's physical appearance also became much more permanent as three brick-and-mortar structures with tiled roofs were soon completed, plus a few low-slung churches, in addition to its original Franciscan convent. The main San Pablo Church was not roofed over and finished until 1584, the year after Venezuela's new bishop, Juan Martínez Manzanillo, arrived and took up residence in Caracas, despite the fact that his see, too, was to remain legally headquartered at Coro for yet another half century. Matters improved further still, once resistance by outlying tribes—already weakened by hunger and fatigue brought on by repeated disruptions of their harvests—collapsed over the next few years. Smallpox swept through their remote encampments in 1580, killing perhaps two-thirds of the 30,000 indigenes living in the Caracas Valley and uncounted thousands beyond.

With hostilities therefore at an end, *Caraqueños* (Caracans) turned to economic pursuits and quickly prospered from a fortunate combination of circumstances that produced a wheat boom. Although unsuitable for vineyards or fruit orchards, the flat landscape and moderate climate of their valley floor meant that cereal cultivation could flourish, crops being typically planted toward the conclusion of every rainy season in early autumn (September–October), then harvested the next spring. The Anauco, Catuche, and Chacao streams running down out of the mountains northeast of the city into the Guaire River became swollen once summer rains resumed, providing hydraulic power for mills erected along their banks to thresh wheat and mill grain into flour. The resultant produce could then be conveyed over the nearby mountain range into La Guaira to be sailed westward upon the prevailing trade winds to Cartagena, where it was sold at a handsome profit in time to resupply the annual plate-fleets arriving from Seville.

During the last two decades of the sixteenth century, Caracas changed from a remote frontier outpost into a significant regional purveyor because of this traffic, a few more migrants even appearing to occupy urban jobs and help clear outlying properties; they were attracted to the city both by its improved prospects—for it was now agriculturally self-sufficient, in addition to exporting bumper crops of wheat and cured meats—as well as by a climate that was more appealing to Castilians than the hot, steamy Caribbean coastline. Unfortunately, such newfound prosperity also enticed foreign enemies, so that the city suffered a devastating attack during Spain's war against Elizabethan England.

On 6 June 1595, eight privateer vessels anchored off Guiacamacuto (modern Macuto), their commanders, Amyas Preston and George Somers, disembarking 300 men—mostly professional soldiers—who marched a mile and a half westward to surprise the tiny, mostly empty Spanish stronghold at La Guaira. Upon receipt of this alarming news, some forty to fifty Caracan riders descended the winding mountain road to confront the invaders the next afternoon, withdrawing when a like number of English musketeers emerged from the captive stronghold to offer battle. Convinced that the rovers must depart without attempting anything further, the Spaniards

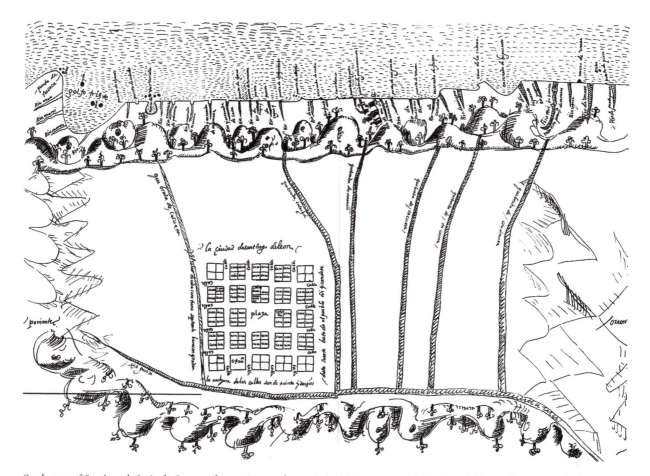

Crude map of Santiago de León de Caracas, the new Venezuelan capital, which accompanied Gov. Juan de Pimentel's report to the king in December 1578. Note that the city has been drawn disproportionately large, as well as the importance accorded to the valuable mountain streams coursing through this fertile agricultural district. (Archive of Indies, Seville)

mustered all their strength along the main road leading up into their capital, but they failed to maintain close watch upon their foes' movements; thus they allowed the English to slip out during a rainstorm that same night and ascend by another little-used track, appearing outside Caracas by the afternoon of 8 June. Since most defenders were gathered along the principal mountain road, only an elderly Spanish rider named Alonso Andrea de Ledesma (one of the city's original founders) remained to check their advance with his lance and shield, being shot dead for his bravery.

The invaders entered the small city at 3:00 P.M. on 8 June 1595, remaining in possession for five days before finally—after failing to extort a ransom—setting its structures ablaze and returning via Catia into La Guaira by noon of 14 June to sail away the following day. Undaunted by this raid and its subsequent outbreak of disease, Caracas's citizenry immediately set about rebuilding their torched dwellings, and their seaborne trade increased further once peace was restored in the spring of 1604; their exports now began reaching as far abroad as Mexico—a development that proved especially timely, as Caracas's

wheat production then plummeted as a result of several years of continuous droughts, coupled with increased competition from Maracaibo as of 1608. *Caraqueño* planters responded by trying tobacco and cacao crops, the former being soon banned but the latter commodity proving so highly marketable that it produced the city's second great economic boom.

During the 1620s, Venezuelan cacao came to displace Central American beans in the lucrative Mexican market, being deemed preferable because of their sweeter natural taste and thus requiring fewer ladlings of expensive sugar to be made into palatable chocolate. A threefold rise in this export traffic, starting as of the early 1630s, in turn financed the importation of the first significant numbers of African slaves into Venezuela, who were used to clear more valley complexes south of Caracas and plant new cacao *arboledas* (groves). As the focal point for the bulk of this traffic, Caracas grew into roughly 220 Spanish households, and Venezuela's bishopric was officially transferred into the capital from Coro as of 1636; a new Mercedarian convent was also completed in Caracas two years afterward and La Concepción Convent in 1639.

Devastation and Recuperation (1641–1751)

However, the tiny city suffered a major setback when a massive earthquake rumbled through much of the region on 11 June 1641, flattening or damaging most buildings. Losses were so dreadful that many *Caraqueños* spoke of moving to a new site and starting again, although they were prevented by truculent opposition from Bishop Mauro de Tovar (who was concerned lest Church titles against destroyed properties would be nullified by such a relocation). Still, Caracas took several decades to recuperate from this calamity, its economy being further debilitated by an *alhorra* blight—which decimated cacao trees—as well as by competition from cheaper cacao exports clandestinely introduced into Mexico from Guayaquil. As a result of such manifold troubles, many *Caraqueños* withdrew to the countryside altogether throughout this difficult interlude, so that even notaries were obliged to close up their offices for lack of work, while the city *cabildo* remained without its requisite complement of *regidores* (councilors) until the Mexican mining revival of the 1670s finally renewed overseas demand for cacao.

As Caracas slowly regained its economic impetus during the latter decades of the seventeenth century, it once more began attracting a few migrants, most coming from the Canary Islands and settling into La Candelaria parish on the city's eastern fringe (where they financed the erection of its church by 1708). The capital was spared the piratical attacks that plagued rival export outlets along the Caribbean coast, so that many plantation owners had resumed living in Caracas by the early eighteenth century. From this central point, they could better manage their scattered rural estates—a policy made more necessary by the shift inland of many operations, most original farms nearer the coast having exhausted their soils by now, so that new and more bountiful estates had to be cleared along inland riverbanks. The number of cacao trees cultivated in Caracas's province rose from 2 million in 1720 to more than 5 million by 1744, about half of them farther southeast in the virgin Tuy River Valley. The city's rebirth was further underscored by the elevation of its seventeenth-century Seminario de Santa Rosa into a royal university by August 1725.

However, such renewed dynamism also tempted a group of investors in the distant Basque province of Guipúzcoa to obtain a license from the Crown in 1728, so that their Real Compañía Guipuzcoana (Royal Guipuzcoan Company) might have exclusive rights to import Caracan cacao into Spain. Technically, such a monopoly would not interfere with the *Caraqueños'* ongoing and more lucrative traffic with Mexico; yet the Basque investors' ulterior motive was to dominate the economy of Venezuela—which despite its recent resurgence still remained a sparsely populated imperial backwater. Since vessels loaded at La Guaira in order of their arrival, a single Guipuzcoan ship could delay all other departures until it had been filled with beans at an extremely low price. Given that most Venezuelan merchants preferred selling their produce for higher profits in Mexico, then reinvesting their gains into purchased goods for resale upon their return, resentment quickly grew against the Guipuzcoans' delaying tactics. That deepened when the Basque Gabriel José de Zuloaga was appointed as Venezuela's royal governor in 1737, exhibiting marked partiality toward the monopolists during his ten-year term in office.

When the Basques attempted to extend their influence into the growing districts of the interior by dispatching officials and "antismuggling" patrols in the 1740s, the *teniente de justicia* (deputy justice) at Panaquire—a wealthy *hacendado* (estate owner) named Juan Francisco de León—spearheaded a popular uprising against the monopoly early in 1749 by marching upon Caracas at the head of 2,000 armed protestors and entering on 20 April. Feelings were so agitated that Gov. Luis de Castellano fled to La Guaira the next day disguised as a friar, and although no great violence thereupon ensued, de León's adherents remained encamped in La Candelaria suburb, threatening Guipuzcoan Company representatives. Venezuela remained uncomfortably devoid of any royal governor until Felipe Ricardos arrived from Spain two years later at the head of 1,200 troops. Local passions having cooled, de León was seized without resistance and deported aboard the man-of-war *Santa Bárbara,* after which his Caracan home was razed, and numerous supporters among the planter elite were arrested as accomplices.

Colonial Heyday (1752–1807)

Ironically, greater Crown scrutiny after this revolt helped solidify Caracas's role as regional capital, the city blossoming thanks to a reinforced royal presence, as well as from the general economic upsurge that swept through all of Spanish America as of the late 1760s. Ensconced behind its coastal mountain barrier, Caracas had long been deemed safe from enemy attacks and thus had been spared the expense of costly fortifications; it furthermore enjoyed—unlike other commercial rivals—a mild, healthful climate, reliable food and water supplies, and its surrounding complex of valleys was by now more densely dotted with satellite towns dependent upon the capital's resources.

Caracas's growth in importance was reflected by an upsurge in its population, which rose from 17,000 inhabitants in 1767 to 19,000 five years later, of whom approximately 75 percent were mulattoes, blacks, or Indians—a racial ratio that would persist well into the nineteenth century. Moreover, its *cabildo* had the distinction of acting on behalf of all Venezuela during a governor's absence, a rare exception to Madrid's otherwise rigid imperial practices, which had seen other such municipal bodies throughout South America shorn of influence.

Bourbon policies that liberalized trade during the last quarter of the eighteenth century helped accelerate Venezuela's economy, whose uncharted jungle borders with Guyana and Brazil were pushed out in the process, precipitating a short-

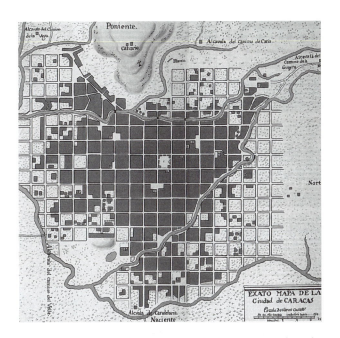

Map of Caracas, prepared in August 1772 by Juan Vicente Bolívar, father of the future Libertador of South America, Simón Bolívar. North is toward right. (Archive of Indies, Seville)

quartered in the capital, while a *real audiencia* (royal tribunal) was added as of 1786 to handle judicial matters. City merchants were furthermore granted the right to form their own *consulado* (merchant guild) in 1793, enhancing their ability to conduct overseas trade.

Thanks to its enhanced status, Caracas began taking on a slightly more imposing appearance, no longer meriting the description penned by an anonymous mid-eighteenth-century visitor who had found a city "without any type of walls, and its structures generally low and made of adobe." Yet despite significant improvements, no major royal buildings were erected specifically to house these new offices; most authorities—from the captain-general, intendant, and justices on down—functioned out of leased premises. When the German naturalist Alexander, Baron von Humboldt, arrived on 29 November 1799 for a stopover during his celebrated South American tour, he estimated that the capital's population was approaching 24,000 residents, with another 16,000 scattered nearby throughout its valley; he was also disappointed to note that no newspaper existed, despite an operating press owned by a Frenchman. (The city's first newspaper—the *Gaceta de Caracas*—was not issued until late October 1808 by the British-born Matthew Gallagher and James Lamb.)

Stirrings of Independence (1808–1811)

Like most other Spanish American vassals, *Caraqueños* were astonished to learn that Napoleon had sent a huge French army into Spain in June 1808 to dislodge its monarch in favor of his own brother Joseph Bonaparte, both Capt.-Gen. Juan de Casas and the city's *cabildo* promptly reaffirming their allegiance to the captive Spanish heir, Ferdinand VII. However, a significant minority among the Caracan *mantuano* elite—a term literally meaning those who wore luxurious lace mantillas (shawls)—

lived conflict against Portugal in 1775–1776. Before these hostilities had even officially concluded, with the signing of a treaty in October 1777, King Charles III issued a royal decree on 8 September that created the new captaincy general of Venezuela by uniting the formerly semiautonomous provinces of Maracaibo, Cumaná, Margarita, Trinidad, and Guiana under Caracas's jurisdiction. Venezuela's civil administration was also placed under the central authority of an *Intendente* head-

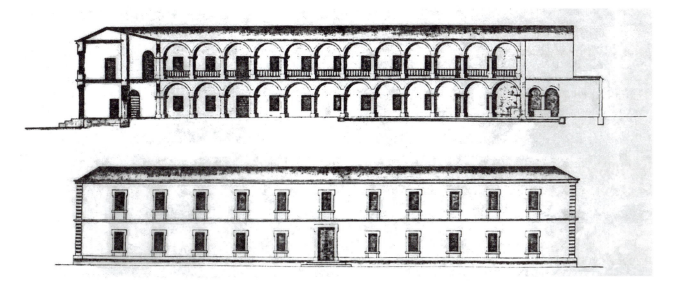

Profile views drawn in September 1785 by Miguel González Dávila of a proposed new barracks to house Caracas's infantry battalion. (Servicio Histórico Militar, Madrid)

also hoped to use this weakening of imperial ties to carve out a more autonomous role for their province and so proposed establishing a local junta (assembly) similar to the emergency body spearheading resistance against the French in Spain. De Casas reluctantly agreed, only to retract his approval and place its leading exponents—including the twenty-five-year-old Simón Bolívar, scion of one of the city's earliest settler families—under house arrest that same November.

The genie of independence had nevertheless been unleashed, so that as Loyalist fortunes in Spain faded against the implacable advance of Bonaparte's troops, the Caracan *cabildo* finally assembled on 19 April 1810 and deposed the new captain-general, Vicente Emparán, in favor of a junta—which although still professing loyalty to Ferdinand VII, began to act increasingly on its own. Emissaries were sent to Dutch Curaçao, the United States, and England, only to be ignored; those dispatched to the sister Venezuelan cities of Maracaibo and Coro were even arrested, although largely because of long-simmering economic rivalries with the capital, as well as jealous resentment against the unilateral *Caraqueño* assumption of a leading national role.

Still, a Congress was held in June 1811 with representatives from Venezuela's next six-largest cities—Barcelona, Cumaná, Margarita, Barinas, Mérida, and Trujillo—which after lengthy debate opted to sever all ties with Spain and declare outright independence on 5 July. Strong opposition immediately appeared at Valencia, requiring that a patriot division be dispatched from Caracas later that same month under Francisco Rodríguez, Marqués del Toro, who was repulsed into Maracay with slight losses. The veteran libertarian Francisco Miranda succeeded him, subduing that fractious city by 12 August, after which a national constitution was promulgated on 21 December—yet which disappointed many lower-class Venezuelans by entrenching the status quo privileges of the elite while leaving other ancient regime practices such as slavery virtually intact. This document marked the beginning of Venezuela's First Republic, also known today as the Patria Boba (False Nation) because of its failure to garner popular support.

Earthquake and Turmoil (1812–1869)

More serious opposition emerged from Coro in early March 1812, when 230 troops began moving eastward under Capt. Juan Domingo de Monteverde, being joined at Siquisique by several hundred Indian auxiliaries under Chief Juan de los Reyes Vargas. Before this Loyalist column could penetrate into the upland valleys and threaten Caracas, an earthquake destroyed much of the capital and other republican-held cities on the afternoon of 26 March—Easter Thursday—while leaving monarchist regions throughout Venezuela largely intact. Demoralized by their 12,000 deaths and the destruction of their capital, patriot survivors soon fell to bickering among themselves, ultimately not granting Miranda the requisite powers to muster an army and check the invasion until 23

April. Meanwhile, the *mantuano* leadership had not only alienated many blacks by their retrograde social dictates; they had also drafted legislation aimed at extending private land ownership into the heretofore unclaimed *llanos* (rangelands), thus reducing the status of its tough *llaneros* (plainsmen) to little more than indentured vassals.

Both groups therefore provided formidable guerrilla contingents for the advancing royalists, the former rising amid the plantations east of Caracas, while the latter revolted on the Calabozo Plains. Monteverde gained Valencia without opposition by 3 May 1812, and after skirmishing with Miranda's larger army around Guaica Pass learned in mid-July that a group of monarchist captives had seized Puerto Cabello. Heartened by such evident patriot disarray, Monteverde resumed his offensive and compelled Miranda to surrender Caracas by 25 July, the patriot leader being further handed over to the Loyalists by his disgruntled subordinates and sent to Cadiz in chains. The First Republic had thus come to an ignominious end, although Monteverde subsequently proved incapable of reimposing royal rule; the devastated capital was doomed to endure more assaults over the next few years.

One republican officer who escaped was young Colonel Bolívar, who after securing promotion to brigadier in the army of neighboring Colombia set out the next spring to reconquer Venezuela from the west in a bitter "war to the death." After a brilliant offensive dubbed the Campaña Admirable (Admirable Campaign), he destroyed a royalist army at Taguanes Plain on 31 July 1813, prompting Monteverde to abandon Valencia, thereby leaving the road into Caracas open. Bolívar reentered the capital in triumph on 6 August, amid scenes of cruel reprisals against defeated Loyalists and their sympathizers, and although proclaimed El Libertador for his reinstallation of a Second Republic, his administration turned out to be little more than a military dictatorship in which Caracan self-interest once again offended many rural blacks and *llaneros*.

The ensuing winter saw an increase in royalist guerrilla raids, the most effective being organized by the former smuggler José Tomás Boves, whose riders eventually numbered 7,000 to 8,000 and crushed a patriot army at La Puerta in Semen Valley southwest of Caracas before finally being checked at La Victoria on 12 February 1814. Frightened republicans had nevertheless executed 800 monarchist captives at La Guaira in anticipation of being overrun, and while Bolívar managed to defeat a royalist army on the Plains of Carabobo on 28 May, it was becoming increasingly difficult for the patriots to hold the capital. When Boves's *llanero* cavalry crushed the combined forces of Bolívar and Santiago Mariño at La Puerta on 15 June, only 1,000 patriot survivors retired into Caracas. The main royalist army turned aside to subdue Valencia, detaching a division to occupy the capital. Believing the latter force to be weak, Bolívar sortied again, only to be defeated once more with even heavier losses on 6 July. Caracas was thereupon abandoned, several thousand republican refugees attempting a pitiful flight toward Barcelona in Bolívar's wake, rather than face the monarchists' vengeance.

The royalist grip on the gutted capital tightened the next year, when Gen. Pablo Morillo y Morillo arrived on 11 May 1815 with a large Spanish expedition to restore Ferdinand VII's rule over all of South America. Before proceeding toward Puerto Cabello on 2 June with his main body, Morillo reintroduced many of the old absolutist policies at Caracas, then furthermore installed a harsh military regime under Brig. Salvador Moxó to ensure a steady flow of provisions and funds for his army. Many black royalists felt acutely disillusioned by these acts, their recent allegiance to the Crown having been so ill rewarded. Still, Morillo's regulars made dissent dangerous within the half-empty capital, and they even sallied successfully three years later to defeat another invasion attempt by Bolívar, surprising his 2,200-man army near La Puerta at 6:00 A.M. on 16 March 1818.

Notwithstanding this setback, the insurgent cause eventually proved inextinguishable, so that a patriot force advancing out of eastern Venezuela under Gen. José Francisco Bermúdez was finally able to reclaim Caracas at dawn on 14 May 1821, while its few remaining Loyalist residents scattered in terror toward La Guaira to sail away aboard a flotilla of vessels. However, with other Spanish armies still operating in the capital's vicinity, Bermúdez merely emptied the arsenal at La Guaira, raised a number of local volunteers, and dug in with his 1,500 men at Márquez between Las Lajas and Las Cocuizas to weather a daylong counterattack on 24 May by 2,800 Loyalists,

who eventually caused him to retire after nightfall and evacuate Caracas two days later.

Less than one month afterward, he returned, only to have his small army crushed while attempting to carry El Calvario Hill just west of Caracas on 23 June 1821. The next morning, however, Bolívar's 6,400 patriots smashed the last big Spanish army at the Battle of Carabobo, so that the Libertador reentered his native city of Caracas by the evening of 28 June. With La Guaira secured the next day, only Puerto Cabello and Cumaná remained in royalist hands, and Venezuela's liberty had been effectively won. Nonetheless, its ruined capital—having changed hands five times, and endured a major earthquake, during slightly less than a decade of conflict—would take many years to recover, its population not regaining colonial-era numbers until the middle of the nineteenth century. Travel accounts from the immediate postindependence period remark upon the desolation and poverty gripping much of Caracas, in stark contrast to its beautiful landscape, while some structural damage would take fifty years to be rectified. (The U.S. naval officer H. E. Sandford, for example, noted numerous ruins still dotting the city during his visit to Caracas in April 1857.)

Great uncertainty was to plague the young nation, starting when Venezuelans bridled at their newfound union with the ineffectual "Republic of Gran Colombia." Although Bolívar's return into Caracas in 1827 briefly placated such complaints, a schism nonetheless occurred two years later, another former

Simón Bolívar's birthplace in Caracas, as it appeared, ca. 1920. (Franck, *Working North from Patagonia*)

Map of Caracas in 1852, as surveyed by the engineers Lino J. Revenga and Gregorio Fidel Méndez; lithograph by W. Stapler, engraved by Jorge Laue. (Cartografía Nacional, Caracas)

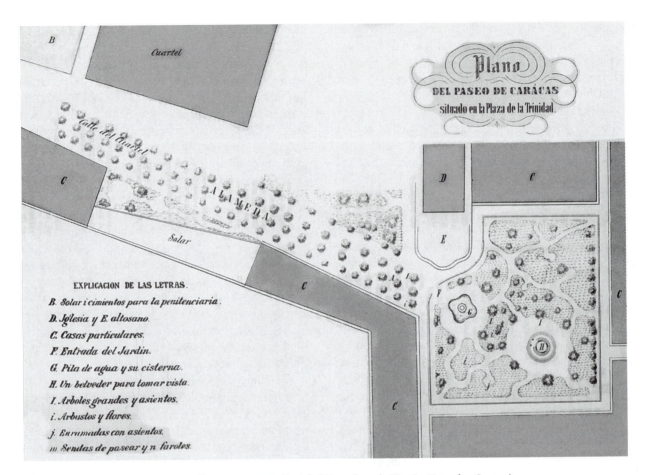

Diagram of the new Paseo or "Boulevard" at Caracas, 1859. (Sociedad Venezolana de Ciencias Naturales, Caracas)

wartime hero—Gen. José Antonio Páez—eventually being elected as Venezuela's first president in April 1831. The Caracan economy was modestly revived by soaring coffee prices on international markets during the 1830s, so that the city reassumed its former commercial role of clearinghouse for regional exports; that brief boom was further bolstered by European investors who reestablished many neglected plantations throughout the central valleys. Yet the capital was also to remain prey to the vagaries of political aggressiveness among the numerous contending factions in the republic, complicating its resurrection.

When Dr. José María Vargas—a well-educated member of the Caracan elite—succeeded Páez as president in 1835, he was quickly toppled by a bloodless uprising of disgruntled independence-era generals on 8 July that became known as the Revuelta de las Reformas (Revolt of the Reforms); despite being restored into office by Páez a few weeks later, this civilian resigned the following year, leaving Venezuelan politics to a succession of strongmen who fought their way in and out of office over the next century. The price of coffee also declined during the 1840s, and debt crises abounded, these political and economic problems eventually culminating with a revolt against the despotic Liberal administration of President José Tadeo Monagas in early March 1858. This rebellion touched off

another five years of hostilities known as the Federal War, because of the federation proclaimed at Coro that following February. The national capital was repeatedly contested throughout this conflict, until finally Gen. Juan Crisóstomo Falcón won Caracas—and thus the presidency—in 1863.

Modernization (1870–Present)

Seven years later, yet another rebel general—Antonio Guzmán Blanco, son of a newspaper publisher—disembarked near Coro and marched upon the capital, rapidly gaining support and fighting his way into Caracas's streets by 27 April 1870. Vain, astute, and avaricious, Guzmán Blanco would cling to power for the next eighteen years; he was the first republican leader to make a concerted effort at beautifying and modernizing the Venezuelan capital.

Aided by a revival of the coffee trade and improved credit abroad, the new dictator sought to showcase his administration's vigor and progressive ideals by launching a feverish construction program, most of his efforts being concentrated in the city's central section: the old colonial core of Santiago de León, whose main square (since renamed Plaza Bolívar) was redesigned and its ancient arcades demolished, while Concepción Convent was displaced by a huge new capitol building; the sixteenth-century San Pablo Church was replaced by

View from the Alameda into the new Paseo at Trinidad Square—modern Panteón Square—as drawn by A. Lutowski, 1859. (Sociedad Venezolana de Ciencias Naturales, Caracas)

a Teatro Municipal (Municipal Theater); and San Francisco Convent became the headquarters for a new Central University. Many lesser public buildings were added, along with broad boulevards and the General del Sur (Southern General) Cemetery, while El Calvario Hill was transformed into a large and elegant public park—most architectural designs being strongly influenced by French concepts, as Guzmán Blanco was an avid Francophile given to protracted vacations in Paris.

Thanks to such endeavors, as well as a rising tide of regional prosperity, Caracas's population rose from roughly 49,000 residents when the first national census was conducted in 1873 to 55,638 eight years later. In addition to Guzmán Blanco's grand construction projects, Caracas's streets also became illuminated by gas; water, sewage, telegraph, and electrical systems were all installed; the federal bureaucracy and army were overhauled; and the 23-mile Caracas-to-La Guaira Railway was inaugurated in 1883 by a private firm (not bought out by the government until 1949), greatly facilitating the transportation of heavy goods to and from the coast.

Guzmán Blanco's tenure was to represent the capital's last major facelift for another six decades, earning him the sobriquet of El Regenerador (The Regenerator). In October 1888, his once-loyal retainer Gen. Joaquín Crespo led a large rebel host into Caracas and bloodlessly seized power, so that the absent Guzmán Blanco was obliged to live out his remaining years in luxurious exile in Paris. Few innovations were attempted during Crespo's reign, one minor exception being the formation of the first baseball club in Caracas in 1895 by students who had returned from the United States. The sport quickly displaced English cricket as the preferred recreation among upper-class youth, then spread rapidly throughout the city and country to become a national passion.

A grassroots rebellion finally exploded in the mountainous regions of western Venezuela at the end of the nineteenth century, sweeping rough and unschooled Gen. Cipriano Castro into power by 1899. His nine-year rule proved to be extremely tumultuous, marred by numerous revolts in outlying districts and an earthquake that rumbled through the capital on 29 October 1900. Inept administration climaxed with fiscal collapse, aggravated by declines in international coffee prices and national gold output. Having defaulted on Venezuela's foreign debts, Castro's government was beset when the British and German ambassadors withdrew on 9 December 1902, paving the way for a combined Anglo-German naval squadron to impose a blockade that same afternoon as a means of exacting payment. Angry street demonstrations exploded in Caracas on 10 December, and more than 200 foreigners were detained in retaliation. Yet although international opinion roundly condemned the heavy-handed Anglo-German intervention, Castro eventually had to accept their terms on 13 February 1903, raising customs duties at La Guaira and Puerto Cabello in order to satisfy the foreign powers' claims. He was glorified by Venezuelans for having resisted such extortionate methods, yet his administration continued to be hampered by mismanagement. After departing to seek medical treatment in Europe for a kidney ailment, he was supplanted by popular demonstrations in the capital in December 1908 in favor of his vice president, Juan Vicente Gómez.

Caracas's municipal theater, as it appeared, ca. 1920. (Franck, *Working North from Patagonia*)

Although more refined than his predecessor, Gómez exceeded him in corruption, so that Caracas remained mired in neglect as he drew freely upon public funds for his personal aggrandizement, granted monopolies to special interests, and used secret police informants and torturers to help maintain his hold on power over the next twenty-seven years. He even appointed his brother Juancho and son Juan Vicente, Jr., as vice presidents and showed scant interest in the capital, preferring to reside amid the security of his military bases 50 miles farther west at Maracay. Caracas's population rose from 72,000 residents in 1905 to a mere 92,212 by 1922, and only massive infusions of revenue after the discovery of petroleum in western Venezuela in 1917 helped to relieve its utter stagnation. Federal government dividends from this windfall skyrocketed from 900,000 bolivares that first year to more than 600 million by 1935, the year in which Gómez—now labeled the "Tyrant of the Andes"—at last died. Mobs ransacked and burned the Caracan homes of his family members, as well as those of Gómez's most notorious henchmen.

Under the relatively more enlightened rule of Gen. Eleázar López Contreras, Caracas at last embarked upon a phase of significant urban expansion and modernization. The Federal District's boundaries having already been extended in 1926 to encompass roughly 147,000 total residents, the number more than doubled to 379,950 by 1941, when López Contreras was

succeeded by Pres. Isaías Medina Angarita. He in turn drew much of his political support from urban workers, especially after Venezuela's petroleum industry was nationalized two years later, proceeds being diverted into public works. Although he was ousted by a military coup in October 1945, policies similar to Medina's were pursued by the populist Pres. Rómulo Betancourt and his successor, Rómulo Gallegos, both members of the socialist Acción Democrática (Democratic Action) Party, until yet another coup occurred in November 1948.

Two years later, Caracas's population stood at 709,464 people, and the capital enjoyed such completed projects as new highways and railways radiating into the Venezuelan interior, plus a huge dam and aqueduct; an international airport was also completed in 1951 to supplement the outdated Maiquetía west of La Guaira. Yet despite such outward manifestations of progress, the capital was also becoming increasingly encircled by vast shantytowns, as impoverished peasants streamed in from the countryside seeking better prospects. The nation's political leadership went into decline again when Gen. Marcos Pérez Jiménez ran for president in November 1952; he assumed office early the next year despite having clearly lost the popular vote. Five years of repressive military rule ensued, culminating with his ouster by fellow officers on 23 January 1958.

Despite such handicaps, the Federal District's population

View of a private home's inner courtyard, ca. 1888. (Curtis, *The Capitals of Spanish America*)

had continued to swell to 1,362,189 residents by June 1961, with another 343,638 living just outside its boundaries; the capital was now spilling over into the neighboring state of Miranda. Over the next few decades, urban sprawl would creep remorselessly throughout the valley and into its foothills, as Caracas engulfed a succession of satellite towns: La Florida, Altamira, La Castellana, Los Caobos, Campo Alegre, San Bernardino (formerly Gamboa), El Paraíso, La Paz, El Pinar, Las Fuentes, Los Rosales, Las Acacias, Los Chaguaramos, Santa Mónica, Las Mercedes, Prados del Este, California Norte and California Sur, La Carlota, Campo Claro, Los Palos Grandes, Los Chorros, Chuao, Bello Monte, Cumbres de Curumo, Los Campitos, El Cafetal, Caurimare, Colinas de los Ruices, Macaracuay, and El Marqués.

Notwithstanding some impressive architectural achievements, and great individual wealth amassed from increased oil sales abroad, the vast metropolitan area came to be blighted by urban problems commonly associated with rapid overdevelopment, such as strained municipal services and resources, crime, slums, traffic congestion, and air pollution. The Federal District's population continued to spiral upward from 1,865,853 inhabitants in 1971 to 2,180,000 five years later and 2,784,042 by 1990. Social unrest festered in many overcrowded neighborhoods, aggravated by sporadic economic collapses

and austerity measures imposed by the government, contributing to outbursts such as the three days of looting in Caracas and sixteen other Venezuelan cities in late February 1989, which resulted in 300 deaths, 2,000 injuries, and 2,000 arrests.

For further reading materials on the history of Caracas and Venezuela, please consult the "Select Bibliography" at the end of this volume.

MARACAIBO

City that has evolved from a minor colonial seaport into Venezuela's second-largest metropolis, thanks to its rich oil fields.

Foundation as "Ulma" (1529–1535)

It is a historical curiosity that Maracaibo has enjoyed German connections from its very earliest days. In the spring of 1528, Habsburg Emperor Charles V—hoping to realize some immediate financial gain from his fast-expanding New World properties—repaid a debt to the German banking concern of Welser headquartered at Augsburg by granting it a lease to colonize hitherto unexplored *Venezuela* (signifying "Little Venice" in Spanish, because of the stilt houses spotted off Maracaibo's shoreline by the first Spanish explorers). This authorization included permission to establish towns, exploit mineral deposits, and import African slaves.

An expedition duly appeared offshore the next year under a tough mercenary named Ambrosio Alfinger, who established his initial base camp in the sandy hills around La Vela de Coro, then struck west-southwestward through the steamy scrubland with a small army of 180 men, cruelly subjugating its inhabitants. On 8 September 1529 he reached the shores of an immense lake, crossing to its more fertile western side and conquering an indigenous town on the site of present-day Maracaibo, which he renamed Ulma in honor of his German birthplace of Ulm. Disease, heat, and a lack of provisions eventually obliged him to retrace his steps toward La Vela de Coro with some booty.

The next summer, however, Alfinger delegated Luis González de Leiva to return into the district as his lieutenant governor and again take up residence at Maracaibo. Alfinger himself joined that ensuing year with more men, and on 1 September 1531 he officially founded a "town" at Maracaibo, Francisco Venegas being designated as its first Welser-appointed mayor. The invaders used this ramshackle collection of thatched huts as a springboard for subsequent ventures farther north and west, but by May 1535 Venegas was transferred to Coro and replaced by Hernando de Beteta, the settlement itself being abandoned that same October to help support Nicolaus Federmann's unsuccessful bid to conquer the Guajira Peninsula farther north. By the mid-1540s, German influence throughout the territory also began to wane as the Spaniards reasserted their monopoly, and the Welser lease was allowed to lapse by 1557.

Panoramic view looking southeastward across Maracaibo's red-tiled rooftops toward its anchorage, ca. 1917; the dark building in right foreground is the recently refurbished Municipal Palace. (*Maracaibo gráfico*)

Revival as Ciudad Rodrigo (1569–1573)

A dozen years later, Alonso Pacheco led a fifty-man expedition across the lake from Trujillo, reestablishing a Spanish outpost called Nueva Ciudad Rodrigo de Maracaibo—after his birthplace of Ciudad Rodrigo in northwestern Spain—on the same spot in July 1569. However, this colony failed as well, being forsaken by its thirty surviving members in December 1573 after an Onoto insurrection that summer.

Evolution as Nueva Zamora (1574–1640)

It was not until Capt. Pedro Maldonado returned the next year with a further thirty-five men from Mérida that a precarious foothold named Nueva Zamora de Maracaibo at last took shape, so dubbed because Zamora was the Spanish birthplace of Venezuela's new royal governor, Diego Mazariegos. Nueva Zamora's hot, torrential climate, plus a lack of mineral riches or a highly advanced indigenous civilization, meant that few settlers were attracted into the area, the census of 1579 listing only thirty property owners in the town. Moreover, its surrounding Indians proved tenaciously hostile, repeatedly attacking isolated farms and boat traffic traversing the lake. By the summer of 1606, a confederacy had even coalesced to drive the Spaniards out, fleets of war canoes prowling the waters and threatening Nueva Zamora itself; its frightened citizenry were thus obliged to erect a stockade and request outside assistance that same September. As a result, Capt. Juan Pacheco Maldonado of Trujillo led a fifty-man counterexpedition across the Lake from Moporo the following spring, smashing the Indian alliance through a series of destructive sweeps.

Maracaibo's citizenry could now look forward to better security and economic prospects, their resolution being bolstered by the offer from wealthy landowners Francisco Ortiz and Inés del Basto to finance the erection of the town's first hospital beside Santa Ana Hermitage in 1607. Agriculture soon flourished as well, Maracaibo's adjacent coastline—especially along the lake's western and southern stretches, now cleared of hostiles—proving remarkably fertile and well irrigated; within a generation, large estates began to be established

Santa Ana Church, as it appeared after its reconstruction in the early twentieth century. (*Maracaibo gráfico*)

there for the cultivation of cash crops such as cacao, which proved so exceptionally profitable as to be exported to Cuba, Mexico, and Spain. The town of San Antonio de Gibraltar (founded in December 1591 near modern-day Bobures in the lake's southeastern corner) was the gathering point for most harvests, which were then shipped some 100 miles northward by boat.

Halfway across the lake, its waters turned from sweet to brackish because of the sea tides pushing gently in from the Gulf of Venezuela and the Caribbean beyond. The lake's outlet to the sea was obstructed by a long neck of islands and sandbars, interspersed by thirteen shallow channels—the main one between San Carlos Peninsula and Zaparas Island having a depth ranging from 7 feet at low tide to 12 feet at high tide. Maracaibo was located only 21 miles south of that line of obstacles and so became the entrepot for transferring cargoes between lake craft and oceangoing ships. Soon the city began to service the entire Andean hinterland, yet the wealth of this traffic also attracted more unwelcome attention. On 11 June 1641 much of Venezuela suffered from a heavy earthquake, and then on 15 October four small Dutch men-of-war, plus a Spanish prize sloop, materialized off the lake's bar under Commo. Hendrik Gerristz. His expedition of 250 to 275 men had been sent by the governor of Curaçao to raid the Spaniards during this period of temporary debility, as the two nations were then at war.

Buccaneer Raids (1641–1678)

After seizing a tiny salvage vessel working on a wrecked Spanish frigate inside the bar, Gerristz piloted his 20-gun flagship *Neptune* and four consorts across, bypassing Maracaibo on 19 October 1641 to surprise Gibraltar two days later, seizing its recently gathered tobacco and cacao harvests. Reversing course, Gerristz then reappeared off Maracaibo by the morning of 31 October to find its garrison of 230 Spanish militiamen, 120 indigenous auxiliaries, and three artillery pieces braced to resist under Lt. Gov. Francisco Cornieles Briceño. A heated artillery exchange ensued from 11:00 A.M. until 3:00 P.M., until Gerristz finally sent a flag of truce inshore to propose a cease-fire. The Spaniards refused, loosing off two more shots, after which the Dutch set their prisoners ashore that same night, sailing back out of the lake three days later.

The next year an English squadron arrived in the West Indies under Commo. William Jackson to retaliate against Spain's American possessions for their extirpation of an English settlement on Providencia Island a year and a half previously. After attacking Margarita, La Guaira, and Puerto Cabello, Jackson hired a Dutch pilot at Curaçao, then reached Maracaibo's bar on 23 December 1642. Leaving his 30-gun flagship with 120 men outside to maintain watch, he worked his remaining seven vessels and almost 1,000 men over its shoals. Spanish lookouts hastened word to Maracaibo's garrison commander, *maestre de campo* Manuel de Velasco, who

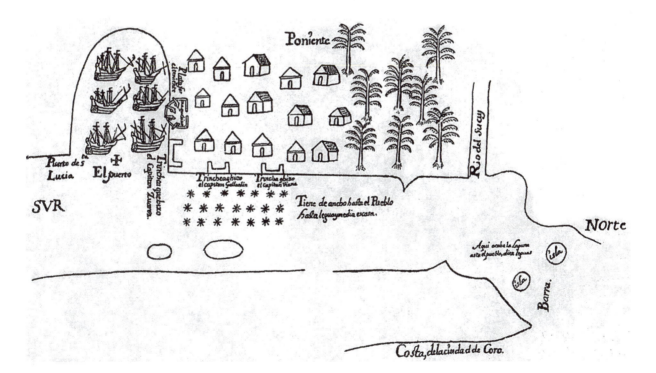

Modern rendering from a crude sketch—not drawn to scale—of Maracaibo and its anchorage in July 1631; north is toward right. Note how the bar across its lake entrance is featured at lower right, although it actually lies more than 20 miles distant from the city. (Archive of Indies, Seville)

mustered his 250 militiamen in anticipation of an assault. The English did not resume their advance until 26 December, seemingly giving the Spaniards time to prepare. But Jackson—aware that most of the city's defenses faced seaward—surprised de Velasco by circling past at 11:00 that same night; he then landed two contingents of 400 men apiece five hours later, 2 to 3 miles farther south at Los Bebederos, to march inland and approach Maracaibo from its rear. The Spanish militia therefore had to abandon their prepared waterfront trenches and fight in the dark jungle, where they were quickly stampeded by fears of superior English numbers. The city fell the following day, de Velasco and most of his followers being driven into its hinterland, while four vessels were also seized from its roads.

The English remained in occupation until 27 January 1643, when they received a ransom payment and departed across the lake, hoping to visit a like treatment upon Gibraltar. The next morning a belated Spanish relief column arrived overland from Coro under Venezuela's royal governor, Ruy Fernández de Fuenmayor, who circled Maracaibo warily until reassured that the city was deserted, then reoccupied it on 29 January and began refurbishing its defenses. The raiders, meanwhile, found scant booty at Gibraltar—its residents having long since fled—so that by 8:00 A.M. on 9 February they reappeared southeast of Maracaibo. Fernández de Fuenmayor sortied that same afternoon with 400 Spanish militiamen and 130 native archers to lay an ambush at El Palmar; Jackson ignored the Spaniards' bait—a cattle herd—and instead anchored out of range, offering to exchange his captives. The transaction was completed by 21 February, when the English proceeded past Maracaibo and exited the bar on 4 March.

Fernández de Fuenmayor stayed on at Maracaibo until September 1643, supervising the construction of a small, 16-gun, pentagonal fort at the lake's entrance to impede future incursions. Unfortunately, the outpost failed to halt the next attack, when a French buccaneer named François Nau "l'Olonnais" (being originally from Les Sables d'Olonne) and his colleague Michel le Basque materialized outside the lake early in 1667, disembarking their *flibustiers,* who quickly overwhelmed its feeble fortification and passed their ships over the bar. Two days later they reached Maracaibo, which lay abandoned by its 3,000 residents (only 265 of whom were actual Spanish property owners). After pillaging and sending out patrols for two weeks, Nau crossed the lake and stormed Gibraltar, holding it for a month before demanding 10,000 pesos to leave its buildings intact upon withdrawing. Once paid, the French recrossed the lake and extorted another 20,000 pesos and 500 head of cattle to spare Maracaibo as well, before quitting the lake altogether two months after entering.

Inspired by this easy success, Henry Morgan arrived outside on 9 March 1669 with eight vessels bearing 500 Jamaican buccaneers, disembarking his freebooters to besiege the tiny keep guarding the San Carlos Peninsula. Having only a single

Spanish officer and eight soldiers left on duty to man 11 guns, they put up a brief show of resistance before slipping out into the night. After spiking its artillery, Morgan's ships navigated across, only to find Maracaibo empty. Three weeks later the Jamaicans proceeded toward Gibraltar, returning into Maracaibo by 17 April with a captive Cuban merchant ship and five smaller piraguas, ready to head back out into the Caribbean.

But while the buccaneers had been ransacking the lakeshore, Spain's West Indian squadron (Armada de Barlovento) had arrived outside the bar under Adm. Alonso de Campos y Espinosa, bottling the interlopers inside with his 412-ton flagship *Magdalena* of 38 guns; 218-ton frigate *San Luis* of 26 guns; plus the 50-ton sloop *Nuestra Señora de la Soledad* (alias *Marquesa*) of 14 guns, manned by a total of 500 men. Having found the San Carlos fortress devastated, Campos reoccupied it with forty harquebusiers, repaired 6 of its guns, and then dispatched messengers inland calling for further local assistance. After several days he had also lightened his warships and had them traverse the bar before finally sending a letter to Morgan in Maracaibo, calling for his surrender.

On 25 April the thirteen English vessels came within sight of the anchored Spaniards, and two days later they rushed Campos's armada at 9:00 A.M.—led by the large Cuban prize, flying an admiral's insignia. It bore down upon Campos's flagship and grappled, but when the Spaniards surged over its bulwarks in a counterattack, they found its decks lined with wooden dummies and twelve buccaneers hastily decamping over its far side. The Cuban ship burst into flames, and *Magdalena* became engulfed, forcing Campos to leap into the water along with his panic-stricken crew. Alarmed by this spectacle, *San Luis* and *Marquesa* cut their cables and ran for the shelter of the fort, pursued by buccaneer craft. Both Spanish vessels grounded and were deliberately set ablaze by their crews, although the latter was soon boarded and saved by the privateers.

Yet despite his victory, Morgan was still unable to get past Fort San Carlos, its garrison having been augmented by seventy militiamen out of the interior, plus most of the surviving Armada crews. When the buccaneers attempted a land assault the next day, it was easily repulsed, so that the Jamaicans retired into Maracaibo. After offering to exchange his Spanish captives for free passage out to sea—which was rebuffed by Campos—Morgan returned to the bar a few days later and began busily plying his boats to and from shore. Convinced that the English were depositing an assault force, Campos's garrison manhandled their few guns into the landward embrasures and braced for a nocturnal attack. But Morgan had again deceived them, his boat movements being merely a feint and no buccaneers having actually disembarked. Instead, his ships weighed and slipped past the undefended side of the Spanish fortress under cover of darkness, depositing their prisoners outside before sailing away in triumph.

Nine years later, another much larger corsair expedition

arrived under François, Sieur de Grammont. Originally, French Vice Adm. Jean, Comte d'Estrées, had reached the West Indies with a royal battle fleet and been reinforced by Grammont and numerous other Caribbean auxiliaries to attack Dutch outposts as part of an ongoing European conflict. However, while sailing against Curaçao, most of the Crown warships had been wrecked on the Aves Islands, and the surviving *flibustiers* had subsequently decided to proceed against the much softer target of Maracaibo.

On 10 June 1678, 2,000 cutthroats materialized in the Gulf of Venezuela aboard six large ships and thirteen smaller ones. Grammont disembarked half this force and marched along the San Carlos Peninsula toward its fort, while the garrison commander, Francisco Pérez de Guzmán, staved off an immediate assault by stationing 100 harquebusiers outside his walls. But when heavy artillery was ferried ashore from the buccaneer flotilla, the Spaniards surrendered after a token exchange of shots. The fort in his power, Grammont thereupon worked his lesser ships over its bar, leaving his six largest to blockade the entrance while his main body pressed on into the lake.

Maracaibo was thrown into panic by this incursion, its ancient and sickly governor, Jorge Madureira Ferreira—in office scarcely a week—being unable to instill any sense of confidence. Citizens therefore fled in every direction, soon followed by Madureira himself, who retired toward Maicao with his handful of regular troops. Grammont entered unopposed on 14 June and gave the empty dwellings over to the sack. After *flibustier* columns had scoured the surrounding countryside, Grammont abandoned Maracaibo's gutted remains on 28 June to fall upon Gibraltar, which he also found largely deserted; he then marched 425 buccaneers almost 50 miles inland to take Trujillo from its rear on 1 September, despite resistance from its fort defended by 350 troops and four artillery pieces.

Finally, the victorious Frenchmen returned into Gibraltar and burned it to the ground on 25 September 1678 before razing Fort San Carlos and quitting the lake altogether on 3 December. Grammont's freebooter ships carried away seventy-seven cannon, much booty, and many captives, arriving to a tumultuous welcome at the Haitian capital of Petit-Goâve on Christmas Eve.

Stagnation (1679–1820)

Such wholesale devastation at last convinced the Venezuelan and Spanish authorities that Fort San Carlos would have to be rebuilt much more strongly than before, with additional outlying batteries to prevent disembarkations and encirclements from its adjoining inlets. Over the next couple of decades, the work was completed, leaving the lake's entrance sufficiently secured by the early eighteenth century as to prevent any further large-scale penetrations. However, regional trade was now being routinely diverted inland toward much safer Bogotá, El Tocuyo, and even Caracas, so that Maracaibo's economy did not revive appreciably. Its reputation for being in such an insalubrious environment—its crushing heat scarcely eased by midday breezes out of the northeast—furthermore discouraged senior government and ecclesiastical authorities from wishing to establish themselves there, blighting its development. Throughout much of the 1700s, the city remained a relatively small backwater, its isolation growing deeper when Venezuela's struggle for independence from Spain erupted in

Road leading north-northeast along the city lakeshore toward El Milagro, ca. 1917; note the dense surrounding vegetation. (*Maracaibo gráfico*)

View along Maracaibo's waterfront, ca. 1917. (*Maracaibo gráfico*)

Botica Vargas or "Pharmacy," a typical storefront at Maracaibo, ca. 1917; note the open sewer in its unpaved street, plus the electric poles and recently laid streetcar tracks. (*Maracaibo gráfico*)

Terminal for Maracaibo's American-owned electric streetcar company, ca. 1917. (*Maracaibo gráfico*)

1810, as it was a Loyalist outpost in a region otherwise gripped with rebel fervor.

When Simón Bolívar began driving eastward from Colombia with a small army early in 1813, Ramón Correa—royalist commander at Maracaibo—deployed his troops far south-southwest at Cúcuta to oppose the insurgent advance. But at dawn on 28 February, Bolívar crossed the Zulia River with 500 patriot soldiers and defeated Correa at San José, driving him back into San Antonio after a four-hour battle. The invader then continued his progression, bypassing Lake Maracaibo and eventually entering Caracas in triumph on 6 August, amid acclamations as El Libertador. The fortunes of war continued to ebb and flow for another seven years, until yet more powerful patriot armies could at last begin closing in upon Maracaibo's district late in 1820.

Independence and Republican Era (1821–1917)

This offensive was suspended when Bolívar and the Spanish commander in chief, Gen. Pablo Morillo y Morillo, signed a six-month truce at Trujillo on 26 November; however, a group of Maracaibo's leading citizens nonetheless conspired to allow patriot general Rafael Urdaneta to close off the lake entrance on 18 January 1821, thereby depriving the city's royalist garrison of seaborne reinforcements. Then, on 26 January, Urdaneta advanced with a battalion of troops, and by the evening of 28 January sent a flying column under Cuban-born Lt. Col. José Rafael de las Heras to support a "spontaneous revolution" within the city itself. Morillo's successor, Gen. Miguel de la Torre, complained to Bolívar about this breach of the truce, but in vain. It was not until the summer of 1822 that the royalists could muster a counterexpedition out of Puerto Cabello under Gen. Francisco Tomás Morales, who disembarked and pushed down the Guajira Peninsula, beating patriot general Lino Clemente at Salina Rica on 6–7 September 1822 and reoccupying Maracaibo the next day. By now, however, the monarchist cause was doomed throughout South America, so that less than a year later—on 3 August 1823—Morales surrendered to patriot besiegers, who had his city hemmed in by both land and sea.

Immediately after gaining its liberty from Spain, Venezuela remained part of the newfangled Republic of "Gran Colombia," along with Colombia and Ecuador. In 1829, though, it split off and consummated full Venezuelan independence. Many years of internal unrest ensued, during which Maracaibo and its surrounding province (renamed the state of Zulia) served as a hotbed for numerous separatist movements yet did not suffer as badly as other regions from the recurrent civil wars. The city's export business gradually revived, boosted by a growing demand for mountain-grown coffee and abetted by descendants of Maracaibo's original German settlers, who constituted a significant portion of its new merchant class. This international trade also entailed certain difficulties, however: during the winter of 1869–1870, for example, the German warships *Arcona, Meteor,* and *Niobe* successfully blockaded Venezuela under Lt. Eduard von Knorr in retaliation for the detention of the merchantmen *Franz* and *Marie Sophie* at Maracaibo.

Still worse followed during the debt crisis of late 1902, when an Anglo-German squadron blockaded Venezuela to pressure the truculent administration of President Cipriano Castro to meet its financial obligations. On 17 January 1903 the crisis escalated when the 962-ton German gunboat *Panther* of Lt. Cmdr. Eckermann dueled with Fort San Carlos—the ancient fortress still guarding its lake entrance—but was compelled to retire when its ordnance could not penetrate the stone battle-

ments. Feeling that he had to reassert German prestige, Commo. Georg Scheder appeared four days later with his much more heavily armed, 5,900-ton cruiser *Vineta,* severely damaging that fortification. Washington responded negatively to this unprovoked and one-sided exchange, lodging formal protests with Berlin, while Adm. George Dewey menacingly conducted maneuvers in the nearby Caribbean with more than fifty vessels. Britain and Italy, Germany's allies in the blockade, were embarrassed by their partner's conduct and so drew apart from its resultant diplomatic furor.

Eventually the standoff was resolved and Maracaibo's fortunes again rose, its population having grown from 22,209 inhabitants in 1881 and approximately 25,000 in 1905 to slightly less than 50,000 by 1915. The first modernization efforts dated from this period, city streets being paved over and the first electric streetlights being lit on 1 March 1913 by the American-owned Maracaibo Electric Light Company. Mule-drawn streetcars were converted over to electric power four years later.

The Baralt Theater, ca. 1917, named in honor of the nineteenth-century man of letters Rafael María Baralt. The building had been recently modernized with the installation of electric fans and other amenities, and the first Venezuelan movies were apparently shown here. (*Maracaibo gráfico*)

Oil Capital (1917–Present)

However, progress truly started when numerous oil fields were discovered around Maracaibo's lakeshore in 1917, creating such a boom that the urban population soared to 110,000 by 1936, 232,000 by 1950, 650,000 by 1976, and more than 750,000 by 1980. Much of this natural resource was initially exported in the form of crude petroleum for refining abroad, most often at nearby Curaçao or Aruba. But when seaborne traffic was interrupted during World War II by U-boat attacks upon the shipping lanes, President Isaías Medina Angarita promulgated a new law in 1943 that was intended to develop Venezuela's own petrochemical infrastructure.

Refineries were duly established just outside the bar at Las Piedras and Punta Cardón on the Paraguaná Peninsula, while during the 1950s the lake's entrance was furthermore dredged to facilitate the passage of heavier vessels. For a time, Venezuela became the largest oil-exporting country in the world—two-thirds of this flow exiting via Lake Maracaibo—a phenomenal upsurge during which most of the city's pre-1910 structures and layout were swept away by an intense wave of modernization and new construction. As one final and curious footnote, this city had also been the cradle of Venezuelan films; following an opera performance in 1897, an entrepreneur presented two locally made films: Manuel Trujillo Durán's *Muchacho bañándose en la Laguna de Maracaibo (Boy Bathing in Lake Maracaibo)* being especially well received.

For further reading on the history of Maracaibo or Venezuela, please consult the Select Bibliography at the end of this volume.

Select Bibliography

General Studies and Specialized Journals

Abrams, Charles. *Housing in the Modern World: Man's Struggle for Shelter in an Urbanizing World.* Cambridge and London: Massachusetts Institute of Technology Press and Faber and Faber, 1964.

Alden, John, editor. *European Americana: A Chronological Guide to Works Printed in Europe relating to the Americas, 1493–1776.* New York: Readex Books, 1980–1988, six volumes.

Bairoch, Paul. *Cities and Economic Development: From the Dawn of History to the Present.* University of Chicago Press, 1988.

Bennett, Ralph, editor. *Settlements in the Americas: Cross-Cultural Perspectives.* Newark: University of Delaware Press, 1991.

Blumenfeld, Hans. *The Modern Metropolis: Its Origins, Growth, Characteristics, and Planning.* Cambridge: Massachusetts Institute of Technology Press, 1967.

Bourne, Larry S. *The Geography of Housing.* London: Arnold, 1981.

Boume, Larry S., editor. *Internal Structure of the City: Readings on Urban Form, Growth and Policy.* New York: Oxford University Press, 1982 re-edition of 1971 original.

Breese, Gerald. *Urbanization in Newly Developing Countries.* Englewood Cliffs, NJ: Prentice-Hall, 1966.

Briggs, Asa. *Victorian Cities.* Harmondsworth: Penguin, 1968.

Buisseret, David J., editor. *Envisioning the City: Six Studies in Urban Cartography.* University of Chicago Press, 1998.

Burnett, John. *A Social History of Housing, 1815–1985.* New York: Methuen, 1986.

Burns, E. Bradford. "Visual History." *Américas [Organization of American States]* 26, Number 8 (August 1974): 5–12.

Calendar of State Papers: Colonial Series, America and West Indies. London: Her Majesty's Stationery Office, 1860–1969, forty-four volumes.

Carter, H. *An Introduction to Urban Historical Geography.* London, 1983.

Castells, Manuel. *City, Class, and Power.* New York: St. Martin's Press, 1978.

———. *The City and the Grassroots: A Cross-Cultural Theory of Urban Social Movements.* Berkeley: University of California Press, 1983.

Chapin, F. S., Jr., and S. F. Weiss. *Urban Growth Dynamics in a Regional Cluster of Cities.* New York: Wiley, 1962.

Conway, D. "Changing Perspectives on Squatter Settlements, Intraurban Mobility, and Constraints on Housing Choice of the Third World Urban Poor." *Urban Geography* 6 (1985): 170–192.

Davis, Kingsley. "The Urbanization of the Human Population." *Scientific American* 213 (September 1965): 40–53.

———. *World Urbanization, 1950–1970, Volume I: Basic Data for Cities, Countries, and Regions.* Berkeley: Institute of International Studies, University of California, 1969.

De la Croix, Horst. *Military Considerations in City Planning: Fortifications.* New York: G. Braziller, 1972.

Duncan, Otis Dudley, et al. *Statistical Geography.* New York: Free Press, 1961.

Eames, Edwin, and Judith Granich Goode. *Anthropology of the City: An Introduction to Urban Anthropology.* Englewood Cliffs, NJ: Prentice-Hall, 1977.

Elliot, James. *The City in Maps: Urban Mapping to 1900.* London: British Library, 1987.

Fox, Richard. *Urban Anthropology: Cities in Their Cultural Settings.* Englewood Cliffs, NJ: Prentice-Hall, 1977.

Gutkind, E. A. *International History of City Development.* New York and London, 1970–1972, six volumes.

Hall, Peter. *The World Cities.* New York: McGraw-Hill, 1966.

Harvey, David. *Consciousness and the Urban Experience: Studies in the History and Theory of Capitalist Urbanization.* Baltimore: Johns Hopkins University Press, 1985.

Hatt, Paul K., and Albert J. Reiss, Jr., editors. *Cities and Society: The Revised Reader in Urban Sociology.* New York: Glencoe, 1957.

Hauser, Philip M., and Leo F. Schnore, editors. *The Study of Urbanization.* New York: Wiley, 1965.

Home, Robert. *Of Planting and Planning: The Making of British Colonial Cities.* London, 1997.

Hughes, Thomas P. *Networks of Power: Electrification in Western Society, 1880–1930.* Baltimore: Johns Hopkins University Press, 1983.

Johnston, R. J. *Urban Residential Patterns: An Introductory Review.* London: Bell, 1971.

Jones, Ronald, editor. *Essays on World Urbanization.* London: George Philip, 1975.

Kidder Smith, G. E. *Source Book of American Architecture: 500 Notable Buildings from the 10th Century to the Present.* Princeton: Princeton University Press, 1996.

Klemp, Egon. *America in Maps Dating from 1500–1856.* New York: Holmes and Meier, 1976.

Knight, Franklin W., and Peggy K. Liss, editors. *Atlantic Port Cities: Economy, Culture, and Society in the Atlantic World, 1650–1850.* Knoxville: University of Tennessee, 1991.

Lavedan, Pierre. *Histoire de l'urbanisme.* Paris: H. Laurens, 1959, two volumes.

Lees, Andrew. *Cities Perceived: Urban Society in European and American Thought, 1820–1940.* Manchester University Press [UK], 1985.

Ley, David. *The New Middle Class and the Remaking of the Central City.* Oxford University Press, 1995.

McGee, T. G. *The Urbanization Process in the Third World.* London: Bell, 1971.

McGrath, Dorn C., Jr., and Manuel Ungaro Zevallos. "A Silence Broken." *Américas [Organization of American States]* 31, Number 2 (February 1979): 16–25.

McShane, Clay. "The Origins and Globalization of Traffic Control Signals." *Journal of Urban History* 25, Number 3 (March 1999): 379–404.

Mora, Gilles. "Walker Evans et la ville." *Revue française d'études américaines [France]* 14, Number 39 (1989): 57–62.

Moses, Robert. *Public Works: A Dangerous Trade.* New York: McGraw-Hill, 1970.

Pinto, John. "Origins and Development of the Ichnographic City Plan." *Journal of the Society of Architectural Historians* 35 (1976): 35–50.

Ports of the World, 1972. London: Benn Brothers, 1971.

Potter, Robert B. *Urbanisation and Planning in the Third World: Spatial Perceptions and Public Participation.* New York: St. Martin's Press, 1985.

Rasmussen, Eiler. *Towns and Buildings.* University of Liverpool Press, 1951.

Rondinelli, Dennis, et al. "The Changing Forces of Urban Economic Development: Globalization and City Competitiveness in the 21st Century." *Cityscape* 3, Number 3 (1998): 71–105.

Santos, Milton. *Les villes du Tiers Monde.* Paris: Génine, 1971.

Schaedel, Richard P., et al., editors. *Urbanization in the Americas from Its Beginnings to the Present.* The Hague: Mouton, 1978.

Sjoberg, Gideon. *The Preindustrial City, Past and Present.* New York: Free Press, 1960.

Taylor, John H., et al., editors. *Capital Cities, Les Capitales: Perspectives Internationales, International Perspectives.* Ottawa: Carleton University Press, 1993.

Thomson, Guy P. C. "America and the Americas: Mexico and Philadelphia." *History Today [UK]* 34 (May 1984): 29–35.

Tooley, Ronald Vere, compiler. *Dictionary of Mapmakers.* New York: Alan R. Liss, 1979.

Turner, John F. C. *Housing by People: Toward Autonomy in Building Environments.* London: Marion Boyars, 1976.

Van Hartesveldt, Fred R., editor. *The 1918–1919 Pandemic of Influenza: The Urban Impact in the Western World.* Lewiston, NY: Edwin Mellen Press, 1992.

Van Vliet, Willem, editor. *The Encyclopedia of Housing.* Beverly Hills, CA: Sage, 1998.

Vance, James E., Jr. *The Continuing City: Urban Morphology in Western Civilization.* Baltimore: Johns Hopkins University Press, 1990.

Weber, Adna Ferrin. *The Growth of Cities in the Nineteenth Century: A Study in Statistics.* Ithaca, NY: Cornell University Press, 1963.

General Works on the Dutch in the Americas

Araúz Monfante, Celestino Andrés. *El contrabando holandés en el Caribe durante la primera mitad del siglo XVIII.* Caracas: Volumes 168–169 of the Series "Fuentes para la Historia Colonial de Venezuela" published by the Academia Nacional de la Historia, 1984.

———. "La acción ilegal de los holandeses en el Caribe y su impacto en las Antillas y Puerto Rico durante la primera mitad del siglo XVIII." *Revista/Review Interamericana [Puerto Rico]* 14, Numbers 1–4 (1984): 67–79.

Böhm, Günther. "The First Sephardic Synagogues in South America and in the Caribbean Area." *Studia Rosenthalia [The Netherlands]* 22, Number 1 (1988): 1–14.

Coolhaas, W. Ph. *A Critical Survey of Studies on Dutch Colonial History.* The Hague: Martinus Nijhoff for the Koninklijk Instituut voor Taal-, Land- en Volkenkunde, 1980 re-edition of 1960 original, revised by G. J. Schutte.

Diepraam, Willem. *The Dutch Caribbean: Foto's uit Suriname en de Nederlandse Antillen.* Amsterdam: Arbeiderspers, 1978.

Gastmann, A. L. *The Politics of Surinam and the Netherlands Antilles.* Rio Piedras: Institute of Caribbean Studies [Monograph Number 3], University of Puerto Rico, 1968.

Goslinga, Cornelis Ch. *Handboekje voor Suriname en Curaçao.* Amsterdam, 1938.

———. *The Dutch in the Caribbean and on the Wild Coast, 1580–1680.* Gainesville: University Presses of Florida, 1971.

———. *A Short History of the Netherlands Antilles and Surinam.* The Hague: Martinus Nijhoff, 1979.

———. *The Dutch in the Caribbean and in the Guianas, 1680–1791.* Dover, NH: Van Gorcum, 1985.

Hiss, Philip Hanson. *Netherlands America: The Dutch Territories in the West.* New York: Duell, Sloan and Pearce, 1943.

Jacobs, H. J., and Fr. Oudschans Dentz. *Onze West in beeld en woord.* Amsterdam: De Bussy, 1929.

Maronier, J. H. *Pictures of the Tropics: A Catalogue of Drawings, Watercolours, Paintings, and Sculptures in the Collection of the Royal Institute of Linguistics and Anthropology in Leiden.* 's Gravenhage: Nijhoff, n.d.

Postma, Johannes. "The Dimension of the Dutch Slave Trade from Western Africa." *Journal of African History* 13, Number 2 (1972): 237–248.

Schrieke, B. J. O., and M. J. Van Heemstra, editors. *Ons Koninkrijk in Amerika: West Indiën.* 's Gravenhage: Van Hoeve, 1947.

Walle, J. van de. *De Nederlandse Antillen; land, volk, cultuur.* Baarn: Wereldvenster, 1954.

General Works on the French in the Americas

Aboucaya, Claude. *Les intendants de la marine sous l'ancien régime.* Gap: Louis-Jean, 1958.

Aboucaya, Claude, and Jacques Merlande, editors. *Documents d'histoire antillaise et guyanaise, 1814–1914.* [No place nor publisher], 1979.

———. *Histoire des communes Antilles-Guyane.* Fort-de-France: Pressplay, 1986, six volumes.

Aldrich, Robert, and John Connell. *France's Overseas Frontier: Départements et territoires d'Outre-Mer.* Cambridge, NY: Cambridge University Press, 1992.

Atlas des Départements d'Outre-Mer. Paris: Centre National de la Recherche Scientifique, 1979.

Balesi, Charles J. *The Time of the French in the Heart of North America, 1673–1818.* Chicago: Alliance Française, 1992.

Bataillon, Claude. *Villes et campagnes.* Paris: Anthropos, 1971.

Berthet, Thierry. *Seigneurs et colons de Nouvelle France: l'émergence d'une société distincte au XVIIIe siècle.* Cachan: L'E.N.S., 1993.

Berthiaume, Pierre. "Le tremblement de terre de 1663: les convulsions du verbe ou la mystification du logos chez Charlevoix." *Revue d'histoire de l'Amérique française [Canada]* 36, Number 3 (1982): 375–387.

Bonnel, Ulane. *La France, les États-Unis et la guerre de course, 1797–1815.* Paris: Éditions Latines, 1961.

Bougaineville, Louis-Antoine de. *Adventures in the Wilderness: The American Journals of Louis-Antoine de Bougaineville, 1756–1760.* Norman: University of Oklahoma Press, 1964 translation by Edward P. Hamilton.

Boyer, Pierre, et al. *Les Archives nationales, état général des fonds [Tome III: marine et outre-mer].* Paris: Archives Nationales, 1980.

Devèze, Michel. *Antilles, Guyanes, la Mer des Caraïbes de 1492 à 1789.* Paris: SEDES, 1977.

"Documents: Journal of a French Traveller in the Colonies, 1765, I." *American Historical Review* 26, Number 4 (July 1921): 726–747.

Dormoy, M. *Architecture française.* Paris: Vincent Fréal, 1951.

Duflot de Mofras, Eugène. *Duflot de Mofras' Travels on the Pacific Coast.* Santa Ana, CA: 1937 translation and re-edition by Marguerite Eyer Wilbur, two volumes.

Eccles, William J. *France in America.* East Lansing: Michigan State University Press, 1990 re-edition of 1972 original published in New York by Harper and Row.

Germain, Annick, and Jean-Claude Marsan. *Aménager l'urbain, de Montréal à San Francisco: politiques et désign urbain.* Montreal: Méridien, 1987.

Goodman, Morris F. *A Comparative Study of Creole French Dialects.* The Hague: Mouton, 1964.

Griffiths, Naomi. *The Acadians: The Creation of a People.* Toronto: McGraw-Hill Ryerson, 1973.

Huetz de Lemps, Christian. *Géographie du commerce de Bordeaux à la fin du règne de Louis XIV.* Paris: Mouton, 1975.

Huret, Jules. *En Amérique.* Paris: "Bibliothèque Charpentier," Eugène Fasquelle, 1904–1905, two volumes.

Julien, Charles-André. *Les français en Amérique au XVIIe siècle.* Paris: SEDES/CDU, 1976.

———. *Les français en Amérique de 1713 à 1784.* Paris: SEDES/CDU, 1977.

Le Moël, Michel, and Claude-France Rochat. *Catalogue général des cartes, plans et dessins d'architecture: Série N, Volume 4.* Paris: Archives Nationales, 1974.

Lussagnet, Suzanne, editor. *Les français en Amérique pendant la deuxième moitié du XVIe siècle.* Paris: Presses Universitaires de France, 1953.

Margry, Pierre, compiler and editor. *Mémoires et documents pour servir à l'histoire des origines françaises des pays d'outre mer: découvertes et établissements des françaises dans l'ouest et dans le sud de l'Amérique Septentrionale.* Paris, 1879–1887, six volumes.

Mollat, Michel. *Les explorations du XIIIe au XVIe siècles: premiers regards sur des mondes nouveaux.* Paris: CTMS, 1992.

Pastoreau, Mireille. *Voies océanes: cartes maritimes et grandes découvertes.* Paris: Bibliothèque Nationale, 1992.

Pluchon, Pierre, and Denise Bouche. *Histoire de la colonisation française.* Paris: Fayard, 1991, two volumes.

Queuille, Pierre. "Les diplomaties anglaise et américaine vis-à-vis de la France vaincue (1940–1942): un schéma d'ensemble." *Revue d'histoire diplomatique [France]* 94, Numbers 1–3 (1980): 230–250.

Rochat, Claude-France, and Michel Le Moël. *Catalogue général des cartes, plans et dessins d'architecture: Série NN.* Paris: Archives Nationales, 1978.

Saussure, Henri de. *Voyage aux Antilles et au Mexique, 1854–1856.* Geneva: Olizane, 1993 re-edition by Louis de Roguin and Claude Weber.

Stein, Robert Louis. *The French Slave Trade in the Eighteenth Century: An Old Regime Business.* Madison: University of Wisconsin Press, 1979.

———. *The French Sugar Business in the Eighteenth Century.* Baton Rouge: Louisiana State University Press, 1988.

Taillemite, Étienne. *Inventaire analytique de la correspondance générale avec les colonies, 1654–1715.* Paris: Ministère de la France d'Outre-Mer, 1959.

Thevet, André. *André Thevet's North America, A Sixteenth-Century View.* Kingston and Montreal: McGill-Queens University Press, 1986 re-edition and translation by Roger Schlesinger and Arthur P. Stabler.

Thwaites, Reuben Gold, editor. *The Jesuit Relations and Allied Documents: Travels and Explorations of the Jesuit Missionaries in New France, 1610–1791.* New York: Pageant, 1959 reprint of 1896–1901 originals published by Arthur H. Clarke in Cleveland, seventy-three volumes.

Villes portuaires, acteurs de l'environnement. Le Havre, France: Association Internationale Villes et Ports, 1994.

Wright, Gwendolyn. *The Politics of Design in French Colonial Urbanism.* University of Chicago Press, 1991.

General Works on Latin America

Acosta, Antonio, and Juan Marchena Fernández, editors. *La influencia de España en el Caribe, la Florida y la Luisiana, 1500–1800.* Madrid: Instituto de Cooperación Iberoamericana, 1983.

Aguilera Rojas, Javier, and Luis J. Moreno Rexach, compilers. *Urbanismo español en América.* Madrid: Editora Nacional, 1973.

Alba, Victor. *Politics and the Labor Movement in Latin America.* Stanford, CA: Stanford University Press, 1968.

Albi, Fernando. *El corregidor en el municipio español bajo la monarquía absoluta: ensayo histórico-crítico.* Madrid, 1943.

Alcedo, Antonio de. *Diccionario geográfico-histórico de las Indias Occidentales o América.* Madrid: Atlas, 1967 reprint of 1786–1789 original published by Benito Cano, four volumes.

Alomar, Gabriel, editor. *De Teotihuacán a Brasilia: estudios de historia urbana iberoamericana y filipina.* Madrid: Instituto de Estudios de Administración Local, 1987.

Altamira y Crevea, Rafael, compiler and editor. *Colección de documentos inéditos para la historia de Ibero-América* [or *Hispano-América*]. Madrid: Ibero-América, 1927–1932, fourteen volumes.

Altamira y Crevea, et al. *Contribuciones a la historia municipal de América.* Mexico City: Instituo Panamericano de Geografía e Historia, 1951.

Altman, Ida. "Immigrants and Society: An Approach to the Background of Colonial Spanish America." *Comparative Studies in Society and History [UK]* 30, Number 1 (1988): 170–190.

———. *Emigrants and Society: Extremadura and Spanish America in the Sixteenth Century.* Berkeley: University of California Press, 1989.

Alvarez Terán, María Concepción. *Mapas, planos y dibujos (1503–1805) del Archivo General de Simancas.* Valladolid: Ministerio de Cultura, 1980.

América colonial: población y economía. Santa Fe, Argentina: Instituto de Investigaciones Históricas de la Universidad Nacional del Litoral, 1967.

América pintoresca: descripción de viajes al nuevo continente, 1884. Madrid: Colección Erisa Ilustrativa, 1980 facsimile reprint of graphic materials.

Andrews, George Reid. "Latin American Urban History." *History Teacher* 19, Number 4 (August 1986): 499–515.

Angulo Iñiguez, Diego. *Planos de monumentos arquitectónicos de América y Filipinas existentes en el Archivo General de Indias.* Seville: Laboratorio del Arte, Universidad de Sevilla, 1933–1940, six volumes.

———. *Bautista Antonelli: las fortificaciones americanas en el siglo XVI.* Madrid: Hauser y Menet, 1942.

———. *Historia del arte hispanoamericano.* Barcelona: Salvat, 1945–1956, three volumes.

Armus, Diego, and John Lear. "The Trajectory of Latin American Urban History." *Journal of Urban History* 24, Number 3 (March 1998): 291–301.

Avellá Vives, Joaquín. *Los cabildos coloniales.* Madrid, 1934.

Ayala, Manuel José de, compiler. *Diccionario de gobierno y legislación de Indias.* Madrid: Cultura Hispánica and the Instituto de Cooperación Iberoamericana, 1988, twenty-two volumes.

Bagú, Sergio. *Economía de la sociedad colonial: ensayo de historia comparada de América Latina.* Buenos Aires, 1949.

———. *Estructura social de la colonia: ensayo de historia comparada de América Latina.* Caracas and Buenos Aires: El Ateneo, 1952.

Barbier, Jacques A., and Allan J. Kuethe, editors. *The North American Role in the Spanish Imperial Economy, 1760–1819.* Manchester University Press, 1984.

Bastide, Roger. *Las Américas negras: las civilizaciones africanas en el Nuevo Mundo.* Madrid: Alianza Editorial, 1969.

Baudot, Georges. *La vie quotidienne dans l'Amérique espagnole de Philippe II, XVIe siècle.* Paris: Hachette, 1981.

Bayitch, S. A. *Latin America and the Caribbean: A Bibliographical Guide to Works in English.* Coral Gables, FL: University of Miami Press, 1967.

Bayle, Constantino. *Los cabildos seculares en la América Española.* Madrid: Sapientia, 1952.

Bayón, Damián. *Sociedad y arquitectura colonial en América Latina.* Madrid: Gustavo Gili, 1975.

Belliter, Erika. *Fotografía latinoamericana: desde 1860 hasta nuestros días.* Madrid: El Viso, 1982.

Beneyto Pérez, Juan. *Historia de la administración española e hispanoamericana.* Madrid: Aguilar, 1958.

Bernaldo de Quirós, Constancio. *La picota en América (contribución al estudio del derecho penal indiano).* Havana, 1947.

Bernales Ballesteros, Jorge. *El urbanismo sevillano de los siglos XVI-XVII y su proyección en Indias.* Seville, 1972.

Beyer, Glenn H., editor. *The Urban Explosion in Latin America: A Continent in Process of Modernization.* Ithaca, NY: Cornell University Press, 1967.

Bonet Correa, Antonio. *Monasterios iberoamericanos.* Madrid: El Viso, 2001.

Borah, Woodrow. "Trends in Recent Studies of Colonial Latin American Cities." *Hispanic American Historical Review* 64, Number 3 (1984): 535–554.

Bourdé, Guy. *Urbanisation et immigration en Amérique Latine.* Paris: Aubier-Montaigne, 1974.

Boyd-Bowman, Peter. *Indice geobiográfico de cuarenta mil pobladores españoles de América en el siglo XVI.* Bogotá and Mexico City: Instituto Caro y Cuervo and Academia Mexicana de Genealogía y Heráldica, 1964–1968 respectively, two volumes.

———. "La procedencia de los españoles de América." *Historia Mexicana* 17, Number 1 (1967): 37–71.

———. *Patterns of Spanish Emigration to the New World, 1493–1580.* Buffalo: Council on International Studies, State University of New York [SUNY], 1973.

———. "Patterns in Spanish Emigration to the Indies, 1579–1600." *The Americas: A Quarterly Review of Inter-American Cultural History [Academy of American Franciscan History]* 33, Number 1 (1976): 78–95.

———. *Indice geobiográfico de 56 mil pobladores españoles de la América Hispánica.* Mexico City: Instituto de Investigaciones Históricas of the Universidad Nacional Autónoma de México [UNAM], and the Fondo de Cultura Económica, 1985.

Boyer, Richard E., and Keith A. Davies. *Urbanization in Nineteenth-Century Latin America: Statistics and Sources.* Berkeley: University of California Press, 1973.

Brading, David A., and Harry E. Cross. "Colonial Silver Mining: Mexico and Peru." *Hispanic American Historical Review* 52, Number 4 (November 1972): 545–579.

Braun, Georg, and Franz Hogenberg [with an introduction by Raleigh A. Skelton]. *Civitates Orbis Terrarum: The Towns of the World, 1572–1618.* Amsterdam: Van Hoeve, 1980 facsimile reprint of 1623 edition, three volumes.

Bronner, Fred. "Urban Society in Colonial Spanish America: Research Trends." *Latin American Research Review* 21, Number 1 (1986): 3–72.

Brown, Jonathan. *The Word Made Image: Religion, Art, and Architecture in Spain and Spanish America, 1500–1600.* Hanover: University Press of New England, 1998.

Burkholder, Mark A., and D. S. Chandler. *From Impotence to Authority: Spain and the American Audiencias.* Columbia: University of Missouri Press, 1977.

———. *Biographical Dictionary of Audiencia Ministers in the Americas, 1687–1821.* Westport, CT: Greenwood, 1982.

Burns, E. Bradford, and Thomas E. Skidmore. *Elites, Masses, and Modernization in Latin America, 1850–1930.* Austin: University of Texas Press, 1979.

Burzio, Humberto F. *Diccionario de la moneda hispanoamericana.* Santiago de Chile, 1958, three volumes.

Buschiazzo, Mario J. *Historia de la arquitectura colonial en Hispano América.* Buenos Aires, 1961 re-edition of 1940 original.

———. *Estudios de arquitectura colonial hispanoamericana.* Buenos Aires, 1943.

Bushnell, David, and Neil Macaulay. *The Emergence of Latin America in the Nineteenth Century.* New York: Oxford University Press, 1988.

Butterworth, Douglas, and John K. Chance. *Latin American Urbanization.* Cambridge, NY: Cambridge University Press, 1981.

Carrière, Jean, et al., editors. *The State, Industrial Relations and the Labour Movement in Latin America.* New York: St. Martin's Press, 1989, two volumes.

Cartografía de ultramar. Madrid: Servicios Geográfico e Histórico del Ejército, 1949–1957, ten volumes.

Casariego Fernández, Jesús Evaristo. *El municipio y las cortes en el imperio español de Indias.* Madrid, 1946.

Casasco, Juan A. "Slums of Hope and Despair." *Américas [Organization of American States]* 21, Number 6 (June 1969): 13–20.

Castañeda, Carlos E. "The Corregidor in Spanish Colonial Administration." *Hispanic American Historical Review* 9 (1929): 446–470.

Castells, Manuel, editor. *Imperialismo y urbanización en América Latina.* Barcelona: Gustavo Gili, 1973.

Chance, John K. "Recent Trends in Latin American Urban Studies." *Latin American Research Review* 15 (1980): 183–188.

Chiaramonte, José Carlos. *Formas de sociedad y economía en Hispanoamérica.* Buenos Aires, 1983.

Chiaramonte, José Carlos , editor. *Pensamiento de la ilustración: economía y sociedad iberoamericanas en el siglo XVIII.* Caracas, 1979.

Chueca Goitia, Fernando. *Invariantes castizos de la arquitectura española.* Madrid: DOSSAT, 1947.

———. *Breve historia del urbanismo.* Madrid: Alianza, 1981 reprint.

Chueca Goitia, plus Leopoldo Torres Balbás and Julio González y González, compilers. *Planos de ciudades iberoamericanas y filipinas existentes en el Archivo de Indias.* Madrid: Instituto de Estudios de Administración Local, Seminario de Urbanismo, 1951, two volumes.

Claro Valdés, Samuel. *La música virreinal en el Nuevo Mundo.* Santiago de Chile, 1970.

Clement, Jean-Pierre. "El nacimiento de la higiene urbana en la América española del siglo XVIII." *Revista de Indias [Spain]* 171 (1983): 77–96.

Cline, Howard F. "The *Relaciones geográficas* of the Spanish Indies, 1577–1648." *Handbook of Middle American Indians* 12 (1972): 183–242.

Colección de documentos inéditos relativos al descubrimiento, conquista y organización de las antiguas posesiones españolas de ultramar. Madrid: Real Academia de la Historia, 1885–1932, twenty-five volumes.

Collier, George A., et al., editors. *The Incan and Aztec States, 1400–1800: Anthropology and History.* New York: Collier 1982.

Collier, Ruth Berins and David. *Shaping the Political Arena: Critical Junctures, the Labor Movement, and Regime Dynamics in Latin America.* Princeton University Press, 1991.

Conniff, Michael L., editor. *Latin American Populism in Comparative Perspective.* Albuquerque: University of New Mexico Press, 1982.

Connolly, Mark. "Adrift in the City: A Comparative Study of Street Children in Bogotá, Colombia, and Guatemala City." *Child and Youth Services* 14, Number 1 (1990): 129–149.

Contribuciones para el estudio de la historia de América: homenaje al doctor Emilio Ravignani. Buenos Aires: Jacobo Peuser, 1941.

Cook, Noble David, and W. G. Lovell, editors. *"Secret Judgements of God": Old World Disease in Colonial Spanish America.* Norman: University of Oklahoma Press, 1992.

Cornelius, Wayne A., and Robert V. Kemper, editors. *Metropolitan Latin America: The Challenge and the Response.* Beverly Hills, CA: Sage, 1978.

Cotler, Julio, editor. *Clases populares, crisis y democracia en América Latina.* Lima: Instituto de Estudios Peruanos, 1989.

Crouch, Dora P., et al. *Spanish City Planning in North America.* Cambridge, NY: Cambridge University Press, 1982.

Cuesta Domingo, Mariano. *Alonso de Santa Cruz y su obra cosmográfica.* Madrid: Instituto "Gonzalo Fernández de Oviedo," Consejo Superior de Investigaciones Científicas, 1983.

Cueto, Marcos, editor. *Salud, cultura y sociedad en América Latina: nuevas perspectivas históricas.* Lima: Instituto de Estudios Peruanos and the Organización Panamericana de la Salud, 1996.

Curtis, William Eleroy. *The Capitals of Spanish America.* New York: Harper and Brothers, 1888.

Das, Man Singh, and Clinton J. Jesser, editors. *The Family in Latin America.* New Delhi: Vikas, 1980.

Dawson, Frank Griffith. *The First Latin American Debt Crisis: The City of London and the 1822–25 Loan Bubble.* New Haven: Yale University Press, 1990.

De la Torre, Carlos. "Génesis y desarrollo de la teoría de la localización." *Revista Interamericana de Planificación* 8, Numbers 28–29 (1973–1974): 63–79.

Díaz Plaja, Fernando. *La sociedad española desde 1500 hasta nuestros días.* San Juan: University of Puerto Rico Press, 1968.

Domínguez, Jorge. *Insurrection or Loyalty: The Breakdown of the Spanish American Empire.* Cambridge, MA: Harvard University Press, 1980.

Domínguez Ortiz, Antonio. *La sociedad española en el siglo XVIII.* Madrid, 1955.

———. "Concesión de 'naturalezas' para comerciar con Indias." *Revista de Indias [Spain]* 19, Number 76 (1959): 227–239.

———. *Sociedad y estado en el siglo XVIII.* Madrid: Ariel, 1976.

Domínguez y Compañy, Francisco. *El urbanismo en las Leyes de Indias: estudio histórico jurídico social.* Havana, 1945.

———. *Los pueblos de indios.* Havana, 1958.

———. *La vida en las pequeñas ciudades hispanoamericanas de la Conquista, 1494–1549.* Madrid, 1979.

———. "Contenido urbanístico de las actas de fundación, 1520–1573." *Revista de Historia de América [Mexico]* 91 (1981): 9–27.

Durston, Alan. "Un régimen urbanistico en la América hispana colonial: el trazado en damero durante los siglos XVI y XVII." *Historia [Chile]* 28 (1994): 59–115.

Elkin, Judith Laikin. *The Jews of Latin America.* New York: Holmes and Meier, 1998.

Encinas, Diego de, compiler. *Cedulario indiano.* Madrid: Cultura Hispánica, 1945–1946 facsimile reprint of 1596 original, published by the Imprenta Real of Madrid, four volumes.

Fernández de Navarrete, Martín, et al., compilers and editors. *Colección de documentos inéditos para la historia de España.* Madrid: Viuda de Calero for the Real Academia de la Historia, 1842–1895, 113 volumes.

Fisher, John R. *Commercial Relations between Spain and Spanish America in the Era of Free Trade, 1778–1796.* Liverpool: Centre for Latin American Studies at the University of Liverpool, 1985.

Florescano, Enrique, editor. *Ensayos sobre el desarrollo económico de México y América Latina.* Mexico City, 1979.

Fox, David John, and David James Robinson. *Cities in a Changing Latin America: Two Studies of Urban Growth in the Development of Mexico and Venezuela.* London: Latin American Publications Fund, 1969.

French, John D., and Daniel James, editors. *The Gendered Worlds of Latin American Women Workers: From Household and Factory to the Union Hall and Ballot Box.* Durham, NC: Duke University Press, 1997.

García, Juan Agustín. *La ciudad indiana.* Santa Fe, Argentina: Editorial Claridad, 1954 re-edition of 1900 original.

García-Baquero, Antonio. *Cádiz y el Atlántico (1717–1778).* Seville: Escuela de Estudios Hispano-americanos, 1976, two volumes.

García Gallo, Alfonso. *Los orígenes de la administración territorial de las Indias.* Madrid, 1944.

García Martínez, Bernardo, et al., editors. *Historia y sociedad en el mundo de habla española.* Mexico City, 1972.

Gibson, Charles. *Spain in America.* New York: Harper and Row, 1966.

Gil Munilla, Ladislao. "La ciudad hispanoamericana." *Anuario de Estudios Americanos [Spain]* 10, Number 48 (1955): 295–310.

Gilbert, Alan. *In Search of a Home: Rental and Shared Housing in Latin America.* London: UCL Press, 1993.

———. *The Latin American City.* New York: Monthly Review Press, 1998 revised edition.

Gilbert, Alan, and Peter M. Ward. *Housing, the State, and the Poor: Policy and Practice in Three Latin American Cities.* Cambridge, NY: Cambridge University Press, 1985.

Gómez Pérez, Carmen. *El sistema defensivo americano: siglo XVIII.* Madrid: MAPFRE, 1992.

Góngora, Mario. *Studies in the Colonial History of Spanish America.* New York: Cambridge University Press, 1975 translation by Richard Southern.

González González, Enrique. "Royal Patronage and Private Support in the Emergence of Spanish American Universities." *Paedagogica Historica [Belgium]* 34, Number 2 (1998): 507–525.

Greenfield, Gerald Michael. "New Perspectives on Latin American Cities." *Journal of Urban History* 15, Number 2 (February 1989): 205–214.

Greenfield, Gerald Michael, editor. *Latin American Urbanization: Historical Profiles of Major Cities.* Westport, CT: Greenwood, 1994.

Greenfield, Gerald Michael, and Sheldon L. Maran, editors. *Latin American Labor Organizations.* Westport, CT: Greenwood, 1987.

Griffin, Charles C., and J. Benedict Warren, editors. *Latin America: A Guide to the Historical Literature.* Austin: University of Texas Press, 1971.

Guarda, Gabriel. *Santo Tomás de Aquino y las fuentes del urbanismo indiano.* Santiago: Academia Chilena de la Historia, 1965.

———. "Tres reflexiones en torno a la fundación de la ciudad indiana." *Revista de Indias [Spain]* 127–130 (January–December 1972).

Guillén y Tato, Julio Fernando. *El fichero fotográfico del Museo Naval.* Madrid, 1933.

———. *Monumenta chartografica indiana.* Madrid, 1942.

Gutiérrez, Ramón. *Notas para una bibliografía hispanoamericana de arquitectura (1526–1875).* Madrid: Resistencia, 1972.

———. *Arquitectura del siglo XIX en Iberoamérica (1800–1850).* Madrid: Resistencia, 1979.

———. *Arquitectura colonial: teoría y praxis.* Madrid: Resistencia, 1980.

———. *Arquitectura y urbanismo en Iberoamérica.* Madrid: Cátedra, 1983.

Gwynne, R. N. *Industrialization and Urbanization in Latin America.* London: Croom Helm, 1985.

Halperín Donghi, Tulio. *Hispanoamérica después de la independencia: consecuencias sociales y económicas de la emancipación.* Buenos Aires, 1972.

———. *Reforma y disolución de los imperios ibéricos, 1750–1850.* Madrid, 1985.

Hamel, P., et al. "Urban Heritage in Puebla and Montreal: Assessment of Strategies and Interpretative Elements." *Canadian Journal of Urban Research* 5, Number 1 (1996): 18–50.

Handbook of Latin American Studies. Austin: University of Texas Press, 1936-.

Hanke, Lewis, and Celso Rodríguez, editors. *Los virreyes españoles en América durante el gobierno de la Casa de Austria.* Madrid: Volumes 273–277 and 280–286 of the "Biblioteca de Autores Españoles," 1976–1980.

Hardoy, Jorge Enrique. *Pre-Columbian Cities.* New York: Walker, 1973 translation of 1964 original *Ciudades precolombinas.*

———. *Urban Planning in Pre-Columbian America.* New York: George Braziller, 1968.

———. "El modelo clásico de la ciudad colonial hispanoamericana." *Actas del XXXVIII Congreso Internacional de Americanistas [Stuttgart 1968],* Volume 4 (1972): 143–182.

Hardoy, Jorge Enrique, editor. *Las ciudades en América Latina: Seis ensayos sobre la urbanización contemporánea.* Buenos Aires: Paidós, 1972.

———. *Urbanization in Latin America: Approaches and Issues.* Garden City, NY: Anchor Books and Doubleday, 1975.

Hardoy, Jorge Enrique, and Carmen Aranovich. "Urbanización de América hispánica entre 1580 y 1630." *Boletín del Centro de Investigaciones Históricas y Estéticas de la Universidad Central de Venezuela* 11 (May 1969): 9–89.

Hardoy, Jorge Enrique, and Richard P. Schaedel, compilers. *Las ciudades de América Latina y sus áreas de influencia a través de la historia.* Buenos Aires: SIAP, 1975.

———. *Asentamientos urbanos y organización socioproductiva en la historia de América Latina.* Buenos Aires: SIAP, 1977.

Hardoy, Jorge Enrique, and Carlos Tobar. *La urbanización en América Latina.* Buenos Aires: Instituto Di Tella, 1969.

Hargreaves-Mawdsley, William N. *Spain under the Bourbons, 1700–1833*. Columbia: University of South Carolina Press, 1973.

———. *Eighteenth-Century Spain, 1700–1788: A Political, Diplomatic and Institutional History*. London and Totowa, NJ: Macmillan, and Rowman and Littlefield, 1979.

Haring, Clarence H. *The Spanish Empire in America*. New York: Oxford University Press, 1947.

Harris, Walter D., Jr., and Humberto L. Rodríguez-Camilloni. *The Growth of Latin American Cities*. Athens: Ohio University Press, 1971.

Hauser, Philip M., editor. *Urbanization in Latin America*. New York, 1961.

Hernández, José, compiler and editor. *Catálogo de los fondos americanos del Archivo de Protocolos de Sevilla*. Madrid: Companía Ibero-americana de Publicaciones for the Instituto Hispano-Cubano de Historia de América, 1930–1932, three volumes.

Higueras Rodríguez, M. D., compiler and editor. *Catálogo crítico de los documentos de la Expedición Malaspina (1789–1794) del Museo Naval*. Madrid: Museo Naval, 1985.

Hoberman, Louisa S., and Susan Migden Socolow, editors. *Cities and Society in Colonial Latin America*. Albuquerque: University of New Mexico Press, 1986.

Howse, Derek, and Norman J. W. Thrower, editors. *A Buccaneer's Atlas: Basil Ringrose's South Sea Waggoner. A Sea Atlas and Sailing Directions of the Pacific Coast of the Americas 1682*. Berkeley: University of California Press, 1992.

Humboldt, Baron Alexander von, and Aimé Bonpland. *Personal Narrative of Travels to the Equinoctial Regions of the New Continent during the Years 1799–1804*. New York: AMS Press, 1966 reprint of translation by Helen M. Williams originally published in London by Longman in 1826, seven volumes.

Humphreys, Robert A. *British Consular Reports on the Trade and Politics of Latin America*. London: Royal Historical Society, 1940.

Jacobsen, Nils, and Hans-Jürgen Puhle, editors. *The Economies of Mexico and Peru during the Late Colonial Period, 1760–1810*. Berlin: Biblioteca Ibero-Americana, 1986.

Jaksic, Ivan. "The Politics of Higher Education in Latin America." *Latin American Research Review [UK]* 20, Number 1 (1985): 209–221.

Johnson, John J. *Political Change in Latin America: The Emergence of the Middle Sectors*. Stanford, CA: Stanford University Press, 1958.

Johnson, Lyman L., and Enrique Tandeter, editors. *Essays on the Price History of Eighteenth-Century Latin America*. Albuquerque: University of New Mexico Press, 1990.

Junquera y Mato, Juan José. "Reflexiones sobre el urbanismo canario y sus relaciones con Hispanoamérica." *Revista de Historia Canaria [Spain]* 37 (1980): 249–251.

Kaplan, Marcos. *Estado y urbanización en América Latina*. Valparaíso: CIDU, 1967.

Karrow, Robert W., Jr. *Mapmakers of the Sixteenth Century and Their Maps: Bio-Bibliographies of the Cartographers of Abraham Ortelius, 1570*. Chicago: Speculum Orbis Press for The Newberry Library, 1993.

Keane, A. H. *Central and South America*. London: Edward Stanford, 1909, two volumes.

Keeler, Mary Frear. "The Boazio Maps of 1585–1586." *Terrae Incognitae [The Netherlands]* 10 (1978): 71–80.

Kelemen, Pál. *Baroque and Rococo in Latin America*. New York: Dover, 1967 reprint of 1951 original published by Macmillan, two volumes.

Kicza, John E. "Patterns in Early Spanish Overseas Expansion." *William and Mary Quarterly*, Third Series, Volume 49, Number 2 (April 1992): 229–253.

———. "The Social and Political Position of Spanish Immigrants in Bourbon America and the Origins of the Independence Movements." *Colonial Latin American Review* 4, Number 1 (1995): 105–128.

Kinsbrunner, Jay. *Petty Capitalism and Spanish America: The Pulperos of Puebla, Mexico, Caracas, and Buenos Aires*. Boulder, CO: Westview, 1987.

Kirkpatrick, F. A. "Municipal Administration in the Spanish Dominions in America." *Transactions of the Royal Historical Society [UK]*, Third Series, Volume 9: 95–110.

Klein, Herbert S. *African Slavery in Latin America and the Caribbean*. New York: Oxford University Press, 1986.

Konetzke, Richard, editor. "Legislación sobre inmigración de extranjeros en América." *Revista Internacional de Sociología [Spain]* 3, Number 9 (1945): 269–299.

Konetzke, Richard, editor. "Documentos para la historia y crítica de los registros parroquiales en las Indias." *Revista de Indias [Spain]* 25 (1946): 581–586.

———. "Las fuentes para la historia demográfica de Hispano-América durante la época colonial." *Anuario de Estudios Americanos [Spain]* 5 (1948): 267–323.

———. *Colección de documentos para la historia de la formación social de Hispanoamérica, 1493–1810*. Madrid: Consejo Superior de Investigaciones Científicas, 1953–1962, four volumes.

Kubler, George A., and Martín S. Soria. *Art and Architecture in Spain and Portugal and Their American Dominions, 1500 to 1800*. Harmondsworth: Penguin, 1959.

Langue, Frédérique. "Hombres e ideas de la Ilustración en dos ciudades consulares: Caracas y Veracruz." *Historia Mexicana* 45, Number 3 (1996): 467–500.

Latorre, Germán, editor. *Relaciones geográficas de Indias*. Seville: Centro Oficial de Estudios Americanistas, 1920.

Lavrín, Asunción. "Women, the Family, and Social Change in Latin America." *World Affairs* 150 (1987): 109–128.

Lavrín, Asunción, editor. *Latin American Women: Historical Perspectives.* Westport, CT: Greenwood, 1978.

León Tello, Pilar. *Mapas, planos y dibujos de la Sección de Estado del Archivo Histórico Nacional.* Madrid: Dirección General de Archivos y Bibliotecas, 1969.

Leonard, Irving A., editor. *Colonial Travellers in Latin America.* New York: Alfred A. Knopf, 1972.

Les villes dans le monde ibérique. Paris: Institut des Hautes Études de l'Amérique Latine or IHEAL, Centre National de la Recherche Scientifique, 1982.

Liagre, Leone, compiler. *Guide des sources de l'histoire de l'Amérique Latine conservées en Belgique.* Brusells: UNESCO, 1967.

Lockhart, James M., and Enrique Otte, editors and translators. *Letters and People of the Spanish Indies: Sixteenth Century.* Cambridge, NY: Cambridge University Press, 1976.

Lockhart, James M., and Stuart B. Schwartz. *Early Latin America: A History of Colonial Spanish America and Brazil.* Cambridge, NY: Cambridge University Press, 1983.

Lohmann Villena, Guillermo. *Los americanos en las ordenes nobiliarias (1529–1900).* Madrid: Instituto "Gonzalo Fernández de Oviedo," 1947, two volumes.

López de Velasco, Juan. *Geografía y descripción universal de las Indias.* Madrid: Ediciones Atlas as Volume 247 of the "Biblioteca de Autores Españoles," 1971 reprint of 1574 original.

Luján Muñóz, Jorge. *Los escribanos en las Indias occidentales.* Guatemala City: Instituto Guatemalteco de Derecho Notarial, 1977 re-edition.

Lynch, John. *The Spanish-American Revolutions, 1808–1826.* London: Weidenfeld and Nicolson, 1973.

Lyn-Hilton, Sylvia. *Bibliografía hispanoamericana y filipina: manual de repertorios bibliográficos para la investigación de la historia y la literatura hispanoamericana y filipina.* Madrid: Fundación Universitaria Española, 1983.

Mangin, William. "Latin American Squatter Settlements: A Problem and a Solution." *Latin American Research Review* 2, Number 3 (1967): 65–98.

Mapas españoles de América, siglos XV–XVII. Madrid: Hauser y Menet for the Real Academia de la Historia, 1951.

Marchena Fernández, Juan, and Carmen Gómez Pérez. *La vida de guarnición en las ciudades americanas de la Ilustración.* Madrid: Ministerio de Defensa, 1992.

Marco Dorta, Enrique. *Fuentes para la historia del arte hispano-americano.* Seville: Escuela de Estudios Hispano-americanos, 1951.

Marichal, Carlos. *A Century of Debt Crises in Latin America: From Independence to the Great Depression, 1820–1930.* Princeton University Press, 1989.

Mellafe, Rolando. *The Latifundio and the City in Latin American History.* University of Toronto Press, 1971.

Menéndez Pidal, Ramón, and Juan Manzano, editors. *Recopilación de leyes de Indias.* Madrid: Cultura Hispánica, 1973 facsimile reprint of 1681 original published by Julián Paredes.

Millares Carlo, Agustín. *Los archivos municipales de Lationamérica: libros de actas y colecciones documentales, apuntes bibliográficos.* Maracaibo, 1961.

Miller, John, and Ralph A. Gakenheimer, editors. *Latin American Urban Policies and the Social Sciences.* Beverly Hills, CA: Sage, 1971.

Molina, Raúl A. *La ciudad hispanoamericana.* Santo Domingo: II Congreso Hispanoamericano de Historia, 1957.

Monteiro, Palmyra V. M. *A Catalogue of Latin American Flat Maps, 1926–1964.* Austin: Institute of Latin American Studies, University of Texas Press, 1967.

Morales Padrón, Francisco. *Fisonomía de la conquista indiana.* Seville: Escuela de Estudios Hispano-americanos, 1953.

———. "Descubrimiento y toma de posesión." *Anuario de Estudios Americanos [Spain]* 12 (1955): 321–380.

Morales Padrón, Francisco, compiler. *Historia y bibliografía americanista, 1967.* Seville: Escuela de Estudios Hispano-americanos, 1969.

Moreno Fraginals, Manuel, editor. *L'Afrique en Amérique Latine.* Paris: UNESCO, 1984.

Mörner, Magnus. *Race Mixture in the History of Latin America.* Boston: Little, Brown, 1967.

———. *La corona española y los foráneos en los pueblos de indios de América.* Stockholm: Almquist and Wiksell for the Instituto de Estudios Ibero-Americanos, 1970.

———. *Estratificación social hispanoamericana durante el período colonial.* Stockholm: Instituto de Estudios Ibero-Americanos, 1980.

———. "Economic Factors and Stratification in Colonial Spanish America with Special Regard to Elites." *Hispanic American Historical Review* 63, Number 2 (1983): 335–369.

Mörner, Magnus, editor. *Race and Class in Latin America.* New York: Columbia University Press, 1970.

Mörner, Magnus, and Harold Sims. *Adventurers and Proletarians: The Story of Migrants in Latin America.* University of Pittsburgh Press, 1985.

Morse, Richard McGee. "Some Characteristics of Latin American Urban History." *Hispanic American Historical Review* 67, Number 2 (1962): 321–322.

————. "Recent Research on Latin American Urbanization: A Selective Survey with Commentary." *Latin American Research Review* 1, Number 1 (fall 1965): 35–74.

————. "Trends and Issues in Latin American Urban Research, 1965–1970." *Latin American Research Review* 6, Number 1 (spring 1971): 3–52 and Number 2 (summer 1971): 19–76.

————. "A Prolegomenon to Latin American Urban History." *Hispanic American Historical Review* 52, Number 3 (1972): 359–394.

————. "Trends and Patterns in Latin American Urbanization, 1750–1920." *Comparative Studies in Society and History [UK]* 16, Number 4 (September 1974): 416–447.

————. "Latin American Intellectuals and the City, 1860–1940." *Journal of Latin American Studies [UK]* 10 (1978): 221–227.

————. "The Urban Development of Colonial Spanish America." Volume 2 of *The Cambridge History of Latin America,* edited by Leslie Bethell. Cambridge, NY: Cambridge University Press, 1984: 67–104.

Morse, Richard McGee, editor. *Las ciudades latinoamericanas.* Mexico City: Volumes 96–97 of the Series "Sep-Setentas" published by the Secretaría de Educación Pública or SEP, 1973.

Morse, Richard McGee, et al., editors. *The Urban Development of Latin America, 1750–1920.* Stanford, CA: Stanford University Press, 1971.

Morse, Richard McGee, and Jorge Enrique Hardoy, editors. *Repensando la ciudad de América Latina/Rethinking the Latin American City.* Baltimore: Johns Hopkins University Press for the Woodrow Wilson Center in Washington, DC, 1992.

Muro Orejón, Antonio, compiler. *Cedulario americano del siglo XVIII: colección de disposiciones legales indianas desde 1680 hasta 1800, contenidas en los cedularios del Archivo General de Indias.* Seville: Escuela de Estudios Hispano-americanos, 1956.

Musset, Alain, and Pablo Emilio Pérez-Mallaína Bueno, editors. *De Séville à Lima.* Paris: Laboratoire de Géographie Urbaine, Université de Paris X-Nanterre, 1997.

Navarro García, Luis. *Intendencias en Indias.* Seville: Escuela de Estudios Hispano-americanos, 1959.

Nutall, Zelia. "Royal Ordinances Concerning the Laying Out of New Towns." *Hispanic American Historical Review* 4 (1921): 743–753 and Volume 5 (1922): 249–254.

Ocaña, Fr. Diego de. *Un viaje fascinante por la América Hispana del siglo XVI.* Madrid: Studium, 1969 re-edition by Fr. Arturo Alvarez, O.F.M.

Ots Capdequí, José María. *Las instituciones sociales de la América española en el período colonial.* Madrid, 1934.

————. *El régimen municipal hispanoamericano del período colonial: concejos y ciudades.* Madrid and Valencia, 1936–1937.

————. *El estado español en las Indias.* Madrid, 1946.

Pacheco, Joaquín F., Francisco de Cárdenas, and Luis Torres de Mendoza, compilers. *Colección de documentos inéditos relativos al descubrimiento, conquista y colonización de las posesiones españolas en América y Oceanía, sacados en su mayor parte del Real Archivo de Indias.* Madrid: Imprenta de Manuel B. de Quirós, 1864–1884, forty-two volumes.

Pastor, José M. F. "Streets and Spaces." *Américas [Organization of American States]* 19, Number 10 (October 1967): 5–11.

Paz, Julián. *Catálogo de manuscritos de América existentes en la Biblioteca Nacional.* Madrid: Tipografía de Archivos for the Patronato de la Biblioteca Nacional, 1934.

Piel, Jean, et al. *Regiones y ciudades en América Latina.* Mexico City: Volume 111 of the Series "Sep-Setentas" published by the Secretaría de Educación Pública or SEP, 1973.

Pierson, W. W. "Some Reflections on the Cabildo as an Institution." *Hispanic American Historical Review* 5 (1922): 573–596.

Pike, Frederick B. "Algunos aspectos de la ejecución de las leyes municipales en la América española durante la época de los Austrias." *Revista de Indias [Spain]* 72 (1958): 201 et seq.

————. "The Municipality and the System of Checks and Balances in Spanish American Colonial Administration." *The Americas: A Quarterly Review of Inter-American Cultural History [Academy of American Franciscan History]* 15 (1958): 139 et seq.

————. "Aspects of Cabildo Economic Regulations in Spanish America under the Hapsburgs." *Inter-American Economic Affairs* 13 (1960): 67–86.

Pineo, Ronn F., and James A. Bayer, editors. *Cities of Hope: People, Protests, and Progress in Urbanizing Latin America, 1870–1930.* Boulder, CO: Westview, 1998.

Ponce Leiva, Pilar. "Publicaciones españolas sobre cabildos americanos, 1939–1989." *Revista de Indias [Spain]* 50, Number 188 (1990): 77–81.

Portes, Alejandro, and John Walton. *Urban Latin America: The Political Condition from Above and Below.* Austin: University of Texas Press, 1976.

Priestley, Herbert Ingram. "Spanish Colonial Municipalities." *California Law Review* (September 1919).

Quesada, Santiago. *La idea de ciudad en la cultura hispana de la edad moderna.* Universitat de Barcelona Publicacions, 1992.

Rabinovitz, F. F., and F. M. Trueblood, editors. *Latin American Urban Research.* Beverly Hills, CA: Sage, 1970–1978, six volumes.

Recopilación de leyes de los reinos de las Indias. Madrid: Consejo de la Hispanidad, 1943, three volumes.

Relaciones históricas de ultramar. Madrid: Servicios Geográfico e Histórico del Ejército, 1955, two volumes.

Ricard, Robert. "La plaza mayor en España y en América española: notas para un estudio." *Estudios geográficos* 11 (1950): 301–327.

Richert, Gertrud. *Johann Moritz Rugendas.* Berlin: Rembrandt, 1959.

Robinson, David James, editor. *Social Fabric and Spatial Structure in Colonial Latin America.* Ann Arbor, 1979.

———. *Studies in Spanish American Population History.* Boulder, CO: Westview, 1981.

———. *Migration in Colonial Spanish America.* Cambridge, 1990.

Roessingh, M. P. H. *Guide to the Sources in The Netherlands for the History of Latin America.* The Hague: Government Publishing Office, under the auspices of UNESCO and the International Council on Archives, 1968.

Romano, Ruggiero, editor. *Governare Il Mondo: L'Impero di Spagna dal XV al XIX secolo.* Palermo, Italy, 1992.

Romero, José Luis. *Latinoamérica: las ciudades y las ideas.* Buenos Aires: Siglo XXI, 1976.

Rothenberg, Irene Fraser. "National Intervention and Urban Development in Colombia and Mexico." *Publius* 12, Number 2 (1982): 111–134.

Rout, Leslie B., Jr. *The African Experience in Spanish America: 1502 to the Present.* New York: Cambridge University Press, 1976.

Rubio Moreno, Luis, compiler. *Colección de documentos inéditos para la historia de Hispanoamérica.* Madrid: Inventario General de Registros de Cedularios, 1928.

Saint-Lu, André, and Marie-Cécile Bénassy-Berling, editors. *La ville en Amérique espagnole coloniale.* Paris: Université de la Sorbonne for the Séminaire Interuniversitaire sur l'Amérique Espagnole Coloniale, 1984.

Sáiz, Blanca, editor. *Alejandro Malaspina: la América imposible.* Madrid: Compañía Literaria, 1994.

Sáiz, Blanca, compiler. *Bibliografía sobre Alejandro Malaspina y acerca de la expedición Malaspina y de los marinos y científicos que en ella participaron.* Madrid: El Museo Universal, 1992.

Sala Catalá, José. "El agua en la problemática científica de las primeras metrópolis coloniales hispanoamericanas." *Revista de Indias [Spain]* 49, Number 186 (1989): 257–281.

Salvatore, Ricardo Donato, and Carlos Aguirre, editors. *The Birth of the Penitentiary in Latin America: Essays on Criminology, Prison Reform, and Social Control, 1830–1940.* Austin: University of Texas Press, 1996.

Sánchez-Albornoz, Nicolás. *The Population of Latin America: A History.* Berkeley: University of California Press, 1974 translation by W. A. R. Richardson of 1973 original *La población de América Latina desde los tiempos precolombinos al año 2000.*

Sánchez Bella, Luis. *Guía del Archivo Histórico Nacional.* Madrid: Dirección General de Archivos y Bibliotecas, 1958.

Sanz Fernández, Jesús, editor. *Historia de los ferrocarriles de Iberoamérica, 1837–1995.* Madrid: Centro de Estudios y Expermientación de Obras Públicas or CEDEX, 1998.

Schaedel, Richard P. "The Anthropological Study of Latin American Cities in Intra and Interdisciplinary Perspective." *Urban Anthropology* 3 (1974): 139–170.

Schteingart, Martha, editor. *Urbanización y dependencia en América Latina.* Buenos Aires: SIAP, 1973.

Segre, Roberto. *América Latina en su arquitectura.* Mexico City: Siglo XXI, 1975.

———. *Las estructuras ambientales de América Latina.* Mexico City: Siglo XXI, 1977.

Serrano y Sanz, Manuel, editor. *Colección de libros y documentos referentes a la historia de América.* Madrid: V. Suárez, 1904–1929, twenty-one volumes.

———. *Relaciones históricas de América, primera mitad del siglo XVI.* Madrid: Sociedad de Bibliófilos Españoles, 1916.

Simposio de geografía urbana. Rio de Janeiro: Instituto de Geografía e Historia, 1968.

Smith, Robert C. "Colonial Towns of Spanish and Portuguese America." *Journal of the Society of Architectural Historians* 14, Number 4 (1953): 1 et seq.

Smith, T. Lynn. "The Changing Functions of Latin Cities." *The Americas: A Quarterly Review of Inter-American Cultural History [Academy of American Franciscan History]* 25 (July 1968): 70–83.

Smith, T. Lynn, editor. *Studies of Latin American Societies.* New York: Anchor, 1970.

Socolow, Susan Migden, and Lyman L. Johnson. "Urbanization in Colonial Latin America." *Journal of Urban History* 8, Number 1 (1981): 27–59.

Sofer, Eugene F., and Mark D. Szuchman. "City and Society: Their Connection in Latin American Historical Research." *Latin American Research Review* 14, Number 2 (1979): 113–129.

Solano Pérez-Lila, Francisco de. "Urbanización y municipalización de la población indígena." *Revista de Indias [Spain]* 127–130 (January–December 1972): 241–268.

———. "Introducción al estudio del abastecimiento de la ciudad colonial." *Atti del XL Congreso Internazionale degli Americanisti [Italy]* 4 (September 1973).

———, editor. *Estudios sobre la ciudad iberoamericana.* Madrid: Instituto "Gonzalo Fernández de Oviedo," Consejo Superior de Investigaciones Científicas, 1975.

———. *Estudios sobre la ciudad americana.* Madrid: Instituto "Gonzalo Fernández de Oviedo," Consejo Superior de Investigaciones Científicas, 1983.

Solaún, Mauricio, and Michael Quinn. *Sinners and Heretics: Patterns of Military Intervention in Latin America.* Urbana: University of Illinois Press, 1973.

Solórzano y Pereyra, Juan de. *Política indiana.* Madrid, 1972, five volumes.

Spalding, Hobart A., Jr. "The Parameters of Labor in Hispanic America." *Science and Society* 36 (summer 1972): 202–216.

———. *Organized Labor in Latin America.* New York University Press, 1977.

Spalding, Karen, editor. *Essays in the Political, Economic, and Social History of Colonial Latin America.* Newark: University of Delaware Press, 1982.

Stanislawski, Dan. "Early Spanish Town Planning in the New World." *Geographical Review* 37 (1947): 94–105.

Stern, Malcolm H. "Portuguese Sephardim in the Americas." *American Jewish Archives* 44, Number 1 (1992): 141–178.

Subero, E. *La ciudad y las ciudades.* Caracas, 1966.

Torres Lanzas, Pedro. *Relación descriptiva de los mapas, planos, etc., de Panamá, Santa Fé y Quito existentes en el Archivo General de Indias.* Madrid, 1904.

Tricart, Jean. "Quelques caractéristiques générales des villes latinoaméricaines." *Annales: économies, sociétés, civilisations [France]* 15, Number 1 (1965): 15–30.

Tudela, José. *Los manuscritos de América en las bibliotecas de España.* Madrid, 1954.

———. *El juego de pelota en ambos mundos.* Madrid, 1957.

"The Urban Population Explosion." *Américas [Organization of American States]* 27, Numbers 11–12 (November–December 1975): 11–16.

Urbanización y proceso social en América. Lima: Instituto de Estudios Peruanos, 1972.

Vázquez de Espinosa, Antonio. *Compendium and Description of the West Indies.* Washington, DC: Smithsonian Institution, 1948 translation by Charles Upson Clark.

Vila Vilar, Enriqueta. *Hispanoamérica y el comercio de esclavos: los asientos portugueses.* Seville: Escuela de Estudios Hispano-americanos, 1977.

Villamarín, Juan A. and Judith E. *Indian Labor in Mainland Colonial Spanish America.* Newark, 1975.

Villes et nations en Amérique Latine. Paris: Institut des Hautes Études de l'Amérique Latine or IHEAL, Centre National de la Recherche Scientifique, 1983.

Villes et régions en Amérique Latine. Paris: Institut des Hautes Études de l'Amérique Latine or IHEAL, Centre National de la Recherche Scientifique, 1970.

Vindel, Francisco. *Mapas de América en los libros españoles de los siglos XVI al XVIII.* Madrid, 1955.

Walter, Richard J. "Recent Works on Latin American Urban History." *Journal of Urban History* 16, Number 2 (February 1990): 205–214.

Ward, James S. *Yellow Fever in Latin America: A Geographical Study.* Liverpool: Centre for Latin American Studies at the University of Liverpool, 1972.

Watriss, Wendy, and Lois Parkinson Zamora. *Image and Memory: Photography from Latin America, 1866–1994.* Austin: University of Texas Press, 1998.

Welch, Thomas L., et al., compilers. *Travel Accounts and Descriptions of Latin America and the Caribbean, 1800–1920: A Selected Bibliography.* Washington, DC: Columbus Memorial Library of the Organization of American States,1982.

Wilhelmy, Herbert. "Appearance and Functions of the Large Latin-American Cities in the Past and Present." *Geoforum* 3 (1970): 31–38.

Yujnosky, Oscar. *La estructura interna de la ciudad: el caso latinoamericano.* Buenos Aires: SIAP, 1971.

Zavala, Silvio. *El mundo americano en la época colonial.* Mexico City, 1967, two volumes.

Zéndegui, Guillermo de. "City Planning in the Spanish Colonies." *Américas [Organization of American States]* 29, Number 2 (February 1977): supplementary pp. 1–12.

NORTH AMERICA
Regional Studies

Benson, Adolph B., editor. *The America of 1750: Peter Kalm's Travels in North America.* New York: Dover, 1964, two volumes.

Buisseret, David J., editor. *From Sea Charts to Satellite Images: Interpreting North American History through Maps.* Chicago, 1990.

Doucet, Michael J. "Urban Land Development in Nineteenth-Century North America: Themes in the Literature." *Journal of Urban History* 8 (1982): 299–342.

Doucet, Michael J., and John Weaver. *Housing the North American City.* Montreal and Kingston: McGill-Queen's University Press, 1991.

Germain, Annick, and Jean-Claude Marsan. *Aménager l'urbain, de Montréal à San Francisco: politiques et désign urbain.* Montreal: Méridien, 1987.

Goldberg, Michael A., and John Mercer. *The Myth of the North American City: Continentalism Challenged.* Vancouver: University of British Columbia Press, 1986.

Huret, Jules. *En Amérique.* Paris: "Bibliothèque Charpentier," Eugène Fasquelle, 1904–1905, two volumes.

Keating, Michael. *Comparative Urban Politics: Power of the City in the USA, Canada, Britain and France.* Aldershot: Edward Elgar, 1991.

Lemon, James T. *Liberal Dreams and Nature's Limits: Great Cities of North America since 1600.* Toronto: Oxford University Press, 1996.

Mitchell, Robert, and Paul Groves, editors. *North America: The Historical Geography of a Changing Continent.* Totowa, NJ: Rowman and Littlefield, 1987.

North American City Plans. London: The Map Collectors' Circle, 1965.

Rothblatt, Donald N. "North American Metropolitan Planning: Canadian and U.S. Perspectives." *Journal of the American Planning Association* 60, Number 4 (1994): 501–520.

Rothblatt, Donald N., and Andrew Sancton. *Metropolitan Governance: American/Canadian Intergovernmental Perspectives.* Berkeley and Kingston: Institute of Governmental Studies at the University of California and Institute of Intergovernmental Relations at Queens University, 1993.

Wells, Robert V. *The Population of the British Colonies in America before 1776.* Princeton University Press, 1975.

Canada
General Studies

Armstrong, Christopher, and H. V. Nelles. *Monopoly's Moment: The Organization and Regulation of Canadian Utilities, 1830–1930.* Philadelphia: Temple University Press, 1986.

Artibise, Alan F. J., and Gilbert A. Stelter, editors. *The Usable Urban Past: Planning and the Politics in the Modern Canadian City.* Toronto: Macmillan, 1979.

———. *Canada's Urban Past: A Bibliography to 1980 and a Guide to Canadian Urban Studies.* Vancouver, 1981.

Bacher, John C. *Keeping to the Marketplace: The Evolution of Canadian Housing Policy.* Montreal and Kingston: McGill-Queen's University Press, 1993.

Balakrishnan, T. R. "Changing Patterns of Ethnic Residential Segregation in the Metropolitan Areas of Canada." *Canadian Review of Sociology and Anthropology* 19 (1982): 92–110.

Ball, Norman R., editor. *Building Canada.* University of Toronto Press, 1991.

Bird, Richard M., and N. Enid Slack. *Urban Public Finance in Canada.* Toronto: Wiley, 1993 re-edition.

Bourne, Larry S. "Close Together and Worlds Apart: An Analysis of the Changes in the Ecology of Income in Canadian Cities." *Urban Studies* 30 (1993): 1293–1317.

Bourne, Larry S., and David F. Ley, editors. *The Changing Social Geography of Canadian Cities.* Montreal and Kingston: McGill-Queen's University Press, 1993.

Broadway, Michael J. "Urban Tourist Development in the Nineteenth-Century Canadian City." *American Review of Canadian Studies* 26, Number 1 (1996): 83–99.

Bunting, Trudi E., and Pierre Filion, editors. *Canadian Cities in Transition.* Toronto: Oxford University Press of Canada, 1991.

Careless, J. M. S. *Frontier and Metropolis: Regions, Cities, and Identities in Canada before 1914.* University of Toronto Press, 1989.

Choko, Marc H., and Richard Harris. "The Local Culture of Property: A Comparative History of Housing Tenure in Montreal and Toronto." *Annals of the Association of American Geographers* 80, Number 1 (1990): 73–95.

Clark, S. D. *The Suburban Society.* University of Toronto Press, 1966.

Dagenais, Michèle. "Political Dimensions to Leisure and Cultural Activities in Canadian Cities, 1880–1940." *Urban History [UK]* 26, Number 1 (1999): 55–70.

Driedger, Leo. *The Urban Factor: Sociology of Canadian Cities.* Toronto: Oxford University Press, 1981.

Du Prey, Pierre de la Ruffinière. "Driving the Last Spike: The Architecture of Edward and W. S. Maxwell." *Queen's Quarterly [Canada]* 99, Number 2 (1992): 400–405.

Ferley, Paul. "The French Cartographer Jacques-Nicolas Bellin's Plans of 18th-Century Urban Settlements in Present-Day Canada." *Urban History Review [Canada]* 25, Number 1 (1996): 36–42.

Filion, Pierre. "The Neighbourhood Improvement Plan, Montreal and Toronto: Contrasts *between* a Participatory Approach to Urban Policy Making." *Urban History Review [Canada]* 17, Number 1 (1988): 16–28.

Forward, Charles N. "The Development of Canada's Five Leading National Ports." *Urban History Review [Canada]* 10, Number 3 (1982): 25–45.

Frisken, Frances, editor. *The Changing Canadian Metropolis: A Public Policy Perspective.* Berkeley and Toronto: Institute of Governmental Studies Press and the Canadian Urban Institute, 1994, two volumes.

Gertler, Leonard O., and Ronald W. Crowley. *Changing Canadian Cities: The Next 25 Years.* Toronto: McClelland and Stewart, 1977.

Goheen, Peter G. "The Changing Bias of Inter-urban Communication in Nineteenth-Century Canada." *Journal of Historical Geography* 16 (1990): 177–196.

———. "Symbols in the Streets: Parades in Victorian Urban Canada." *Urban History Review [Canada]* 18, Number 3 (1990): 237–243.

Goodstein, Ethel S. "Contemporary Architecture and Canadian National Identity." *American Review of Canadian Studies* 18, Number 2 (1988): 127–159.

Harris, Richard. "Working-Class Home Ownership and Housing Affordability Across Canada in 1931." *Social History [Canada]* 19, Number 37 (1986): 121–138.

———. "More American Than the United States: Housing in Urban Canada in the Twentieth Century." *Journal of Urban History* 26, Number 4 (May 2000): 456–478.

Higgins, Donald J. H. *Urban Canada: Its Government and Politics.* Toronto: Macmillan, 1977.

Historical Maps, Canada. Ottawa: Association of Canadian Map Libraries, 1980-, facsimile series.

Hobson, P., and F. St. Hilaire, editors. *Urban Governance and Finance: A Question of Who Does What.* Montreal: Institute for Research on Public Policy, 1997.

Hodge, Gerald. *Planning Canadian Communities: An Introduction to the Principles, Practice and Participants.* Toronto: Methuen, 1986.

Kaplan, Harold. *Reform, Planning, and City Politics: Montreal, Winnipeg, and Toronto.* University of Toronto Press, 1982.

Kazempiur, Abdolmohammad, and Shiva Sitall Halli. "Neighborhood Poverty in Canadian Cities." *Canadian Journal of Sociology* 25, Number 3 (2000): 369–381.

Leacy, F. H., editor. *Historical Statistics of Canada.* Ottawa: Statistics Canada, 1983.

Levine, Gregory J. "Tax Exemptions in Montreal and Toronto, 1870 to 1920." *Cahiers de géographie du Québec* 35, Number 94 (1991): 117–134.

———. "The Single Tax in Montreal and Toronto, 1880 to 1920: Successes, Failures and the Transformation of an Idea." *American Journal of Economics and Sociology* 52, Number 4 (1993): 417–432.

Ley, David, and Heather Smith. "Relations *between* Deprivation and Immigrant Groups in Large Canadian Cities." *Urban Studies [UK]* 37, Number 1 (2000): 37–62.

MacLennan, Hugh. "Canada." *American Heritage* 11, Number 1 (December 1965): 6–45 and 92–99.

Magnusson, W., and Andrew Sancton, editors. *City Politics in Canada.* University of Toronto Press, 1983.

McCann, L. D., editor. *Heartland and Hinterland: A Geography of Canada.* Toronto: Prentice-Hall, 1987.

Miron, John. *Housing in Postwar Canada: Demographic Change, Household Formation and Housing Demand.* Montreal and Kingston: McGill-Queen's University Press, 1988.

Morton, Desmond, and Terry Copp. *Working People: An Illustrated History of Canadian Labour.* Toronto: Deneau and Greenberg, 1980.

Nach, James. *Canada in Pictures.* Minneapolis: The Company, 1989.

Nader, George A. *Cities of Canada.* Toronto: Macmillan, 1975–1976, two volumes.

Piva, Michael J. "Urban Working-Class Incomes and Real Incomes in 1921: A Comparative Analysis." *Social History [Canada]* 16, Number 31 (1983): 145–167.

Porter, John A. *The Vertical Mosaic: An Analysis of Social Class and Power in Canada.* University of Toronto Press, 1965.

Savoie, Donald. *The Politics of Public Spending.* University of Toronto Press, 1990.

Sewell, John. *Houses and Homes: Housing for Canadians.* Toronto: Lorimer, 1994.

Simmons, Jack W. *The Growth of the Canadian Urban System.* Toronto: Centre for Urban and Community Studies, 1974.

Skidmore, Colleen. "'All That Is Interesting in the Canadas': William Notman's *Maple Box Portfolio* of Stereographic Views, 1860." *Journal of Canadian Studies* 32, Number 4 (1998): 69–90.

Stelter, Gilbert A., and Alan F. J. Artibise, editors. *The Canadian City: Essays in Urban History.* Toronto: McClelland and Stewart, 1977.

———. *Shaping the Urban Landscape: Aspects of the City-Building Process.* Ottawa: Carleton University Press, 1982.

———. *Power and Place: Canadian Urban Development in the North American Context.* Vancouver: University of British Columbia Press, 1986.

Stone, Leroy O. *Urban Development in Canada: An Introduction to the Demographic Aspects.* Ottawa: Dominion Bureau of Statistics, 1967.

Taylor, Thomas Griffith. *Canada: A Study of Cool Continental Environments and Their Effect on British and French Settlement.* London: Methuen, 1947.

Teixeira, Carlos. "The Suburbanization of Portuguese Communities in Toronto and Montreal: From Isolation to Residential Integration?" *Canadian Issues* 18 (1996): 181–201.

White, Peter T. "One Canada—Or Two?" *National Geographic* 151, Number 4 (April 1977): 436–465.

Zaslow, Morris. *The Defended Border: Upper Canada and the War of 1812.* Toronto: Macmillan, 1964.

Halifax
British Colonial Era (1749–1860)

Anderson, Beryl L. "List of Books for a Public Library in Halifax, 1793." *Nova Scotia Historical Review* 12, Number 1 (1992): 119–150.

Bains, Yashdip Singh. "The American Company of Comedians in Halifax in 1768." *Dalhousie Review [Canada]* 56, Number 2 (1976): 240–246.

———. "The Articulate Audience and the Fortunes of the Theatre in Halifax in 1816–1819." *Dalhousie Review [Canada]* 57, Number 4 (1977–1978): 726–736.

———. "The Spectator's Eye: Impressions of Halifax Theatre in the Early Nineteenth Century." *Dalhousie Review [Canada]* 59, Number 1 (1979): 40–50.

———. "The New Grand Theatre: Halifax, 1789–1814." *Nova Scotia Historical Quarterly* 10, Number 1 (1980): 1–21.

Barratt, Glynn R. de V. "Halifax through Russian Eyes: Fleet Lieutenant Iurii Lisianskii's Notes of 1794–96." *Nova Scotia Historical Review* 12, Number 2 (1992): 47–65.

Bates, George T. "The Great Exodus of 1749." *Nova Scotia Historical Society Collections* 38 (1973): 27–62.

Beck, J. M. *Joseph Howe.* Montreal and Kingston: McGill-Queen's University Press, 1982–1983, two volumes.

Best, J. Linden. "Box, Pit, and Gallery: The Theatre Royal at Spring Gardens." *Dalhousie Review [Canada]* 53, Number 3 (1973): 520–528.

Buggey, Susan. "Building Halifax, 1841–1871." *Acadiensis [Canada]* 10, Number 1 (1980): 90–112.

———. "Building in Mid-Nineteenth Century Halifax: The Case of George Lang." *Urban History Review [Canada]* 9, Number 2 (1980): 5–20.

Bunbury, Dan. "Safe Haven for the Poor? Depositors and the Government Savings Bank in Halifax, 1832–1867." *Acadiensis [Canada]* 24, Number 2 (1995): 24–48.

Cahill, Barry. "'Ministre des Etrangers Suisses Allemands': A Halifax Letter of 21 September 1750." *Nova Scotia Historical Review* 4, Number 2 (1984): 91–96.

———. "The Treason of the Merchants: Dissent and Repression in Halifax in the Era of the American Revolution." *Acadiensis [Canada]* 26, Number 1 (1996): 52–70.

Candow, James E. "Sir Isaac Coffin and the Halifax Dockyard 'Scandal.'" *Nova Scotia Historical Review* 1, Number 2 (1981): 50–63.

Clark, Andrew Hill. *Acadia: The Geography of Early Nova Scotia to 1760.* Madison: University of Wisconsin Press, 1968.

Crosse, John, compiler. "The Arrival of the *Chesapeake* in Halifax in 1813 as Described by Thomas Haliburton ('Sam Slick')." *American Neptune* 57, Number 2 (1997): 161–165.

Currie, A. W. "Some Eighteenth-Century Observations on Nova Scotia." *Dalhousie Review [Canada]* 47, Number 4 (1967): 567–576.

Cuthbertson, Brian C. U. "Place, Politics and the Brandy Election of 1830." *Collections of the Royal Nova Scotia Historical Society* 41 (1981): 5–19.

———. *The Loyalist Governor: Sir John Wentworth.* Halifax, 1983.

Documents Relating to Currency, Finance and Exchange in Nova Scotia, 1675–1758. Ottawa: I. O. Patenaude for the Board of Historical Publications of the Public Archives of Canada, 1933.

Douglas, W. A. B. "The Sea Militia of Nova Scotia, 1749–1755." *Canadian Historical Review* 47, Number 1 (1966): 22–37.

Ennals, Peter. "The Yankee Origins of Bluenose Vernacular Architecture." *American Review of Canadian Studies* 12, Number 2 (1982): 5–21.

Evans, G. R. "The Annapolis Road: Its Weakest Link." *Nova Scotia Historical Society Collections* 38 (1973): 91–112.

Fergusson, Charles Bruce. "Isaac Hildrith (ca. 1741–1807): Architect of Government House, Halifax." *Dalhousie Review [Canada]* 50, Number 4 (1970–1971): 510–516.

———. "The Establishment of the Consulate of the United States of America in Halifax." *Nova Scotia Historical Quarterly* 3, Number 1 (1973): 5773.

Gouett, Paul M. "The Halifax Orphan House, 1752–1787." *Nova Scotia Historical Quarterly* 6, Number 3 (1976): 281–291.

Greenough, John Joseph. *The Halifax Citadel, 1825–1860: A Narrative and Structural History.* Ottawa: Parks Canada, 1977.

Greiert, Steven G. "The Earl of Halifax and the Settlement of Nova Scotia, 1749–1753." *Nova Scotia Historical Review* 1, Number 1 (1981): 423.

Griffiths, Naomi. *The Acadian Deportation.* Toronto: Copp Clark, 1969.

Guildford, Janet. "'Whate'er the Duty of the Hour Demands': The Work of Middle-Class Women in Halifax, 1840–1880." *Social History [Canada]* 30, Number 59 (1997): 120.

Gutridge, Anthony. "George Redmond Hulbert: Prize Agent at Halifax, Nova Scotia, 1812–1814." *Mariner's Mirror [UK]* 87, Number 1 (2001): 3042.

Gwyn, Julian. "The Culture of Work in the Halifax Naval Yard before 1820." *Journal of the Royal Nova Scotia Historical Society* (1999): 118–144.

Gwyn, Julian, and Pazley Siddiq. "Wealth Distribution in Nova Scotia during the Confederation Era, 1851 and 1871." *Canadian Historical Review* 73, Number 4 (1992): 435–452.

Hall, Frederick A. "A Prince's Sojourn in Eighteenth-Century Canada." *Studies in Eighteenth-Century Culture* 19 (1989): 247–266.

Ingalls, Sharon. "The Duke's Romantic Retreat." *Beaver [Canada]* 76, Number 3 (1996): 2936.

Lohnes, Barry J. "British Naval Problems at Halifax during the War of 1812." *Mariner's Mirror [UK]* 59, Number 3 (1973): 317–333.

Lower, Arthur R. M. *Great Britain's Woodyard: British America and the Timber Trade, 1763–1867.* Montreal and Kingston: McGill-Queen's University Press, 1973.

MacLeod, Malcolm. "Letter from Another World, 1757." *Nova Scotia Historical Quarterly* 3, Number 3 (1973): 197–213.

Major, Marjorie. "The Great Pontack Inn." *Nova Scotia Historical Quarterly* 3, Number 3 (1973): 171–190.

Marble, Allan E. *Surgeons, Smallpox and the Poor: A History of Medicine and Social Conditions in Nova Scotia, 1749–1799.* Montreal and Kingston: McGill-Queen's University Press, 1993.

———. "'To Consummate That Great Desideratum—A General Hospital.'" *Journal of the Royal Nova Scotia Historical Society* (1999): 167–202.

McAleer, J. Philip. "St. Mary's (1820–1830), Halifax: An Early Example of the Use of Gothic Revival Forms in Canada."

Journal of the Society of Architectural Historians 45, Number 2 (1986): 134–147.

McGee, Timothy J. "Music in Halifax, 1749–1799." *Dalhousie Review [Canada]* 49, Number 3 (1969): 377–387.

McNally, Larry. "The *Royal William:* The Saga of a Pioneering Steam-Vessel." *Archivist [Canada]* 17, Number 4 (1990): 24.

Morrison, James H. "The Duke's Innovation: Early Communication Systems in Atlantic Canada, 1794–1815." *Collections of the Royal Nova Scotia Historical Society* 43 (1991): 128–147.

———. "Halifax, 1799: The Duke of Kent's Astonishing Telegraph." *Beaver [Canada]* 71, Number 6 (1991–1992): 2432.

Pacey, E. *Georgian Halifax.* Hantsport, Nova Scotia: Lancelot, 1987.

Picart, Lennox O'Riley. "The Trelawny Maroons and Sir John Wentworth: The Struggle to Maintain Their Culture, 1796–1800." *Collections of the Royal Nova Scotia Historical Society* 44 (1995): 165–187.

Plank, Geoffrey. "The Changing Country of Anthony Casteel: Language, Religion, Geography, Political Loyalty, and Nationality in Mid-Eighteenth Century Nova Scotia." *Studies in Eighteenth-Century Culture* 27 (1998): 5374.

Punch, Terrence M. "Halifax Town: The Census of 1838." *Nova Scotia Historical Quarterly* 6, Number 3 (1976): 233–258.

———. *Irish Halifax: The Immigrant Generation, 1815–1859.* Halifax: St. Mary's University Press for the International Education Centre, 1981.

Richardson, Boyce. "To Halifax with Captain Cook." *Beaver [Canada]* 66, Number 5 (1986): 2730.

Robertson, Allen B. "Bondage and Freedom: Apprentices, Servants and Slaves in Colonial Nova Scotia." *Collections of the Royal Nova Scotia Historical Society* 44 (1995): 57–69.

———. "City upon a Hill: Architecture and Identity in Colonial Halifax." *Journal of the Royal Nova Scotia Historical Society* 2 (1999): 155–166.

Rompkey, Ronald, editor. *Expeditions of Honour: The Journal of John Salusbury in Halifax, N. S., 1749–1753.* Newark: University of Delaware Press, 1982.

Rudachyk, B. E. S. "'At the Mercy of the Devouring Element': The Equipment and Organization of the Halifax Fire Establishment, 1830–1850." *Collections of the Royal Nova Scotia Historical Society* (1982): 165–184.

Smith, Marilyn Gurney. *King's Yard.* Halifax: Nimbus, 1985.

Sutherland, David A. "Halifax Merchants and the Pursuit of Development, 1783–1850." *Canadian Historical Review* 59, Number 1 (1978): 1–17.

———. "Voluntary Societies and the Process of Middle-Class Formation in Early Victorian Halifax, Nova Scotia."

Journal of the Canadian Historical Association 5 (1994): 237–263.

———. "Race Relations in Halifax, Nova Scotia, during the Mid-Victorian Quest for Reform." *Journal of the Canadian Historical Association* 7 (1996): 35–54.

———. "A Prince, the Governor, and Mr. Mayor: Halifax and the Politics of Prestige in 1841." *Journal of the Royal Nova Scotia Historical Society* 1 (1998): 93–103.

Upton, Leslie F. S. *Micmacs and Colonists: Indian-White Relations in the Maritime Provinces, 1713–1867.* Vancouver: University of British Columbia Press, 1979.

Vincent, Thomas B. "'The Inquisition': Alexander Croke's Satire on Halifax Society during the Wentworth Years." *Dalhousie Review [Canada]* 53, Number 3 (1973): 404–430.

Wallace, Annie W. "The History of the Nova Scotia Railway." *Nova Scotia Historical Review* 6, Number 2 (1986): 6772.

Wilson, Alex. "The Public Gardens of Halifax, Nova Scotia." *Journal of Garden History [UK]* 3, Number 3 (1983): 179–192.

Early Maps and Depictions of Halifax, 1749–1819

"Plan of the New Town of Halifax in Nova Scotia," published in Volume 19 of *The Gentleman's Magazine* in London, 1749—available from the Rare Book Collection at Dalhousie University's Killam Library, plus numerous other sources

"A Plan of the Harbour of Chebucto and Town of Halifax," as well as a crude drawing of a porcupine and several other curiosities, all engraved by John Rocque for Volume 20 of *The Gentleman's Magazine* published in London in 1750—available from numerous sources

View of the initial 1750 settlement at Halifax "as drawn from ye topmasthead," published in London by Thomas Jefferys on 25 January 1760—numerous sources

Four panoramic views of Halifax's harbor in 1759 (one as seen from George's Island, the second from Dartmouth opposite, and the third and fourth from atop Citadel Hill), plus a pair of street scenes within the town itself, all six drawn by Richard Short and painted in oils by Dominic Serres "the Elder," being published as a series of engravings in March 1764, April 1777, etc.—numerous sources

Crude drawing of "His Majesty's Dockyard at Halifax," ca. 1760—original held by Parks Canada's Citadel Library, Halifax

French map of "Chibouctou" Bay, plus an insert showing the town of Halifax, published in Paris as Plate 28 in the first volume of Jacques-Nicolas Bellin's *Petit atlas maritime,* 1764—numerous sources

"A View of the Town & Harbour of Halifax, from Dartmouth Shore" and another panorama of the entire bay, both drawn by J. F. W. des Barres and published in London in *The Atlantic Neptune,* 1777–1781—numerous sources

Nine watercolors by Lt.-Col. Edward Hicks of scenes around Halifax, ca. 1780–1782—his view looking toward the Naval Yard and Citadel Hill from Fort Needham, a new redoubt installed to protect against landward assaults out of the northeast, is today held by the Nova Scotia Archives, call number 1979 147.173

Four watercolors around Halifax by G. I. Parkyns (as seen from the gun batteries on George's Island, Fort Needham, Cowie's Hill, and Davis's Hill), April 1801—the first is held by the Nova Scotia Archives, call number 1979 147.166

View of the entrance into Halifax harbor, drawn by Dominic Serres "the Younger" and engraved by Wells for the 31 October 1803 issue of the *Naval Chronicle*—numerous sources

View of the Commissioner's House in the Naval Yard at Halifax, engraved by Wells for the 29 February 1804 issue of the *Naval Chronicle*—numerous sources

Oil painting by J. C. Schetky, lithographed by L. Haghe and published in London by Smith Elder & Co. in 1830, of the captive USS *Chesapeake* being brought to anchor off Halifax's Naval Yard in June 1813—original held by the Nova Scotia Archives, call number 1979 147.606

Engraving by G. I. Parkyns of Halifax, as seen from Dartmouth Point, June 1817—several sources

Detailed chart of Halifax's coastline and approaches—found opposite page 18 in A. Lockwood's *A Brief Description of Nova Scotia,* published in London in 1818

Four etchings by John Elliott Woolford of the Provincial Building in Halifax (architectural elevation and street view out of the northeast), plus Government House (front view from the southwest and rear view from the northeast), 1819—several sources

Civil War Boom (1861–1865)

Jones, Francis I. W. "Treason and Piracy in Civil War Halifax: The Second *Chesapeake* Affair Revisited." *Dalhousie Review [Canada]* 71, Number 4 (1991–1992): 472–487.

———. "A Hot Southern Town: Confederate Sympathizers in Halifax during the American Civil War." *Journal of the Royal Nova Scotia Historical Society* 2 (1999): 5269.

———. "This Fraudulent Trade: Confederate Blockade-Running from Halifax during the American Civil War." *Northern Mariner [Canada]* 9, Number 4 (1999): 3546.

McDonald, R. H. "Second *Chesapeake* Affair: 1863–1864." *Dalhousie Review [Canada]* 54, Number 4 (1974–1975): 674–684.

Winks, Robin W. "The Second *Chesapeake* Affair." *American Neptune* 19, Number 1 (1959): 5172.

Wright, Jeffrey. "The Halifax Riot of April, 1863." *Nova Scotia Historical Quarterly* 4, Number 3 (1974): 299–310.

Early Canadian Era (1867–1916)

Banks, Herbert R. "The Coast Railway: 'Tom Robertson's Wheelbarrow Railroad.'" *Nova Scotia Historical Review* 6, Number 2 (1986): 11–16.

Bilson, Geoffrey. "Two Cholera Ships in Halifax." *Dalhousie Review [Canada]* 53, Number 3 (1973): 449–459.

Carrigan, D. Owen. "The Immigrant Experience in Halifax, 1881–1931." *Canadian Ethnic Studies* 20, Number 3 (1988): 2841.

Davidson, Jonathan H. "*Francklyn v. The People's Heat and Light Company Limited:* A Nineteenth-Century Environmental Lawsuit in Nova Scotia." *Nova Scotia Historical Review* 16, Number 2 (1996): 3448.

Erickson, Paul A. "Yellow Fever in Halifax." *Collections of the Royal Nova Scotia Historical Society* 42 (1986): 5970.

Fingard, Judith. *The Dark Side of Life in Victorian Halifax.* Halifax, 1989.

———. "Race and Respectability in Victorian Halifax." *Journal of Imperial and Commonwealth History [UK]* 20, Number 2 (1992): 169–195.

———. "From Sea to Rail: Black Transportation Workers and Their Families in Halifax, ca. 1870–1916." *Acadiensis [Canada]* 24, Number 2 (1995): 4964.

Hood, David. "Some Fiscal Realities of School Reform in Victorian Halifax." *Nova Scotia Historical Review* 16, Number 1 (1996): 61–80.

Jolliffe, Kyle. "A Saga of Gilded Age Entrepreneurship in Halifax: The People's Heat and Light Company Limited, 1893–1902." *Nova Scotia Historical Review* 15, Number 2 (1995): 1025.

March, William. "Newspaper Competition in Halifax, 1875–1900." *Collections of the Royal Nova Scotia Historical Society* 42 (1986): 7180.

McCann, Larry D. "Staples and the New Industrialism in the Growth of Post-Confederation Halifax." *Acadiensis [Canada]* 8, Number 2 (1979): 4779.

Pulsifer, Cameron. "Winter Comfort and the Use of Storm Sashes in Nineteenth-Century Halifax: The Military Experience." *Material History Bulletin [Canada]* 32 (1990): 65–70.

———. "The Battle of Rockhead, March 1871: Training for War in Mid-Victorian Halifax." *Canadian Military History* 5, Number 1 (1996): 4960.

Roper, Henry. "The Halifax Board of Control: The Failure of Municipal Reform, 1906–1919." *Acadiensis [Canada]* 14, Number 2 (1985): 4665.

Smith, Mary Elizabeth. "People, Place, and Performance: Early Years of the Halifax Academy of Music." *Dalhousie Review [Canada]* 75, Number 3 (1996): 409–439.

Tennant, R. D., Jr. "The Electric Street Railway: Halifax's Symbol of Municipal Worth." *Nova Scotia Historical Society Collections* (1980): 133–159.

Great Explosion (1917)

Armstrong, John G. "Letters from Halifax: Reliving the Halifax Explosion through the Eyes of My Grandfather, a Sailor in the Royal Canadian Navy." *Northern Mariner [Canada]* 8, Number 4 (1998): 55–74.

Bird, Michael J. *The Town That Died: A Chronicle of the Halifax Disaster.* Halifax: Nimbus, 1995 reprint of 1967 original.

Chapman, Harry. "Memories of a Day of Horrors: Dartmouth 1917." *Beaver [Canada]* 73, Number 4 (1993): 3539.

Kitz, Janet. *Shattered City: The Halifax Explosion and Its Aftermath.* Halifax, 1989.

———. "The Halifax Explosion, December 6, 1917." *Canadian Oral History Association Journal* 12 (1992): 611.

MacLeod, Malcolm. "Helping, Unheeded: Newfoundland's Relief Effort and the Historiography of the Halifax Explosion, 1917." *Nova Scotia Historical Review* 2, Number 2 (1982): 6568.

Metson, Graham, compiler and editor. *The Halifax Explosion, December 6, 1917.* Toronto: McGraw-Hill Ryerson, 1978.

Morton, Suzanne. "The Halifax Relief Commission and Labour Relations during the Reconstruction of Halifax, 1917–1919." *Acadiensis [Canada]* 18, Number 2 (1989): 7393.

Richardson, Evelyn M. "The Halifax Explosion: 1917." *Nova Scotia Historical Quarterly* 7, Number 4 (1977): 305–330.

Ruffman, Alan, and Colin D. Howell, editors. *Ground Zero: A Reassessment of the 1917 Explosion in Halifax Harbour.* Halifax: Nimbus, 1994.

Scanlon, Joseph. "Source of Threat and Source of Assistance: The Maritime Aspects of the 1917 Halifax Explosion." *Northern Mariner [Canada]* 10, Number 4 (2000): 3950.

Modern Era (1918–Present)

Bacher, John. "From Study to Reality: The Establishment of Public Housing in Halifax, 1930–1953." *Acadiensis [Canada]* 18, Number 1 (1988): 120–135.

Bobier, Richard. "Africville: The Test of Urban Renewal and Race in Halifax, Nova Scotia." *Past Imperfect [Canada]* 4 (1995): 163–180.

Boudreau, Michael. "Crime and Society in Halifax, 1918–1935." *Collections of the Royal Nova Scotia Historical Society* 44 (1995): 95–103.

Caldwell, R. H. "The VE Day Riots in Halifax, 7–8 May 1945." *Northern Mariner [Canada]* 10, Number 1 (2000): 320.

Cameron, James M. *Murray: The Martyred Admiral.* Hantsport, Nova Scotia: Lancelot, 1981.

Cameron, Silver Donald. "The *Bluenose.*" *Canadian Geographic* 104, Number 2 (1984): 20–25.

———. "'Greatest Harbour': The Port of Halifax Is Confidently Living Up to Its Micmac Name." *Canadian Geographic* 108, Number 6 (1988–1989): 1223.

Collins, Louis W. *In Halifax Town.* Halifax: Self-published, 1975.

Hadley, Michael. "U-Boote vor Halifax im Winter, 1944/45." *Marine Rundschau [Germany]* 79, Number 3 (1982): 138–144 and Number 4: 202–208.

Janelle, Donald, and Michael Goodchild. "Diurnal Patterns of Social Group Distributions in a Canadian City." *Economic Geography* 59, Number 4 (1983): 403–425.

Latta, Peter, and Diane Tye. "Symbols of Change: The Legacy of Two Early Twentieth-Century Nova Scotian Builders." *Nova Scotia Historical Review* 9, Number 2 (1989): 1834.

Little, C. H. "Halifax: Container Port." *Canadian Geographical Journal* 86, Number 4 (1973): 126–133.

McCarry, Charles. "Nova Scotia: The Magnificent Anchorage." *National Geographic* 147, Number 3 (March 1975): 334–363.

Millward, Hugh. "The Spread of Commuter Development in the Eastern Shore Zone of Halifax, Nova Scotia, 1920–1988." *Urban History Review [Canada]* 29, Number 1 (2000): 2132.

Mitic, Trudy Duivenvoorden. "Gateway to Canada." *Beaver [Canada]* 75, Number 1 (1995): 915.

Morton, Suzanne. "Labourism and Economic Action: The Halifax Shipyards Strike of 1920." *Labour [Canada]* 22 (1988): 67–98.

———. *Ideal Surroundings: Domestic Life in a Working Class Suburb in the 1920s.* University of Toronto Press, 1995.

Redman, Stanley R. *Open Gangway: An Account of the Halifax Riots, 1945.* Hantsport, Nova Scotia: Lancelot, 1981.

Sutton, Edward. "Halifax Cabdrivers, 1939–1945." *Nova Scotia Historical Review* 12, Number 2 (1992): 6673.

Watkins, Lyndon. "Halifax-Dartmouth Area: One of the Three Biggest Marine Science Centres in the Western Hemisphere." *Canadian Geographic* 100, Number 5 (1980): 1223.

White, Jay. "Pulling Teeth: Striking for the Check-Off in the Halifax Shipyards, 1944." *Acadiensis [Canada]* 19, Number 1 (1989): 115–141.

———. "The Home Front: The Accommodation Crisis in Halifax, 1941–1951." *Urban History Review [Canada]* 20, Number 3 (1992): 117–127.

General Works

Archibald, Stephen. "Civic Ornaments: Ironwork in Halifax Parks." *Material History Buletin [Canada]* 5 (1978): 111.

Beck, J. Murray. "Ups and Downs of Halifax Influence in Nova Scotia Government, 1749–1981." *Transactions of the Royal Society of Canada* 19 (1981): 6980.

Bell, John, editor. *Halifax: A Literary Portrait.* Halifax, 1990.

Buggey, Susan. "Halifax Waterfront Buildings: An Historical Report." *Canadian Historic Sites* 9 (1975): 119–168.

Cuthbertson, Brian C. "History of the Grand Parade and Halifax City-Hall." *Journal of the Royal Nova Scotia Historical Society* (1999): 7093.

Erickson, Paul A. *Halifax's North End: An Anthropologist Looks at the City.* Hantsport, Nova Scotia: Lancelot, 1986.

Exploring Halifax. Halifax: Greey de Pencier for the Nova Scotia Association of Architects, 1976.

Fergusson, Charles Bruce. "Halifax Has a Winner: Historic Properties." *Canadian Geographic* 97, Number 2 (1978): 3439.

Fingard, Judith, et al. *Halifax: The First 250 Years.* Halifax: Formac, 1999.

Founded on a Rock: Historic Buildings in Halifax and Vicinity. Halifax: Heritage Trust of Nova Scotia, 1971 re-edition.

Girard, Philip. "The Rise and Fall of Urban Justice in Halifax, 1815–1886." *Nova Scotia Historical Review* 8, Number 2 (1988): 57–71.

Hannington, J. Brian. *Every Popish Person: The Story of Roman Catholicism and the Church of Halifax, 1604–1984.* Halifax, 1984.

Hines, Sherman. *Halifax.* Halifax: Nimbus, 1981.

Lochhead, D. G. "Halifax in Canadian Literature." *Transactions of the Royal Society of Canada* 19 (1981): 93–104.

McAleer, J. Philip. *Pictorial History of St. Paul's Anglican Church, Halifax, Nova Scotia.* Halifax: Technical University of Nova Scotia, 1993.

McKay, Ian. *The Craft Transformed: An Essay on the Carpenters of Halifax, 1885–1985.* Halifax: Holdfast, 1985.

Metson, Graham. *An East Coast Port.* Halifax, 1981.

Napier, David. "The Secrets of Halifax Harbour." *Beaver [Canada]* 77, Number 4 (1997): 46.

Payzant, Joan M. *Halifax: Cornerstone of Canada.* Woodland Hills, CA: Windsor, 1985.

Penney, Allen. "Halifax and Nova Scotian Architecture." *Transactions of the Royal Society of Canada* 19 (1981): 105–112.

Piers, Harry. *The Evolution of the Halifax Fortress, 1749–1928.* Halifax: Public Archives of Nova Scotia, 1947.

Raddall, Thomas. *Halifax: Warden of the North.* Toronto, 1971 re-edition of 1948 original.

The Spirit of Africville. Halifax: Africville Genealogical Society, 1992.

Volpi, Charles Patrick de. *Nova Scotia, A Pictorial Record: Historical Prints and Illustrations of the Province of Nova Scotia, Canada, 1605–1878.* Don Mills, Ontario: Longman Canada, 1974.

Waite, P. B. *The Lives of Dalhousie University.* Montreal and Kingston: McGill-Queen's University Press, 1994–1998, two volumes.

Walker, James W. St. G. *The Black Loyalists: The Search for a Promised Land in Nova Scotia and Sierra Leone, 1783–1870.* Halifax: Dalhousie University Press, 1976.

Wallace, A. W. *An Album of Drawings of Early Buildings in Nova Scotia.* Halifax, 1976.

Montreal

French Era (1535–1760)

Allaire, Gratien. "Officiers et marchands: les sociétés de commerce des fourrures, 1715–1760." *Revue d'histoire de l'Amérique française [Canada]* 40, Number 3 (1987): 409–428.

Auger, Roland-J. *La grande recrue de 1653.* Montreal: Société Généalogique, 1955.

Beaudoin, Marie-Louise. *Les premières et les filles du roi à Montréal.* Montreal: Maison Saint-Gabriel, 1996.

Beauregard, Ludger. "Géographie historique des côtes de l'Île de Montréal." *Cahiers de géographie du Québec [Canada]* 28, Numbers 73–74 (1984): 47–62.

Béchard, Henri. *Jérôme de La Dauversière: His Friends and Enemies.* Bloomingdale, OH: AFC, 1991.

Bouchard, Dominique. "Structure et effectifs des métiers du fer à Montréal avant 1765." *Revue d'histoire de l'Amérique française [Canada]* 49, Number 1 (1995): 73–85.

Brault, Jean-Rémi, editor. *Les origines de Montréal.* Montreal: Leméac, 1993.

Cliche, Marie-Aimée. "Fille-mères, familles et société sous le régime français." *Social History [Canada]* 21, Number 41 (1988): 39–69.

Dechêne, Louise. *Habitants and Merchants in Seventeenth-Century Montreal.* Montreal and Kingston: McGill-Queen's University Press, 1992 translation by Liana Vardi of 1974 French-language original.

Dépatie, Sylvie. "La structure agraire au Canada: le cas de l'Île Jésus au XVIIIe siècle." *Historical Papers [Canada]* 1986: 56–85.

Deroy-Pineau, Françoise. *Jeanne Mance: de Langres à Montréal, la passion de soigner.* Montreal: Bellarmin, 1995.

Desjardins, Pauline. "La présence amérindiene à Pointe-à-Callière, Montréal." *Recherches amérindiennes au Québec [Canada]* 24, Numbers 1–2 (1994): 113–118.

Gallat-Morin, Elisabeth. *Jean Girard, musicien en Nouvelle-France: Bourges, 1696-Montréal, 1765.* Montreal: Septentrion, 1993.

Gelinas, Claude. "La nature des attaques iroquoises contre Ville-Marie, 1642–1667." *Recherches amérindiennes au Québec [Canada]* 24, Numbers 1–2 (1994): 119–127.

Grabowski, Jan. "Searching for the Common Ground: Natives and French in Montreal, 1700–1730," *Proceedings of the Annual Meeting of the French Colonial History Society* 18 (1993): 59–73.

———. "Les amérindiens domiciliés et la 'contrebande' des fourrures en Nouvelle France." *Recherches amérindiennes au Québec [Canada]* 24, Number 3 (1994): 45–52.

———. "French Criminal Justice and Indians in Montreal, 1670–1760." *Ethnohistory* 43, Number 3 (1996): 405–429.

Hunter, Douglas. "Virtual Vieux Montréal." *Canadian Geographic* 122, Number 4 (July–August 2002): 88–94.

Jamieson, J. B. "Place Royale: A Prehistoric Site from the Island of Montreal." *Ontario Archaeology [Canada]* 47 (1987): 59–71.

Ladouceur, Jean-Paul. "A la recherche des deux montagnes." *Revue d'histoire de l'Amérique française [Canada]* 52, Number 3 (1999): 383–406.

Lambert, Phyllis, and Alan Stewart, editors. *Opening the Gates of Eighteenth-Century Montreal.* Montreal: Canadian Centre for Architecture, 1992.

Lanctot, Gustave. *Montréal sous Maisonneuve.* Montreal: Beauchemin, 1966.

Landry, Yves. *Orphelines en France, pionnières au Canada: les filles du roi au XVIIe siècle.* Montreal: Leméac, 1992.

Landry, Yves, editor. *Pour le Christ et le Roi: la vie au temps des premiers montréalais.* Montreal: Libre Expression, 1992.

Larocque, Robert. "Les sépultures amérindiennes du Mont-Royal." *Recherches amérindiennes au Québec [Canada]* 20, Numbers 3–4 (1990): 31–41.

Massicotte, Daniel. "Stratification sociale et différenciation spatiale en milieu urbain pré-industrielle: le cas des locataires montréalais, 1731–1741." *Revue d'histoire de l'Amérique française [Canada]* 44, Number 1 (1990): 61–83.

Massicotte, Edouard-Zotique. "Les colons de Montréal de 1642 à 1667." *Memoirs of the Royal Society of Canada* 7: 3–65.

Paterson, T. W. "The Defence of Fort Verchères." *Canadian West* 6, Number 4 (1990): 152–155.

———. "Siege at the Long Sault." *Canadian West* 6, Number 3 (1990): 114–118.

Poirier, Jean. "Origine du nom de la ville de Montréal." *Revue d'histoire de l'Amérique française [Canada]* 46, Number 1 (1992): 37–44.

Simpson, Patricia. *Marguerite Bourgeoys and Montreal, 1640–1665.* Montreal and Kingston: McGill-Queen's University Press, 1997.

Trudel, Marcel. *Montréal: la formation d'une société, 1642–1663.* Montreal: Fides, 1976.

Verney, Jack. "La Folleville's Place: Low Life in the Cabarets of Old Montreal." *Beaver [Canada]* 76, Number 5 (1996): 24–27.

British Era (1761–1866)

Beaudoin, Philippe. "Quelques observations sur les mariages irlandais dans la paroisse Notre-Dame de Montréal, 1840–1861." *Canadian Ethnic Studies* 30, Number 1 (1998): 140–157.

Bélisle, Jean. "Une résidence oubliée: la maison de Louis-Hippolite Lafontaine." *Journal of Canadian Art History* 20, Numbers 1–2 (1999): 46–67.

Black, Robert Merrill. "Anglicans and French-Canadian Evangelism." *Journal of the Canadian Church Historical Society* 26, Number 1 (1984): 18–33.

Bradbury, Bettina, et al. "Property and Marriage: The Law and the Practice in Early Nineteenth-Century Montreal." *Social History [Canada]* 26, Number 51 (1993): 9–39.

Burgess, Joanne. "The Growth of a Craft Labour Force: Montreal Leather Artisans, 1815–1831." *Historical Papers [Canada]* (1988): 48–62.

Chausse, Gilles. *Jean-Jacques Lartigue, premier evêque de Montréal.* Montreal: Fides, 1980.

Collison, Gary. "'Loyal and Dutiful Subjects of Her Gracious Majesty, Queen Victoria': Fugitive Slaves in Montreal, 1850–1866." *Quebec Studies [Canada]* 19 (1994–1995): 59–70.

Courville, Serge. "Le marché des 'subsistances': l'exemple de la plaine de Montréal au début des années 1830: une perspective géographique." *Revue d'histoire de l'Amérique française [Canada]* 42, Number 2 (1988): 193–239.

Courville, Serge, editor. *Paroisses et municipalités de la région de Montréal au XIXe siècle, 1825–1861.* Quebec City: Presses de l'Université Laval, 1988.

Coutu, Joan. "Philanthropy and Propaganda: The Bust of George III in Montreal." *Canadian Art Review* 19, Numbers 1–2 (1992): 59–67.

Dansereau, Bernard. "La fabrication des caractères d'imprimerie à Montréal au milieu du XIXe siècle." *Revue d'histoire de l'Amérique française [Canada]* 47, Number 1 (1993): 83–92.

Dufour, Andrée. "Diversité institutionelle et fréquentation scolaire dans l'Île de Montréal en 1825 et en 1835." *Revue d'histoire de l'Amérique française [Canada]* 41, Number 4 (1988): 507–535.

Epstein, Clarence. "Early Protestant Church Architecture in Montreal." *British Journal of Canadian Studies [UK]* 10, Number 2 (1995): 258–270.

Frost, Stanley Brice. *James McGill of Montreal.* Montreal and Kingston: McGill-Queen's University Press, 1995.

Gagnon-Pratte, France. "Parenté et migration: les cas des canadiens françaises à Montréal entre 1845 et 1875." *Historical Papers [Canada]* 1988: 63–85.

Hamilton, Gillian. "The Market for Montreal Apprentices: Contract Length and Information." *Explorations in Economic History* 33, Number 4 (1996): 496–523.

Lamonde, Yvan. "La sociabilité et l'histoire socio-culturelle: le cas de Montréal, 1760–1880." *Historical Papers [Canada]* 1987: 86–111.

Mackey, Frank. *Steamboat Connections: Montreal to Upper Canada, 1816–1843.* Montreal and Kingston: McGill-Queen's University Press, 2000.

Massicotte, Daniel. "Dynamique de croissance et de changement à Montréal de 1792 à 1819: le passage de la ville préindustrielle à la ville industrielle." *Urban History Review [Canada]* 28, Number 1 (1999): 14–30.

———. "Le marché immobilier locatif à Montréal, 1731–1831: méthodologie d'une enquête à partir des baux notariés." *Histoire et Mesure [France]* 14, Numbers 3–4 (1999): 299–330.

Mayers, Adam. "Montreal's Posh Rebel Rendezvous." *Civil War Times Illustrated* 31, Number 6 (1993): 44–46 and 74.

McCulloch, Michael. "'Dr. Tumblety, the Indian Herb Doctor': Politics, Professionalism, and Abortion in Mid-Nineteenth-Century Montreal." *Canadian Bulletin of Medical History* 10, Number 1 (1993): 49–66.

Monet, Jacques. "La Crise Metcalfe and the Montreal Election, 1843–1844." *Canadian Historical Review* 44, Number 1 (1963): 1–19.

Olson, Sherry. "Occupations and Residential Spaces in Nineteenth-Century Montreal." *Historical Methods* 22, Number 3 (1989): 81–96.

Podruchny, Carolyn. "Unfair Masters and Rascally Servants? Labour Relations among Bourgeois, Clerks and Voyageurs in the Montreal Fur Trade, 1780–1821." *Labour [Canada]* 43 (1999): 43–70.

Ruddel, David-Thiery. "Consumer Trends, Clothing, Textiles and Equipment in the Montreal Area, 1792–1835." *Material History Bulletin [Canada]* 32 (1990): 45–64.

Ruston, Guy J. "Commissioner Thompson's Bizarre War Was Nearly Laughable—Up to a Recently Revealed Point." *Military History* 10, Number 6 (1993): 8 and 79–82.

Senior, Elinor. "The British Garrison in Montreal in the 1840's." *Journal of the Society for Army Historical Research [UK]* 52, Number 210 (1974): 111–127.

Sweeny, Robert C. H., and Grace Laing Hogg. "Land and People: Property Investment in Late Pre-Industrial Montreal." *Urban History Review [Canada]* 24, Number 1 (1995): 42–51.

Thornton, Patricia A., and Sherry Olson. "Family Contexts of Fertility and Infant Survival in Nineteenth-Century Montreal." *Journal of Family History* 16, Number 4 (1991): 401–417.

Young, Brian. *George-Etienne Cartier: Montreal Bourgeois.* Montreal and Kingston: McGill-Queen's University Press, 1981.

Early Canadian Era (1867–1920)

Bliss, Michael. "'Something Terrible': The Odour of Contagion, Montreal 1885." *Beaver [Canada]* 71, Number 6 (1991–1992): 6–13.

Boone, Christopher G. "Language Politics and Flood Control in Nineteenth-Century Montreal." *Environmental History* 1, Number 3 (1996): 70–85.

———. "The Politics of Transportation Services in Suburban Montreal: Sorting Out the 'Mile End Muddle', 1893–1909." *Urban History Review [Canada]* 24, Number 2 (1996): 25–39.

———. "Private Initiatives to Make Flood Control Public: The St. Gabriel Levee and Railway Company in Montreal, 1886–1890." *Historical Geography* 25 (1997): 100–112.

Brault, Jean-Rémi, compiler. *Montréal au XIXe siècle: des gens, des idées, des arts, un ville.* Montreal: Leméac, 1990.

Burley, David G. "The Senator, the Merchant, Two Carpenters, and a Widow: A Survey of Canadian Landlords in 1871." *Urban History Review [Canada]* 25, Number 2 (1997): 5–18.

Collin, Jean-Pierre. "Crise du logement et action catholique à Montréal, 1940–1960." *Revue d'histoire de l'Amérique française [Canada]* 41, Number 2 (1987): 179–203.

Collin, Johanne. "Entre discours et pratiques: les médecins montréalais face à la thérapeutique, 1869–1890." *Revue d'histoire de l'Amérique française [Canada]* 53, Number 1 (1999): 61–92.

Collin, Johanne, and Laurence Monnais-Rousselot. "La communauté médical montréalaise de 1850 à 1890: variations sur la thème d'élite." *Social History [Canada]* 32, Number 64 (1999): 173–207.

Curtis, Bruce. "Expert Knowledge and the Social Imaginary: The Case of the Montreal Check Census." *Social History [Canada]* 28, Number 56 (1995): 313–331.

Dagenais, Michèle. "Vie culturelle et pouvoirs publics locaux: la fondation de la Bibliothèque Municipale de Montréal." *Urban History Review [Canada]* 24, Number 2 (1996): 40–56.

Fougères, Dany. "Les services urbains sous surveillance politique: le pouvoir municipale et l'établissement du service de transport en commun à Montréal, 1860–1880." *Urban History Review [Canada]* 26, Number 1 (1997): 18–31.

Gagnon, Hervé. "Les musées accessibles au public à Montréal au XIXe siècle: capitalisme culturel et idéal national." *Historical Reflections* 22, Number 2 (1996): 351–387.

Gagnon-Pratte, France. *Maisons de campagne des montréalais, 1892–1924: l'architecture des frères Maxwell.* Montreal: Méridien, 1987.

Gilliland, Jason A. "Modeling Residential Mobility in Montreal, 1860–1900." *Historical Methods* 31, Number 1 (1998): 27–42.

Gilliland, Jason A., and Sherry Olson. "Claims on Housing Space in Nineteenth-Century Montreal." *Urban History Review [Canada]* 26, Number 2 (1998): 3–16.

Gordon, Alan. "Ward Heelers and Honest Men: Urban Quebecois Political Culture and the Montreal Reform of 1909." *Urban History Review [Canada]* 23, Number 2 (1995): 20–32.

Gournay, Isabelle, and France Vanlaethem, editors. *Montréal métropole, 1880–1930.* Montreal: Boréal, 1998.

Knott, Leonard L. *Montreal, 1900–1930: A Nostalgic Look at the Way It Used to Be.* Toronto: Nelson, Foster and Scott, 1976.

Lamonde, Yvan, and Raymond Montpetit. *Le parc Sohmer de Montréal, 1889–1919: un lieu populaire de culture urbaine.* Quebec City: Institut Québécoise de Recherche sur la Culture, 1986.

Legault, Réjean. "Architecture et forme urbaine: l'exemple du triplex à Montréal de 1870 à 1914." *Urban History Review [Canada]* 18, Number 1 (1989): 1–10.

Lessard, Michel, editor. *Montréal, métropole du Québec: images oubliées de la vie quotidienne, 1852–1910.* Montreal: Homme, 1992.

Levine, Gregory J. "Class, Ethnicity and Property Transfers in Montreal, 1907–1909." *Journal of Historical Geography [UK]* 14, Number 4 (1988): 360–380.

Lewis, Robert D. *Manufacturing Montreal: The Making of an Industrial Landscape, 1850 to 1930.* Baltimore: Johns Hopkins University Press, 2000.

Linteau, Paul-André. "Le personnel politique de Montréal, 1880–1914: évolution d'une élite municipale." *Revue d'histoire de l'Amérique française [Canada]* 52, Number 2 (1998): 189–215.

Marquis, Dominique. "Une élite mal connue: les avocats dans la société montréalaise au tournant du XXe siècle." *Recherches sociographiques [Canada]* 36, Number 2 (1995): 307–325.

McCann, L. D. "Planning and Building the Corporate Suburb of Mount Royal, 1910–1925." *Planning Perspectives [UK]* 11, Number 3 (1996): 259–301.

McElroy, George E. "High Life and Low Life in Edwardian Montreal." *Beaver [Canada]* 72, Number 1 (1992): 23–28.

Miller, Carman. "The Montreal Militia as a Social Institution before World War I." *Urban History Review [Canada]* 19, Numbers 1–2 (1990): 57–64.

Morrow, Don. "The Knights of the Snowshoe: A Study of the Evolution of Sport in Nineteenth Century Montreal." *Journal of Sport History* 15, Number 1 (1988): 5–40.

———. "Frozen Festivals: Ceremony and the *Carnaval* in the Montreal Winter Carnivals, 1883–1889." *Sport History Review [Canada]* 27, Number 2 (1996): 173–190.

Myers, Tamara. "Women Policing Women: A Patrol Woman in Montreal in the 1910s." *Journal of the Canadian Historical Association* 4 (1993): 229–245.

———. "The Voluntary Delinquent: Parents, Daughters, and the Montreal Juvenile Delinquents' Court in 1918." *Canadian Historical Review* 80, Number 2 (1999): 242–268.

Neilson, Rick. "The Montreal Transportation Company." *Freshwater [Canada]* 4 (1989): 21–24.

Osborne, Brian S. "Constructing Landscapes of Power: The George Etienne Cartier Monument, Montreal." *Journal of Historical Geography [UK]* 24, Number 4 (1998): 431–458.

Poitras, Claire. "Sûreté, salubrité et monolithisme: l'introduction du béton armé à Montréal, de 1905 à 1922." *Urban History Review [Canada]* 25, Number 1 (1996): 19–35.

———. "Construire les infrastructures d'approvisionnement en eau en banlieue montréalaise au tournant du XXe siècle: le cas de Saint-Louis." *Revue d'histoire de l'Amérique française [Canada]* 52, Number 4 (1999): 507–531.

Ramirez, Bruno. *Les premiers italiens de Montréal: l'origine de la Petite Italie du Québec.* Montreal: Boréal Express, 1984.

Remillard, François, and Brian Merrett. *Demeures bourgeoises de Montréal: le Mille Carré Doré, 1850–1930.* Montreal: Méridien, 1986.

Sancton, Andrew. *Governing the Island of Montreal: Language Difference and Metropolitan Politics.* Berkeley: University of California Press, 1985.

Slack, Brian, et al. "Mapping the Changes: The Spatial Development of Industrial Montreal, 1861–1929." *Urban History Review [Canada]* 22, Number 2 (1994): 97–112.

Tremblay, Pierre, and André Normandeau. "L'économie pénale de la société montréalaise, 1845–1913." *Social History [Canada]* 19, Number 37 (1986): 177–199.

Vigneault, Michel. "La diffusion du hockey à Montréal, 1895–1910." *Canadian Journal of History of Sport* 17, Number 1 (1986): 60–74.

Westley, Margaret W. *Remembrance of Grandeur: The Anglo-Protestant Elite of Montreal, 1900–1950.* Montreal: Libre Expression, 1990.

Modern Era (1921–Present)

Agen, Marie Catherine. "The Politics of the *Société Saint-Jean-Baptiste de Montréal.*" *American Review of Canadian Studies* 29, Number 3 (1999): 495–510.

Baillargeon, Denyse. "Gouttes de lait et soif de pouvoir: les dessous de la lutte contre la mortalité infantile à Montréal, 1910–1953." *Canadian Bulletin of Medical History* 15, Number 1 (1998): 27–57.

Beaudet, Gérard. "Domaines 'vides' et structuration morphologique de l'agglomération montréalaise." *Cahiers de géographie du Québec [Canada]* 41, Number 112 (1997): 7–29.

Billard, Jules B. "Montreal Greets the World." *National Geographic* 131, Number 5 (May 1967): 600–621.

Bourassa, Guy, and Jacques Leveille, editors. *Le système politique de Montréal.* Montreal: Cahiers de l'Acfas, 1986.

Bussière, Yves. "L'automobile et l'expansion des banlieues: le cas de Montréal, 1901–2001." *Urban History Review [Canada]* 18, Number 2 (1989): 159–165.

Choko, Marc H. "La 'Boom' des immeubles d'appartements à Montréal de 1921 à 1951." *Urban History Review [Canada]* 23 (1994): 3–18.

———. "Ethnicity and Home Ownership in Montreal, 1921–1951." *Urban History Review [Canada]* 26, Number 2 (1998): 32–41.

Choko, Marc H., Jean-Pierre Collin, and Annick Germain. "Le logement et les enjeux de la transformation de l'espace urbain: Montréal, 1940–1960." *Urban History Review [Canada]* 15, Number 2 (1986): 127–136 and Number 3 (1987): 243–253.

Collin, Jean-Pierre. "City Management and the Emerging Welfare State: Evolution of City Budgets and Civic Responsibilities in Montreal, 1931–1951." *Journal of Policy History* 9, Number 3 (1997): 339–357.

———. "A Housing Model for Lower- and Middle-Class Wage Earners in a Montreal Suburb: Saint-Léonard, 1955–1967." *Journal of Urban History* 24, Number 4 (May 1998): 468–490.

De Bonville, Jean. *Les quotidiens montréalais de 1945 à 1985: morphologie et contenu.* Quebec City: Institut Québécois de Recherche sur la Culture, 1995.

Fahrni, Magda. "The Romance of Reunion: Montreal War Veterans Return to Family Life, 1944–1949." *Journal of the Canadian Historical Association* 9 (1998): 187–208.

Forget, Madeleine. *Les gratte-ciel de Montréal.* Montreal: Méridien, 1990.

Hamel, Pierre. "Mouvements urbains et modernité: l'exemple montréalais." *Recherches sociographiques [Canada]* 36, Number 2 (1995): 279–305.

Hamilton, Janice. "Caughnawaga Perseveres: Forging a Renewed Mohawk Nation in the Shadow of Montreal." *Canadian Geographic* 106, Number 5 (1986): 36–45.

Johnston, David. "The Metamorphosis of Balconville." *Canadian Heritage* 12, Number 2 (1986): 25–31.

Lacasse, Danielle. *La prostitution féminine à Montréal, 1945–1970.* Montreal: Boréal, 1994.

Lanken, Dane. "Drapeau's Montreal: Great Moments, Moun-ments . . . and Excesses." *Canadian Geographic* 106, Number 4 (1986): 10–15 and 18–23.

Lavigne, Gilles, et al. "L'ethnicisation de l'établissement humain en Amérique du Nord: l'exemple du quartier por-tugais à Montréal." *Cahiers de géographie du Québec [Canada]* 39, Number 108 (1995): 417–443.

Lee, Douglas B. "Montreal: Spirited Heart of French Canada." *National Geographic* 179, Number 3 (March 1991): 60–85.

Lessard, Michel, editor. *Montréal au XXe siècle: regards des photographes.* Montreal: Homme, 1995.

Levesque, Robert, and Robert Migner. *Les boss politiques à Montréal: Camillien et les années vingt, suivi de Camillien au goulag: cartographie du houdisme.* Montreal: Brûlés, 1979.

Levine, Marc V. *The Reconquest of Montreal: Language Policy and Social Change in a Bilingual City.* Philadelphia: Temple University Press, 1990.

Macintosh, Donald, et al. "Trudeau, Taiwan, and the 1976 Montreal Olympics." *American Review of Canadian Studies* 21, Number 4 (1991): 423–448.

MacLennan, Anne. "Charity and Change: Montreal English Protestant Charity Faces the Crisis of Depression." *Urban History Review [Canada]* 16, Number 1 (1987): 1–16.

Marois, Claude. "Caractéristiques des changements du paysage urbain dans la ville de Montréal." *Annales de géographie [France]* 98, Number 548 (1989): 385–402.

Morin, Richard. *Réanimation urbaine et pouvoir local: les stratégies des municipalités de Montréal, Sherbrooke et Grenoble en quartiers anciens.* Montreal: Presses de l'Université du Québec for the INRS-Urbanisation, 1987.

Post, Paul V. "Origins of the Montreal Expos." *Baseball Research Journal* 22 (1993): 107–110.

Pothier, Louise, editor. *L'eau, l'hygiène publique, et les infra-structures.* Montreal: Groupe PGV, 1996.

Veilleux, Denis. "Buses, Tramways, and Monopolies: The Introduction of Motor Vehicles into Montreal's Public Transport Network." *Michigan Historical Review* 22, Number 2 (1996): 103–126.

Whelan, Robert K. "The Politics of Urban Redevelopment in Montreal: Regime Change from Drapeau to Dore." *Quebec Studies [Canada]* 12 (1991): 155–169.

General Works

Allard, Michel, et al. *L'Hôtel-Dieu de Montréal, 1642–1973.* Montreal: Hurtubise, 1973.

Brown, Michael. *Jew or Juif? Jews, French Canadians, and Anglo Canadians, 1759–1914.* Philadelphia: Jewish Publishing Society, 1987.

Burgess, Joanne, et al. *Clés pour l'histoire de Montréal: bibliographie.* Montreal: Boréal, 1992.

Choko, Marc H. *Les grandes places publiques de Montréal.* Montreal: Méridien, 1987.

Cinq-Mars, Jean. *Histoire du Collège Sainte-Marie de Montréal, 1848–1969.* Montreal: Hurtubise, 1998.

Debarbieux, Bernard, and Claude Marois. "Le Mont Royal: forme naturelle, paysages et territorialités urbaines."

Cahiers de géographie du Québec [Canada] 41, Number 113 (1997): 171–197.

Demchinsky, Bryan. *Montreal, Then and Now: The Photographic Record of a Changing City.* Montreal: The Gazette, 1985.

D'Iberville-Moreau, Luc. *Lost Montreal.* Toronto: Oxford University Press, 1975.

Drummond, Nichael. *Montreal and Its Countryside.* Toronto: Oxford University Press, 1979.

———. *Montreal.* Toronto: McClelland and Stewart, 1990.

Duquette, Jean-Pierre. *Montréal, 1642–1992.* Ville LaSalle, Ontario: Hurtubise, 1992.

Goulet, Denis, et al. *Histoire de l'Hôpital Notre-Dame de Montréal, 1880–1980.* Montreal: VLB for the "Etudes Québécoises" Series, 1993.

Helly, Denise. *Les chinois à Montréal, 1877–1951.* Quebec City: Institut Québécoise de Recherche sur la Culture, 1987.

Higgins, Benjamin. *The Rise and Fall of Montreal: A Case Study of Urban Growth, Regional Economic Expansion and National Development.* Moncton, NB: Canadian Institute for Research on Regional Development, 1986.

Lamonde, Yvan. *La librairie et l'édition à Montréal, 1776–1920.* Montreal: Bibliothèque Nationale du Québec, 1991.

Linteau, Paul-André. *Histoire de Montréal depuis la Confédération.* Montreal: Boréal, 1992.

Marsan, Jean-Claude. *Montreal in Evolution: Historical Analysis of the Development of Montreal's Architecture and Urban Environment.* Montreal and Kingston: McGill-Queen's University Press, 1981.

Michaud, Josette. *Les oeuvres du temps: le Vieux-Montréal.* Montreal: Guerin, 1991.

Montréal: activités, habitants, quartiers. Montreal: Fides for the Société Historique, 1984.

Montreal in Halftone. Grand Rapids, MI: James Bayne Company for W. J. Clarke of Mount Royal Park, ca. 1900–1910.

Montreal's Century: A Record of the News and People Who Shaped the City in the 20th Century. Montreal: The Gazette, Trecarré and Journal of Montreal, 1999.

Pinard, Guy. *Montréal: son histoire, son architecture.* Montreal: La Presse, 1987.

Prévost, Robert. *Montréal: A History.* Toronto: McClelland and Stewart, 1993 translation by Elizabeth Mueller and Robert Chodos of 1991 French original *Montréal: la folle enterprise* published in Montreal by Alain Stanké.

Robert, Jean-Claude. *Atlas historique de Montréal.* Montreal: Libre Expression, 1994.

Roberts, Leslie. *Montreal: From Mission Colony to World City.* Toronto: Macmillan, 1969.

Terry, Neville. *The Royal Vic: The Story of Montreal's Royal Victoria Hospital, 1894–1994.* Montreal and Kingston: McGill-Queen's University Press, 1995.

Toker, Franklin. *The Church of Notre-Dame in Montreal: An Architectural History.* Montreal and Kingston: McGill-Queen's University Press, 1991 reprint of 1970 original.

Waller, Adrian. "Putting Up at the Ritz." *Canadian Heritage* 12, Number 3 (1986): 18–23.

Williams, Dorothy W. *Blacks in Montreal, 1628–1986: An Urban Demography.* Cowansville, Quebec: Yvon Blais, 1989.

Wolfe, Joshua. *Discover Montreal: An Architectural and Historical Guide.* Montreal: Libre Expression, 1991.

Quebec City
French Era (1535–1758)

Baillargeon, Noel. *Le séminaire de Québec sous l'épiscopat de Mgr de Laval.* Quebec City: Université de Laval, 1972.

Brisson, Réal. *La charpenterie navale à Québec sous le régime français.* Quebec City: Institut Québécois de Recherche sur la Culture, 1983.

Campeau, Lucien. *L'Évêché de Québec, 1694.* Quebec City: Société historique de Québec, 1974.

Charbonneau, André. *The Model of Quebec.* Ottawa: Booklet Number 1 of the "Fortifications of Quebec" Series published by Parks Canada, 1981.

Charbonneau, André, Yvon Desloges, and Marc Lafrance. *Québec: ville fortifiée du XVIIe au XIXe siècle.* Quebec City: Éditions du Pélican and Parks Canada, 1982.

Chénier, Rémi. *Québec: A French Colonial Town in America, 1660 to 1690.* Ottawa: Environment Canada Parks Service, 1991.

D'Allaire, Micheline. *L'hôpital-général de Québec, 1692–1764.* Montreal: Fides, 1971.

Dubé, D., and M. Lacombe. *Inventaire des marchés de construction des Archives nationales à Québec, XVIIe et XVIIIe siècles.* Ottawa: Parks Canada, 1977.

Gauvreau, Danielle. *Québec: une ville et sa population au temps de la Nouvelle-France.* Sillery: Presses de l'Université de Québec, 1991.

Graham, Gerald Sanford, editor. *The Walker Expedition to Quebec, 1711.* Toronto: Champlain Society, 1953.

Lacamp, Olivier, et al. "Quelques caractéristiques des ménages de la ville de Québec entre 1666 et 1716." *Histoire sociale* 23 (1979): 66–78.

LeBlant, Robert. "Les prémices de la fondation de Québec, 1607–1608." *Revue d'histoire de l'Amérique française [Canada]* 20, Number 1 (1966): 44–55.

Léonidoff, G. P. "L'habitat de bois en Nouvelle-France: son importance et ses techniques de construction." *Bulletin d'histoire de la culture matérielle [Canada]* (spring 1982): 13–40.

Mathieu, Jacques. *La construction navale royale à Québec, 1739–1759.* Quebec City: Société historique de Québec, 1971.

Portraits du site et de l'habitat de Place Royale sous le régime français, 1608–1760. Quebec City: Ministère des affaires culturelles, 1984, two volumes.

Rousseau, François. *L'oeuvre de chère en Nouvelle-France: le régime des malades à l'Hôtel-Dieu de Québéc.* Quebec City: Université de Laval, 1983.

Early Maps and Depictions of Quebec City, 1608–1761

Woodcut from an original drawing by Samuel de Champlain, depicting his *Abitation de Quebecq* or "Quebec Residence," built in 1608—published five years later in Paris as part of *Les voyages du Sieur de Champlain,* numerous sources

Accurate hand-drawn map of the town in 1660, by Jean Bourdon—original held by the Archives Nationales in France, plus a copy at the National Archives of Canada (reproduction number: C 15801)

Crude panorama of Quebec as seen from the east, late seventeenth century—original held by the Service Historique de la Marine, at Vincennes in France

Map of the town, ca. 1709, published 35 years later in Pierre-François-Xavier Charlevoix's *Histoire et description générale de la Nouvelle-France*—numerous sources, including the National Archives of Canada (reproduction number: C 42246)

Panoramic view of the town from its opposite shoreline, ca. 1720–1730, engraved in Paris by Chereau—numerous sources, including the National Archives of Canada (reproduction number: C 42)

Panoramic view of the town, engraved in Amsterdam by J. Covens and C. Mortier after an original drawing by J. Condet—published in 1741 as part of *A Map of the British Empire in America,* numerous sources

Map by the royal military engineer Gaspard-Joseph Chaussegros de Léry, depicting the progress on his seven-year upgrade of the town circuit, 1752—original held by the Archives Nationales in France, plus a copy at the National Archives of Canada (reproduction number: C 21779)

Map of the city and its adjacent waterways, published in London in January 1759 by E. Oakley—numerous sources

Two oil paintings by Samuel Scott of French fireships attacking the English fleet anchored off Quebec, 28 June 1759—originals held by the National Maritime Museum at Greenwich, England (reproduction numbers: BHC 0391 and BHC 0393)

Two oil paintings by Dominique Serres the Elder of French fireships attacking the English fleet off Quebec, 28 June 1759—originals held by the National Maritime Museum at Greenwich, England (reproduction numbers: BHC 0392 and BHC 0394)

Oil painting by Francis Swain of the town's bombardment as seen "from the Bason [*sic:* Basin]," based upon an eyewitness drawing by Capt. Hervey Smyth, July–August 1759, then engraved two years later in London by Pierre-Charles Canot to be published by John Bowles—numerous sources

"A Plan of the City of Quebec, the Capital of Canada," plus "An Authentic Plan" of the British siege operations that culminated in its capture, September 1759, both engraved from eyewitness drawings by Capt. Hervey Smyth and published the next January in London in Thomas Jefferys's *The Natural and Civil History of the French Dominions*—numerous sources, including the National Archives of Canada (reproduction number: C 21859)

Panorama of the surrendered city as seen from Point-des-Pères opposite, engraved by Peter Paul Benazech from an eyewitness drawing by Capt. Hervey Smyth, published by Thomas Jefferys in November 1760—numerous sources

Panorama from Pointe-de-Lévis as British boat parties were rowed across toward the surrendered city in September 1759, engraved two years later by Pierre-Charles Canot from an eyewitness drawing by Richard Short, for sale by Thomas Jefferys—numerous sources, including the Metropolitan Toronto Reference Library (call number: T 15732)

Depiction of the badly damaged "Church of Notre Dame de la Victoire [*sic:* des Victoires]" in the Lower Town, engraved by Antoine Benoist from an eyewitness drawing by Richard Short for sale by Thomas Jefferys, September 1761—numerous sources, including the Metropolitan Toronto Reference Library (call number: T 15741)

View of the ruins around the quadrangular Bishop's House "as they appear in going up the Hill from the Lower, to the Upper Town," engraved by Antoine Benoist from an eyewitness drawing by Richard Short for sale by Thomas Jefferys, September 1761—numerous sources, including the Metropolitan Toronto Reference Library (call number: T 31155)

Depiction of the Bishop's House and "the Ruins as they appear in going down the Hill, from the Upper to the Lower Town," engraved by John Fougeron from an eyewitness drawing by Richard Short for sale by Thomas Jefferys, September 1761—numerous sources, including the Metropolitan Toronto Reference Library (call number: T 15734)

View "taken from the Gate of the Governors House [*i.e.,* Château Saint-Louis]," of British troops on parade in the *Place d'Armes* or "Main Square" before the damaged Récollet church and college, with the burnt cathedral shell visible at far right, engraved by Pierre-Charles Canot from an eyewitness drawing by Richard Short for sale by Thomas Jefferys, September 1761—numerous sources, including the National Archives of Canada (call number: C 361) and Metropolitan Toronto Reference Library (call number: T 15745)

View of shrapnel damage to the slate-roofed Jesuit church and its three-storied college, engraved by Charles Grignion from an eyewitness drawing by Richard Short for sale by Thomas Jefferys, September 1761—numerous sources, including the Metropolitan Toronto Reference Library (call number: T 15742)

Detailed view of the damaged interior of the Jesuit church, engraved by Anthony Walker from an eyewitness drawing by Richard Short for sale by Thomas Jefferys, September 1761—numerous sources, including the Metropolitan Toronto Reference Library (call number: T 15743)

Detailed view of the damaged wood-lined interior of the Récollet church, engraved by Charles Grignion from an eyewitness drawing by Richard Short for sale by Thomas Jefferys, September 1761—numerous sources, including the Metropolitan Toronto Reference Library

View of the damaged Treasury and Jesuit college, engraved by Charles Grignion from an eyewitness drawing by Richard Short for sale by Thomas Jefferys, September 1761—numerous sources, including the Metropolitan Toronto Reference Library (call number: T 30421)

View "taken from the Ramparts" on the city's western side, looking over the Orphan's or Urseline Nunnery across Quebec toward the distant Saint Lawrence River, engraved by James Mason from an eyewitness drawing by Richard Short for sale by Thomas Jefferys, September 1761—numerous sources, including the Metropolitan Toronto Reference Library (call number: T 15735)

Depiction of the Intendant's Palace on the city's northern side, engraved by William Elliott from an eyewitness drawing by Richard Short for sale by Thomas Jefferys, September 1761—numerous sources, including the Metropolitan Toronto Reference Library (call number: T 15744)

Panorama of the northwestern section of the city, including the Intendant's Palace and Hospital, as seen "from St. Charles's River" and engraved by Peter Paul Benazech from an eyewitness drawing by Richard Short for sale by Thomas Jefferys, September 1761—numerous sources, including the Metropolitan Toronto Reference Library (call number: T 15733)

Colored manuscript copy of a city map, "enlarged from Bellin's Plan with additions," ca. 1761, by the British military engineer Patrick Mackellar—numerous sources,

including the Metropolitan Toronto Reference Library (call number: JRR 912.71447.B25)

British Era (1759–1866)

Bastien, G., et al. *Inventaire des marchés de construction des archives civiles de Québec, 1800–1875.* Ottawa: Parks Canada, 1975, three volumes.

Bervin, Georges. "Aperçu sur le commerce et le crédit à Québec, 1820–1830." *Revue d'histoire de l'Amérique française [Canada]* 36, Number 4 (1983): 527–533.

———. "Environnement matériel et activités économiques des conseillers exécutifs et législatifs à Québec, 1810–1830." *Bulletin d'histoire de la culture matérielle [Canada]* 17 (1983): 45–62.

Brooke, Frances. *The History of Emily Montague.* Ottawa: Carleton University Press, 1985 re-edition of 1769 London original.

Cameron, Christina, and Jean Trudel. *Québec au temps de James Patterson Cockburn.* Quebec City: Garneau, 1976.

Chartrand, René. *Quebec 1759.* London: Osprey, 1999.

Dagneau, George-H., editor. *Québec, 1800–1835.* Quebec City: Société historique de Québec, 1977.

Dahl, Edward H., et al. *La ville de Québec, 1800–1850: un inventaire des cartes et plans.* Ottawa: Number 13 of "Collection Mercure" issued by the National Museum of Man, 1975.

Dechêne, Louise. "Les entreprises de William Price, 1810–1850." *Histoire sociale* (April 1968): 16–52.

———. "La rente du faubourg Saint-Roch à Québec, 1750–1850." *Revue d'histoire de l'Amérique française [Canada]* 34, Number 4 (1981): 569–596.

Dionne, Hélène. *Contrats de mariage à Québec, 1790–1812.* Ottawa: Number 29 of "Collection Mercure" issued by the National Museum of Man, 1980.

Dufour, Pierre. "La construction navale à Québec, 1760–1825: sources inexplorées et nouvelles perspectives de recherches." *Revue d'histoire de l'Amérique française [Canada]* 34, Number 2 (1981): 231–251.

Hardy, Jean-Pierre. "Niveaux de richesse et intérieurs domestiques dans le quartier Saint-Roch à Québec, 1820–1830." *Bulletin d'histoire de la culture matérielle [Canada]* 17 (1983): 63–94.

Hare, John. "La population de la ville de Québec, 1795–1805." *Histoire sociale* 7 (1974): 23–47.

Harper, J. Russell. *Krieghoff.* University of Toronto Press, 1979.

May, Robin. *Wolfe's Army.* London: Osprey, 1974.

McCulloch, Michael Ernest. "The Defeat of Imperial Urbanism in Quebec City, 1840–1855." *Urban History Review [Canada]* 22, Number 1 (1993): 17–29.

Muller, H. N. "Floating a Lumber Raft to Quebec City, 1805: The Journal of Guy Catlin of Burlington." *Vermont History* 39, Number 2 (1971): 116–124.

Pearson, Michael. "The Siege of Quebec, 1775–1776." *American Heritage* 23, Number 2 (February 1972): 8–15 and 104–108.

Roche, John F. "Quebec under Siege, 1775–1776: The Memorandums of Jacob Danford." *Canadian Historical Review* 50, Number 1 (1969): 68–85.

Ruddel, David-Thiery. "The Domestic Textile Industry in the Region and City of Quebec, 1792–1835." *Bulletin d'histoire de la culture matérielle [Canada]* 17 (1983): 95–126.

———. *Quebec City, 1765–1832: The Evolution of a Colonial Town.* Hull, Quebec: Canadian Museum of Civilization, 1987.

Stacey, Charles Perry. *Quebec 1759: The Siege and the Battle.* Toronto: Macmillan, 1959.

Windrow, Martin. *Montcalm's Army.* London: Osprey, 1973.

Modern Era (1867–Present)

Bland, John. "Preservation and Restoration of Quebec." *Historic Preservation* 16, Number 5 (1964): 190–194.

Brazeau, Diane. "Le role de Gérard Thibault dans le divertissement populaire urbaine à Québec." *Canadian Folklore* 16, Number 1 (1994): 149–156.

Faucher, Albert. "The Decline of the Shipbuilding at Quebec in the Nineteenth Century." *Canadian Journal of Economics and Political Science* 23, Number 2 (1957): 195–215.

Filion, Pierre. "Core Redevelopment, Neighbourhood Revitalization, and Municipal Government Motivation: Twenty Years of Urban Renewal in Quebec City." *Canadian Journal of Political Science* 20, Number 1 (1987): 131–147.

Gilbert, Anne. "Villes, représentations collectives de l'espace et l'identité québécoise." *Cahiers de géographie du Québec* 29, Number 78 (1985): 365–381.

Hulbert, François. *Essai de géopolitique urbaine et régionale: la comédie urbaine de Québec.* Montreal: Meridien, 1994.

Lemelin, André. "Le déclin du port de Québec et la reconversion à la fin du XIXe siècle: une évaluation de la pertinence de l'hypothèse du staple." *Recherches sociographiques* 22, Number 2 (1981): 155–186.

Provost, Honorius. *Notre-Dame-de-la-Garde de Québec, 1877–1977.* Quebec City: Société historique de Québec, 1977.

Rudin, Ronald. "Boosting the French Canadian Town: Municipal Government and Urban Growth in Quebec, 1850–1900." *Urban History Review [Canada]* 11, Number 1 (1982): 1–10.

Sarny, Dominique. "Apprivoiser la ville: le cas des ouvrières de Dominion Corset." *Canadian Folklore* 16, Number 1 (1994): 73–84.

Villeneuve, Paul Y. "Changement social et pouvoir municipal à Québec." *Cahiers de géographie du Québec* 26, Number 68 (1982): 223–233.

General Works

Beaudet, Pierre, editor. *Under the Boardwalk in Québec City: Archaeology in the Courtyard and Gardens of the Château Saint-Louis.* Montreal: Guernica and Septentrion, 1990.

Bergeron, Yves. "Les premieres places de marché au Québec." *Material History Review [Canada]* 35 (1992): 21–34.

Brown, Clément. *Québec: croissance d'une ville.* Quebec City: Presses de l'Université Laval, 1952.

Cameron, Christina, and Monique Trépanier. *Vieux Québec: son architecture intérieure.* Ottawa: Number 40 of "Collection Mercure" published by the National Museum of Man and Parks Canada, 1986.

Cestre, Gilbert. "Québec: évolution des limites municipales depuis 1831–1832." *Cahiers de géographie du Québec* 20, Number 51 (1976): 561–567.

Duval, André. *Québec romantique.* Montreal: Boréal Express, 1978.

———. *La capitale.* Montreal: Boréal Express, 1979.

Hare, John, et al. *Histoire de la ville de Québec, 1608–1871.* Montreal: Boréal and the Canadian Museum of Civilizations, 1987.

La ville de Québec: histoire municipale. Quebec City: Société historique de Québec, 1960–1983, four volumes.

MacLeish, Kenneth. "Quebec: French City in an Anglo-Saxon World." *National Geographic* 139, Number 3 (March 1971): 416–442.

Nickens, Eddie. "City of Walls." *Historic Preservation* 46, Number 4 (1994): 16–19 and 89–90.

Noppen, Luc. *Notre-Dame de Québec: son architecture et son rayonnement.* Quebec City: Pélican, 1974.

Noppen, Luc, Claude Paulette, and Michel Tremblay. *Québec: trois siècles d'architecture.* Quebec City: Libre Expression, 1979.

Ouellet, Fernand. *Histoire de la Chambre de commerce de Québec, 1809–1959.* Quebec City: Université de Laval, 1959.

Richardson, A. J. H. "Guide to the Buildings in the Old City of Quebec." *Bulletin of the Association for Preservation Technology* 2, Numbers 3–4 (1970), 120 pp.

Rousseau, François. *La croix et le scalpel: histoire des augustines et de l'Hôtel-Dieu de Québec.* Quebec City: Septentrion, 1989.

Traquair, R. *The Old Architecture of Quebec.* Toronto: Macmillan, 1947.

Volpi, Charles Patrick de. *Québec, A Pictorial Record: Historical Prints and Illustrations of the City of Quebec.* Sherbrooke, Quebec: Longman Canada, 1971.

Toronto
Early History (1720–1903)
Armstrong, Frederick Henry. *A City in the Making: Progress, People, and Perils in Victorian Toronto.* Toronto: Dundurn, 1988.

Careless, J. M. S. *Toronto to 1918: An Illustrated History.* Toronto and Ottawa: James Lorimer and the Museum of Civilization, 1984.

Firth, Edith G. *The Town of York, 1793–1834.* Toronto, 1962–1966, two volumes.

Goheen, Peter G. *Victorian Toronto, 1850 to 1900: Pattern and Process of Growth.* University of Chicago Press, Department of Geography Research Paper Number 127, 1970.

Harney, Robert F. *Gathering Place: Peoples and Neighbourhoods of Toronto, 1834–1945.* Toronto: Multicultural History Society of Ontario, 1985.

Hounsom, Eric Wilfrid. *Toronto in 1810.* Toronto: Ryerson, 1970.

Illustrated Historical Atlas of the County of York. Toronto, 1969 reprint of 1878 original.

Kalbach, Warren E. *Historical and Generational Perspectives of Ethnic Residential Segregation in Toronto, 1851–1871.* Toronto: Centre for Urban and Community Studies, University of Toronto, 1980.

Kealey, Gregory S. *Toronto Workers Respond to Industrial Capitalism, 1867–1892.* Toronto, 1980.

Litvak, Marilyn M. *Edward James Lennox, "Builder of Toronto."* Toronto: Dundurn, 1995.

Martyn, Lucy Booth. *Toronto, 100 Years of Grandeur: The Inside Stories of Toronto's Great Homes and the People Who Lived There.* Toronto: Pagurian, 1978.

———. *Aristocratic Toronto: 19th Century Grandeur.* Toronto: Gage, 1980.

———. *The Face of Early Toronto: An Archival Record, 1797–1936.* Sutton West, Ontario: Paget, 1982.

———. *View of Original Toronto: The Fabric of York-Toronto, circa 1834.* Sutton West, Ontario: Paget, 1983.

Masters, Donald C. *The Rise of Toronto, 1850–1890.* University of Toronto Press, 1974.

Robinson, Percy James. *Toronto during the French Regime: A History of the Toronto Region from Brûlé to Simcoe.* University of Toronto Press, 1965.

Scadding, Henry. *Toronto of Old.* Toronto: Oxford University Press, 1966.

Volpi, Charles Patrick de. *Toronto: A Pictorial Record, 1813–1882.* Montreal, 1965.

Modern Era (1904–Present)
Arthur, Eric. *Toronto, No Mean City.* University of Toronto Press, 1974.

Bourne, Larry S. *Private Redevelopment of the Central City: Spatial Processes of Structural Changes in the City of Toronto.* Department of Geography, University of Chicago, 1967.

Burton, Lydia, and David Morley. "Neighborhood Survival in Toronto." *Landscape* 23 (1979): 3340.

Caulfield, John. *City Form and Everyday Life: Toronto's Gentrification and Critical Social Practice.* University of Toronto Press, 1994.

Colton, Timothy. *Big Daddy: Frederick C. Gardiner and the Building of Metropolitan Toronto.* University of Toronto Press, 1980.

Conniff, Richard. "Toronto." *National Geographic* 189, Number 6 (June 1996): 120–139.

Dennis, Richard. "Interpreting the Apartment House: Modernity and Metropolitanism in Toronto, 1900–1930." *Journal of Historical Geography* 20, Number 3 (1994): 305–322.

Frisken, Frances. "The Contributors of Metropolitan Government and the Success of Toronto's Public Transit System: An Empirical Dissent from the Public Choice Paradigm." *Urban Affairs Quarterly* 27 (1991): 268–292.

Fulford, Robert. *Accidental City: The Transformation of Toronto.* Toronto: Macfarlane, Walter and Ross, 1995.

Greater Toronto Housing Atlas. Ottawa: Canada Mortgage and Housing Corporation, 1946.

Harney, Nicholas DeMaria. *Eh, Paesan!: Being Italian in Toronto.* University of Toronto Press, 1998.

Harris, Richard. *Unplanned Suburbs: Toronto's American Tragedy, 1900 to 1950.* Baltimore: Johns Hopkins University Press, 1996.

Iacovetta, Franca. *Such Hardworking People: Italian Immigrants in Postwar Toronto.* Montreal and Kingston: McGill-Queen's University Press, 1992.

Kerr, Donald, and Jacob Spelt. *The Changing Face of Toronto.* Toronto, 1965.

Kilbourn, William, editor. *The Toronto Book.* Toronto, 1976.

Kluckner, Michael. *Toronto: The Way It Was.* Toronto: Whitecap, 1988.

Lemon, James T. *Toronto since 1918: An Illustrated History.* Toronto and Ottawa: James Lorimer and the National Museum of Man, 1985.

———. "Plans for Early 20th Century Toronto: Lost in Management." *Urban Historical Review* 18 (1989): 11-31.

———. *The Toronto Harbour Plan of 1912: Manufacturing Goals and Economic Realities.* Toronto: Canadian Waterfront Resource Centre, 1990.

———. "Toronto." *Cities [UK]* 8, Number 4 (1991): 258–266.

Lind, Loren J. *The Learning Machine: A Hard Look at Toronto's Schools.* Toronto: Anansi, 1974.

Lorimer, James. *The Developers.* Toronto: Lorimer, 1978.

Mann, W. E., editor. *The Underside of Toronto.* Toronto: McClelland and Stewart, 1970.

Mays, John Bentley. *Emerald City: Toronto Visited.* Toronto: Viking, 1994.

McMahon, Michael. *Metro's Housing Company: The First 35 Years.* Toronto: The Company, 1990.

Murdie, Robert A. *The Factorial Ecology of Metropolitan Toronto, 1951–1961: An Essay on the Social Geography of the City.* University of Chicago Press, 1969.

Novick, Marvyn. *Metro's Suburbs in Transition.* Metropolitan Toronto Social Planning Council, 1979–1980, two volumes.

Pendergrast, Eudora S. *Suburbanizing the Central City: Analysis of the Shift in Transportation Policies Governing the Development of Metropolitan Toronto, 1959–1978.* Development of Urban and Regional Planning, University of Toronto, 1981.

Rea, K. J. *The Prosperous Years: The Economic History of Ontario.* University of Toronto Press, 1985.

Richmond, John Russell. *Around Toronto: A Look at the City.* Toronto and Garden City, NJ: Doubleday, 1969.

Rose, Albert. *Governing Metropolitan Toronto: A Social and Political Analysis, 1953–1971.* Berkeley: University of California Press, 1972.

Sewell, John. *The Shape of the City: Toronto Struggles with Modern Planning.* University of Toronto Press, 1993.

Struthers, James. *The Limits of Affluence: Welfare in Ontario, 1920–1970.* University of Toronto Press, 1995.

Thompson, Richard H. *Toronto's Chinatown: The Changing Social Organization of an Ethnic Community.* New York: AMS, 1989.

Vass, Benjamin. *Toronto: A Photo-Study of Urban Development.* Toronto: McGraw-Hill Ryerson, 1971.

Williams, Gwyndaf. "Institutional Capacity and Metropolitan Governance: The Greater Toronto Area." *Cities [UK]* 16, Number 3 (June 1999): 171–180.

General Works

Armstrong, Frederick Henry. *Toronto: The Place of Meeting.* Woodland Hills, CA and Toronto: Windsor Publications, 1983.

Benn, Carl, and William Cooke, editors. *The Parish and Cathedral of St. James', Toronto, 1797–1997: A Collaborative History.* University of Toronto Press, 1998.

Dendy, William. *Lost Toronto: Images of the City's Past.* Toronto: McClelland and Stewart, 1993 re-edition of 1978 original published in Toronto by Oxford University Press.

———. *Toronto Observed: Its Architecture, Patrons, and History.* Toronto: Oxford University Press, 1986.

Filey, Mike. *A Toronto Album: Glimpses of the City That Was.* Toronto, 1970.

———. *Discover and Explore Toronto's Waterfront: A Walker's, Jogger's, Cyclist's, Boater's Guide to Toronto's Lakeside Sites and History.* Toronto: Dundurn Press, 1998.

Gee, Marcus. "Toronto: At Home with Strangers." *Américas [Organization of American States]* 52, Number 3 (May–June 2000), 46–52.

Glazebrook, George Parkin de Twenebroker. *The Story of Toronto.* University of Toronto Press, 1971.

Magel, Ralph, coordinator. *200 Years Yonge: A History.* Toronto: Natural Heritage/Natural History, 1998.

McHugh, Susan. *Toronto Architecture: A City Guide.* Toronto: Mercury, 1985.

Relph, Edward Charles. *The Toronto Guide: The City, Metro, the Region.* Centre for Urban and Community Studies, University of Toronto, 1997.

Russell, Victor Loring, editor. *Forging a Consensus: Historical Essays on Toronto.* University of Toronto Press, 1984.

United States
General Studies

Abbott, Carl. *The New Urban America: Growth and Politics in Sunbelt Cities.* Chapel Hill: University of North Carolina Press, 1987.

———. *Urban America in the Modern Age: 1920 to the Present.* Arlington Heights, IL: Harlan Davidson, 1987.

———. *The Metropolitan Frontier: Cities in the Modern American West.* Tucson: University of Arizona Press, 1993.

Abrams, Charles. *The City Is the Frontier.* New York: Harper and Row, 1965.

Adams, John S. *Housing Americans in the 1980s.* New York: Russell Sage Foundation, 1987.

Adams, John S., editor. *Urban Policy Making and Metropolitan Dynamics: A Comparative Geographical Analysis.* Cambridge, MA: Ballinger, 1976.

Arrillaga, José Joaquín. *Diary of His Surveys of the Frontier, 1796.* Los Angeles, 1969.

Attoe, W., and D. Logan. *American Urban Architecture, Catalysts in the Design of Cities.* Berkeley: University of California Press, 1989.

Baar, Kenneth. "The National Movement to Halt the Spread of Multifamily Housing, 1890–1926." *Journal of the American Planning Association* 58 (1992): 3948.

Banfield, Edward C. *The Unheavenly City: The Nature and Future of Our Urban Crisis.* Boston: Little, Brown, 1968.

Bannon, John Francis. *The Spanish Borderlands Frontier, 1513–1821.* New York, 1970.

Barrett, Paul, and Mark H. Rose. "Street Smarts: The Politics of Transportation Statistics in the American City, 1900–1990." *Journal of Urban History* 25, Number 3 (March 1999): 405–433.

Barrows, Robert G. "Beyond the Tenement: Patterns of American Urban Housing, 1870–1930." *Journal of Urban History* 9 (1983): 395–407.

Barth, Gunther. *City People: The Rise of Modern City Culture in Nineteenth-Century America.* New York: Oxford University Press, 1980.

Bauman, John F. "Housing the Urban Poor." *Journal of Urban History* 6 (1980): 211–220.

Beauregard, Robert A. *Voices of Decline: The Post-War Fate of U.S. Cities.* Oxford: Blackwell, 1993.

Beck, Warren A., and Ynez D. Haase. *Historical Atlas of California.* Norman: University of Oklahoma Press, 1974.

Beers, Henry Putney. *Spanish and Mexican Records of the American Southwest: A Bibliographical Guide to Archive and Manuscript Sources.* Tucson: University of Arizona Press, 1979.

Bennett, Larry. *Fragments of Cities: The New American Downtowns and Neighborhoods.* Columbus: Ohio State University Press, 1990.

Berger, Bennett. *Working-Class Suburb: A Study of Auto Workers in Suburbia.* Berkeley: University of California Press, 1960.

Bernstein, Michael A. *The Great Depression: Delayed Recovery and Economic Change in America, 1929–1939.* Cambridge, MA: Harvard University Press, 1987.

Bianco, Martha J. "Technological Innovation and the Rise and Fall of Urban Mass Transit." *Journal of Urban History* 25, Number 3 (March 1999): 348–378.

Biles, Roger. "Thinking the Unthinkable about Our Cities: Thirty Years Later." *Journal of Urban History* 25, Number 1 (November 1998): 5774.

Binford, Henry. *The First Suburbs.* University of Chicago Press, 1985.

Bish, Robert. *The Public Economy of Metropolitan Areas.* Chicago: Markham, 1971.

Blackford, Mansel G. *The Lost Dream: Businessmen and City Planning on the Pacific Coast, 1890–1920.* Columbus: Ohio State University Press, 1993.

Blake, Nelson Manfred. *Water for the Cities: A History of the Urban Water Supply Problem in the United States.* Syracuse, NY: Syracuse University Press, 1956.

Blakely, Edward J., and Mary Gail Snyder. *Fortress America: Gated Communities in the United States.* Washington, DC: Brookings Institution Press, 1997.

Blondheim, M. *News over the Wires: The Telegraph and the Flow of Public Information in America, 1844–1897.* Cambridge, MA: Harvard University Press, 1994.

Blumin, Stuart M. *The Emergence of the Middle Class: Social Experience in the American City, 1760–1900.* New York: Cambridge University Press, 1989.

Bobo, Lawrence, et al., editors. *Urban Inequality in the United States: Evidence from Four Cities.* New York: Russell Sage Foundation, 2000.

Borchert, James. "Residential City Suburbs: The Emergence of a New Suburban Type, 1880–1930." *Journal of Urban History* 22, Number 3 (March 1996): 283–307.

Borchert, John. "American Metropolitan Evolution." *Geographical Review* 57 (1967): 301–332.

Boyer, M. Christine. *Dreaming the Rational City: The Myth of American City-Planning.* Cambridge: Massachusetts Institute of Technology Press, 1983.

———. *The City of Collective Memory: Its Historical Imagery and Architectural Entertainments.* Cambridge: Massachusetts Institute of Technology Press, 1994.

Boyer, Paul. *Urban Masses and Moral Order in America, 1820–1920.* Cambridge, MA: Harvard University Press, 1978.

Bradbury, Katherine L., Anthony Downs, and Kenneth A. Small. *Urban Decline and the Future of American Cities.* Washington, DC: Brookings Institution, 1982.

Bridenbaugh, Carl. *Cities in Revolt: Urban Life in America, 1743–1776.* New York: Alfred A. Knopf, 1955.

———. *Cities in the Wilderness, 1625–1742.* New York: Alfred A. Knopf, 1960 reprint.

Bridges, Amy. *Morning Glories: Municipal Reform in the Southwest.* Princeton University Press, 1997.

Brown, Ralph H. *Historical Geography of the United States.* New York: Harcourt Brace, 1948.

Burnaby, Andrew. *Travels through the Middle Settlements in North America in the Years 1759 and 1760.* Ithaca, NY: Cornell University Press, 1960 re-edition of 1775 original.

Cappon, Lester J., et al., editors. *Atlas of Early American History: The Revolutionary Era.* Princeton University Press for the Newberry Library and Institute of Early American History and Culture, 1976.

Caraley, Demetrius. "Washington Abandons the Cities." *Political Science Quarterly* 107 (1992): 130.

Chudacoff, Howard P., and Judith E. Smith. *The Evolution of American Urban Society.* Englewood Cliffs, NJ: Prentice-Hall, 1988 re-edition.

Cigliano, Jan, and Sarah Bradford Landau, editors. *The Grand American Avenue, 1850–1920.* San Francisco: Pomegranate Artbooks, 1994.

Ciucci, Giorgio, et al. *The American City: From the Civil War to the New Deal.* Cambridge: Massachusetts Institute of Technology Press, 1979.

Clark, Gordon L. *Judges and the Cities: Interpreting Local Autonomy.* University of Chicago Press, 1985.

Clark, Kenneth B. *Dark Ghetto: Dilemmas of Social Power.* New York: Harper and Row, 1965.

Clark, William A. V. "Residential Segregation in American Cities." *Population Research and Policy Review* 5, Number 2 (1986): 95–127.

———. "Understanding Residential Segregation in American Cities: Interpreting the Evidence: Reply to Galster." *Population Research and Policy Review* 7, Number 3 (1988): 113–122.

———. "Residential Segregation in American Cities: Common Ground and Differences in Interpretation." *Population Research and Policy Review* 8, Number 2 (1989): 193–197.

Cleland, Robert G. *California in Our Time.* New York: Knopf, 1947.

Colean, Miles L. *Renewing Our Cities.* New York: Twentieth Century Foundation, 1953.

———. *A Backward Glance in Oral History: The Growth of Government Housing Policy in the United States, 1934–1975.* Washington, DC: Mortgage Bankers' Association of America, 1975.

Colton, Joel, and Stuart Bruchey, editors. *Technology and Society: The American Experience.* New York: Columbia University Press, 1987.

Condit, Carl W. *The Rise of the Skyscraper.* University of Chicago Press, 1952.

Conzen, Michael P. "The Maturing Urban Systems in the United States, 1840–1910." *Annals of the Association of American Geographers* 67 (1977): 88–108.

Crouch, Winston W., and Beatrice Dinerman. *Southern California Metropolis: A Study in Development of Government for a Metropolitan Area.* Berkeley: University of California Press, 1963.

Cummings, William P. *The Southeast in Early Maps.* Princeton University Press, 1958 (plus 1962 re-edition by the University of North Carolina Press at Chapel Hill).

———. *British Maps of Colonial America.* University of Chicago Press, 1974.

Cutler, David M., and Edward L. Glaeser. "Are Ghettos Good or Bad?" *Quarterly Journal of Economics* 112, Number 3 (1997): 827–872.

Cutler, David M., and Jacob L. Vigdor. "The Rise and Decline of the American Ghetto." *Journal of Political Economy* 107, Number 3 (1999): 455–506.

Daniels, Bruce, editor. *Towns and Country: Essays on the Structure of Local Government in the American Colonies.* Middleton, CT: Wesleyan University Press, 1978.

Danielson, Michael N. *Home Team: Professional Sports and the American Metropolis.* Princeton University Press, 1997.

Daunton, Martin J. "Cities of Homes and Cities of Tenements: British and American Comparisons, 1870–1914." *Journal of Urban History* 14 (1988): 283–319.

Davies, Pearl J. *Real Estate in American History.* Washington, DC: Public Affairs Press, 1958.

Davis, Sam. *The Architecture of Affordable Housing.* Berkeley: University of California Press, 1995.

DeCredico, Mary A. "Image and Reality: Ken Burns and the Urban Confederacy." *Journal of Urban History* 23, Number 4 (May 1997): 387–405.

Devens, Carol. *Countering Colonization: Native American Women and Great Lakes Missions, 1630–1900.* Berkeley: University of California Press, 1992.

Documentos para la historia eclesiástica y civil de la provincia de Texas o Nueva Filipinas, 1720–1779. Madrid: Volume 12 of the "Colección Chimalistac" published by José Porrúa Turanzas, 1961.

Domosh, Mona. "Shaping the Commercial City: Retail Districts in Nineteenth-Century New York and Boston." *Annals of the American Association of Geographers* 80 (1990): 268–284.

———. *Invented Cities: The Creation of Landscape in Nineteenth-Century New York and Boston.* New Haven: Yale University Press, 1996.

Downs, Anthony. *Opening Up the Suburbs: An Urban Strategy for America.* New Haven: Yale University Press, 1973.

Du Boff, Richard B. "Telegraph and the Structure of Markets in the United States, 1845–1890." *Research in Economic History* 8 (1983): 253–277.

Duis, Perry R. *The Saloon: Public Drinking in Chicago and Boston.* Urbana: University of Illinois Press, 1983.

Duncan, Otis Dudley, et al. *Social Change in a Metropolitan Community.* New York: Russell Sage Foundation, 1973.

Earle, Carville. *Geographical Inquiry and American Historical Problems.* Stanford, CA: Stanford University Press, 1992.

Eichler, Ned. *The Merchant Builders.* Cambridge: Massachusetts Institute of Technology Press, 1982.

Elkin, S. L. *City and Regime in the American Republic.* University of Chicago Press, 1987.

Elkind, Sarah S. "Building a Better Jungle: Anti-Urban Sentiment, Public Works, and Political Reform in American Cities, 1880–1930." *Journal of Urban History* 24, Number 1 (November 1997): 5378.

Ellis, John H. *Yellow Fever and Public Health in the New South.* Lexington: University Press of Kentucky, 1992.

Engberg, John. "Employment Policy and Urban Economic Development." *Housing Policy Debate* 7, Number 4 (1996): 695–714.

The Exploding Metropolis. Garden City, NJ: Doubleday and the editors of *Fortune* magazine, 1958.

Fairfield, John D. *The Mysteries of the Great City: The Politics of Urban Design, 1877–1937.* Columbus: Ohio State University Press, 1993.

Farley, Reynolds, et al. "Chocolate City, Vanilla Suburbs: Will the Trend toward Racially Separate Communities Continue?" *Social Science Research* 7, Number 4 (1978): 319–344.

Findlay, John M. *Magic Lands: Western Cityscapes and American Culture after 1940.* Berkeley: University of California Press, 1992.

Fishman, Robert. *Bourgeois Utopias: The Rise and Fall of Suburbia.* New York: Basic Books, 1987.

Fleming, Thomas J. "Good-bye to Everything!" *American Heritage* 16, Number 5 (August 1965): 88–95 and 98–99.

Flink, James J. *The Car Culture.* Cambridge: Massachusetts Institute of Technology Press, 1975.

Fogelson, Robert M. *Downtown: Its Rise and Fall, 1880–1950.* New Haven: Yale University Press, 2001.

Foley, Donald L., et al. *Characteristics of Metropolitan Growth in California.* Berkeley: Institute of Urban and Regional Development, University of California, 1965.

Ford, Larry R. *Cities and Buildings: Skyscrapers, Skid Rows, and Suburbs.* Baltimore: Johns Hopkins University Press, 1994.

Foster, Mark. *Henry J. Kaiser: Builder in the Modern American West.* Austin: University of Texas Press, 1989.

Frey, William H. "The New Urban Revival in the U.S." *Urban Studies* 30 (1993): 741–774.

———. "Minority Suburbanization and Continued 'White Flight' in U.S. Metropolitan Areas: Assessing Findings from the 1990 Census." *Research on Community Sociology* 4 (1994): 1519.

Frey, William H., and Alden Speare, Jr. *Regional and Metropolitan Growth and Decline in the United States.* New York: Russell Sage Foundation, 1988.

Fried, Joseph P. *Housing Crisis USA.* New York: Praeger, 1971.

Frieden, Bernard J., and Lynne B. Sagalyn. *Downtown, Inc.: How America Rebuilds Cities.* Cambridge: Massachusetts Institute of Technology Press, 1989.

Fries, Sylvia D. *The Urban Idea in Colonial America.* Philadelphia: Temple University Press, 1977.

Friis, Herman R. *A Series of Population Maps of the Colonies and the United States, 1625–1790.* New York: American Geographical Society, 1968.

Frug, Gerald E. "The City as a Legal Concept." *Harvard Law Review* 93 (1980): 1059–1154.

Funigiello, Philip J. *The Challenge of Urban Liberalism: Federal-City Relations during World War II.* Knoxville: University of Tennessee Press, 1978.

Gad, Gunter, and Deryck Holdsworth. "Corporate Capitalism and the Emergence of the High Rise Office Building." *Urban Geography* (1987): 212–231.

Gallman, Robert E., and John Joseph Wallis, editors. *American Economic Growth and Standards of Living before the Civil War.* University of Chicago Press, 1992.

Gans, Herbert J. *The Urban Villagers: Group and Class in the Life of Italian-Americans.* New York: Free Press, 1962.

———. *People, Plans, and Policies: Essays on Poverty, Racism, and Other National Urban Problems.* New York: Columbia University Press and Russell Sage Foundation, 1991.

———. *The War against the Poor: The Underclass and Anti-poverty Policy.* New York: Basic Books, 1995.

Gardner, Todd. "The Slow Wave: The Changing Residential Status of Cities and Suburbs in the United States, 1850–1940." *Journal of Urban History* 27, Number 3 (March 2001): 293–312.

Garreau, Joel. *Edge City: Life on the New Frontier.* New York: Doubleday, 1991.

Gelfand, Mark I. *A Nation of Cities: The Federal Government and Urban America, 1933–1965.* New York: Oxford University Press, 1975.

Gilchrist, David T., editor. *The Growth of Seaport Cities, 1790–1825.* Charlottesville: University Press of Virginia, 1967.

Glaab, Charles N., and A. Theodore. Brown. *A History of Urban America.* New York: Macmillan, 1976.

Glazer, Nathan, and Davis McEntire, editors. *Studies in Housing and Minority Groups.* Berkeley: University of California Press, 1960.

Glickman, N. J., et al. *State of the Nation's Cities: America's Changing Urban Life.* Washington, DC: U.S. Department of Housing and Urban Development, 1996.

Goering, John, and Ron Wienk, editors. *Mortgage Lending, Racial Discrimination, and Federal Policy.* Washington, DC: Urban Institute Press, 1995.

Goings, Kenneth W., and Raymond A. Mohl, editors. *The New African-American Urban History.* Thousand Oaks, CA: Sage, 1996.

Goldfield, David R. *Region, Race, and Cities: Interpreting the Urban South.* Baton Rouge: Louisiana State University Press, 1997.

Goldfield, David R., and Blaine A. Brownell. *Urban America: A History.* Boston: Houghton Mifflin, 1990 re-edition.

Goldsmith, S. *The Twenty-First Century City: Resurrecting Urban America.* Lanham, MD: Rowman and Littlefield, 1999.

Goldsmith, William W., and Edward J. Blakely. *Separate Societies: Poverty and Inequality in U.S. Cities.* Philadelphia: Temple University Press, 1993.

Gordon, Mitchell. *Sick Cities: Psychology and Pathology of American Urban Life.* New York: Macmillan, 1963.

Gore, Rick. "Living with California's Faults." *National Geographic* 187, Number 4 (April 1995): 217.

Gottdiener, Mark. *Planned Sprawl: Private and Public Interests in Suburbia.* Beverly Hills, CA: Sage, 1977.

Gottlieb, Manuel. *Long Swings in Urban Development.* New York: National Bureau of Economic Research, 1976.

Gottman, Jean. *Megalopolis: The Urbanized Northeastern Seaboard of the United States.* Cambridge: Massachusetts Institute of Technology Press, 1961.

Grebler, Leo, editor. *Metropolitan Contrasts.* Los Angeles: University of California Press, 1963.

Greenberg, Mike. *The Poetics of Cities: Designing Neighborhoods That Work.* Columbus: Ohio State University Press, 1995.

Griffith, Ernest S. *History of American City Government in the Colonial Period.* New York: Oxford University Press, 1958.

Groth, Paul. *Living Downtown: The History of Residential Hotels in the United States.* Berkeley: University of California Press, 1994.

Haar, Charles M. *Suburbs under Siege: Race, Space, and Audacious Judges.* Princeton University Press, 1996.

Halttunen, Karen. *Confidence Men and Painted Women: A Study of Middle-Class Culture in America, 1830–1870.* New Haven: Yale University Press, 1982.

Hamer, David. *New Towns in the New World: Images and Perceptions of the Nineteenth-Century Urban Frontier.* New York: Columbia University Press, 1990.

Hanchett, Thomas W. "Financing Suburbia: Prudential Insurance and the Post–World War II Transformation of the American City." *Journal of Urban History* 26, Number 3 (March 2000): 312–328.

Hardy, Stephen. "Sport in Urbanizing America: A Historical Review." *Journal of Urban History* 23, Number 6 (September 1997): 675–708.

Hayden, Delores. *The Power of Place: Urban Landscapes as Public History.* Cambridge: Massachusetts Institute of Technology Press, 1995.

Hayes, Samuel P. "The Changing Political Structures of the City in Industrial America." *Journal of Urban History* 1 (1974): 622.

Hirsch, Arnold R. "'Containment' on the Home Front: Race and Federal Housing Policy from the New Deal to the Cold War." *Journal of Urban History* 26, Number 2 (January 2000): 158–189.

Historical Statistics of the United States: Colonial Times to 1970. Washington, DC: U.S. Government Printing Office for the Bureau of the Census, Department of Commerce, 1975.

Hodgson, Godfrey. *America in Our Time: From World War Two to Nixon, What Happened and Why.* New York: Random House, 1978.

Holston, James, editor. *Cities and Citizenship.* Durham, NC: Duke University Press, 1999.

Holzman, Robert S. "How Steam Blew the Rowdies Out of the Fire Departments." *American Heritage* 7, Number 1 (December 1955): 66–71.

Hoyt, Homer. *The Structure and Growth of Residential Neighborhoods in American Cities.* Washington, DC: Government Printing Office for the Federal Housing Administration, 1939.

Humphreys, Margaret. *Yellow Fever and the South.* New Brunswick, NJ: Rutgers University Press, 1992.

Hundley, Norris. *The Great Thirst: California and Water, 1770s–1990s.* Berkeley: University of California Press, 1992.

Ihlanfeldt, Keith. "Information on the Spatial Distribution of Job Opportunities within Metropolitan Areas." *Journal of Urban Economics* 41, Number 2 (1997): 218–242.

Ingham, John N. *The Iron Barons: A Social Analysis of an American Urban Elite, 1874–1965.* Westport, CT: Greenwood, 1978.

Isham, Norman M. *Early American Houses.* New York: Da Capo Press, 1967.

Jackson, Kenneth T. *The Ku Klux Klan in the City, 1915–1930.* New York: Oxford University Press, 1967.

———. *Crabgrass Frontier: The Suburbanization of the U.S.* New York: Oxford University Press, 1985.

Jackson, Kenneth T., and Stanley K. Schultz, editors. *Cities in American History.* New York: Knopf, 1972.

Jacobs, Allan B. *Great Streets.* Cambridge: Massachusetts Institute of Technology Press, 1995.

Jaher, Frederic C. *The Urban Establishment: Upper Strata in Boston, New York, Charleston, Chicago and Los Angeles.* Urbana: University of Illinois Press, 1982.

Jakle, John A., and David Wilson. *Derelict Landscapes: The Wasting of America's Built Environment.* Baltimore: Johns Hopkins University Press, 1992.

Jargowsky, Paul. *Poverty and Place: Ghettos, Barrios, and the American City.* New York: Russell Sage Foundation, 1996.

Jencks, Christopher, and Paul E. Peterson, editors. *The Urban Underclass.* Washington, DC: Brookings Institution, 1991.

Jones, David W., Jr. *Urban Transit Policy: An Economic and Political History.* Englewood Cliffs, NJ: Prentice-Hall, 1985.

Kain, John F. "Housing Segregation, Negro Employment, and Metropolitan Decentralization." *Quarterly Journal of Economics* 82, Number 2 (1968): 175–197.

Karsner, Douglas. "Aviation and Airports: The Impact on the Economic and Geographic Structure of American Cities, 1940s–1980s." *Journal of Urban History* 23, Number 4 (May 1997): 406–436.

Kasarda, John D. "Urban Industrial Transition and the Underclass." *Annals of the American Academy of Political and Social Sciences* 501 (1989): 26–47.

———. "Entry Level Jobs, Mobility, and Urban Minority Unemployment." *Urban Affairs Quarterly* 19, Number 1 (1993): 2140.

Kasson, James F. *Rudeness and Civility: Manners in Nineteenth-Century America.* New York: Hill and Wang, 1990.

Katz, Bruce, and Scott Bernstein. "The New Metropolitan Agenda: Connecting Cities and Suburbs." *Brookings Review* 16, Number 4 (1998): 48.

Katz, Michael. *Undeserving Poor: From the War on Poverty to the War on Welfare.* New York: Pantheon, 1989.

———. *Improving Poor People: The Welfare State, the "Underclass," and Urban Schools in History.* Princeton University Press, 1995.

Katz, Michael, editor. *The Underclass Debate: Views from History.* Princeton University Press, 1993.

Katznelson, Ira. *City Trenches: Urban Politics and the Patterning of Class in the United States.* New York: Pantheon, 1981.

Keating, W. Dennis. *The Suburban Racial Dilemma: Housing and Neighborhoods.* Philadelphia: Temple University Press, 1994.

Kennedy, David M. *Over Here: The First World War and American Society.* New York: Oxford University Press, 1980.

Kilbride, Dan. "The Cosmopolitan South: Privileged Southerners, Philadelphia, and the Fashionable Tour in the Antebellum Era." *Journal of Urban History* 26, Number 5 (July 2000): 563–590.

Kirp, David L., et al. *Our Town: Race, Housing, and the Soul of Suburbia.* New Brunswick, NJ: Rutgers University Press, 1995.

Klein, Maury, and Harvey A. Kantor. *Prisoners of Progress: American Industrial Cities, 1850–1920.* New York: Macmillan, 1976.

Knox, Paul L. *Urbanization: An Introduction to Urban Geography.* Englewood Cliffs, NJ: Prentice-Hall, 1994.

Krueckeberg, Donald A., editor. *Introduction to Planning History in the United States.* New Brunswick, NJ: Rutgers University Center for Urban Policy Research, 1983.

Ladd, Helen F., and John Yinger. *America's Ailing Cities: Fiscal Health and the Design of Urban Policy.* Baltimore: Johns Hopkins University Press, 1989.

Langdon, Philip. *A Better Place to Live: Reshaping the American Suburb.* Amherst: University of Massachusetts Press, 1994.

LaVeist, Thomas A. "Linking Residential Segregation to the Infant-Mortality Rate: Disparity in U.S. Cities." *Social Science Review* 73, Number 2 (1989): 9094.

Leach, William. *Land of Desire: Merchants, Power and the Rice of a New American Culture.* New York: Pantheon, 1993.

Lee, Barrett A., and Peter B. Wood. "Is Neighborhood Racial Succession Place-Specific?" *Demography* 28, Number 1 (1991): 2140.

Leigh, Wilhelmina A., and James B. Stewart, editors. *The Housing Status of Black Americans.* New Brunswick, NJ: Transaction Publishers, 1992.

Lemann, Nicholas. *The Promised Land: The Great Black Migration and How It Changed America.* New York: Knopf, 1991.

Lindstrom, Diane, and John Sharpless. "Urban Growth and Economic Structure in Antebellum America." *Research in Economic History* (1978): 161–216.

Lo, Clarence Y. H. *Small Property versus Big Government: Social Origins of the Property Tax Revolt.* Berkeley: University of California Press, 1990.

Logan, John R., and Harvey L. Molotch. *Urban Fortunes: The Political Economy of Place.* Berkeley: University of California Press, 1987.

Logan, John R., and Todd Swanstrom. *Beyond the City Limits: Urban Policy and Economic Restructuring in Comparative Perspective.* Philadelphia: Temple University Press, 1990.

Logan, Michael F. *Fighting Sprawl and City Hall: Resistance to Urban Growth in the Southwest.* Tucson: University of Arizona Press, 1995.

Lotchin, Roger W. *Fortress California, 1910–1961: From Warfare to Welfare.* New York: Oxford University Press, 1992.

Lotchin, Roger W., editor. *The Way We Really Were: The Golden State in the Second Great War.* Urbana: University of Illinois Press, 2000.

Lubove, R. *Community Planning in the 1920s: The Contribution of the Regional Planning Association.* University of Pittsburgh Press, 1963.

Lynch, Kevin. *The Image of the City.* Cambridge: Massachusetts Institute of Technology Press, 1960.

Madden, Janice. "Urban Wage Gradients: Empirical Evidence." *Journal of Urban Economics* 18 (1985): 291–301.

Mahoney, Timothy R. *River Towns in the Great West: The Structures of Provincial Urbanization in the American Midwest, 1820–1870.* Cambridge, NY: Cambridge University Press, 1990.

Marsh, Margaret. *Suburban Lives.* New Brunswick, NJ: Rutgers University Press, 1990.

Martin, James C., and Robert S. Martin. *Maps of Texas and the Southwest, 1513–1900.* Albuquerque: University of New Mexico Press for the Amon Carter Museum, 1984.

Martin, John Stuart. "'He Paints with Lakes and Wooded Slopes . . .'" *American Heritage* 15, Number 6 (October 1964): 14–19 and 84–90.

Marvin, Carolyn. *When Old Technologies Were New: Thinking about Electric Communication in the Late Nineteenth Century.* New York: Oxford University Press, 1988.

Mason, Joseph B. *History of Housing in the United States, 1930–1980.* Houston: Gulf Publishing, 1982.

Massey, Douglas S., and Nancy Denton. *American Apartheid: Segregation and the Making of the Underclass.* Cambridge, MA: Harvard University Press, 1993.

Mathes, William Michael, editor. *Californiana III: documentos para la historia de la transformación colonizadora de California.* Madrid: José Porrúa Turanzas, 1974, three volumes.

Mayer, Harold M., and Clyde F. Kohn, editors. *Readings in Urban Geography.* University of Chicago Press, 1959.

Mayer, Martin. *The Builders: Houses, People, Neighborhoods, Government, Money.* New York: Norton, 1978.

McBain, Howard L. "The Legal Status of the American Colonial City." *Political Science Quarterly* 40 (1925): 177–200.

McEntire, Davis. *Residence and Race: Final and Comprehensive Report to the Commission on Race and Housing.* Berkeley: University of California Press, 1960.

McGovern, Stephen J. *The Politics of Downtown Development: Dynamic Political Cultures in San Francisco and Washington, D.C.* Lexington: University of Kentucky Press, 1998.

McGreevy, John T. *Parish Boundaries: The Catholic Encounter with Race in the Twentieth-Century Urban North.* University of Chicago Press, 1996.

McKelvey, Blake. *The Urbanization of America, 1860–1915.* New Brunswick, NJ: Rutgers University Press, 1963.

McNamara, Kevin R. *Urban Verbs: Arts and Discourses of American Cities.* Stanford, CA: Stanford University Press, 1996.

McShane, Clay. *Down the Asphalt Path: The Automobile and the American City.* New York: Columbia University Press, 1994.

McWilliams, Carey. *Southern California: An Island on the Land.* Santa Barbara, CA: Peregrine Smith, 1973 reprint of 1946 original.

Melosi, Martin V., editor. *Pollution and Reform in American Cities, 1870–1930.* Austin: University of Texas Press, 1980.

———. *Garbage in the Cities: Refuse Reform and the Environment, 1880–1980.* College Station: Texas A&M University Press, 1981.

Mereness, N. D., editor. *Travels in the American Colonies.* New York: Antiquarian Press, 1961.

Miller, Gary. *Cities by Contract: The Politics of Municipal Incorporation.* Cambridge: Massachusetts Institute of Technology Press, 1981.

Mohl, Raymond. *The New City: Urban America in the Industrial Age, 1860–1920.* Arlington Heights, IL: Harlan Davidson, 1985.

Mollenkopf, John Hall. *The Contested City.* Princeton University Press, 1983.

Monkkonen, Eric H. *America Becomes Urban: The Development of U.S. Cities and Towns, 1780–1980.* Berkeley: University of California Press, 1988.

Morrison, Hugh. *Early American Architecture.* New York: Oxford University Press, 1952.

Muller, Edward. "Regional Urbanization and the Selective Growth of Towns in North American Regions." *Journal of Historical Geography* 3, Number 1 (1977): 1–19.

Muller, Peter O. *Contemporary Suburban America.* Englewood Cliffs, NJ: Prentice-Hall, 1981.

Mumford, Lewis. *The City in History: Its Origins, Its Transformation, and the Prospects.* New York: Harcourt, Brace and World, 1961.

Nash, Gerald D. *The American West Transformed: The Impact of the Second World War.* Bloomington: University of Indiana Press, 1985.

Newhall, Beaumont. *The Daguerreotype in America.* New York: Dover, 1975.

Newman, Katherine S. *No Shame in My Game: The Working Poor in the Inner City.* New York: Russell Sage Foundation, 1999.

Noble, David. *America by Design.* New York: Oxford University Press, 1977.

O'Connor, Alice. "Community Action, Urban Reform, and the Fight against Poverty: The Ford Foundation's Gray Areas Program." *Journal of Urban History* 22, Number 5 (July 1996): 586–625.

Ogle, Maureen. "Water Supply, Waste Disposal, and the Culture of Privatism in the Mid-Nineteenth Century American City." *Journal of Urban History* 25, Number 3 (March 1999): 321–347.

Orum, Anthony M. *City-Building in America.* Boulder, CO: Westview, 1995.

Pagano, Michael A. and Bowman, Ann O'M. *Cityscapes and Capital: The Politics of Urban Development.* Baltimore: Johns Hopkins University Press, 1995.

Parrish, Michael E. *Anxious Decades: America in Prosperity and Depression, 1920–1941.* New York: W. W. Norton, 1992.

Patterson, James T. *America's Struggle against Poverty, 1900–1980.* Cambridge, MA: Harvard University Press, 1981.

Paullin, Charles O. *Atlas of the Historical Geography of the United States.* Washington, DC: Carnegie Institution, 1932.

Peattie, Lisa Redfield. *The View from the Barrio.* Ann Arbor: University of Michigan Press, 1968.

Peirce, Neal R., et al. *Citistates: How Urban America Can Prosper in a Competitive World.* Washington, DC: Seven Locks Press, 1993.

Persico, Joseph E. "The Great Swine Flu Epidemic of 1918." *American Heritage* 27, Number 4 (June 1976): 28–31 and 80–86.

Pessen, Edward. *Riches, Class and Power before the Civil War.* Lexington, KY: Heath, 1973.

Peterson, Paul E. *City Limits.* University of Chicago Press, 1981.

Peterson, Paul E., editor. *The Urban Underclass.* Washington, DC: Brookings Institution, 1985.

Peterson, Ruth D., and Lauren J. Krivo. "Racial Segregation and Urban Black Homicide." *Social Forces* 70, Number 4 (1993): 1001–1026.

Peterson, Ruth D. "Racial Segregation, the Concentration of Disadvantage, and Black and White Homicide Victimization." *Sociological Forum* 14, Number 3 (1999): 465–493.

Phillips, Kevin. *Arrogant Capital: Washington, Wall Street, and the Frustration of American Politics.* Boston: Little, Brown, 1994.

Pincetl, Stephanie S. *Transforming California: A Political History of Land Use and Development.* Baltimore: Johns Hopkins University Press, 1999.

Platt, R. H., and R. Macinko. *Beyond the Urban Fringe.* Minneapolis: University of Minnesota Press, 1983.

Pool, Ithiel de Sola, editor. *The Social Impact of the Telephone.* Cambridge: Massachusetts Institute of Technology Press, 1977.

Portillo y Díez de Sollano, Alvaro. *Descubrimiento y exploraciones en las costas de California.* Madrid, 1947.

Pred, A. R. *The Spatial Dynamics of U.S. Urban Industrial Growth, 1800–1914: Interpretive and Theoretical Essays.* Cambridge: Massachusetts Institute of Technology Press, 1966.

———. *Urban Growth and the Circulation of Information: The United States System of Cities, 1790–1840.* Cambridge, MA: Harvard University Press, 1973.

———. *Urban Growth and City Systems in the United States, 1840–1860.* Cambridge, MA: Harvard University Press, 1980.

Price, Jacob M. "Economic Function and the Growth of American Port Towns in the Eighteenth Century." *Perspectives on American History* 8 (1974): 123–186.

Radford, Gail. *Modern Housing for America: Policy Struggles in the New Deal Era.* University of Chicago Press, 1997.

Rainwater, Lee. *Behind Ghetto Walls: Black Families in a Federal Slum.* Chicago: Aldine, 1970.

Rebuilding Inner-City Communities: A New Approach to the Nation's Urban Crisis. Washington, DC: Committee for Economic Development, 1995.

Reps, John W. *The Making of Urban America: A History of City Planning in the United States.* Princeton University Press, 1965.

———. *Town Planning in Frontier America.* Columbia: University of Missouri Press, 1980.

———. *Views and Viewmakers of Urban America: Lithographs of Towns and Cities in the United States and Canada, Notes on the Artists and Publishers, and a Union Catalog of Their Work, 1825–1925.* Columbia: University of Missouri Press, 1984.

———. *Cities of the Mississippi: Nineteenth-Century Images of Urban Development.* Columbia: University of Missouri Press, 1994.

Rice, Roger L. "Residential Segregation by Law: 1910–1917." *Journal of Southern History* 24 (May 1968): 179–199.

Rome, Adam W. "Building on the Land: Toward an Environmental History of Residential Development in American Cities and Suburbs, 1870–1990." *Journal of Urban History* 20, Number 3 (May 1994): 407–434.

Rosen, Christine M. *The Limits of Power: Great Fires and the Process of City Growth in America.* New York: Cambridge University Press, 1986.

Rowe, Peter G. *Modernity and Housing.* Cambridge: Massachusetts Institute of Technology Press, 1995.

Rusk, David. *Cities without Suburbs.* Washington, DC: Woodrow Wilson Center Press, 1993; also republished in 1996 by Johns Hopkins University Press.

Ryan, Mary. *Women in Public: Between Banners and Ballots, 1825–1880.* Baltimore: Johns Hopkins University Press, 1990.

Rybczynski, Witold. *A Clearing in the Distance: Frederick Law Olmsted and America in the Nineteenth Century.* New York: Scribner, 1998.

Sales, Luis. *Noticias de la provincia de California, 1794.* Madrid: Volume 6 of the "Colección Chimalistac" published by José Porrúa Turanzas, 1960.

Schafer, Robert. *The Suburbanization of Multi-Family Housing.* Lexington, KY: Lexington Books, 1974.

Schiesl, Martin J. "City Planning in World War II." *California History* (1980): 126–143.

———. *The Politics of Efficiency: Municipal Administration and Reform in America, 1880–1920.* Berkeley: University of California Press, 1992.

Schlereth, Thomas J. *Victorian America: Transformations in Everyday Life, 1876–1915.* New York: HarperCollins, 1991.

Schnell, J. Christopher. "Chicago Versus St. Louis: A Reassessment of the Great Rivalry." *Missouri Historical Review* 71 (1977): 245–265.

Schnore, Leo F., editor. *The New Urban History: Quantitative Explorations by American Historians.* Princeton University Press, 1975.

Schultz, Stanley K. *American Cities and City Planning, 1800–1920.* Philadelphia: Temple University Press, 1989.

Schultz, Stanley K., and Clay McShane. "To Engineer the Metropolis: Sewers, Sanitation and City Planning in Late Nineteenth-Century America." *Journal of American History* 65 (1978): 389–411.

Schuyler, David. *The New Urban Landscape: The Redefinition of City Form in Nineteenth-Century America.* Baltimore: Johns Hopkins University Press, 1986.

Schwartz, Barry, editor. *The Changing Face of the Suburbs.* University of Chicago Press, 1970.

Scott, Allen J. *Metropolis: From the Division of Labor to Urban Form.* Berkeley: University of California Press, 1988.

Scott, Mellier G. *American City Planning since 1890.* Berkeley: University of California Press, 1969.

Sellers, Charles. *The Market Revolution: Jacksonian America, 1815–1846.* New York: Oxford University Press, 1991.

Sies, Mary Corbin, and Christopher Silver, editors. *Planning the Twentieth-Century American City.* Baltimore: Johns Hopkins University Press, 1996.

Skogan, Wesley. "The Changing Distribution of Big City Crime." *Urban Affairs Quarterly* 13 (1977): 3348.

Smith, Michael Peter, and Joe R. Feagin, editors. *The Bubbling Cauldron: Race, Ethnicity, and the Urban Crisis.* Minneapolis: University of Minnesota Press, 1995.

Smith, Neil, and Peter Williams, editors. *Gentrification of the City.* Boston: Allen and Unwin, 1986.

Smith, Wilson, editor. *Cities of Our Past and Present: A Descriptive Reader.* New York: Wiley, 1964.

Snow, Richard F. "The American City." *American Heritage* 27, Number 3 (April 1976): 26–49.

So, F. S., and Judith Getzelo, editors. *The Practice of Local Government Planning.* Washington, DC: International City Management Association, 1988 re-edition.

Soltow, Lee. *Men and Wealth in the United States, 1850–1870.* New Haven: Yale University Press, 1975.

Sowell, Thomas. *Ethnic America: A History.* New York: HarperCollins, 1981.

Squires, Gregory D., editor. *From Redlining to Reinvestment: Community Responses to Urban Disinvestment.* Philadelphia: Temple University Press, 1992.

Starr, Kevin. *Material Dreams: Southern California through the 1920s.* New York: Oxford University Press, 1990.

The State of the Cities 1998. Washington, DC: Office of Policy Development and Research of the U.S. Department of Housing and Urban Development, 1999.

Sternlieb, George, and Robert W. Burchall. *Residential Abandonment: The Tenement Landlord Revisited.* New Brunswick, NJ: Rutgers University Press, 1973.

Sternlieb, George, et al. "Housing Abandoment in the Urban Core." *Journal of the American Institute of Planners* 40 (1979): 321–332.

Stilgoe, John R. *Borderland: Origins of the American Suburb, 1820–1939.* New Haven: Yale University Press, 1988.

Stokes, I. N. Phelps, and Daniel Haskell. *American Historical Prints: Early Views of American Cities.* Detroit: Gale Research, 1974 reprint of 1933 New York Public Library original.

Strauss, Anselm L. *Images of the American City.* New York: Free Press of Glencoe, 1961.

Strazheim, Mahlon. "Discrimination and the Spatial Characteristics of the Urban Labor Market for Black Workers." *Journal of Urban Economics* 7 (1980): 119–140.

Sugrue, Thomas J. "Crabgrass-Roots Politics: Race, Rights, and the Reaction against Liberalism in the Urban North, 1940–1964." *Journal of American History* 82 (September 1995): 551–578.

Suttles, Gerald. *The Social Order of the Slum.* University of Chicago Press, 1968.

Taylor, George Rogers. *The Transportation Revolution, 1815–1860.* New York: Holt, Rinehart and Winston, 1951.

Teaford, Jon C. *The Municipal Revolution in America: Origins of Modern Urban Government, 1650–1825.* University of Chicago Press, 1975.

———. *City and Suburb: The Political Fragmentation of Metropolitan America.* Baltimore: Johns Hopkins University Press, 1979.

———. *The Unheralded Triumph: City Government in America, 1870–1900.* Baltimore: Johns Hopkins University Press, 1984.

———. *The Twentieth-Century American City: Problem, Promise and Reality.* Baltimore: Johns Hopkins University Press, 1986.

———. *The Rough Road to Renaissance: Urban Revitalization in America, 1940–1985.* Baltimore: Johns Hopkins University Press, 1990.

———. *Cities of the Heartland: The Rise and Fall of the Industrial Midwest.* Bloomington: Indiana University Press, 1993.

Tebbel, John, and Mary Ellen Zuckerman. *The Magazine in America, 1741–1990.* New York: Oxford University Press, 1991.

Thomas, June Manning, and Marsha Ritzdorf, editors. *Urban Planning and the African American Community.* Thousand Oaks, CA: Sage, 1996.

Thomason, Michael. "When Downtowns Were the Thing: On the Streets of Gulf Coast Cities in the 'Roaring Twenties.'" *Gulf Coast Historical Review* 1, Number 1 (1985): 6470.

Thompson, Robert Luther. *Wiring a Continent: The History of the Telegraph Industry in the United States, 1832–1866.* Princeton University Press, 1947.

Thompson, Warren S. *Growth and Change in California's Population.* Los Angeles: Haynes Foundation, 1955.

Vergara, Camilo José. *The New American Ghetto.* New Brunswick, NJ: Rutgers University Press, 1995.

Wade, Richard C. *Slavery in the Cities: The South, 1820–1860.* New York: Oxford University Press, 1964.

———. *The Urban Frontier: The Rise of Western Cities, 1790–1830.* Urbana: University of Illinois Press, 1998 republication of 1967 original published by Harvard University Press.

Wakstein, Allen M. *The Urbanization of America: An Historical Anthology.* Boston: Houghton Mifflin, 1970.

Ward, David. *Cities and Immigrants: A Geography of Change in Nineteenth-Century America.* New York: Oxford University Press, 1971.

———. *Poverty, Ethnicity, and the American City, 1840–1925.* Cambridge, NY: Cambridge University Press, 1989.

———. "Social Reform, Social Surveys, and the Discovery of the Modern City." *Annals of the Association of American Geographers* (1990): 491–503.

Warner, Sam Bass, Jr. *The Urban Wilderness: A History of the American City.* Berkeley: University of California Press, 1995 re-edition of 1972 original.

Weber, Adna F. *The Growth of Cities in the Nineteenth Century: A Study in Statistics.* Ithaca, NY: Cornell University Press, 1963 re-edition of 1899 original.

Weber, Francis J. *The California Missions as Others Saw Them: 1786–1842.* Los Angeles, 1972.

Weiss, Marc A. *The Rise of the Community Builders: The American Real Estate Industry and Urban Land Planning.* New York: Columbia University Press, 1987.

Weiss, Melford S. *Valley City: A Chinese Community in America.* Cambridge, MA.: Schenkman, 1974.

Wexler, Alan. *Atlas of Westward Expansion.* Facts on File, 1995.

Wheat, Carl I. *Mapping the Transmississippi West.* San Francisco: Institute of Historical Cartography, 1957–1963, five volumes.

White, Morton, and Lucia White. *The Intellectual Versus the City.* Cambridge: MIT Press, 1962.

Whitehead, Richard S. "Alta California's Four Fortresses." *Southern California Quarterly* 65, Number 1 (1983): 6794.

Wilbur, Marguerite Eyer, editor. *Vancouver in California, 1792–1794.* Los Angeles, 1954, two volumes.

Williams, Marilyn Thornton. *Washing "The Great Unwashed": Public Baths in Urban America, 1840–1920.* Columbus: Ohio State University Press, 1991.

Willis, Carol. *Form Follows Finance: Skyscrapers and Skylines in New York and Chicago.* Princeton, NJ: Princeton Architectural Press, 1995.

Wilson, James Q., editor. *Urban Renewal: The Record and the Controversy.* Cambridge: Massachusetts Institute of Technology Press, 1966.

Wilson, William H. *The City Beautiful Movement.* Baltimore: Johns Hopkins University Press, 1989.

Wilson, William Julius. *The Truly Disadvantaged: The Inner City, the Underclass, and Public Policy.* University of Chicago Press, 1987.

———. *When Work Disappears: The World of the New Urban Poor.* New York: Alfred A. Knopf, 1996.

Wissink, G. A. *American Cities in Perspective, with Special Reference to the Development of Their Fringe Areas.* Assen, Holland: Van Gorcum, 1962.

The WPA Guide to California. New York: Pantheon, 1984 re-edition of 1939 original.

Wyly, E. K., et al. "A Top 10 List of Things to Know about American Cities." *Cityscape* 3, Number 3 (1998): 732.

Yinger, John. *Closed Doors, Opportunities Lost: The Continuing Costs of Housing Discrimination.* New York: Russell Sage Foundation, 1995.

Boston

Colonial Era (1630–1774)

Bailyn, Bernard. *The New England Merchants in the Seventeenth Century.* Cambridge, MA: Harvard University Press, 1955.

———. "The Ordeal of Thomas Hutchinson." *American Heritage* 25, Number 3 (April 1974): 4–7 and 88–96.

———. *The Ordeal of Thomas Hutchinson.* Cambridge, MA: Harvard University Press, 1974.

Balicki, Joseph F. "Wharves, Privies, and the Pewterer: Two Colonial Period Sites on the Shawmut Peninsula, Boston." *Historical Archaeology* 32, Number 3 (1998): 99–120.

Farmer, Laurence. "When Cotton Mather Fought the Smallpox." *American Heritage* 8, Number 5 (August 1957): 40–43 and 109.

Farmer, Rod. "Instructions of Representatives in Colonial Boston, 1641-1783." *Mid-America* 64, Number 3 (1982): 3–15.

Fischer, David H. *Paul Revere's Ride.* New York: Oxford University Press, 1994.

Fleming, Thomas J. "The Boston Massacre." *American Heritage* 18, Number 1 (December 1966): 6–11 and 102–111.

Menard, Catherine S. "The Things That Were Caesar's: Tax Collecting in Eighteenth-Century Boston." *Massachusetts Historical Review* 1 (1999): 49–77.

Minkema, Kenneth P., editor. "The Lynn End 'Earthquake': Relations of 1727." *New England Quarterly* 69, Number 3 (1996): 473–499.

Nellis, Eric. G. "Misreading the Signs: Industrial Imitation, Poverty, and the Social Order in Colonial Boston." *New England Quarterly* 59, Number 4 (1986): 486–507.

Rutman, Darrett Bruce. *Winthrop's Boston: Portrait of a Puritan Town, 1630–1649.* Chapel Hill: University of North Carolina Press, 1965.

Schutz, John A. *William Shirley: King's Governor of Massachusetts.* Chapel Hill: University of North Carolina Press, 1961.

Sewall, Samuel. *The Diary of Samuel Sewall, 1674–1729.* New York: Farrar, Straus and Giroux, 1973 re-edition by M. Halsey Thomas, two volumes.

Slade, Marilyn M. "Out from Boston." *Early American Life* 18, Number 5 (1987): 66–71 and 86.

Thomas, Veronica. "The Original Boston." *National Geographic* 146, Number 3 (September 1974): 382–389.

Tyler, John W. "The Long Shadow of Benjamin Barons: The Politics of Illicit Trade at Boston, 1760–1762." *American Neptune* 40, Number 4 (1980): 245–279.

Ward, Barbara McLean. "Hierarchy and Wealth Distribution in the Boston Goldsmithing Trade, 1690–1760." *Essex Institute Historical Collections* 126, Number 3 (1990): 129–147.

Webber, Sandra L. "Proud Builders of Boston: The Hallowell Family Shipyard, 1635–1804." *American Neptune* 61, Number 2 (2001): 115–150.

Independence (1775–1783)

Brooks, Victor. *The Boston Campaign: April 1775–March 1776.* Combined, 1999.

Cash, Philip, and Carol Pine. "John Jeffries and the Struggle against Smallpox in Boston (1775–1776) and Nova Scotia (1776–1779)." *Bulletin of the History of Medicine* 57, Number 1 (1983): 93–97.

Labaree, Benjamin Woods. *The Boston Tea Party.* New York: Oxford University Press, 1964.

Early Republican Era (1784–1865)

Bunting, Bainbridge. *Houses of Boston's Back Bay: An Architectural History, 1840–1917.* Cambridge, MA: Harvard University Press, 1967.

Galenson, David W. "Ethnicity, Neighborhood, and the School Attendance of Boys in Antebellum Boston." *Journal of Urban History* 24, Number 5 (July 1998): 603–626.

Handlin, Oscar. *Boston's Immigrants: A Study in Acculturation, 1790–1880.* Cambridge, MA: Harvard University Press, 1959 revised edition.

Holloran, Peter C. *Boston's Wayward Children: Social Services for Homeless Children, 1830–1930.* Boston: Northeastern University Press, 1989.

Kilham, Walter Harrington. *Boston after Bulfinch: An Account of Its Architectural History, 1800–1900.* Cambridge, MA: Harvard University Press, 1946.

Knights, Peter R. *Yankee Destinies: The Lives of Ordinary Nineteenth-Century Bostonians.* Chapel Hill: University of North Carolina Press, 1991.

Modern Era (1866–Present)

The Boston Society of Architects: The First Hundred Years, 1867–1967. Boston: Published by the Society, 1967.

Davidson, Carla. "Boston Painters, Boston Ladies." *American Heritage* 23, Number 3 (April 1972): 4–17.

Ellis, William S. "Breaking New Ground: Boston." *National Geographic* 186, Number 1 (July 1994): 233.

Firey, Walter Irving. *Land Use in Central Boston.* Cambridge, MA: Harvard University Press, 1947.

Formisano, Ronald P. *Boston Against Busing: Race, Class, and Ethnicity in the 1960s and 1970s.* Chapel Hill: University of North Carolina Press, 1992.

Green, Martin Burgess. *The Problem of Boston: Some Reading in Cultural History.* New York: W. W. Norton and Company, 1966.

Halpert, Stephen. "Boston: Looking Backward." *American Heritage* 24, Number 6 (October 1973): 48–55.

———. *Brahmins and Bullyboys: G. Frank Radway's Boston Album.* Boston: Houghton Mifflin, 1973.

———. "Boston's 'Sacred Sky Line': From Prohibiting to Sculpting Skyscrapers, 1891–1928." *Journal of Urban History* 22, Number 5 (July 1996): 552–585.

Holleran, Michael. *Boston's "Changeful Times": Origins of Preservation and Planning in America.* Baltimore: Johns Hopkins University Press, 1998.

Lupo, Alan, et al. *Rites of Way: The Politics of Transportation in Boston and the U.S. City.* Boston: Little, Brown, 1971.

Meyerson, Martin, and Edward C. Banfield. *Boston: The Job Ahead.* Cambridge, MA: Harvard University Press, 1966.

O'Connor, Thomas H. *Building a New Boston: Politics and Urban Renewal, 1950 to 1970.* Boston: Northeastern University Press, 1993.

———. *The Boston Irish: A Political History.* Boston: Northeastern University Press, 1995.

Roos, Robert de. "Massachusetts Builds for Tomorrow." *National Geographic* 130, Number 6 (December 1966): 790–843.

Russell, Francis. "The Last of the Bosses." *American Heritage* 10, Number 4 (June 1959): 20–25 and 85–91.

———. "The Strike That Made a President." *American Heritage* 14, Number 6 (October 1963): 44–47 and 90–94.

———. "Bubble, Bubble—No Toil, No Trouble." *American Heritage* 24, Number 2 (February 1973): 74–80 and 86.

Sarna, Jonathan D., and Ellen Smith, editors. *The Jews of Boston: Essays on the Occasion of the Centenary (1895–1995) of the Combined Jewish Philanthropies of Greater Boston.* Boston: Combined Jewish Philanthropies of Greater Boston, 1995.

Thernstrom, Stephen. *The Other Bostonians: Poverty and Progress in the American Metropolis, 1880–1970.* Cambridge, MA: Harvard University Press, 1973.

Von Hoffman, Alexander. "Weaving the Urban Fabric: Patterns of Residential Real Estate Development in Outer Boston." *Journal of Urban History* 22, Number 2 (January 1996): 191–230.

Warner, Sam Bass, Jr. *Streetcar Suburbs: The Process of Growth in Boston, 1870–1900.* Cambridge: Massachusetts Institute of Technology Press, 1962.

Whitehill, Walter Muir. *The Boston Public Library: A Centennial History.* Cambridge, MA: Harvard University Press, 1956.

———. *Boston in the Age of John F. Kennedy.* Norman: University of Oklahoma Press, 1965.

General Works

Fifty Years of Boston: A Memorial Volume Issued in Commemoration of the Tercentenary of 1930. Boston, 1932.

Haglund, Karl T. *Inventing the Charles River.* Cambridge: MIT Press, 2002.

Judge, Joseph. "Those Proper and Other Bostonians." *National Geographic* 146, Number 3 (September 1974): 352–381.

Kennedy, Lawrence W. *Planning the City upon a Hill: Boston since 1630.* Amherst: University of Massachusetts Press, 1992.

McCord, David. *About Boston.* Boston: Little, Brown and Company, 1973.

Peffer, Randall S. "Massachusetts' North Shore: Harboring Old Ways." *National Geographic* 155, Number 4 (April 1979): 568–590.

Southworth, Michael. *AIA Guide to Boston.* Boston: Globe Pequot Press, 1992.

Taper, Bernard. *The Arts in Boston: An Outsider's View of the Cultural Estate.* Cambridge, MA: Harvard University Press, 1970.

Whitehill, Walter Muir, and Lawrence W. Kennedy. *Boston: A Topographical History.* Cambridge, MA: Harvard University Press, 2000 re-edition of 1959 original.

Charleston
Early History (1670–1860)

Clark, Thomas D. *South Carolina: The Grand Tour, 1780–1865.* Columbia: University of South Carolina Press, 1973.

Crane, Verner W. *The Southern Frontier, 1670–1732.* Ann Arbor: University of Michigan Press, 1954 re-edition of 1928 original.

Hirsch, Arthur H. *The Huguenots of Colonial South Carolina.* Durham, NC: Duke University Press, 1962 reprint of 1928 original.

Hughson, Shirley C. *The Carolina Pirates and Colonial Commerce, 1670–1740.* Baltimore: Johns Hopkins University Press, 1984.

Lawson, John. *New Voyage to Carolina.* Chapel Hill: University of North Carolina Press, 1967 re-edition of 1709 original.

Littlefield, Daniel C. "Continuity and Change in Slave Culture: South Carolina and the West Indies." *Southern Studies* 26 (1987): 202–216.

Merrens, H. Roy, editor. *The Colonial South Carolina Scene: Contemporary Views, 1697–1774.* Columbia: University of South Carolina Press, 1977.

Nash, R. C. "Urbanization in the Colonial South: Charleston, South Carolina, as a Case Study." *Journal of Urban History* 19, Number 1 (1992): 3–29.

Pinckney, Elise, editor. *Letterbook of Eliza Lucas.* Chapel Hill: University of North Carolina Press, 1972.

Rogers, George C., Jr. *Charleston in the Age of the Pinckneys.* Norman: University of Oklahoma Press, 1969.

Saley, Alexander S., compiler and editor. *Journal of the Commons House of Assembly, 1692–1735.* Columbia: 1907–1946, twenty-one volumes.

Sirmans, M. Eugene. *Colonial South Carolina: A Political History, 1663–1763.* Chapel Hill: University of North Carolina Press, 1966.

Smith, David A. "Dependent Urbanization in Colonial America: The Case of Charleston, South Carolina." *Social Forces* 66, Number 1 (1987): 1–28.

Waring, Joseph I. *A History of Medicine in South Carolina, 1670–1825.* Columbia: University of South Carolina Press, 1964.

Weir, Robert M. *Colonial South Carolina: A History.* Millwood, NY: KTO, 1983.

Wood, Peter H. *Black Majority: Negroes in Colonial South Carolina from 1670 to the Stono Rebellion.* New York: Knopf, 1974.

Early Maps and Depictions of Charleston, 1671–1788

Crude chart of the original "Charles-Town" disembarkation area, included as an inset to the 1671 map of Carolina drawn by James Moxon in London, on orders from the Lords Proprietors—originals held by the Library of Congress, plus other sources

"A particular draught" for entering Charleston Harbor, drawn ca. 1685 by Maurice Mathews, accurately depicting the entire estuary—original held by the Library of Congress

"A Plan of the Town and Harbour of Charles-Town" by Edward Crisp, probably drawn ca. 1704, then published seven years later as an inset to a larger coastal map—originals held by the Library of Congress, plus other sources

Map and panoramic view of the Charleston waterfront as seen from its Cooper River anchorage, drawn by Bishop Roberts in 1737 and engraved for publication in London by W. H. Toms in June 1739—originals held by the Henry Francis du Pont Winterthur Museum, plus other sources

Panoramic view of Charleston harbor, published in a 1762 issue of the *London Magazine* and based upon Toms's 1739 engraving—originals held by The Old Print Gallery in Washington, D.C., plus other sources

Panoramic view of Charleston, published in London as part of the 1768 set known as *Scenographia Americana*—originals held by the British Library, plus other sources

Charleston as seen from its sea approaches in 1774, painted by Thomas Leitch—originals held by the Library of Congress, plus other sources

Sketch map of Charleston harbor, showing the disposition of Vice Adm. Mariot Arbuthnot's British fleet during the 1780 attack against Fort Moultrie—original held by the South Carolina Historical Society

"Ichnography of Charleston" as surveyed by Edmund Petrie in 1788, then published two years later in London—originals held by the Library of Congress, plus other sources

Civil War Era (1861–1865)

Bristoll, William Merrick. "Escape from Charleston." *American Heritage* 26, Number 4 (April 1975): 24–27 and 82.

Burton, E. Milby. *The Siege of Charleston, 1861–1865.* Columbia: University of South Carolina Press, 1970.

Foote, Shelby. "Du Pont Storms Charleston." *American Heritage* 14, Number 4 (June 1963): 28–34 and 89.

Halstead, Murat. "Douglas, Deadlock, and Disunion." *American Heritage* 11, Number 4 (June 1960): 56–59 and 80.

———. *Three against Lincoln.* Baton Rouge: Louisiana State University Press, 1960 reedition by William B. Hesseltine of original *The Caucases of 1860.*

Price, Marcus W. "Ships That Tested the Blockade of the Carolina Ports, 1861–1865." *American Neptune* 8 (1948): 196–241.

———. "Blockade Running as a Business in South Carolina during the War between the States, 1861–1865." *American Neptune* (1949): 31–62.

Redding, Saunders. "Tonight for Freedom." *American Heritage* 9, Number 4 (June 1958): 52–55 and 90.

Sims, Lydel. "The Submarine That Wouldn't Come Up." *American Heritage* 9, Number 3 (April 1958): 48–51 and 107–111.

Swanberg, W. A. *First Blood: The Story of Fort Sumter.* New York: Charles Scribner's Sons, 1958.

Modern Era and General Works (1866–Present)

Jarrell, Hampton M. *Hampton and the Negro.* Columbia: University of South Carolina Press, 1949.

Johnson, Elmer D., and Kathleen L. Sloan, compilers and editors. *Documentary Profile of the Palmetto State.* Columbia: University of South Carolina Press, 1971.

Leland, Isabella Gaud. *Charleston, Crossroads of History: A Story of the South Carolina Low Country.* Woodland Hills, CA: Windsor Publications, 1980.

Moltke-Hansen, David, editor. *Art in the Lives of South Carolinians: Nineteenth-Century Chapters.* Charleston, SC: Carolina Art Association, 1979.

O'Neill Verner, Elizabeth. *Mellowed by Time.* Columbia: University of South Carolina Press, 1953.

Peters, Kenneth E. "Economic Consequences of the Charleston Earthquake." *Proceedings of the South Carolina Historical Association* (1986): 70–81.

Powers, Bernard E., Jr. *Black Charlestonians: A Social History, 1822–1885.* Fayetteville: University of Arkansas Press, 1994.

Simkins, Francis B., and Robert H. Woody. *South Carolina during Reconstruction.* Chapel Hill: University of North Carolina Press, 1932.

St. Julien Ravenel, Beatrice. *Architects of Charleston.* Columbia: University of South Carolina Press, 1992 re-edition of 1945 original.

Stockton, Robert P. *The Great Shock: The Effects of the 1886 Earthquake on the Built Environment of Charleston, South Carolina.* Easley, SC: Southern History, 1986.

Tindall, George B. *South Carolina Negroes, 1877–1900.* Columbia: University of South Carolina Press, 1952.

Waddell, Gene. "An Architectural History of Kahal Kadosh Beth Elohim, Charleston." *South Carolina Historical Magazine* 98, Number 1 (1997): 6–55.

Wallace, David Duncan. *South Carolina: A Short History, 1520–1948.* Columbia: University of South Carolina Press, 1951.

Chicago

Early History (1673–1892)

Abbott, Carl. "'Necessary Adjuncts to Its Growth': The Railroad Suburbs of Chicago, 1854–1875." *Journal of the Illinois State Historical Society* 73 (summer 1980): 117–131.

Adler, Jeffrey S. "'If We Can't Live in Peace, We Might as Well Die': Homicide-Suicide in Chicago, 1875–1910." *Journal of Urban History* 26, Number 1 (November 1999): 3–21.

Angle, Paul M., editor. *The Great Chicago Fire.* Chicago Historical Society, 1971.

Avrich, Paul. *The Haymarket Tragedy.* Princeton University Press, 1984.

Bach, Ira J. "Pullman: A Town Reborn." *Chicago History* 4 (spring 1975): 44–53.

Boorstin, Daniel J. "A. Montgomery Ward's Mail-Order Business." *Chicago History* 2 (spring–summer 1973): 142–152.

Clifton, James A. "Chicago, September 14, 1833: The Last Great Indian Treaty in the Old Northwest." *Chicago History* 9 (summer 1980): 86–97.

Cudahy, Brian J. "Chicago's Early Elevated Lines and the Construction of the Union Loop." *Chicago History* 8 (winter 1979–1980): 194–205.

Einhorn, Robin L. *Property Rules: Political Economy in Chicago, 1833–1872.* University of Chicago Press, 1991.

Ekman, Ernst. "Fredrika Bremer in Chicago in 1850." *Swedish Pioneer Historical Quarterly* 14 (October 1968): 234–244.

Fine, Lisa M. *The Souls of the Skyscraper: Female Clerical Workers in Chicago, 1870–1930.* Philadelphia: Temple University Press, 1990.

Frazier, Arthur H. "The Military Frontier: Fort Dearborn." *Chicago History* 9 (summer 1980): 80–85.

Gerwin, Anselm J. "The Chicago Indian Treaty of 1833." *Journal of the Illinois State Historical Society* 57 (1964): 117–142.

Hoy, Suellen. "Caring for Chicago's Women and Girls: The Sisters of the Good Shepherd, 1859–1911." *Journal of Urban History* 23, Number 3 (March 1997): 260–294.

Karamanski, Theodore J. *Rally 'round the Flag: Chicago and the Civil War.* Chicago: Nelson-Hall, 1993.

Keil, Hartmut, and John B. Jentz, editors. *German Workers in Chicago: A Documentary History of Working-Class Culture from 1850 to World War I.* Urbana: University of Illinois Press, 1988.

Lamb, John M. "Early Days on the Illinois and Michigan Canal." *Chicago History* 3 (winter 1974–1975): 168–176.

Lindsey, David. "The Founding of Chicago." *American History Illustrated* 8 (1973): 24–33.

Lowe, David, editor. *The Great Chicago Fire in Eyewitness Accounts and 70 Contemporary Photographs and Illustrations.* New York: Dover, 1979.

Magrath, C. Peter. "A Foot in the Door." *American Heritage* 15, Number 2 (February 1964): 44–48 and 88–92.

Mahoney, Olivia. "Black Abolitionists." *Chicago History* 20 (spring–summer 1991): 22–37.

Markman, Charles W. *Chicago before History: The Prehistoric Archaeology of a Modern Metropolitan Area.* Springfield: Illinois Historic Preservation Agency, 1991.

McGinty, Brian. "Mr. Sears and Mr. Roebuck." *American History Illustrated* (June 1986): 34–37 and 48.

McLear, Patrick E. "'. . . And Still They Come': Chicago from 1832–1836." *Journal of the West* 7 (1968): 397–404.

Meehan, Thomas A. "Jean Baptiste Point du Sable, the First Chicagoan." *Journal of the Illinois State Historical Society* (1963): 439–453.

Miller, Ross. *American Apocalypse: The Great Fire and the Myth of Chicago.* University of Chicago Press, 1990.

Nelson, Bruce C. *Beyond the Martyrs: A Social History of Chicago's Anarchists, 1870–1900.* New Brunswick, NJ: Rutgers University Press, 1988.

———. "Revival and Upheaval: Religion, Irreligion, and Chicago's Working Class in 1886." *Journal of Social History* 25 (1991): 233–253.

Peterson, William S. "Kipling's First Visit to Chicago." *Journal of the Illinois State Historical Society* 63 (1970): 290–301.

Renner, Richard Wilson. "In a Perfect Ferment: Chicago, the Know-Nothings, and the Riot for Lager Beer." *Chicago History* 5 (fall 1976): 161–170.

Sawislak, Karen. *Smoldering City: Chicagoans and the Great Fire, 1871–1874.* University of Chicago Press, 1995.

Schindler, Burton. "The Haymarket Bomb." *American History Illustrated* (June 1986): 20–27.

Schneirov, Richard. "Chicago's Great Upheaval of 1877." *Chicago History* (spring 1980): 2–17.

———. *Labor and Urban Politics: Class Conflict and the Origins of Modern Liberalism in Chicago, 1864–1897.* Urbana: University of Illinois Press, 1998.

Sennett, Richard. *Families against the City: Middle-Class Homes of Industrial Chicago, 1872–1890.* Cambridge, MA: Harvard University Press, 1970.

Smith, Carl S. *Urban Disorder and the Shape of Belief: The Great Chicago Fire, the Haymarket Bomb, and the Model Town of Pullman.* University of Chicago Press, 1995.

Smith, Nina B. "'This Bleak Situation': The Founding of Fort Sheridan, Illinois." *Illinois Historical Journal* 80 (spring 1987): 13–22.

Staudenraus, P. J. "'The Empire City of the West': A View of Chicago in 1864." *Journal of the Illinois State Historical Society* 56 (1963): 340–349.

Swenson, John F. "Chicagoua/Chicago: The Origin, Meaning, and Etymology of a Place Name." *Illinois Historical Journal* 84 (winter 1991): 235–248.

Wade, Louise Carroll. *Graham Taylor: A Pioneer for Social Justice, 1851–1938.* University of Chicago Press, 1964.

———. *Chicago's Pride: The Stockyards, Packingtown, and Environs in the Nineteenth Century.* Urbana: University of Illinois Press, 1987.

Weisberger, Bernard. "The Forgotten Four Hundred: Chicago's First Millionaires." *American Heritage* 38 (November 1987): 34–45.

Williams, Mentor L. "The Chicago River and Harbor Convention, 1847." *Mississippi Valley Historical Review* 35 (1949): 607–626.

The Great Fair (1893)

Burg, David F. *Chicago's White City of 1893.* Lexington: University Press of Kentucky, 1976.

Gilbert, James. *Perfect Cities: Chicago's Utopias of 1893.* University of Chicago Press, 1991.

Lewis, Arnold. *An Early Encounter with Tomorrow: Europeans, Chicago's Loop, and the World's Columbian Exposition.* Urbana: University of Illinois Press, 1997.

Miller, Donald L. "The White City." *American Heritage* (July–August 1993): 70–87.

Shaw, Marian. *World's Fair Notes: A Woman Journalist Views Chicago's 1893 Columbian Exposition.* St. Louis: Pogo Press, 1992.

Progressive Era (1894–1930)

Abbott, Edith. *The Tenements of Chicago, 1908–1935.* University of Chicago Press, 1936.

Allswang, John M. *A House for All Peoples: Ethnic Politics in Chicago, 1890–1936.* Lexington: University Press of Kentucky, 1971.

Barrett, James R. *Work and Community in the Jungle: Chicago's Packinghouse Workers, 1894–1922.* Urbana: University of Illinois Press, 1987.

Barrett, Paul. *The Automobile and Urban Transit: The Formation of Public Policy in Chicago, 1900–1930.* Philadelphia: Temple University Press, 1983.

Best, Wallace. "The Chicago Defender and the Realignment of Black Chicago." *Chicago History* 24 (fall 1995): 4–21.

Bukowski, Douglas. *Big Bill Thompson, Chicago, and the Politics of Image.* Urbana: University of Illinois Press, 1998.

Burnham, Daniel H., and Edward H. Bennett. *Plan of Chicago.* New York: Da Capo, 1970 re-edition by Charles Moore of 1909 original.

Cain, Louis P. "The Creation of Chicago's Sanitary District and Construction of the Sanitary and Ship Canal." *Chicago History* (summer 1979): 98–110.

Condit, Carl W. *The Chicago School of Architecture: A History of Commercial and Public Buildings in the Chicago Area, 1875–1925.* University of Chicago Press, 1964.

———. *Chicago, 1910–1929: Building, Planning and Urban Technology.* University of Chicago Press, 1973.

Diner, Steven J. *A City and Its Universities: Public Policy in Chicago, 1892–1919.* Chapel Hill: University of North Carolina Press, 1980.

Feffer, Andrew. *The Chicago Pragmatists and American Progressivism.* Ithaca, NY: Cornell University Press, 1993.

Flanagan, Maureen A. *Charter Reform in Chicago.* Carbondale: Southern Illinois University Press, 1987.

———. "The City Profitable, the City Livable: Environmental Policy, Gender, and Power in Chicago in the 1910s." *Journal of Urban History* 22, Number 2 (January 1996): 163–190.

Griggs, John. "Excursion to Death." *American Heritage* 16, Number 2 (February 1965): 32–35 and 111.

Hilliard, Celia. "'Rent Reasonable to Right Parties': Gold Coast Apartment Buildings, 1906–1929." *Chicago History* 8 (1979): 66–77.

Hines, Thomas S. *Burnham of Chicago: Architect and Planner.* University of Chicago Press, 1974.

Hogan, David J. *Class and Reform: School and Society in Chicago, 1880–1930.* Philadelphia: University of Pennsylvania Press, 1985.

Horowitz, Helen L. *Culture and the City: Cultural Philanthropy in Chicago from the 1880s to 1917.* Lexington: University of Kentucky Press, 1976.

Johnson, Curt. *The Wicked City: Chicago from Kenna to Capone.* New York: Da Capo, 1998.

Kantowicz, Edward R. *Polish-American Politics in Chicago, 1888–1940.* University of Chicago Press, 1975.

———. *Corporation Sole: Cardinal Mundelein and Chicago Catholicism.* University of Notre Dame Press, 1983.

Kelly, Jack. "Gangster City." *American Heritage* (April 1995): 65–87.

Kenney, William Howland. *Chicago Jazz: A Cultural History, 1904–1930.* New York: Oxford University Press, 1993.

———. "Chicago's 'Black Tans.'" *Chicago History* 26 (fall 1997): 4–31.

Lindberg, Richard. *Chicago by Gaslight: A History of Chicago's Netherworld, 1880–1920.* Chicago: Academy Chicago, 1996.

Lissak, Rivka Shpak. *Pluralism and Progressives: Hull House and the New Immigrants, 1890–1919.* University of Chicago Press, 1989.

McCarthy, Kathleen D. *Noblesse Oblige: Charity and Cultural Philanthropy in Chicago, 1849–1929.* University of Chicago Press, 1982.

Meyerowitz, Joanne J. *Women Adrift: Independent Wage Earners in Chicago, 1880–1930.* University of Chicago Press, 1988.

The Negro in Chicago: A Study of Race Relations and a Race Riot. University of Chicago Press and the Chicago Commission on Race-Relations, 1922.

Nelli, Humbert S. *Italians in Chicago, 1880–1930: A Study in Ethnic Mobility.* New York: Oxford University Press, 1970.

Pacyga, Dominic A. *Polish Immigrants and Industrial Chicago: Workers on the South Side, 1880–1922.* Columbus: Ohio State University Press, 1991.

Parot, Joseph John. *Polish Catholics in Chicago, 1850–1920: A Religious History.* DeKalb: Northern Illinois University Press, 1981.

Philpott, Thomas Lee. *The Slum and the Ghetto: Neighborhood Deterioration and Middle Class Reform, Chicago, 1880–1930.* New York: Oxford University Press, 1978.

Platt, Harold L. *The Electric City: Energy and the Growth of the Chicago Area, 1880–1930.* University of Chicago Press, 1991.

Posados, Barbara. "Suburb into City—the Transformation of Urban Identity on Chicago's Periphery: Irving Park as a Case Study, 1870–1920." *Journal of the Illinois State Historical Society* 76 (1983): 162–176.

Prosser, Daniel J. "Chicago and the Bungalow Boom of the 1920s." *Chicago History* 10 (summer 1981): 86–95.

Schmidt, John. *"The Mayor Who Cleaned Up Chicago": A Political Biography of William E. Dever.* DeKalb: Northern Illinois University Press, 1989.

Siry, Joseph. *Carson Pirie Scott: Louis Sullivan and the Chicago Department Store.* University of Chicago Press, 1988.

Spear, Allan H. *Black Chicago: The Making of a Negro Ghetto, 1890–1920.* University of Chicago Press, 1967.

Stamper, John W. *Chicago's North Michigan Avenue: Planning and Development, 1900–1930.* University of Chicago Press, 1991.

Tarr, Joel. *A Study of Boss Politics: William A. Lorimer of Chicago.* Urbana: University of Illinois Press, 1971.

Trautmann, Frederic. "Arthur Holitischer's Chicago: A German Traveler's View of an American City." *Chicago History* 12 (summer 1983): 36–50.

Tuttle, William M., Jr. *Race Riot: Chicago in the Red Summer of 1919.* New York: Atheneum, 1970.

Watterson, John S. "Chicago's City Championship: Northwestern University versus the University of Chicago, 1892–1905." *Chicago History* 11 (fall–winter 1982): 161–174.

Weiler, N. Sue. "Walkout: The Chicago Men's Garment Workers Strike, 1910–1911." *Chicago History* 8 (1979–1980): 238–249.

Wendt, Lloyd, and Herman Kogan. *Give the Lady What She Wants: The Story of Marshall Field and Company.* Chicago: Rand and McNally, 1952.

———. *Bosses in Lusty Chicago: The Story of Bath-house John and Hinky Dink.* Bloomington: Indiana University Press, 1967.

Wright, Gwendolyn. *Moralism and the Modern Home: Domestic Architecture and Cultural Conflict in Chicago, 1873–1913.* University of Chicago Press, 1980.

Zukowsky, John, editor. *The Plan of Chicago: 1909–1979.* Chicago, 1979.

———. *Chicago Architecture, 1872–1922: Birth of a Metropolis.* Munich, 1987.

Modern Era (1931–Present)

Biles, Roger. *Big City Boss in Depression and War: Mayor Edward J. Kelly of Chicago.* DeKalb: Northern Illinois University Press, 1984.

———. *Richard J. Daley: Politics, Race, and the Governing of Chicago.* DeKalb: Northern Illinois University Press, 1995.

Clavel, Pierre, and Wim Wiewel, editors. *Harold Washington and the Neighborhoods: Progressive City Government in Chicago, 1983–1987.* New Brunswick, NJ: Rutgers University Press, 1991.

Drake, St. Clair, and Horace R. Clayton. *Black Metropolis: A Study of Negro Life in a Northern City.* University of Chicago Press, 1993 revised edition.

Duis, Perry R. "Symbolic Unity and the Neighborhood: Chicago during World War II." *Journal of Urban History* 21, Number 2 (January 1995): 184–217.

Ebner, Michael H. *Creating Chicago's North Shore: A Suburban History.* University of Chicago Press, 1988.

Ehrenhalt, Alan. *The Lost City: Discovering the Forgotten Virtues of Community in the Chicago of the 1950s.* New York: HarperCollins, 1995.

Granger, Bill, and Lori Granger. *Lords of the Last Machine: The Story of Politics in Chicago.* New York: Random House, 1987.

Green, Paul M., and Melvin G. Holli. *The Mayors: The Chicago Political Tradition.* Carbondale: Southern Illinois University Press, 1995.

Grimshaw, William J. *Bitter Fruit: Black Politics and the Chicago Machine, 1931–1991.* University of Chicago Press, 1992.

Grossman, James R. *Land of Hope: Chicago, Black Southerners, and the Great Migration.* University of Chicago Press, 1989.

Guy, Roger. "The Media, the Police, and Southern White Migrant Identity in Chicago, 1955–1970." *Journal of Urban History* 26, Number 3 (March 2000): 329–349.

Hirsch, Arnold R. "Massive Resistance in the Urban North: Trumbull Park, Chicago, 1953–1966." *Journal of American History* 82 (September 1995): 522–550.

Holli, Melvin G., and Paul M. Green, editors. *The Making of the Mayor: Chicago, 1983.* Grand Rapids, MI: Eerdmans, 1984.

Homel, Michael W. *Down from Equality: Black Chicagoans and the Public Schools, 1920–1941.* Urbana: University of Illinois Press, 1984.

Keating, Ann Durkin. *Building Chicago: Suburban Developers and the Creation of a Divided Metropolis.* Columbus: Ohio State University Press, 1988.

Kleppner, Paul. *Chicago Divided: The Making of a Black Mayor.* DeKalb: Northern Illinois University Press, 1985.

Making the Second Ghetto: Race and Housing in Chicago, 1940–1960. New York: Cambridge University Press, 1983.

McMahon, Eileen M. *What Parish Are You From? A Chicago Irish Community and Race Relations.* Lexington: University Press of Kentucky, 1995.

Miranda, Rowan A. "Post-Machine Regimes and the Growth of Government: A Fiscal History of the City of Chicago, 1970–1990." *Urban Affairs Quarterly* 28 (March 1993): 397–422.

Pacyga, Dominic A., and Ellen Skerrett. *Chicago: City of Neighborhoods.* Chicago: Loyola University Press, 1986.

Rakove, Milton L. *Don't Make No Waves, Don't Back No Losers: An Insider's Analysis of the Daley Machine.* Bloomington: Indiana University Press, 1975.

———. *We Don't Want Nobody Nobody Sent: An Oral History of the Daley Years.* Bloomington: Indiana University Press, 1979.

Ralph, James R. *Northern Protest: Martin Luther King, Jr., Chicago, and the Civil Rights Movement.* Cambridge, MA: Harvard University Press, 1994.

Rast, Joel. *Remaking Chicago: The Political Origins of Urban Industrial Change.* DeKalb: Northern Illinois University Press, 2000.

Rivlin, Gary. *Fire on the Prairie: Chicago's Harold Washington and the Politics of Race.* New York: Henry Holt and Company, 1992.

Royko, Mike. *Boss: Richard J. Daley of Chicago.* New York: New American Library, 1971.

Slayton, Robert A. "Labor and Urban Politics: District 31, Steel-Workers Organizing Committee, and the Chicago Machine." *Journal of Urban History* 23, Number 1 (November 1996): 29–65.

Smith, Preston H., II. "The Quest for Racial Democracy: Black Civic Ideology and Housing Interests in Postwar Chicago." *Journal of Urban History* 26, Number 2 (January 2000): 131–157.

Squires, Gregory D., et al. *Chicago: Race, Class, and the Response to Urban Decline.* Philadelphia: Temple University Press, 1987.

Strickland, Arvarh E. *History of the Chicago Urban League.* Urbana: University of Illinois Press, 1966.

Wade, Richard C., Jr. "The Enduring Chicago Machine." *Chicago History* 15 (spring 1986): 4–19.

General Works

Arden, Harvey. "Chicago!" *National Geographic* 153, Number 4 (April 1978): 463–493.

Bach, Ira J. *Chicago on Foot: Walking Tours of Chicago's Architecture.* Chicago Review Press, 1994.

Bluestone, Daniel. *Constructing Chicago.* New Haven: Yale University Press, 1991.

Bowly, Devereux. *The Poorhouse: Subsidized Housing in Chicago, 1895–1976.* Carbondale: Southern Illinois University Press, 1978.

Canetti, Nicolai. *American Photo Album: Chicago.* New York: Haddington House, 1977.

Conniff, Richard. "Chicago: Welcome to the Neighborhood." *National Geographic* 179, Number 5 (May 1991): 50–77.

Cronon, William. *Nature's Metropolis: Chicago and the Great West.* New York: Norton, 1991.

Farr, Finis. *Chicago: A Personal History of America's Most American City.* New Rochelle, NY: Arlington House, 1973.

Furer, Howard B., compiler and editor. *Chicago: A Chronological and Documentary History.* Dobbs Ferry, NY: Oceana, 1974.

Green, Paul M., and Holli Melvin, editors. *The Mayors: The Chicago Political Tradition.* Carbondale: Southern Illinois University Press, 1987.

Handleman, Philip. *Chicago O'Hare: The World's Busiest Airport.* MBI, 1998.

Heise, Kenan, and Baumann Heise, editors. *Chicago Originals: A Cast of the City's Colorful Characters.* Chicago: Bonus Books, 1995.

Heise, Kenan, and Michael Edgerton. *Chicago: Center for Enterprise.* Woodland Hills, CA: Windsor Publications, 1982.

Historic City: The Settlement of Chicago. Chicago: Department of Development and Planning, 1976.

Holli, Melvin G., and Peter d'A. Jones, editors. *Ethnic Chicago: A Multicultural Portrait.* Grand Rapids, MI: Eerdmans, 1984.

Howard, Joseph P. *Chicago O'Hare International Airport: World's Busiest, World's Best.* Cherbo, 1996.

Hoyt, Homer. *One Hundred Years of Land Values in Chicago.* University of Chicago Press, 1933.

Jones, LeAlan, and Lloyd Newman. *Our America: Life and Death on the South Side of Chicago.* New York: Scribner, 1997.

Jordan, Robert Paul. "Illinois: The City and the Plain." *National Geographic* 131, Number 6 (June 1967): 745–797.

Kohl, Johann Georg. "Yesterday's City: Chicago's Geography." *Chicago History* 22 (spring 1993): 62–72.

Mayer, Harold M. *The Railroad Pattern of Metropolitan Chicago.* Department of Geography, University of Chicago, 1943.

Mayer, Harold M., and Richard C. Wade, Jr. *Chicago: The Growth of A Metropolis.* University of Chicago Press, 1969.

McCaffrey, Lawrence J., et al. *The Irish in Chicago.* Urbana: University of Illinois Press, 1987.

Miller, Donald L. *City of the Century: The Epic of Chicago and the Making of America.* New York: Simon and Schuster, 1996.

Monchow, Helen C. *Seventy Years of Real Estate: Subdividing in the Region of Chicago.* Evanston: Northwestern University Press, 1939.

Nash, Jay Robert. *Makers and Breakers of Chicago from Long John Wentworth to Richard J. Daley.* Chicago: Academy Chicago, 1985.

Newell, Barbara Warne. *Chicago and the Labor Movement.* Urbana: University of Illinois Press, 1961.

Pierce, Bessie Louise. *A History of Chicago, 1673–1893.* University of Chicago Press, 1937–1957, three volumes.

Pierce, Bessie Louise, editor. *As Others See Chicago: Impressions of Visitors, 1673–1933.* University of Chicago Press, 1933.

Population of the City of Chicago per Square Mile, 1900–1970. Chicago: Department of Development and Planning, 1975.

Randall, Frank A. *History of the Development of Building Construction in Chicago.* Urbana: University of Illinois Press, 1949.

Slayton, Robert A. *Back of the Yards: The Making of a Local Democracy.* University of Chicago Press, 1986.

Spinney, Robert G. *City of Big Shoulders: A History of Chicago.* DeKalb: Northern Illinois University Press, 2000.

Swanson, Stevenson, editor. *Chicago Days: 150 Defining Moments in the Life of a Great City.* Wheaton, IL: Catigny First Division Foundation Books, 1997.

Terkel, Studs. *Chicago.* New York: Pantheon, 1985.

Detroit

Early History (1701–1966)

Archer, Melanie. "Small Capitalism and Middle-Class Formation in Industrializing Detroit, 1880–1900." *Journal of Urban History* 21, Number 2 (January 1995): 218–255.

Bak, Richard. *Turkey Stearns and the Detroit Stars: The Negro Leagues in Detroit, 1919–1933.* Detroit: Wayne State University Press, 1995.

Boyle, Kevin, and Victoria Getis, editors.. *Muddy Boots and Ragged Aprons: Images of Working-Class Detroit, 1900–1930.* Detroit: Wayne State University Press, 1997.

Bresnahan, Timothy F., and Daniel M. G. Raff. "Intra-Industry Heterogeneity and the Great Depression: The American Motor Vehicles Industry, 1929–1935." *Journal of Economic History* 51, Number 2 (1991): 317–331.

Brown, Henry D., et al. *Cadillac and the Founding of Detroit.* Detroit: Wayne State University Press, 1976.

Burton, Clarence Monroe. *The City of Detroit, Michigan, 1701–1922.* Detroit and Chicago: S. J. Clarke, 1922, five volumes.

Capeci, Dominic J., Jr. *Race Relations in Wartime Detroit.* Philadelphia: Temple University Press, 1984.

Capeci, Dominic J., Jr., and Martha Wilkerson. *Layered Violence: The Detroit Rioters of 1943.* Jackson: University of Mississippi Press, 1991.

Cleland, Charles E. *Rites of Conquest: The History and Culture of Michigan's Native Americans.* Ann Arbor: University of Michigan Press, 1993.

Curcio, Vincent. *Chrysler: The Life and Times of an Automotive Genius.* New York: Oxford University Press, 2000.

Davis, Donald Findlay. *Conspicuous Production: Automobiles and Elites in Detroit, 1899–1933.* Philadelphia: Temple University Press, 1988.

Dunnigan, Brian Leigh. *Frontier Metropolis: Picturing Early Detroit, 1701–1838.* Detroit: Wayne State University Press, 2001.

Fine, Sidney. *Frank Murphy: The Detroit Years.* Ann Arbor: University of Michigan Press, 1975.

Flink, James J., and Glenn A. Niemeyer. "The General of General Motors." *American Heritage* 24, Number 5 (August 1973): 10–17 and 86–91.

Harrigan, Patrick. *The Detroit Tigers: Club and Community, 1945–1995.* University of Toronto Press, 1997.

Hivert-Carthew, Annick. *Cadillac and the Dawn of Detroit.* Davisburg, MI: Wilderness Adventure Books, 1994.

Katzman, David M. *Before the Ghetto: Black Detroit in the Nineteenth Century.* Urbana: University of Illinois Press, 1973.

Kavieff, Paul R. *The Purple Gang: Organized Crime in Detroit, 1910–1945.* New York: Barricade Books, 2000.

Levine, David Allan. *Internal Combustion: The Races in Detroit, 1915–1926.* Westport, CT: Greenwood, 1976.

Lewis, David L. "The Square Dancing Master." *American Heritage* 23, Number 2 (February 1972): 48–51.

Lichtenstein, Nelson. *The Most Dangerous Man in Detroit: Walter Reuther and the Fate of American Labor.* New York: Basic Books, 1995.

Madsen, Axel. *The Deal Maker: How William C. Durant Made General Motors.* New York: John Wiley and Sons, 1999.

Maloney, Thomas N., and Warren C. Whatley. "Making the Effort: The Contours of Racial Discrimination in Detroit's Labor Markets, 1920–1940." *Journal of Economic History* 55, Number 3 (1995): 465–493.

Meier, August, and Elliott Rudwick. *Black Detroit and the Rise of the UAW.* New York: Oxford University Press, 1979.

Mirel, Jeffrey. *The Rise and Fall of an Urban School System: Detroit, 1907–1981.* Ann Arbor: University of Michigan Press, 1993.

Niemeyer, Glenn A. *The Automotive Career of Ransom E. Olds.* East Lansing: Michigan State University Press, 1963.

Palmer, Friend. *Early Days in Detroit.* Detroit: Hunt and June, 1906.

Quaife, Milo Milton, editor. "A Journal of an Indian Captivity during Pontiac's Rebellion in the Year 1763 by Mr. John Rutherford, Afterward Captain, 42nd Highland Regiment." *American Heritage* 9, Number 3 (April 1958): 65–81.

Sugrue, Thomas J. *Origins of the Urban Crisis: Race and Inequality in Postwar Detroit.* Princeton University Press, 1996.

Thomas, June Manning. *Redevelopment and Race: Planning a Finer City in Postwar Detroit.* Baltimore: Johns Hopkins University Press, 1997.

Thomas, Richard W. *Life for Us Is What We Make It: Building Black Community in Detroit, 1915–1945.* Bloomington: University of Indiana Press, 1992.

Vargas, Zaragosa. *Proletarians of the North: A History of Mexican Industrial Workers in Detroit and the Midwest, 1917–1933.* Berkeley: University of California Press, 1993.

Zunz, Olivier. *The Changing Face of Inequality: Urbanization, Industrial Development, and Immigrants in Detroit, 1880–1920.* University of Chicago Press, 1982.

Current Development (1967–Present)

Abraham, Nabeel, and Andrew Shryock, editors. *Arab Detroit: From Margin to Mainstream.* Detroit: Wayne State University Press, 2001.

Chafets, Ze'ev. *Devil's Night and Other True Tails of Detroit.* New York: Random House, 1990.

Darden, Joe T., et al. *Detroit: Race and Uneven Development.* Philadelphia: Temple University Press, 1987.

Farley, Reynolds, et al. "Continued Racial Residential Segregation in Detroit: 'Chocolate City, Vanilla Suburbs' Revisited." *Journal of Housing Research* 4, Number 1 (1993): 1–38.

———. "Stereotypes and Segregation: Neighborhoods in the Detroit Area." *American Journal of Sociology* 100, Number 3 (1994): 750–780.

———. *Detroit Divided.* New York: Russell Sage Foundation, 2000.

Fine, Sidney. *Violence in the Model City: The Cavanagh Administration, Race Relations and the Detroit Riot of 1967.* Ann Arbor: University of Michigan Press, 1989.

Georgakas, Dan, and Marvin Surkin. *Detroit: I Do Mind Dying: A Study in Urban Revolution.* New York: St. Martin's Press, 1975.

Good, David L. *Orvie, the Dictator of Dearborn: The Rise and Reign of Orville L. Hubbard.* Detroit: Wayne State University Press, 1989.

Hartigan, John, Jr. *Racial Situations: Class Predicaments of Whiteness in Detroit.* Princeton University Press, 1999.

Henrickson, Wilma Wood, editor. *Detroit Perspectives: Crossroads and Turning Points.* Detroit: Wayne State University Press, 1991.

Hersey, John. *The Algiers Motel Incident.* New York: Alfred A. Knopf, 1968.

Rich, Wilbur C. *Coleman Young and Detroit Politics: From Social Activist to Power Broker.* Detroit: Wayne State University Press, 1989.

Shogan, Robert, and Tom Craig. *The Detroit Race Riot: A Study in Violence.* Philadelphia: Chilton, 1974.

Smith, Suzanne E. *Dancing in the Street: Motown and the Cultural Politics of Detroit.* Cambridge, MA: Harvard University Press, 1999.

Stolberg, Mary M. *Bridging the River of Hatred: The Pioneering Efforts of Detroit Police Commissioner George Edwards.* Detroit: Wayne State University Press, 1998.

Thompson, Heather Ann. "Rethinking the Politics of White Flight in the Postwar City: Detroit, 1945–1980." *Journal of Urban History* 25, Number 2 (January 1999): 163–198.

Widick, B. J. *Detroit: City of Race and Class Violence.* Detroit: Wayne State University Press, 1989 reprint of 1983 original.

Wolf, Eleanor P. *Trial and Error: The Detroit School Desegregation Case.* Detroit: Wayne State University Press, 1981.

General Works

Dunbar, Willis F., and George S. May. *Michigan: A History of the Wolverine State.* Grand Rapids, MI: Eerdmans, 1995 revised edition.

Eckert, Kathryn Bishop. *Buildings of Michigan.* New York: Oxford University Press, 1993.

Farmer, Silas. *History of Detroit and Wayne County, and Early Michigan: A Chronological Cyclopedia of the Past and Present.* Detroit: Gale, 1969.

Gilpin, Alec R. *The Territory of Michigan.* East Lansing: Michigan State University Press, 1970.

Godzak, Roman. *Make Straight the Path: A 300-Year Pilgrimage: Archdiocese of Detroit.* Strasbourg, France: Editions du Signe, 2000.

Lochbiler, Don. *Detroit's Coming of Age, 1873 to 1973.* Detroit: Wayne State University Press for *The Detroit News,* 1973.

Meyer, Katherine Mattingly, editor. *Detroit Architecture: A. L. A. Guide.* Detroit: Wayne State University Press, 1971.

Poremba, David Lee, editor. *Detroit in Its World Setting: A Three-Hundred Year Chronology, 1701–2001.* Detroit: Wayne State University Press, 2001 re-edition of 250th anniversary version published by the Detroit Public Library in 1951.

Quaife, Milo Milton. *This Is Detroit, 1701–1951: Two Hundred and Fifty Years in Pictures.* Detroit: Wayne State University Press, 1951.

Tentler, Leslie Woodcock. *Seasons of Grace: A History of the Catholic Archdiocese of Detroit.* Detroit: Wayne State University Press, 1990.

Woodford, Arthur M. *This Is Detroit, 1701–2001: An Illustrated History.* Detroit: Wayne State University Press, 2001.

Woodford, Frank B. and Arthur M. *All Our Yesterdays: A Brief History of Detroit.* Detroit: Wayne State University Press, 1969.

New Orleans

French Era (1699–1766)

Allain, Mathé. *"Not Worth a Straw": French Colonial Policy and the Early Years of Louisiana.* Lafayette: Center for Louisiana Studies, 1988.

Bossu, Jean-Baptiste. *Nouveaux voyages en Louisiane, 1751–1768.* Paris: Aubier-Montaigne, 1980 reprint of 1768 original published in Paris by Le Joy.

Brasseaux, Carl A. *L'Officier de Plume: Denis-Nicolas Foucault, Commissaire-Ordonnateur of French Louisiana.* Ruston: Northwestern Louisiana University Press, 1975.

———. "The Administration of Slave Regulations in French Louisiana, 1724–1766." *Louisiana History* 21 (1980): 139–158.

———. "A New Acadia: The Acadian Migrations to South Louisiana, 1764–1803." *Acadiensis [Canada]* 15, Number 1 (1985): 123–132.

Conrad, Glenn R., editor. *The First Families of Louisiana.* Baton Rouge: Louisiana State University Press, 1970, two volumes.

Crouse, Nellis M. *Lemoyne d'Iberville: Soldier of New France.* Ithaca, NY: Cornell University Press, 1954.

De Ville, Winston. *Le grand marquis: Pierre de Rigaud de Vaudreuil et la Louisiane.* Montreal: Fides, 1952.

———. *The New Orleans French, 1720–1733: A Collection of Marriage Records Relating to the First Colonists of the Louisiana Province.* Baltimore, 1973.

Delanglez, Jean. *The French Jesuits in Lower Louisiana, 1700–1763.* New Orleans: Loyola University Press, 1953.

Frégault, Guy. *Pierre Le Moyne d'Iberville.* Montreal: Fides, 1968.

Galloway, Patricia, editor. *La Salle and His Legacy: Frenchmen and Indians in the Lower Mississippi Valley.* Jackson: University Press of Mississippi, 1982.

Giraud, Marcel. *Histoire de la Louisiane française.* Paris: Presses Universitaires de France, 1953–1974, four volumes.

———. *A History of French Louisiana: The Reign of Louis XIV, 1698–1715.* Baton Rouge: Louisiana State University Press, 1974 translation of first volume by Joseph C. Lambert.

Heinrich, Pierre. *La Louisiane sous la Compagnie des Indes, 1717–1731.* New York: Burt Franklin, 1970 reprint of 1904 original.

Ingersoll, Thomas N. *Mammon and Manon in Early New Orleans: The First Slave Society in the Deep South, 1718–1819.* Knoxville: University of Tennessee Press, 1999.

Moore LaRoe, Lisa. "La Salle's Last Voyage." *National Geographic* 191, Number 5 (May 1997): 72–83.

O'Neil, Charles Edward. *Church and State in French Colonial Louisiana: Policy and Politics to 1732.* New Haven: Yale University Press, 1966.

Rowland, Dunbar, et al., editors and translators. *Mississippi Provincial Archives, French Dominion.* Jackson: Mississippi Department of Archives and History, Volumes 1–3, 1927–1932 and Baton Rouge: Louisiana State University Press, Volumes 4–5, 1984.

Silin, Charles I. "The French Theater in New Orleans." *American Society of the Legion of Honor Magazine* 27 (1957): 127–130.

Surry, Nancy M. Miller. *Calendar of Manuscripts in Paris for the History of the Mississippi Valley.* Washington, DC: Carnegie Institution, 1928, two volumes.

Usner, Daniel H., Jr. "The Frontier Exchange Economy of the Lower Mississippi Valley in the Eighteenth Century." *William and Mary Quarterly,* Third Series, Volume 44, Number 2 (1987): 165–192.

Weddle, Robert S. *The French Thorn: Rival Explorers in the Spanish Sea, 1682–1762.* College Station: Texas A&M University Press, 1991.

Spanish Era (1766–1803)

Acosta Rodríguez, Antonio. *La población de Luisiana española.* Madrid: Ministerio de Asuntos Exteriores, 1976.

Arena, Richard C. "Landholding and Political Power in Spanish Louisiana." *Louisiana Historical Quarterly* 36 (1955): 23–39.

Brasseaux, Carl A. *Denis-Nicolas Foucault and the New Orleans Rebellion of 1768.* Ruston: Louisiana Tech University Press, 1987.

Brasseaux, Carl A., and Glenn R. Conrad, editors. *The Road to Louisiana: The Saint-Domingue Refugees, 1792–1809.* Lafayette: University of Southwestern Louisiana Press, 1992.

Burson, C. M. *The Stewardship of Don Estéban Miró.* New Orleans: American Printing Company, 1940.

Caughey, John Walton. *Bernardo de Gálvez in Louisiana, 1776–1783.* Gretna, LA: Pelican, 1972.

Chandler, R. E. "Eyewitness History: O'Reilly's Arrival in Louisiana." *Louisiana History* 20, Number 3 (1979): 317–324.

———. "O'Reilly's Voyage from Havana to the Balize." *Louisiana History* 22, Number 2 (1981): 199–207.

Coutts, Brian E. "Boom and Bust: The Rise and Fall of the Tobacco Industry in Spanish Louisiana, 1770–1790." *The Americas: A Quarterly Review of Inter-American Cultural History [Academy of American Franciscan History]* 42, Number 3 (1986): 289–310.

Din, Gilbert C. "La defensa de la Luisiana española en sus primeros años." *Revista de Historia Militar [Spain]* 22, Number 45 (1978): 151–171.

Din, Gilbert C., and John E. Harkins. *The New Orleans Cabildo: Colonial Louisiana's First City Government, 1769–1803.* Baton Rouge: Louisiana State University Press, 1996.

Ezquerra Abadía, Ramón. "Un presupuesto americano: el del cabildo de Nueva Orleáns al terminar la soberanía española." *Anuario de Estudios Americanos [Spain]* 5 (1948): 675–701.

———. "Un patricio colonial: Gilberto de Saint-Maxent, teniente gobernador de Luisiana." *Revista de Indias [Spain]* 10, Number 39 (January–March 1950): 97–170.

Holmes, Jack D. L. *Honor and Fidelity: The Louisiana Infantry Regiment and the Louisiana Militia Companies, 1766–1821.* Birmingham, AL: "Louisiana Collection," 1965.

Holmes, Jack D. L., editor. *Documentos inéditos para la historia de La Luisiana, 1792–1810.* Madrid: Volume 15 of the "Colección Chimalistac" published by José Porrúa Turanzas, 1968.

Liljegren, Ernest R. "Jacobinism in Spanish Louisiana, 1792–1797." *Louisiana Historical Quarterly* 22 (1939): 47–92.

McConnell, Rolan C. *Negro Troops of Antebellum Louisiana.* Baton Rouge: Louisiana State University Press, 1968.

Moore, John Preston. "Antonio de Ulloa: A Profile of the First Spanish Governor of Louisiana." *Louisiana History* 8, Number 3 (1967): 189–218.

———. *Revolt in Louisiana: The Spanish Occupation, 1766–1770.* Baton Rouge: Louisiana State University Press, 1976.

Morazan, Ronald R., editor and translator. "'Quadroon' Balls in the Spanish Period." *Louisiana History* 14 (1973): 310–315.

Nasatir, Abraham P. *Spanish War Vessels on the Mississippi, 1792–1796.* New Haven: Yale University Press, 1968.

Texada, David Ker. *Alejandro O'Reilly and the New Orleans Rebels.* Lafayette: University of Southwestern Louisiana Press, 1970.

Voorhies, Jacqueline K., editor. *Some Late Eighteenth Century Louisianians.* Lafayette: University of Southwestern Louisiana Press, 1973.

Wood, Minter. "Life in New Orleans in the Spanish Period." *Louisiana Historical Quarterly* 22 (1939): 642–709.

Early American Era (1803–1815)

Brown, Wilbur S. *The Amphibious Campaign for West Florida and Louisiana, 1814–1815: A Critical Review of Strategy and Tactics at New Orleans.* Birmingham: Alabama University Press, 1969.

Carter, Clarence E., editor. *The Territorial Papers of the United States, Volume 9: Territory of Orleans, 1803–1812.* Washington, DC: Government Printing Office, 1940.

Carter, Samuel, III. *Blaze of Glory: The Fight for New Orleans, 1814–1815.* New York: St. Martin's, 1971.

Coker, William S. "How General Jackson Learned of the British Plans before the Battle of New Orleans." *Gulf Coast Historical Review* 3, Number 1 (1987): 84–95.

Dargo, George. *Jefferson's Louisiana: Politics and the Clash of Legal Traditions.* Cambridge, MA: Harvard University Press, 1975.

Everett, Donald. "Emigrés and Militiamen: Free Persons of Color in New Orleans, 1803–1815." *Journal of Negro History* 38 (1953): 377–402.

Forester, Cecil Scott. "Victory at New Orleans." *American Heritage* 8, Number 5 (August 1957): 4–9 and 106–108.

Lachance, Paul F. "The 1809 Immigration of Saint-Domingue Refugees to New Orleans: Reception, Integration and Impact." *Louisiana History* 29, Number 2 (1988): 109–141.

Morazan, Ronald, compiler. *Biographical Sketches of the Veterans of the Battalion of New Orleans, 1814–1815.* Baton Rouge: Louisiana State University Press, 1979.

Murdoch, Richard K. "The Battle of New Orleans and Associated Events." *History Today [UK]* 24 (1964): 172–182.

Nau, Frederick. *The German People of New Orleans, 1850–1900.* Leiden, 1958.

Niehaus, Earl F. *The Irish in New Orleans, 1800–1860.* Baton Rouge: Louisiana State University Press, 1965.

Robertson, James Alexander, editor. *Louisiana under the Rule of Spain, France, and the United States, 1785–1807.* New York: Libraries Press, 1969 reprint of 1911 original published in Cleveland by Arthur H. Clarke, two volumes.

Robin, C. C. *Voyage to Louisiana, 1803–1805.* New Orleans: Pelican, 1966 translation by Stuart O. Landry, Jr.

Roush, J. F. *Chalmette.* Washington, DC: National Park Service, 1958.

Modern Era (1815–Present)

Armstrong, Louis. Satchmo: *My Life in New Orleans.* New York: Prentice-Hall, 1954.

Arnesen, Eric. *Waterfront Workers in New Orleans: Race, Class, and Politics, 1863–1923.* New York: Oxford University Press, 1991.

Chase, John Churchill. *Frenchmen, Desire, Good Children, and Other Streets of New Orleans.* New York: Simon and Schuster, 1997 re-edition.

Connor, William P. "Reconstruction Rebels: The New Orleans Tribune in Post-War Louisiana." *Louisiana History* 21 (spring 1980): 159–181.

Dabney, T. E. *The Industrial Canal and Inner Harbor of New Orleans.* New Orleans: Board of Commissioners of the Port, 1921.

Dawson, Joseph G. "General Phil Sheridan and Military Reconstruction in Louisiana." *Civil War History* 24 (June 1978): 133–151.

———. *Army Generals and Reconstruction: Louisiana, 1862–1877.* Baton Rouge: Louisiana State University Press, 1982.

Heitman, John Alfred. *The Modernization of the Louisiana Sugar Industry, 1830–1910.* Baton Rouge: Louisiana State University Press, 1987.

Helis, Thomas W. "Of Generals and Jurists: The Judicial System of New Orleans under Union Occupation, May 1862–April 1865." *Louisiana History* 29 (spring 1988): 143–162.

Hirsch, Arnold R., and Joseph Logsdon, editors. *Creole New Orleans: Race and Americanization.* Baton Rouge: Louisiana State University Press, 1992.

Hollandsworth, James G. *Pretense of Glory: The Life of General Nathaniel P. Banks.* Baton Rouge: Louisiana State University Press, 1998.

Houzeau, Jean-Charles. *My Passage at the "New Orleans Tribune": A Memoir of the Civil War Era.* Baton Rouge: Louisiana State University Press, 1984 re-edition by David G. Rankin, translated by Gerard F. Denault.

Howard, Perry H. *Political Tendencies in New Orleans, 1812–1952.* Baton Rouge: Louisiana State University Press, 1957.

Latrobe, Benjamin Henry Boneval. *Impressions Respecting New Orleans: Diary and Sketches, 1818–1820.* New York: Columbia University Press, 1951 re-edition by Samuel Wilson, Jr.

Lockett, Samuel H. *Louisiana as It Is: A Geographical and Topographical Description of the State.* Baton Rouge: Louisiana State University Press, 1969 reprint edited by Lauren C. Post.

Marshall, Jessie Ames, editor. *Private and Official Correspondence of Gen. Benjamin F. Butler during a Period of the Civil War.* Norwood, MA: Plimpton Press, 1917.

McConnell, Roland C. *Negro Troops in Antebellum Louisiana: A History of the Battalion of Free Men of Color.* Baton Rouge: Louisiana State University Press, 1968.

Nau, J. F. *The German People of New Orleans.* Leiden: E. J. Brill, 1958.

Persico, Joseph E. "Vendetta in New Orleans." *American Heritage* 24, Number 4 (June 1973): 65–72.

Reinders, Robert C. *End of an Era: New Orleans, 1850–1860.* Gretna, LA: Pelican, 1964.

Rohrer, John H., et al. *The Eighth Generation: Cultures and Personalities of New Orleans Negroes.* New York: Harper and Row, 1960.

Rosenberg, Daniel. *New Orleans Dockworkers: Race, Labor, and Unionism, 1892–1923.* Albany: State University of New York Press, 1988.

Rousey, Dennis C. *Policing the Southern City: New Orleans, 1805–1889.* Baton Rouge: Louisiana State University Press, 1996.

Somers, Dale A. "Black and White in New Orleans: A Study in Urban Race Relations, 1865–1900." *Journal of Southern History* 40 (February 1974): 19–42.

Soulé, Leon Cyprian. *The Know Nothing Party of New Orleans: A Reappraisal.* Baton Rouge: Louisiana State Historical Association, 1961.

Tinker, Edward Laroque. *The Machiavellian Madam of Basin Street and Other Tales of New Orleans.* Austin, TX: Encino Press, 1969.

Tunnell, Ted. *Crucible of Reconstruction: War, Radicalism and Race in Louisiana, 1862–1877.* Baton Rouge: Louisiana State University Press, 1984.

Weisberger, Bernard A. "The Carpetbagger: A Tale of Reconstruction." *American Heritage* 25, Number 1 (December 1973): 70–77.

General Works

Arthur, S. C. *Old New Orleans.* New Orleans: Arthur Publications, 1944.

Asbury, Herbert. *The French Quarter.* Simon's Island: Mockingbird Books, 1979 reprint of 1936 original.

Bell, Caryn Cossé. *Revolution, Romanticism, and the Afro-Creole Protest Tradition in Louisiana, 1718–1868.* Baton Rouge: Louisiana State University Press, 1997.

Binder, Wolfgang, editor. *Creoles and Cajuns: French Louisiana-Louisiane Française.* New York: Peter Lang, 1998.

Cable, George Washington. *The Grandissimes: A Story of Creole Life.* New York: Viking Penguin, 1988 reprint of 1880 original.

———. *The Creoles of Louisiana.* New York: Garrett, 1970 reprint of 1884 original.

Conrad, Glenn R., editor. *A Dictionary of Louisiana Biography.* New Orleans: Louisiana Historical Association, 1988, two volumes.

Evans, Oliver. "Melting Pot in the Bayous." *American Heritage* 15, Number 1 (December 1963): 30–51 and 106–107.

Faulkner, William. *New Orleans Sketches.* New York: Random House, 1968.

Fiehrer, Thomas. "Saint-Domingue/Haiti: Louisiana's Caribbean Connection." *Louisiana History* 30, Number 4 (1989): 419–437.

Haas, Edward, editor. *Louisiana's Black Heritage.* New Orleans: Louisiana State Museum, 1979.

Huber, L. V. *Impressions of Girod Street Cemetery.* New Orleans, 1951.

———. *The Basilica on Jackson Square.* New Orleans, 1966.

Huber, L. V., and Samuel Wilson, Jr. *Baroness Pontalba's Buildings.* New Orleans, 1964.

Judge, Joseph. "New Orleans and Her River." *National Geographic* 139, Number 2 (February 1971): 151–187.

Keating, Bern. "Cajunland: Louisiana's French-Speaking Coast." *National Geographic* 129, Number 3 (March 1966): 352–391.

Kemp, John R. *New Orleans: An Illustrated History.* Woodland Hills, CA: Windsor Publications, 1981.

Lee, Douglas. "Mississippi Delta: The Land of the River." *National Geographic* 164, Number 2 (August 1983): 226–253.

Mathews, Hazel C. *British West Florida and the Illinois County.* Halifax, Nova Scotia, 1977.

McDonald, Robert R., et al., editors. *Louisiana's Black Heritage.* New Orleans: Louisiana State Museum, 1979.

New Orleans City Guide. Boston: Works Project Administration, 1938.

Parkerson, Codman. *New Orleans: America's Most Fortified City.* New Orleans: Quest, 1990.

Saxon, Lyle. *Fabulous New Orleans.* New Orleans: Robert L. Crager, 1947.

Searight, Sarah. *New Orleans.* New York: Stein and Day, 1973.

Sinclair, Harold. *Port of New Orleans.* Garden City, NJ: Doubleday, Doran and Company, 1942.

Smith, Griffin, Jr. "The Cajuns: Still Loving Life." *National Geographic* 178, Number 4 (October 1990): 40–65.

Tallant, Robert. *Mardi Gras.* Garden City, NJ: Doubleday and Company, 1948.

Touchstone, Blake. "Voodoo in New Orleans." *Louisiana History* (1972): 371–386.

Vesilind, Priit. "Upbeat, Downbeat, Offbeat New Orleans." *National Geographic* 187, Number 1 (January 1995): 90–119.

Vieux Carré, New Orleans: Its Plan, Its Growth, Its Architecture. New Orleans: Bureau of Government Research, 1968.

Wilson, Samuel, Jr. *Guide to New Orleans Architecture.* New Orleans, 1959.

New York City
Dutch Era (1624–1663)

Carras, Irmgard. "Who Cared?: The Poor in 17th Century New Amsterdam, 1628–1664." *New York History* 85, Number 3 (2004): 247–263.

deKoning, Joep M. J. "Dating the Visscher, or Prototype, View of New Amsterdam." *Halve Maen* 72, Number 3 (1999): 47–56.

Jacobs, Jaap. "'To Favor This New and Growing City of New Amsterdam with a Court of Justice': Relations between Rulers and Ruled in New Amsterdam." *Halve Maen* 76, Number 4 (2003): 65–72.

Maika, Dennis J. "New York Was Always a Global City: The Impact of World Trade on Seventeenth-Century New Amsterdam." *Magazine of History* 18, Number 3 (2004): 43–49.

Middleton, Simon. "'How It Came That the Bakers Bake No Bread': A Struggle for Trade Privileges in Seventeenth-Century New Amsterdam." *William and Mary Quarterly* 58, Number 2 (2001): 347–372.

Nooter, Eric. "Colonial Dutch Architecture in Brooklyn." *Halve Maen* 59, Number 1 (1985): 1–6, and Vol. 60, Number 1 (1987): 12–16.

Rink, O. A. *Holland on the Hudson: An Economic and Social History of the Dutch New York.* New York, 1986.

Swan, Robert J. "The Other Fort Amsterdam: New Light on Aspects of Slavery in New Netherland." *Afro-Americans in New York Life and History* 22, Number 2 (1998): 1942.

British Colonial Era (1664–1783)

Abbott, Carl. "The Neighborhoods of New York, 1760–1775." *New York History* 55 (1974): 35–54.

Collins, Charles Frederick. "The Artisans' Battle against Political Subordination in Colonial New York City." *UCLA Historical Journal* 2 (1981): 29–55.

Davis, Thomas J. *A Rumor of Revolt: The "Great Negro Plot" in Colonial New York.* New York: Free Press, 1985.

Gold, Nancy Dana. "The End of the Revolution." *American History Illustrated* 18, Number 7 (1983): 10–17.

Goodfriend, Joyce D. *Before the Melting Pot: Society and Culture in Colonial New York City, 1664–1730.* Princeton University Press, 1992.

Harris, Leslie M. "Slavery, Emancipation, and Class Formation in Colonial and Early National New York City." *Journal of Urban History* 30, Number 3 (2004): 339–359.

Hartog, Hendrik. *Public Property and Private Power: The Corporation of the City of New York in American Law, 1730–1870.* Chapel Hill: University of North Carolina Press, 1978.

Hodges, Graham. *New York City Cartmen, 1667–1850.* New York University Press, 1986.

Hoey, Edwin. "Terror in New York—1741." *American Heritage* 25, Number 4 (June 1974): 72–77.

Hoffer, Peter Charles. *The Great New York Conspiracy of 1741: Slavery, Crime, and Colonial Law.* Lawrence: University Press of Kansas, 2003.

Howe, Adrian. "The Bayard Treason Trial: Dramatizing Anglo-Dutch Politics in Early Eighteenth-Century New York City." *William and Mary Quarterly* 47, Number 1 (1990): 57–89.

Kammen, Michael. *Colonial New York: A History.* Oxford University Press, 1996.

Matson, Cathy. *Merchants and Empire Trading in Colonial New York.* Baltimore: Johns Hopkins University Press, 1998.

Middleton, Simon. "The World beyond the Workshop: Trading in New York's Artisan Economy, 1690–1740." *New York History* 81, Number 4 (2000): 381–416.

Narrett, David E. *Inheritance and Family Life in Colonial New York City.* Ithaca, NY: Cornell University Press, 1992.

Nash, Gary B. "The New York Census of 1737: A Critical Note on the Integration of Statistical and Literary Sources." *William and Mary Quarterly* 36, Number 3 (1979): 428–435.

Scott, Kenneth, editor. *Rivington's New York Newspaper: Excerpts from a Loyalist Press, 1773–1783.* New York: New York Historical Society, 1974.

Ultan, Lloyd. "Blacks in the Colonial Bronx." *Bronx County Historical Society Journal* 27, Number 2 (1990): 51–64.

VanBuskirk, Judith. "Crossing the Lines: African-Americans in the New York City Region during the British Occupation, 1776–1783." *Pennsylvanis History* 65 supplement (1998): 74–100.

Voorhees, David William. "The 'Fervent Zeale' of Jacob Leisler." *William and Mary Quarterly* 51, Number 3 (1994), 447–472.

Wright, Esther Clark. "The Evacuation of the Loyalists from New York in 1783." *Nova Scotia Historical Review [Canada]* 4, Number 1 (1984): 5–25.

Early Republican Era (1784–1865)

Albion, Robert G. *Rise of New York Port, 1850–1860.* New York: Charles Scribner's Sons, 1939.

Bernstein, Iver. *The New York City Draft Riots: Their Significance for American Society and Politics in the Age of the Civil War.* New York: Oxford University Press, 1990.

Blackmar, Elizabeth. *Manhattan for Rent, 1785–1850.* Ithaca, NY: Cornell University Press, 1989.

Bobbé, Dorothie. "Philip Hone's New York." *American Heritage* 8, Number 5 (August 1957): 12–23 and 88–93.

Bridges, Amy. *A City in the Republic: Antebellum New York and the Origins of Machine Politics.* New York: Cambridge University Press, 1984.

Chappel, William. "Before Urban Renewal." *American Heritage* 24, Number 4 (June 1973): 28–35.

Dangerfield, George. "The Steamboat's Charter of Freedom." *American Heritage* 14, Number 6 (October 1963): 38–43 and 78–80.

Dolan, Jay P. *The Immigrant Church: New York's Irish and German Catholics, 1815–1865.* Baltimore: Johns Hopkins University Press, 1975.

Ernst, Robert. *Immigrant Life in New York City, 1825–1863.* New York: King's Crown Press, 1949.

Gilfoyle, Timothy J. *City of Eros: New York City, Prostitution, and the Commercialization of Sex, 1790–1920.* New York: Norton, 1992.

Gilje, Paul A. *The Road to Mobocracy: Popular Disorder in New York City, 1765–1834.* Chapel Hill: University of North Carolina Press, 1987.

Gronowicz, Anthony. *Race and Class Politics in New York City before the Civil War.* Boston: Northeastern University Press, 1997.

Gunn, L. Ray. *The Decline of Authority: Public Economic Policy and Political Development in New York, 1800–1860.* Ithaca, NY: Cornell University Press, 1988.

Hill, Marilyn Wood. *Their Sisters' Keepers: Prostitution in New York City, 1830–1870.* Berkeley: University of California Press, 1993.

Lader, Lawrence. "New York's Bloodiest Week." *American Heritage* 10, Number 4 (June 1959): 44–49 and 95–98.

Mohl, Raymond A. *Poverty in New York, 1783–1825.* New York: Oxford University Press, 1971.

Peskin, Lawrence A. "From Protection to Encouragement: Manufacturing and Mercantilism in New York City's Public Sphere, 1783–1795." *Journal of the Early Republic* 18, Number 4 (1998): 589–615.

Pomerantz, Sidney Irving. *New York, an American City, 1783–1803: A Study of Urban Life.* New York: Columbia University Press, 1938.

Scherzer, Kenneth A. *Unbounded Communities: Neighborhood Life and Social Structure in New York City, 1830–1875.* Durham, NC: Duke University Press, 1992.

Spann, Edward K. *The New Metropolis: New York City, 1840–1857.* New York: Columbia University Press, 1981.

Stansell, Christine. *City of Women: Sex and Class in New York, 1789–1860.* New York: Knopf, 1986.

Stott, Richard B. *Workers in the Metropolis: Class, Ethnicity, and Youth in Antebellum New York.* Ithaca, NY: Cornell University Press, 1990.

White, Shane. *Somewhat More Independent: The End of Slavery in New York City, 1770–1810.* Athens: University of Georgia Press, 1991.

Wilentz, Sean. *Chants Democratic: New York City and the Rise of the American Working Class, 1788–1850.* New York: Oxford University Press, 1984.

Wright, Robert E. "The First Phase of the Empire State's 'Triple Transition': Banks; Influence on the Market, Democracy, and Federalism in New York, 1776–1838." *Social Science History* 21, Number 4 (1997): 521–558.

Modern Era (1866–Present)

Allison, Eric William. "Historic Preservation in a Development-Dominated City: The Passage of New York City's Landmark Preservation Legislation." *Journal of Urban History* 22, Number 3 (March 1996): 350–376.

Anderson, J. *This Was Harlem: A Cultural Portrait, 1900–1950.* New York: Farrar, Straus, and Giroux, 1982.

Andrews, Peter. "More Sock and Less Buskin." *American Heritage* 23, Number 3 (April 1972): 48–57.

Auchincloss, Louis. "Images of Elegant New York." *American Heritage* 17, Number 6 (October 1966): 48–65.

Beckert, Sven. *The Monied Metropolis: New York City and the Consolidation of the American Bourgeoisie, 1850–1896.* New York: Cambridge University Press, 2000.

Bellush, Jewel, and Dick Netzer, editors. *Urban Politics, New York Style.* Armonk, NY: M. E. Sharpe, 1990.

Boyer, Christine. *Manhattan Manners: Architecture and Style, 1850–1900.* New York: Rizzoli, 1985.

Brecher, Charles, and Raymond D. Horton. *Power Failure: New York City Politics and Policy since 1960.* New York: Oxford University Press, 1993.

Brooks, Tom. "The Terrible Triangle Fire." *American Heritage* 8, Number 5 (August 1957): 54–57 and 110–111.

Browin, Frances Williams. "When They Built the Big Bridge." *American Heritage* 7, Number 6 (October 1956): 68–73 and 110–112.

Callow, Alexander B., Jr. "The House That Tweed Built." *American Heritage* 16, Number 6 (October 1965): 64–69.

Chauncey, George. *Gay New York: Gender, Urban Culture, and the Making of the Gay Male World, 1890–1940.* New York: Basic Books, 1994.

Condit, Carl W. *The Port of New York: A History of the Rail and Terminal System from the Beginning to Pennsylvania Station.* University of Chicago Press, 1980.

Cray, Robert E. *Paupers and Poor Relief in New York City and Its Rural Environs.* Philadelphia: Temple University Press, 1988.

Daley, Robert. "Alfred Ely Beach and His Wonderful Pneumatic Underground Railway." *American Heritage* 12, Number 4 (June 1961): 54–57 and 85–89.

Danielson, Michael N. *New York: The Politics of Urban Regional Development.* Berkeley: University of California Press, 1982.

Doig, Jameson W. *Empire on the Hudson: Political Power and Progress at the Port of New York Authority.* New York: Columbia University Press, 2001.

Douglas, Ann. *Terrible Honesty: Mongrel Manhattan in the 1920s.* New York: Farrar, Straus, and Giroux, 1995.

Duberman, Martin. *Stonewall.* New York: Penguin, 1994.

Fainstein, Norman, and Susan Nesbitt. "Did the Black Ghetto Have a Golden Age? Class Structure and Class Segregation in New York City, 1949–1970, with Initial Evidence for 1990." *Journal of Urban History* 23, Number 1 (November 1996): 3–28.

Ford, James. *Slums and Housing, with Special Reference to New York City: History, Conditions, Policy.* Cambridge, MA: Harvard University Press, 1936, two volumes.

Gesar, Aram. *New York's Airports: Kennedy, LaGuardia, and Newark.* MBI, 1994.

Gutfreund, Owen D. "The Path of Prosperity: New York City's East River Drive, 1922–1990." *Journal of Urban History* 21, Number 2 (January 1995): 147–183.

Hammack, David C. *Power and Society: Greater New York at the Turn of the Century.* New York: Russell Sage Foundation, 1983.

Hancock, Ralph. *Fabulous Boulevard.* New York: Funk and Wagnalls, 1949.

Homberger, Eric. *Scenes from the Life of a City: Corruption and Conscience in Old New York.* New Haven: Yale University Press, 1994.

Hood, Clifton. *722 Miles: The Building of the Subways and How They Transformed New York.* Baltimore: Johns Hopkins University Press, 1995.

———. "Changing Perceptions of Public Space on the New York Rapid Transit System." *Journal of Urban History* 22, Number 3 (March 1996): 308–331.

Hume, Paul, and Ruth Hume. "Oscar and the Opera." *American Heritage* 24, Number 2 (February 1973): 60–69 and 87–88.

Hurley, Andrew. "Creating Ecological Wastelands: Oil Pollution in New York City, 1870–1900." *Journal of Urban History* 20, Number 3 (May 1994): 340–364.

Johnson, James Weldon. *Black Manhattan.* New York: Atheneum, 1968 reprint of 1930 original.

Kay, Ormonde de, Jr. "His Most Detestable High Mightiness." *American Heritage* 27, Number 3 (April 1976): 60–61 and 89.

Kramer, Rita. "Well, What Are You Going to Do about It?" *American Heritage* 24, Number 2 (February 1973): 17–21 and 94–97.

Landau, Sarah Bradford, and Carl W. Condit. *Rise of the New York Skyscraper, 1865–1913.* New Haven: Yale University Press, 1996.

Lawson, Ronald. *The Tenant Movement in New York City, 1904–1984.* New Brunswick, NJ: Rutgers University Press, 1986.

Lewis, David Levering. *When Harlem Was in Vogue.* Penguin, 1997.

Lockwood, Charles. *Manhattan Moves Uptown: An Illustrated History.* Boston: Houghton Mifflin, 1976.

Lyon, Peter. "The Master Showman of Coney Island." *American Heritage* 9, Number 4 (June 1958): 14–21 and 92–95.

Mandelbaum, Seymour J. *Boss Tweed's New York.* New York: J. Wiley and Sons, 1965.

McCullough, David G. "Hail Liberty!" *American Heritage* 17, Number 2 (February 1966): 22–23 and 96–99.

McNickle, Chris. *To Be Mayor of New York: Ethnic Politics in the City.* New York: Columbia University Press, 1993.

Mitgang, Herbert. *The Man Who Rode the Tiger: The Life and Times of Judge Samuel Seabury.* New York: J. B. Lippincott, 1963.

Moehring, Eugene P. *Public Works as the Patterns of Urban Real Estate Growth in Manhattan, 1835–1894.* New York: Arno, 1981.

Mollenkopf, John Hall. *Power, Culture and Place: Essays on New York City.* New York: Russell Sage Foundation, 1988.

———. *A Phoenix in the Ashes: The Rise and Fall of the Koch Coalition in New York City Politics.* Princeton University Press, 1992.

Monkkonen, Eric H. *Murder in New York City.* Berkeley: University of California Press, 2000.

Morris, John G. "A Century Old, the Wonderful Brooklyn Bridge." *National Geographic* 163, Number 5 (May 1983): 565–579.

Nadel, Stanley. *Little Germany: Ethnicity, Religion, and Class in New York City, 1845–1880.* Urbana: University of Illinois Press, 1990.

Pacelle, Mitchell. *Empire: A Tale of Obsession, Betrayal and the Battle for an American Icon.* New York: John Wiley, 2001.

Sagalyn, Lynne B. *Times Square Roulette: Remaking the City Icon.* Cambridge: Massachusetts Institute of Technology Press, 2001.

Sanders, James. *Celluloid Skyline: New York and the Movies.* New York: Alfred A. Knopf, 2001.

Schlichting, Kurt C. "Grand Central Terminal and the City Beautiful in New York." *Journal of Urban History* 22, Number 3 (March 1996): 332–349.

Schonberg, Harold C. "The Don Quixote of Opera." *American Heritage* 27, Number 2 (February 1976): 48–56 and 97.

Schwartz, Joel. *The New York Approach: Robert Moses, Urban Liberals, and Redevelopment of the Inner City.* Columbus: Ohio State University Press, 1993.

Scobey, David. "Anatomy of the Promenade: The Politics of Bourgeois Sensibility in Nineteenth-Century New York." *Social History* (1994): 203–227.

Shefter, Martin, editor. *Capital of the American Century: The National and International Influences of New York City.* New York: Russell Sage Foundation, 1993.

Snow, Richard F. "A Greeting from Coney Island." *American Heritage* 26, Number 2 (February 1975): 49–55.

Taurenac, John. *The Empire State Building: The Making of a Landmark.* New York: Scribner, 1995.

Taylor, William R., editor. *Inventing Times Square.* New York: Russell Sage Foundation, 1991.

Thomas, Lately. "Tammany Picked an Honest Man." *American Heritage* 18, Number 2 (February 1967): 34–39 and 94–98.

Wallach, Leonard. "The Myth of the Master Builder: Robert Moses, New York and the Dynamics of Metropolitan Development since World War II." *Journal of Urban History* 17 (1991): 339–362.

Webber, Jeanne Curtis. "The Capital of Capitalism." *American Heritage* 24, Number 1 (December 1972): 4–9 and 85–88.

Werner, Walter, and Steven T. Smith. *Wall Street.* New York: Columbia University Press, 1991.

Willis, Carol, editor. *Building the Empire State.* New York: Norton, 1998.

The WPA Guide to New York City. New York: New Press, 1995 reprint of 1939 edition.

General Works

Allen, Irving Lewis. *The City in Slang: New York Life and Popular Speech.* New York: Oxford University Press, 1993.

Bayor, Ronald H., and Timothy J. Meagher, editors. *The New York Irish.* Baltimore: Johns Hopkins University Press, 1996.

Bogart, Michele H. "Public Space and Public Memory in New York City's Hall Park." *Journal of Urban History* 25, Number 2 (January 1999): 226–257.

Burrows, Edwin G., and Mike Wallace. *Gotham: A History of New York City to 1898.* New York: Oxford University Press, 1998.

Buttenweiser, Ann L. *Manhattan Water-Bound: Planning and Developing Manhattan's Waterfront from the Seventeenth Century to the Present.* New York University Press, 1987.

Cohen, Paul E., and Robert T. Augustyn. *Manhattan in Maps, 1556–1990.* New York: Rizzoli, 1998.

Duffy, John. *A History of Public Health in New York City, 1625–1866.* New York: Russell Sage Foundation, 1968.

Foner, Nancy, editor. *Immigrants in New York.* New York: Columbia University Press, 2001.

Geisst, Charles. *Wall Street: A History.* Oxford University Press, 1997.

Gore, Rick. "Broadway: Street of Dreams." *National Geographic* 178, Number 3 (September 1990): 56–87.

Hall, Alice J. "Brooklyn: The Other Side of the Bridge." *National Geographic* 163, Number 5 (May 1983): 580–613.

———. "New Life for Ellis Island." *National Geographic* 178, Number 3 (September 1990): 89–101.

Hercules, Frank. "To Live in Harlem . . ." *National Geographic* 151, Number 2 (February 1977): 178–207.

Jackson, Kenneth T. *The Encyclopedia of New York City.* New Haven: Yale University Press, 1995.

Kouwenhoven, John A. *The Columbia Historical Portrait of New York: An Essay in Graphic History.* New York: Doubleday, 1953.

Lankevich, George J., and Howard B. Furer. *A Brief History of New York City.* Port Washington, NY: Associated Faculty Press, 1964.

Plunz, Richard A. *A History of Housing in New York City: Dwelling Type and Social Change in the American Metropolis.* New York: Columbia University Press, 1989.

Putnam, John J. "Manhattan: Images of the City." *National Geographic* 160, Number 3 (September 1981): 314–343.

Robertson, Archie. "The Island in the Bay." *American Heritage* 17, Number 5 (August 1966): 24–39 and 78–81.

Rosenwaike, Ira. *Population History of New York.* Syracuse University Press, 1972.

Rosenzweig, Roy, and Elizabeth Blackmar. *The Park and the People: A History of Central Park.* Ithaca, NY: Cornell University Press, 1992.

Salins, Peter D., editor. *New York Unbound.* London: Basil Blackwell, 1988.

Schoener, Allon. *New York: An Illustrated History of the People.* New York: Norton, 1998.

Still, Bayrd. *Mirror for Gotham: New York as Seen by Contemporaries from Dutch Days to the Present.* New York University Press, 1956.

Stokes, I. N. Phelps. *The Iconography of Manhattan Island, 1498–1909.* New York: R. H. Dodd, 1915–1928.

Swerdlow, Joel L. "Central Park: Oasis in the City." *National Geographic* 183, Number 5 (May 1993): 2–37.

———. "Under New York." *National Geographic* 191, Number 2 (February 1997): 110–131.

———. "New York's Chinatown." *National Geographic* 194, Number 2 (August 1998): 58–77.

Taylor, Clarence. *The Black Churches of Brooklyn.* New York: Columbia University Press, 1994.

Van Dyk, Jere. "Growing Up in East Harlem." *National Geographic* 177, Number 5 (May 1990): 52–75.

White, Peter T. "The World in New York City." *National Geographic* 126, Number 1 (July 1964): 52–107.

Zwingle, Erla. "New York Harbor: The Golden Door." *National Geographic* 170, Number 1 (July 1986): 1928.

Pensacola

Spanish Era (1689–1763)

Bratten, John R. "Buried Secrets: Analyses in the Emanuel Point Ship Laboratory." *Gulf South Historical Review* 14, Number 1 (1998): 31–45.

Childers, R. Wayne, and Joseph Cotter. "Arrested Development: The Economy at the Royal Presidio of Santa Maria de Galve, 1698–1719." *Gulf South Historical Review* 14, Number 1 (1998): 76–103.

Ford, Lawrence Carrol. *The Triangular Struggle for Spanish Pensacola, 1689–1739*. Washington, DC, 1939.

Griffen, William B. "Spanish Pensacola, 1700–1763." *Florida Historical Quarterly* 37 (January–April 1959): 242–262.

Harris, Norma. "Native Americans at Santa Maria de Galve: Linking the Historical and Archaeological Records." *Gulf South Historical Review* 14, Number 1 (1998): 46–60.

Hunter, James William, III. "Leaden Logs and Broken Ships: Pensacola's First Timber Industry, 1695–1712." *Gulf South Historical Review* 15, Number 2 (2000): 6–20.

Leonard, Irving A., editor and translator. *Spanish Approach to Pensacola, 1689–1693*. New York: Arno Press, 1967 reprint of 1939 original published in Albuquerque by the Quivira Society.

Núñez Cabeza de Vaca, Alvar. *Naufragios y comentarios*. Madrid: Espasa-Calpe, 1971 re-edition.

Oatis, Steven. "'To Eat Up a Village of White Men': Anglo-Indian Designs on Mobile and Pensacola, 1705–1715." *Gulf South Historical Review* 14, Number 1 (1998): 104–119.

Parks, Virginia, editor. *Santa Maria de Galve: A Story of Survival*. Pensacola, FL: Historical Society, 1998.

Smith, Roger C. "Pensacola's Tristan de Luna Shipwreck: A Look at the Archaeological Evidence." *Gulf South Historical Review* 14, Number 1 (1998): 21–30.

Weddle, Robert S. *Wilderness Manhunt: The Spanish Search for La Salle*. Austin: University of Texas Press, 1973.

———. *Spanish Sea: The Gulf of Mexico in North American Discovery, 1500–1685*. College Station: Texas A&M University Press, 1985.

———. *The French Thorn: Rival Explorers in the Spanish Sea, 1682–1762*. College Station: Texas A&M University Press, 1991.

Early Maps and Depictions of Pensacola, 1698–1801

Map of "Santa María de Galve" Bay and its hinterland, drawn in 1698 by the colony's founder, Andrés de Arriola—original held by the Archive of Indies at Seville, old Torres Lanzas call number: Mapas y Planos de México, 91

Diagram of Fort Carlos de Austria, 1699—original held by the Archive of Indies at Seville, old Torres Lanzas call number: Mapas y Planos de México, 93 [archival provenance: Audiencia de México, Legajo 617]

Diagrams of a proposed new harbor castle and its position at the western tip of Santa Rosa Island, drawn in 1728 by the military engineer Bruno Cavallero—originals held as Illustrations 4272–4273 of the Archivo General de la Nación in Mexico City, negatives 978/2011 and 978/2012 [archival provenance: *Reales Cédulas Originales,* Volume 47, Expediente 1, Folios 27–28]

Chart of soundings at the harbor entrance, 1739—original held by the Servicio Geográfico del Ejército in Madrid, call number: LM-8.ª–1.ª-a–15

Cutaway, diagram, and profile view of a proposed new fortification to guard the harbor entrance, 1739—original held by the Servicio Geográfico del Ejército in Madrid, call number: LM-8.ª–1.ª-a–17

View of the town in 1743, published twenty-six years later in Amsterdam as part of Isaac Tirion's *Hedendaagsche historie op tegenwoordinge staat van Amerika,* as well as in such subsequent works as William Roberts's *An Account of the First Discovery and Natural History of Florida* in 1792—numerous sources

Map of the old "Santa Rosa Punta de Sigüenza" island settlement, plus a proposed new "San Miguel de Panzacola" site on the mainland, drawn in August 1755 by the military engineer Felipe Feringán Cortés—original held by the Archive of Indies at Seville, old Torres Lanzas call number: Mapas y Planos de México, 202

Diagram and cutaway view of a proposed new mainland fort by Feringán Cortés, August 1755—original held by the Servicio Geográfico del Ejército in Madrid, call number: LM-8.ª–1.ª-a–16

Map of the new Pensacola establishment, with an insert showing its 10-gun San Carlos Battery, drawn in March 1756 by the military engineer Agustín López de la Cámara Alta—original held by the Servicio Geográfico del Ejército in Madrid, call number: LM-8.ª–1.ª-a–19

Detailed map of Pensacola in the mid-eighteenth century—original held by the Servicio Histórico Militar in Madrid, call number: 5062

Chart of Pensacola Bay in July 1761, by naval Capt. José Porlier of the royal frigate *Tétis*—original held by the Servicio Geográfico del Ejército in Madrid, call number: LM-8.ª–1.ª-a–14

Anonymous Spanish map of the town as surrendered to British control, August–September 1763—original held by the Archive of Indies at Seville, old Torres Lanzas call number: Mapas y Planos de Florida y Luisiana, 64 [archival provenance: Audiencia de Santo Domingo, Legajo 2574]

Pen-and-ink map on vellum of the harbor as "Surveyed in the year 1764 by George Gauld," plus an engraved version issued sixteen years later in London as part of the four-volume *Atlantic Pilot* of Joseph Frederick Wallet Des Barres—both held by the Library of Congress, control numbers: 73691619 and 77693968

View of Pensacola as drawn in 1764 by Gauld, then engraved several years later in London by Thomas Jefferys—originals held in the "P. K. Yonge Library of Florida History" at the University of Florida, as well as Number 37 of the "Mark F. Boyd Collection" of the Otto G. Richter Library, University of Miami

Chart of the bay in November 1768, by Juan José Elixio de la Puente—original held by the Servicio Geográfico del Ejército in Madrid, call number: LM-8.ª-1.ª-a-20

Diagrams of a proposed "new house and offices for the Governor of West Florida," designed in 1770 by Elias Durnford—original held by the Public Record Office in London, England

"Plan and Section of the upper and lower Batteries" atop Red Cliffs, laid out in March 1771—original held in the "P. K. Yonge Library of Florida History" at the University of Florida

Crude chart of the bay, ca. 1780—original held by the Servicio Geográfico del Ejército in Madrid, call number: LM-8.ª-1.ª-a-127

Chart of the bay entrance, 1781—original held by the Archive of Indies at Seville, old Torres Lanzas call number: Mapas y Planos de Florida y Luisiana, 114

Detailed maps of the Spanish siege lines outside Pensacola, May 1781—originals held by the Servicio Geográfico del Ejército in Madrid with call number: LM-8.ª-1.ª-a-13, plus the Archive of Indies at Seville with the old Torres Lanzas call number: Mapas y Planos de Florida y Luisiana, 247

Copy of a map of reconquered Pensacola by Havana's military engineer Luis Huet, dated 30 May 1781 by Francisco de Navas—original held by the Archive of Indies at Seville, old Torres Lanzas call number: Mapas y Planos de Florida y Luisiana, 87 bis [archival provenance: Audiencia de Santo Domingo, Legajo 1232]

Pen-and-ink map with watercolor highlights by José Portillo y Labaggi of recaptured Pensacola and its bay, May 1781—original held by the Archivo General de Simancas in Spain, call number: Mapas, Planos y Dibujos, XII-90 [archival provenance: Marina, Legajo 216]

Chart of the bay in May 1787, by the military engineer Gilbert Guillemard of New Orleans—originals held by the Servicio Histórico Militar in Madrid with call number P-b-10-35 and the Archive of Indies at Seville, old Torres Lanzas call number: Mapas y Planos de Florida y Luisiana, 114 [archival provenance: Audiencia de Santo Domingo, Legajo 2543]

Diagram and cutaway view of Fort San Bernardo, March 1792—original held by the Servicio Geográfico del Ejército in Madrid, call number: LM-8.ª-1.ª-a-18

Proposed plan for fortifying the town against Indian raids, by the military engineer Francisco de Paula Gelabert or Gelavert, February 1797—original held by the Archive of Indies at Seville, old Torres Lanzas call number: Mapas y Planos de Florida y Luisiana, 205 [archival provenance: Capitanía General de la Isla de Cuba, Legajo 2355]

Plan by Gelabert for a more modest palisade around the town, August 1799—original held by the Archive of Indies at Seville, old Torres Lanzas call number: Mapas y Planos de Florida y Luisiana, 204 [archival provenance: Capitanía General de la Isla de Cuba, Legajo 1551]

Diagrams of a new stone and wooden docks, drawn by Gelabert and copied in New Orleans by Guillemard, October 1801—originals held by the Archive of Indies at Seville, old Torres Lanzas call numbers: Mapas y Planos de México, 481 and 482ca.

British Era (1764–1780)

"The Case and Petition of His Majesty's Loyal Subjects, Late of West Florida." *Pensacola History Illustrated* 2, Number 4 (1987): 3–8.

Fabel, Robin F. A. "Governor George Johnstone of British West Florida." *Florida Historical Quarterly* 54, Number 4 (1976): 497–511.

———. "James Thompson, Pensacola's First Realtor." *Florida Historical Quarterly* 62, Number 1 (1983): 62–71.

———. "A Letter from West Florida in 1768." *Florida Historical Quarterly* 74, Number 4 (1996): 461–463.

García de León, Antonio. "Indios de la Florida en La Antigua, Veracruz, 1757–1770: un episodio de la decadencia de España ante Inglaterra." *Estudios de Historia Novohispana [Mexico]* 16 (1996): 101–118.

Gold, Robert L. "The Settlement of the Pensacola Indians in New Spain, 1763–1770." *Hispanic American Historical Review* 45, Number 4 (1965): 567–576.

Howard, Clinton N. "Colonial Pensacola: The British Period." *Florida Historical Quarterly* 19 (October 1940): 109–127.

Mathews, Hazel C. *British West Florida and the Illinois County.* Halifax, Nova Scotia, 1977.

McGovern, James R., editor. *Colonial Pensacola.* Pensacola, FL: Bicentennial Committee, 1974.

Mills, Bill. "Merchant and Naval Shipping of British Pensacola, 1763–1781." *Pensacola History Illustrated* 4, Number 1 (1991): 7–15.

Parks, Virginia. "The British Fort at Pensacola." *Pensacola History Illustrated* 3, Number 4 (1990): 11–18.

Rea, Robert Right. "The King's Agent for British West Florida." *Alabama Review* 16, Number 2 (1963): 141–153.

———. "Military Deserters from British West Florida." *Louisiana History* 9, Number 2 (1968): 123–137.

———. "'Graveyard for Britons': West Florida, 1763–1781." *Florida Historical Quarterly* 47, Number 4 (1969): 345–364.

———. "Brigadier Frederick Haldimand: The Florida Years." *Florida Historical Quarterly* 54, Number 4 (1976): 512–531.

———. "British West Florida Trade and Commerce in the Customs Records." *Alabama Review* 37, Number 2 (1984): 124–159.

———. "Urban Problems and Responses in British Pensacola." *Gulf Coast Historical Review* 3, Number 1 (1987): 43–62.

———. "British Pensacola." *Pensacola History Illustrated* 3, Number 4 (1990): 3–10.

———. "Master James Cook's Gulf Coast Cartography." *Map Collector [UK]* 51 (1990): 34–37.

Spanish Reoccupation (1781–1820)

Baker, Maury, and Margaret Sissler Haas, editors. "Bernardo de Galvez's Combat Diary for the Battle of Pensacola." *Florida Historical Quarterly* 56, Number 2 (1977): 176–199.

Beerman, Eric. "'Yo Solo' Not 'Solo': Juan Antonio de Riaño." *Florida Historical Quarterly* 58, Number 2 (1979): 174–184.

———. "José Solano, marqués del Socorro, y la armada en la batalla de Pensacola en 1781." *Revista General de Marina [Spain]* 204 (June 1983): 903–910.

Clavijo Provencio, Ramón. "España y la conquista de Pensacola." *Historia y Vida [Spain]* 19, Number 224 (1986): 32–41.

Coker, William S. "Religious Censuses of Pensacola, 1796–1801." *Florida Historical Quarterly* 61, Number 1 (1982): 54–63.

Coker, William S., and Rodrigo Fernández Carrión, compilers. "List of the Inhabitants of Pensacola Who Were Householders at the Time of the Capitulation." *Florida Historical Quarterly* 77, Number 1 (1998): 68–72.

Coker, William S., and Hazel P. Coker. *The Siege of Pensacola, 1781, in Maps.* Pensacola, FL: Perdido Bay, 1981.

Coker, William S., and G. Douglas Inglis. *The Spanish Censuses of Pensacola, 1784, 1820: A Genealogical Guide to Spanish Pensacola.* Pensacola, FL: Perdido Bay, 1980.

Coker, William S., and Robert R. Rea, editors. *Anglo-Spanish Confrontation on the Gulf Coast during the American Revolution.* Pensacola, FL: Gulf Coast History and Humanities Conference, 1982.

Fabel, Robin F. A. "Ordeal by Siege: James Bruce in Pensacola, 1780–1781." *Florida Historical Quarterly* 66, Number 3 (1988): 280–297.

Fleming, Thomas. "Bernardo de Galvez." *American Heritage* 33, Number 3 (1982): 30–39.

Gálvez, Bernardo de. *Yo Solo: The Battle Journal of Bernardo de Gálvez during the American Revlution.* New Orleans: Polyanthos, 1978 translation by E. A. Montemayor.

Haarmann, Albert W. "The Siege of Pensacola: An Order of Battle." *Florida Historical Quarterly* 44, Number 3 (1966): 193–199.

Holmes, Jack D. L. "Spanish Treaties with West Florida Indians, 1784–1802." *Florida Historical Quarterly* 48, Number 2 (1969): 140–154.

Mueller, Edward A. "'Fighting Nicolls' of the British Royal Marines." *Pensacola History Illustrated* 5, Number 1 (1996): 2–23.

Murphy, W. S. "The Irish Brigade of Spain at the Capture of Pensacola, 1781." *Florida Historical Quarterly* 38, Number 3 (1960): 216–225.

Owsley, Frank L., Jr. "Jackson's Capture of Pensacola." *Alabama Review* 19, Number 3 (1966): 175–185.

———. "British and Indian Activities in Spanish West Florida during the War of 1812." *Florida Historical Quarterly* 46, Number 2 (1967): 111–123.

Quatrefages, René. "La participación militar de Francia en la toma de Pensacola." *Revista de Historia Militar [Spain]* 21, Number 42 (1977): 7–30.

———. "La collaboration franco-espagnole dans la prise de Pensacola." *Revue historique des armées [France]* 4 (1981): 44–63.

Reparaz, Carmen de. *Yo solo: Bernardo de Gálvez y la toma de Panzacola en 1781: una contribución española a la independencia de los Estados Unidos.* Barcelona: Serbal, 1986.

Rucker, Brian R. "Nixon's Raid and Other Precursors to Jackson's 1814 Invasion of Spanish West Florida." *Gulf South Historical Review* 14, Number 2 (1999): 33–50.

Servies, James A., editor. *The Log of H.M.S. "Mentor," 1780–1781: A New Account of the British Navy at Pensacola.* Gainesville: University Presses of Florida, 1982.

Torneo Tinajero, Pablo. "Estudio de la población de Pensacola, 1784–1820." *Anuario de Estudios Americanos [Spain]* 34 (1977): 537–561.

Watson, Thomas D., and Samuel Wilson, Jr. "A Lost Landmark Revisited: The Panton House of Pensacola." *Florida Historical Quarterly* 60, Number 1 (1981): 42–50.

White, David H. "Commandant Folch at San Fernando de las Barrancas, 1795–1796." *Tennessee Historical Quarterly* 33, Number 4 (1974): 379–388.

Wilkie, Everett C., Jr. "New Light on Galvez's First Attempt to Attack Pensacola." *Florida Historical Quarterly* 62, Number 2 (1983): 194–199.

Wilson, Harry J. "The Americanization of the Second Spanish Period West Florida Interior." *Gulf South Historical Review* 15, Number 1 (1999): 6–17.

Antebelum Era (1821–1860)

Coker, William S. "The Names of Some of West Florida's Citizens, December 1821." *Pensacola History Illustrated* 5, Number 3 (1999): 22–28.

Coker, William S., and Ronald V. Evans. "Poetry and Politics in Pensacola, 1821." *Pensacola History Illustrated* 4, Number 1 (1991): 19–24.

Coleman, James C. "Fort McRee: 'A Castle Built on Sand.'" *Pensacola History Illustrated* 3, Numbers 1–2 (1988): 1–123.

Dawkins, Mary Merritt. "Religion in Early Pensacola: The Birth of Protestantism, 1822–1845." *Pensacola History Illustrated* 3, Number 3 (1989): 22–32.

———. "The West Florida Board of Land Commissioners." *Pensacola History Illustrated* 5, Number 3 (1999): 2–6.

Dibble, Ernest F. *Antebellum Pensacola and the Military Presence.* Pensacola, FL: Pensacola-Escambia Development Committee, 1974.

———. "Slave Rentals to the Military: Pensacola and the Gulf Coast." *Civil War History* 23, Number 2 (1977): 101–113.

Doherty, Herbert J., Jr. "Andrew Jackson's Cronies in Florida Territorial Politics." *Florida Historical Quarterly* 34 (1955): 3–29.

Dunne, W. M. P. "November 7, 1825: The Day Pensacola Nearly Sank the Navy." *Pensacola History Illustrated* 3, Number 3 (1989): 3–11.

Dysart, Jane E. "Another Road to Disappearance: Assimilation of Creek Indians in Pensacola, Florida, during the Nineteenth Century." *Florida Historical Quarterly* 61, Number 1 (1982): 37–48.

Eisterhold, John A. "Lumber and Trade in Pensacola and West Florida, 1800–1860." *Florida Historical Quarterly* 51, Number 3 (1973): 267–280.

Ellsworth, Lucius F. "Raiford and Abercrombie: Pensacola's Premier Antebellum Manufacturer." *Florida Historical Quarterly* 52, Number 3 (1974): 247–260.

Gray, O. Ronald, and Richard V. Calvasina. "The 1826 Contract for Construction of Facilities at the Pensacola Naval Station and Its Implications for Historical Research Using Agency Theory." *Accounting Historians Journal* 22, Number 1 (1995): 35–55.

Knetsch, Joe. "The Canal Era in West Florida: 1821–1845." *Gulf Coast Historical Review* 7, Number 1 (1991): 38–51.

McGovern, James R., editor. *Andrew Jackson and Pensacola.* Pensacola, FL: Bicentennial Committee, 1974.

McInnis, Katherine, editor. "When Smallpox Struck." *U.S. Naval Institute Proceedings* 97, Number 9 (1971): 78–82.

Norris, L. David. "The Squeeze: Spain Cedes Florida to the United States." *Escribano* 25 (1988): 101–133.

"Notes on the Arcadia (Florida) Manufacturing Company." *Cotton History Review* 2, Number 3 (1961): 162–166.

Pearce, George F. "The United States Navy Comes to Pensacola." *Florida Historical Quarterly* 55, Number 1 (1976): 37–47.

Rucker, Brian R. "Dog Days in Old Pensacola." *Pensacola History Illustrated* 4, Number 1 (1991): 25–30.

———. "Hutto the Highwayman." *Pensacola History Illustrated* 4, Number 3 (1995): 13–19.

———. "Pensacola in 1845." *Pensacola History Illustrated* 4, Number 3 (1995): 4–12.

Shelley, Dian Lee. "Tivoli Theatre of Pensacola." *Florida Historical Quarterly* 50, Number 4 (1972): 341–351.

Civil War Era (1861–1865)

Alison, Joseph Dill. "'I Have Been through My First Battle and Have Had Enough War to Last Me.'" *Civil War Times Illustrated* 5, Number 10 (1967): 40–46.

Bearss, Edwin C. "Civil War Operations in and around Pensacola." *Florida Historical Quarterly* 36, Number 2 (1957): 125–165, Volume 39, Number 3 (1961): 231–255, and Number 4: 330–353.

———. "Fort Pickens and the Secession Crisis: January–February 1861." *Gulf Coast Historical Review* 4, Number 2 (1989): 6–25.

Coker, William S. "The Moreno Family of Pensacola and the Civil War." *Gulf Coast Historical Review* 4, Number 2 (1989): 100–125.

Cooley, James. "The Relief of Fort Pickens." *American Heritage* 25, Number 2 (February 1974): 72–77 and 85–88.

DeBolt, Dean. "Life on the Front as Reflected in Soldiers' Letters." *Gulf Coast Historical Review* 4, Number 2 (1989): 26–37.

Holmes, Jack D. L. "Pensacola's Civil War Art: Benjamin Labree and Thomas Nast." *Gulf Coast Historical Review* 4, Number 2 (1989): 50–57.

Lufkin, Charles L. "War Council in Pensacola, January 17, 1861." *Gulf Coast Historical Review* 9, Number 1 (1993): 47–64.

Pearce, George F. *Pensacola during the Civil War: A Thorn in the Side of the Confederacy.* Gainesville: University Presses of Florida, 2000.

Richardson, Joe M. "Some Civil War Letters of a Mississippi Private." *Journal of Mississippi History* 38, Number 1 (1976): 69–74.

Rodgers, Thomas G. "Florida's War of Nerves." *Civil War Times Illustrated* 38, Number 3 (1999): 30–35, 48–50, and 52–53.

Rye, Scott. "Burn the Rebel Pirate!" *Civil War Times Illustrated* 38, Number 3 (1999): 24–28.

Scassellati, Robert R., Jr. "First Shots at Fort Barrancas." *Civil War Times Illustrated* 11, Number 9 (1973): 38–43.

Sullivan, David M. "The Confederate Marines of Pensacola." *Pensacola History Illustrated* 2, Number 4 (1987): 12–21.

Tidball, Eugene C. "The Fort Pickens Relief Expedition of 1861: Lt. John C. Tidball's Journals." *Civil War History* 42, Number 4 (1996): 322–339.

Walker, Henry. "Young Men Go to War: The First Regiment Alabama Volunteer Infantry at Pensacola, 1861." *Gulf Coast Historical Review* 13, Number 2 (1998): 6–34.

Woolsey, Nathan F. "'Conflict at the Water's Edge': Ollinger and Bruce, Frederick G. Howard, and Confederate Naval Gunboat Construction on the Lower Blackwater River, 1861–1862." *Gulf Coast Historical Review* 9, Number 2 (1994): 44–67.

Modern Era (1866–Present)

Bliss, Charles H. "Churches." *Pensacola History Illustrated* 2, Number 3 (1987): 24–32.

———. "Pensacola's Social Features." *Pensacola History Illustrated* 2, Number 3 (1987): 17–23.

———. "A Word to Patrons." *Pensacola History Illustrated* 2, Number 3 (1987): 5–16.

Bowden, Jesse Earle. "The Twenties: Thoughts on the Unruly Jazz Age." *Gulf Coast Historical Review* 12, Number 2 (1996): 6–20.

Bradley, Robert B. "The Role of the Army in Pensacola." *Pensacola History Illustrated* 2, Number 4 (1987): 22–28.

Bragaw, Donald H. "Loss of Identity on Pensacola's Past: A Creole Footnote." *Florida Historical Quarterly* 50, Number 4 (1972): 414–418.

———. "Status of Negroes in a Southern Port City in the Progressive Era." *Florida Historical Quarterly* 51, Number 3 (1973): 281–302.

Coker, William S., and Nathan F. Woolsey. *Commitment to a Community: A History of Sacred Heart Hospital.* Pensacola, FL: Sacred Heart Hospital, 1996.

Coleman, James C. "Gunfire on the Gulf." *Pensacola History Illustrated* 4, Number 1 (1991): 1–6.

Dawkins, Mary Merritt. "Eugene Edwin Saunders: Master of the Fleet." *Pensacola History Illustrated* 4, Number 2 (1993): 11–18.

———. "Robert E. Lee Square: A Memorial to Our Confederate Dead." *Pensacola History Illustrated* 5, Number 2 (1997): 8–13.

Flynt, Wayne. "Pensacola Labor Problems and Political Radicalism, 1908." *Florida Historical Quarterly* 43, Number 4 (1965): 315–332.

Gaines, William. "The Coast Artillery at Pensacola Bay, 1898–1946." *Periodical: Journal of America's Military Past* 23, Number 2 (1996): 25–38.

Hallett, George E. A. "Glenn H. Curtiss' First Off-Water Flight." *Aerospace Historian* 12 (1976): 165–166.

Hamilton, William C. "The Warren Fish Company of Pensacola." *Pensacola History Illustrated* 4, Number 2 (1993): 3–9.

Harmon, Sharon Norris. "The Founding of St. Joseph's Parish: The Catholic Church and Race Relations in Pensacola, Florida, 1865–1900." *Gulf Coast Historical Review* 12, Number 2 (1997): 98–119.

Jackson, John J. "A Student Aviator Discovers Pensacola." *Pensacola History Illustrated* 2, Number 1 (1986): 26–31.

McGovern, James R. "'Sporting Life on the Line': Prostitution in Progressive Era Pensacola." *Florida Historical Quarterly* 54, Number 2 (1975): 131–144.

———. *The Emergence of a City in the Modern South: Pensacola, 1900–1945.* DeLeon Springs, FL: Painter, 1976.

———. "Pensacola, Florida: A Military City in the New South." *Florida Historical Quarterly* 59, Number 1 (1980): 24–41.

McNeil, Charles Robert. "The Fishermen." *Pensacola History Illustrated* 4, Number 2 (1993): 25–31.

Meier, August, and Elliott Rudwick. "Negro Boycotts of Segregated Streetcars in Florida, 1901–1905." *South Atlantic Quarterly* 69, Number 4 (1970): 525–533.

Muir, Thomas, Jr. "1920s East Zaragoza Street, Pensacola, Florida." *Gulf Coast Historical Review* 12, Number 1 (1996): 171–187.

Parks, Virginia. "Jewish Life in Pensacola." *Pensacola History Illustrated* 4, Number 4 (1996): 2–10.

Rucker, Brian R. "It Can't Happen Here?: A History of Earthquakes in West Florida." *Pensacola History Illustrated* 5, Number 2 (1997): 14–27.

Sharpe, Clifford C. "The Spearman Brewing Company." *Pensacola History Illustrated* 5, Number 2 (1997): 1–4.

Shofner, Jerrell H. "The Pensacola Workingman's Association: A Militant Negro Labor Union during Reconstruction." *Labor History* 13, Number 4 (1972): 555–559.

Thompson, Sharyn. "These Works of Mortuary Masonry: The Above-Ground Tombs of St. Michael Cemetery, Pensacola, Florida." *Southern Quarterly* 31, Number 2 (1993): 50–73.

General Works

Bense, Judith A., editor. *Archaeology of Colonial Pensacola.* Gainesville: University Presses of Florida, 1999.

Breetzke, David E. "The Sequence of Military Occupations on the Barrancas." *Gulf South Historical Review* 14, Number 1 (1998): 61–75.

Coker, William S. "Pensacola's Medical History: The Colonial Era, 1559–1821." *Florida Historical Quarterly* 77, Number 2 (1998): 181–192.

Coleman, James C., and Irene S. Coleman. *Guardians on the Gulf: Pensacola Fortifications, 1698–1980.* Pensacola, FL: Historical Society, 1982.

Ellsworth, Lucius F., and Linda. Ellsworth. *Pensacola: The Deep Water City.* Tulsa, OK: Continental Heritage, 1982.

Lloyd, Robert B., Jr. "Development of the Plan of Pensacola during the Colonial Era, 1559–1821." *Florida Historical Quarterly* 64, Number 3 (1986): 253–272.

Marks, Henry S., and William R. Lux. "Pensacola: City under Five Flags." *Américas [Organization of American States]* 24, Number 9 (September 1972): 31–33.

Pearce, George F. "Torment of Pestilence: Yellow Fever Epidemics in Pensacola." *Florida Historical Quarterly* 56 (1978): 448–472.

———. *The U.S. Navy in Pensacola: From Sailing Ships to Naval Aviation, 1825–1930.* Pensacola: University of West Florida and University Presses of Florida, 1980.

———. "Pensacola, the Deep-Water Harbor of the Gulf: Its Development, 1825–1930." *Gulf Coast Historical Review* 5, Number 2 (1990): 128–139.

Pensacola Picture Book. Pensacola: T. T. Wentworth Jr. Museum, 1964–1974, 25 issues.

"Pensacola Quadricentennial Issue." *Florida Historical Quarterly* 37, Numbers 3–4 (January–April 1959): 199–464.

Phillips, John C. "Flood Thy Neighbor: Colonial and American Water-Powered Mills in West Florida." *Gulf South Historical Review* 14, Number 1 (1998): 143–157.

Philadelphia

Colonial and Revolutionary Eras (1683–1800)

Alexander, John K. *Render Them Submissive: Responses to Poverty in Philadelphia, 1760–1800.* Amherst: University of Massachusetts Press, 1980.

Alotta, Robert I. *Another Part of the Field: America's Revolution, 1777–1778.* White Mane, 1990.

Baltzell, E. Digby. *Philadelphia Gentlemen: The Making of a National Upper Class.* Glencoe, IL: Free Press, 1958, reprinted in New Brunswick, NJ, by Transaction Publishers in 1992.

Bishop, Morris. "You Are Invited to a Mischianza." *American Heritage* 25, Number 5 (August 1974): 69–75.

Bridenbaugh, Carl, and Jessica Bridenbaugh. *Rebels and Gentlemen: Philadelphia in the Age of Franklin.* New York: Oxford University Press, 1942.

Burt, Nathaniel. *Perennial Philadelphians: The Anatomy of an American Aristocracy.* Boston: Little, Brown, 1963.

Cotter, John L., et al. *The Buried Past: An Archaeological History of Philadelphia.* Philadelphia: University of Pennsylvania Press, 1993.

Davidson, Marshall B. "Penn's City: American Athens." *American Heritage* 12, Number 2 (February 1961): 10–29 and 103–107.

Diamondstone, Judith. "Philadelphia's Municipal Corporation, 1701–1776." *Pennsylvania Magazine of History and Biography* (1966): 183–201.

Doerflinger, Thomas M. *A Vigorous Spirit of Enterprise: Merchants and Economic Development in Revolutionary Philadelphia.* Chapel Hill: University of North Carolina Press, 1986.

Driver, Clive E., compiler. *Passing Through: Letters and Documents Written in Philadelphia by Famous Visitors.* Rosenbach Museum, 1982.

Dunn, Richard S., and Mary Maples, editors. *The World of William Penn.* Philadelphia: University of Pennsylvania Press, 1986.

———. *The Papers of William Penn.* Philadelphia: University of Pennsylvania Press, 1982–1986, five volumes.

Harris, P. M. G. "The Demographic Development of Colonial Philadelphia in Comparative Perspective." *Proceedings of the American Philosophical Society* 133 (1989): 262–304.

Illick, Joseph. *Colonial Pennsylvania: A History.* New York: Scribners, 1976.

Klepp, Susan E. "Demography of Early Philadelphians." *Proceedings of the American Philosophical Society* 133 (1989): 85–111.

———. *Philadelphia in Transition: A Demographic History of the City and Its Occupational Groups, 1720–1830.* New York: Garland, 1989.

Lindsey, Jack, et al. *Worldly Goods: The Arts of Early Pennsylvania, 1680–1758.* Philadelphia: Museum of Art, 1999.

Miller, Richard G. *Philadelphia, the Federalist City: A Study of Urban Politics, 1789–1801.* Port Washington, NY: Kennikat, 1976.

Nash, Gary B. *Quakers and Politics: Pennsylvania, 1681–1726.* Philadelphia: University of Pennsylvania Press, 1968.

———. "City Planning and Political Tension in the Seventeenth Century: The Case of Philadelphia." *Proceedings of the American Philosophical Society* 112 (1978): 54–78.

Salinger, Sharon. *"To Serve Well and Faithfully": Labor and Indentured Servants in Pennsylvania, 1682–1800.* Cambridge, MA: Harvard University Press, 1987.

Salinger, Sharon, and Charles Wetherell. "Wealth and Poverty in Pre-Revolutionary Philadelphia." *Journal of American History* 71 (1985): 826–840.

Schultz, Ronald. *The Republic of Labor: Philadelphia Artisans and the Politics of Class, 1720–1830.* New York: Oxford University Press, 1993.

Schwartz, Sally. *"A Mixed Multitude": The Struggle for Toleration in Colonial Pennsylvania.* New York: New York University Press, 1987.

Schweitzer, Mary M. *Custom and Contract: Household, Government and the Economy of Colonial Pennsylvania.* New York: Columbia University Press, 1987.

———. "The Spatial Organization of Federalist Philadelphia, 1790." *Journal of Interdisciplinary History* 24 (1993): 31–57.

Siegel, Adrienne, compiler and editor. *Philadelphia: A Chronological and Documentary History, 1615–1970.* Dobbs Ferry, NY: Oceana, 1975.

Smith, Billy G. *"The Lower Sort": Philadelphia's Laboring People, 1750–1800.* Ithaca, NY: Cornell University Press, 1990.

Smith, Billy G., editor. *Life in Early Philadelphia.* University Park: Pennsylvania State University Press, 1995.

Wolf, Stephanie Grauman. *Urban Village: Population, Community, and Family Structure in Germantown, Pennsylvania, 1683–1800.* Princeton University Press, 1976.

Early Maps and Depictions of Philadelphia, 1683–1754
Original town plan as surveyed by Thomas Holme, published in London in 1683 and frequently re-issued—

prints held by numerous sources, such as the Library Company of Philadelphia, Stokes Collection of the New York Public Library, etc.

Toned lithograph depicting Philadelphia as it appeared, ca. 1702; published in 1875 to commemorate America's centennial—prints held by numerous sources such as the Library Company of Philadelphia, etc.

Peter Cooper's 8-foot painting of the city waterfront and anchorage as seen from its southeast, ca. 1720–1723—original held by the Library Company of Philadelphia

Promotional panorama and vignettes commissioned by Thomas Penn and executed by George Heap, "under the Direction of Nicholas Scull, Surveyor General of the Province of Pennsylvania," showing Philadelphia from its eastern or New Jersey side of the Delaware River in 1754, being engraved and published two years afterward in London by Thomas Jefferys—prints held by the Historical Society of Pennsylvania, plus numerous other sources; Heap's view would serve as a model for subsequent versions published in the *London Magazine* of 1761–1762, by Andrew Dury in November 1776, etc.

Modern Era and General Works (1801–Present)

Adams, Carolyn, et al. *Philadelphia: Neighborhoods, Division, and Conflict in a Postindustrial City.* Philadelphia: Temple University Press, 1991.

Beers, Paul B. *Pennsylvania Politics Today and Yesterday.* University Park: Pennsylvania State University Press, 1980.

Cheney, Lynne Vincent. "1876: The Eagle Screams." *American Heritage* 25, Number 3 (April 1974): 15–35 and 98–99.

Clark, Dennis. *The Irish in Philadelphia.* Philadelphia: Temple University Press, 1973,

Clark, Dennis, editor. *Philadelphia, 1776–2076: A Three Hundred Year View.* Port Washington: Kennikat, 1975.

Contosta, David R. *Suburb in the City: Chestnut Hill, Philadelphia, 1850–1990.* Columbus: Ohio State University Press, 1992.

Daughen, Joseph R., and Peter Binzen. *The Cop Who Would Be King.* Boston: Little, Brown and Company, 1977.

Du Bois, W. E. B. *The Philadelphia Negro.* Millwood, NY: Kraus-Thomson Organization, 1973.

Gallery, John Andrew, editor. *Philadelphia Architecture.* Cambridge: Massachusetts Institute of Technology Press, 1984.

Gregg, Robert. *Sparks from the Anvil of Oppression: Philadelphia's African Methodists and Southern Migrants, 1890–1940.* Philadelphia: Temple University Press, 1993.

Hershberg, Theodore, editor. *Philadelphia: Work, Space, Family and Group Experience in the Nineteenth Century.* Oxford Biniversity Press, 1981.

Hutson, James H. "An Investigation of the Inarticulate: Philadelphia's White Oaks." *William and Mary Quarterly,* Third Series, Volume 23 (1971): 3–25.

Lane, Roger. *Roots of Violence in Black Philadelphia, 1860–1900.* Cambridge, MA: Harvard University Press, 1986.

———. *William Dorsey's Philadelphia and Ours.* New York: Oxford University Press, 1991.

Lindstrom, Diane. *Economic Development in the Philadelphia Region, 1810–1850.* New York: Columbia University Press, 1978.

Looney, Robert F. *Old Philadelphia in Early Photographs, 1839–1914.* New York: Dover, 1976.

Maass, John. "When the New World Dazzled the Old." *American Heritage* 27, Number 4 (June 1976): 24–27 and 76–79.

McCabe, James D. *The Illustrated History of the Centennial Exhibition.* Philadelphia: National Publishing, 1975.

Metraux, Stephen. "Waiting for the Wrecking Ball: Skid Row in Postindustrial Philadelphia." *Journal of Urban History* 25, Number 5 (July 1999): 690–715.

Miller, Fredric M., et al. *Still Philadelphia.* Philadelphia: Temple University Press, 1983.

Mires, Charlene. *Memories Lost and Found: Independence Hall in American History and Imagination.* Philadelphia: University of Pennsylvania Press, 2003.

Nash, Gary B. *First City: Philadelphia and the Forging of Historical Memory.* Philadelphia: University of Pennsylvania Press, 2002.

Nash, Gary B., and Jean R. Soderlund. *Freedom by Degrees: Emancipation in Pennsylvania and Its Aftermath.* New York: Oxford University Press, 1991.

Olton, Charles S. "Philadelphia's First Environmental Crisis." *Pennsylvania Magazine of History and Biography* 97 (1974): 90–100.

Richardson, Edgar P. "Centennial City." *American Heritage* 23, Number 1 (December 1971): 17–32.

Scranton, Philip. *Proprietary Capitalism: The Textile Manufacture at Philadelphia, 1800–1885.* New York: Cambridge University Press, 1983.

———. *Worksights: Industrial Philadelphia, 1890–1950.* Philadelphia: Temple University Press, 1986.

Starbird, Ethel A. "They'd Rather Be in Philadelphia." *National Geographic* 163, Number 3 (March 1983): 314–343.

Wainwright, Nicholas B., editor. *Diary of Sidney George Fisher, 1834–1871.* Philadelphia: Historical Society of Pennsylvania, 1967.

Warner, Sam Bass, Jr. *The Private City: Philadelphia in Three Periods of Its Growth.* Philadelphia: University of Pennsylvania Press, 1968.

Weigley, Russell F., editor. *Philadelphia: A 300-Year History.* New York: W. W. Norton, 1982.

Wilson, George. *Yesterday's Philadelphia.* Miami: E. A. Seemann, 1975.

Wolf, Edwin. *"At the Instance of Benjamin Franklin": A Brief History of the Library Company of Philadelphia.* Philadelphia: Library Company of Philadelphia, 1995 revised edition.

Wolf, Edwin, and Kenneth Finkel. *Philadelphia: Portrait of an American City.* Philadelphia: Canio Books and the Library Company, 1990 re-edition.

WPA Guide to Philadelphia. Philadelphia: University of Pennsylvania Press, 1988 reprint of 1937 original *Philadelphia: A Guide to the Nation's Birthplace.*

Early Spanish Maps and Depictions of San Francisco (1772–1803)

Crude map of San Francisco Bay and its adjacent coastline, as reconnoitered in March 1772—original held by the Servicio Geográfico del Ejército in Madrid, call number: LM-?

Map of the bay as reconnoitered by the royal packet *San Carlos* of Lt. Juan Manuel de Ayala in August–September 1775—original held by the Archive of Indies at Seville, old Torres Lanzas citation: Mapas y Planos de México, 305

Another map of the bay and its coastline, 1776—original held by the Servicio Geográfico del Ejército in Madrid, call number: J-?

Diagram by Diego Borica of San Francisco's proposed new cavalry barracks, 1795—original held by the Archivo General de la Nación in Mexico City, photographic negative number: 977/0171 [archival provenance: *Provincias Internas,* Volume 216, Expediente 8, Folio 221]

Diagram by Alberto de Córdoba of the new battery erected at the northernmost tip of San Joaquín Hill to guard the entrance into San Francisco Bay, 1796—original held by the Archivo General de la Nación in Mexico City, photographic negative number: 977/0172 [archival provenance: *Provincias Internas,* Volume 216, Expediente 8, Folio 240]

Diagram by De Córdoba of San Francisco's proposed new presidio, 1796—original held by the Archivo General de la Nación in Mexico City, photographic negative number: 977/0175 [archival provenance: *Provincias Internas,* Volume 216, Expediente 8, Folio 249]

Map by De Córdoba, showing the proposed new presidio's location within the bay, 1796—original held by the Archivo General de la Nación in Mexico City, photographic negative number: 977/0173 [archival provenance: *Provincias Internas,* Volume 216, Expediente 8, Folio 241]

Map by De Córdoba, indicating the geographical position of San Francisco Bay, 1796—original held by the Archivo General de la Nación in Mexico City, photographic negative number: 977/0174 [archival provenance: *Provincias Internas,* Volume 216, Expediente 8, Folio 242]

Map of the bay, as sounded by pilots from the Naval Departament of San Blas, ca. 1803—original held by the Archive of Indies at Seville, old Torres Lanzas citation: Mapas y Planos de México, 487ca.

San Francisco

Hispano-Mexican Era (1775–1845)

Barratt, Glynn. *Russia in Pacific Waters, 1715–1825: A Survey of the Origins of Russia's Naval Presence in the North and South Pacific.* Vancouver: University of British Columbia Press, 1981.

Chamisso, Adalbert von. *A Sojourn at San Francisco Bay, 1816.* San Francisco, 1936.

Colley, Charles C. "The Missionization of the Coast Miwok Indians of California." *California Historical Society Quarterly* 49 (1970): 143–162.

Cook, W. L. *Flood Tide of Empire: Spain and the Pacific Northwest, 1543–1819.* New Haven: Yale University Press, 1973.

Santa María, Fray Vicente de. *The First Spanish Entry into San Francisco Bay, 1775: The Original Narrative, Hitherto Unpublished.* San Francisco: John Howell Books, 1971 translation by John Galvin.

American Conquest and Gold Rush (1846–1905)

Andrist, Ralph K. "Gold!" *American Heritage* 14, Number 1 (December 1962): 6–27 and 90–91.

Bullough, William A. "Eadweard Muybridge and the Old San Francisco Mint: Archival Photographs as Historical Documents." *California History* 68, Numbers 1–2 (1989): 2–13.

Ethington, Philip J. "Vigilantes and the Police: The Creation of a Professional Police Bureaucracy in San Francisco, 1847–1900." *Journal of Social History* 21, Number 2 (1987): 197–227.

———. *The Public City: The Public Construction of Urban Life in San Francisco, 1850–1900.* New York: Cambridge University Press, 1994.

Reinhardt, Richard. "A Nice Piece of Real Estate." *American Heritage* 23, Number 1 (December 1971): 42–47 and 106.

Wollenberg, Charles. "Life on the Seismic Frontier: The Great San Francisco Earthquake of 1868." *California History* 71, Number 4 (1992–1993): 494–509.

Earthquake and Reconstruction (1906–1930)

Anderson, Douglas Firth. "'We Have Here a Different Civilization': Protestant Identity in the San Francisco Bay Area, 1906–1909." *Western Historical Quarterly* 23, Number 2 (1992): 199–221.

Arnstein, Flora, et al. "The Great San Francisco Earthquake Fire, April 18, 1906." *Western States Jewish History* 27, Number 3 (1995): 99–183.

Baker, Simon. "San Francisco in Ruins: The 1906 Aerial Photographs of George R. Lawrence." *Landscape* 30, Number 2 (1989): 9–14.

Bolton, Marie. "An Endless Cycle of Crises? Housing in Post-Earthquake San Francisco, 1906–1915." *Revue française d'études américaines* 64 (1995): 289–297.

Dean, Dennis R. "The San Francisco Earthquake of 1906." *Annals of Science [UK]* 50, Number 6 (1993): 501–521.

"Earthquake." *American Heritage* 34, Number 2 (1983): 36–45.

Egan, Kathryn S. "A Constructivist's View of an Earthquake: Edith Irvine Photographs San Francisco, 1906." *Journalism History* 20, Number 2 (1994): 66–73.

Ewald, Donna, and Peter Clute. "America in Photographs: The Enchanted City." *American History Illustrated* 27, Number 3 (1992): 46–57.

Holm, Ed. "Death of a City." *American History Illustrated* 25, Number 1 (1990): 24–33.

Saul, Eric, and Don Denevi. *The Great San Francisco Earthquake and Fire, 1906.* Millbrae, CA: Celestial Arts, 1981.

Modern Era (1931–Present)

Broussard, Albert S. *Black San Francisco: The Struggle for Racial Equality in the West.* Lawrence: University of Kansas Press, 1993.

Canby, Thomas Y. "Earthquake: Prelude to The Big One?" *National Geographic* 177, Number 5 (May 1990): 76–105.

Deleon, Richard Edward. *Left Coast City: Progressive Politics in San Francisco, 1975–1991.* Lawrence: University of Kansas Press, 1992.

Graves, William. "San Francisco Bay: The Westward Gate." *National Geographic* 136, Number 5 (November 1969): 593–637.

Johnston, Moira. "High Tech, High Risk, and High Life in Silicon Valley." *National Geographic* 162, Number 4 (October 1982): 459–477.

Lee, Anthony W. *Painting on the Left: Diego Rivera, Radical Politics, and San Francisco's Public Murals.* Berkeley: University of California Press, 1999.

Tarpy, Cliff. "The Beauty and the Battles of San Francisco Bay." *National Geographic* 159, Number 6 (June 1981): 814–845.

General Works

Bloomfield, Anne B. "A History of the California Historical Society's New Mission Street Neighborhood." *California History* 74, Number 4 (1995–1996): 372–393 and 446–448.

Choy, Philip P., "The Architecture of San Francisco Chinatown." *Chinese America: History and Perspectives* (1990): 37–66.

Godfrey, Brian J. "Urban Development and Redevelopment in San Francisco." *Geographical Review* 87, Number 3 (1997): 309–333.

Grassick, Mary K. *Fort Point National Historic Site, Presidio of San Francisco, California.* Harpers Ferry, WV: Division of Historic Furnishings of the National Park Service, 1994.

Vance, James E., Jr. *Geography and Urban Evolution in the San Francisco Bay Area.* Berkeley, CA: Institute of Governmental Studies, 1964.

Weber, Francis J. "The San Francisco Chancery Archives." *The Americas: A Quarterly Review of Inter-American Cultural History [Academy of American Franciscan History]* 20 (1964): 313–321.

St. Augustine

Early Spanish Era (1564–1701)

Arana Subirá, Luis Rafael. "The Exploration of Florida and Sources on the Founding of St. Augustine." *Florida Historical Quarterly* 44, Numbers 1–2 (1965): 1–16.

———. *The Building of Castillo de San Marcos.* St. Augustine, FL: Eastern National Park and Monument Association, 1977.

Bennett, Charles E. *Three Voyages: René Laudonnière.* Gainesville: University Presses of Florida, 1975.

Bostwick, John A. "The Plaza II Site Excavation of a Colonial Spanish Well in St. Augustine, Florida." *Historical Archaeology* 14 (1980): 73–81.

Bushnell, Amy. "The Expenses of Hidalguia in Seventeenth-Century St. Augustine." *Escribano* 15 (1978): 23–36.

———. *The King's Coffer: Proprietors of the Spanish Florida Treasury, 1565–1702.* Gainesville: University Presses of Florida, 1981.

Connolly, Matthew J. "Four Contemporary Narratives of the Founding of St. Augustine." *Catholic Historical Review* 51, Number 3 (1965): 305–334.

Coomes, Charles S. "Our Country's Oldest Parish Records." *Escribano* 18 (1981): 74–83.

Corbett, Theodore G. "Migration to a Spanish Frontier in the Seventeenth and Eighteenth Centuries: St. Augustine." *Hispanic American Historical Review* 54, Number 3 (1974): 414–430.

———. "Population Structure in Hispanic St. Augustine, 1629–1763." *Florida Historical Quarterly* 54, Number 3 (1976): 263–284.

Covington, James W. "Drake Destroys St. Augustine: 1586." *Florida Historical Quarterly* 44, Numbers 1–2 (1965): 81–93.

"Don Manuel de Cendoya and Castillo de San Marcos, 1671–1673." *Escribano* 9, Number 1 (1972): 28–43.

Fretwell, Mark E., and Eugenia B. Arana, editors. "Major Ponce and Castillo de San Marcos, 1673–1675." *Escribano* 9, Number 4 (1972): 174–185.

Gillaspie, William R. "Survival of a Frontier Presidio: St. Augustine and the Subsidy and Private Contract Systems, 1680–1702." *Florida Historical Quarterly* 62, Number 3 (1984): 273–295.

"Grammont's Landing at Little Matanzas Inlet." *Escribano* 9, Number 3 (1972): 107–113.

Hann, John H. "Apalachee Counterfeiters in St. Augustine." *Florida Historical Quarterly* 67, Number 1 (1988): 52–68.

———. "Evidence Pertinent to the Florida Cabildo Controversy and the Misdating of the Juan Márquez Cabrera Governorship." *Florida Historical Quarterly* 79, Number 1 (2001): 68–83.

Harris, Sherwood. "The Tragic Dream of Jean Ribaut." *American Heritage* 14, Number 6 (October 1963): 8–15 and 88–90.

Hoffman, Paul E. "St. Augustine 1580: The Research Project." *Escribano* 14 (1977): 5–19.

Hudson, Charles. *The Juan Pardo Expeditions: Exploration of the Carolinas and Tennessee, 1566–1568.* Washington, DC: Smithsonian Institution, 1990.

King, Julia. "Ceramic Variability in 17th Century St. Augustine, Florida." *Historical Archaeology* 18, Number 2 (1984): 75–82.

Lawson, Edward W. *The Discovery of Florida and Its Discoverer, Juan Ponce de León.* Saint Augustine, FL: self-published, 1946.

Lyon, Eugene. "The Captives of Florida." *Florida Historical Quarterly* 50, Number 1 (1971): 1–24.

———. *The Enterprise of Florida: Pedro Menéndez de Avilés and the Spanish Conquest of 1565–1568.* Gainesville: University Presses of Florida, 1976.

———. "The Florida Mutineers, 1566–67." *Tequesta* 44 (1984): 44–61.

———. "Richer Than We Thought: The Material Culture of Sixteenth-Century St. Augustine." *Escribano* 29 (1992): ix–117.

———. "The First Three Wooden Forts of St. Augustine, 1565–1571." *Escribano* 34 (1997): 130–147.

———. "St. Augustine 1580: The Living Community." *Escribano* 14 (1997): 20–33.

Manucy, Albert C. *Menéndez: Pedro Menéndez de Avilés, Captain General of the Ocean Sea.* Sarasota, FL: Pineapple Press, 1992.

———. *Sixteenth-Century St. Augustine: The People and Their Homes.* Gainesville: University Press of Florida, 1997.

Pearson, Fred Lamar, Jr. "Timucuan Rebellion of 1656: The Rebolledo Investigation and the Civil-Religious Controversy." *Florida Historical Quarterly* 61, Number 3 (1983): 260–280.

"Pirates March on St. Augustine, 1683." *Escribano* 9, Number 2 (1972): 51–72.

Reitz, Elizabeth Jean, and C. Margaret Scarry. *Reconstructing Historic Subsistence with an Example from Sixteenth-Century Spanish Florida.* Pleasant Hill: California Society for Historic Archaeology, 1985.

Sluiter, Engel. *The Florida Situado: Quantifying the First Eighty Years, 1571–1651.* Gainesville: University Presses of Florida, 1985.

Thurber Connor, Jeannette. "The Nine Old Wooden Forts of St. Augustine." *Florida Historical Quarterly* 4, Number 3 (January 1926): 103–111 and Number 4 (April 1926): 171–180.

Thurber Connor, Jeannette, editor and translator. *Pedro Menéndez de Avilés, Adelantado, Governor and Captain-General of Florida: Memorial by Gonzalo Solís de Meras.* Deland, FL, 1923.

"Two Letters from Governor Cendoya." *Escribano* 9, Number 3 (1972): 101–106.

Zubillaga, Félix. *La Florida: la misión jesuítica (1566–1572) y la colonización española.* Rome: Institutum Historicum S.I., 1941.

Early Maps and Depictions of St. Augustine, 1586–1817
Accurate and detailed engraving of Sir Francis Drake's raid of June 1586, published two years later in Leyden by Batista Boazio as part of *Le Voyage de Messire François Drake, Chevalier, aux Indes Occidentales,* as well as in Walter Bigges's *A Summarie and True Discourse of Sir Francis Drake's West Indian Voyage,* published in London in 1589—several sources

Four maps and diagrams of the proposed construction of a triangular stone castle, February 1595—originals held by the Archive of Indies at Seville, old Torres Lanzas call numbers: Mapas y Planos de México, 43–46 [archival provenance: 140-7-37]

Three diagrams of the initial stone Castillo de San Marcos, as completed by Gov. Pablo de Hita y Salazar in 1675–1676, plus a later copy—originals held by the Archive of Indies at Seville [old Torres Lanzas call numbers: Mapas y Planos de México, 68–70], as well as by the Servicio Histórico Militar at Madrid, call number: 2-3-3-2-Núm. 3

Six maps and diagrams by the military engineer Antonio Arredondo, of St. Augustine and Castillo de San Marcos, May 1737—originals held by the Archive of Indies at Seville, old Torres Lanzas call numbers: Mapas y Planos de México, 131–136

Map by Pedro Ruiz de Olano of the town after its Anglo-American siege, August 1740—original held by the

Archive of Indies at Seville, old Torres Lanzas call number: Mapas y Planos de México, 137

Map of the town as it appeared when surrendered to the English in 1763 and published three years later in William Stork's *Description of East Florida*—numerous sources

The town and its coastline as they appeared in 1764, apparently engraved from an earlier survey by Juan de Solís—print held by the Library of Congress, plus numerous other sources

Map of the city and its district, published in Madrid by the royal cartographer Tomás López in 1783—prints held by the Servicio Geográfico del Ejército in Madrid [call number: J-9.ª–2.ª-a–59], plus numerous other sources

Map of the city by the military engineer Capt. Mariano de la Rocque or Roque, 1784—original held by the Archive of Indies at Seville [archival provenance: Santo Domingo 2587], plus a copy by the University of Florida Map Collection, call number: R1.1784.003.1997.1481

Diagrams by De la Rocque of the lower and upper floors of the *Casa del Rey* or "Government House," 1787—original held by the University of Florida Map Collection, call number: R1.1787.006.1997.1512

Detailed, three-part map of the city by De la Rocque, 25 April 1788—original held by the U.S. Bureau of Land Management, plus copies in the University of Florida Map Collection, call numbers: R2.1788.002.1997.0571 and ROS.1788.001.1998.0000

Diagram, elevation, and profile views by De la Rocque of the barracks at the San Francisco Convent, 1788—originals held by the Archive of Indies at Seville [archival provenance: Cuba 1395 and 1396], plus copies in the University of Florida Map Collection, call numbers: R1.1788.002.1997.1002 and R1.1788.003.1997.1003

Diagram, elevation, and profile views by De la Rocque of the parish church, 1789—originals held by the Archive of Indies at Seville [archival provenance: Santo Domingo 2589], plus copies in the University of Florida Map Collection, call numbers: R1.1789.001.1997.1005 and R1.1789.002.1997.1006

Diagram by De la Rocque of the main square, 1791—original held by the University of Florida Map Collection, call number: R2.1791.001.1997.0681

Map of the city and its coastline by De la Rocque, December 1791—original held by the Servicio Histórico Militar in Madrid, call number: Sec. de Ultramar, 15

Map of the city and its coastline by Pedro Díaz Berrio, January 1797—original held by the Servicio Histórico Militar in Madrid, call number: K-b-4-38

Map of the city and its coastline by the military engineer Capt. Francisco Cortazar, August 1817—original held by the Servicio Histórico Militar in Madrid, call number: K-b-4-37.

Threatened Outpost (1702–1762)

Arnade, Charles W. *The Siege of St. Augustine in 1702.* Gainesville: University Presses of Florida, Number 3 of the "Social Scienes Monographs," summer 1959.

———. "The Architecture of Spanish St. Augustine." *The Americas: A Quarterly Review of Inter-American Cultural History [Academy of American Franciscan History]* 18 (October 1961): 149–186.

Baine, Rodney E. "General James Oglethorpe and the Expedition against St. Augustine." *Georgia Historical Quarterly* 84, Number 2 (2000): 197–229.

Béthencourt Massieu, Antonio de. "Felipe V y La Florida." *Anuario de Estudios Americanos [Spain]* 7 (1950): 95–123.

Britt, Albert Sidney, Jr. "John Mohr McIntosh, a Prisoner of War in Spain." *Georgia Historical Quarterly* 51, Number 4 (1967): 449–453.

Corbett, Theodore G. "Migration to a Spanish Imperial Frontier in the Seventeenth and Eighteenth Centuries: St. Augustine." *Hispanic American Historical Review* 54, Number 3 (1974): 414–430.

Crane, Verner W. *The Southern Frontier, 1670–1732.* Ann Arbor: University of Michigan Press, 1954.

Deagan, Kathleen A. *Spanish St. Augustine: The Archaeology of a Colonial Creole Community.* New York: Academic Press, 1983.

Deagan, Kathleen A., editor. *America's Ancient City: Spanish St. Augustine, 1565–1763.* New York: Garland, 1991.

Gillaspie, William R. "Sergeant Major Ayala y Escobar and the Threatened St. Augustine Mutiny." *Florida Historical Quarterly* 47, Number 2 (1968): 151–164.

Hann, John H. "St. Augustine's Fallout from the Yamasee War." *Florida Historical Quarterly* 68, Number 2 (1989): 180–200.

Harman, Joyce Elizabeth. *Trade and Privateering in Spanish Florida, 1732–1763.* St. Augustine Historical Society, 1969.

Hoffman, Kathleen S. "The Material Culture of Seventeenth-Century St. Augustine." *Escribano* 32 (1995): 91–112.

———. "Cultural Development in *La Florida.*" *Historical Archaeology* 31, Number 1 (1997): 24–35.

Ivers, Larry E. "The Battle of Fort Mosa." *Georgia Historical Quarterly* 51, Number 2 (1967): 135–153.

Kapitzke, Robert L. "The 'Calamities of Florida': Father Solana, Governor Palacio y Valenzuela, and the Desertions of 1758." *Florida Historical Quarterly* 72, Number 1 (1993): 1–18.

———. *Religion, Power, and Politics in Colonial St. Augustine.* Gainesville: University Presses of Florida, 2001.

Kimber, Edward. *A Relation or Journal of a Late Expedition to the Gates of St. Augustine, on Florida.* Gainesville: University Presses of Florida, 1976 re-edition of 1744 original.

Lanning, John Tate. *The St. Augustine Expedition of 1740: A Report to the South Carolina General Assembly, Reprinted from the Colonial Records of South Carolina.* Columbia: South Carolina Archives Department, 1954.

Marchena Fernández, Juan. "The Defense Structure of East Florida, 1700–1820." *Escribano* 21 (1984): 37–52.

———. "St. Augustine's Military Society, 1700–1820." *Escribano* 22 (1985): 43–77.

Parker, Susan R. "Spanish St. Augustine's 'Urban' Indians." *Escribano* 30 (1993): 1–15.

TePaske, John Jay. *The Governorship of Spanish Florida, 1700–1763.* Durham, NC: Duke University Press, 1964.

———. "Funerals and Fiestas in Early Eighteenth Century St. Augustine." *Florida Historical Quarterly* 44, Numbers 1–2 (1965): 97–104.

British Occupation (1763–1783)

Arana Subirá, Luis Rafael. "A Bicentennial Calendar of British East Florida." *Escribano* 13, Number 1 (1976): 1–18.

Coomes, Charles S. "The Old King's Road of British East Florida." *Escribano* 12, Number 2 (1975): 35–74.

Cummins, Light T. "Luciano de Herrera and Spanish Espionage in British St. Augustine." *Escribano* 16 (1979): 43–57.

Denham, James M. "Denys Rolle and Indian Policy in British East Florida." *Gulf Coast Historical Review* 7, Number 2 (1992): 31–44.

DeVorsey, Louis, Jr. "A Colorful Resident of British St. Augustine: William Gerard de Brahm." *Escribano* 12, Number 1 (1975): 1–24.

Gold, Robert L. "That Infamous Floridian, Jesse Fish." *Florida Historical Quarterly* 52, Number 1 (1973): 1–17.

Griffin, Patricia C. *Mullet on the Beach: The Minorcans of Florida, 1768–1788.* Jacksonville: University of North Florida Press, 1991.

Kennett, Lee. "A French Report on St. Augustine in the 1770's." *Florida Historical Quarterly* 44, Numbers 1–2 (1965): 133–135.

Manucy, Albert C. "Changing Traditions in St. Augustine Architecture." *Escribano* 19 (1982): 1–28.

Mowat, Charles Loch. "St. Augustine under the British Flag." *Florida Historical Quarterly* 20 (October 1941): 131–150.

———. *East Florida as a British Province.* Gainesville: University Presses of Florida, 1964 facsimile reedition of 1943 University of California original.

———. "St. Francis Barracks, St. Augustine: A Link with the British Regime." *Florida Historical Quarterly* 21 (January 1943): 266–280.

Nelson, Paul David. *General James Grant: Scottish Soldier and Royal Governor of East Florida.* Gainesville: University Presses of Florida, 1993.

Rasico, Philip D. *The Minorcans of Florida: Their History, Language, and Culture.* New Smyrna Beach, FL: Luthers, 1990.

Searcy, Martha Condray. *The Georgia-Florida Contest in the American Revolution, 1776–1778.* University of Alabama Press, 1985.

Siebert, Wilbur H., editor. *Loyalists in East Florida, 1774–1785: The Most Important Documents Pertaining Thereto.* Boston: Gregg, 1972 reprint of 1929 original, two volumes.

———. "The Port of St. Augustine during the British Regime." *Florida Historical Quarterly* 24, Number 4 (April 1946): 247–265 and 25, Number 1 (July 1946): 76–93.

Sturgill, Claude C. "The Decision to Re-Arm St. Augustine." *Journal of the Society for Army Historical Research [UK]* 49, Number 200 (1971): 203–211.

———. "John Bull's Stinginess in East Florida." *Florida Historical Quarterly* 50, Number 3 (1972): 292–299.

———. "Troop Utilization in the Garrison at St. Augustine, 1763–1769." *Escribano* 9, Number 1 (1972): 20–27.

Waterbury, Jean Parker. "John Forbes: Man of the Cloth, of His Times, and of St. Augustine." *Escribano* 18 (1981): 1–32.

Williams, Linda K. "East Florida as a Loyalist Haven." *Florida Historical Quarterly* 54, Number 4 (1976): 465–478.

Spanish Reoccupation (1784–1820)

Alexander, J. H. "The Ambush of Captain John Williams, U.S.M.C.: Failure of the East Florida Invasion, 1812–1813." *Florida Historical Quarterly* 56, Number 3 (1978): 280–296.

Arana Subirá, Luis Rafael. "Construction at Castillo de San Marcos, 1784–1821." *Escribano* 25 (1988): 135–145.

Cusick, James Gregory. "Across the Border: Commodity Flow and Merchants in Spanish St. Augustine." *Florida Historical Quarterly* 69, Number 3 (1991): 277–299.

———. "The Importance of the Community Study Approach in Historical Archaeology, with an Example from Late Colonial St. Augustine." *Historical Archaeology* 29, Number 4 (1995): 59–83.

Deagan, Kathleen A. *Archaeology at the National Greek Orthodox Shrine, St. Augustine, Florida: Microchange in Eighteenth-Century Spanish Colonial Material Culture.* Gainesville: University Presses of Florida, 1976.

Emerson, Ann P. "Standards of Nutrition in a St. Augustine Hospital, 1783–1821." *Florida Historical Quarterly* 65, Number 2 (1986): 145–162.

Harper, Robert W., III. "Decorative Arts at the Ximenez-Fatio House: Furnishings Used to Interpret the Past." *Escribano* 16 (1979): 59–75.

Johnson, Sherry. "The Spanish St. Augustine Community, 1784–1795: A Reevaluation." *Florida Historical Quarterly* 68, Number 1 (July 1989): 27–54.

Landers, Jane G. "Jorge Biassou, Black Chieftain." *Escribano* 25 (1988): 85–100.

———. "Acquisition and Loss on a Spanish Frontier: The Free Black Homesteaders of Florida, 1784–1821." *Slavery and Abolition [UK]* 17, Number 1 (1996): 85–101.

———. "Female Conflict and Its Resolution in Eighteenth-Century St. Augustine." *The Americas: A Quarterly Review of Inter-American Cultural History [Academy of American Franciscan History]* 54, Number 4 (1998): 557–574.

Lockey, Joseph B. "The St. Augustine Census of 1786: Translated from the Spanish with an Introduction and Notes." *Florida Historical Quarterly* 18 (July 1939): 11–39.

———. *East Florida, 1783–1785: A File of Documents Assembled, and Many of Them Translated.* Berkeley: University of California Press, 1949.

Norris, L. David. "The Squeeze: Spain Cedes Florida to the United States." *Escribano* 25 (1988): 101–133.

Parker, Susan R. "I Am neither Your Subject nor Your Subordinate." *Escribano* 25 (1988): 43–60.

Quiroga Fernández de Soto, Alejandro. "Military Liberalism on the East Florida 'Frontier': Implementation of the 1812 Constitution." *Florida Historical Quarterly* 79, Number 4 (2001): 441–468.

Rasico, Philip D. "Minorcan Population of St. Augustine in the Spanish Census of 1786." *Florida Historical Quarterly* 66, Number 2 (1987): 160–184.

Romero Cabot, Ramón. *La defensa de Florida en el segundo período español, 1783–1821.* Seville: Escuela de Estudios Hispano-americanos, 1982.

Tanner, Helen Hornbeck. "The 1789 Saint Augustine Celebration." *Florida Historical Quarterly* 38, Number 4 (1960): 280–293.

———. *Zéspedes in East Florida, 1784–1790.* Coral Gables, FL: University of Miami Press, 1963.

———. "The Delaney Murder Case." *Florida Historical Quarterly* 44, Numbers 1–2 (1965): 136–149.

Tornero Tinajero, Pablo. "Sociedad y población en San Agustín de la Florida, 1786." *Anuario de Estudios Americanos [Spain]* 35 (1978): 233–260.

Ware, John D. "Saint Augustine, 1784: Decadence and Repairs." *Florida Historical Quarterly* 48, Number 2 (1969): 180–187.

Antebellum and Civil War Eras (1821–1865)

Arana Subirá, Luis Rafael. "Fort Marion in Civil War Times." *Escribano* 23 (1986): 47–63.

Bearden, Jacqueline K. "'I Wish to Come Home Once More': The Letters of Nathaniel Sherburne." *Escribano* 15 (1978): 37–48.

Buker, George E. "St. Augustine and the Union Blockade." *Escribano* 23 (1986): 1–18.

———. "The Inner Blockade of Florida and the Wildcat Blockade-Runners." *North and South* 4, Number 2 (2001): 70–85.

Clark, Patricia. "'A Tale to Tell from Paradise Itself': George Bancroft's Letters from Florida, March 1855." *Florida Historical Quarterly* 48, Number 3 (1970): 264–278.

Coles, David J. "Ancient City Defenders: The St. Augustine Blues." *Escribano* 23 (1986): 65–89.

Eby, Cecil D., Jr., editor. "Memoir of a West Pointer in Saint Augustine: 1824–1826." *Florida Historical Quarterly* 42, Number 4 (1964): 307–320.

Graham, Thomas. *The Awakening of St. Augustine: The Anderson Family and the Oldest City, 1821–1924.* St. Augustine Historical Society, 1978.

———. "The Home Front: Civil War Times in St. Augustine." *Escribano* 23 (1986): 19–45.

Griffin, John W. "St. Augustine in 1822." *Escribano* 14 (1977): 45–56.

Griffin, Patricia C. "Ralph Waldo Emerson in St. Augustine." *Escribano* 32 (1995): 113–134.

Knetsch, Joe. "A Statesman on the Land: The Multifaceted Career of Benjamin Alexander Putnam." *Escribano* 34 (1997): 98–129.

McGuire, William. "A Connecticut Yankee in St. Augustine, 1863." *Escribano* 28 (1991): 56–80.

Moore, John Hammond, editor. "A South Carolina Lawyer Visits St. Augustine: 1837." *Florida Historical Quarterly* 43, Number 4 (1965): 361–378.

Norris, L. David. "The Squeeze: Spain Cedes Florida to the United States." *Escribano* 25 (1988): 101–133.

Sewall, Rufus K. *Sketches of St. Augustine.* Gainesville: University Presses of Florida, 1976 reprint of 1848 original.

Reconstruction and Modern Era (1866–Present)

Blazek, Ron. "The Development of Library Service in the Nation's Oldest City: The St. Augustine Library Association, 1874–1880." *Journal of Library History* 14, Number 2 (1979): 160–182.

Colburn, David R. *Racial Change and Community Crisis: St. Augustine, Florida, 1877–1980.* New York: Columbia University Press, 1985.

Gibson, Arrell Morgan. "The St. Augustine Prisoners." *Red River Valley Historical Review* 3, Number 2 (1978): 259–270.

Goller, Robert R. "North and South with W. J. Harris, Photographer." *Escribano* 28 (1991): 1–55.

Graham, Thomas. "Flagler's Magnificent Hotel Ponce de Leon." *Florida Historical Quarterly* 54, Number 1 (1975): 1–17.

———. "Flagler's Grand Hotel Alcazar." *Escribano* 26 (1989): 1–32.

Knetsch, Joe. "One of Flagler's Men: William W. Dewhurst." *Escribano* 30 (1993): 16–32.

Mormino, Gary R. "Florida's Gilded Year, 1886." *Gulf Coast Historical Review* 10, Number 1 (1994): 29–43.

Ridolph, Edward A. "Street Railways of St. Augustine." *Escribano* 24 (1987): 85–101.

Stackhouse, H. H. "The Model Land Tract: The Development of a Residential Neighborhood." *Escribano* 16 (1979): 25–32.

General Works

Arana Subirá, Luis Rafael. "Castillo de San Marcos: Three Hundred Years of American History." *National Parks and Conservation Magazine* 46, Number 10 (1972): 4–8.

———. "Defenses and Defenders at St. Augustine." *Escribano* 36 (1999): 1–219.

Conly, Robert L. "St. Augustine, Nation's Oldest City, Turns 400." *National Geographic* 129, Number 2 (February 1966): 196–229.

Coomes, Charles S. "Tolomato Cemetery." *Escribano* 13, Number 4 (1976): 107–138.

———. "The Basilica-Cathedral of St. Augustine, Florida, and Its History." *Escribano* 20 (1983): 32–44.

Dunkle, John R. "Population Change as an Element in the Historical Geography of St. Augustine." *Florida Historical Quarterly* 37, Number 1 (July 1958): 3–22.

Fairbanks, George R. *The History and Antiquities of the City of St. Augustine, Florida.* Gainesville: University Presses of Florida, 1975 reprint of 1958 original.

Halbirt, Carl D. "Of Earth, Tabby, Brick, and Asphalt: The Archaeology of St. Augustine's Historic St. George Street." *Escribano* 34 (1997): 70–97.

Joyce, Edward R. "The St. Francis Barracks: A Contradiction of Terms." *Escribano* 26 (1989): 71–90.

Manucy, Albert C. "The City Gate of St. Augustine." *Escribano* 10, Number 1 (1973): 1–13.

Montequin, François-Auguste de. "El proceso de urbanización en San Agustín de la Florida, 1565–1821: arquitectura civil y militar." *Anuario de Estudios Americanos [Spain]* 37 (1980): 583–647.

Nickens, Eddie. "Colonial Roulette." *Historic Preservation* 47, Number 3 (1995): 44, 46–47, 103, and 109–110.

Reeves, F. Blair. "The Architecture of Historic St. Augustine: A Photographic Essay." *Florida Historical Quarterly* 44, Numbers 1–2 (1965): 94–96.

Seale, William. "History in Houses: The Ximenez-Fatio House in Saint Augustine, Florida." *Antiques* 131, Number 2 (1987): 426–431.

Waterbury, Jean Parker. *The Oldest City, Saint Augustine: Saga of Survival.* St. Augustine Historical Society, 1983.

———. "'The Oldest House,' Its Site and Its Occupants, 1650–1984." *Escribano* 21 (1984): 1–35.

———. "'Long Neglected, Now Restored': The Ximenez-Fatio House (ca. 1797)." *Escribano* 22 (1985): 1–29.

———. "Where Artillery Lane Crosses Aviles Street: The Segui/Kirby Smith House." *Escribano* 24 (1987): 1–37.

———. *Markland.* St. Augustine Historical Society, 1989.

———. "The Treasurer's House." *Escribano* 31 (1994): 1–240.

———. "The Many Lives of the Llambias House." *Escribano* 34 (1997): 5–34.

Wolkomir, Richard and Joyce. "In Search of St. Augustine." *Smithsonian* 32, Number 7 (October 2001): 114–120.

Zéndegui, Guillermo de. "The Oldest City in the United States." *Américas [Organization of American States]* 16, Number 5 (May 1964): 7–14.

———. "Monumental Cities: St. Augustine, U.S.A., 1565." *Américas [Organization of American States]* 25, Number 1 (January 1973): supplementary pp. 7–11.

Washington

Abbott, Carl. *Political Terrain: Washington, D.C., from Tidewater Town to Global Metropolis.* Chapel Hill: University of North Carolina Press, 1999.

Aikman, Lonnelle. "The Nation's Capitol: Under the Dome of Freedom." *National Geographic* 125, Number 1 (January 1964): 4–59.

Blow, Michael. "Professor Henry and His Philosophical Toys." *American Heritage* 15, Number 1 (December 1963): 24–29 and 101–105.

Brown, J. Carter. "Masterwork on the Mall." *National Geographic* 154, Number 5 (November 1978): 680–701.

Caemmerer, H. Paul. *A Manual on the Origin and Development of Washington.* Washington, DC: United States Government Printing Office, 1939.

———. *The Life of Pierre-Charles L'Enfant.* New York: Da Capo Press, 1970 reprint.

"A Capital Education." *American Heritage* 23, Number 4 (June 1972): 26–35.

Clark, Lewis Elizabeth. *Living In, Living Out: African American Domestics in Washington, D.C., 1910–1940.* Washington, DC: Smithsonian Institution Press, 1994.

Cochran, J. O. "District of Columbia Statehood." *Howard Law Journal* 32, Number 2 (1989): 413–425.

Cooling, Benjamin Franklin, and Walton H. Owen. *Mr. Lincoln's Forts: A Guide to the Civil War Defenses of Washington.* Shippensburg: White Mane Press, 1988.

Gillette, Howard, Jr. *Between Justice and Beauty: Race, Planning, and the Failure of Urban Policy in Washington, D.C.* Baltimore: Johns Hopkins University Press, 1995.

Gipe, George A. "Rebel in a Wing Collar." *American Heritage* 18, Number 1 (December 1966): 24–29 and 101.

Green, Constance McLaughlin. *Washington: Village and Capital, 1800–1878.* Princeton University Press, 1962.

Gutheim, Frederick. *Worthy of the Nation: The History of Planning for the National Capital.* Washington, DC: Smithsonian Institution Press, 1977.

Hall, Alice J. "L'Enfant's Washington." *National Geographic* 180, Number 2 (August 1991): 122–134.

Harris, Charles Wesley. *Congress and the Governance of the Nation's Capital: The Conflict of Federal and Local Interests.* Washington, DC: Georgetown University Press, 1995.

Harris, Charles Wesley, and A. Thornton. *Perspectives of Political Power in the District of Columbia.* Washington, DC: National Institute of Public Management, 1981.

Haverstock, Mary Sayre. "George Washington Sat Here . . . and Here . . ." *American Heritage* 24, Number 1 (December 1972): 26–29 and 84.

Jacob, Kathryn Allamong. *Capital Elites: High Society in Washington, D.C., after the Civil War.* Washington, DC: Smithsonian Institution Press, 1995.

Jacobsen, Hugh Newell, editor. *A Guide to the Architecture of Washington, DC.* New York: Praeger, 1965.

Jaffe, Harry, and Tom Sherwood. *Dream City: Race, Power and the Decline of Washington, D.C.* New York: Simon and Schuster, 1994.

Jordan, Robert Paul. "Washington Cathedral: 'House of Prayer for All People.'" *National Geographic* 157, Number 4 (April 1980): 552–573.

Judge, Joseph. "New Grandeur for Flowering Washington." *National Geographic* 131, Number 4 (April 1967): 500–539.

Kousoulas, Claudia, and George Kousoulas. *Contemporary Architecture in Washington, DC.* New York: John Wiley, 1995.

Lessoff, Alan. *The Nation and Its City: Politics, "Corruption," and Progress in Washington, D.C., 1861–1902.* Baltimore: Johns Hopkins University Press, 1994.

Longstreth, Richard, editor. *The Mall in Washington, 1791–1991.* Washington, DC: University Press of New England, 1991.

Lord, Walter. "Humiliation and Triumph." *American Heritage* 23, Number 5 (August 1972): 50–73 and 91–93.

Miller, Fredric M., and Howard Gillette, Jr. "Race Relations in Washington, D.C., 1878–1955: A Photographic Essay." *Journal of Urban History* 21, Number 1 (November 1994): 57–85.

———. *Washington Seen: A Photographic History, 1875–1965.* Baltimore: Johns Hopkins University Press, 1995.

Mitchell, Henry. "Washington, D.C.: Hometown behind the Monuments." *National Geographic* 163, Number 1 (January 1983): 84–125.

Padover, Saul K., editor. *Thomas Jefferson and the National Capital.* Washington, DC: Government Printing Office, 1946.

Reps, John W. *Monumental Washington: The Planning and Development of the Capital Center.* Princeton University Press, 1967.

Taylor, D. R. *Home Rule in the District of Columbia: The First 500 Days.* Washington, DC: University Press of America, 1977.

Weaver, John D. "Bonus March." *American Heritage* 14, Number 4 (June 1963): 18–23 and 92–97.

Weaver, K., and C. Harris. "Who's in Charge Here: Congress and the Nation's Capital." *Brookings Review* 7, Number 3 (summer 1989): 39–46.

Weeks, Christopher. *AIA Guide to the Architecture of Washington.* Baltimore: Johns Hopkins University Press, 1994.

Young, James Sterling. *The Washington Community, 1800–1828.* New York: Columbia University Press, 1966.

SOUTH AMERICA
Regional Studies

Abascal y Sousa, José Fernando de. *Memoria de gobierno.* Seville: Escuela de Estudios Hispano-americanos, 1944 re-edition by Vicente Rodríguez Casado and José Antonio Calderón Quijano, two volumes.

Amat y Juniet, Manuel de. *Memoria de gobierno.* Seville: Escuela de Estudios Hispano-americanos, 1946 re-edition by Vicente Rodríguez Casado and José Antonio Calderón Quijano.

Andrews, Joseph. *Viaje de Buenos Aires a Potosí y Arica en los años 1825 y 1826.* Buenos Aires, 1920 Spanish translation with a preface by Carlos A. Aldao.

Arnold, Samuel Greene. *Viaje por América del Sur, 1847–1848.* Buenos Aires: Emecé, 1951 Spanish translation by Clara de la Rosa.

Balmori, Diana, et al. *Notable Family Networks in Latin America.* Chicago, 1984.

Basadre, Jorge. *Chile, Perú y Bolivia independientes.* Barcelona: Salvat, 1948.

Benavides Rodríguez, Alfredo. *La arquitectura en el virreinato del Perú y en la capitanía general de Chile.* Santiago de Chile: Ercilla, 1961.

Bergquist, Charles W. *Labor in Latin America: Comparative Essays on Chile, Argentina, Venezuela, and Colombia.* Stanford, CA: Stanford University Press, 1986.

Biscay, Acarette du. *Account of a Voyage up the River de la Plata and Thence Overland to Peru.* New Haven, 1968 reprint of 1698 London edition; there also exists a Spanish translation of the 1672 French original, published in Buenos Aires by Alfer y Vays in 1943.

Borget, Auguste. *En las Pampas y los Andes: treinta y tres dibujos y textos sobre Argentina, Chile y Peru.* Buenos Aires, 1960.

Carril, Bonifacio del. *La expedición Malaspina en los mares americanos del sur: la colección Bauza, 1789–1794.* Buenos Aires, 1961.

Carrió de la Vandera, Alonso, *alias* "Concolorcorvo." *El lazarillo de ciegos caminantes: desde Buenos Aires hasta Lima.* Madrid: Volume 122 of the "Biblioteca de Autores Españoles," 1959 re-edition of 1773 original; also republished by Espasa-Calpe in Buenos Aires in 1946, as well as by Emilio Carilla in Barcelona in 1973.

Carrión, Fernando, and Godofredo Sandoval. *Investigación urbana en el área andina.* Quito: Centro de Investigaciones CIUDAD-Institut Français d'Etudes Andines or IFEA, 1988.

Céspedes del Castillo, Guillermo. *Lima y Buenos Aires: repercusiones económicas y políticas de la creación del virreinato de la Plata.* Seville: Escuela de Estudios Hispanoamericanos, 1947; also published in *Anuario de Estudios Americanos [Spain]* 3 (1946): 667–874.

Claro Valdés, Samuel. *Antología de la música colonial en América del Sur.* Santiago de Chile, 1974.

Cole, John P. *Latin America: An Economic and Social Geography.* London: Butterworths, 1965.

Dawson, Thomas Cleland. *The South American Republics.* New York: Putnam's, 1903–1904, two volumes.

Deler, Jean-Paul. "Barrios populares y organización del espacio de las metrópolis andinas: ensayo de modelización." *Bulletin de l'Institut français d'études andines [France]* 17, Number 1 (1988): 239–250.

Demélas, M.-D., and Y. Saint-Geours. *La vie quotidienne en Amérique du Sud au temps de Bolivar, 1809–1830.* Paris, 1987.

D'Orbigny, Alcide. *Viaje a la América meridional.* Buenos Aires: Futuro, 1945 Spanish translation by A. Cepeda of 1846 original *Voyage pittoresque dans les deux Amériques* published in Paris, four volumes.

Franck, Harry Alverson. *Vagabonding Down the Andes: Being the Narrative of a Journey, Chiefly Afoot, from Panama to Buenos Aires.* Garden City, NJ: The Century Company and Garden City Publishing Company, 1917.

Garcés G., Jorge A., compiler. *Documentos inéditos relativos al adelantado capitán don Sebastián de Benalcázar, 1535–1565.* Quito: Archivo Municipal, 1936.

García Martínez, José Ramón. "La escuadra española del Pacífico, 1862–1866." *Revista del Instituto de Estudios Históricos Marítimos del Perú* 8–9 (1987–1990): 81–116.

———. "1866–1991: CXXV aniversario de los bombardeos de Valparaíso y de El Callao." *Revista General de Marina [Spain]* 220 (May 1991): 749–757.

———. "La campaña del Pacífico, 1862–1866: algunos grabados de la época." *Revista de Marina [Chile]* 114, Number 1 (1997): 62–74.

Grimble, Ian. *The Sea Wolf: The Life of Admiral Cochrane.* London, 1978.

Hardoy, Jorge Enrique, et al. *Política de la tierra urbana y mecanismos para su regulación en América del Sur.* Buenos Aires: Centro de Estudios Urbanos y Regionales del Instituto "Torcuato di Tella," 1968.

Harris, Olivia, et al., editors. *La participación indígena en los mercados surandinos: estrategias y reproducción social, siglos XVI a XX.* La Paz, 1987.

Heath, Dwight B., editor. *Contemporary Cultures and Societies of Latin America: A Reader in the Social Anthropology of Middle and South America.* New York, 1974 revised edition.

Heath, Dwight B., and Richard N. Adams, editors. *Contemporary Cultures and Societies of Latin America.* New York, 1965.

Hoffenberg, H. L. *Nineteenth Century South America in Photographs.* New York: Dover, 1982.

Isabelle, Arsène. *Viaje a Argentina, Uruguay, Brasil en 1830.* Buenos Aires: Editorial Americana, 1943 Spanish translation of 1835 French original.

James, Preston E. *Latin America.* New York: Odyssey, 1969 edition.

Jones, Tom B. *South America Rediscovered.* Minneapolis, 1949.

Juan de Santacilia, Jorge, and Antonio de Ulloa. *A Voyage to South America.* New York: Alfred A. Knopf, 1964 abridged version of the John Adams translation of *Relación histórica del viaje a la América Meridional hecho de orden de S.M. para medir algunos grados del meridiano terrestre,* originally published in Madrid by A. Marín in 1748 in two volumes; the latter edition was also reprinted in facsimile in Madrid by the Fundación Universitaria Española in 1978.

———. *Noticias secretas de América.* Madrid: Turner, 1982, two volumes; there also exists a 1953 edition from Buenos Aires, as well as a 1918 one by Editorial América in Madrid.

Lafuente, Antonio. *La geometrización de la tierra: observaciones y resultados de la expedición geodésica hispanofrancesa al virreinato del Perú, 1735–1744.* Madrid: Instituto "Arnau de Villanova," Consejo Superior de Investigaciones Científicas, 1984.

Lafuente, Antonio, and Antonio Mazuecos. *Los caballeros del Punto Fijo: ciencia, política y aventura en la expedición geodésica hispanofrancesa al virreinato del Perú en el siglo XVIII.* Madrid: Serbal, 1987.

Levilier, Roberto, compiler. *Ordenanzas de don Francisco de Toledo, virrey del Perú, 1569–1581.* Madrid, 1929.

Lisboa, Manuel María. *Alias* "el consejero Lisboa." *Relación de un viaje a Venezuela, Nueva Granada y Ecuador.* Caracas: Edime, 1954.

Lloyd, Reginald, et al., editors. *Impresiones de las repúblicas sud-americanas del oeste en el siglo veinte: historia, población, comercio, industria y riqueza.* London: Lloyds Great Britain Publishing Company, 1915.

Martin, Percy F. *Through Five Republics of South America: A Critical Description of Argentina, Brazil, Chile, Uruguay, and Venezuela in 1905.* London: William Heinemann, 1905.

Mason, Tony. *Passion of the People: Football in South America.* London and New York: Verso, 1995.

Memorias del General Guillermo Miller. Lima, 1975 re-edition, two volumes.

Mercier, Roger. "Les français en Amérique du Sud au XVIIIe siècle: la mission de l'Académie des sciences, 1735–1745." *Revue française d'histoire d'Outre-Mer [France]* 56 (1969): 327–374.

Meza Villalobos, Néstor. *Felipe V y el problema ético-político de la provisión de mano de obra a la minería del Perú y Nuevo Reino de Granada.* Valladolid, Spain, 1976.

Moniz de Argão, Pedro, compiler. *Indice dos documentos relativos a América do Sul existentes na Biblioteca da Ajuda.* Rio de Janeiro: Arquivo Nacional, 1968.

Morgan, Michael. "South American Odyssey." *Américas [Organization of American States]* 31, Number 10 (October 1979): 28–34.

Mörner, Magnus. *The Andean Past: Land, Societies, and Conflicts.* New York: Columbia University Press, 1985.

Naylor, B. *Accounts of Nineteenth-Century South America: An Annotated Checklist of Works by British and United States Observers.* London: Athlone, 1969.

O'Phelan Godoy, Scarlett. *Rebellions and Revolts in Eighteenth Century Peru and Upper Peru.* Colgne, 1985.

Pallière, León. *Diario de viaje por la América del Sud.* Buenos Aires, 1945.

Pike, Frederick B. *The United States and the Andean Republics: Peru, Bolivia, and Ecuador.* Cambridge, MA: Harvard University Press, 1977.

Ramos, Demetrio. *Trigo chileno, navieros del Callao y hacendados limeños entre la crisis agrícola del siglo XVII y la comercial de la primera mitad del XVIII.* Madrid: Instituto "Gonzalo Fernández de Oviedo," Consejo Superior de Investigaciones Científicas, 1967 reprint of article originally published in *Revista de Indias* 105–106 (1966).

Robertson, John Parish. *Cartas de Sudamérica.* Buenos Aires: Emecé, 1950 Spanish translation by José Luis Busaniche of 1842 London original *Letters on South America.*

Robinson, David J., editor. *Mil leguas por América, de Lima a Caracas, 1740–1741: diario de don Miguel de Santisteban.* Bogotá, 1992.

Salzano, Francisco M., editor. *The Ongoing Evolution of Latin American Populations.* Springfield, IL, 1971.

Sánchez-Albornoz, Nicolás. *Indios y tributos en el Alto Perú.* Lima, 1978.

Solberg, Carl. *Immigration and Nationalism: Argentina and Chile, 1890–1914.* Austin: University of Texas Press, 1970.

Stern, Steve J., editor. *Resistance, Rebellion, and Consciousness in the Andean Peasant World, Eighteenth to Twentieth Centuries.* Madison: University of Wisconsin Press, 1987.

Stewart, C. S. *A Visit to the South Seas in the U.S. Ship "Vincennes" during the Years 1829 and 1830; with Scenes in Brazil, Peru, Etc.* New York: Praeger, 1970.

Veatch, A. C. *Quito to Bogotá.* London: Hodder and Stoughton, 1923.

Velasco Fito, María de las Mercedes. "En torno a Benalcázar: la discusión sobre su nacimiento y el momento de su incorporación a la hueste de Pizarro." *Revista de Historia Militar [Spain]* 34, Number 68 (1990): 9–22.

Villalobos R., Sergio. "Contrabando francés en el Pacífico, 1700–1724." *Revista de Historia de América [Mexico]* 51 (1961): 49–80.

———. *Comercio y contrabando en el Río de la Plata y Chile, 1700–1811.* Buenos Aires: Editorial Universitaria de Buenos Aires or EUDEBA, 1965.

———. *El comercio y la crisis colonial: un mito de la Independencia.* Santiago, 1968.

Violich, Francis. *Cities of Latin America: Housing and Planning of the South.* New York: Reinhold, 1944.

Violich, Francis, and Juan B. Astica. *Community Development and the Urban Planning Process in Latin America.* Los Angeles, 1967.

Wilhelmy, Herbert. *Südamerika im Spiegel Seiner Städte.* Hamburg, 1952.

Zahm, J. A. *Through South America's Southland.* New York and London: Appleton, 1916.

Argentina
Buenos Aires
Colonial Era (1536–1805)

Barba, Enrique M. *La organización del trabajo en Buenos Aires colonial: constitución de un gremio.* La Plata, 1944.

Baucke, Florian. *Iconografía colonial rioplatense, 1749–1767: costumbres y trajes de españoles, criollos e indios.* Buenos Aires: Viau y Zona, 1935 facsimile re-edition by Guillermo Furlong.

Belotto, Manoel Lelo. "Espanha e o vice-reinado do Rio da Prata: a consolidão do comercio livre no trienio 1787–1789." *Anuario de Estudios Americanos [Spain]* 53, Number 1 (1996): 53–72.

Biedma, Juan José, et al., compilers. *Acuerdos del extinguido cabildo de Buenos Aires, 1589–1821.* Buenos Aires and Barcelona: Archivo General de la Nación, 1907–1934, forty-seven volumes in four series.

Documentos históricos y geográficos relativos a la conquista y colonización rioplatense. Buenos Aires: Jacobo Peuser for the Comisión Nacional del IV Centenario de la Fundación de Buenos Aires, 1941, five volumes.

Domínguez, Luis L. *The Conquest of the River Plate, 1535–1556.* New York: Franklin, 1964.

Gandía, Enrique de, editor. *Crónica del magnífico adelantado don Pedro de Mendoza.* Buenos Aires: L. J. Rosso, 1936.

Garavaglia, Juan Carlos. *Pastores y labradores de Buenos Aires: una historia agraria de la campaña bonaerense, 1700–1830.* Buenos Aires: Ediciones de la Flor, 1999.

García, Juan Agustín. *La ciudad indiana: Buenos Aires desde 1600 hasta mediados del siglo XVIII.* Buenos Aires, 1964 and 1955 reprints of 1900 original.

Haenke, Thaddaeus Peregrinus or Tadeo. "Relación de un viaje al Río de la Plata, ca. 1789–1794." *Anales del Instituto de Etnografía Americana [Argentina]* 3 (1942): 187–247.

Johnson, Lyman L. "The Silversmiths of Buenos Aires: A Case Study in the Failure of Corporate Social Organization." *Journal of Latin American Studies [UK]* 8 (1976): 181–213.

———. "Estimaciones de la población de Buenos Aires en 1744, 1778 y 1810." *Desarrollo Económico [Argentina]* 19, Number 73 (April–June 1979): 107–119.

Lafuente Machain, Ricardo de. *Buenos Aires en el siglo XVII.* Buenos Aires: Emecé, 1944.

———. *Buenos Aires en el siglo XVIII.* Buenos Aires: Municipalidad de la Ciudad, 1946.

Levene, Ricardo. "Historia de la segunda audiencia de Buenos Aires." *Revista de Indias [Spain]* 7 (1946): 239–251.

Levillier, Roberto, compiler. *Correspondencia de los oficiales reales de hacienda de Río de la Plata con los reyes de España.* Madrid: Sucesores de Rivadeneyra, 1915.

———. *Correspondencia de la ciudad de Buenos Aires.* Madrid, 1915–1918, three volumes.

Martínez, Pedro S. *Las industrias durante el virreinato.* Buenos Aires: Editorial Universitaria de Buenos Aires or EUDEBA, 1969.

Memorias de los virreyes del Río de la Plata. Buenos Aires: Bajel, 1943.

Molina, Raúl A. *Don Diego Rodríguez Valdez y de la Banda.* Buenos Aires: Municipalidad de la Ciudad, 1949.

Moreno, José Luis. "La estructura social y demográfica de la ciudad de Buenos Aires en el año 1778." *Anuario del Instituto de Investigaciones Históricas de la Universidad Nacional del Litoral [Rosario, Argentina]* 8 (1965): 151–170.

Outes, Félix F. *Cartas y planos inéditos de los siglos XVII y XVIII y del primer decenio del XIX, conservados en el Archivo de la Dirección de Geodesia, Catastro y Mapa de la Provincia de Buenos Aires.* Buenos Aires: Instituto de Investigaciones Geográficas de la Facultad de Filosofía y Letras, 1930.

Rubio y Esteban, Julián María. *Exploración y conquista del Río de la Plata, siglos XVI y XVII.* Barcelona: Salvat, 1953.

Ruiz Guiñazú, Enrique, compiler. *Garay, fundador de Buenos Aires: documentos referentes a las fundaciones de Santa Fe y Buenos Aires.* Buenos Aires: Municipalidad de la Ciudad, 1915.

Sánchez de Mendeville, María E. or "Mariquita." *Recuerdos del Buenos Aires virreinal.* Buenos Aires: Erre, 1953.

Socolow, Susan Migden. "Religious Participation of the Porteño Merchants, 1778–1810." *The Americas: A Quarterly Review of Inter-American Cultural History [Academy of American Franciscan History]* 32, Number 3 (1976): 372–401.

———. *Merchants of Viceregal Buenos Aires, 1778–1810.* New York: Cambridge University Press, 1978.

———. "Marriage, Birth and Inheritance: The Merchants of Eighteenth-Century Buenos Aires." *Hispanic American Historical Review* 60, Number 3 (1980): 387–406.

———. "Women and Crime: Buenos Aires, 1757–1797." *Journal of Latin American Studies [UK]* 12 (1980): 39–54.

Studer, Elena F. S. de. *La trata de negros en el Río de la Plata durante el siglo XVIII.* Buenos Aires: Editorial Universitaria de Buenos Aires or EUDEBA, 1957.

Tjarks, Germán O. E. *El consulado de Buenos Aires y sus proyecciones en la historia del Río de la Plata.* Buenos Aires: Editorial Universitaria de Buenos Aires or EUDEBA, 1962, two volumes.

Torre Revello, José. *Crónicas del Buenos Aires colonial.* Buenos Aires: Bajel, 1943.

———. *La orfebrería colonial en Hispanoamérica y particularmente en Buenos Aires.* Buenos Aires: Huarpes, 1945.

———. *La casa y el mobiliario en el Buenos Aires colonial.* Buenos Aires: Editorial Universitaria de Buenos Aires or EUDEBA, 1945–1946, two volumes.

———. *La casa cabildo de la ciudad de Buenos Aires.* Buenos Aires, 1951.

———. *La casa en el Buenos Aires colonial.* Buenos Aires: Ministerio de Educación de la Nación, 1952.

Torres Lanzas, Pedro. *Relación descriptiva de los mapas, planos, etc., del Virreinato de Buenos Aires, existentes en el Archivo General de Indias.* Buenos Aires: Sección de Historia, Facultad de Filosofía y Letras, 1921.

Colonial-Era Maps and Depictions of Buenos Aires, 1536–1804

Engraving of the first settlement on the River Plate, ca. 1536—published 31 years later in Frankfurt as part of the memoirs of the Bavarian soldier Ulrich Schmidel, who had participated in this enterprise

Map dated 1583, of the original distribution of 231 *solares* or "city plots" distributed by Juan de Garay three years previously—copy made by the engineer Agustín Ibañez, ca. 1794, held by the Archive of Indies at Seville, old Torres Lanzas call number: Mapas y Planos de Buenos Aires, 11 or Estancia 125, Caja 5, Legajo 4(4)

Anonymous watercolor of Buenos Aires, 1628—from the album of the Dutch cartographer Johannes Vingboons, held by the Apostolic Library at The Vatican

Anonymous diagram of an unidentified fort near Buenos Aires, ca. 1664—original held by the Archive of Indies at Seville, old Torres Lanzas call number: Mapas y Planos de Buenos Aires, 20 or Estancia 76, Caja 3, Legajo 4(1)

Diagram of Buenos Aires' citadel, March 1676—original held by the Archive of Indies at Seville, old Torres Lanzas call number: Mapas y Planos de Buenos Aires, 23 or Estancia 76, Caja 3, Legajo 4(3)

Diagram of a new fort built by Gov. José de Garro, November 1681—original held by the Archive of Indies at Seville, old Torres Lanzas call number: Mapas y Planos de Buenos Aires, 26 or Estancia 74, Caja 6, Legajo 40(1)

Ibid., February 1682—original held by the Archive of Indies at Seville, old Torres Lanzas call number: Mapas y Planos de Buenos Aires, 28 or Estancia 76, Caja 3, Legajo 4(4)

Diagram of a proposed new fort to protect the city, by the military engineer José Bermúdez, June 1701—original held by the Archive of Indies at Seville, old Torres Lanzas call number: Mapas y Planos de Buenos Aires, 37 or Estancia 76, Caja 3, Legajo 4(5)

Map by Bermúdez of the reconstructed citadel (drawn disproportionately large to highlight its details), plus the city and its harbor front, December 1708—original held by the Archive of Indies at Seville, old Torres Lanzas call number: Mapas y Planos de Buenos Aires, 38 or Estancia 76, Caja 3, Legajo 4(6)

Ibid., 1713—original held by the Archive of Indies at Seville, old Torres Lanzas call number: Mapas y Planos de Buenos Aires, 39 or Estancia 76, Caja 3, Legajo 4(7)

Diagram by the Jesuit brother Juan Bautista Prímoli of a proposed new single-story *cabildo* or "city hall," 1719—original held by the Archive of Indies at Seville, old Torres Lanzas call number: Mapas y Planos de Buenos Aires, 40 or Estancia 76, Caja 1, Legajo 38(1)

Anonymous map with watercolor highlights of the city, ca. 1720—original held by the Servicio Geográfico del Ejército at Madrid, call number: J-9-2–25

Diagram and frontal view by the Spanish military engineer Capt. Domingo Petrarca of a new treasury, installed inside Buenos Aires' citadel, 1729—original held by the Archive of Indies at Seville, old Torres Lanzas call number: Mapas y Planos de Buenos Aires, 43 or Estancia 76, Caja 1, Legajos 31(2) y 44

Diagram by Petrarca of a monastery project, left suspended because of the death of Dr. Dionisio de Torre Briceño, 1729—original held by the Archive of Indies at Seville, old Torres Lanzas call number: Mapas y Planos de Buenos Aires, 44 or Estancia 76, Caja 1, Legajo 31(3)

Diagram of San Miguel Castle by Petrarca, ca. 1729–1736—original held by the Archive of Indies at Seville, old Torres Lanzas call number: Mapas y Planos de Buenos Aires, 45 or Estancia 125, Caja 5, Legajo 4(12)

Engraving of Buenos Aires' waterfront, 1734—published fourteen years later in Lisbon as part of Silvestre Ferreira da Silva's *Relação do sitio que o Governador de Buenos Aires, D. Miguel de Salcedo, poz no anno do 1735 a Praça do Nova Colonia do Sacramento*

Diagram and frontal view of the proposed new city cathedral, 1755—original held by the Archive of Indies at Seville, old Torres Lanzas call number: Mapas y Planos de Buenos Aires, 60 or Estancia 76, Caja 4, Legajo 48

Diagram and frontal view of the headquarters for the *Real Renta del Tabaco* or "Royal Tobacco Monopoly" at Buenos Aires, 1779—original held by the Archive of Indies at Seville, old Torres Lanzas call numbers: Mapas y Planos de Buenos Aires, 124 and 125 or Estancia 122, Caja 7, Legajos 14(2) and 14(1)

Anonymous map with watercolor highlights of the city, ca. 1784—original held by the Servicio Histórico Militar at Madrid, call number: 6287

Diagram of a proposed new *real audiencia* or "royal tribunal" courthouse and jail, inside Buenos Aires' citadel, February 1785—original held by the Servicio Histórico Militar at Madrid, call number: 6260

1792 copy by Ozores, of farmlands assigned around the city periphery to residents by Gov. Hernando Arias de Saavedra or "Hernandarias" in 1608—original held by the Archivo General de la Nación, Buenos Aires

Profile views and floor plan by José García Martínez de Cáceres, of a proposed new powder magazine and guardhouse, September 1792—original held by the Archivo General de Simancas in Spain, call number: Mapas, Planos y Dibujos, VII-99 [archival provenance: Guerra Moderna 7241]

Profile views and floor plan by García Martínez de Cáceres, of a proposed new prison, July 1793—original held by the Servicio Histórico Militar at Madrid, call number: 6249

Profile views and floor plan by García Martínez de Cáceres, of a proposed convict barracks, August 1794—original held by the Archivo General de Simancas in Spain, call number: Mapas, Planos y Dibujos, VII-100 [archival provenance: Guerra Moderna 7243]

Profile views and floor plan by García Martínez de Cáceres, of an all-purpose barracks, August 1794—original held by the Servicio Histórico Militar at Madrid, call number: 6249

Profile views and floor plan by García Martínez de Cáceres, of a proposed cavalry base, September 1794—original held by the Archivo General de Simancas in Spain, call number: Mapas, Planos y Dibujos, IX-6 [archival provenance: Guerra Moderna 7243]

Watercolor of Buenos Aires as seen from its anchorage in 1794 by Fernando Brambila, one of the artists who accompanied Malaspina's scientific expedition into the Pacific—original held by the Museo Naval in Madrid, call number: *Colección de láminas de la expedición Malaspina*, Volume 2, Number 64

Watercolor of Buenos Aires as seen from its southern *Camino de las Carretas* or "Wagon Road" in 1794 by José Cardero, another artist from the Malaspina expedition, which was also apparently copied years later in an aquatint by Brambila—original held by the Museo Naval in Madrid, call number: *Colección de láminas de la expedición Malaspina*, Volume 2, Number 55 [aquatint: cliché M-I (53)]

Profile view and diagram by García Martínez de Cáceres, of a proposed new artillery park, February 1795—original held by the Archivo General de Simancas in Spain, call number: Mapas, Planos y Dibujos, VII-92 [archival provenance: Guerra Moderna 7243]

Profile drawings and floor plans by García Martínez de Cáceres, of new structures within Buenos Aires' citadel, June 1798—original held by the Servicio Histórico Militar at Madrid, call number: 6260

Floor plan by García Martínez de Cáceres, of an official residence inside Buenos Aires' citadel, June 1798—original held by the Servicio Histórico Militar at Madrid, call number: 6258

Anonymous map with watercolor highlights of the city, ca. 1800—original held by the Servicio Histórico Militar at Madrid, call number: 6267

Ibid., ca. 1800—original held by the Servicio Histórico Militar at Madrid, call number: 6268

Diagrams submitted by Pedro Arenas of a proposed new *Casa de Comedias* or "Popular Theater" at Buenos Aires, 1802—original held by the Archive of Indies at Seville, old Torres Lanzas call numbers: Mapas y Planos de Buenos Aires, 207 and 208 or Estancia 124, Caja 1, Legajos 5(2) and 5(3)

Diagram by Isidro Lorea of the new *Casa de Comedias*, July 1804—original held by the Archive of Indies at Seville, old Torres Lanzas call number: Mapas y Planos de Buenos Aires, 213 or Estancia 124, Caja 1, Legajo 5(1)

British Invasions (1806–1807)

Costa, Ernestina, Baroness Peers de Nieuwburgh. *English Invasion of the River Plate.* Buenos Aires: Guillermo Kraft, 1937.

Destéfani, Laurio H. *Los marinos en las invasiones inglesas.* Buenos Aires, 1975.

Gillespie, Alexander. *Buenos Aires y el interior: observaciones reunidas durante una larga residencia, 1806–1807.* Buenos Aires: La Cultura Argentina, 1921 Spanish translation by Carlos Aldao of 1818 English original.

Grainger, John D. "The Navy in the River Plate, 1806–1808." *Mariner's Mirror [UK]* 81, Number 3 (August 1995): 287–299.

Pendle, George. "Defeat at Buenos Aires, 1806–1807." *History Today [UK]* Number 6 (June 1952): 400–405.

Roberts, Carlos. *Las invasions inglesas del Río de la Plata (1806–1807) y la influencia inglesa en la independencia y organización de las provincias del Río de la Plata.* Buenos Aires: Jacobo Peuser, 1938.

Torre Revello, José. *El marqués de Sobremonte, gobernador intendente de Córdoba y virrey del Río de la Plata.* Buenos Aires, 1946.

Early Republican Era (1808–1860)

Almanaque politico y de comercio de la ciudad de Buenos Ayres para el año de 1826. Buenos Aires, 1968 facsimile re-edition.

Anonymous English traveler. *Cinco años en Buenos Aires, 1820–1825.* Buenos Aires: Solar Hachette, 1962.

Arquitectura del Estado de Buenos Aires, 1853–1862. Buenos Aires: Instituto de Arte Americano de la Universidad Nacional, 1965.

The British Packet: De Rivadavia a Rosas, 1826–1832. Buenos Aires: Solar-Hachette, 1976 Spanish translation and re-edition by Graciela Lapido and Beatriz Sopta de Lapieza Elli of nineteenth-century Anglo-Argentine newspaper.

Brown, Jonathan C. "Dynamics and Autonomy of a Traditional Marketing System: Buenos Aires, 1810–1860." *Hispanic American Historical Review* 56 (1976): 605–629.

Buschiazzo, Mario J., et al. *La arquitectura de Buenos Aires, 1850–1880.* Buenos Aires: Instituto de Arte Americano de la Universidad Nacional, 1965.

Castagnino, Raúl H. *El teatro en Buenos Aires en la época de Rosas.* Buenos Aires: Instituto Nacional de Estudios de Teatro, 1944.

Forbes, John Murray. *Once años en Buenos Aires, 1820–1831.* Buenos Aires: Emecé, 1956 Spanish translation by Felipe Espil of English original.

García Belsunce, César A., et al. *Buenos Aires, su gente, 1800–1830.* Buenos Aires, 1976 reprint of 1958 original.

———. *Buenos Aires, 1800–1830: salud y delito.* Buenos Aires, 1977 reprint.

Goldberg, Marta B. "La población negra y mulata de la ciudad de Buenos Aires, 1810–1840." *Desarrollo Económico [Argentina]* 16, Number 61 (April–June 1976): 75–99.

Irazusta, Julio, editor. *Vida política de Juan Manuel de Rosas, a través de su correspondencia.* Buenos Aires, 1941–1961, five volumes.

Lattes, Alfredo E., and Raúl Poczter. *Muestra del censo de población de la ciudad de Buenos Aires de 1855.* Buenos Aires: Centro de Investigaciones Sociales del Instituto Torcuato di Tella, 1968.

Levene, Ricardo, editor. *Mensajes de los gobernadores de la provincia de Buenos Aires, 1822–1849.* La Plata: Archivo Histórico de la Provincia de Buenos Aires, 1976, two volumes.

Parish, Woodbine. *Buenos Aires y las provincias del Río de la Plata.* Buenos Aires: Hachette, 1958 Spanish translation by Justo Maeso of the 1852 London original *Buenos Aires and the Provinces of the Rio de la Plata.*

Pellegrini, Charles-Henri. *Tableau pittoresque de Buenos Ayres* or *Recuerdos del Río de la Plata.* Buenos Aires: L'Amateur, 1958 reprint of French original and Spanish translation.

Periódicos de la época de la Revolución de Mayo. Buenos Aires: Academia Nacional de la Historia, 1961, five volumes.

Sáenz Valiente, José María. *Bajo la campana del cabildo: organización y funcionamiento del cabildo de Buenos Aires después de la Revolución de Mayo, 1810–1821.* Buenos Aires, 1952.

Urquiza Almandoz, Oscar F. *La cultura en Buenos Aires a través de su prensa periódica desde 1810 hasta 1820.* Buenos Aires: Editorial Universitaria de Buenos Aires or EUDEBA, 1972.

Immigration Boom (1860–1920)

Armus, Diego, and Juan Suriano. "The Housing Issue in the Historiography of Turn-of-the-Century Buenos Aires." *Journal of Urban History* 24, Number 3 (March 1998): 416–428.

Baer, James A. "Tenant Mobilization and the 1907 Rent Strike in Buenos Aires." *The Americas: A Quarterly Review of Inter-American Cultural History [Academy of American Franciscan History]* 49, Number 3 (January 1993): 343–368.

———. "Street, Block, and Neighborhood: Residency Patterns, Community Networks, and the 1895 Argentine Manuscript Census." *The Americas: A Quarterly Review of Inter-American Cultural History [Academy of American Franciscan History]* 51, Number 1 (July 1994): 89–101.

Blackwelder, Julius Kirk, and Lyman L. Johnson. "Changing Criminal Patterns in Buenos Aires, 1890 to 1914." *Journal of Latin American Studies [UK]* 14 (November 1982): 359–380.

Gorelik, Adrián. *La grilla y el parque: espacio público y cultura urbana en Buenos Aires, 1887–1936.* Buenos Aires: Universidad Nacional de Quilmes, 1998.

Hernando, Diana. *Casa y Familia: Spatial Biographies in Nineteenth Century Buenos Aires.* Los Angeles, 1973.

Hutchinson, Thomas J. *Buenos Aires y otras provincias.* Buenos Aires: Huarpes, 1945 Spanish translation by Luis Varela of 1865 original *Buenos Ayres and Argentine Gleanings* published in London by Edward Stanford.

Moya, José C. *Cousins and Strangers: Spanish Immigrants in Buenos Aires, 1850–1930.* Berkeley: University of California Press, 1998.

Platt, D. C. M. "Who Paid for the Modernization of Cities? The Experience of Buenos Aires, 1880–1910." *Bulletin of Latin American Research [UK]* 2, Number 1 (1982): 106–109.

Sábato, Hilda. *La política en las calles: entre el voto y la movilización, Buenos Aires, 1862–1880.* Buenos Aires: Sudamericana, 1998.

Salvatore, Ricardo Donato. "The Normalization of Economic Life: Representations of the Economy in Golden-Age Buenos Aires, 1890–1930." *Hispanic American Historical Review* 81, Number 1 (February 2001): 1–44.

Sargent, Charles S. *The Spatial Evolution of Greater Buenos Aires, Argentina, 1870–1930.* Tempe: Arizona State University Press, 1974.

Scenna, Miguel Angel. *Cuando murió Buenos Aires: 1871.* Buenos Aires: La Bastilla, 1974.

Scobie, James R. "Buenos Aires as a Commercial-Bureaucratic City, 1880–1910: Characteristics of a City's Orientation." *American Historical Review* 77, Number 4 (October 1972): 1035–1073.

———. *Buenos Aires: From Plaza to Suburb, 1870–1910.* New York: Oxford University Press, 1974.

Suriano, Juan. *La huelga de inquilinos de 1907.* Buenos Aires: Centro Editor de América Latina, 1983.

Szuchman, Mark D. "Childhood Education and Politics in Nineteenth-Century Argentina: The Case of Buenos Aires." *Hispanic American Historical Review* 70, Number 1 (1990): 109–138.

Wilde, Antonio. *Buenos Aires desde setenta años atrás.* Buenos Aires: Editorial Universitaria de Buenos Aires or EUDEBA, 1964 re-edition of 1881 original.

Modern Era (1921–Present) and General Works

Bacle, César Hipólito. *Trages y costumbres de la provincia de Buenos Aires.* Buenos Aires, 1947.

Besio Moreno, Nicolás. *Buenos Aires, puerto del Río de la Plata, capital de la República Argentina: estudio crítico de su población, 1536–1936.* Buenos Aires: Tudurí, 1939.

Billard, Jules B. "Buenos Aires: Argentina's Melting-Pot Metropolis." *National Geographic* 132, Number 5 (November 1967): 662–695.

Bourde, Guy. *Urbanisation et immigration en Amrique latine: Buenos Aires, XIXe et XXe siècles.* Paris, 1974.

Bucich, Antonio J. *La Boca del Riachuelo en la historia.* Buenos Aires, 1971.

Busaniche, José Luis, editor. *Episodios históricos, vida y costumbres de Buenos Aires.* Buenos Aires, 1950, two volumes.

Buschiazzo, Mario J. *Las viejas iglesias y conventos de Buenos Aires.* Buenos Aires: Beutelspacher, 1937.

Caamaño, Roberto. "Temple of the Opera." *Américas [Organization of American States]* 23, Numbers 1–2 (January–February 1971): 17–24.

Casadevall, Domingo F. *Buenos Aires, arrabal, sainete, tango.* Buenos Aires, 1968.

Daufresne, Julio, and Alberico Isola. *Usos y costumbres de Buenos Aires.* Buenos Aires, 1960.

Escardó, Florencio. *Nueva geografía de Buenos Aires.* Buenos Aires: Américalee, 1971.

Evolución institucional del municipio de la ciudad de Buenos Aires. Buenos Aires: Honorable Concejo Deliberante de la Ciudad, 1963.

Gilbert, A. "Moving the Capital of Argentina: A Further Example of Utopian Planning?" *Cities* (1989): 234–242.

Goldhurst, William, "A Yanqui in Buenos Aires." *Américas [Organization of American States]* 24, Number 8 (August 1972): 2–8.

Halperin Donghi, Tulio. *Historia de la Universidad de Buenos Aires.* Buenos Aires: Editorial Universitaria de Buenos Aires or EUDEBA, 1962.

Hardoy, J. Ferrari, et al. "Evolución de Buenos Aires en el tiempo y en el espacio." *Revista de Arquitectura [Argentina]* 40, Number 375 (1955): 25–84 and Numbers 376–377: 25–125.

Keeling, David J. *Buenos Aires: Global Dreams, Local Crises.* Chichester: Wiley, 1996.

La ciudad de Buenos Aires. Buenos Aires: Universidad Nacional, 1966.

Levene, Ricardo, editor. *Historia de la provincia de Buenos Aires y formación de sus pueblos.* La Plata: Archivo Histórico de la Provincia de Buenos Aires, 1940–1941, two volumes.

Llanes, Ricardo M. *La Avenida de Mayo.* Buenos Aires: Guillermo Kraft, 1955.

Martini, José Xavier, and José María Peña. *La ornamentación en la arquitectura de Buenos Aires, 1800–1940.* Buenos Aires: Instituto de Arte Americano e Investigaciones Estéticas, 1966–1967, two volumes.

Míguez, Daniel. *Spiritual Bonfire in Argentina: Confronting Current Theories with an Ethnographic Account of Pentecostal Growth in a Buenos Aires Suburb.* Amsterdam: Centros de Estudio y Documentación Latinoamericanos or CEDLA, 1998.

Molina, Raúl A. *Régimen financiero municipal de la ciudad de Buenos Aires.* Buenos Aires: La Facultad, 1941.

Nadal Mora, Vicente. *Arquitectura tradicional de Buenos Aires.* Buenos Aires: El Ateneo, 1946.

Nogués, Germinal, "Avenida de Mayo: Legendary Avenue of Buenos Aires." *Américas [Organization of American States]* 27, Number 3 (March 1975): 12–18.

Organización del espacio de la región metropolitana de Buenos Aires: esquema director, año 2000. Buenos Aires: Concejo Nacional de Desarrollo, 1969.

Orona, Juan V. *La revolución del 16 de septiembre.* Buenos Aires, 1971.

Pagano, José. *Los templos de San Francisco y Santo Domingo.* Buenos Aires: Academia Nacional de Bellas Artes, 1947.

Putnam, John J. "Buenos Aires." *National Geographic* 186, Number 6 (December 1994): 84–105.

Recchini de Lattes, Zulma L. *La población de Buenos Aires: components demográficos del crecimiento entre 1855 y 1960.* Buenos Aires: Instituto Nacional de Estadística y Censos, 1971.

Romero, José Luis, and Luis Alberto, editors. *Buenos Aires: historia de cuatro siglos.* Buenos Aires: Abril, 1983, two volumes.

Ross, Stanley R., and Thomas F. McGann, editors. *Buenos Aires, 400 Years.* Austin: University of Texas Press, 1982.

Sebreli, Juan José. *Buenos Aires: vida cotidiana y alienación.* Buenos Aires: Siglo Veinte, 1964.

Taullard, Alfredo. *Los planos más antiguos de Buenos Aires, 1580–1880.* Buenos Aires: Jacobo Peuser, 1940.

Walter, Richard J. *The Province of Buenos Aires and Argentine Politics, 1912–1943.* New York: Cambridge University Press, 1985.

———. *Politics and Urban Growth in Buenos Aires, 1910–1942.* New York: Cambridge University Press, 1993.

Zabala, Rómulo, and Enrique de Gandía. *Historia de la Ciudad de Buenos Aires.* Buenos Aires, 1937, two volumes.

Bolivia
General Studies

Abecia Baldivieso, Valentín. *Historiografía boliviana.* La Paz, 1965.

Arnade, Charles W. *The Emergence of the Republic of Bolivia.* Gainesville: University Presses of Florida, 1957.

———. "The Historiography of Colonial and Modern Bolivia." *Hispanic American Historical Review* 42, Number 2 (August 1962): 333–384.

Arze Aguirre, René Danilo. *Paticipación popular en la independencia de Bolivia.* La Paz, 1979.

Balcázar, Juan Manuel. *Historia de la medicina en Bolivia.* La Paz: Juventud, 1956.

D'Orbigny, Alcide. *Viajes por Bolivia.* La Paz: "Biblioteca de Autores Bolivianos" Collection published by the Ministerio de Educación, 1958.

Franqueville, André. "Villes et réseau urbain de Bolivie." *Les cahiers d'Outre-Mer [France]* 43, Number 171 (July–September 1990): 273–288.

Gerstmann, Roberto. *Bolivia.* Paris: Braun and Co., 1928.

Gisbert, Teresa. *Esquema de la literatura virreinal en Bolivia.* La Paz: Universidad Mayor de San Andrés, 1968.

Herreros de Tejada, Luis. *El teniente general D. José Manuel de Goyeneche, primer conde de Guaqui: apuntes y datos para la historia.* Barcelona, 1923.

"Image of Bolivia." *Américas [Organization of American States]* 25, Number 10 (October 1973): 1–24.

Klein, Herbert S. *Bolivia: The Evolution of a Multi-Ethnic Society.* New York, 1982.

Larson, Brooke. *Colonialism and Agrarian Transformation in Bolivia: Cochabamba, 1550–1900.* Princeton University Press, 1988.

Levilier, Roberto, compiler. *Correspondencia de los presidentes y oidores de la audiencia de Charcas, siglo XVI.* Madrid, 1918.

Lofstrom, William Lee. "Attempted Economic Reform and Innovation in Bolivia under Antonio José de Sucre, 1825–1828." *Hispanic American Historical Review* 50, Number 2 (May 1970): 279–299.

———. *The Promise and Problem of Reform: Attempted Social and Economic Change in the First Years of Bolivian Independence.* Ithaca, NY: Cornell University Press, 1972.

López Menéndez, Felipe. *Compendio de historia eclesiástica de Bolivia.* La Paz: El Progreso, 1965.

Marden, Luis. "Titicaca: Abode of the Sun." *National Geographic* 139, Number 2 (February 1971): 272–294.

McIntyre, Loren. "Flamboyant Is the Word for Bolivia." *National Geographic* 129, Number 2 (February 1966): 153–195.

———. "The High Andes: South America's Islands in the Sky." *National Geographic* 171, Number 4 (April 1987): 422–459.

Mesa, José de, and Teresa Gisbert. *Bolivia: monumentos históricos y arquitectónicos.* Mexico City, 1969.

———. *Escultura virreinal en Bolivia.* La Paz: Burillo, 1972.

Paredes Candía, Antonio. *Antología de tradiciones y leyendas bolivianas.* La Paz: J. Camarlinghi, 1968–1969, three volumes.

Peñaloza, Luis. *Historia económica de Bolivia.* La Paz, 1953–1954, two volumes.

Querejazu Calvo, Roberto. *Bolivia y los ingleses: 1825–1948.* Cochabamba, 1973.

René Moreno, Gabriel. *Ultimos días coloniales.* La Paz: Juventud, 1970.

Rivera Cusicanqui, Silvia. "El *mallku* y la sociedad colonial en el siglo XVII: el caso de Jesús de Machaca." *Avances [Bolivia]* 1 (1978): 7–27.

Rodríguez Ostria, Gustavo. "Capchas, trapicheros y ladrones de mineral en Bolivia (1824–1900)." *Siglo XIX: Revista de Historia [Mexico]* 4, Number 8 (1989): 125–140.

Saignes, Thierry. "Las etnias de Charcas frente al sistema colonial (siglo XVII): ausentismo y fugas en el debate sobre la mano de obra indígena, 1595–1665." *Jahrbuch für Geschichte von Staat, Wirtschaft und Gesellschaft Lateinamerikas [Germany]* 21 (1984): 27–75.

Sánchez-Albornoz, Nicolás. "Migraciones internas en el Alto Perú: el saldo acumulado en 1645." *Historia Boliviana* 2, Number 1 (1982): 11–19.

———. "Migración rural en los Andes: Sipesipe (Cochabamba, 1645)." *Revista de Historia Económica* 1, Number 1 (1983): 13–36.

———. "Mita, migraciones y pueblos: variaciones en el espacio y el tiempo: Alto Perú, 1573–1692." *Historia Boliviana* 3, Number 1 (1983): 31–59.

Tandeter, Enrique. "Crisis in Upper Peru, 1800–1805." *Hispanic American Historical Review* 71, Number 1 (February 1991): 35–71.

Wethey, Harold E. *Arquitectura virreinal en Bolivia.* La Paz, 1960.

Wittman, Tibor. *Estudios históricos sobre Bolivia.* La Paz, 1975.

Zulawski, Ann L. "Social Differentiation, Gender, and Ethnicity: Urban Indian Women in Colonial Bolivia, 1640–1725." *Latin American Research Review* 25, Number 2 (1990): 93–113.

La Paz

Colonial Era (1548–1824)

Corte Navarro, Inmaculada de la. "Fray Antonio Sánchez Matas: Obispo de La Paz, 1818–1825." *Archivo Ibero-Americano [Spain]* 57, Numbers 225–226 (1997): 443–450.

Crespo Rodas, Alberto. *Historia de la ciudad de La Paz, siglo XVII.* Lima, 1961.

———. *El corregimiento de La Paz, 1548–1600.* La Paz: Urquizo, 1972.

———. *La vida cotidiana en La Paz durante la Guerra de la Independencia, 1800–1825.* La Paz: Universidad Mayor de San Andrés, 1975.

Díez de Medina, Francisco Tadeo. *Diario del alzamiento de indios conjurados contra la Ciudad de Nuestra Señora de la Paz, 1781.* La Paz: Escuela de Artes Gráficos del Colegio Don Bosco, 1981 re-edition by María Eugenia del Valle de Siles.

Feyles, Gabriel, editor. *Actas capitulares de la ciudad de La Paz, 1548–1562.* La Paz: Alcaldía Municipal, 1965, two volumes.

Klein, Herbert S. "Accumulation and Inheritance among the Landed Elite of Bolivia: The Case of Tadeo Díez de

Medina." *Jahrbuch für Geschichte von Staat, Wirtschaft und Gesellschaft Lateinamerikas [Germany]* 22 (1985): 199–226.

López Beltrán, Clara. "Intereses y pasiones de los vecinos de La Paz en el siglo XVII: la elite provinciana en Charcas, virreinato del Perú." *Anuario de Estudios Americanos [Spain]* 52, Number 1 (1995): 37–56.

———. "El círculo del poder: matrimonio y parentesco en la elite colonial, La Paz." *Revista Complutense de Historia de América [Spain]* 22 (1996): 161–181.

Loza, León M., editor. *Actas capitulares del cabildo de La Paz, 1548–1562.* La Paz: Renacimiento, 1937.

Pinto, Manuel María, et al. *La revolución de la intendencia de La Paz en el virreinato del Río de la Plata con la ocurrencia de Chuquisaca, 1800–1810.* La Paz: "Biblioteca Paceña," Alcaldía Municipal, 1953.

Ponce Sanginés, Carlos, and Raúl Alfonso García, compilers. *Documentos para la historia de la revolución de 1809.* La Paz: "Biblioteca Paceña," Alcaldía Municipal, 1953–1954, four volumes.

Republican Era and General Works (1825–Present)

Acosta, Nicolás. *Guía del viajero de la ciudad de La Paz.* La Paz: Unión Americana, 1880.

Barrenechea, Santiago. *Remembranzas del pasado glorioso de la ciudad de N. S. de La Paz.* La Paz: Centenario, 1948.

Carrión, Fernando, and M. F. Sostres. *La ciudad prometida.* La Paz: SYSTEMA-ILDIS, 1989.

Franqueville, André, and G. Aguilar. *El Alto de La Paz: migraciones y estrategia alimentarias.* La Paz: INAN-ORSTOM, 1988.

Gill, Lesley. "Painted Faces: Conflict and Ambiguity in Domestic Servant-Employer Relations in La Paz, 1930–1988." *Latin American Research Review* 25, Number 1 (1990): 119–136.

González, Nelly S. "Ecclesiastical Archives of the Parroquias de Nuestra Señora de la Paz, Bolivia, 1548–1940: Description and Analysis." *The Americas: A Quarterly Review of Inter-American Cultural History [Academy of American Franciscan History]* 40, Number 1 (1983): 109–117.

Guardia Butrón, Fernando. *La evolución de la forma de la Ciudad de La Paz, Bolivia.* La Paz: Instituto Superior de Administración Pública, 1970.

La Paz en su IV centenario, 1548–1948. Buenos Aires: Imprenta López for the Comité Pro Cuarto Centenario de la Fundación de La Paz, 1948, four volumes.

Leonard, Olen E. "La Paz, Bolivia: Its Population and Growth." *American Sociological Review* 13 (1948).

Lindert, Paul van. "Collective Consumption and the State in La Paz, Bolivia." *Boletín de Estudios Latinoamericanos y del Caribe [The Netherlands]* 41 (1986): 71–93.

———. "Moving Up or Staying Down? Migrant-Native Differential Mobility in La Paz." *Urban Studies [UK]* 28, Number 3 (1991): 433–463.

López Menéndez, Felipe. *Historia del arzobispado de la ciudad de Nuestra Señora de la Paz.* La Paz: Imprenta Nacional, 1949.

Medeiros Anaya, Gustavo, et al. *La Paz: casco urbano central.* La Paz: Centro de Estudios y Proyectos "Nueva Visión," Alcaldía Municipal, 1977.

Siles Salinas, Jorge. *Guía de La Paz.* La Paz: Don Bosco, 1974.

Van Lindert, Paul, and Otto Verkoren. "Segregación residencial y política urbana en La Paz, Bolivia." *Boletín de Estudios Latinoamericanos y del Caribe [The Netherlands]* 33 (1982): 127–138.

Viscarra Monje, Humberto. *Las calles de La Paz.* La Paz: Universidad Mayor de San Andrés, 1965.

Potosí

Early Colonial Era (1544–1626)

Abecia Baldivieso, Valentín. *Mitayos de Potosí, en una economía sumergida.* Barcelona, 1988.

Arzáns Orsúa y Vela, Bartolomé de. *Historia de la villa imperial de Potosí.* Providence: Brown University Press, 1965 reedition by Lewis Hanke and Gunnar Mendoza L., three volumes.

Assadourian, Carlos Sempat. "Acerca del cambio en la naturaleza del dominio sobre las Indias: la mit'a minera del virrey Toledo, documentos de 1568–1571." *Anuario de Estudios Americanos [Spain]* 46 (1989): 3–70.

Bakewell, Peter John. *Miners of the Red Mountain: Indian Labor in Potosí, 1545–1650.* Albuquerque: University of New Mexico Press, 1984.

Barnadas, Josep M. "Una polémica colonial: Potosí, 1579–1584." *Jahrbuch für Geschichte von Staat, Wirtschaft und Gesellschaft Lateinamerikas [Germany]* 10 (1973): 16–70.

Braudel, Fernand. "Du Potosí à Buenos Aires: une route clandestine de l'argent, fin du XVIe, début du XVIIe siècle." *Storiografia [Italy]* 1 (1997): 321–325.

Burzio, Humberto F. *La ceca de la villa imperial de Potosí y la moneda colonial.* Buenos Aires: Peuser, 1945.

———. *"Manifiesto" de la plata extraída del Cerro de Potosí, 1556–1800.* Buenos Aires, 1971.

Campante Patricio, Jaciro. "As minas de prata de Potosí no século XVI: companhias e o comercio das unidades de extrão e de transformão do mineiro em metal." *História [Brazil]* 2 (1983): 39–53.

———. "La 'empresa' argentífera potosina en el siglo XVI." *Historia Boliviana* 4, Number 1 (1984): 15–31.

Capoche, Luis. *Relación descriptiva del asiento y villa imperial de Potosí, 1545–1585.* Madrid: Volume 122 of the

"Biblioteca de Autores Españoles," 1959 Atlas re-edition by Lewis Hanke of 1599 original.

Choque Canqui, Roberto. "El papel de los capitanes de indios de la provincia Pacajes 'en el entero de la mita' de Potosí." *Revista Andina [Peru]* 1, Number 1 (September 1983): 117–125.

Cobb, Gwendolyn Ballantine. *Potosí y Huancavelica: bases económicas del Perú, 1545–1640.* La Paz, 1977.

Crespo Rodas, Alberto. "La 'mita' de Potosí." *Revista Histórica [Peru]* 22 (1955–1956): 169–182.

———. *La guerra entre vicuñas y vascongados.* La Paz, 1969 reprint of 1956 original published in Lima.

Hanke, Lewis. *The Imperial City of Potosí.* The Hague: Nijhoff, 1956.

———. "The Portuguese in Spanish America, with Special Reference to the Villa Imperial de Potosí." *Revista de Historia de América [Mexico]* 51 (1961): 1–48.

Llanos, García de. *Diccionario y maneras de hablar que se usan en las minas y sus labores en los ingenios y beneficios de los metales.* La Paz, 1983 re-edition by Gunnar Mendoza L. of 1609 original.

Moreyra y Paz Soldán, Manuel. "En torno a dos valiosos documentos sobre Potosí." *Revista Histórica [Peru]* 20 (1953): 181–236.

Ruiz Rivera, Julián B. "Potosí: tensiones en un emporio minero." *Anuario de Estudios Americanos [Spain]* 40 (1983): 103–137.

———. "La mita en los siglos XVI y XVII." *Temas Americanistas* 7 (1990): 1–8.

Saignes, Thierry. "Notes on the Regional Contribution to the Mita in Potosí in the Early Seventeenth Century." *Bulletin of Latin American Research [UK]* 4, Number 1 (1985): 65–76.

———. "Potosí et le sud bolivien selon une ancienne carte." *Caravelle: cahiers du monde hispanique et luso-brésilien [France]* 44 (1985): 123–128.

———. "Capoche, Potosí y la coca: el consumo popular de estimulantes en el siglo XVII." *Revista de Indias [Spain]* 48, Numbers 182–183 (1988): 207–235.

Sordo, Emma María. "Las reducciones en Potosí y su carácter urbano." *Revista Complutense de Historia de América [Spain]* 21 (1995): 231–239.

Late Colonial Era (1627–1825)

Arduz Eguía, Gastón. *Ensayos sobre la historia de la minería altoperuana.* Madrid, 1985.

Arze Aguirre, René Danilo. "Un documento inédito de Pedro Vicente Cañete en torno a la controversia de la nueva mita de Potosí." Found in *Estudios bolivianos en homenaje a Gunnar Mendoza L.* La Paz, 1978.

Bakewell, Peter John. *Silver and Entrepreneurship in Seventeenth-Century Potosí: The Life and Times of Antonio López de Quiroga.* Albuquerque: University of New Mexico Press, 1988.

Buechler, Rose Marie. "Technical Aid to Upper Peru: The Nordenflicht Expedition." *Journal of Latin American Studies [UK]* 5 (May 1973): 37–77.

———. "La compañía de azogueros y el banco de rescates de Potosí, 1747–1779." *Boletín del Instituto de Historia Argentina y Americana* 16, Number 26 (1980): 67–116.

———. *The Mining Society of Potosí, 1776–1810.* Ann Arbor, MI: University Microfilms for the Geography Department of Syracuse University, 1981.

Campante Patricio, Jaciro. "As instituiçoes monetária e bancária de Potosí no decurso do século XVIII." *Revista de História [Brazil]* 56, Number 111 (July–September 1977): 51–72.

Cañedo-Argüelles Fábrega, Teresa. "Efectos de Potosí sobre la población indígena del Alto Perú: Pacajes a mediados del siglo XVII." *Revista de Indias [Spain]* 48, Numbers 182–183 (1988): 237–255.

Cañete y Domínguez, Pedro Vicente. *Guía histórica, geográfica, física, política, civil y legal del gobierno e intendencia de la provincia de Potosí.* Potosí: Sociedad Geográfica y de Historia, 1952 re-edition of 1789 original.

Chacón Torres, Mario. *Arte virreinal en Potosí: fuentes para su historia.* Seville: Escuela de Estudios Hispano-americanos, 1973.

———. "Vicente Caba, el último poeta del Potosí virreinal." Found in *Estudios bolivianos en homenaje a Gunnar Mendoza L.* La Paz, 1978.

Chao, María del Pilar. "La población de Potosí en 1779." *Anuario del Instituto de Investigaciones Históricas [Rosario Argentina]* 8 (1965): 171–180.

Cole, Jeffrey A. "An Abolitionism Born of Frustration: The Conde de Lemos and the Potosí Mita, 1667–1673." *Hispanic American Historical Review* 63, Number 2 (1983): 307–333.

———. *The Potosí Mita, 1573–1700: Compulsory Indian Labor in the Andes.* Stanford, CA: Stanford University Press, 1985.

Cortés Salinas, María del Carmen. "Una polémica en torno a la mita de Potosí a fines del siglo XVIII." *Revista de Indias [Spain]* 30, Numbers 119–122 (January–December 1970): 131–215.

Escalera, Saúl J. "A Printed Treasure from Potosí." *Américas [Organization of American States]* 32, Numbers 11–12 (November–December 1980): 53–56.

Fernández Alonso, Serena. "Minería peruana y reformismo estatal: las ordenanzas del Real Banco de San Carlos de la villa de Potosí." *Anuario de Estudios Americanos [Spain]* 47 (1990): 259–277.

Furlong, Guillermo. "Francisco de Paula Sanz: gobernante probo, justo y benéfico." *Boletín de la Academia Nacional de la Historia* 34, Number 2 (1963): 561–588.

González Casasnovas, Ignacio. "Un intento de rectificar el sistema colonial: debates y proyectos en torno a la mita de Potosí a fines del siglo XVII, 1683–1697." *Revista de Indias [Spain]* 50, Number 189 (1990): 431–453.

Helmer, Marie. "Potosí à la fin du XVIII.me siècle." *Journal de la Société des américanistes [France]* 40 (1951): 21–50.

———. "Potosí, un chapitre inédit de l'histoire d'Amérique." *Bulletin hispanique* 58 (1956): 344–352.

La villa imperial de Potosí. Buenos Aires: Volume 1 in the Series "Documentos de Arte Colonial Sudamericano," Academia Nacional de Bellas Artes, 1943.

LeRoy Ladurie, Emmanuel, et al. "Sur les traces de l'argent du Potosí." *Annales: économies, sociétés, civilisations [France]* 45, Number 2 (1990): 483–505.

Mariluz Urquijo, José María. "La situación del *mitayo* en las glosas de Benito de la Mata Linares al código carolino." *Jahrbuch für Geschichte von Staat, Wirtschaft und Gesellschaft Lateinamerikas [Germany]* 14 (1977): 161–198.

Martiré, Eduardo, editor. *El código carolino de ordenanzas reales de las minas de Potosí y demás provincias del Río de la Plata de Pedro Vicente Cañete.* Buenos Aires, 1973–1974 re-edition of 1794 original, two volumes.

———. "Tolerancias, prevenciones y regulación participadora de los indios 'capchas' de Potosí en la explotación del Cerro." Found in Volume 3 of *Estudios sobre política indigenista española en América.* Valladolid, Spain, 1977.

Mendoza L., Gunnar. *El doctor don Pedro Vicente Cañete y su historia física y política de Potosí.* Sucre, 1954.

Mira, Guillermo C. "La provisión de azogue en el virreinato del Río de la Plata." *Cuadernos Hispanoamericanos [Spain]* 2 (1988 Supplement): 209–222.

Molina Martínez, Miguel. "Aspectos de la expedición Nordenflicht en Potosí." *Historia Boliviana* 6, Numbers 1–2 (1986): 103–115.

Noel, Martín S. *Las iglesias de Potosí.* Buenos Aires: Volume 3 in the Series "Documentos de Arte Colonial Sudamericano," Academia Nacional de Bellas Artes, 1945.

Palacio Atard, Vicente. "La incorporación a la corona del banco de rescates de Potosí." *Anuario de Estudios Americanos [Spain]* 2 (1945): 723–737.

Pino Manrique, Juan del. "Descripción de la villa de Potosí y de los partidos sujetos a su intendencia." Found on pp. 7–51 of Volume 7 of *Colección Pedro de Angelis.* Buenos Aires, 1971.

"Relación dada al Virrey de Lima por don Francisco Alvares Reyero del natural de los indios de Potosí, sus vestimentas, las horas que trabajan, etc." *Revista de la Biblioteca Nacional [Argentina]* 9, Number 28 (Fourth Quarter 1943): 336–365.

René Moreno, Gabriel. *La mita de Potosí en 1795, con siete documentos inéditos editados por Guillermo Ovando-Sanz.* Potosí, 1959.

Rodríguez Molas, Ricardo. "Mitayos, ingenios y propietarios en Potosí, 1633." *Runa [Argentina]* 16 (1986): 179–262.

Rovere, Eugenio. "Francisco de Paula Sanz: un discutido intendente de ejército y hacienda." *Administración militar y logística* 36 (July–October 1973): 427–430.

Ruigómez Gómez, Carmen. "La mita de Potosí en tiempos del virrey conde de Alba de Liste: los pareceres de don Juan de Padilla y don Diego de León Pinelo y la visita de fray Francisco de la Cruz." *Cuadernos de Investigación Histórica [Spain]* 13 (1990): 155–166.

Sanz, Francisco de Paula. *Viaje por el virreinato de Río de la Plata: el camino del tabaco.* Buenos Aires, 1977 reedition by Daisy Rípodas Ardanaz.

Tandeter, Enrique. "Forced and Free Labour in Late Colonial Potosí." *Past & Present: A Journal of Historical Studies [UK]* 93 (November 1981): 98–136.

———. "La producción como actividad popular: 'ladrones de minas' en Potosí." *Nova Americana [Turin, Italy]* 4 (1981): 43–65.

———. *Coercion and Market: Silver Mining in Colonial Potosí, 1692–1826.* Albuquerque: University of New Mexico Press, 1993.

Tandeter, Enrique, and Nathan Wachtel. "Precios y producción agraria: Potosí y Charcas en el siglo XVIII." *Desarrollo Económico [Argentina]* 23, Number 90 (1983): 197–232.

Vázquez Machicado, José. *Catálogo de documentos referentes a Potosí en el Archivo de Indias de Sevilla.* Potosí: Colección de la Cultura Boliviana, 1964.

Vidaurre, Enrique. *Potosí: cuartel general de los guerreros de la independencia.* La Paz, 1952.

Independence and General Works (1825–Present)

Capriles Villazón, Orlando. *Historia de la minería boliviana.* La Paz: BAMIN, 1977.

Lindgren, Waldemar, and J. G. Creveling. "The Ores of Potosí, Bolivia." *Economic Geology* 23, Number 3 (May 1928): 233–262.

Lofstrom, William Lee. *Dámaso de Uriburu: A Mining Entrepreneur in Early Nineteenth-Century Bolivia.* Buffalo, NY, 1973.

Mendoza L., Gunnar. "The Imperial City of Potosí." *Américas [Organization of American States]* 18, Number 7 (July 1966): 1–6.

———. "Monumental Cities: Potosí, Bolivia, 1545." *Américas [Organization of American States]* 25, Number 1 (January 1973): supplementary pp. 3–7.

Mitre, Antonio. *Los patriarcas de la plata: estructura socioeconómica de la minería boliviana en el siglo XIX.* Lima: Instituto de Estudios Peruanos, 1981.

Omiste, Modesto. *Crónicas potosinas: estadísticas, biográficas, notas históricas y políticas*. La Paz, 1919, two volumes.

Ovando Sanz, Guillermo. "British Interest in Potosí, 1825–1828: Unpublished Documents from the Archivo de Potosí." *Hispanic American Historical Review* 45, Number 1 (February 1965): 64–87.

———. *La academia de minas de Potosí, 1757–1970*. La Paz, 1975.

Paredes Candía, Antonio. *Folklore de Potosí: algunos aspectos*. La Paz, 1980.

Platt, Tristán. *Estado boliviano y ayllu andino: tierra y tributo en el norte de Potosí*. Lima, 1982.

Potosí: patrimonio cultural de la humanidad. Potosí: Compañía Minera del Sur or COMSUR, 1988.

Prudencio Romecín, Roberto. "Potosí and Charcas." *Américas [Organization of American States]* 22, Number 3 (March 1970): 2–7.

Rudolph, William E. "The Lakes of Potosí." *The Geographical Review* 26, Number 4 (October 1936): 529–554.

Saltillo, Marqués del. *Linajes de Potosí*. Madrid, 1949.

Santamaría, Daniel J. "Potosí entre la plata y el estaño." *Revista Geográfica del Instituto Panamericano de Geografía e Historia [Mexico]* 79 (1973): 71–115.

Subieta Sagarnaga, Luis. *Bolívar en Potosí*. Potosí, 1925.

Brazil
General Studies

Adonias, Isa. *Mapas e planos manuscritos relativos ao Brasil colonial conservados no Ministério das Relações Exteriores (1500–1822)*. Brasilia: Serviço de Documentação, Ministério das Relações Exteriores, 1960.

Adonias, Isa, and Bruno Furrer, editors. *Mapa: imagens da formação territorial brasileira*. Rio de Janeiro: Odebrecht, 1993.

Alden, Dauril. "The Population of Brazil in the Late Eighteenth Century: A Preliminary Study." *Hispanic American Historical Review* 43, Number 2 (May 1963): 173–205.

———. *Royal Government in Colonial Brazil*. Berkeley: University of California Press, 1968.

Alden, Dauril, editor. *Colonial Roots of Modern Brazil*. Berkeley: University of California Press, 1973.

Alden, Dauril, and Joseph C. Miller. "Out of Africa: The Slave Trade and the Transmission of Smallpox to Brazil, 1560–1831." *Journal of Interdisciplinary History* 18, Number 2 (autumn 1987): 195–224.

Amaral Lapa, José Roberto do. *Economia colonial*. São Paulo, 1973.

Andrews, C. C. *Brazil: Its Conditions and Prospects*. New York, 1887.

Azevedo, Aroldo. *Vilas e cidades do Brasil colonial*. São Paulo: FFCL, Universidade de São Paulo, 1956.

"Barlaeus," Caspar van Baerle or. *Nederlandsch Brazilië onder het Bewind van Johan Maurits, Grave van Nassau, 1637–1644*. 's-Gravenhage: Martinus Nijhoff, 1923 translation into Dutch by S. P. l'Honoré Naber of 1647 Latin original *Rerum per octennium in Brasilia et alibi nuper gestarum sub Prefectura Ill. Com. J. Mauritii, Nassoviae, &c . . . historia*, two volumes. (A Portuguese translation by Claudio Brandao also exists, entitled *Historia dos feitos recentemente practicados durante vito anos no Brasil*, published by MEC in Rio de Janeiro.)

Barman, Roderick J. *Citizen Emperor: Pedro II and the Making of Brazil, 1852–1891*. Stanford, CA: Stanford University Press, 1999.

Barman, Roderick J., and Jean Barman. "The Role of the Law Graduate in the Political Elite of Imperial Brazil." *Journal of Interamerican Studies and World Affairs* 18, Number 4 (November 1976): 423–450.

Barreto, Anibal. *Fortificações do Brasil*. Rio de Janeiro: Biblioteca do Exército Ed., 1958.

Bastide, Roger. *The African Religions of Brazil: Toward a Sociology of the Interpenetration of Civilizations*. Baltimore: Johns Hopkins University Press, 1978.

Bello, José Maria. *A History of Modern Brazil, 1889–1964*. Stanford, CA: Stanford University Press, 1968.

Bennassar, Bartolomé. "Une fidélité difficile: les nouveaux chrétiens de Bahia et de Rio de Janeiro aux XVIIe et XVIIIe siècles." *Histoire, économie et société [France]* 7, Number 2 (1988): 209–220.

Bethell, Leslie. *The Abolition of the Brazilian Slave Trade: Britain, Brazil, and the Slave Trade Question, 1807–1869*. Cambridge, UK, 1970.

Borba de Moraes, Rubens. *Bibliographia brasiliana*. Rio de Janeiro, 1958.

Boxer, Charles Ralph. *Salvador de Sá and the Struggle for Brazil and Angola, 1602–1686*. London, 1952.

———. *The Dutch in Brazil*. Oxford University Press, 1957.

———. *Race Relations in the Portuguese Colonial Empire, 1415–1825*. Oxford: Clarendon Press, 1963.

———. *Portuguese Society in the Tropics: The Municipal Councils of Goa, Macao, Bahia, and Luanda, 1510–1800*. Madison: University of Wisconsin Press, 1965.

———. *The Golden Age of Brazil, 1695–1750: Growing Pains of a Colonial Society*. Berkeley: University of California Press, 1969.

"Brazil: Order and Progress." *Américas [Organization of American States]* 27, Numbers 11–12 (November–December 1975): supplementary pp. 1–32.

Bruneau, Thomas. *The Church in Brazil*. Austin: University of Texas Press, 1982.

Buley, E. C. *North Brazil: Physical Features, Natural Resources, Means of Communications, Manufactures and Industrial Development*. London: Pitman and Sons, 1914.

Burns, E. Bradford, editor. *A Documentary History of Brazil.* New York: Alfred A. Knopf, 1966.

Carneiro, Newton. *Rugendas no Brasil.* Rio de Janeiro: Livraria Kosmos, 1979.

Cascuso, Luis da Camara. *Geografia do Brasil holandes.* Rio de Janeiro: Jose Olympio, 1956.

Castro Santos, Lycurgo de, *filho* or "Junior." *Historia geral da medicina brasileira.* São Paulo, 1977.

Censo demográfico do Brasil. Rio de Janeiro: Instituto Brasileiro de Geografia e Estatística, 1991.

Chalhoub, Sidney. *Visões da liberdade: uma história das últimas dêcadas da escravidão na corte.* São Paulo: Companhia das Letras, 1990.

Colson, Roger Frank. "On Expectations: Perspectives on the Crisis of 1889 in Brazil." *Journal of Latin American Studies [UK]* 13, Number 2 (1981): 265–292.

Conniff, Michael L. *Urban Politics in Brazil: The Rise of Populism, 1925–1945.* University of Pittsburgh Press, 1981.

Conrad, Robert. *The Destruction of Brazilian Slavery, 1850–1888.* Berkeley: University of California Press, 1972.

———. "The Planter Class and the Debate over Chinese Immigration to Brazil, 1850–1893." *International Migrations Review* 9, Number 1 (spring 1975): 41–55.

———. *Children of God's Fire: A Documentary History of Black Slavery in Brazil.* Princeton University Press, 1983.

Cooper, Donald. "Brazil's Long Fight against Epidemic Disease, 1849–1917, with Special Emphasis on Yellow Fever." *Bulletin of the New York Academy of Medicine* 51, Number 5 (May 1975): 672–696.

Cortesão, Armando. *History of Portuguese Cartography.* Lisbon: Junta de Investigações do Ultramar, 1969–1971.

Cortesão, Armando, and Avelino Teixeira da Mota, editors. *Portugaliae monumenta cartographica.* Lisbon: Governo Portugues, 1960–1962, six volumes, plus 1987 reprint at reduced size by Imprensa Nacional-Casa da Moeda.

Delson, Roberta Marx. *New Towns for Colonial Brazil: Spatial and Social Planning of the Eighteenth Century.* Ann Arbor, MI: University Microfilms for the Geography Department of Syracuse University, 1979.

Dias, Arthur. *The Brazil of To-Day.* Nivelles, Belgium: Lanneau and Despret, ca. 1907.

Documentos históricos da Biblioteca Nacional do Rio de Janeiro. Rio de Janeiro, 1928-, 120 volumes.

Dundas Graham, Maria [later Lady Maria Calcott]. *Journal of a Voyage to Brazil and Residence There during Part of the Years 1821, 1822, 1823.* New York: Praeger, 1969 reprint of 1824 original published in London by Longman.

Enciclopédia dos municípios brasileiros. Rio de Janeiro: Instituto Brasileiro de Geografia e Estatística, 1957–1959, thirty-six volumes.

Eulálio, Alexandre. "Era of Independence." *Américas [Organization of American States]* 26, Number 1 (January 1974): 30–35.

Ewbank, Thomas. *Life in Brazil, Or a Journal of a Visit.* Detroit: Blaine Ethridge, 1971 re-edition of 1856 original published in New York by Harper and Brothers.

Fausto, Boris. *A revolução de 1930: história e historiografia.* São Paulo, 1970.

———. *Trabalho urbano e conflito social, 1890–1920.* São Paulo, 1976.

Fausto, Boris, editor. *História geral da civilização brasileira.* São Paulo, 1975, four volumes.

Ferrez, Gilberto. *As cidades do Salvadore Rio de Janeiro no século XVIII.* Rio de Janeiro: IHGB, 1963.

———. *O Brasil de Thomas Ender, 1817.* Rio de Janeiro: Fundação Morreira Salles, 1976.

———. *O Brasil do Primeiro Reinado visto pelo botânico William John Burchell, 1825–1829.* Rio de Janeiro: Fundação Morreira Salles and Pró-Memória, 1981.

———. *A fotografia no Brasil, 1840–1900.* Rio de Janeiro: Funarte and Pró-Memória, 1985.

Ferrez, Gilberto, and Weston J. Naef. *Pioneer Photographers of Brazil, 1840–1920.* New York: Center for Inter-American Relations, 1976.

Ferrez, Gilberto, and Robert C. Smith. *Fruehbeck's Brazilian Journey.* University of Pennsylvania Press, 1960.

Fishman, Laura. "Claude d'Abbeville and the Tupinamba: Problems and Goals of French Missionary Work in Early Seventeenth-Century Brazil." *Church History* 58, Number 1 (1989): 20–35.

Flory, Thomas. *Judge and Jury in Imperial Brazil, 1808–1871: Social Control and Political Stability in the New State.* Austin: University of Texas Press, 1981.

Freyre, Gilberto. *The Masters and the Slaves: A Study in the Development of Brazilian Civilization.* Berkeley: University of California Press, 1986 translation by Samuel Putnam of 1933 original *Casa-grande e senzala: formação da familia brasileira sob o regime de economia patriarcal.*

———. *Order and Progress: Brazil from Monarchy to Republic.* New York, 1970 translation by Rod W. Horton of 1959 original *Ordem e progreso: proceso de desintegração das sociedades patriarcal e semipatriarcal no Brazil sob o regime do trabalho livre,* published in two volumes in Rio de Janeiro.

———. *Um engenheiro francês no Brasil.* Rio de Janeiro: José Olympio, 1960 re-edition, two volumes.

———. *Ingleses no Brasil: aspectos da influência britânica sobre a vida, a paisagem e a cultura no Brasil.* Rio de Janeiro: José Olympio/INL/MEC, 1977 re-edition.

Furtado, Celso, et al. *Brasil: hoy.* Mexico City: Siglo XXI, 1968.

Gardel, Luis. *Brazil.* Chicago: Rand-McNally, 1969.

Goulart Reis, Nestor. *Evolução urbana do Brasil.* São Paulo: Pioneira, 1967.

———. *Quadro da arquitetura no Brasil.* São Paulo: Perspectiva, 1969.

Graaf, H. J. de, editor. *De Reis van Z. M. "De Vlieg," Commandant Willem Kreekel naar Brazilië, 1807.* The Hague, 1975, two volumes.

Graden, Dale T. "An Act 'Even of Public Security': Slave Resistance, Social Tensions, and the End of the International Slave Trade to Brazil, 1835–1856." *Hispanic American Historical Review* 76, Number 2 (1996): 249–282.

Graham, Richard. *Britain and the Onset of Modernization in Brazil: 1850–1914.* New York: Cambridge University Press, 1968.

———. *Patronage and Politics in Nineteenth-Century Brazil.* Stanford, CA: Stanford University Press, 1990.

Hahner, June E. *Poverty and Politics: The Urban Poor in Brazil, 1870–1920.* Albuquerque: University of New Mexico Press, 1986.

Harris, Marvin. *Town and Country in Brazil.* New York, 1956.

Hispanic American Historical Review 80, Number 4 (November 2000); entire issue devoted to colonial Brazil.

Hochman, Gilberto. *Era do saneamento: as bases da política de saúde pública no Brasil.* São Paulo: HUCITEC-ANPOCS, 1998.

Katzman, Martin T. *Cities and Frontiers in Brazil.* Cambridge, MA: Harvard University Press, 1977.

Klein, Herbert S. "The Colored Freedmen in Brazilian Society." *Journal of Social History* 3, Number 1 (fall 1969): 30–52.

Larsen, Eric. *Frans Post, interprète du Brésil.* Amsterdam and Rio de Janeiro, 1962.

Le Lannou, Maurice, and Nice Lecoq-Muller. *Le nouveau Brésil.* Paris: A. Colin, 1976.

Leff, Nathaniel. *Underdevelopment and Development in Brazil.* London, 1982, two volumes.

Leite, Serafim. *A história da Companhia de Jesus no Brasil.* Lisbon and Rio de Janeiro, 1938–1950, ten volumes.

Leite Cordeiro, José Pedro. "Algunos documentos sobre medicos e medicina do Brasil seiscentista." *Revista do Instituto Histórico e Geografico do São Paulo* 50 (1953): 271–314.

Lévasseur, E. *Le Brésil.* Paris: H. Lamirault, 1889.

Levine, Robert M. *Brazilian Images: The 1940s Photography of Genevieve Naylor.* New York: Reznikoff Artistic Partnership, 1996.

———. *The Brazilian Photographs of Genevieve Naylor, 1940–1942.* Durham, NC: Duke University Press, 1998.

Lloyd, Reginald, et al., editors. *Twentieth Century Impressions of Brazil: Its History, People, Commerce, Industries,* *and Resources.* London: Lloyd's Greater Britain Publishing Co., 1913 (also published in a Portuguese version).

Lopes, Luís Carlos. *O espelho e a imagem: o escravo na historiografia brasileira, 1808–1920.* Rio de Janeiro, 1987.

Loreto Mariz, Cecília. *Coping with Poverty: Pentecostals and Christian Base Communities in Brazil.* Philadelphia: Temple University Press, 1994.

Ludwig, Armin K. *Brazil: A Handbook of Historical Statistics.* Boston, 1985.

Mainwaring, Scott. *The Catholic Church and Politics in Brazil, 1916–1985.* Stanford, CA: Stanford University Press, 1986.

Malloy, James. *The Politics of Social Security in Brazil.* University of Pittsburgh Press, 1979.

Maram, Sheldon. "Urban Labor and Social Change in the 1920s." *Luso-Brazilian Review* 16 (winter 1979): 215–223.

Marinho de Azevedo, Célia Maria. *Onda negra, medo branco: o negro no imaginário das elites, século XIX.* Rio de Janeiro, 1987.

Markgraf, George. *Historia natural do Brazil.* São Paulo, 1942 translation into Portuguese by José Procopio de Magalhães of 1648 Latin original *Historia rerum naturalium Brasiliae.*

Mauro, Frédéric. *Le Portugal et l'Atlantique au XVIIIe siècle.* Paris, 1960.

Mauro, Frédéric, editor. *L'histoire quantitative au Brésil de 1800 à 1930.* Paris, 1973.

Maxwell, Kenneth. *Conflicts and Conspiracies: Brazil and Portugal, 1750–1808.* New York: Cambridge University Press, 1973.

McDowell, Bart. "Brazil's Golden Beachhead." *National Geographic* 153, Number 2 (February 1978): 246–277.

Mello Leitão, C. de. *O Brasil visto pelos ingleses.* Rio de Janeiro: Edit-Nacional, 1937.

Merrick, Thomas, and Douglas H. Graham. *Population and Economic Development in Brazil: 1800–Present.* Baltimore: Johns Hopkins University Press, 1979.

Monteiro, Salvador, and Leonel Kaz, editors. *Expedição Langsdorff ao Brasil, 1821–1829: iconografia do Arquivo da Académia de Ciéncias da União Soviética.* Rio de Janeiro: Alumbramento, 1988, three volumes.

Murilo de Carvalho, José. *A construção da ordem: a elite política imperial.* Rio de Janeiro, 1980.

———. *Teatro de sombras: a política imperial.* São Paulo and Rio de Janeiro, 1988.

Nero da Costa, Iraci del. *Arraia-miúda: um estudo sobre os não-proprietários de escravos no Brasil.* São Paulo: MGSP Editores, 1992.

Nieuhof, Johan. *Memorável viagem marítima e terrestre ao Brasil.* São Paulo, 1952 translation into Portuguese of 1682 Amsterdam original *Gedenkweerdige Brasiliaense Zee- en Lant-Reize.*

Nizza da Silva, Maria Beatriz. *Cultura no Brasil colônia.* Petrópolis, 1981.

———. *Sistema de casamento no Brasil colonial.* São Paulo, 1984.

Nunes Leal, Victor. *Coronelismo: The Municipality and Representative Government in Brazil.* Cambridge, 1977 translation by June Henfrey of 1949 original.

Oliveira Vianna, Francisco José de. *Resumo histórico dos inquéritos censitários realizados no Brasil.* São Paulo, 1986.

Owensby, Brian. "Domesticating Modernity: Markets, Homes, and Morality in the Middle Class in Rio de Janeiro and São Paulo, 1930s and 1940s." *Journal of Urban History* 24, Number 3 (March 1998): 337–363.

Pandiá Calógeras, J. *Formaçã histórica do Brasil.* Rio de Janeiro: Biblioteca do Exército Ed., 1957.

Pang, Eul-Soo. "Modernization and Slavocracy in Nineteenth-Century Brazil." *Journal of Interdisciplinary History* 9, Number 4 (spring 1979): 667–688.

———. *In Pursuit of Honor and Power: Brazil's Noblemen of the Southern Cross.* Tuscaloosa, AL, 1988.

Pang, Eul-Soo, and Ronald Seckinger. "The Mandarins of Imperial Brazil." *Comparative Studies in Society and History [UK]* 14 (March 1972): 215–244.

Piso, Willem. *Historia natural do Brasil ilustrada.* São Paulo, 1948 translation into Portuguese by Alexandre Correia of 1648 Latin original *Historia naturalis Brasiliae,* published in Leiden.

———. *Historia natural e medica da India Occidental.* Rio de Janeiro, 1957 translation into Portuguese by Mario Lobo Leal of the 1658 Latin original *De Indiae utriusque re naturali et medica libri quatuordecim,* published in Amsterdam.

Porto, José da Costa. *Estatuto das vilas do Brasil colonial.* Recife, 1970.

Prado Júnior, Caio. *The Colonial Background of Modern Brazil.* Berkeley: University of California Press, 1971.

Rago, Margareth. *Do cabaré ao lar: a utopia da cidade disciplinar, Brazil, 1890–1930.* Rio de Janeiro, 1985.

Reis, João José, editor. *Escravidao e invenção da liberdade: estudos sobre o negro no Brasil.* São Paulo: Editora Brasiliense, 1988.

Rodman, Selden. *The Brazil Traveler: History, Culture, Literature, and the Arts.* Old Greenwich, CT: Devin-Adair, 1975.

Rodrigues, José Honorio. *Bibliografia do dominio holandês no Brasil.* Rio de Janeiro, 1949.

Roiter, Fúlvio. *Brazil.* New York: Viking, 1971.

Rugendas, Johann Moritz. *Viagem pitoresca através do Brasil.* São Paulo: Livraria Martins, 1940 translation into Portuguese by Sergio Milliet. (There also exists a paperback version edited by Herculano Gomes Mathias, published by Edições de Ouro in Rio de Janeiro in 1968.)

Russell-Wood, A. J. R. "Women and Society in Colonial Brazil." *Journal of Latin American Studies [UK]* 9, Number 1 (1977): 1–34.

———. *The Black Man in Slavery and Freedom in Colonial Brazil.* New York: St. Martin's Press, 1982.

———. "Brazilian Archives and Recent Historiography on Colonial Brazil." *Latin American Research Review* 36, Number 1 (2001): 75–105.

Russell-Wood, A. J. R., editor. *From Colony to Nation: Essays on the Independence of Brazil.* Baltimore: Johns Hopkins University Press, 1975.

Scheper-Hughes, Nancy. *Death without Weeping: The Violence of Everyday Life in Brazil.* Berkeley: University of California Press, 1992.

Schwartz, Stuart B. "Resistance and Accommodation in Eighteenth-Century Brazil: The Slaves' View of Slavery." *Hispanic American Historical Review* 57, Number 1 (February 1977): 69–81.

———. "Patterns of Slaveholding in the Americas: New Evidence from Brazil." *American Historical Review* 87, Number 1 (1982): 55–86.

———. "Recent Trends in the Study of Slavery in Brazil." *Luso-Brazilian Review* 25, Number 1 (summer 1988): 1–26.

———. "The Voyage of the Vassals: Royal Power, Noble Obligations, and Merchant Capital before the Portuguese Restoration of Independence, 1624–1640." *American Historical Review* 96, Number 3 (1991): 735–762.

———. *Slaves, Peasants, and Rebels: Reconsidering Brazilian Slavery.* Urbana: University of Illinois Press, 1992.

Smith, Anne-Marie. *A Forced Agreement: Press Acquiescence to Censorship in Brazil.* University of Pittsburgh Press, 1997.

Smith, T. Lynn, and Alexander Marchant, editors. *Brazil: Portrait of Half a Continent.* New York, 1951.

Soares de Sousa, Gabriel. *Tratado descritivo do Brasil em 1587.* Rio de Janeiro: Edit-Nacional, 1938 (also republished in São Paulo in 1950 as *Notícia do Brasil*).

Sousa-Leão, J. de. *Frans Post, 1612–1680.* Amsterdam, 1973.

Stein, Stanley. "The Historiography of Brazil, 1808–1889." *Hispanic American Historical Review* 40, Number 2 (May 1960): 234–278.

Striker, Isabel A. "Early Visions of Imperial Brazil." *Américas [Organization of American States]* 29, Number 1 (January 1977): supplementary pp. 1–12.

Teixeira Leite, José Roberto. "Introduction to Brazilian Painting." *Américas [Organization of American States]* 16, Number 5 (May 1964): 21–28.

Thevet, André. *Les singularités de la France antarctique: le Brésil des cannibales au XVIe siècle.* Paris: La Découverte/Maspero, 1983 re-edition by Frank Lestringant of 1557 original.

Tollenare, Louis-François de. *Notes dominicales prises pendant un voyage en Portugal et au Brésil en 1816, 1817, 1818.* Paris, 1971–1973 re-edition by Léon Bourdon, three volumes.

Van der Dussen, Adriaen. *Relatorio sobre os capitanias conquistadas no Brasil pelos holandeses, 1639: suas condições econômicas e sociais.* Rio de Janeiro, 1947 translation into Portuguese by José António Gonsalves de Mello.

Varnhagen, Francisco Adolpho. *História das lutas com os holandeses no Brasil.* São Paulo: Cultura, 1943 reprint.

Vasconcellos, Sylvio de. "The Baroque in Brazil." *Américas [Organization of American States]* 26, Numbers 6–7 (June–July 1974): supplementary pp. 1–16.

Vasquez, Pedro. *Dom Pedro II e a fotografia no Brasil.* Rio de Janeiro: Editora Index, 1985.

Verdonck, Adriaen, and Adriaen Van Bullestrate. *Dois relatorios holandeses.* Recife, 1949 translation into Portuguese by José António Gonsalves de Mello.

Von Spix, Johann Baptist, and Karl F. Von Martius. *Viagem pelo Brasil, 1817–1820: excertos e ilustrações.* São Paulo: Melhoramentos, 1968.

Winter, Nevin O. *Brazil and Her People of To-Day.* Boston: L. C. Page, 1910.

Wirth, John. *The Politics of Brazilian Development, 1930–1954.* Stanford, CA: Stanford University Press, 1970.

Wiznitzer, A. "The Number of Jews in Dutch Brazil, 1630–1654." *Jewish Social Studies [New York]* 16 (1954): 107–114.

Wright, Marie Robinson. *The New Brazil: Its Resources and Attractions, Historical, Descriptive, and Industrial.* Philadelphia: Barrie and Son, 1901.

Recife
General Works

Chacon, Vamireh. *O Capibaribe e o Recife: história social e sentimental de um rio.* Recife: Secretaria de Educação e Cultura de Pernambuco, 1959.

Freyre, Gilberto. *Guia prático, sentimental e histórico da cidade do Recife.* Rio de Janeiro, 1949.

Gondim, Umberto. *Pôrto do Recife: sua história.* Recife, 1968.

Pereira da Costa, F. A. *Anais pernambucanos.* Recife: Arquivo Público Estadual, 1951, ten volumes.

Regueira Costa, José Césio. *O porto do Recife: roteiro de uma viagem através de sua história.* Recife, 1956.

Rocha, Leduar de Assis. *Historia da medicina em Pernambuco, seculos XVI, XVII e XVIII.* Recife, 1960.

Vasconcelos Galvão, Sebastião de. *Dicionário corográfico, histórico e estatístico de Pernambuco.* Rio de Janeiro, 1921 re-edition of 1910 original issued by the Imprensa Nacional.

Dutch Occupation (1630–1654)

Albuquerque Coelho, Duarte de. *Memórias diárias da guerra do Brasil.* Recife, 1944 reprint of 1654 Madrid original.

Blok, G. A. C. *Pieter Post, 1608–1669.* Siegen, 1937.

Bots, Hans, and Pierre E. Leroy. "Le Brésil sous la occupation néerlandaise: douze lettres de Vincent-Joachim Soler, pasteur à Recife, à André Rivet, 1636–1643." *Bulletin de la Société de l'histoire du protestantisme français [France]* 130, Number 4 (1984): 556–594.

Cabral de Mello, Evaldo. *Olinda restaurada: guerra e açucar no Nordeste, 1630–1654.* Rio de Janeiro, 1975.

Gonsalves de Mello, José António. *Tempo dos flamengos: influência da ocupação holandesa na vida e na cultura do norte do Brazil.* Rio de Janeiro, 1947.

———. *João Fernandes Vieira.* Recife, 1956, two volumes.

———. *A cartografia holandesa do Recife: estudo dos principais mapas da cidade, do periodo 1631–1648.* Recife: Parque Histórico Nacional dos Guararapes, 1976.

Jäger, Jens. "Die Schlacht bei Porto Calvo (Matta Redonda) im Januar 1636: Augenzeugenbericht eines Soldaten." *Militärgeschichtliche Mitteilungen [Germany]* 54, Number 2 (1995): 525–533.

Pernambucano de Mello, Ulysses. *O forte das cinco pontas.* Recife: Fundação de Cultura, 1983.

Quatro documentos historicos sôbre as duas batalhas dos Guararapes, 19-4-1648 e 19-2-1649. Recife: Governo do Estado do Pernambuco, 1962.

Richshoffer, Ambrosius. *Diário de um soldado.* Recife, 1977.

Sousa-Leão, J. de. "Palácio dos Tôrres." *Revista do Património Histórico e Artistico Nacional [Brazil]* 10 (1946): 135–167.

Van den Boogaart, Ernst, et al., editors. *Johan Maurits van Nassau-Siegen, 1604–1679, a Humanist Prince in Europe and Brazil: Essays on the Occasion of the Tercentenary of His Death.* The Hague: Johan Maurits van Nassau Stichting, 1979.

Van der Dussen, Adriaen. *Relatório sobre as capitanias conquistadas no Brasil pelos holandeses, 1639.* Rio de Janeiro, 1947.

Warnsinck, J. C. M. "Een mislukte aanslag op Nederlandsch Brazilie, 1639–1640." *De Gids [The Netherlands]* (February 1940): 1–33.

Wolff, Egon and Frieda. "The Problem of the First Jewish Settlers in New Amsterdam, 1654." *Studia Rosenthaliana [The Netherlands]* 15, Number 2 (1981): 169–177.

Early Maps and Depictions of Recife, 1630–1810

Engraved depiction of the Dutch conquest of Olinda and Recife, February 1630—prints held by the Atlas van Stolk Foundation in Rotterdam, plus numerous other sources

Maps of Recife and Antônio Váz Island by the Dutch engineer Andreas Drewisch, July 1631—originals held by the Algemeen Rijksarchief at The Hague, call numbers: Buitenlandse Kaarten 711 and 712

Pen-and-ink maps with watercolor highlights by the royal Portuguese cosmographer João Teixeira Albernaz I, of Pernambuco's coastline in 1631—originals held in the Map Library of the Brazilian Ministry of Foreign Relations, inventory numbers: 774.4a-1631A (2) and (3), as well as 1943-6688/25-IA

Dutch prints and map of Recife and Antônio Váz Island as they appeared "when Mauritius came to Brazil, *anno 1637*"—found in Caspar van Barlaes's or Barlaeus's *Rerum per octennium in Brasiliae gestarum historia*, numerous sources

Drawing of Maurits's first official residence on Antônio Váz Island, ca. 1637–1641, in Zacharias Wagner's *Thierbuch*—original held by the Staatliche Kunstsammlungen at Dresden

Dutch map of Recife and Antônio Váz Island, 1639—prints held by the British Museum [call number: Additional Manuscripts 31,357, UUU]; the University of Leiden Library [Bodel-Nijenhuis Collection, III-9–15]; the Instituo Arqueológico, Histórico e Geográfico Pernambucano at Recife; as well as other sources

Engraving of seventeenth-century sugar mills operating inland from Recife—found in *Reysboeck van het rijcke Brasilien, Rio de la Plata ende Magallanes*, Royal Library at The Hague, call number: (z.p.l. 1624) (Knuttel 3540)

Pen-and-ink map with watercolor highlights by Teixeira Albernaz, of Dutch defenses along Pernambuco's coast, 1640—original held by the Map Library of the Brazilian Ministry of Foreign Relations, inventory numbers: 774.4hkm-1640T and 1898-6691/24-IA, plus copies under 1898-6678/24-IA and 1898-6679/24-IA

Highly detailed map of Recife, Olinda, and environs, ca. 1640, surveyed by Maurits's cartographer Cornelis Sebastiaanszoon Golijath and engraved eight years later by Claes Janszoon Visscher or *Nicolaus Ioannis Piscator*, including small inserts of Mauritsstad and Vrijburg Palace—print held by the Algemeen Rijksarchief at The Hague, plus numerous other sources

Ground plan of Vrijburg Palace, ca. 1642, reputedly drafted a couple of decades later by the German architect Daniel Wolf Dopff—original held by the Staatliche Kunstsammlungen at Dresden

Pen drawing by Frans Post of Vrijburg Palace, ca. 1642–1644, as seen from the Lingueta Peninsula opposite—original held by the British Museum

Maps of Mauritsstad and Olinda, ca. 1645—found in Johan Nieuhof's *Gedenkweerdige Brasiliaanse zee-en land-reize*, published in Amsterdam in 1682, numerous sources

Highly detailed engraving by the Dutch artist Wilhelmus Hondius of Recife under Portuguese siege, ca. 1646–1648—numerous sources

Pen-and-ink map with watercolor highlights by Teixeira Albernaz, of Pernambuco's coast in 1666—original held by the Map Library of the Brazilian Ministry of Foreign Relations, inventory numbers: 774.4a-1666A (2) and 1943-6689/11-IA

Pen-and-ink map with watercolor highlights of Pernambuco's coast between "*Cabo de S: Agostinho*" and "*Maria Farinha*," latter half of the eighteenth century—original held by the Map Library of the Brazilian Ministry of Foreign Relations, inventory numbers: 774.45a-p.1750 and-2356-IA

1799 map of Pernambuco's coast between Cape Santo Agostinho and Olinda, copied from an original in the Arquivo Militar de Lisboa, ca. 1866—copy held by the Map Library of the Brazilian Ministry of Foreign Relations, inventory numbers: 774.49/0–58/R-67 aj-1799 and 1867-191-IA

Map of the city of Santo Antônio do Recife de Pernambuco, ca. 1800, copied sixty years later from an original in the Arquivo Militar de Lisboa—copy held by the Map Library of the Brazilian Ministry of Foreign Relations, inventory numbers: 774.49/R-67 a-c.1800 and 1867-192-IA

1810 map of the city and environs, copied from an original in the Arquivo Militar de Lisboa, ca. 1866—copy held by the Map Library of the Brazilian Ministry of Foreign Relations, inventory numbers: 774.49/R-67 a-1810 and 1867-8427-IA

Late Colonial and Modern Eras (1654–Present)

Cabral, John T., and Alexandrina Sobreira de Moura. "City Management, Local Power, and Social Practice: An Analysis of the 1991 Master Plan Process in Recife." *Latin American Perspectives* 23, Number 4 (1996): 54–70.

Carvalho, Marcos J. M. de. *Liberdade: rotinas e rupturas do escravismo no Recife, 1822–1850*. Recife: Universidade Federal de Pernambuco, 1998.

Cowell, Bainbridge. "Cityward Migration in the Nineteenth Century: The Case of Recife, Brazil." *Journal of Interamerican Studies and World Affairs* 17, Number 1 (February 1975): 43–63.

Eisenberg, Peter L. *The Sugar Industry in Pernambuco: Modernization without Change, 1840–1910*. Berkeley: University of California Press, 1974.

Ferrez, Gilberto. *Iconografia do Recife no século XIX*. Recife: Coleção do Tricentenário da Restauração Pernambucana, 1954.

———. *Velhas fotografias pernambucanas, 1851–1890*. Rio de Janeiro: Campo Visual, 1988 re-edition of 1956 original published at Recife by the Departamento de Documentação Cultural.

―――. *O álbum de Luís Schlappriz: memória de Pernambuco.* Recife: Fundação de Cultura Cidade do Recife, 1981.

Freyre, Gilberto. *The Mansions and the Shanties: The Making of Modern Brazil.* Berkeley: University of California Press, 1986 translation by Harriet de Onís of 1936 original *Sobrados e mucambos: decadência do patriarcado rural e desenvolvimento do urbano,* three volumes.

Galloway, J. H. "The Sugar Industry of Pernambuco during the Nineteenth Century." *Annals of the Association of American Geographers* 58, Number 2 (June 1968): 285–303.

Gonsalves de Mello, José António. *Luiz Schlappriz no Recife, 1858–1865.* Recife, 1962.

―――. *Ingleses em Pernambuco.* Recife: Instituto Arqueológico, Histórico e Geográfico de Pernambuco, 1972.

―――. *Diário de Pernambuco: arte e natureza no Segundo Reinado.* Recife: Fundação Joaquim Nabuco, 1985.

Hendricks, Craig, and Robert M. Levine. "Pernambuco's Political Elite and the Recife Law School." *The Americas: A Quarterly Review of Inter-American Cultural History [Academy of American Franciscan History]* 37, Number 3 (1981): 291–313.

Huggins, Martha Knisely. *From Slavery to Vagrancy in Brazil: Crime and Social Control in the Third World.* New Brunswick, NJ: Rutgers University Press, 1985.

Levine, Robert M. *Pernambuco in the Brazilian Federation, 1889–1937.* Stanford, CA: Stanford University Press, 1978.

Livro do Nordeste. Recife: Diario de Pernambuco, 1925.

Neuhouser, Kevin. "'Worse Than Men': Gendered Mobilization in an Urban Brazilian Squatter Settlement, 1971–1991." *Gender and Society* 9, Number 1 (1995): 38–59.

Outtes, Joel. *O Recife: génese do urbanismo, 1927–1943.* Recife: Editora Massangana for the Fundação Joaquim Nabuco, 1997.

Pereira Callado, Pedro Eloy. *A revolução de 29 de outubro de 1931 em Pernambuco.* Rio de Janeiro, 1944.

Tavares Correia de Lira, José. "A construão discursiva da casa popular no Recife, decada de 30." *Análise Social [Portugal]* 29, Number 3 (1994): 733–753.

Rio de Janeiro
Colonial Era (1565–1822)
Ferrez, Gilberto. "Panorama do Rio de Janeiro, 1775." *Revista do Instituto Histórico e Geográfico Brasileiro* 233 (1957): 3–23.

―――. "João Massé e a sua planta do Rio de Janeiro de 1713." *Revista do Instituto Histórico e Geográfico Brasileiro* 242 (1958): 388–396.

―――. "O Rio de Janeiro no tempo de Bobadela, visto por um padre francês." *Revista do Instituto Histórico e Geográfico Brasileiro* 264 (1967): 155–170.

―――. "Uma arribada francesa ao tempo de Bobadela, 1748." *Revista do Instituto Histórico e Geográfico Brasileiro* 280 (1975): 225–260.

Fragoso, Augusto Tasso. *Os franceses no Rio de Janeiro.* Rio de Janeiro: Biblioteca do Exército Ed., 1950.

McGrath, John. "Polemic and History in French Brazil, 1555–1560." *Sixteenth Century Journal* 27, Number 2 (1996): 385–397.

Moniz de Argão, Pedro, editor. *Tombos das cartas das sesmarias do Rio de Janeiro, 1594–1595, 1602–1605.* Rio de Janeiro: Arquivo Nacional, 1967.

Imperial Era (1823–1888)
Cardozo, Manoel. "The Holy See and the Question of the Bishop-Elect of Rio, 1833–1839." *The Americas: A Quarterly Review of Inter-American Cultural History [Academy of American Franciscan History]* 10 (1953–1954): 3–74.

Chalhoub, Sidney. "Slaves, Freedmen, and the Politics of Freedom in Brazil: The Experience of Blacks in the City of Rio." *Slavery & Abolition [UK]* 10, Number 3 (December 1989): 64–72.

Ferrez, Gilberto. *O velho Rio de Janeiro através das gravuras de Thomas Ender.* São Paulo: Melhoramentos, 1957.

―――. *Aquarelas de Richard Bate: O Rio de Janeiro de 1808–1848.* Rio de Janeiro, 1965.

―――. *Álbum de desenhos antigos dos arredores do Rio de Janeiro de Benjamin Mary, 1792–1846.* Brussels, 1974.

―――. *P. G. Bertichem: o Rio de Janeiro e seus arrabaldes, 1856.* Rio de Janeiro: Kosmos, 1976.

―――. *O sketchbook de Carlos Guilherme von Theremin.* Rio de Janeiro: CBPO, 1982.

―――. *O Rio antigo do fotógrafo Marc Ferrez.* São Paulo: Ex Libris, 1984.

Graham, Sandra Lauderdale. *House and Street: The Domestic World of Masters and Servants in Nineteenth-Century Rio de Janeiro.* Cambridge, 1986.

Greenhaugh, Juvenal. *O arsenal de marinha do Rio de Janeiro na história, 1822–1889.* Rio de Janeiro: Instituto Brasileiro de Geografia e Estatística, 1965.

Holloway, Thomas H. "'A Healthy Terror': Police Repression of *Capoeiras* in Nineteenth-Century Rio de Janeiro." *Hispanic American Historical Review* 69, Number 4 (November 1989): 637–676.

Karasch, Mary C. *Slave Life in Rio de Janeiro, 1808–1850.* Princeton University Press, 1987.

Naro, Nancy. "Customary Rightholders and Legal Claimants to Land in Rio de Janeiro, Brazil, 1870–1890." *The Americas: A Quarterly Review of Inter-American Cultural History [Academy of American Fraciscan History]* 48, Number 4 (April 1992): 485–517.

Soares, Luís Carlos. "Os escravos de ganho no Rio de Janeiro do século XIX." *Revista Brasileira de História* 8, Number 16 (March–August 1988): 107–142.

Modern Era and General Works (1889–Present)

Calderaro, Carlos. *Favelas e favelados do Distrito Federal.* Rio de Janeiro: Instituto de Pesquisas e Estudos de Mercado, 1957.

Conniff, Michael L. "Voluntary Associations in Rio, 1870–1945: A New Approach to Urban Social Dynamics." *Journal of Inter-American Studies and World Affairs* 17, Number 1 (February 1975): 64–82.

Correa de Sousa Costa, Antônio. *Alimentação que usa a classe pobre do Rio de Janeiro e sua influência sobre a mesma classe.* Rio de Janeiro: Perseverança, 1965.

Evenson, Norma. *Two Brazilian Capitals: Architecture and Urbanism in Rio de Janeiro and Brasília.* New Haven: Yale University Press, 1973.

Ferrez, Gilberto. *A mui leal e heróica cidade de São Sebastião do Rio de Janeiro.* Paris, 1965.

———. "O que ensinam os antigos mapas e estampas do Rio de Janeiro." *Revista do Instituto Histórico e Geográfico Brasileiro* 268: 27–42 and 278 (1971): 87–104.

———. *O Rio de Janeiro e a defensa de seu porto, 1555 a 1800.* Rio de Janeiro: Serviço de Documentação General da Marinha, 1972, two volumes.

———. *A Praça 15 de Novembro, antigo Largo do Carmo.* Rio de Janeiro: Riotur, 1978.

———. *O Paço da cidade do Rio de Janeiro.* Rio de Janeiro: Pró-Memória, 1985.

Gay, Robert. *Popular Organization and Democracy in Rio de Janeiro: A Tale of Two Favelas.* Philadelphia: Temple University Press, 1994.

Landau, Alice. "The Gardens of Rio." *Américas [Organization of American States]* 24, Number 5 (May 1972): 30–36.

———. "The Day of Days." *Américas [Organization of American States]* 26, Number 1 (January 1974): 18–24.

Lobo, Eulália Maria. *História do Rio de Janeiro: do capital comercial ao capital industrial e financeiro.* Rio de Janeiro, 1978, two volumes.

Meade, Teresa A. *"Civilizing" Rio: Reform and Resistance in a Brazilian City, 1889–1930.* University Park: Pennsylvania State University Press, 1997.

Murilo de Carvalho, José. *Os bestializados: o Rio de Janeiro e a República que não foi.* São Paulo, 1987.

Nascimento Silva, Fernando, editor. *Rio de Janeiro em seus quatrocentos anos.* Rio de Janeiro: Record, 1965.

Needell, Jeffrey D. "Making the Carioca Belle Epoque Concrete: The Urban Reforms of Rio de Janeiro under Pereira Passos." *Journal of Urban History* 10, Number 4 (August 1984): 382–422.

———. *A Tropical Belle Epoque: Elite Culture and Society in Turn-of-the-Century Rio de Janeiro.* New York: Cambridge University Press, 1987.

Perlman, Janice E. *The Myth of Marginality: Urban Poverty and Politics in Rio de Janeiro.* Berkeley: University of California Press, 1976.

Pinheiro Chaves, Carlos Romero. "Le tourisme dans l'Etat de Rio de Janeiro." *Les cahiers d'Outre-Mer [France]* 41, Number 164 (October–December 1988): 420–423.

Pino, Julio César. "Dark Mirror of Modernization: The Favelas of Rio de Janeiro in the Boom Years, 1948–1960." *Journal of Urban History* 22, Number 4 (May 1996): 419–453.

———. *Family and Favela: The Reproduction of Poverty in Rio de Janeiro.* Westport, CT: Greenwood, 1997.

Sanson, Vitorino. "New Houses for Rio." *Américas [Organization of American States]* 16, Number 12 (December 1964): 32.

Salvador

Colonial Era (1530–1823)

Almanach para a Cidade da Bahia: anno 1812. Salvador da Bahia, 1973 reprint of 1811 original.

Amaral Lapa, José Roberto do. *A Bahia e a carreira da India.* São Paulo, 1968.

Barickman, Bert Jude. *A Bahian Counterpoint: Sugar, Tobacco, Cassava, and Slavery in the Recôncavo, 1780–1860.* Stanford, CA: Stanford University Press, 1998.

Caldas, José António. *Notícia geral desta capitania da Bahia desde o seu descubrimento até o presente ano de 1759.* Salvador da Bahia, 1951 facsimile reedition.

Cerqueira Falcão, Edgar de. *Fortes coloniais da Cidade do Salvador.* São Paulo: Martins, 1942.

Cortês de Oliveira, Maria Inês. *O liberto: o seu mundo e os outros: Salvador, 1790–1890.* São Paulo: Corrupio, 1988.

Costa, Avelino Jesus da. "População da Cidade da Baía em 1775." *Actas do V Colóquio Internacional de Estudios Luso-Brasileiros [Coimbra]* (1964): 191–274.

Denis, Ferdinand. *Lettres familières et fragment du journal intime de Ferdinand Denis à Bahia, 1816–1817.* Coimbra, 1957 re-edition by Léon Bourdon.

Dias Tavares, Luís Enrique. "Escravos no 1798." *Revista do Instituto de Estudos Brasileiros* 34 (1992): 101–120.

Documentos históricos do Arquivo Municipal: atas da Câmara, 1625–1700. Salvador da Bahia, 1944–1945, six volumes.

Flory, Rae Jean Dell, and David Grant Smith. "Bahian Merchants and Planters in the Seventeenth and Early Eighteenth Centuries." *Hispanic American Historical Review* 58, Number 4 (November 1978): 571–594.

Kennedy, John Norman. "Bahian Elites, 1750–1822." *Hispanic American Historical Review* 53, Number 3 (August 1973): 415–439.

Miller, Shawn W. "Fuelwood in Colonial Brazil: The Economic and Social Consequences of Fuel Depletion for the Bahian Recôncavo, 1549–1820." *Forest and Conservation History* 38, Number 4 (1994): 181–192.

Morton, F. W. O. "The Military and Society in Bahia, 1800–1821." *Journal of Latin American Studies [UK]* 7, Number 2 (1975): 249–269.

———. "The Royal Timber in Late Colonial Bahia." *Hispanic American Historical Review* 58, Number 1 (February 1978): 41–61.

Novinsky, Anita. *Cristãos novos na Bahia, 1624–1654.* São Paulo, 1972.

Oliveira França, Eduardo d'. "Enghenos, colonização, e cristãos-novos na Bahia colonial." *Anais do IV Simpósio Nacional dos Professores Universitários de História [São Paulo],* (1969): 181–241.

Oliveira Pinto da França, António d', editor. *Cartas baianas, 1821–1824: subsídios para o estudo dos problemas da opção na independência brasileira.* São Paulo and Rio de Janeiro, 1980.

Parente Augel, Moema. *Visitantes estrangeiros na Bahia oitocentista.* São Paulo, 1980.

Queirós Mattoso, Kátia M. de. "Conjoncture et société au Brésil à la fin du XVIIIe siècle: prix et salaires à la veille de la Révolution des Alfaiates, Bahia 1798." *Cahiers des Amériques Latines [France]* 5 (January–June 1970): 33–53.

———. "Bahia opulenta: una capital portuguesa no Novo Mundo, 1549–1763." *Revista de História [Brazil]* 114 (1983): 5–20.

Russel-Wood, A. J. R. *Fidalgos and Philanthropists: The Santa Casa de Misericordia of Bahia, 1550–1755.* Berkeley: University of California Press, 1968.

Schwartz, Stuart B. "The *Mocambo:* Slave Resistance in Colonial Bahia." *Journal of Social History* 3, Number 4 (summer 1970): 313–333.

———. *Sovereignty and Society in Colonial Brazil: The High Court of Bahia and Its Judges, 1609–1751.* Berkeley: University of California Press, 1973.

———. *Sugar Plantations in the Formation of Brazilian Society: Bahia, 1550–1835.* New York: Cambridge University Press, 1985.

Soeiro, Susan A. "The Social and Economic Role of the Convent: Women and Nuns in Colonial Bahia, 1677–1800." *Hispanic American Historical Review* 54, Number 2 (May 1974): 209–232.

Sousa-Leão, Joaquim de. *Salvador da Bahia de Todos os Santos: iconografia seiscentista desconhecida.* Rio de Janeiro: Kosmos, 1958.

Verger, Pierre. *Trade Relations between the Bight of Benin and Bahia from the 17th to 19th Century.* Ibadan, Nigeria: Ibadan University Press, 1976 translation by Evelyn Crawford of 1968 French original *Flux et reflux de la traite des nègres entre le golfe de Bénin et Bahia de Todos os Santos du dix-septième au dix-neuvième siècle,* published in Paris by Mouton (a 1987 Portuguese translation by Tasso Gadzanis at São Paulo is also available).

Vilhena, Luís dos Santos. *A Bahia no século XVIII.* Salvador da Bahia: Itapuã, 1969 re-edition by Braz do Amaral of 1921–1922 original *Cartas de Vilhena: recopilação de notícias soteropolitanas e brasílicas contidas em XX cartas,* three volumes.

Early Maps and Depictions of Salvador, 1623–1810

Dierick Ruiters's *Toortse der Zee-Vaart,* published in Vlissingen in 1623, contains a rough depiction of the city and its bay—original held by the Algemeen Rijksarchief at The Hague, plus other sources

Adm. Jacob Willekens's capture of São Salvador in May 1624 prompted numerous Dutch engravings, the earliest appearing in the *Reysboeck van het rijcke Brasilien,* followed by others by Claes Janszoon Visscher or *Nicolaus Ioannis Piscator* (his Latinized name) and Hessel Gertiszoon, which were to be often copied or reworked by later artists—numerous examples abound in the Algemeen Rijksarchief at The Hague, plus other sources

Pen-and-ink drawing with watercolor highlights of Salvador as seen from its inner harbor, attributed to the Portuguese military architect Christovão Alvares, ca. 1629—original held by the Algemeen Rijksarchief at The Hague, call number: 2167

Pen-and-ink drawing with watercolor highlights of the Portuguese recapture of Salvador in 1625, plus a highly detailed map of the city itself, both drawn six years later by the royal cosmographer João Teixeira Albernaz I, who was present at this event—original held by the Map Library of the Brazilian Ministry of Foreign Relations, inventory numbers: 776.29/S-71 hkm –1631A and 1943-6688/22-IA (also cited in *Portugaliae Monumenta Cartographica* as 22nd Carta, Estampa 478 B)

Pen-and-ink map with watercolor highlights of Bahia de Todos os Santos in 1631, by Teixeira Albernaz—original held by the Map Library at the Brazilian Ministry of Foreign Relations, inventory numbers: 776.2a-1631A (5) and 1943-6688/21-IA

Detailed map of Maurits's siege of Salvador in 1638, with Portuguese text—original held by the Algemeen Rijksarchief at The Hague, call number: 2166

Pen-and-ink map with watercolor highlights of Bahia in 1640, by Teixeira Albernaz—original held by the Map Library at the Brazilian Ministry of Foreign Relations, inventory numbers: 776.2a-1640T (5) and 1898-6691/18-IA (copies also found in 1898-6678/18-IA and 1898-6679/18-IA)

The Dutch cartographer Cornelis Sebastiaanszoon Golijath apparently drew maps of Salvador's harbor, as well as diagrams of Forts San Felipe, São Bartholomeu, and San Alberto, ca. 1640—originals held by the Archive of the Dutch West-Indische Compagnie

Pen-and-ink map with watercolor highlights of Bahia in 1666, by Teixeira Albernaz—original held by the Map Library at the Brazilian Ministry of Foreign Relations, inventory numbers: 776.2a-1666A (1) and 1943-6689/15-IA

Pen-and-ink diagram with watercolor highlights of São Paulo harbor castle in 1666, by Teixeira Albernaz—original held by the Map Library at Brazilian Ministry of Foreign Relations, inventory numbers: 776.2a-1666A (2) and 1943-6689/16-IA

General map of Bahia, plus a map and panoramic view of the city of Salvador, ca. 1714, by the French visitor Amédée-François Frézier—published in Amsterdam three years later as inserts to his book *Relation du voyage de la mer du Sud aux cotes du Chily et du Perou*, numerous sources

Map and panoramic view of Salvador in 1724, by the Dutch cartographer Gerard van Keulen—original held by the Scheepvaartsmuseum at Amsterdam

Panoramic view of Salvador and its bay, ca. 1786, by the military engineer Capt. Manuel Rodrigues Teixeira—copied in March 1866 from an original in the Arquivo Militar de Lisboa and held in the Map Library of the Brazilian Ministry of Foreign Relations, inventory numbers: 776.29/S-71 a-1788? and 1867-8642-IA

Panoramic view of Salvador and its bay in the 1790s—copied in March 1866 from an original in the Arquivo Militar de Lisboa and held in the Map Library of the Brazilian Ministry of Foreign Relations, inventory numbers: 776.29/S-71 hkcr-179- and 1867-8643-IA

Map of Salvador in 1798, by the military engineer Joaquim Vieira da Silva—copied three years later by the junior naval Lt. José Joaquim Freire and held in the Map Library of the Brazilian Ministry of Foreign Relations, inventory numbers: 776.29/S-71 a-1798S and 1867-98-IA

Map of Bahia, ca. 1810, apparently by the military engineer Colonel Serra—copied thirteen years later, as well as in 1827 and 1865, and held in the Map Library of the Brazilian Ministry of Foreign Relations, inventory numbers: 776.25a-c.1810 and-200-IA; 776.25a-c.1810S and 1867-3013-IA; plus 1867-3012-IAca.

Imperial Era (1824–1888)

A inserção da Bahia na evolução nacional: 1a. etapa, 1850–1889, a Bahia no século XIX. Salvador da Bahia: Centro de Planejamento e Pesquisas, 1978, five volumes.

Butler, Kim D. *Freedoms Given, Freedoms Won: Afro-Brazilians in Post-Abolition São Paulo and Salvador.* New Brunswick, NJ: Rutgers University Press, 1998.

Carvalho Silva, Kátia Maria de. *O Diário da Bahia e o século XIX.* Rio de Janeiro, 1979.

Cerqueira e Silva, Inácio Accioli de. *Memórias históricas e políticas da província da Bahia.* Salvador da Bahia: Impresa Oficial do Estado, 1919–1940 re-edition by by Bras do Amaral, six volumes.

"Devassa do levante de escravos occorido em Salvador em 1835." *Anais do Arquivo do Estado da Bahia [Brazil]* 38 (1968): 1–142.

Ferrez, Gilberto. *Bahia: velhas fotografias, 1858–1900.* Salvador da Bahia and Rio de Janeiro: Banco da Bahia Investimentos and Kosmos, 1988.

Galloway, J. H. "The Last Years of Slavery on the Sugar Plantations of Northeastern Brazil." *Hispanic American Historical Review* 51, Number 4 (November 1971): 586–605.

Kent, R. K. "African Revolt in Bahia: 24–25 January 1835." *Journal of Social History* 3, Number 4 (summer 1970): 334–356.

Kraay, Hendrik. "'As Terrifying as Unexpected': The Bahian Sabinada, 1837–1838." *Hispanic American Historical Review* 72, Number 4 (November 1992): 501–527.

———. "Reconsidering Recruitment in Imperial Brazil." *The Americas: A Quarterly Review of Inter-American Cultural History [Academy of American Franciscan History]* 55, Number 1 (1998): 1–33.

Lovejoy, Paul E. "Background to Rebellion: The Origins of Muslim Slaves in Bahia." *Slavery and Abolition [UK]* 15, Number 2 (1994): 151–180.

Marcílio, Maria Luiza. "The Price of Slaves in XIXth-Century Brazil: A Quantitative Analysis of the Registration of Slave Sales in Bahia." *Studi in Memoria de Federigo Melis* 5 (1978): 83–97.

Maximiliano de Habsburgo (Ferdinand Joseph Maximilian of Austria). *Bahia 1860: esboços de viagem.* Rio de Janeiro and Salvador da Bahia, 1982 translation into Portuguese by Antonieta da Silva Carvalho and others.

Nishida, Mieko. "Manumission and Ethnicity in Urban Slavery: Salvador, Brazil, 1808–1888." *Hispanic American Historical Review* 73, Number 3 (August 1993): 361–391.

Nizza da Silva, Maria Beatriz. *A primeira gazeta da Bahia: a Idade d'Ouro no Brasil.* São Paulo, 1978.

Peard, Julyan G. "Tropical Disorders and the Forging of a Brazilian Medical Identity, 1860–1890." *Hispanic American Historical Review* 77, Number 1 (1997): 1–44.

Queirós Mattoso, Kátia M. de. *Bahia: a cidade do Salvador e seu mercado no século XIX.* São Paulo, 1978.

Queirós Mattoso, Kátia M. de, Klein, Herbert S., and Engerman, Stanley L. "Research Note: Trends and Patterns in the Prices of Manumitted Slaves: Bahia, 1819–1888." *Slavery and Abolition [UK]* 7, Number 1 (May 1986): 59–67.

———. "Au Nouveau Monde: une province d'un nouvel empire, Bahia aux XIXe siècle." *Histoire, économie et société [France]* 6, Number 4 (1987): 535–568.

————. *Família e sociedade na Bahia do século XIX*. São Paulo, 1988.

————. "Slave, Free, and Freed Family Structures in Nineteenth-Century Salvador, Bahia." *Luso-Brazilian Review* 25, Number 1 (summer 1988): 69–84.

————. *Bahia, século XIX: uma província no Império*. Rio de Janeiro: Nova Fronteira, 1992.

Reis, João José. "A elite baiana face os movimentos sociais, 1824–1840." *Revista de História [Brazil]* 108 (1976): 341–384.

————. *Slave Rebellion in Brazil: The Muslim Uprising of 1835 in Bahia*. Baltimore: Johns Hopkins University Press, 1993 translation of original *Rebelião escrava no Brasil: a história do levante dos malês, 1835* published at São Paulo by the Editora Brasilense in 1987.

————. "Slave Resistance in Brasil: Bahia, 1807–1835." *Luso-Brazilian Review* 25, Number 1 (summer 1988): 111–144.

————. "'Death to the Cemetery': Funerary Reform and Rebellion in Brazil, 1836." *History Workshop Journal* 34 (1992): 33–46.

————. "Différences et résistances: les noirs à Bahia sous l'esclavage." *Cahiers d'études africaines [France]* 32, Number 1 (1992): 15–34.

————. "'The Revolution of the Ganhadores': Urban Labour, Ethnicity and the African Strike of 1857 in Bahia, Brazil." *Journal of Latin American Studies [UK]* 29, Number 2 (1997): 355–393.

Ridings, Eugene. "The Merchant Elite and the Development of Brazil: The Case of Bahia during the Empire." *Journal of Inter-American Studies and World Affairs* 15, Number 3 (August 1973): 335–353.

————. "Elite Conflict and Cooperation in the Brazilian Empire: The Case of Bahia's Businessmen and Planters." *Luso-Brazilian Review* 12, Number 1 (summer 1975): 80–99.

Souza, Paulo César. *A Sabinada: a revolta separatista da Bahia, 1837*. São Paulo, 1987.

Sousa Andrade, Maria José de. *A mão-de-obra escrava em Salvador, 1811–1860*. São Paulo: Corrupio, 1988.

Vieira Nascimento, Anna Amélia. *Dez freguesias da Cidade do Salvador: aspectos sociais e urbanos do século XIX*. Salvador da Bahia, 1986.

Wildberger, Arnold. *Os presidentes da província da Bahia, efetivos e interinos, 1824–1889*. Salvador da Bahia, 1949.

Modern Era (1889–Present)

Agier, Michel. "Ethnopolitique: racisme, statuts et mouvement noir à Bahia." *Cahiers d'études africaines [France]* 32, Number 1 (1992): 53–81.

————. "Racism, Culture and Black Identity in Brazil." *Bulletin of Latin American Research [UK]* 14, Number 3 (1995): 245–264.

Alves de Souza, Guaraci Adeodato, and Vilmar Faria, editors. *Bahia de todos os pobres*. Petrópolis, 1980.

Atlas geoeconômico da Bahia. Salvador da Bahia: Instituto de Economia e Finanças, 1959.

Azevedo, Eliane de. "The Anthropological and Cultural Meaning of Family Names in Bahia, Brazil." *Current Anthropology* 21, Number 3 (June 1980): 360–363.

Azevedo, Thales de. *Les élites de couleur dans une ville brésilienne*. Paris, 1953.

————. *Povoamento da Cidade do Salvador*. Salvador da Bahia: Itapuã, 1969 reprint.

————. *Italianos na Bahia e outros temas*. Salvador da Bahia: Empresa Gráfica da Bahia, 1989 reprint.

Barreto de Araujo, Joaquim. *Reminiscências*. Salvador, 1979.

Borges, Dain. *The Family in Bahia, Brazil, 1870–1945*. Stanford, CA: Stanford University Press, 1992.

Caldas Coni, Antônio. *A escola tropicalista bahiana: Paterson, Wucherer, Silva Lima*. Salvador da Bahia, 1952.

Características demográficas do Estado da Bahia. Rio de Janeiro: Instituto Brasileiro de Geografia e Estatística, 1949.

Dias Tavares, Luís Enrique. *O problema da involução industrial da Bahia*. Salvador da Bahia, 1965.

————. *Duas reformas da educação na Bahia, 1895–1925*. Salvador da Bahia, 1968.

Eskelund, Karl. *Drums in Bahia: Travels in Brazil*. London, 1960.

Freyre, Gilberto. *Na Bahia em 1943*. Rio de Janeiro: Companhia Brasileira de Artes Gráficas, 1944.

Guimaraes, Antonio Sergio Alfredo. "Les classes et leurs couleurs à Bahia." *Cahiers d'études africaines [France]* 32, Number 1 (1992): 35–52.

Informações básicas dos municípios baianos, por microregiões. Salvador da Bahia: Centro de Planejamento da Bahia, 1978–1980, six volumes.

Largman, Esther Regina, and Robert M. Levine. "Jews in the Tropics: Bahian Jews in the Early Twentieth Century." *The Americas: A Quarterly Review of Inter-American Cultural History [Academy of American Franciscan History]* 43, Number 2 (1986): 159–170.

Levine, Robert M. *Vale of Tears: Revisiting the Canudos Massacre in Northeastern Brazil, 1893–1897*. Berkeley: University of California Press, 1992.

Machado Neto, Antônio Luís. "A Bahia intelectual, 1900–1930." *Universitas* 12–13 (1972): 261–306.

Madureira de Pinho, Péricles. *São assim os baianos*. Rio de Janeiro, 1960.

Pang, Eul-Soo. "The Revolt of the Bahian *Coronéis* and the Federal Intervention of 1920." *Luso-Brazilian Review* 8, Number 2 (December 1971): 3–25.

————. *Bahia in the First Brazilian Republic: Coronelismo and Oligarchies, 1889–1934*. Gainesville: University Presses of Florida, 1977.

Stepan, Nancy. *The Beginnings of Brazilian Science: Oswaldo Cruz, Medical Research and Policy, 1890–1920.* New York, 1976.

Teixeira, Cid. *Bahia em tempo de Província.* Salvador da Bahia: Fundação Cultural do Estado da Bahia, 1986.

General Works

Alvez de Souza, Wladimir. "The Past Splendor of Pelourinho." *Américas [Organization of American States]* 21, Number 9 (September 1969): 2–8.

Bahia de ontem e de hoje. Salvador da Bahia: Prefeitura Municipal, 1953.

Bibliografia baiana. Salvador da Bahia: Fundação de Pesquisas, Secretaria do Planejamento, Ciência e Tecnologia, 1977, two volumes.

Cerqueira Falcão, Edgar de. *Encantos tradicionais da Bahia.* São Paulo: Martins, 1943.

Crowley, Daniel J. *African Myth and Black Reality in Bahian Carnaval.* Los Angeles: UCLA Museum of Cultural History, Monograph Series 25, 1984.

Evolução física de Salvador. Salvador da Bahia: Universidade Federal da Bahia, 1980.

Levine, Robert M. "The Singular Brazilian City of Salvador." *Luso-Brazilian Review* 30, Number 2 (1993): 59–69.

Megenney, W. *A Bahian Heritage: An Ethnolinguistic Study of African Influence on Brazilian Portuguese.* Chapel Hill: University of North Carolina Press, 1978.

Ott, Carlos. *Formação e evolução étnica da Cidade do Salvador.* Rio de Janeiro, two volumes, 1955.

Pequeno guia das igrejas da Bahia. Salvador da Bahia: Prefeitura Municipal, 1949–1962, seventeen volumes.

Pierson, Donald. *Negroes in Brazil: A Study of Race Contact at Bahia.* Carbondale: Southern Illinois University Press, revised 1967 edition of 1942 original.

Quatro séculos de história da Bahia. Salvador da Bahia: Tipografia Beneditina, 1949.

Queirós Mattoso, Kátia M. de. *To Be a Slave in Brazil, 1550–1880.* New Brunswick, NJ: Rutgers University Press, 1986.

Santos, Milton. *A rêde urbana do Recôncavo.* Salvador da Bahia, 1959.

Teixeira, Cydelmo, editor. *A grande Salvador: posse e uso da terra.* Salvador da Bahia: Governo do Estado, 1978.

Valladares, José. *Beabá da Bahia: guia turístico.* Salvador da Bahia: Progresso, 1951.

Valladares, José, editor. *As artes na Bahia.* Salvador da Bahia: Prefeitura Municipal, 1954.

Viana Filho, Luís. *O negro na Bahia.* Rio de Janeiro: Nova Fronteira, 1988 re-edition.

Vianna, Hildegardes. *A Bahia já foi assim: crônicas de costumes.* Salvador da Bahia, 1973.

Zalamea, Luis. "Bahia's Recôncavo." *Américas [Organization of American States]* 27, Number 1 (January 1975): 30–36.

Chile
General Studies

Alemparte R., Julio. *El cabildo en Chile colonial.* Santiago: Universidad de Chile, 1940.

Amunátegui Solar, Domingo. *La sociedad chilena del siglo XVIII: mayorazgos y títulos de Castilla.* Santiago, 1901–1904, three volumes.

———. *Historia social de Chile.* Santiago, 1932.

Aranguiz, Horacio. "El itinerario ignorado de don Ambrosio O'Higgins." *Boletín de la Academia Chilena de la Historia* 33, Number 74 (1966): 122–129.

Arellano, José Pablo. "Social Policies in Chile: An Historical Review." *Journal of Latin American Studies [UK]* 17 (November 1985): 397–418.

Bibar, Gerónimo de. *Crónica y relación copiosa y verdadera de los reynos de Chile.* Santiago, 1966 re-edition.

Bindis, Ricardo. *Rugendas en Chile.* Santiago: Los Andes, 1989.

Boraiko, Allen A. "Chile: Acts of Faith." *National Geographic* 174, Number 1 (July 1988): 54–85.

Burr, Robert N. *By Reason or Force: Chile and the Balancing of Power in South America, 1830–1905.* Berkeley: University of California Press, 1965.

Campos Harriet, Fernando. *Los defensores del Rey.* Santiago, 1958.

———. *Veleros franceses en el Mar del Sur.* Santiago, 1964.

———. *El teatro en Chile desde los indios hasta los teatros universitarios.* Santiago, 1966.

Cánepa Guzmán, Mario. *Historia del teatro chileno.* Santiago, 1974.

Carmagnani, Marcello. "Colonial Latin American Demography: Growth of the Chilean Population, 1700–1830." *Journal of Social History* 1, Number 2 (1967).

———. *Desarrollo industrial y subdesarrollo económico: el caso chileno (1860–1920).* Santiago: Universidad de Chile, 1999 translation by Silvia Hernández of 1971 Italian original.

———. *Les mécanismes de la vie économique dans une société coloniale: le Chili (1680–1830).* Paris: SEPVEN, 1973.

"Chile: The Land and the People." *Américas [Organization of American States]* 28, Numbers 3 (June–July 1976): supplementary pp. 1–16.

Claro Valdés, Samuel, and Jorge Urrutia Blondel. *Historia de la música en Chile.* Santiago de Chile, 1973.

Collier, Simon, and William F. Sater. *A History of Chile, 1808–1994.* New York: Cambridge University Press, 1996.

Constable, Pamela, and Arturo Valenzuela. *A Nation of Enemies: Chile under Pinochet.* New York: Norton, 1991.

Contreras Arias, Juan, et al. *Fuentes para un estudio de demografía histórica de Chile en el siglo XVIII.* Santiago:

Instituto Central de Historia de la Universidad de Concepción, 1972.

Correa Bello, Sergio. *El "Cautiverio Feliz" en la vida política chilena del siglo XVII*. Santiago, 1965.

Cunill Grau, Pedro. *Atlas histórico de Chile*. Santiago, 1963.

———. *Fuentes cartográficas en la génesis de los tipos de poblamiento chileno, siglos XVI al XVIII*. Santiago, 1972.

DeShazo, Peter. *Urban Workers and Labor Unions in Chile, 1902–1927*. Madison: University of Wisconsin Press, 1983.

Dundas Graham, Maria (later Lady Maria Calcott). *Journal of a Residence in Chile during the Year 1822, and a Voyage from Chile to Brazil in 1823*. New York: Praeger, 1969 reprint of 1824 London original published by Longman.

Encina, Francisco Antonio. *Historia de Chile desde la prehistoria hasta 1891*. Santiago, 1940–1952, twenty volumes.

Espejo, Juan Luis. *Nobiliario de la capitanía general de Chile*. Santiago, 1967.

Esteve Barba, Francisco. *Descubrimiento y conquista de Chile*. Barcelona and Madrid: Salvat, 1946.

Eyzaguirre, Jaime. *Ventura de Pedro de Valdivia*. Santiago, 1963.

———. *Historia de Chile: génesis de la nacionalidad*. Santiago, 1965.

———. *Breve historia de las fronteras de Chile*. Santiago, 1967.

———. *Ideario y ruta de la emancipación chilena*. Santiago, 1972.

Feliú Cruz, Guillermo . *La abolición de la esclavitud en Chile: estudio histórico y social*. Santiago, 1942.

Feliú Cruz, Guillermo, editor. *Colección de antiguos periódicos chilenos*. Santiago: Biblioteca Nacional, 1952–1966, twenty volumes.

García Martínez, José Ramón. "La República de Chile al arribo de la escuadra del Pacífico, mayo de 1863." *Revista de Marina [Chile]* 113, Number 831 (March–April 1996): 194–205.

Geisse G., Guillermo. *Problemas del desarrollo urbano regional en Chile*. Santiago, 1968.

Godoy, Hernán. *Estructura social de Chile*. Santiago: Editorial Universitaria, 1971.

Góngora, Mario. *Origen de los inquilinos de Chile central*. Santiago, 1960.

———. *Vagabundaje y sociedad fronteriza en Chile (siglos XVII a XIX)*. Santiago, 1966.

———. *Encomenderos y estancieros: estudios acerca de la constitución social aristocrática de Chile después de la Conquista, 1580–1660*. Santiago, 1970.

———. "Urban Social Stratification in Colonial Chile." *Hispanic American Historical Review* 55 (1975): 421–446.

Góngora Marmolejo, Alonso de. *Historia de Chile desde su descubrimiento hasta el año 1575*. Madrid: Volume 121 of the "Biblioteca de Autores Españoles," 1960 re-edition.

Greve, Ernesto. *Historia de la ingeniería en Chile*. Santiago: Imprenta Universitaria, 1938, four volumes.

Guarda, Gabriel. *Influencia militar en las ciudades del reino de Chile*. Santiago: Pontifica Universidad Católica, 1957.

———. *La ciudad chilena del siglo XVIII*. Buenos Aires, 1968.

———. *La cultura en Chile austral antes de la colonización alemana, 1645–1850*. Santiago, 1976.

———. *Historia urbana del reino de Chile*. Santiago: Editorial Andrés Bello, 1978.

Haenke, Thaddaeus Peregrinus (or "Tadeo"). *Descripción del reyno de Chile*. Santiago, 1942 reprint.

Heise, Julio. *Las tasas y ordenanzas sobre el trabajo de los indios en Chile*. Santiago, 1929–1930.

Illanes, María Angélica. *"En el nombre del pueblo, del estado y de la ciencia . . .": historia social de la salud pública, Chile, 1880–1973 (hacia una historia social del siglo XX)*. Santiago de Chile: La Unión, 1993.

Jara, Alvaro. *Guerra y sociedad en Chile*. Santiago: Editorial Universitaria, 1972 translation into Spanish of 1961 French original *Guerre et société au Chili*, originally published in Paris by the Institut des Hautes Études de l'Amérique Latine or IHEAL.

———. *Fuentes para la historia del trabajo en el reino de Chile*. Santiago, 1965.

Kinsbruner, Jay. *Chile: A Historical Interpretation*. New York: Harper Torchbooks, 1973.

Korth, Eugene J. *Spanish Policy in Colonial Chile: The Struggle for Social Justice, 1535–1700*. Stanford, CA: Stanford University Press, 1968.

Korth, Eugene J., and Della M. Flusche. "Dowry and Inheritance in Colonial Spanish America: Peninsula Law and Chilean Practice." *The Americas: A Quarterly Review of Inter-American Cultural History [Academy of American Franciscan History]* 43 (1987): 395–410.

Lafond de Lurcy, Gabriel. *Viaje a Chile*. Santiago, 1970.

Lago, Tomás. *Rugendas, pintor romántico de Chile*. Santiago: Universidad de Chile, 1960.

Laval Manrique, Enrique. *Los hospitales fundados en Chile durante la colonia*. Santiago, 1935.

———. *Historia del hospital de San Juan de Dios*. Santiago, 1949.

———. *Botica de los jesuitas en Chile*. Santiago, 1953.

———. *Noticia sobre los médicos en Chile: siglos XVI, XVII y XVIII*. Santiago, 1955.

Lira Montt, Luis. "Padrones del reino de Chile existentes en el Archivo de Indias." *Revista de Estudios Históricos [Chile]* 13 (1965): 85 et seq.

———. *Indice de familias chilenas que han rendido pruebas en la orden de Malta (1783–1970)*. Santiago, 1971.

Lloyd, Reginald, et al., editors. *Twentieth Century Impressions of Chile: Its History, People, Commerce, Industries, and Resources*. London: Lloyds Great Britain Publishing Company, 1915.

Loveman, Brian. *Chile: The Legacy of Hispanic Capitalism*. New York: Oxford University Press, 1988.

Mamalakis, Markos J. *Historical Statistics for Chile: Demography and Labor Force*. Westport, CT: Greenwood, 1980, two volumes.

Mayo, John. *British Merchants and Chilean Development, 1851–1886*. Boulder, CO: Westview, 1987.

Medina, José Toribio. *Biblioteca hispano chilena, 1523–1817*. Santiago, 1963 re-edition, three volumes.

Medina, José Toribio, editor and translator. *Viajes relativos a Chile*. Santiago, 1962 reedition, two volumes.

Medina, José Toribio, compiler. *Colección de documentos inéditos para la historia de Chile, segunda serie*. Santiago, 1956–1963 re-edition, six volumes.

Melcherts B., Enrique. *El arte en la vida colonial chilena*. Valparaíso, 1966.

Mellafe, Rolando. *La introducción de la esclavitud negra en Chile: tráfico y rutas*. Santiago, 1959.

Monumenta peruana. Rome: Istituto Storico della Societatis Iesu, 1954-, eight volumes.

Moreno, Francisco José. *Legitimacy and Stability in Latin America: A Study of Chilean Political Culture*. New York University Press, 1969.

Oña, Pedro de. *Arauco domado*. Madrid: 1944 facsimile reprint of 1596 original published in Lima by Antonio Ricardo.

Ortega, Luis. "The First Four Decades of the Chilean Coal Mining Industry, 1840–1879." *Journal of Latin American Studies [UK]* 14, Number 1 (1982): 1–32.

Ovalle, Alonso de. *Histórica relación del reino de Chile*. Santiago: Instituto de Literatura Chilena, 1969 re-edition of 1646 original published in Rome.

Pabón, Jesús, and Luis Jiménez Placer y Cianriz, compilers. *Algunos documentos del Archivo de Indias sobre ciudades chilenas (fundaciones, títulos de ciudad, de noble y leal, etc.)*. Seville, 1921.

Pereira Salas, Eugenio. *Buques norteamericanos a fines de la era colonial (1788–1810)*. Santiago, 1936.

———. *Apuntes para la historia de la cocina en Chile*. Santiago, 1943.

———. *Juegos y alegrías coloniales en Chile*. Santiago, 1947.

———. *Historia del arte en el reino de Chile, 1541–1776*. Santiago, 1965.

———. *Historia del teatro en Chile desde sus orígenes hasta la muerte de Juan Casacuberta, 1849*. Santiago, 1974.

Pike, Frederick B. *Chile and the United States, 1880–1962*. South Bend, IN: University of Notre Dame Press, 1963.

Randolph, Jorge. *La guerra de Arauco y la esclavitud*. Santiago, 1966.

Rela, Walter. *Contribución a la bibliografía del teatro chileno, 1804–1960*. Montevideo, 1960.

Romano, Ruggiero. *Una economía colonial: Chile en el siglo XVIII*. Buenos Aires, 1965.

Romera, Antonio. *Historia de la pintura chilena*. Santiago, 1960.

Salvat Monguillot, Manuel. "La legislación emanada de los cabildos chilenos en el siglo XVI." *Revista Chilena de Historia del Derecho* 5 (1969): 97 et seq.

Sater, William F. *Chile and the War of the Pacific*. Lincoln: University of Nebraska Press, 1986.

Silva, Jorge Gustavo. *La nueva era de las municipalidades de Chile*. Santiago, 1931.

Spooner, Mary Helen. *Soldiers in a Narrow Land: The Pinochet Regime in Chile*. Berkeley: University of California Press, 1994.

Thayer Ojeda, Tomás. *Formación de la sociedad chilena y censo de la población de Chile en los años 1540 á 1565 con datos estadísticos, biográficos, étnicos y demográficos*. Santiago, 1943, three volumes.

Valdivia, Pedro de. *Cartas de relación de la conquista de Chile*. Santiago: Editorial Universitaria, 1970 edition by Mario Ferrecio.

Varela Münchmeyer, Eugenio. "Manejo de crisis: situación Chile-Estados Unidos en 1891–1892." *Revista de Marina [Chile]* 1 (1992): 56–63.

Véliz, Claudio. *Historia de la marina mercante de Chile*. Santiago, 1961.

———. "Egaña, Lambert, and the Chilean Mining Associations of 1825." *Hispanic American Historical Review* 55, Number 4 (November 1975): 637–663.

Vial Correa, Gonzalo. *El africano en el reino de Chile: ensayo histórico-jurídico*. Santiago, 1957.

Yeager, Gertrude M. "Elite Education in Nineteenth-Century Chile." *Hispanic American Historical Review* 71, Number 1 (1991): 73–105.

Zéndegui, Guillermo de, compiler. "Image of Chile." *Américas [Organization of American States]* 23, Number 3 (March 1971): supplementary pp. 1–24.

Concepción

Colonial Era (1550–1819)

Amunátegui Solar, Domingo. "El cabildo de Concepción, 1782–1818." *Anales de la Universidad de Chile*, Second Series, Volume 8 (January–March 1930): 491–579.

Barrientos Grandon, Javier. "La real audiencia de Concepción, 1565–1575." *Revista de Estudios Histórico-Jurídicos [Chile]* 15 (1992–1993): 131–178.

"Censo del obispado de Concepción en 1812." *Revista Chilena de Historia y Geografía* 23, Number 94 (1939): 266 et seq.

Kinsbruner, Jay. "The Political Status of the Chilean Merchants at the End of the Colonial Period: The Concepción Example, 1790–1810." *The Americas: A Quarterly Review of Inter-American Cultural History [Academy of American Franciscan History]* 29 (1972): 30–56.

Kordic Riquelme, Raïssa. "El terremoto de 1730 visto por el obispo de Concepción, Francisco Antonio de Escandón." *Cuadernos de Historia [Chile]* 10 (1990): 209–225.

Mazzei de Grazia, Leonardo. "La sociedad de la conquista en Concepción." *Atenea [Chile]* 452 (1985): 183–200.

———. "Fundación y supresión de la primera audiencia de Chile: Concepción, 1567–1575." *Revista de Indias [Spain]* 49, Number 185 (1989): 27–89.

Reyes Ramírez, Rocío de los. "Fray Jerónimo de Oré, obispo de Concepción en Chile." *Archivo Ibero-Americano [Spain]* 50, Numbers 197–200 (1990): 1099–1114.

*Early Maps and Depictions of
Concepción, 1687–1801*

Map of the city at its original Penco site from the 1687 sea atlas of William Hack, which was copied from a Spanish pilot's chart book captured in the South Pacific a few years previously by English buccaneers—original held by the British Library

Crude Spanish map of Concepción and its vicinity in the late seventeenth century—original held in the Sala Medina of the Biblioteca Nacional at Santiago

Chart and coastal profile of Talcahuano Bay, plus a map of the city at its Penco site, by the French traveler and military engineer Amédée-François Frézier, ca. 1712—published four years later in Paris to accompany his book *Relation du voyage de la mer du Sud aux cotes du Chily et du Perou,* several sources

Crude French map of Concepción and its coastline in 1713, by Guedeville—copy held by the Central Library of the Universidad de Chile at Santiago, plus other sources

Crude map of the city and its coastline in 1730—original held by the Biblioteca Nacional at Lima

French map of Concepción and Talcahuano Bay during the first half of the eighteenth century, by J.-D. Barbier du Bocage—original held by the British Library

Map of the proposed layout for *Nueva Concepción* or "New Concepción," 1752—original held by the Archive of Indies at Seville, old Torres Lanzas call number: Mapas y Planos de Perú y Chile, 35 [archival provenance: Chile, Legajo 453]

Diagram of the new Trinitarian nunnery to be constructed in the new city, 1752—original held by the Archivo Nacional at Santiago

Map of the old layout at Penco, plus the new site in the Mocha or Mendoza Valley, 1753—original held by the British Library

Eighteenth-century diagram of land plots distributed at Nueva Concepción—original held by the Archive of Indies at Seville

Map of the new city as it appeared in 1765—original held by the Archive of Indies at Seville

Pen-and-ink map with watercolor highlights by Domingo de Boenechea, of a proposed new Talcahuano shipyard, 1768—original held by the Archivo General de Simancas in Spain, call number: Mapas, Planos y Dibujos, XVIII-134 [archival provenance: Marina, Legajo 389]

Diagrams of Concepción's proposed new riverfront citadel to replace Fort Purén on the opposite bank of the Bío-Bío, 1775—originals held by the Archive of Indies at Seville, old Torres Lanzas call numbers: Mapas y Planos de Perú y Chile, 68 [archival provenance: Perú 186, Chile 189, and Chile 435]

Frontal view by the engineer Leandro Badarán of a proposed new cathedral, 1776—original held by the Archive of Indies at Seville

Eighteenth-century diagram of Concepción's new cathedral—original held by the Archive of Indies at Seville

Chart by the naval pilot José Manuel de Moraleda of Talcahuano Bay, Concepción, and the surrounding district in 1782—original held by the Library of Congress in Washington, call number: G 5332.C65 1782.J8 Vault

Map of Talcahuano Bay in 1785, with inserts showing its newly installed "De Gálvez" and "San Agustín" batteries—original held by the Archive of Indies at Seville, old Torres Lanzas call number: Mapas y Planos de Perú y Chile, 80

Map of Talcahuano Bay, Penco, and Concepción as they appeared during the visit by the French Rear Adm. and explorer Jean-François de Galaup, Comte de la Pérouse, February 1786—his *Voyage autour du monde* was published posthumously eleven years later in Paris and today exists in numerous re-editions

Three diagrams of the city's proposed new hospital, 1787—originals held by the Archivo Nacional at Santiago

Diagram of Concepción's cemetery, 1789—original held in the Barros Arana Archive of the Biblioteca Nacional at Santiago

Sketch of Concepción as seen in 1790 from its *almacén de pólvora* or "powder magazine" outside the city limits by José del Pozo, one of the artists contracted during Capt. Alejandro Malaspina's scientific expedition into the Pacific—original held in the Braun Menéndez Collection of the Central Library of the University of Chile at Santiago

Watercolor of the Talcahuano Bay anchorage in 1793 by Fernando Brambila, another artist who accompanied Malaspina's expedition into the Pacific—original held in the Braun Menéndez Collection of the Central Library of the University of Chile at Santiago

Diagram and cutaway views of a prototypical rural chapel to be erected throughout Concepción's bishopric, 1794—original held by the Archivo Nacional at Santiago

Map by Francisco Alvarez of Talcahuano and its surrounding district, 1 July 1801—original held by the Archivo Nacional at Santiago

Independence and General Works (1820–Present)

Campos Harriet, Fernando. *Concepción y su historia.* Santiago, 1971.

———. "Concepción: ayer, hoy y mañana." *Atenea [Chile]* 459–460 (1989): 299–305.

Cruz Barros, Nicolás. "Una contrapropuesta educacional en el Chile del siglo XIX." *Historia [Chile]* 29 (1995–1996): 69–88.

El libro de la provincia de Concepción, 1550–1944. Santiago, 1944.

García Martínez, José Ramón. "El apresamiento del *Paquete de Maule.*" *Revista de Marina [Chile]* 110, Number 814 (May–June 1993): 265–273.

Libro de oro de Talcahuano. Talcahuano, 1964.

López Urrutia, Carlos. "The Chilean Naval Mutiny of 1931." *Derroteros de la Mar del Sur [Peru]* 8 (2000): 51–64.

Mazzei de Grazia, Leonardo. "Orígenes del establecimiento británico en la región de Concepción y su inserción en la molinería del trigo y en la minería del carbón." *Historia [Chile]* 28 (1994): 217–239.

———. "Terratenientes de Concepción en el proceso de modernización de la economía regional en el siglo XIX." *Historia [Chile]* 31 (1998): 179–215.

Mosovich Pont-Lezica, Diana. "Local Politics and Depolitisation in Chile." *Bulletin of Latin American Research [UK]* 16, Number 2 (1997): 197–217.

Muñoz Olave, Reinaldo. *Historia de la diócesis de Concepción.* Santiago, 1973.

Oliver Schneider, Carlos, and Francisco Zapatta Silva. *Libro de oro de la historia de Concepción: IV centenario, 1550–1950.* Concepción, 1950.

Ravest Mora, Manuel. "Narración del combate de Concepción escrita por el soldado Marcos Ibarra Díaz del 2.° de Línea." *Revista Chilena de Historia y Geografía* 150 (1982): 7–13.

Sater, William A. "The Abortive Kronstadt: The Chilean Naval Mutiny of 1931." *Hispanic American Historical Review* 60, Number 2 (1980): 239–268.

Tomic, Patricia, and Ricardo Trumper. "The Contradictions of Neo-Liberalism in Chile, 1973–1989: The Case of the Concepción Region." *Canadian Journal of Latin American and Caribbean Studies* 15, Number 30 (1990): 221–241.

Vivaldi Cichero, Augusto. "De la universidad, la ciudad y los rectores." *Atenea [Chile]* 459–460 (1989): 25–51.

Santiago

Colonial Era (1541–1810)

Antiguos privilegios y documentos de Santiago del Nuevo Extremo. Madrid, 1970.

Carmagnani, Marcello. "Formación de un mercado compulsivo y el papel de los mercaderes: la región de Santiago de Chile, 1559–1600." *Jahrbuch für Geschichte von Staat, Wirtschaft und Gesellschaft Lateinamerikas [Germany]* 12 (1975): 104–133.

———. "Le terre dei conquistadori: le origini della proprietà fondiaria nella regione di Santiago de Cile, 1559–1599." *Quaderni Storici [Italy]* 22, Number 2 (1987): 453–466.

Flusche, Della M. "The Cabildo and Public Health in Seventeenth Century Santiago, Chile." *The Americas: A Quarterly Review of Inter-American Cultural History [Academy of American Franciscan History]* 29 (1972): 173 et seq.

———. "Doña Isabel Osorio de Cáceres: Chilean Matriarch." *Colonial Latin American Historical Review* 3, Number 1 (1994): 39–71.

———. "Church and State in the Diocese of Santiago, Chile, 1620–1677: A Study of Rural Parishes." *Colonial Latin American Historical Review* 4, Number 3 (1995): 241–259.

Flusche, Della M., and Eugene H. Korth. "A Dowry Office in Seventeenth-Century Chile." *Historian* 49, Number 2 (1987): 204–222.

Fuente, Mireya de la. "Formas y calidad de vida ciudadana en el Santiago del siglo XVIII a través de las actas de su cabildo." *Revista Chilena de Historia y Geografía* 157 (1989): 145–163.

Jara, Alvaro. "Los asientos de trabajo y la provisión de mano de obra para los no encomenderos en la ciudad de Santiago, 1586–1600." *Revista Chilena de Historia y Geografía* 125 (1957): 21 et seq.

Klein, Herbert S., and Marcello Carmagnani. "Demografía histórica: la población del obispado de Santiago, 1777–1778." *Boletín de la Academia Chilena de la Historia* 72 (1965): 57 et seq.

Larraín Melo, José Manuel. "Movimiento de precios en Santiago de Chile, 1749–1808: una interpretación metodológica." *Jahrbuch für Geschichte von Staat, Wirtschaft und Gesellschaft Lateinamerikas [Germany]* 17 (1980): 199–259.

Medina, José Toribio. *El escudo de armas de la ciudad de Santiago de Chile.* Santiago, 1910.

Mellafe Rojas, Rolando. "Alma y utopia: Santiago colonial." *Cuadernos de Historia [Chile]* 15 (1995): 37–48.

Pereira Salas, Eugenio. "El abasto de la ciudad de Santiago en la época colonial: la época heróica, siglos XVI y XVII." *Jahrbuch für Geschichte von Staat, Wirtschaft und*

Gesellschaft Lateinamerikas [Germany] 4 (1967): 303 et seq.

Ramón Folch, José Armando de. "Santiago de Chile, 1650–1700." *Historia [Chile]* 12 (1974–1975): 93–373.

Secchi, Manuel Eduardo. *Arquitectura en Santiago: siglo XVII a siglo XIX*. Santiago, 1941.

Stuardo Ortiz, Carlos. "Vecinos de Santiago en 1808." *Boletín de la Academia Chilena de la Historia* 60 (1959): 205 et seq.

Early Maps and Depictions of Santiago during the Colonial Era, 1605–1821

Diagram of the Jesuits' San Miguel College, 1605—original held by the Bibliothèque Nationale in Paris

Diagram of a private home with two patios, 1663—original held by the Archivo Nacional in Santiago

Map of Santiago, ca. 1712, by the French visitor Amédée-François Frézier—published in Amsterdam five years later as part of his book *Relation du voyage de la mer du Sud aux cotes du Chily et du Perou* and repeatedly copied by later cartographers

Crude sketch of some properties at El Salto, just outside Santiago, 1736—original held by the Archivo Nacional in Santiago

Diagram of a private home in San Pablo Street, 1740—original held by the Archivo Nacional in Santiago

Map of the road leading from La Cañada to La Dehesa outside Santiago, 1741—original held by the Archivo Nacional in Santiago

Crude drawing of Santiago and some of its outlying rural hamlets, 1743—original held by the Archivo Nacional in Santiago

1743 drawing of a proposed change to the construction of the San Carlos Canal, initiated eighteen years earlier to divert water from the Maipó into the Mapocho River—original held by the Archivo Nacional in Santiago

Crude drawing of Santiago in the mid-eighteenth century, indicating the position of its churches—original held by the Archive of Indies at Seville

Diagram of a bullring at Santiago, 1760—original held by the Archivo Nacional at Santiago

Crude diagram of some private homes in the city, 1762—original held by the Archivo Nacional at Santiago

Survey of some properties in La Cañadilla, 1762—original held by the Archivo Nacional at Santiago

Diagram and profile view by the engineer José Antonio Birt of a dragoon barracks erected at Santiago, 1764—original held by the Biblioteca Central de Cataluña in Barcelona

Diagram by the engineer Juan Garland y White of its government palace, 1765—original held by the Archive of Indies at Seville

Diagram of part of Santiago's orphanage, 1767—original held by the Archive of Indies at Seville

Diagram of a private home, 1769—original held by the Archivo Nacional at Santiago

Diagram of the foundations for a new stone bridge, eventually called the *Puente Nuevo* or *Puente de Cal y Canto*, 1773—original held by the Archivo Nacional at Santiago

Survey by Antonio Lozada y Carvallo of the Real Universidad de San Felipe, 1778—original held by the Archivo Nacional at Santiago

Diagram by the engineer Leandro Badarán of the government offices at Santiago, 1779—original held by the Archivo Nacional at Santiago

Map of the new stone bridge across Santiago's river, April 1780—original held by the Archivo Nacional at Santiago

Map of the hamlet of La Dehesa outside Santiago, 1781—original held by the Archivo Nacional at Santiago

Map by Badarán, demonstrating some suggested improvements to one of the Mapocho River's *tajamares* or "dykes," 1783—original held by Archivo Nacional at Santiago

Three diagrams by the architect Joaquín Toesca of the Real Audiencia and Cabildo building at Santiago, 1785—original held by the Archivo Nacional at Santiago

Toesca's proposed new façade for the Cabildo, 1785—original held by the Archivo Nacional at Santiago

Toesca diagram of a private home, late eighteenth century—original held by the Archivo Nacional at Santiago

Toesca diagram of some private land plots at Santiago, late eighteenth century—original held by the Archivo Nacional in Santiago

Diagram and profile view by Pedro Rico of Santiago's new dyke, 1787—original held by the Archivo Nacional at Santiago

View of Santiago from the Count of Quinta Alegre's country manor, ca. 1790, by the visiting artist Fernando Brambila—originals held by the Museo Naval at Madrid (call number: *Colección de láminas de la expedición Malaspina*, Volume 2, Number 77), plus the Braun Menéndez Collection of the Central Library of the University of Chile in Santiago

View of one of the *arrabales* or "shantytowns" outside Santiago, ca. 1790, by the visiting artist José del Pozo—originals held by the Museo Naval at Madrid, plus the Braun Menéndez Collection of the Central Library of the University of Chile in Santiago

View by Del Pozo of the Carmen Bajo de San Rafael Monastery outside Santiago, ca. 1790—original held by Braun Menéndez Collection of the Central Library of the University of Chile in Santiago

View by Del Pozo of Santiago's stone bridge, ca. 1790—original held by Braun Menéndez Collection of the Central Library of the University of Chile in Santiago

Toesca diagram of a private home, 1790—original held by the Archivo Nacional at Santiago

Panoramic view of Santiago from atop Blanco Hill by Brambila, 1793—original held by the Braun Menéndez Collection of the Central Library of the University of Chile at Santiago

Map of Santiago, 1793—original held by the British Library

Three eighteenth-century maps of canals running through Santiago—originals held by the Archivo Nacional at Santiago

Eighteenth-century survey of some properties between the Mapocho River and San Cristóbal Hill—original held by the Archivo Nacional at Santiago

Eighteenth-century map of a new street behind the San Francisco Convent—original held by the Archivo Nacional at Santiago

Late eighteenth-century map of Santiago—original held by the Museo Naval at Madrid

Late eighteenth-century diagram by Ignacio de Andía y Varela of the Royal Mint and Assay Office at Santiago—original held by the Archive of Indies at Seville

Late eighteenth-century diagram of the tax offices—original held by the Archive of Indies at Seville

Late eighteenth-century surveys by Antonio Martínez de Matta of the Real Audiencia—original held by the Archivo Nacional at Santiago

Late eighteenth-century map of the San Pablo Mill along Santiago's riverfront—original held by the Archivo Nacional at Santiago

Two profile views and three diagrams by the engineer Agustín Caballero of the Real Palacio de la Moneda, October 1800—original held by the Archive of Indies at Seville

Diagram, plus profile and cutaway views signed by Caballero in August 1800, of a bridge across the San Carlos Canal—original held by the Archive of Indies at Seville

Map by Caballero of the completed San Carlos Canal, December 1800—original held by the Archive of Indies at Seville, call number: Mapas y Planos de Perú y Chile, 141 [or 141bis]

Diagrams, plus profile and cutaway views by Caballero, of the structures diverting water from the Maipó River into the San Carlos Canal, December 1800—originals held by the Archive of Indies at Seville

Drawing of a public water fountain at Santiago, 1801—original held by the Archivo Nacional at Santiago

Early nineteenth-century drawing of the façade for Santiago's Consulado—original held by the Archivo Nacional at Santiago

1803 diagram by Juan José de Goycoechea of a new sports' ground for playing *pelota,* plus public baths, near Santiago's *tajamar*—original held by the Archivo Nacional at Santiago

Two surveys of properties along La Recolecta Street, 1806—original held by the Archivo Nacional at Santiago

Map by de Goycoechea of the powder-mill outside Santiago, February 1817—original held by the Archivo Nacional at Santiago

Views of Santiago drawn by the visiting English Capt. William Waldegrave in 1821, then lithographed three years later in London by Agostino Aglio—several sources

Republican Era (1810–Present)

Bodini Cruz-Carrera, Hugo. "Tendencias recientes en el desarrollo de Santiago de Chile." *Revista Geográfica [Mexico]* 110 (1989): 267–281.

Borde, Jean. "L'essor d'une capitale: Santiago du Chili." *Les cahiers d'Outre-Mer [France]* 7, Number 25 (1954): 5–24.

Brunner, Karl. *Santiago de Chile: su estado actual y su futura formación.* Santiago, 1932.

Cáceres Quiero, Gonzalo. "Urbanistica in Cile, 1910–1934: quattro momenti nell'evoluzione di Santiago." *Storia Urbana [Italy]* 21, Number 78 (1997): 121–132.

Clissold, Stephen. *Bernardo O'Higgins and the Independence of Chile.* New York: Praeger, 1968.

Correas, Edmundo. "Maipú." *Américas [Organization of American States]* 20, Numbers 11–12 (November–December 1968): 23–29.

Donoso, José. "The Old House." *Wilson Quarterly* 9, Number 4 (1987): 152–163.

Feliú Cruz, Guillermo. *Santiago a comienzos del siglo XIX: crónicas de los viajeros.* Santiago: Editorial Andrés, 1969.

Gazmuri, Cristian. "Los artesanos de Santiago en 1850 y el despertar político del sector popular chileno." *Revista de Indias [Spain]* 51, Number 192 (1991): 397–416.

Hojman, David E. "Land Reform, Female Migration and the Market for Domestic Service in Chile." *Journal of Latin American Studies [UK]* 21, Number 1 (1989): 105–132.

Jaksic, Ivan, and Sol Serrano. "In the Service of the Nation: The Establishment and Consolidation of the Universidad de Chile, 1842–1879." *Hispanic American Historical Review* 70, Number 1 (February 1990): 139–171.

Larraín, Patricio. "Néolibéralisme et ségrégation socio-spatiale à Santiago du Chili." *Cahiers des Amériques Latines [France]* 18 (1994): 103–112.

Medina, José Toribio. *Actas del cabildo de Santiago durante el período llamado la patria vieja, 1810–1814.* Santiago: Cervantes, 1910.

Meller, Patricio, et al. "Employment Stagnation in Chile: 1974–1978." *Latin American Research Review* 16, Number 2 (1981): 144–155.

Nickel-Gemmeke, Annegret. "Die Funktion des Sozialen Wohnungsbau im Verstädterungsprozess Lateinamerikanischer Metropolen: Das Beispiel Santiago de Chile." *Ibero-Amerikanisches Archiv [Germany]* 16, Number 3 (1990): 441–460.

Orlove, Benjamin S. "Meat and Strength: The Moral Economy of a Chilean Food Riot." *Cultural Anthropology* 12, Number 2 (1997): 234–268.

Ramón Folch. José Armando de. "Estudio de una perfiferia urbana: Santiago de Chile, 1850–1900." *Historia [Chile]* 20 (1985): 199–294.

Salman, Ton. "Challenging the City, Joining the City: The Chilean Pobladores between Social Movement and Social Integration." *Bulletin of Latin American Research [UK]* 13, Number 1 (1994): 79–90.

Santiago, Jacques. "Urbanisation et sous-développement: Santiago du Chili." *Les cahiers d'Outre-Mer [France]* 30, Number 118 (April–June 1977): 153–177.

———. "Les transports en commun à Santiago du Chili: problèmes et perspectives." *Les cahiers d'Outre-Mer [France]* 31, Number 122 (April–June 1978): 152–170.

Stuardo Ortiz, Carlos, and Juan Eyzaguirre Escobar. *Santiago: contribuyentes, autoridades, funcionarios, agentes diplomáticos y consulares, 1817–1819.* Santiago, 1952.

Thomas, Jack Ray. "Pioneer Chilean Weekly." *Américas [Organization of American States]* 25, Number 2 (February 1973): 13–18.

Uthoff, Andreas W. "Changes in Earnings Inequality and Labour Market Segmentation: Metropolitan Santiago, 1969–1978." *Journal of Development Studies [UK]* 22, Number 2 (1986): 300–326.

Vistas panorámicas de Santiago de Chile, según dibujos originales del Hon. Cap. William Waldegrave, litografiados por Agostino Aglio. Santiago: Sociedad de Bibliófilos Chilenos, 1965 facsimile reprint of 1821 original published in London by John Boosey and Company.

General Works

Amunátegui, Miguel Luis. *El cabildo de Santiago desde 1573 hasta 1851.* Santiago, 1890, three volumes.

Cárcamo, Oscar, et al. *Cuatro siglos de la historia de Santiago.* Santiago: Zig-Zag, 1943.

Espinoza, Vicente. *Para una historia de los pobres de la ciudad.* Santiago: Ediciones Sur, 1988.

Feliú Cruz, Guillermo. *Libro oficial del 4º centenario de Santiago.* Santiago, 1941.

Fuenzalida, Juan B., et al. *La ciudad de Santiago y la celebración de su centenario.* Santiago, 1940.

Gellona, Olga Kliwadenko. "The Flavor of Santiago." *Américas [Organization of American States]* 29, Number 3 (March 1977): 19–25.

Iglesias B., Augusto, and Enrique F. Porte. *La catedral de Santiago: estudio monográfico.* Santiago, 1955.

Latcham, Ricardo A. *Estampas del Nuevo Extremo: antología de Santiago, 1541–1941.* Santiago, 1941.

Lizana, Elías, compiler. *Colección de documentos históricos recopilados del archivo del arzobispado de Santiago.* Santiago, 1919–1921, four volumes.

Martínez Baeza, Sergio. "450 años de Santiago de Chile." *Revista Chilena de Historia y Geografía* 159 (1991): 237–250.

Medina, José Toribio. *Historia de la Real Universidad de San Felipe de Santiago de Chile.* Santiago, 1928, two volumes.

———. *La medicina y los médicos en la Universidad de San Felipe.* Santiago, 1928.

———. *Bibliografía de la imprenta en Santiago de Chile: adiciones y ampliaciones.* Santiago, 1939.

———. *Los matemáticos en la Universidad de San Felipe.* Santiago, 1952 reprint.

Munizaga, Gustavo. *Notas sobre historia urbana.* Santiago, 1966.

Peña Otaegui, Carlos. *Santiago de siglo en siglo.* Santiago: Zig-Zag, 1944.

———. *Una crónica conventual: las agustinas de Santiago, 1574–1951.* Santiago, 1951.

Pereira Salas, Eugenio. *La iglesia y convento mayor de San Francisco.* Santiago: "Cuaderno" Number 4 issued by the Consejo de Monumentos Nacionales, 1953.

Ramón Folch, José Armando de. "Gravitación histórica de Santiago, siglos XVI-XIX." *Revista Universitaria [Chile]* 31 (1990): 30–37.

———. *Santiago de Chile, 1541–1991: historia de una sociedad urbana.* Madrid: Editorial MAPFRE, 1992.

Salinas Meza, René. "Orphans and Family Disintegration in Chile: The Mortality of Abandoned Children, 1750–1930." *Journal of Family History* 16, Number 3 (1991): 315–329.

Secchi, Manuel Eduardo. *La casa chilena hasta el siglo XIX.* Santiago: "Cuaderno" Number 3 issued by the Consejo de Monumentos Nacionales, 1952.

Vicuña Mackenna, Benjamín. *Historia de Santiago.* Santiago: Universidad de Chile, 1938 re-edition, two volumes.

Colombia

General Studies

Acevedo Latorre, Eduardo. *Atlas de mapas antiguos de Colombia, siglos XVI a XIX.* Bogotá: Arco, 1975 re-edition.

Archila Neira, Mauricio. *Cultura e identidad obrera: Colombia, 1910–1945.* Bogotá: CINEP, 1991.

Arrubla, Mario, et al. *Colombia hoy.* Bogotá: Siglo XXI, 1978.

Barling, M. "Rural-Urban Migration in Colombia." *Geography Review* 15, Number 1 (2001).

Bergquist, Charles W. *Coffee and Conflict in Colombia, 1886–1910.* Durham, NC: Duke University Press, 1978.

Berry, R. Albert, et al., editors. *Politics of Compromise: Coalition Government in Colombia.* New Brunswick, NJ: Transaction Books, 1980.

Berry, R. Albert, *Essays on Industrialization in Colombia.* Tempe: Center for Latin American Studies at Arizona State University, 1983.

Berry, R. Albert, and Ronald Soligo, editors. *Economic Policy and Income Distribution in Colombia.* Boulder, CO: Westview, 1980.

Bushnell, David. *The Santander Regime in Gran Colombia.* Newark: University of Delaware Press, 1954.

————. *The Making of Modern Colombia: A Nation in Spite of Itself.* Berkeley: University of California Press, 1993.

Caicedo, Edgar. *Historia de las luchas sindicales en Colombia.* Bogotá: CEIS, 1982.

Camacho Leyva, Ernesto. *Quick Colombian Facts.* Bogotá: Argra, 1962.

Castillo, C., editor. *Vida urbana y urbanismo.* Bogotá: Instituto Colombiano de Cultura, 1976.

Chandler, David C. *Health and Slavery in Colonial Colombia.* New York: Arno, 1981.

Colmenares, G. *Fuentes coloniales para la historia del trabajo en Colombia.* Bogotá, 1968.

————. *Historia económica y social de Colombia, 1537–1719.* Bogotá: Universidad del Valle, 1978.

Colombia: relación geográfica, topográfica, agrícola, comercial y política de este país. Bogotá: Volume 34 of the Archivo de Economía Nacional, 1974 reprint of 1822 London original, two volumes.

Cortés, Vicenta. *Catálogo de mapas de Colombia.* Madrid: Cultura Hispánica, 1967.

Cuervo, Antonio B., compiler. *Colección de documentos inéditos sobre la geografía e historia de Colombia.* Bogotá, 1891, four volumes.

Delpar, Helen. *Red against Blue: The Liberal Party in Colombian Politics, 1863–1899.* University of Alabama Press, 1981.

Dix, Robert H. *Colombia: The Political Dimensions of Change.* New Haven: Yale University Press, 1967.

Escalante, Aquíles. *El negro en Colombia.* Bogotá: Facultad de Sociología of the Universidad Nacional de Colombia, 1964.

Friede, Juan, compiler. *Documentos inéditos para la historia de Colombia.* Bogotá: Academia Colombiana de Historia, 1955–1960, ten volumes.

————. *Fuentes documentales para la historia del Nuevo Reino de Granada.* Bogotá: Editorial Andes, 1975–1976, six volumes.

Fuentes, A. L., and R. Losada. "Implicaciones socioeconómicas de la ilegalidad en la tenencia de la tierra urbana de Colombia." *Coyuntura Económica [Colombia]* 8 (1978).

Gutiérrez Azopardo, Ildefonso. *Historia del negro en Colombia: ¿Sumisión o rebeldía?* Bogotá: Nueva América, 1986.

Gutiérrez de Pineda, Virginia. *Familia y cultura en Colombia.* Bogotá: Tercer Mundo and the Sección de Investigaciones of the Departamento de Sociología of the Universidad Nacional de Colombia, 1968.

Guzmán Campos, Germán, et al. *La Violencia en Colombia.* Bogotá: Tercer Mundo, 1962.

Hartlyn, Jonathan. *The Politics of Coalition Rule in Colombia.* New York: Cambridge University Press, 1988.

Jaramillo Uribe, Jaime. *Ensayos sobre historia social colombiana.* Bogotá: Universidad Nacional de Colombia, 1968.

Kuethe, Allan J. "The Status of the Free Pardo in the Disciplined Militia of New Granada." *Journal of Negro History* 56, Number 2 (April 1971): 105–117.

————. *Military Reform and Society in New Granada, 1773–1808.* Gainesville: University Presses of Florida, 1978.

Kyu, Sik Lee. "Decentralization Trends of Employment Location and Spatial Policies in LDC Cities." *Urban Studies* 22, Number 2 (1985): 151–162.

Loy, Jane Meyer. "Primary Education during the Colombian Federation: The School Reform of 1870." *Hispanic American Historical Review* 51, Number 2 (May 1971): 275–294.

Martínez, Carlos. *Apuntes sobre el urbanismo en el Nuevo Reino de Granada.* Bogotá, 1967.

McFarlane, Anthony. "Civil Disorders and Popular Protests in Late Colonial New Granada." *Hispanic American Historical Review* 64, Number 1 (February 1984): 17–54.

McGreevey, William Paul. *An Economic History of Colombia, 1845–1930.* New York: Cambridge University Press, 1971.

McIntyre, Loren. "Colombia: From Amazon to Spanish Main." *National Geographic* 138, Number 2 (August 1970): 234–273.

Medina, José Toribio. *La imprenta en Bogotá y la Inquisición en Cartagena de Indias.* Bogotá, 1952.

Molina, Gerardo. *Las ideas liberales en Colombia.* Bogotá: Tercer Mundo, 1970–1977, three volumes.

Mörner, Magnus. "Las comunidades de indígenas y la legislación segregacionista en el Nuevo Reino de Granada." *Anuario Colombiano de Historia Social y de Cultura* 1, Number 1 (1963): 63–88.

Oquist, Paul. *Violencia, Conflict, and Politics in Colombia.* New York: Academic Press, 1980.

Ortega Ricarte, Enrique. *Heráldica colombiana.* Bogotá, 1952.

Ospina Vásquez, Luis. *Industria y protección en Colombia, 1810–1930.* Medellín: FAES, 1987.

Palacios, Marco. *Coffee in Colombia, 1850–1970: An Economic, Social, and Political History.* New York: Cambridge University Press, 1980.

Payne, James L. *Patterns of Conflict in Colombia.* New Haven: Yale University Press, 1968.

Pinzón, Martín Alonso. *Historia del conservatismo.* Bogotá: Tercer Mundo, 1983 re-edition.

Ridler, N. "Development through Urbanization: A Partial Evaluation of the Colombian Experiment." *International Journal of Urban and Regional Research* 3 (1979).

Ruiz Rivera, Julián Bautista. *Fuentes para la demografía histórica de Nueva Granada.* Seville: Escuela de Estudios Hispano-americanos, 1972.

———. *Encomienda y mita en Nueva Granada.* Seville: Escuela de Estudios Hispano-americanos, 1975.

Sánchez, Gonzalo, and Donny Meertens. *Bandoleros, gamonales y campesinos: el caso de la Violencia en Colombia.* Bogotá: El Ancora, 1983.

Smith, T. Lynn. "The Racial Composition of the Population of Colombia." *Journal of Interamerican Studies* 8, Number 2 (1966): 213–235.

Sowell, David. "Repertoires of Contention in Urban Colombia, 1760s–1940s: An Inquiry into Latin American Social Violence." *Journal of Urban History* 24, Number 3 (March 1998): 302–336.

Twinam, Ann. *Miners, Merchants, and Farmers in Colonial Colombia.* Austin: University of Texas Press, 1982.

Urrutia, Miguel. *The Development of the Colombian Labor Movement.* New Haven: Yale University Press, 1969.

———. *Winners and Losers in Colombia's Economic Growth of the 1970s.* New York: Oxford University Press, 1985.

Urrutia, Miguel, and Mario Arrubla, editors. *Compendio de estadísticas históricas de Colombia.* Bogotá: Universidad Nacional de Colombia, 1970.

Valenzuela, Jaime G., and Jorge Rodríguez G. *Situaciones de vivienda urbana en Colombia, 1951–1964.* Bogotá: Universidad Nacional de Colombia and CID, 1971.

Wade, Peter. *Blackness and Race Mixture: The Dynamics of Racial Identity in Colombia.* Baltimore: Johns Hopkins University Press, 1993.

Whiteford, Michael B. *The Forgotten Ones: Colombian Countrymen in an Urban Setting.* Gainesville: University Presses of Florida, 1976.

Zéndegui, Guillermo de. "Colombia: Spirit and Progress." *Américas [Organization of American States]* 24, Numbers 6–7 (June–July 1972): supplementary pp. 1–24.

Bogotá
Conquest (1536–1539)

Avellaneda Navas, José Ignacio. "The Men of Nikolaus Federmann: Conquerors of the New Kingdom of Granada." *The Americas: A Quarterly Review of Inter-American Cultural History [Academy of American Franciscan History]* 43, Number 4 (1987): 385–394.

———. *Los compañeros de Féderman: cofundadores de Santa Fé de Bogotá.* Bogotá: Tercer Mundo, 1990.

———. *La expedición de Sebastián de Belalcázar al mar del norte y su llegada al Nuevo Reino de Granada.* Bogotá: Banco de la República, 1992.

Friede, Juan. *Gonzalo Jiménez de Quesada a través de documentos históricos.* Bogotá: Volume 95 of the "Biblioteca de Historia Nacional," Academia Colombiana de Historia, 1960.

———. *Invasión del país de los chibchas: conquista del Nuevo Reino de Granada y fundación de Santafé de Bogotá, revaluaciones y rectificaciones.* Bogotá: Tercer Mundo, 1966.

Galvis Madero, Luis. "Los últimos años del adelantado." *Boletín Cultural y Bibliográfico [Colombia]* 16, Number 3 (1979): 76–80.

Hernández Benavides, Manuel. "*El carnero* hoy: Rodríguez Freyle, cronista de conquista y de ciudad." *Texto y Contexto [Colombia]* 17 (1991): 50–65.

Hernández de Alba, Guillermo. "El momento de don Gonzalo Jiménez de Quesada." *Boletín Cultural y Bibliográfico [Colombia]* 16, Number 2 (1979): 45–50.

Jiménez de Quesada, Gonzalo. "Epítome de la conquista del Nuevo Reino de Granada." *Boletín Cultural y Bibliográfico [Colombia]* 16, Number 3 (1979): 81–97.

Londoño, Eduardo. "La conquista del cacicazgo de Bogotá." *Boletín Cultural y Bibliográfico [Colombia]* 25, Number 16 (1988): 23–33.

Restrepo Canal, Carlos. "Bogotá y el mariscal Gonzalo Jiménez de Quesada." *Boletín de Historia y Antigüedades [Colombia]* 71, Number 744 (1984): 97–101.

Rodríguez Freyle, Juan. *El carnero.* Medellín: Bedout, 1973 re-edition.

Villamarín, Juan A., and Judith E. Villamarín. "Parentesco y herencia entre los chibchas de la sábana de Bogotá al tiempo de la conquista española." *Universitas Humanística [Colombia]* 10, Number 16 (1981): 90–96.

Colonial Era (1539–1809)

Briceño Jáuregui, Manuel. "Santafé en el siglo XVII vista por un jesuita." *Boletín de Historia y Antigüedades [Colombia]* 76, Number 765 (1989): 391–405.

Cacua Prada, Antonio. "De cómo nació el periodismo colombiano hace doscientos años." *Boletín de Historia y Antigüedades [Colombia]* 77, Number 771 (1990): 1003–1015.

———. "El segundo periódico de Santafé de Bogotá." *Boletín de Historia y Antigüedades [Colombia]* 81, Number 786 (1994): 651–667.

Casado Arboniés, Manuel. "La visita general de don Juan Cornejo al Nuevo Reino de Granada: siglo XVII, gobierno." *Boletín de Historia y Antigüedades [Colombia]* 80, Number 782 (1993): 763–794.

Dueñas Vargas, Guiomar. "Sociedad, familia y género en Santafé a finales de la colonia." *Anuario Colombiano de Historia Social y de la Cultura* 21 (1993): 63–113.

———. *Los hijos del pecado: ilegitimidad y vida familiar en la Santafé de Bogotá colonial.* Bogotá: Universidad Nacional, 1997.

Gomez, Thomas. "La république des 'cuñados': familles, pouvoir et société à Santafé de Bogotá, XVIIIe siècle." *Caravelle: cahiers du monde hispanique et luso-brésilien [France]* 62 (1994): 213–226.

Hernández de Alba, Guillermo. "El cedulario del cabildo de Bogotá." *Boletín de Historia y Antigüedades [Colombia]* 30, Numbers 342–343 (April–May 1943): 367–385.

———. "Primer acueducto de la ciudad de Bogotá, el histórico Mono de la Pila." *Boletín de Historia y Antigüedades [Colombia]* 74, Number 758 (1987): 583–591.

Jaramillo de Zuleta, Pilar. "La Casa de Recogidas de Santa Fé: custodia de virtudes, castigo maldades, orígenes de la cárcel del divorcio." *Boletín de Historia y Antigüedades [Colombia]* 82, Number 790 (1995): 631–653.

Libro de acuerdos públicos y privados de la Audiencia Real de Santafé. Bogotá: Archivo Nacional de Colombia, 1947, several volumes.

Lomné, Georges. "Las ciudades de la Nueva Granada: teatro y objeto de los conflictos de la memoria política, 1810–1830." *Anuario Colombiano de Historia Social y de la Cultura* 21 (1993): 115–135.

Mayorga García, Fernando. "La audiencia de Santafé durante los siglos XVI y XVII: desarrollo y conclusiones de un estudio." *Boletín de Historia y Antigüedades [Colombia]* 74, Number 758 (1987): 555–566.

Mesa, Carlos E. "El arzobispado de Santa Fé de Bogotá, 1562–1625." *Missionalia Hispanica [Spain]* 41, Number 120 (1984): 249–291.

Ortiz de la Tabla Ducasse, Javier, et al., compilers and editors. *Cartas de cabildos hispanoamericanos: audiencia de Santa Fe.* Seville: Consejo Superior de Investigaciones Científicas, 1996.

Saldarriaga Vélez, Oscar. "Católicos o ciudadanos: gobierno parroquial en Bogotá, 1780–1853." *Universitas Humanística [Colombia]* 22, Number 37 (1993): 25–34.

Santiestevan, Miguel de. "La Ciudad de Santafé de Bogotá y la economía colonial: visión de un viajero español en 1741." *Boletín de Historia y Antigüedades [Colombia]* 70, Number 742 (1983): 864–876.

Silva Cogollos Amaya, Claudia, and Martín Eduardo Vargas Poo. "Sociedad, muerte y prácticas de enterramiento en el Santafé colonial: la concepción de la muerte en el español." *Universitas Humanística [Colombia]* 22, Number 37 (1993): 35–42.

Silva Olarte, Renan. "La Revolución Francesa en el 'Papel Periódico de Santafé de Bogotá.'" *Caravelle: cahiers du monde hispanique et luso-brésilien [France]* 54 (1990): 165–178.

Uribe Angel, Jorge Tomás. "Testamentos de Santafé: siglos XVI y XVII." *Boletín de Historia y Antigüedades [Colombia]* 82, Number 789 (1995): 417–430.

———. "Datos referentes a la medicina en Santafé de Bogotá." *Boletín de Historia y Antigüedades [Colombia]* 83, Number 792 (1996): 177–186.

Early Republican Era (1810–1919)

Aristizábal, Luis H. "Las tres tazas: 'de Santafé a Bogotá, a través del cuadro de costumbres.'" *Boletín Cultural y Bibliográfico [Colombia]* 25, Number 16 (1988): 61–79.

Díaz Díaz, Oswaldo, editor. *Copiador de órdenes del regimiento de milicias de infantería de Santafé, 1810–1814.* Bogotá: Revista de las Fuerzas Armadas, 1964.

Escobar Rodríguez, Carmen. "Documentos sobre la protesta de los artesanos de Bogotá, 1845–1854." *Anuario Colombiano de Historia Social y de la Cultura* 16–17 (1988–1989): 241–272.

Esguerra Samper, José María. "El detonante de las históricas jornadas del 13 de marzo de 1909 y la caída del general Reyes." *Boletín de Historia y Antigüedades [Colombia]* 74, Number 757 (1987): 363–368.

Esquivel Triana, Ricardo. "Economía y transporte urbano en Bogotá, 1884–1930." *Memoria y Sociedad [Colombia]* 2, Number 4 (1997): 39–61.

Galvis Noyes, Antonio José. "La esclavitud en Bogotá, 1819–1851." *Boletín de Historia y Antigüedades [Colombia]* 67, Number 729 (1980): 333–354.

Guzmán Noguera, Ignacio de. "La revolución de los Supremos." *Boletín de Historia y Antigüedades [Colombia]* 83, Number 793 (1996): 433–457.

Londoño Eduardo, Patricia. "La mujer santafereña en el siglo XIX." *Boletín Cultural y Bibliográfico [Colombia]* 21, Number 1 (1984): 3–24.

Peralta, Victoria. *El ritmo lúdico y los placeres en Bogotá.* Bogotá: Colección Ariel Histórica, 1995.

Pumar Martínez, Carmen, compiler. "Diario de un criollo anónimo sobre el 20 de julio de 1810." *Anuario Colombiano de Historia Social y de la Cultura* 13–14 (1985–1986): 299–317.

Reyes Posada, Carlos José. "El teatro colombiano en el siglo XIX." *Boletín de Historia y Antigüedades [Colombia]* 72, Number 748 (1985): 38–63.

Santa, Eduardo. "El 'Almanaque de Vergara' para 1867." *Boletín de Historia y Antigüedades [Colombia]* 75, Number 763 (1988): 963–970.

Socarrás, José Francisco. "Remembranzas de Bogotá." *Boletín de la Academia Colombiana* 38, Number 159 (1988): 3–17.

Sowell, David. "'La Teoria i la Realidad': The Democratic Society of Artisans of Bogotá, 1847–1854." *Hispanic American Historical Review* 67, Number 4 (1987): 611–630.

———. "The 1893 Bogotazo: Artisans and Public Violence in Late Nineteenth-Century Bogotá." *Journal of Latin*

American Studies [UK] 21, Number 2 (May 1989): 267–282.

———. *The Early Colombian Labor Movement: Artisans and Politics in Bogotá, 1830–1919.* Philadelphia: Temple University Press, 1992.

———. "'La Caja de Ahorros de Bogotá,' 1846–1865: Artisans, Credit, Development, and Saving in Early National Colombia." *Hispanic American Historical Review* 73, Number 4 (1993): 615–638.

Zalamea, Luis. "Bolivar's Villa: A Bogotá Landmark." *Américas [Organization of American States]* 17, Number 12 (December 1965): 20–27.

Modern Era (1920–Present)

Albert, Karsten. "Der Bogotazo: Zu den Ereignissen um den 9 April 1948 in Kolumbien." *Lateinamerika* 25, Number 1 (1990): 80–92.

Aprile Gnizet, Jacques. *El impacto del nueve de abril sobre el centro de Bogotá.* Bogotá: Centro Cultural Jorge Eliécer Gaitán, 1983.

Arbeláez, J. D. "Gobierno local y finanzas municipales en Bogotá." *Bulletin de l'Institut français d'études andines [France]* 17, Number 1 (1988): 123–142.

Assadian, A., and J. Ondrich. "Residential Location, Housing Demand, and Labour Supply Decisions of One- and Two-Earner Households: The Case of Bogotá, Colombia." *Urban Studies* 30, Number 1 (1993).

Badariotti, D., and C. Weber. "La mobilité résidentielle en ville: réalisation par automates cellulaires et système multi-agents, Bogota." *Espace géographique [France]* 31, Number 2 (2002): 97–108.

Beaulac, Willard L. *Career Ambassador.* New York: Macmillan, 1951.

Braun, Herbert. *The Assassination of Gaitán: Public Life and Urban Violence in Colombia.* Madison: University of Wisconsin Press, 1985.

Brown, Susan A. "Housing in Bogotá: A Synthesis of Recent Research and Notes on Anthropological Contributions to the Study of Housing." *Urban Anthropology* 6, Number 3 (1977): 249–267.

Buraglia, P. G. "The Bogotanian Barrio: Return to the Traditional?" *Urban Design International* 3, Number 3 (1998): 101–113.

Cardona Gutiérrez, Ramiro. *Las invasiones de terrenos urbanos.* Bogotá: Tercer Mundo, 1969.

Cardona Gutiérrez, Ramiro, editor. *Urbanización y marginalidad.* Bogotá: ASCOFAME, 1968.

Chambron, Nicole, and Luis De la Torre. "La décentralisation infra municipale comme outil de gestion urbaine: l'exemple de Bogotá en Colombie." *Cahiers des Amériques Latines [France]* 18 (1994): 141–160.

Diederich, Bernard. "Betancur's Battles: A Man of Peace Takes Up the Sword." *Caribbean Review* 15, Number 1 (1986): 10–11 and 35.

Dureau, F. "Les mobilités: géometrie variable des habitants de Bogota." *Espaces, populations, sociétés [France]* 2 (1999): 329–344.

Everett, M. "Evictions and Human Rights: Land Disputes in Bogotá, Colombia." *Habitat International* 25, Number 4 (2001): 453–471.

Gilbert, Alan G. "The Provision of Public Services and the Debt Crisis in Latin America: The Case of Bogotá." *Economic Geography* 66, Number 4 (1990): 349–361.

———. "Employment and Poverty during Economic Restructuring: The Case of Bogotá, Colombia." *Urban Studies [UK]* 34, Number 7 (1997): 1047–1070.

———. "Financing Self-Help Housing: Evidence from Bogotá, Colombia." *International Planning Studies* 5, Number 2 (2000): 165–190.

Goueset, Vincent. "Les élections du 13 mars 1988 à Bogotá." *Problèmes d'Amérique Latine [France]* 92 (1989): 131–143.

———. "La croissance démographique de Bogota au XXe siècle." *Les cahiers d'Outre-Mer [France]* 43, Number 171 (July–September 1990): 289–306.

Goueset, Vincent, and F. Zambrano. "Géopolitique du District Spécial de Bogota et du Haut-Sumapaz (1900–1990)." *Bulletin de l'Institut français d'études andines [France]* 21, Number 3 (1992): 1053–1071.

Hoskin, Gary. "Colombia under Stress: A Presidency Lamed by Instability." *Caribbean Review* 15, Number 1 (1986): 6–9 and 34.

Hudson, Rex A. "Colombia's Palace of Justice Tragedy Revisited: A Critique of the Conspiracy Theory." *Terrorism and Political Violence [UK]* 7, Number 2 (1995): 93–142.

La planificación en Bogotá. Bogotá: Departamento Administrativo de Planificación Distrital, 1964.

Losada, R., and H. Gómez. *La tierra en el mercado pirata de Bogotá.* Bogotá: Fedesarrollo, 1976.

Losada, R., and L. Pinilla. *Los barrios ilegales de Bogotá: su desarrollo histórico y su impacto sobre la ciudad y la Sabana de Bogotá.* Bogotá: Pedro Gómez, 1980.

Mertins, G., and J. M. Muller. "Die Verlangerung Hochrangiger Dienstleistungen aus der Innenstadt von Bogota, Kolumbien: Etappen, Parameter, Auswirkungen." *Erdkunde [Germany]* 54, Number 3 (2000): 189–197.

Mohan, Rakesh. *Work, Wages, and Welfare in a Developing Metropolis: Consequences of Growth in Bogotá, Colombia.* New York: Oxford University Press for the World Bank, 1987.

Psacharopoulos, George, and Eduardo Vélez. "Schooling, Ability, and Earnings in Colombia, 1988." *Economic Development and Cultural Change* 40, Number 3 (1992): 629–643.

Riaño Alcalá, Pilar. "Urban Space and Music in the Formation of Youth Cultures: The Case of Bogotá, 1920–1980." *Studies in Latin American Popular Culture* 10 (1991): 87–106.

Sanger, Jonathan. "Bogotá Builds." *Américas [Organization of American States]* 23, Numbers 6–7 (June–July 1971): 25–30.

Stevens, Marie-Noëlle, and Bartolomé Bennassar. "Bogotá: du paradis à l'enfer." *Histoire [France]* 68 (1984): 58–69.

Udall, Alan. "Urbanization and Rural Labor Supply: A Historical Study of Bogotá, Colombia, since 1920." *Studies in Comparative International Development* 15, Number 3 (fall 1980): 70–83.

Valencia Restrepo, Ricardo. *Santa Fé de Bogotá: guia ilustrada, IV centenario.* Bogotá, 1938.

General Works

Amato, Peter W. *An Analysis of Changing Patterns of Elite Residential Areas in Bogotá, Colombia.* Ithaca, NY: Cornell University Press, 1968.

De la Rosa, Moisés. *Calles de Santafé de Bogotá: Homenaje en su IV Centenario 1938.* Bogotá: Registro Municipal, 1938.

Homenaje del Cabildo a la Ciudad en su IV centenario, 1538–1938. Bogotá: Imprenta Municipal, 1938.

Iriarte, Alfredo. *Breve historia de Bogotá.* Bogotá: Fundación Misión Colombia and the Editorial Oveja Negra, 1988.

Mantilla R., Luis Carlos. *Historia de la arquidiócesis de Bogotá: su itinerario evangelizador, 1564–1993.* Arquidiócesis de Bogotá, 1994.

Martínez, Carlos. *Santafé de Bogotá.* Buenos Aires, 1968.

Samper, Miguel. *La miseria en Bogotá y otros escritos.* Bogotá: Universidad Nacional, 1969.

Sowell, David. "Repertoires of Contention in Urban Colombia, 1760s–1940s: An Inquiry into Latin American Social Violence." *Journal of Urban History* 24, Number 3 (1998): 302–336.

Cartagena
Early Colonial Era (1533–1700)

Anderson, Paul S. "Isla Fuerte on the Juan de la Cosa *Mappamundi* of 1500." *Terrae Incognitae* 16 (1984): 1–13.

Borrego Plá, María Carmen. *Palenque de negros en Cartagena de Indias a fines del siglo XVII.* Seville: Escuela de Estudios Hispano-americanos, 1973.

———. *Cartagena de Indias en el siglo XVI.* Seville: Escuela de Estudios Hispano-americanos, 1983.

De la Matta Rodríguez, Enrique. *El asalto de Pointis a Cartagena de Indias.* Seville: Escuela de Estudios Hispano-americanos, 1979.

Garcés Giraldo, Diego. "Sebastián de Belalcázar y Cartagena de Indias." *Boletín de Historia y Antigüedades [Colombia]* 76, Number 766 (1989): 757–769.

Herráez S. de Escariche, Julia. *Don Pedro Zapata de Mendoza, gobernador de Cartagena de Indias.* Seville: Escuela de Estudios Hispano-americanos, 1946.

Jameson, A. K. "Some New Spanish Documents Dealing with Drake." *English Historical Review* 49 (July 1934): 14–31.

Marco Nieto, Juan José. "Breve noticia histórica de los usos, costumbres y religión de los habitantes del pueblo de Calamar." *Huellas [Colombia]* 28 (1990): 52–59.

Tejado Fernández, Manuel. "Cartagena amenazada: datos para el estudio de las repercusiones en América de la guerra de Sucesión." *Revista de Indias [Spain]* 11, Numbers 43–44 (1951): 179–192.

———. *Aspecto de la vida social en Cartagena de Indias durante el seiscientos.* Seville: Escuela de Estudios Hispano-americanos, 1954.

Téllez, Germán, and Ernesto Moure. "Repertorio formal de arquitectura doméstica en Cartagena de Indias: época colonial." *Boletín de Historia y Antigüedades [Colombia]* 71, Number 745 (1984): 471–478.

Uribe, María Victoria. "Los ocho pasos de la muerte del alma: la Inquisición en Cartagena de Indias." *Boletín Cultural y Bibliográfico [Colombia]* 24, Number 13 (1987): 28–39.

Valtierra, Angel. *San Pedro Claver, el santo que libertó una raza.* Cartagena: Santuario de San Pedro Claver, 1964.

Vila Vilar, Enriqueta. "Extranjeros en Cartagena en el siglo XVII." *Jahrbuch für Geschichte von Staat, Wirtschaft und Gesellschaft Lateinamerikas [Germany]* 16 (1979): 147–184.

Suggested Early Maps and Depictions
of Cartagena, 1570–1808

Crude depiction of the city, ca. 1570–1573—original held by the Real Academia de la Historia in Madrid, inventory number: Colección Muñoz, Manuscrito A-121, Tomo 96

Sketch of the main square and waterfront, 1571—original held by the Archive of Indies at Seville

Engraving of Sir Francis Drake's assault in February 1586, published two years later in Leyden by Batista Boazio as part of *Le Voyage de Messire François Drake, Chevalier, aux Indes Occidentales,* also copied in Walter Bigges's *A Summarie and True Discourse of Sir Francis Drake's West Indian Voyage,* published in London in 1589, as well as Theodore de Bry's *Collectiones peregrinationum in Indiam Orientalem at Indiam Occidentalem,* published ten years later in Frankfurt—several sources

Sketch of Cartagena in April 1594 by the military engineer Batista Antonelli, depicting his proposed new defensive perimeter—original held by the Archive of Indies at Seville, old Torres Lanzas call number: Mapas y Planos de Panamá, 10 [archival provenance: Patronato Real, Legajo 193, R 48]; a copy drawn by the military engineer

Benito León y Canales in November 1851 is also available from the Servicio Histórico Militar in Madrid, call number: 2–3–1–3-no 6007

Two maps of the city and its Getsemaní suburb by the visiting plate-fleet Adm. Luis Fajardo, incorporating his suggestions for a new defensive perimeter, March 1599—original held by the Archive of Indies at Seville, old Torres Lanzas call number: Mapas y Planos de Panamá, 20 [archival provenance: Indiferente General, Legajo 1528]

1602 drawing by the Italian-born military engineer Cristóbal de Roda of the proposed new San Felipe Bastion to protect the city's Santo Domingo land gate—original held by the Archive of Indies at Seville, old Torres Lanzas call number: Mapas y Planos de Panamá, 32

Drawing by De Roda of a portion of Cartagena's northern seawall, running between the Santa Catalina and new San Felipe bastions, 1617—original held by the Biblioteca Nacional in Madrid

Sketch of Cartagena's walls in 1630, showing improvements made by its governor and *maestre de campo* Francisco de Murga—original held by the Real Academia de la Historia in Madrid, inventory number: Papeles de Salazar, Manuscrito 132

Diagram of the proposed "Media Luna" fortified city gate, ca. 1631—original held by the Archive of Indies at Seville, old Torres Lanzas call number: Mapas y Planos de Panamá, 47

Diagram of repairs and improvements made by Governor de Murga to the Santa Catalina ramparts, 1645—original held by the Archive of Indies at Seville, old Torres Lanzas call number: Mapas y Planos de Panamá, 67

Map of Cartagena and its harbor, ca. 1665—original held by the Archive of Indies at Seville, old Torres Lanzas call number: Mapas y Planos de Panamá, 76 or Vitrina 8 [archival provenance: Santa Fe, Legajo 457]

Map of proposed improvements to the defensive perimeter around Cartagena and its Getsemaní suburb, 1688—original held by the Archive of Indies at Seville, old Torres Lanzas call number: Mapas y Planos de Panamá, 100 [archival provenance: Santa Fe, Legajo 457]

Drawing by the *delineador* or "draftsman" José de Figueroa, of new seaside defenses between La Merced and Santa Clara convents, 1725—original held by the Archive of Indies at Seville, old Torres Lanzas call number: Mapas y Planos de Panamá, 128

Three detailed maps of Cartagena and its defenses, by the military engineer Brig. Juan Herrera y Sotomayor, 1730—originals held by the Servicio Geográfico del Ejército in Madrid, call numbers: Ao-J-T-7-C.ª–1.ª–28, –29, and –30

Three detailed maps of the city and its harbor, by the military engineer Carlos Desnaux, 1735—originals held by the Servicio Geográfico del Ejército in Madrid, call number: Ao-J-T-7-C.ª–1.ª–38

Pen-and-ink map with watercolor highlights of the city and its defenses, ca. 1740—original held by the Archivo Histórico Nacional in Madrid, call number: Sección de Estado, Legajo 2335, S.ª 113

Two maps of Cartagena and its harbor by the military engineer Brig. Ignacio Sala, 1742—originals held by the Servicio Geográfico del Ejército in Madrid, call numbers: Ao-J-T-7-C.ª–1.ª–42 and –43

Copy of a map of the city as surveyed in August 1744 by Juan Bautista MacEwan, then redrawn in December 1769 by the military engineer Antonio de Arévalo, MacEwan's original having been intercepted by an English warship while en route to Spain aboard the frigate *Nuestra Señora de Granada*—De Arévalo copy held by the Servicio Histórico Militar in Madrid, call number: E-9-5-1-no 6007

Copy of a map of the city as surveyed in September 1754 by the military engineer Brig. Lorenzo de Solís, then redrawn in December 1769 by De Arévalo—original held by the Servicio Histórico Militar in Madrid, call number: K-B-1-33-no 6005

Two sets of profile views by De Arévalo of a proposed new city jetty, December 1756—originals held by the Archivo General de Simancas in Spain, call numbers: Mapas, Planos y Dibujos, XV-72 and XV-73 [archival provenance: Marina 328]

Diagrams by De Arévalo of a proposed new jetty and wharf to careen large warships, March 1758—originals held by the Archivo General de Simancas in Spain, call numbers: Mapas, Planos y Dibujos, XV-74 and XV-75 [archival provenance: Marina 328]

Map of Cartagena and its harbor, ca. 1763—original held by the Servicio Histórico Militar in Madrid, call number: P-B-11-58-no 6037

Map of the city and its harbor, 1763—original held by the Archive of Indies at Seville, old Torres Lanzas call number: Mapas y Planos de Panamá, 169 [archival provenance: Santa Fe, Legajo 942]

Diagrams and profile views by De Arévalo of the city's north seawall, 12 June 1769—original held by the Servicio Histórico Militar in Madrid, call number: K-B-6-58-no 5999, Hoja Segunda

Maps by De Arévalo of proposed changes to the city defenses, November 1772—originals held by the Servicio Geográfico del Ejército (call number: Ao-J-T-7-C.ª–1.ª–61) and Servicio Histórico Militar in Madrid, call numbers: E-8-23-4-no 5995 (Cuarta Hoja), E-10-5-1-no 6037, and E-10-6-1-no 6038

Map by Juan Ximénez Donoso of suggested changes to Cartagena's defenses, 1 May 1774—original held by the

Servicio Histórico Militar in Madrid, call number: K-M-9-58-no 5949

Nautical chart of the harbor's sea approaches by naval Ens. José de Bertodano, 1776—original held by the Servicio Geográfico del Ejército in Madrid, call number: Ao-J-T-7-C.^{a}-2.ª-66

Engraved and hand-tinted copy of a September 1777 map of Cartagena's province by Antonio de la Torre, reproduced ten years later by Juan López—original held by the Archivo General de Simancas in Spain, call number: Mapas, Planos y Dibujos, IV-27 [archival provenance: Guerra Moderna 7079]

Diagram and profile view by De Arévalo of the proposed new San Lázaro Hospital for lepers at Caño del Loro, near San Mateo Point on Tierra Bomba Island outside the city, ca. 1789—original held by the Servicio Histórico Militar in Madrid call number: E-8-24-1-no 5996

Map by De Arévalo of improvements to the city defenses, June 1789—originals held by the Servicio Geográfico del Ejército (call number: Ao-J-T-7-C.^{a}-2.ª-78) and Servicio Histórico Militar in Madrid, call number: E-7-8-2-no 5945

Highly detailed map by Manuel de Anguiano of Cartagena's wards and main edifices, ca. 1804–1808—original held by the Servicio Histórico Militar in Madrid, call number: E-7-20-1-no 5957

Detailed map of the city by De Anguiano, January 1805—original held by the Servicio Geográfico del Ejército in Madrid, call number: Ao-J-T-7-C.^{a}-2.ª-87

Late Colonial Era (1700–1821)

Bell Lemus, Gustavo. "Un aporte al pensamiento económico de la colonia: informe del último gobernador de Cartagena al virrey Sámano, mayo de 1819." *Huellas [Colombia]* 27 (1989): 58–67.

Gómez Pérez, Carmen. "Los extranjeros en la América colonial: su expulsión de Cartagena de Indias en 1750." *Anuario de Estudios Americanos [Spain]* 37 (1980): 279–311.

Grahn, Lance. "Guarding the New Granadan Coasts: Dilemmas of the Spanish Coast Guard in the Early Bourbon Period." *American Neptune* 56, Number 1 (1996): 19–28.

Jara, Alvaro. "El financiamento de la defensa en Cartagena de Indias: los excedentes de las cajas de Bogotá y de Quito, 1761–1802." *Historia [Chile]* 28 (1994): 117–182.

Lemaitre, Eduardo, compiler and editor. *Antecedentes y consecuentes del once de 1811: testimonios y documentos relacionados con la gloriosa gesta de la independencia absoluta de Cartagena de Indias.* Cartagena, 1961.

Lucena Giraldo, Manuel. "Ciencia y política en los proyectos de obras públicas del Consulado de Cartagena de Indias, 1795–1810." *Memoria y Sociedad [Colombia]* 2, Number 4 (1997): 25–37.

Marchena Fernández, Juan. *La institución militar en Cartagena de Indias en el siglo XVIII, 1700–1810.* Seville: Escuela de Estudios Hispano-americanos, 1982.

Navarro García, Luis. "El privilegio de los regidores en el abasto de Cartagena de Indias." *Anuario de Estudios Americanos [Spain]* 38 (1981): 173–214.

Nowell, Charles E. "The Defense of Cartagena." *Hispanic American Historical Review* 42, Number 4 (November 1962): 477–501.

Parrón Salas, Carmen. "Comercio marítimo y comerciantes de Cartagena en el siglo XVIII." *Revista de Historia Naval [Spain]* 8, Number 29 (1990): 23–61.

Phillips, Carla Rahn. "The Galleon *San José,* Treasure Ship of the Spanish Indies." *The Mariner's Mirror* 77, Number 4 (1991): 355–363.

Porto de González, Judith. "Ataques de Vernon a Cartagena." *Boletín de Historia y Antigüedades [Colombia]* 83, Number 794 (1996): 679–693.

Segovia Salas, Rodolfo. "Las defensas de la canal de Bocachica." *Boletín Cultural y Bibliográfico [Colombia]* 18, Number 1 (1981): 81–85.

———. "El hundimiento del 'San José' en 1708." *Boletín de Historia y Antigüedades [Colombia]* 72, Number 751 (1985): 912–941.

Sourdis Nájera, Adelaida. "Estructura de la ganadería en el Caribe colombiano durante el siglo XVIII." *Boletín de Historia y Antigüedades [Colombia]* 82, Number 790 (1995): 611–629.

Zulueta, Julián de. "Health and Military Factors in Vernon's Failure at Cartagena." *Mariner's Mirror* 78, Number 2 (1992): 127–141.

Modern Era (1821–Present)

Andic, Fuat M., and Ramón J. Cao. "Costs and Benefits of a Free Zone: The Case of Cartagena." *Caribbean Studies [Puerto Rico]* 20, Number 1 (March 1980): 75–96.

Bossa Herazo, Donaldo, editor. *Cartagena independiente: tradición y desarrollo.* Bogotá: Tercer Mundo, 1967.

Desarrollo en Cartagena: filosofía y criterios. Cartagena: Instituto de Crédito Territorial and Oficina de Rehabilitación de Tugurios, May 1969.

Helguera, J. León. "Archives in Cartagena, Colombia." *The Americas: A Quarterly Review of Inter-American Cultural History [Academy of American Franciscan History]* 45, Number 4 (1989): 547–549.

Holguín Pardo, Arturo. "Bocachica." *Boletín de Historia y Antigüedades [Colombia]* 74, Number 758 (1987): 673–683.

McDowell, Bart. "Cartagena Nights." *National Geographic* 175, Number 4 (April 1989): 494–509.

Porto de González, Judith. "El teatro en la historia de Cartagena." *Boletín de la Academia Colombiana* 39, Numbers 164–165 (1989): 82–98.

Restrepo R., Jorge Alberto. "Personajes de la vida económica, política y social de Cartagena a finales del siglo XIX." *Huellas [Colombia]* 26 (1989): 25–39.

Solaún, Mauricio, and Sidney Kronus. *Discrimination without Violence: Miscegenation and Racial Conflict in Latin America.* New York: Wiley, 1973.

Strassmann, Wolfgang Paul. *The Transformation of Urban Housing: The Experience of Upgrading in Cartagena.* Baltimore: Johns Hopkins University Press, 1982.

Streicker, Joel. "Policing Boundaries: Race, Class, and Gender in Cartagena, Colombia." *American Ethnologist* 22 (1995): 54–74.

———. "Spatial Reconfigurations, Imagined Geographies, and Social Conflicts in Cartagena, Colombia." *Cultural Anthropology* 12, Number 1 (February 1997): 109–128.

Triana y Antorveza, Humberto. *Cultura del tugurio en Cartagena.* Bogotá: Italgraf, 1974.

General Works

Bossa Herazo, Donaldo. *Guía artística de Cartagena de Indias.* Bogotá: Retina, 1955.

Castillo Mathieu, Nicolás del. "Cartagena, puerto comercial, 1533–1800." *Boletín Cultural y Bibliográfico [Colombia]* 16, Number 2 (1979): 64–84.

De Castellanos, Juan. *Historia de Cartagena.* Bogotá: Biblioteca Popular de Cultura Colombiana, 1942.

Delgado Camilo, Arcos. *Historia, leyendas y tradiciones de Cartagena.* Cartagena, 1911.

Gutiérrez de Pineda, Virginia. "La familia en Cartagena de Indias." *Boletín Cultural y Bibliográfico [Colombia]* 24, Number 10 (1987): 35–47.

Hinds, James R. "Cartagena de Indias: Shield of the Spanish Main." *Periodical: Journal of the Council on America's Military Past* 13, Number 4 (1985): 47–53.

Lemaitre, Eduardo. *Breve historia de Cartagena, 1501–1901.* Bogotá: Tercer Mundo, 1980.

———. *Historia general de Cartagena.* Bogotá: Banco de la República, 1983, four volumes.

"Los 450 años de la fundación de Cartagena." *Boletín de Historia y Antigüedades [Colombia]* 70, Number 741 (1983): 489–504.

Marco Dorta, Enrique. *Cartagena de Indias: la ciudad y sus monumentos.* Seville: Escuela de Estudios Hispanoamericanos, 1951.

———. *Cartagena de Indias: puerto y plaza fuerte.* Bogotá: Alfonso Amado, 1960.

———. "Ganadería y abastecimiento en Cartagena de Indias, 1766." *Revista de Indias [Spain]* 119–122 (1970): 473 et seq.

Nichols, Theodore E. *Tres puertos de Colombia: estudio sobre el desarrollo de Cartagena, Santa Marta y Barranquilla.* Bogotá: Biblioteca Banco Popular, 1973.

Palacios Preciado, Jorge. *La trata de negros por Cartagena de Indias.* Tunja, 1973.

Porras Troconis, Gabriel. "Heroic Cartagena." *Américas [Organization of American States]* 21, Number 6 (June 1969): 21–30.

Urueta, José P., compiler. *Documentos para la historia de Cartagena.* Cartagena: Gabriel E. O'Byrne, 1890, seven volumes.

Zapatero López, Juan Manuel. *Historia de las fortificaciones de Cartagena de Indias.* Madrid: Cultura Hispánica, 1979.

Ecuador

General Studies

Acosta-Solís, Misael. *Investigadores de la geografía y la naturaleza de América tropical: viajeros, cronistas e investigadores, con especial referencia al Ecuador.* Quito, 1976–1977, two volumes.

Albornoz Peralta, Oswaldo. *Ecuador: luces y sombras del liberalismo.* Quito: El Duende, 1989.

Alchon, Suzanne Austin. *Native Society and Disease in Colonial Ecuador.* New York: Cambridge University Press, 1991.

Andrews, M. L. A. "Land of the Panama Hat." *Geographical Magazine [UK]* 35 (1962): 356–368.

Atlas geográfico de la República del Ecuador. Quito: Instituto Geográfico Militar, 1977.

Ayala Mora, Enrique, editor. *Nueva historia del Ecuador: época republicana.* Quito: Editora Nacional, 1983.

Blanksten, George I. *Ecuador: Constitutions and Caudillos.* Berkeley: University of California Press, 1951.

Bromley, R. J. *Bibliografía del Ecuador: ciencias sociales, económicos y geográficos.* Talence: Centre d'Études de Géographie Tropicale, Centre Nationale de Recherche Scientifique, 1971.

Bromley, Rosemary D. F., and R. J. Bromley. "The Debate on Sunday Markets in XIXth Century Ecuador." *Journal of Latin American Studies [UK]* 7, Number 1 (1975): 85–108.

Carbó, Luis Alberto. *Historia monetaria y cambiaria del Ecuador.* Quito: Banco Central del Ecuador, 1978.

Crawford de Roberts, Lois. *El Ecuador en la época cacaotera.* Quito: Editorial Universitaria, 1980.

Deler, Jean-Paul, et al. *El manejo del espacio en el Ecuador: etapas claves.* Quito: Centro Ecuatoriano de Investigación Geográfica, 1983.

Durán Barba, Jaime, editor. *Pensamiento popular ecuatoriano.* Quito: Banco Central del Ecuador, 1981.

Ecuador pintoresco: acuarelas de Joaquín Pinto. Quito-Barcelona: Salvat, 1977.

El Ecuador: guía comercial, agrícola e industrial de la República. Guayaquil: Compañía "Guía del Ecuador," 1909.

El ferrocarril de Guayaquil a Quito: contratos y otros documentos importantes. Quito: El Comercio, 1912.

Enock, Charles Reginald. *Ecuador: Its Ancient and Modern History, Topography, and Natural Resources, Industries, and Social Developments.* London, 1919.

Estrada Ycaza, Julio. *Historia del Ecuador.* Quito: Salvat, 1982, four volumes.

———. *La lucha de Guayaquil por el estado de Quito.* Guayaquil: Banco Central del Ecuador, 1984–1989, two volumes.

Ferdon, Edwin R. *Studies in Ecuadorean Geography.* Santa Fe, NM: School of American Research, 1950.

Franklin, Albert B. *Ecuador: Portrait of a People.* New York: Doubleday, Doran and Company, 1943.

González Suárez, Federico. *Historia general de la República del Ecuador.* Quito: Casa de la Cultura Ecuatoriana, 1969–1970 reprint of 1890–1903 original published in Quito by the Imprenta del Clero, three volumes.

Guía para investigadores del Ecuador. Quito: Instituto Geográfico Militar and Instituto Panamericano de Geografía e Historia, 1982.

Hallo, Wilson, editor. *Imágenes del Ecuador del siglo XIX: Juan Agustín Guerrero.* Quito-Madrid, 1981.

Hassaurek, Friedrich. *Four Years among the Ecuadorians.* Carbondale: Southern Illinois University Press, 1967 re-edition by C. H. Gardner of 1868 original published by Hurd and Houghton in New York.

Hurtado, Osvaldo. *Political Power in Ecuador.* Boulder, CO: Westview, 1985 translation by Nick D. Mills, Jr.

Kasza, Gregory J. "Regional Conflict in Ecuador: Quito and Guayaquil." *Inter-American Economic Affairs* 35, Number 2 (autumn 1981): 3–41.

Kolberg, Joseph. *Hacia el Ecuador: relatos de viaje.* Quito: Universidad Católica, 1977 reprint of 1897 original.

Lara, A. Darío. *Viajeros franceses al Ecuador en el siglo XIX.* Quito: Casa de la Cultura Ecuatoriana, 1972.

Larrea, Carlos Manuel. *Cartografía ecuatoriana de los sixlos XVI, XVII y XVIII.* Quito: Corporación de Estudios y Publicaciones, 1977.

Linke, Lilo. *Ecuador: Country of Contrasts.* Oxford University Press, 1960.

Maier, Georg. "Presidential Succession in Ecuador: 1860–1968." *Journal of Inter-American Studies and World Affairs* 13 (July–October 1971): 475–509.

Manual de información cultural, educativa, turística, industrial, comercial, agrícola y ganadera de la República del Ecuador. Madrid: Científica Latina, 1980.

Martz, John D. *Ecuador: Conflicting Political Culture and the Quest for Progress.* Boston: Allyn and Bacon, 1972.

McIntyre, Loren. "Ecuador: Low and Lofty Land Astride the Equator." *National Geographic* 133, Number 2 (February 1968): 258–294.

Meggers, Betty J. *Ecuador.* London: Thames and Hudson, 1966.

Middleton, Alan. "Division and Cohesion among the Working Class: Artisans and Wage Labourers in Ecuador." *Journal of Latin American Studies [UK]* 14 (1982): 171–194.

Morales y Eloy, Juan. *Ecuador: atlas histórico-geográfico.* Quito: Ministerio de Relaciones Exteriores, 1942.

Navarro, José Gabriel. *La escultura en el Ecuador (siglos XVI al XVIII).* Madrid, 1929.

Newson, L. "Highland/Lowland Contrasts in the Impact of Old World Disease in Early Colonial Ecuador." *Social Science Medicine* 36 (1993): 1187–1195.

Niles, Blair. *Casual Wanderings in Ecuador.* New York: Century, 1923.

Norris, R. E. *Guía bibliográfica para el estudio de la historia ecuatoriana.* Austin: University of Texas Press, 1978.

Oxandaberro, Roura, and Hugo Cifuentes. *Ecuador: arte, folklore, paisaje.* Quito: Imprenta Argentina, 1969.

Paredes Borja, Virgilio. *Historia de la medicina en el Ecuador.* Quito: Casa de la Cultura, 1963, two volumes.

Pareja Díezcanseco, Alfredo. *Historia del Ecuador.* Quito: Casa de la Cultura Ecuatoriana, 1954, four volumes.

Paz y Miño, Luis Telmo. *Mapas coloniales del Ecuador.* Quito: Academia Nacional de Historia, 1943.

Peñaherrera de Costales, Piedad, and Alfredo Costales Samiego. *Historia social del Ecuador.* Quito: Casa de la Cultura, 1964–1971, four volumes.

Quintero López, Rafael. *El mito del populismo en el Ecuador: análisis del estado ecuatoriano moderno, 1895–1934.* Quito: Universidad Central del Ecuador, 1983.

The Republic of Ecuador. New York: Consulate of Ecuador, 1921.

Robalino Bolle, Isabel. *El sindicalismo en el Ecuador.* Quito: Instituto Ecuatoriano para el Desarrollo Social, 1981.

Robalino Dávila, Luis. *Orígenes del Ecuador de hoy.* Puebla: Cajica, 1967–1970, seven volumes.

Rodríguez, Linda Alexander. *The Search for Public Policy: Regional Politics and Government Finances in Ecuador, 1830–1940.* Berkeley: University of California Press, 1984.

Samaniego, Juan José. *Cronología médica ecuatoriana.* Quito, 1957.

Sampedro V., Francisco, and Clemencia Sampedro de Heredia. *Atlas histórico-geográfico del Ecuador.* Mexico City, 1960.

Saunders, John Van Dyke. *The People of Ecuador: A Demographic Analysis.* Gainesville: University Presses of Florida, 1961.

Schodt, David W. *Ecuador: An Andean Enigma.* Boulder, CO: Westview, 1987.

Spindler, Frank Macdonald. *Nineteenth Century Ecuador: An Historical Introduction.* Fairfax, VA: George Mason University Press, 1987.

Stols, A. M. *Historia de la imprenta en el Ecuador de 1755 a 1830.* Quito, 1953.

Szászdi, Adam. "The Historiography of the Republic of Ecuador." *Hispanic American Historical Review* 44 (November 1964): 503–550.

Townsend, Elizabeth Jane. "Festivals of Ecuador." *Américas [Organization of American States]* 30, Number 4 (April 1978): 9–16.

Van Aken, Mark. "The Lingering Death of Indian Tribute in Ecuador." *Hispanic American Historical Review* 61 (1981): 429–459.

———. *King of the Night: Juan José Flores and Ecuador, 1824–1864.* Berkeley: University of California Press, 1989.

Vargas, José María. *La economía política del Ecuador durante la colonia.* Quito: Editorial Universitaria, 1967.

———. *Patrimonio artístico ecuatoriano.* Quito: Editorial Santo Domingo, 1972.

———. *Historia del Ecuador, siglo XVI.* Quito: Universidad Católica, 1977.

Villacís Verdesoto, Eduardo, compiler. *Grabados sobre el Ecuador en el siglo XIX (Le Tour du Monde).* Quito: Banco Central de Ecuador, 1981.

Villacrés Moscoso, Jorge W. "Cartografía histórica del Ecuador." *Cuadernos de Historia y Arqueología* 22, Number 39 (1973): 29–76.

———. *Geohistoria del estado ecuatoriano.* Guayaquil: Casa de la Cultura Ecuatoriana, 1973.

Von Hagen, Victor Wolfgang. *Ecuador the Unknown.* London: Jarrolds, 1939.

Whitten, Norman E., Jr., editor. *Cultural Transformation and Ethnicity in Modern Ecuador.* Urbana: University of Illinois Press, 1981.

Whymper, Edward. *Travels amongst the Great Andes of the Equator.* London: John Murray, 1892 edition of 1885 original, two volumes.

Wilson, Jacques M. P. *The Development of Education in Ecuador.* Coral Gables, FL: University of Miami Press, 1970.

Wolf, Teodoro. *Geografía y geología del Ecuador.* Quito: Casa de la Cultura Ecuatoriana, 1975 reprint of 1892 original issued in Leipzig by F. A. Brockhaus.

Ycaza, Patricio. *Historia del movimiento obrero ecuatoriano.* Quito: CEDIME, 1984.

Zéndegui, Guillermo de. "Image of Ecuador." *Américas [Organization of American States]* 24, Number 9 (September 1972): supplementary pp. 1–24.

Guayaquil

Colonial Era (1537–1820)

Actas de las sesiones efectuadas por el ilustre consejo municipal de Guayaquil. Guayaquil, 1910–1912, three volumes.

Alsedo y Herrera, Dionisio de. *Compendio histórico de la provincia, partidos, ciudades, astilleros, ríos y puerto de Guayaquil en las costas de la Mar del Sur.* Madrid: Manuel Fernández, 1741 original reprinted by Pedro Carbo in Guayaquil in 1879, as well as in Quito in 1938 and 1946.

Bernal Ruiz, María del Pilar. *La toma del puerto de Guayaquil en 1687.* Seville: Escuela de Estudios Hispano-americanos, 1979.

Cannenburg, W. Voorbeijtel, editor. *De Reis om de Wereld van de Nassausche Vloot, 1623–1626.* 's-Gravenhage: Martinus Nijhoff for the Linschoten Society, 1964.

Castillo, Abel Romeo. *Los gobernadores de Guayaquil del siglo XVIII.* Guayaquil: Archivo Histórico del Guayas, 1978.

Clayton, Lawrence A. *Caulkers and Carpenters in a New World: The Shipyards of Colonial Guayaquil.* Athens: Ohio University Press, 1980.

Conniff, Michael L. "Guayaquil through Independence: Urban Development in a Colonial System." *The Americas: A Quarterly Review of Inter-American Cultural History [Academy of American Franciscan History]* 33, Number 3 (January 1977): 385–411.

Cooke, Edward. *A Voyage to the South Sea and Around the World, Perform'd in the Years 1708–1711.* Bibliotheca Australiana, 1971 reprint of 1712 original.

Dyer, Florence E. "Captain John Strong, Privateer and Treasure Hunter." *The Mariner's Mirror [UK]* 13 (1927): 145–158.

Espinoza Cevallos, Javier. *Aculturación de indígenas en la ciudad de Guayaquil.* Guayaquil: Casa de la Cultura, 1965.

Estrada Ycaza, Julio. "Apuntes para la historia del Hospital Militar." *Revista del Archivo Histórico del Guayas* 1, Number 2 (December 1972): 33–44.

———. "Evolución urbana de Guayaquil." *Revista del Archivo Histórico del Guayas* 1, Number 1 (1972): 37–66.

———. "Desarrollo histórico del suburbio guayaquileño." *Revista del Archivo Histórico del Guayas* 2, Number 3 (June 1973): 14–26.

———. *El puerto de Guayaquil: crónica portuaria.* Guayaquil: Archivo Histórico del Guayas, 1973.

———. *El hospital de Guayaquil.* Guayaquil: Archivo Histórico del Guayas, 1974.

———. *La fundación de Guayaquil.* Guayaquil: Archivo Histórico del Guayas, 1974.

Hamerly, Michael T. *Historia social y económica de la antigua provincia de Guayaquil, 1763–1842.* Guayaquil: Archivo Histórico del Guayas, 1973.

Laviana Cuetos, María Teresa. *Guayaquil en el siglo XVIII: recursos naturales y desarrollo económico.* Seville, 1987.

Madero, Mauro. *Historia de la medicina en la provincia del Guayas.* Guayaquil: Casa de la Cultura, 1955.

Parks, Lois F., and Gustave A. Nuermberger. "The Sanitation of Guayaquil." *Hispanic American Historical Review* 23, Number 2 (May 1943): 197–221.

Rogers, Woodes. *A Cruising Voyage round the World.* London: Cassell, 1928 reprint of 1712 original.

Some Early Maps and Depictions of Guayaquil

Chart of the Gulf of Guayaquil during the late seventeenth or early eighteenth century—original held by the Biblioteca Nacional in Madrid, call number: Manuscritos 2957, folios 70vuelta–71

Crude map of the gulf and city, ca. 1730—published eleven years later in Madrid in Dionisio de Alsedo y Herrera's *Compendio histórico de la provincia, partidos, ciudades, astilleros, ríos y puerto de Guayaquil en las costas de la Mar del Sur,* several sources

Survey of the city by the military engineer Col. Francisco Requena, July 1770—original held by the Servico Histórico Militar in Madrid, call number: 6246, hoja 2/P-b-11–41

Map of Guayaquil's district in September 1779, also by Requena—original held by the British Museum

Diagram of the buildings around Guayaquil's main marketplace in April 1785, by Ramón García de León y Pizarro—original held by the Archivo General de Simancas in Spain, call number: Mapas, Planos y Dibujos, II-24 [archival provenance: Guerra Moderna 6828]

Three watercolors of the city in 1790 by José Cardero, one of the artists who joined Capt. Alejandro Malaspina's scientific expedition into the Pacific—originals held by the Museo Naval in Madrid

Chart of the gulf as surveyed in September 1797 by the engineer José Díaz del Pedregal, then drawn up in December 1798—original held by Ingenieros del Ejército, call number: 674, V. 119

Republican Era and General Works (1821–Present)

América libre: obra dedicada a conmemorar el centenario de la independencia de Guayaquil. Guayaquil, 1920.

Barbosa, Jenaro, editor. *Almanaque ilustrado de Guayaquil 1907.* Guayaquil, ca. 1907.

Beard, Abner H. "The River Port That Became a Seaport." *Américas [Organization of American States]* 15, Number 5 (1963): 17–19.

Bengston, N. A. "Some Essential Features of the Geography of the Santa Elena Peninsula." *Annals of the Association of American Geographers* 14 (1924): 150–158.

Ceriola, Juan B. *Guayaquil a la vista: colección de fototipias con sus explicaciones históricas, artísticas y descriptivas.* Barcelona: Viuda de Luis Tasso, 1910.

Chiriboga, Manuel. *Jornaleros y gran propietarios en 135 años de exportación cacaotera, 1790–1925.* Quito: Consejo Provincial de Pichincha, 1980.

Estrada Ycaza, Julio. *Regionalismo y migración.* Guayaquil: Archivo Histórico del Guayas, 1977.

Gallegos Naranjo, Manuel. *1883 almanaque ecuatoriano guía de Guayaquil.* Guayaquil, 1883.

Gray, William H. "Bolívar's Conquest of Guayaquil." *Hispanic American Historical Review* 27, Number 4 (November 1947): 603–622.

Guerrero, Andrés. *Los oligarcas del cacao.* Quito: El Conejo, 1980.

Hamerly, Michael T. *Trayectoria marítima del Ecuador, 1830–1859.* Quito: Comandancia General de Marina, 1977.

Huerta, Pedro José. *Guayaquil en 1842: Rocafuerte y la epidemia de fiebre amarilla.* Universidad de Guayaquil, 1947.

Jurado Avilés, J. J., editor. *El Ecuador en el centenario de la independencia de Guayaquil.* New York, 1920.

Linke, Lilo. "What's Happening to Guayaquil?" *Américas [Organization of American States]* 9, Number 6 (1957): 3–8.

Masur, Gerhard. "The Conference of Guayaquil." *Hispanic American Historical Review* 31, Number 2 (May 1951): 189–229.

Muñoz Vicuña, Elías. *El 15 de noviembre de 1922.* Guayaquil: Facultad de Ciencias Económicas de la Universidad de Guayaquil, 1978.

Paz Ayora, Vicente. *Guía de Guayaquil y almanaque del comercio ecuatoriano, 1901.* Guayaquil, 1901.

Pineo, Ronn F. "Reinterpreting Labor Militancy: The Collapse of the Cacao Economy and the General Strike of 1922 in Guayaquil, Ecuador." *Hispanic American Historical Review* 68, Number 4 (November 1988): 707–736.

———. "Misery and Death in the Pearl of the Pacific: Public Health Care in Guayaquil, Ecuador, 1870–1925." *Hispanic American Historical Review* 70, Number 4 (November 1990): 609–638.

———. *Social and Economic Reform in Ecuador: Life and Work in Guayaquil.* Gainesville: University Presses of Florida, 1996.

Redclift, Michael R. *Agrarian Reform and Peasant Organization on the Ecuadorian Coast.* London: Athlone, 1978.

Townsend, Camilla. *Tales of Two Cities: Race and Economic Culture in Early Republican North and South America.* Austin: University of Texas Press, 2000.

Quito

Native Origins

Haro Alvear, Silvio Luis. *Mitos y cultos del reino de Quito.* Quito: Editora Nacional, 1980.

Powers, Karen. "Resilient Lords and Indian Vagabonds: Wealth, Migration, and the Reproductive Transformation of Quito's Chiefdoms, 1500–1700." *Ethnohistory* 38, Number 3 (1991): 225–249.

Salomon, Frank. *Native Lords of Quito in the Age of the Incas: The Political Economy of North-Andean Chiefdoms.* New York: Cambridge University Press, 1986.

———. "Indian Women of Early Colonial Quito as Seen through Their Testaments." *The Americas: A Quarterly Review of Inter-American Cultural History [Academy of American Franciscan History]* 44, Number 3 (1988): 325–341.

Early Colonial Era (1534–1764)

Alsedo y Herrera, Dionisio de. *Descripción geográfica de la Real Audiencia de Quito.* Madrid: Hispanic Society of America, 1915 reprint of 1766 original.

Andrien, Kenneth J. *The Kingdom of Quito, 1690–1830: The State and Regional Development.* New York: Cambridge University Press, 1995.

Cushner, Nicholas P. *Farm and Factory: The Jesuits and the Development of Agrarian Capitalism in Colonial Quito, 1600–1767.* Albany: State University of New York Press, 1982.

Descalzi, Ricardo. *La Real Audiencia de Quito, claustro en los Andes: historia de Quito colonial, siglo XVI.* Barcelona: Seix Barrial, 1978.

Garcés G., Jorge A., compiler. *Oficios o cartas al cabildo de Quito por el rey de España o el virrey de las Indias, 1552–1558.* Quito: Archivo Municipal, 1934.

———. *Colección de cédulas reales dirigidas a la Audiencia de Quito, 1538–1600 y 1601–1660.* Quito: Archivo Municipal, 1935–1946, two volumes.

———. *Libro de proveimientos de tierras, cuadras, solares, aguas, etc., por los cabildos de la ciudad de Quito, 1583–1594.* Quito: Archivo Municipal, 1941.

———. *Colección de documentos sobre el obispado de Quito, 1546–1583 y 1583–1594.* Quito: Archivo Municipal, 1946–1947, two volumes.

Herzog, Tamar. "El rescate de una fuente histórica: los libros de visita de cárcel, el caso de Quito, 1738–1750." *Anuario de Estudios Americanos [Spain]* 52, Number 2 (1995): 251–261.

Landázuri Soto, Alberto. *El régimen laboral indígena en la Real Audiencia de Quito.* Madrid: Aldecoa, 1959.

Lavallé, Bernard. *Quito et la crise de l'Alcabala, 1560–1600.* Paris: Collection de la Maison des Pays ibériques, Centre National de la Recherche Scientifique, 1992.

Libros de cabildos de la ciudad de Quito, 1573–1574, 1575–1576, 1593–1597, 1597–1603, 1603–1610, 1610–1616, 1638–1646 y 1650–1657. Quito: Archivo Municipal, 1934–1969, eight volumes.

Minchom, Martin. *The People of Quito, 1690–1810: Change and Unrest in the Underclass.* Boulder, CO: Westview, 1994.

Miño Grijalva, Manuel. *La economía colonial: relaciones socio-económicas de la Real Audiencia de Quito.* Quito: Corporación Editora Nacional, 1984.

Mörner, Magnus. "Aspectos socioraciales del proceso de poblamiento en la Audiencia de Quito durante los siglos XVI y XVII." *Homenaje a don José Maria de Peña y Cámara [Madrid]* (1969): 265–287.

Ortiz de la Tabla Ducasse, Javier. "Obrajes y obrajeros del Quito colonial." *Anuario de Estudios Americanos [Spain]* 39 (1982): 341–365.

———. "De hidalgo castellano a empresario colonial: Rodrigo de Salazar, encomendero y obrajero de Quito, 1510–1584." *Anuario de Estudios Americanos [Spain]* 42 (1985): 43–126.

———. *Los encomenderos de Quito, 1534–1660.* Seville: Escuela de Estudios Hispano-americanos, 1993.

Pareja Díezcanseco, Alfredo. *Las instituciones y la administración en la Real Audiencia de Quito.* Quito: Editorial Universitaria, 1975.

Phelan, John Leddy. *The Kingdom of Quito in the Seventeenth Century: Bureaucratic Politics in the Spanish Empire.* Madison: University of Wisconsin Press, 1967.

Ponce Leiva, Pilar. "La educación disputada: la enseñanza universitaria en la Audiencia de Quito." *Procesos: Revista Ecuatoriana de Historia* 6, Number 2 (1994): 3–21.

———. "El poder del discurso o el discurso del poder: el criollismo quiteño en el siglo XVII." *Procesos: Revista Ecuatoriana de Historia* 10, Number 1 (1997): 3–20.

———. "El poder informal: mujeres de Quito en el siglo XVII." *Revista Complutense de Historia de América [Spain]* 23 (1997): 97–111.

Ponce Leiva, Pilar, editor. *Relaciones histórico-geográficas de la Audiencia de Quito, siglo XVI-XIX.* Madrid, 1991.

Powers, Karen Vieira. *Andean Journeys: Migration, Ethnogenesis, and the State in Colonial Quito.* Albuquerque: University of New Mexico Press, 1995.

Ramos Gómez, Luis J. "La pugna por el poder local en Quito entre 1737 y 1745 según el proceso contra el presidente de la Audiencia, José de Araujo y Río." *Revista Complutense de Historia de América [Spain]* 18 (1992): 179–196.

———. "Algunos datos sobre los abusos e injusticias padecidas en 1737 por los indios de los obrajes de la ciudad de Quito." *Revista Española de Antropología Americana [Spain]* 27 (1997): 153–166.

———. "La situación del indio de obraje en la ciudad de Quito según la visita realizada en 1743 por el presidente José de Araujo." *Revista Española de Antropología Americana [Spain]* 28 (1998): 151–168.

Rodríguez Castro, Hernán. *Literatura en la Audiencia de Quito, siglo XVII.* Quito: Banco Central del Ecuador, 1980.

Rumazo González, José, compiler. *Libros primero y segundo de cabildos de Quito, 1529–1543 y 1544–1551.* Quito: Archivo Municipal, 1934, four volumes.

———. *Documentos para la historia de la Audiencia de Quito.* Madrid: Afrodisio Aguado, 1948–1950, eight volumes.

Super, John C. "Partnership and Profit in the Early Andean Trade: The Experiences of Quito Merchants, 1580–1610."

Journal of Latin American Studies [UK] 11, Number 2 (1979): 265–281.

Szászdi, Adam. "The Economic History of the Diocese of Quito, 1616–1787." *Latin American Research Review* 21, Number 2 (1986): 266–275.

Tobar Donoso, Julio. *Las instituciones del período hispánico, especialmente en la presidencia de Quito.* Quito: Editorial Ecuatoriana, 1974.

Tyrer, Robson Brines. *Historia demográfica y económica de la Audiencia de Quito: población indígena e industria textil, 1600–1800.* Quito: Banco Central de Ecuador, 1988.

Vargas, José María. *El arte quiteño en los siglos XVI, XVII y XVIII.* Quito: Casa de la Cultura Ecuatoriana, 1949.

Early Maps and Depictions of Quito, 1734–1846

Combined drawing and map of the city in 1734, by Dionisio Alsedo y Herrera—original held by the Archive of Indies at Seville, call number: Mapas y Planos de Panamá, 134

Map of the city in 1736, from Jorge Juan de Santacilia and Antonio de Ulloa's *Relación histórica del viaje a la América Meridional,* published a dozen years later—several sources

Depiction of different methods for traversing the Machángara River into this city, ca. 1736—from Juan and De Ulloa's *Relación*

Map of Quito, ca. 1736, by the visiting French scientist Charles-Marie de la Condamine—published in his *Journal d'un voyage fait par ordre du roi à l'équateur,* while a hand-drawn copy is apparently also held by the British Library, call number: Additional Manuscripts 15331

Map of the city, published in Madrid by the royal Spanish geographer and cartographer, Tomás López, in 1786—several sources

Map of the city in 1846, by Salazza—original held by the Bibliothèque Nationale in Paris, call number: Cartes et Plans, C 3593

Late Colonial Era (1765–1822)

Andrien, Kenneth J. "Economic Crisis, Taxes, and the Quito Insurrection of 1765." *Past and Present* 129 (November 1990): 104–131.

Borchart de Moreno, Christiana. "La imbecilidad y el coraje: la participación femenina en la economía colonial, Quito, 1780–1830." *Revista Complutense de Historia de América [Spain]* 17 (1991): 167–182.

———. "Beyond the Obraje: Handicraft Production in Quito toward the End of the Colonial Period." *Americas: A Quarterly Review of Inter-American Cultural History [Academy of American Franciscan History]* 52, Number 1 (1995): 1–24.

Borchart de Moreno, Christiana, and Segundo E. Moreno Yáñez. "Las reformas borbónicas en la Audiencia de Quito." *Anuario Colombiano de Historia Social y de la Cultura [Colombia]* 22 (1995): 35–57.

Büschges, Christian. "Crisis y reestructuración: la industria textil de la Real Audiencia de Quito al final del período colonial." *Anuario de Estudios Americanos [Spain]* 52, Number 2 (1995): 75–98.

———. "La nobleza de Quito a finales del período colonial, 1765–1810: bases jurídicas y mentalidad social." *Procesos: Revista Ecuatoriana de Historia* 10, Number 1 (1997): 43–61.

———. "'Las leyes del honor': honor y estratificación social en el distrito de la Audiencia de Quito, siglo XVIII." *Revista de Indias [Spain]* 57, Number 209 (1997): 55–84.

Hamerly, Michael T. "Selva Alegre, President of the *Quiteña* Junta of 1809: Traitor or Patriot?" *Hispanic American Historical Review* 48, Number 4 (November 1968): 642–653.

Keeding, Ekkehart. *Das Zeitalter der Aufklärung in der Provinz Quito.* Cologne: Böhlau, 1983.

López-Ocón Cabrera, Leoncio. "El protagonismo del clero en la insurgencia quiteña, 1809–1812." *Revista de Indias [Spain]* 46, Number 177 (1986): 107–167.

Lucena Salmoral, Manuel. "La ciudad de Quito hacia mil ochocientos." *Anuario de Estudios Americanos [Spain]* 51, Number 1 (1994): 143–164.

McFarlane, Anthony. "The 'Rebellion of the Barrios': Urban Insurrection in Bourbon Quito." *Hispanic American Historical Review* 69, Number 2 (May 1989): 283–330.

Moreno Yáñez, Segundo E. *Sublevaciones indígenas en la Audiencia de Quito desde comienzos del siglo XVIII hasta finales de la colonia.* Quito: Universidad Católica, 1978.

Navarro, José Gabriel. *La revolución de Quito del 10 de agosto de 1809.* Quito, 1962.

Ponce Ribadeneira, Alfredo. *Quito, 1809–1812, según los documentos del Archivo Nacional de Madrid.* Madrid, 1960.

Ramos Pérez, Demetrio. "El cambio de mentalidades sociales en Quito, en la época del despotismo ilustrado." *Jahrbuch für Geschichte von Staat, Wirtschaft und Gesellschaft Lateinamerikas [Germany]* 26 (1989): 85–113.

Recio, Bernardo. *Compendiosa relación de la cristiandad de Quito.* Madrid: Instituto Santo Toribio de Mogrovejo, 1947 reprint of 1773 original.

Torre Reyes, Carlos de la. *La revolución de Quito del 10 de agosto de 1809: sus vicisitudes y su significación en el proceso general de la emancipación hispano-americana.* Quito: Talleres Gráficos de Educación, 1961.

Velasco, Juan de. *Historia del reino de Quito en la América Meridional.* Quito: Casa de la Cultura Ecuatoriana, 1977–1978, three volumes, reprint of 1789 original.

Modern Era (1822–Present)

Bromley, Rosemary D. F., and Gareth A. Jones. "Identifying the Inner City in Latin America," *Geographical Journal [UK]* 162, Number 2 (1996): 179–190.

Bustamante Y., Marco A., and Víctor M. Madrid A. *Monografía de la provincia de Pichincha.* Quito: Talleres Gráficos del Servicio de Suministros del Estado, 1952.

Colección de oficios y documentos dirigidos por las autoridades del Departamento de Quito al Cabildo de la Ciudad, 1823–1826. Quito: Archivo Municipal, 1972.

Fernández de Castro, María Augusta. "Quito: crecimiento y dinámica de una ciudad andina." *Revista Geográfica [Mexico]* 110 (1989): 121–164.

Godoy, C. C. *Geografía ilustrativa, comercial y turística de la provincia de Pichincha.* Quito: Bona Spes, 1949.

Jones, Gareth A., and Rosemary D. F. Bromley. "The Relationship between Urban Conservation Programmes and Property Renovation: Evidence from Quito, Ecuador." *Cities [UK]* 13, Number 6 (December 1996): 373–442.

Jones Odriozola, Guillermo. *Informe sobre el plan regulador de Quito.* Quito: Biblioteca Municipal, 1941, two volumes.

Monografía ilustrada de la provincia de Pichincha. Freiburg: Herder, 1922.

Quito y sus estadísticas: 1967. Quito: Instituto de Investigaciones Económicas y Financieras de la Universidad, 1969.

Waters, William F. "The Road of Many Returns: Rural Bases of the Informal Urban Economy in Ecuador." *Latin American Perspectives* 24, Number 3 (1997): 50–64.

Weiss, Wendy. "Debt and Devaluation: The Burden on Ecuador's Popular Class." *Latin American Perspectives* 24, Number 4 (1997): 9–33.

General Works

Bravo Aráuz, Bolívar, compiler. *Quito monumental y pintoresco.* Quito: Editorial Universitaria, 1965.

Chiriboga, José R. "Quito: The Legacy from Colonial Times." *Américas [Organization of American States]* 29, Number 4 (April 1977): supplementary pp. 1–12.

El libro de la ciudad de San Francisco de Quito, hasta 1950–1951. Quito: CEGAN, 1951.

Enríquez B., Eliécer. *Quito a través de los siglos.* Quito: Biblioteca Municipal, 1938–1940, two volumes.

Gómez E., Nelson. *El area metropolitana de Quito.* Mexico City: Instituto Panamericano de Geografía e Historia, 1977.

———. *Quito y su desarrollo urbano.* Quito: Camino, ca. 1979.

Morelli, Federica. "Doing Historical Research in Quito: A Guide to Archives and Libraries." *Itinerario [The Netherlands]* 18, Number 2 (1994): 143–147.

Moreno Yáñez, Segundo E., editor and contributor. *Pichincha: monografía histórica de la región nuclear ecuatoriana.* Quito: Consejo Provincial de Pichincha, 1981.

Paz y Miño, Luis Telmo. *Cartografía quiteña: apuntaciones para una geografía urbana de Quito.* Mexico City: Instituto Panamericano de Geografía e Historia, 1960.

Skipper, Dora L. "Restoring Quito's Treasure." *Américas [Organization of American States]* 20, Number 2 (February 1968): 8–15.

Stevenson, R. "Music in Quito: Four Centuries." *Hispanic American Historical Review* 43 (1963): 247–267.

French Guiana
Cayenne

Abonnenc, Emile, et al. *Bibliographie de la Guyane française: ouvrages et articles de langue française concernant la Guyane et les territoires avoisinants.* Paris: Larose, 1957.

Alexandre, Rodolphe. *La Guyane sous Vichy.* Paris: Éditions Caribéennes, 1988.

———. *La révolte des tirailleurs sénégalais à Cayenne: 24–25 février 1946.* Paris: L'Harmattan, 1995.

Bonniol, Jean-Luc, et al. *Immigration et urbanisation en Guyane.* Aix-en-Provence: Institut d'Aménagement Régional, 1985.

Bougard-Cordier, Claudine, et al. *Catalogue des documents concernant la Guyane française conservés à la Bibliothèque nationale, Département des manuscrits.* No place nor publisher, 1952.

———. *Inventaire analytique de la correspondance générale de la Guyane française déposée aux Archives nationales, 1651–1882.* No place nor publisher, 1952–1956, three volumes.

Bourgarel, Sophie. *Santé et géographie en Guyane.* Paris: L'Harmattan, 1994.

Bouyer, Frédéric. *La Guyane française: notes et souvenirs d'un voyage exécuté en 1862–1863.* Cayenne: Delabergerie, 1981 reprint of 1867 original published by Hachette in Paris.

Bruleaux, Anne-Marie, et al., editors. *Deux siècles d'esclavage en Guyane française, 1652–1848.* Cayenne and Paris: Centre Guyanais d'Etudes et de Recherches and L'Harmattan, 1986.

Calmont, André. *La croissance urbaine dans les pays tropicaux: Cayenne, la ville et sa région.* Talence: Centre d'Etudes de Géographie Tropicale, 1978.

Cardoso, Ciro-Flammarion-Santana. *Esclavage coloniale et économie: contribution à l'étude des sociétés esclavagistes d'Amérique à partir du cas de la Guyane française au 18e siècle.* Fort-de-France: Centre d'Etudes Régionales Antilles-Guyane, *Cahier* Number 391, July 1982.

Castor, Elie, and Georges. Othily. *La Guyane: les grands problèmes, les solutions possibles.* Paris: Éditions Caribéennes, 1984.

Cerisier, Charles. *Impressions coloniales, 1868–1892: étude comparative de colonisation.* Paris: Berger Levrault, 1983.

Chaia, Jean. "Science, médecine et état sanitaire en Guyane au XVIIIe siècle." *Mondes et cultures [France]* 39 (1979): 129–143.

Charrière, Henri. *Papillon.* New York: Morrow, 1970 translation of French original published in Paris by Robert Laffont in 1969.

Chérubini, Bernard. *Cayenne, ville créole et polyethnique: essai d'anthropologie urbaine.* Talence: Centre National de Documentation des Départements d'Outre-mer, 1988.

Devèze, Michel. *Cayenne: déportés et bagnards.* Paris: Juillard, 1965.

Donet-Vincent, Danielle. *La fin du bagne.* Ouest-France, 1992.

Drekonja-Kornat, G. "On the Edge of Civilization: Paris in the Jungle." *Caribbean Review* 13 (spring 1984): 26–32.

Fauquenoy, Marguerite. *Bibliographie sur les Guyanes et les territoires avoisinants.* Paris: ORSTOM, 1966.

Henry, Arthur. *La Guyane française: son histoire, 1604–1946.* Cayenne: Le Mayouri, 1981 reprint of 1950 original published by Paul Laporte.

Hurault, Jean-Marcel. *Les noirs réfugiés: Boni de la Guyane française.* Dakar: Institut Français d'Afrique Noire, 1961.

———. *Français et indiens en Guyane, 1604–1972.* Cayenne: Guyane Presse Diffusion, 1989 reprint of 1972 original published by the Union Générale d'Éditions in Paris.

Krakovitch, Odile. "Les antillais et les bagnes de Cayenne: nouvelle approche de la répression dans les Caraïbes." *Revue historique [France]* 285 (1990): 89–100.

Lasserre, Guy, editor. *L'Atlas de la Guyane.* Paris: Centre National de la Recherche Scientifique, 1979.

Lohier, Michel. *Les grandes étapes de l'histoire de la Guyane française: aperçu chronologique.* Cayenne: Clamecy, 1969.

Loker, Zvi. "Cayenne: Perek Behagirah Ubehityashvut Yehudit Ba'olam Hehadash Beme'ah Ha–17." *Zion [Israel]* 48, Number 1 (1983): 107–116.

Malouet, Pierre-Victor. *Collection de mémoires et correspondances officielles sur l'administration des colonies et notament sur la Guyane française et hollandaise.* Paris: Beaudouin, 1802, five volumes.

Mam-Lam-Fouck, Serge. *Histoire de la société guyanaise: les années cruciales, 1848–1946.* Paris: Éditions Caribéennes, 1987.

———. *Histoire de la Guyane contemporaine, 1940–1982: les mutations économiques, sociales et politiques.* Paris: Éditions Caribéennes, 1992.

———. *Histoire générale de la Guyane française: des débuts de la colonisation à l'aube de l'an 2000, les grands problèmes guyanais, permanence et évolution.* Cayenne: Ibis Rouge, 1996.

Marchand-Thebault, Marie-Louise. "L'esclavage en Guyane française sous l'Ancien Régime." *Revue française d'histoire d'Outre-mer* 47, Number 166 (1960): 5–75.

Mirot, Sylvie. *La population de la Guyane française au XVIIe siècle.* Paris: Ecole des Chartes, 1954.

Tarrade, Jean. "Affranchis et gens de couleur libres à la Guyane à la fin du XVIIIe siècle, d'après les minutes des notaries." *Revue française d'histoire d'Outre-mer* 49, Number 174 (1962): 80–116.

Thesée, Françoise. "Une mémoire inédit de Victor Hugues sur la Guyane." *Revue française d'histoire d'Outre-mer* 57, Number 209 (1970): 469–503.

Peru
General Studies

"Adán, Martín" [pseudonym for Rafael de la Fuente Benavides]. *De lo barroco en el Perú.* Lima: Universidad Nacional Mayor de San Marcos, 1968.

Anna, Timothy E. *The Fall of the Royal Government in Peru.* Lincoln: University of Nebraska Press, 1979.

Arden, Harvey. "The Two Souls of Peru." *National Geographic* 161, Number 3 (March 1982): 284–321.

Assadourian, Carlos Sempat. *La organización económica espacial del sistema colonial.* Lima: Instituto de Estudios Peruanos, 1982.

Bakewell, Peter John. "La maduración del gobierno del Perú en la década de 1560." *Historia Mexicana* 39, Number 1 (1989): 41–70.

Ballesteros Gaibrois, Manuel. *Descubrimiento y conquista del Perú.* Barcelona and Madrid: Salvat, 1963.

Boehm, David Alfred. *Peru in Pictures.* New York: Sterling, 1968 re-edition.

Bonilla, Heraclio, compiler. *Gran Bretaña y el Perú, 1826–1919: informes de los cónsules británicos.* Lima: Instituto de Estudios Peruanos, 1975–1977, four volumes.

Bowser, Frederick. *The African Slave in Colonial Peru.* Stanford, CA: Stanford University Press, 1974.

Browning, D. G., and David J. Robinson. "The Origins and Comparability of Peruvian Population Data: 1776–1815." *Jahrbuch für Geschichte von Staat, Wirtschaft und Gesellschaft Lateinamerikas [Germany]* 14 (1977): 199–222.

Bueno, Cosme. *Geografía del Perú virreinal: siglo XVIII.* Lima: Carlos Daniel Valcárcel, 1951 re-edition.

Camp, Roderic A. "Pioneer Photographer of Peru." *Américas [Organization of American States]* 30, Number 3 (March 1978): 5–10.

Campbell, Leon G. *The Military and Society in Colonial Peru, 1750–1810.* Philadelphia, 1978.

Cieza de León, Pedro. *La crónica del Perú, 1555.* Madrid: Biblioteca de Autores Españoles, 1947 reprint; also reissued in Lima in 1973.

Clemence, Stella R., compiler. *The Harkness Collection in the Library of Congress: Calendar of Spanish Manuscripts Concerning Peru, 1531–1651.* Washington, 1932.

Colección documental de la independencia del Perú. Lima: Comisión Nacional del Sesquicentenario, 1971–1975, twenty-seven volumes.

Contreras, Carlos. *Sobre los orígenes de la explosión demográfica en el Perú, 1876–1940.* Lima: Instituto de Estudios Peruanos, 1994.

Cook, Noble David. *Demographic Collapse: Indian Peru, 1520–1620.* Cambridge, 1981.

Descola, Jean. *Daily Life in Colonial Peru, 1710–1820.* New York: Macmillan, 1969 translation by Michael Heron of French original.

Deustúa, Carlos. *Las intendencias en el Perú (1790–1796).* Seville: Consejo Superior de Investigaciones Científicas, 1965.

Diener, Pablo. *Juan Mauricio Rugendas: el Perú romántico del siglo XIX.* Lima: Carlos Milla Batre, 1975.

El siglo XX en el Perú a través de "El Comercio." Lima: Empresa Editora "El Comercio," 1991, several volumes.

Fisher, John R. *Government and Society in Colonial Peru: The Intendant System, 1784–1814.* London, 1970.

———. *Silver Mines and Silver Miners in Colonial Peru, 1776–1824.* Liverpool: Centre for Latin American Studies at the University of Liverpool, 1977.

Gamarra y Hernández, Enrique. *Nobiliario de las ciudades del Perú.* Lima, 1938.

García Barrón, Carlos. "El periodismo peruano del siglo XIX." *Cuadernos Hispanoamericanos [Spain]* 417 (1985): 197–204.

Glave, Luis Miguel. *Trajinantes: caminos indígenas en la sociedad colonial, siglo XVI-XVII.* Lima, 1989.

Hampe Martínez, Teodoro. "En torno al levantamiento pizarrista: la intervención del oidor Lisón de Tejada." *Revista de Indias [Spain]* 44, Number 174 (1984): 385–414.

———. "The Diffusion of Books and Ideas in Colonial Peru: A Study of Private Libraries in the Sixteenth and Seventeenth Centuries." *Hispanic American Historical Review* 73, Number 2 (1993): 211–233.

Helmer, Marie. "Documents pour l'histoire économique de l'Amérique du Sud: commerce et industrie au Pérou à la fin du XVIII.me siècle." *Revista de Indias [Spain]* 10, Number 41 (1950): 519–526.

Hoover, John P. "Sucre in Peru, 1823." *Américas [Organization of American States]* 25, Number 10 (October 1973): 16–23.

Huayhuaca, José Carlos. *Martín Chambi, fotógrafo.* Lima: Centro de Investigación en Comunicación Social de la Universidad de Lima, 1993.

Jiménez de la Espada, Marcos, compiler and editor. *Relaciones geográficas de Indias: Perú.* Madrid: Atlas, 1965 reprint of 1881–1897 originals published by M. G. Hernández for the Ministerio de Fomento, four volumes.

Kapsoli, Wilfrdo. *Sublevaciones de esclavos en el Perú del siglo XVIII.* Lima: Universidad Ricardo Palma, 1975.

Kent, Robert B. "Geographical Dimensions of the Shining Path Insurgency in Peru." *Geographical Review* 83, Number 4 (1993): 441–454.

Kosok, Paul. *Life, Land, and Water in Ancient Peru.* New York: Long Island University Press, 1965.

Kubler, George A. *The Indian Caste of Peru, 1795–1940.* Washington, 1952.

Lastres, Juan. *Historia de la medicina peruana.* Lima: Universidad Nacional Mayor de San Marcos, 1951, two volumes.

Latasa Vasallo, Pilar. *Administración virreinal en el Perú: gobierno del virrey de Montesclaros (1607–1615).* Madrid: Centro de Estudios Ramón Areces, 1997.

Lavalle, José Antonio de, and Werner Lang. *Platería virreinal.* Lima: Banco de Crédito, 1976.

Lazo, Carlos, and Javier Tord. "El movimiento social en el Perú virreinal." *Revista Histórica [Peru]* 1, Number 1 (July 1977): 61–92.

Levilier, Roberto, compiler. *Gobernantes del Perú: cartas y papeles del siglo XVI.* Madrid, 1921–1926, fourteen volumes.

Lissón Chávez, Emilio. *La iglesia de España en el Perú: colección de documentos del Archivo General de Indias.* Seville, 1943–1946, four volumes.

Lockhart, James M. *Spanish Peru, 1532–1560: A Colonial Society.* Madison: University of Wisconsin Press, 1968.

———. *The Men of Cajamarca: A Social and Biographical Study of the First Conquerors of Peru.* Austin: University of Texas Press, 1972.

Lohmann Villena, Guillermo. *El Conde de Lemos, virrey del Perú.* Seville: Escuela de Estudios Hispano-americanos, 1946.

———. *El corregidor de indios en el Perú bajo los Austrias.* Madrid: Cultura Hispánica, 1957.

———. "Juan de Matienzo, autor del 'Gobierno del Perú': su personalidad y su obra." *Anuario de Estudios Americanos [Spain]* 22 (1965): 767 et seq.

Lumbreras, Luis. *De los pueblos, las culturas y las artes del antiguo Perú.* Lima: Moncloa, 1969.

Macera, Pablo. *Noticias sobre la enseñanza elemental en el Perú durante el siglo XVIII.* Lima: Universidad Nacional Mayor de San Marcos, 1967.

Málaga Medina, Alejandro. "Las reducciones en el Perú (1532–1600)." *Historia y Cultura: Revista del Museo Nacional de Historia [Peru]* 8 (1974): 141–172.

Malamud Rikles, Carlos Daniel. *Cádiz y Saint Malo en el comercio colonial peruano (1698–1725).* Cadiz, 1986.

Marco Dorta, Enrique. *La arquitectura barroca en el Perú.* Madrid: Instituto "Diego Velázquez," Consejo Superior de Investigaciones Científicas, 1957.

Martín, Luis. *Daughters of the Conquistadores: Women of the Viceroyalty of Peru.* Dallas, 1989.

Matienzo, Juan de. *Gobierno del Perú.* Paris: Pierre André for the Institut Français d'Etudes Andines (Volume 11), 1967 re-edition by Guillermo Lohmann Villena of the 1567 original.

McCarry, John. "Peru Begins Again." *National Geographic* 189, Number 5 (May 1996): 2–35.

Mejías Alvarez, María Jesús. "Muerte regia en cuatro ciudades peruanas del barroco." *Anuario de Estudios Americanos [Spain]* 49 (1992): 189–205.

Mendiburu, Manuel de. *Diccionario histórico-biográfico del Perú.* Lima: Enrique Palacios, 1931–1935, eleven volumes.

Moore, John Preston. *The Cabildo in Peru under the Bourbons.* Durham, NC: Duke University Press, 1966.

Moral Martín, Victoriano del. "Ultimos años del ejército español en el Perú." *Historia y Vida [Spain]* 22, Number 261 (1989): 63–73.

Moreno Cebrián, Alfredo. *El corregidor de indios y la economía peruana en el siglo XVIII: los repartos forzosos de mercancías.* Madrid, 1977.

Moreyra y Paz Soldán, Manuel. *La moneda colonial en el Perú.* Lima: Banco Central de Reserva del Perú, 1980.

Múzquiz de Miguel, José Luis. *El Conde de Chinchón, virrey del Perú.* Seville: Escuela de Estudios Hispano-americanos, 1945.

Nieto, Armando. *Contribución a la historia del fidelismo en el Perú (1808–1810).* Lima: Instituto "Riva Agüero," 1960.

Núñez, Estuardo y Petersen, Georg. *El Perú en la obra de Alejandro de Humboldt.* Lima: Studium, 1971.

Palacio Atard, Vicente. *Areche y Guirior: observaciones sobre el fracaso de una visita al Perú.* Seville: Escuela de Estudios Hispano-americanos, 1946.

Palmer, David Scott. *Peru: The Authoritarian Tradition.* New York: Praeger, 1980.

Payne, James L. *Labor and Politics in Peru: The System of Political Bargaining.* New Haven: Yale University Press, 1965.

Pearce, Adrian J. "The Peruvian Population Census of 1725–1740." *Latin American Research Review* 36, Number 3 (2001): 69–104.

Rodríguez Casado, Vicente, and José Antonio Calderón Quijano, editors. *Memoria de gobierno de José Fernando de Abascal y Sousa, virrey del Perú.* Seville: Escuela de Estudios Hispano-americanos, 1944, two volumes.

Rodríguez Casado, Vicente, and Guillermo Lohmann Villena, editors. *Memoria de gobierno de Joaquín de la Pezuela, virrey del Perú.* Seville: Escuela de Estudios Hispano-americanos, 1946.

Rodríguez Casado, Vicente, and Florentino Pérez Embid, editors. *Memoria de gobierno de Manuel Amat y Junient, virrey del Perú.* Seville: Escuela de Estudios Hispano-americanos, 1946.

———. *Construcciones militares del virrey Amat.* Seville: Escuela de Estudios Hispano-americanos, 1949.

Rodríguez Pastor, Humberto. *Hijos del celeste imperio en el Perú, 1850–1900.* Lima: Instituto de Apoyo Agrario, 1989.

Roel, Virgilio. *Historia social y económica de la colonia.* Lima, 1970.

Romero, Emilio. *Historia económica del Perú.* Buenos Aires, 1949.

Rostworowski, María. *Etnía y sociedad.* Lima: Instituto de Estudios Peruanos, 1977.

Rowe, John Howland. "Urban Settlements in Ancient Peru." *Nawpa Pacha* 1 (1963): 1–27.

Saenz-Rico Urbina, Alfredo. *El virrey Amat: precisiones sobre la vida y la obra de don Manuel de Amat y de Junyent.* Barcelona, 1967, two volumes.

Salinas y Córdoba, Buenaventura de. *Memorial de las historias del Nuevo Mundo.* Lima: Universidad Nacional Mayor de San Marcos, 1957 reprint of 1630 original.

Sánchez-Albornoz, Nicolás. "Migración urbana y trabajo: los indios de Arequipa, 1571–1645." *De historia e historiadores: homenaje a José Luis Romero.* Mexico City, 1982.

Silva Santiesteban, Fernando. *Los obrajes en el virreinato del Perú.* Lima: Museo Nacional de Historia, 1964.

Spalding, Karen. "Social Climbers: Changing Patterns of Mobility among the Indians of Colonial Peru." *Hispanic American Historical Review* 50, Number 4 (1970): 645–664.

———. *De indio a campesino: cambios en la estructura social del Perú colonial.* Lima, 1974.

Steele, Arthur Robert. *Flowers for the King: The Expedition of Ruiz and Pavon and the Flora of Peru.* Durham, NC: Duke University Press, 1964.

Stein, Steve J. *Populism in Peru: The Emergence of the Masses and the Politics of Social Control.* Madison: University of Wisconsin Press, 1980.

Stepan, Alfred. *The State and Society: Peru in Comparative Perspective.* Princeton University Press, 1978.

Stern, Steve J. *Indian Peoples and the Challenge of Spanish Conquest.* Madison: University of Wisconsin Press, 1982.

Stern, Steve J., editor. *Shining and Other Paths: War and Society in Peru, 1980–1995.* Durham, NC: Duke University Press, 1998.

Tord Nicolini, Javier. "El corregidor de indios del Perú: comercio y tributos." *Historia y Cultura: Revista del Museo Nacional de Historia [Peru]* 8 (1974): 173–214.

———. *Sociedad colonial, fiscalidad e independencia.* Lima, 1974.

Tord Nicolini, Javier, and Carlos Lazo. *Hacienda, comercio, fiscalidad y luchas sociales: Perú colonial.* Lima, 1981.

Vargas Ugarte, Rubén. *Títulos nobiliarios en el Perú.* Lima, 1965.

Vargas Ugarte, Rubén, compiler and editor. *Documentos inéditos sobre la campaña de independencia del Perú (1810–1824)*. Lima: Carlos Milla Batres, 1971.

Varón Gabal, Rafael. *Francisco Pizarro and His Brothers: The Illusion of Power in Sixteenth-Century Peru*. Norman: University of Oklahoma Press, 1997 translation by Javier Flores Espinoza.

Velarde, Héctor. *Arquitectura peruana*. Mexico City: Fondo de Cultura Económica, 1946.

Villarn, Manuel V. *Apuntes sobre la realidad social de los indígenas del Perú ante las leyes de Indias*. Lima, 1964.

Wachtel, Nathan. *La vision des vaincus: les indiens du Pérou devant la conquête espagnole, 1530–1570*. Paris, 1971.

Weaver, Kenneth F. "The Five Worlds of Peru." *National Geographic* 125, Number 2 (February 1964): 212–267.

Wethey, Harold E. *Colonial Architecture and Sculpture in Peru*. Cambridge, MA: Harvard University Press, 1949.

Wiedner, Donald L. "Forced Labor in Colonial Peru." *The Americas: A Quarterly Review of Inter-American Cultural History [Academy of American Franciscan History]* 16 (1959–1960): 357–383.

Zavala, Silvio. *El servicio personal de los indios en el Perú*. Mexico City, 1979, three volumes.

Zéndegui, Guillermo de, compiler. "Eternal Peru." *Américas [Organization of American States]* 23, Number 5 (May 1971): supplementary pp. 1–24.

———. "Engraving in Latin America: Peru." *Américas [Organization of American States]* 28, Number 9 (September 1976): supplementary pp. 1–12.

Cuzco

Native Era (1000–1534)

Agurto, Santiago. *Cuzco: la traza urbana de la ciudad inca*. Lima: "Proyecto PER 39" of UNESCO, 1980.

Iwasaki Cauti, Fernando. "Las panacas del Cuzco y la pintura incaica." *Revista de Indias [Spain]* 46, Number 177 (1986): 59–74.

Rowe, John Howland. "An Introduction to the Archaeology of Cuzco." *Papers of the Peabody Museum [Cambridge, MA]* 27, Number 2 (1944).

———. "What Kind of Settlement Was Inca Cuzco?" *Nawpa Pacha* 7 (1967): 59–77.

———. "Una relación de los adoratorios del antiguo Cuzco." *Revista Histórica [Peru]* 5, Number 2 (1981): 209–261.

———. "La constitución inca del Cuzco." *Revista Histórica [Peru]* 9, Number 1 (1985): 35–73.

Zuidema, Reiner Tom. *The Ceque System of Cuzco*. Leiden, 1964.

———. "The Organization of Sacrifice in the City of Cuzco." *Journal of Latin American Lore* 18, Numbers 1–2 (1992): 63–77.

Early Colonial Era (1534–1780)

"Acta del juramento de amistad entre Pizarro y Almagro, hecho en Cuzco el 12 de junio de 1535." *Revista de Historia Militar [Spain]* 31, Number 63 (1987): 195–202.

Burns, Kathryn. "Nuns, Kurakas, and Credit: The Spiritual Economy of Seventeenth-Century Cuzco." *Colonial Latin American Review* 6, Number 2 (1997): 185–203.

———. "Gender and the Politics of Mestizaje: The Convent of Santa Clara in Cuzco, Peru." *Hispanic American Historical Review* 78, Number 1 (February 1998): 5–44.

———. *Colonial Habits: Convents and the Spiritual Economy of Cuzco, Peru*. Durham, NC: Duke University Press, 1999.

Cahill, David P. "Popular Religion and Appropriation: The Example of Corpus Christi in Eighteenth-Century Cuzco." *Latin American Research Review* 31, Number 2 (1996): 67–110.

Castro, Ignacio de. *Relación del Cuzco*. Lima: Universidad Nacional Mayor de San Marcos, 1978 re-edition of 1795 original.

Colin, Michèle. *Le Cuzco à la fin du XVIIe et au début du XVIIIe siècle*. Paris, 1966.

Cossío del Pomar, Felipe. *Peruvian Colonial Art: The Cuzco School of Painting*. New York: Wiltenborn and Company, 1964 translation by Genaro Abaiza.

Crider, John Alan. "Indians and Artistic Vocation in Colonial Cuzco, 1650–1715." *UCLA Historical Journal* 11 (1991): 51–68.

Cuadros, Manuel. *Historia y arquitectura de los templos de Cuzco*. Lima: Rímac, 1946.

———. "The Virgin and Pachamama: Images of Adaptation and Resistance." *Secolas Annals* 23 (1992): 125–137.

———. "Artist and Patron in Colonial Cuzco: Workshops, Contracts, and a Petition for Independence." *Colonial Latin American Historical Review* 4, Number 1 (1995): 25–53.

———. *The Virgin of the Andes: Art and Ritual in Colonial Cuzco*. Miami Beach, FL: Grassfield, 1995.

Dean, Carolyn. *Inka Bodies and the Body of Christ: Corpus Christi in Colonial Cuzco, Peru*. Durham, NC: Duke University Press, 1999.

Esteras Martín, Cristina. "Aportaciones a la historia de la platería cuzqueña en la segunda mitad del siglo XVII." *Anuario de Estudios Americanos [Spain]* 37 (1980): 709–740.

Fraser, Valerie. "Architecture and Ambition: The Case of the Jesuits in the Viceroyalty of Peru." *History Workshop Journal [UK]* 34 (1992): 17–32.

Gibbs, Donald L. "The Economic Activities of Nuns, Friars, and Their Convents in Mid-Colonial Cuzco." *The Americas: A Quarterly Review of Inter-American Cultural History [Academy of American Franciscan History]* 45, Number 3 (1989): 343–362.

Gómez-Sicre, José. "The Cuzco School." *Américas [Organization of American States]* 17, Number 7 (July 1965): 4–11.

González Pujana, Laura. "Estrategias de actuación sobre las comunidades indígenas en el cabildo de Cuzco." *Revista Complutense de Historia de América [Spain]* 23 (1997): 75–96.

Gutiérrez, Ramón. "Notas sobre organización artesanal en el Cusco durante la colonia." *Revista Histórica [Peru]* 3, Number 1 (1979): 1–15.

Lavallé, Bernard. *Le marquis et le marchand: les luttes de pouvoir au Cuzco, 1700–1730.* Paris: Centre Nationale du Recherche Scientifique, 1987.

Martín Rubio, Carmen. "La caja de censos de indios en Cuzco." *Revista de Indias [Spain]* 39, Numbers 155–158 (1979): 187–208.

———. "Indios y mestizos en Cuzco según dos fuentes inéditas del siglo XVII." *Revista de Indias [Spain]* 43, Number 171 (1983): 59–75.

Pinto Vallejos, Sonia. "Aportes extraordinarios a la Real Hacienda española en el virreino peruano: la región de Cuzco, 1575–1600." *Jahrbuch für Geschichte von Staat, Wirtschaft und Gesellschaft Lateinamerikas [Germany]* 17 (1980): 69–95.

Rowe, John Howland. "El plano más antiguo del Cuzco: dos parroquias de la ciudad vistas en 1643." *Revista Histórica [Peru]* 14, Number 2 (1990): 367–377.

Urteaga, Horacio H., and Carlos A. Romero. compilers. *Fundación española del Cuzco y ordenanzas para su gobierno.* Lima, 1926.

———. "Relación del sitio de Cusco, 1535–1539." *Colección de libros y documentos referentes a la historia del Perú,* Second Series, Volume 10, 1934.

Wightman, Ann M. *Indigenous Migration and Social Change: The Forasteros of Cuzco, 1570–1720.* Durham, NC: Duke University Press, 1990.

Late Colonial Era (1780–1824)

Burns, Kathryn. "Amor y rebelión en 1782: el caso de Mariano Tupác Amaru y María Mejía." *Revista Histórica [Peru]* 16, Number 2 (1992): 131–176.

Cahill, David P. "Curas and Social Conflict in the Doctrinas of Cuzco, 1780–1814." *Journal of Latin American Studies [UK]* 16, Number 2 (1984): 241–276.

———. "Repartos ilícitos y familias principales en el sur andino: 1780–1824." *Revista de Indias [Spain]* 48, Numbers 182–183 (1988): 449–473.

Campbell, Leon G. "Church and State in Colonial Peru: The Bishop of Cuzco and the Tupác Amaru Rebellion of 1780." *Journal of Church and State* 22, Number 2 (1980): 251–270.

———. "Social Structure of the Tupác Amaru Army in Cuzco, 1780–1781." *Hispanic American Historical Review* 61, Number 4 (November 1981): 675–693 and 715–720.

Mörner, Magnus. *Perfil de la sociedad rural del Cuzco a fines de la colonia.* Lima, 1978.

Peralta Ruiz, Victor. "Elecciones, constitucionalismo y revolución en el Cusco." *Revista de Indias [Spain]* 56, Number 206 (1996): 99–131.

Szeminski, Jan. "Del significado de algunos términos usados en los documentos de la revolución tupamarista." *Allpanchis [Peru]* 14, Number 16 (1980): 89–130.

Walker, Charles F. *Smoldering Ashes: Cuzco and the Creation of Republican Peru, 1780–1840.* Durham, NC: Duke University Press, 1999.

Modern Era and General Works (1900–Present)

Azevedo, Paulo O. D. de. *Cusco, ciudad histórica: continuidad y cambio.* Lima: PEISA, 1982.

Brisseau-Loaiza, Jeanine. "Le rôle du camion dans les relations ville-campagne dans la région du Cuzco." *Les cahiers d'Outre-Mer [France]* 25, Number 97 (January–March 1972): 27–56.

Kubler, George. *Cuzco, museos y monumentos: reconstrucción de la ciudad y restauración de sus monumentos.* Paris: UNESCO, 1953.

Porras Barrenechea, Raúl, compiler. *Antología del Cuzco.* Lima, 1961.

Randall, Robert. "Peru's Pilgrimage to the Sky." *National Geographic* 162, Number 1 (July 1982): 60–69.

Reinhard, Johan. "Sacred Peaks of the Andes." *National Geographic* 181, Number 3 (March 1992): 84–111.

Rénique, José Luis. *Los sueños de sierra: Cusco en el siglo XX.* Lima: Centro Peruano de Estudios Sociales, 1991.

Tamayo Herrera, José, and Luis E. Valcárcel. *Historia del indigenismo cuzqueño, siglos XVI-XX.* Lima: Instituto Nacional de Cultura, 1980.

Lima

Early Colonial Era (1535–1745)

Barriga Calle, Irma. "Sobre el discurso jesuíta en torno a la muerte presente en la Lima del siglo XVII." *Revista Histórica [Peru]* 19, Number 2 (1995): 165–195.

Cardona, Francisco Luis. "La Púrpura de la Rosa, primera opera representada en América." *Historia y Vida [Spain]* 24, Number 278 (1991): 22–27.

Carvajal y Robles, Rodrigo. *Fiestas de Lima.* Seville: Escuela de Estudios Hispano-americanos, 1950.

Castañeda Delgado, Paulino, and Pilar Hernández Aparicio. "La visita de Ruiz de Prado al tribunal del Santo Oficio de Lima." *Anuario de Estudios Americanos [Spain]* 41 (1984): 1–53.

Castelli G., Amalia. "La primera imagen del Hospital Real de San Andrés a través de la visita de 1563." *Historia y Cultura: Revista del Museo Nacional de Historia [Peru]* 13–14 (1981): 207–216.

Charney, Paul J. "El indio urbano: un análisis económico y social de la población india de Lima en 1613." *Revista Histórica [Peru]* 12, Number 1 (1988): 5–33.

———. "The Implications of Godparental Ties between Indians and Spaniards in Early Colonial Lima." *The Americas: A Quarterly Review of Inter-American Cultural History [Academy of American Franciscan History]* 47, Number 3 (1991): 295–313.

———. "Negotiating Roots: Indian Migrants in the Lima Valley during the Colonial Period." *Colonial Latin American Historical Review* 5, Number 1 (1996): 1–20.

Dargent Chamot, Eduardo. "La primera ceca de Lima, 1568–1692." *Revista de Indias [Spain]* 48, Numbers 182–183 (1988): 161–186.

Durán Montero, María Antonia. "Lima en 1613: aspectos urbanos." *Anuario de Estudios Americanos [Spain]* 49 (1992): 171–188.

García Morales, Alfonso. "Las fiestas de Lima (1632) de Rodrigo de Carvajal y Robles." *Anuario de Estudios Americanos [Spain]* 44 (1987): 141–171.

González del Riego E., Delfina. "Fragmentos de la vida cotidiana a través de los procesos de divorcio: la sociedad colonial limeña en el siglo XVI." *Revista Histórica [Peru]* 19, Number 2 (1995): 197–217.

González Sánchez, Carlos Alberto. "Consideraciones sobre el comercio de libros en Lima a principios del siglo XVII." *Anuario de Estudios Americanos [Spain]* 54, Number 2 (1997): 665–692.

Hampe Martínez, Teodoro. "Sobre encomenderos y repartimientos en la diócesis de Lima a principios del siglo XVII." *Jahrbuch für Geschichte von Staat, Wirtschaft und Gesellschaft Lateinamerikas [Germany]* 23 (1986): 121–143.

———. "Los testigos de Santa Rosa: una aproximación social a la identidad criolla en el Perú colonial." *Revista Complutense de Historia de América [Spain]* 23 (1997): 113–136.

Harth-Terre, Emilio. "Historia de la casa urbana virreinal en Lima." *Revista del Archivo Nacional del Perú* 26 (1962).

———. *Negros e indios.* Lima: Juan Mejía Baca, 1973.

Heredia Moreno, María del Carmen. "Las ordenanzas de los plateros limeños del año 1633." *Archivo Español de Arte [Spain]* 64, Number 256 (1991): 489–501.

Iwasaki Cauti, Fernando. "Ambulantes y comercio colonial: iniciativas mercantiles en el virreinato peruano." *Jahrbuch für Geschichte von Staat, Wirtschaft und Gesellschaft Lateinamerikas [Germany]* 24 (1987): 179–211.

———. "Toros y sociedad en Lima colonial." *Anuario de Estudios Americanos [Spain]* 49 (1992): 311–333.

———. "Mujeres al borde de la perfección: Rosa de Santa María y las alumbradas de Lima." *Hispanic American Historical Review* 73, Number 4 (1993): 581–613.

———. "Fray Martín de Porras: santo, ensalmador y sacamuelas." *Colonial Latin American Historical Review* 3, Numbers 1–2 (1994): 159–184.

———. "Vidas de santos y santas vidas: hagiografías reales e imaginarias en Lima colonial." *Anuario de Estudios Americanos [Spain]* 51, Number 1 (1994): 47–64.

Lee, Bertram T., and Juan Bromley, editors. *Libros de cabildo de Lima, 1544–1605.* Lima: Impresores Torre Aguirre for the Concejo Provincial, 1935–1946, thirteen volumes.

Lohmann Villena, Guillermo. *El arte dramático en Lima durante el virreinato.* Seville: Escuela de Estudios Hispanoamericanos, 1945.

———. *Las defensas militares de Lima y Callao.* Seville: Escuela de Estudios Hispano-americanos, 1964.

———. *Las ordenanzas municipales de Lima, 1533–1635.* Madrid, 1973.

———. *Los ministros de la Audiencia de Lima, 1700–1821.* Seville: Escuela de Estudios Hispano-americanos, 1974.

Martínez Vidal, Alvar. *El nuevo sol de la medicina en la Ciudad de los Reyes: Federico Bottoni y la evidencia de la circulación de la sangre, Lima, 1723.* Zaragoza, Spain: Comisión Aragonesa "Quinto Centenario," 1990.

Medina, José Toribio. *Historia del tribunal de la Inquisición de Lima.* Santiago de Chile: Fondo Histórico y Bibliográfico, 1956.

———. *La imprenta en Lima, 1584–1824.* Santiago de Chile, 1966 re-edition.

Millar Corbacho, René. "Las confiscaciones de la Inquisición de Lima a los comerciantes de orígen judíoportugués de 'la gran complicidad' de 1635." *Revista de Indias [Spain]* 43, Number 171 (1983): 27–58.

Mugaburu, José, and Francisco Mugaburu. *Diario de Lima, 1640–1694.* Lima: Volumes 1 and 7 of the "Colección de libros y documentos referentes a la historia del Perú," 1927 and 1937.

Paniagua Pérez, Jesús. "Cofradías limeñas: San Eloy y la Misericordia, 1597–1733." *Anuario de Estudios Americanos [Spain]* 52, Number 1 (1995): 13–35.

Pérez, Louis A., Jr. "Academic Culture in Colonial Peru: The Founding and the Secularization of the University of Lima, 1551–1571." *Revista/Review Interamericana [Puerto Rico]* 10, Number 1 (1980): 4–18.

Quiroz, Francisco. *Gremios, razas y libertad de industria: Lima colonial.* Lima: Universidad Nacional Mayor de San Marcos, 1995.

Rodríguez Vicente, María Encarnación. *El tribunal del consulado de Lima en la primera mitad del siglo XVII.* Madrid, 1968.

Sala Catalá, José. "Ciencia y técnica en la metropolización de Lima." *Quipú [Mexico]* 5, Number 3 (1988): 389–412.

San Cristóbal, Antonio. "La portada principal de la catedral de Lima." *Historia y Cultura: Revista del Museo Nacional de Historia [Peru]* 16 (1983): 7–49.

———. "Los puentes de Lima de 1607 y 1608." *Historia y Cultura: Revista del Museo Nacional de Historia [Peru]* 17 (1984): 31–50.

———. "Fray Cristóbal Caballero y la portada de la Merced de Lima." *Anuario de Estudios Americanos [Spain]* 48 (1991): 151–203.

———. "Reconversión de la iglesia del convento de Santo Domingo, Lima, durante el siglo XVII." *Anuario de Estudios Americanos [Spain]* 49 (1992): 233–270.

Sánchez-Albornóz, Nicolás. "La mita de Lima: magnitud y procedencia." *Revista Histórica [Peru]* 12, Number 2 (1988): 193–210.

Schofield, Sophy E., compiler. *Indices de los libros de cabildo de Lima, 1535–1601.* Lima: Impresores Torre Aguirre for the Concejo Provincial, 1946.

Stevenson, Robert. "The First New-World Opera." *Américas [Organization of American States]* 16, Number 1 (January 1964): 33–35.

Tardieu, Jean-Pierre. "Le marronage à Lima, 1535–1650: atermoiements et répression." *Revue historique [France]* 278, Number 2 (1987): 293–319.

———. "La pathologie rédhibitoire de l'esclavage en milieu urbain: Lima, XVIIeme siècle." *Jahrbuch für Geschichte von Staat, Wirtschaft und Gesellschaft Lateinamerikas [Germany]* 26 (1989): 19–35.

———. "L'action pastorale des jésuites auprès de la population noire de Lima, XVIe-XVIIe siècles." *Archivum Historicum Societatis Iesu [Italy]* 58, Number 116 (1989): 315–327.

Torres Saldamando, Enrique, et al., editors. *Libro primero de los cabildos de Lima, 1535–1539.* Paris: Imprimerie Paul Dupont, 1888–1900, three volumes.

Van Deusen, Nancy E. "Defining the Sacred and the Worldly: Beatas and Recogidas in Late-Seventeenth-Century Lima." *Colonial Latin American Historical Review* 6, Number 4 (1997): 441–477.

———. "Determining the Boundaries of Virtue: The Discourse of Recogimiento among Women in Seventeenth-Century Lima." *Journal of Family History* 22, Number 4 (1997): 373–389.

Vergara Ormeño, Teresa. "Migración y trabajo femenino a principios del siglo XVII: el caso de las indias en Lima." *Revista Histórica [Peru]* 21, Number 1 (1997): 135–157.

Williams, Jerry M. *Censorship and Art in Pre-Enlightenment Lima: Pedro de Peralta Barnuevo's "Diálogo de los muertos: la causa académica."* Potomac, MD: Scripta Humanistica, 1994.

———. "Academic and Literary Culture in Eighteenth-Century Peru." *Colonial Latin American Historical Review* 4, Number 1 (1995): 129–152.

Early Maps and Depictions of Lima, 1611–1790

Hand-drawn diagram sent to the Spanish court by Juan de Velveder, depicting the stone bridge that had replaced an earlier brick span across the Rímac River, 18 October 1611—original held by the Archive of Indies at Seville, old Torres Lanzas call number: Mapas y Planos del Perú y Chile, 6

Hand-drawn diagram of the city's central core, accompanying Cristóbal de Espinosa's proposal for improving its defenses, 12 May 1626—original held by the Archive of Indies at Seville, old Torres Lanzas call number: Mapas y Planos del Perú y Chile, 7 [archival provenance: Audiencia de Lima, Legajo 465]

Hand-drawn map of Jean-Raymond Coninck's proposed defensive perimeter, ca. 1682—original held by the Archive of Indies at Seville, old Torres Lanzas call number: Mapas y Planos del Perú y Chile, 11 [archival provenance: Audiencia de Lima, Legajo 299]; another version from 1683 also exists, attributed to the military officer Luis Venegas Osorio

Panoramic view of the city as seen from atop San Cristóbal Hill, ca. 1685, drawn by the Mercedarian friar Pedro Nolasco and engraved three years later in Antwerp by Joseph Wantner, for inclusion in Francisco Echave y Assu's book *La Estrella de Lima convertida en Sol*—versions held by the Archive of Indies at Seville, old Torres Lanzas call numbers: Mapas y Planos del Perú y Chile, 13A and 13bis, or Vitrina, 20 [archival provenance: Audiencia de Lima, Legajo 299], plus numerous other sources

Map of Lima, drawn (with a few errors) in 1712 by the French priest and scientist, Louis Feuillée, then published two years later in his two-volume *Journal des observations physiques et mathematiques de les cotes Orientals de l'Amerique Meridional*—several sources

Map of the city as it appeared in October 1713, by the French visitor, Amédée-François Frézier—published three years later in Paris in his book *Relation du voyage de la mer du Sud aux cotes du Chily et du Perou*, often copied

Hand-drawn map of Lima and El Callao, 1740—original held by the Archive of Indies at Seville, old Torres Lanzas call number: Mapas y Planos de Perú y Chile, 22

Panoramic view of the city, ca. 1744, as seen by the visiting Spanish naval officers, Jorge Juan de Santacilia and Antonio de Ulloa—published four years later in Madrid by A. Marín in the two-volume *Relación histórica del viaje a la América Meridional hecho de orden de S.M. para medir algunos grados del meridiano terrestre,* numerous sources

Map of the city in 1755, as compiled nine years later and published in France by the naval officer and geographer,

Jacques-Nicolas Bellin—frequently copied, numerous sources available

City survey ordered in 1787 by Gov. and Insp.-Gen. Jorge Escobedo y Alarcón, but not published until ten years later by Miguel Antonio de Learreta—original held by the National Library in Lima

Three watercolor views of Lima as seen from its bullring, from the Paseo de los Amancaes, and from the Paseo del Agua, ca. 1790, by the Milanese-born Fernando Brambila, one of the artists who accompanied Capt. Alejandro Malaspina's scientific expedition into the Pacific—originals held by the Museo Naval in Madrid, call numbers: *Colección de láminas de la expedición Malaspina,* Volume 2, Numbers 58, 65, and 78

Late Colonial Era (1746–1823)

Burkholder, Mark A. "From Creole to Peninsular: The Transformation of the Audiencia of Lima." *Hispanic American Historical Review* 52 (1972): 395–415.

———. *Politics of a Colonial Career: José Baquíjano and the Audiencia of Lima.* Albuquerque: University of New Mexico Press, 1981.

Cahill, David. "Financing Health Care in the Viceroyalty of Peru: The Hospitals of Lima in the Late Colonial Period." *The Americas: A Quarterly Review of the Inter-American Cultural History [Academy of American Franciscan History]* 52, Number 2 (1995): 123–154.

Clément, Jean-Pierre. *El "Mercurio Peruano," 1790–1795: estudio y textos.* Frankfurt-am-Main and Madrid: Vervuert and Iberoamericana, 1997, two volumes.

Estabridis Cárdenas, Ricardo. "El grabado colonial en Lima." *Anuario de Estudios Americanos [Spain]* 41 (1984): 253–289.

Estenssoro Fuchs, Juan Carlos. "Música y comportamiento festivo de la población negra en Lima colonial." *Cuadernos Hispanoamericanos [Spain]* 451–452 (1988): 161–168.

Fernández Alonso, Serena. "Condiciones de la sanidad pública en la época virreinal: notas sobre el hospital de Bellavista de Lima en el siglo XVIII." *Asclepio [Spain]* 44, Number 1 (1992): 135–163.

Flores Galindo, Alberto. *La ciudad sumergida: aristocracia y plebe en Lima, 1760–1830.* Lima: Horizonte, 1991.

Haitin, Marcel. "Prices, the Lima Market, and the Agricultural Crisis of the Late Eighteenth Century in Peru." *Jahrbuch für Geschichte von Staat, Wirtschaft und Gesellschaft Lateinamerikas [Germany]* 22 (1985): 167–198.

Laserna Gaitán, Antonio Ignacio. "El último intento de reforma de los monasterios femeninos en el Perú colonial: el auto del arzobispo Parada de 1775." *Anuario de Estudios Americanos [Spain]* 52, Number 2 (1995): 263–287.

Lazo, Carlos, and Javier Tord. *Del negro señorial al negro bandolero: cimarronaje y palenques en Lima, siglo XVIII.* Lima, 1977.

Lohmann Villena, Guillermo. *Los ministros de la Audiencia de Lima, 1700–1821.* Seville: Escuela de Estudios Hispano-americanos, 1974.

Mazzeo, Cristina Ana. "Repercusiones y consecuencias de la aplicación del comercio libre en la elite mercantil limeña a fines del siglo XVIII." *Revista de Indias [Spain]* 55, Number 203 (1995): 101–126.

Molina Martínez, Miguel. *El Real Tribunal de Minería de Lima, 1785–1821.* Seville: Diputación Provincial, 1986.

Moreno Cebrián, Alfredo. "Cuarteles, barrios y calles de Lima a fines del siglo XVIII." *Jahrbuch für Geschichte von Staat, Wirtschaft und Gesellschaft Lateinamerikas [Germany]* 18 (1981): 97–161.

———. "Un arqueo a la hacienda municipal limeña a fines del siglo XVIII." *Revista de Indias [Spain]* 41, Numbers 165–166 (July–December 1981): 499–540.

Pacheco Vélez, César. "La sociedad patriótica de Lima de 1822." *Revista Histórica [Peru]* 2 (1978): 9–48.

Parrón Salas, Carmen. "Religiosidad y finanzas en el Consulado de Lima, 1778–1821." *Hispania Sacra [Spain]* 44, Number 90 (1992): 587–650.

Rabí, Miguel. "Un capítulo inédito: el traslado del Hospital del Espíritu Santo de Lima a Bellavista, 1750." *Asclepio [Spain]* 47, Number 1 (1995): 123–133.

San Cristóbal, Antonio. "Ignacio Martorell y las torres de la catedral de Lima." *Revista Histórica [Peru]* 19, Number 2 (1995): 295–318.

Walker, Charles F. "The Patriotic Society: Discussions and Omissions about Indians in the Peruvian War of Independence." *The Americas: A Quarterly Review of Inter-American Cultural History [Academy of American Franciscan History]* 55, Number 2 (1998): 275–298.

Early Republican Era (1824–1899)

"By Pancho Fierro." *Américas [Organization of American States]* 24, Number 5 (May 1972): 25–29.

García Barrón, Carlos. "El periodismo peruano del siglo XIX." *Cuadernos Hispanoamericanos [Spain]* 417 (1985): 197–204.

Gootenberg, Paul. "Carneros y chuño: Price Levels in Nineteenth-Century Peru." *Hispanic American Historical Review* 70, Number 1 (1990): 1–56.

———. "Los orígenes sociales del proteccionismo y libre comercio en Lima del siglo XIX." *Revista Histórica [Peru]* 14, Number 2 (1990): 235–280.

Hampe Martínez, Teodoro. "Una dinámica de integración social: inmigrantes europeos y norteamericanos en Lima, siglo XIX." *Ibero-Amerikanisches Archiv [Germany]* 17, Number 4 (1991): 343–372.

Miller, Robert R. "New Views of Old Lima." *Américas [Organization of American States]* 30, Number 2 (February 1978): 29–32.

Morse, Richard M. "The Lima of Joaquín Capelo: A Latin-American Archetype." *Journal of Contemporary History* 4, Number 3 (July 1969): 95–110.

Palma, Ricardo. *Cartas a Piérola sobre la ocupación chilena de Lima.* Lima: Carlos Milla Batres, 1979.

Ruiz Zevallos, Augusto. "Dieta popular y conflicto en Lima de principios de siglo." *Revista Histórica [Peru]* 16, Number 2 (1992): 203–220.

Trifilo, S. Samuel. "Lima through British Eyes." *Américas [Organization of American States]* 22, Number 6 (June 1970): 27–34.

Yeager, Gertrude M. "Women and the Intellectual Life of Nineteenth Century Lima." *Inter-American Review of Bibliography* 40, Number 3 (1990): 361–393.

Modern Era (1900–Present)

Austin, Allan G., and Sherman Lewis. *Urban Government for Metropolitan Lima.* New York: Praeger, 1970.

Cameron, Maxwell A. "Political Parties and the Worker-Employer Cleavage: The Impact of the Informal Sector on Voting in Lima, Peru." *Bulletin of Latin American Research [UK]* 10, Number 3 (1991): 293–313.

———. "The Politics of the Urban Informal Sector in Peru: Populism, Class and 'Redistributive Combines.'" *Canadian Journal of Latin American and Caribbean Studies* 16, Number 31 (1991): 79–104.

Collier, David. *Squatters and Oligarchs: Authoritarian Rule and Policy Change in Peru.* Baltimore: Johns Hopkins University Press, 1976.

Cueto, Marcos. "La ciudad y las ratas: la peste bubónica en Lima y en la costa peruana a comienzos del siglo veinte." *Revista Histórica [Peru]* 15, Number 1 (1991): 1–26.

Deler, Jean-Paul. "Croissance accélérée et formes de sous-développement urbain à Lima." *Les cahiers d'Outre-Mer [France]* 23, Number 89 (January–March 1970): 73–94.

———. *Lima, 1940–1970: aspects de la croissance d'une capitale sud-américaine.* Bordeaux-Talence: Institut Français d'Etudes Andines and Centre d'Études de Géographie Tropicale, 1974.

Dietz, Henry A. *Poverty and Problem-Solving under Military Rule: The Urban Poor in Lima, Peru.* Austin: University of Texas Press, 1980.

———. "Political Participation in the Barriadas: A Research Update." *Comparative Political Studies* 22, Number 1 (1989): 122–130.

———. *Urban Poverty, Political Participation, and the State: Lima, 1970–1990.* University of Pittsburgh Press, 1998.

Doughty, Paul. "Perú: . . . y la vida continúa." *América Indígena [Mexico]* 51, Number 4 (1991): 49–79.

Galín, Pedro, et al. *Asalariados y clases populares en Lima.* Lima: Instituto de Estudios Peruanos, 1986.

Glewwe, Paul, and Gillette Hall. "Poverty, Inequality and Living Standards during Unorthodox Adjustment: The Case of Peru, 1985–1990." *Economic Development and Cultural Change* 42, Number 4 (1994): 689–717.

Graham, Carol. "The APRA Government and the Urban Poor: The PAIT Programme in Lima's 'Pueblos Jovenes.'" *Journal of Latin American Studies [UK]* 23, Number 1 (1991): 91–130.

Lloyd, Peter Cutt. *The "Young Towns" of Lima: Aspects of Urbanization in Peru.* New York: Cambridge University Press, 1980.

Lobo, Susan. *A House of My Own: Social Organization in the Squatter Settlements of Lima, Peru.* Tucson: University of Arizona Press, 1982.

Matos Mar, José. "Comas: lo andino en la modernidad urbana." *América Indígena [Mexico]* 51, Numbers 2–3 (1991): 35–74.

———. "El nuevo rostro de la cultura urbana del Perú." *América Indígena [Mexico]* 51, Numbers 2–3 (1991): 11–34.

———. "La experiencia popular en Comas: diez casos." *América Indígena [Mexico]* 51, Numbers 2–3 (1991): 75–105.

———. "Taquileños, quechúas del Lago Titicaca, en Lima." *América Indígena [Mexico]* 51, Numbers 2–3 (1991): 107–166.

Millones, Luis. *Tugurio: la cultura de los marginados.* Lima: Instituto Nacional de Cultura, 1978.

Núñez Rebaza, Lucy, and José A. Lloréns. "La música tradicional andina en Lima metropolitana." *América Indígena [Mexico]* 41, Number 1 (1981): 53–74.

Parker, David S. "White-Collar Lima, 1910–1929: Commercial Employees and the Rise of the Peruvian Middle Class." *Hispanic American Historical Review* 72, Number 1 (1992): 47–72.

Paz Soldán, Carlos Enrique. *Lima y sus suburbios.* Lima: Instituto de Medicina Social, 1957.

Romero Bidegaray, Lucía. "Política salarial y dinámica de las remuneraciones promedio: Lima metropolitana, 1980–1990." *Desarrollo Económico [Argentina]* 33, Number 132 (1994): 587–604.

Stein, Steve. "Popular Culture and Politics in Early Twentieth-Century Lima." *New World* 1, Number 2 (1986): 65–91.

Stein, William W. *Dance in the Cemetery: José Carlos Mariátegui and the Lima Scandal of 1917.* Lanham, MD: University Press of America, 1997.

Stokes, Susan C. "Politics and Latin America's Urban Poor: Reflections from a Lima Shantytown." *Latin American Research Review* 26, Number 2 (1991): 75–101.

Turino, Thomas. "*Somos el Perú:* 'Cumbria Andina' and the Children of Andean Migrants in Lima." *Studies in Latin American Popular Culture* 9 (1990): 15–37.

Uzzell, Douglas. "A Homegrown Mass Transit System in Lima, Peru: A Case of Generative Planning." *City and Society* 1, Number 1 (1987): 6–34.

Young, Grace Esther. "The Myth of Being 'Like a Daughter.'" *Latin American Perspectives* 14, Number 3 (1987): 365–380.

General Works

Banchero Castellano, Raúl. *Lima y el mural de Pachacamilla.* Lima: Aldo Raúl Arias Montesinos, 1972.

Bernales Ballesteros, Jorge. *Edificación de la iglesia catedral de Lima.* Seville: Escuela de Estudios Hispano-americanos, 1969.

———. *Lima, la ciudad y sus monumentos.* Seville: Escuela de Estudios Hispano-americanos, 1972.

Bromley, Juan, and José Barbagelata B. *Evolución urbana de la ciudad de Lima.* Lima: Concejo Provincial de Lima, 1945.

Coloma Porcari, César. "Documentos inéditos para la historia de la Magdalena y el valle de Lima, 1557–1889." *Historia y Cultura: Revista del Museo Nacional de Historia [Peru]* 18 (1990): 9–110.

Córdova Aguilar, Hildegardo. "La ciudad de Lima: su evolución y desarrollo metropolitano." *Revista Geográfica [Mexico]* 110 (1989): 231–265.

Doering, Juan Günther. *Planos de Lima, 1613–1983.* Lima: Municipalidad de Lima Metropolitana, 1983.

Doering, Juan Günther, and Guillermo Lohmann Villena. *Lima.* Madrid: MAPFRE, 1992.

Panfichi, Aldo, and Felipe Portocarreo, editors. *Mundos interiores: Lima, 1850–1950.* Lima: Universidad del Pacífico, 1995.

Quiroz, Alfonso W. "Lima como centro financiero, 1750–1987." *Ibero-Amerikanisches Archiv [Germany]* 17, Number 4 (1991): 331–342.

Welsh, Eileen. *Bibliografía sobre el crecimiento dinámico de Lima, referente al proceso de urbanización en el Perú.* Lima, 1970.

Surinam

General Works

Adhin, J. H., editor. *100 jaar Suriname: Gedenkboek i.v.m. een eeuw immigratie, 1873–1973.* Paramaribo: Varekamp, 1973.

Ankum-Houwink, J. C. "Chinese Contract Migrants in Surinam between 1853 and 1870." *Boletín de Estudios Latinoamericanos y del Caribe [Leiden, The Netherlands]* 17 (1974): 42–68.

Berkel, Adriaan van. *Travels in South America between the Berbice and Essequibo Rivers and in Surinam,* 1670–1689. Georgetown: "Daily Chronicle," 1948 translation by Walter Edmund Roth of 1695 Amsterdam original *Amerikaansche voyagien.*

Blum, Leonor. "Land of Sranang Tongo, Kotto-missie, and Rijsttafel." *Américas [Organization of American States]* 31, Numbers 6–7 (June–July 1979): 6-12.

Bruyning, Conrad Friederich Albert, and Jan Voorhoeve, editors. *Encyclopaedie van Suriname.* Amsterdam-Brusells: Elsevier, 1977.

Chin, H. E., and H. Buddingh'. *Surinam: Politics, Economics, and Society.* London: Frances Pinder, 1987.

Collis, L. *Soldier in Paradise: The Life of Captain John Stedman, 1744–1797.* New York: Harcourt, 1965.

Dew, E. *The Difficult Flowering of Surinam: Ethnicity and Politics in Plural Society.* The Hague: Nijhoff, 1978.

Getrouw, C. F. G. "Suriname en de oorlog." *West-Indische Gids [The Netherlands]* (1946): 129–136.

Goslinga, Cornelis Ch. *The Dutch in the Caribbean and on the Wild Coast, 1580–1680.* Gainesville: University Presses of Florida, 1971.

———. *A Short History of the Netherlands Antilles and Surinam.* The Hague, 1979.

———. *The Dutch in the Caribbean and the Guianas, 1680–1791.* Dover, NH: Van Gorcum, 1985.

Hartsinck, Jan Jacob. *Beschryving van Guiana of de Wilde Kust in Zuid-America.* Amsterdam: S. Emmering, 1974 facsimile reprint of 1770 original, two volumes.

Hoefte, Rosemarijn. *In Place of Slavery: A Social History of British Indian and Javanese Laborers in Suriname.* Gainesville: University Presses of Florida, 1998.

Koeman, C., et al., editors. *Bibliography of Printed Maps of Suriname, 1671–1971.* Amsterdam: Theatrum Orbis Terrarum, 1973.

———. *Schakels met het verleden: De geschiedenis van de kartografie van Suriname, 1500–1971.* Amsterdam: Theatrum Orbis Terrarum, 1973.

Lamur, H. E. *The Demographic Evolution of Surinam, 1920–1970: A Socio-Demographic Analysis.* The Hague: Nijhoff, 1973.

Lier, R. A. J. van. *Frontier Society: A Social Analysis of the History of Surinam.* The Hague: Nijhoff, 1971 translation of 1949 Dutch original *Samenleving in een Grensgebied.*

Lier, R. A. J. van, editor. *Suriname omstreeks 1850: 22 tekeningen en aquarellen door Hendrik Huygens, 1810–1867.* Amsterdam: S. Emmering, 1978.

Locketz, Leslie. "The Photographer's Eye: Suriname." *Américas [Organization of American States]* 31, Number 4 (April 1979): 5–9.

Menezes, M. Noel. "The Dutch and British Policy of Indian Subsidy: A System of Annual and Triennial Presents." *Caribbean Studies* 13, Number 3 (1973): 64–88.

Merian, Maria Sibylla. *Die Reise nach Surinam, 1699.* Stuttgart: Schuler, 1956.

Nagelkerke, Gerard A. *Suriname: A Bibliography, 1940–1980.* The Hague: Smits Drukkers Publishers, for the Department of Caribbean Studies of the Royal Institute of Linguistics and Anthropology at Leiden, 1980.

Poll, Willem van de. *Suriname: Een fotoreportage van land en volk.* Gravenhage: W. van Hoeve, 1949.

————. *Koninklijk bezoek aan Suriname.* 's-Gravenhage: W. van Hoeve, 1956.

————. *Suriname.* Paramaribo: Varekamp, 1959.

Samson, Ph. A. "De Surinaamse pers gedurende het Engelse tussenbestuur." *West-Indische Gids [The Netherlands]* 31 (1950): 80–91.

Schiltkamp, Jacob A., and J. Th. de Smidt, editors. *West Indisch Plakaatboek: Plakaten, ordonnantiën en andere wetten, uitgevaardigd in Suriname, 1667–1761 en 1761–1816.* Amsterdam: S. Emmering, 1973, two volumes.

Siwpersad, J. P. *De Nederlandse regering en de afschaffing van de Surinaamse slavernij, 1833–1863.* Groningen: Bauma's, 1979.

Sluiter, Engel. "Dutch Guiana: A Problem in Boundaries." *Hispanic-American Historical Review* (February 1933).

Sumwalt, Martha Murray, compiler. *Surinam in Pictures.* New York: Sterling, 1971.

Traa, A. van. *Suriname, 1900–1940.* Deventer: W. van Hoeve, 1946.

Waal Malefijt, A. de. *The Javanese of Surinam: Segment of a Plural Society.* Assen: Van Gorcum, 1963.

Westerloo, G. van. *Frimangron, Suriname: Reportages uit een Zuid-amerikaanse republiek.* Amsterdam: Arbeiderspers, 1975.

Paramaribo

Benoit, Pierre-Jacques. *Voyage à Surinam: description des possessions néerlandaises dans la Guyane.* Amsterdam: S. Emmering, 1967 reprint of 1839 original published by the Société des Beaux-Arts in Brusells.

Brana-Shute, Gary. *On the Corner: Male Social Life in a Paramaribo Creole Neighbourhood.* Assen: Van Gorcum, 1979.

Bruijne, G. A. de. *Paramaribo: Stadsgeografische studies van een ontwikkelingsland.* Bussum: Unieboek, 1976.

Buschkens, Willem F. L. *The Family System of the Paramaribo Creoles.* 's-Gravenhage: Nijhoff, 1974.

Cohen, R. *The Jewish Nation in Surinam.* Amsterdam: S. Emmering, 1982.

Fontaine, Jos J. *Zeelandia: De geschiedenis van een fort.* Zutphen: Walburg, 1973.

Helman, Albert, and C. L. Temminck Groll. *Vier eeuwen Paramaribo: Onze nationale hoofdstad.* Amsterdam-Paramaribo: Van Leeuwen, 1963.

Lagerberg, C. S. I. J. *Profiel van een hoofdstad, Paramaribo: Verslag van een onderzoek in een volkswijk.* Tilburg: Instituut voor Ontwikkelingsvraagstukken, 1974.

Oudschans Dentz, Fred. "Een blik op den toestand van Suriname bij den overgang van het Engelsche bestuur op dat van de Bataafsche republiek in 1802." *West-Indische Gids [The Netherlands]* 23 (1941): 379–383.

————. "Wanneer Paramaribo zijn eerste klok kreeg." *West-Indische Gids [The Netherlands]* 28 (1947): 154.

————. "De overneming van de kolonie Suriname van de Engelsen in 1816." *West-Indische Gids [The Netherlands]* 32 (1951): 100–101.

————. "De oorsprong van den naam Combé, de eerste buitenwijk van Paramaribo." *West-Indische Gids [The Netherlands]* 39 (1959): 28–34.

Raat, J. H. *Comfort and Indoor Climate in Paramaribo.* Groningen: Boekdrukkerij, 1958.

Simons, R. D. *Paramaribo: Over de oorsprong en betekenis van de naam.* The Hague: W. van Hoeve, 1947.

Temminck Groll, C. L., et al. *De architektuur van Suriname, 1667–1930.* Zutphen: Walburg, 1973.

Volders, J. L. *Bouwkunst in Suriname: Driehonderd jaar nationale architectuur.* Hilversum: Van Saane, 1966.

Walle, J. van de. *Een oog boven Paramaribo: Herinneringen.* Amsterdam: Querdo, 1975.

Warnsinck, J. C. M. *Abraham Crijnssen; de verovering van Suriname en zijn aanslag op Virginië in 1667.* Amsterdam: Noord-Hollandsche Uitgeversmaatschappij, 1936.

Wit, Y. B. "Is Paramaribo te groot?" *Nieuwe West-Indische Gids [The Netherlands]* 45 (1966–1967): 77–93.

Early Maps and Depictions of Paramaribo, 1690–1880

Detail from a map by A. Maars, ca. 1690, showing Paramaribo's position, seven miles inland from the sea—published in J. D. Herlein's *Beschryvinge van de volkplantinge Zuriname* (Leeuwarden, 1718), available from several sources

Depiction of Paramaribo and Fort Zeelandia during the early eighteenth century—original held by the Atlas van Stolk Foundation in Rotterdam

Sketch of Fort Zeelandia's defenses in 1702, by J. Kleyn—original held by the Algemeen Rijksarchief at The Hague, call number: Inventaris Leupe 2066

Sketch showing proposed improvements to Fort Zeelandia's defenses in 1710, by the engineer I. Tourton—original held by the Algemeen Rijksarchief at The Hague, call number: Inventaris Leupe 2067

French map of Cassard's assault against Paramaribo in October 1712—original held by the Bibliothèque Nationale in Paris

Detail from a survey by G. Palm, showing some suggested improvements to Fort Zeelandia, 1715—original held by the Algemeen Rijksarchief at The Hague, call number: Inventaris Leupe 2069

Engraving of Paramaribo, ca. 1718—published in Herlein's *Beschryvinge van de volk-plantinge Zuriname,* several sources

Proposal to increase Fort Zeelandia's defenses by adding an earthen rampart, ca. 1720—original held by the Algemeen Rijksarchief at The Hague, call number: Inventaris Leupe 2070

Engraving of Fort Zeelandia and Paramaribo, ca. 1750—original held by the *Koninklijk Instituut voor de Tropen* or "Royal Institute of the Tropics" in Amsterdam, call number: 2780–1

Sketchy map of Paramaribo in the mid-eighteenth century, by Mattheus Sager—original held by the Prins Hendrik Maritime Museum in Rotterdam, cited as entry "175 (m. afb.)" in its 1962 *Catalogus tentoonstelling Zuid Zuid West, geschiedenis Nederland-Suriname*

French map of Paramaribo, ca. 1763, drawn from Dutch sources—published in Jacques-Nicolas Bellin's *Description géographique de la Guiane,* several sources

Map of Paramaribo in 1766, sent to Holland five years later with a report by F. Lieftinck—original held by the Algemeen Rijksarchief at The Hague, call number: Inventaris Leupe 1715 (Lieftinck letter dated 22 March 1771); also cited as entry 185 in 1962 *Catalogus tentoonstelling Zuid Zuid West, geschiedenis Nederland-Suriname*

Paramaribo and Fort Zeelandia as they appeared in 1770—engraving by J. V. Schley, published opposite page 567 in the second volume of Jan Jacob Hartsinck's *Beschryving van Guiana of de Wilde Kust in Zuid-America,* reprinted in facsimile in 1974

Diagram and profile views of proposed improvements to Paramaribo's *Gouvernementshuis* or "Government House," 1772—original held by the Algemeen Rijksarchief at The Hague, call number: Gouv. Number 92, Bijlage 516 [accompanying letter from Gov. Jan Nepveu found in S.v.S., Number 248, Folio 16]

Sketch of property grants made to black troops of the Free Corps, 1772—original held by the Algemeen Rijksarchief at The Hague, call number: Inventaris Leupe 1716 (Lieftinck letter dated 17 August 1772); also cited as entry 186 in 1962 *Catalogus tentoonstelling Zuid Zuid West, geschiedenis Nederland-Suriname*

Map showing expansion and beautifaction of Paramaribo beyond Fort Zeelandia in 1775, by the inspector J. C. Hurter—original held by the Algemeen Rijksarchief at The Hague, call number: Gouv. Number 101, Bijlage 1345a (Kaart R 446)

Map showing the governor's gardens outside Fort Zeelandia, 1776—original held by the Suriname Museum, call number: Collecte Fontaine, 1972

Profile views and diagrams of a proposed new barracks inside Fort Zeelandia, 1780—original held by the Algemeen Rijksarchief at The Hague, call number: Collecte Bibl. van Kolonië, Number 350

Profile views and diagrams of a proposed new prison inside Fort Zeelandia, February 1780—original held by the Algemeen Rijksarchief at The Hague, call number: Supl. Leupe, Number 602

Sketch showing proposed improvements to Fort Zeelandia in 1781, by D. van der Mey van Oosterhout—original held by the Algemeen Rijksarchief at The Hague, call number: Inventaris Leupe 2076

Diagrams by Wollant, showing proposed improvements to Fort Zeelandia in 1781—originals held by the Algemeen Rijksarchief at The Hague, call numbers: Inventaris Leupe 2077 and 2078

Cutaway and profile views by Wollant of a proposed new *Commandanthuis* or "Commander's Quarters" at Paramaribo, ca. 1781—original held by the Algemeen Rijksarchief at The Hague, call number: Inventaris Leupe 607

Drawing of a proposed new gallery for Paramaribo's *Gouvernementshuis* or "Government House," 1786—original held by the Algemeen Rijksarchief at The Hague, call number: Collecte van overzeese Rijksd., Number 335

Two sets of profile views and diagrams for a proposed new storehouse inside Fort Zeelandia, the first by the engineer and inspector Capt.-Lt. N. L. Robatel, the second by master carpenter J. van Wijnbergen, September 1788—originals held by the Algemeen Rijksarchief at The Hague, call numbers: Inventaris Leupe suppl. 603 and 604

Profile views and diagram by Maj. J. G. R. Böhm of a proposed new officers' quarters inside Fort Zeelandia, 1789—original held by the Algemeen Rijksarchief at The Hague, call number: Gouv. Number 136, bijlage 957, R 455

Cutaway view and diagrams of a proposed new clock tower/lookout post beside Fort Zeelandia, May 1789—original held by the Algemeen Rijksarchief at The Hague, call number: Inventaris Leupe, suppl. 605

Profile and cutaway views of a proposed new gallery for Paramaribo's military hospital, May 1789—original held by the Algemeen Rijksarchief at The Hague, call number: Inventaris Leupe, suppl. 611

Diagrams, plus profile and cutaway views, of a proposed new 1,200-ton water tank for Paramaribo's military hospital, May 1789—original held by the Algemeen Rijksarchief at The Hague, call number: Inventaris Leupe, suppl. 612

Drawing of the newly completed clock tower inside Fort Zeelandia, 1790—original held by the Algemeen

Rijksarchief at The Hague, call number: Inventaris Leupe, suppl. 605 (kaart R 448), plus another, almost identical version in the Suriname Museum, call number: Collecte Fontaine 1972

Profile views and diagram by Major Böhm of a proposed new storehouse and powder magazine inside Fort Zeelandia, May 1790—original held by the Algemeen Rijksarchief at The Hague, call number: Inventaris Leupe, suppl. 606 [Böhm's accompanying report is in S.v.S., Number 296, Bijlage 170, Rapport van 26 mei 1790]

Diagram by J. H. Rothe of the proposed new layout for Paramaribo's hospital, 1793—original held by the Algemeen Rijksarchief at The Hague, call number: Inventaris Leupe, suppl. 614, also cited as entry 202 in the 1962 *Catalogus tentoonstelling Zuid Zuid West, geschiedenis Nederland-Suriname*

Map of Paramaribo's new "Combé" suburb in 1796, by the engineer A. H. Hiemcke—original held by the Algemeen Rijksarchief at The Hague, call number: Inventaris Leupe 1717 (Hiemcke letter dated 23 November 1796); also cited as entry 203 in the 1962 *Catalogus tentoonstelling Zuid Zuid West, geschiedenis Nederland-Suriname*

Depiction of Paramaribo's *Waterkant* or "Waterfront," ca. 1797—original held by the Scheepvaartmuseum at Amsterdam, also cited as entry 357 in 1962 *Catalogus tentoonstelling Zuid Zuid West, geschiedenis Nederland-Suriname*

Map showing layout of government buildings in central Paramaribo, late eighteenth century—original held by the Algemeen Rijksarchief at The Hague, call number: Inventaris Leupe, suppl. 608 b

Map of Paramaribo, ca. 1800, by J. H. Moseberg—original held by the Algemeen Rijksarchief at The Hague, call number: Inventaris Leupe 1639a

Two aquatints by F. Dieterich of Paramaribo's waterfront, ca. 1803–1804, based upon an eyewitness drawing by Pierre Berranger; both aquatints were subsequently republished in February 1817 by E. Maaskemp of Amsterdam—originals held by the Atlas van Stolk Foundation in Rotterdam, call numbers: 6552 II and 6552 III, also cited as entries 363–364 in 1962 *Catalogus tentoonstelling Zuid Zuid West, geschiedenis Nederland-Suriname*

Map of Paramaribo in 1804, by the engineer A. H. Hiemcke—original held by the University of Leiden Library in The Netherlands, Bodel Nijenhuis Collection, also cited as entry 240 in 1962 *Catalogus tentoonstelling Zuid Zuid West, geschiedenis Nederland-Suriname*

Map of Paramaribo in 1806, by Hiemcke—original held by the Algemeen Rijksarchief at The Hague, call number: Kolonien, Number 348, also cited as entry 241 in 1962 *Catalogus tentoonstelling Zuid Zuid West, geschiedenis Nederland-Suriname*

Model or diorama by G. C. F. Schouten of Paramaribo's Government House and Fort Zeelandia under British occupation, ca. 1812–1813—original held by the Rijksmuseum at Amsterdam, call number: NG 412

Engravings by E. Hoogkamer of the outbreak and aftermath of the conflagration at Paramaribo of 21 January 1821, based upon eyewitness drawings by First Artillery Lieutenant G. Mabé—originals held by the Atlas van Stolk Foundation in Rotterdam, call numbers: Na Muller suppl. 6159A, 1 and 2, also cited as entries 365–366 of 1962 *Catalogus tentoonstelling Zuid Zuid West, geschiedenis Nederland-Suriname*

Engraving by L. Schweikhardt of the 21 January 1821 fire at Paramaribo, also based upon Mabé's drawings—cited as entry 367 in 1962 *Catalogus tentoonstelling Zuid Zuid West, geschiedenis Nederland-Suriname*, wherein it is described as part of the private "collection of Dr. K. Vaandrager of Amsterdam"

Lithograph by Suhr of Hamburg of Paramaribo's *Waag* or "Weighing House," ca. 1824—cited as entry 373 in the 1962 *Catalogus tentoonstelling Zuid Zuid West, geschiedenis Nederland-Suriname*, wherein it is described as part of the private "collection of Dr. K. Vaandrager of Amsterdam"

Drawing of Paramaribo's waterfront in the early nineteenth century—original held by the Suriname Museum, call number: 06–61

Map of Paramaribo in 1827, by the architect Willem de Vroome—original held by the Library of the Ministerie van Binnelandse Zaken at 's-Gravenhage, also cited as entry 308 in the 1962 *Catalogus tentoonstelling Zuid Zuid West, geschiedenis Nederland-Suriname*

Lithographs based upon the 1831 sketches made by the French visitor, Pierre-Jacques Benoit, which were published in Brussels eight years later as part of his book *Voyage à Surinam: description des possessions néerlandaises dans la Guyane*—reprinted in 1967, several sources

Diagram of the grounds around the governor's palace at Paramaribo in 1835, by A. Quisthoudt—original held by the University of Leiden Library in The Netherlands, Bodel Nijenhuis Collection, also cited as entry 310 in *Catalogus tentoonstelling Zuid Zuid West, geschiedenis Nederland-Suriname*

Map of Paramaribo, ca. 1835—published on page 99 of the second volume of M. D. Teenstra's *De Landbouw in de kolonie Suriname* (Groningen, 1835), several sources

Watercolor by P. A. van Rees of Paramaribo's waterfront, ca. 1840—cited as entry 334 in 1962 *Catalogus tentoonstelling Zuid Zuid West, geschiedenis Nederland-Suriname*, wherein it is described as part of the private "collection of Dr. K. Vaandrager of Amsterdam"

Pen-and-ink wash by Soesman of Keizerstraat in 1844, showing Paramaribo's first synagogue at right—original held by the Cur. Handelmij at Amsterdam, also cited as entry 342 of 1962 *Catalogus tentoonstelling Zuid Zuid West, geschiedenis Nederland-Suriname*

Map of Paramaribo in 1850, by Hiemcke—original held by the University of Leiden Library at The Netherlands, Bodel Nijenhuis Collection, also cited as entry 312 in 1962 *Catalogus tentoonstelling Zuid Zuid West, geschiedenis Nederland-Suriname*

Mid-nineteenthth century watercolor by L. Springer of Paramaribo's main hospital, located at 64 Graven-straat—original held by the Suriname Museum, call number: 03–5

Two watercolors by G. W. C. Voorduin of Surinam's Government House and waterfront, later used by J. E. van Heemskerck van Beest to prepare two colored lithographs, ca. 1859—watercolors are today held by the Surinam Museum, inventory number 27–335, while the lithographs are cited as entries 380 and 385 of the 1962 *Catalogus tentoonstelling Zuid Zuid West, geschiedenis Nederland-Suriname*

Watercolor showing rear entrance to the Governor's House, ca. 1860—original held by the Royal Institute of the Tropics in Amsterdam, plus a copy at the Suriname Museum, call number XIX-69

Depiction of Paramaribo's central core, ca. 1863—published in Frédéric Boyer's *La Guyana Française,* several sources

Two nineteenth-century watercolors by Voorduin, of the entrance to the Governor's House—the view from the east is preserved as part of the Schakels Collection of the Vice-Minister President's Kabinet at 's-Gravenhage [citation: "Suriname en de Nederlaandse Antillen, S 51, 1963, Historische Monumenten, Page 9"], while the western view is held by the Scheepvaartmuseum at Amsterdam, cited as entry 345 in the 1962 *Catalogus tentoonstelling Zuid Zuid West, geschiedenis Nederland-Suriname*

Panoramic view of Paramaribo's waterfront, ca. 1880—from a photograph by the French traveler, Dr. Jules Crévaux, published in his book *Voyages dans l'Amérique du Sud* (Paris: Hachette, 1883), several sources

Uruguay
General Studies

Alvarez Lenzi, Ricardo. *Fundación de poblados en el Uruguay.* Montevideo, 1972.

Casal Tatlock, Alvaro. *El automóvil en el Uruguay, 1900–1930.* Montevideo: Ediciones de la Banda Oriental, 1981.

Castellanos, Alfredo. *Uruguay: monumentos históricos y arqueológicos.* Mexico City, 1974.

Collin Delavaud, Anne. "L'Uruguay, un exemple d'urbanisation originale en pays d'élevage." *Les cahiers d'Outre-mer [France]* 25, Number 100 (October–December 1972): 361–389.

———. *Uruguay: moyennes et petites villes, etude de géographie urbaine.* Paris: Institut des Hautes Études d'Amérique Latine or IHEAL, Centre Nationale de la Recherche Scientifique, 1972.

Errandonea, Alfredo, and Daniel Costabile. *Sindicato y sociedad en el Uruguay.* Montevideo: Fundación de Cultura Universitaria, 1969.

Gelman, Jorge. *Campesinos y estancieros: una región del Río de la Plata a fines de la época colonial.* Buenos Aires: Los Libros del Riel, 1998.

Giuria, Juan. *La arquitectura en el Uruguay.* Montevideo, 1955–1958, two volumes.

Lloyd, Reginald, et al., editors. *Twentieth Century Impressions of Uruguay: Its History, People, Commerce, Industries, and Resources.* London: Lloyds Great Britain Publishing Company, 1912 (also available in a Spanish translation).

Lucchini, Aurelio. *Ideas y formas en la arquitectura nacional.* Montevideo, 1969.

Marco, Miguel Angel de. "Méndez Núñez en el Plata." *Revista de Historia Naval [Spain]* 2, Number 5 (1984): 33–63.

Oddone, Juan Antonio. *Una perspectiva europea del Uruguay.* Montevideo: Universidad de la República del Uruguay, 1965.

———. *La formación del Uruguay moderno: la inmigración y el desarrollo económico y social.* Buenos Aires: Editorial Universitaria de Buenos Aires or EUDEBA, 1966.

Rama, Carlos M. *Las clases sociales en Uruguay.* Montevideo: Nuestro Tiempo, 1960.

Rial, Jaime, and Juan Klaczko. *Uruguay: el país urbano.* Montevideo: Ediciones de la Banda Oriental, 1981.

Vanger, Milton I. *The Model Country: José Batlle y Ordóñez of Uruguay, 1907–1915.* Hanover, NH: Brandeis University Press, 1980.

Weinstein, Martin. *Uruguay: The Politics of Failure.* Westport, CT: Greenwood, 1975.

Williams, John Hoyt. "Observations on Blacks and Bondage in Uruguay, 1800–1836." *The Americas: A Quarterly Review of Inter-American Cultural History [Academy of American Franciscan History]* 43, Number 4 (1987): 411–427.

Montevideo
Colonial Era (1723–1828)

Acuerdos del extinguido cabildo de Montevideo (anexos), volúmenes 16–18, del 13 de diciembre de 1776 al 20 de julio de 1795. Montevideo: Archivo General de la Nación, 1942–1943, three volumes.

Acuerdos del extinguido cabildo de Montevideo, volúmenes 12–15, libros XIV a XVIII, del 12 de febrero de 1814 al 29 de agosto de 1829. Montevideo: Archivo General de la Nación, 1934–1941, four volumes.

Apolant, Juan Alejandro. *La ruina de la Ciudadela de Monte-video.* Montevideo: Centro de Estudios del Pasado Uruguayo, 1974.

Ariel Betancur, Arturo. "La provisión de servicios en el puerto colonial de Montevideo: alcances y limitaciones de una fuente local de riqueza." *Anuario de Estudios Americanos [Spain]* 53, Number 2 (1996): 123–145.

Assunçao, Fernando O., and Iris Bombet Franco. *La Aguada.* Montevideo: Fundación Banco de Boston, 1991.

Bertocchi Morán, Alejandro Nelson. "Don José María de Salazar y la banda oriental del río Uruguay." *Revista de Historia Naval [Spain]* 15, Number 56 (1997): 21–30.

Canessa de Sanguinetti, Marta. *La ciudad vieja de Montevideo.* Montevideo: As, 1976.

Capillas de Castellanos, Aurora. *Montevideo en el siglo XVIII.* Montevideo, 1971.

Cooney, Jerry W. "Oceanic Commerce and Platine Merchants, 1796–1806: The Challenge of War." *The Americas: A Quarterly Review of Inter-American Cultural History [Academy of American Franciscan History]* 45, Number 4 (1989): 509–524.

———. "Trials of a Yankee Sailor: Robert Gray in the Río de la Plata, 1798–1802," *American Neptune* 49, Number 4 (1989): 272–277.

Documentos concernientes a la fundación de Montevideo y actas de su cabildo. Montevideo, 1885, five volumes.

Martínez Montero, Homero. *El apostadero de Montevideo, 1776–1814.* Madrid: Instituto Histórico de Marina, 1968.

Olivares, Itamar. "José Ramón Mila de la Roca, un 'afrance-sado' du Rio de la Plata." *Caravelle: cahiers du monde hispanique et luso-brésilien [France]* 51 (1988): 5–21.

Early Maps and Depictions of Montevideo, 1719–1822
Map with watercolor highlights of the uninhabited bay in 1719, by the Spanish military engineer, Capt. Domingo Petrarca—original held by the Servicio Geográfico del Ejército at Madrid, call number: J-9-3-14

Map of San Felipe de Montevideo Bay by Petrarca in 1724, including a side panel detailing its proposed fortifica-tion—original held by the Archive of Indies at Seville, old Torres Lanzas call number: Mapas y Planos de Buenos Aires 41, or Estancia 76, Caja 2, Legajo 25(1)

Map of the bay by Petrarca in 1727, with measurements to plan its overlapping fields of fire, plus a side panel de-tailing some individual strongholds—original held by the Servicio Geográfico del Ejército at Madrid, call num-ber: J-9-3-16

Map of Montevideo's peninsula in 1730 by Petrarca, demon-strating how its settlement would be better protected by a large, new citadel and line of ramparts, rather than the original small fortification—original held by the Servi-cio Geográfico del Ejército at Madrid, call number: J-9-3-18

Anonymous map with watercolor highlights of the bay and its defenses, ca. 1735–1745—original held by the Servi-cio Geográfico del Ejército at Madrid, call number: J-9-3-21

Map with watercolor highlights by the military engineer Diego Cardoso, demonstrating his proposed improve-ments to the harbor defenses, ca. 1741—original held by the Servicio Geográfico del Ejército at Madrid, call number: J-9-3-20

Diagram and profile views by Cardoso, of Montevideo's new *Ciudadela* or "Citadel," October 1746—originals held by the Servicio Geográfico del Ejército at Madrid (call number: J-9-3-22), plus the Archive of Indies at Seville, old Torres Lanzas call number: Mapas y Planos de Buenos Aires 56, or Estancia 125, Caja 3, Legajo 21(1)

Pen-and-ink chart with watercolor highlights of harbor soundings, plus proposals for strengthening city de-fenses, 1752—original held by the Archivo General de Simancas in Spain, call number: Mapas, Planos y Dibu-jos, VII-83 [archival provenance: Estado, Legajo 7380–103]

Chart of Montevideo's harbor soundings, as well as a listing of anchored vessels, 1769—original held by the Archive of Indies at Seville, old Torres Lanzas call number: Mapas y Planos de Buenos Aires 79, or Estancia 125, Caja 3, Legajo 24

Pen-and-ink diagram by the military engineer José Antonio de Borja, suggesting some repairs to the San Fernando Bastion, October 1770—original held by the Archivo General de Simancas in Spain, call number: Mapas, Planos y Dibujos, VI-124 [archival provenance: Guerra Moderna, Legajo 7243]

Cutaway view demonstrating suggested improvements to San Fernando Bastion, November 1770—original held by the Archive of Indies at Seville, old Torres Lanzas call number: Mapas y Planos de Buenos Aires 87, or Estancia 122, Caja 4, Legajo 22(1)

Diagram and profile view of a proposed new defensive cir-cuit around Montevideo, March 1771—original held by the Archive of Indies at Seville, old Torres Lanzas call number: Mapas y Planos de Buenos Aires 93, or Estancia 125, Caja 3, Legajo 24

Four diagrams compiled in June 1771 by Juan Martín Zer-meño, depicting suggested improvements to Monte-video's defenses—originals held by the Archive of Indies at Seville, old Torres Lanzas call number: Mapas y Planos de Buenos Aires 95 through 98, or Estancia 125, Caja 5, Legajos 4(5), 4(6), 4(7), and 4(8)

Map of the city and its harbor in June 1771, showing new batteries being added around its recently completed citadel—original held by the Archive of Indies at Seville, old Torres Lanzas call number: Mapas y Planos de

Buenos Aires 99, or Estancia 125, Caja 5, Legajo 4(9) [archival provenance: Buenos Aires, 555]

Chart of the city and harbor in 1781, enumerating the vessels and artillery pieces available for its defense—original held by the Archive of Indies at Seville, old Torres Lanzas call number: Mapas y Planos de Buenos Aires 140, or Estancia 122, Caja 5, Legajo 15(1)

Pen-and-ink chart with watercolor highlights drawn in July 1781 by Domingo Pallarés, showing how Montevideo's batteries might be supplemented by a defensive line of ships in the event of an attack—original held by the Archivo General de Simancas in Spain, call number: Mapas, Planos y Dibujos, VII-73 [archival provenance: Marina, Legajo 422]

Diagram and profile views of proposed changes to the building that was to serve as military hospital and barracks for Montevideo, June 1781—original held by the Servicio Histórico Militar at Madrid, call number: 6311

Diagram of a proposed new battery on Ratas Island, July 1781—original held by the Servicio Histórico Militar at Madrid, call number: 6295

Diagram and profile drawing by the military engineer Carlos Cabrera, of proposed guard towers for Montevideo's gates, 1782—original held by the Archive of Indies at Seville, old Torres Lanzas call number: Mapas y Planos de Buenos Aires 146, or Estancia 122, Caja 5, Legajo 19(4)

Diagrams and profile drawings, apparently by the military engineer Miguel Juárez, of the new Santa Bárbara Battery erected to cover Estanzuela Beach, November 1783—originals held by the Archive of Indies at Seville, old Torres Lanzas call numbers: Mapas y Planos de Buenos Aires 149 and 150, or Estancia 125, Caja 4, Legajos 4(2) and 4(3), with duplicates in Estancia 122, Caja 5, Legajo 19

Diagram and profile drawing by Cabrera of the newly completed guard towers for Montevideo's gates, December 1783—original held by the Archive of Indies at Seville, old Torres Lanzas call number: Mapas y Planos de Buenos Aires 151, or Estancia 125, Caja 4, Legajo 4(4)

Diagram by Cabrera of proposed improvements to the citadel guarding Montevideo's landward side, August 1784—original held by the Servicio Histórico Militar in Madrid, call number: 6317

Diagram by the military engineer José Antonio del Pozo y Marquy of a proposed new battery on Ratas Island, January 1785—original held by the Servicio Histórico Militar in Madrid, call number: 6295

Diagram and profile views of a proposed new royal hospital for Montevideo, ca. 1780s—original held by the Servicio Histórico Militar in Madrid, call number: 6311

Chart of Montevideo's harbor, drawn by Ibañez during the 1789 visit of the corvettes *Descubierta* and *Atrevida*—original held by the Archive of Indies at Seville, old Torres Lanzas call number: Mapas y Planos de Buenos Aires, 174 or Estancia 125, Caja 4, Legajo 4(14)

View of the city from the *Aguada* or "Watering Spot" at the northern end of its bay in 1794, by Fernando Brambila—originals held by the Municipal Historical Museum of Montevideo and Museo Naval in Madrid, plus other sources

Diagrams and profile drawings by the military engineers Bernardo Lecocq and José García Martínez de Cáceres of improvements to Montevideo's landward defenses, December 1795 and February 1796—originals held by the Servicio Histórico Militar at Madrid (call number: 6364) and the Archive of Indies at Seville, old Torres Lanzas call number: Mapas y Planos de Buenos Aires, 193 and 194 or Estancia 125, Caja 5, Legajo 4(13), plus Estancia 122, Caja 6, Legajos 11(1) and 13

Anonymous map of a proposed new line of fortifications east of the city, ca. 1796—original held by the Servicio Histórico Militar at Madrid, call number: 6329

Diagram and profile views by García Martínez de Cáceres of an arsenal at Montevideo, February 1797—original held by the Servicio Histórico Militar at Madrid, call number: 6364

Diagrams and profile view by García Martínez de Cáceres of a guardhouse at Montevideo, February 1797—original held by the Servicio Histórico Militar in Madrid, call number: 6312

Diagram and profile views by García Martínez de Cáceres of a hilltop powder magazine outside Montevideo, February 1797—original held by the Servicio Histórico Militar in Madrid, call number: 6312

Diagram and profile view by García Martínez de Cáceres of the guardhouse on Montevideo's dock, February 1797—original held by the Servicio Histórico Militar at Madrid, call number: 6327

Drawing by García Martínez de Cáceres of proposed improvements to Montevideo's island battery, February 1797—original held by the Servicio Histórico Militar in Madrid, call number: 6310

Diagram and profile views by García Martínez de Cáceres of a temporary hospital, February 1797—original held by the Servicio Histórico Militar in Madrid, call number: 5311

Diagram and profile view by García Martínez de Cáceres of a cavalry barracks, February 1797—original held by the Servicio Histórico Militar in Madrid, call number: 6331

Diagram and profile view by García Martínez de Cáceres of the governor's palace, February 1797—original held by the Servicio Histórico Militar at Madrid, call number: 6332

Diagrams and profile drawings of the *fanales* or "light towers" to be erected on Flores Island and Cerro Hill, 1791—originals held by the Archive of Indies in Seville, old Torres Lanzas call number: Mapas y Planos de Buenos Aires, 198 and 199 or Estancia 125, Caja 6, Legajos 10(2) and 10(1)

Diagram and profile view by García Martínez de Cáceres of a proposed new stronghold, June 1802—original held by the Servicio Histórico Militar in Madrid, call number: 6338

Diagrams and profile views by Del Pozo and Lecocq of suggested improvements to Montevideo's landward defenses, December 1805—originals held by the Archive of Indies at Seville, old Torres Lanzas call number: Mapas y Planos de Buenos Aires, 218 and 219 or Estancia 122, Caja 6, Legajos 22(1) and 22(2) [archival provenance: Buenos Aires, 93]

Map by Del Pozo of proposed improvements to the city's seaside defenses, December 1808—original held by the Servicio Geográfico del Ejército in Madrid, call number: J-9-3-27

Map by Del Pozo of expansion eastward of Montevideo's defensive perimeter, March 1812—original held by the Servicio Histórico Militar in Madrid, call number: 6325 or P-b-12-35

Diagram and profile view by Del Pozo of Cerro Fortress opposite Montevideo, March 1812—original held by the Servicio Histórico Militar in Madrid, call number: 6309

Diagram and profile view by Del Pozo of the Ratas Island Battery, March 1812—original held by the Servicio Histórico Militar in Madrid, call number: 6295

Views of Montevideo in 1817 by the visiting British naval officer Emeric Essex Vidal, published three years later in his book *Picturesque Illustration of Buenos Ayres and Monte Video*—several sources

1820 map by the military engineer Jozé Cavallo of Montevideo under Portuguese occupation, hand-copied in 1865 from his original in the Arquivo Militar de Lisboa—copy held by the Map Library of the Brazilian Ministry of Foreign Relations, inventory numbers: 786.9/M-55 a-1820C and 1867-118-IA

1822 map of Montevideo's defenses during the Portuguese reign, hand-copied in 1864 from an original in the Arquivo Militar de Lisboa—copy held by the Map Library of the Brazilian Ministry of Foreign Relations, inventory numbers: 786.9/M-55 hkcmf-1822 and 1867-1761-IA

1822 map by the military engineer, Lt.-Col. Jacintho Diziderio Cony, of the deployment of the Portuguese *Voluntários Reais del Rey* Division in Montevideo's suburbs, hand-copied from an original in the Arquivo Militar de Lisboa, ca. 1865—copy held by the Map Library at the Brazilian Ministry of Foreign Relations, inventory numbers: 786.9/M-55 hk-1822C and 1867-1060-IAca.

Modern Era and General Works (1829–Present)

Altezor, Carlos, and H. Baracchini. *Historia urbanística y edilicia de la ciudad de Montevideo.* Montevideo: Junta Departamental, 1971.

Alvarez Lenzi, Ricardo, et al. *El Montevideo de la expansión, 1868–1915.* Montevideo: Ediciones de la Banda Oriental, 1986.

Artucio, Leopoldo C. *Montevideo y la arquitectura moderna.* Montevideo: Nuestra Tierra, 1971.

Azarola Gil, Luis Enrique. *Ayer, 1882–1952.* Lausanne: Imprimeries Réunies, 1953.

Benton, Lauren A. "Reshaping the Urban Core: The Politics of Housing in Authoritarian Uruguay." *Latin American Research Review* 21, Number 2 (1986): 33–52.

Bleil de Souza, Susana. "La construction du port de Montevideo de 1890 à 1913." *Travaux et mémoires de l'institut des hautes études de l'Amérique latine [France]* 33 (1980): 33–45.

Cambareri, Carmen S. "Scuttle the *Graf Spee!*" *U.S. Naval Institute Proceedings* 109, Number 6 (1983): 51–54.

Castellanos, Alfredo. *Historia del desarrollo edilicio y urbanístico de Montevideo, 1829–1914.* Montevideo, 1971.

Daróczi, Isabel. "Area metropolitana de Montevideo." *Revista Geográfica [Mexico]* 110 (1989): 105–120.

Ellis, Roberto J. G. *Del Montevideo de ayer y de hoy.* Montevideo: VYP, 1971.

Ferdinán, Valentín. "Usos sociales de la fotografía en el Montevideo del siglo XIX: aculturación y permisivilidad." *Revista de Historia de América [Mexico]* 108 (1989): 73–130.

Gans, Paul. "Desarrollo económico y sector informal en América Latina: el ejemplo del comercio ambulante en Montevideo." *Revista Geográfica [Mexico]* 113 (1991): 203–222.

Growel, Maria. "Weekend in Montevideo." *Américas [Organization of American States]* 30, Number 8 (August 1978): 7–11.

Kaczko, Jaime. "El Uruguay de 1908: obstáculos y estimulos en el mercado de trabajo, la población económicamente activa." *Revista de Indias [Spain]* 41, Numbers 165–166 (1981): 675–722.

La ciudad vieja de Montevideo: posibilidades de rehabilitación. Montevideo: Ediciones de la Banda Oriental for the Grupo de Estudios Urbanos, 1983.

Montevideo: capital del Uruguay. Paris: Intendencia Municipal, 1980.

Núñez Vilar, Carlos. "Night of Nights in Montevideo." *Américas [Organization of American States]* 29, Numbers 11–12 (November–December 1977): 58–61.

Patrón, Juan Carlos. *Goes y el viejo Café Vaccaro.* Montevideo: Alfa, 1968.

Pérez Montero, Carlos. *Indice cartográfico de la ciudad de Montevideo, 1719–1912.* Montevideo, 1955.

Porzecanski, Arturo C. *Uruguay's Tuparamaros: The Urban Guerrilla.* New York: Praeger, 1973.

Preston, Catherine, and Anton Rosenthal. *"Correo mítico: The Construction of a Civic Image in the Postcards of Montevideo, Uruguay, 1900–1930." Studies in Latin American Popular Culture* 15 (1996): 231–259.

Rial, Juan. "Estilos de desarrollo y primacia urbana en Uruguay, 1852–1933." *Revista de Indias [Spain]* 40, Numbers 159–162 (1980): 337–395.

Rosenthal, Anton. "Streetcar Workers and the Transformation of Montevideo: The General Strike of May 1911." *The Americas: A Quarterly Review of Inter-American Cultural History [Academy of American Franciscan History]* 51, Number 4 (April 1995): 471–494.

———. "The Arrival of the Electric Streetcar and the Conflict over Progress in Early Twentieth-Century Montevideo." *Journal of Latin American Studies [UK]* 27, Number 2 (May 1995): 319–341.

Sisa López, Emilio. *Tiempo de ayer que fue.* La Paz: Vanguardia, 1978.

Vicario, Luis B. *El crecimiento urbano de Montevideo.* Montevideo: Ediciones de la Banda Oriental, 1968.

Venezuela

General Studies

Abercrombie, Thomas J. "Venezuela Builds on Oil." *National Geographic* 123, Number 3 (March 1963): 344–387.

Acosta Saignes, Miguel. *Elementos indígenas y africanos en la formación de la cultura venezolana.* Caracas: Universidad Central de Venezuela, 1956.

———. *Historia de los portugueses en Venezuela.* Caracas, 1959.

———. *Vida de los esclavos negros en Venezuela.* Caracas: Hespérides, 1967.

Alexander, Robert J. *The Venezuelan Democratic Revolution: A Profile of the Regime of Rómulo Betancourt.* New Brunswick, NJ: Rutgers University Press, 1964.

Allen, Loring. *Venezuelan Economic Development.* Greenwich, CT: Fawcett, 1977.

Amezaga Aresti, Vicente de. *Hombres de la Compañía Guipuzcoana.* Caracas: Banco Central de Venezuela, 1963.

———. *El elemento vasco en el siglo XVIII venezolano.* Caracas: Comité de Obras Públicas del Cuatricentenario, 1966.

Amodio, Emanuele. "Curanderos y médicos ilustrados: la creación del protomedicato en Venezuela a finales del siglo XVIII." *Asclepio [Spain]* 49, Number 1 (1997): 95–129.

Andreo García, Juan. "Del 'libre comercio' a la quiebra del sistema colonial, 1789–1796: el comercio exterior de Venezuela." *Anuario de Estudios Americanos [Spain]* 51, Number 2 (1994): 25–60.

Archila, Ricardo. *Historia de la medicina en Venezuela: época colonial.* Caracas: Vargas, 1961.

Arcila Farías, Eduardo. *Economía colonial de Venezuela.* Caracas: Italgráfica, 1973 reprint of 1946 original issued by the Fondo de Cultura Económica in Mexico City, two volumes.

———. *El régimen de la encomienda en Venezuela.* Seville: Escuela de Estudios Hispano-Americanos, 1957.

———. *Historia de la ingeniería en Venezuela.* Caracas: Colegio de Ingenieros de Venezuela, 1961, two volumes.

Arellano Moreno, Antonio, editor. *Fuentes para la historia económica de Venezuela.* Caracas, 1950.

———. *Relaciones geográficas de Venezuela durante los siglos XVI, XVII y XVIII.* Caracas: Volume 70 of the Series "Fuentes para la Historia Colonial de Venezuela" published by the Academia Nacional de la Historia, 1964.

Armas Chitty, José Antonio de. *Origen y formación de algunos pueblos de Venezuela.* Caracas: Tipografía Americana for the Instituto de Antropología e Historia of the Universidad Central de Venezuela, 1951.

Armas Chitty, José Antonio de, compiler. *Documentos para la historia colonial de los Andes venezolanos, siglos XVI al XVIII.* Madrid: Edime for the Instituto de Antropología e Historia of the Universidad Central de Venezuela, 1957.

Arnold, Ralph, et al. *The First Big Oil Hunt: Venezuela, 1911–1916.* New York: Vantage, 1960.

Barbier, Jacques A. "Venezuelan 'Libranzas', 1788–1807: From Economic Nostrum to Fiscal Imperative." *The Americas: A Quarterly Review of Inter-American Cultural History [Academy of American Franciscan History]* 37, Number 2 (1981): 457–478.

Borges, Analola. *Isleños en Venezuela: la gobernación de Ponte y Hoyo.* Santa Cruz de Tenerife: Goya Artes Gráficas, 1960.

———. *La casa de Austria en Venezuela durante la Guerra de sucesión española, 1702–1715.* Santa Cruz de Tenerife: Goya Artes Gráficas, 1963.

Boulton, Alfredo. *Historia de la pintura en Venezuela.* Caracas: Editorial Arte, 1964–1972, three volumes.

Briceño Iragorry, Mario, editor. *Orígenes de la hacienda en Venezuela: documentos inéditos de la época colonial.* Caracas: Imprenta Nacional, 1942.

Brisseau-Loaiza, Jeanine. *Le Venezuela.* Paris: Presses Universitaires de France, 1982.

Brito Figueroa, Federico. *Las insurrecciones de los esclavos negros en la sociedad colonial.* Caracas: Cantaclaro, 1961.

———. *La estructura económica de Venezuela colonial.* Caracas: Imprenta Universitaria for the Instituto de Investigaciones de la Facultad de Economía de la Universidad Central de Venezuela, 1963.

———. *La formación de las clases sociales en Venezuela.* Caracas: Enseñanza Viva, 1976.

————. "Venezuela colonial: las rebeliones de esclavos y la Revolución Francesa." *Caravelle: cahiers du monde hispanique et luso-brésilien [France]* 54 (1990): 263–289.

Brown, Jonathan C. "Why Foreign Oil Companies Shifted Their Production from Mexico to Venezuela during the 1920s." *American Historical Review* 90, Number 2 (April 1985): 362–385.

Burggraff, Winfield J. *The Venezuelan Armed Forces in Politics, 1935–1959.* Columbia: University of Missouri Press, 1972.

Capriles, Alejandro Mario. *Coronas de Castilla en Venezuela.* Madrid: Gráficas Orbe, 1967.

Carl, George Edmund. *First among Equals: Great Britain and Venezuela, 1810–1910.* Syracuse, NY, 1980.

Carrera Damas, Germán. *La sociedad colonial.* Caracas: Universidad Católica Andrés Bello, 1970.

Cartografía y relaciones históricas de ultramar (Volume 6: "Venezuela," two parts). Madrid: Ministerio de Defensa, 1990.

Castillo Lara, Lucas Guillermo. *Las acciones militares del gobernador Ruy Fernández de Fuenmayor (1637–1644).* Caracas: Volume 134 of the Series "Fuentes para la Historia Colonial de Venezuela" published by the Academia Nacional de la Historia, 1978.

————. *Apuntes para la historia colonial de Barlovento.* Caracas: Volume 151 of the Series "Fuentes para la Historia Colonial de Venezuela" published by the Academia Nacional de la Historia, 1981.

————. *La aventura fundacional de los isleños.* Caracas: Volume 163 of the Series "Fuentes para la Historia Colonial de Venezuela" published by the Academia Nacional de la Historia, 1983.

Chaves Vargas, Luis Fernando. *Estructura funcional de las ciudades venezolanas.* Mérida, 1973.

Cisneros, José Luis de. *Descripción exacta de la provincia de Benezuela.* Caracas: Editorial Avila Gráfica, 1950 reprint of 1764 original; also reprinted in 1912 in Madrid.

Crist, Raymond E., and Edward P. Leahy. *Venezuela: Search for a Middle Ground.* New York, 1969.

De la Rosa, Leopoldo. "La emigración canaria a Venezuela en los siglos XVII y XVIII." *Anuario de Estudios Atlánticos [Spain]* 20 (1976): 617–631.

Depons, François. *Viaje a la parte oriental de Tierra Firme en la América Meridional.* Caracas, 1960 two-volume Spanish translation by Enrique Planchart of French original *Voyage à la partie orientale de la Terre Ferme,* published in three volumes in Paris by F. Buisson in 1806; also republished in 1930 by Tipografía Americana in Caracas.

Documentos para los anales de Venezuela desde el movimiento separatista de la unión colombiana hasta nuestros días. Caracas: Academia Nacional de la Historia, 1899–1912, eleven volumes.

Drenikoff, Ivan. *Mapas antiguos de Venezuela: grabados e impresos antes de 1800, con la reproducción del primer mapa impreso en Venezuela y de mapas antiguos.* Caracas: Ediciones del Congreso de la República, 1971.

Duarte, Carlos F., and Graziano Gasparini. *Arte colonial en Venezuela.* Caracas, 1974.

Eastwick, Edward B. *Venezuela o apuntes sobre la vida en una república sudamericana con la historia del empréstito de 1864.* Caracas: Tipografía Vargas for the Banco Central de Venezuela, 1959 Spanish translation.

Encomiendas. Caracas: Archivo General de la Nación, 1945–1958, five volumes.

Febres Cordero, Tulio. *Archivo de historia y variedades.* Caracas: Editorial Sur América, 1930–1931, two volumes.

Federmann, Nicolaus. *Historia Indiana.* Madrid, 1957 translation by Juan Friede.

Figuera, Guillermo, editor. *Documentos para la historia de la iglesia colonial en Venezuela.* Caracas: Volumes 74–75 of the Series "Fuentes para la Historia Colonial de Venezuela" published by the Academia Nacional de la Historia, 1965.

Franco, José Luciano. *Documentos para la historia de Venezuela existentes en el Archivo Nacional de Cuba.* Havana, 1960.

Fuentes para la historia republicana. Caracas: Academia Nacional de la Historia, 1973-, twenty volumes.

Gabaldón Márquez, Joaquín. *Documentos políticos y actos ejecutivos y legales de la Revolución Federal.* Caracas, 1959.

Gacetilla de nombres geográficos. Caracas: Ministerio de Obras Públicas, 1974.

García Chuecos, Hector. *Historia documental de Venezuela.* Caracas: Editorial Rex, 1957.

Gasparini, Graziano. *La arquitectura colonial en Venezuela.* Caracas: Ernesto Armitano, 1965.

————. "Formación de ciudades coloniales en Venezuela, siglo XVI." *Actas del XXXVIII Congreso Internacional de Americanistas [Stuttgart]* (1968), Volume 4 (1972): 225–238.

————. *Las fortificaciones del período hispánico en Venezuela.* Caracas: Ernesto Armitano, 1985.

Gilmore, Robert L. *Caudillism and Militarism in Venezuela, 1810–1910.* Athens: Ohio University Press, 1964.

Gómez Canedo, Lino. *Los archivos históricos de Venezuela.* Maracaibo, 1966.

González y González, Julio. *Catálogo de mapas y planos de Venezuela.* Madrid, 1968.

Grases, Pedro, and Manuel Pérez Vila, editors. *Pensamiento político venezolano del siglo XIX: textos para su estudio.* Caracas: Presidencia de la República, 1960–1962, fifteen volumes.

Grove, Noel. "Venezuela's Crisis of Wealth." *National Geographic* 150, Number 2 (August 1976): 174–209.

Hernández Pino, Andrés. *Papeles coloniales: aporte para la historia de los pueblos del Estado Miranda.* Caracas: Editorial Venezuela, 1948.

Hood, Miriam. *Gunboat Diplomacy, 1895–1905: Great Power Pressure in Venezuela.* London: Allen and Unwin, 1975.

Humbert, Julián. *Los orígenes venezolanos: ensayo sobre la colonización española en Venezuela.* Caracas: Volume 127 of the Series "Fuentes para la Historia Colonial de Venezuela" published by the Academia Nacional de la Historia, 1976.

Keyse, Donna, and G. A. Rudolph. *Historical Dictionary of Venezuela.* Metuchen, NJ: Scarecrow Press, 1971.

Langue, Frédérique. "Les identités fractales: honneur et couleur dans la société venezuelienne du XVIIIe siècle." *Caravelle: cahiers du monde hispanique et luso-brésilien [France]* 65 (1995): 23–37.

Leal, Ildefonso. *Libros y bibliotecas en Venezuela colonial, 1633–1767.* Caracas: Volumes 132–133 of the Series "Fuentes para la Historia Colonial de Venezuela" published by the Academia Nacional de la Historia, 1978.

Lemmo B., Angelina. *La educación en Venezuela en 1870.* Caracas: Imprenta Universitaria for the Instituto de Antropología e Historia de la Universidad Central, 1961.

Levine, Daniel H. *Conflict and Political Change in Venezuela.* Princeton University Press, 1973.

Lieuwen, Edwin. *Petroleum in Venezuela: A History.* New York: Russell, 1967 reprint of 1954 original published by the University of California at Berkeley.

———. *Venezuela.* London, 1965 re-edition.

Llavador Mira, José. *La gobernación de Venezuela en el siglo XVII.* Caracas: Volume 102 of the Series "Fuentes para la Historia Colonial de Venezuela" published by the Academia Nacional de la Historia, 1969.

Llorens Izard. Miguel. *Series estadísticas para la historia de Venezuela.* Mérida, 1970.

Lombardi, John V. *The Decline and Abolition of Negro Slavery in Venezuela, 1820–1854.* Westport, CT: Greenwood, 1971.

———. *People and Places in Colonial Venezuela.* Bloomington: Indiana University Press, 1976.

———. *Venezuela: The Search for Order, the Dream of Progress.* New York: Oxford University Press, 1982.

Lombardi, John V., et al. *Venezuelan History: A Comprehensive Working Bibliography.* New York, 1977.

Marchand, B. *Venezuela: travailleurs et villes du pétrole.* Paris: Institut des Hautes Etudes d'Amérique Latine or IHEAL, Centre Nationale de la Recherche Scientifique, 1971.

Marco Dorta, Enrique. *Materiales para la historia de la cultura en Venezuela, 1523–1828.* Madrid: Gráfica Cóndor, 1967.

Marrero, Levi. *Venezuela y sus recursos.* Caracas: Cultura Venezolana, 1964.

Martínez, Aníbal R. *Chronology of Venezuela Oil.* London, 1969.

Martínez-Mendoza A., Jerónimo. *Venezuela colonial.* Caracas: Editorial Arte, 1965.

Martz, John D. *Acción Democrática: Evolution of a Modern Political Party in Venezuela.* Princeton University Press, 1966.

Martz, John D., and Enrique A. Baloyra. *Electoral Mobilization and Public Opinion: The Campaign of 1973.* Chapel Hill: University of North Carolina Press, 1976.

Martz, John D., and David J. Myers, editors. *Venezuela: The Democratic Experience.* New York, 1977.

Millares Carlo, Agustín, editor. *Protocolos del siglo XVI.* Caracas: Volume 80 of the Series "Fuentes para la Historia Colonial de Venezuela" published by the Academia Nacional de la Historia, 1966.

Morales Padrón, Francisco, and José Llavador Mira, editors. *Mapas, planos y dibujos sobre Venezuela existentes en el Archivo General de Indias.* Seville: Escuela de Estudios Hispano-americanos, 1964–1965, two volumes.

Morón, Guillermo. *Historia de Venezuela.* Caracas: Italgráfica, 1971, five volumes.

Olavarriaga, Pedro José. *Instrucción general y particular del estado presente de la provincia de Venezuela en los años de 1720 y 1721.* Caracas: Volume 76 of the Series "Fuentes para la Historia Colonial de Venezuela" published by the Academia Nacional de la Historia, 1965.

Otte, Enrique, editor. *Cedularios de la monarquía española relativos a la provincia de Venezuela, 1529–1552.* Madrid: Fundación John Boulton y Fundación Eugenio Mendoza, 1959, two volumes.

———. *Cedularios de la monarquía española relativos a la isla de Cubagua, 1523–1550.* Madrid: Fundación John Boulton y Fundación Eugenio Mendoza, 1961, two volumes.

Parra Pérez, Caracciolo. *Mariño y las guerras civiles.* Madrid, 1958–1960, three volumes.

———. *El régimen español en Venezuela.* Madrid, 1964 re-edition.

Perera, Ambrosio. *Historia de la organización de pueblos antiguos de Venezuela.* Caracas, 1964, three volumes.

Pérez de Cáceres, Pedro. "Memorias sobre Venezuela y Caracas." *Boletín de la Academia Nacional de la Historia [Venezuela]* (1939): 133–162.

Petras, James F., et al. *The Nationalization of Venezuelan Oil.* New York, 1977.

Pikaza, Otto. "Don Gabriel José de Zuloaga en la gobernación de Venezuela, 1737–1747." *Anuario de Estudios Americanos [Spain]* (1962): 501–695.

Plá, Alberto. "La formación de la clase obrera en Venezuela: notas introductorias." *Siglo XIX [Mexico]* 3, Number 6 (1988): 163–186.

Polanco Martínez, Tomás. *Esbozo sobre historia económica venezolana.* Madrid: Guadarrama, 1960.

Rodríguez, Ramón Armando. *Diccionario biográfico, geográfico e histórico de Venezuela.* Madrid, 1957.

Salazar Carrillo, Jorge. *Oil in the Economic Development of Venezuela.* New York: Praeger, 1976.

Sangroniz y Castro, José Antonio. *Familias coloniales de Venezuela.* Caracas: Bolívar, 1943.

Sanoja, Mario, and Iraida Vargas. *Antiguas formaciones y modos de producción venezolanos.* Caracas: Monte Avila, 1974.

Santana, Arturo. *La batalla de Carabobo.* Caracas: El Comercio, 1921.

Sección venezolana del Archivo de la Gran Colombia: índice sucinto. Caracas: Fundación Boulton, 1960.

Semple, Robert. *Bosquejo del estado actual de Caracas, incluyendo un viaje por La Victoria y Valencia hasta Puerto Cabello, 1810–1811.* Caracas: Editorial Arte, 1964 Spanish translation by José Nucete Sardi.

Stoan, Steven K. *Pablo Morillo and Venezuela, 1815–1820.* Columbus: Ohio State University Press, 1974.

Sucre, Luis Alberto. *Gobernadores y capitanes generales de Venezuela.* Caracas: Litografía Tecnocolor, 1964 reprint of 1928 original published by El Comercio.

Sucre Reyes, José L. *La capitanía general de Venezuela.* Barcelona, 1969.

Suriño, Jaime. *El eximio prelado doctor Mariano Martí, obispo de Caracas y Venezuela.* Madrid: Juan Bravo, 1962.

Tallenay, Jenny de. *Recuerdos de Venezuela.* Buenos Aires: Biblioteca Popular Venezolana, 1954 translation into Spanish by F. L. Durand of 1884 French original published in Paris.

Terrero, Blas José. *Teatro de Caracas y Venezuela.* Caracas: El Comercio, 1926 publication by Pedro Manuel Arcaya of the original late eighteenth-century manuscript.

Troconis de Veracoechea, Ermila, editor. *Documentos para el studio de los esclavos negros en Venezuela.* Caracas: Volume 103 of the Series "Fuentes para la Historia Colonial de Venezuela" published by the Academia Nacional de la Historia, 1969.

Trujillo, León y sublevación en San Felipe. Madrid: Jaime Villegas, 1955.

Tugwell, Franklin. *The Politics of Oil in Venezuela.* Stanford, CA: Stanford University Press, 1975.

Unceín Tamayo, Luis Alberto. "1772: Semana Santa en Caracas y La Guaira." *Boletín de la Academia Nacional de la Historia [Venezuela]* 68, Number 269 (1985): 169–179.

Vila, Marco Aurelio. *Conceptos sobre geografía histórica de Venezuela.* Caracas, 1971.

———. *Antecedentes coloniales de centros poblados de Venezuela.* Caracas: Universidad Central de Venezuela, 1978.

Vila, Pablo. *Geografía de Venezuela: el paisaje natural y el paisaje humanizado.* Caracas: Ministerio de Educación, 1965.

Wright, Winthrop. *Cafe Con Leche: Race, Class, and National Image in Venezuela.* Austin: University of Texas Press, 1990.

Yanes, Francisco Javier. *Relación documentada de los principales sucesos ocurridos en Venezuela desde que se declaró estado independiente hasta el año de 1821.* Caracas: Elite, 1943, two volumes.

Caracas

Colonial Era (1567–1810)

Actas del cabildo de Caracas, 1573–1842. Caracas: Editorial Elite for the Concejo Municipal del Distrito Federal, 1943–1989, fourteen volumes.

Arcila Frías, Eduardo, editor. *El real consulado de Caracas.* Caracas: Universidad Central de Venezuela, 1957.

Armas Chitty, Antonio de, and Manuel Pinto C., editors. *Juan Francisco de León: diario de una insurgencia, 1749.* Caracas: Tipografía Vargas for the Concejo Municipal del Distrito Federal, 1971.

Blank, Stephanie. "Patrons, Clients and Kin in Seventeenth-Century Caracas: A Methodological Essay in Colonial Spanish American Social History." *Hispanic American Historical Review* 54 (1974): 260–283.

———. "Patrons, Brokers and Clients in the Families of the Elite in Colonial Caracas, 1595–1627." *The Americas: A Quarterly Review of Inter-American Cultural History [Academy of American Franciscan History]* 36 (1979): 90–115.

Canedo, Lino G. "Sobre la llegada de los franciscanos a Venezuela y la fundación de San Francisco de Caracas." *Boletín de la Academia Nacional de la Historia [Venezuela]* 47 (1964): 38–48.

Castillo Lara, Lucas Guillermo. *Los mercedarios y la vida política y social de Caracas en los siglos XVII y XVIII.* Caracas: Volumes 143–144 of the Series "Fuentes para la Historia Colonial de Venezuela," Academia Nacional de la Historia, 1980.

Conjuración de 1808 en Caracas para la formación de una junta gubernativa. Caracas: Comisión de Historia del Instituto Panamericano de Geografía e Historia, 1949.

Díaz, Manuel Guillermo. *El agresivo obispado caraqueño de don Fray Mauro de Tovar.* Caracas: Vargas, 1956.

Documentos relativos a la insurreción de Juan Francisco de León. Buenos Aires: Instituto Panamericano de Geografía e Historia, 1949.

Duarte, Carlos F. "Las fiestas de Corpus Christi en la Caracas hispánica: tarasca, gigantes y diablitos." *Archivo Español de Arte [Spain]* 64, Number 255 (1991): 337–347.

El libro parroquial más antiguo de Caracas. Caracas: Consejo Municipal del Distrito Federal, 1968.

Ferry, Robert J. "Encomienda, African Slavery, and Agriculture in Seventeenth-Century Caracas." *Hispanic American Historical Review* 61 (1981): 609–635.

———. "The Slave Trade, Slavery and Society in Colonial Caracas." *Indian Historical Review [India]* 15, Numbers 1–2 (1988–1989): 63–70.

———. *The Colonial Elite of Early Caracas: Formulation and Crisis, 1567–1767.* Berkeley: University of California Press, 1989.

Gasparini, Graziano. *Caracas colonial.* Buenos Aires, 1969.

Hussey, Roland D. *The Caracas Company, 1728–1784: A Study in the History of Spanish Monopolistic Trade.* Cambridge, MA: Harvard University Press, 1934.

Iturriza Guillén, Carlos, editor. *Matrimonios y velaciones de españoles y criollos blancos celebrados en la catedral de Caracas desde 1615 hasta 1831.* Caracas: Instituto Venezolano de Genealogía, 1974.

Izard, Miguel. "De matadero a las Antillas: los ganaderos caraqueños a finales del período colonial." *Cahiers des Amériques latines [France]* 30 (1984): 13–27.

Langue, Frédérique. "Antagonismo y solidaridades en un cabildo colonial: Caracas, 1750–1810." *Anuario de Estudios Americanos [Spain]* 49 (1992): 371–393.

Leal, Ildefonso. *Historia de la Universidad de Caracas, 1721–1828.* Caracas: Biblioteca de la Universidad Central de Venezuela, 1963.

Leal, Ildefonso, compiler. *Cedulario de la Universidad de Caracas, 1721–1820.* Caracas: Imprenta Universitaria for the Universidad Central de Venezuela, 1965.

López Bohórquez, Alí Enrique. *La Real Audiencia de Caracas en la historiografía venezolana: materiales para su estudio.* Caracas: Volume 187 of the Series "Fuentes para la Historia Colonial de Venezuela," Academia Nacional de la Historia, 1986.

———. "El personal de la Real Audiencia de Caracas: funciones y atribuciones a través de la legislación." *Boletín de la Academia Nacional de la Historia [Venezuela]* 72, Number 286 (1989): 81–113.

———. *La Real Audiencia de Caracas: estudios.* Mérida: Rectorado de la Universidad de los Andes, 1998.

López Falcón, Jorge. "La mujer mantuana: educación y mentalidad." *Boletín de la Academia Nacional de la Historia [Venezuela]* 79, Number 315 (1996): 67–80.

Mago de Chópite, Lila. "La población de Caracas, 1754–1820: estructura y características." *Anuario de Estudios Americanos [Spain]* 54, Number 2 (1997): 511–541.

María, Nectario. *Historia de la conquista y fundación de Caracas.* Caracas: Comité de Obras Públicas del Cuatricentenario, 1966 re-edition.

Martí, Mariano. *Documentos relativos a su visita pastoral de la diócesis de Caracas, 1771–1784.* Caracas: Volumes 95–101 of the Series "Fuentes para la Historia Colonial de Venezuela," Academia Nacional de la Historia, 1969.

Morales Padrón, Francisco. *Rebelión contra la Compañía de Caracas.* Seville: Escuela de Estudios Hispanoamericanos, 1955.

"Nuevos informes realistas sobre el 19 de abril de 1810." *Revista de la Sociedad Bolivariana de Venezuela* 25, Number 87 (1966): 278–300.

Nunes Días, Manuel. *El Real Consulado de Caracas, 1793–1810.* Caracas: Volume 106 of the Series "Fuentes para la Historia Colonial de Venezuela," Academia Nacional de la Historia, 1971–1972.

Otte, Enrique, editor. *Cedularios de la monarquía española de Margarita, Nueva Andalucia y Caracas, 1553–1604.* Caracas, 1959–1967, eight volumes.

Pérez Vila, Manuel, compiler and editor. *Actas del cabildo eclesiástico de Caracas, 1580–1808.* Caracas: Volumes 64–65 of the Series "Fuentes para la Historia Colonial de Venezuela," Academia Nacional de la Historia, 1965.

Piñero, Eugenio. "The Cacao Economy of the Eighteenth-Century Province of Caracas and the Spanish Cacao Market." *Hispanic American Historical Review* 68 (1988): 75–100.

Pinto C., Manuel. *Los primeros vecinos de Caracas.* Caracas: Comité de Obras Públicas del Cuatricentenario, 1966.

Schael Martínez, Graciela. *Vida de don Francisco Fajardo.* Caracas: Concejo Municipal del Distrito Federal, 1956.

Early Maps and Depictions of Caracas, 1578–1801

Crude map of "Santiago de León de Caracas," its waterways, and distant Caribbean coastline, as depicted in the December 1578 report of Gov. Juan de Pimentel—original held by the Archive of Indies at Seville, archival provenance: Patronato Real, Legajo 294, Ramo 12

Diagram of the proposed new layout for market stalls in the city's main square, 1756—original held by the Servicio Geográfico del Ejército in Madrid

Map of Caracas as it appeared in August 1772 by Juan Vicente Bolívar, Simón Bolívar's father—original held by the Archive of Indies at Seville, archival provenance: Audiencia de Caracas, Legajo 81

Map showing the capital's subdivision into barrios or "wards," 1775—original held by the Archive of Indies at Seville, archival provenance: Audiencia de Caracas, Legajo 255

Detailed map attributed to Santiago de Roxas, of San Pablo Parish just west of Caracas, ca. 1775–1776—original held by the Archive of Indies at Seville, archival provenance: Audiencia de Caracas, Legajo 262

Map drawn in May 1778 by the military engineer, Brig. Agustín Crame, of the mountain range lying between La Guaira and Caracas—original held by the Servicio Histórico Militar in Madrid

Profile views and floor diagrams drawn in September 1785 by Miguel González Dávila, of a proposed new barracks to house Caracas's infantry battalion—originals held by the Servicio Histórico Militar in Madrid

Diagram and profile views drawn in March 1801 by José Parreño, of a proposed new arsenal at Caracas—original held by the Servicio Geográfico del Ejército in Madrid

French map of the city in 1801, engraved by J.-B. Tardier to illustrate François Depons's book *Voyage à la partie orientale de la Terre Ferme,* published in three volumes in Paris by F. Buisson in 1806

Republican Era (1811–Present)

Almandoz, Arturo. "European Urbanism in Caracas, 1870s–1930s." *Planning History [UK]* 18, Number 2 (1996): 14–19.

———. "Longing for Paris: The Europeanized Dream of Caracas Urbanism, 1870–1940." *Planning Perspectives [UK]* 14, Number 3 (1999): 225–248.

Bamberger, M. "A Problem of Political Integration in Latin America: The Barrios of Venezuela." *International Affairs* 44, Number 4 (1968): 709–719.

Díaz, José Domingo. *Recuerdos de la rebelión de Caracas.* Madrid: Guadarrama for Volume 38 of the "Biblioteca de la Academia Nacional de la Historia," 1961.

Frechilla, Juan José Martín. "Caracas, 1870–1959: inizio e epilogo dell'urbanistica moderna in Venezuela." *Storia Urbana [Italy]* 21, Number 78 (1997): 133–161.

García de la Concha, José. *Reminiscencias: vida y costumbres de la vieja Caracas.* Caracas: Grafos, 1962.

González Deluca, María Elena. *Los comerciantes de Caracas: cien años de acción y testimonio de la Cámara de Comercio de Caracas.* Caracas: Cámara de Comercio, 1994.

Hernández, Juan Francisco. *Los 75 años de la iglesia de San José, 1889–1964.* Caracas: Imprenta Nacional, 1964.

Karst, Kenneth L., et al. *The Evolution of Law in the Barrios of Caracas.* Los Angeles, 1973.

Lluch, Amalia. "La campaña contra el dictador Juan Vicente Gómez y la implicación del embajador español en Caracas." *Cuadernos de Investigación Histórica [Spain]* 13 (1990): 47–53.

Lucas de Grummond, Jane. *Las comadres de Caracas: historia de John G. A. Williamson.* Barquisimeto: Nueva Segovia, 1955 translation of 1826–1840 diary kept by the American consul.

Maza Zavala, D. F. *Condiciones generales del área metropolitana de Caracas para su industrialización.* Caracas: Comité de Obras Públicas del Cuatricentenario, 1966.

Morris, A. S. "Urban Growth Patterns in Latin America, with Illustrations from Caracas." *Urban Studies* 15, Number 3 (1978): 299–312.

Muñoz Pérez, Antonio, et al. *Plan de desarrollo para Caracas.* Caracas: Oficina Municipal de Planeamiento Urbano, 1956.

Nava, Julián. "The Illustrious American: The Development of Nationalism in Venezuela under Antonio Guzmán Blanco." *Hispanic American Historical Review* 45, Number 4 (1965): 527–543.

Pacanins A., Guillermo. *Siete años en la governación del Distrito Federal.* Caracas: Vargas, 1965.

Penfold, A. "Caracas: Urban Growth and Transportation." *Town Planning Review* 41, Number 2 (1970): 103–120.

Ponte, Andrés F. *Revolución de Caracas y sus próceres.* Caracas: Imprenta Nacional, 1960.

Ray, Talton F. *The Politics of the Barrios of Venezuela.* Berkeley: University of California Press, 1969.

Rondórquez, Rafael Angel. *Guzmán Blanco, el "autócrata civilizador": parabola de los partidos políticos tradicionales en la historia de Venezuela.* Caracas: Garrido, 1943–1944, two volumes.

Taylor, Philip B., Jr. *The Venezuelan Golpe de Estado of 1958: The Fall of Marcos Pérez.* Washington, 1968.

General Works

Abreu, Elena, and Yola Verhasselt. "Quelques aspects géographiques du développement de Caracas." *Les cahiers d'Outre-mer [France]* 34, Number 134 (April–June 1981): 180–188.

Arcaya U., Pedro Manuel. *El cabildo de Caracas.* Caracas: Comité de Obras Públicas del Cuatricentenario, 1965.

Armas Chitty, José Antonio de. *Caracas: origen y trayectoria de una ciudad.* Caracas: Fundación Creole, 1967, two volumes.

Bakkum, Maarten Jan. "Doing Historical Research in Venezuela: A Short Survey on Archives and Libraries in Caracas." *Itinerario [The Netherlands]* 17, Number 2 (1993): 110–114.

Berrizbeitia A., José Ramón, compiler. *Recopilación de ordenanzas municipales.* Caracas: Elite, 1944.

Calcaño, José Antonio. *La ciudad y su música: crónica musical de Caracas.* Caracas: Vargas, 1958.

Compilación legislativa municipal. Caracas: Consejo Municipal del Distrito Federal, 1963–1964, three volumes.

Crónica de Caracas. Caracas: irregular publication of the Consejo Municipal del Distrito Federal, January 1951-.

De-Sola Ricardo, Irma. *Contribución al estudio de los planos de Caracas: la ciudad y la provincia, 1567–1967.* Caracas: Comité de Obras Públicas del Cuatricentenario, 1967.

Gasparini, Graziano. *Caracas: la ciudad colonial y Guzmancista.* Caracas: Ernesto Armitano, 1978.

Gasparini, Graziano, and Juan Pedro Posani. *Caracas a través de su arquitectura.* Caracas: Ernesto Armitano, 1969.

Iturriza Guillén, Carlos. *Algunas familias caraqueñas.* Caracas: Escuela Técnica Industria Salsiana, 1967.

Lecuna, Valentina. *Una casa de Caracas.* Madrid: Afrodisio Aguado, 1962.

Lecuna, Vicente. *La casa natal del Libertador: su historia, logo de cuadros, muebles y reliquias, datos sobre el archivo del Libertador.* Caracas: Imprenta Nacional for the Sociedad Bolivariana de Venezuela, 1954.

Misle, Carlos Eduardo. *Corazón, pulso y huella de Caracas.* Caracas: Servicio Gráfico de Mersifrica, 1964.

Núñez, Enrique Bernardo. *La ciudad de los techos rojos.* Madrid: Edime, 1963 reprint of 1947–1948 originals published in Caracas by Vargas, two volumes.

Schael, Guillermo José. *Imagen y noticia de Caracas.* Caracas: Vargas, 1958.

Suriño, Jaime. *Catálogo del archivo arquidiocesano de Caracas.* Madrid, 1964.

Vila, Marco Aurelio. *Area metropolitana de Caracas.* Caracas: Comité de Obras Públicas del Cuatricentenario, 1965.

———. *Aspectos geográficos del Distrito Federal.* Caracas: Corporación Venezolana de Fomento, 1967.

Maracaibo

Besson, Juan. *Historia del Estado Zulia.* Maracaibo: Hermanos Belloso Rosell, 1943, three volumes.

Cruz Santos, Abel. "Padilla en Maracaibo." *Boletín de Historia y Antigüedades [Colombia]* 71, Number 745 (1984): 355–360.

"El complot de Maracaibo." *Boletín de la Academia Nacional de la Historia [Venezuela]* 66, Number 264 (1983): 1101–1105.

Herwig, Holger H. *Germany's Vision of Empire in Venezuela, 1871–1914.* Princeton University Press, 1986.

Leal, Ildefonso. "La provincia de Maracaibo en 1791, según un informe del segundo intendente de Caracas, don Francisco de Saavedra." *Boletín de la Academia Nacional de la Historia [Venezuela]* 67, Number 267 (1984): 487–503.

Maracaibo gráfico: progresos de esta ciudad durante el período constitucional del general José María García. Maracaibo: Tipografía Panorama, 1917.

María, Nectario. *Los orígenes de Maracaibo.* Madrid: Junta Culutural de la Universidad de Zulia, 1959.

Ojer, Pablo. *El Golfo de Venezuela: una síntesis histórica.* Maracaibo: Corpozulia, 1983.

Unceín Tamayo, Luis Alberto. "Maracaibo y . . . ¡Subida de furros!" *Boletín de la Academia Nacional de la Historia [Venezuela]* 64, Number 254 (1981): 397–400.

———. "Maracaibo: su verdadero cuatricentenario." *Boletín de la Academia Nacional de la Historia [Venezuela]* 64, Number 254 (1981): 401–404.

———. "El Carmen de Maracaibo: capilla con historias." *Boletín de la Academia Nacional de la Historia [Venezuela]* 68, Number 269 (1985): 181–183.

Vaccari, Letizia. "Una ordenanza del siglo XVII." *Boletín de la Academia Nacional de la Historia [Venezuela]* 67, Number 265 (1984): 105–115.

Index

Aztecs
conquest by Cortés, 209, 226,
249–250
conquest of Totonacs, 301
in Oaxaca area, 276
under Spanish rule, 251–252,
253–254, 255
at Veracruz, 301–302

Baas-Castelmore, Jean-Charles de,
78–79, 169
Báez, Buenaventura, 99, 101
Bahamas
derivation of name, 3
and English, 4–5
and French, 4
major hurricanes, 6
See also Nassau, Bahamas
Balaguer, Joaquín Antonio, 104–106
Balmaceda, José Manuel, 734
Bananas, 338
Guatemala, 344
Bank of the Bahamas, 13
Bannister, James, 809
Baranda, Pedro, 226
Barbados, 17, 22, 25
abolition of slavery, 27
Charter of, 19
derivation of name, 17
and Dutch, 19, 20–21
and English Civil War, 18–19
and North America, 22–23
and Panama Canal, 29, *29*
population figures, 24, 27, 28, 30
"Starving Time," 18
See also Bridgetown, Barbados
Barrera, Antonio Imbert, 105
Barreto de Meneses, Francisco,
688–689
Barrio Nuevo, Francisco de, 348
Barrios, Justo Rufino, 343–344
Barros de San Millán, Manuel, 772
Barton, Clara, 544
Batista, Fulgencio, 53–54, 69–70, 103
Bayamo, Cuba, 58
Beauharnais, Alexandre, Vicomte de,
179
Beauharnois, François de Beaumont,
Comte de, 173
Beauregard, Pierre G. T., 541, 542
Beckwith, George, 178
Beeston, William, 153

Béhague, Jean-Pierre Antoine de, 176,
177
Bejarano, Lázaro, 74
Belalcázar, Sebastián de, 759, 769–771
Beltrán de Guzmán, Nuño, 226–227,
278
Berbeo, Juan Francisco, 739
Beresford, William Carr, 657–658
Bermúdez, José Francisco, 835
Berrio y Oruña, Antonio de, 198–199
Biassou, Georges, 114
Bienville, Jean-Baptiste Le Moyne,
Sieur de, 565–567, 593–594
Bird, Vere, 30
Blackbeard. *See* Teach, Edward
(Blackbeard)
Blakeley (U.S. destroyer), 182–183, *182*
Blanchelande, Philibert François de
Rouxel de, 126–127
Blénac, Charles de Courbon, Seigneur
de Romegeux and Comte de,
170–171
Blénac Courbon, Charles, Comte de,
111–112
Block, Adriaen, 580
Bobo, Rosalvo, 118–119
Bogotá, Colombia, 737, *737*
and assassination of Gaitán, *743,*
744, *744*
Calle Real, *742,* 743–744
and Chibchas, 737–738, 739
colonial era, 737–741
early and mid-20th century,
743–745
early republican era, 741–743
epidemics, 738
and independence, 739–741
maps, *738, 741*
modern era, 745–746
population figures, 739, 742, 743,
744, 745, 746
viceregal palace, *740*
and *La Violencia,* 744–745
young woman resident, *745*
Bolívar, Simón
birthplace, *835*
and Bolivia, 673, 682
and Colombia, 740–741, 755–756
and Curaçao, 84–85
and Ecuador, 763–764, 775
and Panama City, 354
and Peru, 801

and Santo Domingo, 98
and Venezuela, 834–836, 845
Bolivia. *See* La Paz, Bolivia; Potosí,
Bolivia
Bonaparte, Joseph, 48, 63, 84, 97, 242,
258, 293, 312, 325
Bonaparte, Louis, 83
Bonaparte, Napoleon. *See* Napoleon I
Bontemps, Jean, 74
Boot, Adrian, 212, 254–255
Borel, Auguste, former Marquis de, 127
Borno, Louis, 142, 143
Bosch, Juan D., 105
Boston, Massachusetts, 521, *521*
and American Revolution, 526–529
Beacon Hill, 522
Boston Bay, *527*
earthquakes, 522, 524
epidemics, 524
fires, 524, 526, 530
founding, 522
and Glorious Revolution, 523–524
Harvard University, 525
and Irish, 530
and King Philip's War, 523
and Long Wharf, 524, *526*
maps, *525, 527, 528, 529*
and Massachusetts Bay, 522
modern era, 530–531
population figures, 524, 529, 530,
531
postrevolutionary era and 19th
century, 529–530
post–World War II revival, 530
precolonial era, 521–522
and Puritans, 522–523, 524–525
as seaport, 522, 523, 524, 525–526,
526, 529
Shawmut Bay and Peninsula, *521,*
522
under crown control, 523–528
Boucaniers. See Privateers and pirates
Bouterese, Desi, 814–815
Boves, José Tomás, 834
Boyer, Jean-Pierre, 98–99, 117, 132
Bragg, Braxton, 601–602
Bravo, Nicolás, 216, 312–313
Brayne, William, 151
Brazil. *See* Olinda, Brazil; Recife, Brazil;
Rio de Janeiro, Brazil; Salvador,
Brazil
Brice, Broussais, 136, *136*